MW01492285

THE ROUTLEDGE INTERNATIONAL HANDBOOK OF SOCIAL WORK SUPERVISION

This handbook provides a comprehensive overview of social work supervision internationally and presents an analytical review of social work supervision theory, practice, and research.

Presented in seven parts:

- International perspectives
- Supervision settings
- Roles, responsibilities, and relationships
- Models and approaches
- The interactional process
- Leading and managing supervision
- Emerging areas

The book examines how supervision contributes to the well-being, development, and practice of social workers. It also sets the agenda for the future development of social work supervision internationally. Social work supervision is examined across countries, practice settings, and in terms of participants' roles, relationships, and responsibilities. Contributors show how and why social work supervision is integral to social work and the rich diversity of ways supervision can be practiced.

Bringing together an international team of social work supervision scholars, researchers, supervisors, and practitioners, this handbook is essential reading for social workers, supervisors, managers, policy advisors, and professional leaders.

Kieran O'Donoghue (PhD, RSW) is an Associate Professor in the School of Social Work at Massey University, Aotearoa New Zealand. He has published extensively on social work supervision and been a practicing supervisor for over twenty-five years.

Lambert Engelbrecht (MA *Cum Laude*, DPhil in Social Work) is a Professor of Social Work and Chair of the Department of Social Work at Stellenbosch University, South Africa. He started his professional career as a front-line social worker in 1986 and has extensive experience as a supervisor, manager, and academic in social work.

THE ROUTLEDGE INTERNATIONAL HANDBOOK OF SOCIAL WORK SUPERVISION

Edited by Kieran O'Donoghue and Lambert Engelbrecht

Routledge
Taylor & Francis Group

LONDON AND NEW YORK

First published 2021
by Routledge
2 Park Square, Milton Park, Abingdon, Oxon OX14 4RN

and by Routledge
605 Third Avenue, New York, NY 10017

Routledge is an imprint of the Taylor & Francis Group, an informa business

© 2021 selection and editorial matter, Kieran O'Donoghue and Lambert Engelbrecht; individual chapters, the contributors

The right of Kieran O'Donoghue and Lambert Engelbrecht to be identified as the authors of the editorial material, and of the authors for their individual chapters, has been asserted in accordance with sections 77 and 78 of the Copyright, Designs and Patents Act 1988.

All rights reserved. No part of this book may be reprinted or reproduced or utilised in any form or by any electronic, mechanical, or other means, now known or hereafter invented, including photocopying and recording, or in any information storage or retrieval system, without permission in writing from the publishers.

Trademark notice: Product or corporate names may be trademarks or registered trademarks, and are used only for identification and explanation without intent to infringe.

British Library Cataloguing-in-Publication Data
A catalogue record for this book is available from the British Library

Library of Congress Cataloging-in-Publication Data
Names: O'Donoghue, Kieran, editor. | Engelbrecht, Lambert K.
(Lambert Karel), 1961- editor.
Title: The Routledge international handbook of social work supervision
/ edited by Kieran O'Donoghue and Lambert Engelbrecht.
Description: New York : Routledge, 2021. | Series: Routledge
international handbooks | Includes bibliographical references and index.
Identifiers: LCCN 2020056316 (print) | LCCN 2020056317 (ebook) |
ISBN 9780367250867 (hardback) | ISBN 9780429285943 (ebook)
Subjects: LCSH: Social workers--Supervision of.
Classification: LCC HV40.54 .R68 2021 (print) | LCC HV40.54
(ebook) | DDC 361.3068/3--dc23
LC record available at https://lccn.loc.gov/2020056316
LC ebook record available at https://lccn.loc.gov/2020056317

ISBN 13: 978−0−367−25086−7 (hbk)
ISBN 13: 978−1−03−200925−4 (pbk)

Typeset in Bembo
by Deanta Global Publishing Services, Chennai, India

CONTENTS

Contents

FIGURES

TABLES

CONTRIBUTORS

Mari Alschuler is Associate Professor of Social Work at Youngstown State University Ohio, United States. She teaches supervision, advanced clinical practice, creative arts therapies, practice with LGBTQIA clients, and integrated field seminars and capstone courses. She is a mentor/practitioner through the International Academy of Poetry Therapy and is a therapist in private practice in north-eastern Ohio.

Liz Beddoe is Professor of Social Work at the University of Auckland in New Zealand. Her research interests include critical perspectives on social work education and supervision, social work professional identity, and the experiences of migrant social workers. Liz has published widely in international journals and has written several books on the practice of professional supervision.

Godfred Boahen is a National Safeguard Policy and Development Lead. Previously the Policy, Research, and Practice Development Lead at BASW (British Association of Social Workers), he led projects commissioned by the Department of Health and Social Care in digital "capabilities" and social work in learning disability and autism. He also supported BASW members to form communities of practice called Special Interest Groups.

Marion Bogo is Professor at the Factor-Inwentash Faculty of Social Work, University of Toronto, Canada. Her long-standing program of research focuses on social work field education, the conceptualization and assessment of professional competence, and more recently, simulation-based education. She has published over 140 journal articles and book chapters and seven books and disseminated her research in invited presentations internationally.

Alistair Brown is the immediate past National Director of the Scottish Association of Social Work and past company director of BASW. He has extensive local authority and NGO experience in Aotearoa New Zealand and the UK in managerial, therapeutic, and statutory mental health roles. As an independent consultant, he develops training and resources on supervision and professional development for regulatory authorities.

Stefan Busse is the Chair of Psychology at the Faculty of Social Work at Mittweida University, Germany, and Head of the certificate courses in Supervision and Coaching. He is also the Academic Director of the Institute for Competence, Communication and Languages (IKKS) at the University of Applied Sciences, Mittweida. He is the founder of the Psychological Centre, Leipzig and of Basta Fortbildungsinstitut für Supervision und Coaching.

Lareen Cooper is the Associate Head, School of Social Work, Massey University in Palmerston North, Aotearoa New Zealand. She teaches and writes in social policy and management. She has an extensive background in health services executive management in District Health Boards in New Zealand. She has served for five years as a Member of the Social Workers Complaints and Disciplinary Tribunal.

Carolyn Cousins has postgraduate degrees in social work and adult education and has worked in the trauma and mental health sectors in Australia and the UK. She provides individual and group supervision in a range of fields and is the Convener of the Clinical Division of the Australian College of Social Work.

Beth Crisp is Professor and Discipline Leader of Social Work at Deakin University in Australia, where her responsibilities include managing several academic staff. She has been actively involved in health and human services research for the past 30 years. Her interests include professional development; social inclusion; and interface of religion, spirituality, and social work practice.

Michael Dale is a Senior Lecturer in Social Work at the School of Social Work, Massey University, New Zealand. He teaches and writes in social work practice, social services leadership, management, and practice development. Michael has an extensive senior management background in the Department of Corrections, child welfare, and non-government organizations.

Allyson Davys works part time as Senior Lecturer at the University of Auckland in New Zealand and conducts a private supervision practice. Her professional and research interests include supervision practice development and education and evaluation in supervision. She has recently completed a Doctoral study on inter-professional supervision.

Ronnie Egan has specialized in research about supervision and practice for social workers and students, has published widely in these areas, and has extensive and active networks in the human service sector. Her relationships with the field span her career as a practitioner and academic, and this has enabled the development of innovative ways of understanding and facilitating the nexus between universities and the community.

Lambert Engelbrecht is the Chair of the Department of Social Work at Stellenbosch University, South Africa. He started his professional career as a front-line social worker in 1986 and has extensive experience as a manager, supervisor, and professor of social work. He publishes widely on topics related to social work: social development, management, and supervision of social workers; social work education; and the impact of a neoliberal discourse on social welfare.

Moana Eruera is an indigenous Māori wāhine/female of Ngāpuhi, Ngāti Ruanui, and Ngāti Rangiwewehi descent from Aotearoa New Zealand. Moana has more than 30 years' experience in social and community work. She has made a significant contribution in whānau violence prevention, child protection, Indigenous training and framework development, youth restorative justice, tribal projects/research, intimate partner relationships, and indigenous approaches to child protection.

Luke Geoghegan is the Head of Policy and Research at the British Association of Social Workers (BASW). As a qualified and registered social worker, Luke has over 30 years of experience of being supervised, supervising others, and leading a variety of teams and organizations. He writes in a personal capacity.

Trish Hafford-Letchfield is Professor of Social Work at the University of Strathclyde, Scotland. She is a qualified social worker and nurse and her research interests focus on the experience of ageing in marginalized communities, sexual and gender identities in social work, leadership and management in health and social care, and arts-based pedagogies to engage service users in social work education.

Tracey Harris is the CEO of Amovita International, a PhD Candidate at the School of Human Services and Social Work, Griffith University, Australia, and a leader in organizational performance and supervision. Her research interests include clinical and professional supervision, organizational performance and neuro-social science. She is a social worker and is currently developing a capability instrument for social work supervisors.

Staffan Höjer is Professor of Social Work at the Department of Social Work, University of Gothenburg, Sweden. His research interest focuses on knowledge, professionalization, and organization of social work. He was an Honorary Doctor at the University of Finland, was appointed as Research Associate at Stellenbosch University, South Africa, and as Professor Catedratico at the University of Lisbon.

Ephrat Huss is Professor of Social Work at Ben-Gurion University Israel and is a Chair of a MA degree in art for social workers. She has researched and published extensively on arts-based research methods with marginalized groups, arts and sense of coherence, creative community and place-making through arts, and social and critical theories in art therapy.

Richard Ingram is a Reader in Social Work at the University of Dundee, Scotland. His teaching and research interests include emotions, relationship-based practice, student experience, and internationalization. He is currently a co-editor of the Social Work Education journal.

Priscalia Khosa is a Lecturer at the Department of Social Work at Stellenbosch University, South Africa. She has published widely in her fields of research interests, which include social work supervision, social work education, and social policy. She received a Social Work Emerging Educator Award by the Association of South African Social Work Education Institutions (ASASWEI) in 2019.

Carolyn Knight is a social worker with more than 30 years of experience with adult survivors of childhood trauma. She has been teaching generalist social work practice and has served as a faculty field liaison for more than 25 years. She has written about and presented workshops and training on the trauma-informed conceptualization and its application to clinical practice and supervision.

Sharon Lambley is a part-time Lecturer in Public Services Management and Leadership at the University of the West of Scotland in the UK, and a freelance social work lecturer in London. Her research and teaching interests focus on the interface between professional and managerial worlds and how to navigate these worlds in organizations successfully, whilst keeping service users at the heart of practice.

John Lawler qualified and practiced as a social worker before moving into academia. He has wide-ranging research experience and qualifications in the areas of leadership and management and public service and has published extensively in these areas. He has considerable experience internationally in management and leadership development.

Charles Tong Lit Leung is a Hong Kong registered social worker and supervisor and trains social workers in mainland China. He is currently an Assistant Professor of Social Work and Social Administration Programme at Beijing Normal University-Hong Kong Baptist University, United International College, Zhuhai GZ.

Cynthia Lietz is the President's Professor at Arizona State University's School of Social Work, United States. She developed Strengths-Based Supervision (SBS), a model of clinical supervision that supports the effective implementation of family-centered practice. Prior to coming to ASU, she worked as a family therapist and supervisor with youth and families involved in the child welfare system.

Noel Macnamara is a social worker with over 35 years of experience as a clinician, supervisor, and executive with a wide range of services with children, adolescents, and families in Australia and the UK. Noel is currently the Deputy Director of the Centre of Excellence in Therapeutic Care and Executive Manager Policy and Research ACF.

Lynne McPherson has practiced as a social worker and as a social work academic in Australia since 1981. She joined Southern Cross University, Australia in 2016 where she has teaching and research interests in supervision, children and trauma, and out of home care.

Fiona Mainstone practiced as a social worker in Scotland, London, and Sussex before teaching at Brighton University, England, as a Senior Lecturer. She has engaged with the development of over 2000 social work supervisors, managers, and leaders, and has worked independently as a social work consultant, facilitator and educator since 2003.

Kitty Yuen Han Mo is a social work educator in Hong Kong who writes extensively in the area of supervision. She is an external supervisor of social work organizations in mainland China. Currently, she is doing research concerning job satisfaction and turnover of social workers. She has obtained the National One Hundred Social Worker Award, Outstanding Supervisor Award, and Outstanding Trainer Award.

Ksenija Napan is Associate Professor at the School of Social Work, Massey University in Auckland, Aotearoa New Zealand. She is an experienced social work supervisor who initiated and participated in several peer supervision groups. She believes in the transformational power of a group process for improvement of wellbeing and quality of life of individuals, groups, families, and communities.

Mpumelelo Ncube is a Lecturer at the University of Johannesburg, South Africa. He specializes in social work supervision and community development. He has published various articles on supervision within a social development context and serves on national task teams regarding supervision of social workers and social service professions in South Africa.

Agnes Kwok Tung Ng is a practitioner, consultant, trainer, and researcher in social work supervision. She is currently the supervisor of the Australia Monash University's Master of Counselling Program and the Supportive Supervision Scheme Honorary Director of the Hong Kong Social Workers Association.

Amanda Nickson is a social worker with over 30 years of experience and has expertise in supervision. She completed her PhD on exploring peer group supervision in virtual teams in rural Australia. She is passionate about helping individuals and organizations to reach their full potential. She runs a business and consultancy in interactive solutions in Queensland, Australia.

Kieran O'Donoghue is an Associate Professor in the School of Social Work at Massey University, Aotearoa New Zealand. He has published extensively on social work supervision and been a practicing supervisor for over twenty-five years. Kieran is the coordinator of the Post Graduate Diploma in Social Service Supervision at Massey University.

Abigail Ornellas was a postdoctoral fellow at the Department of Social Work, Stellenbosch University, South Africa. She is involved in several international research projects and has published widely on mental health, the impact of neoliberalism on social welfare and social work, socioeconomic and political policies, micro and macro linkages, and the role of social workers in social welfare.

Frances Patterson is a Senior Lecturer at the University of Stirling, Scotland, and is involved in post-qualifying learning and development for managers and practitioners in health and social services. She began practicing as a social worker in 1981, and her professional background spans statutory and voluntary sector settings, focusing particularly on work with adults who have a learning disability.

Keely Phillips has worked in peer support for over a decade. She has created and led the implementation of peer support programs in diverse settings and has authored numerous resources on peer support. She is a Certified Peer Support Mentor through Peer Support Canada and works at the Canadian Mental Health Association, Waterloo, Wellington as the peer support services manager.

Matt Rankine is a Lecturer and Program Director of the Post-graduate Professional Supervision program at the University of Auckland, New Zealand and provides external supervision for practitioners. He is a registered social worker with 20 years' experience working with children and families. Matt is interested in critical approaches to practice and has published in the areas of field education and supervision.

Frederic Reamer is Professor at the School of Social Work, Rhode Island College, United States. His teaching and research focus on professional ethics, criminal justice, mental health, and health care. He chaired the National Task Force that wrote the Code of Ethics adopted by the National Association of Social Workers in 1996 and recently served on the Code Revision Task Force.

Leland Ruwhiu is an indigenous Māori tāne/male of Ngāpuhi, Ngāti Porou, Ngāti Kahungunu, and Ngāi Tahu o Mohaka Waikare descent from Aotearoa New Zealand. Leland was the first Māori to complete a Doctorate in Social Work and Social Policy. He is committed to Indigenous frameworks for whānau wellbeing. Leland is married to Nicky Haeata-Ruwhiu and they have 6 children and 14 grandchildren.

Glen Schmidt has been a social worker for over 40 years, and he worked as a supervisor in the fields of child welfare, mental health, and medical social work. He is a Professor Emeritus at the University of Northern British Columbia, Canada.

Karen Sewell is an Assistant Professor in the School of Social Work at Carleton University in Ottawa, Canada. Her research interests stem from her practice in children's mental health, including clinical supervision, evidence-supported interventions, and program development. She is also interested in social work education, including field education and simulation in teaching/learning and research.

Lawrence Shulman is Dean Emeritus at the University at Buffalo School of Social Work, United States. He received the Council on Social Work Education's Significant Lifetime

Contribution to Social Work Education award. He is the author of numerous articles and eight books, including "The dynamics and skills of group counseling," "The skills of helping individuals, families, groups and communities," and "Interactional supervision."

Maddy Slattery is a Senior Lecturer in mental health in the School of Human Services and Social Work at Griffith University, Australia. Her teaching and research interests include clinical supervision, consumer engagement in health service provision and research, and peer workers with lived experience. Maddy is a clinical psychologist and provides supervision for clinicians.

Ming-sum Tsui is a practitioner, teacher, and researcher in social work supervision. He has published 3 books and more than 25 refereed journal articles in supervision in the last 40 years. He is currently Professor and Felizberta Lo Padilla Tong Dean of Social Sciences, Caritas Institute of Higher Education, Hong Kong, and co-editor of the International Social Work journal.

Nicki Weld has worked in a variety of social work roles in the health, statutory child protection, government, and non-government sectors in Aotearoa New Zealand. She has been providing supervision for over 23 years. Nicki is the author and co-author of six books, and the primary creator of the Three Houses Tool that is used internationally.

Jane Wexler is a consultant in leadership development, supervision, and coaching in Australia and Asia. She has designed and delivered supervision training to thousands of human service professionals across diverse settings, using multiple delivery modes. She previously lectured in social work at Deakin, RMIT, and Monash universities in Australia, and in business studies at Shanghai Holmes Chang le College, China.

David Wilkins is a Senior Lecturer in Social Work and Assistant Director of the Children's Social Care Research and Development Centre, Cardiff University, Wales. His research interests are professional supervision in child and family social work and decision-making, with a focus on what difference supervision makes for children and parents, and how to define and support good decision making in practice.

Peace Yuh Ju Wong is a Senior Lecturer at the Department of Social Work, National University of Singapore. She excels in her teaching and has been awarded the Faculty Teaching Excellence Awards since 2014 and Annual Teaching Excellence Award (2018, 2019). She actively promotes social work supervision by chairing workgroups to organize seminars and to develop a Supervision Guide and Competency Framework in Singapore.

Jane Wonnacott is a social worker, safeguarding consultant, and Director of In-Trac Training and Consultancy in the UK. She has been involved in the development and delivery of supervision training for over 25 years and has published materials as well as overseeing large scale supervision training contracts for central government.

INTRODUCTION

Supervision in social work

Kieran O'Donoghue and Lambert Engelbrecht

In this introduction, we start by discussing the role of supervision in social work and the key developments over the past fifty years that have contributed to its emerging internationalization. Following this we outline the structure of the Handbook and explain how it is organized and overview the parts of the book.

Supervision in social work

Twenty-first century social work supervision has been shaped by the influence of past scholars, researchers, practitioners, social service organizations, and by the professionalization of social work (O'Donoghue 2015). Since the 1930s, when Robinson (1936) linked supervision with social casework and conceptualized it as an educational process involving administration, teaching, and helping, it has become integral to social work. Supervision subsequently became a pillar of casework practice and inseparable from the casework method (Rabinowitz 1987). The professionalization of social work across the period of the 1950s to 1970s saw supervision challenged by the idea that professional social workers, like other professionals, should practice autonomously and consult their peers when they need advice or support, rather than have continuous career-long supervision. Consequently, during this period there was a tendency amongst practitioners to be supervised for a time limited period after qualifying and then to engage in autonomous practice and consult peers on cases (Tsui 1997). Innovations such as peer group supervision and case consultation developed during this time and occurred alongside traditional organizational supervision (Rabinowitz 1987).

During the 1970s, supervision in social work was influenced by fiscal pressure and a focus on accountability within social service organizations, as well as the scholarship and research of two US scholars, Alfred Kadushin and Carlton Munson. The impact of the fiscal pressure and focus on accountability resulted in an increased emphasis on administrative supervision (O'Donoghue 2015). Meanwhile the influence of the scholarship and research of Kadushin (1974, 1976) and Munson (1975, 1979a) set the empirical foundation for social work supervision theory and practice. Kadushin (1974) completed the first national survey of social work supervision which provided the first descriptive overview of supervisory practices, processes, and challenges. Munson (1975) completed the first empirical doctoral thesis about social work supervision and examined the structural, authority, and teaching models of social work supervision. Munson (1975) found that supervisors whose authority was derived from competence had a greater influence upon their supervisees than those who derived authority from agency sanction. He also noted that a dual model that separated administrative supervision from case consultation deserved further consideration particularly if used in conjunction with an interactional approach to clarify issues of structure, authority, and roles.

Building upon their research, both Kadushin (1976, 1985, 1992) and Munson (1979b, 1983, 1993) produced leading texts in the field of social work supervision. Kadushin's (1976, 1985, 1992) administrative, educative, and supportive functions and his organizational-based definition of social work supervision has influenced the conceptualization of social work supervision internationally for the past fifty years. Similarly, Munson's (1983, 1993) conceptualization of clinical social work supervision has contributed to keeping a focus on clinical aspects (i.e. the supervision of direct practice and the supervision of the practitioner) of social work supervision, as well as resulting in social work contributing to and drawing from the interdisciplinary field of clinical supervision.

A managerialist and managed cost environment dominated social service organizations in the 1980s and 1990s. The impact of this on social work supervision was to make it an accountability process, with the administrative or managerial function being strengthened using contracts, task completion, and job performance (Engelbrecht 2015, O'Donoghue 2015). This period also saw further advances in social work supervision research and scholarship, with Shulman et al. (1981) conducting a study focused on the content, context, and skills of supervision in Canada, from which he and his colleagues developed a scale of supervisory skills, which he used to test an interactional model. Shulman (1982, 1993, 2010) subsequently used this scale to identify the influence of parallel process within social work supervision. Shulman's (1993) interactional model has continued to provide the foundation for interactional skills in supervision, as well as how supervisors mediate between the management and practice systems.

In the 1980s and 1990s, serious questions were being raised about whether supervision had beneficial outcomes for workers, organizations, and clients. These questions were addressed by studies which found: a) that supervisory support may reduce the psychological stress and relieve burnout and job dissatisfaction among frontline social workers (Himle et al. 1989), b) that supportive supervision could improve worker morale when the supervisor attended to workload demands (Rauktis and Koseske 1994), and c) that supervision focused on client problems resulted in improvements in clients' generalized contentment and client satisfaction with their goal attainment, the worker helpfulness, and the partnership between worker and client (Harkness and Hensley 1991). Despite the emerging evidence base that supervision contributed to worker, organizational, and clients' outcomes, supervision in social work was at turning point in the 1990s. This turning point was aptly described by Payne (1994) when he outlined three possible futures for supervision, namely: 1) the separation of the professional and managerial components as part of a professional resurgence; 2) the integration of the professional and managerial components through supervision becoming a quality assurance process; or 3) the elimination of the professional component with social work supervision becoming purely managerial.

The response to this turning point involved firstly an argument to separate line-management and professional supervision (Erera and Lazar 1995, Gibelman and Schervish 1998). The idea of separating the management and professional roles within supervision and locating each role with a different person was also a response to the increase in generic managers who did not have a social work background in social service organizations (Rees 1999). It also contributed to the development of clinical supervision undertaken within an organization by a professional peer, as well as external clinical supervision provided by a private consultant not employed by the organization, where the manager or team leader was not a social worker (O'Donoghue 2015). The second response was to emphasize the clinical aspects of supervision through situating social work supervision within the wider interdisciplinary field of clinical supervision. This resulted in the literature from other disciplines being incorporated into social work, as well as the beginning of cross-disciplinary and interprofessional supervision (O'Donoghue 2004). The third response came via regulatory authorities and professional bodies. Regulatory authorities linked a period of supervision with licensure or registration (Gray 1990, Barretta-Herman 1994), whereas professional bodies established national supervision policies and linked supervision with competent practice, professional development, and professional ethics (Engelbrecht 2013, O'Donoghue 1998). The outcome of this response was the recasting of social work supervision as professional supervision. Supervision was linked to the well-being, development, and practice of the professional social worker and enshrined as a core artifact of professional social work (Engelbrecht 2010, O'Donoghue 2012).

During the late 1980s and 1990s, it was identified that traditional supervision was aligned with a white, male, Western, hierarchical perspective, which did not address the power issues identified in the structural, political, and socio-cultural discourses within social work and was silent about the effects of gender and cultural differences (Chernesky 1986, Morrison 1993, Hipp and Munson 1995, Brown and Bourne 1996, Kaiser 1997, Matheson 1999). The feminist and cultural critiques that emerged suggested new approaches and contributed to the development of feminist models (Chernesky 1986, Hipp and Munson 1995, Matheson 1999); approaches that were anti-discriminatory and anti-oppressive (Morrison 1993, Brown and Bourne 1996); and the questioning of assumptions regarding power, authority, and culture differences in the supervisory relationship (Engelbrecht 2006, Kaiser 1997, Tsui and Ho 1997).

The late 1990s and first decade of the 21st century was a period of significant change internationally due to the emergence and influence of information and communications technology and the resulting globalization (O'Donoghue 2001, 2003). In this period, social workers and supervisors were introduced to the mobile phone, pagers, the personal computer, the electronic file, the caseload database, email, voicemail, teleconferencing, videoconferencing, the internet, and world wide web (O'Donoghue 2003). The most significant impact on social workers and supervisors was arguably the introduction of the personal computer, computer servers, and database software. The effect of this on social work and supervision has been an increased emphasis on the electronic accounting and recording of the work that is done with clients, which has resulted in a greater amount of time spent engaged in data entry rather than direct client or practitioner contact. It also resulted in increased surveillance and monitoring of client records and the viewing of these records as the most valid form of evidence of social work or supervision practice (O'Donoghue 2003). These developments coupled with a focus on risk management saw social work supervision being juxtaposed as both a means of surveillance, as well as a process of reflection (Beddoe 2010).

The information and communication technology developments in the 21st century have arguably also advanced supervision scholarship internationally through enabling scholars to search and access colleagues' work from other countries and to collaborate (e.g. Bradley and Höjer 2009, Hair and O'Donoghue 2009, Bradley et al. 2010). Other international developments during the first decade of the 21st century were international supervision conferences in Aotearoa New Zealand and the United States (O'Donoghue and Tsui 2012). Since 2000 the evidence-base for social work supervision grew markedly with O'Donoghue and Tsui (2015) identifying 44 journal articles reporting empirical research between 2000 and 2010. This was a significant increase on the 25 published in 1990s. According to O'Donoghue and Tsui (2015), the research in the 2000s reflected the increasing internationalization of social work supervision, with articles coming from the United States, Hong Kong, Aotearoa New Zealand, Canada, Australia, UK, and Sweden.

In the most recent decade, 2011 to 2020, the international focus upon social work supervision has increased. This has been illustrated by the following list of international journals dedicating special issues focused on supervision:

- *2012 – Australian Social Work 65 (2)*
- *2012 – Smith College Studies in Social Work 82 (2–3)*
- *2015 – Practice: Social Work in Action 27 (4): The Supervision of Social Work Practice*
- *2015 – China Journal of Social Work 8 (2)*
- *2018 – Clinical Social Work Journal 46 (4)*
- *2018 – European Journal of Social Work 21 (3): Contemporary practices in social work supervision: Time for new paradigms?*
- *2019 – Aotearoa New Zealand Social Work 31 (3)*

There has been a growing internationalization of social work supervision with publications of both theoretical and empirical articles across the continents of Europe, Asia, Australasia, Africa, and North America (Sewell 2018). Reviews of the empirical research and literature indicate that the main themes in the literature are: 1) the differing perspectives of supervision internationally; 2) the differing practices of supervision across specific settings or areas of social work practice; 3) the roles, responsibilities, and relationships enacted in supervision; 4) the models and approaches used in practice and a growing call for evidence-informed supervision; 5) the interactional process and its importance in managing emotions, enabling reflection, and containing stress and conflict; 6) the role leadership and management have through supervision both organizationally and professionally; and 7) the emerging areas of the use of information technology in supervision, the engagement of service users, and the future research agenda (Carpenter et al. 2013, O'Donoghue and Tsui 2015, Sewell 2018). The development of social work supervision internationally is now at the point where a comprehensive overview of social work supervision internationally is needed.

The structure of the Handbook

This Handbook aims to provide a comprehensive overview of social work supervision internationally. The Handbook is structured in seven parts with each part focusing on a specific theme within the literature and research.

Part I: International perspectives

The differing perspectives of social work supervision from ten countries across the continents of Europe, North America, Africa, Asia, and Australasia are discussed in this group of chapters. Each chapter situates supervision within the local context and discusses how supervision has developed and responded to its professional and organizational context. The chapters as a group provide insights into what is common or core within social work supervision internationally. They also show a range of local and Indigenous developments occurring in specific locations.

Part II: Supervision settings

Social work supervision is practiced across a range of settings. In this part there are seven chapters that discuss supervision in the following specific settings: students, newly qualified social workers, child and family social work, social work with adults in care, social work in isolated and rural areas, the supervision of peer workers, and within the specific setting of Māori culture. These chapters illustrate how the focus of supervision, and the methods and approaches used are influenced by each setting.

Part III: Roles, responsibilities, and relationships

In this part, the chapters examine the roles, responsibilities, and relationships and start with the learning journey of the supervisee and the experience of becoming a supervisor. The chapters that follow examine the supervisor's perspective and positioning in dual role, external, peer, and group supervision. This part concludes with a discussion of the ethical issues in supervision and the supervisor's responsibility for ethical social work and supervision practice.

Part IV: Models and approaches

In this part, a selection of ten current models and approaches used in social work supervision practice internationally is discussed. The models and approaches included range from those that are comprehensive and integrated, to specific models and approaches developed from research in child and family settings, to theoretical approaches informed by social work practice theory, to an ethical evidence informed model.

Part V: The interactional process

The interactional process is the primary medium of social work supervision, and in this part the six chapters explore interactional supervision, the supervision session, emotional sensitivity, the thinking out loud reflective process, live observation and feedback, and the management of conflict and challenging processes.

Part VI: Leading and managing supervision

In this part the leadership and management of supervision within an organizational setting is examined. The eight chapters discuss supervisory leadership and management, the enhancement and management of performance, the facilitation of flourishing through supervision, effective supervision and organizational culture, how strength-based supervision supports effective family social work practice, evaluating supervision, and the development of evidence informed supervision policy and practices.

Part VII: Emerging areas

In the final part there are four chapters which describe emerging areas for social work supervision practice. The emerging areas we have identified are arts-based methods in social work supervision, the service user's voice, and supervision and information and communications technology. The final chapter of the Handbook identifies a future research agenda for social work supervision following a review of the 115 research articles published between 1 January 2011 and 30 September 2020.

In conclusion, we are grateful to our contributors for working with us to achieve the goal of an international handbook of social work supervision. We have learned a lot from each of their contributions and have noted the common features of social work supervision as well as the variety and diversity of practices across cultures, settings, and countries. One of the strengths of this Handbook is the diversity of perspectives, experiences, and views expressed about social work supervision and how to practice it. Finally, in editing the Handbook we were mindful of Munson's (2004, p. 94) comments regarding the challenges facing supervision in the 21st century, being for supervisors to find "a balance between the general and specific in practice to achieve the best possible outcomes for clients," and to develop new models that pass on the values, knowledge, and skills of the profession and relay "a sense of social work's heritage" to the next generation of practitioners and supervisors. It is our hope that in this book you will find a new supervision that has grown out of the old, or new wine from old wineskins.

References

Barretta-Herman, A., 1994. On the development of a model of supervision for licensed social work practitioners. *The Clinical Supervisor*, 11 (2), 55–64. doi:10.1300/J001v11n02_05.

Beddoe, L., 2010. Surveillance or reflection: professional supervision in 'the risk society'. *British Journal of Social Work*, 40 (4), 1279–1296.

Bradley, G., Engelbrecht, L.K., and Höjer, S., 2010. Supervision: a force for change? Three stories told. *International Social Work*, 53 (6), 773–790. doi:10.1177/0020872809358401.

Bradley, G., and Höjer, S., 2009. Supervision reviewed: reflections on two different social work models in England and Sweden. *European Journal of Social Work*, 12 (1), 71–85. doi:10.1080/13691450802220990.

Brown, A., and Bourne, I., 1996. *The social work supervisor: supervision in community, day care, and residential settings*. Buckingham: Open University Press.

Carpenter, J., Webb, C.M., and Bostock, L., 2013. The surprisingly weak evidence base for supervision: findings from a systematic review of research in child welfare practice (2000–2012). *Children and Youth Services Review,* 35 (11), 1843–1853. doi:10.1016/j.childyouth.2013.08.014.

Chernesky, R., 1986. A new model of supervision. *In*: N. Van Den Bergh and L. Cooper, eds. *Feminist visions for social work*. Silver Spring, MD: NASW Press, 128–48.

Engelbrecht, L.K., 2006. Cultural friendliness as a foundation for the support function in the supervision of social work students in South Africa. *International Social Work*, 49 (2), 256–266.

Engelbrecht, L.K., 2010. Yesterday, today and tomorrow: is social work supervision in South Africa keeping up? *Social Work/Maatskaplike Werk*, 46 (3), 224–242.

Engelbrecht, L.K., 2013. Social work supervision policies and frameworks: playing notes or making music? *Social Work/Maatskaplike Werk*, 49 (4), 456–468.

Engelbrecht, L.K., 2015. Revisiting the esoteric question: can non-social workers manage and supervise social workers? *Social Work/Maatskaplike Werk*, 51 (3), 311–331.

Erera, I.P., and Lazar, A., 1995. The administrative and educational functions in supervision: indications of incompatibility. *The Clinical Supervisor*, 12 (2), 39–56. doi:10.1300/J001v12n02_04.

Gibelman, M., and P.H. Schervish, 1998. Supervision in social work: characteristics and trends in a changing environment. *The Clinical Supervisor*, 16 (2), 1–15. doi:10.1300/J001v16n02_01.

Gray, S.W., 1990. The interplay of social work licensure and supervision. *The Clinical Supervisor*, 8 (1), 53–65. doi:10.1300/J001v08n01_05.

Hair, H.J., and O'Donoghue, K., 2009. Culturally relevant, socially just social work supervision: becoming visible through a social constructionist lens. *Journal of Ethnic and Cultural Diversity in Social Work*, 18 (1/2), 70–88. doi:10.1080/15313200902874979.

Harkness, D., and Hensley, H., 1991. Changing the focus of social work supervision: effects on client satisfaction and generalized contentment. *Social Work*, 37, 506–12.

Himle, D.P., Jayaratne, S., and Thyness, P.A., 1989. The buffering effects of four types of supervisory support on work stress. *Administration in Social Work*, 13 (1), 19–34.

Hipp, J., and Munson, C., 1995. The partnership model: a feminist supervision/consultation perspective. *The Clinical Supervisor*, 13 (1), 23–38.

Kadushin, A., 1974. Supervisor-supervisee: a survey. *Social Work*, 19 (3), 288–298.

Kadushin, A., 1976. *Supervision in social work*. New York: Columbia University Press.

Kadushin, A., 1985. *Supervision in social work*. 2nd ed. New York: Columbia University Press.

Kadushin, A., 1992. *Supervision in social work*. 3rd ed. New York: University of Columbia Press.

Kaiser, T.L., 1997. *Supervisory relationships: exploring the human element*. Pacific Grove, CA: Brooks/Cole.

Matheson, J., 1999. *The process of social work supervision: women's perspectives.* Dissertation (PhD), University of Calgary.

Morrison, T., 1993. *Staff supervision in social care: an action learning approach.* Harlow: Longman.

Munson, C., 1975. *The uses of structural, authority and teaching models in social work supervision.* Dissertation (DSW), University of Maryland.

Munson, C., 1979a. An empirical study of structure and authority in social work supervision. *In*: C. Munson, ed. *Social work supervision: classic statements and critical issues.* New York: Free Press, 286–296.

Munson, C., ed., 1979b. *Social work supervision: classic statements and critical issues.* New York: Free Press.

Munson, C., 1983. *An introduction to clinical social work supervision.* New York: Haworth Press.

Munson, C., 1993. *Clinical social work supervision.* 2nd ed. New York: Haworth Press.

Munson, C., 2004. The evolution of protocol-based supervisory practice. *In*: M. Austin and K. Hopkins, eds. *Supervision as collaboration in the human services: building a learning culture.* Thousand Oaks, CA: SAGE, 85–96.

O'Donoghue, K., 1998. *Supervising social workers.* Palmerston North: School of Policy Studies and Social Work, Massey University.

O'Donoghue, K., 2001. Surfing the world wide web and social work practice in Aotearoa New Zealand. *Social Work Review*, 13 (2), 43–48.

O'Donoghue, K., 2003. *Restorying social work supervision.* Palmerston North: Dunmore Press.

O'Donoghue, K., 2004. Social workers and cross-disciplinary supervision. *Social Work Review*, 16 (3), 2–7.

O'Donoghue, K., 2015. Issues and challenges facing social work supervision in the twenty-first century. *China Journal of Social Work*, 8 (2), 136 149. doi:10.1080/17525098.2015.1039172

O'Donoghue, K., and Tsui, M.S., 2012. Towards a professional supervision culture: the development of social work supervision in Aotearoa New Zealand. *International Social Work*, 55 (1), 5–28. doi: 10.1177/0020872810396109

O'Donoghue, K., and Tsui, M.S., 2015. Social work supervision research (1970–2010): the way we were and the way ahead. *British Journal of Social Work*, 45 (2), 616–633. doi:10.1093/bjsw/bct115

Payne, M., 1994. Personal supervision in social work. *In*: A. O'Connor, and S. Black, eds. *Performance review and quality in social care*, London: Jessica Kingsley Publishers, 43–58.

Rabinowitz, J., 1987. Why ongoing supervision in social casework. *The Clinical Supervisor*, 5 (3), 79–90. doi:10.1300/J001v05n03_07.

Rauktis, M.E., and Koseske, G.F., 1994. Maintaining social worker morale: when supportive supervision is not enough. *Administration in Social Work*, 18 (1), 39–60.

Rees, S., 1999. Managerialism in social welfare: proposals for a humanitarian alternative-an australian perspective. *European Journal of Social Work*, 2 (2), 193–202.

Robinson, V., 1936. *Supervision in social casework.* Chapel Hill, NC: University of North Carolina Press.

Sewell, K.M., 2018. Social work supervision of staff: a primer and scoping review (2013–2017). *Clinical Social Work Journal*, 46 (4), 252–265. doi:10.1007/s10615-018-0679-0.

Shulman, L., 1982. *Skills of supervision and staff management.* Itasca, IL: F. E. Peacock.

Shulman, L., 1993. *Interactional supervision.* Washington, DC: NASW Press.

Shulman, L., 2010. *Interactional supervision.* 3rd ed. Washington, DC: NASW Press.

Shulman, L., Robinson, E., and Luckj, A., 1981. *A study of the content, context and skills of supervision.* Vancouver, BC: University of British Columbia.

Tsui, M.S., 1997. The roots of social work supervision. *The Clinical Supervisor*, 15 (2), 191–198. doi:10.1300/J001v15n02_14.

Tsui, M.S., and Ho W.S., 1997. In search of a comprehensive model of social work supervision. *The Clinical Supervisor*, 16 (2), 181–204.

PART I

International perspectives

1

DEVELOPING REFLECTIVE MODELS OF SUPERVISION

The role of the United Kingdom professional association

Godfred Boahen, Luke Geoghegan, and Alistair Brown

This chapter explores models of supervision adopted by members of the British Association of Social Workers (BASW) in response to the "triumph of managerialism" in UK supervision. It starts with a discussion of the role of professional associations, positioning peer-to-peer reflection, and supervision as one element of their knowledge generation functions. This contextualizes an exploration of the changing nature of supervision in the UK. It is argued that the development of "UK Supervision Policy" (BASW 2011) and member-led communities of practice (Wenger 1998) for peer-led and group supervision were responses to the dominance of managerialist approaches in the UK. Attention will be paid to the role of supervision in human rights-based practice. While most of the literature on supervision addresses concerns about the *frequency*, *quality*, and *effectiveness* of supervision (Wilkins et al. 2018), there is a gap about how social work professional associations – custodians of professional identity (Boahen and Wiles 2018) – can provide alternative models to performance and risk management.

Professional associations: Knowledge generation and reflective practice

While there is a consensus that globally, social work supervision has taken a managerialist, performance management turn (Engelbrecht 2013, Tsui 1997) which is not always desirable, the role of professional associations in providing reflective models remains unexplored. O'Donoghue et al. (2006) and O'Donoghue et al. (2005) respectively surveyed members of the Aotearoa New Zealand Association of Social Workers for their experiences of supervision. In the former study, it was noted that one of the "best things" about supervision, according to survey respondents was "interactional processes (e.g. 'being listened to,' 'working with the whole person,' providing 'perspective, guidance and clarification'), receiving feedback, and a strengths-based process." (O'Donoghue et al. 2006, p. 83). Taken from the perspectives of employees of the British Association of Social Workers (BASW), this chapter extends this latter finding, and explores how member-led interactional processes *within* the professional association provides reflective supervision.

Professional associations are collectives of people with shared expertise who organize to represent their mutual interests. One of these is supervision, which is necessary for effective practice and social workers' wellbeing (Wilkins 2019). Professional associations are linked to professionalization, whereby occupational groups are formed through the activities of individuals who lay claim to their unique specialities, or for their political recognition as legitimate representatives of them (Freidson 2001). The fluidity of processes of professionalization has been recognized since the post war period – "professional does not earn his status once and for all. Rather, it is a continuous process in which his [sic] claims to competence are being tested every day in interaction with others and he can lose the respect of others." (Bucher and Stelling 1969, p. 4). This highlights the role of members in maintaining their professional standards through their interactions, drawing attention to the role of supervision.

Freidson (1994, 2001) suggested that professional associations can engender (high) quality standards in the delivery of public services. This arises from their own self-interest. In order to lay claim to specialization and hence foreground their legitimacy, associations must ensure that their members are skilled. This can be achieved through formal and informal avenues – for instance through dissemination of literature and through their networking and physical interaction, knowledge can be exchanged (Carter and Mahallati 2019). Seeing themselves as custodians of professional standards, associations may consult their members to determine practice benchmarks, communicate these (internally and externally), and provide training or continuous professional development.

In the UK, BASW (The British Association of Social Workers) is the professional association of social workers and currently has some 20,000 members. There are national offices in Scotland, Wales, and Northern Ireland. Members provide formal and informal supervision through their interactional processes, and they seek to represent the professional status of social work.

In the literature it is posited that professional associations desire professional status, however how this is achieved reflects how power is exercised over them. Evetts (2003) distinguishes between organizational and occupational professionalism. In the former, professionalization is initiated or imposed by external and powerful actors – for instance governments or regulators – to "control" the profession and set (high) standards. This can entail central regulations about training standards and supervision. As an example, in England (General Social Care Council 2004) the social work regulator stipulated that employers had to provide supervision to staff, and employees were obliged to participate. More desirably, occupational professionalism can arise from a quest by group members to improve professional standards. In the latter framework, it is members of the occupational group that establish the standards, and this implies more democratic ownership and accountability by the members over the process of professionalization. Historically, BASW has experienced the two models of professionalization discussed here.

BASW was formed following the amalgamation in 1970 of professional associations which represented discrete areas of social work practice. The impetus for merger was the 1970 Local Authority Social Services Act (LASSA), which established generic social work practice in England under Social Services Departments. The legislation was a move by central government to improve professional standards through increased regulation and the elevation of the status of social work as a profession (Harris 1970). Throughout its history, BASW has responded to such policy initiatives through its own programs for professionalization. These have included development of practice standards, such as a Code of Ethics (BASW 2018), Professional Capabilities Framework (BASW 2018), and practice frameworks for autism and learning disability (BASW 2019, a, b). Historically, BASW has demonstrated another function of professional associations – communities of practice – as forums for peer-led and informal supervision.

Professional associations and supervision: communities of practice

Professional associations can also promote knowledge generation through their activities as communities of practice – "…groups of people who share a concern, a set of problems, or a passion about a topic, and who deepen their knowledge and expertise in this area by interacting on an on-going basis" (Wenger et al. 2002, p. 4). Situated within a social learning perspective, the concept of communities of practice (CoP) proposes that individuals within a group gain knowledge and expertise from meaning making through their interactions. Wenger (1998) suggested that interactions, engagement, and participation of members within the group lead to the creation (and negotiation) of explicit knowledge and development of a tacit understanding and shared world view. Through "engagement in action, interpersonal relations, shared knowledge, and negotiation of enterprises, such communities hold the keys to real transformation" (Wenger 1998, p. 85). Due to the emphasis on collective learning and knowledge transmission (Jagasia et al. 2015), models of CoPs are widely adopted in social work, for instance in reflection (Staempfli et al. 2016) and in virtual communities of practice (Adedoyin 2016). The theoretical framework can also explain the work of professional associations that seek to enhance the knowledge of their members, for example, through the development of practice standards and other forms of learning such as supervision (Weller 2017). Within BASW these communities of practice exist in several forms. There are member-led Special Interest Groups; Policy, Practice and Education Groups; or groups that meet to reflect and provide peer-to-peer supervision. It is argued that the communities of practice on supervision have developed in response to the UK policy context of managerialism – in the face of this, members meet to provide each other with the reflective supervision that they desire but which is not provided by their employers. This thesis is developed further in the next section through an exploration of the history of supervision in the UK.

Supervision in UK social work: Historical overview of models

In the UK, the practice of supervision has been shaped by the policy, organizational, and practice contents, exemplifying global developments (O'Donoghue and Tsui 2012). Following Tsui (1997), we argue that there are historically distinct models of supervision in the UK: the case-work / psychoanalytic period from post-war to the late 1970s–80s; the rise of managerialism (1980s–2000); and the "the triumph of managerialism" (2000–present). These periods are not neatly delineable – for example, psychoanalytic models of supervision are still in use in some settings (Bower 2005). However, being dominant models at the time, they shaped social workers' experiences of supervision.

Social work is a registered profession in the UK, meaning that to practice, a formal social work qualification and registration with a national regulator is required (Bamford 2015). Often described as "statutory," it involves managing conflicts *between* competing human rights (Harms-Smith et al. 2019), needs-led resource allocation, and making fine ethical judgements (Banks 2008). Accordingly, supervision is not simply an optional dialogue between social workers but must often address life-changing issues. Historically, different models have been dominant, starting with the case work approach, which is discussed next.

The case-work and psychoanalytic period

From the post-war period until the 1970s / 80s, case work and psychoanalytic models dominated social work practice. Key influences were (Perlman 1957), (Biestek 1957), and (Rogers 1951). The focus on individuals was complemented by groupwork (Bion 1961), and these also influenced the nature of supervision. However, psychoanalytic models came under increasing criticism. First, there was a change to the organizational context of supervision. The Seebohm report in England and its corollary in Scotland, the Kilbrandon Report of 1964 (Turbett 2018), resulted in the creation of Social Services Departments delivering generic social work through local authorities. Social work also moved away from a series of specialisms delivered from different agencies to a generic profession working from one agency (Bamford 2015). These developments undermined clinical social work undertaken in psychoanalytic settings and with this, models of psychoanalytic supervision. Alongside this, the case work approach was increasingly criticized by academics. In "The Client Speaks," Mayer and Timms (1970) noted the lack of client involvement in casework approaches. Brake and Bailey (1980) also argued that social work should seek to change social structures to make them more equitable instead of assisting people to adapt to them. The casework / psychoanalytic model was undermined and with it, psychoanalytic models of supervision, with the discussion shifting from the need for individual change to the need for structural societal change.

One response to this polarization between case work / psychoanalytic models and radical models was the partial emergence of a pragmatic middle ground for example (Pincus and Minahan 1973). However, these models were soon swept away by the new model of managerialism.

The rise and triumph of managerialism

From the 1980s, UK social work practice was increasingly defined by child abuse scandals and sustained criticism of the profession (Parton 1985). In the "Cleveland Crisis" in 1987, large numbers of children were removed for reasons of sexual abuse – only for the allegations to be subsequently overturned. These scandals occurred at a time of debates about the quality and quantity of public services. While this reflected neo-liberal desires to scale back the role of the state, there were also legitimate concerns about poor professional practice (Dickens 2016). A result was "New Public Management" which emphasized performance and risk management.

Since the late 1990s in the UK, policy has emphasized supervision as "social workers' rights" (Godden 2011), however this is underpinned by managerialism. Reflecting developments in other Anglo-Saxon countries, performance management has become the central purpose of supervision (O'Donoghue and Tsui 2012) alongside a quest to increase social work practice standards. This has included the creation of a regulator for social work, the General Social Care Council, and stipulation of a university degree as the minimum qualification standard for social work. The agenda has also included emphasis on supervision as an "administrative function" within a managerialist framework (Tsui 1997).

However, a positive by-product of this managerialist orientation from the 2000s onwards was the establishment of the consensus that supervision was indispensable to safe practice. For instance, employers of social workers were required to have policies and procedures for "Effectively managing and supervising staff to support effective practice and good conduct and supporting staff to address deficiencies in their performance" (General Social Care Council 2004, p. 6). Within this regulatory context, supervision was intrinsic to "good" social work performance. Against this background, the death of another child, Peter Connelly, in 2007 reignited the debate about poor social work practice. This resulted in policy initiatives to embed supervision into practice but largely underpinned by performance management rather than solutions to the complex emotional impact of child protection practice on social workers (Warner 2015).

BASW developed its Supervision Policy (BASW 2011) in response to this turbulent political context. The Policy set out the purposes and definition of supervision, contextualizing it as a prerequisite for high standards to fulfil needs and human rights of people using services (BASW, 2011). The Policy aimed to highlight the wider contextual issues that affected social workers' performance, such as high workload, lack of services, and de-professionalization, thus moving the debate beyond the focus on individual professional skills. The policy proposed a *normative model* that social workers should demand from their employers and what should be provided. Internally, BASW members increasingly practiced their desired model of supervision within a framework of communities of practice, focused on their emotional wellbeing. This contrasted with the managerialist and administrative approaches that they experienced in their employment settings.

Communities of practice and supervision within BASW

This section describes a three-stage model adopted by some members of BASW for peer-to-peer reflective supervision. The first stage is a reflection by members to understand their learning styles (Honey and Mumford 1992), the second purposively focuses on addressing the emotional demands of their role and their psychological wellbeing based on the work of Proctor (2000). The third is the use of action learning sets (Ravens 1998).

It is recognized that social work practice can be stressful, and this must be addressed within supervision. Beddoe et al. (2014) argued that work stress, burnout, and vicarious trauma contribute to high staff turnover, "compassion fatigue," and "compassion satisfaction" which affect social workers' motivation and relationships with people needing services. These emotions can adversely affect psychological wellbeing and decision-making if unaddressed (Boahen and Wiles 2018). Consequently during reflective supervision within their communities of practice, BASW members' reflection seeks to address these issues.

The overarching framework for the model is communities of practice. Although it may require a facilitator, overall the underpinning ethos is mutual learning through individual reflection within a group context. Within these settings, the emphasis is on social workers learning from sharing their experiences with colleagues instead of primarily being concerned with accountability for their practice decisions. The attention to learning provides a safe space for people to engage and explore situations which may not necessarily have led to a desired outcome but nevertheless provide learning opportunities.

This model has been adopted by some BASW members because it engenders reflective supervision and thus contrasts sharply with the managerialist approaches, which currently dominate in social work and are concerned with performance appraisal and risk management. BASW members report that unlike the supervision provided by their employers, this three-stage model described here enables them to identify and address the emotional dimensions of their work and, in the process, provide them with a powerful toolkit of self-management methods to maintain their psychological wellbeing. In order to derive the maximum benefit from these models, members are encouraged, as a starting point, to understand their learning styles, drawing on the work of Honey and Mumford (1982).

Stage 1: Member self-reflection on learning styles

Honey and Mumford (1982) proposed that there are four distinct adult learning styles which should match the learning activity for effectiveness. According to Honey and Mumford, adults fall into four categories of learning types:

1. Activists – learn by doing and therefore find experiential approaches more beneficial.
2. Reflectors – learn by observing and thinking about their experiences. These individuals therefore like to listen and take their time to explore issues in-depth.
3. Theorists – are more interested in understanding the concepts and theories that underpin phenomena.
4. Pragmatists – are mainly problem solvers and are keen to experiment with ideas with the most efficient ways of addressing the issues at hand.

BASW members using this approach have reported that this stage enables them to understand their learning styles and, in the process, they are empowered to identify the learning opportunities that they will gain most from within the reflective supervision model. The next stage of the process is for members to reflect on the purpose of supervision: by exploring models different to the dominant managerialist approaches, members can envisage and thereby explore alternatives underpinned by reflection.

Stage 2: Reflecting on the purpose of supervision

This stage draws on the work of Brigid Proctor, which is well-known in counseling and increasingly applied in social work.

Proctor (2000) proposed that there are three main functions of supervision:

- Formative – sharing knowledge, skills, and experience leading to problem solving
- Restorative – offering support for morale and confidence as well as personal development
- Normative – providing a structure for practice and everyday working

The noteworthy point about this model is that the three functions are interactional. It has been suggested that the formative aspect of supervision is about the need for the supervisee to acquire new knowledge and skills, and the restorative is about the supervisor addressing the impact of work on the supervisees' wellbeing. The final part of the model refers to the "managerial" purpose of supervision, whereby supervisors address the "compliance with agency and organisational procedures and professional standards for the well-being of clients." Proctor argued that both supervisee and supervisor have responsibility for the success of their supervisory relationship:

> Both [supervisor and supervisee] carry some degree of responsibility for the development of the student or worker (the formative task). Both carry some share of the responsibility for the ongoing monitoring and evaluating of the student or worker and at certain times – at the end of the course or the point of promotion, for instance – either may carry responsibility for assessment (the normative task). Each carries a share of the responsibility for ensuring that the student or worker is adequately refreshed and re-creative (the restorative function).
>
> *(Proctor 1987; cited in Sloan and Watson, 2002, p. 41)*

As well as its usefulness during the group reflection within the communities of practice, the model described above can be drawn upon by BASW members in their discussions with their managers about their *expectations* of how supervision should be conducted.

At this stage, some BASW members also adopt the six-category intervention analysis (Heron 1975) developed within nursing but widely used in social work. First proposed as a model for understanding interpersonal relationships, this is now applied in supervision to conceptualize the relationship dynamic between the supervisee and supervisor. Heron separates supervision functions into two main types, authoritative and facilitative, and each has its sub-categories.

Heron suggested that the authoritative category includes:

- Prescriptive interventions – for example, advising and directing the supervisee
- Informative interventions – for example, instructing and guiding the supervisee
- Confronting interventions – for example, challenging behaviors and/or attitudes which are counter to social work practice and conduct

Under a facilitative approach, the supervisee retains more control and power in the supervision relationship as a way of encouraging self-reflection, professional discretion, and autonomy. The sub-categories of this type are:

- Cathartic – this allows the supervisee to express troubling thoughts, ethical conflicts, or vicarious traumatization processes arising from their work.
- Catalytic interventions – through reflection processes, social workers are encouraged to think of important areas of practice, thus enabling their self-development and self-reflection.
- Supportive processes – these help build confidence and focus on competence and the social worker's positive qualities.

While Heron did not prioritize either the facilitative or authoritative approaches, BASW members who practice six-category analysis of supervision appear to prefer the former. This may be because it is less hierarchical and is similar to processes of reflection familiar to most social workers. However, another advantage is that in these times of reduced capacity, social workers can draw on their emotional skills, for mutual support. This also allows for the safety that comes from peer-to-peer contact and without a manager or expert facilitator.

Stage 3: Action learning sets

Created by Professor Reg Revans, action learning is based on the principle that people learn by doing. Revans (1998) argued that there is no learning without action and that adults acquire most knowledge when they are directly involved in their own learning about a current life situation. The key feature of this model is that learning occurs when people are involved in "real life" situations, often in a group in which they have the opportunity for mutual exchange of learning. Adults who voluntarily choose a learning experience usually gain more readily, and applying this in the workplace makes it more personally meaningful and of greater benefit to the organization.

Action Learning Sets involve five components:

- The individual – this individual voluntarily joins the group with the view to learning and contributing to the process.
- The set – this comprises a group of four to eight people who meet regularly having agreed their ground rules and ways of working.
- The issue or task – each member identifies a practice issue important to them that they want to address within the group.
- The processes of questioning, reflection, and learning – this is about how each member of the group presents their issues for discussion; how the group clarifies and questions to

understand the nature of the problem; and sometimes challenging the member to identify creative solutions. This element is also about how the group support each other and agree action points and their method for providing feedback about successes.

- The facilitator – this person assists the group to agree its processes, assists with group reflection and problem solving, and facilitates with group cohesion.

During the group's formation, BASW members agree "ground rules" or a "group contract." This may be written on a whiteboard or flipchart and cover confidentiality and the need for a non-judgmental ethos by all members. Psychologically and emotionally, members position themselves appropriately to engage with the discussions within the group rather than simply seek solutions to problems encountered at work.

The action learning sets themselves usually start with a member presenting the key points of the issues that they want the group to discuss. Each person then offers their initial reflective solution and the presenter recaps and summarizes the learning gained from their colleagues' reflections. As mutual learning is central to the action learning set, the focus throughout is on how each member has benefitted from the processes of presentation and reflection. Another aim is for group members to focus on emotional processing, as described above. It is important that the facilitator assists the group to create a culture and ethos of reflection, thereby resisting the urge to default to the prevailing task-centred and managerialist models of supervision. Furthermore, the group should be mindful of power (im)balances between them – groups turn to reflect prevailing structural issues – and members who are less confident of speaking in public should be supported to share their thoughts.

Overall, the three stages of peer-led and group supervision show that within the context of a professional association where members can seek learning and mutual support to address the emotional demands of social work, reflection and mutual learning are preferred over managerialist models of supervision. While not providing evidence of impact, this first-hand account is therefore a useful addition to the literature on supervision which to date has not fully addressed the role of professional associations in providing alternative frameworks to contemporary dominant supervision approaches.

Conclusion

There is a consensus that supervision is desirable, however prevailing evidence of benefits is sparse (Wilkins 2019). Notwithstanding this, there is general opposition to dominant administrative and performance management approaches and a preference for reflection in supervision (Rankine 2017). However, while professional associations act as communities of practice that can support reflection and learning, their role in reflective supervision is unexplored in the literature. This chapter has addressed this gap by explaining how BASW members engage in a three-stage model of reflective supervision within the context of the professional association. The argument has been based on a discussion of the historical development of supervision models in the UK. It has been shown that from the late 1980s to present, managerialist approaches to supervision became policy prescriptions in the UK, ostensibly to increase accountability and performance levels. Against this background, BASW members asked for development of a supervision policy based on reflection, supervision as social workers' "right," and a concomitant responsibility on employers to provide them. Alongside this, some BASW members used the "safe space" of their interactions to practise supervision as they desire but do not receive at work. These are also part of a campaign for better working conditions in social work. Nonetheless there are ongoing challenges. First, the models of collective and reflective practice are not universally practiced by all members, therefore access is an issue. Second, accountability and performance management may have been over-emphasized in the managerialist models of supervision but that does not mean they are not legitimate elements of the supervision process. The risk is that a model evolves where reflective group supervision among professionals sits separately from the models of performance and accountability practiced among employers. However, it is difficult to avoid the conclusion that if supervision was practiced in a way that addressed emotional support and fostered individual and collective learning, this could not but have a positive impact on social work sickness levels and vacancy rates. In this sense, effective appropriate supervision could be an entirely practical action for even for the most "managerialist" of managers.

References

Adedoyin, A.C., 2016. Deploying virtual communities of practice as a digital tool in social work: a rapid review and critique of the literature. *Social Work Education*, 35 (3), 357–370.

Bailey, R. and Brake, M., 1980. *Radical social work and practice*. London: Edward Arnold.

Bamford, T., 2015. *A contemporary history of social work: learning from the past*. Bristol: Policy Press.

Banks, S., 2008. Critical commentary: social work ethics. *British Journal of Social Work*, 8 (6), 1238–1249.

Beddoe, L., Davys, A.M., and Adamson, C., 2014. Never trust anybody who says "I don't need supervision"': practitioners' beliefs about social worker resilience. *Practice*, 26 (2), 113–130.

Biestek, F., 1957. *The casework relationship*. Chicago, IL: Loyola University Press.

Bion, W.R., 1961. *Experiences in groups, and other papers*. New York: Basic Books.

Boahen, G., and Wiles, F., 2018. *Professionalism and self-management*. London: McGraw-Hill Education.

Bower, M., ed., 2005. *Psychoanalytic theory for social work practice: thinking under fire*. London: Routledge.

British Association of Social Workers, 2011. *UK supervision policy*. Available from: https://www.basw.co.uk/system/files/resources/basw:73346-6_0.pdf [Accessed 6 April 2020].

British Association of Social Workers, 2018. *Professional capabilities framework*. Available from: https://www.basw.co.uk/system/files/resources/PCF%20CHART%20update%2011-7-18.pdf [Accessed 24 August 2019].

British Association of Social Workers, 2018. *Professional capability framework – social work level capabilities*. Available from: https://www.basw.co.uk/pcf/PCF05SocialWorkLevelCapabilities.pdf [Accessed 10 January 2018].

British Association of Social Workers, 2019. *Capabilities statement for social work with adults who have learning disabilities*. Available from: https://www.basw.co.uk/capabilities-social-work-adults-who-have-learning-disability [Accessed 7 April 2020].

British Association of Social Workers, 2019. *Capabilities statement for social work with autistic adults*. Available from: https://www.basw.co.uk/capabilities-statement-social-work-autistic-adults [Accessed 7 April 2020].

Bucher, R., and Stelling, J., 1969. Characteristics of professional organizations. *Journal of Health and Social Behavior*, 10 (1), 3–15.

Carter, D.P., and Mahallati, N., 2019. Coordinating intermediaries: the prospects and limitations of professional associations in decentralized regulation. *Regulation & Governance*, 13 (1), 51–69.

Dickens, J., 2016. *Social work and social policy: an introduction*. 2nd ed. London: Routledge.

Engelbrecht, L., 2013. Social work supervision policies and frameworks: playing notes or making music? *Social Work/Maatskaplike Werk*, 49 (4), 456–468.

Evetts, J., 2003. The sociological analysis of professionalism: occupational change in the modern world. *International Sociology*, 18 (2), 395–415.

Freidson, E., 1994. *Professionalism reborn: theory, prophecy and policy*. Cambridge: Polity.

Freidson, E., 2001. *Professionalism, the third logic*. Chicago, IL: University of Chicago Press.

General Social Care Council, 2004. *Code of practice for social care workers and code of practice for employers of social care workers*. Available from: https://www.whatdotheyknow.com/request/104671/response/253327/attach/4/Codes%20of%20Practice%20GSCC.pdf [Accessed 30 January 2020].

Godden, J., 2011. *BASW/CoSW England research on supervision in social work, with particular reference to supervision practice in multi-disciplinary teams*. Available from: https://www.basw.co.uk/system/files/resources/basw:13955-1_0.pdf [Accessed 30 January 2020].

Harms-Smith, L., Martinez-Herrero, M., Arnell, P., et al., 2019. *Social work and human rights: a practice guide.* Birmingham: BASW.

Harris, J., 1970. Local authority social services act 1970. *The Modern Law Review*, 33 (5), 530–534.

Heron, J., 1975. *Six category intervention analysis.* Guildford: University of Surrey.

Honey, P., and Mumford, A., 1992. *The manual of learning styles.* 3rd ed. Maidenhead: Peter Honey.

Jagasia, J., Baul, U., and Mallik, D., 2015. A framework for communities of practice in learning organizations. *Business Perspectives and Research*, 3 (1), 1–20.

Mayer, J.E., and Timms, N., 1970. *The client speaks: working class impressions of casework.* London: Routledge & Kegan Paul.

O'Donoghue, K., Munford, R., and Trlin, A., 2005. Mapping the territory: supervision within the association. *Social Work Review*, 17 (4), 46–64.

O'Donoghue, K., Munford, R., and Trlin, A., 2006. What's best about social work supervision according to association members. *Social Work Review*, 18 (3), 79–91.

O'Donoghue, K., and Tsui, M., 2012. Towards a professional supervision culture: the development of social work supervision in Aotearoa New Zealand. *International Social Work*, 55 (1), 5–28.

Parton, N., 1985. *The politics of child abuse.* London: Macmillan.

Payne, M., 2002. The role and achievements of a professional association in the late twentieth century: British Association of Social Workers 1970–2000. *British Journal of Social Work*, 32 (8), 969–995.

Perlman, H.H., 1957. *Social casework: a problem-solving process*, Chicago, IL: University of Chicago Press.

Pincus, A., and Minahan, A., 1973. *Social work practice: model and method.* Itasca, IL: F. E. Peacock.

Proctor, B., 1987. Supervision: a co-operative exercise in accountability. *In:* M. Marken, and M. Payne, eds. *Enabling and ensuring: supervision in practice.* Leicester: National Bureau and Council for Education and Training in Youth and Community Work, 21–23.

Proctor, B., 2000. *Group supervision: a guide to creative practice.* London: SAGE.

Rankine, M., 2017. Making the connections: a practice model for reflective supervision. *Aotearoa New Zealand Social Work*, 29 (3), 66–78.

Revans, R.W., 1998. *ABC of action learning.* 3rd ed. London: Lemos and Crane.

Rogers, C.R., 1951. *Client-centered therapy: its current practice, implications and theory.* London: Constable.

Sloan, G., and Watson, H., 2002. Clinical supervision models for nursing: structure, research and limitations. *Nursing Standards*, 17 (4), 41–46.

Staempfli, A., Tov, E., Kunz, R., and Tschopp, D., 2016. Improving professionalism through reflection and discourse in communities of practice: the key situations in social work model and project. *Journal of Practice Teaching and Learning*, 14 (2), 59–79.

Tsui, M., 1997. The roots of social work supervision: an historical review. *The Clinical Supervisor*, 15 (2), 191–198.

Turbett, C., 2018. *Social work across the UK: legal and policy differences from a Scottish perspective.* Available from: https://www.basw.co.uk/system/files/resources/Acrobat%20Document.pdf [Accessed 6 April 2020].

Warner, J., 2015. *The emotional politics of child protection.* Bristol: Policy Press.

Weller, A., 2017. Professional associations as communities of practice: exploring the boundaries of ethics and compliance and corporate social responsibility. *Business and Society Review*, 122 (3), 359–392.

Wenger, E., 1998. *Communities of practice: learning, meaning.* Cambridge: Cambridge University Press.

Wenger, E., McDermott, R.A., and Snyder, W., 2002. *Cultivating communities of practice: a guide to managing knowledge.* Harvard Business Press.

Wilkins, D., 2019. Social work supervision in child and family services: developing a working theory of how and why it works. *Aotearoa New Zealand Social Work*, 31 (3) 7–19.

Wilkins, D., Khan, M., Stabler, L., Newlands, F., and Mcdonnell, J., 2018. Evaluating the quality of social work supervision in UK children's services: comparing self-report and independent observations. *Clinical Social Work Journal*, 46 (4), 350–360.

2

A GERMAN PERSPECTIVE ON SUPERVISION

Supervision between maintenance of, emancipation from, or abnegation of the origins of social work?

Stefan Busse

This chapter will look into the relationship between supervision and social work as it has developed in German-speaking countries following the Second World War. From a historical viewpoint, it will become clear that social work was the origin of supervision in Germany. Since its inception, supervision has moved away from its origin due to far-reaching horizontal and vertical expansions (Kühl 2006). Supervision is conceptually no longer solely implemented in social work, but rather in other professional fields as well. This development has been the subject of controversial and ambivalent commentary within the supervising community. It can be viewed as being caught in the tension between an expansion effort and self-limitation, as a progressive and at the same time endangered professionalization of supervision (Kühl 2006). One could even consider it to be a renouncement and abandonment of supervision's roots in social work (Gaertner 2004). Whatever the case may be, supervision has not been solely implemented in social work for a long time. Today it is a generalized counseling format for work environments and professionals and must share this claim with other formats, above all organizational counseling and coaching (see below). The situation is somewhat paradoxical: social work is the origin of supervision and still a central field for counseling, and at the same time, supervision has moved away from social work conceptually. Simultaneously, supervision and supervisors have been working through the central developmental contradictions in social work, which have been both hurdles and milestones, and continue to do so. Either way, social work and supervision are concerned at different levels with central questions of a social service oriented toward effectiveness and efficiency in the late-modern working world. This chapter will trace supervision's ties to and departure from its origin, social work. Current discussions about the future of supervision and its identity, the challenge posed by coaching, and strategic organizational development can only be understood against this backdrop (Busse 2009, DGSv 2011).

What exactly is a German perspective on supervision?

When the German perspective on supervision is referred to below, it refers mainly to the development of supervision in Germany following the Second World War. However, supervision in German-speaking countries will also be discussed because supervisors in Austria and Switzerland have provided important and essential stimulation to the field. Additionally, since Germany has been a reunified country since 1989, the relationship and dynamics between the former East Germany and West Germany resulting from the differing biographies and work histories of both supervision providers and clients must not be underestimated (Busse and Fellermann 1998, Busse and Tietel 2009). Furthermore, in the past 20 years, the German perspective has become integrated in European discussions within the Association of National Organisations for Supervision in Europe (ANSE) as part of the clarification of standards and of supervision's self-concept and quality. In this way, the German, Austrian, and Swiss perspectives may well have become increasingly European. Nevertheless, discourse around supervision in Germany and in German-speaking countries has been primarily a matter of a rather German discussion with occasional reference to international discourse since its inception following the end of the Second World War (Belardi 1994). This is at least the case for the community of practitioners and has also been noted in the research community (Schigl et al. 2020). This means that unique developments may have taken place within the supervision community in German-speaking countries, but parallel developments may have also occurred on an international scale. (Here there are interesting parallels but also clear differences to the developments in German-speaking countries which can be observed.)

Social work – Supervision's central counseling field

I will begin with an overview of the figures: for over a decade, at least a portion of the German supervision scene has spoken of a lower demand for supervision in the fields of social work, that supervision processes are becoming shorter, and that the available budgets are being reduced. Furthermore, there seems to be the impression that supervisors are leaving the field of social work one by one. Social work is fleeing supervision and conversely, supervisors are fleeing social work. In a study, Herbert Effinger traced this double flight (Effinger 2015, 2017). A representative survey of the approximately 4300 members of supervision's largest professional association, the German Association for Supervision and Coaching (*Deutsche Gesellschaft für Supervision und Coaching e. V.* – DGSv) (Effinger 2017, p. 10), did not confirm this impression. According to its results, it cannot be said that a double flight is occurring between social work and supervision. 88% of the survey participants stated that supervising assignments in the field of social work have remained stable or even increased. Only 10% of respondents reported that interest in supervision had decreased, while 70% reported stable interest and 19% reported an increase in interest (Effinger 2017, p. 9). A 2018 DGSv member survey about the job market for supervisors indicated that nearly half of the supervisors and coaches surveyed offered three quarters or more of their services in socially oriented fields (Brutzer de Palma 2019, p. 31). Three quarters (77.4%) of those surveyed conduct one quarter of their business in companies (Brutzer de Palma 2019). This means that a clear majority of supervisors attain a small portion of their work from outside the social economy. However, it is not clear whether they are providing supervision or coaching.

Overall, the results demonstrate supervisors' high level of engagement in social work as a classic counseling field (Drüge and Schneider 2015, Knaier 2017, Hamburger 2017). Social work and supervision still have a special relationship (Schorn 2017); this is surely related to the professional backgrounds of the organization's members. The current composition of the 4247 supervisors who were members of the DGSv as of 17 February 2020 has hardly changed over the course of the past ten years. The 2009 study reveals that 42% of members work in the field of social work, 23% in education, and about 15% in the field of psychology. Effinger's 2017 findings are nearly identical with 44% social workers, 25% educators, and 12% psychologists

(Effinger 2017, p. 10). This indicates that social work is still the primary occupational field for the supervisors organized in the DGSv. Similar membership proportions can be observed in the Swiss professional organization *Berufsverband für Coaching, Supervision und Organisationsberatung* (bso) and the Austrian association *Österreichische Vereinigung für Supervision und Coaching* (ÖVS) (Belardi 2015, p. 142). However, the fact that the majority of supervisors also now view themselves as coaches – there are 3012 coaches in the DGSv (DGSv 2017, p. 20) – indicates less a shift in the understanding of counseling than a change in the market strategy of supervisors and the DGSv's claim of being the largest professional organization for supervision and coaching in Germany. Accordingly, the DGSv has named itself the German Association for Supervision and Coaching. Nevertheless, according to the numbers, supervisors provide counseling primarily in the fields of social work. Several transformations have taken place since the beginning of German supervision following the Second World War and the development of its self-concept today as a counseling format for the working world. However, these transformations are not reflected in the numbers just reported about the counseling market.

Supervision's developmental phases, lines, and contradictions

At least three phases of supervision's development in Germany can be observed at a glance (Lohl 2019).

1. An *initial or constitutional phase*, which lasted mainly from the end of the Second World War until about the middle of the 1960s. It was strongly influenced by Dutch and North American social workers and supervisors. It can be said that they mentored the first generation of German supervisors, who promoted the following phase.
2. A *pioneer or dawning phase* in which the first generation of supervisors set the course for important conceptual, institutional, and occupational developments and shifted the focus from the original concept. This phase led to a quantitative expansion, consolidation of competence, and differentiation of supervisors. Finally, it resulted in the foundation of the first German professional organization for supervisors, the DGSv, in 1989.
3. A *professionalization or consolidation phase* which has spanned from the founding of the DGSv to today. Supervisors have to face the consequences of their own development and success and at the same time are confronted with fast social change among their clients and customers as well as with an expanding, competitive counseling market particularly in the field of consulting and coaching within organizations. This leads supervisors to critically question their own identity and ask, "What is supervision or what is a supervisory role?" (Weigand 2007).

This kind of division into developmental phases is helpful since it eases understanding and the reconstruction of history. However, phases like those outlined above also simplify the actual developments which took place. Contrary to this phase logic, there is also a logic of lines of development and contradictions, with which one can consider and describe certain problems, conflicts, and tasks the community of supervisors has addressed. This has been occurring across the phases. I will attempt to represent both logics accurately and demonstrate how they are interconnected.

Social work as the origin of supervision in Germany

The history of supervision is actually originally the history of social work (Wieringa 1990, p. 34). This describes the essence of American and German developments in the relationship between supervision and social work after the Second World War (Weigand 1989, Belardi 1992). Re-emigrated psychoanalysts, social workers, and social work educators from the United States and England were the fathers of this development in the 1950s and 1960s (e.g. Louis Lowy, Stenzel 2019). They were active in re-education programs for the citizens of West Germany following the Second World War.[1]

In that respect, supervision had an early connection to the democratization project in the Federal Republic of Germany. Dutch social workers and supervisors (e.g. Cora Baltussen, cf. Austermann 2019, or Cornelis F. Wieringa and Henk Foole) offered supervision as an exercise in methodical practice and as a reflection of helper-client-interaction in German vocational schools in the context of casework (individual support services) or group work. In this way supervision became a special form of teaching and conveying the practice of social work. It was a way of "case working the caseworker" (Huppertz 1975, p. 57). A reflective understanding of supervision only gradually developed through the differentiation of directing practice, advising practice, and reflecting on practice (Hege 2011, p. 60). The conceptual spectrum understood under the term supervision shifted at that time between the pragmatism of a distinct self-image of social workers, conceptual orientations toward group dynamics and psychoanalysis, and an early awareness of the organizational and societal context of social work and supervision (Leuschner and Weigand 2011, p. 42).

Early training institutes for social work and supervision brought forth the first generation of German supervisors. They became pioneers and were a driving force in the further institutionalization of supervision. They were also the protagonists of the difficult process of finding a platform for professional exchange and a common special interest group which finally led to the founding of the DGSv (Lippenmeier 2011, p. 12). A high level of gratitude and solidarity with the first generation and a desire to secure the early democratic roots of supervision still exist today (Lohl 2019[2]).

The origin changes as do the aspirations of supervision

Social work as the origin of supervision changed during the reform movement in the 1960s and hereafter took on a form paralleling that of a social welfare state. A welfare system has developed in which the social economy (Effinger 2018) has formed as a third sector between the state and the market. The basic philosophy of this system is subsidiarity. The state has legally established a right for individuals to receive help and guarantees aid through laws for social benefits. However, the provision of services is delegated to service providers which are more closely intertwined in the living environment of their clients. Service providers are professionally autonomous, but their services are state-controlled. Thus, social work exists in a legal triangle between state social services such as family services, service providers or private agencies, and the people who are eligible for benefits (von Schubert 1999, Pattar 2012). Social work or even the whole of care work is still being provided in this triadic structure. The so-called double mandate has become an important discourse figure for critical social work as influenced by the 1968 generation (Böhnisch and Lösch 1973). However, it not only mediates between two parties, society or the state and individuals, but a third professional mandate is also involved, comprizing a triple mandate (Staub-Bernasconi 2013). From this point reflection needs arise which go beyond practical instruction for methodical action and reflecting on practice.

This inevitably expanded supervision's horizon. In the context of a general politicization of society and the debate about German history during the student movement (the so-called '68 movement), supervision too was driven to question its own role as social work's role in society was being questioned. The demand to develop individual support services into an engaged dialog and its counterpart, case supervision, into an emancipatory understanding of a case was linked with criticism of individual support services in social work as individual introspection on matters of the soul (Althoff 2018). Supervision was considered by some, but not all, purveyors of social work to be a problematic chapter of social work that was thought to have more of a sedative effect as a magic potion of American origin keeping social workers in a marginal situation (Huppertz 1975). This was directed particularly at individual supervision (Ibid.) and was linked with a call to make supervision an instrument of emancipatory politicization.

The question that arose from this is still virulent today, namely, in the midst of the contradiction between emancipation and integration, can or should social work, or respectively supervision, be a wrench or oil in the works (Weigand 2011)? Separation from the American-influenced origins led to a connection to a critical professionalism, where German social work began to see itself. Supervision should have become a critical accompaniment to social work's professional self-control (Huppertz 1975). A critical-emancipatory claim was formed which clashed strongly with conservative bureaucratic practice (Blinkert and Huppertz 1974). This self-image still holds today in large parts of the community of supervisors; it includes the question of supervision having its own professional mandate. Still, it must be acknowledged today with some historical distance, that viewing supervision as an institution of critical self-reflection or a reflective supervision project (Gröning 2016) was not a uniformly shared understanding within the first pioneer generation (Lohl 2019). Nevertheless, a series of changes started from this point; these questions confront supervision repeatedly as central questions with specific themes, conflicts, and contradictions.

Leaving the field of origin and entering other fields

Despite the two-fold influence of American and then German social work on supervision, it has separated from social work as a primary or sole field of counseling. Although the two even appear to be seemingly best friends (to borrow the allusive title of the special issue of *Supervision*, Issue 2, from 2017), supervision has expanded to other professions and fields. This is true both for supervisors and supervisees.

The concept that supervision could be used in other professions and adjusted for use with other occupational groups or supervisees can be traced back to Louis Lowy (1983) (Stenzel 2019). Conceptual impulses from social group work, work with groups inspired by group dynamics, and group psychoanalysis flowed into team supervision in which social workers cooperated with other occupational groups.

Other professionals, such as psychotherapists and doctors, had already worked in parallel formats such as psychoanalytical control supervision and Balint groups. In this way, other professional groups, such as psychotherapists, educators, theologians, psychologists, and sociologists, entered the supervision market and made the social workers' new and prestigious field of work contestable. For that reason, resistance from the community of supervisors had to be overcome to allow non-social workers (above all psychologists) into the DGSv (Weigand 2012).[3]

With this two-sided vertical expansion of supervision (Kühl 2006) – admitting clients and service providers from outside social work and other professional groups to the organization – the DGSv was no longer an organization for social workers. This generalized orientation to professional and work fields (Gotthardt-Lorenz and Walther 1998) led to a critical limit, at which not only the field of social work was exceeded, but also the field of professionals and with that the non-profit sector. This accessibility for the for-profit sector was observed ambivalently as a fascination with money and a new field (Weigand 1993) and was viewed as a rocky road into other fields of work (Fürstenau 1995). Supervision was not only confronted with a different professional logic, but also with the logic of a different and contrary societal functional system. Thus, it was about the difficult or hopeless question, depending on the supervisor's standpoint, whether supervision was well-placed here (Diebäcker, 1995, Buchinger 1999). Confronted with its own emancipatory self-image, the central question of this development was not only regarding the relationship between counseling and field expertise, but also where the division between self-reflective and instrumental or strategic counseling lies (Leuschner and Diebäcker, 1995).

The departure from and return to social organizations

Breaking away from the American form of supervision involved, above all, giving up the model of administrative supervision. External supervision became a standard model in Germany and has become a standard offer in social services. The supervisor is neither a superior nor a direct member of the organization, but rather an autonomous contractor. This has significantly moved supervision's professionalization project forward. The integration of supervision into training programs for social workers in the form of practice reflection and casework teaching has been strongly relativized (Pühl 1994). It is still present today in various forms in social work programs at universities of applied sciences; however, it is marginalized as a protected area and has an extraterritorial niche existence (Geißler-Pilz 2017). Likewise, internal supervision is not connected to any managerial or superior role. Rather, it is connected to management through staff units in a partially autonomous way. Alongside internal offers by the organization, it serves the procurement and coordination of external supervisors (Becker 1994).

Further, the German translation of "supervision" to "mentorship" or "practical counseling" was intended to semantically relativize the supervisor's function as a superior and trainer. However, the misleading term "supervision" has become established in Germany and German-speaking countries (Belardi 2015).

The structural coupling between supervision and organizations or supervision's re-entry into social organizations is regulated by the so-called triangular contract between the contracting party, the supervisee, and the supervisor. This contract is an agreement among the involved parties regarding focus, framework, setting, and payment (Gröning 2016). An exact, detailed contract is considered the gold standard of professional supervision today (DGSv 2012). It is no coincidence that the triangular contract reflects the social policy triangle, in which supervision assumes the role of the service provider. In this case, supervision is no longer part of a social organization, but rather part of an institutional triad. With this departure from the organization of social work, the explicitly controlling aspect is settled and the reflective and innovative potential for social work is significantly strengthened by its re-entry (Weigand 1987a). The central question of how supervision should take on an important, triangulating role as an external third party and handle various tasks and expectations arose from this development (Busse and Tietel 2018).

The discovery of the organization and the encounter with organizational counseling

The confrontation with the organization was already at the top of the agenda in 1968 (Leuschner and Weigand 2011, p. 51). The organization became a dominating theme in the 1990s. Sources of complex reflection tasks in organizations included distress related to bureaucracy, reduced professional autonomy due to administrative restrictions, societal expectations of the normalization of those in need of help, increasingly limiting demands —also of an economic nature – on social organizations, experiencing bad or good leadership, and the limits of institutionalized help

(Buchinger 1997, Pühl 2000). Team supervision (Weigand 1994a), organizational counseling (Gotthard-Lorenz 1989) and organizational supervision (Gotthardt-Lorenz 2020), leadership counseling (Weigand 1994b), and complex counseling designs in which supervision is implemented alongside other formats are an expression of an extended and more complex understanding of supervision (Heltzel and Weigand 2012).

Not only facing the clients and turning their backs on organizations (Hege and Weigand 1997 p. 5) is an expression of an increased awareness of institutions and organizations in the supervising community. It has relativized the earlier global criticism of the institution and the organization and its fixation on the helper-client relationship in supervision. The conceptual framework is the understanding that supervision is always concerned with the triad of person, role, and institution (organization) (Weigand 1985, 1987b); the primary task of the organization is a fixed point of action in social work and thereby supervisory reflection. The primary orientation to the psychotherapeutic concepts of the so-called "psychoboom" in the 1970s also receives a type of sociological correction.

The horizon of supervisory knowledge expanded because the complexity of the purpose of supervision increased or, rather, because awareness of that complexity increased. Integrative concepts (Schreyögg 1991, Petzold 1998) and the reception of system-theoretical approaches have substantially contributed to this broadening perspective (Ebert 2001, Schiersmann and Thiele 2012). Classic psychotherapeutic formats also take organizational phenomena into view, for example as psychoanalysis of an organization (Lohmer and Möller 2014, Giernalczyk and Möller 2018). Although supervisors still define their identity against the backdrop of psychotherapeutic schools today, the question of what supervisors must know and be able to do is moving toward competence profiles which span across different schools of thought and integrate various methods (Judy and Knopf 2016, Busse and Jahn 2020). This development is still expanding in view of the social and professional contexts of organizations (see below).

Another question remains virulent with this broadened perspective: at whose table is supervision sitting in its role as the guest within an organization? Who should be served is a question that was already encountered at the origin of supervision. The relationship with the organization, above all in social work, was and still is ambivalent. Social work's general mistrust of organizations can be viewed as a misguided (one-sided) professionalization of the helper-client interaction (Gschosmann 2017). This hostility toward organizations then opposes or challenges the established triadic thinking of supervision. However, one should also take note of changes in social services, such as in the classic field of community services. The attempt here is to relate administrative and help logic in case work to one another and to pass on expectations to supervision (Hege 2011). The tendency in large social organizations such as family services is to view these as learning organizations and to seek organizational sources of success in social services (Busse and Ehlert 2017).

Not only is the organization a challenge for supervision, but so is the confrontation with organizational counseling. Due to a stronger awareness of the organization in social service organizations, organizational counseling has become established as a rival to supervision. It has entered the organization from the top and stems from the for-profit sector, having arisen in the course of the human relations movement and in the context of corporate consulting (von Ameln, Kramer and Stark 2009). This has caused the question of competition for authority and the markets of supervision and other formats to come into focus. The pragmatic and theoretical question of setting boundaries has resulted: isn't supervision always organizational development? But when is it organizational counseling? It has always applied in day-to-day counseling to keep the difference between reflexive counseling in and counseling of organizations in mind. That means clarifying, again and again, which format is suitable and what focus on the person, the role, the team, and the organization is appropriate. An almost Solomonic solution to that question is the idea that organizational counseling could function as a kind of supervision-oriented diplomatic negotiator of interests and perspectives of different stakeholders within an organization (Jahn and Nolten 2017). A more radical response is the concept of independent organizational supervision, which conceptualizes all professional and work-related action as organizational action (Gotthardt-Lorenz 2020). The question of setting boundaries between the two counseling formats holds yet another even more serious question about the relationship between profession and organization (Buer 2010). With that, we arrive at a basic conflict of social work: that organizations both threaten and secure professional helping action. This dilemma cannot really be solved. Supervision's central question of how it positions itself between humanity and functionality arises from that dilemma (Buer 2010).

The discovery of the global world of work and its need for reflection

The horizontal and vertical expansion of supervision, initiated in the 1990s, continued into the mid-2000s (Kühl 2006). It addresses global phenomena and consequences of structural change in the world of work. This extends beyond the professional and organizational orientation and expands the reflexive terrain (Hausinger 2008, Haubl, Hausinger and Voß 2013). The general sociological characteristics of the second modernist movement since the 1980s have become noticeable in the world of work as increasing knowledge work, through the confrontation with phenomena related to subjectification and the elimination of boundaries in life and work, and the digitalization of work and life. They have led to a new type of salary-dependent employee: the hybrid figure of the entreployee (Pongratz and Voß 2004). Work must notoriously be carried out under conditions of unknowing and uncertainty. Work increasingly becomes relationship building and with the expansion of the service sector it becomes interactive work, in which tasks are approached co-constructively and emotional regulation is a standard of competence. Working contexts, and above all, organizations, lose their retention and binding power in large part (Tietel 2003, Busse 2018) and become a volatile, uncertain, complex, and ambiguous (VUCA) world. Tolerance of ambiguity and the ability to be ambivalent become new key competences. This requires permanent reflexivity and reflexive self-regulation and indicates the for-profit sector as a future field for supervision (Buchinger 1999). The new character of work is marked by attributes that social work is very familiar with: reflexivity and self-reflexivity as an inner moment of work (Effinger 2018). If one views only the chances of this societal change through the naive lens of modernization, then the differences between the non-profit and the for-profit sectors appear increasingly obsolete, irrelevant, and equalized (Belardi 2018). This is in line with the motto: "Wherever reflecting is going on, we have always been there."

The true challenge lies in the confrontation with the negative aspects and the risks of this development – including exhaustion due to constant change, new forms of alienation due to self-optimization, the psychosocial costs such as burnout, and a lowered capacity and willingness for bonding, especially in the form of commitment to organizations. In this sense, supervision has become a literal mirror and seismograph of the dangerous world of work and has followed up directly on supervision's self-conception as a type of critical field investigation (Haubl and Voß 2011, Haubl, Voß, Alsdorf and Handrich 2013).[4] Supervision's strong orientation to the world of work has led to the confrontation with the central question of how critical reflection *of the reflection imperative* is positioned in a world where reflectivity is in fashion and at the same time is subject to capitalist exploitation logic.

This includes yet another crisis, when one considers that the outlined changes in the world of work have reached the social sector – above all in its economization (Hammerschmidt,

Sagebiel and Yollu-Tok 2017). The introduction of private-sector-oriented new management to public administration since the middle of the 1990s brought social management, controlling, and other business-related concepts into social service organizations. The VUCA phenomena (volatility, uncertainty, complexity, and ambiguity) were supposed to become more controllable through management concepts and increased market and customer orientation (Effinger 2018). Conservative, neoliberal criticism of social organizations overshadowed and perhaps even made the original emancipatory criticism of the inflexible bureaucracy of social organizations obsolete. This was even more sweeping than every emancipatory hope from below. It led to a change in the dynamics of the social policy triangle in social organizations and in the continuation of old bureaucracy with new entrepreneurial means. For employees in many social organizations this increasingly meant that they not only were driven to the limits of what was professionally still manageable, but rather that they had to go to the limits of what was still bearable in terms of stress. It became increasingly clear, even in the social sector, that it was not only important to do one's work well in professional terms, but also to have a good position (Kunkel and Tietel 2018). A new contradiction between *profession* and *economy* joined the classic contradiction between *profession* and *organization*. This had the result that reflection on the relationship with the client has taken a backseat to the immediate working conditions (Fritsch 2011).

Social work is no longer work on and for clients, but also paid work for social workers. Consequently, the question of how the societal and sociopolitical context can be connected with social management that does not simply copy economic concepts into social organizations arose (Grunwald 2009, Wöhrle 2015). Thus, it is sensible to address the factual structural problems of social work action beyond social technology and enlightenment pathos (Dewe and Otto 2002) or rather the real facilitation of critical reflection and action in everyday social work practice. In order to escape the old either-or stance, social service organizations have begun to be viewed as hybrid organizations in which different rationalities must be negotiated (Schedler 2012, Uebelhart 2014). That connects well with professional sociological concepts, which describe professionalism as the ability to bridge structural paradoxes (Schütze 1992). This central question for supervision becomes virulent: how to reflectively assist professionals at their origin in mediating paradoxical action and how professionals handle the paradoxes they encounter.

Supervision encounters coaching

With that, we arrive at the final chapter of the changes that supervision has gone through both alongside and in distancing itself from social work. As described above, changes in the working world have made reflection necessary, especially for work in the for-profit sector because rational, hierarchy-based, and linear management logic has reached its limits. The subject's role has changed from that of a disturbance to that of a useful source of production and productivity, and this has led to a high need for counseling. This initiated the coaching boom which started in the 1990s (Böning 2005, Fellermann 2011). Thus, following the confrontation and encounter with organizational counseling, supervision is having a second borderline experience. The attempts and offers to establish supervision in industry have been thwarted and overrun by an excessive and expanding coaching market. It is a matter of competition and, even more, identity and the self-concept of supervision and supervisors.

Coaching's different origins (sports, training, mentoring at universities, and as counseling for managers (von Schumann 2014)) make it more compatible both culturally and logically with a world of efficiency, industrial logic, and strict orientation to results and goals. But meanwhile, coaching has entered the origin of supervision. It has become customary for management personnel to receive coaching in organizations active in the social economy due to a strong orientation toward organizational and leadership questions, while lower-level employees receive supervision. That constitutes more than a silent hierarchization of the counseling formats. But also, the central tasks of social work are being absorbed by the coaching format – corporate social work is now called corporate coaching, long-term unemployed people receive psychosocial coaching, parent counseling becomes parent coaching, and so on (Belardi 2015). It is almost logical to think that social work needs coaching more than supervision or even that supervision *is* actually coaching for helping professions (Loebbert 2016) because helping action is itself goal- and result-oriented and would even be hindered by too much reflection. That is jarring. Supervision and coaching are not only two counseling formats that have different origins and characters but also different rationales. Supervision's priority is complex professional relationship building, while coaching's priority is more linear, product-, goal-, and result-oriented work. This corresponds to the difference between critical context reflection and performance-oriented pragmatics of action. Different basic values are behind this: on the one hand, an orientation to general well-being with its emancipatory pretense and on the other hand, capitalist exploitation logic and the growth imperative. In short, this corresponds to the difference between moral and market. But can this contradiction be reduced to the simple formula that coaching means making one fit, and supervision means making one reflect, as Buer provocatively and pointedly expressed (Buer 2005)?

Accordingly, there have been a series of attempts by supervision to position itself toward coaching. At the beginning there was harsh defense and denial. Was coaching an attempt to cry with the wolves rather than bleating with the sheep (Bauer 2004)? The multi-dimensional methods of interpretation and work as well as the professional-ethical view does not exist in coaching (Buer 2010). This changed to the demand for a peaceful cooperation between the formats (Buer 2005). That was followed by the attempt to integrate coaching into the qualitatively more demanding and more valuable format of supervision. A powerful advertising slogan used by the DGSv in 2009 was: "My coach is a supervisor. And yours?" Coaching was thought to be simply a method while supervision was a concept (Weigand 2002).

In the meantime, these attempts at defense, assimilation, and integration have been replaced by the attempt to promote the professionalization of both supervision and coaching (Hausinger and Volk 2013). This is accompanied by visible efforts at professionalization in coaching: through a strong research orientation and through questions regarding its status as an autonomous profession (Fietze 2011, Schmidt-Lellek 2004) and its societal and political effectiveness (Böning and Strikker 2014). The DGSv is a founding member of the round table of various coaching organizations (RTC)[5] where standards governing counseling in the work world are the central focus. As mentioned above, "coaching" has been a part of the DGSv's name since 2017. Thus, the sameness and difference of supervision and coaching are asserted. But wherein lie the links and divisions between the two formats? Will there be a common professionalization story in the future, in which the sameness and difference will endure and be implemented? Or will supervision, which has left its origin in social work, return as coaching? What remains of supervision in a comprehensively VUCA world?

These are questions that define the current debate in the community of supervisors (Bentele and Fellermann 2012). A long overdue detailed discussion about the professional and ethical foundations of supervision and coaching is pending (Austermann 2019). This debate, at least about the strategic orientation of the DGSv, has already long begun, above all regarding moral and market, job and profession, and old and young (Austermann et al. 2018). These are questions which will be answered by the coming generation, a generation who is currently being trained where the formats of supervision, coaching, and organization counseling overlap, and not by the pioneer and following generations.

Conclusion: Six theses

If we look back upon German or German-language supervision over the course of about the past 50 years, the at times contradictory lines of development can be summarized into the following theses:

1. Supervisors' central field of counseling remains institutions and the fields of social work. However, supervision is no longer primarily social work supervision. Its range is far broader than a general offer for professions in need of reflection. Supervision serves the expansion and safeguarding of professional empowerment. This can be described and understood as its horizontal expansion.
2. Supervision's focus has become increasingly contextualized from the methodical treatment and reflection of immediate helper-client interaction and relations. Teams, organizations, and ultimately, the social, political, and cultural context can be reflected as variables which structure helping and professional action. Changes in the late modern working world are a central focus in the current German-language discourse. Supervision serves to make work good (professionally) and provide good (paid) work. This can be described and understood as its vertical expansion.
3. In the course of this development, supervisory knowledge has expanded. Attachment to schools of psychotherapeutic thought is decreasing and making space for a general orientation to competences.
4. The model of external supervision (or the extensive independence of internal supervision) has become accepted. The relationship among supervisor, supervisee, and organizational client is regulated in a triangular contract. This requires the supervisor to assume a triangulating role and to reflect that role against the backdrop of the organization's dynamics (power, loyalty, independence, entanglement, etc.).
5. Beyond social work, professional action is in need of reflection due to it being embedded in contradictory, paradoxical, multi-rational, and hybrid expectations and logics which exist between interaction and bureaucracy, profession and organization, emancipation and conformity, market and moral, etc. Supervision is a helpful reflective method for clients and customers. At the same time, these contradictions make up the central challenges to the professionalization of supervision.
6. Supervision has not only expanded its settings during its development, moving from individual to case supervision, and further to group, team, and finally to organizational supervision, but has also needed to position and define itself with regard to other reflective formats, such as psychotherapy, mediation, moderation, team development, and above all, organizational counseling. Currently, coaching has become a competitor on the counseling market. Coaching is the central challenge, chance, and danger to the further professionalization of supervision.

Notes

1 There were also several exchange programs in which young West German educators and social workers came into contact with American social work and supervision through continued education courses in the USA (Müller, 2006).
2 Jan Lohl interviewed 26 members of supervision's founding generation using an oral history approach. The aim was to reconstruct the social history of supervision. Everyday supervisors (practicing supervisors) and so-called knowledgeable authorities of supervision participated in his study due to his theoretical orientation (Ibid. p. 23).

3 Weigand referred to the psychologist rule as a fighting word since it was difficult to accept those who insisted on their academic supremacy over social work in a supervision organization (Weigand 2012).
4 The research project entitled "Work and life in organizations" was conducted from 2008 to 2011 in cooperation with the DGSv, the Sigmund-Freud-Institut in Frankfurt a.M., and the Chemnitz University of Technology.
5 Cf. RTC position paper: http://www.roundtable-coaching.eu/wp-content/uploads/2015/03/RTC -Profession-Coach-2015-03-19-Positionspapier.pdf, 2 September 2019.

References

Althoff, M., 2018. Fallverständnis in der Sozialen Arbeit und seine Relevanz für Fallsupervision. *Forum Supervision*, 51, 6–19. doi:10.4119/fs-2328.

Ameln von, F., Kramer, J., and Stark, H., 2009. *Organisationsberatung beobachtet. Hidden Agendas und Blinde Flecke.* Wiesbaden: Springer VS Verlag für Sozialwissenschaften.

Austermann, F., 2019. Zu den demokratischen, emanzipatorischen und intentionalen Wurzeln der Profession Supervision am Beispiel von Cora Baltussens Beratungsverständnis. *Forum Supervision*, 52, 6–16. doi:10.4119/fs-2320.

Austermann, F., Beyer, P., Bond, K., Jahn, R., Krammer, I., Fortmeier, P., and Mulkau, A., 2018. Wesentlich, dass zukünftig die Orientierung an der Praxis der Supervision den Ton angibt. Eine Debatte über die strategische Ausrichtung der DGSv. *Journal Supervision. Informationsdienst der Deutschen Gesellschaft für Supervision und Coaching e.V.*, 4, 12–19. Available from: https://www4.dgsv-warp.de/wp-content/uploads/2018/12/Journal_Supervision_4_2018.pdf [Accessed 3 May 2020].

Bauer, A., 2004. "Lieber mit den Wölfen heulen als mit den Schafen blöken?" Anmerkungen zur Kontroverse Supervision und Coaching. *In*: F. Buer and G. Stiller, eds. *Die flexible Supervision. Herausforderungen − Konzepte − Perspektiven. Eine kritische Bestandsaufnahme.* Wiesbaden: Springer VS Verlag für Sozialwissenschaften, 121–142.

Becker, P., 1994. Externe supervision − interne supervision. *In*: Pühl, H., ed. *Handbuch der Supervision 2.* Berlin: Edition Marhold, 344–352.

Belardi, N., 1992. *Supervision. Von der Praxisberatung zur Organisationsentwicklung.* Paderborn: Junfermann.

Belardi, N., 1994. Supervision in den USA − heute. *Organisationsberatung, Supervision, Clinical Management (OSC)*, 2, 107–121.

Belardi, N., 2015. *Supervision für helfende Berufe.* Freiburg i. Brsg: Lambertus Verlag.

Belardi, N., 2018. *Supervision und Coaching. Grundlagen, Techniken, Perspektiven.* Munich: Verlag C.H. Beck.

Bentele, M., and Fellermann, J., eds., 2012. *Womit Supervision und Coaching zu tun haben werden. Schlaglichter auf Veränderungen in Gesellschaft, Arbeit und Beratung.* Kassel: Kassel University Press.

Blinkert, B., and Huppertz, N., 1974. Der Mythos der Supervision. Kritische Anmerkungen zu Anspruch und Wirklichkeiten. *Neue Praxis*, 2, 117–132.

Böhnisch, L., and Lösch, H., 1973. Das Handlungsverständnis des Sozialarbeiters und seine institutionelle Determination. *In*: Otto, H.-U., and Schneider, S. eds., *Gesellschaftliche Perspektiven der Sozialarbeit.* Neuwied: Luchterhand, 21–40.

Böning, U., 2005. Coaching: Der Siegeszug eines Personalentwicklungs-Instrumentes − Eine 15-Jahres-Bilanz. *In*: Rauen, C., ed., *Handbuch coaching.* Göttingen: Hogrefe, 21–55.

Böning, U., and Strikker, F., 2014. Ist Coaching nur Reaktion auf gesellschaftliche Entwicklungen oder auch Impulsgeber? *Organisationsentwicklung, Supervision, Coaching (OSC)*, 21 (4), 483–496.

Brutzer de Palme, N., 2019. Wie, wo und für wen arbeiten Sie? Die Ergebnisse der Mitgliederbefragung "Ihre Tätigkeit im Markt 2018". *Journal Supervision. Informationsdienst der Deutschen Gesellschaft für Supervision und Coaching e.V.*, 1, 30–33.

Buchinger, K., 1997. *Supervision in organisationen.* Heidelberg: Carl-Auer-Verlag.

Buchinger, K., 1999. *Die Zukunft der Supervision. Aspekte eines neuen "Berufs".* Heidelberg: Carl-Auer-Systeme Verlag.

Buer, F., 2005. Coaching, Supervision und die vielen anderen Formate. Ein Plädoyer für ein friedliches Zusammenspiel. *Organisationsentwicklung, Supervision, Coaching (OSC)*, 12 (3), 278–297.

Buer, F., 2010. Gefährdet Organisation Profession? *In*: A. Schreyögg and C. Schmidt-Lellek, eds., *Die organisation in supervision und coaching.* Wiesbaden: Springer VS Verlag, 41–60.

Busse, S., 2009. Supervision between critical reflection and practical doing. *Journal of Social Work Practice*, 23 (2), 159–175.

Busse, S., 2018. Bindung(en) in der Arbeitswelt. *Gruppe. Interaktion. Organisation. Zeitschrift für Angewandte Organisationspsychologie (GIO)*, 49 (4), 305–317.

Busse, S., and Ehlert, G., 2017. Organisationsveränderungen im ASD – auf der Suche nach Gelingensbedingungen. *Supervision. Mensch, Arbeit, Organisation*, 35 (2), 49–55.

Busse, S., and Fellermann, J., eds., 1998. *Gemeinsam in der Differenz - Supervision im Osten*. Münster: Votum-Verlag.

Busse, S., and Jahn, R., (2020). Excellence in Supervision and Coaching Training: Considerations. *European Journal of Supervision and Coaching*, 3.

Busse, S., and Tietel, E., eds., 2009. 20 Jahre beisammen – Beratung im vereinten Deutschland. *Supervision. Mensch, Arbeit, Organization*, 27 (3).

Busse, S., and Tietel, E., 2018. *Mit dem Dritten sieht man besser: Triaden und Triangulierung in der Beratung*. Göttingen: Vandenhoeck & Ruprecht.

Dewe, B., and Otto, H.U., 2002. Reflexive Sozialpädagogik. Grundstrukturen eines neuen Typs dienstleistungsorientierten Professionshandelns. *In*: W. Thole, ed. *Grundriss Soziale Arbeit. Ein einführendes Handbuch*. Opladen: Leske + Budrich, 179–198.

DGSv (Deutsche Gesellschaft für Supervision e.V.), 2011. Das Ende eines unerklärlichen Unterschieds. *Journal Supervision. Informationsdienst der Deutschen Gesellschaft für Supervision und Coaching e.V.*, 3, 3.

DGSv, ed., 2012. *Supervision ein Beitrag zur Qualifizierung beruflicher Arbeit*. Cologne: DGSv.

DGSv, 2017. *Journal Supervision. Informationsdienst der Deutschen Gesellschaft für Supervision und Coaching e.V.*, 1, 20.

Diebäcker, H., 1995. Chancen und Risiko der Personalentwicklung mit Supervision in Profit-Unternehmen. *Supervision, Zeitschrift für berufsbezogene Beratung, Sonderheft*, 21–37.

Drüge, M., and Schleider, K., 2015. Supervision in pädagogischen Kontexten. Ein Vergleich von Supervision in der Sozialen Arbeit und Schule. *Forum Supervision*, 46, 98–101. doi:10.4119/fs-2285.

Ebert, W., 2001. *Systemtheorien in der Supervision*. Wiesbaden: Springer VS Verlag für Sozialwissenschften.

Effinger, H., 2015. Über Supervision, Soziale Arbeit und eine doppelte Flucht. *Journal Supervision. Informationsdienst der Deutschen Gesellschaft für Supervision und Coaching e.V.*, 3, 10–11.

Effinger, H., 2017. Flüchten oder Standhalten? Reflexionen über Supervision in der Sozialen Arbeit. *Journal Supervision. Informationsdienst der Deutschen Gesellschaft für Supervision und Coaching e.V.*, 2, 6–15.

Effinger, H., 2018. *Beratung in der Sozialwirtschaft. Ungewissheit als Chance kreativer Problemlösungsstrategien*. Göttingen: Vandenhoeck & Ruprecht.

Fellermann, J., ed., 2011. *Supervision und Coaching auf dem Beratungsmarkt. Eine explorative Studie als Beitrag zur Marktforschung*. Göttingen: Vandenhoeck & Ruprecht.

Fietze, B., 2011. Profilbildung und Strukturkonkurrenz. Zur Bedeutung der Distinktionsstrategien im Professionalisierungsprozess von Supervision und Coaching. *In*: E.-M. Graf, Y. Aksu, I. Pick, and S. Rettinger, eds. *Beratung, coaching, supervision. Multidisziplinäre Perspektiven vernetzt*. Wiesbaden: Springer VS, 23–36.

Fritsch, J., 2011. Supervision 2008. Schlaglichter auf Veränderungen in der Profession. *In*: Haubl, R., and Voß, G.G., eds., *Riskante Arbeitswelt im Spiegel der Supervision. Eine Studie zu den psychosozialen Auswirkungen spätmoderner Erwerbsarbeit*. Göttingen: Vandenhoeck & Ruprecht, 68–74.

Fürstenau, P., 1995. Supervision auf dem steinigen Weg zu neuen Arbeitsfeldern. *Supervision, Zeitschrift für berufsbezogene Beratung, Sonderheft*, 10–21.

Gaertner, A., 2004. Supervision in der Krise – Expansionismus, Unschärfeprofil und die Ausblendung der Selbstreflexion. In: F. Buer and G. Stiller, eds. *Die flexible Supervision. Herausforderungen – Konzepte – Perspektiven. Eine kritische Bestandsaufnahme*. Wiesbaden: Springer VS Verlag für Sozialwissenschaften, 79–100.

Geißler-Piltz, B., 2017. Statt Marginale: Integration von Supervision im Studium der Sozialen Arbeit. *Supervision. Mensch Arbeit Organisation*, 35 (2), 16–26.

Giernalczyk, T., and Möller, H., 2018. *Entwicklungsraum: Psychodynamische Beratung in Organisationen*. Göttingen: Vandenhoeck & Ruprecht.

Gotthardt-Lorenz, A., 1989. *Organisationsberatung. Hilfe und Last für die Sozialarbeit*. Freiburg: Lambertus Verlag.

Gotthardt-Lorenz, A., 1994. "Organisationssupervision": Rollen und Interventionsfelder. *In*: Pühl, H., ed. *Handbuch der Supervision 2*. Berlin: Edition Marhold, 365–379.

Gotthard-Lorenz, A., 2020. *Organisationssupervision – Ein Konzept*. Göttingen: Vandenhoeck & Ruprecht.

Gotthardt-Lorenz, A., and Walther, I., 1998. Berufs- und Arbeitsfeldorientierung – der Blickwinkel, der Supervision zur Supervision macht. *Supervision, Osterreichische Vereinigung für Supervision*, 2, 7–11.

Gröning, K., 2016. *Sozialwissenschaftlich fundierte Beratung in Pädagogik, Supervision und Sozialer Arbeit.* Gießen: Psychosozial-Verlag.

Grunwald, K., ed., 2009. Vom Sozialmanagement zum Management des Sozialen? Eine Bestandsaufnahme. *Grundlagen der Sozialen Arbeit*, Bd. 21, Baltmannsweiler: Schneider Verlag Hohen Gehren.

Gschosmann, A., 2017. Das Unbehagen mit dem Dreieckskontrakt. Überlegungen zu einer Konstante in der Teamsupervision von Sozialorganisationen. *Supervision*, Mensch Arbeit Organisation, 2, 27–36.

Hamburger, A., 2017. Supervision in der Jugendhilfe. *In*: A. Hamburger, W. Mertens (Hrsg.). *Supervision – Konzepte und Anwendungen. Band 1: Supervision in der Praxis – ein Überblick.* Stuttgart: Verlag Kohlhammer.

Hammerschmidt, P., Sagebiel, J., and Yollu-Tok, A., eds., 2017. *Die Soziale Arbeit im Spannungsfeld der Ökonomie.* Schriftenreihe Soziale Arbeit der Fakultät für angewandte Sozialwissenschaften der Hochschule München.

Haubl, R., Hausinger, B., and Voß, G.G., 2013. *Riskante Arbeitswelten: Zu den Auswirkungen moderner Beschäftigungsverhältnisse auf die psychische Gesundheit und die Arbeitsqualität.* Frankfurt a.M.: Campus.

Haubl, R., Voß, G.G., eds., 2011. *Riskante Arbeitswelt im Spiegel der Supervision. Eine Studie zu den psychosozialen Auswirkungen spätmoderner Erwerbsarbeit.* Göttingen: Vandenhoeck & Ruprecht.

Haubl, R., Voß, G.G., Alsdorf, N., and Handrich, C., eds., 2013. *Belastungsstörung mit System.* Göttingen: Vandenhoeck & Ruprecht.

Hausinger, B., 2008. *Supervision: Organisation - Arbeit - Ökonomisierung: Zur Gleichzeitigkeit des Ungleichzeitigen in der Arbeitswelt (Arbeit und Leben im Umbruch).* Mering: Rainer Hamp Verlag.

Hausinger, B., and Volk, T., 2013. Erneuerung statt Imagepflege. *Sonderpublikation zum Journal Supervision. Informationsdienst der Deutschen Gesellschaft für Supervision und Coaching e. V.*, 4.

Hege, M., 1979. *Engagierter Dialog. Ein Beitrag zur sozialen Einzelhilfe.* 2nd ed. München: Ernst Reinhardt.

Hege, M., 2011. Supervision im Prozess der Veränderung beruflicher Arbeit im Allgemeinen Sozialdienst (ASD). *Forum Supervision*, 37, 58–71. doi:10.4119/fs-2147.

Hege, M., and Weigand, W., 1997. "Ich sitze immer dazwischen und bemühe mich, auch dort zu bleiben". Marianne Hege im Gespräch mit Wolfgang Weigand. *Supervision. Zeitschrift für berufsbezogene Beratung*, 31, 4–16.

Heltzel, R., and Weigand, W., 2012. *Im Dickicht der Organisation: komplexe Beratungsaufträge verändern die Beratungsrolle.* Göttingen: Vandenhoeck & Ruprecht.

Huppertz, N., 1975. *Supervision. Analyse eines problematischen Kapitels der Sozialarbeit.* Neuwied: Luchterhand.

Jahn, R., and Nolten, A., 2017. Diplomaten im Dienste der Organisation. Psychoanalytisch orientierte Überlegungen zur Beratung von Organisationen. *Supervision. Mensch Arbeit Organisation*, 1, 21–25.

Judy, M., and Knopf, W., eds., 2016. *In the mirror of competences.* Wien: facultas.

Knaier, D., 2017. Supervision in der Sozialen Arbeit. *In*: Hamburger A., and Mertens, W., eds. *Supervision – Konzepte und Anwendungen. Ban 1: Supervision in der Praxis – ein Überblick.* Stuttgart: Kohlhammer.

Kunkel, R., and Tietel, E., 2018. "Gute Arbeit" als professions- und arbeitspolitisches Projekt. *Positionen, Beiträge zur Beratung der Arbeitswelt, hrsg. von Stefan Busse, Rolf Haubl, Heidi Möller und Christiane Schiersmann*, 1. Kassel: University Press.

Kühl, S., 2006. Die Supervision auf dem Weg zur Profession? Professionalisierung im Spannungsfeld zwischen Expansionsbestrebung und Selbstbescheidung. *Organisationsberatung, Supervision, Coaching (OSC)*, 13 (1), 5–19.

Leuschner, G., and Diebäcker, H., 1995. Briefwechsel: supervision in profit-unternehmen. *Supervision. Zeitschrift für berufsbezogene Beratung, Sonderheft*, 37–47.

Leuschner, G., and Weigand, W., 2011. Wege zur Professionalisierung – Über die Anfänge der Supervision in Deutschland. *Forum Supervision*, 37, 38–58. doi:10.4119/fs-2146 [Accessed 15 March 2020].

Lippenmeier, N., 2011. Der Entwicklungsprozess der Supervision in Deutschland und wie es zur Gründung der DGSv kam. *Forum Supervision*, 37, 8–16. doi:10.4119/fs-2141

Loebbert, M., 2016. *Wie Supervision gelingt. Supervision als Coaching für helfende Berufe. essentials.* Berlin: Springer.

Lohl, J., 2019. "…und ging ins pralle Leben" Facetten der Sozialgeschichte der Supervision. Göttingen: Vandenhoeck & Ruprecht.

Lohmer, M., and Möller, H., 2014. *Psychoanalyse in Organisationen: Einführung in die psychodynamische Organisationsberatung* (Psychoanalyse im 21. Jahrhundert). Stuttgart: Kohlhammer.

Lowy, L., 1983. Social work supervision: from models toward theory. *Journal of Education for Social Work*, 19(2), 55–62. Available from: http://www.jstor.org/stable/23038537 [Accessed 16 April 2020].

Mack, O., Khare, A., Krämer, A., and Burgartz, T., eds., 2015. *Managing in a VUCA World.* Heidelberg: Springer.

Müller, W.C., 2006. *Wie Helfen zum Beruf wurde. Eine Methodengeschichte der Sozialen Arbeit*. Weinheim: Beltz.

Pattar, A.K., 2012. Sozialrechtliches Dreiecksverhältnis – Rechtsbeziehungen zwischen Hilfsbedürftigen, Sozialhilfeträgern und Einrichtungsträgern. *SozialRecht aktuell. Zeitschrift für Sozialberatung*, 3, S, 85–132.

Petzold, H., 1998. *Integrative Supervision, Meta-Consulting, Organisationsentwicklung: Ein Handbuch für Modelle und Methoden reflexiver Praxis*. Paderborn: Junfermann Verlag.

Pongratz, H.J., and Voß, G.G., eds., 2004. *Typisch Arbeitskraftunternehmer? Befunde der empirischen Arbeitsforschung*. Berlin: Edition sigma.

Pühl, H., 1994. Supervision in der (Fach-) Hochschul-Ausbildung. In: Pühl, H., ed. *Handbuch der Supervision 2*. Berlin: Edition Marhold, 406–418.

Pühl, H., ed., 2000. *Supervision und Organisationsentwicklung*. Opladen: Leske + Budrich.

Schedler, K., 2012. Multirationales Management. *dms – der moderne Staat – Zeitschrift für Public Policy. Recht und Management*, 5 (2), 361–376.

Schiersmann, C., and Thiele, H.U., 2012. *Beratung als Förderung von Selbstorganisationsprozessen: Empirische Studien zur Beratung von Personen und Organisationen auf der Basis der Synergetik*. Göttingen: Vandenhoeck & Ruprecht.

Schigl, B., et al., 2020. *Supervision auf dem Prüfstand. Wirksamkeit, Forschung, Anwendungsfelder, Innovation*. 2nd ed. Wiesbaden: Springer.

Schmidt-Lellek, C.J., 2004. Anmerkungen zur Professionalisierung des Coaching auf dem Hintergrund des klassischen Professionsbegriffs. *Organisationsentwicklung, Supervision, Coaching (OSC)*, 11 (2), 183–192.

Schorn, A., 2017. Ein besonderes Verhältnis: Soziale Arbeit und Supervision. *Supervision. Mensch Arbeit Organisation*, 2, 60–62.

Schreyögg, A., 1991. *Supervision. Ein integratives Modell*. Paderborn: Junfermann Verlag.

Schubert von, H., 1999. Unternehmenskultur in der freien Wohlfahrpflege – Fragen eines Mitarbeiters an den Träger. *System Familie*, 12, 109–119.

Schütze, F., 1992. Sozialarbeit als "bescheidene" Profession. *In:* B. Dewe, W. Ferchhoff, and F.-O. Radtke, eds. *Erziehen als Beruf. Zur Logik professionellen Handelns in pädagogischen Feldern*. Opladen: Leske + Budrich, 132–170.

Schumann von, K., 2014. *Coaching im Aufwind. Professionelles Business-Coaching: Inhalte, Prozesse, Ergebnisse und Trend*. Wiesbaden: Springer VS Verlag für Sozialwissenschaften.

Staub-Bernasconi, S., 2013. Der Professionalisierungsdiskurs zur Sozialen Arbeit (SA/SP) im deutschsprachigen Kontext im Spiegel internationaler Ausbildungsstandards. Soziale Arbeit – eine verspätete Profession? *In:* Roland Becker-Lenz, Stefan Busse, Gudrun Ehlert und Silke Müller, eds. *Professionalität in der Sozialen Arbeit*. Wiesbaden: Springer VS Verlag für Sozialwissenschaften, 24–32.

Stenzel, H., 2019. Louis Lowy - erlebte Geschichte(n) als Entwicklungsimpuls der Supervision in Deutschland. *Forum Supervision*, 52, 17–32. doi: 10.4119/fs-2321.

Tietel, E., 2003. *Emotion und Anerkennung in Organisationen. Wege zu einer triangulären Organisationskultur*. Münster: Lit-Verlag.

Uebelhart, B., 2014. Warum lösen sich historisch gewachsene Grenzen zwischen Wohlfahrtorganisationen, klassischen For-Profit-Organisationen und hybriden Organisationsformen auf? *Jugendhilfe*, 52 (4), 260–266.

Weigand, W., 1985. Des Supervisors Gang in die Organisation. *Supervision, Zeitschrift für berufsbezogene Beratung*, 7, 1–8.

Weigand, W., 1987a. Supervision als Innovationsinstrument sozialer Arbeit. *In:* B. Maelicke, ed. *Soziale Arbeit als soziale Innovation*. Weinheim/München: Juventa Verlag, 151–164.

Weigand, W., 1987b. Zur beruflichen Identität des Supervisors. *Supervision, Zeitschrift für berufsbezogene Beratung*, 11, 19–35.

Weigand, W., 1989. Sozialarbeit – das Ursprungsland der Supervision. *Integrative Therapie*, 3–4, 248–259.

Weigand, W., 1993. Die Faszination des Geldes und des fremden Feldes –Supervision in Wirtschaftsunternehmen. *Supervision, Zeitschrift für berufsbezogene Beratung*, 24, 3–11.

Weigand, W., 1994a. Teamsupervision: Ein Grenzgang zwischen Supervision und Organisationsberatung. *In:* H. Pühl, ed. *Handbuch der Supervision 2*. Berlin: Edition Marhold, 112–131.

Weigand, W., 1994b. Leitungsberatung. In: H. Pühl, ed. *Handbuch der Supervision 2*. Berlin: Edition Marhold, 406–418.

Weigand, W., 2002. Coaching eine Methode – Supervision ein Konzept. *In:* L.v. Kessel and J. Fellermann, ed. *Supervision und Coaching in europäischer Perspektive. Beiträge der ANSE-Konferenz 2000*. Cologne: Association of National Organisations for Supervision in Europe (ANSE), 45–54.

Weigand, W., 2007. Das eigentlich Supervisorische – Eine Einführung in dieses Heft. *Supervision. Mensch Arbeit Organisation. Die Zeitschrift für Berater/innen*, 2, 4–5.

Weigand, W., 2012. Die DGSv in ihren (historischen) Spannungsfeldern. *Forum Supervision*, 39, 18–28. doi:10.4119/fs-2112.

Wieringa, C.F., 1990. Entwicklungsphasen der Supervision (1860–1950). *Supervision, Zeitschrift für berufsbezogene Beratung*, 18, 36–44.

Wöhrle, A., 2015. Beratung unter Bedingungen des Umbruchs sozialer Organisationen: Plädoyer für ein forschende Haltung. *In:* St. Busse, R. Haubl, H. Möller and Chr. Schiersmann, eds. *Positionen, Beiträge zur Beratung der Arbeitswelt, 1.* Kassel: Univers.

3

EXTERNAL REFLECTIVE SUPERVISION IN SWEDEN

Staffan Höjer

Introduction

One aim of this chapter is to present and discuss the main arguments for external supervision in Sweden and to compare these with what we know of its outcomes more than 30 years later. Another is to discuss some of the challenges facing external supervision in Swedish social work. The chapter builds mostly on the empirical work done in the most recent study of social work supervision in Sweden conducted more than ten years ago (Höjer et al. 2007). In 13 municipalities, 193 social workers who had supervision answered a survey, 53 managers were interviewed, and there were different focus groups with managers, social workers, and supervisors.

Evolution of social work supervision in Sweden

There have been calls for external supervision in Nordic social work practice since the 1980s, and since the beginning of the 2000s it has become something that every social worker in Sweden, as in the other Nordic countries, expects to have. It is not clear how this tradition developed; it contradicts the role models of the UK and United States, which have traditionally played a pivotal role in the development of social work as a profession in Sweden (Pettersson 2001). The practice of supervision in Sweden, as in other countries, does of course also have predecessors. The first form of supervision in Sweden was through a kind of "master-apprentice" system in which more experienced social workers supervised their colleagues (Bernler and Johnsson 1985; Höjer et al. 2007). With the development of social work education, the first school of social work was founded in Stockholm in 1921. The supervision of social work students became, and still is, an important part of social work education. Similar historical trends have been seen in many other countries, and more comprehensive descriptions of the history of social work supervision can be found in Mo et al. (2020) and the seminal work of Kadushin and Harkness (2002).

Both of the above-mentioned forms of supervision, which still exist in Swedish social work, are mainly individualized and conducted from one supervisor to one supervisee. In social work practice, the first form is usually referred to as "internal" supervision and is given by a first-line manager (or subordinate to him/her). Supervision serves managerial and administrative as well as educational and supportive functions. It is important to ensure that clients receive treatment in accordance with rules and laws. This is part of the induction and managerial support provided to new social workers in relation to the difficult decisions they need to take. This kind of external supervision is part of a tradition of reflective group supervision in Swedish social work focused on support and professional development intended to prevent burnout and on the feelings and perceptions of social workers in their professional development. Accordingly, it is perhaps better to describe supervision in Swedish social work as a "dual" system which offers both individual supervision from the line manager and supervision from an external consultant.

In seeking to understand the call for external group-based supervision in Nordic social work, there are at least four leads. First, social work supervision followed in the footsteps of psychology and psychotherapy in which having external supervisors was standard practice. Supervisors from this background have claimed that supervision for social workers would be one way of expanding their professional and commercial turf (see, for instance, Boalt, Boetsius and Ögren 2000). Second, in 1986 the first education for supervisors in social work was started, and its purpose was to promote private practitioners or, at least, people working independently of certain educational backgrounds. The first important book on supervision in Swedish social work (a PhD in social work) presented a non-linear organizational relationship between supervisors and groups of supervisees as one of its criteria for supervision in social work (Bernler and Johnsson 1985). In this book, a distinction was made between Anglo-Saxon supervision, which was claimed to be mostly managerial and supportive, and reflective external supervision. Third, over time, external supervision has become part of the professional project for social work to further professionalize its work. A later section of this chapter elaborates on this.

Evidence of the need for supervision in social work

This book is in itself evidence of the claim that supervision is important for social work, and of course there are many studies in which social workers themselves have asked for supervision as a means to handle difficult professional tasks (e.g. Baldschun et al. 2019; Tham and Lynch 2019). Supervision seems to be important to prevent social workers from suffering burnout and secondary stress, and in some cases leaving the profession, for instance in child protection (Cearley 2004; Jacquet Clark, Morazes and Withers 2008; Westbrook, Ellis and Ellett 2006). It is also claimed to enhance emotional resilience (Rose and Palattiyil 2020). Group supervision does also seem to conform to the decision-making process in certain parts of social work, such as child protection (Björkenheim 2007). Collegial discussion and supervision is claimed to be the most important source of knowledge in the handling of child protection cases (Iversen and Heggen 2016).

When social workers are asked about the impact of supervision on clients, they are positive. As many as 88% of social workers receiving external supervision in Sweden believe that it leads to increased understanding of service users' situations, and 70% think that their service users would be affected if external supervision were to be stopped (Höjer et al. 2007). Social work managers were asked the same question in the study, and they expressed the same positive attitudes towards supervision (Bradley and Höjer 2009). However, a number of reviews of supervision have concluded that there is a general lack of evidence that supervision actually provides better social work practice for clients (Carpenter et al. 2013; Beddoe et al. 2016). There is also a lack of studies in which different supervision systems are compared (see Bradley et al. 2010 for an exception). While there are a number of practical and ethical difficulties in attaining such evidence, the mere fact of its absence presents a problem for those claiming its importance.

Theoretical perspective on supervision

The provider of social work supervision in Sweden is normally a human service organization (HSO) within the statutory sector. According to Hasenfeld (2010), the attributes of HSOs are vague and ambiguous goals and uncertainty about methods and values, and yet moral issues play an important role in the activities of their personnel and the people they serve. The relationship between these two groups is of great importance to HSOs, as a consequence, they are dependent on professionals who can solve the problems arising in complex organizations by drawing on professional expertise and discretion (Evans and Harris 2002). Social workers are expected to exercise considerable professional discretion to adapt to a complex professional reality and respond effectively to the needs of the service users, whilst being cognizant of the rules and regulations of the HSO. Supervision is claimed to play an important role in helping not only social workers but also managers to handle these uncertainties, moral dilemmas, and complex relations. Exercising professional discretion and striving for status and authority is referred to in sociological terms as the "professional project" (Abbot 1988). The endeavors of professionals to exercise discretion based on their knowledge and expertise may be in conflict with the aims of bureaucratic organizations in terms of their rules and regulatory systems. Within today's paradigm of New Public Management (NPM), such conflicts are likely to arise. Ideas concerning value for money and managerial control are likely to be in contrast with the professional perspective and logic as presented by social workers (Freidson 2004). The claim that legitimacy is an overarching value of modern organizations, including HSOs, and that supervision has a role to play when it comes to providing legitimacy for the organization that it serves (Höjer et al. 2007) gives the concept and the activity an important place within the organization, in this case the social work agency.

Supervision in Swedish social work is clearly linked to professionalization in both individual and collective terms. For individuals it offers continuous education in the job and the opportunity to learn from more experienced peers and supervisors. In this sense, supervision is seen as one of the most important sources of knowledge in social work practice (Dellgran and Höjer 2005; Iversen and Heggen 2016). In terms of collective professionalization, the mere fact that supervision is considered a legitimate activity for creating better social work has given it status. There is also specific post-graduate education for supervisors in social work, which confers the right to provide supervision, a well-paid career path within social work. Supervision has become an alternative expert career for social workers alongside the linear progression towards being a manager or developing expertise through further study and attaining a master's or PhD (Kullberg 2011). Among social workers involved in their own independent private practice, being a supervisor is the most common activity, followed by providing psychotherapy and/or consultations (Dellgran and Höjer 2005).

The role of supervision in the professional project of social work can be seen in its authorization system, administered by one of the main professional organizations in Sweden (Akademikerförbundet SSR). In order to be authorized, a practitioner needs three years of social work practice, to follow ethical rules, to provide two independent letters of recommendation from a manager, colleague and/or supervisor, and have had 100 hours of external supervision. This emphasizes the role of supervision in social work as part of the professional project.

A closer look at some of the traits of external reflective supervision

The seven traits of external reflective supervision, according to the first book on the matter in Sweden, have been discussed elsewhere by the author (see Bernler and Johnsson 1985; Bradley and Höjer 2009, p. 75). They are

1. Continuity. Supervision should be a continuous activity, with contracts fixed for at least one year ahead.

2. A global objective. Supervision should help social workers to integrate all aspects of their work.

3. Process aim. Supervision should help the social worker to reflect on ways of using him-/ herself as an instrument, and monitor his/her reactions and feelings in treatment situations.

4. A non-linear organizational relationship between the supervisor and group of social workers is encouraged.

5. Supervisors have a process responsibility, that is for the process of the supervision not for the direct work with clients.

6. Facultative obligatory, meaning that all social workers should have supervision. It should not be an optional activity.

7. Expertise. The supervisor should have expertise, here meaning (i) personal experience of social work, (ii) knowledge about supervision theory and techniques, and (iii) cultural competence, i.e. knowledge about the work tasks and conditions that supervisees have.

Starting with no. 6 – it should be for everyone and not be optional. This can be seen as both a call for resources to give social workers supervision and a demand that all social workers participate. There are no grounds for refusing supervision, and social workers are expected to reflect on their own reactions and feelings in their work. Trait no. 4 – there should be a non-linear organization relationship – referred to in this chapter as external supervision – between the supervisor and group of supervisees. The reason for this is to avoid administrative and managerial control and enhance openness and reflexiveness. No. 7 – the claim for expertise – is also important. Own expertise and cultural competence of the work was positively received in the call for "social workers supervising social workers" and education on supervision. The first post-graduate education for supervisors in social work had just started, at the University of Gothenburg in Sweden.

When it comes to the content of supervision in social work, there is a clear distinction between supervision and management. Supervision is not to do with accountability, managerial control, or decisions on individual cases. It has a global objective (no. 2) with a process aim (no. 3), and supervisors are responsible for the process not the direct work with the clients (no 5).

The relative importance of these traits may be debated; nonetheless, it should be noted that many of them are embraced by supervisors in Sweden (Höjer et al. 2007). Some reject the idea that supervisors require cultural competence and claim that an outside perspective in relation to this can sometimes be positive (Cajverts 1998). For a comprehensive discussion of the pros and cons of external supervision see Beddoe (2012).

The map and the terrain – How is external social work supervision performed in Sweden?

In Sweden there is still much more literature on the need for supervision and how it should be performed than research on how it is actually being performed. This is also true of Denmark where one study of social work supervision practice was undertaken recently (Magnussen 2018). The study refers to the concept of "dirty supervision" as a pragmatic adaptation of group-based supervision. It is termed "dirty" because "in terms of strict theoretical understanding it deviates from the recommended method" (p. 370). The study also asserts a need to narrow the gap between what is and what ought to be with regard to supervision. In response, an evaluation of what is known of Swedish social work supervision is presented below.

Obligatory for everyone?

Until recently, the call for supervision for everyone had been very successful in Sweden. It is probably not possible to advertise a position in social work practice and claim that there is no supervision. It has been something that social workers in Sweden expect. In a study of 1000 social workers in Sweden, 78% reported that they had supervision (external). Of those participants working in social services related to child protection, over 90% responded that they "always" had supervision, as did 84% of those working with abuse and 80% in social assistance. Of the participants working with disabilities or adult protection (elderly persons), 67% had external supervision (Dellgran and Höjer 2005). The afore-mentioned professional organization, Akademikerförbundet SSR, regularly asks its members if they have external supervision. The figures for the above-mentioned groups remain at the level reported. For school social workers, the level was 77% as of 2016. The most common way of implementing supervision at that time was via the same external supervisor, two or three hours twice a month on a contract renewed once a year (Höjer et al. 2007). However, recent anecdotal evidence from practicing supervisors suggests that contracts are becoming shorter and the time between meetings longer.

The fact that external supervision has been seen as a resource for all, not only beginners or newly educated social workers, increases the expectations of what supervisors should contribute. More than ten years ago, when the empirical study was undertaken, half of the participants had already had external supervision with four supervisors or more and for longer than six years. A recurring discussion is whether specific external supervision should be included as part of the induction into the profession. So far, anecdotal evidence suggests that most groups are mixed with social workers with differing amounts of experience.

Educated supervisors with cultural competence?

Do supervisors have the expertise claimed? Today, there is post-graduate education for supervisors in social work at several universities in Sweden, so the number of supervisors with specific education in the discipline is much higher now than before. Acceptance on the first social work supervision course, besides a bachelor's degree in social work (or equivalent), was dependent on an applicant having at least five years' experience of social work practice and having received personal therapy (at least 40 hours of individual therapy or 80 hours of group therapy). This was claimed to be a way of ensuring that supervisors had reflected on internal feelings that could influence their supervisory practice. This demand can also be seen as evidence of the historic psychotherapeutic tradition in Swedish social work supervision. Today, having a specific education in supervision is often included among the criteria when new procurement agreements are constructed. In the afore-mentioned study, social workers were asked about the professional backgrounds of their supervisors. One out of five did not know what professional background their supervisor had. About four out of ten said the supervisor had a degree in social work, and more than three out of ten said that theirs had one in psychology. Therefore, it cannot be claimed that social workers in Sweden are being supervised exclusively by social workers (Höjer et al. 2007).

What then of the theoretical perspective of supervisors? For the supervisees it was not always clear. When asked about the theoretical perspective of their supervisor, about 30% claimed it that it was "eclectic," 25% said "systemic," 17% "psycho dynamic," 10% "solution focused," and more than 10% answered that they did not know. For some managers, a certain theoretical perspective could be identified (such as a system-oriented one). It is therefore interesting to note that the managers in the same study and groups as the previous respondents on the whole answered that they thought their supervisors' theoretical orientations were mainly systemic when asked the same question. Their views on the importance of a supervisor's perspective also differed:

> Right now systemic theory is "modern" in our organisation. The worst thing in our business is that some methods become popular and then everyone has to work in this specific way. Supervision should be an oasis where cases should be discussed with an open mind, irrespective of today's modern theory
>
> *(social worker)*[1]

> The social services are conducting a systems-theory education for all its staff. It is important that this perspective goes all the way from the management to the social workers.
>
> *(social workers – examples from Höjer et al. 2007 p. 88)*

Independent from the organization

In Swedish social work, the defense of the system of external supervision has been of paramount importance among social workers. Naturally, the supervisor is not entirely independent of the organization: he/she is employed by the organization on a contract. Some years back it was predominantly up to social workers themselves to contact potential supervisors, after which their manager simply signed the contract (Egelund and Kvilhaug 2001). Today, the process is more controlled. Management is more involved in the choice of supervisor, and recruitment is not up to any one group or manager but rather conducted according to contract rules and procurement policy. Nonetheless, in most cases, social workers are involved in both taking the initiative to change supervisor and contacting and arranging an interview with a potential candidate before making a recommendation to their manager. For some time, securing the resources for independent reflection has been seen as a victory for the profession, and any discussion about supervision can be seen as a threat that these will be taken away. This is an idea that will be returned to under the challenges below.

A global perspective – What is going on in external supervision?

When asked to tick off what they had discussed during their sessions, supervisors identified the following themes most often:

1. The social workers' feelings when meeting a client
2. Approaches and methods in the work
3. Client cases and appropriate work procedure
4. Client cases, in order to understand his/her actions
5. The social workers' own conceptions and possible prejudices
6. Ethical dilemmas in work

All of these had been part of the supervision for more than 90% of the social workers.

Issues related to the organization, such as "organizational issues" or "leadership of managers" and "cooperation within the work group," had been part of more than 80% of supervision groups. Much more unusual was the fact that "the discussion of research reports" or "sessions resembling therapy for personal development" had been part of 25% of sessions according to the social workers themselves. Normally, a line is drawn between personal therapy and professional supervision when contracts about supervision are created (Höjer et al. 2007); nonetheless, one out of four participants reported that the sessions had resembled therapy at least once.

Enlightenment – The value of supervision

The overall response among both social workers and managers in Swedish social work towards external reflective supervision is very positive. There is unanimous agreement that social workers need a dual form of supervision, an internal one which focuses on accountability and solving cases, and an external one which focuses on the feelings and reactions of the social workers themselves. It is about the creation of a reflexive space where a practitioner is able to discuss anything that is happening in his/her daily work (the global objective, see above). One social worker said:

> Supervision is a way of reflecting on your competence, to have it more grounded in the daily work. The link between the theory you learned as a new graduate of social work education and what it takes to apply it in daily practice. It is a kind of searching in which I see supervision as an important tool in order to find the right approach that allows you to endure entering meetings with individuals who have great difficulties.
>
> *(Social worker in Höjer et al. p. 81)*

Supervision is also perceived by many managers as providing protection for the clients, with social workers being encouraged to discuss their difficult cases with each other, which may lead to more transparent decisions, and prevent social workers from letting their own feelings influence their decisions in an improper way. Some managers also claim supervision actually calms things down in the organization.

> It has a calming effect. When working in human service work there are so many feelings involved and so many parallel processes, so it will be a kind of sorting as well. It will be a calmer and hopefully more open climate.
>
> *(Manager in Höjer et al. p. 83)*

However, a calming influence is not always seen as positive for everyone in an organization. If it leads to reduced claims for resources for clients or a better working environment for social work as a whole, it would be a technique employed for control and governmentality. This study did not identify this kind of experience amongst the social workers surveyed. Nonetheless, the fact that there were some claims by a few of the managers to restrict and control the supervision more could be a warning in this direction; see also Lauri (2019). It is important to remind the reader that this chapter does not try to evaluate the effects of social work supervision but capture the perceived experiences of a number of Swedish social workers and managers.

A third value (besides enlightenment in reflection over practice and calmness in the organization) is strengthening cooperation within the team. Since supervision encourages joint responsibility and interaction between social workers, with regard to the cases and themes they discuss, it can often help to create a better working environment within a group.

Some challenges

Although there is huge support within the profession for this external form of supervision, it does of course also pose several challenges. One is financial, resulting from a situation of restricted resources. Supervision, for any group of social workers in Sweden, is normally the greatest (and sometimes only) expenditure in the budget for competence development. Other ventures may be put on hold. Another challenge is the independence of external supervision and its relation to management. A third arises when supervision does not work well, or in some cases could even be considered abusive.

Over the last 20 years of Swedish social work, NPM has had a huge effect on social work both in general terms and with regard to supervision more specifically. There is plenty of research on its effects on social work in Sweden (see, for example, Höjer et al. 2011, Sallnäs and Wiklund 2018), however the effects of social work supervision have been studied much less. On the one hand, it could be assumed that NPM, with its focus on marketization and privatization, would enhance the quality of external supervision provided by private practitioners within their own firms, and in one way it has. It is not at all unusual that social services contract out different forms of care to private providers including services for professional development. This has been the case for a number of years, especially with regard to supervision. Over the last ten years, regulatory changes to the way services that are contracted out are to be organized with reoccurring procurement processes and the creation of general agreements for providers of supervision have made it almost impossible to function as an independent private practitioner. In order to complete the necessary paperwork and be accessible on the lists of supervisors from which municipal social work organizations are allowed to choose contractors, it is necessary to be part of a bigger organization. This has led to mergers between supervisors and the creation of bigger firms and corporations. Anecdotal evidence suggests that a number of supervisors actually left the industry due to this development.

Another effect of NPM is its focus on value for money, local and decentralized budget responsibility, and local management to fulfil budget strategies. As a result, the responsibilities, even of first-line managers, in the governance of social service organizations have increased over time. Supervision is an appreciated form of staff support and development, but as has been noted above, there is no clear evidence that it actually improves the outcomes of services. As has also been shown, the Swedish external reflective supervision tradition has substantial independence from the organization and is part of the professionalization process of social work in both individual and collective terms. There have been attempts to govern and control supervision in different ways. From time to time, different social work organizations in Sweden have tried to replace external supervision with different forms of supervision by representatives of their own organizations (not necessarily the first-line manager). So far, these attempts have been met with great resistance from social workers and in most cases stopped. Another management strategy has been to decrease the time for external supervision, either by number of hours or how often the groups meet. Unfortunately, no recent national study of supervision in Sweden has been conducted, but this picture is quite clear in discussions with many of the active supervisors today.

In the study that underlines this chapter, the reasons for control were not only financial. There was unease among some managers over supervisors coming in and discussing organizational issues such as social workers' relations to their managers or how they handled reorganization topics. Both managers and social workers evidenced that supervisors and managers did not always pull in the same direction on several issues, and for some managers this was not acceptable and needed to be controlled.

Abusive supervision

In the international dialogue on supervision, there are new discussions about abusive supervision and how this may lead to subordinate silence (Xu, et al. 2020). This relates mostly to situations in which supervisors are also managers with power over social workers' daily work, which leads to silence and lower retention rates. External supervision may now be seen as one solution to situations such as these, but external supervision is not without its challenges. In the afore-mentioned study, social workers and managers where asked if they had any experience of supervisors exceeding their authority. Almost half of all the social workers asked said that they had experienced this at least once in their professional lives. This included: (i) formal breaches of contracts, (ii) role conflicts, (iii) unethical or improper behaviour, and (iv) conflicts over the content of supervision. Examples of these different forms are given in Bradley and Höjer (2009).

> One example from the first category is the supervisor that on his own account prolonged the supervision contract with the group without consulting the manager. Examples of inappropriate behavior have been given, for instance when a supervisor physically left the group in the middle of a supervision session claiming that it was too difficult, or another who fell asleep during a session, and then on waking blamed the group for being too boring.
>
> *(ibid. p. 80)*

It can thus be seen that external supervision may also have abusive elements. As has been commented upon before, both social workers and managers in Swedish social work are content with the way external supervision normally works – a number of social workers could relate to some kind of abusive event in the history of supervision. More commonly was of course dissatisfaction with individual supervisors or periods of supervision. Then the discontent was not about abusive elements but merely that the needs of the group were not met or that the supervisor was not active enough or did not help the group during the supervision.

Conclusion

On the whole, the situation for external supervision in Swedish social work is still strong, despite some recent challenges. The defense of external supervision is solid among social workers, and there are few stories about social workers wanting to discontinue having supervision. In Sweden, reflective external supervision nonetheless bears traces of the historic foundations from psychodynamic psychotherapeutic practice: the ideas of openness, reflective space, that the inner world of social workers also matters when it comes to their handling of cases, and creating an alliance between supervisors and supervisees, etc. (see, for example, Norberg et al. 2016). The supervision given also seems to follow the idea of a "global objective" in which different parts of the social work experience may form part of the supervision content.

The last decade has seen different kinds of threats against external supervision in the footsteps of NPM. The time for supervision has been restricted, and there has been regular control from management in relation to the choice of supervisors and reducing costs. Many issues in relation to external supervision need further study.

Note

1 The translations of the quotes in this chapter from Swedish into English have been made by the author.

References

Abbot, A., 1988. *The systems of professions*. Chicago, IL: University of Chicago Press.
Baldschun, A., Hämälääinen, J., Töttö, P., Rantonen, O., and Salo, P., 2019. Job-strain and well-being among Finnish social workers: exploring the differences in occupational well-being between child protection

social workers and social workers without duties in child protection. *European Journal of Social Work*, 22 (1), 43–58.

Beddoe, L., 2012. External supervision in social work: power, space, risk, and the search for safety. *Australian Social Work*, 65 (2), 197–213.

Beddoe, L., Karvinen-Niinikoski, S., Ruch, G., and Tsui, M., 2016. Towards an international consensus on a research agenda for social work supervision: report on the first survey of a delphi study. *British Journal of Social Work*, 46, 1568–1586.

Bernler, G., and Johnsson, L., 1985. *Handledning i psykosocialt arbete*. Stockholm: Natur och Kultur.

Björkenheim, J., 2007. Knowledge and social work in health care – the case of Finland. *Social Work in Health Care*, 44, 261–278.

Boalt Boetsius, S., and Ögren, M.-L., 2000. *Grupphandledning. Den lilla gruppen som forum för lärande*. Stockholm: Mareld.

Bradley, G., Engelbrecht, L., and Höjer, S., 2010. Supervision: a force for change? Three stories told. *International Social Work*, 53 (6), 773–790.

Bradley, G., and Höjer, S., 2009. Supervision reviewed: reflections on two different social work models in England and Sweden. *European Journal of Social Work*, 12 (1), 71–85.

Cajverts, L., 1998. *Behandlarens kreativa rum. Om handledning*. Lund: Studentlitteratur.

Carpenter, J. Webb, and Bostock, L., 2013. The surprisingly weak evidence base for supervision. Findings from a systematic review of research in child welfare practice (2000—2012). *Children and Youth Services Review*, 35 (11), 1843–1853.

Cearley, S., 2004. The power of supervision in child welfare services. *Child & Youth Care Forum*, 33 (5), 313–327.

Dellgran, P., and Höjer, S., 2005. Privatisation as professionalisation? Attitudes, motives and achievements among Swedish social workers. *European Social Work*, 8 (1), 41–64.

Egelund, T., and Kvilhaug, A., 2001. Supervisionens organisering. *Socialvetenskaplig Tidskrift*, 3, 180–198.

Evans, T., and Harris, J., 2002. Street-level bureaucracy, social work and the (exaggerated) death of discretion. *British Journal of Social Work*, 34 (6), 871–895.

Freidson, E., 2004. *Professionalism. The third logic*. Chicago, IL: University of Chicago.

Hasenfeld, Y., 2010. *Human services as complex organizations*. 2nd ed. Los Angeles, CA: SAGE.

Höjer, S., Beijer, E., and Wissö, T., 2007. *Varför handledning? Handledning som professionellt projekt och organisatoriskt verktyg inom handikappomsorg och individ och familjeomsorg*. Göteborg: FoU i Väst.

Höjer, S., and Forkby, T., 2011. Care for sale: the influence of new public management in child protection in Sweden. *British Journal of Social Work*, 41 (1), 93–110.

Iversen, A.C., and Heggen, K., 2016. Child welfare workers use of knowledge in their daily work. *European Journal of Social Work*, 19 (2), 187–203.

Jacquet, S.E., Clark, S.J., Morazes, J.L., and Withers, R., 2008. The role of supervision in the retention of public child welfare workers. *Journal of Public Child Welfare*, 1 (3), 27–54.

Kadushin, A., and Harkness, D., 2002. *Supervision in social work*. 4th ed. New York: Columbia University Press.

Kullberg, K., 2011. *Socionomkarriärer: Om vägar genom yrkeslivet i en av välfärdsstatens nya professioner*. Göteborgs universitet: Institutionen för social arbete.

Lauri, M., 2019. Mind your own business: technologies for governing social worker subjects. *European Journal of Social Work*, 22 (2), 338–349.

Magnussen, J., 2018. Supervision in Denmark – an empirical account of experiences and practices. *European Journal of Social Work*, 21 (3), 359–373.

Mo, K.Y., O'Donoghue, K., Wong, P.Y., and Tsui, M., 2020. The historic development of knowledge in social work supervision: finding new directions from the past. *International Social Work*. doi:10.1177/0020872819884995.

Norberg, J., Axelsson, H, Barkman, N., Hamrin, M., and Carlsson, J., 2016. What psychodynamic supervisors say about supervision: freedom within limits. *Clinical Supervisor*, 35 (2), 268–286.

Pettersson, U., 2001. *Socialt arbete, politik och professionalisering. Den historiska utvecklingen i USA och Sverige*. Stockholm: Natur och Kultur.

Rose, S., and Palattiyil, G., 2020. Surviving or thriving? Enhancing the emotional resilience of social workers in their organizational settings. *Journal of Social Work*, 20 (1), 23–42.

Sallnäs, M., and Wiklund, S., 2018. *Socialtjänstmarknaden*. Stockholm: Liber.

Tham, P., and Lynch, M., 2019. Lost in transition? – Newly educated social workers' reflections on their first months in practice. *European Journal of Social Work*, 22 (3), 400–411.

Westbrook, T.M., Ellis, J., and Ellett, A.J., 2006. Improving retention among public child welfare workers: what we can learn from the insights and experiences of committed survivors. *Administration in Social Work*, 30 (4), 37–62.

Xu, Q., Zhao, Y., Xi, M., and Li, F., 2020. Abusive supervision, high-performance work systems and subordinate silence. *Personal Review*, 49 (8), 1637–1653. doi:https://www.emerald.com/insight/content/doi/10.1108/PR-01-2019-0029/full/pdf

4

SOCIAL WORK SUPERVISION IN WESTERN CANADA

Glen Schmidt

This chapter will examine social work supervision in Western Canada, specifically the four provinces of Manitoba, Saskatchewan, Alberta, and British Columbia. For those unfamiliar with Canada, the chapter begins with some brief geographic and economic description followed by basic information on Canadian government and the organization and regulation of social work. A short commentary on Western Canadian settlement and the relationship between social work and Indigenous people is also provided. The limited research on supervision of practicing social workers in the Western Canadian context is discussed along with challenges, opportunities, and future directions for social work supervision.

The Canadian context

Canada is the second largest country in the world and the largest in the western hemisphere. The last official census in 2016 reported a population of 35,121,728 (Statistics Canada 2016). About two-thirds of the Canadian people live within 100 kilometers of the border with the United States, an area that represents four percent of total Canadian territory (Statistics Canada 2016). Given the territorial size of Canada and the concentration of population near the Canadian and American border, it goes without saying there are vast areas of the country that are sparsely populated. The Canadian population is increasingly urban although large parts of the economy are dependent on resource-based industries that are typically located in more remote, rural, and northern regions. During the last census period from 2011 to 2016, the highest growth in population occurred in the four western provinces of Manitoba, Saskatchewan, Alberta, and British Columbia. The 2016 census data found that the four western provinces made up 31.6% of Canada's total population (Statistics Canada 2016). Natural resource extraction represents an important part of the western Canadian economy. Collectively, the four western provinces accounted for 38% of Canada's real GDP in 2017, and the per capita GDP in the four western provinces was 18% higher than the national average (Government of Canada 2019).

The Canadian political system operates under federalism with legislative responsibility shared and divided between the federal and provincial governments. This model of governance has some strengths but it also creates challenges. For example, there are universal health and social welfare programs but new initiatives are difficult to develop given the varied interests and needs of the provincial and federal governments. Despite the somewhat cumbersome nature of policy development, Canada is a highly democratic country and ranks sixth among the world's countries on the Democracy Index (The Economist Intelligence Unit 2019).

Social work services are delivered through various mechanisms and structures including the federal government, provincial governments, municipal governments, health authorities, Indigenous organizations, non-government organizations, and private for-profit individuals and companies. There is variation from province to province, as many of the services fall under provincial legislation and standards as established by the individual provinces. There are also differences between provinces in the organization and regulation of social workers, as the enabling legislation falls under provincial jurisdiction. For example, in some provinces, registration of social workers is mandatory while in others it is voluntary. In provinces such as British Columbia, a social worker employed with some organizations is exempt from mandatory registration while other organizations require registration. This makes it difficult to know the exact number of social workers in every province, as non-control of title, excluded employment categories, and voluntary registration obscure the number of social workers and where they work. Similarly, it is impossible to identify exact numbers of social workers employed in a supervisory capacity. As noted, many social workers are not registered. As a result, the data from regulatory bodies is not complete. Similarly, Statistics Canada uses occupational categories rather than professional designations for numeric counts and these categories do not provide a reliable indicator of the number of social workers.

Historical context

At confederation in 1867, Canada was comprised of four eastern provinces: Nova Scotia, New Brunswick, Quebec, and Ontario. Unlike its neighbor to the south, Canada's independence from Britain was achieved through a relatively orderly and peaceful process that didn't involve violent revolution. However, there was conflict with Indigenous populations as Canadian settlers moved west. The Red River Insurrection in 1870 and the North West Rebellion in 1885 were conflicts between the Dominion or federal government and Indigenous people. The Indian Act of 1876, the creation of reserves, and the development of residential school policies after 1880 served to marginalize and oppress Indigenous populations and contributed in a major way to the current challenges of poverty, high rates of unemployment, substance misuse, violence, and lower life expectancy. Social work was involved in moving children to residential schools and, through its professional association, the Canadian Association of Social Work, there was a call to assimilate Indigenous people (Jennissen and Lundy 2011 p. 138). During the 1960s, social workers working in the area of child welfare removed thousands of Indigenous children from their communities and placed them with non-Indigenous families, separating the children from their extended families, community, and culture. Many of the adoptive families lived in the United States and Europe, further complicating the situation. The mass removals were brought to public attention by Patrick Johnson in his report for the Council on Social Development (1983), and social work as a profession has struggled with the legacy of its involvement in the aptly named "sixties scoop."

Western Canada

Many of the settlers who came to the four western provinces left oppressive situations in their homelands. Although British settlers accounted for a significant portion of the in-migration, many Europeans such as Belgians, Germans, Dutch, Poles, Romanians, Ukrainians, and Hungarians were among the newcomers (Gagnon 2019). There were also Chinese and Indian newcomers as well as groups who suffered persecution because of religious beliefs and ethnic identity. These included Jews, Mennonites, and Hutterites from eastern Europe as well as Mormons and African Americans from the United States (Gagnon 2019). Most of the settlers engaged in agriculture, as the government offered 160 acres of free land as an incentive to settle the prairie provinces of Manitoba, Saskatchewan, and Alberta. Unlike the established eastern provinces, the four western provinces had a more diverse population, albeit one that was predominantly European in origin. There was a hierarchy among the settler populations with English-speaking people of British and American origin holding positions of power and influence. This was reflected in eastern Europeans being excluded from some organizations, and it was also evident during the Winnipeg General Strike of 1919 when "foreign agitators" were blamed for the large labor action. The Canadian West reflected a high level of diversity even during the early years of European settlement. The population diversity has continued though many of the newcomers that arrived after World War II chose to settle in the larger cities such as Vancouver, Edmonton, Calgary, Regina, Saskatoon, and Winnipeg.

Social workers have to deal with a challenging legacy in relation to their work with Indigenous people, and social workers also have to be adept at ensuring a level of cultural safety for populations from diverse backgrounds. Social work supervisors have to be mindful of and sensitive to these realities, not only in terms of the populations they serve, but also in terms of the social workers they supervise.

Social work supervision

O'Donoghue, Wong Yuh Ju, and Tsui (2018) examined social work literature published between 1958 and 2015 looking for research articles that focused on supervision of practicing social workers. Most of the published research dealt with supervision of social work field education students, and only 130 articles in the specified time period examined supervision of practicing social workers. In Canada, published research pertaining to supervision of practicing social workers is sparse, as the work on supervision also largely deals with supervision of students in field education. The few studies that examine supervision of practicing social workers focus on Ontario, Canada's most populous and largest province (Hair 2013, Vito 2017).

In order to gain a better understanding of social work supervision in Western Canada, I applied for a grant from the Social Sciences and Humanities Research Council of Canada. The application was successful, and through the research project I recruited 27 social work supervisors from different fields of social work practice. The participants included 8 males and 19 females, with 10 practicing in British Columbia, 8 in Alberta, 2 in Saskatchewan, and 7 in Manitoba. The average age of the supervisors was 47.12 years, with a range from 27 to 61 years. The participants worked an average of 6.7 years in a supervisory role, and the range was from 1 to 20 years. The supervisors averaged 12.3 years on the front-line prior to moving into a supervisory role. The range in front-line experience prior to supervision was from 1 to 30 years. There were no significant differences between the male and female participants.

The participants completed a brief questionnaire and participated in a personal interview. The questionnaire generated descriptive information while the personal interviews elicited in depth responses to prepared questions. The questions were intended to gather information related to how people became social work supervisors; the type of education and training they received before and during their time as a supervisor as well as the value or lack of value in the training and education they received; the sources of support for supervisors; the challenges faced by supervisors; and the rewards and opportunities associated with supervision. The personal interviews were recorded, transcribed, and analyzed using the method of thematic analysis as described by Braun and Clarke (2006). A more detailed account of the methodology can be found in Schmidt and Kariuki (2019).

Becoming a supervisor

Only 5 of the 27 participants started their social work career with a clear goal of becoming a social work supervisor. In most instances the participants developed an interest in becoming a supervisor through what I call "task exposure." Task exposure refers to work opportunities that allow a person to take on the supervisory role or some aspects of the supervisory role. For example, this might involve serving as an acting supervisor while the permanent supervisor is absent for things like training, holiday, medical leave, or parental leave. A senior social worker might also be asked to provide some mentorship to a newly hired social worker. Through this experience some of the participants began to develop an interest in supervision and sought other opportunities to supervise.

Another example of task exposure is the supervision of field education students. This served as a trigger of interest for a number of the supervisors who participated in this research. All of the supervisors who supervised field education students reported that this was a very positive experience and one that promoted their own learning and professional growth. Becoming a supervisor of field education students creates a relationship with a university, and normally there is training and education offered by the university to field education supervisors.

There was also a third group of supervisors who became supervisors through a process of default that I call "happenchance." In this process, a supervisor often left their job without a lot of notice. In some cases there was forewarning but poor planning for replacement on the part of the organization. The vacancy had to be filled and people were recruited quickly even though they lacked a strong interest and may have been reluctant to move into the supervisor role.

The youngest supervisor in the research did not plan to become a supervisor but described the situation this way:

> I guess what had happened is the position unexpectedly became available and I was worried about someone else from the outside coming in because we had a really tight knit group and I definitely had encouraged other seasoned social workers to apply, like I would've respected it if they wanted to step up to the plate and take this position, but none of them were really interested just because within healthcare, especially as a social work lead, it's very dynamic and challenging and stressful. Lots of politics involved. I kind of felt better having someone that I knew would be supporting us as a profession and an advocate and so I think that's ultimately why I applied because no one else wanted to apply. I kind of wanted to make sure we were looked after as a team.

The stereotypical idea of career development – starting as a new graduate, gaining experience over a period of time, planning, then applying to become a supervisor did hold true for some participants in this study. One of the supervisors in Indigenous child welfare who decided early on to become a supervisor said this:

> I found as a frontline worker that I was frustrated with a lot of the standards and the regulations and I felt that it limited my practice. It was one of the reasons I decided to do my Master's. It was my impression that when you have a BSW, no one really cares about your opinion about broad policy. It was really early on in my career, that I felt

that I needed to be at a level to make policy changes and for someone to listen to you; listen to your suggestions.

The role of field education and the relationship with universities was an important factor. Organizations that struggle with resource shortages and workload may decline to take field education students, but it is clear that having a relationship with university field education programs can provide some benefits to the host organization. One supervisor described the importance of the relationship with a university as a pathway to supervision this way:

I would say probably as I became more and more involved with the University doing the field piece for them, I think more by default than anything I developed an interest in supervision.

Education and training

There are currently 43 accredited social work programs across Canada (CASWE-ACFTS 2019). Social work education programs are accredited by the Commission on Accreditation, a body that operates within the Canadian Association for Social Work Education. Of the 43 accredited programs, 41 offer a Bachelor of Social Work (BSW) degree, 29 offer the Master of Social Work (MSW) degree as well as the BSW, and two only offer the MSW degree. There are 30 anglophone programs, 11 are francophone, and 1 program is francophone and anglophone. There are 14 programs located in Western Canada. One of these programs is francophone (Université de St. Boniface) and the remainder are anglophone.

Most of the MSW degrees offer at least one course on supervision and leadership but it is usually an elective course. There are some exceptions, such as the University of Calgary, which has a series of courses called the Leadership in the Human Services Specialization. Courses in leadership and supervision are rare at the BSW level. However, a couple of programs such as MacEwan University in Alberta and the Nicola Valley Institute of Technology in British Columbia offer a single course on leadership.

The lack of courses on social work supervision at the BSW level is a problem in that it is fairly common for Canadian social workers to become supervisors without completion of a graduate degree or specialized training in supervision. This is most evident in rural and remote practice locations, Indigenous organizations, and smaller NGOs and non-profit organizations (Schmidt 2008). For example, I practiced and supervised social work in Northern Manitoba for more than twelve years. The services were provided by the Manitoba Provincial government and included programs in child welfare, community mental health, and disabilities. Five supervisors worked in these programs, and during my period of employment 11 different people moved through the supervisory positions. Only three held MSW degrees while the remainder were people with a BSW degree.

Most of the 27 social work supervisors recruited for the research practiced in urban communities (Schmidt and Kariuki 2019). Among this group 15 held the MSW degree but 12 held undergraduate degrees. There isn't research data to indicate whether this is a precise representation of the qualifications of social work supervisors but it is probably safe to say that substantial numbers of Western Canadian social work supervisors do not hold graduate degrees.

In the research, supervisors were asked about specific training and education that focused on supervision. Nine of the participants reported that they received some training in supervision and leadership before they became a supervisor but eighteen reported no specific training in the area of supervision. Of the nine participants who reported receiving education and training before becoming a supervisor, four indicated that they had taken a course or courses on supervision while doing their MSW degree; three stated that their employer had sponsored them to take a workshop or training course on supervision; and two participants had acted on their own to find supervisory training opportunities. All 27 participants reported that they had received formal training sponsored by their employer after becoming a supervisor.

Reactions of the research participants to training and education varied with no clear pattern regarding the effectiveness or satisfaction with the training received. BSW qualified supervisors indicated that it would have been helpful to have taken a course on leadership and supervision while studying for their undergraduate degree. Supervisors in this study as well as previous research (Blackman and Schmidt 2013) were divided in terms of where they'd like to see supervisory training developed and delivered. Some believed that it should be the responsibility of the Schools of Social Work but others believed it to be the responsibility of employers and professional associations.

Supervisory training is systematic and structured within some larger organizations, but it is more random in smaller NGOs and private agencies that don't have extensive budgets for staff development. In some cases, the training is generic in nature and focused on supervision in a general sense rather than focused on social work supervision. This was certainly my experience when I received training as a supervisor. The training was provided through the Manitoba government's Civil Service Commission and the material used to train social work supervisors was the same as that used to train supervisors in the Department of Highways and Transportation.

Sources of support for supervisors

Research and literature on support of social work supervisors and sources of support for social work supervisors that supervise practicing social workers is virtually non-existent. Most of the published material examines how supervisors can be supported in field instruction or how supervisors working with practicing social workers can support their workers and their clients.

In the research that I did, the 27 supervisors were asked a number of questions pertaining to support in their role as a supervisor. Participants were asked if they felt supported by their supervisees, by other supervisors (if there were other supervisors in the organization), and by senior managers and administrators. They were also asked about mentorship and what form that mentorship took.

All the supervisors who had colleagues in similar supervisory roles felt very supported by their peer group. Not surprisingly, fellow supervisors had a shared understanding of the challenges and frustrations, and fellow supervisors served as a safe source to discuss mutual concerns. Most of the supervisors also felt supported by their supervisees. However, the 27 supervisors did not feel supported by administration and management. Some pointed to individual managers who were supportive but believed the overall management structure was not very supportive or understanding. The lack of understanding often related to prioritizing different goals, as the administrators were focused on budgets and efficiency while supervisors were primarily concerned about the welfare of their clients and workers. One supervisor in an Indigenous child welfare agency put it this way:

> I don't think Finance and Human Resources understand the stress of being a frontline worker because you know if payments are missing or child maintenance or anything like that then Finance will say, well we're busy and you should see all the work we have to do. It's the same on our end but we deal with lives and I've actually confronted our former Director of Finance. I said your dollars can be replaced but our children can't.

A supervisor working in community mental health for a very large urban health authority had this to say about senior management:

> They focus a lot on the numbers and not on the challenges of the work. Clients are not the same. Like I can tell you one of my staff has only 25 clients but she's got the most difficult 25 clients. Another of my staff has 35 clients and they're not so difficult. But administration would only look at the number difference. They don't see the magnitude of the difference and don't realize that the worker with the 25 challenging clients is working a lot harder. Management only looks at the dollar numbers and wants efficiencies.

Mentorship, and the support derived from having a mentor, was important for 12 of the supervisors but among that number those who supervised for a longer period of time lost contact with their mentors and did not rely on mentorship to the same extent as when they first started supervising. Even those who reported not having a mentor thought it would be a valuable resource that could support them in their work as a supervisor. One supervisor who never had a mentor said:

> It's important to look for people doing similar work. I found it quite lonely when I started work as a supervisor. Suddenly I felt that I wasn't a part of a team. My feelings have sort of changed but I think it is important to seek mentorship early on.

None of the supervisors reported an organized or formal system of mentorship in their agency or organization. The mentorship that occurred developed informally and through the personal initiative of the supervisor or the person who became a mentor to a supervisor.

Challenges faced by supervisors

Social work supervisors are stuck in the middle of competing goals and dynamic tensions. On the one hand they are expected to meet organizational goals, but they are also expected to support and advocate for their supervisees as well as the people served by the organization. The aspirations and goals of administrators, supervisees, and clients are not necessarily the same, and the supervisor is often the focal point of dynamic tensions. This was evident in the language some of the supervisors used to describe the challenges they faced. One supervisor working in a large hospital said, "Some days I feel like a punching bag." The supervisor was referring to the sense of feeling caught between administration and the workers they supervised. Another supervisor who worked in a child welfare organization described the sense of being caught in the middle and also used the metaphor of being a target for punishment.

> I don't want to sound overly dramatic, right, but I think dramatic metaphors are probably more accurate. I mean you feel like a whipping boy, a whipping person, as a supervisor. I really think it's interesting because when you look at a lot of research in social work, they talk about the team lead supervisory position as one of the most challenging positions. You're kind of sandwiched, right. You get the garbage from beneath and the garbage from up top.

Technology and access were also noted as challenges for many of the supervisors. One supervisor working for a large health care authority expressed their frustration this way:

> There are no options. So, I think in this job, I think the timelines are tight and the expectations have gotten higher and emails – we'd like to blow up our email system. Everyone emails far too often. I have a notorious reputation in eHealth of having the largest hard drive space of any supervisor in the system and it's because everyone comes looking for an answer. And anyone who sends me back a thank you, I never want to talk to them again. You do not have to say thank you on an email. I got it you know. I think I weaned myself down to zero on Friday. I have 84 today. I'll have 300 by the end of the day.

The application of business models to human service organizations was also seen as a challenge. A number of the supervisors working in health care described the practical effects of working with business models like Lean. Lean is a model germane to business as it focuses on continuous improvement, total quality management, and the development of just-in-time inventory systems. The goals are to reduce or cut wasteful spending while improving the quality of service. Two of the supervisors working in health care described the practical effects of working with this model as an exercise in downloading. They used the specific example of the Human Resources department in their respective organizations. In order to reduce costs and demonstrate greater efficiency, the Human Resources department passed on some of their functions to program supervisors. The end result was that while the Human Resources department could claim greater efficiency and boast about meeting its targets, social work supervisors were expected to manage additional work.

This drive for efficiency was evident in many of the interviews but it was especially noticeable among social work supervisors in health care. For example, supervisors in hospitals face constant pressure to ensure their workers develop discharge plans so that patients can be moved out of beds as quickly as possible. Canada has a public health care system but hospital beds are a costly component of the system. One can understand the desire of administrators to move patients into less expensive community care options as quickly as possible. However, this is a major challenge faced by supervisors in health care. The desire to move a patient out of a hospital bed surfaced as a key ethical dilemma faced by hospital social work supervisors. A supervisee might say that the resources aren't in place or the support situation with family is such that it would not be a good idea for the person to go home at this stage. At the same time administrators put pressure on supervisors to move patients as quickly as possible.

Most of the supervisors raised concerns about the lack of resources available to their workers. One supervisor in a large child welfare organization with responsibility for remote communities had this to say:

> I get frustrated about the availability of support, like resources in the community. We deal with a population that doesn't always have the ability to plan in advance so we have a lot of crises and not a lot of our resources have the ability to deal with a crisis because they want to have everything planned in advance; so it doesn't mesh well with the communities that we serve. There are lots of budget constraints and an inability to spend money on things that make sense when there's other spending that doesn't make sense.

Child welfare organizations face constant public scrutiny. This is not unique to Canada – it is widely seen in other developed countries with formal child welfare systems. Serious injury to a child or the death of a child results in media attention and even public backlash against social workers. For example, the murder of a five-year-old child by his mother in British

Columbia resulted in a public inquiry that dominated the media for months. Social workers were heavily criticized and blamed in the media (Callahan and Callahan 1997). Supervisors can be the focus of blame when there is a tragedy, but they also face additional work in that organizations responsible for child protection develop multiple check and balance systems to try and avoid mistakes.

Rewards and opportunities

All of the social workers believed their job as a supervisor was important and while they expressed frustration and described many challenges, they also talked about the rewards that came with supervision. For example, one supervisor said:

> I feel very lucky and really grateful to be able to provide supervision and be in a supervisory role to so many outstanding social workers. Supervision really does give you the opportunity to support people in their role as a social worker making a difference for people and creating positive social change.

Relationships with their supervisees were especially important. One supervisor put it this way:

> I don't know if enjoy is the right word but I certainly find at the end of the day that I feel like I've made a valuable contribution if I've been able to support the staff that work for me to be able to do their jobs. I don't always like the people management side and you know in a group of ten staff, you're always going to have one or two that may not be following the organizational procedures and that kind of thing and certainly some of the internal politics I could do without, but I think the actual practical work, either helping out where I can or supporting my staff to do a good job, I find value in that.

While the work of supervision is challenging and demanding, the supervisors were able to point to the benefits that derive from the job. Helping staff to develop their skills and being able to support people in difficult work can be rewarding and satisfying.

Summary

Within Western Canada social work supervisors face many challenges. Lack of resources, working within business models that aren't a good fit with the human services, and intense media and public scrutiny in some fields of practice such as child welfare, represent a few of the challenges. University social work education and research tends to concentrate on the supervision of field education students. While there are courses and program options regarding supervision at the graduate level, undergraduate programs seldom provide courses on supervision and this is problematic, as BSW-qualified social workers do become supervisors. Employers provide training for practicing social work supervisors but this training is often generic in nature and lacks a specific social work focus. Mentorship was seen as a useful resource by the participants in this research but there is no systematic system of mentorship that is widely available to social work supervisors. Despite the challenges, supervisors derive value from their work and understand its importance. Educators, employers, professional associations, and regulators need to come together to celebrate social work supervision and provide stronger and more systematic mechanisms for people to grow in the supervisory role.

Note: The research for this work was made possible through funding from the Social Sciences and Humanities Research Council of Canada.

References

Blackman, K., and Schmidt, G., 2013. The development of child protection supervisors in Northern British Columbia. *Child Welfare*, 92 (5), 87–105.

Braun, V., and Clarke, V., 2006. Using thematic analysis in psychology. *Qualitative Research in Psychology*, 3 (2), 77–101.

Callahan, M., and Callahan, K., 1997. Victims and villains. *In*: J. Pulkingham, and G. Ternowetsky, eds. *Child and family policies: struggles, strategies and options*. Halifax: Fernwood Publishing, 40–57.

CASWE-ACFTS, n.d. *Accredited programs*. Available from: https://caswe-acfts.ca/commission-on-accreditation/list-of-accredited-programs/ [6 August 2019].

Gagnon, E., 2019. Settling the west: immigration to the prairies from 1867 to 1914. Canadian Museum of Immigration at Pier 21, Halifax. Available from: https://pier21.ca/research/immigration-history/settling-the-west-immigration-to-the-prairies-from-1867-to-1914 [5 August 2019].

Government of Canada, 2019. *Economic overview*. Available from: https://www.wd-deo.gc.ca/eng/243.asp [6 August 2019].

Hair, H., 2013. The purpose and duration of supervision, and the training and discipline of supervisors: what social workers say they need to provide effective services. *British Journal of Social Work*, 43 (8), 1562–1588. doi:10.1093/bjsw/bcs071.

Jennissen, T., and Lundy, C., 2011. *One hundred years of social work: a history of the profession in English Canada 1900–2000*. Waterloo, ON: Wilfred Laurier Press.

Johnson, P., 1983. *Native children and the child welfare system*. Ottawa, ON: Council on Social Development.

O'Donoghue, K., Wong Yuh Ju, P., and Tsui, M.S., 2018. Constructing an evidence-informed social work supervision model. *European Journal of Social Work*, 21 (3), 348–358. doi:10.1080/13691457.2017.1341387.

Schmidt, G., 2008. Geographic location and supervision in child welfare. *Journal of Public Child Welfare*, 2 (1), 91–108.

Schmidt, G., and Kariuki, A., 2019. Pathways to social work supervision. *Journal of Human Behavior in the Social Environment*, 29 (3), 321–332. doi:10.1080/10911359.2018.1530160

Statistics Canada, 2016. *Population size and growth in Canada: key results from the 2016 census*, Available from: https://www150.statcan.gc.ca/n1/daily-quotidien/170208/dq170208a-eng.htm [6 August 2019].

The Economist Intelligence Unit, January 8 2019. *Democracy index 2018: me too?* Available from: https://www.eiu.com/public/topical_report.aspx?campaignid=Democracy2018 [6 August 2019].

Vito, R., 2017. The impact of service system transformation on human service agencies: competing Ministry directives and strategic innovative leadership adaptations. *Human Service Organizations: Management, Leadership & Governance*, 41 (5), 477–491.

5

SUPERVISION OF SOCIAL WORKERS WITHIN A SOCIAL DEVELOPMENT PARADIGM

A South African perspective

Lambert Engelbrecht

Supervision of social workers has been practiced in South Africa for more than half a century. This chapter presents an integrated overview of the evolution of social work supervision practices in South Africa, as well as a process model with actionable steps towards authentication of supervision within the country's social development paradigm. Based on contemporary local qualitative research findings, a comprehensive synthesized and authentic definition of supervision is compiled and unpacked with distinct determinants. Some challenges for future supervision practices in South Africa are posed. The definition of social work supervision, determinants, and challenges may be applicable to other contexts across the world.

The evolution of social work supervision in South Africa

Differences in understanding and experiences of colonialism, apartheid, and democratization are shaping the narrative of the evolution of social work supervision in South Africa. For this reason, the exposition below will be based chiefly on the interpretation of, and integration with, specific markers of the history of social work and the socio-economic development of the country.

Emerging and predominantly administrative years (1960–1980)

As a response to poverty aggravated by a war and colonization by England at the beginning of the twentieth century, several non-governmental organizations were established after 1904 and a government department of social welfare was constituted in 1937. These developments resulted in a fairly sophisticated social service delivery system, despite fragmented welfare services along racial lines, owing to the political discourse of the apartheid era. One of the first social work supervision-related articles, published in an academic journal in South Africa, focused on supervision in a group work context (Pieterse 1961) and referred to supervision as field guidance. This was followed by the view held by social work scholars in the country that both administration and education should be included as functions of supervision in their quest for the training of supervisors at South African universities (Du Plessis 1965). The interest in supervision in social work was fueled by articles by Barette (1968a, 1968b) in *Social Work/Maatskaplike Werk*, which was the first professional journal for the social worker in South Africa. Although the emphasis of supervision during this era was chiefly rooted in administrative practices, Botha's (1971) exposition of administration, education, and support as integrated functions of supervision, with reference to the problem-solving process of Perlman (1957), sparked an interest in the expansion of the sole focus on the administrative function of supervision to include education and support (Dercksen 1973, Hoffmann 1976). This happened at a time when supervision of social workers was statutorily mandated with the promulgation of a Social and Associated Workers Act (110 of 1978) (RSA 1978), which made provision for a statutory council to regulate the conduct, training, and registration of social and associated workers, and which stipulated that a social worker may only be supervised by another competent social worker.

Period of integrated supervision functions and escalation of knowledge base (1981–1993)

The seminal work of Botha (1985) on an education model for efficient supervision eventually laid the foundation for the practice and training of supervisors in South Africa. During this period, postgraduate supervision courses were offered at several South African universities at honors and master's degree levels, finally acknowledging the integration of administration, education, and support as essential functions of supervision. A plethora of academic theses followed during the next decade or more and at least 40 postgraduate theses in social work supervision were produced during this period (NRF 2019). This timeframe, in which was founded the current body of supervision knowledge in South Africa, may be regarded as a period when research and practices in supervision flourished (Engelbrecht 2019).

Times of social change (1994–2014)

With the transition towards a new political dispensation and welfare system in South Africa in 1994, the focus on supervision as a mainstay in social work veered gradually to priorities of service delivery rather than to issues of human resources and supervision of social workers. A white paper for social welfare (RSA 1997) was introduced with the aim of shaping social welfare services in the new political dispensation, ushering in a developmental approach towards social welfare. This marked a fundamental movement away from a residual and institutional welfare approach, and is a rights-based, people-centered welfare approach, which is largely based on Midgley's (1995, p. 25) definition as "a process of planned social change designed to promote the well-being of the population as a whole in conjunction with a dynamic process of economic development." More specifically, the developmental approach to social welfare recognizes the need for integrated strengths and rights-based interventions in social service delivery, and emphasizes appropriate services to all, particularly the poor, vulnerable, and those with special needs. It recognizes that social work, among other social service professions, plays a major role in addressing the developmental needs of the South African society (DSD 2006). The distinctive type of social work that has evolved from the social development approach has become known as "developmental social work" (Midgley and Conley 2010, p. xiii). Developmental social work can be defined as an integrated, holistic approach to social work that responds to the interconnections between the person and the environment, links micro and macro practice, and utilizes non-discriminatory models, approaches and interventions, and partnerships to promote social and economic inclusion and well-being (Gray 2006, Patel and Hochfeld 2008). An integration of case work, group work, and community work is regarded as primary methods of developmental social work service delivery.

Significantly, the new political dispensation resulted in a massive migration of South African social workers to other countries and employment outside the social work domain, and this consequently had a tremendous impact on the deterioration of supervision knowledge and skills as a whole (Engelbrecht 2006a). Also, the newly established Department of Social Development did not regard supervision of social workers as a priority and acknowledged in a recruitment and retention strategy (DSD 2006, p. 33) that "…the dearth of supervisors in practice is exacerbated by the perception that trained supervisors are not necessary." This recruitment and retention strategy specifically referred to "…poor quality supervisors, who themselves also lack capacity to conduct professional supervision" (p. 33). The "lost generation" and "brain drain" of supervisors (Engelbrecht 2006a, p. 141), intensified when all universities in the country who offered structured postgraduate courses in supervision in the past discontinued their programs (Engelbrecht 2010), chiefly owing to the lack of interest and demand. Only some five postgraduate theses on supervision of social workers were produced during this period in the country (NRF 2019). This decline in both the theory and practice of supervision in the country gave momentum to the development of a national Supervision Framework for the social work profession in South Africa (hereafter referred to as the Supervision Framework) by both the National Department of Social Development (DSD) and the South African Council for Social Service Professions (SACSSP) (DSD and SACSSP 2012). The aim of this Framework was to set norms and standards for effective supervision in the country and was designed by means of public consultations with government departments, non-governmental organizations, and social workers in private practice.

The emergence of an authentic inclination (2015 and beyond)

A campaign towards the decolonization of university curricula in South Africa was launched in 2015 by students and academics from all over South Africa (Molefe 2016). The implication for social work, and specifically supervision of social workers, was that such a dismantling would entail the revisiting of the initial work and practices of primary authors who conceptualized supervision in South Africa (see Hoffmann 1976, Botha 1985, Pelser 1988), and who largely drew on the work of North American authors such as Kadushin (1976), Austin (1981), Middleman and Rhodes (1985), Bunker and Wijnberg (1988), Shulman (1993), and Munson (1993). This transmission of knowledge from North America to the South African context was based on the premise that knowledge in social work (and thus also supervision) is universally applicable. However, in order to conceptualize a body of supervision knowledge and practices in South Africa's social development paradigm, which is regarded by the Department of Social Development as an antithesis of the country's previous institutional social welfare approach (DSD and SACSSP 2012), the Department (DSD) contracted a private service provider to compile a manual for supervision of social workers. Supervisors were also trained by the DSD and private service providers on the national Supervision Framework. The DSD furthermore activated some schools of social work in the country to offer a postgraduate diploma in supervision. Parallel to these initiatives, the SACSSP embarked on a process to regulate supervision as a registered field of specialization in social work in the country. In addition, the DSD contracted a private service provider to compose a consolidated national Supervision Framework with norms, standards, and theoretical components for all social service professions in the country (including child and youth care and community development workers). As part of the consultations on this document, several academic scholars in the field of social work supervision, together with scholars of different social service professions, the SACSSP, and the DSD, continue with efforts to develop and refine authentic supervision practices in South Africa (Engelbrecht 2019).

Towards defining authentic supervision in South Africa

Against the backdrop of the evolution of supervision in South Africa, and as an effort to define supervision of social workers in the country, Engelbrecht (2019) proposed a process model of stages in decolonization and steps in authentication of social work supervision practices. The stages in decolonization are principally based on Walton and Abo-El-Nasr's (1988) exposition thereof and refer to transmission as an initial stage in the development of social work and the emergence of supervision in countries outside the West. The work of the founders of supervision in South Africa, such as Botha (1971, 1985, 2002), may serve as an example. The Supervision Framework of the country (DSD and SACSSP 2012), furthermore, may be regarded as an effort towards indigenization, as a second identifiable stage towards decolonization. This Framework featured some form of modification to suit Indigenous needs and contexts with specific norms and standards, and engendered a third stage, namely authentication. Within this context, authentication (compare Abo-El-Nasr and Eltaiba, 2016) refers to the development of a local model of social work supervision within a social development paradigm. An example of such a model is Ncube's (2018) model of social work supervision in a social development approach. However, Engelbrecht (2019) suggests, in addition, an explicit dissection of the authentication stage in the process of decolonization of supervision knowledge and practice, with specific actionable steps, in order to derive a comprehensive definition of supervision in South Africa. These actionable steps may be regarded as a prerequisite for an authentic model of supervision in South Africa's social development paradigm. The steps are the following:

Step 1: Examine the local context and professional status of social work and supervision practices.

Step 2: Identify essential determinants of supervision based on local empirical research.

Step 3: Analyze the identified determinants of supervision against available frameworks (such as the Supervision Framework for the social work profession in South Africa), professional status of social work and supervision, and contemporary local research findings on supervision of social workers in South Africa.

Step 4: Compose a comprehensive, synthesized definition of social work supervision, encapsulating the identified determinants of supervision.

Step 5: Use the composed definition of supervision to engender future nationally relevant enquiries into the ongoing development of an authentic body of supervision knowledge and practices.

The execution of the steps of authentication of social work supervision in South Africa's social development paradigm, however, begged for a scholarly methodology in order to eliminate, inter alia, cultural and experiential biases. In order to employ such a methodology, and as a first and second step of authentication, a secondary analysis (Strydom and Delport 2011) was performed of relevant local statutory documents and legislation, and research publications by both authoritative international and South African authors. Seventeen determinants of supervision in South Africa were ultimately identified through a process of thematic analyses (Fouché and De Vos 2011). These determinants are analyzed below as part of a third step in the authentication process, based on sixteen purposively selected (Strydom 2011) qualitative studies on supervision of Southern African social workers (see Cloete 2012, Jacques 2014, Engelbrecht 2013, 2015,

Mokoka 2016, Shokane 2016, Joseph 2017, Mamaleka 2018, Parker 2017, Silence 2017, Chibaya 2018, Goliath 2018, Ncube 2018, Ornellas 2018, Brandt 2019, Wynn 2020). The main criterion for inclusion of these studies was that they should have been executed after the introduction of the country's national Supervision Framework in 2012. As a fourth step in the authentication process, the 17 identified determinants are synthesized in a comprehensive definition of supervision in South Africa (compare Engelbrecht 2019). However, for the purpose of this chapter and ease of comprehension, the definition is presented first and will then be followed with an analysis of each of the determinants of the definition. The fifth step of the authentication process is elucidated in the last section of this chapter dealing with the future challenges for supervision in South Africa.

Definition of social work supervision in South Africa

The definition is demarcated in terms of a brief (a set of detailed directives of supervision), the operationalization of supervision (how to put supervision in action), and the scope of supervision (what determines supervision).

> The *brief* of supervision of social workers is a mandated, formal arrangement by an agency supervision policy, which entails the execution of supportive, educational, and administrative functions by a designated authoritative and trained supervisor, with the ultimate goal to render the best possible services to the user system. Supervision is *operationalized* by means of structured, interactional supervision sessions; directed by adult education principles in a cyclical process with associated tasks, methods, and activities according to a predetermined time-span; based on appropriate theories, perspectives, and practice models; and guided by distinct values and ethical conduct. The *scope* of supervision is determined by a professional, constructive supervisor-supervisee relationship, context of the work environment, and resultant roles, which the supervisor has to fulfil
>
> *(Engelbrecht 2019, p. 318).*

Determinants of social work supervision in South Africa

The following determinants, generated through the actionable steps of authentication as indicated above, are examined against social work supervision practices as extrapolated in the sample of South African research reports. The determinants encompassing the brief of supervision (mandate, policy, functions, designation, and goal) will be examined in greater depth than the determinants regarding the operationalizing and scope of supervision, since the brief of supervision encapsulates more detailed directives of supervision practices. However, it should be noted that the respective determinants of supervision are all interconnected, with a disequilibrium in one affecting another.

Mandate of supervision

Supervision of all social workers as a mandatory practice in South Africa is stipulated by the Policy guidelines of the SACSSP (2016). Specifically, point 5.4.5 (c) of the Policy guidelines states that social workers should take reasonable steps to ensure that adequate agency or organizational resources are available to provide appropriate staff supervision. This statement should be seen in tandem with stipulations of the Social Work Act (RSA 1978) and the requirement of the Supervision Framework (DSD and SACSSP 2012) that only registered social workers may act as supervisors of social workers. This requirement by an Act and a statutory body may be regarded as the hallmark of social work supervision in South Africa. However, in practice, many social workers are not being supervised, although most agencies employ supervisors on a middle management position to adhere to legislative regulations (Chibaya 2018, Brandt 2019, Wynne 2020). Supervisors, in many instances (specifically in designated child protection agencies), act merely as signatories to statutory reports, but do not render meaningful support and education to social workers (Parker 2017, Ornellas 2018, Wynne 2020). Engelbrecht (2015) and Silence (2017) furthermore found that many social workers are managed and supervised by non-social workers.

Agency supervision policy

The Supervision Framework (DSD and SACSSP 2012, pp. 67–68) extensively prescribed the content of a supervision policy to employers of social workers in terms of aspects such as the ratio of supervisor to supervisees, statement on non-discriminatory practices, requirements of the performance management system, and methods for resolving disagreements. This potentially could be a significant strength of supervision practices in South Africa. However, in practice, agency supervision policies are either absent or merely address managerial aspects of supervision (Engelbrecht 2015, Parker 2017, Ornellas 2018).

Functions of supervision

Drawing on the work of Kadushin (1976), Botha (1985) established the core of social work supervision in South Africa in terms of its functions. It seems that administration, education, and support are generally accepted in South Africa as the primary functions of supervision, despite efforts by some scholars to add additional functions or to rename or merge the functions (Engelbrecht 2013, Jacques 2014, Parker 2017, Silence 2017, Chibaya 2018, Goliath 2018, Ornellas 2018). The administrative function ensures that the supervisee's work is professionally executed in accordance with agency and statutory norms; the educational function implies continuing staff development; and the supportive function enables supervisees to mobilize their emotional energy required for effective work performance. In spite of that, all the research reports that were included in the sample as described above suggest that supervision in South Africa is primarily concerned with managerial/administrative functions, that education in supervision is not structured but rather impromptu and informal, and that supervisees experience the support by supervisors as inadequate. This conundrum is mainly ascribed to (i) limited resources owing to insufficient financial allocations to social work *per se* (Cloete 2012), (ii) the kind of social work within the social development paradigm (Joseph 2017), and (iii) the current inadequate academic knowledge of supervision theories of government policy makers, agency managers, and supervisors alike (Brandt 2019). These tenets are engendered by a hidden neoliberal discourse imposed by the DSD on the social work profession in the country (Ornellas 2018), which results in multiple managerial measures, and directing accountability and compliance to do more with less (Engelbrecht 2015), based on three discrete practice realities. First, the limited resources are causing unfavorable working conditions and unmanageable workloads of both supervisors and supervisees, which turn supervision into a crisis-driven and reactive coaching of supervisees, with insufficient time to spend on support of supervisees (Ornellas 2018, Wynne 2020). Second, the bulk of social work service delivery in South Africa tends to focus more on child protection and family perseverance, despite (or because of) the social development approach of the country (Joseph 2017). The implication for supervision is that the Children's Act (RSA 2006) of South Africa requires certain supervision actions (for example to sign off all statutory reports), which is a strictly managerial action, leaving little time for supervision functions other than administration (Chibaya 2018, Brandt 2019). Third, the relative questionable academic and practice supervision knowledge and experience of government policy makers, agency managers, and supervisors alike, is evident in the recent managerially inclined policy documents, frameworks, and manuals, which are academically contested and aimed primarily at administrative compliance and control, rather than at knowledge transfer to and support of the supervisee (Brandt 2019, Wynne 2020). This is an enduring situation in South African social work, alerted by scholars throughout the distinct time periods in the evolution of supervision in South Africa (compare Pieterse 1961, Botha 1971, 1985, Botha 2002, Engelbrecht 2015), and is a direct consequence of the decline in supervision knowledge and experiences after the "times of social change era" in South African social work.

Designated authoritative and trained supervisor

The detrimental impact of untrained supervisors on the wellbeing of supervisees, owing to the power vested in their authority is significant in the analyses of supervisees' experiences of supervision (Joseph 2017, Parker 2017, Mamaleka 2018, Ornellas 2018, Ncube 2018, Brandt 2019, Wynne 2020). This tendency is exacerbated by the fact that a benchmark level of supervision knowledge is not a requirement to take up a position as supervisor at most agencies (Parker 2017). The inherited complex racial, gender, generational, and cultural divides of the country are also proposed as reasons for authoritarian supervision styles (Engelbrecht 2015, Wynne 2020). To this end, captured discourses of supervisees (Chibaya 2018, Mamaleka 2018, Brandt 2019, Wynne 2020) clearly indicate that many supervisors act from an authoritarian stance (e.g. insist that their authority not be questioned, demand compliance, use punishment and threats, and are rule driven) as opposed to an authoritative disposition (e.g. the supervision dyad is based on respect, supervisors are transparent, warm, and nurturing). Notable research findings (Chibaya 2018, Brandt 2019, Wynne 2020) also reveal that newly qualified supervisees experience that they have more in-depth and well-founded academic knowledge on the processes, functions, techniques, and models of supervision than their supervisors, and that this contributes inter alia to the authoritarian stance of their supervisors (many schools of social work currently offer undergraduate courses in supervision and management).

Goal of supervision

The goal of supervision is a vital determinant to demarcate as it is a dependent variable impacting on the definition of supervision as a whole, and it has an influence specifically on the timespan of supervision. The primary goal of supervision is generally defined as enabling supervisees to deliver to service users the best possible services (Engelbrecht 2010, 2015, Parker 2017, Ncube 2018). This primary goal correlates with the postulation of Kadushin (1976), which Botha (1985) initially employed in the development of her model for supervision in South Africa. However, Ornellas (2018) found that some social work agencies across the board (private and public agencies) regard the primary goal of supervision as basically to develop autonomous workers in the shortest time possible. This suggests that cost-effectiveness is the determining driver for supervision, due to decreasing government funding, organizational budget cuts, and overall austerity measures owing to neoliberal socio-economic implications. As a result, findings of Chibaya (2018), who focused specifically on the supervision experiences of intermediate frontline social workers (with three to seven years of work experience), suggested that some supervisees experience supervision after two years as a constraint and an affirmation of their incompetencies, which need management control, and detracting from their professionality. In the same vein, many social workers throughout their professional careers, do not regard supervision as essential to the benefit of service users, and in some scenarios even experience supervision as more harmful than helpful (Wynne 2020).

Structured, interactional supervision sessions

Although Botha (1985), in her exposition of the education model of supervision, and specifically in her accounts of the structure of supervision sessions (2002), detailed that supervision sessions should in essence be based on the supervisee's personal development plan (with specific outcomes) and an associated agenda, Chibaya (2018) found that supervision sessions, in many instances, take the form of inspection and control of supervisees' administrative and statutory compliance (specifically in report writing), and the provision of collegial advice or instruction on what to do and how to do it. This may in general be defined as managerial coaching rather than clinical supervision, which is typified by reflection and support. These practices are supported by research findings of Wynne (2020), which suggest that more often than not, supervision contacts are reduced to impromptu and unstructured "open door, on the run" practices, which may not meet any determinant of the definition of supervision as expounded in this chapter.

Adult education principles

Brandt (2019) found in her study on supervisees' experiences of their supervisors' utilization of adult education principles in supervision, that this is a contentious issue owing to supervisors' lack of knowledge of adult education. This finding supported Parker's (2017) assertion that adult education is an unknown area for many supervisors, as they do not study this in their social work training, nor are any competencies in this specialized area linked to an expectation of holding a position of supervisor. Nevertheless, both supervisors and supervisees regard the utilization of adult education principles as essential in supervision and aver that it should be part of any definition of supervision (Engelbrecht 2015, Brandt 2019).

Cyclical supervision process

A supervision process should consist of progressive phases (compare Botha 2002, Kadushin and Harkness 2014, Tsui 2005). These phases are directed by the agency's goal of supervision (Parker 2017). Engelbrecht (2015) and Silence (2017) proposed a cyclical supervision process, consisting of engagement, assessment, planning, contracting, implementation, and evaluation, as also prescribed by the South African Supervision Framework (DSD and SACSSP 2012). Nevertheless, Ornellas (2018), Goliath (2018), Brandt (2019), and Wynne (2020) revealed that many supervisees do not experience any progressive phases of supervision, with the supervision process remaining stuck in an implementation phase, without proper engagement, assessment, planning, or evaluation.

Supervision tasks

Engelbrecht (2019) and Parker (2017) conceptualized five associated supervision tasks, based on the primary work of Botha (1985), but redefined the tasks in a human resources context:

an inventory of job-specific competencies as part of an engagement phase; a personal development assessment as part of a general assessment phase; a personal development plan as part of a planning phase; specific planned and structured supervision sessions as part of the implementation phase, based on essential tasks in the supervision process; and finally an official summative performance appraisal of the total work functioning of the social worker over a given period of time as part of an evaluation phase. The performance appraisal may ultimately result in the launching of the supervision process into a new cycle by redefining the development plan and contract as associated tasks of the process. These tasks are also described by the Supervision Framework (DSD and SACSSP 2012) and implied by Ncube (2018) in his process model of social development supervision in social work. However, only anecdotal evidence exists that these tasks are being completely and comprehensively performed during supervision of social workers in South Africa (Chibaya 2018, Ncube 2018).

Supervision methods

It seems that individual supervision remains the preferred method of supervision in South Africa, probably owing to the administrative orientation of most supervision practices (Engelbrecht 2013, 2015, Parker 2017, Silence 2017, Goliath 2018). Group supervision is replaced in many instances by training opportunities provided by private service providers, which serve to accumulate points for Continuing Professional Development (CPD) as determined by the SACSSP (Cloete 2012; Ornellas 2018). It appears that peer supervision, distance supervision, or supervision performed via the internet and social media is not the norm (Wynne 2020).

Supervision activities

Cloete (2012), Engelbrecht (2012), and the Supervision Framework (DSD and SACCSP 2012) identified coaching, mentoring, and consultation as supervision activities in a developmental process in South Africa. Although these activities share overlapping foundations, the primary focus of coaching is characterized by high levels of instruction; mentoring implies activities in supervision through identification, internalization, and imitation; and consultation suggests that experienced social workers require input only on specific practice issues. Although not defined as activities in supervision, Ornellas (2018), Brandt (2019), and Wynne (2020) indicate that the characteristics of coaching are in many instances overriding the primary supervision functions, process, and tasks.

Timespan of supervision

Consultation, as originally conceptualized by Botha (2002) in the South African context, is also regarded as a supervision activity (as mentioned in the previous section), and does not entail administrative control (Cloete 2012). However, the practice reality reveals that frontline social workers remain under the auspices of a supervisor regarding administrative matters throughout their careers, and never reach a consultation stage in their supervision (Parker 2017). This feeds the notion that supervision is reduced to an interminable time-span, with the focus on control to the detriment of the other functions of supervision (Ornellas 2018, Silence 2017).

Theories, models, and perspectives underlying supervision

Although the Supervision Framework (DSD and SACSSP 2012) determines that all social work agencies should identify supervision models, theories, and perspectives to be utilized in their supervision policies, no evidence indicates that this is the case in practice. Chibaya (2018) specifically found in his research that supervisors and agency managers are not able to identify any process model or perspective in their supervision practices. An attempt by Ncube (2018), for example, to compose a model for social work supervision in a social development approach alludes to a certain type of supervision within a specific paradigm, viz. a social development paradigm, and does not draw, for example, on acknowledged practice theories, organizational, structural-functional models, or specific perspectives (compare Tsui 2005, Bradley, Engelbrecht and Höjer 2010, Engelbrecht 2019). The research findings of Mokoka (2016), Shokane (2016), Parker (2017), Silence (2017), Chibaya (2018), and Ornellas (2018) indicate that it appears that supervisors merely "do" supervision intuitively (without any theoretical substantiation). However, efforts to authenticate supervision in South Africa, such as those by Ncube (2018), and Mamaleka (2018) who introduced a specific supervision model, and collaborative social work supervision based on a strengths perspective respectively, are nevertheless laudable and may guide supervisors and future research regarding context-specific theories, models, and perspectives underlying supervision in South Africa.

Values and ethical conduct

Values and ethical conduct are an under-researched area in social work supervision in South Africa (Chibaya 2018, Wynne 2020). Although the Supervision Framework (DSD and SACSSP 2012) refers to the upholding of professional values and ethical standards in supervision, it does not clarify relevant content. A broad-based ethical conduct in supervision is provided by the policy guidelines for course of conduct, code of ethics, and the rules for social workers of the SACSSP (2016) in terms of certain practicalities. The absence of specific ethical pointers in supervision in South Africa is an area of grave concern, as is alerted to by the research findings of Wynne (2020) on harmful supervision practices in South Africa. Nevertheless, African principles such as *ubuntu* are referred to, but not comprehensively conceptualized in Indigenous texts on supervision (compare Mamaleka 2018) and may augment the values and ethical conduct in a supervision context in future.

Professional, constructive supervisor-supervisee relationship

The Ethical Code of the SACSSP (2016) refers to specific aspects regarding the nature of the professional supervisor-supervisee relationship in South Africa. This is also a determinant that is pertinent in research findings by researchers such as Mamaleka (2018), Ncube (2018), Brandt (2019), and Wynne (2020). However, within the context of South Africa's complex history of apartheid and cultural discrimination, the only research publication so far that refers specifically to the impact of culture on supervision practices was released twelve years after the country's first democratic elections (Engelbrecht 2006b). Research on power differences influencing the supervision dyad is also scant, with general anecdotal references by Mamaleka (2018) and Engelbrecht (2019).

Context of the work environment

Although the importance to take into consideration the unique differentiations of the contexts of work environments in the supervision of social workers is emphasized by Joseph (2017), Silence (2017), and Parker (2017), the inclination to standardize supervision practices in social work remains prevalent (compare the Supervision Framework of the DSD and SACSSP 2012).

This was specifically critiqued by Engelbrecht (2013), but the multiple neoliberal tenets influencing the social work profession, as identified and described by Ornellas (2018), persist and diminish social work supervision to a one-size-fits-all orientation in South Africa.

Roles of the supervisor

The roles a supervisor has to fulfill cannot be seen in isolation, as pertinent roles affect all the determinants of supervision (Engelbrecht 2019). For instance, the mandate of the supervisor, and the functions and goals of supervision determine whether the supervisor fulfills roles of, for example, administrator, facilitator, or activist. It is evident from frontline social workers' narratives that supervisors in South Africa do not generally have clarity on their role differentiation, although they express a need that the scope of their roles should be defined in a situation-specific way (Chibaya 2018, Ornellas 2018).

Some future challenges for supervision in South Africa

The analysis of the determinants in this chapter, flowing from the compiled definition of social work supervision within South Africa's social development paradigm, clearly indicates that some crucial challenges remain, specifically on how to bridge the gap and discrepancies between the intended brief, operationalization and scope of supervision, and practice realities. If supervision is regarded as a mainstay of social development service delivery in South Africa, mandatory supervision of social workers should be efficiently imposed, not by requiring that social workers themselves should take reasonable steps to ensure supervision, but by regulating that no agency can employ a social worker without availing of adequate resources, including supervision. Therefore, (i) it should be a mandatory practice that any agency employing social workers should have a supervision policy in place for supervision practices, which meets minimum standards regulated by the South African Council for Social Service Professions; (ii) supervision practice in agencies should adhere to the national Supervision Framework under the auspices of the Department of Social Development; and (iii) the clinical orientation of supervision should not be forsaken to meet mere managerial expectations: specifically, the clinical elements of the supervision process and actual supervision sessions should be the primary focus of supervision and training in supervision, rather than managerial accountability and compliance. Hence, it is imperative for social work researchers and academics in South Africa to address these challenges as a point of departure, through a collaborative upscaling of academic supervision knowledge held by government policy makers, agency managers, and supervisors in future – otherwise authentication endeavors of supervision practices in the South African social development paradigm are senseless, as supervision potentially becomes merely mechanical, and a managerial surveillance practice, which will not serve the best interest of the social work profession in the country. Be that as it may, as illustrated in this chapter by research evidence and practice realities, the significance of supervision is well-acknowledged on all levels of social development in the country – by frontline social workers, middle and top managers of both private and public organizations, and government policy makers. With progressive structures and systems in place such as (i) a Social Work Act, (ii) a Council for Social Service Professionals, (iii) provision for registration at the Council as specialist in supervision, (iv) a national Supervision Framework, and (v) numerous government and private efforts towards training of supervisors, supervision of social workers may potentially flourish in future to benefit social development in the country.

Reference list

Abo-El-Nasr, M.A., and Eltaiba, N., 2016. Social work in Egypt: experiences and challenges. *British Journal of Education, Society & Behavioural Science*, 16 (1), 1–11.

Austin, M.J., 1981. *Supervisory management in the human services*. Englewood Cliffs, NJ: Prentice-Hall, Inc.

Barette, J., 1968a. A few thoughts on supervision as a learning experience 1. *Social Work/Maatskaplike Werk*, 4 (2), 85–90.

Barette, J., 1968b. A few thoughts on supervision as a learning experience 2. *Social Work/Maatskaplike Werk*, 4 (3), 131–135.

Botha, N.J., 1971. Supervisie in maatskaplike werk met besondere klem op drie partikuliere Welsynsorganisasies [Supervision in social work with special emphasis on three private welfare organisations]. *Social Work/Maatskaplike Werk*, 8 (2), 72–82.

Botha, N.J., 1985. Onderrigmodel vir doeltreffende supervisie [The educational model for effective supervision]. *Social Work/Maatskaplike Werk*, 21 (4), 239–248.

Botha, N.J., 2002. *Supervision and consultation in social work*. Bloemfontein: Drufoma.

Bradley, G., Engelbrecht, L.K., and Höjer, S., 2010. Supervision: a force for change? Three stories told. *International Social Work*, 53 (6), 773–790.

Brandt, S., 2019. Beginner maatskaplike werkers se ervaring van volwasseneonderrig in supervisie [Beginner social workers' experiences of adult education principles in supervision]. Unpublished thesis. Stellenbosch University.

Bunker, D.R., and Wijnberg, M.H., 1988. *Supervision and performance: managing professionals in human service organizations*. San Francisco, CA: Jossey-Bass.

Chibaya, N.H., 2018. The execution of individual reflective supervision sessions: experiences of intermediate frontline social workers. Unpublished thesis. Stellenbosch University.

Cloete, V., 2012. The features and use of mentoring as an activity in supervision of newly qualified social workers. Unpublished thesis. Stellenbosch University.

Dercksen J.W., 1973. Die onderhoud as hulpmiddel by supervisie van gevallewerk as metode in die maatskaplike werk [The interview as aid in supervision of case work as method in social work]. Unpublished thesis. University of Pretoria.

DSD (Department of Social Development), 2006. *Draft recruitment and retention strategy for social workers*. Pretoria: Department of Social Development.

DSD (Department of Social Development) and SACSSP (South African Council for Social Service Professions), 2012. *Supervision framework for the social work profession*. Department of Social Development. [online] Available from: https://www.westerncape.gov.za/assets/departments/social-development/supervision_framework_for_the_social_work_profession_in_south_africa_2012.pdf [Accessed 6 November 2019].

Du Plessis, G.A., 1965. Supervisie as hulpmiddel in maatskaplike werk met besondere aandag aan die Departement van Volkswelsyn en Pensioene. [Supervision as aid in social work with specific attention to the Department of Social Welfare and Pensions]. Unpublished thesis. University of Pretoria.

Engelbrecht, L.K., 2006a. Plumbing the brain drain of South African social workers migrating to the UK: challenges for social service providers. *Social Work/Maatskaplike Werk*, 42 (2), 101–121.

Engelbrecht, L.K., 2006b. Cultural friendliness as a foundation for the support function in the supervision of social work students in South Africa. *International Social Work*, 49 (2), 256–266.

Engelbrecht, L.K., 2010. Yesterday, today and tomorrow: is social work supervision in South Africa keeping up? *Social Work/Maatskaplike Werk*, 46 (3), 224–242.

Engelbrecht, L.K., 2012. Coaching, mentoring and consultation: the same but different activities in supervision of social workers in South Africa? *Social Work/Maatskaplike Werk*, 48 (3), 357–368.

Engelbrecht, L.K., 2013. Social work supervision policies and frameworks: playing notes or making music? *Social Work/Maatskaplike Werk*, 49 (4), 456–468.

Engelbrecht, L.K., 2015. Revisiting the esoteric question: can non-social workers manage and supervise social workers? *Social Work/Maatskaplike Werk*, 51 (3), 311–331.

Engelbrecht, L.K., 2019. Towards authentic supervision of social workers in South Africa. *The Clinical Supervisor*, 38 (2), 301–325.

Fouché, C.B., and De Vos, A.S., 2011. Formal formulations. *In*: A.S. de Vos, H. Strydom, C.B. Fouché, and C.S.L. Delport, eds. *Research at grass roots. For the social sciences and human service professions*. 4th ed. Pretoria: Van Schaik Publishers, 376–389.

Goliath, J., 2018. Management functions of frontline social workers supervising social auxiliary workers. Unpublished thesis. Stellenbosch University.

Gray, M., 2006. The progress of social development in South Africa. *International Journal of Social Welfare*, 15 (1), 53–64.

Hoffmann, W., 1976. Performance of undergraduate students in field instruction in social work education. Unpublished thesis. University of the Witwatersrand.

Jacques, G., 2014. Supervision functions: African echoes. *In*: L.K. Engelbrecht, ed. *Management and supervision of social workers: issues and challenges within a social development paradigm*. Andover: Cengage Learning EMEA Limited, 124–142.

Joseph, D., 2017. Perceived contributing factors impeding job satisfaction of social workers in non-government organisations. Unpublished thesis. Stellenbosch University.

Kadushin, A., 1976. *Supervision in social work*. New York: Columbia University Press.

Kadushin, A., and Harkness, D., 2014. *Supervision in social work*. 5th ed. New York: Columbia University Press.

Mamaleka, M.M., 2018. Towards collaborative social work supervision: your voice or our voices? *In*: A.L. Shokane, J.C. Makhubele, and L.V. Blitz, eds. *Issues around aligning theory, research and practice in social work education (knowledge pathing: multi-, inter- and trans-disciplining in social sciences series), Volume 1*. Cape Town: AOSIS, 213–235.

Middleman, R.R., and Rhodes, G.B., 1985. *Competent supervision. Making imaginative judgements*. Englewood Cliffs, NJ: Prentice-Hall.

Midgley, J., 1995. *Social development. The developmental perspective in social welfare*. London: SAGE Publications.

Midgley, J., and Conley, A., eds., 2010. *Social work and social development: theories and skills for developmental social work*. New York: Oxford University Press.

Mokoka, L., 2016. The experiences of social work supervisees in relation to supervision within the Department of Social Development in the Johannesburg region. Unpublished thesis. Pretoria: University of South Africa.

Molefe, T.O., 2016. Oppression must fall: South Africa's revolution in theory. *World Policy Journal*, 33 (1), 30–37.

Munson, C.E., 1993. *Clinical social work supervision*. 2nd ed. New York: Haworth Press.

Ncube, M.E., 2018. A model of social work supervision in a social development approach. Unpublished thesis. University of Johannesburg.

NRF, 2019. Nexus [online]. Available from : http://stardata.nrf.ac.za/starweb/CCRPD/servlet.starweb [Accessed 6 November 2019].

Ornellas, A., 2018. Social workers' reflections on implications of neoliberal tenets for social work in South African non-governmental organisations. Unpublished thesis. Stellenbosch University.

Parker, L., 2017. Essential professional competencies of social work supervisors in a non-profit welfare organisation. Unpublished thesis. Stellenbosch University.

Patel, L., and Hochfeld, T., 2008. Indicators, barriers and strategies to accelerate the pace of change to developmental welfare in South Africa. *The Social Work Practitioner-Researcher*, 20 (2), 192–211.

Pelser, M.F., 1988. Supervisie in maatskaplike werk. Riglyne vir die praktyk [Supervision in social work. Guidelines for practice]. Unpublished thesis. University of Pretoria.

Perlman, H.H., 1957. *Social casework. A problem-solving process*. Chicago, IL: University Press.

Pieterse, J.E., 1961. Praktykleiding in groepwerk [Practice guidance in groupwork]. *Mens en Gemeenskap*, 11 (3/4),155–162.

RSA (Republic of South Africa), 1978. *Act on social and associated workers, Act 110 of 1978*. Pretoria: Government Printers.

RSA (Republic of South Africa), 1997. Ministry of Welfare and Population Development. *White Paper for Social Welfare*. Notice 1108 of 1997, Government Gazette, vol. 386, No. 18166 of 8 August. Pretoria: Government Printers.

RSA (Republic of South Africa), 2006. *Children's Act*, No. 38 of 2005. Government Gazette, vol. 492, 19 June. No 28944. Pretoria: Government Printers.

SACSSP (South African Council for Social Service Professions), 2016. *Policy guidelines for course of conduct, code of ethics and the rules for social workers*. Available from: http://www.sacssp.co.za/ [Accessed 6 November 2019].

Shokane, F.F., 2016. An evaluation of the implementation of the supervision framework for the social work profession in Mopani District, Limpopo Province. Unpublished thesis. University of Limpopo.

Shulman, L., 1993. *Interactional supervision*. Washington, DC: NASW Press.

Silence, E., 2017. The significance of social work supervision in the Department of Health, Western Cape: social workers' experiences. Unpublished thesis. Stellenbosch University.

Strydom, H., 2011. Sampling in quantitative paradigm. *In*: A.S. De Vos, H. Strydom, C.B. Fouché and C.S.L. Delport, eds. *Research at grass roots. For the social sciences and human service professions*, 4th ed. Pretoria: Van Schaik Publishers, 222–235.

Strydom, H., and Delport, C.S.L., 2011. Information collection: document study and secondary analyses. *In*: A.S. de Vos, H. Strydom, C.B. Fouché and C.S.L. Delport, eds. *Research at grass roots. For the social sciences and human service professions*. 4th ed. Pretoria: Van Schaik Publishers, 376–389.

Tsui, M., 2005. *Social work supervision. Contexts and concepts*. London: SAGE.

Walton, R.G., and Abo-El-Nasr, M.M., 1988. Indigenization and authentization in terms of social work in Egypt. *International Social Work*, 31 (2), 135–144.

Wynne, T., 2020. Potential factors contributing to harmful supervision of social workers. Unpublished thesis. Stellenbosch University.

6

SOCIAL WORK SUPERVISION IN SINGAPORE

Historical development and the way forward

Peace Yuh Ju Wong

In recent years, there has been a keen interest in focusing on social work supervision in Singapore. This interest in social work supervision is related to an urgent need to recruit, sustain, and develop social workers. The strong demand for competent social workers in Singapore, which is a small island located in South East Asia, is not a surprise, given that the first social work program was established in the 1950s (Department of Social Work). The Social Work Accreditation and Advisory Board (SWAAB) has been advancing social work supervision in the local context through recognizing that social work supervision is an important area of social work practice, which develops competent social workers and ensures the quality of service to clients (Kadushin and Harkness 2014). Since 2015, SWAAB has initiated biennial supervision seminars, as well as developed Social Work Supervision Guidelines in 2017. More recently, a study on the state of social work supervision in Singapore was conducted (Wong and Chua 2019). This study is of significance and informs the local supervisory practice, by suggesting that there is no one "fixed" supervisory model being practiced across sectors, with the supervisory model being dependent on three "C"s – choice, context, and collaboration. This chapter discusses the evolution of social work supervision from the 1990s to 2019 in Singapore and provides recommendations to advance social work supervision from 2021 onwards.

The evolution of social work supervision from the 1990s to 2019 in Singapore

Since the 19th century, the early years of charity organizations, social work supervision has been embedded in social work practice (Kadushin and Harkness 2014, Tsui 2005). Whilst being more administrative in nature in the early years, supervision also contributes to the development of professional identity and should "convey the mission and vision" of social work (Tsui 2005, p. 11). When social work evolved into a mature profession, there existed an array of autonomous practice among social workers, which called for greater accountability, especially in the last two decades (Beddoe 2010, Tsui 2005). In Singapore, as the professional practice of social work develops, there is a parallel development in the practice of social work supervision. The following section documents the development of social work supervision before 1991 until 2019.

Before 1995: Managerialist dominance

This period saw the dominance in the administrative function in supervision (O'Donoghue and Tsui 2015). This has been echoed in countries such as the UK (Manthorpe et al. 2015, Wilkins and Antonopoulou 2019) and Australia (Egan et al. 2016) where research indicates a focus on management oversight and accountability. It is also noted that in Australia, line managers may also function as supervisors (Australian Association of Social Workers 2014). Such arrangements have, in some cases, resulted in the managerial aspect substituting the professional (Beddoe 2012). New Zealand sees a broader spectrum where the primary focus is management of work and practice with clients, while personal well-being and professional development is secondary (O'Donoghue 2019).

Similarly, in Singapore, the supervisor's role was administrative in nature, ensuring accountability and adopting a task-oriented stance. Supervision took the form of case consultations where the supervisor would take the expert position to provide advice and problem solving. Peer supervision – the consulting and advising of peers, was also present within this time-frame. There was a scarcity of both supervisors and resources for supervisory reference during this period. Literature on supervision is scarce, consisting of a report on a series of seminars on supervision of social workers by the National University of Singapore (then University of Singapore) in 1968 (Wong 2014).

From 1996 to 2005: A greater emphasis towards education purpose

The supervisor's role shifted from expert problem solving to directive guidance in developing the practical skills and meeting learning needs of supervisees. During this period, supervision was intended for administrative and educational purposes. Examples of the educational emphasis in supervision was the use of "live" supervision, influenced by the family therapy courses run by Counselling and Care Centre (CCC), as well as the family therapy course that was developed in the late 1990s by the Family Resource Training Centre (FRTC) at the Singapore Association of Social Workers (SASW) and the Ministry of Social and Family Development (then Ministry of Community Development). The late Dr Myrna Blake supervised the participants, who were mainly social workers, in honing their knowledge and skills in family therapy. A Manual on Supervision for Social Work Supervisors was launched by SASW in 2010. Since then, there was some interest in the area of supervision, with some academic research that focused on supervision as a secondary concern, and one by Chinniah (2006) that discussed "Practice Issues of Social Work Supervision among Family Service Centres" (Wong 2014).

From 2005 to 2015: Moving towards a more balanced and collaborative supervision

During this period, supervisory practice shifted towards the supervisee and was based on the supervisee's professional development and needs. The stance of the supervisor shifted from a "top-down" approach towards one that was collaborative in nature, facilitating and empowering supervisees in making decisions in problem-solving. Technology had also enabled new types of supervision formats, such as video-recordings and "live" supervision. Many agencies with social workers who were trained in family therapy utilized the one-way mirror, as well as video recordings to supervise their social work supervisees. In addition, the development of social workers was supported by an increase in the engagement of external supervisors from CCC to enhance the competency of social workers in casework management and skills development

(Chua 2017). In similar vein, there was also an increase in training resources for supervisors. This was seen by the launch of a "Certificate in Supervision Training for Social Services," that was organized by SASW twice annually and targeted at supervisors who may or may not have been trained in social work but who were supervising social workers. Other courses related to supervision included the "Diploma in Clinical Supervision" offered by CCC, introduced by the late Anthony Yeo.

Such resources were needed to support the social workers and their supervisors at the agencies, as it was during the same period that there was a greater call for accountability and sound governance structures, due to the National Kidney Foundation (NKF) (Foo 2013) and Renci Hospital saga (Khalik 2007), where public funds were misappropriated. Supervisors at the agencies had to respond to various inquiries by the funding body to account for their work through the Programme Evaluation System (PES) and Outcome Management (OM). Whilst useful to monitor outcomes and ensure effective allocation of resources, these inquiries may have the unintended effects of aligning supervisors towards managerialism. This means favoring fiscal expediency and efficiency, instead of best supervision practice driven by professional values and ethical consideration to ensure the best interests of the clients (Wong and Lee 2015). This move towards managerialism gives rise to an increased focus on compliance, prioritizing efficiency, and fiscal management, instead of the best interests of clients.

From 2015 to 2019: Greater recognition and an evolvement of a more professional supervision culture

This period saw a greater recognition and an evolvement of a more professional supervision culture. At the practice level, supervision saw the person/self of the supervisor being introduced in the supervisory context of both supervisor and supervisee. At the same time, more varied supervision types were available, i.e., individual, group, peer, and external, in comparison to the predominant use of individual and group supervision during the time period before 1991 (Chua 2017). At the sectoral level, there were various milestones, which were (a) the initiation of bi-annual social work supervision seminars; (b) the launch of social work supervision guidelines and availability of local resources on supervision; (c) the development of supervision of supervisory practice; and (d) the completion of the study on the state of social work supervision.

The initiation of bi-annual social work supervision seminars

Supervision became increasingly recognized, with the synergy by the SWAAB, SASW, and the Department of Social Work at the National University of Singapore (NUS), as a core part of social work to be advanced. Since 2015, bi-annual social work supervision seminars were organized to discuss and share ideas about social work supervision, as practiced in local and overseas contexts. In 2015, the inaugural supervision seminar on "Social Work Supervision: Challenges and Advances" was well attended by 300 participants, with workshops being conducted by overseas/local practitioners on topics related to ways of advancing the different challenges faced in social work supervision. The second biennial Social Work Supervision Seminar in 2017 focused on the theme on "Innovative Ways to Chart the Bare Essentials." Attended by 350 participants, interesting topics were featured, such as "Issues and Challenges facing Social Work Supervision in the 21st century" (O'Donoghue 2015), as well as workshops conducted by local/overseas practitioners to discuss pertinent concerns in supervisory practice, such as "Supervision of groupwork practice" and "Supporting the conscious use of self in supervision." In 2019, the third biennial Social Work Supervision Seminar looked at the theme on "Intentional supervision: Impacting

Singapore Social Work Supervision," with 400 participants. The seminar examined the landscape of social work supervision, with representatives from various sectors, such as health, social services, and rehabilitation sectors taking stock of the current state of their social work supervision, in terms of their respective milestones, challenges, needs, and future possibilities.

The launch of Social Work Supervision Guidelines and availability of local resources on supervision

An aspect that signals the level of development is the pace of recognition of supervision and extent of governance from institutional frameworks. In particular, the Social Work Supervision Guidelines (SWAAB 2017) was developed by a group of passionate social work scholar/practitioners after reviewing several supervision guidelines and policies from various countries. Intending to set supervision policy direction and support the development of supervisory practice, the Social Work Supervision Guidelines (SWAAB 2017) outlined the frequency of supervision for supervisees with different years of experience and included different templates/forms that could be used by social work supervisors and supervisees during supervision. It is worth noting that countries with developed social work supervision landscapes have set forth their supervision policies which establish supervisory guidelines and make supervision mandatory for social workers, such as the UK Supervision Policy (British Association of Social Workers 2011), the Australian Supervision Standards (Australian Association of Social Workers 2014), and ANZASW Supervision Policy (Aotearoa New Zealand Association of Social Workers 2015).

Concurrently, the movement towards good social work supervisory practice is growing, with more practitioners and organizations recognizing the importance of social work supervision. This is seen by the availability of funding and supervision services through the SASW Supervision Service, where supervisors would be matched with social workers who do not have social work supervisors in their organizations. At the same time, Master Practice Leaders were appointed and deployed as external supervisors for organizations that require support for supervision.

During this period, there was also an increase in local literature on supervision, such as the doctoral thesis on "A grounded understanding of social work supervisors with dual roles" (Wong 2014), "Clinical Supervision: Clinician's perspectives and practices – Towards Professionalising Counselling" (Lim and Sim 2014), and "Superecipe – The Montfort Care Guide to Supervision" (Chia et al. 2016).

The development of supervision of supervisory practice (SOSp)

A noteworthy piece during this period is the development of supervision of supervisory practice. In 2019, the SASW invited three experts to look at supervision of supervisory practice. This is an important milestone in the development of social work supervision as more senior social work supervisors recognize the need to be supervised themselves for their supervisory practice. This is consistent with a paper on the development of supervisors by Stoltenberg and Delworth (1987), which proposes that supervisors move along different stages of development. In social work supervisory practice where supervisors tended to take on a more specialized role in management or a clinical track, one of the developments for supervisors is a recognition of the importance of integrating both management/clinical perspectives. Hence, a workgroup with social work supervisors from community-based and health sectors, as well as academia, was formed to look into the development of a training curriculum that synthesizes the management and clinical perspectives for SOSp.

The completion of the study on the state of social work supervision

Using a questionnaire that was adapted from the national survey used by New Zealand (O'Donoghue 2010), a survey was conducted to understand the state of social work supervision in Singapore. A total of 267 social work supervisees and 135 social work supervisors completed the surveys in two waves of data collection. The first wave began in October 2017 and ended in January 2018. A second wave of data collection was conducted from June to July 2018. Respondents were recruited using the convenient method of emailing potential heads of departments/social workers using various sources such as SASW, NCSS, and PI's own contacts to ensure a wider reach and a larger sample for the survey. The sample consisted mainly of social workers who were registered social workers (RSWs) with SASW. The data collected were used and kept in accordance with the University's Research Data Management Policy, with IRB clearance being obtained in October 2017. The data collected were analyzed using SPSS software and kept in a password-protected PC. The section that follows highlights the key themes and summarizes the current state of development of social work supervision in Singapore, namely (i) nature of social work supervision; (ii) value of individual supervision; and (iii) impact of supervision on one's motivation to stay in the organization and social services sector.

Nature of social work supervision – Move from administrative focus to professional considerations

The findings suggested that social work supervision in Singapore had moved beyond the administrative focus to consider supervisory practices which are geared towards enhancing supervisees' competence and well-being, safeguarding of competent and professional practice in the best interests of clients. On average, supervisees received three types of supervision, with about one-quarter receiving four types of supervision. The most frequent types of supervision received were individual supervision, group supervision, and team supervision. Of those who received individual and group supervision, 69% and 68% received at least an hour or more supervision per session. However, about 9% of the respondents mentioned that they did not receive individual supervision (Wong and Chua 2019).

In terms of amount of time spent, about two-thirds (69%) of the supervisees had one to two hours of individual supervision per month, with 46% having one to two hours of supervision, 14% having two to three hours of supervision, and 9% having more than three hours of supervision per month. About one-third (31%) had less than one hour of individual supervision per month, although this may have excluded other types of supervision arrangements. Considering the recommendations of the Social Work Supervision Guidelines (SWAAB 2017) is for supervisees with at least three to ten years of working experience to have at least one and a half hours of supervision per month, it seems like supervisees are in general receiving sufficient supervision. It is however interesting to note that when asked about their perception of the adequacy of supervision using a scaling response of inadequate, somewhat adequate, and highly adequate, 13% of the supervisees indicated that their supervision received is inadequate, 26% somewhat adequate, and 60% highly adequate (Wong and Chua, 2019).

Value of individual supervision

An interesting finding pertains to the importance given to individual supervision, as supervisees who received individual supervision reported significantly higher adequacy, satisfaction, and effectiveness, as compared to those who did not receive any individual supervision. Based on the findings, the number of types of supervision available to supervisees and the amount of time spent on individual supervision were significantly correlated to adequacy, satisfaction, and effectiveness. In particular, supervisees who receive individual supervision reported being significantly more satisfied and feeling that the supervision received was adequate and effective. It appears that regardless of the number of types of supervision received, having access to individual supervision is important to supervisees, and has an impact on their perception of supervision received.

The continued value placed on individual supervision can be attributed in part to the nature of the social work profession, in which interventions are often based on one-on-one relationships (Bogo 2006, Kadushin 1992, Ray and Altekruse 2000). There is thus a present expectation that a one-on-one setting would facilitate the development and growth of the social worker (Zeira and Schiff 2009). The social work practice is also largely relationship-based (O'Leary and Tsui 2019), thus highlighting the importance of individual supervision, which allows for a stronger supervisory relationship (Zeira and Schiff 2009). The supervisory relationship is crucial in the effectiveness of supervision, providing a safe space for which concerns can be explored (Egan et al. 2016). The affective aspect of the supervisory relationship, pivotal to supervision (Tsui 2006), would be better achieved through individual supervision, as it allows for a certain level of comfort in exposing vulnerabilities (Bogo 2006). This holds especially true in an Asian context, where relational mobility is generally lower (Falk et al. 2009, Schug et al. 2009, Yuki et al. 2013, Yuki et al. 2007), and the motivation to self-disclose diminishes to prevent negative evaluations from others (Kito et al. 2017). Therefore, it can be postulated that individual supervision would be more beneficial in Asian societies, where individuals can discuss personal affects without fear of criticism from their peers (Kadushin 1992).

Impact of supervision and one's motivation to stay in the organization and social services sector

Based on the findings, perceived adequacy, satisfaction, and effectiveness of supervision by supervisees are significant predictors of motivation to remain in the organization, while only perceived satisfaction and effectiveness of supervision are significant predictors of motivation to stay in the social services sector, after controlling for age, years of experience, and the type of sector (Wong and Chua, 2019). Numerous studies have recognized the importance of regular and supportive supervision in staff retention (Brewer and Shapard, 2004, Chiller and Crisp, 2012). Smith and Shields (2013) have highlighted that social services workers are motivated by non-monetary aspects of the work environment, such as a positive supervisory relationship. It is therefore not surprising that respondents highlighted that quality supervision impacts their decision to stay in the organization and social services sector.

What's Next? 2021 and beyond

The development of social work supervision in Singapore has moved from an administrative focus to one that is integrative, with the various administrative, supportive, and educational functions being demonstrated through various types of supervisory arrangements. In the past few years, the social work fraternity across sectors was united in propelling the progress of social work supervision, seen by the organization of bi-annual seminars, the launch of Social Work Supervision Guidelines, as well as the initiation of SOSp.

Moving forward to the next five years and beyond, the following are the proposed recommendations in advancing social work supervision in Singapore and these are focused on (a) supervisory practice; (b) organizational level; (c) professional level; and (d) research possibilities.

Supervisory practice

In general, supervision is often conceived as beneficial for supervisees' development and quality outcomes for clients. It will be helpful to pay greater attention to the provision of individual supervision and the creation of safe reflective supervisory space, as well as to ensure that helpful rather than harmful supervision is being provided.

Valuing individual supervision and the safe reflective space

Depending on the resource availability, there may be different types of supervisory arrangements in terms of the format and frequency of supervision. Given that there is no one "fixed" supervisory model practiced by social workers across the social services sector, one needs to consider three "C"s – choice, context, and collaboration – in determining "the question of fit." Collaboratively, supervisees and supervisors need to find a "fit" in the supervisory relationship within the organizational context, based on the choices of supervisees/supervisors, and within the parameters of the Social Work Supervision Guide (SWAAB 2017). It would be important to support more supervisees to move towards the ideal guide of at least one and a half hours of supervision hours per month, especially for those without individual supervision.

In addition, when revisiting the ideas of effective supervisory practice where one strives towards balancing the supportive, educational, and administrative functions, it makes sense that supervision, amidst uncertainties and competing interests of the various systems we are working with, provides the space for critical reflection in the best interests of our clients. Invariably, in the process of supervision, there may be a realization that one's personal issues tend to impact the way one works with clients. However, recognizing that supervisees and supervisors are engaged in a professional relationship/context, it is important to note that supervision is not a therapy session for supervisees. Supervisors could facilitate a process of self-discovery, since self-awareness contributes to professional growth, by embedding therapeutic elements into the supervisory relationship, such as being warm and non- judgmental to facilitate a safe working relationship.

(In)Adequacy of supervision – Harmful or helpful?

In the light of the increasing attention being paid to bad supervision in recent years (Beddoe 2017, Goodyear et al. 2006), it is worth examining the effects of harmful supervision on social workers and their work. This is especially important, given that 13% of supervisees indicated that the supervision received is inadequate and almost one-third of the supervisees had not received individual supervision. This is because harmful supervision could also be the provision of inadequate supervision (Ellis et al. 2015). Ellis et al. (2014, p. 440) have suggested that harmful supervision exists, and this it has been defined as the following:

> Supervisory practices that result in psychological, emotional, and/or physical harm or trauma to the supervisee ... The two essential components of harmful supervision are (a) that the supervisee was genuinely harmed in some way by the supervisor's actions or inactions, or (b) the supervisor's behavior is known to cause harm, even though the supervisee may not identify the action as harmful.

Organizational level

The recommendation to improve supervisory practice at the organizational level includes (i) recognizing social work supervision as an organizational and professional responsibility and (ii) setting up organization structure and processes to support good supervisory practice.

Recognizing social work supervision as an organizational and professional responsibility

Social work supervision in Singapore seemed to embrace consistent ideas with the literature to enhance clients' outcomes and develop supervisees' competence. With that, supervisors exercised leadership to creatively manage the tension of dual roles and organizational resource constraints. One such example is the engagement of external supervisors to develop supervisees' competence in clinical and micro-skills. Whilst the educational function of supervision is being fulfilled to some extent by these consultants, the efficacy of external supervision arrangement remains unclear (Beddoe 2012). This is especially so for the social work profession, since developing social workers is not a matter of only developing their knowledge and skills for practice. It involves developing their identity as social workers and embracing the commitment and the soul of the profession to devote their best to enhance the well-being of clients. The improper socialization of social workers into the profession and equating supervision with technical competence has the risk of reducing social workers from professionals to technicians. Hence, supervision must not be seen as an educational tool, lest the perceived benefits with fulfilling the educational learning needs (as narrowly defined as skills development) of supervisees risk robbing the supervisees of a more holistic professional development. Furthermore, it cannot be used as an administrative tool, with emphasis on the organizational, rather than a client-focused or professionally driven ideology. Therefore, different supervision structures, processes, and strategies must be considered in totality to address the administrative demands of organizations and the professional needs of social workers. One such possibility is a re-definition of supervision by considering the portfolio model (O'Donoghue, 2015), which consists of management and professional supervision (such as peer and clinical supervision) being delivered separately.

Setting up an organization structure and process to support good supervisory practice

In view that support from the organization has an impact on supervisory practice, social workers would need to engage the organizational leadership in advancing supervisory practice. It would be helpful to consider supervisory structures and processes by stipulating minimum standards, such as qualifications and frequency of supervision. In addition, it is important to develop career pathways that may be more aligned to the interests and capabilities of social workers, since some may have preference for clinical work more than administrative work, and vice versa. Equipping supervisors with relevant supervisory knowledge/skills is critical, as the role requires different ethical considerations, such as competencies and management of professional boundaries as peer/supervisor.

Professional level

The recommendations to advance supervision at the professional and sector level include (i) mandating supervision as part of social work professional regulatory systems and (ii) supporting the developmental pathways of supervisors through training and accreditation.

Mandating supervision as part of social work professional regulatory systems

As the social work profession matures, there is a need to mandate supervision as part of the social work professional regulatory systems. According to Beddoe (2016, p. 157),

even in the absence of licensing, major employers of social workers may set requirements for supervision, and it has become a tool of quality assurance in managed
systems. The practice of supervision is thus mandated by the professional and organisational systems (both regulatory and managerial).

The mandating of supervision into social work professional regulatory systems mirrors the
supervisory development in many parts of the world, with the growth of licensing or regulation
of social work. In our local context, it may be helpful to consider having minimum supervision
hours for social workers in their applications to renew their work licenses, especially for those
in their earlier years of social work practice.

Supporting the developmental pathways of supervisors through training and accreditation

It is important to prepare supervisors who transition from social worker to a managerial role to
mitigate the stress of changing their role (Wong and Lee, 2014). The availability of training for
social work supervisors, such as peer supervisors' groups and SOSp could be considered. This
helps to address the challenges for supervisors, who would need support and may be lacking in
resources to develop their supervisory skills. In addition, it is worth considering the accreditation of social work supervisors to ensure a minimum standard of supervision for supervisees. To
do that, there must be a proper training roadmap in place in developing supervisors at different
stages of their supervisory development.

Research Possibilities

Given the lack of local studies and that there exists much practice wisdom concerning supervisory practice in Singapore, it would be helpful to continue the documentation of good supervisory practice. Future studies could examine supervisees' views and the longitudinal experiences
of the supervisory process to examine if the intended supervisory goals of supporting the supervisees and developing their professionalism are met, in addition to having good client outcomes.
In addition, it would be interesting to examine cross-national studies of the construction, delivery, satisfaction, and effectiveness of supervision (O'Donoghue 2015), as a local study on the state
of social work supervision has already been completed (Wong and Chua 2019). This will contribute to a better knowledge base and advance the practice of social work supervision. Given
that there are different types of supervision arrangements that are being practiced, it would be
helpful to conduct comparative research that compares supervision using the traditional model
where one supervisor performs all functions, as compared to supervision undertaken through
a portfolio model where the management and professional supervision are delivered separately.

Conclusion

In Singapore, as the social work profession gains greater recognition, there is a parallel recognition of the value of supervision in developing competent social workers in service delivery.
This chapter has documented the state of social work supervision from the 1990s to the present
day. It is evident that over the years, standards of supervisory practice have been raised through
different initiatives, such as the development of supervision guidelines, training opportunities,
and local resources on supervision. The nature of social work supervision in Singapore is one
that is focused on enhancing the competency of supervisees and enhancing professional practice towards the best interest of clients. There is a preference for individual supervision and a

suggestion that supervision serves to motivate social workers to remain in the organization and social services sector. At present, there is no one "fixed" supervisory model and one needs to consider three "C"s – choice, context, and collaboration – in determining "the question of fit." Recommendations were made to advance supervisory practice in Singapore through enhancing supervision at the practice, organizational, and professional levels, as well as further research considerations.

References

Aotearoa New Zealand Association of Social Workers, 2015. Supervision policy. [online]. Available from: https://anzasw.nz/wp-content/uploads/ANZASW-Supervision-Policy-Updated-February-2015.pdf [Accessed 3 March 2020].

Australian Association of Social Workers, 2014. Supervision standards—2014. [online]. Available from: https://www.aasw.asn.au/document/item/6027 [Accessed 3 March 2020].

Beddoe, L., 2010. Surveillance or reflection: professional supervision in 'the risk society'. *British Journal of Social Work*, 40 (4), 1279–1296.

Beddoe, L., 2012. External supervision in social work: power, space, risk, and the search for safety. *Australian Social Work*, 65 (2), 197–213.

Beddoe, L., 2016. Supervision in social work in Aotearoa New Zealand: challenges in changing contexts. *The Clinical Supervisor*, 35 (2), 156–174.

Beddoe, L., 2017. Harmful supervision: a commentary. *The Clinical Supervisor*, 36 (1), 88–101.

Brewer, E.W., and Shapard, L., 2004. Employee burnout: a meta-analysis of the relationship between age or years of experience. *Human Resource Development Review*, 3 (2), 102–123.

Bogo, M., 2006. Field instruction in social work. *The Clinical Supervisor*, 24 (1–2), 163–193.

British Association of Social Workers, 2011. UK supervision policy. [online]. Available from: https://www.basw.co.uk/resources/basw-uk-supervision-policy [Accessed 3 March 2020].

Chia, S.G.A., et al., 2016. *Superecipe – the Montfort care guide to supervision*. Singapore: Montfort Care.

Chiller, P., and Crisp, B.R., 2012. Professional supervision: a workforce retention strategy for social work? *Australian Social Work*, 65 (2), 232–242.

Chinniah S., 2006. Practice issues of social work supervision among family service centres in Singapore. Academic Exercise, National University of Singapore, Department of Social Work.

Department of Social Work, *Our rich heritage*. Singapore. [online]. [Accessed 5 March 2020].

Egan, R., Maidment, J., and Connolly, M., 2016. Who is watching whom? Surveillance in Australian social work supervision. *British Journal of Social Work*, 46 (6), 1617–1635.

Ellis, M.V., Berger, L., Hanus, A.E., Ayala, E.E., Swords, B.A., and Siembor, M., 2014. Inadequate and harmful clinical supervision: testing a revised framework and assessing occurrence. *The Counseling Psychologist*, 42, 434–472.

Ellis, M.V., Creaner, M., Hutman, H., and Timulak, L., 2015. A comparative study of clinical supervision in the Republic of Ireland and the United States. *Journal of Counseling Psychology*, 62, 621–631.

Falk, C.F., Heine, S.J., Yuki, M., and Takemura, K., 2009. Why do westerners self-enhance more than East Asians? *European Journal of Personality*, 23, 183–203.

Foo, T., 2013. National Kidney Foundation financial scandal (2005). *Singapore Infopedia* [online]. Available from: https://eresources.nlb.gov.sg/infopedia/articles/SIP_2013-07-01_120748.html.

Goodyear, R.K., Bunch, K., and Claiborn, C.D., 2006. Current Supervision Scholarship in Psychology. *The Clinical Supervisor*, 24 (1–2), 137–147.

Kadushin, A., and Harkness, D., 2014. *Supervision in social work*. 5th ed. New York: Columbia University Press.

Kadushin, A., 1992. Whats wrong, whats right with social work supervision. *The Clinical Supervisor*, 10 (1), 3–19.

Khalik, S., 2007. Ren Ci under probe for financial discrepancies. *The Straits Times*. Available from: https://www.asiaone.com/News/The+Straits+Times/Story/A1Story20071108-35171.html#:~:text=Ren%20Ci%20under%20probe%20for%20financial%20discrepancies&text=ANOTHER%20charity%20has%20come%20under,companies%20in%20the%20past%20decade. [Accessed 7 June 2020].

Kito, M., Yuki, M., and Thomson, R., 2017. Relational mobility and close relationships: a socioecological approach to explain cross-cultural differences. *Personal Relationships*, 24 (1), 114–130.

Lim, C., and Sim, E., 2014. *Clinical Supervision: Clinician's perspectives and practices – Towards Professionalising Counselling* Singapore: Counselling and Care Centre.

Manthorpe, J., Moriarty, J., Hussein, S., Stevens, M., & Sharpe, E., 2015. Content and Purpose of Supervision in Social Work Practice in England: views of Newly Qualified Social Workers, Managers and Directors. *British Journal of Social Work*, 45 (1), 52–68.

Mo, Y.H., 2019. An exploration of social work supervision in Mainland China. *China Journal of Social Work*, 12 (1), 70–89.

O'Donoghue, K., 2010. Towards the construction of social work supervision in Aotearoa New Zealand: a study of the perspectives of social work practitioners and supervisors. PhD thesis. Massey University.

O'Donoghue, K., 2015. Issues and challenges facing social work supervision in the twenty-first century. *China Journal of Social Work*, 8 (2), 136–149.

O'Donoghue, K., 2019. The supervision of registered social workers in Aotearoa New Zealand: a national survey. *Aotearoa New Zealand Social Work*, 31 (3), 58–77.

O'Donoghue, K., and Tsui, M.S., 2015. Social work supervision research (1970–2010): the way we were and the way ahead. *British Journal of Social Work*, 45 (2), 616–633.

O'Leary, P., and Tsui, M.-S., 2019. The base of social work: relationship, client, evidence or values? *International Social Work*, 62 (5), 1327–1328.

Ray, D., and Altekruse, M., 2000. Effectiveness of group supervision versus combined group and individual supervision. *Counselor Education and Supervision*, 40, 19–30.

SASW, *SASW Supervision Service*. Available from: https://www.sasw.org.sg/index.php?option=com_content&view=article&id=228&Itemid=205 [Accessed 4 March 2020].

Schug, J., Yuki, M., Horikawa, H., and Takemura, K., 2009. Similarity attraction and actually selecting similar others: how cross-societal differences in relational mobility affect interpersonal similarity in Japan and the USA. *Asian Journal of Social Psychology*, 12, 95–103.

Singapore Association of Social Workers, 2017. *Social work supervision guidelines*. Available from: http://www.sasw.org.sg/docs/SWD_SocialWorlSupervisionGuidelines_FINAL.pdf [Accessed 4 March 2020].

Smith, D.B., and Shields, J., 2013. Factors related to social service workers' job satisfaction: revisiting Herzberg's motivation to work. *Administration in Social Work*, 37 (2), 189–198.

Stoltenberg, C.D., and Delworth, U. 1987. *Supervising counselors and therapists*. San Francisco: Jossey-Bass.

Tsui, M.S., 2005. *Social work supervision: contexts and concepts*. Thousand Oaks, CA: SAGE Publications, Inc.

Tsui, M.S., 2006. Hopes and dreams ideal supervision for social workers in Hong Kong. *Asia Pacific Journal of Social Work and Development*, 16 (1), 33–42.

Wilkins, D., and Antonopoulou, V., 2019. What does supervision help with? A survey of 315 social workers in the UK. *Practice*, 31 (1), 21–40.

Wong, P.Y.J., and Chua, J., 2019. *The state of social work supervision in Singapore*. Singapore: National Council of Social Service.

Wong, P.Y.J., and Lee, A.E.Y., 2015. Dual roles of social work supervisors: strain and strengths as managers and clinical supervisors. *China Journal of Social Work*, 8 (2), 164–181.

Wong, Y.J., 2014. A grounded understanding of challenges and responses of social work supervisors with managerial and clinical roles. Thesis (PhD).

Yuki, M., Sato, K., Takemura, K., and Oishi, S., 2013. Social ecology moderates the association between self-esteem and happiness. *Journal of Experimental Social Psychology*, 49, 741–746.

Yuki, M., Schug, J., Horikawa, H., Takemura, K., Sato, K., Yokota, K., and Kamaya, K., 2007. *Development of a scale to measure perceptions of relational mobility in society (Working Paper Series No. 75)*. Sapporo, Japan: Center for Experimental Research in Social Sciences.

Zeira, A., and Schiff, M., 2009. Testing group supervision in fieldwork training for social work students. *Research on Social Work Practice*, 20 (4), 427–434.

7

SOCIAL WORK SUPERVISION IN HONG KONG

Agnes Kwok Tung Ng, Ming-Sum Tsui,
and Charles Tong Lit Leung

Introduction

Hong Kong is a tiny place around 1,100 km² (Survey and Mapping Office 2020) in East Asia, but it has been playing significant roles in blending the political, socio-cultural, and professional contexts between the West and the East. Since 1842, Hong Kong was governed by the British until the handover in June 1997. Hong Kong has since then been a Special Administrative Region of the People's Republic of China, operating under the principle of "one country, two systems." This means that while China is governed by the communist party and the values of socialism, the region of Hong Kong is still operating under a political system of capitalism as before. The Hong Kong Special Administrative Region's constitutional document, the Basic Law, ensures that the current political situation remains in effect until 2046. The rights and freedom of people in Hong Kong are derived from the impartial rule of law and an independent judiciary (The Basic Law 2008). Despite applying the political system like Anglo-American countries, more than 92% of the population in Hong Kong are ethnically Chinese (Census and Statistics Department 2016). Therefore, the influences of Chinese culture to the practices of social work, certainly including supervision, can be seen in the literature (Tsui 2001, 2003, 2004, 2006, 2008, Tsui et al. 2014). Under this mixed and dynamic context, the profession of social work has developed in Hong Kong for more than six decades (Lai and Chan 2009). The direct practice of social work in Hong Kong has reached a new milestone in terms of the diversity of service delivery and the intensity of professional intervention. However, supervision has been viewed as a promise of service quality, a type of support for social workers, and a recognition of the importance of professionalization in the social work academy (Maidment and Beddoe 2012). Supervisory research and practice in Hong Kong have been viewed as an emerging issue and distinct interest since the late 1990s.

The earliest study regarding supervisory practice in Hong Kong was published in the 1980s (Ko 1987). This area of study becoming a trend conducted on a local level was identified around the early part of this century (e.g. Chan 1998, Fu 1999, Tsui 2001, 2003, 2004, 2005, 2006, 2008, Social Worker Registration Board 2006, Leung 2012, Ng 2016). These studies reported that the supervisors in Hong Kong tended to adopt task-centered approaches, rather than worker-oriented approaches, for supervising staff members. The findings also discovered that the supervisory practice proportionally performed more on administrative functions. Although Tsui et al. (2017) had commented that educational and supportive roles of supervisors have been constrained by administrative obligations, these results partially align with the research evidence concerning supervision's contribution to worker outcomes. This evidence suggests that task assistance, high level of social and emotional supports, and constructive supervisory interpersonal interaction were related to beneficial outcomes for social workers (Mor Barak et al. 2009).

Against the overview above, it has been shown that there is great room in Hong Kong for further developing the supervisory practice. This chapter thus intends to firstly highlight the significant studies related to the local context throughout the years, and then portray those recent initiatives in the social work sector of Hong Kong.

Historical development of social work supervision in Hong Kong

The historical development of social work supervision in Hong Kong could be reported in three developmental phases: the year 2000 and before; 2001 to 2010; and 2011 to present. All of the phases will be further illustrated by its recognition, establishment, achievement, and the trend of development.

Year 2000 and before: Supervision was formally recognized and first practiced in social casework

The level of recognition of social work supervision was relatively undeveloped during this period. Most of the supervision providers had no formal training, and there were also no official rules and standards required to social work supervision practice. According to the study by Ko (1987), which was a pioneering study in the local context, there was only attention given to the issue of supervision because the social welfare policy of Hong Kong eventually began to require more intensive services of casework counseling. The demand for improving professional knowledge and skills of the social workers was thus increasing. In Ko's study, he explored four areas of the issue related to supervision work. They were: (1) characteristics of casework supervisors and workers in the voluntary family service agencies; (2) the functions performed by casework supervisors; (3) the forms, frequencies, approaches, and problems of supervision; and (4) the supervisor-worker relationship.

Ko (1987) found that although the supervisors were trained in social work practice, they had limited experience in their supervisory position during the period of study. The forms of supervisory practice found included individual sessions, case conferences, group supervision, staff development programmes, and "pop-in" (ad-hoc and unplanned) consultation. It was also found that 14% of the workers examined in the study did not receive any individual supervision sessions in the designated one-month period. 55% of the workers expressed that they preferred to receive supervision every three to four weeks. 37% of the workers showed their preference to "pop-in" consultations when they encountered difficulties. All these findings reflected a demand for social work supervision in Hong Kong in which the availability of supervisory advice and support was valued by the frontline workers. In addition, it was also reported in the same study that there are three related factors – the experience of the supervisor, the clinical competence of social workers, and supervisor-worker relationships – that influenced the performance of the supervisory function. It was not surprising that the social work supervisor, who is a professional worker and a manager or administrator at the same time, devoted large portions of time to administrative clarification, monitoring, and workload management during a supervisory session. Nonetheless, Ko's study indicated that social work, i.e. casework, was the first type of professional work that affirmed supervision's existence in the social work profession.

A study conducted by Tsui and Ho (1998), however, could be viewed as an academic foundation for developing the models of social work supervision in Hong Kong. In this study, they reviewed the approaches and models of supervision that set the foundation for social work supervision practice in Hong Kong. From this review, the conceptualization of the supervisory relationship and supervisory process was redefined, and the influence of culture as the major context for supervision was highlighted. This re-conceptualization provides a wider perspective for research and theory building. As a result, they proposed a comprehensive model of social work supervision in which a holistic view of the context of social work supervision was illustrated. Tsui and Ho (1998) identified that social work supervision should be based on four aspects: the format, the purpose, the nature of supervisory relationship, and the use of supervisory authority. The format of supervision in Hong Kong was characterized by its loose structure: it relied on a verbal agreement; supervision sessions were infrequent. Regarding the purposes and functions of supervision, the supervisor and the supervisee had the same professional goals. Supervision sessions were also used to address personal matters and encourage team building. The most distinctive feature of the supervisory relationship in Hong Kong was the dual perspective of both the personal and professional. The tension inherent in the supervisor-supervisee relationship was mitigated by Chinese cultural values that stress reciprocity: qing (affective attachment), yuan (being determined by fate), and "face" (assign of respect to the senior). As a result, the supervisory relationship was maintained without much tension and friction. Four cultural factors influence the four aspects of social work supervision. These factors are the time perspective, the concept of space, value orientations, and attitudes. However, since Chinese social workers in Hong Kong tend to respect hierarchy and treasure harmony, relationships are maintained by reciprocity and consensus.

According to Tsui and Ho (1998), a social work supervision model was no exception in practice, with assumptions and principles which reflected the underlying philosophy. Thus, they identified seven basic principles that govern model building. The details were as follows:

1. Supervision is an interpersonal transaction between two or more persons. The premise of supervision is that the experienced and competent supervisor may help the supervisee and ensure the quality of service to the clients.
2. The work of the supervisee must be related to the agency objectives through the supervisor.
3. In this interpersonal transaction, there is a use of authority, and exchange of information, and an expression of emotion.
4. As an indirect practice of social work, supervision reflects the professional values of social work.
5. The supervisor monitors job performance, teaches knowledge and skills, and provides emotional support to the supervisee.
6. To reflect the short-term and long-term objectives of supervision, the criteria for evaluating supervisory effectiveness include staff satisfaction with supervision, job accomplishments, and client outcomes.
7. From a holistic point of view, supervision involves four parties, namely, the agency, the supervisor, the supervisee, and the client. All of them are strongly influenced by the context of supervision, that is, the prevailing culture.

The models in Table 7.1 below are those that Tsui and Ho (1998) highlighted for social work professionals of Hong Kong as references. Following this work, the supervision practice began to have some concepts and frameworks.

Table 7.1 Models of social work supervision

Name of model	Sources
Practice theory as model: to adopt therapy theories as models for supervision.	Liddle and Saba 1983, Russell et al. 1984, Storm and Heath 1985, Olsen and Stern 1990, Bernard and Goodyear 1992
Structural-functional models: to focus on objectives, functions, and authority structure of supervision.	
a. Supervisory function model	Erera and Lazar 1994, Kadushin and Harkness 2002, Tsui 2005
b. Integrative model	Gitterman 1972, Lowy 1983
c. Models of authority	Munson 1976, 1979, 1981, 2002, Tsui 2005
Agency models: to reflect different levels of administrative accountability and professional autonomy within the agency.	
a. Casework model	Gitterman 1972, Gitterman and Miller 1977, Stoltenberg 1981, Hart 1982, Worthington 1984, Latting 1986, Shulman 1993
b. Group supervision model	
c. Peer supervision model	
d. Team service delivery model	Kadushin 1974, 1992, Ko 1987
e. Autonomous practice	Sales and Navarre 1970, Watson 1973, Brown and Bourne 1996, Kadushin and Harkness 2002, Tsui 2005
	Watson, 1973 Epstein 1973, Watson 1973, Kadushin 1974, Kutzik 1977, Wax 1979, Rock 1990, Veeder 1990, Barretta-Herman 1993, Kadushin and Harkness 2002
Interactional process model: to focus on the interaction between the supervisor and the supervisee.	Gitterman 1972, Gitterman and Miller 1977, Stoltenberg 1981, Hart 1982, Worthington 1984, Latting 1986, Shulman 1993
Feminist partnership model: to propose an alternative feminist partnership model which assumes that social workers can be self-directing, self-disciplined, and self-regulating.	Chernesky 1986, Hipp and Munson 1995

To conclude, Tsui and Ho (1998) commented that the new model of social work supervision showed the past research on supervision was too narrowly focused. In fact, a supervisory process should put the supervisor-supervisee relationship at the core. This notion led to the foundation of their work focusing on the theoretical building of social work supervision in Hong Kong in the following years.

From 2000–2010: Theoretical establishment of social work supervision

The literature during this period was directly related to the development of social work supervision in Hong Kong. A series of studies conducted by Tsui (2001, 2003, 2004, 2006, 2008) significantly contributed to this field of study by revealing how Chinese culture played a role in the local context. The model for understanding supervisory practice of social work (Tsui and Ho 1998) in the Chinese context of Hong Kong was further elaborated upon by Tsui (2001). Traditionally, supervision has been recognized as a practice embedded in an organizational setting. Tsui (2001) emphasized that this approach is valid only when supervision is perceived as a process taking place between two employees (i.e., the supervisor and the frontline worker) of a human service organization. Tsui (2001) also explored the non-administrative element and relationship in supervisory practice. Tsui (2005) further examined the format, purpose, relationship, use of authority, and ideal of social work supervision in the cultural context of Hong Kong. He found that both supervisors and supervisees view successful client outcomes as the major purpose of supervision, but supervisors see the process as a rational and systematic tool for safeguarding standards and quality of service, whereas supervisees hope that supervision will provide emotional support and foster teamwork.

Most of the research during this period was mainly related to the format and functions of social work supervision in Hong Kong. There was little empirical investigation concerning the utility of this perspective involving a matched supervisee and supervisor dyad to determine its significance for supervision effectiveness. Tsui (2004) further developed the understanding of how traditional Chinese culture influenced the supervisory relationship in Hong Kong through the emphasis on harmony and compromise. Thus, this strengthened the understanding of the supervisor and supervisee alliance in relation to "quanxi (relationship)," "harmony," and "reciprocity" concepts in Chinese culture. This in turn was helpful in enhancing supervisory practice through reinforcing the importance of the traditional values of Chinese reciprocity as the guiding principle. To maintain this, Tsui (2003, p. 114) further indicated that the supervisory relationship of social workers in Hong Kong is a complicated mix of (1) hierarchical, (2) collegial, and (3) familial relationships. The first, "hierarchical relationship," would be seen as a "rational authority" for determining the behavior of both the supervisor and the supervisee(s). The second is the "collegial relationship" between two staff members working in the same or other units of the human service organization. The professional culture of social work provides the dominant norms for the behavior of the supervisor and the supervisee. The third is the "familial relationship," which reflects a psychological transference arising from interpersonal interaction between the supervisor and the supervisee(s). The two parties may treat each other as members of the same extended family. Thus, we can imagine how complicated and difficult it would be when the supervisor and their supervisee(s) interact with each other within the organizational context, professional culture, and Chinese values.

Exploratory empirical studies also occurred in this period. Tsui (2006) examined the hopes and dreams of social work supervision perceived by local frontline workers. This study found that social workers, whether they are supervisors or supervisees, wish to make better use of their supervision sessions in order to promote professional growth and effective decisions for clients. Social workers prefer regular, practice-based, and action-oriented supervision sessions. Supervision should aim to solve practice problems, recognize staff efforts, and encourage future professional development. Another study by Tsui (2008) provided similar results in which the supervisors in Hong Kong perceived supervision as a rational and systematic process, whereas the supervisees expected emotional support and collaborative teamwork. The voices for harm reduction and managing social risk have further enforced the management role in determining the nature of the social work supervision provided. It often results in the emergence of more therapeutic type interventions aimed at the individual as the favored practice modality at the expense of community development, social policy, and social change work. Thus, the practice of social work supervision encountered many constraints that social workers had frequently complained about, such as "lack of time," "administrative focus," and "incompetent supervisor." Thus, the demands for studying the phenomena of social work supervision, especially regarding professional development and satisfaction, had increased significantly during the period.

The professional bodies in Hong Kong have also focused their efforts in relation to supervision. In 2006, the Social Workers Registration Board (SWRB) re-visited social work supervision practice by conducting a comprehensive study exploring supervision practice in Hong

Kong. The purpose of the study aimed at getting professionals' support for making social work supervision a mandated practice. The result showed that the social work professionals agreed that supervision was important and necessary. However, they showed great resistance to make supervision a mandated practice because there was no proper training for supervisors, who had a heavy workload that hindered regular supervision, and immediate and/or on-site consultation was reportedly available to help social workers. Subsequently though, the SWRB devised recommended supervision guidelines, which cover the objectives and functions of social work supervision, supervision structure, required standards, and code of ethics, and several promotional forums were conducted to introduce these recommendations.

Though there was significant support to regulate proper social work supervision, Ng and Tsui (personal communication, 9 June 2020) found that there was no strong view from the Social Welfare Department in Hong Kong, who was the main source of funding for social welfare organizations to provide social services. In addition, the SWRB considered the social work supervision guidelines had been well written and social work professionals were well governed under the current system. There was no obvious disagreement from social welfare organizations since supervision was available regardless of whether it was mandated or self-regulated, and many frontline social workers welcomed this supervision practice. It was decided that it was too difficult to make supervision a mandated practice because many small non-government organizations lacked the resources to hire qualified supervisors to carry out the task. Eventually, the recommended supervision standards and code of ethics became a reference for supervision practice since no mandate for supervision could be established and supervision practice currently depends on the good will and self-regulation of organizations. SWRB as a social work regulatory authority has put this requirement in Guidelines on Code of Practice for Registered Social Workers (2013). However, the practice of supervision in Hong Kong remained as a recommendation only, and thus the issue of supervision effectiveness remains unclear.

From 2011–2020: Further support and work undertaken towards better supervision practice

Tremendous progress has been achieved over this period with regard to the research, policy, and practice of social work supervision in Hong Kong.

Research advancement

To follow Tsui's work in building social work supervision theory, Ng (2016) conducted research regarding how the supervisor-supervisee dyad formed and maintained a working alliance with each other in the context of Chinese culture. The study addressed the research gap, concerning the fact that no empirical evidence existed on how the "supervisory working alliance relationship" was formed across four dimensions including agency, supervisor, supervisee, and the client, within the Chinese cultural context. Basically, if the context was taken into consideration, both in theory and in practice, a more sensitive and effective supervision could be achieved. The study's core focus was on professional-focused supervision with an emphasis on supervisory working alliance relationships. This relationship needs to span from novice to maturity across four stages of learning, in a multi-dimension context. The cultural context referred to the values, norms, customs, and patterns of society in which the supervision takes place. The study had explored the interplay between professional values (i.e., social work codes of ethics) and Chinese values (i.e., harmonious relationship – *qing*, *yuan*, and *face*). The agency context explored supervisors' monitoring roles in the supervisory process and supervisees' practice in conforming to agency goals through supervision practice. It also investigated supervisors' professional competence in creating the supervision contract, the supervision format, attachment styles, the use of power and authority, transaction and transformation behaviors, and cultural sensitivity. For the supervisees, the study was focused on looking at their needs, job performance and satisfaction, attachment styles and behaviors. In terms of the client, this study did not involve them because of the sensitivity of clients' encountered problems, complexity of problem nature, and confidential control, as the cases might involve too many people's issues. Apart from this, to keep clients to stay in the study loop is also difficult, and looking for replacements would have impacted upon the study's progress.

The study's results indicated that the supervision practice of our professionals is greatly influenced by Chinese culture. In fact, supervision is a collaborative and co-constructive journey between the supervisor and supervisee(s). The good or bad "supervisory relationship" is a product of the interaction and intervention results of their co-created efforts. Ng (2016) reported nine types of supervisory relationships that further developed Tsui's (2003) three relationship groups, i.e. (1) hierarchical – (i) master and apprentice, (ii) gate keeper and articulation of responsibility, and (iii) regulator and devotion alignment; (2) collegial – (iv) buddy and professional aspiration, (v) supporter and creator of togetherness, and (vi) "*Yin*" and "*Yang*" partner; and (3) familial relationships – (vii) support and retention, (viii) nurturer and self-reframing and (ix) commander and troops.

Ng (2016) reported that the professional context of Hong Kong supervision is unique, because the social workers are torn between two cultures. They are trained in a Western professional framework, but their practice is greatly influenced by Chinese culture. Nonetheless, the study also identified the awareness of the social workers regarding the responsibility to set and enforce explicit and appropriate professional boundaries within their context. "Professional boundaries" are emphasized in social work training, especially concerning boundaries with clients (Chu and Tsui, 2008). Clearly boundaries should also be applied to supervisor-supervisee relationships, although the desire to do this is not as strong as it is for "worker-client" relationships. Similarly, some supervisors in this study also stated that they preferred clear "professional boundaries" with supervisees to avoid expectations from unclear reciprocal relationships. Therefore, when considering connection or disconnection, and the complexities of supervisory relationships, a clear approach to professional boundaries cannot be underestimated. The other concern regarding supervision's effectiveness is that supervisors' inadequate use of their power and authority has been considered to be poor supervision and had a negative effect on supervisees' job performance and satisfaction (Leung 2012). Hofstede (1980) and Martinsons (1996) both claimed that Hong Kong was still regarded as a high-power country, which was strongly influenced by Confucianism. They reported that Chinese leadership styles might be more autocratic than those found in the West. This means that supervisors expected their subordinates to show respect and obedience to them, and thus apply tighter controls. Under these circumstances, subordinates were not expected to confront their supervisors. This situation was identified in some supervisor-supervisee dyads. Consequently, supervisees were found to be more accepting of supervisors' power and authority and accepted it as part of the Chinese management style. If the Chinese management style is seen as more autocratic, it needs to be modified to meet supervisees' requests. This is because the supervisees in this study have clearly stated that competent supervisors: (1) are available and responsive, (2) are knowledgeable about tasks and skills and can relate them to theory, (3) have practice expectations about service delivery similar to their supervisees', (4) provide support and encouragement for supervisees' professional growth and development, (5) trust and allow supervisees to try new initiatives, (6) are demonstrative of professional role models, and (7) interact with supervisees in a mutually respective style. Undeniably, "trust" is the key construct of supervisory working alliance relationships, and it the result of a number of relational behaviors including reflection, acceptance, listening, modesty, cooperation, and mutual exchange. These important components became relevant to effective social work supervision practice in Hong Kong.

Supportive Supervision Scheme

The SWRB (2006) study on the supervision for social workers also recommended improved training for supervisors, the development of peer supervision from experienced workers, and re-focusing supervisory support to new entrants of social work field. Very limited work was made advancing these recommendations until official support was eventually shown. The Social Welfare Department of Hong Kong granted a three-year project named "Supportive Supervision Scheme" (SSS) for promoting supervision practice in Social Work Service (HKSWA, 2014). Although this project was granted much later than initially expected, it followed years of requests and advocacy by social work professionals. As such we still value it because supervision is viewed as a promise of service quality, a type of support for the social workers, and a recognition of the importance of social work supervision. The major target of the scheme was for social work supervisors who had five or more years of experience in supervisory practice. All of them were recommended by their employers, and they were allowed to take time off from work to attend ten training sessions related to supervision knowledge, attitudes, and skills. The important messages that the trainers wanted to deliver to the trainees was that supervision should be co-constructed between the supervisor and supervisee(s); it needs to be structured with regular, set times and planned agendas so that both parties are well prepared to make full use of the session. Both supervisors and supervisees shared an understanding of supervision as a relationship and reflective process that was concerned with organizational and professional accountabilities, development and support. The agenda should cover discussions, reflections upon practice, policy and skills development, as well as giving attention to organizational behaviors, cultures, and practices. The supervision structure was in line with those practices in different countries. Noble (1999) describes supervision sessions as a unique opportunity to focus on linking the "thinking" with the "doing," and the "doing" with the "thinking" in order to articulate the particular practice approach and/or issue. In fact, trainers had been reminded that supervision needs to be seen as complex work. The complexity is often continued or formalized through the development of a supervision contract which emphasizes goals and action plans.

Apart from that, organizations also needed to provide not fewer than two social workers for the training, and each trainee to complete 20 hours supervision practice under the guidance of a consultant supervisor assigned by the Steering Committee of the Supportive Supervision Scheme. On top of that, a reflective journal needed to be submitted to the session trainer or Project Director of SSS regarding each session's training. A certificate was awarded upon completion of all the above requirements, with satisfactory performance approved by their consultant supervisors and the Steering Committee. An evaluation of the project was done by a researcher and the outcome was positive. At the end of the project, 100 certified social work supervisors were trained. Overall, all the certified social work supervisors found the training valuable, as the training provided them with very good support and experience-sharing from the consultant supervisors; they also identified further development possibilities through reflective journal writing. Eventually, a supportive group was formed among the certified social work supervisors for continued mutual learning. Meanwhile, up to May 2020, the project continues to be conducted, with its 7th batch of trainees. Even though the SSS is now running on a self-financing basis, there are many local practitioners eager to participate. The feedback from the sector in general is also very encouraging.

Discussion

Based on the foregoing achievements throughout the years, the social work sector in Hong Kong remains keen on further promoting the development of supervisory practice. While numerous initiatives were observed, various challenges and hurdles are also being faced in the local context.

Continual professional development

Compulsory continuing professional development is needed for capacity building and to promote resilience among social workers, in order to both strengthen the profession and to safeguard the interests of service recipients. Currently, professionals, human service organizations, and social work training sectors are more alert to the importance of supervision and making an effort to provide adequate supervision to their supervisees. One of the most significant contributors, The Hong Kong Social Workers Association, has set up The Hong Kong Academy of Social Work (HKASW 2020a) to promote matters of social work professional advancement. The major works cover creating a "Professional Development System for Social Workers" to enforcing "Accreditation & Credentialing of Social Work Practice" and developing "Professional Competence Framework for Social Workers." It is hoped that with the multidisciplinary efforts, the quality of our social work practice can be improved and/or advanced with the continued professional advancement and effective social work supervision practice.

Social workers in Hong Kong have reported encountering great stress, frustration, and poor job satisfaction due to downsizing, salary cuts, and increased pressures on work output and outcomes (Leung 2012). It is optimistic to consider that effective supervision would improve this situation. However, there were numerous complaints from social workers that they did not have proper supervision, in terms of it being infrequent, having no formal structure, having an over-emphasis on administrative supervision etc. The administrative function of supervision over-emphasizes evaluating social workers' work performances in organizational terms, rather than supporting and paying more attention to professional practice and skill development. If organizational priorities, such as performance evaluation and accountability, become the core of supervision at the expense of professional development, a new challenge to supervision will emerge.

Ng (2016) reported that social workers did not dare to oppose their supervisors' instructions or seek help from supervisors, as doing so might highlight the social workers' perceived incompetencies, and because those supervisors had the power to determine the social workers' professional recognition or employment. It was commonly said that supervisors "have the licence to kill." Tsui (2005) noted that there is a strong need for researchers to conduct qualitative studies that explore the functions of social work supervision in various cultural contexts. In light of social workers in Hong Kong being born into and educated in two cultures, what is recommended here is a study that gains better understanding of cultural competence, especially ideal supervision and its application in blended Western and Chinese cultures, in terms of growth-producing supervisory relationships in supervisor-supervisee dyads.

The way ahead

Obviously, there is a perceived need for additional professional training and education on the topic of supervision, specifically for social work supervisors. O'Donoghue et al. (2005) demonstrated that supervision, rather than the social work code of ethics, is more often the primary source of ethical decision-making for social workers. This further supports the increasing importance of the provision of adequate and quality supervision to social workers in order to secure effective and competent social work practice. Apart from getting outside assistance, professionals should play an active role in securing and advancing their knowledge, which will bring effective supervision outcomes. Cournoyer and Stanley (2002, p. 4) offer what appears to be the most comprehensive definition for "Lifelong Learning." Lifelong learning for social work refers to ongoing processes associated with the acquisition or construction of information, knowledge, and understanding; the development, adoption, and reconsideration of values and attitudes; and the development of skills and expertise… from the time someone first explores social work as an educational or professional career choice to the time that person no longer considers him or herself a social worker.

Tsui et al. (2017) also provided a clear typology to illustrate how the four different aspects, namely supervision, mentorship, consultation, and coaching, can mix together to have supplementary and even complementary effects on each other for lifelong learning during supervision practice. However, according to Ng (2016), the supervisors commonly shared some worries and resistance regarding training. They expressed that they would be too busy for their practice, as well as doubts about the quality of trainers. They even used some quotations like "work comes first" and "doubts regarding training adequacy and quality"! All these appeared to be the most common excuses from the social workers for seeing continued development practice as a low priority. Social work practice exists in the context of rapidly changing community needs and theoretical developments. It is necessary to encourage social workers to engage in personal lifelong learning practice outside of the support from their workplace. External help can provide them with tools and opportunities to engage in continuous learning and professional growth. Lifelong learning and self-reflective exercises on their daily work practice enable professionals to continually update their knowledge and skills in order to provide relevant and effective services.

Against the foregoing working environment in Hong Kong, external supervision may be an alternative for consideration. The key of the question here should be how this move could be effectively done. Beddoe (2012) illustrated a number of contributing factors that hinder the use and development of external supervision including: the perceived imposition of managerial agendas on supervision; the problem of power dynamics within organizations; and a growing "risk" conceptualization of practitioners' wellbeing. Without taking risk, we can never go beyond our existing capability. For example, Shenzhen was one of the pioneering cities in using external supervision from Hong Kong. Though it was reportedly not entirely smooth, the new attempt took social work practice into a fast-tracked development. For better results, precautions need to be taken, by defining the roles and responsibilities of the external supervisors. External supervisors are supposed to devote their efforts to enhancing the professional development of the supervisees, rather than the organizational concerns. Mo and Tsui (2016) identified three critical issues that needed to be addressed for external supervisors who were conducting supervision for social workers in Shenzhen. These issues were: how external supervisors integrate the international core values of the social work profession into the local indigenous practice; how to instill a postmodern perspective of social work practice into a society which is still entering into the era of modernity; and how to earn the space and autonomy for individual choices for both clients and frontline social workers within a collective socio-political system. Therefore, the exploration of these safeguarding measures should be studied to encourage the use of external supervision which would meet the real needs in supervision practice.

Apart from formal external supervision, "Peer Group Supervision" is another form of support that we found to be a viable mechanism for providing consultation and continuing education for experienced clinicians. In fact, it is common practice in response to a discernible need of social work practitioners, especially in counseling services. It is also found to be a safe yet challenging environment in which to continue the learning process and thereby enrich our professional development and our relationships with colleagues. This is the model of leader-led peer supervision, long used in other mental health professions in Western countries like the United States, England, and Australia. It has proven to be a rewarding format for this group of genetic counsellors. It is well suited to the professional development needs of genetic counselors and is a particularly appropriate way to address growth in counseling skills; many avenues already exist for keeping up to date in the scientific component of our profession (Hiller and Rosenfield 2000, p. 399–410). The Australian Association of Social Work (AASW) set up guidelines Supervision Standards in 2014. With these kinds of actions, the quality of peer supervision practice can be secured.

Supervision demands are growing and pose challenges for time pressured, geographically isolated, and/or rural and remote professionals. It seems necessary to explore and develop new formats of supervision, i.e. online supervision, instead of only being able to conduct supervision on-site. However, this is a long debated issue, and there has been resistance brought about by issues of online security, confidentiality, and verification of users etc (APA 2013, HKASW 2020b). However, the current Covid-19 period has allowed this resistance to be broken down. Our communication has been forced to go online through Skype, Zoom, and other video communication software, for business meetings, school teaching, and even medical consultations. In the field of social work, the Council on Social Work Education (CSWE 2020) announced a statement in which remote field activities, including online supervision, could be counted as part of the field hours for social work students in the United States. The first and third authors of this chapter also mainly use the format of online supervision for facilitating their supervisees' learning in the field practice. Thus, developing online communication has great potential, is another solution to meet supervision demands, and is worth further exploration. Any solution for online supervision needs to be recognized, and issues that are legally sensitive or confidential should be dealt with appropriately with proper guidance, including the clarification of the nature of services and verification of supervisory users. User perceptions of security and utility will ultimately determine uptake of online supervision services, and further investigations of user perception is required.

Finally, constructing an evidence-based supervision model is also recommended, as this can enhance the effectiveness of social work supervision practice. Hong Kong social work professionals are recommended to take a serious look at the model of social work supervision that O'Donoghue et al. (2017) synthesized from the findings of empirical peer-reviewed journal articles. The model is seen as a practical application of social work supervision research and an attempt to advance the previous work undertaken in this area as well as to address the lack of empirically supported models of supervision currently available to social workers. Another reason for the authors to recommend this to professional social workers is because we found the model to express a new theoretical understanding of supervision, which incorporates the tasks, processes, and context of supervision, and which is responsive to the plurality of supervision arrangements found internationally.

Social work, as a learning profession, has been striving for continual improvement in the past decades. The provision of effective supervisory practice is an essential element in maintaining and enhancing the quality of our services to the community. The development of a comprehensive mechanism which comprises supervised practice, independent practice, and a more balanced supervision involving peer learning and professional guidance is the way ahead. This will not only strengthen our professional intervention, but also benefit our clients in need.

Social work supervision in Hong Kong began as an administrative practice of charity organizations. At the beginning of the 20th century, universities set up training programs, and gradually a body of knowledge and a theoretical framework for social work supervision emerged. Unsurprisingly, supervision became an educational process. At the same time, the impact of psychoanalytic theory and its treatment methods led to the casework-oriented format and structure of supervision. When social work evolved into a mature profession, support grew for independent autonomous practice among social workers. However, due to the increasing demand for accountability in the last decade, supervision is now back to the circle of administrative necessity, as well as a means to ensure quality of service to clients and to satisfy regulating bodies. The development of social work supervision can be perceived as the result of the influence of external funding bodies and the forces of professionalization over the last 125 years (Tsui, 1997a, 2004b, 2005a; Tsui and Ho, 2003).

Bibliography

American Psychology Association (APA), 2013. Guidelines for the practice of telepsychology. *American Psychologist*, 68 (9), 791–800.

Australian Association of Social Workers (AASW), 2014. Supervision Standards – 2014. Available from: https://www.aasw.asn.au/document/item/6027 [Accessed 1 March 2021].

Barretta-Herman, A., 1993. On the development of a model of supervision for licensed social work practitioners. *The Clinical Supervisor*, 11(2), 55–64.

Bennett, P., Evans, R., and Tattersall, A., 1993. Stress and coping in social workers: a preliminary investigation. *British Journal of Social Work*, 23, 31–44.

Beddoe, L., 2012. External supervision in social work: power, space, risk, and the search for safety. *Australian Social Work*, 65 (2), 197–213.

Bernard, J. M., and Goodyear, R. K., 1992. *Fundamentals of clinical supervision*. Boston, MA: Allyn and Bacon.

Brown, A., and Bourne, I., 1996. *The social work supervisor: Supervision in community, day care, and residential settings*. Buckingham: Open University Press.

Chan, D., 1998. Functional relations among constructs in the same content domain at different levels of analysis: a typology of composition models. *Journal of Applied Psychology*, 83 (2), 234–246.

Census and Statistics Department, 2016. Population by-census: main results [online]. Hong Kong Special Administrative Region of the People's Republic of China. Available from: https://www.bycensus2016 .gov.hk/data/16bc-main-results.pdf [Accessed 9 June 2020].

Chernesky, R. H., 1986. A new model of supervision. *In*: N. Van Den Bergh, and L. B. Cooper, eds. *Feminist visions for social work*. Silver Spring, MD: National Association of Social Workers, 128–148.

Cogan, M., 1953. Toward a definition of profession. *Harvard Educational Review*, 23 (1), 33–50.

Collings, J., and Murray, P., 1996. Predictors of stress amongst social worker: an empirical study. *British Journal of Social Work*, 26 (3), 375–387.

Council on Social Work Education (CSWE), 2020. CSWE statement on field hour reduction [online]. Available from https://www.cswe.org/News/General-News-Archives/CSWE-Statement-on-Field -Hour-Reduction?from=singlemessage [Accessed 25 March 2020].

Cournoyer, B.R., and Stanley, M.J., 2002. *The social work portfolio: planning, assessing, and documenting lifelong learning in a dynamic profession*. Pacific Grove, CA: Brooks/Cole.

Ellis, M.V., 2001. Harmful supervision, a cause for alarm: comment on Gray et al., 2001 and Nelson and Friedlander, 2001. *Journal of Counseling Psychology*, 48 (4), 401–406.

Epstein, L., 1973. Is autonomous practice possible. *Social Work*, 18, 5–12.

Erera, I. P., and Lazar, A., 1994. The administrative and educational functions in supervision: Indications of incompatibility. *The Clinical Supervisor*, 12(2), 39–56.

Fu, K., 1999. Supervisory practice in medical social service setting of scheduled II hospital in Hong Kong. MA in Social Work Dissertation, Department of Applied Social Studies, The Hong Kong Polytechnic University.

Gitterman, A., 1972. Comparison of educational models and their influences on supervision. In: F. W. Kaslow, ed. *Issues in human services*. San Francisco, CA: Jossey-Bass, 18–38.

Gitterman, A., and Miller, I., 1977. Supervisors as educators. *In*: F.W. Kaslow, ed. *Supervision, consultation, staff training in the helping professions*. San Francisco, CA: Jossey-Bass, 100–114.

Hart, G. M., 1982. *The process of clinical supervision*. Baltimore, MD: University Park Press.

Hiller, E., and Rosenfield, J.M., 2000. The experience of leader-led peer supervision: genetic counselors' perspective. *Journal of Genetic Counseling*, 9 (5), 399–410.

Hipp, J. L., and Munson, C. E., 1995. The partnership model: a feminist supervision/consultation perspective. *The Clinical Supervisor*, 13(1), 23–38.

Hofstede, G., 1980. *Culture's consequences*. Beverly Hills, CA: SAGE.

Hong Kong Academy of Social Work (HKASW), 2020a. About HKASW [online]. Available from: https:// www.facebook.com/Hong-Kong-Academy-of-Social-Work-100248694989216 [Accessed 9 June 2020].

Hong Kong Academy of Social Work (HKASW), 2020b. Reference guide to the application of information and communication technology in social work services [online]. Available from: https://www.hkswa .org.hk/%e3%80%8c%e6%87%89%e7%94%a8%e8%b3%87%e8%a8%8a%e5%8f%8a%e9%80%9a%e8 %a8%8a%e7%a7%91%e6%8a%80%e6%96%bc%e7%a4%be%e5%b7%a5%e6%9c%8d%e5%8b%99%e3 %80%8d%e5%8f%83%e8%80%83%e6%8c%87%e5%bc%95/ [Accessed 9 June 2020; In Chinese].

Hong Kong Council of Social Service (HKCSS), 2010. Survey on turnover and wastage of social work personnel. Advisory Committee on Social Work Training and Manpower Planning [online]. Available from http://www.hkcss.org.hk [Accessed 9 June 2020].

Hong Kong Social Workers Association (HKSWA), Support supervision scheme. Available from http:// hkswa.sss.org.hk/about-us.html [Accessed 9 June 2020].

Kadushin, A., 1974. Supervisor-supervisee: a survey. *Social Work*, 19(3), 288–298.

Kadushin, A., 1992. *Supervision in social work*, 3rd ed. New York: Columbia University Press.

Kadushin, A., and Harkness, D., 2002. *Supervision in social work*, 4th ed. New York: Columbia University Press.

Ko, G.P., 1987. Casework supervision in voluntarily family services agencies in Hong Kong. *International Social Work*, 30, 171–184.

Kutzik, A. J., 1977. The social work field. *In*: F. W. Kaslow, ed. *Supervision, consultation, and staff training in the helping professions*. San Francisco, CA: Jossey-Bass, 25–60.

Lai, F.W.H., and Chan, T.K.T., 2009. Social work in Hong Kong: from professionalization to 're-professionalization'. *China Journal of Social Work*, 2 (2), 95–108.

Latting, J. E., 1986. Adaptive supervision: a theoretical model for social workers. *Administration in Social Work*, 10(1) 15–23.

Leung, K.K., 2012. An exploration of the use of power in social work supervisory relationships in Hong Kong. *Journal of Social Work Practice*, 26 (2), 151–162.

Liddle, H., and Saba, G., 1983. On context replication: the isomorphic relationship of training and therapy. *The Journal of Strategic and Systematic Therapies*, 2, 3–11.

Lloyd, C., King, R., and Chenoweth, L., 2002. Social work stress and burnout: a review. *Journal of Mental Health*, 11 (3), 255–265.

Lowy, L., 1983. Social work supervision: From models toward theory. *Journal of Education for Social Work*, 19(2) 55–62.

Magnuson, S., Norem, K., and Wilcoxon, A., 2000. Clinical supervision of relicensed counselors: recommendations for consideration and practice. *Journal of Mental Health Counseling*, 22 (2), 176–188.

Martinsons, M.G., 1996. Michael Hammer meets Confucius: re-engineering Chinese business processes. *The Managers*, (May–June), 6–17.

McMahon, M.L., and Patton, W.A., 2002. Supervision: life long learning for career counselors. *In*: M.L. McMahon and W.A. Patton, eds. *Supervision in the helping professions: a practical approach*. Frenchs Forest, NSW: Pearson Education, 234–248.

Mo, Y.H., and Tsui, M.S., 2016. External supervision for social workers in another socio-political context: a qualitative study in Shenzhen, China. *China Journal of Social Work*, 9 (1), 67–74.

Mor Barak, M.E., et al., 2009. The impact of supervision on worker outcomes: a meta-analysis. *Social Service Review*, 83 (1), 3–32. doi:10.1086/599028.

Munson, C. E., 1976. Professional autonomy and social work supervision. *Journal of Education for Social Work*, 12(3) 95–102.

Munson, C. E., ed., 1979. *Social work supervision: Classic statements and critical issues*. New York: The Free Press.

Munson, C. E., 1981. Style and structure in supervision. *Journal of Education for Social Work*, 17(1) 65–72.

Munson, C. E., 2002. *Clinical social work supervision*, 3rd ed. New York: The Haworth Press, Inc.

Ng, K.T., 2016. Exploring the professional supervisory dyad working alliance in children and family integrated services in Hong Kong (Unpublished Thesis).

Noble, C., 1999. The elusive yet essential project of developing field education as a legitimate area of social work inquiry. *Issues in Social Work Education*, 19 (1), 2–16.

O'Donoghue, K., Munford, R., and Trlin, A., 2005. Mapping the territory: supervision within the association. *Social Work Review*, 17 (4), 46–64.

O'Donoghue, K., Wong, P.Y.J., and Tsui, M.S., 2017. Constructing an evidence-informed social work supervision model. *European journal of Social Work*, 21 (3), 348–358.

Olsen, D. C., and Stern, S. B., 1990. Issues in the development of a family supervision model. *The Clinical Supervisor*, 8(2), 49–65.

Perlman, B., and Hartman, E.A., 1982. Burnout: summary and future research. *Human Relations*, 35 (4), 283–305.

Rock, B., 1990. Social worker autonomy in the age of accountability. *The Clinical Supervisor*, 8(2), 19–31.

Russell, R. K., Crimmings, A. M., and Lent, R. W., 1984. Counselor training and supervision: theory and research. *In*: S. D. Brown, and R. W. Lent. eds. *Handbook of counseling psychology*. New York: John Wiley, 625–681.

Sales, E., and Navarre, E., 1970. *Individual and group supervision in field instruction: a research report*. Ann Arbor, MI: School of Social Work, University of Michigan.

Shulman, L., 1993. *Interactional supervision*. Washington, DC: NASW Press.

Social Welfare Department of Hong Kong, 2016. Statistics on child abuse, spouse/cohabitant battering and sexual violence cases [online]. Available from http://www.swd.gov.hk/vs/english/stat.html [Accessed 18 October 2019].

Social Workers Registration Board, 2006. Study on the current state of supervision for social workers in Hong Kong. Available from http://swrb.org.hk/Documents/research2006.pdf [Accessed 9 June 2020].

Social Workers Registration Board, 2013. Guidelines on code of practice for registered social workers. Available from: https://www.swrb.org.hk/documents/Guidelines%20on%20Code%20of%20Practice _Eng.pdf [Accessed 19 June 2020].

Social Workers Registration Board, 2019. The statistics on complaints cases [online]. Available from http://www.swrb.org.hk/EngASP/statistic_com_c.asp [Accessed 17 October 2019].

Stein, D.M., and Lambert, M.J., 1995. Graduate training in psychotherapy: are therapy outcomes enhanced? *Journal of Consulting & Clinical Psychology*, 63 (2), 182–196.

Stoltenberg, C., 1981. Approaching supervision from a developmental perspective: the counselor complexity model. *Journal of Counseling Psychology*, 28(1) 59–65.

Storm, C. L., and Heath, A. W., 1985. Models of supervision: using therapy theory as a guide. *The Clinical Supervisor*, 3(1) 87–96.

Survey and Mapping Office, 2020. Total land and sea area of Hong Kong [online]. Hong Kong Special Administrative Region of the People's Republic of China. Available from: https://www.landsd.gov.hk /mapping/en/publications/total.htm [Accessed 9 June 2020].

Tam, S.K., and Mong, P.K., 2005. Job stress, perceived inequity and burnout among school social workers in Hong Kong. *International Social Work*, 48 (4), 467–483.

The Basic Law, 2008. Some facts about the Basic Law [online]. Hong Kong Special Administrative Region of the People's Republic of China. Available from: https://www.basiclaw.gov.hk/en/facts/index.html [Accessed 9 June 2020].

Tromski, D.K., 2007. Should the clinical supervisor be the administrative supervisor. *The Clinical Supervisor*, 25 (1–2), 53–67.

Tsui, M.S., 1997. The root of social work supervision: an historical review. *The Clinical Supervisor*, 15 (2), 191–198.

Tsui, M.S., 2001. Towards a culturally sensitive model of social work supervision in Hong Kong. Unpublished doctoral Thesis. Toronto, ON: University of Toronto.

Tsui, M.S., 2003. The supervisory relationship of Chinese social workers in Hong Kong. *The Clinical Supervisor*, 22 (2), 99–120.

Tsui, M.S., 2004. Supervision model in social work: from nature to culture. *Asian Journal of Counselling*, 11 (1&2), 7–55.

Tsui, M.S., 2005. *Social work supervision: content and concepts*. Thousand Oaks, CA: SAGE.

Tsui, M.S., 2006. Hopes and dreams: Ideal supervision for social workers in Hong Kong. *Asia Pacific Journal of Social Work and Development*, 16 (1), 34–42.

Tsui, M.S., 2008. Adventures in re-searching the features of social work supervision in Hong Kong. *Qualitative Social Work*, 7 (3), 349–362.

Tsui, M.S., and Cheung, F.C.H., 2004. Gone with the wind: the impacts of managerialism on human services. *British Journal of Social Work*, 34, 437–442.

Tsui, M.S., O'Donoghue, K.B., and Ng, A., 2014. Cultural competent and diversity-sensitive clinical supervision: an international perspective. *In:* C. Watkins and D. Milne, eds. *The Wiley International handbook of clinical supervision*. Chichester: John Wiley & Sons, 238–254.

Tsui, M.S., et al., 2017. From supervision to organizational learning: a typology to integrate supervision, mentorship, consultation and coaching. *British Journal of Social Work*, 47 (8), 2406–2420.

Tsui, M.S., and Ho, W.S., 1998. In search of a comprehensive model of social work supervision. *The Clinical Supervisor*, 16 (2), 181–205.

Veeder, N. W., 1990. Autonomy, accountability, and professionalism: The case against close supervision in social work. *The Clinical Supervisor*, 8(2) 33–47.

Vondracek, F.W., and Corneal, S., 1995. *Strategies for resolving individual and family problems*. Pacific Grove, CA: Brooks/Cole Publishing Company.

Watson, K.W., 1973. Differential supervision. *Social Work*, 8(3) 37–43.

Wax, J., 1979. The pros and cons of group supervision. *Social Casework*, 40, 307–313.

Worthington, E. L., 1984. Empirical investigation of supervision counselors as they can experience. *Journal of Counseling Psychology*, 31(1) 63–75.

8

THE EMERGENCE OF SOCIAL WORK SUPERVISION IN CHINA

Kitty Yuen Han Mo

This chapter examines how social work supervision is developing in mainland China. One perspective suggests that government policies and the organizational context in mainland China play an important role in the development of supervision. Another perspective suggests that the presence of external supervision support and technology will enhance the development of supervision. The contemporary problems facing the development include (1) insufficient supply of experienced supervisors; (2) lack of supervision qualification standards; (3) lack of incentive mechanism for the position of supervisors; (4) no established supervision approach; (5) insufficient understanding of the effectiveness of supervision; and (6) inadequate policy and financial support from government. The above problems indicate that social work supervision is still in its initial stage of development. In addition, the culturally diverse country of China reflects a need to develop its indigenous culturally sensitive approach to supervision. A critical review of supervision in a rapidly changing practice situation in mainland China echoes challenges facing international social workers.

Background information about social work development in mainland China

The People's Republic of China is a country in East Asia with a population is around 1.43 billion (World Population Review 2019). The country consists of 56 ethnic groups, and the official spoken language is Putonghua (Mandarin). In total, it has twenty-two provinces, five autonomous regions, four direct-controlled municipalities, and two special administrative regions. Politically speaking, the term mainland China does not include the special administrative regions of Macau and Hong Kong. This chapter mainly discusses the development of social work and social work supervision in mainland China.

The history of social work in mainland China can be dated back to mid-1920s. As indicated by Li, Han, and Huang (2013), social work was first introduced by academics as an educational program in universities. Later, social work was suspended because it was considered a means of spreading capitalism (Wu 2015). With the rise of state-owned enterprises and public institutions, the social and welfare needs of employees were satisfied by their working units and the services provided by public institutions (Yan and Tsang 2005). Until 1987, the Ministry of Civil Affairs was responsible for developing social work (Gao and Yan 2015). Subsequently, a series of government policies and measures were issued to support the development of social work, for example, the Guidance on Purchasing Services from the Social Forces (China Philanthropy Times 2015), the Medium-to-Long Term Talents Development Plan 2010–2020, the 1 + 7 policy documents of Shenzhen (Chan, Ip, and Lau, 2009), and the Regulations on the Social Workers Occupational Standard System (Leung 2007). All these policies and measures are used to regulate and monitor the implementation of social work in the country.

Shanghai was the first city to develop a social workers association in 1993. Social work has since been recognized as a profession (Sigley 2011). Another city, Shenzhen, followed as a major social work service developer in the southern region (Wang and Jiang 2013). Various types of government bodies have been established at central and provincial levels to facilitate the development of social work in the country (Gao and Yan 2015, Wang and Jiang 2013). The social work service system is a system of programs that are funded by government to address social needs. Most regions adopt a contracted service approach to establish social work service in the community level or within government institutions (Wei and Tsui 2018). Many universities offer social work education programs with a wide range of professional courses (Zhang 2017). The standardization of social work undergraduate programs is the responsibility of the Chinese Association of Social Work Education (Law and Gu 2008). However, the process towards the development of a standardized curriculum is not easy. The central government adopts a nation-wide accreditation examination to measure a person's knowledge (Tsui and Pak 2013). The exam is used in professional certification and is part of the requirements of accreditation.

The development of social work supervision in mainland China

Social work supervision is an important component of social workers' development in mainland China. In examining the development of social work supervision, one perspective suggests that government policies and organizational culture in mainland China play an important role in the development of supervision. Another perspective suggested that the presence of external supervision support and technology will enhance the development of supervision.

The role of government policies in the development of supervision

Government policies and organizational context play an important role in the development of supervision. The occurrence of many social issues such as city renewal, poverty, and aging, and natural disaster push the government to consider social work as an intervention method for these problems (Sigley, 2011). Against this background, supervision is viewed as an effective means to support the development of social work. According to Zhang (2017), the mid-term and long-term plan for the Construction of Social Work Professionals 2011–2020 proposed to train 80,000 local supervisors. There are over 30 supervision related policies and guidance notes to promote the development of social work supervision. These include supervisor's qualifications, selection methods, training, responsibilities, assessment, salary, and other benefits. For example, Li (2015) examines the Administrative Measures for Selection of Social Work Supervisors in Nanjing and discovers that there are strict regulations on the selection process, supervision role, and job duties of the supervisors.

The accreditation of supervisors varies, for example in the two cities in the southern provinces, Shenzhen and Dongguan, it is conducted by two different authorities. In Shenzhen (a special economic zone and a major city in Guangdong Province) accreditation is conducted by the Shenzhen Association of Social Workers (SASS) (Li, 2017). The SASS selects and assesses the local supervisors in accordance with the Shenzhen Social Workers' Primary Supervisor and Selection Management Measures. Then the SASS issues qualification certificates to the accredited supervisors. Those who do not obtain the qualification certificate are not allowed to engage in supervision services. In Dongguan (a major city in Guangdong Province and adjacent to Shenzhen), the selection, accreditation, and assessment of supervisors is coordinated by the Municipal Bureau of Civil Affairs (MBCA) (Dongguan government 2016). The MBCA selects and assesses the local supervisors in accordance with the Dongguan Municipal Bureau of Civil Affairs Social Workers Supervisors Selection and Management Measures. Participants in supervisor selection must have at least two years of social work experience.

Concerning the training of supervisors, some local governments have issued policies to regulate the practice. For example, the Xiamen Government uses both classroom training and mentorship to train their local supervisors in accordance with the Notice of the Xiamen Municipal Bureau of Civil Affairs on the Training Plan for Xiamen Social Work Supervisors (PKULAW 2016). Other major milestones in relation to training and development of supervisors include: a) the establishment of the China Social Work Education Association Social Work Supervision Professional Committee and b) the first national social work supervision conference which was held at Shandong University.

In general, social work organizations do not have adequate financial resources to develop the supervision system. Instead they depend on government financial support. The attitude and behaviors of different local governments towards the development of supervision range from wait-and-see to actively supporting it. Although the central government highly advocates the development of a social work service, many local governments only follow their own pace to develop it. Overall, the development of social work or social services is regionalized and decentralized (Ngok and Chan 2016). Moreover, the number of social workers distributed throughout the country is mainly concentrated in particular cities or provinces such as Guangdong, Shanghai, Zhejiang, Chongqing, Beijing etc. Some cities like Heilongjiang and Hunan cannot recruit social workers (China Philanthropy Times 2016). Because of the uneven distribution of social workers, it is difficult to develop social work supervision across different regions.

The role of organizational culture in the development of supervision

Organizational culture plays an important role in the development of supervision. Tsui (2008) acknowledges that the supervision process in Chinese culture is multifaceted. Chinese culture emphasizes the importance of balance, relationship, and harmony among different parties. A harmonious and warm working relationship in a team is highly appreciated by Chinese social workers (Mo and Lai 2018; Tsui, Ho, and Lam 2005). Relationship building (in another words: guanxi building) among team members is considered as good practice (Law, Wong, Wang, and Wang 2000). Therefore, the supervisory relationship is highly prioritized and protected in a Chinese organizational context (Tjosvold, Poon, and Yu, 2005). Apart from discussing working issues, supervisors are expected to show concern to a supervisee's emotional and life issues (Ng 2014). Supervisors are expected to play the role of father, mother, big brother, or big sister in an organizational culture. This demonstrates a coexistence of benevolence and authority in a supervisory relationship.

In addition, China is a culturally diverse country, and most often a working team is composed of people with different regional languages and cultures. Cultural sensitivity and cultural awareness by supervisors is highly recommended by Mo and Tsui (2016). Supervisors need to also maintain a culturally-friendly attitude to their supervisees, because there are regional varieties of cultural traditions (Engelbrecht 2006, Gao 2016) which supervisors have to respect in order to facilitate the social workers with different cultural background in order to work as a team.

The impact of Confucian values on organizational culture is still prevalent (Fan 1995). Confucian values emphasize the importance of a set of mutual obligations and defined roles in human relationships (Tamai and Lee 2002). The accepted norms of individual behavior in an organization includes respect for seniority, conformity, maintenance of social hierarchy, and group harmony (Wang, Ruona, and Rojewski 2005). Social workers are expected to be loyal and respectful of hierarchy in handling the relationship with their superiors. Tsui, Ho, and Lam (2005) reveal that managers in Chinese organizations have dominant power in decision-making. If a social worker is working in a secondary service setting such as a school, hospital, or government unit, he or she will be requested to comply with institutional rules (Mo, Leung, and Tsui 2019). Therefore, social workers experience ethical conflicts when the client's interest is different from the institution's requirements. Overall, supervisors must be sensitive to these ethical and value conflicts.

The role of external supervisors in the development of supervision

External supervisors play an important role in the initial establishment of supervision systems because there are not enough experienced internal supervisors, and the development of social work is still in the initial stage. With the support from government, social work organizations employ external supervisors to provide educational support for their young social workers. In the past ten years (2008–2018), various forms of external supervision support services appear in Guangdong regions, Chengdu, Xiamen, and Zhejiang etc. For example, some social work organizations in Zhejiang employ external supervisors from Hong Kong and Taiwan. However, due to insufficient funds, most social work organizations mainly employ local university teachers as their external supervisors (The Research Team of Zhejian League College 2016). Hung, Ng, and Fung (2010) investigated the nature of the external supervision scheme in Shenzhen and discovered that the input from external supervisors was to provide educational and emotional support to frontline social workers.

Another the study, Mo and Tsui (2018), found that external supervisors adopted an indigenized supervision approach to address the needs of Chinese social workers. This was due to the social workers who were the supervisees being for the most part young, inexperienced, inadequately trained, and not widely recognized by the general public. The indigenized approach the external supervisors used consisted of four characteristics: a) an educational approach in supervisory sessions because the social workers needed to learn social work knowledge and skills; b) tailor-made supervision content to assess the developmental needs of individual social workers; c) the reflective element in supervision was emphasized to facilitate critical reflection of supervisees; and d) the cultural, political, and contextual issues which may affect supervision were highly emphasized. The supervisors needed to maintain a balance between professional values and bureaucratic values in traditional Chinese culture and ensure cooperation occurred between internal and external supervisors, with the latter being essential to successful supervision.

The role of technology in the development of supervision

Technology plays a special role in assisting the development of social work supervision. There have been increasing demands for professional supervision support in the remote and rural areas. Traditional face-to-face supervision in these difficult contexts seems to be difficult or even impossible. The e-supervision method is supported by Chinese scholars and practitioners (Chan 2016; Mo and O'Donoghue 2019). Chan (2016) examines a cyber supervision program conducted by a national social workers association in mainland China. The program which has been in place since 2013 aimed to train local supervisors in performing their roles. Since all the participants come from different cities, each of them is matched and paired up with an experienced distance supervisor in Hong Kong or the southern cities of the country. The supervisees and supervisors use technology-assisted methods to communicate monthly. Supervision was conducted online, and it lasted for five months. All participants in the program were satisfied with the online supervision.

Supervision needs to keep pace with the latest technological developments. In particular, social workers in remote and rural areas are not able to receive supervision provided by competent supervisors. Borrowing from Western experiences, advances in technology allow distance supervision to occur where supervisor and supervisee are in different locations (Rousmaniere and Renfro-Michel 2016). Cyber supervision, e-supervision, or technological-assisted supervision – all these terms refer to the use of technologies in synchronous and asynchronous supervision practice (Barnett 2011).

Research conducted by Mo and O'Donoghue (2019) identified the use of information and technology in the above-mentioned national supervision training program. They discovered that a series of "e-supervision skills" are used on cyber supervision platforms. The skills include questioning, immediate response, clarification, listening, empathy, and preparation before supervision. Because a distance supervisor may not be familiar with the context and culture facing supervisee, the issue of cultural sensitivity may be ignored or neglected in the cyber supervision process. Moreover, in China it is important that supervisors use appropriate cyber security, abide by the law, and take measures to protect confidentiality. Overall, there is an urgent need to address the ethical issues of online supervision in China including the development of ethical guidelines to inform e-supervision practice.

Local studies about developmental needs of supervisees and related supervision strategies

Consideration of the supervisee's needs has increasingly become important in the development of supervision in China. Social workers vary in their needs and level of development. The educational and emotional needs of each social worker require special attention. Supervision is best when tailored to match with the supervisee's needs. This section discuss several Chinese studies concerned with the developmental needs of supervisees and the strategies their supervisors employed. The first study is that of Mo (2015) who studied the developmental needs of Chinese social workers in Shenzhen (a city in south China), who found that social work was at an initial stage of development, with most of the social workers' development progressing from stages of inexperience to having greater autonomy and stable professional skills. Supervisors met their supervisees' needs according to their developmental level. For example, many young inexperienced social workers had a higher degree of anxiety because of their insufficient knowledge and skills. They wanted professional support from senior colleagues or mentors. They also had a greater attachment to a supportive supervisor. In addition, there was an inadequate supply of organizational supervisors, with many social workers being promoted to a supervisory role after they had three or four years' experience. These experienced social workers were promoted to the role of group leader, team leader, manager, or mentor. They had accumulated knowledge and skills in practice, but they lacked the skills in management and supervision. They felt the pressure from the role transition, and they hoped to learn advanced management knowledge. They were independent in this stage and did not need frequent supervision. Therefore, their supervisors taught them supervision and management knowledge.

An earlier study by Hung, Ng, and Fung (2010) indicated that young and inexperienced social workers feel powerless when they deal with the demands from their administrative heads. This was because some social workers are working in governmental units or quasi-governmental units, and the administrative heads of these units did not have an adequate understanding about the roles and responsibilities of social workers. Apart from these governmental units, the social workers also worked in a variety of settings such as schools and hospitals where their line managers did not understand the social work task. Moreover, the novice social workers had little knowledge and experiences about the social welfare system and the resources available in the community. They expected their supervisors could provide them with emotional support and practical guidance. The supervisors provided emotional support by showing appreciation of the work of supervisees, encouraging and understanding their difficulties, and acceptance of their weaknesses.

The third study which was conducted by Mo & O'Donoghue (2018) explored ten supervision strategies employed by external supervisors. The ten strategies included: attentive listening, performance coaching, reflective listening, role modeling, consultative advice, emotional support, conflict mediation, practice teaching, culturally friendly attitudes, and practice teaching. A quite special and generic supervision strategy in the Chinese context was the promotion of social work values. The promotion of social work values in supervision was due to the Ministry of Personnel and the Ministry of Civil Affairs having developed criteria for taking licensing examinations since 2008. According to the Interim Provisions on the Evaluation of the Professional Level of Social Workers and the Implementation Measures for the Professional Level Examination of Assistant Social Workers and Social Workers, all candidates must have at least four years of working experiences in social services plus a high school certificate; or two years of working experiences in social services plus a college degree in social work; or be recent graduates with a bachelor degree in social work; or two years of working experiences in social services plus a bachelor degree in other majors (Yan and Lu, 2013). The examinations are used across the country in making licensing decisions. No other factor is included in licensing requirements. From this special context, anyone who passes the accreditation examination can register as a social worker. Because some of the registered social workers are not formally trained in social work knowledge and social work values (Xu 2013), the education and promotion of social work values was needed in their supervision. To achieve this, a reflective supervision process was used with the aim of facilitating supervisees to be more reflective in their professional practice (Mo and O'Donoghue 2018).

Apart from social work values, the non-trained social workers needed to equip themselves with professional social work knowledge and knowledge of social policies (Chow 2019). This was reinforced by An and Ng's (2014) study of social workers' educational background, who found that more than 49% of social workers do not have a professional social work background, and this implies that they do not understand actual social work practices and have little social work practice knowledge. As a result, supervisors must provide a lot of structured practice teaching like fieldwork practice teaching. In particular, the new social work graduates require a systematic way of teaching and instruction. Methods used include demonstration, discussion, role-playing, and on-site observation.

In recent years, the government has vigorously developed community work and has more specific requirements to ensure the ability of social workers to perform their duties in the community. According to Zhu (2019), the policy documents about community work request a social worker to organize and guide social organizations in the community, facilitate community residents to participate in community activities and community governance, promote social work methods, and support government's work in the community. In addition, the Community Social

Work Service Guide requires community social workers to participate in the mediation of residents' conflicts, to prevent and resolve community conflicts, to provide various professional services for social assistance projects, and to provide emergency support after accidental injuries. All these documents clearly state that community social workers should have the professional knowledge required to carry out community social work services and continuously improve their professional competencies. As a result, supervisors must address these service needs and equip social workers with necessary community knowledge. Moreover, supervisors must train social workers with knowledge and skills in handling emergency cases.

In summary, the contemporary problems facing the development of social work supervision in mainland China are: (1) an insufficient supply of experienced supervisors; (2) a lack of supervision qualification standards; (3) a lack of incentives for supervisors; (4) no established supervision approach; (5) insufficient understanding of the effectiveness of supervision; and (6) inadequate policy and financial support from government. The above problems indicate that social work supervision is still in its initial stage of development. In addition, the culturally diverse country of China reflects a need to develop its indigenous culturally sensitive approach to supervision. A critical review of supervision in the rapidly changing practice situation of mainland China to some extent also echoes the challenges facing international social workers.

Challenges to the development of supervision in mainland China

There are five further challenges to the development of supervision in mainland China. The first is the varied understanding of the effects of supervision. Gao (2018) notes that the importance of supervision as a driving force for the professional development of the frontline social worker is underestimated. According to a qualitative study conducted by Mo (2019), some local governments take a positive stance towards supervision development, with some cities in Fujian and Guangdong provinces developing the supervisor's promotion system through which senior social workers can be promoted to the role of supervisors. This is in contrast to some other cities which have been slow to develop social work supervision. In these regions such as Inner Mongolia Autonomous Region and Xinjiang Uyghur Autonomous Region, frontline social workers seldomly receive supervision from their seniors or supervisors. Moreover, the recruitment of experienced supervisors is not easy in these remote regions (Xing 2015).

The second challenge is the inadequate supply of experienced supervisors. Li (2017) indicates that many local supervisors have insufficient self-confidence in their abilities to supervise frontline social workers. Moreover, every supervisor needs to supervise too many frontline social workers, and the supervision policies cannot keep up with the development needs. Given the lack of experienced supervisors, many social workers believe that the local supervisors lack the relevant professional experiences to supervise social workers effectively. The lack of experienced supervisors and the high turnover rate of experienced social workers have become real challenges facing the development of supervision in the country (Cheng and Wai 2011).

The third challenge is non-professional supervision practice conducted by non-social work supervisors. As indicated by Mo (2019), many social workers are supervised by non-social workers. This occurs because some social workers are working in government departments or quasi-governmental units, and their team managers are non-social workers. In these situations, the social workers cannot get enough professional support from their immediate heads. Therefore, Ng (2014) suggests they adopt a dual supervision model. The dual model is characterized by a combined supervision effort of an internal administrative supervisor and an external professional supervisor. Some prosperous cities in southern China take the lead and adopt a dual supervision model in social work organizations. Internal supervisors mainly support administrative management within an organization. External supervisors are recruited and employed from outside sources.

The fourth challenge is due to inadequate financial resources to support the development of supervision. For example, Li and Zhang (2018) examined the current situation of supervision in Chengdu. They found that the supervision system within a social work organization was not effective because only large social work organizations have the resources to set up a complete internal supervision system. This is compared to small organizations which can only look for short-term supervision services provided by external supervisors. Although there are many small social work organizations, most of them rely on government social work projects to survive. These projects have short durations and are unstable sources of funds, which leads to the loss of social workers. Since there is no way to retain experienced social workers, it is very difficult for an organization to establish its internal supervisory system. The example of Chengdu also reflects similar situations in other cities.

The fifth challenge concerns insufficient training provided to supervisors. Tse (2015) expresses that it is of great importance to establish mandatory qualifications and the provision of supervision training. Some local government have conducted supervisors training courses for their local supervisors (Baijiahao 2018; Hunan Daily 2017; SWCHINA 2013). Further attention to supervisor training is required to address the learning needs of local supervisors.

Future research agenda

The situations mentioned in the above paragraphs indicate that social work supervision in mainland China is still in its infancy. The culturally diverse characteristics of the country reflect a need to develop its indigenous culturally sensitive approach to supervision. A critical review of supervision in this rapidly changing practice environment echoes challenges facing international social workers. First, the dual supervision model practiced within social work organizations reveals that the administrative, educational, and support functions of supervision should be emphasized within a healthy organizational setting (O'Donoghue 2015). The practice of a dual supervision model could be further explored within the context of social work in mainland China.

A second area of research relates to the components of successful supervision, the process of supervision, and the supervisory relationship which greatly affects the effectiveness of supervision. The outcomes of the supervision will affect the future development of supervision in different areas of the country. This requires a more systematic measurement of the supervision outcomes. In addition, it reinforces the need for evidence-based supervision practice and innovative methodologies that identify the outcomes from supervision.

Third, a culturally sensitive supervision approach is greatly needed for attending to multiple cultural identities of supervisees, clients, and supervisors (Falender, Burnes, and Ellis, 2013). Therefore, the need for multicultural supervision research to answer those questions raised from multicultural supervision practice from the social work field is critical.

Fourth, the effectiveness of supervision in retaining social workers in the Chinese social work context can be further explored. A study conducted by Mo and Lai (2018) in different cities of Guangdong Province discovered that organizational strategies include supervision, mentoring, training, career ladder, an orientation program, career counseling, and team building activities adopted by NGOs can increase the retention of social workers. This is consistent with Western findings that peer supervision, mentoring, and a supportive supervision environment can reduce stress level of junior social workers (Csiernik 2010, Lloyd, King, and Chenoweth 2015).

Conclusion

NGOs often face a competitive environment, and they need to constantly restructure and improve their strength. Some NGOs demonstrate an ability to retain their social workers, exercise various organizational management strategies, cooperate with stakeholders, and maintain good relationships with funders (Lu 2003). Supervision is seen as one of the important measures to retain social workers in an organization. In addition, appreciation and recognition of work by supervisors and the provision of training are possible measures to increase job satisfaction (Coffey, Dugdill, and Tattersall 2004). Factors affecting supervision development in mainland China include government policies, organizational context, external supervision support, and technology. Still, supervision practice faces various challenges, and further research studies in local supervision practice are needed.

References

An, Q.L., and Wu, S.Y., 2014. The development of social work specialization in China: based on employment information. *Chinese Social Work Research*, 2, 23–24.

Baijiahao, 23 March 2018. *Jiangsu excellent social worker case story 4: constructing a "pyramid" of social workers - the first phase of social work supervisors in Suzhou.* [online] Available from https://baijiahao.baidu.com/s?id =1595736853967135354&wfr=spider&for=pc&isFailFlag=1 [Accessed 22 March 2019].

Barnett, J.E., 2011. Utilizing technological innovations to enhance psychotherapy supervision, training and outcomes. *Psychotherapy*, 48 (2), 103–108.

Chan, K.T., Ip, F.K.D., and Lau, S.M.A., 2009. Social work professionalization in China: the case of Shenzhen. *China Journal of Social Work*, 2 (2), 85–94.

Chan, O.F., 2016. Explore supervision and training from the social work supervision training class of the Chinese Mainland. *China Social Work*, 280 (10), 62.

Cheng, L.P., and Wai, H.D., 2011. A report on cultivating supervision talents: the practice of localization of social work in China--taking Pearl River Delta Area as an example. *Journal of East China University of Science and Technology (Social Science Edition)*, 6, 15–30.

China Philanthropy Times, 18 March 2015. *The ten major events in the development of social work in China in 2014.* [online] Available from http://www.gongyishibao.com/html/yaowen/7848.html [Accessed 28 June 2018].

China Philanthropy Times, 22 November 2016. *More than 5,000 licensed social workers in 17 provinces.* [online] Available from http://www.gongyishibao.com/html/gongyizixun/10722.html [Accessed 29 Apr 2018].

Chow, W.K., 2019. Research on the necessity and path of social workers' learning social policy. *Society and Public Welfare*, 12, 25–27.

Coffey, M., Dugdill, L., and Tattersall, A., 2004. Stress in social services: mental well-being, constraints and job satisfaction. *British Journal of Social Work*, 34 (5), 735–746.

Csiernik, R., 2010. Supporting new workers in a child welfare agency: an exploratory study. *Journal of Workplace Behavioral Health*, 25, 218–232.

Dongguan Government, 2016. *Dongguan Municipal Bureau of Civil Affairs Social Workers Supervisors Selection and Management Measures.* [online] Available from http://www.dg.gov.cn/007330088/0801/201611 /42b4b59ea23f4e9a9073bbfcfe4adcaf.shtml [Accessed 20 May 2018].

Engelbrecht, L.K., 2006. Cultural friendliness as a foundation for the support function in the supervision of social work students in South Africa. *International Social Work*, 49 (2), 267–276.

Falender, C.A., Burnes, T.R., and Ellis, M.V., 2013. Multicultural clinical supervision and benchmarks: empirical support informing practice and supervisor training. *The Counseling Psychologist*, 41 (1), 8–27.

Fan, X., 1995. The Chinese cultural system: implications for cross-cultural management. *SAM Advanced Management Journal*, 60 (1), 14–20.

Gao, J.G., and Yan, M.C., 2015. Social work in making: the state and social work development in China. *International Journal of Social Welfare*, 24, 93–101.

Gao, Q.Y., 2018. *Demand-based social work project supervision research.* Nanjing University. Master Thesis Dissertation. [online] Available from http://cdmd.cnki.com.cn/Article/CDMD-10284-1018150176 .htm [Accessed 20 Apr 2019].

Gao, X.S., 2016. Linguistic instrumentalism and national language policy in Mainland China's state print media coverage of the protecting Cantonese movement. *Chinese Journal of Communication*, 10, 157–175.

Hunan Daily, 26 August 2017. *Changsha: 10 local supervisors finish the local supervisor's training scheme and report for duty.* [online] Available from http://hnrb.voc.com.cn/hnrb_epaper/html/2017-08/26/content_1241092.htm?div=-1 [Accessed 13 March 2018].

Hung, S.L., Ng, S.L., and Fung, K.K., 2010. Functions of social work supervision in Shenzhen: insights from the cross-border supervision model. *International Social Work*, 53 (3), 366–378.

Law, K.C., and Gu, J.X., 2008. Social work education in Mainland China: development and issues. *Asian Social Work and Policy Review*, 2, 1–12.

Law, K.S., Wong, C.S., Wang, D.X., and Wang, L.H., 2000. Effect of supervisor-subordinate guanxi on supervisory decisions in China: an empirical investigation. *The International of Human Resource Management*, 11, 751–765.

Leung, C.B., 2007. An international definition of social work for China. *International Journal of Social Welfare*, 16 (4), 391–397.

Li, D., 2017. Analysis of the role of social work supervision: take Shenzhen as an example. *Réncái zīyuán kāifā*, 14 (7), 43–44.

Li, F., 2015. Nanjing social work supervisor development system gets started – interpretation of administrative measures for selection of social work supervisors in Nanjing (trial). *China Social Work*, 22, 10–11.

Li, X.L., and Zhang, R., 2018. Problems in social work supervision of Chengdu and their countermeasures. *Tsinghua Social Work Review*, 6, 77–80.

Li, Y.S., 2016. *Social work development in the new era: needs, challenges and counter-measures.* [online] Available from http://big5.xinhuanet.com/gate/big5/news.xinhuanet.com/gongyi/2016-03/29/c_128830876.htm [Accessed 20 August 2018].

Li, Y.S., Han, W.J., and Huang, C.C., 2013. Development of social work education in China:Background, current status, and prospects. *Journal of Social Work Education*, 48, 635–653.

Lu, Y.Y., 2003. *The limitations of NGOs: a preliminary study of non-governmental social welfare organisations in China.* International Working Paper Series 13. [online] Available from http://eprints.lse.ac.uk/29218/1/IWP13LuYiyi. pdf. [Accessed 22 Apr 2018].

Lloyd, C., King, R., and Chenoweth, L., 2015. Social work, stress and burnout: a review. *Journal of Mental Health*, 11 (3), 255–265.

Mo, Y.H., 2015. *In search of a knowledge map of external social work supervision in Shenzhen, China.* Thesis (Doctoral). Hong Kong Polytechnic University.

Mo, Y.H., 2019. An exploration of social work in Mainland China. *China Journal of Social Work*, 12 (1), 70–89.

Mo, Y.H., and Lai H.S., 2018. Social worker turnover issue in Mainland China: organizations can do something, *The Hong Kong Journal of Social Work*, 52 (1/2), 63–83.

Mo, Y.H., Leung, T.L., and Tsui, M.S., 2019. Chaos in order: the evolution of social work supervision practice in the Chinese Mainland. *The Clinical Supervisor*, 38 (2), 345–365.

Mo, Y.H., and O'Donoghue, K., 2018. Nurturing a budding flower: external supervisors' support of the developmental needs of Chinese social workers in Shenzhen, China. *International Social Work*, 1–15.

Mo, Y.H., and O'Donoghue, K., 2019. A snapshot of cyber supervision in Mainland China. *Qualitative Social Work*, 1–18.

Mo, Y.H., and Tsui, M.S., 2016. External supervision for social workers in another socio-political context: a qualitative study in Shenzhen, China. *China Journal of Social Work*, 9 (1), 62–73.

Mo, Y.H., and Tsui, M.S., 2018. Toward an indigenized external supervision approach in China. *International Social Work*, 1–18.

Ng, K.F., 2014. Comparison of practice in Hong Kong supervisors and supervisors of the Mainland. *Journal of Zhangjiang Normal University*, 35 (4), 33–37.

Ngok, K.L., and Chan, K.C., 2016. *China's social policy: transformation and challenges.* Abingdon: Routledge.

O'Donoghue, K., 2015. Issues and challenges facing social work supervision in the twenty-first century. *China Journal of Social Work*, 8 (2), 136–149.

PKULAW, 2016. *Notice of the Xiamen Municipal Bureau of Civil Affairs on the training plan for Xiamen social work supervisors.* [online] Available from https://www.pkulaw.com/lar/ff3c23af01551778c24cc4d6b44 7841dbdfb.html [Accessed 9 January 2019].

Rousmaniere, T., and Renfro-Michel, E., 2016. *Using technology to enhance clinical supervision.* United States: American Counselling Association.

Sigley, G., 2011. Social policy and social work in contemporary China: an interview with Xu Yongxiang. *China Journal of Social Work*, 4, 103–113.

SWCHINA, 30 December 2013. *Weifang's opinions on strengthening the construction of professional talents in social work.* [online] Available from http://laws.swchina.org/policy/2013/1230/3442.shtml [Accessed 17 April 2018].

Tamai, K., and Lee, J., 2002. Confucianism as cultural constraint: a comparison of Confucian values of Japanese and Korean university students. *International Education Journal*, 3 (5), 33–49.

The Research Team of Zhejian League College, 2016. Study on the supervision system in social work in Zhejiang Province under the perspective of talents construction of social work. *Youth and Children Research and Practice*, 2, 68–75.

Tjosvold, D., Poon, M., and Yu, Z.Y., 2005. Team effectiveness in China: cooperative conflict for relationship building. *Human Relations*, 3, 341–367.

Tse, M.S., 2015. A study about supervisory alliance between social work supervisors and supervisees. *China Social Welfare*, 3, 47–52.

Tsui, M.S., Ho, W.S., and Lam, C.M., 2005. The use of supervisory authority in Chinese cultural context. *Administration in Social Work*, 29, 51–68.

Tsui, M.S., 2008. Adventures in re-searching the features of social work supervision in Hong Kong. *Qualitative Social Work*, 7 (3), 349–362.

Tsui, M.S., and Pak, C.M., 2013. Professional development: social work education in China: the way we were and the way ahead. *The International Journal of Continuing Social Work Education*, 16, 62–70.

Wang, G.G., Ruona, W.E.A., and Rojewski, J.W., 2005. Confucian values and the implications for international HRD. *Human Resource Development International*, 8 (3), 311–326.

Wang, W.L., and Jiang, T.J., 2013. The development of social work in Shenzhen and Shanghai. *Practice and Theory of SEZS*, 4, 36–45.

Wei, A.T., and Tsui, M.S., 2018. Conjuncture and cultural reproduction in the process of embedding: social work practice in the context of government purchase of services in China. *China Journal of Social Work*, 11 (1), 18–40.

World Population Review, 2019. *China population 2019.* [online] Available from http://worldpopulation review.com/countries/china-population/ [Accessed 21 Apr 2019].

Wu, W., 19 March 2015. *Struggling to serve: the challenges faced by social workers in China.* [online] Available from http://www.thatsmags.com/shenzhen/post/9060/struggling-to-serve-the-challenges-faced-by -social-workers-in-china [Accessed 29 Apr 2018].

Xing, W., 2015. Investigation on the status quo of social work development in Inner Mongolia. *Management Observer*, 576, 1–10.

Xu, Y.B., 2013. Analysis of the impact of vocational level examinations on the construction of social work professionals. *Journal of Social Work*, 3, 138–144.

Yan, M.C., and Tsang, K.T., 2005. A snapshot on the development of social work education in China: a delphi study. *Social Work Education*, 24, 883–901.

Yan, Q.S., and Lu, Q.C., 2013. On the connection between the professional education level of social work and the vocational examination. *Journal of Social Work*, 5, 134–138.

Zhang, H.Y., 2017. The status quo and future development of social work supervision in China. *China Social Work*, 4, 1–1.

Zhang, Y., 10 December 2017. *There are 339 universities and colleges in China that set up social work majors and 105 MSW colleges.* [online] Available from https://www.060694.com/p/clrm20.html [Accessed 29 Apr 2018].

Zhu, T.Y., 2019. Research on the evaluation index system of community social workers' competence - intensive reading based on the perspective of policy documents. *Society and Public Welfare*, 11, 22–25.

9

THE EVOLUTION OF SOCIAL WORK SUPERVISION IN AOTEAROA NEW ZEALAND

Kieran O'Donoghue

This chapter discusses the evolution of social work supervision within Aotearoa New Zealand since 1994, through a review of three distinct periods. The first period, from 1994–1997, is characterized by the influence of managerialism. The second (1998–2007) details the professional response to strengthen supervision, whereas the most recent period (2009–2019) explores the evolving professional culture. Prior to discussing the periods, the scene will set by briefly outlining the relevant historical and social context of Aotearoa New Zealand social work.

Setting the scene

Surrounded by water, approximately 1500 kilometers east of Australia and 1000 kilometers south of the Pacific Islands, Aotearoa New Zealand is relatively remote and far from other countries. The development of Aotearoa New Zealand society has been shaped by the interactions and relationship between Māori and the Crown, encapsulated in the Treaty of Waitangi 1840 (see Taylor, 1976). The historical relationship between Māori and non-Māori is the background against which a national identity and nationhood have emerged (Belich 2001, Ruwhiu 2001, 2009). This has included a history of settler colonization and oppression of Māori, the mono-cultural dominance of Pākeha (non- Māori) New Zealand culture, and the prevalence of the Westminster system of law and government. The mono-cultural dominance of Pākeha New Zealand culture also had prejudicial effects on the Pacific Island peoples who had migrated to New Zealand in response to a high demand for labor (Ministry of Pacific Island Affairs, 1999). The last quarter of the twentieth century saw Aotearoa New Zealand as a nation starting to acknowledge its colonial past and the impact this has had on Māori, through settlements by the government of Treaty of Waitangi land claims, the recognition of Māori as an official language, and the emergence of Iwi (tribal) social services (Bradley 1996, Cheyne et al. 2004). Nonetheless, Māori and Pacific Island peoples feature disproportionately across a wide range of social and health indicators, and are significant users of welfare, health, social service, and criminal justice services (Pega et al. 2010). The social work profession as part of Aotearoa New Zealand society has reflected the mono-cultural dominance of Pākeha New Zealand culture and has been an instrument of colonization, oppression, and institutional racism. Since the mid-1980s, the New Zealand Association of Social Workers (NZASW) has been on bicultural journey, with developments including a bicultural code of practice, competency standards, and the inclusion of Te

Tiriti o Waitangi (The Treaty Waitangi) in its constitution and Code of Ethics (O'Donoghue 2003). In 2000, the Association changed its name to the Aotearoa New Zealand Association of Social Workers (ANZASW) to reflect its bicultural aspirations. The development of social work supervision has paralleled the development of social work and was mono-cultural until the mid-1980s (O'Donoghue and Tsui 2012). The New Zealand Social Work Training Council (NZSWTC) *Supervision Resource Package* (1985) marked the first steps towards decolonizing supervision, with the inclusion of a bicultural model that challenged non-Māori supervisors and practitioners to develop an understanding of Māori culture, by placing an emphasis on "the concepts of 'whanaungatanga' (relationships), 'mana' (respect), and 'rangatiratanga' (leadership)" in the supervision of Māori staff and social work practice with Māori clients (NZSWTC 1985, p. 79). Towards the end of the 1980s, the neoliberal social policy introduced by the government started to influence the social services through the introduction of the purchaser-provider split, the contracting of services and the introduction of private sector business management practices. The effects of these changes were felt by supervisors who were perceived by their organizations to be managers and expected to change their case-work supervision to a more managerially focused approach (O'Donoghue, 1999).

Managerial dominance (1994–1997)

The market-led reforms of the late 1980s were reinforced throughout 1990s, through neoliberal social policy and the wholesale application business management practices in the form of new public management for health and social services (O'Donoghue 1999). The professionalization of social work profession at this time was low, with less than 30% of practicing social workers holding formal qualifications, and their social work identity was aligned to their organization, rather than the profession (Taverner 1989). The effect this had on social work supervision, which had a traditional casework and educative focus, was devastating (O'Donoghue 2010). Supervision was reduced to managerial oversight, with performance management and accountability systems replacing education, development, and critical reflection upon the practitioner's use of self and their practice (Beddoe and Davys 1994, O'Donoghue 1999). This situation is summarized in the editorial of a special issue of *Social Work Review*, on management and supervision, which stated:

> ...A decision had been made to emphasize the crucial role that supervision plays in ensuring social workers maintain professional and ethical standards in their practice. Supervision can be a way of ensuring that social work is not undermined by the imperatives of organizational efficiency
>
> *(Barrett and Munford 1994, p. 1)*

The special issue was a catalyst for a professional resistance to the managerialist takeover of supervision. It contained articles on supervision from a training perspective (Beddoe and Davys 1994), a qualitative study regarding the supervision of care and protection of workers in a statutory social work agency (Young 1994), and a brief outline of the essential features of social work supervision process (Cockburn 1994).

In the mid-1990s, the statutory child welfare agency (Child, Youth and Family (CYF)) engaged Tony Morrison, the author of *Supervision in Social Care* and from the United Kingdom, as a consultant to train supervisors and practice consultants (Morrison 1993). Morrison's model was based on adult learning theory and was applied to the functions of management, education, support, and mediation (Morrison 1993). This model arguably provided a compromise by making supervision a quality assurance process in which the supervisor facilitated the workers' reflection on their work. Other notable efforts during this period included an annotated bibliography of local and international literature (Bennie 1995), and the NZASW, Massey University, and the Auckland College of Education discussing the development of postgraduate supervision qualifications. Beddoe (1997a) reveals some of the behind the scenes work that was occurring when she refers to the development of a supervision policy within CYF and the development of the NZASW policy. Beddoe also proposed a credentialing system for professional supervision in the form of portfolios submitted by supervision in a fashion similar to the NZASW competency process (Beddoe 1997b).

Professional response (1998–2008)

Professionalization was to the forefront in Aotearoa New Zealand social work from 1998 to 2008 (O'Donoghue 2010). The primary emphasis from 1998 to 2004 was the establishment of social worker registration, whereas the period after 2004 concerned the implementation of social worker registration. It was notable that across the whole period, the proportion of formally qualified social workers rose markedly because of the requirement for social worker registration to hold a recognized qualification (Dale et al. 2017).

The period begins with NZASW publishing a *Supervision Policy Statement* (1998) and explicitly linking supervision to competent social work practice and its competency assessment process (NZASW 1998). The same year, both Massey University and Auckland College of Education launched their postgraduate supervision qualifications, and the monograph *Supervising Social Workers* was published by Massey University (O'Donoghue 1998). This monograph was made widely available within New Zealand with every supervisor in CYF and every non-government child and family support service organization receiving a copy. Two articles detailing indigenous approaches to supervision for Māori practitioners by Māori were published in 1999 (Bradley et al. 1999, Webber-Dreadon 1999). These articles set the groundwork for later research and reflection in relation to the role of culture within supervision and the development of Kaupapa Maori and bicultural supervision approaches. In 2000, the first of three supervision conferences was held in Auckland and attended by 175 participants (Beddoe and Worrall 2001). The 2000 conference provided the impetus for a marked increase in both supervision research and publications (Cooper and Anglem 2003, Davys 2002, Hirst 2001, Kane 2001, Morrell 2001, 2003, O'Donoghue 2001, 2002, 2003, Shepherd 2003, Tisdall and O'Donoghue 2003). Also in the year 2000, the Ministry of Social Development entered into a contract with Massey University and the Auckland College of Education to provide clinical supervision training to supervisors in CYF, non-government child and family support services and Māori and Pasifika providers. The Auckland College of Education withdrew from the contract in 2002, leaving Massey University to deliver the training through to 2009 (O'Donoghue 2010).

The Social Workers Registration Act (SWRA) (2003) became law in April 2003 and established the Social Workers Registration Board (SWRB) as the regulatory authority for a voluntary system registration of state registration for social workers (O'Donoghue 2004). The SWRB consulted widely throughout 2004, concerning the development of the code of conduct and policies related to experience, competence, and recognized qualifications. During the same year, the ANZASW reviewed its Code of Ethics and inserted a new section on social workers' responsibility in supervision relationships (ANZASW 2004). This clause was timely and contributed to the SWRB reinforcing the importance of supervision in the Code of Conduct (2005), Code Conduct Guidelines (2006), and policies concerning the role supervision has in obtaining and maintaining full registration, practicing certificates, and competency (O'Donoghue 2010).

The second supervision conference was held in Auckland in 2004, this conference was attended by 261 delegates. The resulting conference proceedings had more international contributors and was more interdisciplinary that the previous one (Beddoe et al. 2005). Between 2004 and 2008, there was a further strengthening of supervision through the increasing literature and research base with seventeen journal articles, four book chapters and three master's theses (Bell and Thorpe 2004, Cooper 2006, Davys 2005, Eruera 2005, 2007, Field 2008, Garland and Ellis 2006, Gillanders 2005, Hutchings 2008, Morrell 2005, 2008, O'Donoghue 2004, 2006, 2007, 2008, O'Donoghue et al. 2005, 2006, Ruwhiu et al. 2008, Simmons 2006, Simmons et al. 2007, Su'a Hawkins and Mafile'o 2004, Thomas 2005, Thomas and Davis 2005, Walsh-Tapiata and Webster 2004). This period was also notable for the further advancement of Kaupapa Māori and cultural supervision, with eight publications occurring during this period (Bell and Thorpe 2004, Davys 2005, Eruera 2005, 2007, Ruwhiu et al. 2008, Su'a Hawkins and Mafile'o 2004, Thomas and Davis 2005, Walsh-Tapiata and Webster 2004). There was also widespread delivery of supervision education and training, ranging from postgraduate diplomas and courses offered by universities through to short courses offered by private trainers (O'Donoghue 2010). Also during this period, the first national survey of social work supervision practice occurred (O'Donoghue 2008, O'Donoghue et al. 2005, 2006). This survey of 209 full members of ANZASW found that their supervision was professionally focused, and on average of a very good standard. There were significant differences between the supervision practice of Māori and non-Māori, particularly in regard to how supervision sessions were conducted and the approaches and models used. O'Donoghue et al. (2005) also raised serious questions about the extent to which the supervision involving non-Māori was bicultural. The survey also identified that what was best about supervision was a conducive environment in which progressive, effective, interactive, and safe practice occurred within a supportive, trusting, honest, and open relationship with a supervisor who demonstrated professionalism and shared practice expertise, knowledge, and experience (O'Donoghue et al. 2006). On the other hand, the improvements identified included having more time for supervision, better agency support, greater choice, better accessibility and availability of supervision, a culturally responsive environment, better organization and management of supervision sessions, and improvements in their supervisors' knowledge, skills, development, training, and professionalism (O'Donoghue 2008).

An evolving professional culture (2009–2019)

Since 2009, Aotearoa New Zealand has faced the impact of the global financial crisis and natural disasters in the form of the Christchurch and Kaikoura earthquakes. The government's social policy approach was neoliberal and promoted fiscal restraint and social investment policies in the face of growing inequality, a housing crisis, rising homelessness, child poverty, an increased demand upon health, mental health services, and child and family services. At the same time a greater demand was made by government for evidence in its social investments and results in the form of demonstrable outcomes (Dale et al. 2017). The first notable effect on social work supervision was that the contract to provide training to MSD and others finished, and there was less emphasis put on supervision. This was contrasted with both ANZASW and SWRB revising the supervision policies in 2009 and the widespread establishment of supervision policies across social service providers (O'Donoghue 2010). The 2010 supervision conference examined the tensions in the current environment, particularly regarding regulation, surveillance, and risk, and cautioned against supervision being promoted as the solution to all of the current issues (Beddoe and Davys 2011).

Since 2009, scholars from Aotearoa New Zealand have made a leading contribution to the international social work supervision literature (Sewell 2018). This contribution consists of three books published in the United Kingdom (Beddoe and Davys 2016, Davys and Beddoe 2010, Weld 2012), seven chapters in internationally published edited books (Beddoe 2015a, Beddoe and Egan 2009, 2013, Davys and Beddoe 2015a, O'Donoghue 2015a, 2019a, Tsui, O'Donoghue et al. 2014) and 29 articles in international peer-reviewed journals (Adamson 2012, 2018, Beddoe 2010, 2011, 2015b, 2016, Beddoe et al. 2014, Beddoe and Howard 2012, Beddoe et al. 2016, Davys et al. 2019, Davys et al. 2017, Hair and O'Donoghue 2009, O'Donoghue 2012, 2014, 2015b, O'Donoghue and O'Donoghue 2019, O'Donoghue and Tsui 2011, 2012, 2015, O'Donoghue et al. 2018, Pack 2009, 2011, 2015, Rankine 2013, 2018, 2019, Rankine et al. 2018, Rankine and Thompson 2015, Tsui, O'Donoghue et al. 2017).

Locally, there are two areas of focus for supervision, namely cultural responsiveness and fields of practice. In regard to culture responsiveness, new indigenous and bicultural approaches to supervision emerged, from six articles published by Māori practitioners (Eketone 2012, Elkington 2016, Eruera 2012, King 2016, Lipsham 2012, Murray 2012) to Te Wananga o Aotearoa offering the kaitiakitanga (guardianship) postgraduate diploma in bicultural supervision, which has Māori approaches as the core of its supervision curriculum.

In regard to fields of practice, there has been an increased recognition of the differences in the provision of supervision across different fields and the unique challenges of each field. The variations across fields of social work practice was identified from a survey of registered social workers supervision conducted in 2015 (n=278), which found significant differences (p<.001) in supervision pertaining to areas of practice and ethnicity. There were also significant mean differences in the supervisees overall satisfaction and overall evaluation of their supervision, with those in private practice, health, and non-government organizations all having higher means than those in the statutory (child welfare) field. The survey results also identified that there is a need to improve supervision overall, particularly in statutory social work (O'Donoghue 2017). Since 2015, statutory child welfare in Aotearoa New Zealand has been involved in a major change which resulted in a new organization, Oranga Tamariki, the Ministry for Children (Dale et al. 2017). As a consequence of this change, Oranga Tamariki revised and updated its supervision policy and has provided training for its supervisors (Oranga Tamariki, 2017). To date, there is no evidence available to indicate whether supervision in this organization has improved or not. The other major area of improvement for social work supervision concerned cultural competence and building capacity and capability towards more culturally supportive supervision practice and environments (O'Donoghue 2019b, 2019c).

On 27 February 2019, the Social Workers Registration Legislation Act (2019) became law. This Act amended the SWRA (2003) and made social worker registration mandatory through protection of the title of social worker, with a scope of practice to be established over the following two years. The implications for the future of social work supervision in Aotearoa New Zealand are that it is important that supervision is included in the general scope of practice, as a practice the social workers are required to participate in, as well as a practice that social workers provide as supervisors. The scope of the practice approach also raises the future possibility of the supervisor scope of practice, which could lead to a form of supervisor accreditation. A supervisor scope of practice would also assist the SWRB and the profession in strengthening the professional development pathway for becoming a supervisor and would ensure that all supervisors had a baseline level of supervisory education and training. This strengthening is needed, with O'Donoghue (2019c) identifying gaps between the SWRB expectations, policy, Code of Conduct, and supervisors' backgrounds and supervision practices. O'Donoghue (2019c) also identified the need to further develop the supervisory workforce in regard to increasing the proportion of Māori and Pasifika supervisors.

Conclusion

This chapter has reviewed the evolution of social work supervision in Aotearoa New Zealand since 1994 and has identified three specific periods. Across the periods, three key themes have been present in the evolution of supervision. The first is the ongoing challenge of decolonizing supervision so that it is culturally responsive in relation to Māori and Pacific practitioners and culturally safe in relation social workers' practice with clients who are Māori or Pacific people. The second theme is the influence of social service organizations, the professional association (ANZASW), and regulatory authority (SWRB) in shaping the policy and practice of supervision by way of providing a foundational infrastructure that supports supervision. The third theme is the influence of an active social work supervision community of practice, which has developed a research and practice base for supervision locally, as well as made an important international contribution to the field of social work supervision.

In conclusion, this chapter, through reviewing the evolution of social work supervision over a 25 year period has also shown the importance of looking to the past as one lives the present and envisages the future. Over 25 years, the evolution of supervision has paralleled that of the social work profession, thus highlighting the important relationship between professional social work practice and supervision. Furthermore, social work supervision, like social work practice, has resisted the managerial takeover through developing a professional culture and community of practice. In terms of the future, social work supervision in Aotearoa New Zealand needs to improve its quality so that it enhances practitioners' well-being, development, and facilitates best practice with clients and better outcomes for both clients and the wider community.

References

Adamson, C., 2012. Supervision is not politically innocent. *Australian Social Work*, 65 (2), 185–196. doi:10.1080/0312407X.2011.618544

Adamson, C., 2018. Trauma-informed supervision in the disaster context. *The Clinical Supervisor*, 1–20. doi:10.1080/07325223.2018.1426511

Aotearoa New Zealand Association of Social Workers, 2004. *Code of Ethics (revised)*. Dunedin: ANZASW.

Barrett, P., and Munford R., 1994. Focusing on management and supervision of social workers. *Social Work Review*, 6 (5/6), 1.

Beddoe, L., 1997a. A new era for supervision. *Social Work Now*, 7, 10–15.

Beddoe, L., 1997. Best practice in social work supervision- education and accreditation issues. *Social Work Review*, 9 (4), 37–43.

Beddoe, L., 2010. Surveillance or reflection: professional supervision in 'the risk society'. *British Journal of Social Work*, 40 (4), 1279–1296.

Beddoe, L., 2011. External supervision in social work: power, space, risk, and the search for safety. *Australian Social Work*, 65 (2), 197–213. doi:10.1080/0312407x.2011.591187

Beddoe, L., 2015a. Social work supervision for changing contexts. *In:* Liz Beddoe and Jane Maidment, eds. *Supervision in social work: contemporary issues*. London: Routledge, 82–95.

Beddoe, L., 2015b. Supervision and developing the profession: one supervision or many? *China Journal of Social Work*, 8 (2), 150–163. doi:10.1080/17525098.2015.1039173

Beddoe, L., 2016. Supervision in social work in Aotearoa New Zealand: challenges in changing contexts. *The Clinical Supervisor*, 35 (2), 156–174. doi:10.1080/07325223.2016.1217497

Beddoe, L., and Davys, A., 1994. The status of supervision-reflections from a training perspective. *Social Work Review*, 6 (5/6), 16–21.

Beddoe, L., and Davys, A., eds., 2011. *2010 professional supervision: common threats, different patterns: conference proceedings*. Auckland. Available from https://cdn.auckland.ac.nz/assets/education/about/schools/chsswk/docs/2010-Supervision-Conference-Proceedings.pdf [Accessed 4 May 2019].

Beddoe, L., and Davys, A., 2016. *Challenges in professional supervision: current themes and models for practice*. London: Jessica Kingsley.

Beddoe, L., Davys, A.M., and Adamson, C., 2014. 'Never trust anybody who says "I don't need supervision": practitioners' beliefs about social worker resilience. *Practice*, 26 (2), 113–130. doi:10.1080/09503153.2014.896888

Beddoe, L., and Egan, R., 2009. Social work supervision. *In:* Marie Connolly and Louise Harms, eds. *Social work: contexts and practice*, 2nd ed. Melbourne, VIC: Oxford University Press, 410–422.

Beddoe, L., and Egan, R., 2013. Social work supervision. *In:* Marie Connolly and Louise Harms, eds. *Social work: contexts and practice*, 3rd ed. Melbourne, VIC: Oxford University Press, 371–382.

Beddoe, L., and Howard, F., 2012. Interprofessional supervision in social work and psychology: mandates and (inter) professional relationships. *The Clinical Supervisor*, 31 (2), 178–202. doi:10.1080/07325223.2013.730471

Beddoe, L., Karvinen-Niinikoski, S., Ruch, G., and Tsui, M.S., 2016. Towards an international consensus on a research agenda for social work supervision: report on the first survey of a Delphi study. *British Journal of Social Work*, 46 (6), 1568–1586. doi:10.1093/bjsw/bcv110

Beddoe, L., and Worrall, J., eds., 2001. *Supervision conference 7–8 July 2000 from rhetoric to reality:* keynote address and selected papers. Auckland: Auckland College of Education.

Beddoe, L., Worrall, J., and Howard, F., eds., 2005. *Supervision conference 2004 "Weaving together the strands of supervision": conference proceedings of the supervision conference*. Auckland: University of Auckland.

Belich, J., 2001. *Making peoples: a history of the New Zealanders from Polynesian settlement to the end of the nineteenth century*. Auckland: Penguin.

Bell, H., and Thorpe, A., 2004. External supervision: what is it for a social worker in schools? *Te Komako VII, Social Work Review*, 16 (2), 12–14.

Bennie, G., 1995. *Social work supervision: an annotated bibliography*. Palmerston North: Department of Social Policy and Social Work, Massey University.

Bradley, J., 1996. Iwi and cultural services policy: the state's best kept secret. *Te Komako II Social Work Review*, 8 (4), 3–5.

Bradley, J., Jacob, E., and Bradley, R., 1999. Reflections on culturally safe supervision, or why Bill Gates makes more money than we do. *Social Work Review*, 11 (4), 3–6.

Cheyne, C., O'Brien, M., and Belgrave, M., 2004. *Social policy in Aotearoa New Zealand: a critical introduction*. 3rd ed. Auckland: Oxford University Press.

Cockburn, G., 1994. Supervision in social work: a brief statement of the essentials. *Social Work Review*, 6 (5/6), 37.

Cooper, L., and Anglem, J., 2003. *Clinical supervision in mental health*. Adelaide, SA: ACCSR.

Cooper, L., 2006. Clinical supervision: private arrangement or managed process? *Social Work Review*, 18 (3), 21–30.

Dale, M., Mooney, H., and O'Donoghue, K., 2017. *Defining social work in Aotearoa: forty years of pioneering research and teaching at Massey University*. Auckland: Massey University Press.

Davys, A., 2002. *Perceptions through a prism: three accounts of 'good' social work supervision*. Palmerston North: Massey University, MSW Thesis. Available https://mro.massey.ac.nz/handle/10179/5754 [Accessed 4 May 2019].

Davys, A., 2005. At the heart of the matter: culture as a function of supervision. *Social Work Review*, 17 (1), 3–12.

Davys, A., and Beddoe, L., 2010. *Best practice in professional supervision: a guide for the helping professions*. London: Jessica Kingsley Publishers.

Davys, A., and Beddoe, L., 2015. Interprofessional supervision: opportunities and challenges. *In:* Lisa Bostock, ed. *Interprofessional staff supervision in adult health and social care services*. Brighton: Pavilion, 37–41.

Davys, A.M., Howard, F., Rankine, M., and Thompson, A., 2019. Supervision under the microscope: critical conversations in a learning community. *Practice*, 31, 1–16. doi:10.1080/09503153.2018.1558196

Davys, A.M., O'Connell, M., May, J., and Burns, B., 2017. Evaluation of professional supervision in Aotearoa/New Zealand: an interprofessional study. *International Journal of Mental Health Nursing*, 26 (3), 249–258. doi:10.1111/inm.12254

Eketone, A., 2012. The purposes of cultural supervision. *Aotearoa New Zealand Social Work*, 24 (3/4), 20–30 .doi:10.11157/anzswj-vol24iss3-4id104

Elkington, J., 2016. A Kaupapa Māori supervision context – cultural and professional. *Aotearoa New Zealand Social Work*, 26 (1), 65–73. doi: 10.11157/anzswj-vol26iss1id56

Eruera, M., 2007. He korero korari. *In:* Dianne Wepa, ed. *Clinical supervision Aotearoa/New Zealand: a health perspective.* Auckland: Pearson Education, 141–151.

Eruera, M., 2012. He kōrari, he kete, he kōrero. *Aotearoa New Zealand Social Work Review*, 24 (3/4), 12–19. doi: 10.11157/anzswj-vol24iss3-4id103

Eruera, M.M., 2005. *He kōrero kōrari: supervision for Māori: weaving the past, into the present for the future.* MPhil Thesis. Albany, NY: Massey University. Available http://mro.massey.ac.nz/handle/10179/6471 [Accessed 4 May 2019].

Field, J., 2008. Rethinking supervision and shaping future practice. *Social Work Now*, 40, 11–18.

Garland, M., and Ellis, G., 2006. Synergistic supervision. *Social Work Review*, 18 (3), 31–42.

Gillanders, M., 2005. The hidden power of the written word: record-keeping in supervision. *Social Work Review*, 17 (3), 2–9.

Hair, H.J., and O'Donoghue, K., 2009. Culturally relevant, socially just social work supervision: becoming visible through a social constructionist lens. *Journal of Ethnic and Cultural Diversity in Social Work*, 18, (1/2), 70–88. doi:10.1080/15313200902874979

Hirst, V., 2001. *Professional supervision for managers: an effective organisational development intervention: an inquiry based on the perceptions and experiences of managers of social work.* MCom Thesis. Auckland: University of Auckland.

Hutchings, J., 2008. Does social worker registration have implications for social work supervision? *Aotearoa New Zealand Social Work Review*, 20 (1), 2–9.

Kane, R., 2001. Supervision in New Zealand social work. *In:* Marie Connolly, ed. *New Zealand social work contexts and practice.* Auckland: Oxford University Press, 291–303.

King, L., 2016. KIAORA – the emerging construction of a bicultural professional supervision model. *Aotearoa New Zealand Social Work*, 26 (1), 20–28. doi:10.11157/anzswj-vol26iss1id51

Lipsham, M., 2012. Āta as an innovative method and practice tool in supervision. *Aotearoa New Zealand Social Work*, 24 (3–4), 31–40. doi:10.11157/anzswj-vol24iss3-4id122

Ministry of Pacific Island Affairs, 1999. *Pacific directions report: a report to government on a possible pathway for achieving Pacific people's aspirations.* Wellington: Ministry of Pacific Island Affairs.

Morrell, M., 2001. External supervision- confidential or accountable? An exploration of the relationship between agency, supervisor and supervisee. *Social Work Review*, 13 (1), 36–41.

Morrell, M., 2003. Forethought and afterthought - two of the keys to professional development and good practice in supervision. *Social Work Review*, 15 (1/2), 29–32.

Morrell, M., 2005. Supervision – an effective partnership: the experience of running workshops for supervisees in 2004–2005. *Social Work Review*, 17 (4), 39–45.

Morrell, M., 2008. Supervision contracts revisited – towards a negotiated agreement. *Aotearoa New Zealand Social Work Review*, 20 (1), 22–31.

Morrison, T., 1993. *Supervision in social care.* Harlow: Longman.

Murray, V., 2012. Hoki ki tōu maunga kia purea ai e koe ki ngā hau o Tāwhirimātea – a supervision model. *Aotearoa New Zealand Social Work*, 24 (3–4), 3–11. doi:10.11157/anzswj-vol24iss3-4id102

New Zealand Association of Social Workers., 1998. *Policy statement on supervision.* Dunedin: NZASW.

New Zealand Social Work Training Council., 1985. *Supervision resource package.* Wellington: New Zealand Social Work Training Council.

O'Donoghue, K., 1998. *Supervising social workers.* Palmerston North: School of Policy Studies and Social Work, Massey University.

O'Donoghue, K., 1999. *Professional supervision practice under new public management: a study of the perspectives of probation officers and service managers in the community probation service.* Palmerston North: Massey University, MPhil Thesis. Retrieved from http://mro.massey.ac.nz/handle/10179/751.

O'Donoghue, K., 2001. The future of social work supervision within New Zealand. *Social Work Review*, 13 (1), 29–35.

O'Donoghue, K., 2002. Global-vision, local-vision, personal-vision and social work supervision. *Social Work Review*, 14 (4), 20–25.

O'Donoghue, K., 2003. *Restorying social work supervision.* Palmerston North: Dunmore Press.

O'Donoghue, K., 2004. Social workers and cross-disciplinary supervision. *Social Work Review*, 16 (3), 2–7.

O'Donoghue, K., 2006. An introduction to social work supervision practice: defining and describing the terrain towards an ideal practice. *Today's Children are Tomorrow's Parents*, 17–18, 93–103.

O'Donoghue, K., 2007. Clinical supervision within the social work profession in Aotearoa New Zealand. *In:* Dianne Wepa, ed. *Clinical supervision in Aotearoa New Zealand: a health perspective.* Auckland: Pearson, 12–25.

O'Donoghue, K., 2008. Towards improving social work supervision in Aotearoa New Zealand. *Aotearoa New Zealand Social Work Review*, 20 (1), 10–21.

O'Donoghue, K., 2010. *Towards the construction of social work supervision in Aotearoa New Zealand: a study of the perspectives of social work practitioners and supervisors.* PhD Thesis. Palmerston North: Massey University. Retrieved from http://mro.massey.ac.nz/handle/10179/1535

O'Donoghue, K., 2012. Windows on the supervisee experience: an exploration of supervisees' supervision histories. *Australian Social Work*, 65 (2), 214–231. doi:10.1080/0312407x.2012.667816

O'Donoghue, K.B., 2014. Towards an interactional map of the supervision session: an exploration of supervisees and supervisors experiences. *Practice*, 26 (1), 53–70. doi:10.1080/09503153.2013.869581

O'Donoghue, K., 2015a. Towards an evidence-informed approach to clinical social work supervision. *In:* Margaret Pack and Justin Cargill, eds. *Evidence discovery and assessment in social work practice.* Hershey, PA: IGI Global, 289–301. doi:10.4018/978-1-4666-6563-7.ch014

O'Donoghue, K.B., 2015b. Issues and challenges facing social work supervision in the twenty-first century. *China Journal of Social Work*. 8 (2), 136–149.

O'Donoghue, K., 2017. *Draft report on the supervision of registered social workers.* Unpublished Report. Palmerston North: Massey University.

O'Donoghue, K., 2019a. Supervision and Evidence-Informed Practice. *In:* Robyn Munford and Kieran O'Donoghue, eds. *New theories for social work practice: ethical practice for working with individuals, families and communities.* London: Jessica Kingsley Publishers, 271–288.

O'Donoghue, K., 2019b. The supervision of registered social workers in Aotearoa New Zealand: a national survey. *Aotearoa New Zealand Social Work Review*, 31 (3), 58–77. doi:10.11157/anzswj-vol31iss3id648

O'Donoghue K., 2019c. Registered social workers who are supervisors: a national survey. *Aotearoa New Zealand Social Work Review*, 31 (3), 97–115. doi:10.11157/anzswj-vol31iss3id651

O'Donoghue, K., Munford, R., and Trlin, A., 2005. Mapping the territory: supervision within the association. *Social Work Review*, 17 (4), 46–64.

O'Donoghue, K., Munford, R., and Trlin, A., 2006. What's best about social work supervision according to association members. *Social Work Review*, 18 (3), 79–91.

O'Donoghue, K., and O'Donoghue, R., 2019. The application of ethics within social work supervision: a selected literature and research review. *Ethics and Social Welfare*, 1–21. doi:10.1080/17496535.2019.1590438

O'Donoghue, K.B., and Tsui, M.S., 2011. In search of an informed supervisory practice: an exploratory study. *Practice*, 24 (1), 3–20. doi:10.1080/09503153.2011.632678

O'Donoghue, K., and Tsui, M.S., 2012. Towards a professional supervision culture: the development of social work supervision in Aotearoa New Zealand. *International Social Work*, 55 (1), 5–28. doi:10.1177/0020872810396109

O'Donoghue, K., and Tsui, M.S., 2015. Social work supervision research (1970–2010): the way we were and the way ahead. *British Journal of Social Work*, 45 (2), 616–633. doi:10.1093/bjsw/bct115

O'Donoghue, K., Wong, Y.J., and Tsui, M.S., 2018. Constructing an evidence-informed social work supervision model. *European Journal of Social Work*, 21 (3), 348–358. doi:10.1080/13691457.2017.1341387

Oranga Tamariki, 2017. *Professional supervision: policy and standards.* Available from https://practice.orangatamariki.govt.nz/practice-standards/use-professional-supervision/professional-supervision-practice-standards/ [Accessed 12 June 2019].

Pack, M., 2009. Clinical supervision: an interdisciplinary review of literature with implications for reflective practice in social work. *Reflective Practice*, 10 (5), 657–668. doi:10.1080/14623940903290729

Pack, M., 2011. Two sides to every story: a phenomenological exploration of the meanings of clinical supervision from supervisee and supervisor perspectives. *Journal of Social Work Practice*, 26 (2), 163–179. doi:10.1080/02650533.2011.611302

Pack, M., 2015. 'Unsticking the stuckness': a qualitative study of the clinical supervisory needs of early-career health social workers. *British Journal of Social Work*, 45 (6), 1821–1836. doi:10.1093/bjsw/bcu069

Pega, F., Valentine, N., and Matheson, D., 2010. *Social determinants of health discussion paper 3 (Case Studies)*. Geneva: World Health Organization. Monitoring Social Well-being to Support Policies on the Social Determinants of Health: the case of New Zealand's Social Reports/TePūrongoOrangaTangata. Available from https://www.who.int/sdhconference/resources/who_monitoring_sdh_newzealand.pdf [Accessed 12 June 2019].

Rankine, M., 2013. Getting a different perspective: piloting the 'group consult' Model for supervision in a community-based setting. *Practice*, 25 (2), 105–120. doi:10.1080/09503153.2013.786696

Rankine, M., 2018. How critical are we? Revitalising critical reflection in supervision. *Advances in Social Work and Welfare Education*, 20 (2), 31–46.

Rankine, M., 2019. The 'thinking aloud' process: a way forward in social work supervision. *Reflective Practice*, 20 (1), 97–110. doi:10.1080/14623943.2018.1564651

Rankine, M., Beddoe, L., O'Brien, M., and Fouché, C., 2018. What's your agenda? Reflective supervision in community-based child welfare services. *European Journal of Social Work*, 21 (3), 428–440. doi:10.108 0/13691457.2017.1326376

Rankine, M., and Thompson, A., 2015. 'Swimming to shore': co-constructing supervision with a thinking-aloud process. *Reflective Practice*, 16 (4), 508–521. doi:10.1080/14623943.2015.1064377

Ruwhiu, L., 2001. Bicultural issues in Aotearoa New Zealand. *In:* Marie Connolly, ed. *New Zealand social work: contexts and fields of practice*. Auckland: Oxford University Press, 54–71.

Ruwhiu, L., 2009. Indigenous issues in Aotearoa New Zealand. *In:* Marie Connolly and Louise Harms, ed. *Social work: contexts and practice*. Melbourne, VIC: Oxford University Press, 107–120.

Ruwhiu, P., Ruwhiu, L.A, and Ruwhiu, L.II., 2008. To Tatou Kupenga. Mana Tangata supervision a journey of emancipation through heart mahi for healers. *Aotearoa New Zealand Social Work* 20 (4), 13–34. Available from https://anzasw.nz/wp-content/uploads/Issue-4-Te-Komako-Articles-Ruwhiu -Ruwhiu-and-Ruwhiu1.pdf [Accessed 12 June 2019].

Sewell, K.M., 2018. Social work supervision of staff: a primer and scoping review (2013–2017). *Clinical Social Work Journal*, 46 (4), 252–265. doi:10.1007/s10615-018-0679-0

Shepherd, S., 2003. *An exploratory study of social work supervision and the health sector*. Christchurch: University of Canterbury, MA Thesis.

Simmons, H., 2006. *Out of the closet: experiences and expressions of spirituality in supervision*. MPhil Thesis. Palmerston North: Massey University. Available from http://mro.massey.ac.nz/handle/10179/6726 [Accessed 12 June 2019].

Simmons, H., Moroney, H., Mace, J., and Shepherd, K., 2007. Supervision across disciplines: fact or fantasy? In Dianne Wepa, ed. *Clinical supervision in Aotearoa/New Zealand: a health perspective*. Auckland: Prentice Hall New Zealand, 72–86.

Social Workers Registration Act, 2003. Available from http://www.legislation.govt.nz/act/public/2003 /0017/latest/DLM189915.html [Accessed 12 June 2019].

Social Workers Registration Board, 2005. *Code of conduct*. Wellington: SWRB.

Social Workers Registration Board, 2006. *Code of conduct guidelines*. Wellington: SWRB.

Social Workers Registration Legislation Act, 2019. Retrieved from http://www.legislation.govt.nz/act/ public/2019/0003/22.0/DLM7396614.html [Accessed 12 June 2019].

Su'a-Hawkins, A., and Mafile'o, T., 2004. What is cultural supervision? *Social Work Now*, 29, 10–16.

Taverner, P., 1989. Supervision. *Social Work Review*, 1 (3&4), 20–21.

Taylor, C., 1976. *Facsimilies of the declaration of independence and the Treaty of Waitangi*. Wellington: Government Printer.

Thomas, C., 2005. *What's in a name strengths based supervision reality or rhetoric an analysis*. Palmerston North: Massey University MSW Thesis. Available from http://hdl.handle.net/10179/5656 [Accessed 12 June 2019].

Thomas, C., and Davis, S., 2005. Bicultural strengths-based supervision. *In:* Mary Nash, Robyn Munford, and Kieran O'Donoghue, eds. *Social work theories in action*. London: Jessica Kingsley Publishers, 189–204.

Tsui, M.S., O'Donoghue, K., Boddy, J., and Pak, C.M., 2017. From supervision to organisational learning: a typology to integrate supervision, mentorship, consultation and coaching. *The British Journal of Social Work*, 47 (8), 2406–2420. doi:10.1093/bjsw/bcx006

Tsui, M.S., O'Donoghue, K., and Ng, A.K.T., 2014. Culturally competent and diversity-sensitive clinical supervision. *In:* Clifton Edward Watkins Jr and Derek Milne, eds. *The Wiley International handbook of clinical supervision.* Chichester: John Wiley & Sons, Ltd., 238–254.

Webber-Dreadon, E., 1999. He taonga mo o matou tipuna (A gift handed down by our ancestors): an indigenous approach to social work supervision. *Social Work Review,* 11 (4), 7–11.

Walsh-Tapiata, W., and Webster, J., 2004. Do you have a supervision plan? *Social Work Review,* 16 (2), 15–19.

Weld, N., 2012. *A practical guide to transformative supervision for the helping professions: amplifying insight.* London: Jessica Kingsley Publishers.

Young, G., 1994. Critical components in the supervision of child protection social workers in a statutory agency. *Social Work Review,* 6 (5/6), 23–29.

10

SOCIAL WORK SUPERVISION IN AUSTRALIA

Ronnie Egan and Jane Wexler

In this chapter, we begin by locating the Australian socio-political context for the international audience, followed by an overview of social work supervision practice in Australia, including discussion of key discourses informing supervision practice and research over time. We position social work supervision within the context of the Australian Association of Social Work (AASW), supervision education and training, and identify different approaches to supervision in Australia, highlighting the need for developing a social work specific approach to Aboriginal and Torres Strait Islander supervision in the context of cultural needs and knowledge. The chapter concludes with an examination of the links between supervision and leadership, and identifies themes and challenges facing Australian social work supervision practice today and into the future.

Locating the Australian context for an international audience

Australia is a continental island, the largest country in Oceania, located between the Indian and South Pacific Oceans and south of its South East Asian neighbors with a population of 25.3 million (Australian Bureau of Statistics 2019). First Nation's include Aboriginal and Torres Strait Islander people who represent one of the world's oldest living cultures, estimated between 50,000 and 120,000 years. There were between 300,000 to 950,000 Aboriginal people living in Australia when the British arrived, and approximately 260 distinct language groups and 500 dialects (Working with Indigenous Australians, Australia's First Peoples 2019). The first contact between Indigenous and British people occurred in 1788 when Australia was taken over as a colony by British settlers, under the premise of "terra nullius," a legal term which claimed Australia was deemed to be unoccupied and belonged to no one (Tatz 1999). Massacres, frontier wars, disease, starvation, and policies of kidnapping and re-educating Indigenous children followed, resulting in a massive decline in the Indigenous population by the early 20th century. Despite more recent changes such as the overturning of terra nullius in 1991, the granting of land rights, pursuing reconciliation, and increased service delivery and policies, the colonization of Australia continues to have a devastating effect on Aboriginal and Torres Strait Islander peoples, their cultures, and identities. In areas such as health, housing, education, employment, child removal, deaths in custody, and income, basic human rights have not been realized (Briskman 2014, Westbury and Dillon 2019).

Increasingly, it is recognized that policymaking in Australia reflects colonial ideas, attitudes, and institutions that continue to work against Indigenous peoples and their rights (Dodson & Cronin 2011). Social work in Australia has a negative history in relation to the implementation of policies which reinforce colonial and patriarchal approaches to Australia's First Nation peoples. The most recent iteration of Australian Association of Social Workers Code of Ethics (2010) sought to redress this through the central location of Aboriginal and Torres Strait Islander people within its principles and practice responsibilities, Practice Standards and Information Sheets related to Culturally Responsive Practice (AASW 2014, 2015). This remains an ongoing project for the Australian social work profession.

Immigration has been a driving force of economic and social development for more than two centuries in Australia, which is now reflected in the country's ethnically and culturally diverse population. In 2018, there were 7.3 million migrants living in Australia, which represented 29% of the population that were born overseas. In 2018, every country from around the world was represented in Australia's population. People born in England (992,000) continue to be the largest group of overseas-born living in Australia, followed by China (651,000), India (592,000), and New Zealand born (568,000) (Australian Bureau of Statistics, 2019). In 2018, Australia ranked third among top refugee resettlement countries worldwide. However, its controversial hardline policies and treatment of asylum seekers arriving by boat in recent years have sullied its reputation as a country that supports people in need (Inglis 2018).

The development and current practice of Australian social work supervision

There are varied definitions of social work supervision, which emphasize its different aspects and reflect the changing political nature of social work practice over time. In Australia, conflicting stories about social work supervision represent different discourses and competing interests. On the one hand, despite massive changes experienced in social work practice as a result of neoliberalism, the practice of social work supervision remains largely uncontested (Jones 2004, Noble et al. 2016, Noble and Irwin 2009, O'Donoghue 2003, Peach and Horner 2007, Phillipson 2002). On the other, there is evidence that managerial discourses have focused on aligning supervision practices more closely with market or market-like modes of organization, with a greater emphasis on compliance and regulation (Beddoe 2010, Cooper and Anglem 2003). Both positions highlight how social work supervision sits within broader contexts that influence how it is thought about, practiced and experienced. Davys' (2007) definition of social work supervision effectively incorporates the two discourses:

> Supervision provides us with the chance to stand back from our work and reflect on what we do, the context of what we do and the impact that this has on ourselves. It provides the opportunity to evaluate our work in terms of positive and negative performance so that we can learn from experience.
>
> *(Davys 2007, p. 27)*

In 2014, the AASW adopted a similar definition of professional supervision in social work, which explicitly names supervision as "a forum for reflection and learning" (AASW 2014). We note however, that the service user is absent from these definitions, which reflects a lack of attention paid to the relationship between supervision and service user outcomes, and a lack of research about supervision and its effect on outcomes for service users.

In reviewing material from the Australian, New Zealand, British, and North American contexts, it is evident that the development of social work supervision practice in Australia closely parallels the history of social work supervision in other English speaking countries (Baglow 2009, Baine 2009, Bruce Austin 2000, Clare 1991, Grauel 2002, Tsui 1997). There are two Australian empirical studies of note, the Pilcher and Egan studies (Pilcher 1984, Egan 2012).

Pilcher's 1984 Victorian survey was the first empirical one on social work supervision and was undertaken during a period of increasing pressures on service delivery in a neo-liberal context. This study set the agenda for the establishment of the Australian Association of Social Workers Standing Committee on Social Work Supervision (Pilcher 1984, AASW 2000, Scott and Farrow 1993). During 1988, the Standing Committee originally published "Recommended Standards for Social Work Supervision" as Victorian Standards. These Standards were subsequently endorsed by the AASW Board of Directors as National Standards (Australian Association of Social Workers 2000). At the time, the Standards represented "a balance between agency resource constraints and ideal professional standards," which acknowledged the ambivalent place of social work supervision in the current managerial context (Scott and Farrow 1993, p. 33).

Egan's national study in 2007 (Egan 2012) was the first comprehensive empirical analysis of social work supervision practice in Australia. This research identified that social work supervision practice had a long way to go before it reflected either the rhetoric within the literature or met the AASW Supervision Standards (2000). This was highlighted when in 2011, a Victorian Government report (Department of Human Services, 2011) investigating the Department of Human Services Child Protection Program (Brouwer 2009) identified a drop in supervision compliance rates, noting that supervision was being sacrificed for day-to-day service delivery. This report led to significant shifts in supervision practice within the Child Protection program.

Limited Australian empirical studies make it difficult to gain a detailed picture of social work supervision practice during the 1990s (Spence et al. 2001). In the 20 studies that we looked at regarding Australian research into social work supervision from the 1990s to 2018, a common theme was the impact of the neoliberal environment on social work supervision, and the contradictions between managerial and professional discourses informing practice. It was acknowledged that the neoliberal environment had shifted the focus in supervision, whilst also lamenting the loss of its professional aspects (Egan 2012, Egan, Maidment, and Connolly 2016, 2017, and 2018, Hough 2003, Ife 1997, Jones 2004, King et al. 2017, McPherson, Frederico, and McNamara 2016, Nickson 2015, Noble and Irwin 2009, Phillipson 2002). The Australian research, in line with international studies, calls for an increase in knowledge and evidence concerning the construction and practice of social work supervision, and the growth of compliance procedures, which reflect a greater emphasis on managerial supervision (Beddoe 2010, Clare 2001, Jones 2004, Noble and Irwin 2009, Phillipson 2002).

A key difference between Australia and other countries relates to the overall statutory regulation of social work, and therefore social work supervision. Social work in Australia is a self-regulated profession. It is not legally registered in any of Australia's eight states or territories, despite a long, ongoing campaign by the AASW for inclusion in the National Registration and Accreditation Scheme (NRAS), which is the government authority that oversees the regulation of qualifications, standards, and practice for health practitioners in Australia. Recently, the state of South Australia introduced a private members bill to the South Australian Parliament for the registration of social work in South Australia (AASW 2019). However, at the time of writing there was no further progress on this. Of significant concern is that without regulation, Australian social workers do not have a statutory framework that mandates ongoing professional development in accordance with Practice Standards.

The parameters of Australian social work supervision and the profession

The AASW is the professional representative body for social workers in Australia, which sets the standards for social work practice and professional social work education, promotes the profession, and regulates the professional conduct of its members. It accredits undergraduate and post graduate degrees in Australian universities and international social work qualifications, which it assesses as comparable to an AASW accredited qualification in order for people to gain entry into the profession and to meet the minimum eligibility requirements for AASW membership (AASW 2014). In 2019, the Association had in excess of 11,500 AASW voluntary members (AASW 2019), which represents less than half the estimated numbers of social workers in the country.

In the absence of a government regulatory body, Association members are guided by regulatory documents and processes set by the AASW. These include a Code of Ethics (currently under review) and complaints process; education standards and university accreditation processes; practice and supervision standards; accreditation and credentialing processes; international qualification assessment processes; and continuing professional development (CPD) requirements. AASW members who meet ongoing CPD requirements are eligible for status as an "Accredited Social Worker" and an Accredited Mental Health Social Worker (AASW 2014). Accredited Mental Health Social Workers are registered providers with Medicare Australia, and have been assessed by the AASW on behalf of the Commonwealth Government, as having specialist mental health expertise. An Accredited Mental Health Social Worker (AMHSW) is eligible to provide services through some of the Commonwealth-funded programs. Accredited social workers can also provide services under the Access to Allied Psychological Services program (AHPA 2019).

In addition to accredited social worker and accredited mental health social worker credentials, the AASW has recently developed a new credentialing for members to gain recognition for other specialized practice areas. In part, this aims to assure the public, employers, and funding bodies that accredited social workers have acquired a distinguished level of expertise in their field of practice. One of the new credentials soon to be available is "Accredited Supervisor." At the time of writing, the AASW had not yet released information about the criteria for this credential.

The AASW considers social work supervision as integral to professional social work practice and maintaining best practice in Australia. Supervision is a core Practice Standard, which is described as essential for "enhancing the skills and competence of social work practitioners, ongoing professional learning, and supporting and resourcing practitioners to provide quality, ethical and accountable services" (AASW 2014). In addition to Practice Standards, the Association has a set of Supervision Standards for social workers who engage in supervision as both supervisees and supervisors of social workers or other professionals. Supervision Standards apply to all modes of delivery, including individual, group, peer, face-to-face, and other technology-enhanced supervision. The Australian Association of Social Workers Supervision Standards describe the purpose, functions, responsibilities, and values of professional supervision; what is considered good supervision practice in varied contexts across Australia; and acceptable supervision modes and processes under CPD guidelines (AASW 2014). There are ten Standards and a series of Indicators for each Standard. A summary of the key Standards is shown in Table 10.1.

All Association members are required to undertake and record supervision as part of CPD requirements, which vary depending on the level of accreditation. Supervisors must have a minimum of three years post qualifying experience relevant to the field of the supervisee. Supervision by a social worker is preferred, although another professional is acceptable when

Table 10.1 The Australian Association of Social Workers Supervision Standards, 2014

9.1.1 Supervisors uphold their professional ethical responsibilities when engaging in the supervisory relationship.

9.1.2 Supervisors establish a supervision contract/agreement and maintain a record of supervision maintained for the duration of the supervisory relationship.

9.1.3 Supervisors are appropriately trained and experienced to provide supervision and demonstrate a commitment to professional practice and currency of knowledge.

9.1.4 Supervisors manage the dynamics of a supervisory relationship appropriately

9.1.5 Supervisors facilitate a process designed to achieve the purpose and functions of supervision, as outlined in the Supervision Standards.

9.1.6 Supervisors manage any suspected or actual misconduct or unethical behavior of supervisees in line with ethical responsibilities outlined in the Code of Ethics (AASW, 2010).

9.2.1 Social workers maintain their professional ethical responsibilities when engaging in the supervisory relationship.

9.2.2 Social workers actively participate in the supervisory process

9.2.3 Social workers take an active role in establishing supervisory processes that meet their needs

9.3 Recommended frequency and duration of supervision

- Supervision may comprise one-on-one, group/peer supervision, and informal/in vivo supervision. Formal supervision should account for at least half of the minimum supervision time.
- New social work graduates with 2 years or less experience. Fortnightly. A minimum of half of the supervision comprises one-on-one formal supervision. 60 minutes
- Social workers entering a new field of practice, facing particular challenges, or re-entering workforce. Fortnightly. 60 minutes
- Social work practitioners with 2+ years' experience. Monthly. Some social workers that do not work in direct practice roles with clients may require less regular supervision. A minimum frequency of quarterly is recommended. 60 minutes

Source: AASW Supervision Standards 2014

this is the most suitable option. This flexibility is interesting to note in light of recent research that suggests a growth in inter-professional supervision and increased numbers of supervisors seeking supervision from a range of colleagues within and outside the profession and their organizations (Beddoe 2016, King et al. 2017). The AASW also hosts a Supervisor's Register on their website where supervisors offer supervision on a private fee-paying basis.

Given the lack of regulation of social work in Australia, the Australian Association of Social Workers Practice and Supervision Standards become the only guidelines which frame supervision practice in Australian. In light of this, there is a strong need for Australian research that examines how Association members and non-members use the Standards to inform their practice and decision-making.

Ethics in social work supervision

Like many countries, Australia is rightly concerned with the ethics of social work supervision. This is reflected in the AASW Supervision Standards (AASW 2014), which state that social work supervisors must meet their ethical responsibilities outlined in the 2010 Australian Code of Ethics (currently under review). The AASW Code of Ethics also states that supervisors adhere to a set of values, which underpin their practice, shown in Table 10.2. It publishes 17 sets of ethi-

Table 10.2 AASW Code of Ethics: Key Values, 2010

4.1 *Respect for persons* – This value relates to the nature of supervisory relationships and in the manner in which client issues and workplace relationships are addressed in supervision. In particular, efforts should be made to understand different viewpoints.

4.2 *Social justice* – As a core obligation of social work, social justice principles should guide content, choices, processes, and goals of supervision, with special regard for those who are vulnerable, disadvantaged, or oppressed.

4.3 *Professional integrity* – The principles of honesty, transparency, reliability, empathy, reflective self-awareness, discernment, competence, and commitment are expected to underlie professional supervision relationships and processes. Professional supervision is part of the social worker's ongoing responsibility for the quality of practice performance.

---

cal guidelines for social work practice related to specific practices and client groups, and offers a free Ethics and Practice Standards Consultation Service for Association members to assist with ethical dilemmas and practice issues.

The AASW Supervision Standards refer to "upholding professional ethical responsibilities when engaging in the supervisory relationship, managing the dynamics of a supervisory relationship appropriately, and managing any suspected or actual misconduct or unethical behavior of supervisees in line with the *Code of Ethics*"(AASW, 2010; 9.1.1 & 9.1.4). They articulate the need to maintain professional boundaries, to avoid inappropriate sexual, personal, social, business, and therapeutic relationships, to maintain confidentiality, and to be transparent about and manage any conflicts of interests.

Whilst providing social workers with a guide for ethical social work practice, the AASW Supervision Standards and Code of Ethics tell us little about how ethics are integrated into supervision practice in Australia, which varies widely across diverse regions, contexts, and disciplines. We are unaware of any reports published by the Australian Association of Social Workers Ethics and Practice Standards Consultation Service which indicate the types of ethical issues that AASW members bring to the Service, how often the Service is used, by whom it is used, for example supervisors and non-supervisors, and what type of ethical issue is identified. This is a cause for concern, particularly as only voluntary members of the AASW can be investigated for alleged breaches of the Code of Ethics, with loss of membership being the most severe penalty imposed. For non-registered members, whom the Association has no jurisdiction over, there is no legal penalty (Swain 2001).

In their review of social work supervision and ethics literature, O'Donoghue and O'Donoghue (2019) identify significant key gaps in our knowledge of ethics, which are applicable to the Australian context. These include knowledge of how supervision actually contributes to ethical practice, how supervisors assist supervisees to identify, explore, and manage ethical issues, how supervisors act ethically, and how organizations influence the application of ethics (O'Donoghue and O'Donoghue 2019). Anecdotal evidence, consistent with these findings, comes from the author's eight years' experience of training over a thousand Australian professional supervisors, which suggests that some supervisors pay minimal attention to how ethics are integrated into supervision, unless a significant ethical dilemma or issue related to risk arises. Some case examples are provided in Table 10.3.

Consistent with the literature (O'Donoghue and O'Donoghue 2019, Reynolds 2013) there is a need to move beyond thinking of ethics as dilemmas, or difficult risk related issues that

Table 10.3 Case example – Perceptions of ethics and supervision

During training, supervisors are asked what they think about ethics and how they incorporate ethics into supervision. Common responses include:

- *At the end of a meeting we can ask the question: did we cover the ethics?*
- *We don't really talk about ethics unless there is a complaint or a concern that someone is behaving unethically.*
- *We put ethics in the too hard basket unless there's an obvious breach.*
- *We never talk about what is ethical in group supervision. You can't criticize a colleague's practice in a group setting.*
- *There is no formal structure in our organization to deal with ethical issues.*
- *It's an area I feel is out of my depth.*
- *I had an ethical question but got no help with it. There's not enough guidance about this area.*
- *I would follow the organization's line if I had an ethical problem*

arise from time to time. Rather, ethics should be located at the heart of supervision practice as Reynolds (2013) suggests:

> We need to know a lot more than the I am interested in helping workers practice in accord with their ethics, because what matters most in our work with clients is that we enact our ethics, not how we talk about them. It is in the doing that ethics are revealed. Theory, the ideas that support our work, is revealed through an examination of practice, or what we do. Both theory and practice exist in relationships with our ethical stances.
>
> *(Reynolds 2013, p. 5)*

A key tenant of ethical supervision practice in Australia should be that ethics are held at the centre of supervision and that as supervisors, we promote client-centred supervision. This is a contentious issue and one that requires further research to better understand its implications.

Education and training in Australian social work supervision

The AASW does not require social workers to have formal qualifications in supervision. However, it is expected that social work supervisors are social work qualified and engage in continuing professional development for the provision of professional supervision (AASW Supervision Standards 2014, 9.1.3a & 9.1.3d). In general, most supervisors learn how to supervise on the job, once they are promoted to a senior position such as senior practitioner, team leader, case manager, or coordinator. Prior to this, they may have no or limited supervision training, which is similar to the experience of our neighbors in Aotearoa New Zealand (Beddoe 2016).

There is no current national data and independent research on supervision training in Australia which would tell us how many social workers have been trained in supervision, the nature and scope of the training, or its effectiveness. This represents a significant gap in our knowledge and understanding of supervisor education in this country. We do know that in the last few years, the Australian Association of Social Workers has actively developed its entire continuing professional development program, which includes supervision training. In order to receive CPD endorsement for an activity, external providers must submit an application form that addresses a range of criteria related to Quality Content, and Educational and Ethical

Standards. All endorsed activities are required to be evaluated internally (for example by course participants).

The AASW contracts external providers to provide content and facilitate online and face-to-face supervision short courses, which are offered as accredited continuing professional development Association Branch Events (AASW Annual Report 2017–2018). These providers may be the same or different to external private providers, of which there are a handful, who currently offer Australian Association of Social Workers CPD endorsed and non-endorsed supervision training courses in most States. The Association lists these courses on their website. Supervision training also occurs onsite, within small and large organizations, such as the Department of Human Services, which, independently from the AASW, contract educators to provide onsite supervision training, sometimes to large numbers of their staff. For example, the authors of this chapter deliver online and in-person onsite supervision training to social work, health and human service professionals from government, not-for profit, community based, and private organizations (Wexler 2019).

There continues to be strong interest from social workers in supervision training, but limited training opportunities to meet the demand across Australia, particularly in rural regions (Harris, Slattery, Fowler 2019, Beddoe 2015). Australian universities provide a range of online and face-to-face supervision training options for supervisors of social work students on placement, including the delivery of student supervision as a single subject (for example Charles Sturt University). However, the same priority has not been given to training social work practitioners in supervision, which remains a significant gap in supervision education.

Approaches to social work supervision

Similar to a number of other countries, supervision in Australia is typically delivered and configured in a variety of ways (Beddoe, Karvinen-Niinikoski, Ruch, and Tsui 2016; O'Donoghue, Wong Yuh Ju, and Tsui 2018). These include internally by an employee within an organization to an individual or group; by an external person contracted to provide individual or group supervision; by a peer within or outside an organization; through line management; and provided by someone from within or outside an organization, who is from another profession. Supervision occurs as individual, group, and peer in-person meetings, meetings by phone, and meetings using telecommunications applications that provide video chat, voice calls and messaging between computers, tablets, and mobile devices via the internet. Isolation, disadvantage, and lack of services are significant in rural Australia, and rurally based social workers often lack opportunities for professional supervision. One study suggests that technology-enhanced group and peer supervision is used successfully in rurally disadvantaged settings, although unreliable internet connections, which are a common problem in rural Australia, influence the type of technology used and reliability of supervision (Nickson 2015).

There is, however, no national data that tells us which configurations of supervision currently dominate Australian supervision and why. An interesting South Australian study found that professional human service workers from three human service organizations were no longer relying on a single supervisor from their field. Seeing themselves as self-managing agents, they were ensuring their supervision needs were met by workers in their own fields and own organizations, in other fields and organizations and, interestingly, by friends and family members, including Indigenous communities (King et al. 2017). Other writers have also identified a possible growth in inter-professional supervision as a response to the current climate (Beddoe 2016, Davys 2017).

This brings us to the appropriateness of supervision for First Nations social workers in Australia, which we believe is an area that requires urgent attention. Unlike our Aotearoa New Zealand neighbors, Australia does not have a strong tradition of Indigenous supervision, culturally responsive supervision practice, or research in the area (Bennett et al. 2018, Uniting Care 2011). Indeed, despite us knowing the importance of embedding supervision in "…an Aboriginal/indigenous space that is supportive and culturally safe for Aboriginal and non-Aboriginal social workers" (Bennett et al. 2018, p. 76), there appears to have been little done to develop an approach to supervising Aboriginal staff, which would meet their professional development needs in the context of cultural needs and knowledge (Uniting Care 2011). One exception is the work of Dr Tracy Westerman, an Njamal woman from the Pilbara in Western Australia and finalist in the 2018 Australian of the Year. Westerman's extensive contribution to work in Aboriginal mental health, cultural competency, and suicide prevention includes Cultural Competency for Supervisors of Aboriginal people training, using Westerman's Cultural Competency Profiles and Assessment Tools (Westerman 2019). One of the chapter authors, Jane Wexler, is currently working in collaboration with Gunditjmara Aboriginal Cooperative Ltd in rural Victoria, to develop a culturally appropriate supervision model that combines the Aboriginal Healing Model with strengths based frameworks.

Despite the AASW strongly advocating for culturally responsive and inclusive practice in Australia, there are obvious gaps in research and knowledge to inform supervision practice with Aboriginal and Torres Strait Islander communities. There is no AASW Supervision Standard dedicated to cultural supervision for example, and only one Indicator out of more than forty that are applicable to AASW Supervision Standards which specifically refers to cultural supervision but in the broadest of terms, as shown:

"Supervisors recognize cultural influences on practice and the diversity of knowledge and meanings that supervisees bring, collaborating with supervisees to access culturally relevant supervisory arrangements that serve to strengthen practice from cultural perspectives" (AASW Practice Standards 2013, 9.1.5g)

Our understanding of commonly used supervision approaches in Australia comes from Egan's (2012) Australian study, other international literature, and from our own observations as supervisors and supervisor educators. This suggests that individual, internal managerial, and individual internal reflective supervision, which make use of strengths based approaches, are likely to be commonly used approaches in Australia, followed by external professional supervision and internal group supervision. This parallels international research findings (O'Donoghue and Tsui 2015). Supervision training that is listed on the AASW CPD Events Calendar appears consistent with this (AASW 2019). Other approaches (that may still draw on strengths frameworks) include solutions focused, narrative, mindfulness, and use of specific models such as "Seven Eyed." Art therapy and other approaches are also used.

Another approach to supervision which links leadership to supervision (Wonnacott 2012) is explored and currently presented by one of the chapter's authors, within supervision training.

Supervision as leadership

Becoming a supervisor is often a social worker's first step in taking on a leadership role in an organization. Indeed, a common job title for a supervisor is team "leader." Yet social work supervision and leadership are often conceptualized as two distinctly separate practices.

There are a multitude of approaches to leadership and no universal agreement about what it is. The social work literature identifies some approaches such as transformational models of leadership as being consistent with social work (Hughes and Wearing 2013, Tafvelin et al. 2014).

A useful way of conceptualizing leadership comes from Kouzes and Posner (2016) who define leadership as "….having a vision, which inspires and motivates others… and makes a difference in people's levels of engagement, commitment and performance" (Kouzes and Posner 2016, p. 1). They argue that leadership is a mindset and a set of skills and capabilities that can be learnt, rather than an innate talent. Like supervision skills, leadership skills and attitudes can be acquired and modeled to others.

The AASW defines social work leadership in terms of having a vision, empowering others to produce useful change, and something that can be practiced by anyone in an organization (AASW 2016). However, supervision is described as one of a number of functions of leadership and management rather than part of leadership itself. The AASW Supervision Standards rely heavily on the Functions Model as a supervision framework (Kadushin and Harkness 2014). This model is useful for delineating between roles and tasks, and for distinguishing between management and other functions, but it and similar models (Hawkins and Shohet 2012, Beddoe 2016) don't conceptualize supervision as a form of leadership in its own right.

Wonnacott's Integrated Model (2012) moves beyond functions to focus on both management and professional aspects of work, locating the supervisor as a leader of practice. Here, a supervisor is concerned with how good practice can thrive, ensuring that emerging practice issues, knowledge, skill gaps, and context are taken into account within supervision (Wonnacott 2012). However, leadership is limited to social work practice, which prevents us from viewing supervision as leadership for all practice within organizations.

How supervisors think about and use authority and power is also relevant, particularly as evidence suggests that supervisors struggle with power and authority within the supervisory role (Hawkins and Shohet 2012, Egan 2012, Beddoe and Davys 2016). Adopting a broader, leadership mindset in organizations that is not limited to the sphere of social work enables supervisors to shift their thinking away from themselves, to others. The question becomes not what is my authority and power in this situation as a social work supervisor, but what is my authority and power here as a leader of all practice in the organization? This approach sits well with the principles, ethics, and practice of social work supervision and the notion, as Sinclair (2007) argues, that leadership should liberate and support people to make thoughtful choices about what to do and how to influence. She says:

> Leadership can liberate us from oppressive conditions imposed by structures, others and ourselves….it can invite us to imagine, initiate and contest, requiring leaders to be acutely conscious of power relations, to commit to using power and authority ethically, not in competitive self-interest or to control others.
>
> *(Sinclair 2007; xix)*

It is beyond the scope of this chapter to develop this discourse in any depth. However, future research that examines how supervisors in Australia carry out their "higher purpose role" as leaders in the organizational context would provide greater understanding of the important links between supervision and leadership, and its potential to provide vision for Australian supervision into the future.

Conclusion

On the surface, supervision in Australia parallels broad developments in other English-speaking countries, particularly our neighbors in Aotearoa New Zealand. Supervision is considered a high priority for social work practice in Australia and is strongly endorsed by the Australian Association of Social Workers. Similarly, there is recognition of the need for an increase in evidence and knowledge regarding social work supervision practice and in particular, the need for research about the use and effectiveness of different approaches. However, there are some key differences, which shape Australian social work supervision practice and highlight the competing discourses informing social work supervision in this country.

Research and knowledge of culturally appropriate supervision practice models in the context of Aboriginal and Torres Strait Islander cultural needs and knowledge is not reflected in the AASW Supervision Standards (2014), which has Indicators about cultural safety in supervision but no specific cultural supervision Standard. The significance of the cultural dimension of supervision in a country such as Australia can't be ignored, and this gap in knowledge and practice requires urgent attention.

The lack of statutory regulation of the social work profession in Australia has an impact on the mandating of ongoing professional development in supervision, and for non-members of the Association, the Standards serve as a guideline only. Like others, we are concerned that clients are not located at the centre of ethical supervision practice. However, in the unregulated Australian context, this has a different and potentially significant impact. Given that the AASW only has jurisdiction over members, there needs to be far greater understanding of how all social work supervisors use the Standards to guide practice and decision making.

Finally, whilst there are competing discourses and interests in the Australian social work supervision context, the links being made in the training space between supervision and leadership are hopeful. Such a reorientation within a managerial context suggests moving beyond seeing supervision as leadership of practice, to leadership for both the profession and human service organizations more broadly.

Acknowledgements

The authors would like to acknowledge our colleagues in the field for their valuable insights into this complex area of practice. In particular, we would like to thank Frederika Davies and Sussan Visser from Relationships Australia Western Australia, and Robyn Van Ingen from Barwon Health and Genus.

References

Allied Health Professions Australia, 2019. Available from: https://ahpa.com.au/our-members/australian-association-of-social-workers [Accessed 4 December 2019].

Australian Association of Social Workers, (AASW), 2000. *National practice standards of the Australian association of social workers: supervision.* Victoria: Standing Committee on Professional Supervision.

Australian Association of Social Workers (AASW), 2010. *Code of ethics.* Canberra, ACT: Australian Association of Social Workers.

Australian Association of Social Workers (AASW), 2013. *Practice standards.* Canberra, ACT: Australian Association of Social Workers.

Australian Association of Social Workers (AASW), 2014. *AASW submission to the review of the national registration and accreditation scheme for health professions.* Available from: https://www.aasw.asn.au/document/item/6692 [Accessed 4 December 2019].

Australian Association of Social Workers (AASW), 2014. *Practice standards for mental health social workers.* Canberra, ACT: Australian Association of Social Workers.

Australian Association of Social Workers (AASW), 2014. *Supervision standards.* Canberra, ACT: Australian Association of Social Workers. Available from: https://www.aasw.asn.au/document/item/6027 [Accessed 4 December 2019].

Australian Association of Social Workers (AASW), 2015. *Preparing for culturally responsive and inclusive social work practice in Australia: working with aboriginal and torres strait islander peoples - January 2015.* Updated April 2016. Available from: https://www.aasw.asn.au/document/item/7006 [Accessed 4 December 2019].

Australian Association of Social Workers (AASW), 2016. *Scope of social work practice: leadership and management.* Canberra, ACT: Australian Association of Social Workers.

Australian Association of Social Workers (AASW), 2018. *Annual report 2017–2018.* Canberra, ACT: Australian Association of Social Workers.

Australian Association of Social Workers (AASW), 2019. *National registration and accreditation scheme.* Available from: https://www.aasw.asn.au/social-policy-advocacy/national-registration-and-accreditation-scheme/national-registration-and-accreditation-scheme [Accessed 4 December 2019].

Australian Bureau of Statistics, 2019. *3101.0 - Australian demographic statistics.* Available from: https://www.abs.gov.au/ausstats%5Cabs@.nsf/mediareleasesbyCatalogue/CA1999BAEAA1A86ACA25765100098A47?Opendocument [Accessed 4 December 2019].

Baglow, L., 2009. Social work supervision and its role in enabling a community visitor program that promotes and protects the rights of children. *Australian Social Work*, 62 (3), 353–368.

Baine, D., 2009. If we don't get back to where we were before: working in the restructured non-profit social services. *British Journal of Social Work*, 40 (3), 928–945.

Beddoe, L., 2010. Surveillance or reflection: professional supervision in 'the risk society'. *British Journal of Social Work*, 40 (4), 1279–1296.

Beddoe, L., 2015. Supervision and developing the profession: one supervision or many? *China Journal of Social Work*, 8(2), 150–163. doi:10.1080/17525098.2015.1039173

Beddoe, L., 2016. Supervision in social work in Aotearoa New Zealand: challenges in changing contexts. *The Clinical Supervisor*, 35(2), 156–174.

Beddoe, L., and Davys, A., 2016. *Challenges in professional supervision: current themes and models for practice.* London: Jessica Kingsley.

Bennett, B., Redfern, J., and Zubrzycki, J., 2018. Cultural responsiveness in action: co-constructing social work curriculum resources with aboriginal communities. *The British Journal of Social Work*, 48 (3), 808–825. doi:10.1093/bjsw/bcx053

Briskman, L., 2014. *Social work with Indigenous communities: a human rights approach.* 2nd ed. Annandale, NSW: Federation Press.

Brouwer, G., 2009. *Investigation into the Department of Human Services Child Protection Program.* Available from: https://www.bing.com/search?q=Brouwer%2C+G.%2C+%282009%29.+Investigation+into+the+Department+of+Human+Services+Child+Protection+Program+&form=EDNTHT&mkt=en-au&httpsmsn=1&msnews=1&plvar=0&refig=0a3e8fcbb83d4dcdd05debae48d28066&PC=ASTS&sp=-1&pq=&sc=8-0&qs=n&sk=&cvid=0a3e8fcbb83d4dcdd05debae48d28066 [Accessed 19 February 2020].

Bruce, E.J., and Austin, M.J., 2000. Social work supervision: assessing the past and mapping the future. *Clinical Supervisor*, 19 (2), 85–107.

Clare, M., 1991. Supervision and consultation in social work: a manageable responsibility? *Australian Social Work*, 44 (1), 3–10.

Clare, M., 2001. Operationalising professional supervision in this age of accountabilities. *Australian Social Work*, 54 (2), 69–79.

Cooper, L., and Anglem, J., 2003. *Clinical supervision in mental health.* Adelaide, SA: Australian Centre for Community Services Research, Flinders University.

Davys, A., 2007. Active participation in supervision: a supervisee's guide. *In*: D. Wepa, ed. *Clinical supervision in Aotearoa/New Zealand: a health perspective.* Auckland: Pearson Eduction New Zealand, 26–42.

Davys, A., 2017. Interprofessional supervision: a matter of difference. *Aotearoa New Zealand Social Work*, 29 (3), 79–84.

Department of Human Services, Victoria, 2011. *Child protection workforce: the case for change.* Melbourne, VIC: State of Victoria.

Dodson, P., and Cronin, D., 2011. Australian dialogue decolonising the country. *In*: Maddison, S and Brigg, M., eds. *Unsettling the settler state, creativity and resistance in indigenous settler-state governance.* Annandale, NSW: Federation Press, 189–201.

Egan, R., 2012. Australian social work supervision practice in 2007. *Australian Social Work*, 65 (1), 171–184.

Egan, R., Maidment, J., and Connolly, M., 2016. Who is watching whom? Surveillance in Australian social work supervision. *British Journal of Social Work*, 46 (6), 1617–1635.

Egan, R., Maidment, J., and Connolly, M., 2017. Trust, power and safety in the social work supervisory relationship: results from Australian Research. *Journal of Social Work Practice*, 31, 307–321.

Egan, R., Maidment, J., and Connolly, M., 2018. Supporting quality supervision: insights into organisational practice. *International Social Work*, 61(3), 353–367.

Grauel, T., 2002. Professional oversight: the neglected histories of supervision. *In*: M. McMahon and W. Patton, eds. *Supervision in the helping professions: a practical approach*. Frenchs Forest, NSW: Pearson Education, 3–15.

Harris, T., Slattery, M., and Fowler, J., 2019. *How is social work supervision being practiced in Australia?* ePoster, Workforce Development. Available from: http://www.nahc.com.au/2716 [Accessed 6 December 2019].

Hawkins, P., and Shohet, R., 2012. *Supervision in the helping professions*. 4th ed. Maidenhead: Open University Press.

Hough, G., 2003. Enacting critical practice in public welfare contexts. *In*: J. Allan, B. Pease, and L. Briskman, eds. *Critical social work*. St. Leonards, NSW: Allen and Unwin, 214–227.

Hughes, M., and Wearing, M., 2013. *Organisations and management in social work*. 2nd ed. Los Angeles, CA: SAGE.

Ife, J., 1997. *Rethinking social work: towards critical practice*. Melbourne, VIC: Longman.

Inglis, C., 2018. *Australia: a welcoming destination for some*. Migration Policy Institute. Available from: https://www.migrationpolicy.org/article/australia-welcoming-destination-some [Accessed 6 December 2019].

Jones, M., 2004. Supervision, learning and transformative practices. *In*: N. Gould and M. Baldwin, eds. *Social work, critical reflection and the learning organisation*. Aldershot: Ashgate Publishing, 11–22.

Kadushin, A., and Harkness, D., 2014. *Supervision in social work*. 5th ed. New York: Columbia University Press.

King, S., Carson, E., and Papatraianou, L., 2017. Self-managed supervision. *Australian Social Work*, 70 (1), 4–16.

Kouzes, J.M., and Posner, B.Z., 2016. *Learning leadership: the five fundamentals of becoming an exemplary leader*. San Francisco: John Wiley & Sons.

McPherson, L., Frederico, M., and McNamara, P., 2016. Safety as a fifth dimension in supervision: stories from the frontline. *Australian Social Work*, 69 (1), 67–79. doi: 10.1080/0312407X.2015.1024265

Nickson, A., 2015. *Exploring peer group supervision in virtual teams in rural and remote Australia*. PhD Thesis. James Cook University. Available from: https://researchonline.jcu.edu.au/46579/12/46579-nickson-2015-thesis.pdf [Accessed 6 December 2019].

Noble, C., Gray, M, and Johnston, L., 2016. *Critical supervision for the human services: a social model to promote learning and values-based practice*. London: Jessica Kingsley.

Noble, C., and Irwin, J., 2009. Social work supervision: an exploration of the current challenges in a rapidly changing social, economic and political environment. *Journal of Social Work*, 9 (3), 345–358.

O'Donoghue, K., 2003. *Restorying social work supervision*. Palmerston North: Dunmore Press.

O'Donoghue, K., and O'Donoghue, R., 2019. The application of ethics within social work supervision: a selected literature review. *Ethics and Social Welfare*. doi: 10.1080/17496535.2019.1590438

O'Donoghue, K., and Tsui, M.-S., 2015. Social work supervision research (1970–2010): the way we were and the way ahead. *British Journal of Social Work*, 45 (2), 616–633. doi:10.1093/bjsw/ bct115

O'Donoghue, K., Wong, Y.J., and Tsui, M.-S., 2018. Constructing an evidence-informed social work supervision model. *European Journal of Social Work* 21(3), 348–358. doi:10.1080/13691457.2017.1341387

Peach, J., and Horner, N., 2007. Using supervision: support or surveillance. *In*: M. Lymbery and K. Postle, eds. *A companion to learning*. London: SAGE, 228–239.

Phillipson, J., 2002. Supervision and being supervised. *In:* R. Adams, L. Dominelli, and M. Payne, eds. *Critical practice in social work*. Basingstoke: Palgrave, 244–250.

Pilcher, A., 1984. The state of social work supervision in Victoria according to the practitioners. *Australian Social Work*, 37 (3), 33–43.

Reynolds, V., 2013. Centering ethics in group supervision. *International Journal of Narrative Therapy and Community Work*, 4, 1–13.

Royal Commission into Aboriginal Deaths in Custody, 2017. *Working with Indigenous Australians, Australia's first peoples*. Available from: http://www.workingwithindigenousaustralians.info/content/History_2_60,000_years.html [Accessed 6 December 2019].

Scott, D., and Farrow, J., 1993. Standards of social work supervision in child welfare and hospital social work. *Australian Social Work*, 46 (2), 33–41.

Sinclair, A., 2007. *Leadership for the disillusioned. Moving beyond myths and heros to leading that liberates*. Sydney, NSW: Allen and Unwin.

Spence, S., Wilson, J., Kavanagh, D., Strong, J., and Worrall, L., 2001. Clinical supervision in four mental health professions: a review of the evidence. *Behaviour Change*, 18 (3), 135–155.

Tafvelin, S., Hyvö̈nen, U., and Westerberg, K., 2014. Transformational leadership in the social work context: the importance of leader continuity and co-worker support. *British Journal of Social Work*, 44, 886–904.

Tatz, C., 1999. *Genocide in Australia*. Canberra, ACT: Australian Institute of Aboriginal and Torres Strait Islander Studies.

Tsui, M-S., 1997. The roots of social work supervision: an historical review. *Clinical Supervisor*, 15 (2), 191–198.

Uniting Care. Children, Young People and Families, 2011. *Models of supervision for aboriginal staff. A review of the literature*. Dr. Natalie Scerra. Research Paper Research and Program Development Social Justice Unit.

Westbury, N.D., and Dillon, M.C., 2019. Overcoming Indigenous exclusion: very hard, plenty humbug. *The Centre for Aboriginal Economic Policy Research*. *CAEPR Policy Insights Paper 1/2019*, Canberra, ACT: ANU.

Westerman, T., 2019. Available from: https://indigenouspsychservices.com.au [Accessed 6 December 2019].

Wexler, J., 2019. *Executive coaching, leadership development, training, supervision*. Available from: https://janewexler.com [Accessed 6 December 2019].

Wonnacott, J., 2012. *Mastering social work supervision*. London: Jessica Kingsley.

PART II

Supervision settings

11

SUPERVISION OF STUDENTS IN FIELD EDUCATION

Marion Bogo

Introduction

Recognizing the importance of field education to prepare the next generation of social workers, scholars, and researchers has identified theoretical concepts and practices that inform learning and teaching in practice settings. The aim of this chapter is to present this information in order to support field instructors as they engage with students. The chapter draws on educational concepts to identify dynamics and practices for student supervision. Findings from studies on students' perceptions of approaches that support their learning provide further support for key principles. Structural issues facilitating or impeding the provision of quality field education are also presented.

The purpose of field education

Internationally, social work graduates and instructors are united in describing field education as a critical component for preparing for one's professional practice. Accrediting bodies in many countries have developed policies and standards for implementing the field program, recognizing its central role in socializing and preparing students for the profession. For example, in the United States, the Council on Social Work Education, in its Educational Policy and Accreditation Standards (EPAS) in 2008, and reaffirmed in 2015, declared field education as the signature pedagogy of social work (CSWE 2018. Lee Shulman, an education scholar, coined the term "signature pedagogy" to capture the essential ways in which professions use specific educational approaches to teach students the fundamental elements of their profession (Shulman 2005). Importantly Shulman pointed out that unlike education in traditional disciplines, education for human service professions socializes students "to think, to perform, and to act ethically" (p. 52) in order to serve clients. The Council on Social Work Education recognized the crucial impact of field education in this regard as follows:

> The intent of field education is to integrate the theoretical and conceptual contribution of the classroom with the practical world of the practice setting. It is a basic precept of social work education that the two interrelated components of curriculum—classroom and field—are of equal importance within the curriculum, and each

contributes to the development of the requisite competencies of professional practice. Field education is systematically designed, supervised, coordinated, and evaluated based on criteria by which students demonstrate the Social Work Competencies.

(CSWE 2015, p. 12)

Shulman's perspective is consistent with a view of holistic competence in that it integrates critical thinking and the use of judgment in applying knowledge to practice (Bogo 2018). In addition, that professionals must act in the service of others, using ethical principles, is underscored.

Experiences in field education achieve many goals. Through participating in a service organization and providing social work interventions to clients, students are exposed to, what is referred to as, the "real world." Social work values, theoretical frameworks, and empirical findings taught in university courses come alive when students observe the way in which these dimensions are evident in practice. In addition, they can observe and critique the gap between theory and practice: when abstractions do not fully explain the phenomena encountered nor when following principles and processes they still do not achieve the anticipated goals. Students see the artistry of social work in action as they witness the ways in which experienced professionals draw upon their practice wisdom.

In course work, students are exposed to the knowledge base of social work as they learn about practice, specifically concepts that contribute to understanding and intervening. They may also have opportunities to see how this knowledge base is enacted in practice. This can occur through watching video-recordings of experienced practitioners while instructors clearly point out how theory informs what is actually done when meeting with a client. Increasingly, active learning through participating in role-play and simulation brings students' learning closer to how to do practice (Bogo et al. 2014). When de-briefing stimulates critical thinking, the links between how we think and what we do as social workers are reinforced. These are all worthy educational activities. But it is only in interacting with clients and the challenges presented that students have an authentic experience and one that requires learning the competencies and skills needed for practice (Lager and Robbins 2004).

Finally, it has long been a tradition of the profession that students develop, what has been called, professional use of self. The early pioneers of social work education in the United States, leaders such as Reynolds (Reynolds 1942) and Towle (Towle 1954), discussed the importance of personality development of the student. This notion evolved to a consideration of how the personal attributes of students – such as for example, one's values, attitudes, implicit biases, characteristics – find expression in professional activities (Farber and Reitmeier 2019; Larrison and Korr 2013). Through in-depth reflection on the way they think and feel when engaged in practice situations students are expected to develop self-awareness. The aim is to be cognizant of factors that interfere with productively using personal attributes, such as warmth, empathy, and genuineness in the service of assisting clients. Also of great importance is the ability to engage in self-regulation to contain and modify convictions that lead to unproductive emotional arousal. When students are involved in intense interactions with clients these experiences can stir up strong reactions. This is in contrast to classroom discussions that are one-step removed from the palpable feelings elicited when faced with complex and challenging client situations. Hence, developing professional use of self is likely best achieved through field education.

In summary, field education is highly valued, as it plays the central role in socializing students to the profession. This occurs through interactions with social workers in organizations serving clients. Field learning provides opportunities for students to link and apply knowledge to practice, including theoretical concepts and practices derived from empirical studies. Critical thinking and the exercise of judgment are developed when general principles are examined in relation to the contingencies presented by individual client situations. Competencies and the specific skills needed for building relationships with clients, conducting assessments, and providing interventions are learned through engaging in active learning. Moreover, consistent with a continuing focus on the humanistic tradition in social work, students are assisted in developing professional use of self. When instructional activities are present that address all of these dimensions then we can confidently state that field education is the signature pedagogy of social work (Bogo 2015; Wayne et al. 2010).

For those social workers who volunteer to serve as field educators and for faculty members carrying out roles in the field, a shared vision of the purpose of field learning provides an important framework to guide our efforts. Field education administrators can, understandably, become preoccupied with producing administrative guidelines; they also need to pay attention to developing the pedagogical foundation. The purposes of field education discussed thus far are presented as they can serve as an important touchstone as we endeavor to offer the best learning experience for students and prepare them to become competent, effective, and committed social workers.

Effective educational practices

Over many decades social work education researchers have produced a substantial body of knowledge about what students perceive as helpful approaches in field education. While contributing important data, the lack of studies examining outcomes of students' learning is limited. Fortune and her colleagues are an exception, conducting studies linking preferences and outcomes (see for example Fortune and Abramson 1993; Fortune et al. 1985; Fortune and Kaye 2002; Lee and Fortune 2013a, b). There is a need for more such studies to develop an evidence-base for social work field education. In the absence of substantial literature in this regard currently, field educators must rely on a range of studies, mainly using qualitative methods that can provide guidance for a quality experience. This chapter presents practices derived from this body of literature, discussed in relation to the purposes of field education identified above. The focus on best practices was chosen as a recent survey of articles published in the online journal *Field Educator* found it to be the most salient topic of interest to those involved in field education (Gushwa and Harriman 2019).

Opportunities to observe experienced social workers

Social learning theory proposes that new behaviors can be acquired by observing and imitating others, modeling one's own actions based on others (Bandura 1977, 1986). This process is not a simple transfer, rather it involves cognitive processes. These processes include directing attention to what is important, remembering the behavior, being able to perform the behavior, and having the motivation to perform the behavior.

These theoretical concepts come to life when the field instructor guides students' observation of the instructor's interactions with team members and clients through discussion before, during, or after the observation. Moreover, the field setting provides an excellent environment for students to observe the practice not only of their own field instructor but also of other social workers (Barretti 2007). Through seeing social workers in action as they perform their roles with clients, teams, and other professionals, students can see the "real world" of practice. Learning is potentiated when practitioners discuss their actions with the student – pointing out what is important to observe. Providing a rationale for their stance and specific interventions helps students understand the way implicit constructs can guide practice; it provides a window into the way in which practitioners use knowledge, critical thinking, and judgment to decide how to proceed. Open and critical discussion can also highlight when theory and research guide practice, when values and a humanistic stance predominate, when practice wisdom is used, and when practice comes closer to art – that is, the underpinnings are not easily articulated. Shadowing a number of social workers demonstrates how personal style influences the performance of a professional service. Such experiences approach the goal of socializing students to the way social workers think, feel, and act in the complex client situations and service environments they encounter.

Students have multiple opportunities to practice

Social learning theory (Bandura 1977, 1986), experiential learning theory (Kolb 1984), and neuroscience research contribute to understanding how learning to practice comes about (Schenck and Cruickshank 2015). Learners need to engage in a cognitive process whereby they construct new knowledge and find meaning in it for themselves; knowledge needs to make sense to the learner, they need to make it their own. One optimal way for this to occur is through the active use of that knowledge in relevant situations. Experiential learning theory proposes that concepts are learned and re-learned through experience (Kolb and Kolb 2005). Learners engage in a cycle moving from concrete experience, to reflective observation, abstract conceptualization, and active experimentation. For example, learning about the various ways in which a helping relationship can be constructed will be stimulated by the student interacting with a range of clients. Through reflecting on the dynamic interaction occurring in each dyad, the student can recognize the impact of various needs and styles on building relationships. This concept can then be acted upon through experimenting with offering different approaches based on the nature of the client. Such learning can only occur if the student has multiple opportunities to apply this new knowledge to a range of clients, tailoring their own professional stance to the contingencies presented by different individuals. Studies repeatedly find that students value diverse assignments where they can engage in active learning making personal and professional meaning out of concepts, as they apply them (Katz et al. 2014; Lee and Fortune 2013a).

Students are observed and receive feedback

Through a long-standing program of research on the development of expertise, Anders Ericsson (Ericsson et al. 1993; Ericsson 2004) established the importance of focusing in a deliberate manner on specific areas of practice that needed improvement. Knowing what to focus on depends upon receiving specific feedback from knowledgeable coaches. Field instructors can provide such information only if they actually see students' practice in real time or through review of video-recordings. In many schools of social work the reliance on process recordings of sessions has taken on a "sacred status." Given the extensive research in health science professions on the human tendency to distort when recalling interactions with clients (see for example Baxter and Norman 2011; Davis et al. 2006; Eva and Regehr 2005), it is unfortunate if we continue to rely on written records, or verbal reports, as the basis of field instruction sessions. In our research on students' written reflections immediately after completing an interview with a simulated client we noted many instances where these reflections did not accurately capture what direct observation by a rater and video recordings actually showed transpiring (Bogo et al. 2014). Written recollections can be interesting and useful as a way of journaling impressions, reflections, and self-presentation, and especially, about students' perceived responses in practice. They do not however provide an accurate account on which to base feedback about practice.

Unfortunately numerous studies in a number of countries, over the years, have found a dearth of observation of students' field practice (see for example in Australia (Smith et al. 2015), in Canada, (Rogers and McDonald 1995), in England (Domakin 2018), and in New Zealand (Maidment 2000)). Review and discussion of actual performance appears as foundational for achieving a number of the goals for field education as reviewed above. Without access to practice data, instructors are providing supervision "in the dark."

Similar to Ericsson (2004), social learning theory (Bandura 1977, 1986) posits that for learning to take place attention needs to be directed to learning what is important. Neuroscience research further supports this principle noting that when individuals are in complex situations they are bombarded with multiple stimuli (Schenck and Cruickshank 2015). Furthermore, cognitive load theory suggests that when students have not yet developed professional knowledge and concepts to enable them to use existing knowledge to integrate new experiences, students can become overwhelmed (Sweller 1994). Assignments in the field present such challenges. Students confront situations that usually are multi-dimensional and, despite eliciting strong emotional reactions, require students' engagement and commitment to connect with clients and offer assistance. Drawing on concepts regarding learning, one can see the need for field instructors to draw students' attention to particular client phenomena to help students distinguish key elements to address.

Feedback from the field instructor is another crucial element of quality field education (Davys and Beddoe 2015; Kanno and Koeske 2010; Miehls et al. 2013; Saltzburg et al. 2010). Again, field instructors must observe students' practice so that they can provide instruction based on actual events and interactions. The concept of deliberate practice is useful in this regard. As noted above, based on extensive research on the achievement of expertise, Ericsson (2004) recommends numerous cycles where the student learns what they need to improve, focuses attention on specific competencies and skills, practices in a deliberate or intentional manner to learn those skills, and reviews each instance of such practice to determine whether progress has occurred. Additional support for this approach comes from implementation science, where a study found when supervision included modeling, role-play, and feedback there was higher overall use of the evidence-based model than when supervision only involved discussion (Bearman et al. 2013). Further, when modeling was used in supervision the intervention approach was more likely to be used in the next session.

In a recent study on simulation-based learning, our research team found students reported that feedback enhanced all aspects of holistic competence – that is, increased their use of knowledge, improved their practice skills, developed their professional judgment, and increased self-reflection. The study highlighted the central role of feedback in learning to practice, and illuminated teaching practices that can also be used in field education (Kourgiantakis et al. 2019). These practices include "articulating clear competencies, identifying focused practice opportunities upon which to scaffold learning, observing practice, guiding student reflections, and providing specific, immediate, constructive feedback related to these competencies" (Kourgiantakis et al. p. 131). When used in the field, not only can the instructor discuss the needed practice behaviors, they can use role-play to demonstrate the preferred behaviors. When these practices are accompanied with reflective discussion, connections can be made to concepts and values that provide the underpinnings of the recommended behavior.

One caveat to the need for observation and feedback in the field relates to the competing demands on agency-based instructors who carry a range of responsibilities and their own caseload. It is therefore unrealistic to expect that all student assignments can receive the intense level of attention suggested. Instructors should however aim to include this powerful pedagogy in a selected sample of student experiences over the span of students' placements.

In summary, there is theoretical and empirical support for field instructors to observe student practice and to provide feedback and coaching. For their part, students will engage in active learning, consciously focusing their attention, finding opportunities to practice, and to review and evaluate that practice. These activities are specific examples of active learning that facilitate students' competence development. When instructors also use reflective discussion, the integration of theory and practice occurs, leading to a knowledge-directed practitioner.

Reflective discussion

The crucible of field education is the supervision session. Ideally, instructor and student mutually discuss a wide range of topics. Since field instructors hold accountability for effective service provision, understandably an important agenda item in the supervision session should address progress in meeting the clients' needs. For the session to maintain an *educational focus* however, integration of knowledge should be included. This involves field instructors articulating concepts and, when applicable, empirical findings informing their practice. Students are also encouraged to make linkages between ideas they are learning in academic courses and practice phenomena. The Integration of Theory and Practice Loop provides a process model that is ongoing and loops back on itself as the activities of thinking, feeling, and acting are drawn together (Bogo 2010, 2018). A cumulative looping process accesses practice data, examines students' personal reflections, and then makes links to the professional knowledge base. Factors at the societal, organizational, interpersonal, and personal level are considered. In an iterative fashion, the integration of these dimensions guide planning for the next professional response.

Positive field instructor and student relationship

Numerous studies over time have highlighted the enduring importance of a positive and supportive relationship as crucial to quality field education (Ellison 1994; Fortune and Abramson 1993; Fortune et al. 2001; Homonoff 2008; Lefevre 2005; Miehls et al. 2013). Drawing on concepts from adult learning theory (Knowles 1980) and psychodynamic theory (Brandell 2004), we recognize that learning to become an effective social worker involves aspects of self. In common with education in all helping professions that include a practicum or internship, students deliver a service while they are developing the competence to do so effectively. This circumstance provokes concerns and doubts about one's competence and affects self-esteem. Studies have found student anxiety about whether clients will have confidence in working with a student, feeling emotionally overwhelmed, and uncertainty about how to respond to diversity and difference in client populations (Gelman and Baum 2010). Bennett and colleagues (Bennett et al. 2008, 2012) suggested that the supervisory relationship in field education can be seen as similar to an attachment relationship. This occurs when a supportive supervisor is available as a secure base where students can express their anxieties, concerns, and challenges, receive help in understanding their thoughts and emotional reactions, and find support and encouragement to venture out again into difficult situations. The supervisor's stance and behavior in such a relationship provides a model that students can transfer into their practice with clients. Not only do core conditions for helping come alive, but also the student experiences the impact of such an approach on their own learning and development.

Positive learning environments

Thus far the focus on quality field education has been the central dyadic relationship between the student and field instructor. The larger context within which field learning occurs must be accounted for as well. The field setting can exert a positive influence when the organization and service team welcome students, view student teaching and learning as their responsibility, not only that of the field instructor, and enjoy sharing the unique aspects of their programs. Such settings, called learning organizations, value staff development and recognize that teaching is often the best way of learning. Conversely, in part due to resource limitations, some organizations do not embrace learning. Staff may experience overload, burnout, a culture of blame, and may develop coping mechanisms contrary to social work values. Students experience a gap between values and approaches course instructors explicitly teach and implicit messages in the practice setting. A recent study on field education in New Zealand reports students' examples of the difference between reflective supervision expected by the school and experiences with supervisors who have high workloads and emphasize case management "…I'm not actually a reflective person, I just do the job." (Hay et al. 2019, p. 28).

Thus far educational processes are presented at a general level without consideration of salient unique factors on the part of the student that influence the way these principles are enacted. Factors to consider are age, previous experience in helping roles, developmental stage, and placement level (Coohey et al. 2017) in relation to how much emotional support, challenge, and autonomy each student needs.

The macro context

Despite agreement on the importance of best practices for quality field instructors, social workers who agree to take on this role largely do it on a volunteer basis with no workload adjustment. They value contributing to the development of the next generation of practitioners as well as feel a commitment to give back to their profession. Field directors use a range of strategies to recruit, support, and show value for their contributions. Developing the next generation of the profession should not however be left to the initiatives of these committed faculty members and administrators. The entire sector must be concerned with workforce preparation and find ways to collaborate as partners since it is to their benefit to have competent and effective practitioners. This requires innovation and partnerships from those leading government health and mental health departments, social services, child and family programs, agency administrators, deans and directors of social work schools, national social work organizations, and regulators concerned with quality. As so clearly stated in the Field Education Survey conducted by CSWE, "[b]ecause students become practitioners, the functioning of social systems, the needs of clients and consumers, and the fabric or society are at stake" (CSWE 2018, p. 6).

Conclusion

The purpose of social work education is to prepare ethical, competent, effective social workers to meet the needs of vulnerable populations. Field education provides the crucible for achieving this goal, as it provides opportunities for students to link and apply knowledge to practice, develop critical thinking and good judgment, advance use of self in a professional role, and master communication skills and intervention techniques. This chapter reviewed conceptual and empirical literature that supports key educational practices that field instructors can use to prepare the next generation of social workers. Such practices include: opportunities to observe experienced social workers, giving students multiple opportunities to practice, ensuring students are observed and receive feedback, and facilitating reflective discussions. These approaches are effective when nested in positive learning environments, especially the field instructor and student relationship, as well as the organization. Structural issues however have resulted in fewer quality practicum available in social service and health community settings and organizations. It is imperative that leaders of the sector come together to support agencies, social workers, schools of social work, and students so that what we know works to promote effective practice learning can actually be offered.

References

Bandura, A., 1977. *Social learning theory*. Englewood Cliffs, NJ: Prentice Hall.

Bandura, A., 1986. *Social foundations of thought and action: a social cognitive theory*. Englewood Cliffs, NJ: Prentice-Hall.

Barretti, M.A., 2007. Teachers and field instructors as student role models: a neglected dimension in social work education. *Journal of Teaching in Social Work*, 27 (3/4), 215–239. doi: 10.1300/J067v27n03_14

Baxter, P., and Norman, G., 2011. Self-assessment or self deception? A lack of association between nursing students' self-assessment and performance. *Journal of Advanced Nursing*, 67 (11), 2406–2413. doi: 10.1111/j.1365-2648.2011.05658.x

Bearman, A.K., Weisz, J.R., Chorpita, B.F., Hoagwood, K., Ward, A., Ugueto, A.M., and Bernstein, A., 2013. More practice, less preach? The role of supervision processes and therapist characteristics in EBP implementation. *Administrative Policy in Mental Health*, 40 (6), 518–529. doi: 10.1007/s10488-013-0485-5

Bennett, S., Mohr, J., Deal, K.H., and Hwang, J., 2008. General and supervision-specific attachment styles: relations to student perceptions of social work supervisors. *Journal of Social Work Education*, 42 (2), 75–94. doi.org/10.5175/JSWE.2008.200700016

Bennett, S., Mohr, J., Deal, K.H., and Hwang, J., 2012. Supervisor attachment, supervisory working alliance, and affect in social work field instruction. *Research on Social Work Practice*, 23 (2), 199–209. doi: 10.1177/1049731512468492

Bogo, M., 2010. *Achieving competence in social work through field education*. Toronto, ON: University of Toronto Press.

Bogo, M., 2015. Field education for clinical social work practice: best practices and contemporary challenges. *Clinical Social Work Journal*, 43 (3), 317–324. doi: 10.1007/s10615-015-0526-5

Bogo, M., 2018. *Social work practice: integrating concepts, processes, and skills*. 2nd ed. New York, NY: Columbia University Press.

Bogo, M., Rawlings, M., Katz, E., and Logie, C., 2014. *Using simulation in assessment and teaching: OSCE adapted for social work*. Alexandria, VA: Council on Social Work Education.

Brandell, J., 2004. *Psychodynamic social work*. New York, NY: Columbia University Press.

Coohey, C., Dickinson, R., and French, L., 2017. Student self report of core field instructor behaviors that facilitate learning. *Field Educator*, 7 (1), 1–15.

Council on Social Work Education CSWE 2018. *Field education survey: final report*. Alexandria, VA: Council on Social Work Education.

Davis, D.A., Mazmanian, P.E., Fordis, M., v. Harrison, R., Thorpe, K.E., and Perrier, L., 2006. Accuracy of physician self-assessment compared with observed measures of competence: a systematic review. *Journal of the American Medical Association*, 296, 1094–1102. doi:10.1001/jama.296.9.1094

Davys, A.M., and Beddoe, L., 2015. 'Going Live': a negotiated collaborative model for live observation of practice. *Practice: Social Work in Action*, 27 (3), 177–196. doi: 10.1080/09503153.2015.1032234

Domakin, A., 2018. Grading individual observations of practice in child welfare contexts: a new assessment approach in social work education. *Clinical Social Work Journal*. doi: doi.org/10.1007/s10615-018-0691-4.

Ellison, M.L., 1994. Critical field instructor behaviors: student and field instructor views. *Arete*, 18 (2), 12–20.

Ericsson, K.A., 2004. Deliberate practice and the acquisition and maintenance of expert performance in medicine and related domains. *Academic Medicine*, 79 (October 10, Suppl.), 570–581.

Ericsson, K.A., Krampe, R.T., and Tesh-Romer, C., 1993. The role of deliberate practice in the acquisition of expert performance. *Psychological Review*, 100, 363–406.

Eva, K.W., and Regehr, G., 2005. Self-assessment in the health professions: a reformulation and research agenda. *Academic Medicine*, 80 (10 suppl), S46–S54.

Farber, N., and Reitmeier, M.C., 2019. (Re) Capturing the wisdom of our tradition: the importance of Reynolds and Towle in contemporary social work education. *Clinical Social Work Journal*, 47 (1), 5–16. doi: https://doi.org/10.1007/s10615-018-0666-5

Fortune, A.E., and Abramson, J.S., 1993. Predictors of satisfaction with field practicum among social work students. *The Clinical Supervisor*, 11 (1), 95–110.

Fortune, A.E., Feathers, C.E., Rook, S.R., Scrimenti, R.M., Smollen, P., Stemerman, P., and Tucker, E.L., 1985. Student satisfaction with field placement. *Journal of Social Work Education*, 21 (3), 92–104.

Fortune, A.E., and Kaye, L., 2002. Learning opportunities in field practica: identifying skills and activities associated with MSW students' self-evaluation of performance and satisfaction. *The Clinical Supervisor*, 21, 5–28.

Fortune, A.E., McCarthy, M., and Abramson, J.S., 2001. Student learning processes in field education: relationship of learning activities to quality of field instruction, satisfaction, and performance among MSW students. *Journal of Social Work Education*, 37 (1), 111–124.

Gelman, C.R., and Baum, N., 2010. Social work students' pre-placement anxiety: an international comparison. *Social Work Education*, 29 (4), 427–440.

Gushwa, M., and Harriman, K., 2019. Paddling against the tide: contemporary challenges in field education *Clinical Social Work Journal*, 47 (1), 17–22. doi: 10.1007/s10615-018-0668-3

Hay, K., Maidment, J., Ballantyne, N., Beddoe, L., and Walker, S., 2019. Feeling lucky: the serendipitous nature of field education. *Clinical Social Work Journal*, 47 (1), 23–31.

Homonoff, E., 2008. The heart of social work: best practitioners rise to challenges in field instruction. *The Clinical Supervisor*, 27 (2), 135–169.

Kanno, H., and Koeske, G.F., 2010. MSW students' satisfaction with their field placements; The role of preparedness and supervision quality. *Journal of Social Work Education*, 46 (1), 23–38.

Katz, E., Tufford, L., Bogo, M., and Regehr, C., 2014. Illuminating students' pre-practicum conceptual and emotional states: implications for field education. *Journal of Teaching in Social Work*, 34, 96–108. doi: 10.1080/08841233.2013.868391

Knowles, M.S., 1980. *The modern practice of adult education*. Chicago: Association Press/Follett.

Kolb, A.Y., and Kolb, D.A., 2005. Learning styles and learning spaces: enhancing experiential learning in higher education. *Academy of Management Learning and Education*, 4 (2), 193–212.

Kolb, D.A., 1984. *Experiential learning: experience as the source of learning and development*. Englewood Cliffs, NJ: Prentice Hall.

Kourgiantakis, T., Sewell, K.M., and Bogo, M., 2019. The importance of feedback in preparing social work students for field education. *Clinical Social Work Journal*, 47 (1), 124–133. doi: https://doi.org/10.1007/s10615-018-0671-8

Lager, P.B., and Robbins, V.C., 2004. Field education: exploring the future, expanding the vision. *Journal of Social Work Education*, 40 (1), 3–11.

Larrison, T.E., and Korr, W.S., 2013. Does social work have a signature pedagogy? *Journal of Social Work Education*, 49 (2), 194–206.

Lee, M., and Fortune, A.E., 2013a. Do we need more "doing" activities or "thinking" activities in the field practicum? *Journal of Social Work Education*, 49 (4), 646–660.

Lee, M., and Fortune, A.E., 2013b. Patterns of field learning activities and their relation to learning outcome. *Journal of Social Work Education*, 49 (3), 420–438.

Lefevre, M., 2005. Facilitating practice learning assessment: the influence of relationship. *Social Work Education*, 24 (5), 565–583.

Maidment, J., 2000. Methods used to teach social work students in the field: a research report from New Zealand. *Social Work Education*, 19 (2), 145–154.

Miehls, D., Everett, J., Segal, C., and du Bois, C., 2013. MSW students' views of supervision: factors contributing to satisfactory field experiences. *The Clinical Supervisor*, 32 (1), 128–146.

Reynolds, B.C., 1942. *Learning and teaching in the practice of social work*. New York, NY: Rinehart.

Rogers, G., and McDonald, P.L., 1995. Expedience over education: teaching methods used by field instructors. *The Clinical Supervisor*, 13 (2), 41–65.

Saltzburg, S., Greene, G.J., and Drew, H., 2010. Using live supervision in field education: preparing social work students for clinical practice. *Families in Society*, 91 (3), 293–299. doi: 10.1606/1044-3894.4008

Schenck, J., and Cruickshank, J., 2015. Evolving Kolb: experiential education in the age of neuroscience. *Journal of Experiential Education*, 38 (1), 73–95.

Shulman, L.S., 2005. Signature pedagogies in the profession. *Daedalus*, 134 (3), 52–59.

Smith, D.C., Cleak, H., and Vreugdenhil, A., 2015. "What are they really doing?" An exploration of student learning activities in field placement. *Australian Social Work*, 68 (4), 515–531.

Sweller, J., 1994. Cognitive load theory, learning difficulty, and instructional design. *Learning and Instruction*, 4, 293–312.

Towle, C., 1954. *The learner in education for the professions*. Chicago: University of Chicago Press.

Wayne, J., Bogo, M., and Raskin, M., 2010. Field education as the signature pedagogy of social work education: congruence and disparity. *Journal of Social Work Education*, 46 (3), 327–339.

12

SUPERVISION OF NEWLY QUALIFIED SOCIAL WORKERS

Lambert Engelbrecht and Mpumelelo Ncube

Introduction

Field instruction in social work is the training mode through which students put their learnt skills, knowledge, and values into practice (Schmidt and Rautenbach 2016). This may be viewed as the signature pedagogy that strengthens the social work profession's scientific footprint (Nadesan 2019). Ross and Ncube (2018) contend that supervision in the context of field instruction provides an opportunity for skills development and accelerates the progression of supervisees to becoming social work professionals. This however does not mean that the objectives of field instruction and those of the supervision of social work practitioners are the same, despite numerous similarities. Bates et al. (2010) and Hunt et al. (2016) assert that complexities of moving from a relatively well-protected position of being a student to that of an employed social worker are challenging and at times, may even be contradictory. While field instruction has transfer of knowledge, skills, and attitudes as its main goal, supervision of practitioners is chiefly focused on social service delivery (Ncube 2019). Furthermore, unlike in field instruction, supervision of practitioners involves organizational dynamics, hierarchies of administrative authority, and several accountabilities both within and outside the agency. Bogo and McKnight (2006) argue that for these reasons, it is important that a distinction in the terminology referencing to social work students and professional social workers as staff members should be made. Therefore, the delineation of the differences between social work students in field practice and professional social workers as staff members of an organization begs the question on the challenges that may emerge as a result of the transition from field instruction as a student to practice as a newly qualified social worker (NQSW). It has been observed that these challenges are not always sufficiently addressed in supervision across the globe, despite the fact that supervision of NQSWs can be regarded as the most intense in terms of content and scope spanning a social worker's whole career (cf. Beddoe et al. 2020; Bates et al. 2010; Carpenter et al. 2015; Engelberg and Limbach-Reich 2016; Grant et al. 2017; Hunt et al. 2017; Hussein et al. 2014; Jansen 2017; Manthorpe et al. 2015; Moorhead 2019; Patterson and Whincup 2018; Pretorius 2020; Tham and Lynch 2019). Indeed, supervision of NQSWs lays the foundation not just for the rest of their careers, but also of their capacity to make a difference in the lives of vulnerable people, arguably the initial reason they entered the social work profession.

This chapter propounds characteristics of NQSWs, the transition from student to professional social worker, typical challenges of NQSWs, and how these challenges are being addressed in supervision. In conclusion, a synthesis is presented of specific components in supervision, as drawn from a range of recent research findings, and valued by NQSWs.

Characteristics of NQSWs

NQSWs are generally defined as such by the period spent in the profession since qualification. However, to typify NQSWs based merely on the duration of their experience, may be controversial (Engelbrecht 2019a), as there seem to be some discrepancies that commentators ascribe to the length of time in practice before one could be regarded as a seasoned practitioner. Moorhead et al. (2016) indicate that the length of time required to define a NQSW begins after graduation and ends 12 months later. While Hussein et al. (2014) and Pretorius (2020) posit that NQSWs are treated as such for up to 24 months, some governing bodies extend this period to 36 months (South African Department of Social Development [DSD] and South African Council for Social Service Professions [SACSSP] 2012). Nevertheless, whatever the length of time determined by different employers or national welfare policies, the defining feature across the board is the NQSWs' lack of field experience. Second, irrespective of the nature of field instruction they have had, and against the backdrop of their inexperience, NQSWs need socialization into the profession (Engelberg and Limbach-Reich 2016). Socialization into the profession may include the worker's ability to practice across different fields with various service user population groups and diverse challenges (Hay et al. 2019), aiming at a trajectory to establish a professional identify consisting inter alia of a professional self-concept, based on attributes, beliefs, values, motives, and experiences (Engelbrecht 2019b). This professional identity furthermore entails an understanding of the parameters within which social workers operate in an organization and how they relate to various aspects of the profession, such as how policy directives and legislation impact on social workers' service delivery on all levels of work vis-à-vis micro to macro level intervention. Although the challenge of insufficient field experience may extend to seasoned practitioners who are newly employed in a particular field setting, it is nevertheless an explicit determining factor in the overall occupational functioning of NQSWs. Notwithstanding the absence of field experience, NQSWs are varyingly exposed to unfamiliar and diverse service users, and organizational and environmental systems, which may differ completely from their practice and perceptions as social work students. This eventually leads to heightened anxiety and impaired work efficiency, resulting in work apathy and even compassion fatigue (Hunt et al. 2017). Against this backdrop, Pretorius (2020) reflects on the lack of professional confidence among NQSWs as one of their primary identifying characteristics.

Engelbrecht (2019b) identifies additional critical characteristics of NQSWs as an integral part of a developmental theory of social workers' professional identity. He posits that NQSWs' motivation for supervision is in the main characterized by high levels of anxiety owing to their need to gain skills and experience. Second, he notes that NQSWs, whom he refers to as beginner social workers, are highly dependent on supervision to meet their work demands. As such, the intensity of supervision which they are subjected to becomes focal in the effective execution of their duties. Third, NQSWs may have a limited awareness of their work-related strengths and limitations and may rely on external sources (such as an experienced supervisor) to provide them with opportunities for professional development. It is however important to note that the context of Engelbrecht's (2019b) exposition regarding the developmental stages of social workers' professional identity cannot be interpreted merely in terms of a social worker's duration of work experience, but should be seen rather within the context of progression based on innate

Table 12.1 Developmental stages of professional identity in supervision (partially adapted from Engelbrecht 2019b and Stoltenberg et al. 1998)

BEGINNER	INTERMEDIATE	ADVANCED
Motivation		
Motivation for supervision may be driven by high anxiety levels owing to the need to gain knowledge and skills appropriate to a new professional environment; professional identity is yet to be established in the current or anticipated professional life.	Fluctuating confidence and motivation for supervision owing to practice realities, demands and complexity of work; professional identify may be ambivalent.	Stable motivation and acceptance of cooperative supervision owing to an established professional identity.
Autonomy		
Is dependent on supervision in order to fulfil work requirements.	Is ambivalent about the need for supervision to fulfil work requirements.	Is self-confident and self-directed in work requirements and knows when to seek and use supervision.
Awareness		
Limited awareness of work-related strengths and challenges and may rely on external sources to provide opportunities for continuing education and support.	Identifies work-related strengths and challenges, and opportunities for continuing education and support.	Aware of work-related strengths and challenges and takes ownership of continuing education and support.

characteristics such as motivation, autonomy, and awareness. In reality, it may thus be that some social workers with more than 12-, 24-, or 36-month's experience are still functioning in the mode of a beginner social worker in supervision. Table 12.1 illustrates the different stages of professional identity relevant to supervision.

The characteristics ascribed to NQSWs in Table 12.1 are not meant to be complete, exhaustive, and a stereotyping of their knowledge, skills, and attitudes, determined by the duration of their practice experiences. The different stages rather provide a hypothetical continuum to pitch the supervision engagement with social workers based on their professional identity, which may be helpful in the transition of NQSWs from being students to being professional social workers.

Transition from being a student to the workplace as a qualified social worker

The move from being a student to the realities of a professional work environment implies a transition from a training institution where academic performances were graded towards obtaining a qualification, to a work environment with accountability towards making a difference in the lives of services users; and moving from being a trainee in a designated agency or even variously approved field placements, to being an employee in an employment of choice. Moreover, the implication is that in training of social work students, the focus is on the attainment of learning outcomes and to gain optimum intervention experiences with service users, and not on the day-to-day organizational and managerial issues in the workplace. Beddoe et al. (2020) are mindful of this fact when observing that students' field placements are to some extent a protected environment and not the real world. The segue from student placement to the first professional appointment may thus be marked by an unexpected disruption into new roles, environments, and responsibilities as an employee (Donnellan and Jack 2015), which may differ from how NQSWs envisioned social work practice. The work environment and conditions are major push factors, impeding retention of NQSWs. In certain instances, work conditions do not only lead to NQSWs leaving their jobs, but that they exit the social work profession as well (Bates et al. 2010; Hussein et al. 2014). The specific realities of social work practice, which NQSWs may not have been exposed to as students, may include for instance, meagre salaries, restricted upward occupational mobility, health and safety challenges, and lackluster forms of management (Joseph 2017). Although these practice realities may have been obliquely referred to in the training institutions' classrooms, by seasoned social workers' narratives in field placements, and especially by the media, it is still in many instances a reality shock for social work students to experience social work in all its dimensions as an employee (Pretorius 2020). It specifically appears not to be the social work practice and interventions with service users itself, but rather distinct organizational and managerial issues such as poor work facilities and conditions, power plays by staff and resultant ramifications, constant limited funding, scarce resources, excessive time spent on report writing and administrative record keeping, mismatch between policies and practice, and political interference, and its implications for social work practice in turn, that hinders a seamless transition from student to professional social worker.

However, NQSWs may adapt quickly to the organizational culture of their employer and workplace, and this culture may either facilitate or restrict an employee's professional growth (Pretorius 2020). This is an additional challenging dynamic in retaining NQSWs, together with the diversity and unpredictability of social work. For instance, in countries influenced drastically by neoliberal-inspired managerial implications for social work and social care, and resultant socio-political issues (Ornellas and Engelbrecht 2020) where it is expected of supervisors to exercise "market logic" (Bradley et al. 2010, p. 785), retention of NQSWs would need extra effort from the employer agency to soften the adverse impact of both managerial and service user challenges on the transition of an NQSW to the workplace.

A case in point would be of social workers practicing in areas severely affected by the Covid-19 pandemic. This virus has caused significant panic, and patients have been stigmatized in some communities. As this is a novel pandemic on a global scale, even seasoned social workers have to learn to deal with the unprecedented effects on communities. As such, NQSWs may find it difficult to traverse the plethora of challenges brought about by this pandemic in their social work interventions, while they grapple with other layers of managerial and structural challenges accompanying their transition to occupational practices. For instance, in some provinces of South Africa, the Department of Social Development has failed to transfer contracted financial subsidies to non-profit social welfare organizations (NGOs) during crucial stages of the country's Covid-19 lockdown. Many NQSWs employed by the affected NGOs were financially vulnerable as new entries into the labor market where they had no financial resources as backup. These NQSWs had to rely on food parcels in the same way that their service users did, as they did not receive full or any remuneration, despite working as essential workers (Vetten and Grobbelaar 2020). Hence, these NQSWs did not just have to contend with the anxieties and complexities of a novel pandemic and resultant service user dynamics, but also had to endure organizational and managerial turmoil affecting their own wellbeing.

In another example in the United States, exposed in the same timeframe in social media and popular world news as the South African example above, social movements such as the *#BlacklivesMatter* were born out of perceived experiences of systematic and intentionally targeted attacks against black people by law enforcement officers (Garza 2014). Yancy (2020) posits that many black people in the United States reside in high-density residential areas where fighting Covid-19 through social distancing was the biggest challenge, leading to a high mortality rate. That situation might have presented a scenario with an intersectionality of race, social work practice, and the transitioning of NQSWs to occupational employment, where their own safety and even that of their supervisors could not be guaranteed. Even where practitioners are assured of safety at work, the thought of intervening in communities where similar conditions abound may exacerbate the concerns of NQSWs who must perform essential services as professional practitioners.

The realities mentioned above may not have surfaced during the NQSWs' studies if the focus of their field placements was in the main to provide them with optimal, selected experiences of the integration of theory and practice. Ncube (2019) reflects on the shortage of trained supervisors in a South African context and the lack of quality social work supervision of NQSWs. This is surely also applicable in other country contexts (Ornellas et al. 2019). Yet, NQSWs are expected, in many instances, to have a fully developed and coherent professional identity when they enter the workplace (Engelbrecht 2015), and they are also expected to have the requisite knowledge, skills, and expertise to practice independently (Moorhead et al. 2016). Within the neoliberal, managerially infiltrated work environment of social workers, the demand for "ready-made," independent (from supervision) social workers is thus the norm in many agencies across the world, with the primary goal of a supervisor being to develop the NQSW as speedily as possible into a cost-effective, self-contained social worker (Engelbrecht 2019b). In some contexts, it is preferred that social workers function officially on a consultation basis as soon as possible after their appointment, which means that they themselves have to determine if, when, and what support, education, and administration they need (Engelbrecht 2019c). In these instances, structured and regular supervision is not a given as part of a social worker's appointment. It is rather a nice-to-have activity, and if it is available, it is merely a compliance checking designed for those social workers who struggle to work, independent from the instructions and support of a manager (who may not necessarily be a social worker) (Engelbrecht 2015). These practice realities should be seen in light of the conclusion by Reuven Even Zahav et al. (2020) that social work students consider supervision to be the most crucial component of their preparation to practice in social work. Without a regular, structured continuation of supervision into professional practice, the tension between NQSWs' expectations of practice as they have visualized it as students, and the eventual work conditions as elucidated above, may create conflicting challenges that threaten the retention of NQSWs (Pretorius 2020). Therefore, taking cognizance of the unique, typical challenges of NQSWs is essential in order to address this in supervision.

Typical challenges of NQSWs

The transition from field instruction to professional employment, as highlighted above, presents a bleak picture that has a significant bearing on the transitional process. Contributing factors are multifaceted and may range from the academic and personal attributes of NQSWs, to their lived experiences of field placements, and to the operational modalities of the new workplace (cf. Hay et al. 2019; Pretorius 2020). The training institution may not be able to prepare student social workers in field placements to exactly match the organizational design and demands of new workplaces. In general, social work training institutions offer generalist social work training, in preparation for a range of workplace contexts, leaving the responsibility to the new workplace to introduce NQSWs to their context-specific, specialized interventions. Most institutions that offer social work qualifications in various parts of the world include both a rigorous theoretical, and a field instruction program in their training (Nadesan 2019). However, regardless of the number of years, level, and content of social work training that is offered by social work training institutions, it remains a worldwide phenomenon that social work agencies prefer NQSWs who are "ready-made" (as explained in the previous section), and thus do not need regular, specialized, and structured input to master their employment brief. The blame apportioned to social work training institutions by social work agencies, that their curricula are not on a par with requirements and developments in practice, and that their training is not effective, is an ongoing debate with much rhetoric in the social work profession (Engelbrecht 2015, 2019c; Pretorius 2020).

Parallel to the debate regarding the mismatch between social work academic training and practice, Bates et al. (2010, p. 154) advance a view that "… professional knowledge becomes more concerned with 'being' a professional rather than just 'having' the requisite factual knowledge…This implies an iterative process to development into and beyond qualified practice." There is, however, more to being a professional than just having the requisite knowledge in a particular profession. It entails proper application of skills, knowledge, and values that govern a spectrum of behaviors. Kanter et al. (2013), in their definition of professionalism, bemoan knowledge without the ability to apply it. They state that professionalism requires a consistent demonstration of professional behavior under the pressures of practice with conflicting demands and multiple priorities. Nevertheless, it is debatable whether field instruction alone, where social work students are spending a prescribed number of hours to reach predetermined outcomes or standards according to an accredited curriculum, may be sufficient to attain the required level of professionalism in social work practice, without granting the student the opportunity to fully experience the field and organizational dynamics as an employee, as explained above. Most importantly, social work students doing field practice should not be regarded as a primary workforce in an organization. Such a misconception of the principal goal of a social work student's field practice and a qualified social worker's employment may defeat the purpose of social work training (Engelbrecht 2019b, c). This may even result in neither the training institution's objectives nor the practice organization's expectations being achieved, leaving graduates with a meagre understanding of both theory and practice, and the integration thereof. In the midst of the global novel Covid-19 pandemic, many social work agencies and training institutions alike have been demonstrating this confusion by classifying the field practice of social work students as essential social services and are in fact joining neoliberal discourses on their preoccupation with individualized, cost-effective, and business-driven operating standards and procedures instead of focusing on academically sound teaching, learning, and reflection (Ornellas and Engelbrecht 2020).

In the same vein, Engelbrecht (2015, 2019a) avers that increasingly, supervision in a neoliberal environment, is depriving NQSWs of the opportunity to reflect on their real needs and challenges in their new professional role, as they are expected to demonstrate swiftly that they can meet organizational and managerial demands without continuous emotional support and education, which are regarded by some social service governing bodies as unnecessary and even improper for professionals (arguing that a professional should be able to work without supervision). The expression of the need for education and support by NQSWs in supervision is thus seen as either personal incompetence or a failure in the training institution's curriculum to prepare students adequately for practice.

The following extract from a poem by well-known Scottish psychiatrist Laing (1972, p. 55), who wrote extensively on people's lived experiences, may be echoed by NQSWs:

> *There is something I don't know*
> *that I am supposed to know.*

I don't know what it is I don't know
and yet am supposed to know,
and I feel I look stupid
if I seem both not to know it
and not know what it is I don't know.
Therefore, I pretend I know it.
This is nerve-racking
since I don't know what I must pretend to know.

This sentiment was overtly expressed by participants in Pretorius's (2020) study on compassion fatigue and self-care of NQSWs in South Africa. The constant struggle by NQSWs to prove that they are independent and fit for purpose, that they can master unfamiliar and new expectations quickly, and that they do not need regular and structured supervision and support, may result in classical symptoms of compassion fatigue. This is despite the fact that most NQSW participants in the study of Pretorius (2020) found the sudden higher caseload in professional practice unmanageable. The content of their supervision was also based merely on supervisors' reviews of their written intervention reports and notes (and statutory administration when working in such a context), with little evidence of clinical features and elements. In consequence, the participants presented symptoms of compassion fatigue and acknowledged that they did not follow up on critical cases, their engagements with service users were rushed, and that they did not have genuine compassion for vulnerable people anymore, which originally had attracted them to social work as a profession. Many of them were now considering leaving the social work profession, ready to embark on another career (cf. Pretorius 2020, pp. 109–110).

These retention issues of NQSWs are however not unique to South Africa. All over the world, governing bodies and researchers in social work are interested in challenges facing NQSWs. In a UK-based study, Keen et al. (2016) developed a practice guide to assist NQSWs during their first year of employment. This was done against the backdrop of comprehensively documented challenges imbued in their initial period of employment as social workers. Following a survey on the importance of supervision of social workers in the UK, Wilkins and Antonopoulou (2019) documented a number of findings related to the supervision of NQSWs, which to some extent point to the persistence of the same challenges that Keen et al. (2016) sought to address. The study surveyed more than 300 social workers in the UK and listed several critical findings. It reflected on the inadequate amount of time spent on supervision and lack of detail in the supervision process due to other competing duties of supervisors. It was also found that supervisors were insufficiently trained, which had a negative impact on their supervision practice and on the clinical progression of NQSWs. Supervisors largely executed supervision based on their own experiences as supervisees. The study also suggested that while supervisors do resort to mentoring activities, it is done on an informal basis.

In a longitudinal study conducted by Weaver et al. (2007) in the USA, factors affecting the newly employed public child welfare workers were explored, with which the abovementioned studies correlated. The study reflected on the predictors of the intention to quit the job, and predictors of actually quitting the job. In their exploration, the researchers highlighted factors such as work conditions and caseloads either as determinants that generate the inclination to leave the job or actually leaving the job. They furthermore reflected on individual factors such as the workers' psychological well-being, as pivotal in their job retention. All these factors oblige the employer of social workers to provide supervision as a mechanism to quell the occupational tensions experienced by NQSWs.

A recent study on coping and work-related stress reactions in the UK (Cummings et al. 2020) also explored workplace-related burnout, secondary traumatic stress, and vicarious trauma among protective service workers as three highly prevalent work-related stress reactions experienced in helping professions. The study confirmed the hypothesis on the susceptibility of protective service workers to one or more types of work-related stress. It further revealed that workers may adopt maladaptive coping mechanisms to some extent. Although time spent in the profession since graduation was not one of the study variables, it can reasonably be deduced that given the complexities of transitioning from field instruction to the workplace, NQSWs suffer equally from similar stressors, which indeed correlated with findings in the study of Pretorius (2020) in South Africa. To this end, the latter author found, through the lived experiences of NQSWs, that supervision may effectively act as a buffer to alleviate the challenges they experience when they enter professional social work practice.

Addressing the challenges faced by NQSWs

In response to the challenges faced by NQSWs, recent research findings regarding programs and policies, guidelines, or frameworks addressing the challenges faced by NQSWs emerged from countries such as Aotearoa New Zealand (Beddoe et al. 2020), Australia (Moorhead 2019), England (Scourfield et al. 2020), Israel (Reuven Even Zahav et al. 2020), Scotland (Grant et al. 2017; Patterson and Whincup 2018), South Africa (Pretorius 2020), and Sweden (Tham and Lynch 2019).

One example of a comprehensive program of support for NQSWs, correlating with most programs in other countries, is a Newly Qualified Social Worker program, established in 2008 in England (Carpenter et al. 2012, 2015). While the focus of the program was on NQSWs, their supervisors were equally targeted as enablers of competent social work services. The program inter alia purposed to help NQSWs improve their skills, competence, and confidence as social workers in a systematic manner during their first year of practice. It also enabled employers to provide focused supervision, support, and guidance. The program intended to contribute towards NQSWs' post-registration training and learning, to improve job satisfaction and to promote retention. Key findings of the evaluation of this program are supported by findings of several recent studies on challenges of NQSWs in different contexts (cf. Allcock 2019), which indicates that specific programs focusing on the support of NQSWs may indeed have a positive impact on recruitment and retention; supervisory skills of supervisors can be enhanced; specific actions are required to support the professional development of NQSWs; and these actions are generally appreciated by NQSWs. Significantly, NQSWs throughout the world generally report that receiving regular, structured supervision to reflect on their practice bears the greatest benefit of all actions to support them, followed by having a protected caseload. Ultimately, conclusions regarding specific programs tailored to address challenges faced by NQSWs indicate that there is a significant decrease in stress levels among those NQSWs who are supervised, compared to those who received partial supervisory attention or who were not supervised at all.

The supervision framework for the social work profession of the South African national Department of Social Development (the department responsible for welfare services) and the South African Council for Social Service Professions (SACSSP) may also serve as an example of a governing policy, guideline, or framework with specific regulations for supervision of NQSWs (DSD and SACSSP 2012). This framework addresses supervision in general and specifies norms and standards for supervision of NQSWs. It implores social work employers to develop organization specific supervision policies regarding NQSWs. Such policies should include requisites for the process of supervision, methods, frequency, performance appraisal, and continued professional development. In essence, the framework calls for a mandatory induction program for new appointees and makes provision for at least three years of regular, structured supervision. On completion of the entry years the NQSWs should be ready to move to a supervision level where they could exercise a greater level of independence. Moreover, the framework states that compulsory supervision during the first year of practice should be at least on a fortnightly basis, after which the frequency may be contracted to at least once a month. It further requires that assessments of performance be done quarterly in line with a personal development plan. Upon completion of the initial structured supervision period, a final assessment should be conducted to determine the renewal of a supervision contract in terms of the format and frequency of further supervision (DSD and SACSSP 2012).

However, despite these specifications, qualitative research by Pretorius (2020), reflecting the voices of South African NQSWs on their experiences of compassion fatigue and self-care, reveals that supervision of NQSWs does not occur as prescribed by the country's national supervision framework, owing to a myriad of reasons. The main reason appears to be the under-funding of supervision posts by national and provincial governments, impacting negatively on both public and private social work organizations, with the result that supervisors are over-burdened by managerial and practice demands. A NQSW participant in this study observes: "…they said that we should look after ourselves, but they didn't say how we should look after ourselves" (Pretorius 2020, p. 114). Another participant affirms that "…the supervision we learnt about in theory doesn't happen in the organization. There is an open-door policy, it isn't structured with a date and time" (p. 97).

These accounts are certainly not unique to South Africa, as concurrent research findings in a different context, reveal that "…despite the substantial investment made in social work education, little is done in Aotearoa New Zealand to support the needs of newly qualified practitioners…." (Beddoe 2020, p. 19). Consequently, and on a global level, social work agencies struggle to retain NQSWs, which may be regarded as one of the major reasons for the generation of a multitude of programs of support and policies, frameworks, or guidelines by national governing bodies all over the world. In the absence of special attention to NQSWs in a demanding new aspect of employment, a participant in the study of Pretorius (2020, p. 105) confesses:

> It impacted me physically, having headaches and high blood pressure. I saw others suffering from depression because of it. Your relationships suffer, you don't give time to others, including your family, your boyfriend; you don't have the energy for them. You are so physically drained you don't feel like doing anything…. emotionally, it can make you feel low where you can't look after yourself, because you are so drained. You may also no longer even want to go to work.

Based on these accounts captured by Pretorius (2020), she concludes that supervision of NQSW is an essential part of social work and care, and that this supervision should take on a distinct form with specific content, tailored by the integration of the administrative, educational, and support functions of supervision.

Specific content of supervision of NQSWs

In order to circumscribe the specific content of supervision of NQSWs, a synthesis will be presented below, structured in terms of the typical functions of supervision (Kadushin 1976; Kadushin and Harkness 2014). However, it should be noted that the functions of administration, education, and support are operationalized in an integrated manner (Bradley et al. 2010), as opposed to a mere boxed-in, tick-box exercise, and that the exposition below is not exhaustive. The specific content in supervision of NQSWs should be adapted to be context and situation specific and is presented with the purpose to illustrate the unique content of supervision valued by NQSWs, as obtained from a myriad findings, conclusions, and recommendations of recent relevant research studies all over the world (cf. Allcock 2019; Beddoe et al. 2020; Bates et al. 2010; Carpenter et al. 2015; Cummings et al. 2020; Donellan and Jack 2015; Grant et al. 2017; Hay et al. 2019; Hunt et al. 2017; Hussein et al. 2014; Jansen 2017; Keen et al. 2016; Manthorpe et al. 2015; Moorhead et al. 2016; Moorhead 2019; Patterson and Whincup 2018; Pretorius 2020; Reuven Even Zahav et al. 2020; Scourfield et al. 2020; Tham and Lynch 2019; Wilkins and Antonopoulou 2019; Yu et al. 2016).

Administrative content

First, a comprehensive induction program to introduce NQSWs at the onset of employment seems to be the point of departure of their supervision. During this program, in addition to an introduction to the total work environment, the supervisor should specifically introduce the NQSW to the agency's supervision policy or related documents and practices to set expectations and requirements of supervision. Tasks in supervision, as indicated in the agency's supervision policy or practices, should be executed as soon as possible by the supervisor, which may entail the planning, organizing, leading, and controlling of a supervision process in terms of a supervision agreement with the NQSW, the design of a personal development/supervision plan, and the format, goal, and use of performance evaluations. Determining the nature of supervision sessions in respect of content, frequency, time, duration, and record keeping is particularly essential. An understanding should be established that supervision will pertain to more than just the day-to-day case management issues, and that it (essentially) will include critical reflections on practices as well. Concrete measures should be taken by the supervisor to arrange protected caseloads for NQSWs, and to assist them in managing their time and workload by setting priorities. Practicalities to enable NQSWs to do their job in a positive and secure environment, with specific health and safety measures, should be in place, as well as sufficient office space, computer/IT access, and transport arrangements (surprisingly, these practicalities do not seem to be commonplace, based on feedback by NQSWs in diverse contexts). Time and resources for structured continuing professional development activities should also be organized, in addition to, and not replacing, supervision. To cultivate the professional growth of NQSWs, senior co-workers may be assigned as mentors to be shadowed by NQSWs and with whom they can work together on challenging cases or projects. This may also be a way to initially reduce the administration and paperwork of NQSWs as an initiative to be gradually immersed in their workloads. The organizing and coordination of a peer group of the NQSW who may take co-responsibility in supplementary support and education was also found to be effective.

Educational content

The generic educational content of supervision of NQSWs centers on what to do when, where, and how, for the benefit of the service user. Training of social workers is usually offered at an accredited training institution, where the entire educational content is guided by a program consisting of generic outcomes, standards, and/or competencies, which must be demonstrated before a qualification can be awarded. Social work practice however, is a response to a multitude of behaviors, events, and phenomena on diverse levels of society, hence intervention requires specialized knowledge, skills, and attitudes. This indeed, and not mere accountability, justifies primarily the extended education of social workers in the form of supervision when they enter professional practice. However, understanding this rationale and making optimal use of the educational opportunities that supervision can offer may not come naturally to NQSWs, as they may have preconceived perceptions about supervision, based on the "performance-grading" nature of their field practice as students, on a scale of fail and pass. NQSWs may thus transfer this "grade-orientation" into the supervision dyad and respond accordingly to the educational content of supervision, specifically where they have had a negative or conflicting experience around their grades as students, or where their academic grading was inflated above their actual practice performance. This "practice self-concept" of NQSWs may have a significant bearing on how they present themselves in the initial supervision dyad. Kadushin (1968) originally articulated a multitude of blockages and power games in the supervision dyad, which were enlarged upon by commentators such as Tsui (2005).

Therefore, the educational content of supervision should, first of all, be clarified with NQSWs in terms of how to utilize supervision optimally and what supervision within the specific work environment and job context will entail. Hence, defining and clarifying the goal of supervision as a specialized professional developmental activity, which stretches beyond mere caseload management and compliance oversight, is an essential point of departure. The NQSWs should furthermore understand that their supervision would still focus on the application of theory and its integration with practice. Consequently, NQSWs will get the opportunity to apply their acquired critical, analytical, and academic skills under the supervision of a designated supervisor with more experience to interpret and respond to practice complexities in a systematic way. In this regard, supervisors should first clarify their own roles in the supervision dyad, and second, reveal the theoretical underpinning and practice models in use in the particular setting. Third, applicable legislation, policies, and procedures which guide the social work service delivery should also be clarified in the same manner as the theoretical conceptualization. Fourth, introducing NQSWs to resources in the work environment and the development of skills to create and utilize resources, should be a priority in the education of the NQSWs, especially within an inter- and multidisciplinary environment to enable them to be assertive in such contexts. These aspects may hold that the generalist social work skills that NQSWs acquired in their training should be refined to fit their new specific and/or specialized environment. Since NQSWs may be unfamiliar with their new work environments, they might need to be prepared on how to describe and explain their professional role to specific systems in the community (ranging from service users to other professionals). This denotes, in addition, that their cultural competencies must also be refined, with specific emphasis on all sorts of communication on all levels. Report writing forms part of this communication, which may take up the most energy in supervision, as the NQSWs may spend considerable time on written communication as record keeping according to the requirements of the organization.

Supportive content

The supportive content of supervision depends on the level of understanding and empathy that supervisors have for NQSWs. Feedback from NQSWs suggests that many supervisors pride themselves on being seasoned and tough and that these supervisors proclaim that retention in social work practice is a matter of survival of the fittest – and these "fittest" are the social workers that deserve to remain. Therefore, many supervisors subscribe to the idea that NQSWs should be thrown in at the deep end of social work practice, based on a reflection of their own experiences as NQSWs. In contrast, the supportive content of supervision should rather nurture NQSWs through the emotional quicksand they may initially experience, to enable them to mobilize the motivation, resilience, and energy required for their work in a mutually respectful relationship, and in a safe space. By its very nature, social work in most contexts requires multiple diverse roles and tasks, which may initially be overwhelming owing to the immediacy, intensity, frequency, urgency, and specialization required for intervention. This uncertainty and unpredictability form part of the daily grind in social work practice and may either contribute to or impede the job satisfaction of NQSWs – depending on the support available in supervision. Moreover, support at all levels of practice fosters the development of professional confidence in NQSWs and strengthens their professional identity within their organizational setting. In turn, this augments the NQSWs' identification with professional values and ethical conduct.

Additional aspects unique to social work, which need special support, include the emotional strain of NQSWs due to resistance from service users and resultant conflict, and the concomitant fear of making mistakes in interventions. The modeling of collaborative decision-making processes by supervisors is thus a tangible way to support NQSWs. Ultimately, the supervisor's modeling of self-care and coping mechanisms against the multiple work stressors peculiar to a specific social work setting is paramount in the support of NQSWs. This modeling includes the manner in which the supervisor provides feedback to the supervisee. Feedback should not only be specific and frequent, but particularly developmental and supportive, considering that the tasks NQSWs are performing may be a first, new experience. NQSWs have not "been there and done that," despite organizational managerial demands for "ready-made" social workers to enter practice seamlessly.

Conclusion

It has been affirmed in this chapter that supervision of NQSWs is indispensable and that the employment of a social worker without professional practice experience should not be considered by social work agencies if supervision by a senior social worker with scholarly knowledge, skills, and values is not available. However, supervision of NQSWs consists of more than just knowledge and skills transfer by a senior social worker, given the unique challenges posed by the transition from student to professional practitioner. These challenges point to the differences between supervision of seasoned workers and NQSWs in terms of their motivation, autonomy, and awareness. It has been globally observed that neoliberal, managerial practices result in meagre budget allocations for social services and care, which in turn impede supervision of social workers in general, with the most detrimental effect on supervision of NQSWs. To ensure retention and a more seamless transition of NQSWs to the workplace, national programs, frameworks, and policies have been put in place in various countries across the world to ensure basic norms and standards in supervision of NQSWs. Evaluations of these programs suggest that NQSWs in diverse contexts appreciate certain content in supervision, as synthesized in this chapter. This lateral thinking may encourage both supervisors and their newly qualified supervisees to timeously develop bottom-up knowledge from practice. Ultimately, supervisors may use "market logic" to calibrate the cost of staff recruitment and supervision, but they should also apply "professional logic" (Bradley et al. 2010, p. 785) to ensure that supervision of NQSWs be given priority in social work agencies.

References

Allcock, A., 2019. *ESSS outline: newly qualified social workers, supervision and child protection.* Iriss. Available from: https://doi.org/10.31583/esss.20190408 [Accessed 2 February 2020].

Bates, N., Immins, T., Parker, J., Keen, S., Rutter, L., Brown, K., and Zsigo, S., 2010. Baptism of fire: the first year in the life of a newly qualified social worker. *Social Work Education*, 29 (2), 152–170.

Beddoe, L., Ballantyne, N., Maidment, J., Hay, K., and Walker, S., 2020. Supervision, support and professional development for newly qualified social workers in Aotearoa New Zealand. *Aotearoa New Zealand Social Work*, 32 (2), 17–31.

Bongo, M., and McKnight, K., 2006. Clinical supervision in social work. *The Clinical Supervisor*, 24 (1–2), 49–67.

Bradley, G., Engelbrecht, L.K., and Höjer, S., 2010. Supervision: a force for change? Three stories told. *International Social Work*, 53 (6), 773–790.

Carpenter, J., Patsios, D., Wood, M., Platt, D., Shardlow, S., McLaughlin, H., Scholar, H., Haines, C., Wong, C., and Blewett, J., 2012. *Newly qualified social worker programme: final evaluation report (2008 to 2011)*. London: Department for Education. Available from: https://dera.ioe.ac.uk/15065/1/DFE-RR229.pdf [Accessed 1 July 2020].

Carpenter, J., Shardlow, S.M., Patsios, D., and Wood, M., 2015. Developing the confidence and competence of newly qualified child and family social workers in England: outcomes of a national programme. *British Journal of Social Work*, 45 (1), 153–176.

Cummings, C., Singer, J., Moody, S.A., and Benuto, L.T., 2020. Coping and work-related stress reactions in protective services workers. *The British Journal of Social Work*, 50 (1), 62–80.

Department of Social Development (DSD) and South African Council for Social Services Professions (SACSSP) 2012. *Supervision framework for the social work profession*. Pretoria: DSD and SACSSP. Available from: https://www.westerncape.gov.za/assets/departments/social-development/supervision_framework_for_thc_social_work_profession_in_south_africa_2012.pdf [Accessed on 1 August 2020].

Donellan, H., and Jack, G., 2015. *The survival guide for newly qualified social workers: hitting the ground running*. 2nd ed. London: Jessica Kingsley.

Engelberg, E., and Limbach-Reich, A., 2016. Prepared enough to practise? Evaluating a study programme in social work. *Journal of Social Work*, 16 (5), 561–577.

Engelbrecht, L.K., 2015. Revisiting the esoteric question: can non-social workers manage and supervise social workers? *Social Work/Maatskaplike Werk*, 51 (3), 311–331.

Engelbrecht, L.K., 2019a. Towards authentic supervision of social workers in South Africa. *The Clinical Supervisor*, 38 (2), 301–325.

Engelbrecht, L.K., 2019b. Fundamental aspects of supervision. *In*: L.K. Engelbrecht, ed. *Management and supervision of social workers: issues and challenges within a social development paradigm*. 2nd ed. Andover: Cengage Learning EMEA Limited, 150–173.

Engelbrecht, L.K., 2019c. Processes, tasks, methods and activities in supervision. *In*: L.K. Engelbrecht, ed. *Management and supervision of social workers: issues and challenges within a social development paradigm*. 2nd ed. Andover: Cengage Learning EMEA Limited, 174–191.

Garza, A., 2014. A herstory of the #BlackLivesMatter movement [online]. *The Feminist Wire*. Available from: https://thefeministwire.com/2014/10/blacklivesmatter-2/ [Accessed 31 May 2020].

Grant, S., Sheridan, L., and Webb, S.A., 2017. Newly qualified social workers' readiness for practice in Scotland. *British Journal of Social Work*, 47 (2), 487–506.

Hay, K., Maidment, J., Beddoe, L., Ballantyne, N., Walker, S., and Mayhew, Z., 2019. *Enhancing the readiness of newly qualified social workers in Aotearoa New Zealand*. The national centre for tertiary teaching excellence. Ako Aotearoa. Available from: https://ako.ac.nz/assets/Knowledge-centre/NPF16-003-Enhancing-the-readiness-to-practice-of-newly-qualified-social-workers/Literature-Scan-3.pdf [Accessed 1 August 2020].

Hunt, S., Lowe, S., Smith, K., Kuruvila, A., and Webber-Dreadon, E., 2016. Transition to professional social work practice: the initial year. *Advances in Social Work and Welfare Education*, 18 (1), 55–71.

Hunt, S., Tregurtha, M., Kuruvila, A., Lowe, S., and Smith, K., 2017. Transition to professional social work practice: the first three years. *Advances in Social Work and Welfare Education*, 19 (2), 139–154.

Hussein, S., Moriarty, J., Stevens, M., Sharpe, E., and Manthorpe, J., 2014. Organisational factors, job satisfaction and intention to leave among newly qualified social workers in England. *Social Work Education*, 33 (3), 381–396.

Jansen, A., 2017. 'It's so complex!': understanding the challenges of child protection work as experienced by newly graduated professionals. *British Journal of Social Work*, 48 (6), 1524–1540.

Joseph, D., 2017. *Perceived contributing factors impeding job satisfaction of social workers in non-government organisations*. Unpublished thesis. Stellenbosch University.

Kadushin, A., 1968. Games people play in supervision. *Social Work*, 13 (3), 23–32.

Kadushin, A., 1976. *Supervision in social work*. New York: Columbia University Press.

Kadushin, A., and Harkness, D., 2014. *Supervision in social work*. 5th ed. New York: Columbia University Press.

Kanter, M.H., Nguyen, M., Klau, M.H., Spiegel, N.H., and Ambrosini, V.L., 2013. What does professionalism mean to the physician? *The Permanente Journal*, 17 (3), 87–90.

Keen, S., Parker, J., Brown, K., & Galpin, D., eds., 2016. *Newly-qualified social workers: a practice guide to the assessed and supported year in employment*. 3rd ed. London: SAGE.

Laing, R.D., 1972. *Knots*. New York: Vintage Book Company.

Manthorpe, J., Moriarty, J., Hussein, S., Stevens, M., and Sharpe, E., 2015. Content and purpose of supervision in social work practice in England: views of newly qualified social workers, managers and directors. *British Journal of Social Work*, 45 (1), 52–68.

Moorhead, B., 2019. Transition and adjustment to professional identity as a newly qualified social worker. *Australian Social Work*, 72 (2), 206–218.

Moorhead, B., Bell, K., and Bowles, K., 2016. Exploring the development of professional identity with newly qualified social workers. *Australian Social Work*, 69 (4), 456–467.

Nadesan, V.S., 2019. *A systems analysis of field instruction in social work education*. Unpublished thesis. University of Johannesburg.

Ncube, M., 2019. Conceptualising social development supervision in social work. *The Indian Journal of Social Work*, 80 (1), 31–46.

Ornellas, A., and Engelbrecht, L.K., 2020. Neoliberal impact on social work in South African Non-Governmental Organisations. *Southern African Journal for Social Work and Social Development*, 32 (1), 1 21.

Ornellas, A., Spolander, G., Engelbrecht, L.K., Sicora, A., Pervova, I., Martínez-Román, M., Law, A.K., Shajahan, P.K., Das Dores Guerreiro, M., Casanova, J.L., Garcia, M.L.T, Acar, H., Martin, L., and Strydom, M., 2019. Mapping social work across 10 countries: structure, intervention, identity and challenges. *International Social Work*, 62 (4): 1183–1197.

Patterson, F., and Whincup, H., 2018. Making the transition from practitioner to supervisor: reflections on the contribution made by a post-qualifying supervisory course. *European Journal of Social Work*, 21 (3), 415–427.

Pretorius, T., 2020. *Compassion fatigue and self-care: voices of newly qualified social workers*. Unpublished thesis. Stellenbosch University.

Reuven Even Zahav, R., Refaeli, T., Shemesh, S., Gottlieb, S., and Ben-Porat, A., 2020. Supervision satisfaction among social work students in Israel: supervision components, peer support, and trauma-related factors. *Research on Social Work Practice*. Available from: https://doi.org/10.1177/1049731520936755 [Accessed 10 August 2020].

Ross, E., and Ncube, M., 2018. Student social workers' experiences of supervision. *The Indian Journal of Social Work*, 79 (1), 31–54.

Schmidt, K., and Rautenbach, J.V., 2016. Field instruction: is the heart of social work education still beating in the Eastern Cape? *Social Work/Maatskaplike Werk*, 52 (4), 589–610.

Scourfield, J., Maxwell, N., Venn, L., Carpenter, J., Stepanova, E., and Smith, R., 2020. *Social work fast track programmes: tracking retention and progression*. Interim Report. Department of Education. Government social research. Available from: https://assets.publishing.service.gov.uk/government/uploads/system/uploads/attachment_data/file/902442/Fast_track_Interim_report_July_2020.pdf [Accessed 1 August 2020].

Stoltenberg, C.D, McNeil, M.W., and Delwarth, U., 1998. *IDM supervision: an integrated development model for supervising counsellors and therapists*. San Francisco: Jossey-Bass.

Tham, P., and Lynch, D., 2019. 'Lost in transition?' – Newly educated social workers' reflections on their first months in practice. *European Journal of Social Work*, 22 (3), 400–411.

Tsui, M., 2005. *Social work supervision: contexts and concepts*. London: SAGE.

Vetten, L., and Grobbelaar, M., 2020. *Rapid assessment on the financial status of non-profit organisations providing social care services*. Available from: https://www.groundup.org.za/media/uploads/documents/npofinancingreport072020.pdf [Accessed 10 August 2020].

Weaver, D., Chang, J., Clark, S., and Rhee, S., 2007. Keeping public child welfare workers on the job. *Administration in Social Work*, 31 (2), 5–25.

Wilkins, D., and Antonopoulou, V., 2019. What does supervision help with? A survey of 315 social Workers in the UK. *Practice*, 31 (1), 21–40.

Yancy, C.W., 2020. COVID-19 and African Americans. *American Medical Association*, 323 (19), 1891–1892.

Yu, N., Moulding, N., Buchanan, F., and Hand, T., 2016. How good is good enough? Exploring social workers' conceptions of preparedness for practice. *Social Work Education*, 35 (4), 414–429.

13

SUPERVISION IN CHILD AND FAMILY SETTINGS

David Wilkins

Supervision in child and family settings may be said to epitomize the wider challenges of child and family social work – how to balance help and support for families with the need to safeguard vulnerable children and prevent significant harm? The answer to this challenge in recent years and decades has been to increase modes of control, whether of families by workers or of workers by their managers. In some extreme cases, supervision has been replaced entirely by managerialism. Yet there are also signs that supervision in child and family settings is undergoing a renaissance, with forms of reflective and group supervision in particular becoming increasingly popular. This chapter offers a summary of these debates before concluding with a consideration of evidence-informed supervision, and the need to establish more rigorous theoretical models of how supervision in this context ultimately benefits children and their families.

Supervision as a form of surveillance

Supervision has always been at the core of social work with children and families, from the earliest history in which volunteers were supervised in their work by more experienced workers (Tsui 1997), to current sophisticated systems of child protection in which the work of qualified social workers in statutory settings must be overseen by their managers (National Association of Social Workers 2013). Inevitably, the nature of the supervision provided has changed over the decades. More recently it has been suggested that supervision in this context is increasingly focused not on the provision of support for workers or achieving best outcomes for families but on management oversight and surveillance of practice (Beddoe 2010). This prioritization of accountability has taken place in various jurisdictions, including England (Munro 2011, p. 53), Australia (Egan 2012), and New Zealand (Beddoe 2016). This suggests that common factors between the different countries may be at least partially responsible. One such factor is the increasing distrust by policy-makers and perhaps the public at large of social workers (Heyes 2014), itself in part the result of a series of high-profile child deaths – particularly when the families of those children have been in close contact with social services (Brandon et al. 2010; Shoesmith 2016). This lack of trust has contributed to the implementation of new approaches to public management, with the aim of ensuring consistency and compliance with procedural guidelines (Heffernan 2005; O'Donoghue and Tsui 2011).

Yet there is something a little odd about the belief that without close scrutiny, social workers would not aim to do the right thing. Munro (2009) has argued that when reviewing disasters in the aerospace industry, such as plane crashes, we hold an inherent assumption that the pilots involved would have avoided disaster if they could. As the pilot is usually killed in such tragic events, we assume that unless he or she wanted to die, they would have done everything possible to avoid a crash. Munro contrasts this with what often happens in relation to the death of abused or neglected children. In England, when a child dies and abuse or neglect are suspected as contributory factors, a Serious Case Review is held to try and understand what happened and to generate useful learning for future casework. Some very helpful recommendations have emerged from such Reviews. Yet many have also suggested, whether implicitly or explicitly, that social workers need to be encouraged, beseeched, or otherwise mandated to do their best for vulnerable children and families – and that without constant scrutiny and management oversight, social workers may do otherwise. As Munro (2009) says, "we might consider if there is any point in repeatedly asking why staff do not follow procedures and ask instead what hampers them from doing so" (unpaginated).

Partly as a result of these pressures, in England and in other countries, an increasing amount of resources have been dedicated to various forms of surveillance, including burdensome inspections of service providers, a requirement for practitioners to record in writing much of what they do, the collection and reporting to central government of vast quantities of administrative data – and in the form of supervision.

Thus, we can see the context in which supervision has become for many child and family services part of a system of oversight and surveillance of practice, if not exclusively then certainly as a core function (Baginsky et al. 2010). None of which is to suggest that supervision should not contain any element of oversight. As defined by Watkins and Milne (2014), supervision without accountability is not really supervision and there is nothing inherently wrong with management oversight of practice. Given the powers invested in many statutory child and family social workers, it is essential that their work and decision-making is subject to both internal and external scrutiny. Yet when supervision becomes little more than a forum for accountability, then it stops being what most practitioners, supervisors, and academics in the field would recognize to be high-quality supervision.

Rebalancing supervision within child and family services so that it can include accountability alongside rather than instead of other more supportive functions is not a straightforward task. (Although as discussed below, there are examples from England and elsewhere in which this rebalancing effort is already underway.) It is not straightforward in part because supervision reflects as much as it informs the nature of the wider service. As statutory child and family social work in the UK and in other places has become ever-more focused on risk, predicting future harm to children, and policing relatively minor aspects of family life (Featherstone et al. 2013), it is unsurprising that what passes for supervision in many settings has followed the same trend with respect to practitioners themselves. As many parents cannot, apparently, be trusted to want and do their best for their own children, so workers cannot be trusted to do their best without near-constant scrutiny by their managers.

What happens in child and family supervision?

What do we find when either observing what happens in supervision or asking what child and family social workers and supervisors think about it? Most of what we know comes from self-report surveys or interviews rather than from direct observation, and there is a relatively limited diversity of methods used within the field (Sewell 2018). Having said that, some more recent studies have included direct observations, and some have also sought to correlate what happens in supervision with what social workers do in direct practice with families and what families think about the services they receive. Despite these efforts, we actually know relatively little. There are few if any representative surveys of social workers, although there are various non-representative surveys available, and observational studies have tended to be based in only a small number of different services and to involve only a small number of case studies. With these limitations in mind, what do these various different studies show?

Wilkins et al. (2017) observed 34 supervision discussions in one local authority in England and found a relatively consistent approach. Most sessions would start with a brief "check in" between worker and supervisor. The supervisor might ask about workload or how the worker was feeling. The worker and supervisor would then agree a list of families to be discussed in turn. In relation to each family, supervisors would typically ask the worker to provide an update of their activity since the previous supervision session. The supervisor would ask clarifying questions and almost always type written notes to record the discussion on the child's file. The supervisor and worker would at some point identify a particular dilemma or challenge to be resolved. The supervisor would then typically provide a solution in the form of agency-oriented or procedural actions, before moving on to discuss the next family. The following relatively extensive extract shows the flavor (if not the extent) of this approach (Wilkins et al. 2017, p. 945):

Social worker (SW): I said, are you worried about anything in terms of the children being in their dad's care, do you feel that they'd be safe, she did say she was concerned about the dad's shouting around the children, about dad's use of shish and also khat, so that's another thing, she also was concerned he has cut off contact [with] the children and she felt makes them sad and they've got no money and he's cleared out her bank account.

Supervisor (S): How did he do that?

SW: When she went into hospital, she said he took the card.

S: Why would he take out all the money?

SW: We talked about that, the outcome was that the care coordinator was going to have a further discussion with her about whether she wants the police involved in an investigation of financial abuse but, I mean, the dad's been calling me constantly, to say I've got no money, I've got no money, I need money for the children and she's cut off the money and he's furious, obviously he needs money to pay for the children's things.

S: In the interim, we can give money, food vouchers. What does he need other than food vouchers?

SW: I need to meet up with both of them and think about contact, these children have not had contact with their mum for two weeks. So much work to be done with this family. Getting to the bottom of it.

S: Ok. Father has said he has no money, it's hard to figure out how much there is. He gets Jobseeker's Allowance. [Job Seekers Allowance or JSA is an unemployment benefit payable in England and Wales.] 4 kids to feed. We'd have to look at what we do there, I think feeding a family of four, £60 is not too bad, it's quite low, £60 of food vouchers if you can get it.

SW: He's getting his JSA, so he can feed himself, as long as the kids have got something.

S: I expect they get free school meals, but you need to check on that.

SW: Maybe a bit more to take account of nappies and things...they're quite expensive, aren't they? I'm wondering if maybe £80?

S: Find out from him how much he feels he needs to buy food and nappies. That's the only action I've got. Did I say anything else?

SW: I've also got down that I should contact the ward to request the benefits advisor make contact with mum.

S: Ok. We have time for one more.

There are two main things happening within this extract (and within the supervision discussions observed more generally). First, the majority of the time is spent by the social worker reporting to the supervisor what they have been doing and the supervisor typing a summary note onto the child's file (if you could listen to the audio recording of these discussions, you would hear the sound of typing almost continuously). Second, the supervisor adopts a problem-solving stance, in this case by helping decide what problem to focus on (the father's lack of money rather than, say, the lack of contact between the children and the mother) and giving advice about what the worker should do (check whether the children receive free school meals and apply for food vouchers).

There is generally an absence of reflection and in-depth analysis and there is no meaningful discussion about the children's experiences, about their needs, or about possible risk and harm. There is also no meaningful focus on practice (what the worker might do *with* the family) as opposed to a focus on task completion by the worker.

These observational findings reflect those from various surveys. For example, in a survey of more than 300 social workers and supervisors in England, Wilkins and Antonopoulou (2018) found that the majority of time in supervision was spent by social workers reporting information to their managers, with limited time for reflection and analysis. Baginsky et al. (2010) found that managers considered supervision to be a way of gathering information from workers, rather than a way of providing support to workers. Similar findings have been reported consistently by different researchers, across different periods of time, and in different jurisdictions (Egan et al. 2015; Manthorpe et al. 2013).

The relationship between high-quality supervision, practice skills, and family-outcomes

Although there is limited evidence for any relationship between high-quality supervision, practice skills, and family-outcomes, there is some. Wilkins et al. (2018) and Bostock et al. (2019) have both reported how certain forms of group supervision are associated with more advanced practice skills in the child and family context. Although the two studies used different methods for assessing the quality of supervision, they employed the same approach for assessing the quality of practice skills (while Wilkins et al. also reported on the views of parents and young people). Despite the studies being undertaken separately and in different locations, the findings are strikingly similar. Wilkins et al. found a strong association between supervision that focused on practice and good authority skills, while Bostock et al. found a modest association between more systemic supervision and good authority skills and a strong association between systemic supervision and care and engagement skills.

Before describing what is meant by practice-focused and systemic supervision, it is important to be clear about the nature of these practice skills. Using an analytical framework based in part on Motivational Interviewing (Whittaker et al. 2017), Forrester et al. (2018, 2019) observed more than one hundred meetings between child and family social workers and parents – and established a relationship between particular skills and outcomes for families. The skills within this framework are set out in Table 13.1. Each skill is rated on a scale from 1 (very low skill) to

Table 13.1 An overview of the practice skills evaluated by Wilkins et al. and Bostock et al. in relation to supervision in the context of child and family social work

Low	2	3	4	High
1				5

Evocation (behavior change)

Actively provides reasons for change	Relies on education and advice	Shows no interest or awareness of carer's reasons for change	Accepts carer's reasons and ideas for change when offered	Actively evokes carer's own reasons and ideas for change

Collaboration (care and engagement)

Assumes expert role, collaboration is absent	Responds superficially to opportunities to collaborate	Incorporates carer's goals and ideas in a lukewarm fashion	Fosters power sharing so carer's ideas impact the discussion	Actively fosters power sharing so that carer's ideas substantially impact the discussion

Autonomy (care and engagement)

Actively denies parent's choice and control	Discourages carer's perceptions of choice and control	Is neutral about carer's choice and control	Accepts and support carer's choice and control	Expands carer's perceptions of choice and control

Empathy (care and engagement)

Has no apparent interest in carer's perspective	Makes sporadic efforts to understand carer's perspective	Tries to understand carer's perspective with limited success	Accurate understanding of carer's perspective	Deep understanding of carer's perspective

Purposefulness (good authority)

No clear aim to the discussion	There is some sense of purpose but mainly formulaic	Sense of purpose imposed by the worker	Clear sense of purpose, worker remains flexible to carer's responses	Clear sense of purpose, negotiated between worker and carer

Clarity about risk and need (good authority)

Fails to cover significant issues	Fails to provide sufficient clarity	Issues or concerns are raised but not discussed	Issues or concerns raised, attempts made to explore carer's perspective	Issues or concerns raised, carer engaged in a meaningful discussion

Child focus (good authority)

Fails to consider child	Issues related to the child are raised superficially and briefly	Child is considered but in a generic fashion	Child is meaningfully considered with some attempt to draw on carer's perspective	Child is consistently and meaningfully considered, carer's understanding of the child is enhanced

Table 13.2 An overview of Wilkins et al.'s concept of "practice-focused" supervision and Bostock et al.'s model of systemic fidelity

Wilkins et al. "practice focused" supervision	Analysis and critical thinking	Clarity about risk and need	Focus on the child and family	Support for practice (how and why things are being done)
Bostock et al. "systemic supervision"	Curiosity and flexibility	Risk talk	Voice of the family *and* relational nature of problems	Intervention (including clarity about purpose and how these will effect change)

5 (very high skill) and can be grouped into "care and engagement" skills, "good authority" skills, and "evocation" (relating to behavior change; Forrester et al. 2020).

Care and engagement skills were found by Forrester et al. (2019) to be strongly associated with parental engagement (but no other outcome measure within their study). Good authority skills were weakly associated with parental engagement but more strongly associated with improved family functioning, increased family cohesion, and reductions in family conflict. Overall, Forrester et al. found that the skills of good authority were more influential than the skills of care and engagement, particularly when families were visited more often (possibly serving as a proxy indicator that the level of concern about these families was relatively high). This suggests that good practice within the context of child and family social work is dependent not simply on developing positive working relationships with families, important though this is. In addition, more skillful workers balance their care and engagement skills with purposefulness, clarity about risk, and need and child focus (as well as evocation, if and when the family's difficulties relate to behavior-change issues such as substance misuse).

Returning to Wilkins et al. and Bostock et al.'s studies, both found that certain kinds of supervision were associated with better demonstrations of these skills. Wilkins et al. refer to "practice-focused" supervision while Bostock et al. assessed how closely the sessions they observed adhered to a systemic model of practice. Table 13.2 gives a snapshot of each of these different approaches. They both share some key similarities, particularly a focus on families, a clear discussion of risk (and/or need), and a consideration of how and why (and not just *what*) things need to be done. These two approaches, developed in separate studies, indicate how supervision in the child and family context in particular can be associated with a higher quality of practice for families.

The green shoots of different approaches

Despite the apparent dominance of managerial oversight within many statutory child and family settings, it would be inaccurate to suggest that other approaches are not possible. Within the UK, for example, there is something of a supervisory renaissance taking shape in some places, and a growing interest in how supervision might be provided differently and more effectively for all concerned. First, many authorities are embedding forms of group supervision, most often but not always based on systemic models of practice. Second, a number of authorities are adopting psycho-dynamic principles and approaches as a way of providing more effective social and emotional support for workers. Third, some authorities are trialing new ways of meeting the needs of the workforce, outside of what might traditionally be seen as supervision. And finally, many individual supervisors are undergoing specialist training.

Systemic group supervision – the most widely known example is probably that of Reclaiming Social Work, first used in the London Borough of Hackney, and now more often referred to as systemic social work. In this model, groups of workers and managers meet together to discuss families, alongside individual meetings between workers and line-managers. A large-scale evaluation of this approach, across ten local authority areas, found that systemic group supervision was associated with enhanced practice skills demonstrated by workers in their meetings with families (Bostock et al. 2017). These findings, while being far from definitive in relation to cause-and-effect, suggest that this kind of supervision may be particularly suited for child and family settings.

Reflective practice groups – as an alternative to systemic approaches, other settings have adopted psychodynamic principles instead, often described as relationship-based practice (Lees and Cooper 2017). These approaches prioritize the emotional and social needs of the workforce, suggesting that "if social workers feel safe and contained, they can [then] build relationships with families and use these relationships to affect change" (p. 8). In one authority in England, reflective practice groups have been provided since 2015. Groups of staff meet together to discuss their work, with a focus on "the emotional and relational challenges arising from the direct experience of participants' practice with service users, supervisees or…the organisational systems for which they are responsible" (p. 11). Each group has a facilitator, sometimes from within the organization and sometimes provided externally. This is significant in relation to Lees and Cooper's finding that participants in externally facilitated groups rated the impact of reflective practice groups on their practice more positively than those who attended internally facilitated groups.

Schwartz Rounds – as an example of the provision of support outside traditional supervision, several areas in England have trialed the use of Schwartz Rounds (Wilkins and Forrester 2019). These originate from the healthcare sector, and are structured, monthly meetings, open to staff at all levels and from all backgrounds (Goodrich 2012). At each Round, a panel of volunteers share a story about their working life, usually based on a theme, for example "a child or family I will never forget" or "a day my work made a difference." Rounds are not designed to replace traditional supervision and indeed, part of the model is to provide a different kind of space for reflection, without the need to make decisions or audit casework. There is some evidence from healthcare settings that they help staff to feel more compassionate about people who use services and to feel more connected with one another (Maben et al. 2018).

Firstline and the Practice Supervisor Development Programme (PSDP) – finally, in England there are now two national training programs available for supervisors and other managers. Despite the complexity and specialist skills needed for the supervisory role, most supervisors in child and family settings report having received no formal training and having to rely instead primarily on their own experience as a supervisee to inform how they supervise others (albeit training is not necessarily a straight-forward solution; Kavanagh et al. 2011). Firstline (funded by the Department for Education and provided by the Frontline organization) and the PSDP (also funded by the Department for Education and provided by a consortium including the Tavistock and Portman NHS Foundation Trust, Goldsmiths University of London, the University of Sussex, and Research in Practice) are helping to address this training gap. While the PSDP has yet to be formally evaluated, a recent evaluation of Firstline found that the first cohort of participants "gave overwhelmingly positive feedback [saying that] it represented the best training and professional development they had received as managers and leaders" (Holmes et al. 2017, p. 8). Positive effects of the program were said to include learning how to promote professional development, effectively holding workers to account, and analysis and decision-making. In any event, the significance of these two programs may not (yet) be their tangible results, but simply their very existence, showing that at long last, the question of what training and support are needed by supervisors is being addressed.

In the use of Schwartz Rounds, and various forms of group supervision, we see an example of how supervision can be diverse and pluralistic, meeting the needs of workers, and those of the wider organization, not simply through one-to-one supervision but via a range of different methods working in tandem (O'Donoghue 2015).

Theorizing supervision for child and family social work

As important as it is to consider the empirical evidence and practice innovations being realized in relation to child and family supervision, it is as important to develop good theories about how and why supervision works (or not) in this context. As the old saying has it, there is "nothing so practical as a good theory" (McCain 2015). A context-specific theory of child and family supervision need not however start from a blank slate. There are many good existing models and theories of supervision (e.g. O'Donoghue et al. 2017), and any specific theories adapted to child and family settings can be developed from these helpful starting points.

One such foundational idea is that supervision has three primary functions – administration, education, and support (Kadushin 1992). The administrative function means ensuring that workers adhere to agency policies and procedures (p. 20). The education function means to develop the worker's knowledge, attitudes, and skills in order for them to perform their job to a high-standard. Support means to ensure the worker's well-being, including to maintain their morale and job satisfaction. To provide support, "the supervisor seeks to prevent the development of potentially stressful situations, removes the worker from stress, reduces stress impinging on the worker, and helps her [sic] adjust to stress." (Kadushin 1992, p. 292). A good starting point is to compare these (universal?) functions of good supervision with what child and family social workers say about their own experiences.

In a recent study in England, Pitt et al. (in press) interviewed 50 social workers and supervisors and asked them about the function and purpose of their supervision. From these interviews, four primary functions were identified – oversight and accountability, support and guidance, providing an outside perspective, and keeping a focus on the child. In another study, this time of 300 social workers and supervisors via an online survey, respondents said that supervision helped with seven key aspects of practice – management oversight, clarity about task (what to do), clarity about timescales (by when), professional development, analysis and reflection, and emotional support (Wilkins and Antonopoulou 2018). Table 13.3 shows how these various functions compare with those previously identified by Kadushin.

Table 13.3 A comparison between Kadushin's model of supervisory functions and the results of empirical interviews and surveys with social workers and supervisors

Kadushin's model of supervision	*Social worker and supervisor interviews*	*Social worker and supervisor survey*
Administration	Management oversight *and* accountability	Management oversight *and* clarity about task and timescales
Education	Outside perspective *and* support and guidance	Professional development *and* analysis and reflection
Support	Outside perspective *and* support and guidance Child-focus	Emotional support

These findings indicate that the functions identified by Kadushin are broadly similar to those identified in practice by social workers and supervisors. However, they also show how some of these universal functions of good supervision need to be adapted or added to for this specific context. In Pitt et al.'s (in press) study, the additional function of child-focus was considered to be critical by many of the workers and supervisors alike. Child-focus here refers to the role that supervision plays in ensuring that the child's needs and experiences remain at the heart of everything the worker does. This suggests that a theory of child and family social work supervision would need to take account of the particular legal context in which it takes place. In a variety of ways, all modern systems of child protection provide for the paramountcy of the child's welfare, over and above all other considerations. Good supervision in this context must therefore contribute towards this end, by ensuring the worker's focus remains on the child and his or her welfare.

From a review of previously published papers (Wilkins 2019), other potential nuances and areas for development in our existing theoretical ideas can be identified (Figure 13.1). For example, much more thought has been given to the qualities of a good supervisor than to the qualities of a good supervisee. This is especially significant when we consider that just as "you cannot force people to learn by bringing them into a classroom" (Lees and Cooper 2017, p. 7), so you cannot make someone think reflectively, or analytically, simply by inviting them (or mandating them) into a supervisory space. Equally, there is potential for further theoretical development linking what happens in supervision with outcomes for children and families. As outlined above, there are now some empirical studies that have considered this relationship. Yet the question of outcomes in children's services is much more complicated than these studies have so far suggested (Forrester 2017). Child and family social workers are not solely concerned with changing (behavioral or otherwise measurable) outcomes, for example the child's school attendance or family functioning (important those these kinds of outcomes can be). Just as importantly (or even more so), child and family social workers are promoters and enablers of human rights (Mapp et al. 2019). Deciding not to intervene in the private life of a family is a critical decision, and just as important as any decision to intervene. But by definition, not-intervening is unlikely to make much different to the family's outcomes. Understanding more about how good supervision can inform ethical decision-making and help embed and sustain a human rights approach in practice is key. In nursing, for example, certain approaches to supervision have been associated with more ethical decision-making (Magnusson et al. 2002). The same may well be true for child and family services – but as noted by O'Donoghue and O'Donoghue (2019) there is a distinct lack of research evidence in this area. As further suggested by the same authors, ethics could be integrated within the supervision process based on a model of care ethics, whereby moral action is achieved via the provision of benevolent care within the context of interpersonal relationships (something that would appear a priori to be a good fit with wider social work values).

Summary

Although there is a widespread consensus about the need for high-quality supervision within the context of child and family social work, a consensus is not the same as an evidence base (Beddoe and Wilkins 2019). And an evidence base is not the same as a robust and explanatory theoretical model. As we have seen in this chapter, there are many challenges to the contemporary practice of supervision within child and family settings (at least in many of them, if not all). As the system overall has taken an increasingly investigative turn (Bilson and Martin 2017), so supervision has become more and more about the managerial surveillance of practice. These challenges are echoed in many observational and self-report empirical studies. And however

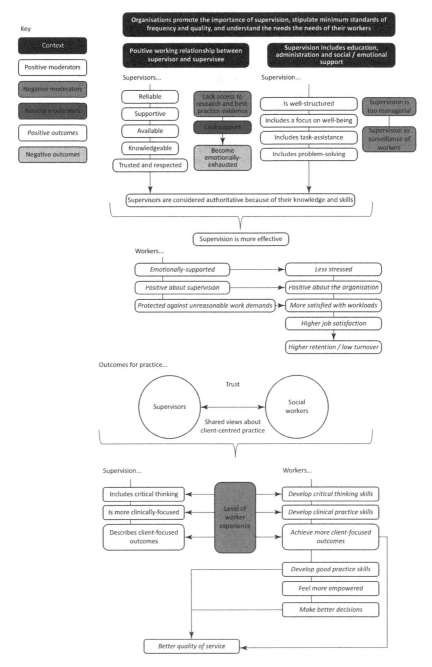

Figure 13.1 A preliminary model of good supervision for child and family services. Source: (Wilkins 2019, p.13) reprinted with permission of the Editor of the *Aotearoa New Zealand Social Work Journal*

highly we might rate the potential influence of supervision, it seems probable that it is supervision which has been influenced by the changing nature of the system, rather than supervision which is responsible for leading the change. If so, any efforts to improve supervision that do not also attempt to make more general improvements in practice and culture are likely to fail or at most achieve a modest success. Efforts to introduce portfolio approaches to meeting the needs of workers are one potential avenue. Whole-system changes, such as the introduction of systemic models of practice, are another. But we still have some way to go before we can truly say we have achieved the necessary level of empirical and theoretical knowledge of when, where, and why such approaches work, for workers certainly, but primarily for children and their families.

References

Baginsky, M., Moriarty, J., Manthorpe, J., Stevens, M., MacInnes, T., and Nagendran, T., 2010. *Social workers' workload survey, messages from the frontline*. London: Social Work Task Force.

Beddoe, L., 2010. Surveillance or reflection: professional supervision in the risk society. *British Journal of Social Work*, 40 (4), 1279–1296.

Beddoe, L., 2016. Supervision in social work in Aotearoa New Zealand: challenges in changing contexts. *The Clinical Supervisor*, 35 (2), 156–174.

Beddoe, L., and Wilkins, D., 2019. Does the consensus about the value of supervision in social work stifle research and innovation?. *Aotearoa New Zealand Social Work*, 31 (3), 1–6.

Bilson, A., and Martin, K., 2017. Referrals and child protection in England: one in five children referred to children's services and one in nineteen investigated before the age of five. *British Journal of Social Work*, 47 (3), 793–811.

Bostock, L., Forrester, D., Patrizo, L., Godfrey, T., Zonouzi, M., Antonopoulou, V., Bird, H., and Tinarwo, M., 2017. *Scaling and deepening the reclaiming social work model*. London: Department for Education.

Bostock, L., Patrizo, L., Godfrey, T., and Forrester, D., 2019. What is the impact of supervision on direct practice with families?. *Children and Youth Services Review*, 105. Available from: https://www.sciencedirect.com/science/article/pii/S0190740919303561 [Accessed 14 February 2020].

Brandon, M., Sidebotham, P., Bailey, S., Belderson, P., Hawley, C., Ellis, C., and Megson, M., 2010. *New learning from serious case reviews: a two-year report in 2009–2011*. London: Department for Education.

Egan, R., 2012. Australian social work supervision practice in 2007. *Australian Social Work*, 65 (2), 171–184.

Egan, R., Maidment, J., and Connolly, M., 2015. Who is watching whom? surveillance in australian social work supervision. *British Journal of Social Work*, 46 (6), 1617–1635.

Featherstone, B., Morris, K., and White, S., 2013. A marriage made in hell: early intervention meets child protection. *British Journal of Social Work*, 44 (7), 1735–1749.

Forrester, D., 2017. Outcomes in children's social care. *Journal of Children's Services*, 12 (2/3), 144–157.

Forrester, D., Killian, M., Westlake, D., and Sheehan, L., 2020. Patterns of practice: an exploratory factor analysis of child and family social worker skills. *Child & Family Social Work*, 25 (1), 108–117.

Forrester, D., Westlake, D., Killian, M., Antonopoulou, V., Mccann, M., Thurnham, A., Thomas, R., Waits, C., Whittaker, C., and Hutchison, D., 2018. A randomized controlled trial of training in motivational interviewing for child protection. *Children and Youth Services Review*, 88, 180–190.

Forrester, D., Westlake, D., Killian, M., Antonopolou, V., McCann, M., Thurnham, A., Thomas, R., Waits, C., Whittaker, C., and Hutchison, D., 2019. What is the relationship between worker skills and outcomes for families in child and family social work?. *The British Journal of Social Work*, 49 (8), 2148–2167.

Goodrich, J., 2012. Supporting hospital staff to provide compassionate care: do Schwartz Center Rounds work in English hospitals?. *Journal of the Royal Society of Medicine*, 105 (3), 117–122.

Heffernan, K., 2005. Social work, new public management and the language of service user. *British Journal of Social Work*, 36 (1), 139–147.

Heyes, L., 2014. Social work needs positive news stories – why are they so hard to tell? *The Guardian*, 10 Jan.

Holmes, L., Thomas, C., Hyde-Dryden, G., and Williams, A., 2017. *Firstline Evaluation Report*. London: Department for Education.

Kadushin, A., 1992. *Supervision in Social Work*. 3rd ed. New York: Columbia University.

Kavanagh, D., Spence, S., Sturk, H., Strong, J., Wilson, J., Worrall, L., Crow, N., and Skerrett, R., 2011. Outcomes of training in supervision: randomised controlled trial. *Australian Psychologist*, 43 (2), 96–104.

Lees, A., and Cooper, A., 2017. *Evaluation of reflective practice group project*. London: Centre for Social Work Practice.

Maben, J., Taylor, C., Dawson, J., Leamy, M., Mccarthy, I., Reynolds, E., Ross, S., Shuldham, C., Bennett, L., and Foot, C., 2018. A realist informed mixed-methods evaluation of Schwartz Center Rounds in England. *Health Services and Delivery Research*, 6 (37), 1–260.

Magnusson, A., Lutzen, K., and Severinsson, E., 2002. The influence of clinical supervision on ethical issues in home care of people with mental illness in Sweden. *Journal of Nursing Management*, 10 (1), 37–45.

Manthorpe, J., Moriarty, J., Hussein, S., Stevens, M., and Sharpe, E., 2013. Content and purpose of supervision in social work practice in England: views of newly qualified social workers, managers and directors. *British Journal of Social Work*, 45 (1), 52–68.

Mapp, S., Mcpherson, J., Androff, D., and Gabel, S.G., 2019. Social work is a human rights profession. *Social Work*, 64 (3), 259–269.

McCain, K., 2015. "Nothing as practical as a good theory" does Lewin's maxim still have salience in the applied social sciences?. *Proceedings of the Association for Information Science and Technology*, 51 (1), 1–4.

Munro, E., 2009. Beyond the blame culture. *The Guardian*, 3 Nov.

Munro, E., 2011. *The munro review of child protection, interim report: the child's journey*. London: Stationary Office.

National Association of Social Workers 2013. *Best practice standards in social work supervision*. Washington, DC: National Association of Social Workers.

O'Donoghue, K., 2015. Issues and challenges facing social work supervision in the twenty-first century. *China Journal of Social Work*, 8 (2), 136–149.

O'Donoghue, K., and O'Donoghue, R., 2019. The application of ethics within social work supervision: a selected literature and research review. *Ethics and Social Welfare*, 13 (4), 340–360.

O'Donoghue, K., and Tsui, M.-S., 2011. Towards a professional supervision culture: the development of social work supervision in Aotearoa New Zealand. *International Social Work*, 55 (1), 5–28.

O'Donoghue, K., Wong Yuh Ju, P., and Tsui, M.-S., 2017. Constructing an evidence-informed social work supervision model. *European Journal of Social Work*, 21 (3), 348–358.

Pitt, C., Addis, S., and Wilkins, D., in press. What do social workers and supervisors think about their supervision? *Child and Family Social Work*.

Sewell, K.M., 2018. Social work supervision of staff: a primer and scoping review (2013–2017). *Clinical Social Work Journal*, 46 (4), 252–265.

Shoesmith, S., 2016. *Learning from Baby P*. London: Jessica Kingsley.

Tsui, M.-S., 1997. The roots of social work supervision. *The Clinical Supervisor*, 15 (2), 191–198.

Watkins, C.E., and Milne, D.L., 2014. Clinical supervision at the international crossroads. *In*: C.E. Watkins and D.L. Milne, eds. *The Wiley international handbook of clinical supervision*. West Sussex: John Wiley & Sons, 671–696.

Whittaker, C., Forrester, D., Killian, M., and Jones, R., 2017. Can we reliably measure social work communication skills? Development of a scale to measure child and family work direct practice. *International Journal of Child and Family Welfare*, 17 (1–2), 47–63.

Wilkins, D., 2019. Social work supervision in child and family services: developing a working theory of how and why it works. *Aotearoa New Zealand Social Work*, 31 (3), 7–19.

Wilkins, D., and Antonopoulou, V., 2018. What does supervision help with? A survey of 315 social workers in the UK. *Practice*, 31 (1), 21–40.

Wilkins, D., and Forrester, D., 2019. *Trial evaluation protocol, Schwartz Rounds*. London: What Works for Children's Social Care.

Wilkins, D., Forrester, D., and Grant, L., 2017. What happens in child and family social work supervision? *Child & Family Social Work*, 22 (2), 942–951.

Wilkins, D., Lynch, A., and Antonopoulou, V., 2018. A golden thread? The relationship between supervision, practice, and family engagement in child and family social work. *Child & Family Social Work*, 23 (3), 494–503.

14

SUPERVISION IN ADULT CARE SETTINGS

Sharon Lambley

In this chapter supervision research from national studies are used to examine our understanding of supervision in adult care settings. Three propositions are examined. The first proposition is that supervision is primarily a professional concern that it is not affected by the setting in which it takes place. The second proposition is that the setting for supervision is an important concern because it can negatively and/or positively affect supervision in adult care settings. The third proposition is that interactions between adult care settings and individuals need to be considered together because this is where the most interesting aspects of supervision can be found. This chapter concludes by identifying the emerging challenges for supervision in adult care settings.

The international context

The first observation to make when reviewing the supervision literature is that there is a lack of international comparative research. Secondly, qualitative research studies into supervision tend to focus on supervision in children and family settings, where the professional discourse informing supervision has remained strong. Thirdly, supervision in adult care settings may differ to supervision in children and family settings because workers may not be trained in social work supervision, and the relationships between workers and citizens are often determined by neo-liberal and citizen rights discourses, rather than professional ones (Lambley 2018). Supervision in adult care settings therefore, is a complex topic to research because of the diversity of provision, multiple worker roles, and the variety of supervision approaches and practices. Demonstrating outcomes from supervision is a significant research challenge because of this complexity. For example, an adult care setting could be a person's home, a hospital, nursing or residential home, a day care facility, hostel, supervised housing, a mental health assessment unit, etc. An adult care setting could be tailored for specific groups such as adults with learning disabilities, autism, or mental health or physical disabilities. Some services only target adults of a particular age or adults with more than one care need, for example older adults with a learning disability in sheltered housing. Adult care services are often provided by many types of professionals that work together to deliver a service. These settings may or may not employ social workers and/or social work supervisors. Ornellas et al. (2019) investigated social work settings in ten countries and suggested that "greater employment through the state is found in England, Spain, Italy, Russia and Turkey, whereas India, China and South Africa demonstrate a higher concentration of social workers in the non-governmental and private sectors" (Engelbrecht and Strydom 2013). Takeda et al. (2005, p. 119) found Japanese social workers employed in "health facilities, psychiatric units, services for public assistance, the disabled, the elderly, families and children." Supervisors of social workers are not always employed in the organization where the supervisee works (Rankine 2019). Belardi (2002, p. 316) found some self-employed social work supervisors in Germany provided supervision in counseling, education, and many other fields of practice, because they viewed "themselves as all round supervisors for many fields and problems". In New Zealand, Rankine (2019) conducted research that highlighted the benefits and challenges of using external supervisors. In the United States, supervisors must be licensed to supervise, whilst in some countries untrained social workers in line management positions with no fieldwork experience may also supervise social workers (Engelbrecht 2019). To add to this picture, new care worker roles have emerged in many adult care settings in response to the development of care markets (Ornellas et al. 2019). These new workers often complete tasks which social workers may have undertaken previously and these "other professionals or less skilled/qualified individuals are being employed at a lower rate for social work functions" (Ornellas et al. 2019. p 1188). As supervision in adult care settings evolves, research from comparative studies into supervision in adult care settings could help us to understand how supervision continues to evolve at a global level. Studies to date are largely nationally based, but they have examined *how* social work supervision has developed, *what* knowledge and practices *inform* supervision, and *why* supervisors do what they do (Mo et al. 2020; Fortune 2014; Harkness and Poertner 1989). Three key points have emerged from the research.

Firstly, how supervision is conceptualized matters. For example, a first conceptualization of social work is as a professional project (McDonald 2006). From this perspective, professional associations and groups establish professional authority and legitimacy for social work through a variety of mechanisms, for example the International Federation of Social Work (IFSW) "promotes the idea of social work as a set of processes (doing social work), an identity (a social worker), and a coherent entity (the profession of social work) which transcends national borders" (McDonald 2006, p. 14). Professional social work and supervision is defined in international and national standards in many countries, although many supervisors find themselves in roles that are at odds with these standards. A second conceptualization of supervision is by way of an historical analysis, in which early adopter countries (for example UK, United States, Canada, Australia etc.) developed social casework and practice knowledge providing a blueprint for social work and supervision practice, which was later transmitted around the world. The contribution of human and social science theories in social work and supervision has encouraged conflictual and contested approaches to emerge, but in recent years the knowledge base for the supervision of social work has become increasingly focused on evidence informed interventions. The appropriateness of having one international blueprint for supervision has been challenged in recent years in some countries (Engelbrecht 2019; Mo et al. 2019) whilst supervision knowledge and practice continues to be challenged by management and citizen rights discourses that require professional accountability and the evaluation of outcomes. This is a particular issue for supervision in adult care settings because there has been a growth in care markets around the world so many adult care settings are not supported by social work for care, as new assistant and support roles have emerged, which has created the conditions for many conceptualizations of supervision to emerge (Lambley 2019). This can be a challenge for social workers who may be the only professional employed in a work setting, and their supervisor could be a manager from another professional group or not professionally trained. In these situations how supervision is conceptualized in very important for social workers.

Secondly, the purpose of supervision matters. Harkness and Poertner (1989, p. 115) suggest that social work was built on the foundations of supervision, because supervisors supervised volunteers and "the belief was that supervised practice would result in better client outcomes" (Burns 1958). However, Harkness and Poertner (1989, p. 115) suggest that supervisors shifted the purpose of supervision from delivering better client outcomes to training workers. Today, the Australian Association of Social Workers (2014, p. 2) describes the purpose of supervision as enhancing the professional skills and competence of social workers to "achieve positive outcomes for the people with whom they work," which is a view that is widely accepted. Supervisors seek to enable the delivery of better outcomes through processes supported by critical reflection and learning. For Harkness and Poertner (1989) research into supervision became too focused on the professional development needs of social workers and practice, and feedback on client outcomes were routinely provided by professionals on behalf of service users (Lambley 2019). The professional discourses that support service user experiences being provided by professionals is being challenged by citizen and human rights discourses (Healy 2014), international research standards that require service users to validate research outcomes (Goldman 2013), management discourses that seek evaluation evidence and accountability for practice, and research agendas that seek to evidence "what works" (Pawson and Tilley 2004). All of these challenges are contested, not least because they threaten long accepted professional discourses and practices, but they also challenge the professional construction of the purpose of supervision.

Thirdly, what supervisors do, matters. Research by Kadushin (1976) produced a model of supervision with three functions, which included administration, education, and support. This, and later models, have been used to de-construct supervisor activities, leading to research that suggests supervisors in many adult care settings spend a lot of time on addressing management concerns in supervision, thereby distorting professional supervision (Dustin 2007; Harris 2014). In other studies, where management and professional supervision is separated, there is research that suggests supervision can focus on professional concerns and providing personal support, although dual models of supervision are not without challenges (Davys et al. 2017; Beddoe 2010; Bradley and Hojer 2009). What supervisors do in the supervisory relationship has been explored by Ellis et al. (2015) who identified three types of supervision: inadequate, harmful, and exceptional, and found little differences between occurrence rates of each across the United States and the Republic of Ireland. Given conflict will arise in supervision, it is important to be concerned with what supervisors do and the dynamics of supervision. New models of supervision have emerged (O'Donoghue et al. 2018; Lambley 2018) but many are untested (Carpenter et al. 2012) although they can enable greater understanding of what is happening in supervision and how this impacts on client outcomes.

To explore what is happening in supervision in adult care settings, the first proposition will now be considered, drawing on two examples from mental health social work supervision in hospital settings in South Korea and Australia.

Supervision is a professional concern that is not affected by its setting

The supervision of social workers in South Korea emerged in the 1950s after the Vietnam war. As South Korea moved towards developing a system of welfare, social work emerged as part of this project. Fieldwork supervision was integral to educational developments to train social workers in basic social welfare, human behavior, and social sciences. Professional social work was heavily influenced by psychosocial approaches in casework, which were imported from the USA. Whilst variations in quality and the content of courses have emerged, the focus of social work training was on the development of professional knowledge and practices. Specialty courses in mental health, medical, and school social work were created, supported by training programs and certification. Supervisors were expected to be qualified social workers with one year practice experience. They were expected to have been supervised by someone with a doctorate degree, and to have gained a supervision certificate to practice. Supervision curricula also was imported from the United States and included topics such as supervision theory, casework, attitudes and roles of fieldwork supervisors, resource development, organization management, and administration etc. (Han and Lim 2014). Specialist social work training was also developed with employers. During the 1960s, hospital social workers delivered psychosocial services, which provided "emotional support to patients and families to alleviate the potential impact of the diagnosis and the treatment process" (Nam et al. 2019, p. 703). Social workers were integral to multi-disciplinary treatment teams and took part in hospital ward rounds. By the 1970s the legal and institutional basis for social work in hospital settings was established and "[p]sychosocial problem solving was the most important role of South Korean hospital social workers by the late 1990s" (Nam et al. 2019, p. 706). However, in the late 1990s South Korea introduced welfare policies supporting the marketization of care, which led to changes in social worker roles (Chon 2019). Nam et al.'s (2019) survey of 198 South Korean hospital social workers concluded that social work priorities had changed, as providing finance and community support was now more significant than psychosocial work because it was ranked by participants as fourth out of eight social work activities. Nam et al. (2019, p. 713) suggested that "[i]n the 1990s, efforts to reduce escalating costs were more urgently required. When cost reduction became the most important issue, the roles of the traditional hospital social worker were reduced, and the middle management system, which played the supervisory role, collapsed" (Neuman 2003). Psychosocial interventions were re-prioritized at a time when "supervisory responsibilities shifted from social work based professions to other disciplines, such as physicians, nurses or others" (Nam et al. 2019, p. 713). When comparing these changes with hospital social work in the United States, Nam et al. (2019, p. 713) suggest that hospital social workers in the United States also became less involved in psychosocial social work interventions having become more focused on discharge planning "in order to ensure full re-imbursement for hospital services." They suggest that hospital social workers were needed to safeguard hospital income and to mobilize community resources. Lymbery (2006) argues that the status and power of social work in hospital settings in the UK, when examined alongside other professional groups, was transformed when power shifted from practitioners to managers.

> A major part of the problem was that hospital staff particularly valued the social workers ability to gain access to resources, placing them under pressure to resolve practical problems and arrange for the provision of services. Whilst practitioners maintained the importance of counseling skills to their work, their practice was more in accordance with the administrative priorities that governed the hospital – particularly in respect of hospital discharge.
>
> *(Lymbery 2006, p. 1126)*

This insight is helpful when considering what has been happening in South Korea. In Australia, Renouf and Bland (2005) caution against social work complacency in mental health workplace settings, because, they suggest, these are contested environments where other professionals could colonize traditional social work practice areas. In Australia, threats to the supervision of mental health social workers also emerged in the 1990s in response to policy developments which emphasized the need for evidence-based interventions and professional accountability. According to Renouf and Bland (2005) the reforms were based on two principles: participation is a right (i.e., consumers have the right to be fully involved in planning, delivering, and evaluating services) and participation ensures better services (i.e., participation can strengthen accountability mechanisms and increase responsiveness). These principles are informed by managerialist ideas, which Trevithick (2014) has identified as the three M's: market, managers, and measurement (Ferlie et al. 1996) and the three E's: economy, efficiency, and effectiveness (Audit Commission 1983, p. 8). However, Renouf and Bland (2005, p. 421) suggest that such ideas are not at odds with social work because "[t]he emphasis upon human rights, and providing services for the most needy groups, accord strongly with the social justice principles of the profession." However, tensions have arisen with regards to what changes have been made and how changes have been introduced including new social worker roles, practices, and the need to evaluate outcomes, and all of this must be supported by supervision. Renouf and Bland (2005, p. 421) suggest that social workers have participated in "new models of service provision as case managers, therapists, disability support workers, and sometimes consultants and community workers, but there has been no well-articulated identification of the distinctive social work contribution within modern mental health services." As many mental health social workers are located in multi-disciplinary teams, there are many supervision arrangements to be found in practice settings (O'Donoghue 2015). The Australian Association of Social Workers supports the use of external social work supervisors, but where social workers are supervised by other professionals, the advice is that "[i]n all circumstances, the goal of social work supervision is to ensure that the purpose, functions and standards of supervision are achieved" (AASW 2014, p. 2). The use of external social work supervisors takes place within challenging work environments. Cosgrave et al. (2015) identified a range of challenges in multi-professional teams including conflicts over models of care, role confusion, gaps in training, and challenges to decision-making. Some mental health social workers have responded with "ambivalence and caution to the requirement that interventions in mental health should be evidence based" (Renouf and Bland 2005, p. 426). However, the predominantly clinically based settings require social workers to develop a viable paradigm for practice that supports effective psychosocial interventions in mental health, and to affirm the role and purpose of social work in multi-professional practice settings (Renouf and Bland 2005). Whilst evidence is emerging of effective social work practice interventions (Renouf and Bland 2005), supervisors of social work practice are also required to support social workers to challenge medical models and medically based interventions where social models may be more appropriate, to ensure better outcomes for service users. This can be most helpfully achieved in group supervision where clinical and professional discourses are encouraged to co-exist, but this can also be a challenge.

The degree to which the marketization of care is impacting on the conceptualization, purpose, and practice of supervision in mental health settings will vary within countries and around the world, but what is evident is that social work supervision is under threat. The threats not only include losing supervisor roles (and social workers), but where social work supervision remains, the work environment may be as hostile to social work practice knowledge, and the low status and power of social workers in these environments can also undermine practice. Professional supervision appears to be less protected in some settings whilst it has been changed in others, although the supervision of social work remains a professional concern. To understand what is happening to professional supervision, we now need to examine the second proposition.

The supervision setting can negatively or positively impact on supervision

Changes to the conceptualization and purpose of social work in adult care settings has impacted negatively on professional supervision in some adult care settings because some supervisors have become overseers of care manager assessments to establish if adults are eligible for care services, rather than supervisors of social work practice to deliver better client outcomes (Dustin 2007). The introduction of customers, consumers, and co-producers in adult care settings has provided managers with narratives that enable them to replace social work. There have been mixed-responses to new service developments in the UK from service users (Lambley 2018), and research from around the world suggests that in adult care settings many managers of professional supervision have been changing what supervisors do, and this is largely unwelcome (Engelbrecht 2019; Nam et al. 2019; Egan 2012; Noelker et al. 2009; Beddoe 2012). The introduction of international and national standards and dual, peer, or group supervision models, however, has enabled some social work supervisors to retain control over professional supervision (O'Donoghue 2015), and therefore not all work settings have been negatively impacted by managerialism, particularly where management and supervisors have been able to collaborate (Evans 2010; Lambley 2010). These developments are now examined in research from Canada and Sweden.

In Canada, Hair (2012, p. 1563) observed that "throughout the world social workers and social work supervisors have been expressing growing concerns about the diminishing availability and decreased quality of supervision and the potentially negative effects for service delivery" (Beddoe 2010; Bogo and McKnight 2005; Noble and Irwin 2009). In a study of 636 Canadian social workers who worked in hospitals, adult mental health, community health, child welfare, or children mental health centers in Ontario, social workers were asked what they needed from supervisors. They said that supervisors needed to support knowledge and skills development in supervision (96%) and emotional support (90%) as well as address administration tasks (80%) to enable them to maintain accountability for their work. Respondents said that "supervision conversations are needed to help social workers 'self-reflect' and think about their own personal and professional functioning (p. 33), engage in critical thinking and dialogue (p. 260), and to work through ethical challenges of the work I do (p. 319)" (Hair 2012, p. 1574). Concerns were raised about a lack of trust when management agendas dominated professional supervision, and it was suggested that two supervisors (one management and one professional) or a line manager and external supervisors could address this issue. Respondents asked for new systems of accountability for supervisor practice, which they wanted to be informed by feedback from social workers on the performance of supervisors. Social workers wanted supervisors to demonstrate appropriate ethics, skills, and knowledge to support social work practice, and a positive approach to accountability. These results are not untypical of research findings from around the world where the introduction of care by markets has undermined professional supervision (Engelbrecht 2019; Rankine 2019; Wong and Lee 2015; Egan 2012; Beddoe 2012). What is significant is the call for supervisors to behave ethically and within the professional standards that inform social work practice, rather than adopt management discourses, which impact negatively on supervisor behavior and practices (Hair 2012).

In Sweden, "the call for supervision was strong in the latter part of the 1980s as part of the drive for professional recognition. One of the mottos at the time was social workers should be supervised by social workers, a response to the fact that psychologists dominated the scene" (Bradley and Hojer 2009, p. 75). Seven principles were developed for supervision. They included offering continuous contracted supervision that is obligatory, that integrates all aspects of social work, and helps social workers to reflect on themselves and their practice. The supervisor was to be part of the group supervision and offer expertise but had the responsibility for the process of supervision rather than direct practice with clients (Bradley and Hojer 2009, p. 75). External supervision was highly rated in this study in Sweden because external supervisors provide work related and emotional support and "although it is not the remit of external supervision, the format is used to make decisions on individual cases, to improve understanding and find new approaches to the tasks." Some respondents however, were critical of external supervision saying that supervisors could be too passive, not able to facilitate or lead group sessions or not sensitive enough to the group needs. Beddoe (2012) raises issues about contracting out supervision and accountability issues, suggesting that external supervision could compromise the safety of social worker, manager, professional supervisor, or service user if not provided at a high standard. Bradley and Hojer (2009, p. 76) noted that some managers were critical of external supervision too because they felt that external supervisors were sometimes overpaid when compared to line managers, that they sometimes exceeded their authority, and that some interfered in areas of management practice. Rankine (2019) found that external supervision had an important role to play in supporting social work discourses, facilitating reflection and critical thinking, empowering social workers to engage in professional thinking and practice, and being helped to help others. These research studies suggest that in order understand the interactions between adult care settings and individuals in supervision, we need to examine a third proposition.

Interactions between adult care settings and individuals need to be considered together

To examine the third proposition, it is helpful to use a model constructed by O'Donoghue et al. (2018), which was developed using research evidence from around the world. The model consists of five elements. The first element refers to how social work supervision is constructed. O'Donoghue et al. (2018) found that administration, education, and support, which define the three functions of supervision (Kadushin 1976), dominate the supervision literature, but how these three functions are balanced within supervision varies, which suggests that there are many "supervisions." The second element is the supervision of the practitioner. The research suggests workers prefer supervisors that are helpful, informative, supportive, and enabling (O'Donoghue et al. 2018). The third element is the supervisory relationship which involves trust, support, honesty, openness etc. Where these aspects are lacking, individuals can employ tactics to avoid, subvert, or undermine the authority of the supervisor. The fourth element is the interactional process, where supervision "moves through phases of preparation, engagement, planning, working and endings. It also involves constructive interactive discursive exchanges between the supervise and supervisor" (O'Donoghue et al. 2018, p. 351). The fifth element is the supervision of practice, where supervisors develop "a constructive, considerate, culturally competent and caring relationship with their supervisees" (O'Donoghue et al. 2018, p. 351). O'Donoghue (2018, p. 352) suggests that these elements are dynamic and contingent upon "the organizational and professional practice setting, the supervisee, supervisor and issues presented in supervision." Using this framework, it is possible to review the research findings from China and South Africa.

Mo et al. (2019) argues that all the supervision functions are present in social work supervision in China. However, there is no requirement for agency-based supervisors to be professionally qualified social workers, or to have relevant practice experience (Xiong and Wang 2007). In addition, some social workers did not have formal social work training and they were very dependent upon supervisor support and learning in practice settings (Shen and Wang 2013). This situation means that in some settings, supervision is largely constructed by managers. Pilot projects are underway in parts of China, as the need for good supervision of practice has merged as the training and education of supervisors remains patchy (Mo et al. 2019). Cultural considerations in supervision have led to a focus on indigenized supervision relationships and practices. "Chinese culture emphasizes the importance of building the supervisor relationship and creating a harmonious and warm relationship among team members. Moreover, a supervisor needs to ensure a balance between authority and kindness to cope with different situations and the needs of supervisees" (Mo et al. 2019, p. 353). Adding a cultural dimension to how supervision is constructed enables the supervision of practice to be respectful, and culturally competent, and an acceptance of the authority of the supervisor. However, Wong and Lee (2015, p. 165) suggest that conflict can emerge between social workers and managers, which can create tensions that leave "social work supervisors feeling caught in the middle." The administration requirements of the supervisory role can undermine professional supervision. For example, it can be very challenging to address capability issues whilst trying to motivate and develop social workers (Wong and Lee 2015). Dual supervision models are emerging in some regions which focus on separating administration from education and support functions, and this has enabled external supervisors to focus on the training and development needs of workers, and the delivery of good client outcomes. Feedback from supervised social workers has been very positive, and there is evidence of peer support activities emerging in some regions of China. The professional process of reflection and learning in supervision impacted positively on social workers who have received support in pilot projects. The model developed by O'Donoghue et al. (2018), when applied to the Chinese situation, highlights the challenge posed by untrained social work supervisors, who have management and supervision responsibilities. However, even where supervisors are trained social workers, the demands of the management role can create tension. This situation is not unique to China.

In South Africa, after the African National Congress party came to power in 1994, social work became part of a welfare system where social development was adopted as the means to achieve purposeful and equitable redistribution of resources to bring about social justice. Developmental social work was part of an overall strategy to achieve social cohesion and system transformation. However, two areas have emerged as problems: supervision in employment settings, and the social work curricula. A review of largely South African supervision literature in employment settings was undertaken with a view to analyze the evidence, and to de-colonize the literature. Engelbrecht (2019) proposed a South African conceptualization of supervision, and a definition of supervision was developed from the literature. The purpose of supervision was to "render the best possible services to the user system" (Engelbrecht 2019, p. 318). Using O'Donoghue et al.'s (2018) supervision model to evaluate the findings, supervision was constructed in terms of functional activities which include administration, education, and support (Kadushin 1976), but it was suggested that the balance of these functions needed to change because "Western-infused and neo-liberal features, are contributing to the fact that social work supervision practices in South Africa are generally more managerially driven than clinically orientated" (Engelbrecht 2019, p. 301). In terms of the supervision of the practitioner, the Social Services Professions Act (RSA 1978) stipulates that only a "competent and registered social worker may supervise another social worker. In reality, however, non-social workers often perform this task much to the detriment of social work practice" (Engelbrecht 2019). This weak employer compliance is an issue for the profession. The supervisor relationship and the interactional process needs to be "a professional, constructive supervisor-supervisee relationship," and the supervision of practice needs to provide a structured, interactional supervision session that is "directed by adult education principles in a cyclical process with associated tasks, methods, and activities, according to a predetermined time-span, based on authoritative theories, perspectives, and practice models" (Engelbrecht 2019, p. 318). However, the research suggests that this is not currently happening in many work settings, as staff are overworked, not adequately supervised, and struggling to deliver the outcomes required. Drawing from Lambley's (2018) semi-open supervision systems model, a developmental program for supervision could identify and address gaps in work settings supported by curricula developments, which would contribute to the development of national supervision system in South Africa and improve the interactions between adult care settings and individuals, which need to be considered together.

Conclusion

The emerging challenges for social work supervision focus around understanding how supervision can be delivered in adult care settings in ways that enable social workers to improve outcomes for adults. The three propositions demonstrate that supervision is a professional concern, but it is under threat from neo-liberal ideologies, management discourses, and practices. In adult care settings, citizen rights discourses also have an impact on policy and legislative developments, which is challenging social work and supervision discourses. There is much that needs to change to improve supervision in adult care settings. Evans' (2010) research into supervision in an older people and a mental health team in an English Local Authority organization, found supervision could be a site of collaboration or conflict, depending on how supervisors (who were first line managers) *and* social workers, responded to issues that affected outcomes for adults, for example service eligibility, the use of professional discretion, resource decisions, etc. One social work team experienced conflict because managers took decisions without consulting social workers whilst a second group worked together to find solutions (Evans 2010). In the second group, the supervisors (who were also first line managers) were professionally trained social workers and they used their professional training to inform their management role, which included the supervision of social workers. These different responses are interesting. Whittington (2015) uses structuration theory to explain how structure provides the resources that make action happen, and the rules that guide it. He suggests that managers are agents by virtue of their control over resources and their powers are shared in the system . Where social workers and first line managers can work together there is scope for professional supervision to be supported. However, Evans (2010) noted that organizational fractures were evident in the Local Authority because middle and senior managers were focused on organizational survival, whilst front line managers were focused on professional issues. There is an argument to be made therefore, that professional concerns need to be integral to all parts of supervision systems (Lambley 2018) if supervision in adult care settings is to survive the current threats.

References

Audit Commission 1983. *Performance review in local government: a handbook for auditors and local authorities.* London: Audit Commission.

Australian Association of Social Workers (AASW) 2014. *Supervision standards.* Available from: http://www.aasw.asn.au/document/item/6027 [Accessed 21 June 2020].

Beddoe, L., 2010. Surveillance or reflection: professional supervision in "the risk society". *British Journal of Social Work*, 40 (4), 1279–1296.

Beddoe, L., 2012. External supervision in social work: power, space, risk, and the search for safety. *Australian Social Work*, 65 (2), 197–213.

Belardi, N., 2002. Social work supervision in Germany. *European Journal of Social Work*, 5 (3), 313–318.

Bogo, M., and McKnight, K., 2005. Clinical supervision in social work: a review of the research literature. *The Clinical Supervisor*, 24 (1/2), 49–67.

Bradley, G., and Hojer, S., 2009. Supervision reviewed: reflections on two different social work models in England and Sweden. *European Journal of Social Work*, 12 (1), 71–85.

Burns, M., 1958. *The historical development of the process of casework supervision as seen in the professional literature of social work.* Unpublished doctoral dissertation, University of Chicago.

Carpenter, J., Webb, C., Bostock, L., and Coomber, C., 2012. *SCIE research briefing 43: effective supervision in social work and social care.* London: Social Care Institute of Excellence.

Chon, Y., 2019. The marketization of childcare and elderly care, and its results in South Korea. *International Social Work*, 62 (4), 1260–1273.

Cosgrave, C., Hussain, R., and Maple, M., 2015. Factors impacting on retention amongst community mental health clinicians working in rural Australia: a literature review. *Advances in Mental Health*, 13 (1), 58–71.

Davys, A., May, J., Burns, B., and O'Connell, M., 2017. Evaluating social work supervision. *Aotearoa New Zealand Social Work*, 29 (3), 108–121.

Dustin, D., 2007. *The mcdonaldization of social work*. London: Routledge.

Egan, R., 2012. Australian social work supervision practice in 2007. *Australian Social Work*, 65 (2), 171–184.

Ellis, M.V., Creaner, M., Hutman, H.B., and Timulak, L., 2015. A comparative study of clinical supervision in the Republic of Ireland and the US. *Journal of Counseling Psychology*, 62, 621–631.

Engelbrecht, L.K., 2019. Towards authentic supervision of social worker in South Africa, *The Clinical Supervisor*, 38 (2), 301–325.

Engelbrecht, L.K., and Strydom, M., 2013. *Social work in South Africa: context, concepts and some critical reflections*. Stellenbosch, South Africa: Department of Social Work, Stellenbosch University.

Evans, T., 2010. *Professional discretion in welfare services, beyond street-level bureaucracy*. Surrey: Ashgate.

Ferlie, E., Ashburner, L., Fitzgerald, L., and Pettigrew, A., 1996. *The new public management in action*. Oxford: Oxford University Press.

Fortune, A.E., 2014. How quickly we forget: a historical analysis of evidence-based practice in social work; the unfinished journey towards an empirically grounded profession. *Social Services Review*, 88 (2), 217–233.

Goldman, R., 2013. *Narrative summary of the evidence review on the supervision of social workers and social care workers in a range of settings included integrated settings*. London: SCIE.

Hair, H., 2012. The purpose and duration of supervision, and the training and discipline of supervisors: what social works say they need to provide effective services. *British Journal of Social Work*, 43, 1562–1588.

Han, I., and Lim, J., 2014. The current status and future challenges of social work education in South Korea. *In*: C. Noble, H. Strauss, and B. Littlechild, eds. *Global social work: crossing borders, blurring boundaries*. Sydney, Australia: University of Sydney Press, 156–168.

Harkness, D., and Poertner, J., 1989. Research and social work supervision: a conceptual review. *Social Work*, 34 (2), 115–119.

Harris, J., 2014. (Against) neo-liberal social work. *Critical and Radical Social Work*, 2 (1), 7–22.

Healy, K., 2014. *Social work theories in context, creating frameworks for practice*. 2nd ed. London: Palgrave McMillan.

Kadushin, A., 1976. *Supervision in social work*. New York: Columbia University Press.

Lambley, S., 2010. Managers: are they really to blame for what's happening to social work?, *Social Work and Social Sciences Review*, 14 (2), 6–19.

Lambley, S., 2018. A semi-open supervision systems model for evaluating staff supervision in adult care settings: a conceptual framework. *European Journal of Social Work*, 21 (3), 389–399.

Lambley, S., 2019. A semi-open supervision systems model for evaluating staff supervision in adult-care organisational settings: the research findings. *British Journal of Social Work*, 49, 391–410.

Lymbery, M., 2006. United we stand? Partnership working in health and social care and the role of social work in services for older people. *British Journal of Social Work*, 36, 1119–1134.

McDonald, C., 2006. *Challenging social work, the context of practice*. London: Palgrave McMillan.

Mo, K.Y., O'Donoghue, K., Wong, P.Y., and Tsui, M., 2020. The historical development of knowledge in social work supervision: finding new directions from the past. *International Social Work*. https://doi.org/10.1177/0020872819884995 .

Mo, Y.K., Leung, T.L, Tsui, M.S., 2019. Chaos in order: the evolution of social work supervision practice in the Chinese mainland. *The Clinical Supervisor*, 38 (2), 345–365.

Nam in Seok Choi, K., and Kim, J., 2019. Role changes of hospital social workers in South Korea. *Social Work in Health Care*, 58 (7), 703–717.

Neuman, K., 2003. The effect of organizational reengineering on job satisfaction for staff in hospital social work departments. *Social Work in Health Care*, 36 (4), 19–33.

Noble, C., and Irwin, J., 2009. Social work supervision: an exploration of the current challenges in a rapidly changing social, economic and political environment. *Journal of Social Work*, 9 (3), 345–358.

Noelker, L.S., Ejaz, F.K., Menne, H.L., and Bagaka, J.G., 2009. Factors affecting frontline satisfaction with supervision. *Journal of Aging and Health*, 21 (1), 85–101.

O'Donoghue, K., 2015. Issues and challenges facing social work supervision in the twenty-first century. *China Journal of Social Work*, 8 (2), 136–149.

O'Donoghue, K., Wong, P.Y., and Tsui, M., 2018. Constructing and evidence-informed social work supervision model. *European Journal of Social Work*, 21 (3), 348–358

Ornellas, A., Spolander, G., Sicora, A., Pervova, I., Martinez-Roman, M., Law, A.K, Shajahan, P.K., and Guerreiro, M., 2019. Mapping social work across 10 countries: structure, intervention, identify and challenges. *International Social Work*, 62 (4), 1183–1197.

Pawson, R., and Tilley, N., 2004. *Realist evaluation*. London: Cabinet Office.

Rankine, M., 2019. The internal/external debate: the tensions within social work supervision. *Aotearoa New Zealand Social Work*, 31 (3), 32–45.

Renouf, N., and Bland, R., 2005. Navigating stormy waters: challenges and opportunities for social work in mental health. *Australian Social Work*, 58 (4), 419–430.

Republic of South Africa 1978. *Social services professions act, act 110 of 1978*. Pretoria, South Africa: Government Printers.

Shen, L., and Wang, A.Q., 2013. The operation of indigenous social work supervision in Shanghai. *Social Work*, 1, 86–97.

Takeda, F., Ibaraki, N., Yokoyama, E., Miyake, T., and Ohida, T., 2005. The relationship of job type to burn-out in social workers at social welfare offices. *Journal of Occupational Health*, 47, 119–125.

Trevithick, P., 2014. Humanising managerialism: reclaiming emotional reasoning, intuition, the relationship, and knowledge and skills in social work. *Journal of Social Work Practice*, 28 (3), 287–311.

Whittington, R., 2015. Giddens, structuration theory and strategy-as-practice. *In*: D. Golsorkhi, L. Rouleau, D. Seidl, and E. Vaara eds. *Cambridge handbook of strategy as practice*. Cambridge: Cambridge University Press, 109–126.

Wong, P.Y.J., and Lee, A.E.Y., 2015. Dual roles of social work supervisors: strain and strengths as managers and clinical supervisors. *China Journal of Social Work*, 8 (2), 164–181.

Xiong, Y.G., and Wang, S.B., 2007. Development of social work education in China in the context of new policy initiatives: issues and challenges. *Social Work Education*, 26, 560–572.

15

SUPERVISION IN ISOLATED AND RURAL SETTINGS

Amanda Nickson

Introduction

Social work practice in isolated and rural settings in Australia faces many challenges and rewards. One of the challenges is the provision of supervision. A lack of supervision and professional development opportunities contribute to recruitment and retention difficulties. Social work practice in rural Australia faces high staff turnover, burnout, and difficulties in recruitment and retention (Cuss 2005; Symons 2005; Chisholm et al. 2011).

Social work supervision is a cornerstone to accountable and ethical practice and provides opportunity for support, ongoing professional development, and reflection on practice. Social work practice in isolated and rural settings can be very rewarding. There are also challenges working in small communities where high visibility, lack of anonymity, dual roles, and boundary dilemmas are more common than in practice in metropolitan areas. These challenges can be managed well when good supervision is readily available. Accessing supervision can be especially difficult in isolated and rural areas due to large distances between a possible supervisor and the supervisee.

This chapter will discuss some of the characteristics of rural and remote social work practice, the challenges to accessing supervision in these locations, some research regarding a way to provide peer group supervision using technology and other options for supervision in rural and isolated places.

Alston (2009, pp. 15–16) describes some of the challenges of rural practice:

> Communities may not readily accept workers, workers may have fewer colleagues, supervision may be patchy or non-existent, resources may be more stretched, ... telecommunication infrastructure such as mobile phone and broadband coverage is very poor in many areas, the geographical areas workers are expected to cover are much more extensive, driving long distances is expected and can be hazardous as a result of kangaroos and other wildlife on the roads, because of distance, workers may not be able to see as many clients, regional and city-based managers may not understand the difficulties associated with rural practice…, anonymity is impossible, separating professional and personal space may be difficult.

In this context, rural practice is discussed in some more detail.

Rural practice

Welfare practices in rural and isolated areas create many rewards, challenges, and ethical dilemmas for social workers (Green and Lonne 2005). However, factors like high visibility, lack of anonymity, and managing dual and multiple roles results in high levels of stress for rural workers.

"Australia is one of the most urbanised countries in the world, with over two-thirds (69%) of the population living in major cities. It also has one of the lowest population densities outside of its major cities" (Baxter et al. 2010, p. 2). The remaining one-third of Australia's population lives outside major cities in regional, rural, and remote Australia. Alston described rural as:

> Those areas outside major metropolitan areas that are more commonly in the Outer Regional, Remote and Very Remote classification, where accessibility to services is moderate to remote, where the main industries are agriculture, mining and to a lesser extent tourism, and where people generally relate to the notion of a shared set of values loosely defined as rural.
>
> *(2009, p. 9)*

Access to services has been recognized by the Australian government (Australian Bureau of Statistics 2011) as diminished the further one is located from a capital city or major regional center. It is in this context that social workers practice.

On the whole, Australia's rural and remote populations have poorer health than those in the city. Life expectancy declines with increasing remoteness (more so amongst men than women). The gap is widening between urban and rural people, with life expectancy increasing more than 20% faster for residents of metropolitan local government areas (LGAs), compared to rural LGAs (Cresswell cited in Vines 2011).

The poor health of rural Australians is compounded by the fact that Indigenous Australians, more frequently residing in rural locations, die more at a younger age than non-Indigenous Australians (Glover et al. 2004; Australian Institute of Health and Welfare 2014). In addition, there is some indication that more vulnerable older Australians migrate to rural and remote areas while young people migrate to the cities (National Rural Health Alliance and Aged Community Services Australia 2004). "Remote communities in Australia have small groups of people, vast areas; changing socio-economic conditions; unpredictable ecological conditions (fire, drought, flood, salinity); lack of facilities [and] outmigration [of] younger people" (Rajkumar and Hoolahan 2004, p. 78). As well, there is some evidence of higher levels of health-related risk which can exacerbate health disadvantage in rural environments (Smith et al. 2008).

Smith (2016, p. 19) stated that "Rural people and their forebears have endured considerable hardship, extreme isolation and tough geographical conditions to produce some of Australia's greatest economic resources. They have done this through hard work, resourcefulness, self-reliance, mateship and stoicism." These characteristics contribute to the resilient image and many people's understanding of life in rural Australia (Alston 2009). However, as Pugh and Cheers noted, there are other factors that feature widely in the literature on rurality and the context for rural social work. These included that

> ...the existence and needs of some rural dwellers tend to be unrecognised or understated; rural populations are typically underserved by welfare services; rural infrastruc-

tures are weaker – that is the availability or presence of other services such as affordable housing, effective transport systems and so on is reduced; employment opportunities are restricted, either because of rural location and / or the changing rural labour market; poverty and poorer life chances are more common in most rural areas; and rural services usually cost much more to deliver.

(Pugh and Cheers 2010, p. xvi)

Alston identified that "rural Australia is in crisis"(Alston 2005, p. 276) and little seems to have changed since then. According to Alston (2005) and others, the loss of population to the cities for work, years of crippling drought, financial stress, and the loss of services through state and federal re-structuring of services to cities or large regional centers has created a social crisis in rural and remote Australia (Alston 2005; Quinney 2006). Alston (2010) stated that a number of studies in Australian rural communities over a lengthy period reveal that rural people are suffering significant hardship, alienated from governments that have moved away from addressing poverty alleviation, particularly in relation to the rural context, and feel their citizenship rights are eroded – that they have no avenue to address their needs.

Humphreys and Gregory (2012) and Harvey (2014) noted the poor health status of rural and remote Australians, despite the existence of over a decade of increased rural health policies and programs. Rural social work practice exists within this context.

In summary, rural and remote Australia has diverse populations and industries, characterized by increasing disadvantage. This has created particular challenges for social work practice in these areas, characterized by the personal challenges of living and working in small communities, often involving the overlap of personal and professional life, having few or limited access to other services, presenting particular challenges to working with rural populations. Added to this are harsh and extreme climatic conditions, geographic and professional isolation – in all, what can be a very challenging and taxing working and living environment.

Recruitment and retention in rural and remote areas

A number of authors have written about concerns with recruitment and retention of human service workers in rural and remote areas. Chisholm, Russell, and Humphreys (2011) analyzed human resources data on rural allied health workforce turnover and retention on 901 allied health staff in Western Victoria over a six year period from 2004–2009. They found "...differences in crude workforce patterns according to geographical location emerge 12 to 24 months after commencement of employment" (Chisholm et al. 2011, p. 81). The profession, employee age, and grade upon commencement were significant determinants of turnover risk. Remote health services had the highest annual turnover rates, lower stability rates after two, three, and four years, and lower retention probabilities after second and subsequent years of employment. This study did not consider supervision as a factor in retention, despite supervision being identified as a core retention strategy in health and allied health services. There is a need to discuss the need for supervision options for rural and remote workers as a priority.

Technology and social work supervision in a rural and remote context

Technology is becoming more important in social work practice and supervision. Hitchcock, Sage, and Smyth (2018) suggest the ability to interpret both verbal and nonverbal communication requires adequate training and competence to use telephone and videoconferencing well in remote supervision. Regardless of what modality of technology is used for supervision, the importance of protection of confidential information is a responsibility to be considered.

In considering ways to overcome the tyranny of distance, often a problem in accessing supervision for social workers in rural and remote Australia, it is helpful to consider the use of technologies in seeking ways to remedy this problem. Technologies used in social work can include telephone, video-links, Skype, Zoom, email, and social media such as Facebook and Twitter. Technology is in some ways providing the missing supervisory link and would appear to provide possible solutions to the lack of social work supervisors on the ground in rural communities. Literature on technology in social work is examined in the following section.

Crago and Crago (2002) in their conceptual discussion of literature on technology in social work, noted that "telephone supervision is perhaps the most obvious alternative to local face-to-face supervision for rural and remote area practitioners." They noted that there is already an established body of practice wisdom, based on telephone counseling, that can assist supervisors and supervisees, and also noted that "phone supervision is reasonably cost effective and provides for immediate feedback and real-time dialogue (unlike tape, letter or email supervision)" (Crago and Crago 2002, p. 85). Its limitations include the absence of non-verbal cues, which can mean the possibilities for mistrust and temporary miscommunication may be greater.

Counseling by telephone has in the past been seen as "the poor relation compared with face –to face counseling in terms of professional recognition" (Rosenfield and Sanders 1998, p. 5). However, an analysis of social work services provided via telephone call centers identified a range of difficult and complex issues being referred to call center social workers. This analysis identified that the call center social workers were able to follow up using crisis intervention frameworks, with good outcomes being reported by customers (Humphries and Camilleri 2002). This analysis of the work of social workers using the phone showed good outcomes.

Crago and Crago (2002) talk about alternatives to the face-to-face model. They noted that "a peer supervision group can function extremely well if it attains a level of trust, honesty and mutual respect sufficient to allow all members to expose both their doubts and their competencies" (2002, p. 82). Trust remains a core requirement and a commonly repeated ingredient for effective supervision.

Types of supervision

Davys and Beddoe (2010) challenged the need for an expert role in supervision and suggested that:

> When supervision is regarded as a reflective learning process, a shift occurs which moves the supervisor from an "expert" to a "facilitator" in the supervision forum. As a facilitator the supervisor's role becomes one of ensuring the space and context for learning.
>
> *(p. 88)*

This shift in positioning of the supervisor as a facilitator opens up possibilities of other modes of supervision. Davys and Beddoe (2010, p. 88) suggested a reflective learning model of supervision in which "solutions which emerge from the supervision process are discovered and owned by the supervisee rather than 'taught' by the supervisor." The reflective learning model of supervision combines reflective practice and adult learning. While this model was designed for one-on-one supervision and not for group or peer group supervision, the notions of reflective practice, adult learning, and solutions being discovered and owned by the supervisee sit well with group and peer supervision.

Pack, in her qualitative research study, using semi-structured interviews with twelve early-career mental health professionals working in their first year as social workers and occupational therapists, found that the relationship in clinical supervision was one of the most important features that supervisees valued. She noted that a positive, trusting relationship is one in which "difficulties related to practice could be raised without fear of censure" (Pack 2013, p. 12). When the supervisory relationship was "safe," supervisees could explore difficulties related to the workplace that were personally distressing. She concluded that "for clinical supervision to be 'successful' from the clinical supervisee's perspective, opportunities for learning from clinical supervisors in a 'safe' relationship need to be available" (Pack 2015, p. 1835). Pack's research indicated that the relationship between supervisor and supervisee must be marked by traits of support and safety.

Peer supervision

A peer is defined as "one that is of equal standing with another, equal" (Anon. 2012). This is the key factor of a peer relationship – each person is of equal standing. Peer supervision is defined by the Australian Association of Social Workers as a "collaborative learning and supervisory forum for a pair, or a group, of professional colleagues of equal standing" (Australian Association of Social Workers 2014, p. 13) in which the "participants move between the roles of supervisor, supervisee and collaborative learner" (Australian Association of Social Workers 2014, p. 6). This definition leaves scope to cover all the usually expected aspects of supervision – support, education, administration, and reflection on practice.

Proctor further defined peer group supervision when she identified peer group supervision as one of four styles of group supervision. The four types of groups and leadership styles are: the authoritative group, the participative group, the co-operative group, and peer group supervision. Peer group supervision features members taking shared responsibility for supervising and being supervised (Proctor 2008, p. 32). Proctor described peer group supervision as potentially ground-breaking, because there is a freedom from a fixed authority figure.

Hawken and Worrall's term "reciprocal mentoring supervision" clearly described what is considered by other authors to be peer supervision. Hawken and Worrall noted "a reciprocal mentoring supervisory relationship creates an environment of increased trust because it is based on mutuality and equality. Such a relationship implicitly recognises the wisdom, skills and knowledge of each person" (2002 p. 43). They suggested that this relationship based on mutuality is a catalyst for learning. They go on to define reciprocal mentoring supervision as

> …a structured, reciprocal learning relationship between peers (two or three) who wish to work together, where trust, support and challenge encourage honesty, in-depth reflection and constructive analysis on practice and related personal and contextual issues, enhancing self-confidence, personal and professional learning and promoting best practice.
>
> *(Hawken and Worrall 2002 p. 43)*

For social workers in rural and remote areas, considering peer supervision, whether with one other social worker or a small group, would give options for supervision where there is limited or no access to more traditional supervision arrangements.

The choice to consider supervision in a group context rather than an individual context may suit some social workers more than others. In a peer supervision group situation, where the roles of supervisor and supervisee are shared amongst all members, there appears to be the possibility of optimizing the benefits for participants through group processes.

Reporting on research that combined peer group supervision and technology

The research of the author for her PhD was on the topic of exploring peer group supervision in virtual teams in rural and remote Australia: linking individual social workers together virtually using teleconference calls and video link technology to enable geographically isolated social workers to access supervision.

One of the challenges in the Australian context is professional isolation and a lack of supervision exacerbated by geographic isolation and remote locations involving large distances from regional centers. Gradually more social workers are looking to technology as a way of overcoming this barrier of large distances. Options more readily accessible include phone, Skype, and Zoom technology, making it possible to access supervision where none is available in the rural areas in which a social worker is based.

Methodology

The chosen methodology incorporated a qualitative, interpretive social science theoretical framework. Interpretive interactionism provided a framework to analyze the lived experiences of participants. Action research was chosen as the vehicle for this interpretive approach. A strengths-based approach was the philosophy that guided the action research activities. In this research, the processes involved in undertaking peer supervision with virtual teams in rural and remote Australia over a 12-month period is reported. Pre- and post-trial individual interviews; monthly group supervision sessions; online evaluations of the peer group supervision experiences; and focus groups all provided a rich landscape of the experiences of participants.

Participants' demographics

The sample consisted of twenty social workers from six Australian states who contributed to five virtual peer supervision groups. There were no new graduates in the sample, with years of experience ranging from 1.5 years to 30 years. The researcher was located in Townsville in North Queensland. The trials were undertaken across 2006 and 2007.

The use of the telephone as the main medium for the interviews was essential as participants were from geographically dispersed areas all over Australia.

Research informed practice models in supervision

A number of structured models are found in the literature on supervision. The researcher chose a strengths-based approach and a structured model from the New Zealand Mentoring Centre (2000) for the structured peer supervision groups.

"Strengths-based supervision aims to enhance and develop practice through meaningful reflection that focuses on the worker's practice and activity as opposed to the client's issues and stories" (McCashen 2005, p. 139). Strengths-based practices and processes are characterized by transparency, respect, collaboration, inclusion, and consultation; self-determination; an emphasis on strengths and capacities; the sharing of resources; the removal of constraints; and the right to safety (McCashen 2005, p. 125).

An example of a strengths-based process is presented in what Heron (1993) and the New Zealand Mentoring Centre (2000) termed the Good News Story. A suggested modification to consider is naming this process as a "Good Practice Story," where a practitioner can describe something that went well, recognizing a lot of social work is not in circumstances of good news, but dealing well in crisis and other life events.

This process worked well in building trusting relationships for peer group supervision groups, where supervisees were able to share good practice (Nickson et al. 2016). The same technique can be used in peer supervision and group supervision as a way for colleagues to get to know each other and build trust.

What the research found

First, connection with like-minded professionals at a peer level within a safe (virtual) space was key to the success of these peer supervision groups. Second, structure and process were vital to the success of the groups. Third, supervision with peers in groups using teleconference technology works, and facilitates good quality supervision.

Other strengths in this way of doing supervision included giving and receiving support; learning; reflection on practice; finding value in the diversity of social work contexts; the impact of structure or no structure; technology and the challenges of priority, preparation, and time.

Peer group supervision worked, and the reasons included that there was connection with like-minded people, participants experienced unconditional support in a peer supervision space, there was learning taking place, and there was reflection on practice. The connection with like-minded professionals was one of the strongest messages participants voiced. It is a message that is new to the literature on supervision.

This message was demonstrated in the following quotes from participants.

> I guess for me it was that trust, the trust that this person who was on the other end of the telephone. Yep, I couldn't put a face to the name but just that they were from a similar background and have an understanding and I was, **I'm not talking Chinese** when I'm talking to another group member.
>
> *(Jillene) (emphasis added)*

As described by Mary:

> One of the things that really came home to me was the fact that I'm a social worker working in a unit with other Allied Health staff, that all deal with the physical aspects of a person's health whereas I deal with the social and emotional aspects of a person's health so often one can feel misunderstood ..... It's great to actually be in a group of **like-minded people**. It's just really good to talk to other social workers and listen to their ideas and just that support.
>
> *(emphasis added)*

The shared understanding and common ground expressed by participants facilitated a sense of trust and safety, which was reported by a number of participants.

A number of factors were identified by participants that contributed to the sense of connectedness and safety. These included group identity and a sense of belonging and purpose, the idea that participants had "permission to talk," having common or shared professional values, and the safety that was felt in the groups because of the connection between participants. This connection provided an environment where trust was readily established and a safe place became available. The connectedness with like-minded people that created a safe, trustworthy space demonstrably provided the platform or essential foundation for support, learning, and professional development. This connectedness and safety appeared to be important prerequisites for the development of good peer supervision groups and linked directly to the outcome that supervision with peers in groups worked.

Participants across the different groups reported that being able to share and listen, the sense of non-judgmental support, encouragement, and the positive affirmation was highly valued.

> I found the feedback very useful for a current issue I am trying to manage at the moment. The opportunity to discuss the issue openly and without bias helped me to look at it from a new perspective. The group members actively participated and the discussion flowed for the allocated time.
>
> *(anonymous online feedback)*

Hearing about other people's practice across a number of contexts was highlighted by participants as helpful to learning and a positive attribute of the peer group supervision experience. Many participants came wanting to learn and build on their knowledge.

"I came into the peer supervision wanting to learn first and foremost." (Liz)

Most groups in this research comprised social workers who held different professional interests working from varied fields of practice. The common denominator for most was that their employment was primarily in a rural area. Participants repeatedly provided comments on the value of diversity to their peer group supervision experiences. Several participants described getting a "slice across organisations," which they stated was beneficial.

What this suggests is that for all workers in rural areas, being able to link with another social worker, even in a totally different field of practice, was very beneficial. The common understanding of another social worker was greater than the potential differences being in a different practice context.

The opportunity to learn and reflect on practice was commented on and valued by numerous participants. For some participants this was in the period leading up to and preparing for the scheduled peer supervision session. For some participants it was during the session, while for others, reflection on practice continued in the days after the peer supervision group met.

In considering what assisted the peer supervision groups to work, having a prescribed structure appears to have contributed to the longevity of the groups.

Significantly, the two groups that discontinued after only a few months into the trial were the two groups who were not given a specific structure to use at the start of the peer supervision groups. While general guidance and support was provided, the lack of a specific model to follow appeared to make a difference.

Having a model provided a sense of security and safety, and in some ways relief, as participants knew exactly what was required of them, in both sharing and responding. Another benefit of the prescribed model was the ability to make the best use of the time available to maximize the benefit. Participants in the structured groups also provided positive feedback about the availability of a range of prescribed processes, offering flexibility, and the fact that the choice of the process was driven by the supervisee

This research deliberately used technology to address these issues and sought specific feedback from participants about the effectiveness or otherwise of the technological medium used – teleconference phone links. Feedback was overwhelmingly positive. Some other technological options existed and were not used. Video conference links for the peer group supervision sessions were considered, and the possibilities actively explored with all participants during the pre-trial interviews. Because most of the participants lacked videoconferencing facilities, this was not a feasible option. A basic landline phone was the preferred and easiest reliable means to access supervision.

Other ways to access supervision

At the time of this research trial, Skype was not widely available and therefore was not explored as an option. It was considered to have limited application for many parts of rural and remote Australia where internet connections are slow and drop out from time to time.

Skype and Zoom are more prevalent for accessing supervision in recent years and are accessible options for social workers in rural and isolated locations. There are a number of compelling reasons that accessing supervision by Skype from a remote community can be especially helpful. These are described by Maire (Molly) Hall (a practitioner in a small remote community in the Northern Territory) in Nickson, Carter, and Francis:

> One is to be able to speak to an experienced social worker who understands the context of remote work, but isn't themselves swamped by the endless need, or part of the complex relationship web. Another is the insight that can be offered from a social worker working in another context. Finally, Skype supervision sessions aren't dependent on my ability to leave the community, something that has prevented me from accessing supervision in the past.
>
> *(2019, p. 164)*

Hall goes on to describe being able to access Skype supervision as a "game changer" in her practice (Nickson et al. 2019, p. 164).

Whilst traditional models of supervision suggest face to face in the same location, successful supervision can be accessed using available technologies including phone, Skype, Zoom, and emerging technologies. The connection with a like-minded and trusted social worker, who could be a peer or an external supervisor gives social workers many more options than those available in rural and isolated areas a decade ago.

Peer supervision, whether with one other social worker or in a group has been found to have positive benefits for the supervisees. This opens up a number of supervision possibilities for social workers in rural, isolated, and remote contexts.

In conclusion, whilst the challenges of working in rural and isolated areas remain, supervision in these areas is more possible with the increasing availability of reliable technologies. Greater acceptance of the value of external supervision, whether by an experienced supervisor or by a social work peer with peer supervision means there are more options to have regular supervision even when living and working in rural and isolated areas where a supervisor may not be in the same location. Just as in social work practice there is a need to be flexible and try new approaches, the same could be said for supervision in rural and isolated areas. If social workers are willing to try something new in the way they do supervision, the resulting support and growth through supervision could surpass expectations.

References

Alston, M., 2005. Forging a new paradigm for Australian rural social work practice. *Rural Society*, 15 (3), 277–284.

Alston, M., 2009. *Innovative human services practice: Australia's changing landscape*. South Yarra, VIC: Palgrave Macmillan.

Alston, M., 2010. Australia's rural welfare policy: overlooked and demoralised. *In*: Milbourne, P. ed. *Welfare reform in rural places: comparative perspectives*. Bingley, UK: Emerald Group, 199–217.

Anon 2012. *peer. Merriam-Webster's collegiate dictionary*. 11th ed. Springfield, MA: Merriam-Webster.

Australian Association of Social Workers 2014. *Supervision standards 2014* [online]. North Melbourne, VIC: AASW. Available from: https://www.aasw.asn.au/practitioner-resources/supervision-standards.

Australian Bureau of Statistics 2011. *Australian statistical geography standard (ASGS) remoteness structure* [online]. Canberra, ACT: ABS. Available from: https://www.abs.gov.au/websitedbs/D3310114.nsf/home/remoteness+structure.

Australian Institute of Health and Welfare 2014. *Mortality and life expectancy of Indigenous Australians: 2008 to 2012* [online]. Canberra, ACT: AIHW Available from: https://www.aihw.gov.au/reports/indigenous-australians/mortality-life-expectancy-2008-2012/contents/summary.

Baxter, J., Gray, M., and Hayes, A., 2010. *Families in regional, rural and remote Australia* [online]. Canberra, ACT: Australian Institute of Family Studies. Available from: https://aifs.gov.au/publications/families-regional-rural-and-remote-australia.

Chisholm, M., Russell, D., and Humphreys, J., 2011. Measuring rural allied health workforce turnover and retention: what are the patterns, determinants and costs?. *Australian Journal of Rural Health*, 19 (2), 81–88.

Crago, H., and Crago, M., 2002. But you can't get decent supervision in the country! *In*: McMahon, M., and Patton, W. eds. *Supervision in the helping professions: a practical approach*. Frenchs Forest NSW: Pearson Education Australia, 79–90.

Cuss, K., 2005. *Professional supervision of allied health professionals in the central Hume region*. Melbourne, VIC: Victoria Department of Health & Human Services.

Davys, A., and Beddoe, L., 2010. *Best practice in professional supervision*. London: Jessica Kingsley.

Glover, J.D., Tennant, S.L., and Page, A., 2004. *The impact of socioeconomic status and geographic location on Indigenous mortality in Australia, 1997–99*. Adelaide: Public Health Information Development Unit, the University of Adelaide.

Green, R., and Lonne, B., 2005. 'Great lifestyle, pity about the job stress': occupational stress in rural human service practice. *Rural Society*, 15 (3), 253–267.

Harvey, D., 2014. Exploring women's experiences of health and well-being in remote northwest Queensland, Australia. *Qualitative Health Research*, 24 (5), 603–614.

Hawken, D., and Worrall, J., 2002. Reciprocal mentoring supervision. Partners in learning: a personal experience. *In*: McMahon, M., and Patton, W. eds. *Supervision in the helping professions: a practical approach*. Frenchs Forest NSW: Pearson Education Australia, 43–53.

Heron, J., 1993. *Group facilitation: theories and models for practice*. London: Kogan Page.

Hitchcock, L.I., Sage, M., and Smyth, N.J., 2018. *Technology in social work education: educators' perspectives on the NASW Technology Standards for Social Work Education and Supervision*. Buffalo, NY: State University of New York at Buffalo. School of Social Work.

Humphreys, J.S., and Gregory, G., 2012. Celebrating another decade of progress in rural health: what is the current state of play?. *Australian Journal of Rural Health*, 20 (3), 156–163.

Humphries, P., and Camilleri, P., 2002. Social work and technology: challenges for social workers in practice: a case study. *Australian Social Work*, 55 (4), 251–259.

McCashen, W., 2005. *The strengths approach: a strengths-based resource for sharing power and creating change*. Bendigo, VIC: St Luke's Innovative Resources.

National Rural Health Alliance and Aged Community Services Australia 2004. *Older people and aged care in rural, regional and remote Australia: a discussion paper* [online]. Canberra: Aged and Community Services Australia Melbourne. Available from: https://www.ruralhealth.org.au/sites/default/files/position-papers/position-paper-04-07-26.pdf.

New Zealand Mentoring Centre 2000. *The power of peer supervision: enhancing your ability to learn from experience*. Auckland, NZ: New Zealand Mentor Centre.

Nickson, A., Gair, S., and Miles, D., 2016. Supporting isolated workers in their work with families in rural and remote Australia: exploring peer group supervision. *Children Australia*, 41 (4), 265–274.

Nickson, A.M., Carter, M.-A., and Francis, A.P., 2019. *Supervision and professional development in social work practice*. Los Angeles, CA: SAGE.

Pack, M., 2013. The relationship in clinical supervision: models preferred by allied mental health professionals who work with traumatic disclosures. *Advances in Clinical Supervision Conference*, June 4–6 2013. Sydney, NSW.

Pack, M., 2015. 'Unsticking the stuckness': a qualitative study of the clinical supervisory needs of early-career health social workers. *British Journal of Social Work*, 45 (6), 1821–1836.

Proctor, B., 2008. *Group supervision: a guide to creative practice*. 2nd ed. London: SAGE.

Pugh, R., and Cheers, B., 2010. *Rural social work: an international perspective*. Bristol, UK: Policy Press.

Quinney, A., 2006. Social work theories in action by Mary Nash, Robyn Munford and Keiran O'Donaghue (eds.), London, Jessica Kingsley, 2005, pp. 272, ISBN: 1843102498. (Book review). *British Journal of Social Work*, 36, 165–166.

Rajkumar, S., and Hoolahan, B., 2004. Remoteness and issues in mental health care: experience from rural Australia. *Epidemiology and Psychiatric Sciences*, 13 (2), 78–82.

Rosenfield, M., and Sanders, P., 1998. Counselling at a distance: challenges and new initiatives. *British Journal of Guidance & Counselling*, 26 (1), 5–10.

Smith, J.D., 2016. *Advance rural Australia. Australia's rural, remote and indigenous health*. Chatswood, NSW: Elsevier Australia, 1–22.

Smith, K.B., Humphreys, J.S., and Wilson, M.G., 2008. Addressing the health disadvantage of rural populations: how does epidemiological evidence inform rural health policies and research?. *Australian Journal of Rural Health*, 16 (2), 56–66.

Symons, J., 2005. Applying the evidence: recruiting and retaining Allied Health Professionals in a remote area. *Paper presented at the Mount Isa Centre for Rural and Remote Health (MICRRH) Remote Health Conference*. Mt Isa, QLD.

Vines, R., 2011. Equity in health and wellbeing: why does regional, rural and remote Australia matter? *InPsych* [online], October. Available from: https://www.psychology.org.au/for-members/publications/inpsych/2011/oct/Equity-in-health-and-wellbeing-Why-does-regional.

16

SUPERVISION OF PEER
SUPPORT WORKERS

Keely M. Phillips

Introduction

There is a story told in peer support circles to highlight the power of peer support to someone recovering from mental health or addiction issues. The story goes: a person is walking down the street and falls into a hole. The person calls for help. A priest comes by and offers to pray for them, tosses them a book of faith, and then the priest goes on his way. Then a psychiatrist comes by and provides some pills to make being stuck in the hole more bearable. Next a therapist comes by and talks to the person about how their life choices led them to this moment and explored with them how being stuck in the hole feels emotionally. Finally, a peer worker comes by and jumps into the hole. The person says "why did you jump into the hole? Now we are both stuck." The peer worker responds, "but I have been down here before and can show you the way out." This is peer support: walking alongside someone during their journey to wellness, the peer supporter intentionally using their experiences with illness and recovery like a lantern on a dark path. The lantern is loaded with strategies, new perspectives, and hope for the person who is struggling. The peer supporter is reassuring, honest, and connects with a level of authenticity, having been through a similar life experience.

This chapter will discuss supervision of peer support workers within the scope of social work settings. While effort is made to take an international perspective, the author acknowledges much is written from a Canadian perspective. The chapter begins with developing an understanding of what peer support is (and what it is not) and its roots within mental health and addictions systems. A review of the evidence for peer support within mental health and addictions fields is presented. Next, we explore how peer support aligns with and differs from clinical services. The final sections of the chapter focus on a shared model of supervision: the peer worker having an administrative supervisor and a separate peer support supervisor who provides supportive and educational supervision. The role of each supervisor in creating a successful peer worker role is explored.

What is peer support?

Peer support is the practice of people who share similar life experiences providing each other encouragement and emotional support, sharing information and coping strategies. It is not unique to mental health or addictions services. In everyday life, people access informal peer support for issues such as parenting, grief, disability, divorce, and more. Formal peer support positions tend to exist for the following life experiences:

- People living with mental health and/or addiction issues
- People living with homelessness
- Equity-seeking populations such as: refugees, sex workers, LGBTQ people
- People who are/have been incarcerated
- Specific physical health conditions: HIV, diabetes, chronic pain, cancer
- Specific health behaviors: breastfeeding, harm reduction, smoking cessation
- Involvement with child welfare systems
- Disenfranchised grief (suicide, HIV, drug overdose/poisoning)
- Being a caregiver/family member of people living with disenfranchised life experiences such as dementia, mental illness, addiction, physical or mental disability
- All forms of disability and neural diversity

A peer supporter is most effective when they are working with a disenfranchised population when there is a level of stigma or prejudice from greater society, which influences the quality of life of the individual. A peer supporter always has first-hand experience living with similar issues of the people they are supporting. Informal peer support occurs outside of the system, often between patients/clients of services. Many peer support roles may also be volunteer. Formal peer support occurs when a person is trained and employed to provide peer support to others. This chapter focuses on formal paid peer support roles.

Recovery

Traditionally, recovery has meant a person is no longer troubled by their issues, or no longer "suffering." Within addiction services, "recovery" historically indicates abstinence from substance use. Today the term recovery is evolving to embrace values of harm reduction, resilience, and growth. Today, recovery is defined by living well, despite illness, with "living well" being defined by the individual. For example: a person who lives with a diagnosis of addiction and schizophrenia can be "in recovery" and still hear voices and may use substances sometimes but their overall quality of life is improved. Maybe the voices they hear are less distressing or they are better able to self-manage their illness, maybe they use less harmful substances. Recovery is not a static state, it is a journey, and what recovery means to an individual changes over time. Peer workers believe that everyone, regardless of their issues or circumstances, can recover from the challenges they are facing.

History of peer support

Informal peer support is not new. Community based peer support such as indigenous healing-circles have long supported people going through challenging times to learn from one another. However, paid and formalized peer support is relatively novel to the past 30 years. Paid peer support roles began to emerge in the 1980s as a product of the consumer-survivor ex-patient (C/S/X) movement of the 1970s. In the 1970s, European groups such as Clientenbond, the Federation of Mental Patients Unions, and the European Network of Alternatives to Psychiatry pushed for human rights of mental patients, and the creation of alternative healing communities (Starkman 2013). In North America, the closing of the mental asylums in the 1960s and 1970s left thousands of people under-housed, living in poverty, and without adequate community mental health supports. This situation combined with a mental health system continuing to exercise forced treatment and confinement led the "ex-patients" or "consumer-survivors" to organize against the system, demanding alternatives. C/S/X activists around the world demanded user-run (peer) community services. These services utilized a self-help and mutual-aid approach and were operated by and for consumer-survivors.

Within addictions services, peer support work has a different history. Due to addiction being viewed as a moral failing, the treatment and helping system, for much of the 20th century, has consisted of people with lived experience being the helpers. The addiction system includes a strong focus on mutual aid (a component of peer support) since the creation of Alcoholics Anonymous in the 1930s. In the 1980s, addiction treatment became professionalized, and valuing of lived experience became confined to 12 Step programming, with social workers, doctors, and other professions holding all the power in the addiction system.

Peripheral to addiction treatment services, the HIV/AIDS harm reduction movement of the 1980s and the present-day drug-user movements continue to put lived experience front and center in their models of care. Today, harm reduction services such as supervised injection sites, needle exchanges, and hepatitis C and HIV education and prevention use peer workers with lived experience of addiction as a best practice to engage and support people marginalized by their substance use.

The presence of paid peer support workers continues to grow in North America, with professionalized designations such as "Certified Peer Specialist" (America) and "Certified Peer Supporter" (Canada) becoming more common. As the practice has grown, the creation of standards for peer support practice (see Sunderland et al. 2013) have helped to formalize peer support work. This professionalization of peer support has its criticism. People fear peer workers working in treatment-focused programs can become co-opted and drift into clinical approaches or become agents of coercion and oppression. These fears can be addressed by effective supervision.

Theory

Peer support acknowledges that people who have overcome life challenges have cultivated a "lived expertise" which is valuable in helping others. Peer support workers focus on walking alongside others as they navigate the detours and bumps of the recovery journey. Peer workers emphasize helping people uncover and utilize their strengths, and improving self-awareness and self-management, over an end-state of being symptom free. A peer worker shares parts of their lived experience that enhanced their recovery journey, being open-minded and nonjudgmental. Peer support is grounded in values of mutuality and reciprocity, recovery, meaningful choice, dignity of risk, intentional use of lived experience, empowerment, and self-management of illness. In North American contexts, peer support also values self-determination and harm reduction. Table 16.1 highlights the core elements of peer support.

Are peer workers social workers?

Certainly, there is overlap between the social justice values of peer support work and social work. Social workers and peer support workers share common practices such as supportive listening, system navigation, and helping people meet basic needs. These overlaps occur in other helping professions. In places where social work requires a specific post-secondary education and/or being part of a regulatory college, it is unlikely to find peer workers identifying as social workers. Regulatory colleges may dislike social workers using their personal lived experiences in their work and in some jurisdictions social workers are barred from doing so. In these contexts, a peer worker cannot also be a social worker.

Table 16.1 Core elements of peer support

Peer support is...	Peer support is not...
Thoughtful sharing of relevant lived experience	Telling ones illness story over and over again
Walking beside someone in their recovery, whatever direction they take. Focus on empowerment.	Assessing, therapy or case management, keeping people on one path (e.g., sobriety)
Sharing coping and wellness strategies	Giving advice, or interpreting someone's experiences for them
A relationship built on trust and mutuality	Exercising power over people supported, using clinical terms or other language that can disconnect

Most importantly, peer support is not clinical and differs from clinical social work and therapy in several ways. Peer supporters use mutuality and intentional use of lived experience as their knowledge base, not formal education. Peer supporters do not give advice and are not prescriptive; they do not emphasize one path to wellness over another path. In therapy, the helper uses specific modalities and extensive training to assess, guide, and assist people to achieving wellness. In peer support, there is no clinical assessment, and support is not based on diagnosis or on helping people work towards goals defined by anyone other than the individual.

Evidence of efficacy

Peer support, although less researched than clinical interventions, has a growing body of evidence. Recent meta-analyses and systemic reviews have found evidence that peer support is helpful to people living with mental health and addiction issues in a variety of quality of life domains. Accessing peer support leads to improved self-management and healthier behaviors (Nasland et al. 2016), decreased substance use (Bassuk et al. 2016; Mental Health America 2019), improved hope for recovery and the future (Fuhr et al. 2014), decreased internalized stigma (Bellamy et al. 2017; Boevink 2018), improved social connection (Nasland et al. 2016), deceased loneliness (Boevink 2018), improved engagement with treatment services (Mental Health America 2019), and overall improved quality of life (Bellamy et al. 2017; Mental Health America 2019).

Compared to clinical interventions, peer support tends to have the same impact on re-hospitalization and relapse rates with better outcomes in measurements of hope, empowerment, engagements, and self-efficacy (Bellamy et al. 2017; Boevink 2018). There is some evidence that accessing peer support reduces number of days spent in hospital (Mental Health America 2019). When looking at how peer support complements clinical care, there is no evidence that accessing peer support negatively affects an individual's psychosocial or clinical outcomes or symptoms (Fuhr et al. 2014). Peer support is as effective as cognitive behavioral therapy and other therapies at reducing symptoms of depression (Pfeiffer et al. 2011). Peer support interventions are also cost effective, due to people utilizing more outpatient treatments and needing shorter and less intensive mental health services (Mental Health America 2019).

Scope of peer support roles in mental health and addiction services

So, what does a peer worker do? How does a supervisor know what to expect from the peer worker? The tasks a peer worker carries out can be organized by five areas: emotional support, instrumental support, affiliation support, educational support, and informational support (Reif et al. 2014). All peer work needs to allow for the use of the peer worker's lived experience. For example, peer workers may provide transportation to appointments as other workers do, but with the intention of the trip to and from the appointment having a conversation where the peer worker shares their lived experience of communicating with medical professionals or navigating the doctor-patient power imbalances. If the peer worker simply drove the person to and from the appointment, it would not be peer support.

Peer supporters often deliver both individualized and group peer support programs. Ideally, only peer staff run peer support groups, as the presence of clinical staff can lessen the peer connection in a group setting. Psychoeducational groups can be co-facilitated by peer and clinical staff.

When working in interdisciplinary teams, peer workers should be valued as any other member of the team, with the same opportunities to participate in workplace training, team meetings, access to supervision and accommodations, and access to the information they require to support people, such as client files. There are some definitive out of scope activities for peer workers including providing clinical services such as assessment, diagnosis, or treatment protocols, but peer workers work alongside practitioners who do so. Peer workers should not do medication monitoring or participate in coercive practices such as physical or chemical restraint. Depending on setting of work, peer workers may do basic information gathering and risk screening. Peer workers should avoid being directive or advice giving with the people they support.

The level of education and training a peer worker requires varies by the scope of their role. Peer workers delivering psychoeducational support groups often require education in adult learning and facilitation. Those working in crisis services require suicide intervention training, de-escalation skills, etc. All peer workers need an awareness of the population they are working with, beyond their own experiences with illness, recovery, and accessing help. Some peer workers will gain this through informal learning, and others will benefit from formal education. Finally, not all peer roles are direct support; peer roles may also include policy, public speaking, system advocacy, research, or management.

Supervisors, especially those working in clinical settings, may encounter common myths about peer workers. These include that peer workers are anti-system/anti-psychiatry, they are less skilled than other disciplines of staff, they lack boundaries, they will be triggered by their work, and peer workers were never "that" sick if they are able to be effective helpers.

A possible explanation for some of the misconceptions and reluctance to embrace peer support may be "disruptive innovation" (Deegan 2011). Peer support, and the presence of a peer worker, challenges whose knowledge is valued and is an attempt to shift power from being held by clinicians, "the experts," to those who are living with the condition. Simply, peer support values lived experience knowledge as equal to professionalized knowledge. Despite decades of reluctance of the field of mental health and addictions care to fully embrace peer support as a legitimate form of support, strides are being made. Notably in 2018, the American Psychiatric Association (at long-time odds with the consumer-survivor movement) stated peer support is "an essential component of recovery-oriented care" (American Psychiatric Association 2018).

Supervision for peer support workers

As peer roles have grown in the social and healthcare settings, the supervision of peer workers has become a contemporary topic. Supervision is possibly the most critical ingredient to the success of a peer support role (Orwin 2008). However, supervisors may overestimate their level of understanding of peer roles. Depression and Bipolar Support Alliance (2010) found that 94% of supervisors felt strongly that they understand the role of peer staff, but only 64% of peer workers felt their supervisors understood the peer role. A supervisor's understanding of the peer role has a strong impact on a peer worker's job satisfaction (Kuhn et al. 2015). Supervisors need a superior understanding of peer work, as the supervisor sets the tone for the relationship between the peer worker and other management in the organization and brokers the relationship between the peer worker and their colleagues (Kuhn et al. 2015).

Supervisors of peer workers benefit from training on recovery philosophy, peer support history and values, the scope of peer roles, how to implement peer roles, and funding requirements for peer roles (Minehart et al. 2014). Peer workers (and all staff) need to have accountability structures in place and be aware of how their work is monitored and evaluated; a written job description, performance appraisals, and regular supervision are helpful (Phillips et al. 2019). It may be difficult for supervisors to assess whether a peer worker is performing their role with fidelity to peer support's best practices. A lack of standardization and the newness of many peer support roles contribute to this issue. To address these issues supervisors can focus on encouraging and facilitating peer support workers to demonstrate eleven competencies in their work.

First, peer workers use their lived experience with ease and with intentionality, focus on wellness instead of illness or symptoms, and demonstrate they value the person's lived experiences. Peer workers offer validation of the hard work of recovery, authentically demonstrate and share their wellness skills with people supported, and encourage people to self-advocate and help them gain the skills to do so. Peer workers help people supported to learn self-management skills and are harm reduction focused, viewing any positive change as helpful to the individual. It is essential for peer workers to discuss boundaries, confidentiality, and the scope of their support and use an empowerment and capacity building approach. Finally, peer workers will explore what illness, disability, and recovery mean to the individual; with a goal of helping the individual find meaning and purpose in their experiences and life overall.

Part of the role of the supervisor is to help the peer worker stay grounded in the scope of peer support; this is more difficult for non-peer supervisors (Grey and O'Hagan 2015). This is why it is best practice for peer workers to have both an administrative supervisor and a peer support supervisor who provides mentorship and coaching specific to peer support (Swarbick and Nemec 2010; Daniel et al. 2015). This peer support specific supervision helps peer workers maintain integrity in their practice (Orwin 2008) and clearly delineates between the administrative supervision provided by the employer and the supportive/educational supervision provided by a peer support supervisor within or outside the organization (Tucker et al. 2013).

The practice of separate administrative and supportive/educational supervisors is common in clinical social work, with many social workers accessing clinical supervision. However, there is no consensus on peer support specific supervision as necessary, with some (e.g., Chinman et al. 2008) believing peer workers having different supervision than other staff can contribute to further challenges with workplace integration.

The remainder of this chapter presents a model of shared supervision depicted using the three functions of supervision (Kadushin and Harkness 2002). By clearly delineating administrative supervision from supportive and educational supervision, this model attempts to address Chinman and colleagues concern (2008) of workplace integration challenges created by separate supervision.

Kadushin's model of supervision and peer support work

Alfred Kadushin articulates three distinct functions of supervision: administrative, educational, and supportive (Kadushin and Harkness 2002). "Administrative supervision provides a model of an efficient worker; educational supervision provides a model of a competent worker; sup-

Table 16.2 Model of shared supervision for peer workers

Type of supervisor	Administrative supervisor	Peer support supervisor
Professional experience of supervisor	Often regulated health professionals such as social worker, nurse, doctor, occupational therapist.	Experienced peer supporter with lived experience similar to peer workers they are supporting. Training, coaching, and mentoring skills and advanced knowledge of peer support practices.
Tasks of supervisor	Overall performance targets and performance management, employee workload and schedule. Often leads a team of interdisciplinary staff.	Supportive supervision focuses on avoiding drift and dealing with stress such as stigma and micro-aggression. Strong focus on self-awareness and reflective practice.
	In-service training and staff development opportunities focus on benefiting all agency staff.	Educational supervision focuses on practices of peer support, including intentional use of lived experience, communicating boundaries, and how to demonstrate wellness strategies with people supported.
Goal of supervision	Peer worker functions as an effective team member, helping the team to meet its goals.	Peer worker functions as an effective peer supporter – staying grounded in peer support values and best practices.

portive supervision provides a model of a compassionate, understanding worker" (Kadushin and Harkness 2002, p. 220). Rich (1993) considers both educational and supportive supervision to be functions of clinical supervision. The same is true for peer support specific supervision. Table 16.2 defines the professional experience, tasks, and goals of this shared model of supervision.

Administrative supervision of peer workers

Administrative supervision of peer workers is similar to that of other social service workers with some particularity in the planning, hiring, documentation, and ongoing integration of peer roles into agency teams and services.

Planning for the peer role

Organizations often implement peer worker roles without full organizational support or in an inconsistent manner, giving rise to peer role implementation issues. A recent literature review identified many of the implementation issues peer workers face throughout their career journey, these include: a lack of role clarity and defined scope of practice, discrimination and stigma in the workplace, difficulty accessing accommodations, a lack of pay equity, challenges with co-worker relationships, peer workers drifting into clinical approaches, and supervisors not understanding or valuing the peer supporters role (Harrison and Read 2016). Many implementation issues can be avoided by thorough planning prior to role implementation.

When planning for a peer worker role, organizations and supervisors should ensure the organization is clear on why they are hiring a peer worker and how the peer role will align with the organizations purpose and vision. The organization should define the intended impact of a successful peer role and how the role will be evaluated (Jorgenson and Schmook 2014). Hiring a peer supporter is not a replacement for client engagement. Clarity between the role of peer supporters and of organization clients who participate in committees or design services is necessary.

Planning for a peer worker role also includes the organization reviewing its policies to eliminate unnecessary barriers faced by peer staff during hiring or once in their roles. For example, organizations seeking to hire peer workers with lived experience of addiction and street involvement need to be prepared for how to deal with the potential of a peer worker having a history of criminal charges. It is best practice to involve service users in the design of the peer role, as they may identify peer worker tasks others miss (Hino 2014). Whenever possible peer roles should be implemented in pairs, to reduce isolation. Furthermore, all levels of the organization from senior management down need to develop an understanding and appreciation for peer roles, and there needs to be a plan to educate and train staff on understanding peer support. A successful peer role begins with a clear job description with identified "peer only duties" such as leading peer support groups, or engagement with the most difficult to reach clientele. The job description also includes clear core competencies for the peer worker (Daniel et al. 2015). During this planning stage, the agency addresses ethical issues presented by the presence of peer workers, such as boundaries with people supported, confidentiality, duty of report, and how a peer worker's previous history with the organization will be protected (Minehart et al. 2014). Importantly, the agency needs to ensure applicability to all employees when adapting policies to address these ethical areas. This avoids discrimination towards peer workers. Finally, accessibility issues such as where a job advertisement is posted (e.g., only internally at a hospital vs through a peer-run service), the rate of pay being a living wage, the need for the peer to have a car, attendance policies, and access to extended health benefits should be taken into consideration when designing the role.

Peer workers often experience a lack of role clarity, and both supervisors and peer workers may be challenged as to "what does peer support work look like?" Compounding the lack of role clarity is a lack of formalized training and lack of consensus in the scope of peer support work, leading to a diversity in how peer work is practiced.

> As an example, at one organization a peer worker many be a fully imbedded member a professional team, taking on a workload similar to that of a social worker or recreation therapist. Whereas in another organization, a peer worker role may be a casual position where people still engaged as service recipients work for a low-hourly wage providing harm reduction supplies or driving people to appointments.
>
> *(Phillips 2018, p. 1)*

Role clarity can be enhanced by defining peer support, core principles, variations, differentiation from other roles, and value of peer support; identifying both peer specific tasks and tasks which overlap with other roles; and having standardized job descriptions and organization's sharing peer job descriptions (Harrison 2015).

Hiring a peer worker

During the hiring phase, many supervisors wonder how to ask about lived experience and what indicates that someone will be an effective peer worker. A peer worker job posting should state the requirement that peer workers have a lived experience similar to those they will be providing support to (such as lived experience of addiction, or of accessing hospital mental health services). The hiring committee should look for candidates who state they have lived experience in their application. In addition, the level of education and past work experience required, specifics of certification or previous training in peer support required, whom the position reports to, the vision for the role, and how it aligns with the organization should be stated. A robust job posting will also include a brief list of duties the peer worker will perform and the setting or team the peer worker will work within. At the application stage candidates should be notified of the accommodation process and be assured the process is no different for peer staff than for other staff.

Interview questions should assess the candidates understanding of peer support and their experience delivering and receiving peer support. A strong candidate will be at ease talking about their lived experience in a trauma-informed way and communicate the uniqueness and boundaries of peer support. Supervisors often struggle with how to ask about lived experience in an interview setting. This is because in many jurisdictions asking directly may be discrimination. Interviewers can instead ask how candidates would use a peer support approach to elicit responses that demonstrate intentional use of lived experience. Questions relevant to all social service roles such as how candidate will navigate conflict, problem solve, and communicate with the team and supervisor should also be asked.

Another common challenge in hiring is if time "in recovery" (abstinence) is required. Employers need to be clear with candidates as to why abstinence is required and, to avoid discrimination, abstinence policies should apply to all staff. Finally, if someone is moving from a clinical role to a peer support role the hiring committee needs to explore how the candidate will stay grounded in a peer approach (additional training and peer support supervision can help with this).

Documentation

Supervisors are also commonly confused about whether peer supporters need to document their work and if so how. Overall, if the service the peer supporter works in documents its interactions with people supported, so should the peer worker. Documentation should reflect peer support values in that it is brief, co-written with the person supported, and reflective of the strengths-based nature of peer support work (Phillips et al. 2019). Documenting peer support interactions often requires peer workers to contribute to the clinical file of the person supported. This can be conflicting for peer workers and supervisors: some peers and supervisors prefer peer workers to not have access to clinical files out of fear the peer worker will be influenced by the clinical view. Conversely, peer workers who do not contribute to the clinical file may lack a means of capturing their work. This can cause challenges with reporting the impact of peer support to funders, communication with team members, and how supervisors measure the work of a peer supporter.

Ensuring integration of the role

The administrative supervisor also provides the peer worker with opportunities to grow and move into other roles within their organizations, ensures the peer worker is integrated as an equal part of the team, and models the use of recovery-oriented and person-centered language. One of the most impactful tasks of the administrative supervisor peer worker is to embrace any tension that exists between clinical and peer services: focusing on finding ways that peer support and clinical care complement one another and building recovery-oriented alliances with clinical colleagues with the end goal of more person-centered care for people supported.

While peer workers tend to have access to administrative supervision, they often lack adequate essential educational and supportive supervision. Administrative supervisors of peer workers need to express their support for the ongoing learning and support that peer support specific education and supervision can bring. In this model of shared supervision, the task of education and supportive supervision aligns with the peer support supervisor role.

Educational supervision of peer workers

Peer support supervisors are experts in the practice of peer support. They have several years of practical experience working as a peer supporter and additional development in coaching, supporting, and educating people about peer support. These supervisors are attuned to emerging practices and trends in peer support and provide those they supervise a connection to other peer workers in the field. Peer worker communities of practice are one modality peer support supervisors use to provide connection to other peer workers and educational supervision.

While it may be more cost-effective for a non-peer supervisor or colleague to attempt to train a peer worker, it is unethical and ineffective. Practitioners with years of experience working in peer support should deliver peer support training. Peer worker training courses are offered online for those who do not have access to local training. Training for a peer worker should include the following topics: bio-psycho-social-spiritual understanding of mental health and addiction issues, common treatments and a critique of the disease model of mental health/ addiction, recovery philosophy, intentional use of lived experience, and how peer support complements and fits with other social services. A history of peer support, person-centered language, negotiating boundaries, avoiding drift, and demonstrating wellness strategies are also essential training components. Training on conflict resolution, communication skills, active listening and soft counseling skills, and providing trauma-informed support does not need to be delivered by a peer support trainer. However, including these topics as part of peer support training will allow for intentional used of lived experience to be woven into the application of these skills. Ideally, training should also include a supervised practicum with opportunities for reflective practice.

Supportive supervision of peer workers

Supportive supervision aides the worker in dealing with job-related stress (Kadushin and Harkness 2002). Supportive supervision for peer workers often focuses on reducing stress in three areas of peer support work: burnout, drift, and challenges with colleagues.

Burnout

Like other staff in social services, peer workers are at risk of burnout. However, peer workers have developed resiliency and demonstrate their wellness in their work, both protective factors in preventing burnout. Burnout in peer workers can be avoided by administrative supervisors helping the peer to manage a fair workload and peer support supervisors ensuring regular access to supportive supervision and a peer worker community of practice. Reducing isolation and ensuring peer workers have access to the same resources as other staff, such as employee health programs, can also reduce burnout.

It is helpful for supervisors to be able to distinguish between a peer worker being too unwell to work versus a peer worker who is having a temporary tough time. A peer worker having a tough time will likely use their experience intentionally with people supported to model how they stay well when challenged. For example, a peer worker may state to someone supported "I had a hard time getting to work today, my sleep is off. I had to be gentle with myself and allow myself stay in bed ten extra minutes." This is different from a peer worker who cannot perform the regular duties of their job due to illness and may require accommodation or a leave of absence. Peer support supervisors should encourage administrative supervisors to deal with this as they would any other employee.

Drift

By far the most common issue supervisors of peer workers encounter is drift. Drift occurs when a peer worker takes on the language and approach of their clinical colleagues, stepping outside of the scope of peer support. Drift is often a byproduct of role strain, where the peer worker feels torn in different directions, creating stress. To manage this stress the peer worker often drifts into clinical approaches. Best practices in addressing and avoiding drift are to have the peer worker regularly connect with other peer support workers and have both administrative and peer support supervisors be aware of and able to identify issues of drift. Peer support supervisors may enhance a peer worker's training in areas related to anti-oppressive practice and empowering a peer worker to stay grounded in peer support values.

Minimizing drift can be accomplished by peer and administrative supervisors ensuring the peer worker's tasks are in scope of the role. Tasks which allow for intentional use of peer worker lived experience, build rapport with people supported and help the peer worker learn about the individual, and encourage participant connections to resources and new perspectives are ideal. Tasks which conflict with peer support values, principles, or ethics (such as monitoring medication adherence or conducting urine drug screening) are not suitable to peer workers and will cause drift and role strain (Phillips et al. 2019).

Challenges with colleagues

Finally, peer workers sometimes encounter resistance from other staff in embracing a peer support approach. This may take the form of outright stigma and discrimination but is often more subtle, in the form of micro-aggressions. It may also be a simple lack of understanding. Best practice to prevent this conflict between peer workers and non-peer colleagues is to have the peer support supervisor train all team members on the scope of the peer role and the evidence for peer support approaches. This training ideally allows non-peer staff an opportunity to express any fears they have with the implementation of a peer role. Conflict may also arise between peer and non-peer colleagues when there is a lack of role clarity. Mapping scope of all team members' roles may be beneficial in this instance. When peer and non-peer staff conflicts are not due to implementation factors they should be addressed as regular staff-staff conflicts.

Conclusion

As the presence of peer support work grows in mental health and addiction systems and beyond, so does our understanding of peer support best practices and how to best integrate peer support roles into mainstream services. When peer workers have effective supervision, their ability to provide this unique form of support to individuals is enhanced. By utilizing the shared model of supervision outlined in this chapter, the success of a peer support worker role can be strengthened.

References

American Psychiatric Association 2018. *Position statement on peer support services*. Available from: https://www.psychiatry.org/File%20Library/About-APA/Organization-Documents-Policies/Policies/Position-2018-Peer-Support-Services.pdf [Accessed 24 September 2019].

Bassuk, E., Hanson, J., Green, N., Richard, M., and Laudet, A., 2016. Peer-delivered recovery support services for addictions in the United States: a systematic review. *Journal of Substance Abuse Treatment*, 63, 1–9.

Bellamy, C., Schmutte, T., and Davidson, L., 2017. An update on the growing evidence base for peer support. *Mental Health and Social Inclusion*, 21 (3), 161–167.

Boevink, F., 2018. Peer delivered services in mental health care in 2018: infancy or adolscence?. *World Psychiatry*, 17 (2), 222–224.

Chinman, M., Hamilton, A., Butler, B., Knight, E., Murray, S., and Young, A., 2008. *Mental health consumer providers: a guide for clinical staff*. Santa Monica, CA: RAND Corporation.

Daniel, A., Turner, T., Powell, I., and Fricks, L.A., 2015. *Pillars of peer support - VI: peer specialist supervision*. Available from: http://www.pillarsofpeersupport.org/POPS2014.pdf [Accessed 4 December 2019].

Deegan, P., 2011. *Peer staff as disruptive innovators*. Available from: https://www.commongroundprogram .com/blog/peer-staff-as-disruptive-innovators [Accessed 29 September 2019].

Depression and Bipolar Support Alliance 2010. *A report on peer support supervision in VA mental health services*. Depression and Bipolar Support Alliance.

Fuhr, D., Taylor Salisbury, T., De Silva, M., Atif, N., van Ginneken, N., Rahman, A., and Patel, V., 2014. Effectiveness of peer delivered interventions for severe mental illness and depression on clinical and psychosocial outcomes: a systematic review and meta-analysis. *Social Psychiatry*, 49, 1691–1702.

Grey, F., and O'Hagan, M., 2015. *The effectiveness of services led by consumers in mental health: rapid review of evidence for recovery-oriented outcomes*. Mental Health Commission of New South Wales.

Harrison, J., 2015. *Peer support consultations: summary*. Kitchener, ON: Ontario Peer Development Initiative (OPDI).

Harrison, J., and Read, J., 2016. *Literature review: challenges associated with the implementation of peer staff roles in mainstream mental health and addiction agencies*. Available from: http://cmhawwselfhelp.ca/wp -content/uploads/2016/11/Harrison-Read-2016-Literature-review-Challenges-Associated-With-the -Implementation-of-Peer-Staff-Roles-in-Mainstream-Mental-Health-and-Addiction-Agencies.pdf [Accessed 29 September 2019].

Hino, S., 2014. *What is a mental health peer specialist's role in a care team?* Available from: http://peers-forprogress.org/pfp_blog/what-is-a-mental-health-peer-specialists-role-in-a-care-team [Accessed 20 December 2016].

Jorgenson, J., and Schmook, A., 2014. *Enhancing the peer provider workforce: recruitment, supervision and retention*. Alexandria: National Association of State Mental Health Program Directors.

Kadushin, A., and Harkness, D., 2002. *Supervision in social work*. 4th ed. New York: Columbia University Press.

Kuhn, W., Bellinger, J., Stevens-Manser, S., and Kaufman, L., 2015. Integration of peer specialists working in mental health service settings. *Community Mental Health Journal*, 51, 453–458.

Mental Health America 2019. *Peer services*. Available from: https://www.mentalhealthamerica.net/peer-services [Accessed 24 September 2019].

Minehart, M., White, W., Cantwell, A., Combs, M., Glazer, H., Korczykowski, J., Skipworth, K., Stewart-Taylor, P., Uffner, E., and Vernig, P., 2014. *The integration of peer recovery supports within Philadelphia's crisis response centers: an in progress report from the field*. Available from: http://www.williamwhitepa-pers.com/pr/2014%20Integration%20of%20Peer%20Recovery%20Support%20Services%20within %20Philadelphia%27s%20Crisis%20Response%20Centers.pdf [Accessed 4 December 2019].

Nasland, J., Aschbrenner, K., Marsch, L., and Bartels, S., 2016. The future of mental health care: peer-to-peer support and social media. *Epidemiology and Psychiatric Services*, 25, 113–122.

Orwin, D., 2008. *Thematic review of peer supports: literature review and leader interviews*. Wellington, New Zealand: Mental Health Commission.

Pfeiffer, P., Heisler, M., Piette, J., Rogers, M., and Valenstein, M., 2011. Efficacy of peer support interventions for depression: a meta-analysis. *General Hospital Psychiatry*, 33 (1), 29–36.

Phillips, K., 2018. *Supervising peer staff roles: literature and focus group results*. Kitchener: Canadian Mental Health Association, Waterloo, Wellington.

Phillips, K., Jabalee, C., and Harrison, J., 2019. *Supervising peer workers: a toolkit for implementing and supporting successful peer staff*. Available from: https://cmhawwselfhelp.ca/wp-content/uploads/2016/11/ Supervising-Peer-Workers-Toolkit-CMHA-WW-2019.pdf [Accessed 29 September 2019].

Reif, S., Braude, L., Lyman, D., Doughtery, R., Daniels, A., Ghose, S., Salim, O., and Delphin-Rittmon, M., 2014. Peer recovery support for individuals with substance use disorder: assessing the evidence. *Psychiatric Services*, 65 (7), 853–861.

Rich, P., 1993. The form function and content of clinical supervision. *The Clinical Supervisor*, 11 (1), 137–178.

Starkman, M., 2013. The movement. *In*: B. LeFrancois, R. Menzies, and G. Reaume, eds. *Mad matters: a critical reader in Canadian mad studies*. Toronto: Canadian Scholars' Press Inc, 27–37.

Sunderland, K., Mishkin, W., Peer Leadership Group, Mental Health Commission of Canada 2013. *Guidelines for the practice and training of peer support*. Calgary, AB: Mental Health Commission of Canada. Available from: https://www.mentalhealthcommission.ca/sites/default/files/peer_support_guidelines .pdf.pdf [Accessed 4 December 2019].

Swarbick, P., and Nemec, P., 2010. *Practices in peer specialist supervision and employment*. Available from: http:// www.patnemec.com/pdfs/NJPRA-HO-2010-Swarbrick-Nemec.pdf [Accessed 23 January 2016].

Tucker, S., Tiegreen, W., Toole, J., Banathy, J., Mulloy, D., and Swarbrick, M., 2013. *Supervisor guide: peer support whole health and wellness coach*. Decatur, GA: Georgia Mental Health Consumer Network.

17

AN INDIGENOUS[1] EYE GLASS ON SUPERVISION IN AOTEAROA NEW ZEALAND[2]

Moana Eruera and Leland A. Ruwhiu

The defining of supervision as a protective measure to advance quality practice and its function-alities, roles, and ethical guiding principles has often been the past time of western accountability sentinels tasked with supporting and promoting mainstream notions of professionalism espe-cially within the human welfare and health services. In the past three decades, the profession of social work, within Aotearoa and in particular Indigenous (Māori) practitioners, has vigorously critiqued this phenomenon to claim space for Indigenous knowledge and models of supervi-sion that reinforce Māori practice frameworks. Worldwide, the challenge posed here is for all Indigenous peoples to tell "their working stories" on this phenomena of "Supervision."

Claiming space for Indigenous supervision

In making sense of the supervision discourse from an Indigenous perspective, a continuum of supervision critical thinking and practice has emerged. At one end of the spectrum there is mainstream supervision that is generic, based on Western professional knowledge, skills, values, and ethical considerations. This is often presented as acultural by nature, that actualizes Western theory, practice, safety, protection, and development/learning connections (Chinnery et al. 2004). These mainstream models are dominant within the global supervision discourse and are generically used to supervise any practitioner regardless of culture/ethnicity and often without consideration of the culture/ethnicity of those client groups they are practicing with.

A strong middle positioning on the continuum can be described as supervision that focuses on "working alliances" (Ellis and Garland 2004), that acknowledges cross cultural engagement. These are built on collaborative and participatory elements, use adult learning cycles of experi-ence, reflection, conceptualizing, and acting, that mitigate transference and countertransference in order to strengthen meaningful engagements between supervisor/supervisee. Again, these are founded on Western theoretical framings that seek to be more culturally responsive. Grey et al. (2013) contend that within this space the development of decolonizing social work saw progress in the use of some traditional cultural practices being applied into contemporary set-tings. Supervision therefore was a means of providing practice accountability and competency for practitioners engaged in these activities.

Taking into account the social, cultural, economic, environmental, political, and historical environments influencing this critique of supervision within Aotearoa New Zealand, it is not surprising to see as one moves to the other end of the continuum there is a very clear message that supervision is culturally founded and by its very nature incorporates "indigenous and cultural forms of supervision" (Eketone 2012). O'Donoghue (2003) also identified the importance of culturally competent supervision as critical in defining the maintenance of cultural boundaries and ethics; protection from unsafe practices; providing a form of quality assurance; and reassuring clients that practitioners engaging with them are culturally competent and accountable. However, the most significant point within his critique was the recognition in Aotearoa New Zealand that Indigenous Māori critical voices were missing from narratives about supervision (Hair and O'Donoghue 2009; O'Donoghue and Tsui 2012).

Underpinning this positioning on the continuum are foundational rights and obligations that need to be addressed when guiding practitioners working with Indigenous and or other cultural realities. These are evidenced both internationally through the United Nations Declaration on the Rights of Indigenous Peoples, UNDRIP (2007) and nationally within Aotearoa New Zealand in Te Tiriti O Waitangi[3] (1840) rights and obligations between the Crown representing Tauiwi[4] (those who have made New Zealand their home) and Tangata Whenua[5] Māori (Indigenous peoples of the land). Eruera (2012) thus contends that:

"With the increase in the development of Māori frameworks, whānau ora policies, whānau-centred approaches and the delivery of iwi/tribal social services, the practice of supervision to support these processes is imperative" (p. 13).

At this end of the supervision continuum in Aotearoa New Zealand, there is a clear articulation of Kaupapa Māori[6] supervision, that places Māori critical theoretical thinking and practices as foundational in caring for Tangata whenua healers, and accountable best practice for Indigenous peoples/Māori that is delivered by Tangata whenua for Tangata whenua (Eketone 2008; Ruwhiu et al. 2008; Elkington 2014). Furthermore, Kaupapa Māori supervision has been described as, "an agreed supervision relationship by Māori for Māori with the purpose of enabling the supervisee to achieve safe and accountable professional practice, cultural development and self-care according to the philosophy, principles and practices derived from a Māori worldview" (Eruera 2005, p. 64).

Surprisingly, while there is the plethora of diverse cultural supervision approaches/models of practice guided by Indigenous relational tenets that creates form, ideation, and praxis of this phenomenon, still that voice appears to be muted. It is not our intention to try to critically examine the entire supervision continuum outlined here, but rather to concentrate specifically on airing that missing Indigenous Tangata Whenua Māori voice.

Whakatakoto te kaupapa[7]

Subsequently, the purpose of this chapter is three-fold: first to critically summarize key elements within Tangata whenua/Māori Indigenous social/community workers and pāwhakawairua[8]/mentor voices, culturally mapping this praxis space of supervision. Second, to introduce a specific Tangata whenua/Māori (Indigenous) model of supervision thinking and praxis unique to Aotearoa New Zealand called "Ngā mahi whakakoi te wairua."[9] Third and finally, to provide clear illustrations of this in action/practice from both an Indigenous māreikura[10] (female) Māori and an Indigenous whatukura[11] (male) Māori eye/lens, paradigm and/or perspective.

Throughout this chapter we have used both Māori and English languages which reflect the nature of its use in our contemporary society and which are both acknowledged as official languages in Aotearoa New Zealand. As Māori, our cultural beliefs and customs are transferred through our language, and the nuances of our tribal diversity is often recognized and reflected through the uniqueness of tribal language and customs. The terms "kaiārahi"[12] for supervisor and "kaitiaki"[13] for supervisee have been adopted for this article and were gathered through a Ngāpuhi tribal supervision research project (Eruera 2005) that showed these as the most commonly used Māori words to name the supervision roles.

However, critical to claiming Māori space and identity within the Aotearoa supervision discourse it is important to explore, reclaim, and promote tribal uniqueness by using "te reo o te kainga"[14] or significant words relevant within different tribal areas in which supervision is practiced.

Indigenous (Māori) voices in supervision in Aotearoa New Zealand

In critically assessing Tangata whenua/Māori Indigenous social/community workers and pāwhakawairua/mentor voices within this praxis space of supervision, a number of common elements are identifiable. Tangata whenua supervision is grounded in Kaupapa Māori (Kohere 1951; Te Kaunihera 1979; Ngata 1959, 1961, 1970, 1980; Te Pani Manawatu 1989; Barlow 1991; Ruwhiu 1999; Halbert 2012; Durie 2001; Mead 2003; Royal 2003; Eketone 2008; Eruera 2012; Welsh-Sauni 2018; Ruwhiu 2019), that privileges as foundational Māori philosophies, traditions, values/beliefs, paradigms, theories, perspectives, whānau,[15] hapū,[16] iwi[17] Māori histories, te reo Māori (Māori language), and tikanga Māori (Māori practices) as a base line for providing ways to effectively work with Maori using human services and for supporting practitioners delivering their services to Māori clientele. Gaining space for "Kaupapa Māori paradigms" has taken many years. It comes with a clearly acknowledged evidence base in Aotearoa New Zealand and aligns strongly with global Indigenous development.

Another element displayed within tangata whenua supervision was a common explanatory method about the composition of Māori models of supervision through using direct metaphors from Te Ao Tūroa[18] (the natural environment/dimensions) that humans are strongly connected to.

E ai ki te Māori he hononga ita tō te tangata ki te whenua me te taiao

According to the Māori, humans are tightly connected to the land and to the natural world (Royal 2013)

There are many illustrations of Māori Indigenous social work leaders, researchers, writers, movers and shakers claiming and valuing their cultural voices using metaphors in mapping Māori supervision. For example, Dreadon (1997) and Webber-Dreadon (1999) used the Awhiowhio Poutama[19] designs reflected in the koru of native ferns to map out supervision with a Māori lens. Awhiowhio (spiral) embraces all and implies the art of reflection needed in supervision, while Poutama (steps) implies connection and action. Ruwhiu et al. (2008) build a picture of supervision as a mana-enhancing emancipatory journey using the metaphor of a fishing net. Lipsham (2012) built a reflective supervision method and practice tool in supervision based on Pohatu's social work practice model name "Āta." Murray (2012) used metaphorical sites of significance identified in her whakapapa to name her model of Indigenous supervision:

Hoki ki tōu maunga kia purea ai e koe ki ngā hau o Tāwhirimatea – as a supervision model, offers time and place for Kaupapa Māori practitioners to develop, extend, and reflect on their person and practice from a tangata whenua perspective. Accessing the taha wairua and recognizing the atua in participants of supervision is a step on the journey towards mauri ora (p. 10).

Furthermore, Eruera (2012) discussed her model of supervision named "he kōrero korari" by aligning it to the traditional process and customs undertaken when weaving a flax kete (woven basket) and the skills and knowledge required to competently undertake the supervision process.

He kōrero Kōrari is a tangata whenua supervision framework that uses the analogy of weaving a kete as a guide for developing responsive supervision for tangata whenua. It supports kaiārahi when constructing their supervision philosophy, principles, and practice for working with Māori supervisees towards "best practice" with whānau Māori. "He Kōrari" is the natural resource or your innate attributes and skills, "he kete" is your supervision practice made up of strands of your knowledge, experiences, values, and skills woven together to form a safe, competent, and responsive supervision process. "He Kōrero" enables Māori practitioners to openly share and contribute their stories so that the kaiārahi can facilitate a process for them to reflect, learn, develop, and seek support to enhance practice (p. 12).

The third and final common element reflected in Tangata whenua supervision are "notions of oranga"[20] or wellbeing, commonly identified throughout Indigenous tangata whenua Māori best social work practice and supervision discourses, and collectively captured in the writings and narratives of Durie (1994, 1998, 2001, 2006), Walsh-Tapiata and Webster (2004), Pohatu (2004, 2008, 2011), Ruwhiu and Ruwhiu (2005), Munford and Walsh-Tapiata (2006), Eruera et al. (2006) Paniora (2008), Eketone (2008), Hollis-English (2012), Cram and Williams (2012), Cram (2012, 2014, 2019), Cram and Wilson (2014), Dobbs (2015), Eruera and Ruwhiu (2015, 2016), Ruwhiu et al. (2016), King (2017), and Webster, Munford, and Saunders (2019).

Tangata whenua/Māori (Indigenous) supervision by its very nature champions notions of oranga – wellbeing/wellness as both a key outcome in its delivery but also a central facilitator advancing our cultural wisdom in practice. This promotes cultural safety for both Tangata whenua supervisors/practitioners and ultimately whānau Māori engaged in their service. Likewise, it places an onus on identifying clearly what the Indigenous Tangata whenua Māori supervision matrix on "oranga" looks like from the onset in terms of matauranga Māori (Māori knowledge) and tikanga Māori (Māori customs and practices). More importantly, to continue advancing oranga demands that practitioners in the supervision space should be engaging in "mana enhancing" practice and also quality assure and measure that practice in the same fashion. As Ruwhiu (2009) summarizes, triangulated by the works of Webster et al. (2019) plus King (2017):

> Mana enhancing practice pays attention to and respects history, the role of narratives and cultural concepts related to Māori wellbeing . . . Throughout social work's short history in New Zealand its theoretical foundations have largely been devoid of any Māori understandings of healing and wellness. Understanding concepts that are important for Māori wellbeing such as wairuatanga[21] and whakapapa[22] reinforces the importance of cultural identity and its constant presence in all we do including social work [inclusive of supervision].
>
> *(pp. 117, 118)*

In summary, with these foundational Tangata whenua supervision elements in mind, we introduce a specific Tangata whenua/Māori (Indigenous) model of supervision thinking and praxis called "Ngā mahi whakakoi te wairua."

Ngā mahi whakakoi te wairua – Development of the model

Ngā mahi whakakoi te wairua emerged through development of a working paper that combined Tangata whenua experiences (our own and those of Tangata whenua practitioners we engaged with throughout New Zealand) supported by the existing Tangata whenua supervision evidence base. The information was then tested in various forums including a national webinar in August 2014 for the ANZASW (Aotearoa New Zealand Association of Social Workers) called "Honouring Mokopuna in Supervision" (Eruera and Ruwhiu 2014) and a conference presentation called "Ngā mahi whakakoi te wairua" at the inaugural Te Wānanga O Raukawa symposium on "Supervision through Māori eyes" (2017).

The model was framed by its name/metaphor, guiding principles, and its nine phases, while its application is shared through examples from māreikura (female) and whatukura (male) perspectives. This framing reflects what the evidence shared earlier tells us about Tangata whenua supervision; that it is grounded in Kaupapa Māori, it uses Māori imagery/metaphor and is based on Māori concepts of wellbeing.

Name – *Ngā mahi whakakoi te wairua*

Ngā mahi (significant work/support), whakakoi (to sharpen), and te wairua (Tangata Whenua values and beliefs) combine to highlight the centricity of Māori cultural engagement processes founded in "te reo me ōna tikanga Māori,"[23] that applies Indigenous principles to support healing and development, reflection, and safe, accountable practices with whānau Māori. Ngā mahi whakakoi te wairua has for convenience sake been shortened to "Whakakoi te wairua" (Ruwhiu, P. T. O. Personal communications, July/Aug 2014).

Guiding principles

Within the context of Tangata whenua supervision, the principle of "Kaitiakitanga"[24] highlights the significance of protecting, making safe, and caring for and supporting the development of Tangata whenua healers. The principle of "Whakapiki oranga" emphasizes the "core essence" of supervision-type engagements, that healers should be supported using notions of Indigenous wellbeing and wellness. Such interventions have been well documented by Durie (1994, 1998, 2001, 2006, 2011) and embellished further through healthy supervisory practices with whānau Māori social service practitioners in Te Moanaui-Makirere et al. (2014). The final principle of "Wairuatanga" in "ngā mahi whakakoi te wairua," places the validity and legitimacy of Māori values, beliefs, concepts, paradigms, perspectives, ideologies, philosophies, frameworks, theories, and models of practice at the center of this critical engagement space of healing and wellbeing.

Māreikura/Whatukura applied exemplars

One unique aspect emphasized here is that for Māori, balance is reflected in the value of combining both māreikura (female) and whatukura (male) knowledge and understandings. Critiquing supervision is no different. This is provided using applied exemplars untainted by justification references to demonstrate how "whakakoi te wairua" has been implemented. As the following whakatauki[25] states:

Ko ngā wehewehe ngā tō reo, ko ngā wehewehe ngā tō Ao

Reflections of your language, are reflections of your world

Ngā tikanga whakahaere

There are nine phases/stages (ngā tikanga whakahaere) of "Whakakoi te wairua." The nine stages are not linear by nature but occur dynamically. They are:

- Hononga (connecting, relationship building, bonding)
- Whakawātea (to clear up, to free up, to make way, dislodge)

- Whakatika (to set out on a journey, to straighten)
- Whakatara/Whakamanawa (to provoke and prompt critical thinking, to challenge/to encourage, inspire, instill confidence, reassure, stimulate, support, and assess at a particular point in time)
- Āta (Intentional and thoughtful reflection, to pause, to breathe, be gentle)
- Ako wairua (an epiphany, an "aha moment," when a light goes on, when learning occurs)
- Turanga whakairo (revisiting your foundation – in this case principles guiding your mahi)
- Mauri ora (I breathe it is life, a plan of wellness and wellbeing)
- Whakairo kaupapa (learned patterns to engage in this work)

We now share the phases of "whakakoi te wairua" and apply examples to support understanding.

Hononga

Hononga is a process of physical and spiritual connection that requires participants to both give and receive and can be applied in a myriad of different practices. In other words, it can be defined as a "union, connection, and/or relationship, a joint, joining place or link"[26] but in this context, it reemphasizes the importance of taking time to really connect with someone. This phase requires spending quality time building meaningful purposeful relationships with people. In "whakakoi te wairua," this phase is underpinned by placing "tikanga Māori" (processes) and "me oritenga" (reasonings) at the center of all engagement. This hononga process is very much like a cementing or joining together of a whakapapa weave. Often in this phase, the subtle differences between Tangata whenua and Tauiwi practitioners involves the quality of "wā"[27] allocated for such a joining. The space involves active sharing by both in attendance concerning their lives, work lives, their whānau, hāpu, and iwi whakapapa, their historical whānau pūkorero,[28] and successful or difficult moments that surround their experiences of "supervision."

Hei Tauira (māreikura) – There are times when kaitiaki come and have an urgency about wanting to start straight into the session, particularly when they have things they want to resolve or are impacting them. In sessions such as this it is the art of the kaiārahi to implement a process of hono with them while still addressing their resolve.

Hei Tauira (whatukura) – Having karakia before proceeding with the other components of the healing support process was significant for because it broke us away from the worldly daily grind and emphasized that we would be sharing some personal matters and exploring better ways to navigate in the work space as indigenous practitioners. Tane Māori (whatukura/mana tane) may well seek environmental spaces to facilitate advancing that sense of connectedness and affirmation to being committed in this "whakakoi te wairua" journey. I can remember deciding with a fellow Māori practitioner that we would use going to the movies to shift our thinking into a wellbeing space where friendship (Hoatanga) resided. In Palmerston North, this hononga process was also illustrated in my involvement in peer supervision with a group of Tāne Māori meeting at the lido in the spa pool. Having to strip down to "bare-bones" so to speak connected us all together under a common reality – this mahi wasn't about hiding behind stuff, it was about being clear that we wanted to be in a healing space, both physically and spiritually – we wanted soul, heart and real action conversations to assist us in working with whānau Māori.

Whakawātea

The term whakawatea most commonly refers to a cultural process that takes the time to clear, free or dislodge a Kaupapa from anything residual that is attached to enable participants to move forward from that situation and resume normal activities. Within "te mahi whakakoi te wairua," this whakawātea practice prioritizes space and time to ground oneself in the session, freed from anything preoccupying. It would allow the kaitiaki to share their current state with the kaiārahi (a feeling, issue, attitude, event, success, or other) that is distracting their ability to fully engage in the session or in practice in general (sometimes it is offloading). The purpose of whakawātea is to collectively and formally acknowledge the state (on a continuum between "ora" and "kahu po"[29]) the kaitiaki has arrived in, gain understanding about the reason they are so, and in doing so activate a releasing process that enables them to continue into the session and/or practice.

Hei Tauira (māreikura) – Two wāhine Māori had asked for cultural supervision to discuss issues of discrimination and racism by their manager. The whakawātea process allowed them to verbalize what had occurred, culturally reframe the actions as a violation of their tapu[30] and mana, and recognize the disruption it had caused to their "ora" or personal wellness. Equally important, they were able to share in a safe space how these behaviors had made them feel. The prolonged culmination of these feelings and emotions triggered a physical and emotional response to these oppressive behaviors through "tangi" or crying together and releasing some of the tension stored up over a prolonged period of time. This process opened a healing pathway to begin to address and restore their tapu and mana.

Hei Tauira (whatukura) – In the rōpū pool (puna) session, the conversations with other tāne, then placing it in front of all present, helped to separate the whānau issues from best practice professionally. The challenge was to value the space to ground oneself in. The kaitiaki tane had a clear understanding after this process about how issues with his daughter as she was leaving home were impacting on his judgements professionally with the whānau dynamics of a situation he was key worker for. Being able to speak candidly with other tāne, and still feel the tinana responding to the healing waters of the spa pool, culminated in shifting his practice. He felt the physical release as he relaxed in the pool, but at the same time could see the way forward in his hinengaro to address the complicated issues facing the whānau and mokopuna ora issues he was assisting in.

Whakatika

The whakatika phase contextualized within this process enacts the notion of claiming space to prepare or set out on a journey. The kaitiaki introduces the kaupapa for discussion and will have identified, to varying degrees, those things they hope to achieve from the session. Kaitiaki come with their practice wisdom intact from a range of sources and often have already applied some of this knowledge to the kaupapa. The whakatika period of "whakakoi te wairua" would facilitate a process through "hono a wairua,"[31] to openly discuss the situation and begin processing it through an organizationally contextualized lens.

Hei Tauira (māreikura) – A wahine[32] Māori introduced a kaupapa korero for the session, common to that experienced by many Māori working within mainstream organizations. She was being called upon regularly to do karanga,[33] reo Māori translations, and cultural coaching for the organizations manager, as in teaching mihi and as such was acting as a cultural advisor. She had already considered the dilemmas and tensions for herself and these were twofold. While she considered that these requests were appropriate identification of her cultural leadership skills by the organization, they were also an added expectation over and above her formal role of employment and had begun to affect her performance, as she had less time to undertake her own role. These knowledge and skills were also not acknowledged and compensated formally as part of her professional competency base. She felt an added burden and obligation as she was the only wahine Māori on staff that was able to speak reo Māori and was committed to upholding tikanga to ensure whānau Māori receive the practices they are entitled, while also being aware that it was beginning to impact on her ability to manage her workload, and she was starting to feel resentful about tokenistic requests. When asked what kind of support she wanted from the session she said that she wanted to check what other kaimahi Māori in this situation had done (both inside the same organization and external) so she could consider and explore all options.

Hei Tauira (whatukura) – One kaitiaki tane[34] Māori, just came to our session without preparing. Subsequently, his expectation was that he was going to just talk about what was happening with the whānau he was working with. He never considered that this time might also be about looking at what was happening around him personally. Nor that he might well be able to plan his own continuing professional development journey and this space might be one source of meeting his goals. My response to him was that there were new opportunities available to him to strengthen his practice, and the wero[35] was to put "wā" into preparing about what he felt needed to happen so that we could negotiate an agenda jointly to address those various terrains.

Whakatara/whakamanawa

This section of the process can be described as the exploration phase facilitated through activities that apply the concepts of whakatara and whakamanawa. The whakatara role is renowned within the Dynamics of Whanaungatanga[36] framework. The main function of whakatara is to provoke alternative thought patterns, prompt critical thinking, facilitate challenge, prick the conscience, and assist the kaitiaki to ensure rigor in their exploration of the kaupapa. This role is enhanced further through the process of whakamanawa. This concept can best be understood by examining the segments of the word whaka-mana-wa. "Whaka" means to cause or effect change, "mana" is about understanding the potential of a person and supporting them to positively express that potential, and "wa" is within a defined space and time. Therefore, whakamanawa can be understood within this context as emancipatory practice applied by assisting the kaitiaki to identify barriers, obstacles, and forms of oppression that restrict positive progress of the kaupapa so that mana can be restored and/or enhanced. The Kaiārahi role also involves providing encouragement, inspiration, reassurance, stimulation, and support that instils confidence in the Kaitiaki.

Hei Tauira (māreikura) – The skills of whakatara to constructively challenge the thinking of the kaitiaki in a supportive way is a critical part of good supervision. In a session with a tane Māori practitioner, there was an exploratory kōrero[37] with him about how his "whatukura" (mana tane) perspective informed and applied to a kaupapa for mokopuna. I shared a "māreikura" (mana wahine) view about the situation that challenged him to consider and gain insights into the mother's view which he hadn't thought about prior. He then moved to the "whakamanawa" stage by identifying the barriers for this mahi and how he might challenge and advocate on the mokopuna's behalf. He reviewed his rationale about his decision and actions moving forward and used a different approach with the mother.

Hei Tauira (whatukura) – In a one-to-one session with a tane Māori practitioner, the impression I got was that there were several matters weighing heavily on his mind concerning a whānau. Scratchy details had appeared on his case notes, but using the art of questioning all aspects of this situation helped open up and create an in-depth clearer understanding of his responsiveness to the whānau he was working with. It felt like he had exhausted all avenues, but in being a kaiārahi and feeling the situation, it prompted me to ask those questions that automatically came from within and meant that he could voice these issues creating blockages for him. We used a symbols exercise to map out exactly what those issues were (the whakamanawa component). The Tāne Māori tendencies of providing minimal detail or depth on issues (letting things slide "like water off a duck's back"), and to sidestep heartfelt korero was managed by using the art of questioning with intent to allow him to really explore those concerns creating a physical heaviness on his hinengaro. Respecting a whatukura positioning does not limit being brave enough to explore his knowingness in a different fashion.

Āta

Pohatu (2004) and Pohatu and Pohatu (2007) founded and described the concept of "āta" as a cultural tool, shaped to inform and guide understandings of respectfulness in relationships within social and community practice. "Āta" focuses on respectful relationships, negotiating boundaries, and creating ahurutanga or safety within those relationship engagements (Lipsham 2012). Within te reo Maori, "āta" is often the prefix used to emphasis thoughtful, contemplative, careful, and reflective states such as ata rongo (reflection using all the senses) and āta haere (safe, careful, and intentional movement). Commonly within social and community work, kaitiaki often fail to create time to indulge in "āta" processes, which are critical in gaining personal insights to improve practice delivery. The "āta" phase in the context of "te mahi whakakoi wairua" (supervision) intentionally creates the space and time whereby the kaitiaki is given the opportunity to stop, breathe, ponder, consider, and reflect on the personal and professional insights gained so far throughout the process. This is often a time of comfortable silence to prompt intentional and thoughtful reflection.

Hei Tauira (māreikura) – A māreikura "āta" space that fondly frequents my memories is a time where we were asked to intentionally contemplate what "kaitiakitanga" means to us. I was transfixed quickly back to the experiences of birthing my two sons and the complete awe of new life, te tapu o te tangata,[38] and the kaitiakitanga roles, responsibilities, and obligations to care for and nurture the potential of a newborn soul manifested into our physical realm. When transposing this concept of kaitiakitanga into the practice context, it reinforced to me the reasons why I have unwavering commitment to the safety of mokopuna at all times and those practices that support and maintain their improved wellbeing and safety.

Hei Tauira (whatukura) – The essence of "āta" in all its variation is that, as a cultural tool of engagement, it challenges tāne to breathe, to pause, to create spaces, to hold and capture time, and to ponder and reflect on the actions prior to these actually occurring. The natural tendency for tāne is to react, but this adds a dimension of thoughtfulness and measured informed responsiveness. In one peer session with my colleague I raised an issue about being asked to provide cultural advice on the spot. She reminded me to think long term, and to emphasize the protocols we needed to engage in which involve linking back to those in our region who had the capacity to provide regional support. Āta for me are those critical teeth of reflective practice. I remember on one occasion as a kaiārahi, thoughtfully listening with intent to kaitiaki Tāne Māori as we did a group healing circle. Structured by tikanga, as one member of the group took centre stage while the rest of us listened with our hearts, the tears of understanding, of sorrow or hope flowed. The impact of practicing āta was opening the session into the realm of mōtoi.[39] Not shallow but deep, meaningful diving into the roots of the issues impacting on best practice.

Ako wairua

"Ako" infers learning and "wairua" emphasizes our values and beliefs. So, given this position on "Ako wairua," there is acknowledgement that realizations will occur. This is having an epiphany: an "aha moment" when a light goes on, so to speak, about something that has been troubling you, continually pressing on your mind, doesn't fit, or leaves you feeling rangi-rua.[40] Ako wairua involves recognizing that a paradigm shift has occurred for you. There are levels of Ako wairua.

Sometimes it feels like the penny drops and you get it, or your tinana responds – for example, your body affirms to your wairua that something special has happened or that a burden has been released, e.g. "kua heke ngā roimata me ngā hupe."[41] In other words, it can occur with huge fanfare or in a quiet, still moment as a realization manifests itself to you about what is pono and tika, about what necessary actions and deeds need to be taken in a situation to support whānau shifting from kahupō to oranga states of wellbeing.

Hei Tauira (mareikura) – When discussing the impact of emotionally heavy social work, a wahine Māori wanted to talk about how to cleanse herself from the weight of this. Our kōrero drew parallels with our Māori cultural process of tapu/noa, of entering and leaving a state of "tapu" or restriction. There are tikanga or processes that enable us to do this, for example the use of water, food, karakia/takutaku (incantations) to remove yourself from a tapu state. She had an "ako wairua" when she drew these parallels and thought about her issue from a Māori worldview. She also realized that it requires Māori cultural knowledge and skills to perform these processes, and while she is Māori, she did not feel confident to do so as she was still reclaiming our language. We discussed what she could manage and found a way for her to do so.

Hei Tauira (whatukura) – I remember a time when I was struggling as a child health social work practitioner with a particular dilemma concerning a young ten-year-old boy. His whānau were finding his sexual exploration behavior (masturbating) difficult to cope with, especially when having guests over etc. Informing them of the fact that this was quite normal behavior (as indicated in all the texts on human development) still did not ease the embarrassment this was causing. The "aha moment" in this situation came when hearing a korero say, "natural doesn't mean to say that it's acceptable and right." In talking this through with my kaiārahi I was able to use that learning to support the mātua in their mokopuna ora management strategy.

Turanga whakaaro

Turanga whakaaro highlights the importance of revisiting ngā takepu (those principles) inform-ing whakapiri oranga/whakakoi te wairua mahi. This phase is characterized by making sense of our supporting principles that guide best practice in working with mokopuna and whānau Māori. There are three key principles guiding this journey: kaitiakitanga, whakapiki oranga, and wairuatanga. Protection of those we work with and ourselves, having a strong sense of wellbe-ing and wellness, and grounding these experiences of engagement with our cultural values and beliefs intact summarize the power of those principles. A time to reflect and connect to turanga whakaaro is often missed in this space, and our wero is that these should be continually revisited. They provide sense and depth to your practices of supporting the journey between kaiārahi and kaitiaki. The overall outcome should be better informed services to mokopuna and whānau Māori.

Hei Tauira (mareikura) – Many kaitiaki Māori I supervise want to discuss how they experi-ence racism and discrimination in the workplace because they are Māori. Within this discussion I use these cultural principles of kaitiakitanga, whakapiki oranga, and wairuatanga as prompts for them to describe how this makes them feel and how they may address it.

Hei Tauira (whatukura) – Whenever we meet there is always a space to align our actions with ngā takepu, ngā ūaratanga, ngā matapono[42] (our principles). So why did you support that type of mahi with your whānau you are working with? One of my kaitiaki Tane Māori highlighted that it reinforced the shift from kahupō to oranga, and that was actively manifested in developing with whānau a strategy to have "whānau time."

Mauri ora

"Mauri ora" infers supporting kaitiaki in the constructing of their "ora plan" to shift them on from just talking about wellbeing and wellness into active action to meet those aspirations. This is a space for supporting whānau shifts of aspirational thinking into real action that they are the key architects of.

Hei Tauira (māreikura) – Self-care is a recurring topic with kaitiaki which needs active planning and reviewing within supervision to maintain consistency and develop habits. This part of the session allows time for this to happen, e.g. these are generally simple, practical plans such as leaving space between appointments to move safely from one whānau visit/ interaction to another, maintaining the time to adequately disconnect and prepare for the next visit.

Hei Tauira (whatukura) – a Tane Māori came to the wānanga, held in Ngā Tai E Rua Marae, on whānau violence prevention, and when he along with his whānau were asked to construct an ora plan, I remember the advice I got from my kaiārahi that reinforced the view that they should be the owners of their oranga plan. They asked me what this might look like and I reminded them about looking at areas they could improve on to move towards oranga. That Tane Māori said "I need to get my head sorted out" …so in that mauri ora plan he committed to attending a 14-week Tāne Māori violence-free course run in Papakura by Tāne Māori.

Whakairo kaupapa

As with "tā moko or moko kauwae,"[43] there are etched and embedded patterns that provide a whakapapa to learn in our contact with each other and with those we work with. "Whakairo kaupapa" highlights the reflective ponderings of patterns that influence our engagements with our fellow beings. And the challenge is to be able to clearly signpost those learnings in our development as "competent Tangata whenua Pou" in supporting, strengthening, and nurturing our healers who share their puna with our mokopuna and whānau Māori.

Hei Tauira (māreikura) – Often within supervision there is a lot of discussion, and this part of the process creates the space for the kaitiaki to articulate what they have learned, discovered, and reflected on in the session. In a cultural supervision session, we were debating the differences in understandings between whakapapa whānau. I described this as descendants from the same genealogical or bloodline, and my colleague described this as those who you have strong relationships with including those who are not bloodline related. When we unpacked this, we realized that our learning was our belief system, and this had a strong influence on how we understood this concept. While we may not agree, we could understand each other's view more deeply.

Hei Tauira (whatukura) – In this engagement space, the kaiārahi and kaitiaki exchange gifts. I have been in both roles, and what has been a learning that I've valued is that pono, tika, and aroha are continually exchanged when there is a strong relational foundation established at the onset of our time with each other. I was challenged about not completely opening up to my kaiārahi but then explained to her that as a Tane Māori I ticked differently. And my silence was often not about not wanting to share. I needed to have time to think in acting. That emphasized the importance to me of working in something and then talking. So gathering kaimoana, going to the movies, being part of a tāne rōpū in a spa pool, preparing kai in the kāuta …were all manifestations of "time to think in acting." That was a huge learning for me, and I continue to practice that today.

Māreikura final words

We hear the cry of our Māori practitioners in Aotearoa New Zealand. They are seeking healing, restoration, guidance, support, acknowledgement, and challenges through supervision that is grounded in a Kaupapa Māori worldview, that promotes an oranga or wellbeing approach, that understands, affirms, and finds meaning in Māori ways of thinking, being, and feeling. Our language and customs are practiced as a normal part of the model to continue to strengthen the validity of working with our people in ways that reclaim our traditions. We no longer leave our culture at the Western supervision door or hide our practices as unevidenced or subjective and therefore non-professional. Our supervision is professionally and culturally accountable, safe, evidenced; and practiced equally within the supervision discourse. Tihei mauri ora … and there was life.

Whatukura final words

As a teenager in my first full time working experience I was introduced to "supervision" at the Tomoana meat works in Hastings. In the mid-1970s, all new prospective workers would line up on the floor and a "hard hat" or supervisor of the mutton chain[44] would, in view of those already working on the chain, walk down the line of those seeking employment and give you the nod. When it came to me, I remember this supervisor looking at me — he turned to my father on the chain and my father nodded at him, then I got a job. So you can imagine that in my "mind's eye," I thought that supervisors were like "gods" who determined whether you worked or not. That "boss/worker mentality" power relationship image of supervision where your voice meant very little remained with me, until I entered the profession of social work. In my first supervision experience, suddenly the focus was on me, my interpretation of matters in the work I was engaged in, and my needs in terms of personal and professional development. Culture wasn't even a consideration to me, I was just eager to become a social work professional, a change agent, a mover and shaker, a people whisperer. However, my first supervisors were tauiwi, and both emphasized to me that they were inadequate in meeting my needs fully. My kaumatua and kuia became my cultural supervisors, and straight away there were differences in delivery, in focus, in language, in directional maps, and in wisdom and knowledge with practice experience shared. Questions arose for me about mainstream supervision paradigms, and my growth accelerated. As a Māori kaitauwhiro,[45] and more particularly a whatukura, I have realized just how powerfully embracing it is to be able to deconstruct and culturally reconstruct supervision, with regard to the processes of supporting, invigorating, and challenging Tangata whenua practitioners/healers in the arts of strengthening their delivery of servicing Māori with their cultural eye/lens actively functioning. It's like opening up ones pūmotumotu[46] so that "being Māori, thinking Māori, feeling Māori, acting Māori" become the central drivers for mapping out the bracing and strengthening of our healers through the art of "whakakoi te wairua."

Concluding summary

1. "Ngā mahi whakakoi te wairua" promotes and advances the paramountcy of Tangata whenua cultural integrity and balance.
2. "Ngā mahi whakakoi te wairua" is where Tangata whenua meet Tangata whenua at our ideological borderlands to "exchange and receive gifts" of learning and development.
3. "Ngā mahi whakakoi te wairua" is Kaupapa Māori driven. Our voice, our experience, our understanding, our wisdom, our theories, our processes guiding our healing.

4. "Ngā mahi whakakoi te wairua" opens the sharing of Indigenous bodies of wisdom (practiced knowledge) concerning this phenomena of "supervision."

Notes

1 Indigenous refers to the original inhabitants of a country. The country in this case is New Zealand. The Indigenous peoples of this country are referred to as Tangata whenua – peoples of the land. Since contact history, these tribal nations were categorised as Māori. Tangata whenua/Māori are the Indigenous peoples of New Zealand.

2 Aotearoa, land of the long white cloud, is a traditional name given to New Zealand by its Indigenous inhabitants. New Zealand was coined initally by Abel Tasman, a Dutch Explorer, who was the first European to discover the country in 1642.

3 Te Tiriti O Waitangi – The Treaty of Waitangi – is a founding document that gave birth to the southern seas nation of New Zealand. Signed by a multiplicity of Māori tribal nations, and leadership and representatives of the English Crown (on behalf of all settlers and future migrants), the Treaty embedded the Indigenous rights of Māori and nationhood development with the Tauiwi arriving in Aotearoa New Zealand.

4 Tauiwi is irrevocably connected to the term Tangata whenau. When talking about Indigenous people of the land (Tangata whenau), the term Tauiwi describes all other people who have settled here, after leaving their homelands, thus making roots in Aotearoa New Zealand. They will always be Tauiwi (having genealogical origins in other countries), but the beautiful thing is that Tauiwi also can develop a sense and notion of belonging here. In other words, this new homeland becomes embedded in their intergenerational DNA, as it reinforces their right to participate as full citizens of Aotearoa New Zealand.

5 Tangata whenua – Tangata (people), whenua (land). Put together: "people of the land." Often attached to Tangata whenua are land occupation rights, and these are more about roles of being caretakers of the land not land ownership. Furthermore, Tangata whenua reflects the indigeneity of being First Nations People. In this case, the Indigenous people of Aotearoa.

6 Kaupapa Māori – Kaupapa (purpose, topic), Māori (emerged as an identifier in contact history with Tauiwi Pākehā). In this context, Pākehā is a relational term to Māori to describe white European settlers within their townships and settlements). Combined together, "Kaupapa Māori" reflects Māori ideology. A philosophical doctrine, incorporating as a priority the knowledge, skills, attitudes, and values of Māori society.

7 Whakatakoto te kaupapa is defined in this context as laying down the subject/topic of this chapter.

8 Pa-whaka-wairua translates in this context to mean significant people and places that remind you of or mentor you about those things that are invaluable in building and strengthening your sense of value as a Māori. "Pa" refers to a traditional fortress made of wooden pallisades, "whaka" highlights an invigorating sense of activity, and "wairua" is defined as those values and beliefs that are significant to being Māori. Put together, the question asked "is who is the person or people or what natural entity or entities provide you with inspiration to be Māori, to maintain your cultural integrity, to use as an exemplifer of being at peace with one's Māori-ness."

9 "Ngā mahi whakakoi te wairua" was coined by Pirihi Te Ohaki Ruwhiu as a name for supervision, after being approached in July/August 2014. Ngā (plurality), mahi (work), whaka (active causation), koi (sharp), te wairua (the values/beliefs, perspectives, paradigms, etc). Joined together "Ngā mahi whakakoi te wairua" can be defined as practice that involves sharpening ones values/beliefs/perspectives (knowledge sources of wisdom) in practice.

10 Māreikura is a term that comes out of Māori esoteric folklore concerning the Journey of Tane (God of the forests) who ascended to the highest heaven seeking support for humanity. On his arrival he was given three baskets of knowledge and two stones as gifts to assist humanity in obtaining wellness and wellbeing. One of the stones was called Māreikura, that came out of the house of Rauroha, and exemplified the mana (power, honour, prestige, authority, self-esteem, voice, level of influence, and humility) of womanhood.

11 The second stone called Whatukura, that originated from the house of Rangiatea, exemplified the mana (power, honour, prestige, authority, self-esteem, voice, level of influence, and humility) of manhood. With the three baskets of knowledge, these two stones provided balance to help humanity

in seeking oranga – wellness/wellbeing (one needs to take into consideration that there are diverse Tangata whenua narratives regarding the creation of humanity and the natural environment).

12 Kai (in this context refers to the role of a person) and ārahi (guide or lead). When combined, "Kaiārahi" in this space is defined as "supervisor."

13 Kai (the role of a person) and tiaki (to care for, look after, protect). When combined "Kaitiaki" in this space is defined as "supervisee."

14 "te reo o te kainga" also referred to as "te mita o te reo" is used to identify the specific unique local dialects of the Māori language. It is important to remember that in New Zealand there are nations (iwi) of diverse Māori realities, each with their own language, practices, and ways of viewing the world, who are genealogically able to trace their lineage to each other.

15 Whānau (Family inclusive of extended family). The notion of whānau – family groups – in Māori culture is more inclusive of connecting with others based on bloodlines (whakapapa – cousins, both close and distant, etc.) and purpose (kaupapa – church, sports, school, work, interests-based whānau).

16 Hapū – sub tribes, large extended families who are tied genealogically to an eponymous ancestor.

17 Iwi – a tribal nation made up of numerous hapū, who all genealogically connect to each other through their migration canoe (waka) to Aotearoa. On landing they took up residence in parts of Aotearoa. Thus they have kaitiakitanga (caretaker) obligations to whenua.

18 Te Ao Tūroa also referred to as Te Taiao is defined as the natural dimension, nature, the natural environment.

19 Awhiowhio Poutama is a combination of two distinctive Māori designs that feature in Māori cultural art. Awhiowhio is a spiral that draws from the koru of the natural fern plant, while Poutama is depicted as a stairway or steps. Both are used to depict growth and development.

20 Oranga can be broken down to three words for interpretation and understanding. "O" was used in the past to infer "supplies/sustenance," "ra" is defined as day/daily, and "nga" highlights plurality/more than singular. Within this context, it emphasizes more than one aspect to consider. When looking at the basic level of needs to consider, a Māori framework and model of practice known as Te Whare Tapa Whā (Durie 1994) highlights four significant areas: one's physical, mental, spiritual, and family wellness. Together "oranga" in this context highlights "providing sustenance on a daily basis to meet the overall wellbeing welfare and wellness of a person."

21 "Wairua" (values/beliefs, spiritual, ideological, conceptualizations, paradigms, theories, perspectives), "tanga" (collective). Together "Wairuatanga" highlights the collective values/beliefs, spiritual, ideological, conceptualizations, paradigms, theories, and perspectives of the Māori culture.

22 Whaka (invigorate/activate) papa (Papatuanuku – mother earth). Together this reflects the significance of genealogical connections (to tangata – people, to te ao tūroa/te taiao – the natural terrain, to our wairuatanga – to our culture knowledge, wisdom, traditions, and aspirations).

23 "te reo me ōna tikanga Māori" means "Māori language and practices/process."

24 Kaitiakitanga – the collective sense of people who carry the responsibilities of caring for, protecting, safeguarding, and supporting the health and wellbeing of people, places, and values/beliefs.

25 Whakatauki is defined as a "proverb." A form of messaging in cultural codes.

26 http://www.maoridictionary.co.nz/

27 Wā – time

28 Whānau pūkorero – family historical stories, narratives.

29 "kahupō" – defined as "a cloak of darkness." Within the Māori healing terrain it is used to describe moments where someone is in a state of confusion, feeling lost. There is also alignment to experiencing symptoms of ill health or unwellness such as depression etc.

30 Tapu – sacredness, protective factors.

31 Hono a wairua – connection to our values, beliefs, spirituality, conceptualizations, perspectives, ideology, theories, and paradigms.

32 Wahine – singular for "a woman." Note the plural, wāhine, for more than one woman.

33 Karanga – is a ceremonial call that occurs in Māori processes, when people are brought onto a marae, into a significant event. The karanga is performed by māreikura.

34 Tane is singular for "a man/male." Note the plural, tāne, for more than one man/male.

35 Wero in this context infers "a challenge."

36 Dynamics of Whanaungatanga (DOW) – In recent times this role has been strongly promoted within a Tangata Whenua framework called the "Dynamics of Whanaungatanga" (DOW) by Pa Henare Tate, Te Hiku o te Ika Trust, and kaumatua of Te Tai Tokerau. This framework was mandated by Iwi of Te

Taitokerau and is well known to those who are leaders in Tangata Whenua Social Work Practice, not only within Tai Tokerau but throughout Aotearoa New Zealand.

37 Kōrero – to speak, a narrative, to talk.

38 Te tapu o te tangata – the sacredness of humanity/people

39 Mōtoi – within Māori movements, wānanga the tōhunga Beez Ngarino te Waati talks of mōtoi being the subconscious space where the roots of much of our trauma reside – the roots to our behaviors.

40 Rangirua – is defined as confusion, doubt, in two minds, ambiguous etc.

41 Kua heke ngā roimata me ngā hūpē – both tears and muscus will fall (a physical response to emotional trauma or joy).

42 Ngā takepu, ngā ūaratanga, ngā matapono are all kupu Māori (Māori words) – dialectical ways of defining principles.

43 Tā moko – full facial tattoos depicting status and whakapapa for Tāne Māori; moko kauwae – jawbone facial tattoos depicting genealogical connections for wāhine Māori.

44 In charge of hiring and firing people who worked on the production line (chain that began with slaughtering sheep to finally meat ready for the freezers.

45 Kaitauwhiro broken into three words: kai – a person fulfiling a role/function; tau – settled; whiro – conflict, evil, bad. Joined together within this context – the role of a social worker.

46 Pūmotumotu – at birth it is evident that a baby's skull has a soft opening that eventually closes as they mature into childhood. In Māori traditional narratives, when Tane (god of the forests) was tasked with traveling through the various esoteric spaces to the highest heaven (each heaven was depicted as a whare tupuna – ancestral house), he used incantations to travel up the chimneys to ascend to that heaven where he was given those three baskets of knowledge and two stones to help humanity to deal with being on earth.

References

Barlow, C., 1991. *Tikanga Whakaaro: key concepts in Māori culture.* Auckland: Oxford University Press.

Chinnery, S., Worrall, J., and Beddoe, L., 2004. Actualising the theory-practice connection. *Oral presentation at supervision conference – weaving together the strands of supervision,* 9–11 July Centra, Auckland Airport.

Cram, F., 2012. *Safety of subsequent children, Māori Children and Whanau, a review of selected literature.* Wellington: Families Commission. Available from: https://thehub.sia.govt.nz/assets/Uploads/SoSC-Maori-and-Whanau.pdf [Accessed 24 February 2020].

Cram, F., 2014. Measuring Māori wellbeing. *MAI Journal – A New Zealand Journal of Indigenous Scholarship,* 3 (1), 18–32. Available from: http://www.journal.mai.ac.nz/sites/default/files/MAI_Jrnl_V3_Iss1_Cram.pdf [Accessed 24 February 2020].

Cram, F., 2019. Measuring Māori children's wellbeing: a discussion paper. *MAI Journal – A New Zealand Journal of Indigenous Scholarship,* 8 (1), 16–32. doi:10.20507/MAIJournal.2019.8.1.2.

Cram, F., and Williams, L., 2012. *What works for Māori – synthesis of selected literature.* Wellington, New Zealand: Department of Corrections.

Cram, F., and Wilson, M., 2014. *Disparities paper/systemic bias – internal report.* Ministry of Social Development (unpublished).

Dobbs, T., 2015. *Te Ao Kohatu – principled framing of best practice with mokopuna Māori: a literature review of indigenous theoretical and practice frameworks for mokopuna and whānau well-being.* Available from: https://practice.orangatamariki.govt.nz/assets/resources/Documents/te-ao-kohatu-literature-review-of-indigenous-theoretical-and-practice-frameworks.pdf [Accessed 24 February 2020].

Dreadon, E., 1997. Mātua whakapai tōu whare, ka whakapai ae i te marae o te tangata: first set in order your marae before you clean another. *Social Work Review Te Komako,* 8 (1), 6–8.

Durie, M., 1994. *Whaiora: Māori health development.* Auckland: Oxford University Press.

Durie, M., 1998. *Whaiora: Māori health development.* 2nd ed. Auckland: Oxford University Press.

Durie, M., 2001. *Mauri ora: the dynamics of Māori health.* Auckland: Oxford University Press.

Durie, M., 2006. *Measuring Māori well-being.* New Zealand Treasury, Guest Lecture Series. Avaliable from: https://treasury.govt.nz/sites/default/files/2007-09/tgls-durie.pdf [Accessed 25 February 2020].

Durie, M., 2011. *Ngā Tini Whetu: navigating Māori futures.* Palmerston North, New Zealand: Huia Publishers.

Eketone, A., 2008. Theoretical underpinning of kaupapa Māori directed practice. *Mai Journal – A New Zealand Journal of Indigenous Scholarship,* 3 (1), 1–11. Available from: https://ndhadeliver.natlib.govt.nz/delivery/DeliveryManagerServlet?dps_pid=FL1050971 [Accessed 25 February 2020].

Eketone, A., 2012. The purposes of cultural supervision. *Aotearoa New Zealand Social Work*, 24 (3–4), 20–30. doi:10.11157/anzswj-vol24iss3-4id104.

Ellis, G., and Garland, M., 2004. Integrating models for clinical supervision training. *Workshop presentation at supervision conference – weaving together the strands of supervision*, 9–11 July Centra, Auckland Airport.

Elkington, J., 2014. A Kaupapa Māori supervision context – cultural and professional. *Aotearoa New Zealand Social Work*, 26 (1), 65–73. doi:http://dx.doi.org/10.11157/anzswj-vol26iss1id56

Eruera, M., 2005. He korero korari. *In*: L. Beddoe, J. Worrall, and F. Howard, eds. *Weaving together the strands of supervision. Proceedings of the 2004 conference.* Auckland, New Zealand: Faculty of Education, University of Auckland, 59–66.

Eruera, M., 2012. He kōrari, he kete, he kōrero. *Aotearoa New Zealand Social Work*, 24 (3–4), 12–18. doi:10.11157/anzswj-vol24iss3-4id103.

Eruera, M., Huata, P., King, L., Pere, R., Ruwhiu, L.A., and Tule, C., 2006. Transcripts of Think Tank on Oranga Whānau for Hei Tauira & Kaahukura, held at Clarks Beach, South Auckland on 9 and 10 of May 2006.

Eruera, M., and Ruwhiu, L.., 2014. *Honoring mokopuna ora through supervision*. Available from: https://anzasw.nz/webinar-moana-eruera-dr-leland-ruwhiu-honoring-mokopuna-ora-through-supervision/ [accessed 1 March 2021]

Eruera, M., and Ruwhiu, L.A., 2015. Eeny, meeny, miny, moe catch hegemony by the toe: validating cultural protective constructs for indigenous children in Aotearoa. *In*: C. Fejo-King, and P. Mataira, eds. *Expanding the conversations: international indigenous social workers' insights into the use of indigenist knowledge and theory in practice.* Torren, ACT Australia: Magpie Goose Publishing, 131–174.

Eruera, M., and Ruwhiu, L.A., 2016. Ngā kārangaranga o te ngākau o ngā tūpuna tiaki mokopuna: ancestral heartfelt echoes of care for children. *In*: M.A. Hart, A.D. Burton, K. Hart, G. Rowe, D. Halonen, and Y. Pompana, eds. *International indigenous voices in social work.* Newcastle on Tyne, UK: Cambridge Scholars, 115–132.

Grey, M., Coates, J., Yellow Bird, M., and Hetherington, T., eds., 2013. Decolonizing social work. Abingdon, Oxon: Routledge.

Hair, H.J., and O'Donoghue, K., 2009. Culturally relevant, socially just social work supervision: becoming visible through a social constructionist lens. *Journal of Ethnic & Cultural Diversity in Social Work*, 18 (1–2), 70–88.

Halbert, R., 2012. *Horouta: the history of the Horouta canoe, Gisborne and East Coast.* Auckland: Oratia Books.

Hollis-English, A., 2012. *Māori social workers: experiences with social service organisations.* Thesis (PhD), Otago University, Dunedin. Available from: http://hdl.handle.net/10523/2127 [Accessed 25 February 2020].

King, L.F., 2017. *Indigenous social work practice development: the contribution of manaakitanga to mana-enhancing social work practice theory.* Thesis (MSW) Otago University, Dunedin. New Zealand.

Kohere, R.T., 1951. *The autobiography of a Maori.* Wellington, New Zealand: A. H. & A.W. Reed.

Lipsham, M., 2012. Āta as an innovative method and practice tool in supervision. *Aotearoa New Zealand Social Work*, 24 (3–4), 31–40. doi:10.11157/anzswj-vol24iss3-4id122.

Mead, H., 2003. *Tikanga Māori: living by Māori values.* Whakatane: New Zealand Huia Publishers.

Munford, R., and Walsh-Tapiata, W., 2006. Community development: working in the bicultural context of Aotearoa New Zealand. *Community Development Journal*, 41 (4), 426–442.

Murray, V., 2012. Hoki ki tōu mauna kia purea ai e koe ki ngā hau o Tāwhirimātea – a supervision model. *Aotearoa New Zealand Social Work*, 24 (3–4), 49–64. doi:10.11157/anzswj-vol24iss3-4id102.

Ngata, A.T., 1959, 1961, 1970, 1980. *Nga moteatea: He marama rere no nga waka maha, parts i, ii, iii.* Wellington: A. H. Reed & A.W. Reed.

O'Donoghue, K., 2003. *Restorying social work supervision.* Palmerston North: New Zealand Dunmore Press.

O'Donoghue, K., and Tsui, M.S., 2012. Towards a professional supervision culture: the development of social work supervision in Aotearoa New Zealand. *International Social Work*, 55 (1), 5–28.

Paniora, R., 2008. Ko wai au?. *Aotearoa New Zealand Social Work, Te Komako*, 20 (4), 52–55.

Pohatu, T.W., 2004. Āta: growing respectful relationships. *He pukenga kōrero*, 8 (1), 1–8.

Pohatu, T.W., 2008. Tākepu: principled approaches to healthy relationships. *In*: J. Te Rito, and S. Healy, eds. *Proceedings of the traditional knowledge conference 2008, Te Tatau Pounamu: the greenstone door.* Auckland: Ngā Pae o te Māramatanga, 241–247.

Pohatu, T.W., 2011. Mauri – rethinking human wellbeing. *MAI Journal – A New Zealand Journal of Indigenous Scholarship*, 3 (1), 1–12. Available from: https://ndhadeliver.natlib.govt.nz/delivery/DeliveryManager Servlet?dps_pid=FL10697584 [Accessed 25 February 2020].

Pohatu, T.W., and Pohatu, H.R., 2007. Names: distance travellers. *In*: S. Edwards, and R Hunia, eds. *Toroa te Nukuroa Vol 2: traditions and values of frameworks of being*. Te Wānanga o Aotearoa, 13–25. Available from: https://ndhadeliver.natlib.govt.nz/delivery/DeliveryManagerServlet?dps_pid=IE2581558 [Accessed 25 February 2020].

Royal, Te A.C., ed., 2003. *The woven universe: selected writings of Rev. Māori Marsden*. Otaki: Estate of Rev. Māori Marsden.

Royal, Te A.C., 2013. *Kaitiakitanga - Connected to nature*. Te Ara - the Encyclopedia of New Zealand. Available from: http://www.TeAra.govt.nz/mi/kaitiakitanga/page-2 [accessed 21 February 2020].

Ruwhiu, L.A., 1999. *Te puawaitanga o te ihi me te wehi: the politics of Māori social policy development*. Thesis (PhD), Massey University, New Zealand. Available from: http://hdl.handle.net/10179/3529 [Accessed 25 February 2020].

Ruwhiu, L.A., 2009. Indigenous issues in Aotearoa New Zealand. *In*: M. Connolly, and L. Harms, eds. *Social work: context and practice*. South Melbourne, VIC: Oxford University Press, 107–120.

Ruwhiu, P.A., 2019. *Emancipate yourself from mental slavery, none but ourselves can free our minds: wetekia te mau here o te hinengāro, ma tātou e whakaora, e whakawātea te hinengāro*. Thesis (PhD), Massey University, New Zealand. Available from: http://hdl.handle.net/10179/15109 [Accessed 25 February 2020].

Ruwhiu, P.T., and Ruwhiu, L.A., 2005. Ko te pae o te atua mai i ngā whakaaro hōhonu nei, hei oranga mo te ira tangata. *Social Work Review Te Komako*, 17 (2), 4–19.

Ruwhiu, P.T., Ruwhiu, L.A., and Ruwhiu, L.L.H., 2008. Tō Tātou kupenga: Mana tangata supervision a journey of emancipation through heart mahi for healers. *Aotearoa New Zealand Social Work Te Komako*, 20 (4), 13–34.

Ruwhiu, L.A., Te Hira, L., Eruera, M., and Elkington, J., 2016. Borderland engagements in Aotearoa New Zealand: Te Tiriti and social policy. *In*: J. Maidment, and L. Beddoe, eds. *Social policy for social work and human services in Aotearoa New Zealand: diverse perspectives*. Christchurch, New Zealand: Canterbury University Press, 79–93.

Te Kaunihera, 1979. *He Matapuna: some Maori perspectives: Wellington*. New Zealand: Planning Council.

Te Pani Manawatu, 1989. Personal Communication.

Te Moananui-Makirere, J., King, L., Eruera, M., Tukukino, M., and Maoate-Davis, S., 2014. Te Ara Whakapikorang. *Aotearoa New Zealand Social Work*, 26 (1) 10–19.

UN General Assembly, *United Nations declaration on the rights of indigenous peoples: resolution / adopted by the general assembly*, 2 October 2007, A/RES/61/295. Available at: https://www.refworld.org/docid /471355a82.html [Accessed 2 March 2021]

Walsh-Tapiata, W., and Webster, J., 2004. Do you have a supervision plan? *Social Work Review, Te Komako*, 16 (2), 15–19.

Webber-Dreadon, E., 1999. He taonga mo o mātou tīpuna (A gift handed down by our ancestors): an indigenous approach to social work supervision. *Social Work Review Te komako*, 11 (4), 7–11.

Webster, J., Munford, R., and Sanders, J., 2019. *Tōu ake mana: an approach to practice with vulnerable rangatahi Māori. Pathways to resilience and youth transitions research*. Available from: http://www.youthsay.co .nz/massey/learning/departments/centres-research/resilience-research/t%C5%8Du-ake-mana/t%C5 %8Du-ake-mana_home.cfm [Accessed 8 March 2020].

Welsh-Sauni, M., 2018. *Tiaki mana mokopuna: protecting the rights of mokopuna Māori*. Thesis (MA Indigenous Knowledge) Te Wānanga o Aotearoa, Te Awamutu, Waikato, New Zealand.

PART III

Roles, responsibilities, and relationships

18

THE SUPERVISEE'S LEARNING JOURNEY

Kieran O'Donoghue

This chapter explores the supervisee's learning journey within and through supervision. It does this by firstly discussing the role of the supervisee and then explores how supervisees learn to understand, participate, and use supervision for professional accountability, development, and support across the span of their careers. This is followed by a discussion concerning how changes in their professional development, organization, and supervisor influence supervisees' learning journeys within and through supervision.

The role of supervisee

The role of supervisee is integral to the practice of supervision. Social workers first engage as supervisees in field education, and in most countries, continue to participate in supervision throughout their career (O'Donoghue 2010). Despite this, limited attention has been given to the role and contribution of the supervisee to supervision within the social work supervision literature (Barretta-Herman 2001). For example, most of the social work supervision books since 2000 have been written for and from the perspective of the supervisor (Austin and Hopkins 2004; Beddoe and Davys 2016; Caspi and Reid 2002; Davys and Beddoe 2010; Engelbrecht 2014; Howe and Gray 2013; Kadushin and Harkness 2014; McKitterick 2012; Morrison 2006; Munson 2002; Noble et al. 2016; O'Donoghue 2003; Pecora et al. 2010; Shulman 2010; Tsui 2005; Weld 2012; Wonnacott 2012). The small amount of literature that focuses on the role of the supervisee is in the form of guides and manuals which are designed to assist supervisees to actively participate, make the most of their supervision, understand their role, and contribute to the interactive process of supervision (Carroll and Gilbert 2006; Davys 2007; Knapman and Morrison 1998; Morrell 2013). The few exceptions to this are Morrell's (2005) report on her experience of running workshops for supervisees and an Aotearoa New Zealand based qualitative study that explored the influence supervisees' histories had on development, understanding, and participation within supervision as well as how their histories also influenced their role development as supervisees (O'Donoghue 2012).

Supervisees primarily develop their understanding of their supervisee role and identity through the lived experience of participating in supervision, rather than from formal education and training (O'Donoghue 2012). This includes the limited preparatory training they have prior to field education (Moorhouse et al. 2014). The supervisees' experiences shape their expectations and inform them when processing and responding within supervision. They also form the basis of their evaluations of the supervision and supervisor (O'Donoghue 2010). Each experience of a supervision relationship contributes to a supervisee's development of a mental map of supervision and supervisory relationships. This in turn, shapes their expectations about the relationship, the interactional process, and the use of power and authority by the supervisor (Hanna 2007). Supervisees' also bring their history, personality, gender, social and cultural background, and professional practice experiences to the role of supervisee, as well as their personal constructions of authority relationships (O'Donoghue 2003). The combination of the supervisee's background, mental map of supervision, expectations regarding the supervisor, and lived experiences of supervision, influence how the supervisee perceives and participates in supervision (O'Donoghue 2012). In other words, each supervisee has their own personal construction of their supervisee role, supervision, and their supervisor. This highlights the importance of exploring and understanding a supervisee's supervision history, as well as their background as a person and practitioner when establishing a new supervision relationship (Morrison 2006; O'Donoghue 2003, 2012). Supervisees prefer supervision that is socially and emotionally supportive, helpful for their professional practice with clients, and enhances their professional development (O'Donoghue and Tsui 2015; O'Donoghue et al. 2018). Supervisees also prefer supervisors who are socially and emotionally intelligent, culturally competent, and who help them with their practice, as well as help them develop professionally (O'Donoghue and Tsui 2015; O'Donoghue et al. 2018). For supervisees, supervision is ideally an activity and place in which their practice, development, and well-being are able to be explored, reflected upon, and processed within a professional relationship that is safe, supportive, and sensitive to their diverse backgrounds and needs (O'Donoghue 2010; O'Donoghue and Tsui 2015). In other words, it is a secure base for professional advice, support, education, and development (Hanna 2007; O'Donoghue 2012). The foundation of this secure base is derived from a constructive supervision alliance, interactional process, and emotionally competent organizational culture (Morrison 2007; O'Donoghue 2012). From this base the supervisee is empowered to act as the protagonist in supervision, through bringing items for exploration or review in supervision. These items are derived from their experiences with clients, organizational matters affecting them, and their professional learning and development needs. The supervisee's part in supervision consists of planning for supervision by creating an agenda or list of items, prioritizing and presenting these items in supervision, then interactively processing each item through a reflective conversation, which leads to decisions and actions (O'Donoghue 2014). The final aspect of the supervisee's part is reviewing and implementing the actions in their practice or workplace (O'Donoghue 2010).

Supervisee's learning, participation, and use

The supervisee's learning, participation, and use of supervision occurs in parallel with their learning and growth as a professional practitioner. The supervisees' learning journey within supervision is progressive through the following stages: a) being supervised, b) the supervision of client practice, and c) supervision as part of professional practice (O'Donoghue 2012).

Being supervised

The first stage, being supervised, begins during field education and continues into the supervisee's initial employment as a beginning practitioner. It is characterized by the supervisee being overseen by the supervisor and relying on the supervisor's expertise and leadership to lead, manage, and guide the supervision process (O'Donoghue 2012). Supervision at this stage primarily involves instruction, support, learning, and guidance as the supervisee is socialized into supervision and their role and identity as a social worker. The supervisee's primary learning in this stage is about how to use supervision to help them develop confidence and competence through performing job tasks and learning how to practice as a social worker (Tsui 2005). Supervisees at this stage have concrete needs such as how to make a referral, complete an assessment, and write a court report or affidavit. In their supervision meetings, supervisees are usually responding to enquiries from their supervisors regarding their caseload and their understanding of particular types of procedures. In general, the supervisee is primarily focused on obtaining direct guidance, advice, and support as they learn to practice in their organizational setting (Brown & Bourne 1996). In other words, the "being supervised" stage corresponds with the social workers induction, orientation, and entry into practice. This stage is often described as the self-focused stage, with the practitioner being concerned with their job performance, with their focus being on the individual and specific tasks in front of them, whilst cognizant of their limited confidence and competence and aware how much they need to be supported in their learning and development as beginning practitioner (Hawkins and Shohet 2012; Stoltenberg 2005). Throughout this stage, the supervisor provides the holding environment and secure base that assists the supervisee to move beyond their initial concerns, fears, and worries. The supervisors interventions during this stage are often directive and prescriptive with some facilitative and conceptual interventions to support the supervisee and assist them to make connections between theory, research, and practice (Stoltenberg 2005).

Supervision of client practice

The second stage, the supervision of client practice, marks a shift from the reliance upon supervisory oversight, leadership, and support to the supervisee becoming a more proactive participant in supervision by bringing and discussing matters concerning clients (O'Donoghue 2012). During this stage, the supervisee is learning that supervision involves reviewing their practice with clients and that it is a place where they can work through ways to manage and resolve challenges their clients face. The supervisee's experiences of focusing on their clients in supervision starts to deepen their reflection on client situations and takes them beyond descriptive narratives about clients to exploring the connections between a client's personal situation and its relationship to wider social issues. It also starts to raise for the supervisee the limitations they face with regard to community and social supports and resources, as well as the limits of their organizational and professional role. Another change that occurs concerns the leadership within the supervision session with this becoming more interchangeable and shared. In short, in this stage the supervisee learns to use their supervision for client consultations, and how to prepare, present, explore, and reflect on their practice within supervision (O'Donoghue 2012).

The social worker's learning and development through supervision at this stage is conceptual as they start to make connections between their client's issues, their practice, the organizational and professional context, and the policy environment (Brown and Bourne 1996). In other words, they are putting the pieces of this jigsaw together and starting to glimpse aspects of the whole.

As a practitioner, the supervisee has developed in confidence, competence, and independence to the extent that they will engage in debate and discussion and disagree with their supervisor. These changes mark a transition from their previous dependence on their supervisor to a greater level of autonomy as a practitioner (Hawkins and Shohet 2012). In other words, the supervisee has moved from being directed and overseen by their supervisor to consulting their supervisor. For supervisors, this change means that their interventions are more reflective and catalytic. In this stage, the supervisor is also able to be more challenging with their interventions through questions and reflective responses concerning the supervisees perceptions, blind spots, and assumptions (Stoltenberg 2005).

Supervision as part of professional practice

The third stage, supervision as part of professional practice, occurs when the supervisee has ownership of their supervision and knows how supervision works, what they expect and want from it, and how to use it to get their needs met (O'Donoghue 2012). In other words, their understanding of the supervisee role, and how to participate in supervision and use supervision has developed to the point where they are aware of the supervision process, and understand the supervisee role and their own needs as a professional practitioner. They also have the motivation and confidence to proactively pursue their needs within the supervision forum (O'Donoghue 2012). Supervision is supervisee-led with the supervisee driving the agenda and discussion and the supervisor following and responding. The process is more conversational, reflective and direct, with the supervisee being more willing and comfortable to scrutinize what is informing their practice and to explore their blind spots. For the supervisee, supervision is concerned with their ongoing growth, development, and learning as a practitioner and how they can best use their strengths and capabilities in their practice (Brown and Bourne 1996; Hawkins and Shohet 2012). Supervisees in this stage are mature practitioners who have developed an integrated approach to practice; are informed by their practice wisdom; and understand the complexity of social work practice, the organizational and professional context, and the influence of the policy environment. They seek to use supervision for meaning making, reflection, refreshment, and to be challenged and grow. For supervisors, the challenge when supervising these experienced practitioners is to ensure that the reflective conversations do not become abstract and removed from their practice and continued growth (Brown and Bourne 1996). Supervisors also have be careful not to become too comfortable and complacent when supervising advanced practitioners and ensure that they do not get stuck in one area of the reflective learning process (Brown and Bourne 1996; Morrison 2006).

Developmental and contextual influences

The supervisee's journey described above from "being supervised" to "supervision as part of professional practice" is also influenced by the supervisee's professional development, their experiences within their organization, and relationships with supervisors (O'Donoghue 2012). These factors can influence the supervisee's learning, use, and participation both positively and negatively. Positive influences advance the supervisee's development, while negative experiences may result in the supervisee stagnating or regressing to a previous stage of development.

Supervisee's professional development

O'Donoghue (2012) identified two positive professional development influences, the first occurred when a supervisee undertook professional development that enhanced their practice skills or learnt a specific practice approach, such as learning solution focused practice or dialectical behavior therapy. This resulted in the supervisee developing more awareness of the supervision process, a better understanding of their role as supervisees, and increasing the level of responsibility they took for their supervision. In other words, it resulted in a developmental movement from supervision of their client practice to using supervision for their professional development. According to O'Donoghue (2012), the main reason for this change was that the practitioner's learning and development became the focus of their supervision and this contributed to increased ownership and self-efficacy within their supervisee role.

The second positive influence was the completion of supervision training by supervisees. Supervision training increased the supervisee's understanding of supervision and motivation to act to meet their own needs through supervision (O'Donoghue 2012). For some supervisees, completing supervision training also increased their expectations to the extent that they advocated for and obtained external supervision in order to ensure their needs were met (O'Donoghue 2012).

In contrast to the positive influence of supervision training, the professional development experience of becoming a supervisor had a mixed influence on supervisees' supervision. According to O'Donoghue (2012), those in his study who became peer clinical supervisors or external supervisors reported having their awareness raised concerning their own needs within supervision and gaining an increased understanding of the potential of supervision. These revelations occurred as a consequence of trying to provide supervision that met their supervisees' needs. The effect of this on their supervisee role in their own supervision was that they took greater responsibility for having their own needs met (O'Donoghue 2012).

In contrast, supervisees who became internal line management supervisors described this change as negatively influencing their supervisee role (O'Donoghue 2012). For these supervisees, their manager became their supervisor and their supervision was focusing on management tasks and staffing matters with their work essentially being overseen by their manager. In other words, their supervision had reverted back to the "being supervised" stage.

Organizational experiences

Studies have indicated that organizational culture has an influence on supervision (Collins-Camargo and Royse 2010; Dill and Bogo 2009; O'Donoghue and Tsui 2015). It is therefore not surprising that supervisees' experiences of organizational policies, practices, and decisions regarding supervision have an influence on their use, participation, and motivation in supervision. O'Donoghue (2012) notes that decisions made about the type of supervision, and the availability, approval, and choice of supervisors affected supervisees. The decisions that allowed supervisees to access external supervision and choose their supervisor enabled supervisees to take greater ownership of their supervision, be more proactive in their use of it, and participate fully in order to further their professional and practice development. In contrast, decisions that emphasized an organization's control of supervision through restricting the availability of supervision to internal line management supervision, with no or very limited choices of supervisor seemed to result in more reactive and passive supervisee participation that was indicative of a regression to "being supervised" (O'Donoghue 2012). To some extent the decisions of organizations in their supervision policies and practices indicate whether the culture of supervision is one that is of high trust and learning and development focused, or low trust and orientated towards control and compliance. For supervisees, the former culture aids the development of a secure base within the supervision alliance, and promotes ownership of the supervisee role and self-efficacy. The latter, however, contributed to a less secure base within the relationship and a less engaged and more circumspect supervisee whose use and participation in supervision had regressed to a stage of being instructed and directed.

Relationships with supervisors

The relationships supervisees had with their supervisors influenced supervisees' development and behavior in supervision, as well as their development as a practitioner. Constructive and supportive relationships that attended to the supervisee's development needs advanced a supervisee's level of engagement, use, and participation in supervision and their overall professional development (O'Donoghue 2012). In contrast, relationships where supervisees perceived the supervision to be inconsistent or sub-standard, or where there was a difficulty in the relationship, or the supervisor micro-managed a supervisee at an advanced stage of development had a negative effect on a supervisee's level of engagement, participation, and motivation within supervision (O'Donoghue 2012). Amongst the supervisees, in O'Donoghue's (2012) study, several of the relationship difficulties occurred following a change of supervisor, particularly when the supervisee had little choice or say in the change, and their experience of the interactional process with the new supervisor did not meet the supervisee's expectations. For these supervisees, their use and participation regressed to the point where they had actively disengaged and subverted the process to protect themselves from a perceived threat and that this primarily occurred in relationships where the supervisor was also the line manager (O'Donoghue 2012). In other words, their learning through supervision was focused on their protection and survival rather than their own professional and practice development.

Towards a conceptual map of the supervisee learning journey

The supervisee's learning journey from "being supervised" to "supervision as part of professional practice" is a complex journey that involves the interaction between the personal and professional development of the supervisee, their relationships with their supervisors, and the supervision culture of their organization. Table 18.1 below presents an emerging conceptual map of supervisee development that outlines the key features of each stage together with the positive and negative developmental influences. It clearly identifies that supervisees' growth and development within supervision is signposted by increases in their participation, motivation, ownership, and proactivity both within supervision and as a professional social worker (O'Donoghue 2012). The map shows the important role supervisors play in positive supervisee and practitioner development.

The implications of the emerging conceptual map for supervisees are that it shows that their participation, learning, and development within and through supervision is progressive and how their development can be positively and negatively influenced. For supervisors, the map can assist them by applying a developmental lens to their supervision and considering how they can positively support and assist their supervisees, as well as be mindful when the supervisee has had to change supervisor and has had limited options or voice in this process. In such cases, they would be wise to explore the supervisee's history and feelings about the change in supervision arrangements and diligently attend to the supervisee throughout the interactional process (O'Donoghue 2012). The implications for organizations primarily concern the decisions organizations make regarding their supervision policies and practices. The conceptual maps highlights that where these decisions provide supervisees with opportunities and options for supervision that contribute to their ongoing professional development, these in turn enhance their proactivity, participation, and use of supervision. Conversely, when organizations use supervision for surveillance, control, and risk management, this is arguably counterproductive because of the negative effect it has on supervisees' participation and ownership of their supervision (O'Donoghue 2012). Finally the emerging conceptual map highlights the need for

Table 18.1 Emerging conceptual map of supervisee development

Stage	Key features	Positive developmental influences	Negative developmental influences
Being supervised	• Socialization into supervisee role • Development of social worker identity • Supervision involves instruction, support, learning, and guidance.	• Supportive supervisor who is a secure base for supervisee • Meeting of supervisees concrete needs • Holding environment for supervisee's worries and fears. • Directive, prescriptive, facilitative, and conceptual interventions.	• Unsupportive and inattentive, inconsistent supervisor. • No attention to supervisee's needs. • Demanding, watch your back environment. • Command and control-based interventions.
Supervision of client practice	• Supervisee is more proactive. • Uses supervision for client consultation. • Deeper reflection on self, situations, client, and context. • As a practitioner, the supervisee connects client's situation, social issues, and resourcing. • They also understand the limits of organizational and professional role. • The supervisee has developed confidence, competence, and independence. • Engages in debate, discussion, and can disagree with supervisor.	• Supervisor who uses reflective and catalytic interventions. • Supervisor challenges perceptions, blind spots, and assumptions. • Supervisee undertakes professional development for practice skills development. • Supervision training and becoming peer or external supervisor. • The provision of external supervision for the supervisee.	• Supervisor who is directive and prescriptive. • Supervisor's interactional skills do not match with supervisees expectations. • Becoming a supervisor who is line-manager. • Change from external supervisor to internal or line-manager supervisor. • Supervision being perceived by supervisee as a threat or something to survive.

(Continued)

Table 18.1 Continued

Stage	Key features	Positive developmental influences	Negative developmental influences
Supervision part of professional practice	• Supervisee takes ownership of supervision. • Understands their role and responsibilities as a supervisee • Knows how to use the supervision to meet their professional needs. • Supervision is supervisee-led. • Process is conversational, reflective, and direct. • The supervisee is an integrated practitioner, informed by their practice wisdom and understanding of the complexity of social work practice, the organizational and professional context, and the influence of the policy environment. • Supervision is concerned with supervisees ongoing growth, development, and learning and how they can best use their strengths and capabilities in their practice.	• Supervisors who assist supervisee with meaning making, reflection, refreshment, and challenges them to grow. • The supervisee's own continuing professional development.	• Supervisors who do not challenge • Reflection that is either stuck or abstracted from practice and the practitioner. • Changes of supervisor • Change to type of supervision. • Micro-management by supervisor of supervisee. • Supervision being perceived by supervisee as a threat or something to survive.

research regarding supervisees' perspectives, experiences, roles, participation, development, and behavior within supervision.

Conclusion

This chapter has explored the supervisee's learning journey within and through supervision. It has identified that whilst this journey is progressive through the stages of "being supervised" to "supervision as part of professional practice," it is also influenced by the supervisee's professional development as a social worker, their organization's supervision culture, and by their supervisors. An emerging conceptual map of supervisee development has been proposed which identifies the key features of each stage and both the positive and negative developmental influences. The implications of this map for supervisees, supervisors, and social work organizations have been discussed, together with the need for research regarding the supervisee's role, participation, and development in supervision. In conclusion, this chapter illustrates the importance of conceptualizing and theorizing supervision from the perspective of the supervisee and considering the influence that professional development, organizations, and supervisors have on supervisees' participation and behavior within supervision.

References

Austin, M., and Hopkins, K., eds., 2004. *Supervision as collaboration in the human services: building a learning culture.* Thousand Oaks, CA: SAGE.

Barretta-Herman, A., 2001. Fulfilling the commitment to competent social work practice through supervision. *In*: L. Beddoe and J. Worrall, eds. *Supervision conference from rhetoric to reality: keynote address and selected papers.* Auckland, New Zealand: Auckland College of Education, 1–10.

Beddoe, L., and Davys, A., 2016. *Challenges in professional supervision: current themes and models for practice.* London: Jessica Kingsley Publishers.

Brown, A., and Bourne, I., 1996. *The social work supervisor: supervision in community, day care, and residential settings.* Buckingham, UK: Open University Press.

Carroll, M., and Gilbert, M., 2006. *On being a supervisee: creating learning partnerships.* Kew, VIC, Australia: PsychOz.

Caspi, J., and Reid, W., 2002. *Educational supervision in social work: a task-centred model for field instruction and staff development.* New York: Columbia University Press.

Collins-Camargo, C., and Royse, D., 2010. A study of the relationships among effective supervision, organizational culture promoting evidence-based practice, and worker self-efficacy in public child welfare. *Journal of Public Child Welfare,* 4 (1), 1–24.

Davys, A., 2007. Active participation in supervision a supervisee's guide. *In*: D. Wepa, ed. *Clinical supervision in Aotearoa New Zealand : a health perspective.* Auckland: Pearson Education, 26–42.

Davys, A., and Beddoe, L., 2010. *Best practice in professional supervision: a guide for the helping professions.* London: Jessica Kingsley Publishers.

Dill, K., and Bogo, M., 2009. Moving beyond the administrative: supervisors' perspectives on clinical supervision in child welfare. *Journal of Public Child Welfare,* 3 (1), 87–105.

Engelbrecht, L.K., (ed.) 2014. *Management and supervision of social workers: issues and challenges within a social development paradigm.* Andover, UK: Cengage Learning EMEA Limited.

Hanna, S., 2007. Not so strange! An application of attachment theory and feminist psychology to social work supervision. *Aotearoa New Zealand Social Work Review,* 19 (3), 12–22.

Hawkins, P., and Shohet, R., 2012. *Supervision in the helping professions.* 4th ed. Milton Keynes: Open University Press.

Howe, K., and Gray, I., 2013. *Effective supervision in social work.* London: SAGE.

Kadushin, A., and Harkness, D., 2014. *Supervision in social work.* 5th ed. New York, NY: Columbia University Press.

Knapman, J., and Morrison, T., 1998. *Making the most of supervision in health and social care: a self-development manual for supervisees.* Brighton, UK: Pavilion.

McKitterick, B., 2012. *Supervision*. Maidenhead, UK: Open University Press.

Moorhouse, L., Hay, K., and O'Donoghue, K., 2014. Listening to student experiences of supervision. *Aotearoa New Zealand Social Work*, 26 (4), 37–52. doi:10.11157/anzswj-vol26iss4id25.

Morrell, M., 2005. Supervision an effective partnership: the experience of running workshops for supervisees in 2004–5. *Social Work Review*, 17 (4), 39–45.

Morrell, M., 2013. *You deserve good supervision! A guide for supervisees*. Fullarton, SA, Australia: Margaret Morrell & Associates Ltd.

Morrison, T., 2006. *Staff supervision in social care: making a real difference for staff and service users*. 3rd ed. Brighton, UK: Pavilion.

Morrison, T., 2007. Emotional intelligence, emotion and social work: context, characteristics, complications and contribution. *British Journal of Social Work*, 37 (2), 245–263.

Munson, C., 2002. *Handbook of clinical social work supervision*. 3rd ed. Binghamton, NY: Haworth Press.

Noble, C., Gray, M., and Johnston, L., 2016. *Critical supervision for the human services: a social model to promote learning and value-based practice*. London: Jessica Kingsley Publishers.

O'Donoghue, K., 2003. *Restorying social work supervision*. Palmerston North, New Zealand: Dunmore Press.

O'Donoghue, K., 2010. *Towards the construction of social work supervision in Aotearoa New Zealand: a study of the perspectives of social work practitioners and supervisors*. Thesis (PhD), Massey University. Available from http://mro.massey.ac.nz/handle/10179/1535.

O'Donoghue, K., 2012. Windows on the supervisee experience: an exploration of supervisees' supervision histories. *Australian Social Work*, 65 (2), 214–231. doi:10.1080/0312407x.2012.667816.

O'Donoghue, K.B., 2014. Towards an interactional map of the supervision session: an exploration of supervisees and supervisors experiences. *Practice*, 26 (1), 53–70. doi:10.1080/09503153.2013.869581.

O'Donoghue, K., and Tsui, M.S., 2015. Social work supervision research (1970–2010): the way we were and the way ahead. *British Journal of Social Work*, 45 (2), 616–633. doi:10.1093/bjsw/bct115.

O'Donoghue, K., Wong Yuh Ju, P., and Tsui, M.S., 2018. Constructing an evidence-informed social work supervision model. *European Journal of Social Work*, 21 (3), 348–358. doi:10.1080/13691457.2017.134 1387.

Pecora, P.J., Cherin, D., Bruce, E., Arguello, T. de J., 2010. *Strategic supervision: a brief guide for managing social service organizations*. Los Angeles: SAGE.

Shulman, L., 2010. *Interactional supervision*. 3rd ed. Washington, DC: NASW Press.

Stoltenberg, C., 2005. Enhancing professional competence through developmental approaches to supervision. *American Psychologist*, 60 (8), 857–864.

Tsui, M., 2005. *Social work supervision: contexts and concepts*. Thousand Oaks, CA: SAGE.

Weld, N., 2012. *A practical guide to transformative supervision for the helping professions: amplifying insight*. London: Jessica Kingsley.

Wonnacott, J., 2012. *Mastering social work supervision*. London: Jessica Kingsley Publishers.

19

BECOMING A SUPERVISOR

Frances Patterson

Introduction

The journey of "becoming a supervisor" is a varied one shaped by diverse personal, professional, and organizational factors. It may be a consciously chosen step of career progression or an unplanned "acting-up" position of indeterminate length. Working with students as a practice educator can provide experienced social workers with an opportunity to dip their toe into supervisory waters, or a senior practitioner may be assigned a specific remit for staff supervision without line management responsibilities. For many, however, the roles of supervisor and manager are closely intertwined, and balancing the dual aspects of professional and organizational accountability is a dynamic tension.

This chapter aims to identify and explore some of the issues supervisors grapple with as they adjust to a shift in role and identity. Experiences will diverge depending on job remit and context but hopefully there is sufficient commonality for certain themes to resonate. Integrated services and interprofessional working are impacting on models of supervision in the United Kingdom (UK), but it is still the norm that a single supervisor, usually the worker's line manager, holds responsibility for the administrative, supportive, and developmental functions. For that reason, the assumption underpinning this chapter's discussion is that the process of becoming a supervisor simultaneously involves transition into a formal management post.

Change and transition is the lens through which this chapter will examine what becoming a supervisor involves, what strategies may be helpful for a new supervisor, and what challenges are likely to arise. This perspective on the supervisory journey is chosen for specific reasons. First and foremost, to emphasize that becoming a manager, leader, and supervisor is a significant transition (Gilmore 2010; Patterson 2015). Linked to that is the awareness that there are internal and external dimensions to a change process: adjustment on a psychological as well as a practical level. Secondly, transition theory suggests that endings are as important as new beginnings (Bridges 2009). Acknowledging what is being given up as well as what can be carried forward helps mark the distinction between a practitioner and a management role. This clarity is particularly important if role boundaries are blurred and supervisors are carrying a caseload as well as supervising others or covering staff vacancies within their team. And thirdly, the dichotomy between planned and emergent models of change serves as mirror for the new supervisor's evolving journey. Planned approaches to change (Lewin 1947;

Kotter 1996) can support new managers adapting to an altered role and identity. They provide a degree of security, some sense of order and direction when confidence may be shaky. In contrast, principles of emergence require adaptability and an acceptance that outcomes are uncertain. Becoming more at ease with what is unknown and unpredictable is often a challenging developmental task.

Endings and letting go

Bridges' (2009) model of transition outlines three phases which in some respects parallel Lewin's (1947) three-step model of change. The key difference lies in the distinction he makes between change and transition, describing the former as "situational" and the latter as a "psychological" process. Someone may occupy a supervisor's position and be accorded whatever formal title belongs to that role while below the surface they are still adjusting to what that means on a personal and professional level. One of the tasks to be undertaken before transition is possible is to "let go of the old reality and the old identity you had before the change took place" (Bridges 2009, p. 7), and for new supervisors there are multiple factors which can impede that internal shift. Within the social work profession, the basis for promotion to a supervisory post is often practice experience and competence. Progression into management is more an evolutionary journey than a distinct career choice and as a result, the significance of that shift may not be immediately obvious. This blurring of transition is exacerbated when promotion occurs within the worker's existing team or when it is a temporary acting-up position with the prospect of returning to their substantive post of practitioner.

Letting go of old ways requires inner motivation and effort and represents loss even when there is a readiness for change. Taking up a supervisory role in a new workplace involves a fracture with the past, and this discontinuity can be helpful when stepping into a management position. For those whose work environment is unchanged, it can be harder to resist the pull of familiar ways, particularly when these are reinforced by the expectations of others. A lack of preparation for supervisory responsibilities has been widely recognized (Cousins 2004; Bartoli and Kennedy 2015; Patterson 2015; White 2015; Beddoe and Davys 2016), and in the UK, projects such as the Practice Supervisor Development Programme (Research in Practice 2018) are in progress to address that gap. While formal training or other developmental opportunities are important (Harlow 2016), supporting new supervisors to reflect on the emotional as well as practical dimensions of transition is also of value.

Becoming a supervisor and a first line manager does not sever the connection to social work practice, but it necessitates a different relationship. To be one step removed is necessary in order to provide a supervisory space where practice can be explored, assumptions challenged, and alternative perspectives considered. But standing back takes effort if one's identity as a practitioner feels secure in comparison with the uncertainty of a novice supervisor. Clearly there are situations where direct engagement is appropriate, for example, accompanying a worker on a joint visit, but it is useful to acknowledge the part played by one's own needs. Whether this is to relieve an office-bound routine, to prove oneself as a supportive manager, or allay the anxiety generated by feeling accountable without hands-on involvement, understanding the pull factor of direct practice better equips a supervisor to fulfil their role. For many people, transition is compromised because they occupy a hybrid position spanning practice and management, carry a legacy caseload from being a practitioner in the team, or are covering staff vacancies and unallocated work. Gray et al. (2010, p. 44) describe the negative rip-tide effect when a manager gets caught in the current of front-line practice. For a new supervisor it is important to know where to locate themselves in the system to be most effective and to hold to that position as consistently as they can.

Social work practitioners are well accustomed to problem solving and bring this capacity to their new supervisory role. There is a place for such intervention but not when this becomes a habitual response to workers' concerns. Learning to hold back from offering solutions and instead creating a reflective space where supervisees are encouraged to dig deeper into their own resources and reach independent conclusions about the best way forward is a more crucial skill. There is something intriguing about the way in which supervisors are, in theory at least, committed to the value of reflection but often struggle to put this into practice. There is no lack of guidance on models of reflective supervision (Morrison 2005; Davys and Beddoe 2010) but studies have shown how social work managers more commonly give directive advice than spend time exploring ideas or emotions (Wilkins et al. 2017). Time pressures are an obvious contributory factor as are legitimate concerns about accountability in situations of high risk. In addition to these factors, however, new supervisors can feel pressured to offer something tangible, to have useful knowledge to impart, or expertise to share. The desire to be helpful can foster dependency in less experienced staff while limiting the development of reflective skills in both supervisor and supervisee. Letting go of having answers, becoming more comfortable with not knowing, and learning to trust in the value of listening and asking good questions – these all belong to the supervisor's transition.

The art of adaptive change (Heifetz and Laurie 1997) lies in discerning what shift is required and will make a positive difference. It may be an apparently minor adjustment but, if successful, its impact will be significant. This insight can be applied to the contested arena of transferable skills from social work practice to management where some emphasize commonality (Coulshed and Mullender 2006; Tolleson Knee and Folsom 2012), and others question the usefulness of managers' practice experience (Saltiel 2017). An array of capabilities including interpersonal skills, communication skills, and problem solving are undoubtedly relevant across both contexts. They are not merely replicated, however, but adapted in order to fit the demands of a new situation. One way of marking transition is to take stock of what has been learned as a practitioner, reflecting on strengths and weaknesses, weighing up what to leave behind and what to carry forward. That process enables a new supervisor to identify knowledge, skills, and values which represent continuity as well as gaps to be addressed. Included in such a review is one's own experience on the receiving end of supervision. Supervision history shapes the way that people supervise others, and being conscious of that influence is beneficial (Morrison 2005; O'Donoghue 2012; Kadushin and Harkness 2014). It supports a more nuanced approach than simply emulating the style of supervisors one has appreciated and rejecting what has been difficult. Closer scrutiny and reflection can reveal what was needed at different stages of development, what facilitated new learning, or what obstacles got in the way of a constructive supervisory relationship. The complexity of supervision begins to reveal itself and the diversity of approaches which may be employed (Beddoe 2015).

Becoming a supervisor of former colleagues brings particular challenges whether this is a temporary position or permanent post. In addition to letting go of the "doer role" and one's identity as a practitioner, this represents a dislocation in terms of peer support and the friendship of colleagues (Stoner and Stoner 2013, p. 8). At one extreme there may be rivalry and resentment over a promoted post, but even if team members are supportive there is a shift in power dynamic which cannot be side-stepped. Relationships are no longer equal and it is more damaging to pretend that nothing has changed than to negotiate a different way of relating. Some managers will handle this dilemma by consciously separating personal and professional worlds, but it is hard to avoid some degree of constraint bringing a potential sense of loss and isolation.

Moving through transition

A three-phase model of transition implies a more consistent sequential process than most people experience. Ibarra et al. (2010, p. 666) convey a sense of the confusing flux as different stages overlap and overlay one another, speaking of the "process of leaving one thing, without having fully left it, and at the same time of entering something else, without fully being a part of it." Bridges (2009) describes the middle phase of transition as a place of limbo and discomfort where familiar orientation is lost, and the destination is not always clear. While the temptation is to move through as fast as possible, he suggests that latent creative forces are at work if given time and patience.

> "One doesn't discover new lands without consenting to lose sight of the shore for a very long time."
>
> *(Andre Gide, quoted in Bridges 2009, p. 39)*

There are aspects of becoming a supervisor which resonate with this sense of disorientation and insecurity. While some may adapt with ease to a shift in personal and professional identity, others can feel conflicted and uncertain.

The issue of belonging versus isolation affects supervisors whether in a new work environment or a familiar team. Being in the team but not of the team can be a lonely place regardless of whether one sits in a separate office or an open plan workspace. While it is wholly acceptable for team members to have closer connection to some colleagues than others, similar affiliation on the part of a manager risks being interpreted as favoritism. Not only is it important to demonstrate parity across the staff group, but workers also need to trust their supervisor's confidentiality. A first line manager is inextricably bound up in the work of their team and the decisions being made by practitioners. The balance of proximity and distance, involvement and separation is not straightforward, and every supervisor has to find their own way through this terrain. One newly promoted supervisor encapsulated the emotional impact of becoming an outsider through an evocative analogy. Initially included in the invitation "we're going for lunch, do you want to come?", she soon experienced "we're going for lunch, do you want anything brought back?", and subsequently, a backwards call, "we're going for lunch. We'll be back at 2," as people left the office (Walls 2011, cited in Patterson 2015, p. 2081). While quite conceivable that exclusion was never a conscious intent, the sense of being displaced from "one of us" to "one of them" (White 2009, p. 140) remains potent.

Becoming "one of them" has a range of connotations for the supervisor and those around them. It may be perceived as a shift of allegiance from professional to managerial priorities or that the supervisor has "sold out" (Cousins 2004) by climbing the hierarchical ladder instead of holding true to core values of equality and social justice. Rather than being on the side of those who are disadvantaged and advocating on their behalf, a manager must juggle competing priorities and weigh up different needs in allocating finite resources. If there is residual ambivalence about joining the managerial ranks, a supervisor can struggle to establish a balanced relationship with the authority they hold. Power imbalance is inherent in social work practice, but handling power dynamics in a supervisory context is new territory for which people are often unprepared. Role insecurity can lead to an authoritarian approach (Wonnacott 2012) which is overly directive and undermines both the autonomy of an established practitioner and an inexperienced worker's need to develop greater independence. Alternatively, lack of confidence to exercise appropriate authority may result in "permissive" supervision (Wonnacott 2012) which fails to adequately oversee professional practice or manage risk.

Coming to terms with power and authority can be explored through the "dual role" of a social work supervisor (Wong and Lee 2015; Beddoe and Davys 2016). There are parallels with the tensions of care versus control in a practice context, but managing this potential splitting when supervising staff is a less familiar challenge. Although widely accepted that there are at least three core functions of supervision: administrative, developmental, and supportive (Kadushin 1976; Hawkins and Shohet 2012), some would argue that the divide between professional and managerial concerns is more revealing (Hughes and Pengelly 1997; Noble and Irwin 2009). The emphasis of new public management on target-setting, accountability, and performance management has changed the culture of supervision across sectors and specialisms (Noble and Irwin 2009; Bartoli and Kennedy 2015; White 2015). An administrative approach and the surveillance of risk gained dominant hold, leaving minimal space for reflective discussion and exploration of the emotional dimensions of working with people (Peach and Horner 2007; Beddoe 2010). While the limitations of a narrow technical-rational approach to complex social work practice are now widely recognized (Munro 2011; Ruch 2012), the influence of managerialism casts a long shadow and consequently "negotiating or mediating between practice and managerial worlds is crucial" (Lawler 2015, p. 271). It is interesting to note that reviews both in England (Munro 2010; 2011) and Scotland (Scottish Executive 2006) raised the possibility of separating line management from the support and development functions of supervision, mirroring the divide between clinical supervision and managerial accountability which is the norm for health professionals in the UK and is an established model for social work supervision in other parts of Europe (Bradley and Hojer 2009; O'Donoghue 2015). Supervisors' anxiety about being held accountable can lead to micro-management and many struggles with the tension between supporting staff and managing their performance. In the early stages of becoming a supervisor there is a need both to win trust and earn credibility. It can be hard to feel confident in one's own skills and what one has to offer particularly in relation to experienced staff or those who are skeptical about the value of supervision. As a result, the need to be liked or seen as helpful can take precedence, undermining the supervisor's capacity to provide challenge as well as support.

It seems self-evident that a supervisor's own supervision is critical is they are to fulfil their role effectively. Ideally this is the space where it is safe to be uncertain, to acknowledge vulnerability, and to explore what it means both personally and professionally to be overseeing the practice of others. In this respect, however, the experience of first line supervisors is variable, and it is not uncommon for reflective supervision to be replaced by "one-to-one meetings" where a business focus and management priorities dominate the agenda (Ruch 2008; Ward 2012). Lack of congruence between what is espoused in supervision policy and what happens in practice is problematic on many levels, not least of all the modeling of consistent and containing supervision across an organization (Patterson 2019). Potentially, it can also mean that new supervisors have limited opportunity for thoughtful reflection on the complexity of their task and the dilemmas they encounter. In situations where line management does not fully address those needs, it may be necessary to pursue alternative options whether that be peer supervision, group supervision, or some form of external consultancy. This is preferable to the "tendency to go on one's own as a supervisor" highlighted as a risk by Stoltenberg and Delworth (1987, cited in Hawkins and Shohet 2012, p. 83). A supervisor's continuing development, in addition to their wellbeing, is reliant on being able to step back from the immediacy of their day-to-day work and receive supervision which both supports and challenges their management practice.

Heron's (1975) typology of helping interventions offers a framework which supports supervisors to reflect on their preferred style of interaction. There is no ranking of style but a recognition that too narrow a repertoire is likely to limit a manager's effectiveness. Starting from the premise that supervisors draw on two distinct categories of intervention – facilitative or authoritative – a new manager can identify which of these feels instinctively familiar and which is less comfortable territory. Within each of these broad groupings are three further domains revealing a subtler range of skills and their distinctive contribution. A novice supervisor is unlikely to move effortlessly between the diverse types of intervention but can use these as a developmental tool to extend their practice and become more adept at sensing what the situation needs. Areas that are avoided in supervision, consciously or otherwise, are often those where anxiety is located, another reason for supervisors to pay attention to their habitual ways of responding and be alert to the invisible dynamics which may play out within a supervision relationship (Hughes and Pengelly 1997).

Power and authority are present in every supervisory relationship but not always discussed openly. Power imbalance can be an uncomfortable topic to raise and hard to gauge when or how to broach the issue. "Advantage blindness" describes the way in which those who hold positions of power or advantage often fail to recognize the impact this has on other people. It is not so much willful blindness as a taking for granted of the privileges afforded. It requires conscious effort to "recognise how the subtle and not-so-subtle forms of advantage operate" and to question "what's it like to be on the receiving end of me?" (Fuchs 2019).

Power dynamics within supervision are tricky because the balance of power does not consistently reside with the supervisor. Myriad factors may undermine a manager's role security, but they are nonetheless mandated with delegated authority from their organization and hold position power greater than that of their supervisees. For that reason, and without underestimating the challenge involved, it is incumbent on the supervisor to ensure that power and authority are openly addressed. A contract for supervision is an obvious starting place offering a structure within which standards and expectations can be clearly articulated. Pro forma templates have limited value as they invite a tokenistic approach, but spending time developing an individualized working agreement allows meaningful discussion to take place. This is an opportunity to talk about aspects of difference, such as gender, sexuality, age, ethnicity, which impact on the supervisory relationship or, at the very least, to demonstrate awareness of these issues and the constraints they may impose. The space may not yet feel safe enough for in-depth disclosure, but the intent is to make power dynamics discussable in the same way that practitioners need to acknowledge the impact of role authority on their relationships with people using services. Raising the issue of power is likely to be less challenging when the supervisor feels relatively secure in their own position than in situations where they feel intimidated by a worker's expertise or their dismissive attitude towards supervision. Naming the issue is important, however, and marks the beginning of a process aimed at honest and forthright dialogue.

Failure to name what is going on below the surface is a feature of collusive relationships and supervision an arena highly susceptible to different kinds of collusion. A new supervisor's wish to belong; discomfort at being seem as "one of them"; desire to be liked or to be helpful; all of these can contribute to supervisory games where habitual patterns become established and critical issues are avoided. The game of "treat me, don't beat me" is explored in depth by Cousins (2010)

Table 19.1 Supervisory approaches (adapted from Heron's six categories of helping interventions)

Authoritative	Telling or directing
	Sharing information
	Challenging or confronting
Facilitative	Encouraging the expression of feelings
	Stimulating the person's own problem-solving capacity
	Offering support

to show how supervisors in the helping professions can lose focus on outcomes for service users when they are drawn into a quasi-therapeutic relationship with those they supervise. Games in supervision are obvious once identified, but their greatest potency lies in the fact that they often remain hidden. The destructive dynamic of the drama triangle is probably the most well-known, playing itself out repeatedly in both professional and personal relationships (Karpman 1968). For a supervisor, an area for development is becoming attuned to games as they are in process, a version of reflection-in-action, which may not provide immediate answers but allows one to observe what is happening rather than be submerged in the drama (Schon 1983). Another form of collusion which can go unrecognized is the close identification a supervisor may have with a worker whose practice causes them no concern and with whom they feel a natural affinity. This is not necessarily about favoritism but acknowledgment that some supervisees are easier to get along with than others because of shared history, common interests, sense of humor, or other factors. While supervision may be enhanced by mutual understanding there is also a need for caution. Support and challenge are essential components in every supervisory relationship and the balance is easier to sustain when there are elements of difference between both parties. Mirroring the detrimental impact of groupthink on decision-making, the necessary rigor of questioning assumptions or challenging certitude can be compromised if there is too little dissent and disagreement (Janis 1972). At the opposite end of the spectrum to relationships which become too cozy, there can be collusion involving crossed rather than supportive transactions when a supervisee seems to do nothing right and the dynamic becomes one of critical parent and rebellious child. The sense of slipping out of an adult-adult interaction provides early warning that some type of collusion may be present and that attention needs to be directed towards surfacing the underlying issue (Berne 1961).

It will be clear from all that has been said about power, authority, and collusion that becoming a supervisor involves difficult conversations. It takes bravery to initiate "courageous conversations" (Beddoe and Davys 2016) and skill to handle these so that people feel heard and can expose their vulnerability rather than reacting defensively. There is limited practice ground to rehearse such conversations, so it is hardly surprising when they are avoided or delayed until a situation is critical. Work on dialogue (Burson 2002) explores the balancing act between advocacy and inquiry and how conscious awareness of these elements can enhance the quality of a conversation. Within social work practice and supervision there is taken-for-granted recognition of the value of active listening but far less evidence that this is put into practice consistently. When one is on the receiving end of genuine active listening, the difference is palpable. This is the quality of attention that is needed in a difficult conversation along with clarity of intent. Rock (2006, cited in Beddoe and Davys 2016) offers three guiding principles: to be succinct, to be specific, and to be generous. If that generosity incudes the readiness to listen and to hear then there is potential for a transformative conversation. There is no formula that can be learned for difficult conversations, but opportunities for new (and established) supervisors to practice these skills in a low-stakes environment can only be beneficial. The value of the supervisor's own supervision is again apparent as this can offer a safe environment in which to prepare for challenging dynamics or interpersonal conflict. It is a place where anxieties can be owned and different scenarios anticipated so that the supervisor is better resourced to manage their own emotions and avoid defensive responses.

New beginnings

The transition period for a new supervisor is of no fixed duration and, as Bridges (2009) suggests, there may be value in not pushing "prematurely for certainty and closure" (p. 57) during this time of "reorientation and redefining" (p. 43) which holds rich potential for learning along-side whatever challenges are encountered. But marking a new beginning is also a critical stage when one takes ownership of the shift in professional identity and commits on an emotional as well as a practical level to the supervisory role. Beginnings are undermined when posts are temporary, and it is not possible to ratify the ending of what came before. Beginnings are also muddied when someone occupies a hybrid practitioner-manager role and the discipline of holding clear boundaries between these separate identities is a near impossible feat.

Regardless of whether a supervisor is in an acting-up position, a senior practitioner role, or a permanent management post there are caveats to be addressed in relation to the phased process of transition which has been presented. As with other planned models of change there is something appealing about the clarity of progressive stages and a sense of inherent order. But the limitations of a planned approach become readily apparent when the context is neither stable nor predictable, necessitating a more emergent understanding of change. There are many variables which cannot be controlled when stepping into a supervisory role. Having an overarching map of the terrain can be helpful but not if one is then blindsided by the unexpected. Kanter (1983, p. 305) identified the paradox: "there needs to be a plan and the plan has to acknowledge that it will be departed from," and it is this degree of adaptability and responsiveness which is part of the new supervisor's journey.

Gradually and almost imperceptibly a supervisor will become more at ease in their role as they progress towards conscious competence. This is the time for thinking about how to develop and resource oneself going forward. Formal training opportunities are only rarely available to new supervisors with learning on the job a typical experience. The chance to step back and reflect in a more detached way on different aspects of professional supervision brings benefits at whatever stage of development. Supervision practice is brought into a shared arena where diverse approaches can be explored and there is safe space for trying out new skills. Some managers will be able to use their own supervision to engage with the dilemmas that confront them in their supervisory practice. The supportive and developmental functions will be attended to, not subsumed by pressing managerial demands, and "positive containing supervision" (Toasland 2007, p. 202) will be available to first line supervisors who are on the receiving end of practitioners', referrers', and senior managers' cumulative anxieties (Patterson 2019). Others will experience line management supervision where reflective dialogue is superseded by a primary focus on administrative concerns requiring them to seek out alternative options such as external consultancy, peer or group supervision, if they are to sustain and develop their supervisory practice and their own wellbeing.

Carroll (2009, p. 218) lays strong emphasis on mutuality within the supervisory process: "moving from 'I-learning' to 'we-learning.'" There is much in the experience of supervising others which enables managers to become more skilled in responding to different individuals and adapting their approach to match varying levels of experience, confidence, professional, or cultural background. But there are also risks of falling into detrimental habits such as being too ready to give advice or offer a solution rather than fostering the supervisee's own strengths and reflective capacity. Carroll (2009, p. 212) sees it as the supervisor's job to "manufacture uncertainty" in order to stimulate disagreement, debate, and learning. Arguably, the degree of volatility, uncertainty, complexity, and ambiguity (VUCA) in the contemporary environment and in social work practice renders it unnecessary to "manufacture' such conditions, but rather a key task for the supervisor is to be able to tolerate uncertainty. Reluctance to accept that there are risks which cannot be measured and problems which have no obvious solution exists at many levels: societal, organizational, and personal, and a supervisor needs strong resolve if they are to hold out against the implicit pressure to collude. This can only be achieved if there is a level of self-knowledge about how one responds to uncertainty, what personal defense mechanisms are triggered by insecurity, and how one maintains inner equilibrium in the face of hostility. Developing as a supervisor includes trying out different approaches and practicing new skills or "helping interventions" (Heron 1975). Fundamentally, however, it involves commitment to self-awareness and trust in the two-way interaction between supervisor and supervisee. The ability to supervise oneself both "in-action and on-action" (Schon 1983) is essential and best supported by a reflective space where the *process* of supervision is understood to be as important as the *content*. Whether this is offered by the supervisor's line manager as an integral aspect of professional supervision or needs to be sourced elsewhere, what matters most is realizing that one's capacity to meet the supervisory needs of others needs support, challenge, and continuous development if it is to be sustainable over time.

Conclusion

This chapter has explored the journey of "becoming a supervisor" through the frame of change and transition, believing that this does justice to the significant emotional and psychological dimensions of shifting from a practitioner to a managerial role. It has identified the different phases of: detaching from an established professional identity; moving through a period of flux and uncertainty; and laying down roots in a new place and moving forward. Within this process there are predictable challenges to be met such as balancing the dual role of managing performance and supporting staff; working openly and honestly with issues of power and authority; acknowledging and addressing one's own professional supervisory needs; and committing to ongoing development as a reflective supervisor. There are also unknown and unforeseen events which serve as reminder that there is no "right" way of supervising or "becoming a supervisor." Whether as supervisee or supervisee, we bring ourselves to the process and draw deeply from that resource when building meaningful relationships in a supervisory context as in direct practice.

References

Bartoli, A., and Kennedy, S., 2015. Tick if applicable: a critique of a national UK social work supervision. *Policy & Practice*, 27 (4), 239–250.

Beddoe, L., 2010. Surveillance or reflection: professional supervision in 'the risk society'. *British Journal of Social Work*, 40 (4), 1279–1296.

Beddoe, L., 2015. Supervision and developing the profession: one supervision or many?. *China Journal of Social Work*, 8 (2), 150–163.

Beddoe, L., and Davys, A., 2016. *Challenges in professional supervision*. London: Jessica Kingsley.

Berne, E., 1961. *Transactional analysis in psychotherapy*. New York: Grove Press.

Bradley, G., and Hojer, S., 2009. Supervision reviewed: reflections on two different social work models in England and Sweden. *European Journal of Social Work*, 12 (1), 71–85.

Bridges, W., 2009. *Managing transition*. 3rd ed. Philadelphia: Da Capo Press.

Burson, M.C., 2002. Finding clarity in the midst of conflict: facilitating dialogue and skillful discussion using a model from the Quaker tradition. *Group Facilitation*, 4, 23–29.

Carroll, M., 2009. Supervision: critical reflection for transformational learning, part 1. *The Clinical Supervisor*, 28 (2), 210–220. https://doi.org/10.1080/07325220903344015

Coulshed, V., and Mullender, A., 2006. *Management in social work*. 3rd. ed. Basingstoke: Palgrave Macmillan.

Cousins, C., 2004. Becoming a social work supervisor: a significant role transition. *Australian Social Work*, 57 (2), 175–185.

Cousins, C., 2010. "Treat me don't beat me" …. exploring supervisory games and their effect on poor performance management. *Practice*, 22 (5), 281–292.

Davys, A., and Beddoe, L., 2010. *Best practice in supervision: a guide for the helping professions*. London: Jessica Kingsley Publishers.

Fuchs, B., 2019) *Talking* leadership: ben fuchs on 'advantage blindness'. Kings Fund. Available from: https://www.kingsfund.org.uk/publications/talking-leadership-advantage-blindness. [Accessed 23 July 2019].

Gilmore, T., 2010. Challenges for physicians in formal leadership roles: Silos in the mind. *Organisational and Social Dynamics*, 10 (2), 279–96.

Gray, I., Field, R., and Brown, K., 2010. *Effective leadership, management and supervision in health and social care*. Exeter: Learning Matters.

Harlow, L., 2016. The management of children and family social workers in England: reflecting upon the meaning and provision of support. *Journal of Social Work*, 16 (6), 674–687.

Hawkins, P., and Shohet, R., 2012. *Supervision in the helping professions*. 4th ed. Berkshire: Open University Press.

Heifetz, R.A., and Laurie, D.L., 1997. The work of leadership. *Harvard Business Review*, Jan–Feb, 124–134.

Heron, J., 1975. *Six*-category intervention analysis. Human Potential Research Project, University of Surrey, Surrey, UK.

Hughes, L., and Pengelly, P., 1997. *Staff supervision in a turbulent environment: managing process and task in front-line service*. London: Jessica Kingsley.

Ibarra, H., Snook, S., and Ramo, L.G., 2010. Identity-based leader development. *In*: N. Nohria, and R. Khurana, eds. *Handbook of leadership theory and practice*. Boston: Harvard Business Press, 657–678.

Janis, I.L., 1972. *Victims of groupthink: a psychological study of foreign-policy decisions and fiascoes*. Oxford: Houghton Mifflin.

Kadushin, A., 1976. *Supervision in social work*. New York: Columbia University Press.

Kadushin, A., and Harkness, D., 2014. *Supervision in social work*. 5th ed. New York: Columbia University Press.

Kanter, R.M., 1983. *The change masters*. New York: Simon and Schuster.

Karpman, S., 1968. Fairy tales and script drama analysis. *Transactional Analysis Bulletin*, 7 (26), 39–43.

Kotter, J.P., 1996. *Leading change*. Boston: Harvard Business School Press.

Lawler, J., 2015. Motivation and meaning: the role of supervision. *Practice*, 27 (4), 265–275.

Lewin, K., 1947. Frontiers in group dynamics: concept, method and reality in social science; social equilibria and social change. *Human Relations*, 1 (1), 5–41.

Morrison, T., 2005. *Staff supervision in social care: making a real difference for staff and service users*. 3rd ed. Brighton: Pavilion Publishing.

Munro, E., 2010. *The Munro review of child protection, part one: a systems analysis*. Norwich: Stationery Office, Department for Education.

Munro, E., 2011. *The Munro review of child protection, final report: a child-centred system*. London: Stationery Office.

Noble, C., and Irwin, K., 2009. Social work supervision: an explorations of the current challenges in a rapidly changing social, economic and political environment. *Journal of Social Work*, 9 (3), 345–358.

O'Donoghue, K., 2012. Windows on the supervisee experience: an exploration of supervisees' supervision histories. *Australian Social Work*, 65 (2), 214–231.

O'Donoghue, K., 2015. Issues and challenges facing social work supervision in the twenty-first century. *China Journal of Social Work*, 8 (2), 136–149.

Patterson, F., 2015. Transition and metaphor: crossing a bridge from direct practice to first line management in social services. *British Journal of Social Work*, 45 (7), 2072–2088.

Patterson, F., 2019. Supervising the supervisors: what support do first-line supervisors need to be more effective in their supervisory role?. *Aotearoa New Zealand Social Work*, 31 (3), 46–57. doi: 10.11157/anzswj-vol13iss3id647.

Peach, J., and Horner, N., 2007. Using supervision: support or surveillance. *In*: M. Lymbery, and K. Postle, eds. *Social work: a companion to learning*. London: SAGE, 228–239.

Research in Practice 2018. *Practice supervisor development programme*. Available from: http://psdp.rip.org.uk/overview.html, [Accessed 20 July 2019].

Ruch, G., 2008. Developing 'containing contexts' for the promotion of effective direct work: the challenge for organisations. *In*: B. Luckock and M. Lefevre, eds. *Direct work: social work with children and young people in care*. London: BAAF, Adoption & Fostering, 295–305.

Ruch, G., 2012. Where have all the feelings gone? developing reflective and relationship-based management in child-care social work. *British Journal of Social Work*, 42 (7), 1315–1332.

Saltiel, D., 2017. Supervision: a contested space for learning and decision making, *Qualitative Social Work*, 16 (4), 533–549.

Schon, D., 1983. *The reflective practitioner*. New York: Basic Books.

Scottish Executive 2006. *Changing lives: 21st century review of social work*. Edinburgh: Scottish Executive.

Stoner, C.R., and Stoner, J.S., 2013. *Building leaders*. Abingdon: Routledge.

Toasland, J., 2007. Containing the container: an exploration of the containing role of management in a social work context. *Journal of Social Work Practice*, 21 (2), 197–202.

Tolleson Knee, R., and Folsom, J., 2012. Bridging the crevasse between direct practice social work and management by increasing the transferability of core skills. *Administration in Social Work*, 36 (4), 390–408.

Ward, J., 2012. 1 once knew a team where all the workers called the manager "mother" 'Some reflections on supervision within an integrated leadership and management programme. *Social Work and Social Sciences Review*, 16 (3), 65–80.

White, V., 2009. Quiet challenges? Professional practice in modernised social work. *In:* J. Harris, and V. White, eds. *Modernising social work: critical considerations*. Bristol: Policy Press, 129–143.

White, V., 2015. Reclaiming reflective supervision. *Practice*, 27 (4), 251–264.

Wilkins, D., Forrester, D., and Grant, L., 2017. What happens in child and family social work supervision?. *Child and Family Social Work*, 22 (2), 942–951.

Wong, Y.J.P., and Lee, Y.A.E., 2015. Dual roles of social work supervisors: strain and strengths as managers and clinical supervisors. *China Journal of Social Work*, 8 (2), 164–181.

Wonnacott, J. 2012. *Mastering social work supervision*. London: Jessica Kingsley Publishers.

20

PEACE PROCESS-IN-CONTEXT SUPERVISORY MODEL FOR MAINTAINING BALANCE AS DUAL ROLE SUPERVISOR

Peace Yuh Ju Wong

Introduction

Supervisors with dual roles tend to face tension between management control and providing space and autonomy for their supervisees in developing professional judgment. The dual role of supervisors is being discussed in the literature by social work and other related professions such as counseling and psychotherapy and marital and family therapy (Wong and Lee 2015). While the discussion is focused on the impact of managerialism and ethical considerations, there is a lack of literature that documents the way social work supervisors manage their supervisory sessions. This chapter proposes a clinical supervisory model that highlights the PEACE process-in-context as a way forward for supervisors in maintaining balance of their dual roles. Using systemic ideas and building on the seven-eyed supervision model by Hawkins and Shohet (2012), this supervisory model balances the administrative, educational, and supportive functions of supervisors by looking at different stages, namely, PEACE (**P**lace and Priority; **E**vent Recounting; **A**ppreciative Analysis; **C**ollaborative Planning; and **E**xperimentation and Evaluation) across nine different contexts, i.e., (i) client, (ii) supervisee, (iii) client-supervisee, (iv) supervisor, (v) supervisee-supervisor, (vi) client-supervisor, (vii) client-supervisee-supervisor, (viii) organization, and (ix) culture, professional values and ethics, socio-political/economic realities, and spiritual contexts.

The dilemma of the dual role of supervisors

Supervision is a supportive activity that helps to strengthen both the professional capabilities of the individual and professional developments of the profession (Bernard and Goodyear 2019). It is used widely in the health and social services sector for accountability of services provided to our service users. However, the dual roles of supervisors pose many potential ethical challenges during supervision (Falvey 1987; Kaiser 1997). This happens when supervisors are conducting both clinical supervision and administrative supervisions. Clinical supervision in this case is referred to as face-to-face supervision that promotes the professional development of the supervisee, involving the development of professional skills in assessment, intervention, and clinical skills (Tromski-Klingshirn 2007). Administrative supervision refers to the promotion and evaluation of staff and program members, with the purpose to help the supervisee function better as an employee in the organization (Hart 1982; Kenfield 1993). This can include assessment of the supervisee that aids in hiring, firing, or reprimanding clinical staff and/or completing performance evaluations of supervisee (Tromski-Klingshirn 2007). Learning about organizational life and preparing workers for opportunities to advancement is one important administrative supervision aim. It is ideal that supervisors with multiple roles should minimize and mitigate potential conflicts of interest. As an extension, mixing administrative supervision with clinical supervision can inadvertently affect the ethical treatment to clients, as the supervisee may choose not to disclose important problems that may reflect potential professional incompetence, since they are being evaluated by the supervisors with administrative and clinical roles (Tromski-Klingshirn 2007).

Across the various disciplines, it is found that supervisory relationships are frequently experienced as uncomfortable and relatively unproductive when the dual role of relationships appear (Beddoe 2012; Tromski-Klingshirn 2007). Tromski-Klingshirn (2007) has suggested that some research studies have found that in counseling, approximately one-half of practicing counselors receive clinical supervision from supervisors who are also their administrative supervisors (Evan 1993; Kenfield 1993). In occupational therapy, anxiety is often experienced by supervisees as they have to present a professional front to their supervisors to prove their competence (Sweeney et al. 2001). In social work, supervision is increasingly getting sourced externally due to the dual roles of supervision and power dynamics in the organization (Beddoe 2012).

Despite the challenges of dual roles, it has been observed that supervision in social work has two unique features which may be different from other disciplines. Firstly, social workers experience supervision throughout their entire career, and secondly, supervision is conducted in the same organization, which necessitates the presence of both administrative and clinical supervision roles in their supervisors (Beddoe 2012; Davys and Beddoe 2010). The dual roles of supervision mean that power dynamics between supervisors and supervisees are inevitable and it is crucial they are addressed to minimize possible ethical challenges (Cousins 2010).

While there is an extant literature that suggests the use of external supervision to minimize the conflict of interest of the dual roles in supervision (Beddoe 2012; Mo and Tsui 2019), there seems to be a dearth of literature that looks into the way social work supervisors manage dual roles (Wong and Lee 2015). Seen in this light, an exploratory study was conducted to gain a better understanding of the way social work supervisors manage the dual roles during supervisory sessions (Wong 2014). Using a constructivist grounded theory (Charmaz 2006, 2008, 2011) as a method, the researcher interviewed a total of 27 respondents with managerial and clinical roles in community-based agencies with different years of supervisory experience, gender, and in single and multi-centre agencies. The researcher also observed 13 "live" supervisory sessions conducted by these respondents. Based on the rich set of data from the interviews and observation sessions, a theoretical model, named PEACE process-in-context supervisory model was constructed. This supervisory model documents the process in which the supervisors embraced both the managerial and clinical roles in educating/supporting the supervisees, as well as made administrative demands. The following sections highlight the PEACE process-in-context supervisory model by indicating the theoretical underpinnings, the contextual map of social work supervision, PEACE supervision process, and assumptions as well as limitations of the supervisory model.

PEACE Process-in-context supervisory model

This section will highlight (a) the theoretical underpinning of the supervisory model and present the social work process-in-context supervision model that looks at how social work supervisors manage the demands of dual roles in casework supervision by looking at (b) the contextual map of social work supervision, (c) the PEACE supervision process, and (d) the assumptions, practice implications, and critique of the supervisory model.

Theoretical underpinnings of the PEACE process-in-context supervisory model

The PEACE process-in-context supervisory model is informed by systems theory, strengths-based orientation, David Kolb's (1984) cycle of experiential learning, Integration of Theory and Practice (ITP) loop developed by Bogo and Vayda (1989, 1998), as well as the seven-eyed supervision model by Hawkins and Shohet (2012).

Systems theory

The systems theory originates from general systems theory by von Bertanlanffy (1968). Systems theory posits that systems are "various activities of the body [that] are composed of interconnected but distinct systems of components that operate together in an integrated and coordinated way to maintain stability." As an outgrowth of general systems theory, systemic thinking incorporates some of the original ideas from general systems theory, as well as new concepts. Systemic theory emphasizes going beyond causality (cause-and-effect thinking or linear thinking) to observe and understand the multi-layered processes within an organization. The term *circularities*, as developed by Watzlawick et al. (1967, 1974, cited Dallos and Draper 2007, p. 25) further our understanding of supervision by allowing one to consider the interconnectedness of the client, supervisee, and supervisor systems within an organization and the larger environment. Using systemic thinking in supervision, supervisors could direct supervisees to consider the impact/effects of an event encountered in the client-supervisee system on their perspectives and intervention. In addition, systemic thinking will influence our understanding of supervision, since a change in the supervisor-supervisee context will impact the client-supervisee context, and in turn influence the client context.

Furthermore, the evolution of systemic thinking has directed one away from the mechanistic concept of a closed system to one that is "goal-directed" and "meaning driven." According to Campbell et al. (1994, p. 15), having "purpose creates a context that in turn gives meaning to all of the activity that takes place in that context." The use of systemic thinking enables one to appreciate the contexts people are in and the meaning attributed to various activities. In this regard, there is an emphasis on contexts and meanings, and contextual variables such as ethnicity, gender, and religion need to be considered and acknowledged as a meaning system for clients and supervisees (Lappin and Hardy 2002). Applying the concepts in systemic thinking is relevant as it enables supervisors to examine the dynamic interaction of supervision from the perspective of the individual in context.

Strengths-based orientation

The use of a strengths-based orientation in supervision is believed to be useful because the strengths-based orientation was first developed to assess clients' capacities, talents, competencies, possibilities, vision, values, and hopes (Saleeby 2013; Walsh 2006). Such an approach can be reinforced by supervisors during supervision, such as facilitating supervisees to find strengths in their clients and also in themselves as they consider different possibilities to work with clients.

Kolb's cycle of experiential learning

Kolb's (1984) cycle of experiential learning comprises four stages, namely concrete experience, reflective observation, abstract conceptualization, and active experimentation. The first stage, the "concrete experience" stage, is where the learner actively experiences an activity. Seen in supervision, supervisees might have conducted a session with the client(s). The reflective observation stage represents the phase in which the learner reflects on the experience. Similarly, practitioners could be viewing their experiences from the position of the "hawk in the mind" by examining their feelings, thoughts, actions, values, and beliefs (Scaife 2010). This is followed by the abstract conceptualization stage, in which the learner identifies patterns and seeks to apply theories. The active experimentation stage involves the "doing" aspect, where decisions are made to act on the reflection that has taken place in the previous stages. Seemingly useful as a framework to guide one's thinking about learners, some authors have criticized it for its simplicity (Moon 2001; Rowland 2000 cited Scaife 2010), whereas others have further developed it, for example, Davys (2000) described supervision as a cycle of experience, reflection, conceptualization, and active experimentation. In addition, Gibbs (1998) provided a more detailed and prescriptive guidance for the reflective cycle, which consists of description, feelings, evaluation, analysis, conclusion, and action plan.

ITP loop

The ITP loop was developed as a teaching model to promote the linkage between classroom learning and field education (Bogo and Vayda 1989). The ITP loop was an adaptation of Kolb's (1984) cycle of experiential learning and the adapted model, that is, the ITP loop, could be applied to social work practice. There are four stages of the ITP loop: retrieval, reflection, linkage, and professional response. The retrieval stage is the recall of information and description of any given practice situation, for example, the student could recall facts/observations of a professional encounter both as a participant and observer. The reflection loop starts with one's personal associations to the situation and contains elements of self-awareness. The main purpose of this phase to allow one to "gain self-knowledge so that we are wary of the influence of assumptions that are culture-based and thus biased, and of beliefs that are perceived as truths and not as cultural constructs that belong to a personal world view and are not universal" (Bogo and Vayda 1991, p. 275). The linkage stage of the loop uses cognitive associations of both the student and educator to the retrieved data and the associations elicited through reflection, with the intention of identifying and labeling knowledge to explain practice experience and subjective reactions (Bogo and Vayda 1991). The process is analytical, and there is a search for concepts and theories to make sense of one's experience. The professional response stage is the action planning aspect of the loop, where one selects a plan that will inform the next encounter with the specific situation.

The seven-eyed supervision model

According to Hawkins and Shohet (2012), all supervision situations involve at least five elements, namely a supervisor, a supervisee, a client, a work context, and the wider systemic context. In addition, the supervision process involves two interlocking systems, and these are the client-supervisee and supervisee-supervisor contexts. These five contexts, together with the two interlocking systems must be considered during the supervision process. This will be further illustrated in the following section, under (c) the contextual map of social work supervision.

Contextual map of social work supervision

Similar to the seven-eyed model proposed by Hawkins and Shohet (2012), the contextual map of the social work supervision consists of at least five contexts, namely, (i) client (C1); (ii) a supervisee (C2); (iii) a supervisor (C4); (iv) work context (C8); and (v) wider systemic context (C9), such as professional values and ethics, spirituality, and socio-political/economic realities. In addition, the contextual map of social work supervision involves three interlocking contexts, which are the (i) client-supervisee (C3); (ii) supervisee-supervisor (C5); and (iii) client-supervisor (C6) contexts. As an extension to the seven-eyed supervision model, the client-supervisee-supervisor (C7) context is proposed as the reflective supervisory space with its own process, named as PEACE supervision process, which will be discussed in the next section. Furthermore, the aspects of culture and spirituality need to be considered under the other systemic contexts (C9).

This following segment presents the elements to be considered in each of the different contexts.

Focus on client (C1)

In C1, there is a focus on client's context, in particular, the clients' profiles during the supervisory sessions. Social work supervisors and supervisees could utilize tools such as genograms and ecomaps to facilitate the discussions on the clients' profiles and their formal and informal systems. It is important to reflect on questions such as "What are client's microsystems – such as family, social, and peer systems – like?", "Are there resources in the formal and/or informal systems which clients have tapped on in managing their difficulties?", and "In what manner

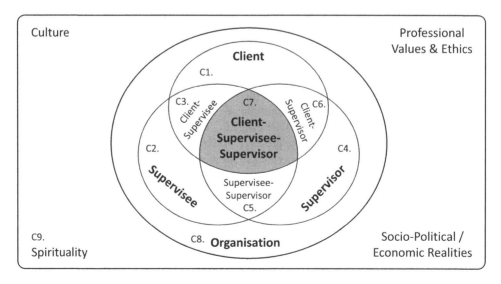

Figure 20.1 Contextual map of social work supervision

can we further tap on their internal/external resources now?" These questions helped supervisors gain a better understanding of the client's systems and is consistent with the ecosystem or person-in-environment perspective adopted by social workers (Compton and Galaway 2005; Sheafor and Horejsi 2006).

Focus on supervisee (C2)

In supervision, supervisors need to be mindful of their own and their supervisees' profiles (e.g., gender, age, years of work experience, prior supervisory experience), learning characteristics (i.e., learning attitudes and styles) and their impact on the supervisory process. In addition, supervisors could attune to the values, beliefs (including theoretical orientation), and feelings of supervisees during supervisory sessions.

In the supervisee context (C2), the focus is on the "internal process of the supervisee and how these are affecting and being affected by the work and their relationship" (Hawkins and Shohet 2012, p. 95). It is therefore helpful to look at transference and counter-transference processes during supervision. For example, the supervisor could explore the supervisee's frustration and impact of transference on her work with clients. The supervisor could further lead the supervisee into an exploration of the latter's frustration and develop an awareness/understanding of its impact on her work. Such discussions are designed to lead to better self-awareness, with supervisors facilitating the connection of the supervisees' transference and counter-transference processes with their work with clients. This linkage with clients' work is important, since supervisees are neither clients, nor supervisors, therapist, or social workers to the supervisees.

Focus on client-supervisee (C3)

The client-supervisee context could be divided into two dimensions, namely client-supervisee relationship and client-supervisee interaction. For the client-supervisee relationship, supervisors could enquire about the referral source and its impact on the client-supervisee relationship, and the supervisee's roles in case management with respect to different stakeholders and/or organizations. Hence, questions that might be useful for consideration are, "How was the client referred to you?" and "How may their choice of you as a social worker and/or an organization – or a lack of choice thereof – influence the help seeking relationship?"

In addition, supervisors could consider supervisees' reactions and/or interaction with client(s) during and/or after their sessions with client(s). For example, supervisors could attend to the supervisee's frustrations and address the impact of transference. This could be facilitated by helping the supervisee to consider one's interaction pattern with the client, especially regarding the way the client might have triggered the supervisee's emotions and how this might impact the way he/she works with her client. The questions for consideration in this client-supervisee context include "Where do the thoughts and/or emotions (about the client) come from?" and "In what manner does it impact the way you work with this particular client?"

Focus on supervisor (C4)

In the supervisor context, supervisors could use their intuition to make sense of the here-and-now experiences in the supervisory session. According to Hawkins and Shohet (2012), supervisors should strive to be more aware of, and attuned to, their own shifts in sensation and even peripheral thoughts and fantasies while attending to the content and process of the supervisory session. Supervisors could intentionally present their own feelings, thoughts, and reactions during supervisory sessions to their supervisees.

Focus on supervisee-supervisor (C5)

In the supervisee-supervisor context, there are three dimensions to look at in the supervisee-supervisor relationship, and these are (a) structure, quality, and relational element of supervisory relationship; (b) the exploration of supervisees' knowledge and/or skills in engagement, assessment, and intervention in the casework process; and (c) parallel processes in the supervisory session.

The first dimension on supervisory relationship considers (a) the structure (format and frequency of supervision); (b) quality (warmth and perceived safety); and (c) relational element (gender, cultural similarities and differences, influence of power and authority) of the relationship. In this context, it is important for supervisors to be mindful of the characteristics of supervisees, such as developmental stages, gender, and prior supervisory experiences, as these influence supervisees' views about the supervisory relationship. Questions that might be helpful for consideration are "How might our similarities and differences facilitate our supervisory relationship?" and "To what extent would I as a supervisor be seen as potentially biased, and in what manner could I be more aware of these possible biases and the impact on our supervisory relationship?"

The next dimension looks at the "thinking behind the doing" of the supervisees in their work with clients. This implies facilitating supervisees to consider their theories and/or skills used in assessment and intervention with clients. Questions that might be helpful for consideration in this dimension include "What were you thinking about when you decided to intervene in this manner?" and "What are the theories that guide your assessment and subsequent intervention?"

The third dimension in the supervisory relationship looks at the parallel process, which is "the process at work currently in the relationship between client and supervisee [that is] uncovered through the way they are reflected in the relationship between supervisee and supervisor" (Hawkins and Shohet 2007, p. 93). It is a re-enactment of the client-supervisee interaction in the here-and-now supervisory relationship.

One of the skills highlighted by Hawkins and Shohet (2007) involves the ability to notice one's reaction and feed them back to the supervisee in a non-judgmental way. For example, if the supervisor feels "stuck" during the supervision session, he/she might use the here-and-now experience and share with the supervisee, "I am sensing that you are experiencing a lot of 'stuckness' in working with the client and I am feeling the same 'stuckness,' as it seems difficult to progress in our discussion. I wonder to what extent do you experience 'stuckness' in your work with your clients of this nature?" By so doing, the supervisee would feel safe to discuss the difficulties and explore different ways to handle one's 'stuckness' for the case, which might have been contributed by the client, him/herself, and/or other contexts such as organizational and state- and/or national-legal contexts.

Focus on client-supervisor (C6)

In the client-supervisor context, supervisors focus on their own thoughts and/or emotional processes, as they may have some hunches and/or assumptions about the client(s) (or issues surrounding clients) based on supervisees' sharing. Supervisors utilize such information to facilitate discussions on supervisees' work with clients. The utilization of intuition is important in supervision (Rowan 2010). This idea is also supported by Charles (2004, p. 189) in her book on intuition, where she suggested that "supervisors are indeed sometimes presented with a 'hunch' or a 'gut feeling' about a client, a strong sense of something, but without the supervisee being able to clarify it, or pinpoint the origin of the impression."

Additionally, a supervisor could highlight to his/her supervisee that he/she became more switched off during a supervisory session as the supervisee went into a detailed description of the case. Since there may be similar parallel processes in the client-supervisee and/or supervisee-supervisor contexts, they could jointly examine the effects of this interaction pattern on the client-supervisee interaction and/or the supervisory relationship.

Focus on client-supervisee-supervisor – Termed the PEACE supervisory process (C7)

The supervisory session takes place in the client-supervisee-supervisor context, since it concerns supervisees' work with clients, in joint consultation with supervisors. Supervisees can present their work with clients through videotape and/or verbal presentations. The client-supervisee-supervisor context is the reflective space where supervisors and supervisees examine supervisee's work with clients. The PEACE supervisory process involves the following phases, namely, **P**lace and Priority; **E**vent Recounting; **A**ppreciative Analysis; **C**ollaborative Planning; and **E**xperimentation and Evaluation. This will be elaborated in the next section under PEACE Supervision Process.

Focus on organizational context (C8)

Since supervision takes place within an organizational context (C8), one needs to pay attention to the agency's mission, policies, and guidelines, since these impact supervisory practice and service delivery. Another consideration is the funding sources, as it involves accountability to funders, and hence, this will influence the content of the supervision sessions. Oftentimes, the specifications by funders on the nature/type of work that could be done with clients would impact how social workers deliver their services/programs. For example, a mandatory six-month program with young offenders would mean that the social workers would need to work closely with clients on fulfilling the program's objective, and supervisors would need to check in on the progress of the case development within the stipulated time frame.

Focus on other systemic contexts (C9)

Finally, supervision is also subjected to influences from other contexts (C9), namely, culture, spirituality, professional values/ethics, and socio-political and economic realities. Consideration of the wider environment and its impact is consistent with the person-in-environment or eco-system theories adopted by social workers (Bronfenbrenner 1999; Compton and Galway 2005; Kirst-Ashman and Hull 2009). Some of these contexts may impact the clients, supervisees, and supervisors in similar ways (e.g., socio-political and economic realities, such as in the case of a country affected by an economic downturn), while others affect them dissimilarly (e.g., culture, religion, spirituality, such as the case of an ethnically diverse population in a country). Specifically, the ideas of culture and spirituality need to be considered, in addition to the ideas of socio-political and economic realities, as proposed by Hawkins and Shohet (2012).

The idea to consider culture was proposed by Tsui (2005), who deemed it an important context for social work supervision. Despite the different definitions of culture, it is easy to identify culture, as it is "the way of life and the way of viewing the world of a specific social group" (Tsui 2005, p. 46). Hence, culture influences social work supervision, since supervisees, supervisors, and clients interpret and make sense of their experiences (that is, experiences with the client, supervisee, or supervisor; and between client-supervisee and between supervisee-supervisor) using their respective cultural lens. For example, help-seeking may be perceived as a "face" issue by clients, and this has to be considered in assessing the client's help-seeking behavior and the way the supervisee and/or supervisor approach the idea of service provision in the organizational context. Hence, questions such as "How is help-seeking behavior being perceived in the client's culture?" and "How might one's perception of help-seeking impact the utilization of services?" may be helpful for supervisees and supervisors.

In addition, it is noted that spirituality has gained prominence in clinical work, as well as organizational management, and it is timely to contextualize and examine the relevance of spirituality in social work supervision. The attention given to spirituality is consistent with Tsui's (2005) framework on social work supervision, as spirituality includes the consideration of one's culture (Canda and Furman 2020). In addition, some supervisors see faith and spirituality as resources in managing challenges that arise in supervisory relationships and in organizational management.

PEACE supervision process (C7)

As discussed, the PEACE process-in-context supervisory model consists of two parts, namely, the contextual map of supervision, as well as the PEACE supervision process. The PEACE supervision process was developed based on the observations of supervisors with dual roles conducting their casework supervision (Wong 2014). It mirrors the flow of supervision, with distinctive stages, namely, the beginning, middle, and end stages. It is similar to the process of conducting individual supervisory conference with phases proposed by Kadushin and Harkness (2014). Similarly, Davys and Beddoe (2010), in their development of a reflective learning model for social work students, have also suggested a structure to guide the supervisory process from the beginning to end. The PEACE supervisory process involves the following phases, namely, **P**lace and Priority; **E**vent Recounting; **A**ppreciative Analysis; **C**ollaborative Planning; and **E**xperimentation and Evaluation.

Figure 20.2 PEACE supervision process

PEACE supervision process: Place and Priority

"Place" in the PEACE supervision process refers to the identification of a suitable location to provide a physical contextual cue to the supervisee and supervisor (Tsui 2008). The "Priority" of the session refers to the way in which supervisors and/or supervisees set goals for the supervisory session to steer the session in the desired direction. A priority or priorities could be identified at the beginning or during the session, and the focus is to develop the competence of supervisees to work with clients.

PEACE supervision process: Event Recounting

The Event Recounting phase is similar to the concrete experience phase in Kolb's (1984) experiential learning cycle and the description stage in Gibbs' (1998) prescription of the reflective cycle. In the Event Recounting phase, the supervisor listens to the situation and/or case as perceived and experienced by the supervisee. Typically, this would involve the supervisee presenting to his/her supervisor the case and the nature of the client's involvement with the supervisee and the agency. In this phase, client, client-supervisee, and organizational contexts are often considered during the discussion about the case.

PEACE supervision process: Appreciative Analysis

In the Appreciative Analysis phase, supervisors need to both appreciate the supervisees and be engaged in the analysis of materials being presented in the Place and Priority and Event Recounting phases. The purpose of the Appreciative Analysis phase is to move from the specifics of the situation being presented to generalizations, using research, theories, personal experience, professional values, or cultural and socio-political contexts. Typically, the Appreciative Analysis phase leads towards an expansion of supervisees' understanding of the self, of supervisees' knowledge/skills in the case management process, and of supervisees' application of professional values and ethics in practice. By so doing, it addresses the clinical role of the supervisor in educating and supporting the supervisees.

Depending on the priority of the session, the supervisor might use the Appreciative Analysis phase to address the issues raised during the Place and Priority phase. For example, if the supervisee was struggling to understand client's perspectives and behaviors, the supervisor might attempt to analyze the supervisees' lack of understanding. This might result in an increased understanding of the supervisee's self. Of equal importance is the need to be appreciative of the supervisee; hence, support is rendered through encouragement and/or affirmation of supervisee's work. The utilization of active listening skills such as attending, paraphrasing, summarizing, clarifying, and reflective listening are needed in this phase, as the use of these skills conveys to the supervisee that his/her supervisor is genuinely interested in developing and educating the supervisee in his/her work with clients. However, it is important to note that whilst being supportive, supervisors need to be aware of the limits of the professional supervisor-supervisee boundary as well as the supervisees' personal-professional boundaries so as to avoid engaging the supervisee in personal therapy, but rather, should the need arise, to refer the supervisee for therapy.

PEACE supervision process: Collaborative Planning

The overriding goal of the Collaborative Planning phase is for supervisors and supervisees to jointly decide on the intervention plans for clients. For example, after supervisees have developed an expanded understanding of the self at work, have developed their knowledge and skills in practice during the earlier phases of the supervisory process, the supervisor could guide the supervisee to consider how this new understanding, knowledge, and/or skills could be used in their work with clients. Apart from conceiving intervention work in the domain of counseling, it is helpful for supervisor-supervisee pairs to conceive of intervention in other domains, using the different professional roles of social workers, such as brokerage, case management, and even advocacy to help clients (Hepworth et al. 2017; Kirst-Ashman and Grafton 2012). And in addition to conceiving of intervention as solely derived from the case worker, supervisor-supervisee pairs could also explore the multitude of developmental and/or preventive programs offered by social service agencies to provide the necessary resources to clients. Intervention plans could also be developed to involve client's informal support systems whenever possible, as this will address the issue of over-reliance on formal support systems.

Similar to the Appreciative Analysis phase, different contexts are also involved in the Collaborative Planning phase, and these contexts are client, supervisee, supervisor, supervisee-supervisor, client-supervisor, and organizational and wider contexts, such as culture and spirituality. In particular, where the enhancement of knowledge in intervention work was concerned, there seemed to be greater emphasis on the education function of the supervisor in enhancing supervisees' knowledge in intervention work by facilitating supervisees to look at theories that informed their work with clients.

Two different contexts in the Collaborative Planning phase deserve further discussion: the client-supervisor and cultural contexts. The client-supervisor context involves the supervisors' beliefs, the theories supervisors subscribe to, and their personal/practice knowledge gained from their work experience and using the latter to formulate intervention plans for clients. The cultural dimension involves examining taboo/sensitive topics during supervision, such as discussing the concept of "face" in help-seeking behavior for clients. In addition, it also involve the consideration of Chinese cultural values of reciprocity as proposed by Tsui (2008), by examining the concepts of *qing* (a primary and intense relationship), *yuan* (a predetermined relationship), and "face" (mutual respect). These values impact how supervisees may approach their supervisors in the unbalanced power relationship, since supervisors tend to assume a more powerful position due to their appraisal roles. Taken together, these values serve to maintain the supervisory relationship in a more harmonious and stable manner (Tsui 2008).

PEACE supervision process: Experimentation and Evaluation

The "experimentation" in this phase is like the active experimentation stage, or "doing" of Kolb's (1984) experiential learning or professional response phase of the Integration of Theory and Practice (ITP) loop by Bogo and Vayda (1989). It involves making decisions for an action plan, based on insights, knowledge and/or skills gained, or theories identified, in the earlier phases of Appreciative Analysis and Collaborative Planning. The term "experimentation" is appropriate and fitting because it suggests that one is unable to determine the consequence, given the unpredictable nature of working with people. Examples of "experimentation" or "doing" involve supervisors jointly doing a home visit with supervisees or being involved in the implementation of the plan as identified in the earlier Collaborative Planning phase.

The evaluation aspect involves assessing the effectiveness of one's work and this may involve examining "What works?" Evaluation may also involve supervisees providing feedback to supervisors about the usefulness of the supervisory session. Most importantly, evaluation signifies the accountability aspect of a social worker's work with clients by updating his/her supervisor of the progress of the case and planning for closure.

Case illustration

The following case is an illustration of the PEACE process-in-context supervisory model. The case illustrates the PEACE process, as well as the various contexts that need to be considered during supervision.

		PEACE process-in-context
Supervisee:	*A young supervisee sees supervisor in the office corridor.* Hey supervisor, I need to consult you urgently over a crisis case.	
Supervisor:	Sure, let's discuss this in a more private place. How would you want me to help you with this case?	Place and Priority
Supervisee:	Help me to know what to do as I am at a loss.	
Supervisor:	Tell me more about the case.	Event Recounting
Supervisee:	My seven-year-old client just told me that she was abused by her father. In school, we were taught to tell our supervisor. Now I come to you for help. What should I do? I am freaking out already.	
Supervisor:	I am hearing that you are worried about a client who told you about being abused by her father.	
Supervisee:	Yes, what should I do?	
Supervisor:	Ok, what did you tell the client when she told you she was abused by the parent?	Appreciative Analysis; client-supervisee
Supervisee:	I just stared at her and said, "Don't joke that. How can it be true." Inside, I was afraid that it might be true.	context (C3)
Supervisor:	I am hearing that you have some fear. What is your	Appreciative Analysis;
Supervisee:	concern?	supervisee context (C2)
	I have fear whenever I think of people being abused. I am afraid I may not do a good job.	
	Supervisor and supervisor continue the exploration of the case.	
Supervisor:	Based on your description of where there are high risks	Appreciative Analysis;
Supervisee:	of abuse, what makes it difficult for the child's father to recognize that he is abusing the child?	other systemic contexts (C9), such as culture and faith
	He thinks that because this was how he was brought up in the past , disciplining the child by caning is acceptable, since this was normal for him growing up. His religion also suggests that he needs to discipline the child.	
	Supervisor and supervisor continue the exploration of the case.	
Supervisor:	Based on your description and that there is a high probability of abuse, how do you think you can access the client's informal support systems in looking out for signs of abuse? Who might the child feel safe with?	Collaborative Planning; client context (C1)
Supervisee:	Maybe her grandmother? Perhaps I need to work with Child Protection?	
	Supervisor and supervisee continues the conversation.	
Supervisor:	Would you want to do a joint assessment together with me?	Experimentation and Evaluation
Supervisee:	Yes, that will be most useful since this is my first case.	

(Continued)

(Continued)

		PEACE process-in-context
Supervisor:	Sure. How do you think this session has been for you in helping you manage this case?	Experimentation and Evaluation supervisee- supervisor context (C5)
Supervisee :	I think I have gained a lot of insight on the kinds of questions to ask. I also feel very supported because you will do the joint session with me.	
Supervisor:	That is good to hear. I am glad that despite your fear of handling potential child abuse cases, you are proactive in seeking supervision. I appreciate that as I think it is courageous and professional of you to do that.	

Based on the case, the supervisor has identified a suitable place for case discussion, and it would be conducted in a room and not in the corridor which is an open space where others could listen to the conversation. This is an ethical consideration, and it is important for social workers to respect the confidentiality of a client's information. The goal(s) of the session was/were established when the supervisor asked the supervisee "How would you want me to help you with this case?" Subsequently, the supervisee narrated the client's case (termed Event Recounting) and in the process, the supervisor has attempted to appreciate the thinking of the worker and examine the impact of "self" on the supervisee regarding her work with clients (termed Appreciative Analysis). The Collaborative Planning process takes place when the supervisor facilitates the planned intervention for the clients by considering the engagement of various formal/informal support networks in managing both the presenting and underlying issues. Invariably, various contexts of the clients have to be considered other than the client-supervisee-supervisor context (termed as PEACE supervision process, C7). These include client's context (C1); supervisee's context such as age and developmental stage of supervisee (C2); client-supervisee context, such as interaction between client and supervisee (C3); supervisee-supervisor context (C5), such as the relationship dimension; and wider systemic contexts (C9), such as the influence of culture and one's faith on their views of the problems.

PEACE supervision process across time and stages

Having illustrated the PEACE supervision process, Figure 20.3 highlights the process across the time dimension and contexts.

It has a spiral shape, suggesting that there is constant movement and balance. The spiral (of the PEACE supervision process) symbolizes evolution and represents the cycles of growth and change of the supervisees and clients through the supervision process.

The PEACE supervision process across the time dimension

The PEACE supervision process takes place across the time dimension. Typically, the Event Recounting tends to relate to the past, when the supervisee narrates about the case encounter with the client. As the session supervision session progresses, there is a movement from the present to the future, when the supervisor and supervisee pair discuss the intervention plan and implement the plan subsequently. Whilst the Place and Priority phase focuses on the present

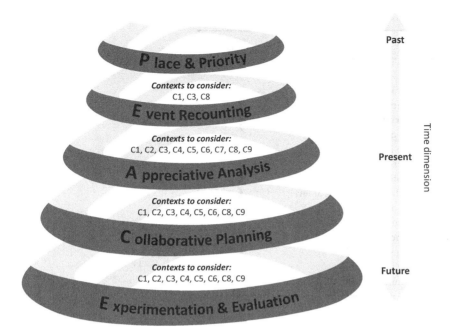

Contexts to consider:
C1, C3, C8

Contexts to consider:
C1, C2, C3, C4, C5, C6, C7, C8, C9

Contexts to consider:
C1, C2, C3, C4, C5, C6, C8, C9

Contexts to consider:
C1, C2, C3, C4, C5, C6, C8, C9

Figure 20.3   PEACE supervision process across time and contexts. Source: A grounded understanding of challenges and responses of social work supervisors with clinical and managerial roles (p. 303), by Wong Y.J. (2014). Thesis (PhD). National University of Singapore

during the supervisory session, the Event Recounting phase looks at past events, concerning itself with occurrences and/or interactions that took place between client and the supervisee.

In the Appreciative Analysis phase, there is a movement between the past and present, depending on the focus and intent of supervisors. For example, the supervisor, upon sensing the supervisees' anxiety during the supervisory session (i.e., the present), could explore the source of anxiety with the supervisee. As the supervisee recounts her interaction with the client (i.e., the past), the supervisee reveals that the source of anxiety concerned her own insecurities and unresolved family issues (i.e., the past and present).

In the Collaborative Planning phase, the focus tends to be on the future as supervisor-supervisee pairs examine intervention plans for clients. However, information about the past and present and about the client-supervisee relationship is important when the future plans for clients are considered, since what might happen in future has to be linked to what transpired in the past and what is happening in the present. Similarly, the Experimentation and Evaluation phase focuses on the future, as it is concerned with planning the joint client-supervisee-supervisor session, as well as considering plans for case closure.

The PEACE supervision process across stages

It appears that supervisory sessions parallel the helping process, covering aspects such as engagement, assessment, intervention, and evaluation (Hepworth et al. 2017; Kirst-Ashman and Grafton 2012). This is inevitable, since supervision has to address issues related to how supervisees make assessments, which will influence their intervention. It supports the process as highlighted in the C5P5A5 model which suggests that there are stages to be worked through in "an approximately chronological order" (Hay 2007, p. 69). The C5P5A5 model is illustrated in Table 20.1 below.

Table 20.1 C5P5A5 model

C5P5A5	Stages
What is the **content**?	
How clear is the **contract**?	
How well are we in **contact**?	C5
Is the content **appropriate**?	
How are we using our **contrasts**?	
Whose **paradigms** are in effect?	
How are we at the **personal** level?	
How are we at the **professional** level?	P5
What is happening at the **psychological** level?	
Are there any **parallel** processes?	
Are we being **autonomous**?	
Are we being **authentic**?	
Are **alternatives** being generated?	A5
Whose **aims** are being worked on?	
Are **actions** being committed to?	

The assumptions, practice implications, and critique of the PEACE process-in-context supervisory model

Having articulated the contextual map and PEACE supervision process, Figure 20.4 depicts the PEACE process-in-context supervisory model. Influenced by my own professional and personal experiences, the PEACE process-in-context supervisory model is inspired by insights and ideas from the research study in observing how supervisors managed the dual role challenges (Wong 2014). The following section highlights the assumptions, practice implications, and critique of the model.

Assumptions of the PEACE process-in-context supervisory model

In this proposed PEACE process-in-context supervisory model, it is assumed that there are nine different contexts for consideration during supervision. One of the contexts (C7) consists of a PEACE supervision process with its different phases that take place across the time dimension.

Taking a reflexive stance in using the model

Whilst the model seeks to provide greater clarity in terms of the supervisory process and contexts, it may be limited in its ability to capture different realities and truths, as experienced by different people. Therefore, a critical stance in examining social work supervision together with the adoption of a similar reflexive stance in the utilization and further development of the model is proposed. According to D'Cruz et al. (2007, p. 83), reflexivity can be described as a "critical approach to knowledge generation" that operates in the moment, with a constant process of questioning (self-monitoring) their own knowledge claims and those of others as he/she engages in social interaction and the micro processes of knowledge/power. This is similar to the "reflection-in-action" as proposed by Schon (1983, p. 69), who advocated for the development of an "epistemology of practice which places technical problem solving within a broader context of reflective inquiry." The development of a curious mind, with its rigor and non-complacent attitude, would allow one to know why one is doing what one is doing and be

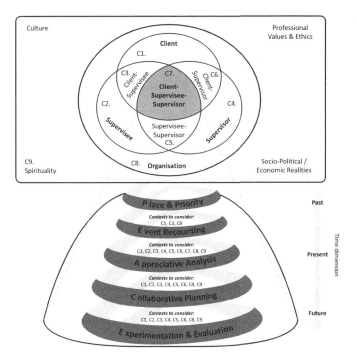

Figure 20.4   PEACE process-in-context supervisory model. Source: A grounded understanding of challenges and responses of social work supervisors with clinical and managerial roles (p. 314), by Wong Y.J. (2014). Thesis (PhD). National University of Singapore

more informed about the effect of one's doing. This is helpful in one's search to infuse one's self more consciously into professional practice.

More importantly, taking a reflexive stance challenges the traditional, positivist way of knowing and blind adherence to "truth." Rather than proposing that social work supervisors distant themselves from their emotions and be objective in applying the model, it is suggested that they acknowledge the influences of their experiences and their *being* in supervision by utilizing their subjective experience and awareness of tacit knowledge in informing their practice.

Fluidity of the different phases

Even though there are unique phases in the PEACE supervision process, there is no fixed flow and sequence since supervisors are free to begin from any phase. For example, supervisors could begin with the Experimentation and Evaluation phase by touching base with supervisees about the case progress and then move back to a previous phase to examine what had been done well. Alternatively, supervisors could commence with the Place and Priority phase, with the supervisee setting the goal(s) for the supervisory session.

Movement between contexts in the PEACE supervision process

During supervisory sessions, the content and process could potentially span across the nine different contexts. Since there is often a movement of content and process between different contexts during supervisory sessions, it is helpful for supervisors to utilize information from different contexts in case discussion. This will enable and help supervisors not to get stuck relying on information based on certain contexts, such as client and client-supervisee

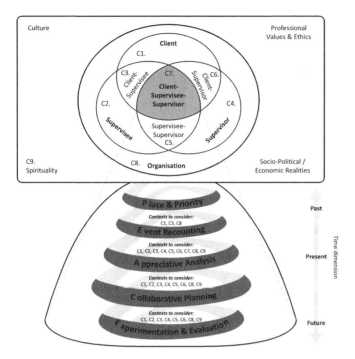

Figure 20.5 Different emphasis in the PEACE process-in-context supervisory model. Source: A grounded understanding of challenges and responses of social work supervisors with clinical and managerial roles (p. 319), by Wong Y.J. (2014). Thesis (PhD). National University of Singapore

contexts. For example, it helps when a supervisor relies on his/her own judgment or hunches about the supervisee and/or client during the here-and-now supervisory session to facilitate the case discussion, since there is a parallel process that takes place between client-supervisee and supervisee-supervisor contexts. Furthermore, supervisors' hunches about clients in the client-supervisor context could be harnessed further during supervisory sessions, since supervisors may have different insights, given their own experience in working with certain clientele and issues. In some instances, there may be a greater emphasis on certain phases, for instance, if a supervisee indicates that his/her goal is to learn more about the impact of their assessment on intervention plans, supervisors could therefore devote more time at the Appreciative Analysis phase.

Practice implications of PEACE process-in-context supervisory model

The PEACE process-in-context supervisory model with its distinctive PEACE supervision process contributes and expands our understanding of social work supervisors in managing the challenges with dual roles. Based on the aforementioned discussion, the practice implications of the PEACE process-in-context supervisory model highlights the performance of the supervision functions of supervisors and ways in balancing the managerial and clinical roles of supervisors.

Performance of supervision functions

Supervisors perform different educational, supportive, and administrative supervisory functions at different phases of the PEACE supervision process. For example, the educational function of the supervisor could be seen in the Appreciative Analysis, Collaborative Planning, and Experimentation and Evaluation phases. In the Appreciative Analysis phase, social work supervisors were observed to be educating their supervisees and facilitating the consideration of knowledge/skills in working with clients. In the Collaborative Planning phase, supervisor-supervisee pairs generated the intervention plan and considered ways to mobilize resources and coordinate services with different stakeholders. The supervisor may educate the supervisees concerning ways to conduct a joint session and/or home visit.

The supportive function of social work supervisors is seen by the affirmation and encouragement they give to their supervisees. In addition, many supervisors were observed to be using their reflective listening skills when they took the time to reflect with their supervisees on the transference and counter-transference issues that had arisen from their work with clients. There were ample examples of summarizing, paraphrasing, and clarification skills. These supervisory skills used by the supervisors were similar to the skills used in the workplace as proposed by Shulman (2010), such as elaboration skills and empathic skills.

The administrative function, on the other hand, with its implications for the accountability of social work to clients, agency, funding organization(s), and to the social work profession, is evident when supervisors monitored, reviewed, and evaluated the work of their supervisees. For example, supervisors would check with their supervisees concerning the progress of their cases and what their plans for closure were.

Balancing the managerial and clinical roles of supervisors

As mentioned, the evolvement of the supervisory model was based on the observed "live" sessions of supervisors with managerial and clinical roles (Wong 2014). There are two ways in which the supervisory model could facilitate a better balance of the dual roles of supervisors, and these are related to (i) mindfulness of Place and Priority during the supervisory session, (ii) being systemic and appreciating the idea of isomorphism, and (iii) harnessing the strengths of dual roles.

Mindfulness of Place and Priority during supervisory session

Using the PEACE process which begins with Place and Priority, it is helpful if the supervisors could determine the setting to conduct the supervisory space, based on the purpose of the supervisory session. Hewson and Carroll (2016) have highlighted six supervisory spaces, and these are Directive (Office), Evaluative (Exam Room), Passive (Lecture Theatre), Restorative (Sitting Room), Active (Studio), and Reflective (Observatory). Determining the purpose of the session and choosing an appropriate space for the supervisory session help to clarify the roles of the supervisor in session. If the purpose of the session is to generate collaborative solutions, the supervisor may want to move into the "Active Space" so that they can have a place for meaningful learning and discussion. On the other hand, the supervisor can choose to move into the evaluative space to evaluate performance and provide necessary feedback, if the supervisor decides to take on the managerial role. With the view that each "room" provides a relational space with its own role, supervisors could help supervisees to be clearer about the priority of the session and move between "spaces." In this manner, supervisees would feel safer as they would be assured that they are not being evaluated when they honestly share their struggles in managing the difficult cases.

Being systemic and appreciating the idea of isomorphism

In adopting PEACE process-in-context supervisory model, supervisors are encouraged to appreciate the realities of the nine contexts in impacting one's work. Specifically, the organization (C8) and wider systemic contexts (C9) are aspects of realities which supervisors and supervisees need to be mindful of during supervision. Having a systemic perspective broadens one's understanding of the inter-relatedness of the systems in impacting the various contexts under discussion. One important systemic concept is that of isomorphism. This refers to the replication of similar patterns and interactional sequences across different levels of a system and its sub-systems (Liddle 1988). Isomorphism could be observed in supervisory sessions, where the supervisory relationship mirrors the therapeutic relationship (Lo 2014; Low 2019). For example, certain emotional themes and patterns, such as anxiety present in the client's life, could surface during the supervision session, where the supervisee becomes anxious and the supervisor realizes the impact of this anxiety in the supervisory relationship. As Liddle (1988, p. 155) suggests, the interactional processes across subsystems could be altered and shaped through "intentional supervisory intervention and change." This requires the supervisors to pay attention to the spoken/unspoken emotions/thinking as expressed by supervisees during the "here-and-now" of the supervisory session. It may involve influencing the process by a more reflexive process and even direct guidance, which indirectly impact the client-supervisee relationship. For example, using the earlier case as an illustration, the supervisor, upon noticing the anxiety of the supervisee about the potential child abuse, could attend to the supervisee by checking whether the supervisee has noticed any similar patterns of interaction in the client and the client-supervisee relationship. The supervisor could then directly address this anxiety by helping the supervisee to better manage such emotions and their impact on the interaction/relationship with the client(s).

In addition, supervisors with dual roles could collaborate with supervisees to address the realities and demands as experienced in their managerial and clinical roles. For example, in supervising clinical work, the supervisors could facilitate supervisees' in developing competencies and at the same time, help supervisees to have an expanded view of management's perspective concerning accountability at work.

Harnessing the strengths of dual roles

The dual roles of supervisors could be seen as both a strength and a possible strain. Instead of adopting a dichotomized view where one chooses an "either/or" paradigm, it would be helpful to harness the strengths of the dual roles, whilst attempting to minimize the strains through various role management strategies (Wong and Lee 2015). For example, supervisors in their managerial role could develop wide angle empathy (Hawkins 2019) that is not just for the clients, but for the staff, management, as well as stakeholders in the external systems. Simply put, this means that the supervisors could train themselves to be appreciative of multiple perspectives and the interests of different systems, as opposed to holding the perspectives of either the clinical or the manager role. This appreciation and suspension of certainty or absolutism of a discourse would allow both the supervisees and supervisors to develop different understanding and develop possibilities towards changes (Chua 2019).

Critique of the PEACE process-in-context supervision model

Whilst the PEACE process-in-context supervision model is useful for supervisory practice, it is limited by the format and context of practice, i.e., casework supervision in community-based organizations. Largely conceptualized and developed for supervisors with dual roles, the model addresses both the managerial and clinical concerns of the supervisor. Supervisors need to be familiar with the ecological systems theory by Bronfenbrenner (1989), eco-systems perspective (Compton et al. 2005; Hepworth et al. 2017), systems perspective, and the phases of problem solving in the social work process (namely, engagement, assessment, intervention, and evaluation) to guide social work supervisees. Conversely, a lack of such knowledge/skills may limit the use of the model in supervisory practice.

Conclusion

Supervisors with dual roles tend to face tension between management control and providing space and autonomy for their supervisees in developing professional judgment. This chapter has proposed a clinical supervisory model that highlights the PEACE process-in-context as a way forward for supervisors in maintaining balance of their dual roles. The supervisory model is informed by a variety of theoretical underpinnings, including systems theory, strengths-based orientation, Kolb's (1984) cycle of experiential learning, ITP loop, and the seven-eyed supervision model. The PEACE process-in-context supervisory model builds on the seven-eyed model of supervision by Hawkins and Shohet (2012) by including the PEACE supervision process. Hence, the PEACE process-in-context supervision model goes beyond looking at different contexts, since it involves the process of supervision. The model recognizes that social work supervision involves the client, supervisee, and supervisor within an organizational context, with influences from the wide systemic contexts. The model acknowledges the relevance and possible utilization of faith and spirituality in supervision sessions, both for clients and supervisees. In using the PEACE process-in-context supervisory model, supervisors are able to perform the various supervision functions and be mindful of their dual roles. By so doing, it is believed that the use of the PEACE process-in-context supervisory model will provide social work supervisors with a more informed way to manage the conflicts that may arise in their clinical and managerial roles.

References

Beddoe, L., 2010. Surveillance or reflection: professional supervision in 'the risk society'. *British Journal of Social Work*, 40 (4), 1279–1296.

Beddoe, L., 2012. External supervision in social work: power, space, risk and the search for safety. *Australian Social Work*, 65 (2), 197–213.

Bernard, J.M., and Goodyear, R.K., 2019. *Fundamentals of clinical supervision*. 6th ed. Boston: Pearson.

Bogo, M., and Vayda, E., 1989. Developing a process model for field instruction. *Canadian Social Work Review*, 6 (2), 224–232.

Bogo, M., and Vayda, E., 1991. A teaching model to unite classroom and field. *Journal of Social Work Education*, 27 (3), 271–278.

Bogo, M., and Vayda, E., 1998. *The practice of field instruction in social work: theory and process*. 2nd ed. New York: University of Toronto Press.

Bronfenbrenner, U., 1989. Ecological systems theory. *In*: R. Vasta, ed. *Annals of child development: six theories of child development: revisited formulations and current issues*. Greenwich, CT: JAI Press, 187–247.

Bronfenbrenner, U., 1999. Environments in developmental perspective: theoretical and operational models. *In*: S.L. Friedman, and T.D. Wachs, eds. *Measuring environments across the lifespan: emerging methods and concepts*. Washington, DC: American Psychological Association, 3–28.

Campbell, D., Coldicott, T., and Kinsella, K., 1994. *Systemic work with organizations: a new model for managers and change agents*. London: Karnac Books.

Canda, E., Furman, L., and Canda, H., 2020. *Spiritual diversity in social work practice: the heart of helping*. New York: Oxford University Press.

Charles, R., 2004. *Intuition in Psychotherapy and Counselling*. London: Whurr.

Charmaz, K., 2006. *Constructing grounded theory: a practical guide through qualitative analysis*. London: SAGE.

Charmaz, K., 2008. Grounded theory. *In*: J.A. Smith, ed., *Qualitative psychology: a practical guide to research methods*. 2nd ed. London: SAGE Publications Ltd, 81–110.

Charmaz, K., 2011. Grounded theory methods in social justice research. *In*: N.K. Denzin, and Y.E. Lincoln eds. *The SAGE handbook of qualitative research*. 4th ed. Thousand Oaks, CA: SAGE, 359–380.

Compton, B.R., Galaway, B., and Cournoyer, B.R., 2005. *Social work processes*. Pacific Grove: Brooks/Cole.

Cousins, C., 2010. "Treat me don't beat me": exploring supervisory games and their effect on poor performance management. *Practice: Social Work in Action*, 22, 281–292.

Chua, R., 2019. The transition from a clinical role to management: a journey to the dark side?. *In*: E. Sim and S. Sng eds. *Weaving compassion: relational understandings and practices*. Singapore: Counselling & Care Centre, 51–72.

Dallos, R., and Draper, R., 2007. *An introduction to family therapy: systemic theory & practice*. London: Open University Press.

Davys, A., 2000. Reflective learning in supervision. *In*: L. Beddoe, and J. Worrall, eds. *From rhetoric to reality: proceedings of the supervision conference*. Auckland College of Education.

Davys, A., and Beddoe, L., 2010. *Best practice in professional supervision: a guide for the helping professions*. London: Jessica Kingsley Publishers.

D'Cruz, H., Gillingham, P., and Melendez, S., 2007. Reflexivity, its meanings and relevance for social work: a critical review of the literature. *British Journal of social work*, 37, 73–90.

Evans, W.N., 1993. *An analysis of the job satisfaction of substance abuse counsellors certified by the Commonwealth of Virginia*. Thesis (PhD). Virginia Polytechnic Institute and State University.

Falvey, J.E., 1987. *Handbook of administrative supervision*. Baltimore, MD: University Park Press.

Gibbs, G., 1998. *Learning by doing: a guide to teaching and learning methods*. Oxford: Further Education Unit, Oxford Brookes University.

Hart, G., 1982. *The process of clinical supervision*. Baltimore, MD: University Park Press.

Hawkins, P., and Shohet, R., 2007. *Supervision in the helping professions*. 3rd ed. London: Open University Press.

Hawkins, P., and Shohet, R., 2012. *Supervision in the helping professions*. 4th ed. London: Open University Press.

Hawkins, P., 2019. Resourcing: the neglected third leg of supervision. *In*: E. Turner and S. Palmer eds. *The heart of coaching supervision: working with reflection and self care*. Abingdon, England: Routledge, 61–82.

Hay, J., 2007. *Reflective practice and supervision for coaches*. Maidenhead, Berkshire: Open University Press.

Hepworth, D.H., et al., 2017. *Direct social work practice: theory and skills*. 10th ed. Canada: Thomson.

Hewson, D., and Carroll, M., 2016. *Reflective practice in supervision*. Australia: Moshpit Publishing.

Kadushin, A., and Harkness, D., 2014. *Supervision in social work*. 5th ed. New York: Columbia University Press.

Kaiser, T.L., 1997. *Supervisory relationships: exploring the human elements*. Pacific Grove, CA: Brooks/Cole.

Kenfield, J.A., 1993. *Clinical supervision of licensed psychologist: nature of and satisfaction with the supervisory relationship*. Unpublished thesis. University of Minnesota, Minneapolis.

Kirst-Ashman, K.K., and Hull, G.H., 2009. *Understanding generalist practice*, (5th ed.) Belmont, CA: Thomson Brooks/Cole, Cengage Learning.

Kirst-Ashman, K., and Hull, G.H., 2012. *Understanding generalist practice*. 6th ed. Belmont: Brooks/Cole.

Kolb, D., 1984. *Experiential learning: experience as the source of learning and development*. New Jersey: Prentice-Hall.

Lappin, J., and Hardy, K.V.H., 2002. Keeping context in view: the heart of supervision. *In*: T.C. Todd, and C.L. Storm eds. *The complete systemic supervisor: context, philosophy & pragmatics*. USA: Allyn & Bacon.

Liddle, H.A., 1988. Systemic supervision: conceptual overlays and pragmatic guidelines. *In*: H.A Liddle, D.C. Breunlin, and R.C. Schwartz eds. *Handbook of family therapy training and supervision*. New York: Guilford Press.

Lo, R., 2014. Isomorphism and parallel processes in clinical supervision. *In*: C. Lim and E. Sim eds. *Clinical supervision: clinicians' perspectives and practices: towards professionalising counselling*. Singapore: Counselling & Care Centre, 36–58.

Low, J., 2019. Compassion through the isomorphic process. *In*: E. Sim and S. Sng eds. *Weaving compassion: relational understandings and practices*. Singapore: Counselling & Care Centre, 96–111.

Mo, K.Y, and Tsui, M.S., 2019. Toward an indigenized external supervision approach in China. *International Social Work*, 62 (4), 1286–1303.

Rowan, J., 2010. *Personification: using the dialogical self in psychotherapy and counselling*. London: Routledge.

Saleebey, D., 2013. *Strengths perspective in social work practice*. 6th ed. Upper Saddle River, NJ: Pearson.

Scaife, J., 2010. *Supervising the reflective practitioner: an essential guide to theory and practice*. USA: Routledge.

Schon, D.A., 1983. *The reflective practitioner: how professionals think in action*. New York: Basic Books.

Sheafor, B.W., and Horejsi, C.R., 2006. *Techniques and guidelines for social work practice*. Boston: Allyn and Bacon.

Shulman, L., 2010. *Interactional supervision*. 3rd ed. Washington: NASW Press.

Sweeney, G., Webley, P., and Treacher, A., 2001. Supervision in occupational therapy, part 1: the supervisor's anxieties. *British Journal of Occupational Therapy*, 64 (7), 337–345.

Tromski-Klingshirn, D., 2007. Should the clinical supervisor be the administrative supervisor? *The Clinical Supervisor*, 25 (1–2), 53–67.

Tsui, M.S., 2005. *Social work supervision: contexts and concepts*. USA: SAGE Publications.

Tsui, M.S., 2008. Adventures in re-searching the features of social work supervision in Hong Kong. *Qualitative Social Work*, 7 (3), 351–362.

Von Bertalanffy, L., 1968. *General systems theory: foundation, development, application*. New York: Brazillier.

Walsh, J., 2006. *Direct social work practice*. USA: Brooks/ Cole.

Wong, Y.J., 2014. *A grounded understanding of challenges and responses of social work supervisors with managerial and clinical roles*. Thesis (PhD). National University of Singapore.

Wong, P.Y.J., and Lee, A.E.Y., 2015. Dual roles of social work supervisors: strain and strengths as managers and clinical supervisors. *China Journal of Social Work*, 8 (2), 164–181.

21

EXTERNAL SUPERVISION IN SOCIAL WORK

Liz Beddoe

Introduction

External supervision as a form of supervision in social work developed initially from two motivating forces. First was the desire to separate clinical or professional supervision of social workers from "line" or managerial supervision. The thinking behind this separation of functions was that provision of supervision by an external supervisor would free it from overly managerial concerns and enable the supervisory dyad to focus on the educative and supportive elements of supervision. The second motivation has more pragmatic origins. In a growing social services marketplace, supervision can be contracted out to external self- employed or consultant supervisors, enabling employing agencies to meet regulatory requirements for registered social workers without investing in supervisory education for their own staff. Supervision is thus privatized alongside a growing market in for-profit and not-for-profit social services.

A third motivation has emerged over time. Within a relationship freed from the problem of power manifest in organizations, external supervision is seen to better attend to staff wellbeing by providing a safety valve for highly stressed practitioners (Hair 2014). Such a motivation draws upon the concerns for risk, safety, wellbeing, and the securing of professional identity and professional autonomy, all of which are omnipresent elements in social work. Supervision thus located away from the busy office setting is conceptualized within an interplay of three dimensions of safety: the temporal, the locational, and the relational.

This chapter will explore the three motivations driving the growth of external supervision: the separation of functions, the growth of markets for private practice, and lastly the focus on safety and wellbeing within a professional framework

The growth of external supervision

For the purpose of clarity, in this chapter external supervision is defined as professional supervision of a social worker by a supervisor who is not employed in the agency where the supervisee practices (Beddoe 2011). A review of literature reveals that external supervision began to be noted as a practice within social work in the 2000s, often interpreted as reflecting an expanding market discourse in social work and public services wherein professional supervision is just another service outsourced to external private contractors (Busse 2009;

Beddoe 2011; O'Donoghue 2015). Another common interpretation of the growth of external supervision is that it is a response to the problematization of the dual roles of supervisor and manager (Wong and Lee 2015). The inclusion of the administrative function within traditional descriptions of supervision in social work had tended to underpin an assumption that the supervisory role was at least partially inclusive of management (Kadushin 1976). External supervision enables the separation of this function from the educative and supportive functions. O'Donoghue (2015) states that the growth of this phenomenon of external supervision was a demonstration that "the paradigm of social work supervision has shifted and that the characteristics of this change have been the separation of the line management and professional aspects of supervision" (p. 142). The separation of functions also overlaps with growing focus in social work supervision on reflective practice and the personal professional development aspects of supervision rather than just casework (Jones 2004; Davys and Beddoe 2010; Harvey and Henderson 2014).

In considering the phenomenon of external supervision in the international context it is important to reiterate that "in its purest form, it might be hoped that supervision could transcend its 'local' contexts," however supervision is increasingly "legitimated via professional and organizational systems (regulation and management)" (Beddoe 2015a, p. 152). Professional regulation has led to mandates and rules about supervision (Beddoe 2015b). Indeed, in the current environment for social work in many Western countries, and those where Western models of professionalization have been adopted, traditional discourses of social work "street level" autonomy and discretion may be perceived to have weakened (Karvinen-Niinikoski et al. 2019). External supervision may be seen by many as an antidote to an overly managed and regulated social work.

The separation of supervisory functions

Supervision in social work has traditionally been inclusive of functions of education, support, and case administration. The problematizing of the dual role of supervisor and line manager began to emerge in the 1990s. In 1994 Malcolm Payne noted the proliferation of managerial roles and the impact on more traditional casework supervision, invoking a scenario of social work at risk of becoming captured by "unthinking adherence to politically and bureaucratically defined roles" (Payne 1994, p. 55). The confluence of New Public Management in health and social services and highly risk-averse environments (Connell et al. 2009) was deemed to have pushed supervision away from its educative emphasis, towards greater focus on accountability (Noble and Irwin 2009). Noble and Irwin argued that the managerialism that accompanied the neoliberal transformation of social services led to changed priorities: "the changing context of supervision has meant that supervision had changed from being a priority of the profession to a priority of management" (2009, p. 352). Anxiety about risk management may have been a significant driver of this growth of the provision of external supervision. Playing "into the accountability agenda," supervision was "rendered a compliance activity to be checked off on the list of mechanisms that aim to ensure safe practice" (Beddoe 2011, p. 200).

The motivations underlying supervisees' own desire for external supervision and managers' willingness to contract it out were not particularly well aligned. Audit, quality assurance, and targets all required the supervisory oversight of front-line professionals in a manner that many social workers feared threatened professional autonomy and demonstrated reduced trust in professionals' ability to self-manage (Peach and Horner 2007; Karvinen-Niinikoski et al. 2019). While Payne (1994) hoped for a reconciliation of managerial and professional supervision models as a consequence of the growing focus on quality assurance, others were rightly concerned about threats to supervision's integrity as a learning-focused activity (Peach and Horner 2007; Beddoe 2010). Fears in nursing and other professions that supervision was a kind of Trojan horse for a "predominance of appraisal, censure and managerial control – linked with a concomitant erosion of professional autonomy" (Peach and Horner 2007, p. 9) led to models of supervision, in those professions, where supervision was explicitly separate from the managerial relationship, even if provided internally (Bond and Holland 2010; Carroll 2014).

In Australasia, external supervision seems to be utilized by roughly a quarter of social workers. Egan's (2012) study of Australian social workers, where 81.6% of respondents did not have a choice of supervisor, found that nearly two-thirds of respondents identified their supervisor as internal to their team and were also line managers, while 22.3% had supervisors external to their team (Egan 2012, p. 177). O'Donoghue (2019) reported that in a survey of 240 social workers in Aotearoa New Zealand, 28.3% reported participation in external supervision. The same study found that a surprisingly large number of social workers (49.5% n = 136) had more than one supervisor. Of these, a third of respondents (33.5%, n = 92: the largest group) had two supervisors. External supervision is the common model of social work supervision in China (Mo 2016; Mo and Tsui 2019) where supervision is seen as an important component in ensuring the development of a strong professional identity in social work (Liu et al. 2012). South Africa and the Republic of Ireland allow for external supervision where internal line management supervision is not available. Bogo and McKnight (2006) reported variable arrangements for supervision in the United States, from internal to external, or not available at all.

Many professional associations seem to assume that one supervisor can provide administrative and clinical supervision, although power dynamics may be acknowledged. The US National Association of Social Workers "Best Practice Standards in Social Work Supervision" (2013, p. 12) emphasizes the role of the contract in ensuring responsibilities are clarified:

> In circumstances in which a supervisee is being administratively or clinically supervised simultaneously by more than one person, it is best practice to have a contractual agreement or memorandum of understanding delineating the role of each supervisor, including parameters of the relationships, information sharing, priorities, and how conflicts will be resolved. If no agreement exists, the immediate employment supervisor may have the final say.

Thus, while there is an assumption of line management supervision there is some awareness of the power dimension which will be explored further in this chapter. For example, the 2014 "Supervision Standards" policy published by the Australian Association of Social Workers (AASW) includes a suggestion for supervisors to be alert to "issues related to power dynamics, surveillance and control if the line manager assumes different supervision functions" (Australian Association of Social Workers 2014, p. 6).

Bradley and Höjer (2009) reported on two very different kinds of supervision systems, in England and Sweden, respectively. Examining the two systems reveals that supervision within child protection in Sweden supervision typically occurs in groups away from the employing agency, which is facilitated by an external consultant in order to focus on the educative aspects. In the English system supervision happens within the agency on a one-to-one basis between the practitioner and a supervisor who is a line-manager. In statutory social work this supervision is closely aligned to audited targets for practice activity (Turner-Daly and Jack 2014) and is thus more aligned with a managerial focus.

The mandate for supervision

It is difficult to consider the separation of supervision from the workplace without considering the mandate for supervision. External supervision raises the issue of the mandate and accountability for supervision practice and what kind of relationship it implies between internal and external stakeholders. To some extent the practice seems to have developed over time without much focus on research or evaluation, particularly when associated with interprofessional supervision (Davys et al. 2017). O'Donoghue (2015) notes that the scholarship of supervision lagged behind in identifying the changes taking place: "the theory of social work supervision has been slow in incorporating the empirical research evidence about the practice of supervision which constructs peer and external supervision" (p. 141). O'Donoghue argues these increasingly common forms of supervision have "been constructed as 'consultation' rather than as 'supervision', in accordance with the traditional organization-based paradigm of social work supervision" (p. 141), with the assumption made that external and peer supervision are not hierarchical and lack an authorized authority accountability mechanism.

However, O'Donoghue asserts that practice agencies do provide a mandate in the delegation of authority to external clinical supervisors to supervise their staff, via supervision contracts and agreements. Social workers may very likely also have professional accountability through their registration or licensing by, or membership of, professional bodies. O'Donoghue helpfully delineates four sources of a mandate or tacit right to act as a supervisor. Furthermore, he suggests that the supervision mandate comes from "the same four sources that a social worker's mandate for work with clients comes from; namely, from their agency, profession, by law and from people to whom the service is provided" (p. 145).

Agency authority derives either from the supervisor being an agency employee or as an external supervisor under contract to provide supervision for social workers in the organization. The professional mandate is conferred through membership of a professional body that requires social workers to be supervised and/or a statutory mandate derived from the obligations inherent in professional regulation, registration, or licensing.

The fourth mandate in the case of supervision is conferred by the practitioner who participates in the supervision. This may be related to a choice made by the social worker themselves when they have had options and some freedom to choose, or by their acknowledgement of a supervisor who has been assigned to them by their organization or professional bodies (O'Donoghue 2015). A survey of health professionals in a mental health service in New Zealand revealed supervision to be a private arrangement: "practitioners within the organisation see supervision as a predominantly private arrangement between two individuals to ensure the highest possible quality of care and professional standards, which equates to the highest quality of service for their clients." The choice of supervisor was "driven by the supervisees," with mainly verbal agreements and the "general feeling that they do not need to give line managers any feedback about supervision" (Cooper 2006, p. 29).

It is this last source of mandate where choice is a significant factor. Davys (2017) and Davys and Beddoe (2015) note that choice is of particular significance in interprofessional supervision, allowing supervisees to exercise some agency over this important part of their professional identity and accountability. Danish researcher Magnussen (2018) reviewed 15 studies of supervision in Scandinavia and noted that employees can take the initiative to ask for supervision and often choose their own supervisor though this may be subject to management approval. His review found a fairly homogenous picture of the practice of supervision which mainly consisted of group-based supervision with external supervisors, along the lines of that described by Bradley and Höjer (2009). The European and Scandinavian models which emerged have created a kind of supervision that was distinct from the systems familiar in Anglophone countries, where supervision was much more closely aligned to management, as noted above. The developing models have allowed creativity in developing models such as use of video for supervision for statutory youth workers in Denmark, reported by Antczak et al. (2019).

There is little published research about the extent to which external supervision has become formally mandated in a more regulated social work environment. It certainly seems likely that where supervision is a legal requirement, some auditing occurs, and it is certainly considered best practice that formal supervision agreements or contracts are in place that address boundaries, the limits of confidentiality, and the requirements for reporting and evaluation (Beddoe and Davys 2016). The risk of unhealthy triangulation of practitioner, line manager, and clinical supervisor is often discussed with the best practice suggested to include a clear contract (Davys and Beddoe 2010). A strong three-way contract with the supervisee, the organization, via the line manager, and the external supervisor can ensure sufficient attention is paid to the clarity of the mandate for supervision and lines of communication. Reporting of supervision need not impact on trust if the limits of confidentiality, the nature of information provided, and agreement on matters such as external supervisor input into annual appraisals are all clarified and noted in the contract.

The growth of the market

To examine the phenomenon of external supervision as a manifestation of marketization, it is useful to include in the analysis reference to the wider changes heralded by neoliberal ideology as it has influenced social work. The shift towards a more mixed market for social service has seen privatization become an option for social work (van Heugten and Daniels 2001; Lord and Ludice 2012). Supervision is a significant component of what those who "go private" do in their practice. In the United States for example, Lord and Ludice report that 35.3% of their survey sample provided consultation or supervision to other professionals (2012, p. 89). It thus provides an income stream for those in private practice.

The more extensive development of supervision as separate from social work was initially promoted in Europe and Scandinavia where supervision as a private practice had developed (Belardi 2002; Busse 2009). O'Donoghue (2015, p. 139) asserts that with this shift towards separation of functions, supervision becomes an independent activity:

> where private practitioners from a range of disciplines provided supervision as a professional, educational and organizational development intervention (Belardi 2002; Bradley and Höjer 2009; Busse 2009). This in turn has resulted in a number of European countries professionalizing supervision in its own right, separately from social work
>
> *(Belardi 2002; Busse 2009).*

Social work has frequently eschewed private models of service delivery, though the critique rests more on profit making enterprise. A large survey of social workers in three Nordic countries and Italy, for example, found social workers perceived privatization, in terms of for-profit organizations, more critically than services privatized by non-governmental sector not-for-profit agencies (Kallio et al. 2015). Supervision stands out as being an area of social work practice privatization that is viewed less critically than other services, most likely as it is seen as self-employment rather than a "business" (Kallio et al. 2015). In an investigation of Swedish social workers' attitudes towards privatization in social services, it is reported there was relatively strong support for private external supervision (Dellgran and Höjer 2005). Social workers were asked, "In what organisational form do you think the following activities are best carried out?" Among other examples, supervision received the highest percentage (24%) of support by those who thought it is best executed in private practice. Only 3% thought supervision is best done under public management (Dellgran and Höjer 2005, p. 48). This study found support for a hypothesis that "privatisation is a professional strategy for status, legitimacy, autonomy and control ('pull factors'), as well as for the discontent hypothesis ('push factors')" (Dellgran and Höjer 2005, p. 57). While research that explores supervision in the context of private practice is scarce, it seems reasonable to assume that pull factors might operate, given the growing requirement and demand for supervision, the consensus that supervision is good (Beddoe and Wilkins 2019), and the growth of supervision qualifications and the desire to employ these skills fully to promote reflective practice (Beddoe 2011). The push factors may be the same as for other kinds of self-employment: discontent with practice constraints, family circumstances requiring flexibility, and opportunities for professional development (Dellgran and Höjer 2005).

A critical examination of the privatization of supervision is provided by Busse (2009), who begins his analysis of supervision with a brief historical survey. Supervision's "country of origin" (Weigand 1991, cited in Busse 2009, p. 159) is social work, and the two practices, social work and supervision, were linked over the development of the profession from the late 19th century. Busse regards supervision "in the course of its own history" to have "emancipated itself, or has been unfaithful to its origins, separating from social work" (2009, p. 159). This unfaithfulness can in large part be attributed to the growth of a market in his view; the separation represented an ideological shift from the traditional embedded model of supervision where it is seen as a core part of social work practice, rather than a separate activity. This in turn represents an extension of the separation from an internal separation of management and supervision allowing the growth of a market for private or independent supervision.

Belardi (2002), who describes German supervision as holding the most advanced position "in the entire world with regard to conceptual development, variety of methods, instruction and practical relevance" (p. 313), describes self-employment in supervision as "a chance for career promotion and a means to exit for disappointed social workers" (p. 316). While this may seem cynical, supervision is often seen as a way of continuing one's professional contribution, especially when continuing in direct clinical work no longer holds great appeal. The growth of supervision education perhaps represents the desire to raise supervision standards, but also to meet the needs of a market that has been created, because if organizations are to outsource their supervision then it is almost inevitable that credentialing supervision follows.

Supervision space and place: The focus on safety and wellbeing

In a small study, Beddoe (2011) explored the development of external supervision though a lens of risk. Discourses of risk and vulnerability about social work practice and in particular the very negative impacts of prominent child abuse deaths and anxious, risk-averse governments have sought to enhance supervision. Supervision "can be harnessed to technologies of risk minimisation and, where this appropriation occurs, a shift from a focus on the development of practitioners to the monitoring of their practice" means that the separation of functions noted above encourages dual systems to occur (Beddoe 2011, pp. 199–200). The provision of external supervision can thus be conceptualized as a response to managerial anxiety, with supervision rendered a compliance activity to be checked off on the list of mechanisms that aim to ensure safe practice. Internal supervision can become unashamedly organizationally focused and managerial, while more professional aspirations to reflective practice can be outsourced to private practice. Such practice also reflects the shift in administrative systems to more generic management, where professionals may no longer be managed by a clinician of their profession (Cooper 2006). Difficulties of access to social work supervision within organizations were noted by McAuliffe and Sudbery (2005) as another factor driving the external model, and interprofessional supervision (Davys 2017).

While the pursuit of safety can be located in the anxieties of risk averse practice, a further reading of this conceptualizes this search as aiming for a stronger focus on the practitioner, linked to self, growth, and professional identity. Rankine's recent research, for example, found practitioners viewed external supervisors "more invested in the supervisory relationship and the social worker's development" (Rankine 2019, p. 41). Safety, in what is commonly called "safe place" or "safe space" has emerged over time as an element of external supervision that offered an enhanced experience for practitioners (Beddoe 2011; McPherson et al. 2016). From this perspective supervision offers more opportunity for reflection and exploration of ethical challenges, for professional development freed from the organizational preoccupations of line management: a place with *room* for uncertainty and *not knowing*. Research in Australia found that participants with external supervisors were more likely to have raised ethical dilemmas in supervision having sought "dedicated time for clarification of ethical dimensions and problem solving" (McAuliffe and Sudbery 2005, p. 28).

Conceptualizations of space and place frequently occur in the supervision literature. The notions of both space as protected time (temporal) and place (locational) are often bracketed with safety (Beddoe 2011). Supervision was described for example as "sacred time" by a participant in Benton, Dill, and Williams (2017) study. Magnussen (2018) raises the idea that fear of self-censorship is diminished by the sense of safety in the space and place provided in the external supervision relationship. Beddoe (2011) noticed many references to space and place in earlier literature, where space and place are almost interchangeably used to explain a state of *being between*, in different aspects: professional self and personal self, the "office" and other places. External supervision can act as a safety-zone, away from the busy workplace, removed from the stresses in crisis teams. It offers both a refuge and a boundaried time: "The respondents described [supervision] as the place where they connected with their supervisor, profession, peer and group; shared their frustrations and successes; could be challenged; and could learn and develop" (O'Donoghue et al. 2006, p. 84). For Busse (2009, p. 162) the location of external supervision away from the social service workplace is an attempt to achieve a more reflective, democratic space: "Supervision, as has become clearer, is an exclusive space for the reflexive achievement of distance from working life."

There are locational and temporal considerations in this making room for reflection. Schön's (1983) work on "reflection-in-action" has been fairly dominant in social work education with educators aspiring to develop social workers who can "think on their feet" with the capacity for both rapid decision-making and critical refection while *in situ* in practice, that is where practice happens. Ferguson (2018) has discussed the challenges of such reflection "in action," arguing that "research shows that there are times and situations in which practitioners find that it is better *not* to reflect in the manner advocated in the literature" (p. 417). Furthermore, Ferguson is concerned that there is a "failure to recognise the limits to reflection" because the self has been "conceptualised as a coherent unproblematic entity, as something distinct and unified that the worker accesses and goes into in order to connect to themselves and their service users" (p. 417). This model of reflection, as being on tap, ready in every social worker's "self" to make good decisions on the move suggests a somewhat perverse and contradictory approach to a more traditional notion of reflection as contemplation.

Conclusions

External supervision, freed from the shackles of management, provides a safe space in which social workers can be "reflective and inquisitive about their own cases without having to censor themselves in order to avoid potential ramifications" (Magnussen 2018, p. 366). Research is needed to determine whether there are empirical certainties that external supervision is better able to offer this safe space and place for professional reflection and growth. The research we do have, drawn upon in this chapter, suggest that practitioners highly value it.

In his book entitled *Space and Place*, humanist geographer Tuan (1977) writes: "Place is security, space is freedom: we are attached to the one and long for the other" (1977, p. 3). In such a conceptualization, effective external supervision can hold this tension providing both the security of sanctuary and the freedom to be uncertain, to be creative, and to be one's authentic self. At this point we can add the relational element to the mix. Trust is essential for this kind of critically reflective supervision to flourish because, while uncertainty is ubiquitous in social work, excellent supervisors can listen, probe, and critically question while retaining respect and care as conditions of trust (Egan, Maidment, and Connolly 2017; Noble et al. 2016). The research suggests that what makes supervision effective is the relational. It is the relationship that makes the difference (McPherson et al. 2016; Rankine 2019). Supervision can provide a bulwark to strengthen practice confidence in the face of uncertainty and conflict.

Against background debates about reflection, external supervision offers a sanctuary, away from the busy workplace, where there is time to make room to think about practice moments and to process emotions which may have been overwhelming. It helps social workers address risk, anxiety, and uncertainty. It is growth oriented. The external supervision room and external supervisor can provide a quiet space where critical inquiry and the exploration of the unpredictable aspects of social work practice can be held in a creative tension.

References

Antczak, H.B., Mackrill, T., Steensbæk, S., and Ebsen, F., 2019. What works in video-based youth statutory caseworker supervision – caseworker and supervisor perspectives. *Social Work Education*, 1–16. doi:10.1080/02615479.2019.1611757.

Australian Association of Social Workers AASW 2014. *AASW supervision standards*. Canberra: Author.

Beddoe, L., 2010. Surveillance or reflection: professional supervision in 'the risk society'. *British Journal of Social Work*, 40 (4), 1279–1296. doi:10.1093/bjsw/bcq018.

Beddoe, L., 2011. External supervision in social work: power, space, risk, and the search for safety. *Australian Social Work*, 65 (2), 197–213. doi:10.1080/0312407x.2011.591187.

Beddoe, L., 2015a. Supervision and developing the profession: one supervision or many?. *China Journal of Social Work*, 8 (2), 150–163. doi:10.1080/17525098.2015.1039173.

Beddoe, L., 2015b. Social work supervision for changing contexts. *In*: L. Beddoe and J. Maidment, eds. *Supervision in social work: contemporary issues*. London: Routledge, 82–95.

Beddoe, L., and Davys, A., 2016. *Challenges in professional supervision: current themes and models for practice*. London: Jessica Kingsley.

Beddoe, L., and Wilkins, D., 2019. Does the consensus about the value of supervision in social work stifle research and innovation?. *Aotearoa New Zealand Social Work*, 31 (3), 1–6.

Belardi, N., 2002. Social work supervision in Germany. *European Journal of Social Work*, 5 (3), 313–318. doi:10.1080/714053162.

Benton, A.D., Dill, K., and Williams, A.E., 2017. Sacred time: ensuring the provision of excellent supervision. *Journal of Workplace Behavioral Health*, 32 (4), 290–305. doi:10.1080/15555240.2017.1408416.

Bogo, M., and McKnight, K., 2006. Clinical supervision in social work. *The Clinical Supervisor*, 24 (1), 49–67.

Bond, M., and Holland, M., 2010. *Skills of clinical supervision for nurses*, 2nd ed. Maidenhead: Open University Press.

Bradley, G., and Höjer, S., 2009. Supervision reviewed: reflections on two different social work models in England and Sweden. *European Journal of Social Work*, 12 (1), 71–85. doi:10.1080/13691450802220990.

Busse, S., 2009. Supervision between critical reflection and practical action. *Journal of Social Work Practice*, 23 (2), 159–173.

Carroll, M., 2014. *Effective supervision for the helping professions*. 2nd ed. London: SAGE.

Connell, R., Fawcett, B., and Meagher, G., 2009., Neoliberalism, new public management and the human service professions: introduction to the special issue. *Journal of Sociology*, 45 (4), 331–338. doi:10.1177/1440783309346472.

Cooper, L., 2006. Clinical supervision: private arrangement or managed process? *Social Work Review*, 18 (3), 21–30.

Davys, A.M., 2017. Interprofessional supervision: a matter of difference. *Aotearoa New Zealand Social Work*, 29 (3), 79–94. doi:10.11157/anzswj-vol29iss3id278.

Davys, A., and Beddoe, L., 2010. *Best practice in professional supervision: a guide for the helping professions*. London: Jessica Kingsley.

Davys, A., and Beddoe, L., 2015. Interprofessional supervision: opportunities and challenges. *In*: L. Bostock, ed. *Interprofessional staff supervision in adult health and social care services*. Vol. 1. Brighton, England: Pavilion Publishing, 37–41.

Dellgran, P., and Höjer, S., 2005. Privatisation as professionalisation? Attitudes, motives and achievements among Swedish social workers. *European Journal of Social Work*, 8 (1), 39–62. doi:10.1080/1369145042 000331369.

Egan, R., 2012. *Social work supervision practice in Australia: does the rhetoric match the practice?* Thesis (PhD), University of Melbourne. Available from: http://hdl.handle.net/11343/37891 [Accessed 19 December 2019].

Egan, R., Maidment, J., and Connolly, M., 2017. Trust, power and safety in the social work supervisory relationship: results from Australian research. *Journal of Social Work Practice*, 31 (3), 307–321. doi:10.1080 /02650533.2016.1261279.

Ferguson, H., 2018. How social workers reflect in action and when and why they don't: the possibilities and limits to reflective practice in social work. *Social Work Education*, 37 (4), 415–427. doi:10.1080/026 15479.2017.1413083.

Hair, H.J., 2014. Power relations in supervision: preferred practices according to social workers. *Families in Society: The Journal of Contemporary Social Services*, 95 (2), 107–114.

Harvey, A., and Henderson, F., 2014. Reflective supervision for child protection practice – Reaching beneath the surface. *Journal of Social Work Practice*, 28 (3), 343–356. doi:10.1080/02650533.2014.925862.

Jones, M., 2004. Supervision, learning and transformative practices. *In*: N. Gould and M. Baldwin, eds. *Social work, critical reflection and the learning organisation*. Aldershot: Ashgate, 11–22.

Kadushin, A., 1976. *Supervision in social work*. New York, NY: Columbia University Press.

Kallio, J., Meeuwisse, A., and Scaramuzzino, R., 2015. Social workers' attitudes to privatization in five countries. *Journal of Social Work*, 16 (2), 174–195. doi:10.1177/1468017314568850.

Karvinen-Niinikoski, S., Beddoe, L., Ruch, G., and Tsui, M.S., 2019. Professional supervision and professional autonomy. *Aotearoa New Zealand Social Work*, 31 (3), 87–96.

Liu, Y., Lam, C.-M., and Yan, M.-C., 2012. A challenged professional identity: the struggles of new social workers in China. *China Journal of Social Work*, 5 (3), 189–200. doi:10.1080/17525098.2012.721166.

Lord, S.A., and Ludice, J., 2012. Social workers in private practice: a descriptive study of what they do. *Clinical Social Work Journal*, 40 (1), 85–94. doi:10.1007/s10615-011-0316-7.

Magnussen, J., 2018. Supervision in Denmark – an empirical account of experiences and practices. *European Journal of Social Work*, 21 (3), 359–373. doi:10.1080/13691457.2018.1451827.

McAuliffe, D., and Sudbery, J., 2005. 'Who do I tell?': support and consultation in cases of ethical conflict. *Journal of Social Work*, 5 (1), 21–43. doi:10.1177/1468017305051362.

McPherson, L., Frederico, M., and McNamara, P., 2016. Safety as a fifth dimension in supervision: stories from the frontline. *Australian Social Work*, 69 (1), 67–79. doi:10.1080/0312407X.2015.1024265.

Mo, K.Y., and Tsui, M.S., 2019. Toward an indigenized external supervision approach in China. *International Social Work*, 62 (4), 1286–1303. doi: 10.1177/0020872818778104.

Mo, Y.H., 2016. In search of a professional supervisory practice: external social work supervision in China. *Asian Social Work and Policy Review*, 10 (3), 349–357. doi:10.1111/aswp.12103.

National Association of Social Workers 2013. *Best practice standards in social work supervision*. Washington, DC: Author. Available from: https://www.socialworkers.org/LinkClick.aspx?fileticket=GBrLbl4BuwI%3D &portalid=0 [Accessed 19 December 2019].

Noble, C., Gray, M., and Johnston, L., 2016. *Critical supervision for the human services: a social model to promote learning and values-based practice*. London, UK: Jessica Kingsley Publishers.

Noble, C., and Irwin, J., 2009. Social work supervision: an exploration of the current challenges in a rapidly changing social, economic and political environment. *Journal of Social Work*, 9 (3), 345–358. doi:10.1177/1468017309334848.

O'Donoghue, K.B., 2015. Issues and challenges facing social work supervision in the twenty-first century. *China Journal of Social Work*, 8 (2), 136–149. doi:10.1080/17525098.2015.1039172.

O'Donoghue, K.B., 2019. The supervision of registered social workers in Aotearoa New Zealand: a national survey. *Aotearoa New Zealand Social Work*, 31 (3), 58–77. doi:http://dx.doi.org/10.11157/anzswj-vol31iss3id648.

O'Donoghue, K., Munford, R., and Trlin, A., 2006. What's best about social work supervision according to association members. *Social Work Review*, 18 (3), 79–91.

Payne, M., 1994. Personal supervision in social work. *In*: A. Connor and S.E. Black, eds. *Performance review and quality in social care*. London, UK: Jessica Kingsley, 43–58.

Peach, J., and Horner, N., 2007. Using supervision: support or surveillance. *In*: M. Lymbery and K. Postle, eds. *Social work: a companion to learning*. London, UK: SAGE, 228–239.

Rankine, M., 2019. The internal/external debate: the tensions within social work supervision. *Aotearoa New Zealand Social Work*, 31 (3), 32–45. doi:http://dx.doi.org/10.11157/anzswj-vol31iss3id646.

Schön, D., 1983. *The reflective practitioner*. London: Temple Smith.

Tuan, Y.-F., 1977. *Space and place: the perspective of experience*, Minneapolis: University of Minnesota Press.

Turner-Daly, B., and Jack, G., 2014. Rhetoric vs. reality in social work supervision: the experiences of a group of child care social workers in England. *Child & Family Social Work*, 22 (1), 36–46. doi:10.1111/cfs.12191.

van Heugten, K., and Daniels, K., 2001. Social workers who move into private practice: the impact of the socio-economic context. *British Journal of Social Work*, 31 (5), 739–755. doi:10.1093/bjsw/31.5.739.

Wong, P.Y.J., and Lee, A.E.Y., 2015. Dual roles of social work supervisors: strain and strengths as managers and clinical supervisors. *China Journal of Social Work*, 8 (2), 164–181. doi:10.1080/17525098.2015.1039168.

22

THE SPIRIT OF PEER SUPERVISION

Ksenija Napan

Introduction

Peer-supervision is a collegial process where practitioners can reflect, better understand, and explore professional, personal, political, and spiritual issues that emerge while working with people. It is an alternative and an addition to managerial and one-to-one professional supervision. As such, it is distinctive as it is non-hierarchical – tending to develop a liberating culture which is self-determining, self-directing and self-renewing, allowing participants to learn from one another in areas they believe they need to develop. In literature (Golia and MGovern 2013), (Counselman and Weber 2004), (Christensen and Kline 2001) peer supervision is defined as any facilitated, planned, or ad hoc interactions with colleagues of similar experience levels, particularly clinical social workers, psychologists, and other mental health counsellors-in-training, in both dyadic and group contexts, for the purposes of clinical training, professional development, and mutual aid and affinity. Some (Bailey et al. 2014) refer to those groups as consultation groups, as individual participants retain the legal and ethical responsibility for their own client work and also reflect teams originated in a framework of narrative therapy (Brownlee et al. 2009). In this context, peer supervision is a planned and structured activity and not an ad hoc interaction nor a casual chat about professional practice. The three vignettes that follow focus on three different ways of conducting peer supervision with a common aim of enabling participants to cooperatively explore challenging issues that inevitably emerge in any kind of social practice and facilitate their autonomous and holistic learning in order to become empowered and equipped to work to the best of their potential. Peer-supervision in this context accommodates for people from various professions where transdisciplinary nature enables participants to explore professional issues from a range of different professional lenses. It is also possible that participants share the same profession. The main principle is that there is no leader, roles and participation are equally shared, and there is no monetary exchange. The focus is on the development of the sense of coherence (Antonovsky 1993) which results in a sense of wellbeing and enhanced ability to work to the best of one's potential.

This chapter explores the life enriching spirit of peer-supervision while reflecting on three different ways of conducting a peer-supervision group. The first vignette explores effectiveness of a specific peer supervision model by John Heron (1999), that requires a structured approach and a use of a booklet of peer supervision tools described in detail in the Complete Facilitator's

Handbook (Heron 1999) used by a range of helping professionals. The second vignette focuses on a transdisciplinary group of women who were involved in learning, teaching, and practicing Choice Theory within the International William Glasser Institute (Glasser 1999) blended with Jean Shinoda Bolen's work on feminine Greek goddess archetypes (Bolen 1984). The final vignette reflects on a cooperative inquiry research group initiated as an antidote to detachment experienced within a neoliberal academia (Napan et al. 2018). These three examples are reflected on through a lens of social work values and principles based on Aotearoa New Zealand Association of Social Workers Code of Ethics in order to integrate the professional, personal, political, and spiritual aspects of peer-supervision, examining how it enhances wellbeing of professionals and consequently communities they serve.

Although distinct, all three modalities are permeated with same characteristics and abide by same or similar rules to ensure effectiveness.

Main characteristics

1. Non-hierarchical
2. Reciprocal
3. Trust, honesty, and transparency (no hidden agendas or benefits)
4. Content and the process equally important
5. Non-judgmental and non-evaluative
6. Self-directed, participants determining their own needs, choosing processes that will meet them, using the group as a resource for learning and enabling different perspectives, viewpoints, and ideas that emerge to enable to tap into hidden resources
7. Confidential

Simple but essential rules

1. Meetings every two to three weeks, at least once a month for two to three hours
2. A closed group of two to twelve members (when more than six in a group, a group can split into two smaller groups for a particular session)
3. Confidentiality (with no exclusions) and activity
4. No "post mortems" (no questions asked after the group unless participant in focus initiates it)
5. Being supportive, non-competitive, and authentic (and being open to be challenged when not)
6. Focus on strengths in others and find strength in acceptance of own vulnerability and growing moments
7. Giving a person in focus full attention by listening, observing, and by looking for their strengths
8. Giving positive and negative feedback with an equal sense of respect for the person who is receiving it
9. Avoiding pussyfooting and sledgehammering; saying and owning your truth
10. No advice giving
11. Commitment to attendance
12. Sticking to allocated time and structure

The main philosophy is that quality can always be improved (Glasser 1998) and that lifelong learning is essential for effectiveness of all social practitioners. In these groups, professional, personal, political, and spiritual lives are perceived as closely interrelated and the peer-supervision process provides a forum where these artificial separations can be deconstructed in order to bring more coherence in professional actions and activities practitioners undertake, including addressing challenges and cognitive dissonances. Perception of these dissonances as learning opportunities enable participants to bring forth the world (Capra 1997) and contribute to their communities to the best of their potential. Peer-supervision makes practice more intentional and enables necessary space and time for reflection and reflexivity that can transform good practitioners into exceptional ones.

I have noticed in my professional practice that the higher one is on a hierarchy of power in any organization, the less likely it is that they would be openly challenged. When minds become clouded with power, humans somehow tend to lose touch with their own inadequacies. On the other hand, when feeling disempowered or challenged, humans often become defensive and miss the opportunity to learn and grow. Peer-supervision enables practitioners to explore their practice in a way they see fit and suitable while exposing their vulnerabilities or arrogancies. These acts of exposure that often lead to growth enable other group members to grow, either through resonances, notice of differences, or through opening a group space for speaking about the unspeakable. Its reciprocal and non-hierarchical nature and the fact that there is no monetary exchange but a focus on one another's strengths and abilities, enables participants to go where "angels fear to tread" (Bateson 1987) and following a proper process, insights emerge that have implications for all aspects of practitioners' lives.

Vignette one: Peer supervision – John Heron style

My involvement with John Heron started in 2000 when he was my individual professional supervisor and encouraged me to start a peer supervision group at my work. He shared with me his readings (Heron 1999) which included a comprehensive chapter on a specific peer supervision model that resonated with my way of thinking, being, teaching, and learning. I organized a first training at my place of work and gathered a group of teaching academics who committed to meet monthly and follow a specific prescribed process. The peer-group wisdom enhanced my individual supervision process with John and finally completely replaced it. The training for my first peer supervision group lasted for a day and was facilitated by NZ Coaching and Mentoring Centre who produced a booklet of processes called The Power of Peer Supervision: Tools for supervision & mentoring groups (New Zealand Coaching and Mentoring Centre 2012).

The process

A group meets for two to three hours, every two to three weeks, or at least once a month.

Stage 1 – Participants meet and greet while pouring refreshments or bringing their lunch (some groups prefer shared lunches or dinners). Sharing food and refreshments is important as it creates a context of comfort and collaboration.

Stage 2 – Some groups like to have an opening ritual that may involve a *karakia* (invocation or a prayer), a poem, or some acknowledgement of everyone's presence.

A timekeeper is appointed who keeps participants to agreed time (this role needs to be rotated).

Stage 3 – Check-in round: participants share how they are, what is alive for them. If they want to take a turn, they indicate how much time they need and choose a tool[1] that would be most appropriate for the issue they want to focus on. They can suggest a new peer-supervision tool too that can be added to a tool book.

Stage 4 – The agenda with timing is set.

Stage 5 – The process starts. A booklet of tools is used without deviations. Timekeeping for each section of the process is important.

Stage 6 – Check-out round: the final 15 minutes are reserved for a process review and possibly to a closing *karakia* (an invocation or a prayer), a quote, *waiata* (a song to affirm the process), or a thank you round.

The agenda set at the beginning of the meeting may cover challenges, difficulties, problems, affirmations of joys, successes, and achievements. Themes can reflect on the past, focus on the present, or plan for the future. Work is focused on various aspects of transformation while working with people in a range of settings. Each participant indicates which tool they would like to use. The tools are simple, structured activities that a participant in focus can choose from. This enables a self-directed process to emerge where a person taking a turn is fully responsible for the way the process is going to occur. A list of peer supervision tools is published in The Complete Facilitator's Handbook (Heron 1999) and in a booklet by NZCMC (New Zealand Coaching and Mentoring Centre 2012) facilitators who provide training. Attending training is important and enables the group to be disciplined in applying these tools and following the process thoroughly in order to avoid becoming a mere complaint session, advice giving, or deteriorate into gossip or running in circles. These tools enable participants to maximize their use of time and be focused and are constructed in a way that when one person is the focus of attention, everybody is deeply engaged in the process. At a first meeting ground rules are established and in consequent meetings participants take turns in facilitation. One person is assigned as a facilitator for a day. The facilitator's job is to keep time and monitor the process, enabling participants to stick to agreements and follow the routine. A booklet with tools is used and strictly adhered to. When everybody who wants to completes their turn, a "check-out" round closes the meeting. Confidentiality and focus on the benefit of the supervisee is paramount, and supervisees are supported to be the experts of their own session, their needs, and their learning, which reflects the principle of self-determination so essential for social work practice.

Benefits and unique features

Just having time set aside to focus on potential problems or challenges at work is beneficial, and the tools and processes enable participants to rapidly grow professionally and at the same time hone their social work skills of giving and receiving feedback, being focused, emphasizing strengths, being aware of the risks, and being clear and precise. This model of peer supervision provides clarity, focus, and time efficiency. It is also a disciplined approach to peer supervision, and trusting a process enables participants to develop a sense of confidence in its effectiveness. Although well structured, it allows for creativity because it is based on voluntary disclosure, a person taking a turn being responsible for a choice of a tool that is going to be used, and how they will utilize what they have heard from other participants. The way tools are structured enable a person in focus to sift and sort what they receive from other participants, and insights and responses are often surprising and creative. A process of transformation of thinking or shift of perspective is visible to all participants. As there is no advice giving, no complaining and no "post mortems," a person in focus feels in charge of the process which enables them to self-evaluate, adopt an alternative perspective on the issue, and find solutions to complex dilemmas while taking full responsibility for actions that will follow.

Another benefit of this model is that it requires no preparation apart from each participant bringing an issue they would like to work on, but even that is not required as sometimes not all participants will want to take a turn. However, when one person is working, the whole group is fully engaged and reflections empathically reverberate throughout the group.

It is a professional approach which enables group members to work together even when they do not like one another or even when there are dual relationships. I participated in peer supervision groups with people from a range of cultural backgrounds and have not noticed any cultural discord, however, white, middle class female members outnumber others. Its directness and structure may be not acceptable for all, but modifications of the model to suit any particular group would only enrich it. The model requires a minimum of a day of training in order to explain principles and philosophy that underpins it as well as the experience of the tools used in a session. Only after the experience can a group commit to engage in regular meetings. A review day with a facilitator, after trying it as a group, is recommended as it enhances proper application of this deceptively simple approach.

Challenges

Full commitment is essential for effectiveness of the group, also emotional maturity and openness to expose vulnerabilities. Dual relationships, potential conflicts of interest, and hidden agendas need to be declared, as they may jeopardize the openness and full engagement of members. Sticking to a rigid structure may be challenging for undisciplined or divergent thinkers. "Stars," "divas," and people with dominating personalities are likely to drop out, as the process will not give them the attention and admiration they may crave. Longer training may be required for practitioners who are not social workers or counsellors and without prior knowledge and experience in dynamics of group processes.

Vignette two: The Goddesses group

After completing my Bachelor of Social Work education in Croatia, which was predominantly theoretical with a "thrown in at the deep end" type of fieldwork placement, I did not feel competent to practice social work, and I engaged in training provided by William Glasser Institute, where there was teaching about his philosophy and its practical application in work with people (Glasser 2011). I befriended a transdisciplinary group of fascinating women who were yearning to learn how to work with people effectively. In the same year, a book by a Jungian therapist Jean Shinoda Bolen came out, and as we were focused on the application of William Glasser's choice theory in a range of settings, we wanted to enrich Glasser's theory with the spirit of an open minded mystical woman of Asian origin who expressed her knowledge in the book Goddesses in Every Woman: Powerful Archetypes in Women's Lives (Bolen 1984). We started as an informal group of colleagues that later evolved into peer supervision meetings once a month on Fridays, after work. We would meet for a shared meal and then we would split in small groups of mutual interest and talk about work. Each of us completed Jean Shinoda Bolen's questionnaire, and were delighted to learn that none of us was a clear type, but a combination of at least two to three Goddess archetypes. We were surprised at the accuracy of the questionnaire results, which enabled us to get to know one another better and dive into deep personal exploration of archetypes. During peer supervision we spontaneously started playing to each other's strengths and archetypes as they manifested in everything we did, whether our personal life, our social practice, or in the peer supervision group itself. We laughed with each other when we would spot an archetype in action and supported one another to move when our own archetypes would keep us stuck. The group gathered psychologists, social workers, social pedagogues, psychiatrists, and mental health nurses. We all had in common our interest in Choice theory (Glasser 1999), all of us have completed the full training and many of us were offering accredited William Glasser Institute training to other helping professionals all around the country. The group continued meeting when I left Croatia in 1995 and is still meeting but in a more informal way. We became friends, and the group currently serves the purpose of self-care, fun, engagement, and support, particularly relevant at the time of writing this chapter during the Covid-19 pandemic. This support manifests in almost daily contact through a closed group on social media, haiku poetry, joint outings to theatre, dinners, holidays, general self-care, and direct support in personal and professional issues. Two members visited me in Aotearoa New Zealand, and after 24 years of not seeing each other, we just continued from where we stopped. Some members have retired but remain active in the group and provide professional support to those who are still in paid employment. For more focused professional supervision members have an option of booking individual free sessions with one another as well.

Benefits and unique features

This groups serves to support and understand specific personality traits and how they manifest in professional practice. Good knowledge of Choice theory (Glasser 1999) that underpins its existence is essential, as well as familiarity with Jean Shinoda Bolen's work (Bolen 1984). This knowledge prevents participants from engaging in what Glasser calls the seven deadly habits destructive for every relationship:

- Criticizing
- Blaming
- Complaining
- Nagging
- Threatening
- Punishing
- Bribing or rewarding for control

Replacing them with seven caring habits:

- Supporting
- Encouraging
- Listening
- Accepting
- Trusting
- Respecting
- Negotiating differences (Glasser 2011).

Cognitive practicalities of human helping were enhanced with a spiritual component linked to Jungian archetypes through metaphors of Greek goddesses (Bolen 1984). Calling on one another's natural strengths enables participants to see a practice issue from a range of different perspectives. For example, "Demeter" (whose strengths are being motherly, determined, well-organized, nurturing, self-sacrificing, and deeply caring) would approach a practical issue from a different perspective than "Aphrodite," who is all about the importance of self-love, enjoyment in life, playfulness, and generosity; or "Persephone," who is deeply spiritual, tends to live in two worlds, and is imaginative, innovative, empathetic, and reflective. During a discussion on a specific issue, "Artemis" may pop up with a confident, unconventional, innovative, and decisive solution. Specific goddess archetypes may play out as a dominant trait from each participant in the course of a group discussion or as an internal dilemma that one participant may harbor. An open discussion through a Goddesses metaphor externalizes personality traits and allows a playful approach to serious situations. These discussions enable participants to explore alternative pathways to challenging situations yet retaining their core beliefs and acting in harmony with their calling and personality. This also enables respect of differences and an open exploration of various manifestations of a certain archetype. The transdisciplinary nature of the group enriched the collaboration across disciplines retaining a strong focus on William Glasser's philosophy, theory and practice, and how it manifested in practitioners' personal and professional lives. This group was initiated 30 years ago, and participants are still meeting regularly.

Challenges

It is a women's group and because of female archetypes included in the initial questionnaire, it is not likely that it would be suitable for men. However, various gender and cultural modifications would be possible to cater for any culturally specific way people relate to one another. The richness of history, personal growth, major life events, and deep trust that developed over years makes this unique group a model that is deeply resonant with Croatian culture where lasting female friendships are deeply interwoven in the fabric of society. Professional and personal boundaries are blurred in this model, and soon after its conception this peer supervision group became a self-care support group or simply, a group of friends with a common professional interest. With advances in technology, a WhatsApp virtual group was created for exchange of current events, jokes, haiku poetry, and organizing joint outings. After 30 years of its existence the group has ten members and in that period, only one new member joined and only one left.

Vignette three: Cooperative inquiry group as an alternative to peer supervision for academics within a neoliberal university

When I joined one of the major universities in Aotearoa New Zealand, I wondered if peer supervision could enhance our teaching and researching. In 2014, a Massey University teaching developer, Jane Terrell, and I initiated a group called Learning Spirals, a support group for academics passionate about teaching and interested in collaborative research into enhancement of their practice. This group later evolved into a Cooperative Inquiry for Reflection and Collaboration on Learning Effectiveness (CIRCLE). It is a closed group that meets monthly with the aim of improvement of our teaching practices, research, and publications. The model started by initiating a cooperative inquiry group (Heron 1996) where each participant committed to improve one specific aspect of their teaching. At the same time, the whole group critically evaluated and appreciatively enquired into effectiveness of being engaged in such a group and into cooperative inquiry as a method of improvement of creativity in teaching and support in research outputs. As a cooperative inquiry, similarly to action research with cycles between action and reflection, the action was happening between group meetings in our respective classrooms with reflection occurring during monthly group meetings. It is also important to note that reflection in action was happening all the time and all participants reported becoming more reflexive and mindful about their teaching processes and ways they reach students who struggled with various aspects of their courses. Co-operative inquiry is a way of working with other people who have similar concerns and interests to yourself, in order to understand the way they operate in their world and learn how to do things better (Heron 1996). When effective, it leads to a deep personal transformation which happens through development of cooperative and empowering relationships and commitment to tasks related to purposeful research into effectiveness of teaching. All participants are co-researchers and research cycles among four different types of knowledge: propositional knowing (related to findings from literature and science), practical knowing (that comes through experimenting with new ways of teaching), experiential knowing (personal experience from feedback from interaction with environment), and presentational knowing (which relates to the artistic rehearsal process through which we create new practices) (Heron and Reason 2004; Reason and Bradburry-Huang 2008). The research participants cycle through four stages of the process, being fully committed to undertaking agreed actions between group meetings and examining challenges they encountered between and during group meetings. This sense of accountability and support enhances the readiness to experiment and development of novel teaching/learning methods and processes.

The first stage of reflection determined the focus of our inquiry which was initially about enhancing effectiveness of teaching and which later evolved into survival of primacy of teaching within neoliberal academia. At this stage, our primary focus was on presentational knowing.

The second stage involved individual actions outside of the group that included some radical transformation of courses or joint projects between participants. This stage was predominantly about practical knowing. The third stage combined action and reflection by participants becoming deeply immersed in the process and reflecting in action, exploring transformations in our teaching. This stage mainly involved experiential knowing and supporting one another through the process of raising awareness of the nature of neoliberal academia and ways of coping with its performative nature. In stage four, we reflected on our experiences and decided to use the group to start documenting our findings and start publishing in academic journals and present at conferences. These four ways of knowing are not linear nor do they appear in a singular way. They are all interrelated and are presented here as stages for the sake of clarity. None of the ways of knowing is more nor less important in relation to transformations that occur during the life of a cooperative inquiry group.

Benefits and unique features

The group so far produced eleven research outputs directly related to the group and six subsequent research collaborations beyond the group but involving group members. Most group members have been nominated as lecturers of the year and are known as exceptional teachers. Innovations ranged from minor course improvements to a complete transformation of the way they taught. Camaraderie and collegiality are main features of this group as well as mutual support and development of academic rigor. The group has been meeting for five years and presents an example of collaboration across disciplines within a competitive neoliberal university often separated with departmental and disciplinary boundaries. At the end of 2018 we decided to focus on collaboration as an act of resistance and transformation within a neoliberal performative university. Data from our findings have been transcribed, and we are currently engaged in extracting themes and writing about it. The uniqueness of this group is in its dual focus on individual innovation in teaching, collaborative research, and publications, and the development of a meta research process on evaluating cooperative inquiry and its suitability for transformation of academia from inside.

Challenges

The main challenge of this endeavor is a context of neoliberal academia which often reduces all academic activities to measurable commodities, attempting to subject our work with students and research to market calculations that maximize exploitation and profit (Morley et al. 2017). Finding time for a voluntary activity (that we found essential for the quality of our work as academics) on top of ever-increasing demands from university was challenging. None of this valuable work is included in the elusive "workload formula" that attempts to quantify deeply qualitative contributions academics make. We all agreed that being an academic implies doing more than a bare minimum, and this activity being not "work-loaded" guaranteed deep internal motivation and commitment of all participants that goes beyond prescribed academic tasks. However, finding time and synchronizing diaries of busy academics can be a challenge. Having it noted in a workload would be beneficial, as participation in this group enabled us to publish more, teach better, and it inspired some members to take on various committee duties in order to transform the university from inside and make our voices heard. Our role as critics and conscience of society was highlighted in several discussions, and given that social work is a practice-based academic discipline with a strong commitment to critical analysis and practices of social change (Morley et al. 2017), group members from the School of Social Work were often leaders in suggesting responses to curriculum development, resistant to impositions from management, and they provided ideas for creative communication with students to promote social transformation and critical thinking.

Discussion and reflection on the relevance of peer supervision within Aotearoa New Zealand social work practice, research, and education

In Aotearoa New Zealand, all practicing social workers are required to have supervision. The local Association of Social Workers (Aotearoa New Zealand Association of Social Workers, ANZASW 2015) stipulates the requirement of minimum monthly meetings and equates individual, group, peer, and virtual supervision. Internal and external supervisions are usually contracted by the agency, but social workers often have a choice of their external supervisor and the modality they prefer and need.

My understanding of social work in Aotearoa New Zealand is based on incorporation of seven value-based principles deeply embedded in Māori culture and relevant to social work internationally. In this discussion, special focus is put on those relevant to social work and embedded in Aotearoa New Zealand Association of Social Workers Code of Ethics (Aotearoa New Zealand Association of Social Workers 2019) and also, in more detail, exemplified in the work of Rangatahi Tū Rangatira (R2R) a national training provider that promotes cultural and physical wellbeing of young people to enable them to become strong, competent, and resilient leaders while utilizing Kaupapa Māori approaches (Kokiri Hauora 2019).

Rangatiratanga relates to the notion of self-determination, autonomy, and empowerment through leadership and ethical guidance when needed. It is about being in control, and it relates to making informed choices and determining the outcomes, our power, and influence in the world. In a peer supervision group this is upheld by appreciating cultural, positional, or age differences without imposing a hierarchical approach. Each member holds their power and competence related to their expertise and life experience. Being (or becoming) an autonomous human being inevitably impacts the practitioner's social practice. An effective peer supervision group enables vulnerabilities to transform into challenges and continuous growth without a hierarchical disempowerment or need for performativity. A peer supervision group can also become a vehicle for social change, promotion of socially just policies, and improvement of social conditions.

Aroha is a principle that relates to unconditional love in a widest possible sense. It closely relates to a Greek word, *agape*, which is about universal unconditional love and which is more in a form of life force or energy that inspires and gives life to life. Christianity adopted the word *agape* in relation to love for a single God, whereas *aroha* relates to love for all that is in the universe. Translated to social work jargon, it is about unconditional positive regard and acknowledgement of mutual responsibility for wellbeing, use of professional judgment in risk assessment without being judgmental, shedding light on people's strengths and abilities, and learning to perceive possibilities and unique abilities in every person.

The principle of *manaakitanga* is a practitioner's ability to express *aroha*. It is about hospitality, ability to hold space in uncomfortable situations and when challenging emotions are expressed. It is about politics of kindness in action (Magnet et al. 2014) and a true measurement of social worker's ability to extend *aroha*. In a peer supervision group, this is manifested through helping and supporting each other, lobbying for meaningful change, being fully present and engaged, and often sharing food and academic resources.

As all principles are deeply interconnected, *whanaungatanga* follows, which is about a sense of belonging, reciprocity, and creation of long term and sustaining relationships. It is about reciprocal relationships embedded in the Māori word *ako*, which depicts teaching and learning, acknowledging the reciprocal two-way process of holistic learning particularly evident in a peer supervision group where roles of a teacher and learner quickly change, emphasizing the mutuality of the endeavor. Most peer supervision groups evolve into deep friendships, and informal gatherings outside of the group often blur professional and personal boundaries. This blurring is a process that needs to be accompanied with awareness and transparency which minimize the damage that dual relationships and power games within professional and academic hierarchies can cause. Voluntary participation enhances the principle of *whanaungatanga*, which is about the shared experience of working together, providing participants with a deep sense of belonging. The fact there is no monetary exchange for this valuable service emphasizes the value of reciprocity and kinship relationships (one does not charge friends or family for support!).

Kotahitanga is about unity and sense of community, solidarity, and global oneness which springs from *aroha* (compassion, love in a widest possible sense, and empathy) and *wairuatanga* that relates to the sense of spiritual wellbeing, soul connections, being in tune with one's life contribution, and development of the sense of calling, including purposeful action.

Mātātoa is a value principle of being fearless or feeling fear and doing it anyway. In social work contexts, this value is about having moral courage in situations that are uncomfortable and uncertain. It relates to the ability to stand with complexity and address "wicked problems" (Wexler 2009) with grace and integrity.

Wairuatanga relates to holistic wellbeing encompassing the spirit of social work, the spirit of respectful relationships, and awareness of a sense of calling and being an agent of social transformation through our unique, idiosyncratic, culturally, and personally determined agency in this world. It relates to relationships permeated with respect, courtesy, honesty, and integrity in order to enhance professional practice by being in tune with our main tool that is our human instrument. Wairuatanga can be equally expressed through beliefs that subscribe to organized religion or being secular, humanistic, or directly connected to nature and the universe. It is about not imposing these beliefs but respectfully attending to differences and expanding participants' views during that process.

The list of principles that inform an effective peer supervision group and depicts its spirit is not exhaustive and limited to the Aotearoa New Zealand social work principles listed above. Additional values in practice that are embedded in the spirit of peer supervision are *mohiotanga*, which manifests through generous sharing of information, as knowledge is there to be shared, not copyrighted. Peer supervision enhances generosity, and participants have a chance to experience how sharing of information contributes to creation of new knowledge and shifts of perception. This generous sharing leads to the manifestation of the principle of *maramatanga* where participants see the relevance of the new learning and how it can be applied in new situations. All these lead to the manifestation of the principle of *kaitiakitanga* (Science Learning Hub Pokapū Akoranga Pūtaiao 2019), which is a deeply spiritual principle meaning much more than mere guardianship. It encompasses all principles mentioned above in order to maintain a reciprocal relationship between the spiritual realm, humans, and nature. Humans are part of the land they live on, part of the planet and the universe, and they are not in any way superior. Our existence is interrelated, and only through collaborative reciprocal relationships can we advance our professional practice and existence. There is saying that poetically summarizes the principle of *kaitiakitanga*:

> E rere kau mai te awa nui nei
> Mai i te kāhui maunga ki Tangaroa
> Ko au te awa
> Ko te awa ko au.

> The river flows
> From the mountains to the sea
> I am the river
> The river is me (Young 2019).

The experience of these three peer supervision modalities expanded my intellectual sphere as much as it enriched my heart while creating respectful connectedness, leading to transformation. Participants in these groups agreed that these processes holistically held the space while enabling them to focus on the issue of their interest in order to enhance their understanding and explore the relevance of novel ways of approaching it. When these universal values (for the purpose of this chapter humbly borrowed from Indigenous wisdom of Aotearoa New Zealand Māori) underpin the peer supervision group, mutuality, trust, self-directedness, equality, and self-determination thrive. This often leads to the excitement about practice, transparency, bravery into exploring ethically challenging issues, and "know-it-allness" and professional arrogance get replaced with a sense of humbleness, connectedness, and curiosity.

Note

1 A list of peer supervision tools is published in The Complete Facilitator's Handbook (Heron, 1999) and also by NZCMC (New Zealand Coaching and Mentoring Centre, 2012) facilitators who provide training.

References

Antonovsky, A., 1993. The structure and properties of the sense of coherence scale. *Social Science & Medicine*, 36 (6), 725–733.

Aotearoa New Zealand Association of Social Workers ANZASW 2015. *Supervision policy*. Available from: https://anzasw.nz/wp-content/uploads/ANZASW-Supervision-Policy-Updated-February-2015.pdf [Accessed 26 July 2019].

Aotearoa New Zealand Association of Social Workers 2019. *Code of ethics 2019.* [online]. Available at: https://anzasw.nz/wp-content/uploads/ANZASW-Code-of-Ethics-Final-1-Aug-2019.pdf [Accessed 1 October 2019].

Bailey, R., Kalle, W., Pawar, M., and Bell, K., 2014. Restoring meaning to supervision through a peer consultation group in rural Australia. *Journal of Social Work Practice*, 28 (4), 479–495.

Bateson, G.B.M., 1987. *Angels fear: towards an epistemology of the sacred (advances in systems theory, complexity, and the human scienc) (advances in systems theory, complexity & the human sciences)*. 1st ed. New York: Macmillan Pub Co.

Bolen, J.S., 1984. *Goddesses in every woman: powerful archetypes in women's lives*. New York: Harper Collins.

Brownlee, K., Vis, J.A., and McKenna, A., 2009. Review of the reflecting team process: strengths, challenges, and clinical implications. *The Family Journal*, 17 (2), 139–145.

Capra, F., 1997. *The web of life: a new scientific understanding of living systems*. London: Flamingo.

Christensen, T.M., and Kline, W.B., 2001. The qualitative exploration of process-sensitive peer group supervision. *The Journal for Specialists in Group Work*, 26 (1), 81–99.

Counselman, E.F., and Weber, R.L., 2004. Organizing and maintaining peer supervision groups. *International Journal of Group Psychotherapy*, 54 (2), 125–143.

Glasser, W., 1998. *The quality school managing students without coercion*. 3rd ed. New York: Harper Collins.

Glasser, W., 1999. *Choice theory: a new psychology of personal freedom*. New York: Harper Collins.

Glasser, W., 2011. *Take* charge of your life: how to get what you need with choice theory psychology. Bloomington, IN: iUniverse.

Golia, G.M., and MGovern, A.R., 2013. If you save me, I'll save you: the power of peer supervision in clinical training and professional development. *British Journal of Social Work*, 45 (2), 634–650.

Heron, J., 1996. *Co-operative inquiry: research into the human condition*. London: SAGE Ltd.

Heron, J., 1999. *The complete facilitator's handbook*. London: Kogan Page.

Heron, J., and Reason, P., 2004. The practice of co-operative inquiry: research with rather than on people. *In*: P. Reason, and H. Bradbury, ed. *The Handbook of action research*. London: SAGE, 179–189.

Kokiri Hauora 2019. *R2R* [online]. Available from: https://www.r2r.org.nz/maori-health/tikanga-maori-values.html [Accessed 8 August 2019].

Magnet, S., Mason, D., and Trevenen, K., 2014. Feminism, pedagogy, and the politics of kindness. *Feminist Teacher*, 25 (1), 1–22.

Morley, C., Macfarlane, S., and Ablett, P., 2017. The neoliberal colonisation of social work education: a critical analysis and practices for resistance. *Social Work Education*, 19 (1), 25–40.

Napan, K., Green, J.K., Thomas, J.A., Stent, W.J., Jülich, S.J., Lee, D., and Patterson, L., 2018. Collaborative transformations: cooperative inquiry as a catalyst for change. *Journal of Transformative Education*, 16 (3), 246–267. https://doi.org/10.1177/1541344617736636.

New Zealand Coaching and Mentoring Centre 2012. *The power of peer supervision: tools for supervision & mentoring groups*. Auckland: NZCMC.

Reason, P., and Bradburry-Huang, H., 2008. *Handbook of action research: participative inquiry and practice*. 2 ed. London: SAGE.

Science Learning Hub Pokapū Akoranga Pūtaiao 2019. *Understanding kaitiakitanga* [online]. Available from: https://www.sciencelearn.org.nz/resources/2544-understanding-kaitiakitanga [Accessed 14 August 2019].

Wexler, M.N., 2009. Exploring the moral dimension of wicked problems. *International Journal of Sociology and Social Policy*, 29 (9/10), 531–542.

Young, D., 2019. Whanganui tribes – Ancestors. *Te Ara - the Encyclopedia of New Zealand* [online]. Available from: http://www.TeAra.govt.nz/en/whanganui-tribes/page-1 [Accessed 2 October 2019].

23

SOCIAL WORK GROUP SUPERVISION

Mari Alschuler

Group supervision has grown as both an adjunctive approach to individual supervision and as a stand-alone practice for social work students in field placement, agency staff, and in external clinical supervision. In a group setting, students and staff learn to develop their clinical skills, experientially understand group dynamics, to give and receive peer feedback, listen to multiple perspectives, and use reflective thinking. This chapter will review the history of group supervision and several contemporary theories, including relational, attachment, narrative, solution-focused, trauma-informed, and mindfulness-based approaches to group supervision. It will explore issues related to group dynamics and parallel process; the power differential; trainee anxiety and nondisclosure; reflective, present moment, process-oriented approaches; and self-care strategies to decrease anxiety and avoid burnout.

Social work group supervision

Bernard and Goodyear (2019) defined group supervision as

> the regular meeting of a group of supervisees (a) with a designated supervisor or supervisors; (b) to monitor the quality of their work; and (c) to further their understanding of themselves as clinicians, of the clients with whom they work, and of service delivery in general. Supervisees achieve these goals with the help of their supervisor(s) and the feedback from and interactions with one another.
>
> *(pp. 190–191)*

The tasks of social work group supervision include ensuring that clinical work is performed competently and without harm to clients. Supervisees learn how to apply theory to practice, become socialized to the social work profession, and develop clinical skills as they become more effective practitioners.

The role and tasks of the group supervisor

Group supervision is used to train social work interns as an adjunctive approach to individual supervision; it is offered as a stand-alone practice in some organizations. The role of the supervisor is to "establish a holding learning climate" (Ögren and Sundin 2009, p. 130). Group supervisors' theoretical orientations impact how they operate in a group setting and which aspects of group dynamics they attend to. Other group supervisory tasks are to explore conflicts among supervisees (p. 71). Typical group supervision activities include: critiquing videos of client sessions; case conceptualization; discussing case studies or assigned readings; tuning in to one's internal thoughts, images, and feelings as a session is described; or Socratic questioning (Alschuler et al. 2015; Bransford 2009; Schauss et al. 2017).

Additional challenges in a group format include: "to establish and maintain a good working relationship with the group,...to carefully identify the trainees' learning issues and evaluate [their] capacity to meet their clients' needs in an ethically defendable way," and to "allow the trainees to develop their skills in a variety of different ways," including allowing a certain amount of conflict to develop (Ögren and Sundin 2009, pp. 136–137). The authors concluded that group supervision provides a variety of perspectives from supervisees as well as from the supervisor.

Differences between group therapy and group supervision

Group supervision permits supervisees to experience group dynamics and processes firsthand. They can develop additional clinical skills for leading therapy or psychoeducation groups, treatment team meetings, or committees. Supervisees learn to manage their emotions and reactions during group supervision and can begin to work on their own emotional regulation (Bernard and Goodyear 2019).

One difference between group therapy and group supervision is that group norms and rules may be held to a higher standard in group supervision, as the latter implies accountability, evaluation, and gatekeeping: "The supervisor has to take into account the competence of the supervisee" (Melnick and Fall 2008, p. 57). A major difference, of course, is that one does not give therapy clients a performance evaluation.

Another way to look at the differences between supervision and therapy groups is that some techniques might be unethical or disruptive if conducted during group therapy. For example, Paré (2016) developed a group supervision protocol premised on the concepts of "acknowledgment" and "generativity" (p. 277). Acknowledgment relates to the intention of the therapist who is describing her or his work, and reflection upon that content by the therapist, supervisor, and peers. Generativity relates to the multiple perspectives held by those present. The "sharing therapist" recounts the clinical episode to peers and supervisor and then becomes silent as the episode is discussed by everyone around her or him. This would be terribly uncomfortable, if not unethical, in the course of a group therapy session (p. 277).

Differences between group and individual supervision

There are basic differences between individual and group supervision, such as cost, time, and evaluative aspects. Group supervision in organizations is impacted by administrative requirements for accountability, adherence to the agency's preferred evidence-based practices, clients served, and socio-political influences.

Similarities between group and individual supervision include the evaluative aspect. Advantages to group over individual supervision include: receiving multiple perspectives; universalization of experiences; and vicarious learning about group process and group dynamics (Bernard and Goodyear 2019, pp. 191–192). In contrast, the supervisee in a supervisory dyad may receive a biased understanding of social work, limited exposure to varying theories and interventions, and limited multicultural knowledge and experience.

Melnick and Fall (2008) remarked that group supervision, as compared to individual supervision, includes some negatives: "a less intimate relationship between supervisor and supervisee, and being known more intimately by one's peers. At the same time, group supervision offers different points of view, learned compassion and empathy toward others, and familiarity among group members and leader" (p. 56). Another difference is that group "supervisors need to pay attention to rules, group norms, and group process" compared to individual supervisors (p. 57). Melnick and Fall described group supervision as an "opportunity to deal with the increased complexity and chaos that results when group dynamics and development are added to the variables present in supervision" (p. 56). This added complexity stems from new relationships between group members themselves and between the leader and group members.

Advantages and disadvantages of group supervision

Advantages

The most important advantages include the provision of peer feedback, learning from various perspectives, and broadening one's scope of client presentations. The ability to facilitate and foster peer feedback is central to the growth of cohesion and the ability of supervisees to develop their own "self-supervision skills" (Wahesh et al. 2017, p. 275). Trainees gave "a broad range of feedback on conceptualization, therapeutic alliance, and the use of skills and structured interventions observed in their peers' counseling sessions" (p. 282).

Positive attributes of group supervision have been described as "vicarious learning [and the] universality of learning issues" (Borders et al. 2012, p. 281). Other advantages include "peer-to-peer learning, exposure to a greater number of clients, and [a reduction in] supervisee anxiety" (Mastoras and Andrews 2011, p. 102). Mehr et al. (2015) found the most helpful supervisors were able to help trainees build skills, confidence, and self-awareness. Fleming et al. (2010) described how group members develop the ability to "learn about group dynamics…through attention to group process…group cohesion, interpersonal relationships within groups, trust, norms, multicultural issues" (p. 194).

Disadvantages

Group supervision has no single method or form, no set of best practices, and varies "from very structured activities to unstructured and free form supervision" (Schauss et al. 2017, p. 105). Fleming et al. (2010) listed four hindrances to groups that were unrelated to group process: "physical/environment problems; absent peer; distraction; and time constraints" (p. 198).

Disadvantages of group supervision include conflict and competition among supervisees and confidentiality concerns (Mastoras and Andrews 2011, p. 102). Bernard and Goodyear (2019) listed several limitations of group supervision as including that some supervisees might feel they did not receive enough attention, time, or support; "insensitivity to individual and cultural differences"; and "negative experiences in childhood with corrective feedback" which may impede how supervisees accept feedback (p. 192).

Fleming et al. (2010) listed several negative group processes that have to be managed so they do not interfere with the group's functioning: "ongoing or unresolved conflicts between members or supervisors, failure to provide constructive feedback, different backgrounds of students, individual differences, and personality conflicts" (p. 195). Supervisors also need to pay attention to multicultural issues and supervisee anxiety and nondisclosure and take risks by bringing up what may be uncomfortable subjects.

Concerns about group supervision include "peer matching, challenges giving and receiving negative feedback, and having to share supervision time" (Borders et al. 2012, p. 281). Supervisors who had logistical problems, lacked technical ability, did not manage time well, or who monopolized case discussions without promoting peer-to-peer feedback were seen as the least helpful (see Enyedy et al. 2003; Reiser and Milne 2017).

Cohesion, trust, and safety

Schauss et al. (2017) stated that the more group members feel they are in a safe and supportive environment, the more they will be able to develop group cohesion. Over time, supervisees develop trust in the supervisor and in one another as they move toward cohesion. Factors that "facilitated feelings of safety…included cohesion, fluid leadership, and discussion of group process" (Fleming et al. 2010, p. 198). Cohesion is important to developing a felt "sense of belonging" to a group (p. 198). Effectively leading the group toward cohesion is achieved by discussing group process and supervisee anxiety openly. Other supervisory tasks which may help enhance group cohesion include "self-disclosure, sharing emotions, resolving conflict, and engaging in the group" (p. 198).

Navigating supervisee anxiety

Supervisors recognize that supervisees often experience mounting anxiety and a sense of vulnerability as they begin to reveal more and more in the supervision group. Having "positive peer relations may help in reducing the withholding of crucial information or errors made during client or supervisory sessions, such as 'personal/countertransference reactions to clients' for fear of how supervisors will view them" (Schauss et al. 2017, p. 103).

The skill of the supervisor in managing supervisees' anxiety is paramount. The supervisor can help trainees understand how to use "their anxiety as a motivator" as they "intentionally developed safe interpersonal relationships" and to view anxiety "as part of the learning process" (Fleming et al. 2010, p. 201). Supervisees bear witness to clients' suffering and require support and empathy. Supervisors need to make proactive efforts to help their supervisees avoid burnout, "a condition consisting of emotional exhaustion, depersonalization, and a decreased sense of personal accomplishment." Some administrative concerns affecting staff include "heavy caseloads, long workdays, low salaries, unsupportive peers, or inadequate supervision" (Ohrt et al. 2015, p. 42).

Supervisors can assist supervisees by teaching and modeling wellness and self-care techniques to promote wellness and avoid burnout, according to Ohrt et al. (2015). They created an intervention to help trainees in "(a) maintaining a sense of purpose in their work, (b) exploring their creativity in coping, (c) expressing their subjective experiences related to wellness, (d) developing a positive relationship with their supervisors and other supervisees, and (e) developing holistic wellness goals" (p. 45). This intervention was provided in a group format and thus is suitable for group supervision.

Mehr et al. (2015) stated that nondisclosure is a barrier to effective supervision. They identified factors that contribute to trainees' willingness to disclose, such as the strength of the working alliance and a sense of emotional safety among and between the group members and the supervisor. Elements of emotional safety include "building trust, listening, reflecting, and deepening" as well as "sharing, witnessing, and supporting the reflections of others" (Heffron et al. 2016, p. 631). Alliances and cohesion are closely monitored as supervisees "come into frequent contact with extreme states of vulnerability, dependency, and anxiety" (p. 631).

Rethinking parallel process

Parallel process describes an unconscious re-enactment in supervision of what had occurred during a therapy session. In counseling this is referred to as "isomorphism," meaning that what "happens at one level (i.e., supervision) might be repeated at another (i.e., during counseling)" (Edwards and Chen 1999, p. 352). "Transference is present when feelings and behaviors meant for one person are directed at someone else," including the supervisor (Zeligman 2017, p. 9). This concept also relates to systems theory: "A change in one part of the interconnected system will correspondingly change that part of the other system" (p. 352).

A relational view of parallel process understands that the supervisory relationship is one of mutuality. It is possible that the supervisor may also be re-enacting and then "exporting" his or her own trans- or countertransferential events onto the supervisee and their relationship (Bransford 2009, p. 121). Countertransference, acting out phenomena, and projective identification are ways of understanding what may be re-enacted in group supervisory sessions (p. 121).

Techniques used in group supervision that address parallel process include "the attitude of non-expert, transparency, respect, expanding frames, and the tentative offer of idea" (Edwards and Chen 1999, p. 352). The authors called this "nonaction supervision: Wu-Wei," a Zen concept which is "a metaphor for action/nonaction" (p. 349).

The reflective process and relational approaches to group supervision

Heffron et al. (2016) defined reflective functioning (RF) as "a process by which we understand, interpret, and make meaning of others' behavior in light of the thoughts, feelings, beliefs, wishes, desires, and plans that underlie and motivate that behavior" (p. 630). The authors suggested that a reflective frame be used to create both physical and emotional safety. They recommended that the supervisor begin with "clarifying the frame at the outset, including agreements about time, confidentiality, and intentions of the group" (p. 631). These structural aspects free supervisees to take a stance of "curiosity and receptivity" as they "attend to shifting internal states and responses to clinical material" (p. 631). By reflecting together and focusing on one's internal states, such as thinking, feeling, bodily sensations, beliefs, attitudes, and meanings, trainees can develop the ability to regulate themselves (pp. 631–632).

A relational model of supervision decenters the role of the supervisor and posits "a more egalitarian, less hierarchical focus," stated Ganzer and Ornstein (2004, p. 436). Ganzer and Ornstein advised that supervisors consider how "reciprocity and mutual influence are intrinsic to the supervisory relationship" (p. 432). The relational model "looks at a dialogic approach that pays particular attention to how the personalities of the supervisor and supervisee interact" (p. 434). Other elements of this approach include "active exploration of the interpenetration of intrapsychic, interpersonal, environmental, and organizational influences on the treatment" (p. 435).

Postmodernist and social constructionist approaches to group supervision

Postmodernism is a paradigm whose central principle is that reality is generated and produced through language in historical, social, and environmental contexts. There is no one "reality" or objective truth. Social constructionism suggests reality is a social construct co-created by humans through language and culture. Zeligman (2017) pointed out that in postmodern supervision "the focus is less so on the individual supervisee and more so on the process of understanding the world, the language we use, and their stories we choose to tell" (p. 9).

Postmodern supervision includes process-centered, strength-based, and mindfulness approaches. Narrative and solution-focused theories derive from social constructionism, with its emphasis on the use of language and how our culture affects our language and thoughts about ourselves and others. These postmodern approaches are used to assist supervisees in co-constructing "new realities through the deconstruction of old narratives…to replace them with new, more useful ones that do not pathologize people" (Edwards and Chen 1999, p. 351). Strengths are highlighted rather than challenges. The power differential is flattened so the supervisory relationship is more egalitarian (see feminist supervisory models).

Process-centered group supervision

Supervisors who foster the affective processes of group supervision help group supervisees work through deeper reactions and emotions as they develop self-awareness. Process-oriented supervisors are aware of their own thoughts, reactions, and feelings and can respond authentically, share his or her own countertransference, clinical mistakes, and model open discussion of these. By creating a safe space in which everyone can divulge mistakes and be vulnerable, members are encouraged to verbalize their reactions, feelings, bodily sensations, and thoughts about cases as they are being discussed (Bransford 2009).

In Bransford's (2009) experiential approach, members listen attentively as a peer presents a case while attending to their own feelings, thoughts, and bodily sensations. Trainees learn to listen "with 'the third ear,'" to develop attending skills "in order to help create more emotionally attuned relationships with clients" (p. 126). Peers listen actively "for metaphors, images, beliefs… and how language is uniquely used by each storyteller" (p. 123). The goal is for members "to be more open to their own inner experience as a way of making greater contact and achieving a deeper understanding of the client being presented" (pp. 123–124).

Strength-based group supervision

In strength-based supervisory groups, the supervisor empowers, motivates, and supports, with a goal of encouraging members' resilience and self-efficacy (Alschuler et al. 2015, p. 38). The supervisor creates a climate that is safe, trustworthy, accepting, and non-pathologizing of both clients and supervisees. In such a climate, trainees are empowered to risk, be vulnerable, and manage their anxiety.

Bransford (2009) described the importance of taking on a "not-knowing stance" to "better able to hear and appreciate the many instances of resilience and perseverance" (p. 119). Edwards and Chen (1999) focused on "the language trainees use to talk about clients," discouraging pathology-laden language and encouraging them to "identify strengths and assets in their clients." The "not-knowing" position is one way to be more transparent with trainee groups, deflecting the power differential while still acknowledging "the power we have in the evaluative position" p. (354).

Narrative supervision

Narrative supervision emphasizes "externalizing problems, finding unique outcomes, and deconstructing problem-saturated stories" (Edwards and Chen 1999, p. 352). Narrative supervision is seen as "emphasizing multiple voices of the team members and thereby illuminating and transforming ideas, rather than criticizing or disqualifying." Narrative concepts "help people access resources and cocreate alternative stories," producing a sense of personal agency (p. 356).

Alschuler et al. (2015) described the use in narrative supervision of "active listening to narratives" that supervisees tell about their clients' and their own problem-saturated narratives (pp. 45–46). In narrative supervision, hope is instilled through the re-storying of a clinical narrative by group members. Narrative supervision is another method that may lower supervisee anxiety and nondisclosure about

> sharing mistakes, uncertainty, or other concerns, such as fear of judgment or a personal history of oppression…or fears of discrimination. Supervisors can help supervisees break these silences and ensure that voices silenced in the past are released and heard in the safe space of the supervision group.
>
> *(p. 47)*

Zeligman (2017) developed a postmodern, developmental narrative model (DNM) for use in supervision, meant to "provide an integrative clinical supervision model aimed at enhancing counseling competencies" (p. 5). The group supervisor can utilize re-storying to identify learning needs or problems, address oppression, empower supervisees, identify causes for their anxiety, gain confidence in their abilities, and to assess their "socially constructed views" (p. 7).

The DNM model draws upon both developmental supervision and narrative therapy (Zeligman 2017). This approach "is comprised of three primary theoretical tenets: (a) awareness, (b) storying and language, and (c) social advocacy" (p. 5). Supervisors collaborate with supervisees to help them develop their identities as clinicians "through a storying process," through helping them in "(a) developing awareness, (b) focusing on [their] language and storying, and (c) enhancing [their] role as a social advocate" (p. 3). According to Zeligman, "four mechanisms guide the work done with clients" and with supervisees: "(a) externalizing the problem, (b) identifying socially constructed messages, (c) maintaining a strengths focus, and (d) re-authoring the client's story" (p. 4).

Solution-focused group supervision

Solution-focused therapy is premised on the concept that individuals can identify and use their own solutions to solve their problems. The solution-focused supervisor emphasizes what supervisees are doing well (Knight 2004, p. 165), using a strengths perspective. Strength-based social work supervision is the foundation for incorporating solution-focused techniques into group supervision. The therapist/supervisor is in a collaborative relationship with their clients/supervisees. This model is considered an evidence-based strategy whether used separately or when used in conjunction with other theoretical frameworks (Knight 2004, p. 154).

Basic assumptions include a focus on the present; that "individuals have the resources and abilities to solve their own problems"; that reality "is socially and linguistically constructed"; and that the act of asking for help by itself is a precursor to actively seeking solutions (Knight 2004, pp. 155–156). Solution-focused therapy is purposefully time limited. Solution-focused techniques include the miracle question, asking about exceptions (when the problem did/does not exist), searching for solutions, using compliments, scaling questions, and coping questions (Knight 2004, pp. 156–163). The miracle question might be used in supervision to help trainees develop a sense of mastery or confidence, and to improve in areas they have identified as needing attention (p. 169).

Edwards and Chen (1999) suggested that solution-focused supervisors use supervision to search for exceptions when the supervisee did something well or better, to "take the lead in defining goals, using scaling questions," and using the miracle question (p. 353). By asking about exceptions, the supervisor assists supervisees in discovering and building upon her strengths (Knight 2004, p. 166). The supervisor might inquire about trainee strengths by asking these questions:

What about your work with clients would be most productive for us to focus on today?
What aspects of your work with clients have you noticed getting better?
What is the best thing that you did in your work since we last met? (p. 166)

In group supervision using solution-focused techniques, the supervisor may choose to take on a "not-knowing" stance, recognizing that the supervisee is the expert—just as the supervisee relies on clients as experts of their own lives. The supervisor attends to both the clinical work as well as how trainees react to feedback and how they use reflection to help the client achieve his or her goals.

Mindfulness approaches to group supervision

The multiple perspectives of a cohesive social work supervision group provide a perfect vehicle for helping trainees develop their self-awareness and emotional regulation. Mindfulness "is popularly defined as moment-to-moment awareness or paying attention to the moment without judgment" (Lynn 2010, p. 290). Additional values of mindfulness are the development of "the practitioner's resilience and well-being, as a means of improving empathy, compassion, and listening or as an intervention method with clients—all of which are significant skills for the social work professional" (Lynn 2010, p. 297).

Lynn (2010) posited that training in mindfulness techniques of social work school students might result in greater self-awareness, empathy, and compassion as one develops into a reflective practitioner (pp. 294–295). However, the type of critical reflection taught in social work programs is derived from an empiricist "epistemology that separates body from mind and subjugates bodily knowledge and sensory experience to the intellect" with the "phenomenology of experience" that reunites body and mind during mindfulness practices (p. 290).

Schauss et al. (2017) highlighted the importance of mindful self-awareness: "Because attitudes and experiences affect views and beliefs about self and others," it is imperative that supervisees "become aware of their attitudes and beliefs as well as being mindful of their own worldview and the worldview of clients" (p. 104). The role of the supervisor is to help trainees develop their awareness of "the automatic thoughts, views, and implicit biases they have regarding their clients," themselves, and others (p. 105). According to the authors, integrating mindfulness into group supervision can increase trainees' "empathy for clients' emotional and physical experiences" and enhance their "awareness of their functions as therapists, which leads to more efficacious practice" (p. 108).

In a study by Lynn (2010), students' awareness and identification of "the moment of discomfort" during a mindfulness meditation exercise was "significant in terms of change… [as] they became more conscious of their habitual mental reactivity, more aware of categorizing and labelling their experiences, more aware of judging others and themselves…and [able] to detach from the habitual patterns of the mind" as they took on an "observer stance" (pp. 296–297). Lynn concluded that teaching mindfulness can be used "as additional pedagogies to develop students' self-awareness, reflective capacity, transform values and beliefs and handle field and academic stresses, as well as enhance educators' use of reflection in their teaching" (p. 297).

Mindfulness as well as the use of free association can be used in group supervision to address issues of trainee anxiety and nondisclosure, transference, and countertransference. Schauss et al.

(2017) created a clinical group supervisory protocol which asks supervisees to both use mindfulness meditation techniques as well as free association. Both mindfulness and free association as techniques employ the present moment.

Trainees first received a guided meditation exercise to ground them in the here-and-now. They then listened to an audio recording of a peer's client session during which they were asked to free associate. In this context, free association was "intended to prime implicit memory, tapping into a [trainee's] values, beliefs, customs and their exposure to culture" (p. 109). As in parallel processes, this technique can be used with clients. Schauss et al. (2017) concluded that trainees benefited from this approach as they gained "insight and awareness into their automatic thoughts, beliefs, values, and biases" (p. 111).

Concluding remarks

As early as the 1990s, authors have discussed the need for supervisors to be more "real" and to use the personhood of the supervisor as ways to model use of self, reflection, self-awareness, emotional regulation, strengths, and competence for their supervisees. Edwards and Chen (1999) felt that the client's personal agency and voice should be reflected in the self-efficacy, personal agency, and voice of their therapist, as promulgated by the supervisor (p. 356).

Models that employ mindful reflection, focus on both trainees' and clients' strengths, attend to group process and dynamics, and take a relational, more non-hierarchical approach to the supervisor/supervisee relationship are some of the current approaches for social work group supervision. Specific interventions such as mindfulness meditation can lead to transformational social work education and clinical work. Strengths-based, narrative, solution-focused, and mindfulness approaches to group supervision are currently undergoing additional research, but so far studies support their effectiveness in developing well-rounded social work practitioners.

References

Alschuler, M., Silver, T., and McArdle, L., 2015. Strengths-based group supervision with social work students. *Groupwork*, 25 (1), 34–57.

Bernard, J.M., and Goodyear, R.K., 2019. *Fundamentals of clinical supervision*. 6th ed. New York: Pearson.

Borders, L.D., Welfare, L.E., Greason, P.B., Paladino, D.A., Mobley, A.K., Villalba, J.A., and Wester, K.L., 2012. Individual and triadic and group: supervisee and supervisor perceptions of each modality. *Counselor Education & Supervision*, 51, 281–295.doi:10.1002/j.1556-6978.2012.00021.x.

Bransford, C., 2009. Process-centered group supervision. *Clinical Social Work Journal*, 37 (2), 119–127.

Edwards, J.K., and Chen, M., 1999. Strength-based supervision: frameworks, current practice and future directions: a Wu-Wei method. *Family Journal: Counseling & Therapy for Couples & Families*, 7, 349–357.

Enyedy, K.C., Arcinue, F., Puri, N.N., Carter, J.W., Goodyear, R.K., and Getzelman, M.A., 2003. Hindering phenomena in group supervision: implications for practice. *Professional Psychology: Research & Practice*, 34 (3), 312–317. doi: 10.1037/0735-7028.34.3.312.

Fleming, L.M., Glass, J.A., Fujisaki, S., and Toner, S.L., 2010. Group process and learning: a grounded theory model of group supervision. *Training & Education in Professional Psychology*, 4 (3), 194–203. doi: 10.1037/a0018970.

Ganzer, C., and Ornstein, E., 2004. Regression, self-disclosure, and the teach or treat dilemma: implications of a relational approach for social work supervision. *Clinical Social Work Journal*, 32 (4), 431–449.

Heffron, M.C., Reynolds, D., and Talbot, B., 2016. Reflecting together: reflective functioning as a focus for deepening group supervision. *Infant Mental Health Journal*, 37 (6), 628–639. doi: 10.1002/imhj.21608.

Knight, C., 2004. Integrating solution-focused principles and techniques into clinical practice and supervision. *The Clinical Supervisor*, 23 (2), 153–173.

Lynn, R., 2010, Apr. Mindfulness in social work education. *Social Work Education*, 29 (3), 289–304.doi: 10.1080/02615470902930351.

Mastoras, S.M., and Andrews, J.J., 2011. The supervisee experience of group supervision: implications for research and practice. *Training & Education in Professional Psychology*, 5 (2), 102–111. doi: 10.1037/a0023567.

Mehr, K.E., Ladany, N., and Caskie, G.I.L., 2015. Factors influencing trainee willingness to disclose in supervision. *Training & Education in Professional Psychology*, 9 (1), 44–51. doi:10.1037/tep0000028.

Melnick, J., and Fall, J., 2008, Sept. A gestalt approach to group supervision. *Counselor Education & Supervision*, 48, 48–60.

Ögren, M-L., and Sundin, E.C., 2009, May. Group supervision in psychotherapy: main findings from a Swedish research project on psychotherapy supervision in a group format. *British Journal of Guidance & Counselling*, 37 (2), 129–139. doi:10.1080/03069880902728614.

Ohrt, J.H., Prosek, E.A., Ener, E., and Lindo, N., 2015. The effects of a group supervision intervention to promote wellness and prevent burnout. *Journal of Humanistic Counseling*, 54 (1), 41–58. doi:10.1002/j.2161-1939.2015.00063.x.

Paré, D., 2016. Creating a space for acknowledgement and generativity in reflective group supervision. *Family Process*, 55 (2), 270–28 doi: 10.1111/famp.12214.

Reiser, R.P., and Milne, D.L., 2017. A CBT formulation of supervisees' narratives about unethical and harmful supervision. *The Clinical Supervisor*, 36 (1), 102–115. doi:10.1080/07325223.2017.1295895

Schauss, E., Steinruck, R.E., and Brown, M.H., 2017. Mindfulness and free association for multi-cultural competence: a model for clinical group supervision. *Journal of Counselor Practice*, 8 (2), 102–119. doi: 10.22229/xpw610283.

Schön, D., 1983. *The reflective practitioner*. New York: Basic Books.

Wahesh, E., Kerner, G., Willis, B.T., and Schmidt, C.D., 2017, Dec. An analysis of peer feedback exchanged in group supervision. *Counselor Education & Supervision*, 56, 274–288. doi: 10.1002/ceas.12085.

White, M., and Epston, D., 1990. *Narrative means to therapeutic ends*. New York: Norton.

Zeligman, M., 2017. Supervising counselors-in-training through a developmental, narrative model. *Journal of Creativity in Mental Health*, 12 (1), 2–14. doi: 10.1080/15401383.2016.1189370.

24

ETHICAL ISSUES IN SUPERVISION
Essential content

Frederic G. Reamer

Meaningful supervision has been a vital component of social work practice since the profession's formal inauguration in the late nineteenth century. For more than a century, social workers have understood that supervision is essential for quality control, supportive, educational, and administrative purposes.

Historically, nearly all of the profession's scholarship on supervision has focused on key issues related to models and theories of supervision, supervision goals, supervision styles and techniques, the role of authority, supervisor stress, supervision contracts, and supervision evaluation (Bogo and McKnight 2005; Kadushin and Harkness 2014; Munson 2002; O'Donoghue 2003, 2015; Tsui 2005). Relatively little scholarship has focused explicitly on ethical issues germane to social work supervision. Following their comprehensive literature review, O'Donoghue and O'Donoghue (2019) concluded that there is "a dearth of research pertaining to supervisory ethics" (p. 16). Yet, social work educators and practitioners clearly recognize that social work supervision broaches a wide range of complex ethical issues (Banks 2012; Barsky 2010; Cohen 1987; Copeland et al. 2011; Frunza and Sandu 2017; Hair 2015; Hugman and Carter 2016; Jacobs 1991; McAuliffe and Sudbery 2005; O'Donoghue and O'Donoghue 2019). Ethical issues in social work supervision concern several major themes: (1) ethics consultation; (2) ethics training and education; and (3) ethics quality control.

Ethics consultation

One of the key features of competent social work supervision is the provision of sound ethics consultation to supervisees. Ideally, supervisees bring challenging ethical dilemmas to the attention of their supervisors. In clinical contexts, examples include ethical decisions about the limits of clients' confidentiality rights, boundary issues and dual relationships, informed consent, conflicts of interest, use of technology to deliver services, documentation, and termination of services. In administrative and policy contexts, examples include ethical decisions about compliance with troubling laws and regulations, fraudulent practices, and the allocation of limited resources.

Skilled ethics consultation provided in the context of supervision requires specialized knowledge and skill. It should not be a casual "add on" to other supervisory duties. In fact, ethics consultation has become a specialty in its own right.

Ethics consultation – first provided in hospitals – began in the United States in the late 1960s and early 1970s at Pennsylvania State University, the New Jersey College of Medicine (now the University of Medicine and Dentistry of New Jersey), and the University of Wisconsin. In 1978 and 1979, bioethicists Edmund Pellegrino and Mark Siegler published several influential papers that proposed a role for "clinical ethics" as a separate field of expertise, and in 1985, the University of California, San Francisco, and the National Institutes of Health cosponsored a conference on ethics consultation. Over the years, ethics consultation – which is especially prominent in healthcare settings – has assumed various forms and tasks that can be usefully incorporated into supervision provided in many social work settings. Ideally, social work supervisors who provide ethics consultation have obtained formal education in ethical theory, practical ethics, and professional ethics to supplement their substantive social work expertise. Ethics consultants are trained to identify, analyze, and help resolve difficult ethical issues.

On occasion, a social work supervisor may serve as a mediator to help resolve differences of opinion involving a supervisee and other parties who have a vested interest in a particular case's outcome. Also, an ethics consultant can serve as an effective advocate, particularly in instances where a supervisee believes he or she would benefit from added support to address an ethical concern.

To carry out these various roles, supervisors who serve as ethics consultants need extensive knowledge and a variety of skills. They must have a firm grasp of key concepts related to ethical theory and the field of practical and professional ethics, particularly related to conceptual frameworks used for analyzing ethical issues and making ethical decisions. Also, consultants must have refined interpersonal skills that enable them to negotiate agreements or mediate ethics-related disputes. In addition, supervisors must be able to model appropriate ethical behavior and ethical decision-making.

In settings that feature formal ethics committees, social work supervisors can look for opportunities for supervisees to participate; this, too, can greatly enhance supervisees' ethics expertise. Ethics committees, which originated in the 1970s and have been most prominent in healthcare settings (such as hospitals, nursing homes, rehabilitation facilities, hospices, and home healthcare programs), typically include representatives from various disciplines and positions, such as nursing, medicine, social work, the clergy, and agency administration. Some ethics committees include an ethicist – either an agency employee (for instance, in large teaching hospitals) or an outside consultant – who has formal training in applied and professional ethics, moral philosophy, and ethics consultation.

Although ethics committees are not always able to provide definitive advice or guidance about complex ethical issues, they can offer colleagues and clients with a forum for organized, focused, explicit, and principled exploration of ethical dilemmas that arise in their work settings. This can provide participating supervisees with a greater understanding of the ethical issues and options they face and enhance the quality of their ethical decision making.

Many ethics committees also serve other functions which offer valuable opportunities for supervisees. Some ethics committees are responsible for reviewing existing ethics-related policies and suggesting revisions, sometimes in response to controversial case-related issues that arise in the agency. For example, an ethics committee in a family service agency may review agency policies and guidelines related to complicated confidentiality issues (such as disclosure of confidential information to the parents of clients who are minors, disclosure of information about deceased clients, and disclosure of information in response to subpoenas or informal requests from law enforcement officials). An ethics committee in a community mental health center may review and suggest revisions of the agency's policies concerning the termination of services to clients who do not comply with treatment recommendations.

Ethics committees also draft new ethics-related policies and procedures for more formal review and approval by agency administrators and boards of directors. For example, a supervisee in a program that serves clients who have serious drug and alcohol problems may be able to participate in the ethics committee that drafts new boundary-related guidelines concerning the hiring of former clients as staff members. An ethics committee in a nursing home may draft new guidelines concerning consensual sexual relationships among residents, and an ethics committee in a residential treatment program for children with serious physical and mental disabilities may draft new guidelines concerning the handling of gifts given to staff by the children's parents (Bonosky 1995).

Supervisors who serve as ethics consultants must understand the complex relationship between ethical issues and social work practice issues (that is, ethical issues that arise related to the delivery of services to individuals, couples, families, groups, organizations, communities, and in policy arenas). Often, an ethics consultant's most effective intervention involves the adept use of clinical instincts and communication skills to manage group process and interpersonal conflict.

Supervisors who want to enhance their ethics consultation skills can seek formal ethics education offered by various universities and continuing education programs. Ideally, supervisors would become well versed in basic ethical theory (for example, theories related to what ethicists label deontology, teleology, consequentialism, utilitarianism, virtue ethics, the ethics of care, and feminist ethics); the history of professional and practical ethics; ethical standards in social work; and ethical decision-making frameworks and protocols.

As valuable as ethics consultation provided by supervisors can be, supervisees should not assume that they should always defer to consultants' judgment. Supervisees should regard ethics consultation as a useful supplement and complement to their own ethics expertise, not a replacement. Supervisees should continue to assume primary responsibility for their own ethical judgments and acquire the knowledge and cultivate the conceptual skills necessary to make those judgments.

Ethics education and training

Supervisors are often in a key position to provide ethics education and training to their direct supervisees and other agency staffers. Ideally, ethics education and training provided by supervisors – either one-on-one or in a group context – should (1) identify pertinent ethical issues and dilemmas in the work setting; (2) enhance supervisees' ethical decision-making skills and protocols; and (3) impart knowledge about ethics risk management.

Ethical issues and dilemmas

Situations sometimes arise in social work in which core values within the profession conflict, and this leads to ethical dilemmas (Banks 2012; Barsky 2010; Congress 1999; Reamer 2018a, d). An ethical dilemma is a situation in which professional duties and obligations, rooted in core values, clash (Dean and Rhodes 1992). This is when supervisees must decide which values – as expressed in various duties and obligations – take precedence.

Supervisors are in a critically important position to help supervisees identify and address challenging ethical dilemmas. In one case, a supervisee informed her supervisor that her client, who had been diagnosed with bipolar disorder, had threatened to harm his estranged girlfriend who, the client reported, was involved with another man. The supervisee told the supervisor that the client was hospitalized recently during a manic episode; the supervisee said that she was concerned that the client's erratic behavior, which had included domestic violence, posed a threat to his estranged girlfriend. The supervisee sought the supervisor's advice about possible clinical strategies, the nature of the client's confidentiality rights, and whether there is any duty under social work's ethical standards and relevant laws to disclose confidential information to the client's estranged girlfriend or the police to protect her from harm.

In another case, a social worker provided counseling services to a 16-year-old client who struggled with anxiety and clinical depression. The minor's parents consented to the counseling at the local community mental health center. Several weeks after the counseling began, the teen disclosed to the social worker that she was engaged in high-risk, unprotected sex with a 32-year-old man she had met online. The social worker recognized the conflict between her duty to respect her client's confidentiality and the parents' right to know about their child's high-risk behavior. In addition to discussing clinical options designed to enhance the client's judgment, the supervisee and supervisor reviewed pertinent code of ethics standards and laws governing the limits of minors' rights to privacy and confidentiality. The case provided a valuable opportunity for the supervisee to learn about systematic ethical decision-making.

Other ethical issues that arise in supervision concern macro social work. In one case, a social worker employed as a policy analyst on a legislator's staff was assigned responsibility for drafting a bill that would provide funding for services to assist children who are aging out of the government-sponsored foster care program. The social worker knew that the funds that were likely to be allocated would not cover the need and demand for services for vulnerable youths. The social worker met with his supervisor to develop criteria that would be used to distribute the limited funds ethically. The supervisor outlined various resource distribution options, based on ethical principles related to severity of client need and equality of opportunity, that the social worker used to develop legislatively sanctioned policy guidelines.

In another case, a social work supervisor in a prominent adoption agency collaborated with her supervisee to develop policies governing adult adoptees' requests to gain access to their adoption records. This challenge raised complex ethical issues because the adoption records had been sealed many years earlier, during a time when secrecy dominated adoption proceedings. The supervisor and social worker struggled to develop policy guidelines that would balance adult adoptees' right to information about their origins and birth parents' privacy rights.

Most recently, it has been incumbent among supervisors to address ethical issues related to supervisees' and clients' increasing use of technology (Reamer 2017, 2018b). Supervisees are increasingly using digital and other electronic technology to provide information to the public, deliver services to clients, communicate with and about clients, manage confidential information and case records, and search online for information about clients. Examples include electronic tools for communication with and delivery of services to clients – some of whom social workers may never meet in person – including social media, online chat and social networks, text (SMS), email, smartphones, and video technology. As such, supervisors must ensure that supervisees are very familiar with new technology-related ethical standards concerning practitioner competence; informed consent; privacy and confidentiality; boundaries, dual relationships, and conflicts of interest; records and documentation; collegial relationships; and social work practice across jurisdictional boundaries (NASW, ASWB, CSWE, & CSWA 2017).

Ethical decision-making

The phenomenon of ethical decision-making in social work has matured considerably. Today's social workers and supervisors have far more access to helpful literature and concepts related to ethical decision-making than did their predecessors.

Supervisors who confer with supervisees about challenging ethical dilemmas can model sound decision making by helping them (1) identify the key ethical issues, including the values and duties that conflict; (2) identify individuals, groups, and organizations who are likely to be affected by the decision; (3) tentatively identify all possible courses of action and the participants involved in each, along with the possible benefits and risks for each; (4) thoroughly examine the reasons in favor of and opposed to each possible course of action, considering relevant ethical theories and principles, codes of ethics, social work practice standards, theories and principles, legal guidelines, and personal values; (5) consult with colleagues and appropriate experts, such as supervisors, agency administrators, colleagues, ethics experts, and, when warranted, attorneys; (6) make the decision and document the decision-making process; and (7) monitor, evaluate, and document the decision (Barsky 2010; Dolgoff et al. 2009; Reamer 2018a, c).

Ethics risk management

Social workers and their supervisors must be concerned about the risk-management ramifications of their ethical decisions and actions, particularly the possibility of legal exposure in the form of litigation and disciplinary proceedings (Houston-Vega et al. 1997; Reamer 2015; Strom-Gottfried 2016). Contemporary supervisors are much more sensitive to these issues than earlier generations of supervisors, primarily due to increases in litigation and licensing board complaints. It is important for both supervisees and supervisors to fully understand the ways in which ethical issues and judgments occasionally lead to malpractice claims and ethics complaints.

It is especially important for supervisors to ensure that supervisees adhere to prevailing ethical standards related to management of confidential information, informed consent, boundaries and dual relationships, conflicts of interest, documentation, use of technology, termination of services, and allocation of resources, among others. Supervisors must ensure that supervisees receive comprehensive in-service training concerning pertinent ethical issues.

In one case, both a social worker and her supervisor were named in a lawsuit filed by one of the supervisee's former clients. The client alleged that the supervisee disclosed confidential information about the client to a police detective without the client's consent. The disclosure violated strict laws governing the management of confidential information about clients who are treated for substance abuse issues. In addition to the claim against the supervisee, the lawsuit claimed that the supervisor failed to provide the supervisee with proper supervision and training related to client confidentiality. In another case, a supervisor was sanctioned by a licensing board because she engaged in an inappropriate dual relationship with her supervisee; the supervisee filed the licensing board complaint after the relationship ended.

Supervisors should be particularly aware of the legal concepts of respondeat superior (Latin for "let the master respond") and vicarious liability. It is not unusual for legal complaints filed against social workers to include their supervisors, claiming that proper supervision would have prevented unethical or negligent conduct on the part of a practitioner. Ordinarily, these claims are based on the legal principles of respondeat superior and vicarious liability. According to these concepts, supervisors may be held partly responsible for the actions or inactions of their supervisees, although the supervisors were involved only indirectly. These legal cases typically involve assessments of the adequacy of supervision.

Formal complaints filed against social workers and their supervisors can take several different forms. In principle, a single case could lead to four different types of formal complaints against a social worker that are filed with (1) a government licensing board, (2) a professional social work organization to which the social worker belongs, (3) a civil court of law (lawsuit), and (4) a criminal court of law.

Lawsuits brought against social workers typically allege both negligence and malpractice. In general, malpractice occurs when evidence exists of the following:

1. At the time of the alleged malpractice, the social worker had a legal duty to the client.
2. The practitioner was derelict in that duty, either through omission (the failure to perform one's duty) or through commission (an action taken by the practitioner).
3. The client suffered some harm or injury.
4. The social worker's dereliction of duty was the direct and proximate cause of the harm or injury.

Lawsuits can include allegations that the supervision provided to social workers was negligent in that it fell below supervision standards of care and caused harm.

Ethics quality control

Social work is among the most values based of all professions. Social work is deeply rooted in a fundamental set of values that ultimately shapes the profession's mission and its practitioners' priorities (Abbott 1988; Allen-Meares 2000; Levy 1976; Varley 1968; Vigilante 1974). Supervisees are expected to embrace social work's explicit values and explore the relationship between their values and the profession's values.

Occasionally, field supervisors encounter challenging circumstances where these values clash. Examples are when a supervisee's religious beliefs conflict with social work values or agency policy (Doyle et al. 2009; Reamer 2018a), or when a supervisee questions social work's venerable commitment to addressing issues of discrimination and social injustice (Gil 1998). In one prominent case, a social work student who was being supervised sued the university in which she was enrolled, claiming she was retaliated against because she refused to support gay adoption as part of a class project (Keegan 2017). In another highly publicized case, a social work student filed a lawsuit against her field instructor, the agency in which she was a field student, and her university, alleging that she was terminated from her field placement unlawfully when her supervisors became concerned about how the student managed her religious beliefs and values in the field placement (Huntington 2007). When such conflicts arise, it is incumbent upon supervisors to help supervisees examine their values and related conduct in light of the profession's core values and assist supervisees in their efforts to reconcile these conflicts in a manner consistent with social work's values and ethical standards.

Impairment

Many cases that lead to ethics complaints and lawsuits arise out of practitioner impairment (Barsky 2010; Reamer 2012, 2015). Often, social workers who engage in egregious ethical misconduct, especially cases involving inappropriate dual relationships and incompetent practice, are impaired in some manner. Supervisors are in a unique position to identify supervisees who may be struggling with impairment.

Both the seriousness of practitioner impairment and the forms it takes vary. Impairment may involve failure to provide competent care or violation of social work's ethical standards. Impairment may also take such forms as providing flawed or inferior services to a client, sexual involvement with a client, failure to carry out one's duties as a result of an addiction (alcohol, drug, gambling, sex, etc.), or mental illness. Research suggests that distress among human service professionals generally falls into two categories: environmental stress, which is a function of employment conditions (e.g., stressful working conditions and the broader culture's lack of support of the human services mission) or inadequate professional training, and personal stress, caused by problems with one's marriage, relationships, emotional and physical health, legal difficulties, and finances (Fausel 1988; Kilburg et al. 1988; Reamer 2015).

Research on impairment among professionals suggests that many struggling practitioners do not seek assistance, and colleagues who are concerned about them may be reluctant to share their concerns (Kilburg et al. 1988). Supervisors may be in a position to encourage supervisees to seek help when they are struggling. Some impaired professionals may find it difficult to seek help because of their mythological belief in their competence and invulnerability, they believe that an acceptable therapist is not available or that therapy would not help, they prefer to seek help from family members or friends or work problems out by themselves, they fear exposure and the disclosure of confidential information, they are concerned about the amount of effort required and about the cost, they have a spouse or partner who is unwilling to participate in treatment, or they do not admit the seriousness of the problem; they believe that they should be able to work their problems out by themselves; and/or they believe that therapy would not help.

Supervisors should do what they can to make collegial-assistance programs available to supervisees, when warranted. Although some serious cases of impairment must be dealt with through formal discipline and adjudication procedures, many cases can be handled primarily by arranging therapeutic or rehabilitative services for distressed practitioners. Impaired social workers should have access to competent service providers who are trained to understand professionals' special concerns and needs. For instance, regulatory bodies and professional social work organizations can enter into agreements with local employee assistance programs, to which impaired practitioners can be referred.

Whistleblowing

Supervisors who are concerned about supervisees' alleged impairment, unethical conduct, or incompetence must sometimes make ethical judgments about disclosing their concerns. This raises what ethicists refer to as whistle-blowing issues (Reamer 2019). When attempts to resolve unethical behavior through direct discussion with supervisees who appear to be impaired or to have behaved unethically are impossible or ineffective, supervisors must consider the possibility of blowing the whistle. This decision can be difficult. While whistleblowing may be necessary to protect clients and social service agencies, it also can have powerful and harmful ramifications on supervisees' careers, agency morale, and even whistleblowers themselves.

Before blowing the whistle, supervisors should ask themselves several compelling questions: First, "What are my motives? Am I disclosing information to authorities about my supervisee because of my genuine and sincere concern for clients and the agency, or is it a convenient opportunity for retribution—to 'pay back' a supervisee with whom I have had some conflict?" To justify whistleblowing, supervisors must be confident that their motives are noble, not self-serving.

Second, potential whistleblowers should ask themselves, "How strong is the evidence of misconduct?" Supervisors should allocate greater weight to compelling, incontrovertible evidence and exercise caution in the face of equivocal, circumstantial, and hearsay evidence. In light of the often serious consequences of whistleblowing, supervisors should feel confident that their allegations rest on a solid evidentiary foundation.

Third, "Have I pursued every feasible and reasonable alternative to full-scale whistleblowing?" Supervisors should carefully consider the extent to which they have made genuine, forthright attempts to discuss concerns with supervisees who are or appear to be impaired or involved in misconduct. Intermediate steps – which may involve mediation and various forms of corrective action, such as strict supervision, restitution, and continuing education – are sometimes reasonable alternatives to formal whistleblowing.

The final question concerns the extent to which social workers' whistleblowing is likely to be effective and produce meaningful reform and change. "Are outside parties in a position to address the issue, or would the whistleblowing result only in toxic publicity and bruised reputations?"

On a more practical note, supervisors who consider blowing the whistle on a supervisee should keep in mind the liability risk associated with defamation of character. Such defamation occurs when a supervisor makes a statement about a supervisee that is false, the supervisor knew or should have known that the statement was false, and the communication caused some kind of injury (for example, the supervisee was fired or disciplined, or the supervisee's professional reputation was sullied).

Defamation can take two forms: libel and slander. Libel refers to harmful written statements (for example, if a supervisor circulates a written memo falsely accusing a supervisee of impairment or ethical misconduct). Slander is when the information is conveyed orally (for example, when a supervisor makes accusing statements about a supervisee during the course of a staff meeting in the presence of other agency employees). Thus, for risk-management purposes, supervisors who consider blowing the whistle should be certain that any written or oral statements are factual.

One of the unpleasant facts of any profession is that supervisors occasionally encounter supervisees who appear to be impaired or involved in some kind of unethical behavior. In many instances, constructive incremental steps short of formal whistleblowing successfully resolve the problem; supervisees acknowledge errors and take sincere, meaningful steps to address them and to protect clients and the agency. In extreme circumstances, when intermediate steps are not feasible or are likely to be ineffective, supervisors may need to consider whistleblowing. Before doing so, however, responsible supervisors carefully examine their motives, the quality of the evidence of misconduct, the extent to which they have pursued reasonable alternatives, and the likelihood that whistleblowing will produce significant results.

Supervisor-supervisee boundaries

It is essential that supervisors serve as role models for ethical behavior. In particular, supervisors should model clear maintenance of professional boundaries in their relationships with supervisees. The most obvious violation entails intimate relationships between supervisors and supervisees (Jacobs 1991). More subtle challenges, which do not necessarily entail blatantly unethical behavior, involve supervisors entering into friendships with supervisees, socializing with supervisees, and sharing personal information with supervisees. Given the power differential between supervisors and supervisees, supervisors should be careful to avoid engaging in behaviors that might be misinterpreted by supervisees, constitute a conflict of interest, and compromise supervisors' professional judgment and objectivity.

Moral injury and moral courage

On a broader note, supervisors should be mindful of two overarching ethical issues that can arise in their work. First, supervisors should be aware that supervisees may need support when they encounter what has become known as moral injury. The concept of moral injury is receiving increased attention in health and human services professions (Briggs and Fronek 2019;

Campbell et al. 2016; Fantus et al. 2017; Jinkerson 2016; Weinberg 2009). It is ordinarily defined as the sort of harm that results when someone has perpetrated, failed to prevent, or witnessed acts that transgress deeply held moral beliefs. Social workers in many settings are well versed in the ravages, symptoms, and treatment of the complicated forms of posttraumatic stress that accompany moral injury. Moral injury experienced by supervisees may be the result of witnessing deliberate mistreatment of clients, inadvertent mistreatment of clients, and unjust/discriminatory organizational and public policies. Also, it can be the result of intimidating agency performance mandates, draconian funding and insurance company mandates, poor employee compensation, poor working conditions, inadequate supervision, and onerous legal regulations. Witnessing moral injury can lead supervisees to experience secondary trauma, existential angst, and workplace conflict.

To enhance supervisees' willingness and ability to address ethical concerns in the workplace and beyond, supervisors should do what they can to promote supervisees' moral courage. Moral courage is a concept rooted in the German concept of Zivilcourage, which entails a willingness to challenge authority and, when necessary, take on unpopular causes in the name of justice (Comer and Vega 2011; Kidder 2006; Kidder and Bracy 2001; Osswald et al. 2010; Pianalto 2012; Strom-Gottfried 2016).

In their efforts to define moral courage, Kidder and Bracy (2001) ask a question whose answer has profound implications for social work supervisors:

> What, then, is moral courage? It can be defined as the quality of mind and spirit that enables one to face up to ethical dilemmas and moral wrongdoings firmly and confidently, without flinching or retreating … It enables us to "face up" to problems—not necessarily to resolve them, and certainly not to promise that we will master them, but to address them squarely, frontally, and with determination … It requires action that is both firm in its persistence and confident that its tools—the moral, mental, and emotional elements of argumentation and persuasion—are sound enough to weather serious resistance.

For more than a century, the social work profession has been filled with morally courageous practitioners who have used their passion and values-based determination to challenge oppression, injustice, poverty, and exploitation. For social workers, moral courage entails identifying social injustice and unethical conduct, rallying colleagues and the citizenry to confront it, and inspiring them to sustain the effort over time. Moral courage often entails risk, especially the risk of opposition and failure. This is risk that social work demands in the name of social justice, and quality supervision can play a critical role in supervisees' willingness to cultivate this profoundly important instinct.

Conclusion

Knowledge about social work supervision has expanded exponentially since the profession's modest beginnings in the late 1800s. Over time, social work scholars and practitioners have added to the profession's fund of knowledge related to models and theories of supervision, supervision goals, supervision styles and techniques, the role of authority, supervisor stress, supervision contracts, and supervision evaluation. More recently, students of social work supervision have focused more explicitly on pertinent ethical issues.

Clearly, quality supervision must pay close attention to the ethical dimensions of social work practice. One of the principal goals of supervision is to enhance supervisees' awareness of the ethical dimensions of their work and their ability to reflect deliberately on ethical issues as they arise.

In the early 1980s, Massachusetts Institute of Technology scholar Donald Schon (1983) wrote a powerful book entitled *The Reflective Practitioner: How Professionals Think in Action*. In an imaginative study, Schon examined practitioners in five professions – engineering architecture, management, psychotherapy, and town planninto show how professionals go about solving problems. The best professionals, Donald Schön maintains, are those who have a unique ability to reflect on their conduct, and the way they practice their professions, at the very same time they are engaged in that conduct. In this regard, reflective supervisors have the compelling ability to reflect on the way they are supervising as they are actively engaged in supervisory tasks. Reflective supervisors are keenly aware that during encounters with supervisees, they are serving as ethical role models and, as it were, modeling the art of ethical decision making, ethics consultation, and ethics instruction. This is at the heart of what it means to be a professional.

References

Abbott, A.A., 1988. *Professional choices: values at work*. Silver Spring, MD: National Association of Social Workers.

Allen-Meares, P., 2000. Our professional values and the changing environment. *Journal of Social Work Education*, 36, 179–182.

Banks, S., 2012. *Ethics and values in social work*. 4th ed. London: Palgrave.

Barsky, A., 2010. *Ethics and values in the social work profession*. New York: Oxford University Press.

Bogo, M., and McKnight, K., 2005. Clinical supervision in social work. *The Clinical Supervisor*, 24 (1/2), 49–67.

Bonosky, N., 1995. Boundary violations in social work supervision: clinical, educational, and legal implications. *The Clinical Supervisor*, 13, 79–95.

Briggs, L., and Fronek, P., 2019. Incorporating demoralization into social work practice. *Social Work*, 64, 157–164.

Campbell, S.M., Ulrich, C.M., and Christine, G., 2016. A broader understanding of moral distress. *American Journal of Bioethics*, 16, 2–9.

Cohen, B., 1987. The ethics of social work supervision revisited. *Social Work*, 32, 194–196.

Comer, D.R., and Vega, G., eds., 2011. *Moral courage in organizations: doing the right thing at work*. Armonk, NY: M.E. Sharpe.

Congress, E.P., 1999. *Social work values and ethics: identifying and resolving professional dilemmas*. Chicago: Nelson-Hall.

Copeland, P., Dean, R., and Wladkowski, S.P., 2011. The power dynamics of supervision: ethical dilemmas. *Smith College Studies in Social Work*, 81, 26–40.

Dean, R.G., and Rhodes, M.L., 1992. Ethical-clinical tensions in clinical practice. *Social Work*, 39, 28–32.

Dolgoff, R., Loewenberg, F., and Harrington, D., 2009. *Ethical decisions for social work practice*. 8th ed. Belmont, CA: Thomson/Brooks Cole.

Doyle, O.Z, Miller, S.E., and Mirza, F.Y., 2009. Ethical decision-making in social work: personal and professional values. *Journal of Social Work Values and Ethics*, 6 (1). Available from: http://jswve.org/download /2009-1/JSWVE-Spring-2009-Complete.pdf [Accessed 5 July 2019].

Fantus, S., Greenberg, R.A., Muskat, B., and Katz, D., 2017. Exploring moral distress for hospital social workers. *British Journal of Social Work*, 47, 2273–2290.

Fausel, D.F., 1988. Helping the helper heal: co-dependency in helping professionals. *Journal of Independent Social Work*, 3 (2), 35–45.

Frunză, A., and Sandu, A., 2017. Ethical values in social work practice: a qualitative study. *Journal of Social Work Values and Ethics*, 14, 40–58.

Gil, D., 1998. *Confronting injustice and oppression: concepts and strategies for social workers*. New York: Columbia University Press.

Hair, H.J., 2015. Supervision conversations about social justice and social work practice. *Journal of Social Work*, 15, 349–370.

Houston-Vega, M.K., Nuehring, E.M., and Daguio, E.R., 1997. *Prudent practice: a guide for managing malpractice risk*. Washington, DC: NASW Press.

Hugman, R., and Carter, J., eds., 2016. *Rethinking values and ethics in social work*. London: Palgrave.

Huntington, D., 2007, April 3. Trial to begin for fired intern who shared faith. *Christian Post Reporter*. Available from https://www.christianpost.com/news/trial-to-begin-for-fired-intern-who-shared-faith.html [Accessed 5 September 2019].

Jacobs, C., 1991. Violations of the supervisory relationship: an ethical and educational blind spot. *Social Work*, 36, 130–135.

Jinkerson, J., 2016. Defining and assessing moral injury: a syndrome perspective. *Traumatology*, 22, 122–130.

Kadushin, A., and Harkness, D., 2014. *Supervision in social work*. 5th ed. New York: Columbia University Press.

Keegan, H., 2017, January 9. MSU settles lawsuit with student who wouldn't counsel gay couples. *Springfield News-Leader*. Available from: https://www.news-leader.com/story/news/local/2017/01/09/msu-settles-lawsuit-student-who-wouldnt-counsel-gay-couples/96340566/ [Accessed 5 September 2019].

Kidder, R.M., 2006. *Moral courage*. New York: Harper.

Kidder, R.M., and Bracy, M., 2001. *Moral courage: a white paper*. Available from: https://ww2.faulkner.edu/admin/websites/jfarrell/moral_courage_11-03-2001.pdf. [Accessed July 5, 2019].

Kilburg, R.R., Kaslow, F.W., and VandenBos, G.R., 1988. Professionals in distress. *Hospital and Community Psychiatry*, 39, 723–725.

Levy, C.S., 1976. *Social work ethics*. New York. Human Sciences Press.

McAuliffe, D., and Sudbery, J., 2005. Who do I tell? Support and consultation in cases of ethical conflict. *Journal of Social Work*, 5, 21–43.

Munson, C., 2002. *Handbook of clinical social work supervision*. 3rd ed. Binghamton, NY: Haworth.

National Association of Social Workers, Association of Social Work Boards, Council on Social Work Education, and Clinical Social Work Association 2017. *Standards for technology in social work practice*. Washington, DC: National Association of Social Workers.

O'Donoghue, K., 2003. *Restorying social work supervision*. Palmerston North, New Zealand: Dunmore Press.

O'Donoghue, K., 2015. Issues and challenges facing social work supervision in the twenty-first century. *China Journal of Social Work*, 8, 136–149.

O'Donoghue, K., and O'Donoghue, R., 2019. The application of ethics within social work supervision: a selected literature and research review. *Ethics and Social Welfare*. doi:10.1080/17496535.2019.1590438.

Osswald, S., Greitemeyer, T., Fischer, P., and Frey, D., 2010. What is moral courage? Definition, explication, and classification of a complex construct. *In*: C. Purey and S. Lopez, eds. *The psychology of courage: modern research on an ancient virtue*. Washington, DC: American Psychological Association, 149–164.

Pianalto, M., 2012. Moral courage and facing others. *International Journal of Philosophical Studies*, 20 (2), 165–184.

Reamer, F.G., 2012. *Boundary issues and dual relationships in the human services*. New York: Columbia University Press.

Reamer, F.G., 2015. *Risk management in social work: preventing professional malpractice, liability, and disciplinary action*. New York: Columbia University Press.

Reamer, F.G., 2017. Evolving ethical standards in the digital age. *Australian Social Work*, 70 (2), 148–159.

Reamer, F.G., 2018a. *Social work values and ethics*. 5th ed. New York: Columbia University Press.

Reamer, F.G., 2018b. Ethical standards for social workers' use of technology: emerging consensus. *Journal of Social Work Values and Ethics*, 15 (2), 71–80.

Reamer, F.G., 2018c. *Ethical standards in social work: a review of the NASW Code of Ethics*. Washington, DC: NASW Press.

Reamer, F.G., 2018d. *The social work ethics casebook: cases and commentary*. 2nd ed. Washington, DC: NASW Press.

Reamer, F.G., 2019. The ethics of whistle blowing. *Journal of Ethics in Mental Health*, 10, 1–19. Available from https://jemh.ca/issues/v9/documents/JEMH%20article%20final%20Whistle%204.pdf [Accessed 14 July 2019].

Schon, D., 1983. *The reflective practitioner: how professionals think in action*. New York: Basic Books.

Strom-Gottfried, K., 2016. *Straight talk about professional ethics*. 2nd ed. New York: Oxford University Press.

Tsui, M., 2005. *Social work supervision: contexts and concepts*. Thousand Oaks, CA: SAGE.

Varley, B.K., 1968. Social work values: changes in value commitments from admission to MSW graduation. *Journal of Education for Social Work*, 4, 67–85.

Vigilante, J.L., 1974. Between values and science: education for the profession; Or, is proof truth?. *Journal of Education for Social Work*, 10, 107–115.

Weinberg, M., 2009. Moral distress: a missing but relevant concept for ethics in social work. *Canadian Social Work Review*, 26, 139–151.

PART IV

Models and approaches

25

THE COMPREHENSIVE MODEL OF SOCIAL WORK SUPERVISION

Ming-sum Tsui

Introduction

Social work supervision has a long history of practice, but a short period of time in theory and model building. According to the classical classification by Tsui (1997), the history of supervision in social work can be divided into five stages. First, administrative roots of social work supervision are established (1878–1910). In this stage, the duty of the volunteer supervisors is to monitor, not teach the frontline service helpers. Second, there was change of context from the community to the universities, supervisory training programs were set up and a literature base emerged (1911–1945). Third, the influence from other disciplines such as psychoanalysis and sociology on practice theory and methods in supervision occurred (1956–1970). They have shaped the format of orientation of the modern supervisory practice. Fourth, there was a heated debate between interminable supervision versus autonomous practice (1956–1970s), while the former supported that supervision should be a long lasting effort to monitor the frontline social workers to establish the indirect accountability to the client(s), the latter asserted that we should follow the model of the medical profession to allow a certain degree of professional autonomy and responsibility in the internship. Fifth, social work supervision came back to the administrative function in the age of accountability (1980s–1990s) as both the government and the service users request the helping professions to demonstrate the effectiveness and efficiency in a "more output for less resource input" approach instead of a "more or less" manner.

In fact, starting from the 1990s, following the path of the three founders in social work supervision – (1) Kadushin's foundation of three supervisory functions: administrative, educational, and supportive (Kadushin 1976, 1985, 1992a, b, c; Kadushin and Harkness 2014), (2) Munson's emphasis on supervisor's competence instead of use of power and sanction (1976, 1979, 1981, 1993), and (3) Shulman's interactional approach to social work supervision (1982, 1993) – a group of scholars followed their paths and put much effort in examining and conceptualizing the supervisory practice, for example Rich (1993) looked into the form, functions, and contents of clinical supervision and tried to set up an integrated model. Tsui (2001) conducted a study in Hong Kong and formulated a cultural model. He advocated that supervision is not a professional practice, but also a personal practice. It is not only an organizational practice, but also a cultural practice (Tsui 2001, 2005). O'Donoghue and his friends attempted to build up an evidence-based supervision model (O'Donoghue et al. 2018).

The joint effort has become a milestone of theory and knowledge building in social work supervision. The author is lucky to have the honor to take part in this journey. In the 21st century, we are entering the sixth stage of "theory exploration and knowledge building" (2000 to 2020s). The scholars, researchers, and practitioners are trying to formulate and test different models which may facilitate the supervisory process and make the supervisory process more innovative, interactive, and productive. In the following sections, the author is going to review the existing models of social work supervision, formulate the comprehensive model of social work supervision and highlighting their implications for further research.

Existing models of social work supervision

Before we go into the discussion of models of social work supervision, we have to figure out what a model is. A model is a simplified abstract map to act as a guide to the explorers to understand the reality and the contents in the real world (Dechert 1965; Galt and Smith 1976; Tsui 2001, 2005; Tsui and Ho 1998). Sergiovanni (1983) suggested that model building should be concerned with the reality of the context, the ideal, the components, and the action guidelines for practicing supervisors. Models can add clarity to the supervisory process and are usually useful to apply. Models are more flexible and specific than theories. A model of supervision can be just a package of inter-related ideas of techniques that are useful in supervisory practice. They are easier to modify and to test (Bernard and Goodyear 2019). In the supervisory process, models can serve as a common language between the supervisor and the supervisee(s). Of course, it may be possible for a supervisor to learn how to supervise through imitation or by a "trial and error" approach. However, without a model, the supervisor may not be able to understand the rationale and the process of social work supervision in a holistic manner.

Practice theory as a guide to supervision model

A group of scholars in counseling (Liddle and Saba 1983; Olsen and Stern 1990; Storm and Heath 1985) have suggested that supervisors may adopt therapy theories as models for supervision for a number of reasons. First, there is a lack of formal and well-established supervision theories. Second, theories on therapy and counseling are relatively well developed in terms of stages, format, and components. Third, there is an existing collection of literature on therapy and counseling which provides a clear description of why, what, and how in supervision. Fourth, therapy theories provide useful guidance on step-by-step intervention and practice skills. Fifth, the use of therapy as a model of supervision enables social work supervisors to build on what we already know. Sixth, the format of therapy and supervision is similar in terms of structure, for example, the individual supervision looks like a therapeutic session to a certain extent.

The parallel linkage between therapy and supervision is defined as "isomorphism," referring to two complex structures which are mapped on to each other (Bernard and Goodyear 1992). However, if we assume supervision looks like a kind of therapy, there will be some issues. First, no formal models of social work supervision can be really established. Second, this assumption may also discourage the effort in viewing and defining supervision in a holistic and integrative manner. Third, it is rather difficult to operationalize and hypotheses in therapy and counselling theories, this will create complicated issues in conducting meaningful and useful research studies to verify and test the proposed theories. Fourth, this may explain why Bernard and Goodyear (1992) asserted that the emergence of models of supervision is a mature sign of the development of theory and models in supervisory practice.

Structural-functional models

Structural-functional models of supervision are traditional models widely used by supervisors in the social work field. The focus is on the objectives, structures, and functions of supervision. Three models belong to this category: (1) models of authority, (2) integrative models, and (3) supervisory function models.

Models of authority

Models of authority are formulated by Munson (1976, 1979, 1981, 1993) from his research on the use of supervisory authority. In Munson's study, he paired up 64 dyads of supervisors and supervises, which was the first attempt in conducting research on supervision dyads. From the study, Munson found there were two major approaches in using the supervisory authority: first, the sanction style which is used by supervisors who believe the authority comes from their position in the organizational hierarchy. Second, there is another style – competence – adopted by supervisors who think that their authority comes from internal sources, that means, their own job performance and practice skills. As a conclusion, Munson (1979, 1981) asserted that the competence model is the most effective model in enabling and enhancing the supervisor-supervisee interaction and job satisfaction among frontline social workers.

Integrative model

Regarding the focus and emphasis of supervision, Gitterman (1972) identified three models in social work supervision, namely (1) organization-oriented model, (2) worker-centred model, and (3) integrative model. As expected, Gitterman preferred the integrative model, which is a combination model to strike a balance between the organizational model and worker model. After a decade, Lowy (1983) also formulated three models, namely (1) the work-oriented model which focuses on the frontline social worker's performance according to the demands from the organization and the profession; (2) the theory and method-oriented model which emphasizes the understanding of relevant theories and application of useful models, and (3) the learning model which emphasizes the educational aspects of supervision. In fact, in the context of supervisory practice, we always combine the three kinds of models in our supervisory practice. The classification can only serve as a guide in conceptualizing social work supervision.

Supervisory functions model

Supervision functions models illustrate the three different functions of supervision: administrative, educational, and supportive (Erera and Lazar 1994; Kadushin 1976, 1985, 1992a, b, c; Kadushin and Harkness 2014). Each function deals with its own set of problems and achieves related objectives. The administrative function is to monitor the frontline social workers to fulfill the requirements from the human service organizations, including organizational mandate, managerial policies and regulations, as well as the administrative procedures. The educational function is to enable and enhance the capability and capacity of the frontline social workers to address the client's problems with adequate knowledge and skills. The supportive function is to maintain the staff morale and to encourage the staff to achieve high motivation and job satisfaction. It is suggested by the scholars in supervision that the three functions are complementary to one another (Kadushin and Harkness 2014; Tsui 2005; Tsui and Ho 1998).

Organizational models

In the daily operations, social work supervision models often reflect the demands of organizational structure and procedures of the human service organizations (Kadushin 1992a; Kadushin and Harkness 2014; Skidmore 1995; Watson 1973). The use of specific supervision models, in fact, is an effort to establish a certain extent of the administrative accountability and ensure that professional autonomy can be achieved. We can formulate this category of organizational models on a continuum. At one extreme, there is the casework model in which a high level of administrative accountability is built in. At another end, the autonomous practice model allows the supervisees to enjoy a high level of professional autonomy (Epstein 1973; Rock 1990; Veeder 1990). Between the two, there are the group work supervision model (Getzel et al. 1971; Kaplan 1991; Kaslow 1972; Shulman 1993), the team service delivery model (Payne and Scott 1982), and the peer supervision model (Skipmore 1995).

Casework model

As indicated by Kadushin (1992a) and Tsui (1997), the "theories" of social work supervision have been much influenced by the theories of social work practice, especially social casework practice. This may explain why the format of individual supervision sessions looks like the casework interviews. The casework model engages a supervisor and a supervise in a one-to-one and face-to-face interview. Everything discussed is kept confidential and private. The functions of the supervision cover administrative, educational, and supportive functions (Kadushin 1976, 1992a, b, c; Ko 1987). Even though there are numerous supervision models adopted in the social work profession, the casework model is still the most popular model of supervision, especially for those newly recruited frontline social workers.

Group supervision model

The next model in the continuum is the group supervision model, which is the second most popular model of supervision in the social work field. The group supervision model is often taken as a supplement, rather than a substitute for individual supervision (Kadushin 1992a; Kadushin and Harkness 2014; Tsui 2005). In this model, the supervisor serves as the group leader to facilitate the interaction among the frontline social workers as group members. Since the discussion focuses on the common needs and problems of the colleagues, the levels of the professional training and practice experience of participants should not be too diverse, otherwise staff members may not fully benefit from the group process (Watson 1973). Within the group supervision session, the power between the group leader and members are more equal and balanced. Then the members can be exposed to a wider variety of professional knowledge and practice wisdom in a more natural and comfortable atmosphere. Emotional support does not only come from the supervisor as the group leader, but also from the colleagues. However, there are two pre-conditions for the success of group supervision, that is, the group work skills of the supervisor and the readiness of the staff members. Obviously, group supervision is more efficient than individual supervision as it saves a lot of time, however, it cannot be used to discuss the private issues of the supervisee(s) and the staff relationships and conflicts.

Peer supervision models

Next to group supervision on the continuum is the peer supervision model. In peer supervision, there is no designated supervisor, and all staff participate equally (Tsui 2005; Watson 1973). Each staff member takes the responsibility for his/her own work. There are only regular case conferences among all the staff. Collegial consultation among the staff is the major format of the discussion and interaction. As indicated by Tsui and Ho (1998), peer supervision can make the staff more sensitive to the needs and difficulties of others by creating an atmosphere of sharing, peer support, and mutual help. However, Tsui and Ho also reminded us that the peer supervision model only fits those staff with a certain level of practice experience. Another model of supervision developed from the peer supervision model is the "Tandem Model" (Watson 1973). When there are two staff members who would like to have a mutual consultation and co-reflection away from the peer group, they can form a "tandem." Both colleagues should be well-experienced practitioners, and neither of them is designated as the supervisor. As a tandem, the two staff members meet occasionally and informally to discuss the caseloads and recent working experiences. Whenever a tandem member is on leave, they can cover each other's duties, thereby exposing themselves to different learning opportunities. However, there is no obligation for the partners in the tandem to be accountable to the other's job performance.

Autonomous practice

At another end of the continuum is autonomous practice. In fact, this is not really a model, but a kind of staff development in ensuring and enhancing professional practice. In the social work profession, there is a group of advocates who argue that for the professionally trained and well-experienced practitioners, there is no need to provide regular supervision (Epstein 1973; Kutzik 1977; Veeder 1990). Definitions of "experienced" range from two to six years of practice after graduation (Kadushin 1992a; Kadushin and Harkness 2014; Tsui 2005; Veeder 1990; Wax 1979). Epstein (1973) further elaborated that the two pre-conditions for autonomous practice are decentralization of bureaucratic authority and abandonment of the obligatory teaching process as a means of monitoring professional practice. Barretta-Herman (1993) also suggested using a model of supervision for licensed social work practitioners. In this model, as the licensed practitioners are well trained, licensed, and experienced, the primary responsibility for continual professional development and accountability will be shouldered by individual practitioners instead of their immediate supervisors. The supervisor is no longer "super" in terms of professional knowledge and skills. The supervisor only plays the role of a facilitator. Group supervision will be adopted as the major mode of supervision. The supervisory relationship will become more interactive, independent, and more equal. Of course, there is a drawback, as pointed out by Veeder (1990) – the absence of measurable evaluation criteria and concrete objectives for planning in direct social work practice – which will make the self-accountable nature of the truly autonomous professional blunted.

Interactional process models

Interactional process models focus on the interaction and communication between the supervisor and the supervisee(s) during the supervisory process (Tsui and Ho 1998). For example, Latting (1986) proposed an adaptive supervision model which uses four categories to illustrate different interactional patterns between the supervisor and the supervisee(s). In this model, instrumental behavior denotes the administrative and educational functions while expressive behavior refers to the supportive function. The supervisor may instruct, collaborate, encourage, or entrust the supervisee(s) in different practice contexts. In the field, there are two types of interactional process models. First, developmental models of supervision focus on the stage of development in supervisory process in which supervisees acquire hands-on skills for their professional practice (Hart 1982; Stoltenberg 1981; Worthington 1984). Second, there are growth-oriented models of supervision which are supervisee-oriented. They focus on the enhancement of supervisees' understanding and reflection of their personal self and professional self (Gitterman 1972; Gitterman and Miller 1977).

Feminist partnership model

Just like other areas in social work practice, feminism has played a significant role and has had an impact on supervision in social work. Some feminists are critical of the traditional social work supervision model and see the power hierarchy of the supervisor-supervisee relationships, interminable supervision, and administrative control as manifestations of a patriarchal model of power.

A few scholars (Chernesky 1986; Hipp and Munson 1995) proposed an alternative feminist partnership model which assumes that the frontline social worker can be self-directing, self-disciplined, and self-regulating. The relationship between the supervisor and the supervisee(s) can be a more equal sharing relationship between equal partners. In this context, the hierarchy of power will be re-conceptualized as a professional affiliation to a human service organization. Direct supervision as a performance monitoring mechanism should be replaced by indirect mechanism such as group norms and peer approval. The advocates for the feminist partnership model claim that it is more compatible with the values, objectives and functions of the social work profession than the traditional authority model (Tsui and Ho 1998).

Postmodern models in supervision

After reviewing the traditional social work supervision models, let us move our mind and eyes to other newly constructed models in the last two decades. We may classify them as "postmodern models in supervision." They widen the scope of supervision and extend its functions. First, there is "external supervision" in which the supervisor is not a senior member of the organization, but a professional consultant outside the organization or even outside the institutional context. The supervisor is not the administrator who serves as the boss of the frontline social workers, but an expert who focuses mainly on the educational function. However, from the empirical findings (Mo and Tsui 2018), the supportive function is still the entry point in the supervisory process and the function most valued by the supervisee(s), especially the newly recruited frontline social workers.

Second, there is "online supervision" which provides supervision from a long distance. It involves the compression of time and space and innovative use of information technology in the postmodern age. This supervision facilitates the continuity of the operations of human services during a natural disaster (e.g., pandemic, tsunami, or earthquake). In addition, the supervisory practice can be done across cultures located in different parts of the world (Tsui et al. 2014). Thus, "online supervision" can compress time and space as well as shorten the physical distance, organizational distance, and cultural distance. In the future, it has the potential to be widely used as it is a more efficient supervision in terms of time and money.

Third, there is an attempt to build up evidence-based supervision which is a stream of the evidence-based social work practice. In fact, it is also a research-informed model of social work supervision (O'Donoghue and Tsui 2015) It consists of five areas, namely the construction of social work supervision, supervision of the practitioner, the supervision alliance, the interactional process, and the supervision of direct practice. The model provides supervisors with an integrated approach to social work supervision. Then the supervisors can: (1) apply knowledge about social work supervision, and clarify roles, responsibilities, and accountabilities, (2) attend to the professional development and emotional needs of their supervisee(s) as frontline social workers, (3) effectively engage with the interactional and rational processes involved in supervision, as well as (4) seek to improve the supervisee's practice with clients (O'Donoghue et al. 2018).

Last but not least, supervision can also be reframed into a typology of organizational learning in which supervision is one of the self-directed efforts in the organizational learning, consisting of (1) supervision, (2) coaching, (3) mentoring, and (4) consultation (Tsui et al. 2017). It is envisaged that the future path of social work supervision will be a new form of self-initiated, self-motivated, and proactive organizational learning for professional practitioners. Other than supervision, coaching as an intensive teaching in practice knowledge and hands-on skill, mentoring as learning among peers with different seniority, and consultation as advice and feedback provided by an external expert should be adopted and used in an integrated synergy. A typology as a guide in organizational learning is also provided by Tsui et al. (2017). In the future, when social work has become a more mature profession, these four kinds of organizational learning measures will be used, not only in a supplementary way, but also a complementary manner.

Seven principles of social work supervision

After reviewing the existing and developing models in social work supervision, it is time for us to think about formulating a comprehensive model of social work supervision. The following seven basic principles of social work supervision are identified by the author (Tsui 2001, 2005).

1. Supervision is an interpersonal transaction between two or more staff. The premise of supervision is that an experienced and competent supervisor enables the supervisee(s) and ensures the quality of service to clients (Kadushin and Harkness 2014; Tsui 2001, 2005).
2. As part of indirect practice of social work, supervision reflects the professional values of social work (Kadushin and Harkness 2014; Munson 1993; Shulman 1982, 1993; Tsui 2001, 2005).
3. In this interpersonal transaction, there is a use of authority (the organizational/ administrative function), an exchange of information and ideas (the professional/educational function), and expression of feelings (the emotional/supportive function) (Munson 1976, 1979a, b, 1981, 1993, 2002; Tsui 2001, 2005).
4. The work of the supervisee is related to the organizational objectives through the supervisor (Kadushin and Harkness 2014; Shulman 1995; Tsui 2005).
5. The supervisor monitors job performance; conveys professional values, knowledge, and skills; and provides emotional support to the supervisee (Kadushin and Harkness 2014; Tsui 2005).
6. Staff satisfaction with supervision, job satisfaction, job accomplishment, and client outcome are the criteria for evaluating the effectiveness of supervision (Harkness 1995; Harkness and Hensley 1991; Kadushin and Harkness 2014; Tsui 2001, 2005).
7. From a holistic point of view, supervision involves four parties: the service agency, the supervisor, the supervisee, and the client (Kadushin 2014; Shulman 1993; Tsui and Ho 1998).

A comprehensive model of social work supervision

Traditionally, social work supervision has been conceptualized as an indirect social work practice embedded in an organizational context (Austin 1957; Holloway and Brager 1989; Miller

1987; Munson 1993). For this reason, investigations in the past have focused their mind on factors related to the supervisor-supervisee relationship within an organizational setting. However, this narrow mindset limited the focus on the supervisor and the supervisee. If we take a more multifaceted interactionalist view, the four parties – the agency, the supervisor, the supervisee, and the client – will be included. As an enabling social work process, these four parties in social work supervision are embedded in the same specific cultural context. It involves the interaction of personal values and cultural values. This is why Tsui (2005) asserted that social work supervision is not only a professional practice, but also a personal practice (Tsui 2003). It is not only an organizational practice, but also a cultural practice (Tsui 2001, 2005; Tsui et al. 2005). Unfortunately, culture is something easy to identify, distinguish, and discuss, but difficult to define. It is a shared system of concepts or mental representations established by convention and reproduced by transmission (Berry and Laponce 1994; Goodenough 1996; Geertz 1973; Ingold 1994).

Taking the supervisory relationship as involving four parties explains their behavior in a more precise manner. In the supervisory process, supervisees have to be accountable to the client, but not directly. They are accountable to the client through the supervisor and the agency. Thus, as long as the frontline social worker is not employed by the client, some kind of supervision is necessary. This comprehensive model explains why supervision in private practice, for example, the third-party payment, has different features.

The comprehensive model here provides a holistic view of supervisory practice in social work (See Figure 25.1, Tsui 2001, p. 62). The culture, not the organization, is taken as the major context. In addition, a wider perspective is adopted in the components. In this model, the effectiveness of supervision depends on a few factors: the relationship among the four involving parties, the supervisory contract, supervision format and development stages of the supervisory

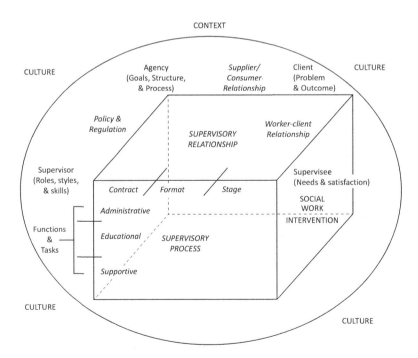

Figure 25.1 The comprehensive model of social work supervision

316

process, the balance among various supervisory functions, and the relationship between the features of supervision and the culture of the external environment.

Research agenda in the future

After formulating the comprehensive model, it is time for us to look at the research agenda in supervision. O'Donoghue and Tsui (2015) did a good job in reviewing the state of the art in social work supervision research – they reviewed the research on the supervision of frontline social workers published in peer-reviewed social work journals over a 40-year period (1970–2010). Eighty-six articles were located and analyzed by decade, location, research design, research participants, research focus, and findings. O'Donoghue and Tsui discussed the current state of knowledge in relation to the foundation of theory and practice in social work supervision. They recommended that future efforts should focus on the development of empirically based supervision models, the evaluation of the impact of supervision on client outcomes, as well as comparative cross-national studies (O'Donoghue and Tsui 2015, p. 616).

Time goes so fast. After ten years, since 2010, with the effort of the second-generation scholars in social work supervision, the above recommendations have been partially achieved. What we are going to do can be summarized in six major points. First, regarding research methodology, it is an intellectual pursuit to use different research methods and designs. Up to now, there has still been a lack of longitudinal studies, in particular panel studies, to investigate the same set of respondents at different points in time. Even though the attempt is time-consuming and expensive, it will certainly enable, ensure, and enrich the practice of social work supervision with evidence. Second, the research subject should be focused on interpersonal interaction (Tsui 2008). Based on this direction, the focus of research studies should be moved from investigating supervisors alone to the dyads of supervisor and the supervisee, and then to the triads including the supervisor, the supervisee, and the client, and eventually to the four parties involved in the supervisory process (that is, the client, frontline social worker, the supervisor, and the organization) (Tsui 2008; Tsui and Ho 1998).

Third, the context for conducting the studies on supervision should also be extended from the organizational context to the societal culture and then across different cultures (Tsui et al. 2014), that is, from institutional to inter-cultural, and then international (Beddoe et al. 2015). Fourth, research studies should also be focused on the content of supervision sessions, which is the investigation on the interventional strategies in the supervisory process (Tsui 2004a). This effort will make the research on social work supervision inform and improve the supervisory practice and make it more down-to-earth, practical, and competent. Fifth, the research effort should also be inter-disciplinary, which would take other disciplines as references and partners in summing up the experience and developing the expertise in supervising frontline professional practitioners. In this regard, other forms of organizational learning in learning organizations, such as coaching, mentorship, and consultation, should be adopted and incorporated.

References

Austin, L., 1957. Supervision in social work. *In*: R.H. Kurtz, ed. *Social work year book*. New York: National Association of Social Workers, 569–573.

Barretta-Herman, A., 1993. On the development of a model of supervision for licensed social work practitioners. *The Clinical Supervisor*, 11 (2), 55–64.

Beddoe, L., Karvinen-Niinikoski, S., Ruch, G., and Tsui, M.S., 2015. Towards an international consensus on a research agenda for social work supervision: report on the first survey of a delphi study. *British Journal of Social Work*, 46 (6), 1568–1586. doi:10.1093/bjsw/bcv110.

Bernard, J.M., and Goodyear, R.K., 1992. *Fundamentals of clinical supervision*. Boston, MA: Allyn and Bacon.

Bernard, J.M., and Goodyear, R.K., 2019. *Fundamentals of clinical supervision*. New York: Pearson.

Berry, J.W. and Laponce, J.A. (Eds.), 1994. Ethnicity and culture in Canada: the research landscape. Toronto: University of Toronto Press.

Chernesky, R.H., 1986. A new model of supervision. *In*: N. Van Den Bergh and L.B. Cooper, eds. *Feminist visions for social work*. Silver Spring, MD: National Association of Social Workers, 128–148.

Dechert, C., 1965. Cybernetics and the human person. *International Philosophical Quarterly*, 5, 5–36.

Epstein, L., 1973. Is autonomous practice possible?. *Social Work*, 18, 5–12.

Erera, I.P., and Lazar, A., 1994. The administrative and educational functions in supervision: indications of incompatibility. *The Clinical Supervisor*, 12 (2), 39–56.

Galt, A., and Smith, L., 1976. *Models and the study of social change*. New York: John Wiley & Sons.

Geertz, C., 1973. *The interpretation of cultures: selected essays*. New York: Basic Books.

Getzel, G.S., Goldberg, J.R., and Salmon, R., 1971. Supervising in groups as a model for today. *Social Casework*, 52, 154–163.

Gitterman, A., 1972. Comparison of educational models and their influence on supervision. *In*: F.W. Kaslow et al., eds. *Issues in human services*. San Francisco, CA: Jossey-Bass, 18–38.

Gitterman, A., and Miller, I., 1977. Supervisors as educators. *In*: F.W. Kaslow et al., eds. *Supervision, consultation, and staff training in the helping professions*. San Francisco, CA: Jossey-Bass, 100–114.

Goodenough, W., 1996. Definition. *In*: D. Levinson and M. Ember, eds. *Encyclopedia of cultural anthropology*. New York: Henry Holt & Company, 291–299.

Harkness, D., 1995. The art of helping in supervised practice: skills, relationships, and outcomes. *The Clinical Supervisor*, 9 (2), 31–42.

Harkness, D., and Hensley, H., 1991. Changing the focus of social work supervision: effects on client satisfaction and generalized contentment. *Social Work*, 36 (6), 506–512.

Hart, G.M., 1982. *The process of clinical supervision*. Baltimore, MD: University Park Press.

Hipp, J.L., and Munson, C.E., 1995. The partnership model: a feminist supervision/consultation perspective. *The Clinical Supervisor*, 13 (1), 23–38.

Holloway, S. and Brager, G., 1989. *Supervising in the human service: the politics of practice*. New York: Free Press.

Ingold, T., (Ed.), 1994. *Companion encyclopedia of anthropology: humanity, culture and social life*. London: Routledge.

Kadushin, A., 1976. *Supervision in social work*. New York: Columbia University Press.

Kadushin, A., 1985. *Supervision in social work*. 2nd ed. New York: Columbia University Press.

Kadushin, A., 1992a. *Supervision in social work*, 3rd ed. New York: Columbia University Press.

Kadushin, A., 1992b. What's wrong, what's right with social work supervision?. *The Clinical Supervisor*, 10 (1), 3–19.

Kadushin, A., 1992c. Social work supervision: an updated survey. *The Clinical Supervisor*, 10 (2), 9–27.

Kadushin, A., and Harkness, D., 2014. *Supervision in social work*. 5th ed. New York: Columbia University Press.

Kaplan, T., 1991. A model for group supervision for social work: implementations for the profession. *In*: D. Schneck, B. Grossman, and U. Glassman, eds. *Field education in social work: contemporary issues and trends*. Dubuque, IA: Kendall/Hunt, 141–148.

Kaslow, F.W., 1972. Group supervision. *In*: F.W. Kaslow, ed. *Issues in human services: a sourcebook for supervision and staff development*. San Francisco: Jossey-Bass.

Ko, G.P., 1987. Casework supervision in voluntary family service agencies in Hong Kong. *International Social Work*, 30, 171–184.

Kutzik, A.J., 1977. The social work field. *In*: F.W. Kaslow et al., eds. *Supervision, consultation, and staff training in the helping professions*. San Francisco, CA: Jossey-Bass, 25–60.

Latting, J.E., 1986. Adaptive supervision: a theoretical model for social workers. *Administration in Social Work*, 10 (1), 15–23.

Liddle, H., and Saba, G., 1983. On context replication: the isomorphic relationship of training and therapy. *The Journal of Strategic and Systematic Therapies*, 2, 3–11.

Lowy, L., 1983. Social work supervision: from models to wards theory. *Journal of Education for Social Work*, 19 (2), 55–62.

Miller, I., 1987. Supervision in social work. *In*: A. Minahan et al., eds. *Encyclopedia of social work*. Vol 2, 18th ed. Silver Spring, MD: NASW Press, 748–756.

Mo, K.Y.H., and Tsui, M.S., 2018. External supervision for social workers in another socio-political context: a qualitative study in Shenzhen, China. *China Journal of Social Work*, 9 (1), 62–74.

Munson, C.E., 1976. Professional autonomy and social work supervision. *Journal of Education for Social Work*, 12 (3), 95–102.

Munson, C.E., 1981. Style and structure in supervision. *Journal of Education for Social Work*, 17 (1), 65–72.

Munson, C.E., 1993. *Clinical social work supervision*. 2nd ed. New York: Haworth Press.

Munson, C.E., ed., 1979. *Social work supervision: classic statements and critical issues*. New York: Free Press.

Munson, C.E., 2002. *Handbook of clinical social work supervision* (3rd ed). Binghamton, NY: Haworth Social Work Practice.

O'Donoghue, K., and Tsui, M.S., 2015. Social work supervision research (1970–2010): the way we were and the way ahead. *The British Journal of Social Work*, 45 (2), 616–633. doi:10.1093/bjsw/bct115

O'Donoghue, K., Wong Yuh Ju, P., and Tsui, M.S., 2018. Constructing an evidence-informed social work supervision model. *European Journal of Social Work*, 21 (3), 348–358. doi:10.1080/13691457.2017.134 1387.

Olsen, D.C., and Stern, S.B., 1990. Issues in the development of a family supervision model. *The Clinical Supervisor*, 8 (2), 49–65.

Payne, C., and Scott, T., 1982. *Developing supervision of team in field and residential social work*. London: National Institute for Social Work.

Rich, P., 1993. The form, function, and content of clinical supervision: an integrated model. *The Clinical Supervisor*, 11 (1), 137–178.

Rock, B., 1990. Social worker autonomy in the age of accountability. *The Clinical Supervisor*, 8 (2), 19–31.

Sergiovanni, T.J., 1983. *Supervision: a perspective*. 3rd ed. New York: McGraw-Hill.

Shulman, L., 1982. *Skills of supervision and staff management*. Itasca, IL: Peacock Publishers.

Shulman, L., 1993. *Interactional supervision*. Washington, DC: NASW Press.

Shulman, L., 1995. Supervision and consultation. *In*: R. Edwards, and J. Hopps, eds. *Encyclopedia of Social Work*. 19th ed. Silver Spring, MD: NASW Press, 2373–2379.

Skipmore, R., 1995. *Social work administration: dynamic management and human relationships*. 3rd ed. Boston, MA: Allyn and Bacon.

Stoltenberg, C., 1981. Approaching supervision from a developmental perspective: the counselor complexity model. *Journal of Counseling Psychology*, 28 (1), 59–65.

Storm, C.L., and Heath, A.W., 1985. Models of supervision: using therapy theory as a guide. *The Clinical Supervisor*, 3 (1), 87–96.

Tsui, M.S., 1997. The roots of social work supervision: an historical review. *The Clinical Supervisor*, 15 (2), 191–198.

Tsui, M.S., 2001. *Towards a culturally sensitive model of social work supervision in Hong Kong*. Unpublished PhD Thesis, Toronto: University of Toronto. Available from: http://hdl.handle.net/1807/16196 [Accessed 12 July 2020].

Tsui, M.S., 2003. The supervisory relationship of Chinese social workers in Hong Kong. *The Clinical Supervisor*, 22 (2), 99–120.

Tsui, M.S., 2004. Charting the course of future research on supervision. *In* Austin, M.J., and Hopkins, K.M., eds. *Supervision as collaboration in the human services: building a learning culture*. Thousand Oaks, CA: SAGE, 272–280.

Tsui, M.S., 2005. *Social work supervision: contexts and concepts*. Thousand Oaks, CA: SAGE.

Tsui, M.S., 2008. Adventures in re-searching the features of social work supervision in Hong Kong. *Qualitative Social Work*, 7 (3), 349–362.

Tsui, M.S., and Ho, W.S., 1998. In search of a comprehensive model of social work supervision. *The Clinical Supervisor*, 16 (2), 181–205.

Tsui, M.S., Ho, W.S., and Lam, C.M., 2005. The use of supervisory authority in Chinese cultural context. *Administration in Social Work*, 29 (4), 51–68.

Tsui, M.S., O'Donoghue, K., and Ng, A.K.T., 2014. Culturally-competent and diversity-sensitive clinical supervision: an international perspective. *In*: Watkins, C.E. Jr., and Milne, D.L., eds. *International handbook of clinical supervision*. Oxford: John Wiley & Sons, 238–254.

Tsui, M.S., O'Donoghue, K., Boddy, J., and Pak, C.M., 2017. From supervision to organisational learning: a typology to integrate supervision, mentorship, consultation and coaching. *The British Journal of Social Work*, 47 (8), 2406–2420. doi:10.1093/bjsw/bcx006

Veeder, N.W., 1990. Autonomy, accountability and professionalism: the case against close supervision in social work. *The Clinical Supervisor*, 8 (2), 33–47.

Watson, K.W., 1973. Differential supervision. *Social Work*, 8 (3), 37–43.

Wax, J., 1979. The pros and cons of group supervision. *Social Casework*, 40, 307–313.

Worthington, E.L., 1984. Empirical investigation of supervision counselor as they can experience. *Journal of Counseling Psychology*, 31 (1), 63075.

26

THE INTEGRATED SUPERVISION MODEL

The 4×4×4

Fiona Mainstone and Jane Wonnacott

The 4×4×4 supervision model of supervision was developed organically over time by Tony Morrison, a well-respected social work trainer, educator, manager, and practitioner. The model emerged as he reflected on the experience of working with hundreds of supervisors and their organizations, both in the UK and elsewhere. Morrison first articulated this model in his seminal text *Staff Supervision in Social Care*, (Morrison 2005) and from the start there was an integrated approach which drew on theories of practice, management, and adult learning.

The model was developed by Morrison as a result of his work, which he later described as that of a "scholar-facilitator" (Morrison 2010). As a result, the model is derived from both formal and reflective knowledge: i.e. "practice wisdom" and as such, it is not set in stone but continues to develop and adapt to the ever changing social work environment as it is used by social work supervisors and trainers in their day to day work (Sturt and Rothwell 2019). Morrison (2010) asserted that theory can and should be generated by practice, placing practitioners as active producers of knowledge rather than merely as passive recipients of ideas published by academic researchers and theorists.

As a result, this model is practice-led as a matter of principle. Trainers and consultants working with social workers and organizations to implement the model do not impose knowledge, theory, and frameworks but instead share ideas and invite participants to consider how they might be relevant to them in their day to day practice, and to test and refine ideas in new practice and socio-cultural contexts. These explorations in turn elicit new conversations about how the ideas could be extended or expanded or adapted.

Another fundamental principle is that ideas should be understood using plain English without relying on jargon or esoteric vocabulary. One practical development has been to replace the term "4 × 4 × 4 model" by renaming it the "integrated model." This title describes the purpose and intention of the model within today's social work environment.

This chapter aims to describe the model, reflect on its relevance to contemporary social work practice, and consider future developments.

What is the integrated model?

The core purpose of the integrated model is to promote effective practice across the whole field of social work. The crucial significance of supervision reached professional consciousness in the UK with the publication of the Laming Report (2003). This report followed an inquiry into the death of Victoria Climbié in February 2000, whose circumstances were assessed repeatedly by both health and social care professionals but nevertheless died in London aged eight as a result of sustained harm inflicted by her carers. In the UK, Serious Case Reviews (now called Child Safeguarding Practice Reviews), which are conducted into child deaths and serious injury in England, have continued to reflect on the difference that supervision can make to the safety of both children and adults, with 44 of the 139 reviews published by the National Society for the Prevention of Cruelty to Children in 2018–19 mentioning supervision as a learning point or recommendation. Even where reviews of practice do not explicitly make the link with supervision, the repeated calls for more "professional curiosity," "respectful uncertainty," and the avoidance of bias and assumptions all give credence to the importance of supervision as an opportunity to stop, think, and to be challenged if effective practice is to flourish.

The small (but growing) body of academic research into the impact of supervision on practice suggests that this approach to supervision does increase job satisfaction, worker retention, and worker effectiveness (Carpenter et al. 2012, 2013; Wilkins and Antonopolou 2019). Combined with evidence from practice, this research indicates the value of an approach to supervision that enables effective social work practice to flourish.

Social work does not take place within a vacuum, and supervision needs to manage many layers of complexity and relationships with service users and colleagues within and outside the organization (Mainstone 2014). The importance of the model is that it moves beyond a focus on the supervisor/supervisee dyad, to a position which acknowledges complexity, the multi-faceted nature of the work, and the need for a whole organizational approach to supervision practice.

The integrated model enables us to bring together three quite different ways of conceptualizing the supervision process, each of which has four components:

- The four functions of supervision
- The four key stakeholders in supervision
- The four elements of the supervision cycle

This reflects the need for supervision to address a range of requirements on behalf of different stakeholders and involves a complex set of practical and cognitive activities. The model helps us understand the interdependence of the functions, the impact of supervision on four key stakeholders, and the need to think both reflectively and analytically about each family's unique story before forming a plan of action.

A functional approach to supervision was discussed within the supervision literature for many years. Kadushin (2002) identified three functions: management, support, and education. Subsequently, Richards et al. (1990) added mediation as the fourth function. Supervision policies and training often used to focus solely on the need for supervisors to deliver these functions during their supervision sessions. Indeed, Morrison (1993) initially replicated this approach, describing four functions. These functions are:

- Management: ensuring competent accountable practice and performance
- Development: supporting continuing professional development, promoting learning
- Support: providing a secure, restorative relationship

- Mediation: engaging the individual practitioner/team with the organization and serving as a bridge between the world of direct practice and the world of senior management/ politics

These four functions rely on each other to give a balanced approach to the supervision process. One cannot be performed effectively without the others, but supervisors can find it hard to pay equal attention to all four functions, especially where employing organizations impose specific procedural expectations. It is therefore not uncommon for the management function to dominate. Sometimes however, supervisors compensate for this by emphasizing the support function. This can lead to poor performance going unchallenged.

In discussions between supervisors and their organizations it became apparent that this functional, static approach to supervision did not reflect the aspiration of social work to make a positive difference to families. A more dynamic idea of the four "stakeholders" developed, and the model progressed from simply supporting supervisors to delivering the four functions. Training programs began to emphasize the need for individual supervisors *and the organization* to grasp the role that supervision should play in making a positive impact on service users, practitioners, partner organizations, and the organization itself.

Alongside this shift, working with supervisors, and drawing on knowledge derived from the field of adult learning (Schön 1983; Kolb 1984), Morrison (2005) introduced and developed the "supervision cycle," positioning this as the central point in the model. Morrison re-conceptualized stages of Kolb's original cycle as experience, reflection, understanding, plans, and action. He used the idea of "story" as a narrative metaphor describing the practitioner's engagement with the service user as they journey together through the cycle and integrated this practice cycle within the supervision cycle. This conscious integration of the two stories highlights the parallels between the practitioner's journey with the service user and the supervisor's journey with the practitioner.

With the addition of these four stages of the cycle (experience, reflection, analysis, and action) the supervision model became colloquially known as the 4×4×4 model. It was this model that was subsequently used as the foundation for a national supervisors training program in the UK in 2009 (Morrison and Wonnacott 2010). The development of this model has continued, and it is used in local and national training programs in the UK.

Figure 26.1 below aims to depict the dynamic nature of the model with all twelve components being interdependent on each other. This is a crucial aspect of the model that is not always fully conveyed in the supervision literature (Sturt and Rothwell 2019). Nor, indeed, is it always found in practice. For example, several research projects have found that practice supervisors in England often focus almost exclusively on case-management, while their managers, in turn, emphasize supervision's role in quality assurance and performance management (Baginsky et al. 2010; Turner-Daly and Jack 2017; Wilkins 2019).

Case-management discussions can, and should, be a vehicle for supporting the practitioner, identifying development needs and reflecting on the interface between the various parts of the system. Similarly, performance-management and support are not mutually exclusive with good management of performance including consideration of factors that might impact on practice and the member of staff's support needs. In the integrated model this is not a matter of either/or.

It is through:

- exploration of the day to day practice experience of the supervisee that oversight, and quality assurance of their work can take place, the service users voice be heard, and gaps in

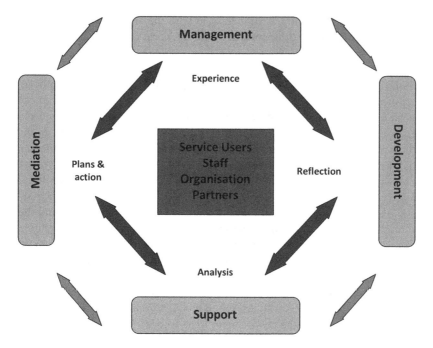

Figure 26.1 The integrated supervision model © Morrison and Wonnacott 2010, used with permission

information identified including issues that might relate to communication and relationships with partner organizations;

- the use of reflection that the emotional impact of the work can be explored, supervisee support needs identified, factors that might be affecting practice discussed and impact on work with service users considered;
- analysis that defensible decision making develops – important for all within the system;
- action planning that accountability is clear, service users can be properly involved, and barriers to delivery can be brought to the attention of the organization and partners.

The danger for practitioners and supervisees alike is that, under pressure to be seen to work quickly and efficiently (especially in times of austerity), reflection and analysis can come to feel like an unaffordable luxury. The reverse is true. When supervision bypasses reflection and analysis, judgments and plans based on superficial, incomplete, and unprocessed information are likely to be naïve and simplistic. This "quick fix" is far from being cost effective: it creates misguided intervention, poor outcomes, increased workloads, and unmanaged risk-taking.

Implicit within the diagram of the model is the crucial importance of a safe supervisory relationship. The model will not work unless time and attention is paid to the development of a contained space where the supervisee feels safe to explore sometimes difficult issues, and the boundaries between that space and the rest of the system are clearly understood. It is here that, once again, the organizational context is crucial. For example, organizations can promote and support the development of effective supervisory relationships by creating an explicit expectation that each practitioner will enter into an individualized "bespoke" supervision agreement negotiated with their supervisor to meet their own and the service needs.

Why is the integrated model relevant today?

Social workers face the dual challenge of managing profoundly complex and uncertain situations with access to only limited resources. Individuals and families that need the most social work support usually experience multiple problems such as poverty, physical and mental health concerns, engagement with the criminal justice system, and relationship difficulties. Alongside this, systems and services are often fragmented, individual organizations may work only with one service user, or with a single aspect of the problem. Social workers routinely work at the interface of many different systems and relationships. There will always be tensions, but the task of the social worker is to manage these, understand differing perspectives and holding multiple factors in mind throughout their day-to-day work. Disagreements between individuals and agencies will happen and social workers need to avoid becoming part of the problem through increased polarization and adversarial approaches.

The integrated model provides a framework for exploring and navigating the treacherous "swampy lowlands" of contemporary practice (Schön 1983). Working with this model, supervisors readily recognize that the complexity of the supervision process mirrors the complexity of contemporary humanistic social work practice.

How is the integrated model helpful today?

The next three sections of this chapter highlight how the integrated model of supervision contributes to effective supervision in each of the practice approaches which are commonly in use across different social work settings.

Relationship-based practice

The principles of relationship-based social work as social work's "vital thread" are widely espoused but may not always inform practice, let alone supervision (Ruch et al. 2018). The integrated model revolves around the supervisory relationship because, as Trevithick (2005) argued, the harnessing of the relationship as the vehicle for change is the defining characteristic of the social work profession. While many might agree with this assertion on a surface level, few, perhaps, have thought through its implications. Relationship based practice collides with and poses a fundamental challenge to managerial approaches to social work, foregrounding relationships, in all their ambiguity and messiness, above the bureaucratic, instrumental, and ostensibly rational foundations of contemporary practice" (Ingram and Smith 2018).

The supervision agreement describes a working alliance: a covenant between supervisor and supervisee that recognizes the psychological dimension of the work, and the significance of their relationship (Mena and Bailey 2007). When supervisors explore their own experiences of being supervised, the enduring impact of both dissonant and congruent relationships is evident. Exploring the cultural, personal, and organizational factors that can affect the supervisory relationship highlights the inevitable ambiguity within relationships that offer support and development functions alongside management and mediation. Personal, professional, and sociocultural factors intersect to create challenges that are unique to each supervisory relationship. Supervisors must acknowledge their legitimate role-authority and take responsibility for creating an authentic and trusting relationship, so that the working alliance transcends any disparities of privilege between them (Burnham 2014).

At best, trusting relationships support practitioners to utilize personal experiences of disadvantage, enhancing their work with people facing life difficulties, whilst also "mediating" their transition into their professional role in public service. Critical engagement with the Kolb cycle from within a safe supervisory relationship can

- check confirmatory bias;
- develop practitioners' willingness to acknowledge their own assumptions; and
- empower practitioners to challenge others.

This is crucial since the literature generated by service-user's perspectives suggests that toxic social work interventions arise where supervision has not been anchored to an empathic understanding of their lived experience (Wiffin 2010).

When supervisors in training rooms consider the personal qualities they especially value in a good supervisor, discussions almost invariably start with reflections on the heart, articulating the centrality of care and compassion, "heart-felt" connection, wisdom, spirituality, humanity, and generosity.

The secure-base model describes how carers can best look after the needs of traumatized children (Beek and Schofield 2017). Biggart et al. (2016) have applied the same idea to the needs of teams. Supervisors employ an impressive range of strategies to promote strong team relationships: from perk of the week to pay day breakfast, from clinical supervision to a stuffed toy that can be claimed and placed on the desk of anyone who is feeling vulnerable to alert others to their need for a bit of nurture. It seems that sharing food, rituals, and symbolism are as important in teams as they are in families and friendships.

The inevitable anxiety generated by working with trauma, loss, uncertainty, and complexity puts to the test supervisees' tried and trusted strategies for coping with stress. Supervisors need to be mindful of how habitual patterns of behavior play out in teams. When supervisors enable practitioners to process and manage their anxiety and distress, all is well. By contrast, where either or both bring less healthy strategies for managing anxiety, the relationship may be compromised. For example, the supervisor who feels it is always best to put on a brave face and resolve problems alone, may not warm to the supervisee who seems to need constant reassurance and support. Meanwhile, that same supervisee may experience this stoical supervisor as unresponsive and "hard-nosed" (Baim and Morrison 2011).

Using the reflective cycle to promote reflection in and on practice (Kolb 1984; Morrison 2010) helps ensure that the emotional impact of social work is harnessed as a positive force, develops practitioners' capacity for critical thinking, and supports them to build constructive relationships (Ruch 2007). Without reflective opportunities practitioners struggle to inform their work with all the sources of knowledge and insight available to them (Munro 2008). Moreover, when supervisors model reflective practice, and validate supervisees' willingness to empathize and reflect, this contributes to the resilience of individual workers and teams (Kinman and Grant 2011; McFadden et al. 2015).

When they investigate the synergy of these processes, supervisors usually come to the startling realization that reflection within the supervisory alliance is essential and not a luxury. Time invested in developing critical thinkers provides three benefits "for the price of one":

- improved outcomes for service users,
- personal and professional development,
- increased resilience …and therefore retention.

Where supervision provides a safe space, and supervisors engage in emotional listening, its impact goes well beyond simply enabling the individual to cope with adversity. It enables clarity, insight, harnesses hope, and promotes a sense of instrumentality (Ghaye 2000). The complex, fractured, and conflicted relationships social workers encounter within service-users' lives, teams, and professional networks demand high levels of emotional literacy (Howe 2008). Ruch (2002) emphasizes the potency of reflective supervision for what Trevithick (2018) describes as "use of self." When practitioners are encouraged to recognize and name their own emotions, to read the feeling state of others, self-regulate, and manage other people's feelings, their influence extends across the lives of service-users, professional networks, and organizations.

There are numerous examples from reviews of practice as to the importance of paying attention to the emotional impact of the work as a foundation for effective relationship-based practice. For example, a serious case review into the death of a young man from a drug overdose whilst in the care of the local authority (Barnet Safeguarding Children Board 2018) found that although on the surface relationships with him were good, supervision had not helped practitioners to recognize the underlying dynamics and the way their emotional reactions to him had prevented a focus on risky behavior. For example, professionals felt that he was probably exaggerating his use of Class A drugs, because they perceived him as routinely over-dramatizing events.

At the other end of the spectrum, working with fear and hostility without effective support and supervision has been found to lead to hostage-like behavior (Stanley and Goddard 2002) on the part of practitioners who form alliances with the violent family member, with relationships becoming unhealthily skewed and a loss of focus on risks to vulnerable people within the family.

Strengths-based practice and restorative social work

The integrated model is congruent with strengths-based approaches but is not aligned to any one specific practice model. Encouraging supervisors to consider their role in developing practitioners' full potential does not negate or undermine any of the managerial/organizational functions associated with supervision, but it does draw a distinction between supervising the practitioner and micro-managing social work tasks. Since everyone has the wisdom and skill to resolve the problems they encounter, the supervisor's task is to illuminate this expertise.

The integration of all four management functions means that, like parents, supervisors must achieve the right balance of support and demand for each of their charges (Calder and Hackett 2003). This support-demand dynamic resonates with the emphasis in strengths-based approaches on amplifying peoples' unique resources and potential alongside challenging them to commit to achieving specific goals for change. The structure of the supervision cycle supports supervisors' attention to each individual practitioner's developmental needs, while still insisting on criticality and independence.

Restorative Practice rests on the premise that people are happier, more productive, and more likely to change when those in authority work "with" them (Kelly 2014). A supervisor and supervisee sitting down to puzzle their way through the supervision cycle together is a clear example of committed "working with," in contrast to the linear and one-dimensional case management approach that Wilkins (2017a) has identified as commonplace in the UK. Developing practitioners' instrumentality empowers them to embrace professional autonomy and discourages them from feeling entitled to continuous direction.

Strengths-based tools that focus on identifying and progressing towards specific goals support the managerial tasks of audit and quality assurance (Mainstone 1998; Davys and Beddoe 2010). The supervision cycle concludes with a focus on action plans to secure best outcomes for service users. Encouraging practitioners to identify specific named goals creates clarity of purpose, driving active engagement with service-users and the professional network. Developing practitioners' use of the supervision cycle to think creatively, experiment, and manage complexity generates confidence to take constructive risks and live with "safe uncertainty" (Mason 1993; Duguid and Mayhew 2016).

The ethos of challenge without blame is implicit in the supervision cycle's rigorous pursuit of reflection and analysis. The offer of emotional listening balanced with the expectation that the supervisee will take responsibility for robust analysis, positions the supervisor as a "critical friend." This provides a context that supports supervisors to fulfil all four management functions in equal measure. This stance echoes the aspiration in Appreciative Inquiry to help people "realize their sleeping skills" and achieve optimal performance (Turner 2012).

The principle behind the supervision cycle is that although we might have an individual preference to dwell in just one part of the cycle, social work requires practitioners to develop their capacity to engage with all four ways of thinking. This demands the will to step outside habitual comfort zones, commitment to personal/professional development, and an openness to change. The guidance supervisors offer within the supervision cycle enables the practitioner to embrace that challenge. This mirrors the message within the five-factor model of personality that peoples' strengths are the flip side of their vulnerabilities, and that practitioners can transform their weaknesses by understanding them as potential resources (John et al. 2008).

Strengths-based approaches generally encourage us to identify the exceptions to problem-behavior, expand all existing assets, and promote resilience (Berg 2009; Department of Health and Social Care 2019). These perspectives are especially relevant wherever supervisors need to develop a practitioner whose work is compromised by poor capability (Mainstone 1998). Where performance concerns arise out of non-compliance, a focus on setting achievable time-limited goals (Turnell and Edwards 1999; McCarthy 2002; Wahab 2005) is compliant with performance management principles and procedures.

Tragically, practitioners working in strengths-based services have reported an unintentional negative consequence of naively espousing this approach: identifying people's innate resourcefulness and potential can lead to benefits, care, support, or services being withdrawn or withheld. Just as the Recovery Model (Bonney and Stickley 2008) should not disadvantage people with enduring emotional and psychological distress, strengths-based supervision must not bring with it the unfair expectation that practitioners should be tireless and resilient in the face of overwhelming challenges. The integrated model helps us to move beyond a focus on individual resilience to achieve an understanding of how the supervisor can mediate between the workforce and senior management: "managing-up" to build organizational resilience.

Systemic social Work

The integrated model rests on the systemic principle that supervision is a process that takes place within, and is affected by multiple contexts, and simultaneously influences them (Brown and Bourne 1996; Burnham 2010). Effective supervision hinges not only on what happens within timetabled one-to-one conversations behind a closed door, but also on the supervisory relationship within the context of the team, organization, and professional network. The integrated model encourages supervisors to embrace systemic support, and learning and development fora outside the one-to-one, such as action learning and peer supervision. The value of wider opportunities for reflection alongside individual supervision is endorsed by recent research (Wilkins 2017b).

Where management of task, and compliance with procedures is privileged over an integrated, holistic approach to supervision, practitioners have difficulty in moving from simply gathering facts towards evaluating the significance of information, synthesizing different perspectives, and forming professional judgment (Brown and Turney 2014; Wilkins 2017a). This mechanistic and linear approach to decision-making is not only detrimental to practice which is less likely to manage multiple layers of complexity across the family and professional system but also to individual professional progress and workforce development.

Mindful practice of the Kolb cycle puts supervisors "on the spot" to consider why and how they ask questions. Conceptualizing every inquiry as an intervention demands that supervisors consciously design questions intended to address the practitioner's developmental need, and influence their cognitive process, as well as inform casework decisions. The rich repertoire of questioning styles developed in the field of family therapy are integral to this approach to supervision since they equip supervisors with tools to encourage critical reflection.

When they reflect on relationship dynamics within their team, challenges and difficulties within the professional network, and indeed their own connection with supervisees, supervisors often begin by applying their understanding of the "drama triangle" and "games people play" to the challenges they encounter (Berne 1964; Karpman 1968). These were explored in the first iteration of the integrated model (Morrison 1993) and continue to be relevant as social work practice has continued to develop and embrace systemic practice which encourages supervisors to examine the uncertainties and complexities of all interpersonal communication.

"Containment," the experience of attentive supervision that affords exploration of difficult feelings and conflicted states of mind, impacts directly on the quality of relationship practitioners can offer to service-users (Ferguson 2010). This psycho-dynamic concept is sometimes misunderstood as something that the supervisor does "to" or "for" the supervisee. It is more helpful to understand containment as a process that arises out of engagement with each other. Systems theorists refer to this as "relational reflexivity" (Burnham 1993). Reflective supervision allows practitioners to have their needs met, resolve and heal from the impact of painful experiences, and then focus on service-users' needs and uniquely difficult life experiences. This capacity then extends into the often fraught inter-disciplinary dynamic and can sustain their sense of agency as part of a large organization (Menzies-Lyth 1988). Three different dimensions of containment: personal, epistemological, and organizational, come together, intersect, and potentiate each other to orchestrate a secure base from which social workers can develop best practice (Beek and Schofield 2016; Toasland 2007).

When we are asked to design supervision development programs intended to support whole system change, we often incorporate action learning sets, inter-professional supervision, peer observations of supervisory practice. These enable the supervisor to develop in a more rounded way, responding incrementally to different approaches and influences. This holistic approach generates multiple opportunities for supervisors to expand their own capacity for reflection and analysis. As these programs unfold, it becomes clear that fundamental changes in attitude and understanding take place as supervisors assimilate their personal experience and professional expertise.

Morrison used the term "mirroring" as a metaphor that expands upon the phenomena understood by systemic family therapists as "parallel process" and referred to in the psycho-dynamic tradition as "transference and countertransference." The relationship between a supervisor and their supervisee can provide a positive model for the relationship between the practitioner and the people they serve. This relationship, in turn, is mirrored again in the relationship between the parent and their child or a vulnerable adult and their carer. When the supervisor offers

- a relationship that conveys empathy, care, compassion, and generosity
- an authoritative balance of support/demand
- insightful questions that act as interventions

- the message that people can generate their own solutions to difficulties they encounter
- commitment to eliciting expertise through experience
- acknowledgement of advantage/disadvantage
- flexibility to adapt to and meet differing needs
- approachability
- cultural competence
- emotional literacy
- a can-do mindset
- honesty and authenticity as the source of trust
- containment

the supervisee can internalize these positive experiences and then create a benign cycle that replicates them in their own direct work with people. Conversely, poor supervision is mirrored in flawed practice, for example, where resistance arises it is usually a product of dissonance whether between supervisor and supervisee or in the practice relationship. An organizational "culture of no challenge" to poor performance arises out of the failure of role authority in the same way as "disguised compliance."

In this understanding of mirroring, the relationship dynamic enacted in supervision has a powerful impact on the supervisee's practice. This is more than a simple, observable parallel process. When the supervisor models best practice this ripples down and through the whole system. Systemic leadership recognizes the power of integrated, holistic supervision to influence and improve practice.

The future of the integrated supervision model

The fundamental purpose of the integrated model is to empower practitioners to, in turn, empower people to achieve lives that are safe, fulfil potential, and ensure well-being. It is intended to serve as a foundation for humane, ethical social work practice.

Unfortunately, the profession has achieved only limited understanding of how supervision contributes to effective social work. This gap in our knowledge deserves focused investigation. Across the past ten years or so social work academics have taken a long overdue and very welcome new interest in supervision processes. The opening paragraphs of this chapter outlined the principles of a practice epistemology where practitioners, supervisors, and scholar-facilitators generate and test knowledge (Morrison 2010). We hope that future investigations will be designed from this perspective and will help to unravel some of the most immediate challenges, so that supervision can make a real difference to practice outcomes.

Whether and how supervision influences positive outcomes for service users (Wilkins 2019) is one of the most significant gaps in our understanding. Future investigations will need to actively harness the insights and wisdom of service users, so that we can reach a clearer understanding of how they perceive the influence of supervision in social work intervention, and how social work impacts on their lives. We know that supervision has always felt crucially important within this profession. There is a need to explore the experience and expertise of social work practitioners, supervisors, and leaders, in order to understand why this sense of its significance endures.

Solutions to the challenges of "working together" across the professional network remain elusive. Poor inter-agency communication, fractured relationships, and failures of coordinated planning still compromise practice despite the proliferation of procedures and protocols. Scholar-facilitators using the integrated model are passionate about working with practitioners and supervisors to continue developing the model. Interdisciplinary initiatives offer rich opportunities to support the best possible practice solutions, as well as understand the challenges and barriers that may need to be overcome for this to happen. (Sturt and Rothwell 2019).

The integrated model has been used extensively throughout the UK for more than a decade, and it has been widely adopted in other English-speaking jurisdictions. An innovative training program based on this model was recently piloted with four cohorts in South-East Asia. Since practice knowledge is always emergent and provisional, we look forward to testing and refining the integrated model in new practice and socio-cultural contexts across the continents.

Bibliography

Baginsky, M., Moriarty, J., Manthorpe, J., Stevens, M., MacInnes, T., and Nagendran, T., 2010. Social workers' workload survey: messages from the frontline: findings from the 2009 survey and interviews with senior managers. Department for Children, Schools and Families. http://dera.ioe.ac.uk/1945/1/SWTF%20Workload%20Survey%20(final).pdf [Accessed 4 March 2021]

Baim, C., and Morrison, T., 2011. *Attachment-based practice with adults*. Brighton: Pavilion.

Barnet Safeguarding Children Board 2018. *Serious case review Child E.* https://library.nspcc.org.uk/HeritageScripts/Hapi.dll/search2?searchTerm0=C7457.

Beek, M., and Schofield, G., 2014. *The secure base model: promoting attachment and resilience in foster care and adoption*. London: British Association of Adoption and Fostering.

Berg, C.J., 2009. A comprehensive framework for conducting client assessments: highlighting strengths, environmental factors and hope. *Journal of Practical Consulting*, 3 (2), 9–13.

Berne, E., 1964. *Games people play: the psychology of human relationships*. Middlesex: Penguin.

Biggart, L., Ward, E., Cook, L., and Schofield, G., 2016. Team as secure base. Copyright © 2018 (Team as Secure Base) University of East Anglia (UEA). All rights reserved.

Bonney, S., and Stickley, T., 2008. Recovery and mental health: a review of the British literature. *Journal of Psychiatric & Mental Health Nursing*, 15, 140–153.

Bowyer, S., and Roe, A., 2015. *Social work recruitment and retention*. Dartington: Research in Practice.

Brown, A., and Bourne, I., 1996. *The social work supervisor*. Buckingham and Philadelphia: Open University Press.

Brown, L., and Turney, D., 2014. *Analysis and critical thinking in assessment*. Dartington: Research in Practice.

Burnham, J., 1993. Systemic supervision: the evolution of reflexivity in the context of the supervisory relationships. *Human Systems. The Journal of Systemic Consultation and Management*, 4 (3–4), 349–381.

Burnham, J., 2010. Creating reflexive relationships between practices of systemic supervision and theories of learning and education. *In*: C. Burck and G. Daniel, eds. *Mirrors and reflections: processes of systemic supervision*. London: Karnac, 49–78.

Burnham, J., 2014. "Which aspects of social GGRRAAACCEEESSS grab you most?" The social GGRRAAACCEEESSS exercise for a supervision group to promote therapists' self-reflexivity. *Journal of Family Therapy*, 36, 1S.

Calder, M.C., and Hackett, S., 2003. *Assessment in child care. Using and developing frameworks for practice*. Lyme Regis: Russell House Publishing.

Carpenter, J., Webb, C., and Bostock, L., 2013. The surprisingly weak evidence base for supervision: findings from a systematic review of research in child welfare practice (2000 - 2012). *Children and Youth Services Review*, 35, 1843–1853.

Carpenter, J., Webb, C., Bostock, L., and Coomber, C., 2012. *Effective supervision in social work and social care. (SCIE research briefing 43)*. London: Social Care Institute for Excellence.

Chen, S., and Scannapieco, M., 2010. The influence of job satisfaction on child welfare worker's desire to stay: an examination of the interaction effect of self-efficacy and supportive supervision. *Children and Youth Services Review*, 32 (4), 482–486.

Davys, A., and Beddoe, L., 2010. *Best practice in professional supervision: a guide for the helping professions*. London: Jessica Kingsley.

Department of Health and Social Care 2019. *Strengths-based approach: practice framework and practice handbook*. London: Stationery Office.

Duguid, A., and Mayhew, E., 2016. *Safe uncertainty*. Essex Safeguarding Children Board.

Earle, F., Fox, J., Webb, C., and Bowyer, S., 2017. *Reflective* supervision resource pack. Dartington: Research in Practice.

Ellett, A.J., 2009. Intentions to remain employed in child welfare. The role of human caring, self-efficacy beliefs, and professional organizational culture. *Children and Youth Services Review*, 31 (1), 78–88.

Fairclough, A., 2017. *Professional leadership for social work practitioners and educators.* Abingdon and New York: Routledge.

Ferguson, H., 2010. Walks, home visits and atmospheres: risk and the everyday practices and mobilities of social work and child protection. *The British Journal of Social Work*, 40 (4), 1100–1117. doi:10.1093/bjsw/bcq015

Ferguson, H., 2011. *Child protection practice.* Basingstoke: Palgrave MacMillan.

Ferguson, H., 2018. How social workers reflect in action and when and why they don't: the possibilities and limits to reflective practice in social work. *Social Work Education*, 37 (4), 415–427.

Forrester, D., Westlake, D., and Glynn, G., 2012. Parental resistance and social worker skills: towards a theory of motivational social work. *Child and Family Social Work*, 17 (2), 118–129.

Ghaye, T., 2000. Into the reflective mode: bridging the stagnant moat. *Reflective Practice*, 1 (1), 5–9.

Gibbs, J., Dwyer, J., and Vivekananda, K., 2014. *Leading practice: a resource guide for child protection leaders.* Melbourne: Child Protection, Victorian Government Department of Human Services.

Horwath, J., and Morrison, T., 2007. Collaboration, integration and change in children's services: critical issues and key ingredients. *Child Abuse and Neglect*, 31 (6), 1, 55–9.

Howe, D., 2008. *The emotionally intelligent social worker.* Basingstoke: Palgrave MacMillan.

Ingram, R., and Smith, M., 2018. Relationship-based practice: emergent themes in social work literature. *IRISS, Insight*, 41.

John, O.P., Naumann, L.P., and Soto, C.J., 2008. Paradigm shift to the integrative big five trait taxonomy: history, measurement, and conceptual issues. *In*: O.P. John, R.W. Robins, and L.A. Pervin, eds. *Handbook of personality: theory research*. New York: Guilford, 114–158.

Kadushin, A., 2002. *Supervision in social work.* New York: Columbia University Press.

Karpman, S., 1968. Fairy tales and script drama analysis. *Transactional Analysis Bulletin*, 7 (26), 39–43.

Kelly, V., 2014. *The psychology of emotion in restorative practice.* London: Jessica Kingsley.

Kinman, G., and Grant, L., 2011. Exploring stress resilience in trainee social workers: the role of emotional and social competencies. *British Journal of Social Work*, 41 (2), 261–275.

Kinman, G., and Grant, L., 2016. *Building emotional resilience in the children and families workforce. An evidence-informed approach.* Dartington: Research in Practice.

Koenig, T., and Spano, R., 2007. The cultivation of social workers' hope in personal life and professional practice. *Journal of Religion and Spirituality in Social work: Social Thought*, 26 (3), 45–61.

Kolb, D., 1984. *Experiential learning: experience as the source of learning and development.* Englewood Cliffs, NJ: Prentice-Hall.

Laming, W.H., 2003. *The Victoria Climbie inquiry report.* London: Stationery Office.

Laming, W.H., 2009. *The protection of children in England.* London: Stationery Office.

Mainstone, F., 1998. Practice teaching: a solutions focused approach. *In*: H. Lawson, ed. *Practice teaching changing social work*. London: Jessica Kingsley.

Mainstone, F., 2014. *Mastering whole family assessment. Balancing the needs of children, adults and their families.* London: Jessica Kingsley.

Mason, B., 1993. Towards a position of safe uncertainty. *Human Systems*, 4, 189–200.

McArthy, J.C., 2002. Motivational interviewing in the workplace. *In*: D.S. Sandu, ed. *Counselling employees: a multi-faceted approach*. Alexandria VA: American Counselling Association.

McCold, P., and Wachtel, T., 2001. Restorative justice in everyday life. *In*: J. Braithwaite and H. Strang, eds. *Restorative justice and civil society*. Cambridge: University Press.

McFadden, P., Campbell, A., and Taylor, B., 2015. Resilience and burnout in child protection social work: individual and organizational themes from a systematic literature review. *British Journal of Social Work*, 45 (5), 1546–1563.

Mena, K., and Bailey, J., 2007. The effects of the supervisory working alliance on worker outcomes. *Journal of Social Service Research*, 34 (1), 55–65.

Menzies-Lyth, I., 1988. *Containing anxiety in institutions.* London: Free Association Books.

Morrison, T., 1993. *Staff supervision in social care.* Essex: Longman.

Morrison, T., 2005. *Staff supervision in social care.* Brighton: Pavilion.

Morrison, T., 2010. *The role of the scholar-facilitator in generating practice knowledge to inform and enhance the quality of relationship-based social work practice with children and families. A critical review and analysis.* PhD by Publication: University of Huddersfield. http://eprints.hud.ac.uk/id/eprint/9005/1/Tmorrisonfinalthesis.pdf.

Morrison, T., and Wonnacott, J., 2010. *Supervision: now or never.* Reclaiming reflective supervision in social work. http://www.in-trac.co.uk/supervision-now-or-never/.

Munro, E., 2008. *Effective child protection.* London: SAGE.

Munro, E., 2010. *Munro review of child protection: interim report – the child's journey.* London: Stationery Office.

O'Sullivan, N., 2018. Creating space to think and feel in child protection social work; a psychodynamic intervention. *Journal of Social Work Practice*, 1–11.

Office for Standards in Education, Children's Services and Skills 2012. *High expectations, high support and high challenge.* Manchester: OFSTED. http://www.ofsted.gov.uk/resources/110120.

Richards, M., Payne, C., and Sheppard, A., 1990. *Staff supervision in child protection work.* London: National Institute of Social Work.

Rothwell, B., and Sturt, P., 2019. Implementing the integrated model of supervision: a view from the training room. *Aotearoa New Zealand Social Work Journal*, 31 (3), 116 –121.

Ruch, G., 2002. From triangle to spiral: reflective practice in social work education, practice and research. *Social Work Education*, 21 (2), 199–216.

Ruch, G., 2005. Relationship based practice and reflective practice: holistic approaches to contemporary childcare social work. *Child and Family Social Work*, 10 (2), 111–123.

Ruch, G., 2007. Reflective practice in contemporary child-care social work: the role of containment. *British Journal of Social Work*, 37 (4), 659–680.

Ruch, G., Turney, L., and Ward, A., 2018. *Relationship-based social work. Getting to the heart of practice.* 2nd ed. London: Jessica Kingsley.

Schon, D.A., 1983. *The reflective practitioner. How practitioners think in action.* New York: Basic Books.

Stanley, J., and Goddard, C., 2002. *In the firing line: violence and power in child protection work.* Chichester: Wiley.

Toasland, J., 2007. Containing the container: an exploration of the containing role of management in a social work context. *Journal of Social Work Practice*, 21 (2), 197–202.

Trevithick, P., 2005. *Social work skills: a practice handbook. so, what can we do to help social workers to help families to enact change?* Milton Keynes: Open University Press.

Trevithick, P., 2018. The "self" and "use of self" in social work: a contribution to the development of a coherent theoretical framework. *British Journal of Social Work*, 48 (7), 1836–1854.

Turnell, A., and Edwards, S., 1999. *Signs of safety: a solution and safety oriented approach to child protection casework.* New York: Norton.

Turner, S., 2012. *Appreciative scrutiny. A guide to using appreciative inquiry to add value to overview and scrutiny.* London: Centre for Public Scrutiny.

Turner-Daly, B., and Jack, G., 2017. Rhetoric vs. reality in social work supervision: the experiences of a group of child care social workers in England. *Child & Family Social Work*, 22 (1), 36–46. doi:10.1111/cfs.12191

Wahab, S., 2005. Motivational interviewing and social work practice. *Journal of Social Work*, 5 (1), 45–60.

Wiffin, J., 2010. *Family perspectives on safeguarding and on relationships with children's services.* London: Office of the Children's Commissioner.

Wilkins, D., 2017a. Does reflective supervision have a future in English local authority child and family social work?. *Journal of Children's Services*, 12 (2/3), 163–173.

Wilkins, D., 2017b. How is supervision recorded in child and family social work? An analysis of 244 written records of formal supervision. *Child & Family Social Work*, 22 (3), 1130–1140. doi:10.1111/cfs.12330

Wilkins, D., 2019. Social work supervision in child and family services: developing a working theory of how and why it works. *Aotearoa New Zealand Social Work Journal*, 31 (3), 7–19.

Wilkins, D., and Antonopoulou, V., 2019. What does supervision help with? A survey of 315 social workers in the UK. *Practice: Social Work in Action*, 31 (1), 21–40.

Wilkins, D., Forrester, D., and Grant, L., 2017. What happens in child and family social work supervision?. *Child and Family Social Work*, 22 (2), 942–951.

Wilkins, D., Lynch, A., and Antonopoulou, V., 2018. A golden thread? The relationship between supervision, practice and family engagement in child and family social work. *Child and Family Social Work*, 23 (3), 494–593.

Wonnacott, J., 2012. *Mastering social work supervision.* London: Jessica Kingsley.

27

EFFECTIVE SUPERVISION IN CHILD PROTECTION

An integrative Australian model

Lynne McPherson and Noel Macnamara

Supervision in child protection social work is a "hot" topic, with calls for improvements in this area typically recommended by major inquiries, across Australia and internationally. Such recommendations assume that what constitutes effective supervision in child protection is known and that evidence informed implementation strategies can be drawn upon. This chapter reports on emerging evidence in relation to "what works" in child protection supervision. The project built on previous research which culminated in the development of a new conceptual model of supervision. Recently, more than 100 Australian child protection supervisors were trained in the conceptual model, known as the Integrative Model of Supervision. Participants' use of the model was tracked over time. A primarily qualitative research design enabled the gathering of stories from the participants who were invited to reflect upon the application of this model in the workplace. The chapter presents some surprising findings, concluding that enhanced supervision and leadership in this turbulent field of practice, is possible.

Child protection practice across the world is a highly contested, politically sensitive field of practice. Formal inquiries are commonly commissioned by governments to examine the service system and to make recommendations for change, in a bid to address intractable problems (Cummins Scott and Scales 2012; House of Commons Committee of Public Accounts 2016; Munro 2011; Queensland Child Protection Commission of Inquiry 2013; Swain 2014). Typically, these multimillion-dollar investigations make comments about supervision of the child protection workforce and recommend improved implementation of supervision arrangements for practitioners (Cummins Scott and Scales 2012; Munro 2011). Calls for improvements to supervision practice and implementation are routinely identified as one of several panaceas for a troubled service system. These recommendations assume that there is a consensus about models of supervision which are known to strengthen child protection practice. In addition, they assume that current knowledge exists about the ways in which new models of supervision can be effectively implemented within organizations. The literature on staff supervision in social work illuminates different approaches to and processes of support (Davys and Beddoe 2010) and has only begun to explore the link between supervision, the quality of practice, and service-user outcomes (Wilkins et al. 2018).

Supervision has been identified as both "context dependent" and "context specific," posing a challenge for the development of a universally accepted supervision framework or conceptual model of supervision (Davys and Beddoe 2010). An emphasis on context is consistent with an understanding that social work practice itself is committed to a person-in environment perspective and as such, is ensconced in local conditions as a "place based" profession. The organizational and socio-political context within which supervision takes place may also be seen as a critical influence on the quality of practice, in what has been identified as an emotionally charged environment in child protection (Gibbs 2001; McPherson et al. 2016; McPherson and Macnamara 2017). An organizational culture, for example, that promotes learning and reflection may be more likely to value the educative functions of supervision and to promote the integration of theory, research, and practice at the frontline (Collins et al. 2010; McPherson and Macnamara 2017).

The nature of the work in child protection practice is well established as that which is uncertain, distressing, and at times positively dangerous for frontline practitioners. Anxiety, stress, secondary stress, compassion fatigue, vicarious trauma, and burnout are among the potential negative outcomes of practicing in this field (Gibbs 2001; McPherson and Macnamara 2017). An emerging body of knowledge focused on complex trauma is paving the way for a new appreciation of the potential neurobiological impact of toxic stress (Cozolino 2017; Seigal 2012) with the subsequent identification of the risk of secondary trauma to professionals, relevant to child protection practice and consequently supervision of practice. Vicarious trauma has been defined as those negative or traumatic emotional experiences where "observers and listeners have not actually been exposed to the event, though they can really feel it" (Rothschild 2006, p. 4). The role of supervision becomes even more complex when we consider the importance of the supervisory relationship and relational interactions between supervisor and supervisee as essentially at the heart of what is often described as the support function of supervision (Kadushin and Harkness 2002; Morrison 2005). Ironically, it is the relationship between supervisor and supervisee that emerges in the literature as a key contested issue (McPherson et al. 2016). Issues of power and politics are cited as important contextual issues leading to the potential for tension "within the role, function and purpose of supervision…" in particular where supervisors are also line managers of their supervisees (Adamson 2012, p. 185). It was within this complex and contested context that a conceptual model of supervision evolved. The evolution of the model and the model itself are outlined below.

A social ecological lens to report on findings: What is effective supervision?

A small, exploratory study was undertaken involving experienced and post graduate qualified supervisees and supervisors engaged in child and family practice in Australia. The central question addressed in this study was "what is effective supervision?" In-depth interviews were conducted with 20 purposively selected supervisees and supervisors in child and family practice using a semi structured interview schedule. A qualitative methodology was adopted to ensure that the voices of participants were captured and the data interrogated for an in-depth exploration allowing for consideration of the context within which participants constructed their responses (Liamputtong 2017). Data were analyzed using a thematic inductive approach which drew upon the six stage model of thematic analysis developed by Braun and Clarke (2006, 2012). Ethical clearance was granted to conduct the research by La Trobe University (11–082).

The findings of this study were reported using a social ecological lens (Belsky 1980) identifying implications for child protection supervision spanning four levels; the individual, relational, organizational, and community levels (McPherson 2014).

At the individual level, that of ontological development (Belsky 1980), findings indicated that in order for supervision to be effective, attention should be paid to what each of the individual players, supervisee and supervisor, bring to the relationship. In particular, a focus on the developmental and socio-cultural histories of each individual is seen as important, including personal and professional experiences, that may influence individual values and beliefs about childhood, parenting, and attitudes toward supervision. Consideration of these issues at the commencement of a supervisory relationship may promote an understanding of mutual expectations and responsibilities within supervision. Findings also suggested that this required a preparedness on the part of supervisees to identify and share their perceived knowledge "gaps" and areas of personal and professional vulnerability. The latter brings the issue of supervisory relationship into sharp focus (McPherson 2014).

At this second, micro level, findings in respect of the nature, purpose, and quality of the supervisory relationship indicated a strong theme of "safety" as being of paramount importance. This will be elaborated upon in presenting the model of supervision that was developed, however noted here is the central purpose of supervision in child protection practice. The purpose is to enhance the quality of service delivery to vulnerable children and their families, using the vehicle of an effective supervisory relationship. Findings suggested that effective supervisors actively consider and work with issues of power, gender, culture, and "difference" in the context of a safe relationship (Davys and Beddoe 2010; Wonnacott 2012). The powerful impact of unbearable levels of complexity and anxiety on social workers requires much greater recognition (Ferguson 2017). Theories of social neuroscience were seen to make a useful contribution to the construction of the supervisory relationship, highlighting the critical importance for supervisors in their "use of self" as an empathetic listener who is emotionally regulated, calm, and considered (Cozolino 2017).

At the third level of consideration, the exo system, the focus here is on the "world of work," or organizational context within which supervision takes place. Findings suggested a need for organizational congruence between relationships at the micro level and wider organizational behaviors. This congruence included the need for managers to promote reflective practice, to minimize requirements for compliance to procedure, and to facilitate professional growth and development of knowledge.

Organizations enabling effective supervision were seen to be those that developed a dominant organizational culture that was experienced as "trauma informed" (Bloom and Farragher 2011) and therefore was nurturing, healing, and supportive of strong team relationships and networks. These organizations facilitated open communication, were open to critical feedback, and valued diversity.

Fourthly, the findings drew attention to the relevance of the macro system or wider social and political context within which social work supervision in child protection operates. Neoliberal constructions which may enable individual "pathologizing" of social issues including poverty and structural disadvantage were found to disempower social workers at the front line of practice, in what is experienced by them as a highly complex context. Conversely, a community which demonstrated a commitment to social justice, evidenced by resourcing and policy and which valued the professionalism of social workers charged with responsibility to practice in child protection, was identified as one which would enable organizations supervising practitioners to flourish (McPherson 2014).

The integrative model of supervision (IMS)

The findings summarized above have been reported elsewhere (McPherson 2014). They informed and formed the basis of the Integrative Model of Supervision (IMS). The IMS is an aspirational model, comprising five dimensions of supervision of child protection practice. Each of the five dimensions is integrated and enacted within the context of child protection practice, recognized as a turbulent and potentially traumatizing field of social work. What follows is an overview of each of the five dimensions.

Dimension one: Keeping the child in mind

At the heart of the model is the child, seen in the context of their family, culture, and community. This first dimension establishes the ultimate purpose of supervision in child protection to ensure a well-informed, culturally responsive focus on the child. Supervisors are challenged to empower child protection practitioners to maintain a focus on children's developmental needs whilst working to strengthen and empower families and communities to care for them. It has been suggested that in the child protection system, children can all too easily become objects of concern rather than living breathing individuals:

> "Reviews of cases in which children have died invariably contain scenes where professionals were in the presence of abused children, most often in their home, but the workers did not get close enough to them to discover the abuse."
>
> *(Ferguson 2017, p. 1009)*

This dimension is consistent with the United Nations Convention on the Rights of the Child (UNCROC 1989). Article 3 (1) of the Convention states:

> "In all actions concerning children, whether undertaken by public or private social welfare institutions, courts of law, administrative authorities or legislative bodies, the best interests of the child shall be a primary consideration." (UN General Assembly 1989, p. 3, 1). The principle of children's best interests and subsequent calls for child centered practice have been contested over time in their application to child protection practice. Concern about who the primary "client" in child protection is, can cause division and conflict amongst professional groups seeking to serve and strengthen the child and family, often focusing on debates in relation to the dichotomy of individual children's safety versus prevention and family strengthening (McPherson 2014). The IMS locates the vulnerable child as the central focus as primary client, however, articulates that the child must be seen in the context of their family, culture, and community. In doing this the critical importance of family and cultural connections are articulated as integral to the child's identity and wellbeing.

Reflecting that this first dimension is "at the heart" of the IMS (McPherson and Macnamara 2017, p. 28), supervision aims to promote and maintain "child centered practice" in accordance with practice principles which seek to: strengthen children's development, promote family decision making, facilitate children's participation in decisions about their lives, and share knowledge across networks and promote a collaborative approach (Winkworth and McArthur 2006). Social workers are supported to develop collaborative and empowering relationships with children and young people, using the practice of "exquisite empathy" as a practice tool which is founded on deep listening and "empathetic attunement" (Harrison and Westwood 2009).

Dimension two: Knowledge and skill development

This second dimension promotes a wide perspective and multiple sources of knowledge, including theoretical and research knowledge, cultural knowledge, self-knowledge, and practice wisdom (Thompson and West 2013). Contemporary approaches to learning involve a collaborative process that does not assume that the supervisor holds all expertise. Rather, an active exploration of case related material that is under discussion, enables opportunity for critical reflection and an examination of ambiguity, uncertainty, and complexity. Within this second dimension a three-staged model of critical reflection was designed to respond to the unique context of child protection practice. The phases identified build on the work of Gardner's two phases of critical reflection (2014), offering additional "scaffolding" for child protection practitioners to pause and to work through each of the phases. This important distinction recognizes the difficulty that child protection practitioners may have in integrating what may be overwhelming and at times traumatizing practice experiences with relevant theory, research, and practice wisdom. The addition of a guided phase in the reflective process offers an opportunity to child protection practitioners to co-regulate, debrief, and ultimately to learn.

Phase one in critical reflection is an initial analysis and exploration of issues. Here the supervisee/practitioner leads the discussion, taking responsibility to identify the purpose of the reflection and to name what the objective for them in deconstructing this case material might be. The practitioner is invited to begin to explore, as part of this presentation, their own initial reflections and reactions, taking care to consider relevant issues of power, culture, gender, and values and beliefs that may impact on the perspective that they are taking. Supervisors in this first phase are respectfully curious and endeavor to facilitate a conversation which will promote a deeper understanding of the prevailing information.

Phase two involves a guided reflection by the supervisor through forms of knowledge. Here the supervisor leads the supervisee through various forms of knowledge, promoting reflection on the presenting case material through the lens of theory, research, practice wisdom, and other forms of knowledge. This phase involves the active generation of fresh hypotheses and new ways of seeing the material in a context that may be uncertain and ambiguous. An important assumption in this phase is that the supervisor and supervisee will each make an important contribution to the co-creation of new knowledge about the case in this phase. Supervisees will bring their firsthand observations and direct experience of the situation to the discussion whilst supervisors may introduce knowledge that will build upon these observations. An objective of the supervisor in this phase is to contain the supervisees' anxiety (Ruch 2007) whilst assisting less experienced practitioners to build their own "pattern recognition" over time, thus accelerating their learning (Munro 2011).

Finally, phase three is based on Gardner's second phase and involves change and reconstruction (Gardner 2014). Here both the supervisee and supervisor collaborate to rebuild a new story on the basis of these reflections and to articulate the personal and professional implications and outcomes, including any identified actions that may have been identified (McPherson and Macnamara 2017).

In summary, the knowledge and skill dimension of the IMS involves teaching and learning methodologies that are respectful of the supervisees' existing knowledge and seek to accelerate learning in a collaborative and empowering manner. A three phased approach to critical reflection is tailored to the complex and at times distressing context of child protection practice, enabling practitioners to reflect, debrief, and to learn within a safe and respectful learning environment.

Dimension three: Leadership and management

Leadership and management are the third dimension. Leadership behavior, utilizing the IMS, is consistent with ethical principles and values of social work, promoting social justice, and distributing power. Leaders practice with professional integrity and a high level of self-awareness and self-regulation. The consistent, predictable demonstration of these leadership traits are pivotal within the context of the turbulent environment of child protection practice. Effective leaders in this context seek to be transformational in their influence on the workplace, shaping organizational culture, managing meaning for staff, and inspiring professionals by building hope and generating enthusiasm. At the same time, sound governance arrangements, natural justice principles within the workplace (for example, staff recruitment and promotion practices), and effective and efficient systems and processes are the responsibility of leaders who manage service systems. The potential for role tension for leaders who are managers is mitigated by the priority in the first dimension to keep the child at the center of all supervisory reflections.

Dimension four: Advocacy

Advocacy is the fourth dimension and enables supervisors as middle managers to maintain their role as an "agent of change" whilst taking on supervisory responsibilities. As undergraduates, students are routinely introduced to their responsibilities as social workers of the future, to develop a professional identity which is strongly inclusive of the need to promote social justice, to practice ethically, and to advocate on behalf of disempowered and disadvantaged individuals groups and communities as part of one's core business (Connolly et al. 2018). Interestingly, advocacy is not a function that is routinely identified in the literature documenting social work supervision.

Within the context of an operating environment in child protection, advocacy may be undertaken in response to emerging direct practice issues, for example in relation to access for vulnerable persons to essential services or safe housing. At another level, advocacy may come into play for supervisors within an organizational context, for example practitioner workloads, policy, or other organizational issues. More broadly, supervisors may advocate on a wider scale in terms of issues that impact on society as social policy advocates who might take the role of "change agent" nationally or globally. Issues of sustainability and "green" social work practice are becoming part of the international discourse (AASW 2020) about advocacy and social work practice.

Dimension five: Safety

The final, overarching dimension of the Integrative Model of Supervision is of "safety." The establishment of safety within the supervisory relationship is facilitated by the creation of a safe, empathic, and supportive environment built on the knowledge of the impact of secondary trauma. This term refers primarily to relational safety and is premised on the supervisor-supervisee relationship being collaboratively co-created. Power, culture, diversity, and context are actively considered and worked with in the context of a trusting relationship with transparent parameters. The emotional impact of child protection practice is recognized and worked with in supervision, with the creation of a safe supervisory relationship seen as a pivotal strategy to ameliorate vicarious trauma. Emerging theories of social neuroscience are very helpful in an understanding of the need to and strategies for the creation of safety in child protection supervision (Cozolino 2017). For example, an understanding of the impact of threat and sustained stress on the neurobiological systems of human beings, enables supervisors to counter the risk of practitioners becoming immobilized in a flight/fright/freeze response to the distressing case material encountered in child protection practice. Developing preventative strategies that are designed to promote a safe, calm relationship, that are predictable and maintain routines amidst chaos and crisis, help to form a safe work environment. A proactive approach to self-care is an

Figure 27.1 The Integrative Model of Supervision (McPherson and Macnamara 2017). Reproduced with permission from Springer Nature. License number 4791001073543

important component of this dimension. This may include the development of preventative self-care plans in supervision with practitioners, attending to the risk of secondary stress, compassion fatigue, and vicarious trauma (Rothschild 2006).

These five key dimensions are conceptualized as integrative in Figure 27.1.

Implementing the model

A multi-faceted learning and development strategy was recently developed for implementation of the Integrative Model of Supervision in an Australian government child protection department. One hundred and twelve supervisors undertook intensive in-depth training in the model over a six-month period. Ninety-nine of these supervisors completed all four two-day workshops.

The identified purpose of the workshop series, commissioned by the state government authority was to strengthen leadership capabilities, to build supervisor capacity to use and to lead critically reflective practice, and to enable supervisors to develop critically reflective, trauma informed child protection practitioners.

In response to the identified purpose, the content of the workshop series was designed to build knowledge and to develop micro skills enabling supervisors to apply the Integrative Model of Supervision into their day to day practice. The identified learning outcomes for the supervisor workshop series were agreed as follows:

At the completion of this development program participants will demonstrate:

- knowledge with understanding of the Integrative Model of Supervision and the skills to apply the model in their practice as supervisors
- a stronger identity as a leader in child protection with an enhanced capacity to use emerging evidence to inform supervision
- capacity to initiate and maintain relationship-based supervision
- enhanced capability to facilitate learning and critically reflective practice in child protection
- greater capacity to ameliorate the impact of secondary stress and vicarious trauma in the workplace (McPherson 2018)

Based on these identified learning outcomes, a series of intensive workshops spanning four days were inclusive of the theoretical and research underpinnings of the IMS and skill development sessions, allowing participants to translate the theoretical material into their practice as supervisors.

To ensure wider organizational support for the learning strategy, all senior executives overseeing the child protection program were briefed in the model, including ways in which they might support the implementation of enhanced supervision in the workplace. A briefing session and collaborative question and answer session was offered to all supervisees, who were case workers, across the department. The pedagogical model drew upon inquiry based and blended learning strategies (Aditomo et al. 2011). The design of the learning and development strategy drew upon implementation science, informed by a five-factor conceptual map of evidence-informed implementation. These five factors operate in concert and include transparent planning and communication, commitment by managers to the innovation, a reflective organizational culture, a perceived "fit" between what is needed and what is offered, and workers who are motivated and open to change (Atkins and Frederico 2017).

Early implementation and early results

One hundred and twelve participants commenced the learning strategy with ninety nine completing all three phases over a six month period. All participants consented to take part in an evaluation. Participants ranged in age from 20 to 59 years of age with various educational backgrounds. A majority indicated that they had either a bachelor or qualifying master's degree in social work (n=51). Human Ethics approval was obtained from the Southern Cross University Ethics Committee: ECN-16-191.

Based on this initial implementation strategy, early results are encouraging. Participants indicated motivation to learn and to apply the concepts to their day to day practice as supervisors. Several participants reported that in the months following the development sessions, they had systematically implemented the IMS and had developed a community of practice within their local areas to support ongoing implementation and learning. A selection of responses from participants illustrates their use of the model following the workshop series:

In formal, scheduled supervision session I am utilising the model as well as critical reflection in a high level of detail. My formal and informal supervision now focuses on safety, knowledge and skill development and "giving power" to the supervisee to come prepared to supervision and take ownership of case tasks, professional development needs etc. It is more a sense of "us" in this relationship…

(Jessie)

I am building a sense of safety in supervision and in the team… we share responsibility for the team climate and focus on articulating ways in which we have operationalised the IMS each time we meet

(Maree)

I no longer see myself as needing to have all of the expertise or to hold all of the power. My new supervisory relationships have begun with extended conversations about how we will work together. My long standing supervisory relationships have been revisited and are reforming…

(Jane)

One surprising finding was that, prior to the development strategy, the concept of critical reflection was seen as a threat rather than an opportunity by a number of the supervisors participating. This view changed over the course of strategy implementation.

At the completion of the workshop series, supervisors shared new stories:

I have started using critical reflection in supervision and team meetings and I advocate for it to be used more often. A complete shift from the current way of doing critical reflection can be challenging. At the moment it appears to be "criticism" and (identification of) gaps in the work and hence it needs a conscious approach to change that

(Louise)

Using critical reflection is such a lovely way to learn and to promote learning in others…it has definitely had bad press here in the past but in fact it is the best way to encourage autonomous and creative thinkers…

(Marg)

The complexity and demands of the work combined with the emotional and visceral experiences of social workers must be understood in terms of the interaction of organizational processes, the practitioner's knowledge and qualities, and the context within which the practice occurs. At the center is supervision. Supervision that provides relational safety, space for critical thought and exploration, organizational containment, and emotionally attuned support can, as Ruch argues, transform experiences of fear, anxiety, anger, and frustration into "a resource for practice" (Ruch 2007, p. 377). More research is required into the impact that supervision has on direct practice with children and families.

Conclusion

The Integrative Model of Supervision (IMS) was developed as a conceptual model, emerging from a small exploratory study examining the perceptions and experiences of supervisors and supervisees in child and family practice of "effective supervision" (McPherson and Macnamara

2017). The newly developed model was recently introduced to a cohort of supervisors in child protection, offering a series of intensive workshops and briefing sessions for senior executives. The learning and development strategy disseminated the research findings and communicated the five dimensions of the IMS, including the integrative and holistic way in which it might be implemented. Early indications are that, in the context of a turbulent work environment, it is possible to enhance the practice of child protection supervision by refocusing, prioritizing a safe supervisory relationship, advocating, leading with integrity, and enabling practitioners to think creatively and critically.

References

AASW 2020. *World social work day*. Available from: https://www.aasw.asn.au/social-policy-advocacy/world -social-work-day-2020 [Accessed 12 April 2020].

Adamson, C., 2012. Supervision is not politically innocent. *Australian Social Work*, 65 (2), 185–196. doi:10. 1080/0312407x.2011.618544.

Aditomo, A., Goodyear, P., Bliuc, A., and Ellis, R., 2011. Inquiry-based learning in higher education: prin- cipal forms, educational objectives and disciplinary variations. *Studies in Higher Education*, 38 (9), 1239– 1258. doi:10.1080/0375079.2011.616584.

Atkins, P., and Frederico, M., 2017. Supporting implementation of innovative social work practice: what factors really matter?. *The British Journal of Social Work*, 47 (6), 1723–1744. doi:10.1093/bjsw/bcx091.

Belsky, J., 1980. Child maltreatment: an ecological integration. *American Psychologist*, 35 (4), 320–335.

Bloom, S.L., and Farragher, B., 2011. *Destroying sanctuary: the crisis in human service delivery systems.* Oxford University Press.

Braun, V., and Clarke, V., 2006. Using thematic analysis in psychology. *Qualitative Research in Psychology*, 3 (2), 77–101.

Braun, V., and Clarke, V., 2012. Thematic analysis. *In*: H. Cooper, P.M. Camic, D.L. Long, A.T. Panter, D. Rindskopf, and K.J. Sher, eds. *APA handbook of research methods in psychology, Vol. 2. Research designs: quan- titative, qualitative, neuropsychological, and biological.* Washington, DC: American Psychological Association, 57–71. doi:10.1037/13620-004.

Collins-Camargo, C., and Millar, K., 2010. The potential for a more clinical approach to child welfare supervision to promote practice and case outcomes: a qualitative study in four states. *The Clinical Supervisor*, 29 (2), 164–187. doi:10.1080/073252232010.517491.

Connolly, M., Harms, L., and Maidment, J., 2018. *Social work contexts and practice.* 4th ed. South Melbourne, VIC, Australia: Oxford University Press.

Cozolino, L., 2017. *The neuroscience of psychotherapy. healing the social brain.* 3rd ed. New York: WW Norton and Company.

Cummins, P., Scott, D., and Scales, B., 2012. *Protecting Victoria's vulnerable children inquiry.* State Government of Victoria: Australia. Available from: Available at http://www.childprotectioninquiry.vic.gov.au/report -pvvc-inquiry.html [Accessed 17 April 2020].

Davys, A., and Beddoe, L., 2010. *Best practice in supervision: a guide for the helping professions.* London: Jessica Kingsley Publishers.

Ferguson, H., 2017. How children become invisible in child protection work: findings from research into day-to-day social work practice. *The British Journal of Social Work*, 47 (4), 1007–1023. doi:10.1093/bjsw/ bcw065.

Gardner, F., 2014. *Being critically reflective: engaging in holistic practice.* Basingstoke: Palgrave McMillan.

Gibbs, J., 2001. Maintaining front-line workers in child protection: a case for refocusing supervision. *Child Abuse Review*, 10 (4), 323–335.

Harrison, R., and Westwood, M. 2009. Preventing vicarious traumatization of mental health therapists: identifying protective practices. *Psychotherapy: Theory, Research, Practice, Training*, 46 (2), 203–219.

House of Commons 2016. *House of commons committee of public accounts.* Available from: https://publications .parliament.uk/pa/cm201617/cmselect/cmpubacc/713/713.pdf [Accessed 17 April 2020].

Kadushin, A., and Harkness, D., 2002. *Supervision in social work* (4th ed.). New York: Columbia University Press.

Liamputtong, P., 2017. *Research methods in health. Foundations for evidence based practice.* 3rd ed. London, UK: Oxford University Press.

McPherson, L., 2014. *Supervision in* child and family practice: what works? Thesis (PhD). La Trobe University.

McPherson, L., 2018. *Response to* invitation to tender. Unpublished, commercial in confidence state government documentation.

McPherson, L., Frederico, M., and McNamara, P., 2016. Safety as the fifth dimension in supervision: stories from the front line. *Australian Social Work*, 69 (1), 67–79. doi:10.1080/0312407X.2015.

McPherson, L., and Macnamara, N., 2017. *Supervising child protection practice: what works? an evidence informed approach*. Zurich, Switzerland: Springer International Publishing. doi: 10.1007/978-3-319-50036-2.

Morrison, T., 2005. *Staff supervision in social care*. Brighton: Pavilion.

Munro, E., 2011. *The Munro review of child protection: final report*. A child centred system London, United Kingdom: Department for Education. Available from: https://assets.publishing.service.gov.uk/government/uploads/system/uploads/attachment_data/file/175391/Munro-Review.pdf [Accessed 17 April 2020]

Rothschild, B., 2006. *Help for the helper*. New York: Norton Publishing.

Ruch, G., 2007. Reflective practice in contemporary child care social work: the role of containment. *British Journal of Social Work*, 37 (4), 659–680.

Seigal, D., 2012. *The Developing Mind*. New York: Guildford Productions.

State of Queensland 2013. *Queensland child protection commission of inquiry*. Brisbane, Queensland: Department of Child Safety, Youth and Women.

Swain, S., 2014. *History of inquiries reviewing institutions providing care for children*. Royal Commission into Institutional Responses to Child Sexual Abuse. Sydney, Australia. Available from:http://www.childabuseroyalcommission.gov.au/documents/published-research/historical-perspectives-report-3-history-of-inquir.pdf [Accessed 17 April 2020].

Thompson, L., and West, D., 2013. Professional development in the contemporary educational context: encouraging practice wisdom. *Social Work Education: The International Journal*, 31 (1), 118–133. doi:10.1080/02615479.2011.648178.

Wilkins, D., Lynch, A., and Antonopoulou, V., 2018. A golden thread? The relationship between supervision, practice, and family engagement in child and family social work. *Child & Family Social Work*, 23 (3), 494–503. doi:10.1111/cfs.12442.

Winkworth, G., and McArthur, M., 2006. Being 'child centred' in child protection: what does it mean?. *Children Australia*, 31 (4), 13–21. doi:10.1017/s1035077200011305.

Wonnacott, J., 2012. *Mastering social work supervision*. London: Jessica Kingsley Publishers.

UN General Assembly, Convention on the Rights of the Child 1989, November 20. United Nations, Treaty Series, vol. 1577, p. 3. Available from: https://www.refworld.org/docid/3ae6b38f0.html [Accessed 15 April 2020].

28

THINKING CRITICALLY

A four-layered practice model in supervision

Matt Rankine

Introduction

Internationally, social work has changed in response to the management of risk and surveillance of practice in services from a neoliberal government-controlled agenda (Gray and Webb 2013). The dominance of this agenda has led the social worker to be preoccupied with meeting targets and outcomes on caseloads, at the expense of professional relationships with colleagues, managers, supervisors, service users, and communities. Moreover, social workers struggle to find the appropriate space to critically explore their position and understand the environment in which they are practicing.

Reflective practice and critical reflection are processes (defined later) commonly championed by social work educators and practitioners but are more problematic to implement within the day-to-day pressures in practice. Comparing the "espoused theory" with "theory-in-use" in practice (Argyris and Schön 1974) reveals inconsistencies in professional standards due to the dominant managerial discourses which preoccupy a social worker's time rather than sufficient critical reflection related to social justice issues and analysis of the wider environment. For social work to maintain a level of professionalism in practice, practitioners are required to maintain a commitment to their codes of ethics, values, and to develop their skill-base over their careers (Gray and Webb 2013). Reflective practice and critical reflection become crucial for a practitioner to holistically bring together knowledge, experience, and theory in the day-to-day encounters they have when working with others (Davys and Beddoe 2010). Supervision provides the obvious space for social workers to reflect upon their practice and critically reflect on the wider social work environment.

Supervision has been established in social work for 150 years and is the space for developing professionalism, providing support, and ensuring organizational commitments are met by practitioners (Davys and Beddoe 2010; O'Donoghue and Tsui 2011; Weld 2012). In order for supervision to be effective for learning and the development of practice, it is necessary for the supervisor to facilitate a reflective process and exhibit a range of skills to enable the supervisee to critically consider their practice (Hawkins and Shohet 2012). The supervisee also needs to be active in this process in how they plan and participate within the session. According to Davys and Beddoe (2010), supervision is most effective as a place for reflection and learning when the agenda is led by the supervisee. Within the current climate of neoliberalism, the development of reflective supervision models that are context-specific and stimulate critical reflection are essential in order for social workers to pro-actively work with communities and service users (Rankine 2017).

A four-layered practice model of reflective supervision is presented in this chapter, outlining a framework for critically reflecting on practice. Four intersecting layers are identified as essential for exploration within supervision and assist with understanding the interrelationship between the social worker, the organization, service users, and professionals, and the wider environmental context which influences practice. Both the supervisee and supervisor have key tasks to perform in the process of critical reflection within the session. The supervisee is responsible for preparing for the session with an agenda for the purpose of critical thinking whilst the supervisor facilitates the process of analysis through inquiry and supporting the supervisee's development of inclusive practice strategies. The application of the four-layered practice model by the supervisee and supervisor is demonstrated through the use of vignettes which emphasize the co-constructed partnership within supervision.

Reflective practice and critical reflection

Reflective practice and critical reflection are both essential aspects of a social worker's professional development and necessitate a critical understanding of the world. Literature in this area has generated interest in professional and organizational learning within many different professions, including social work (Fook and Gardner 2007). Reflective practice and critical reflection are terms that are often used interchangeably and, often, incorrectly, by practitioners and educators due to the subjective nature of each experience. These terms can be described as interconnected through a process of deeper thinking or as completely different concepts altogether where critical reflection illuminates the impact of the wider environment on practice (Rankine 2018). In addition, critical reflection and reflective practice are commonly espoused by professional bodies, organizations, and individual practitioners as important professional concepts but are often forgone within a social worker's busy schedule to meet organizational targets related to caseload and performance.

Reflective practice is the basis for all professionals to develop their learning from assessment, exploration, adaptation, and change (Carroll 2011; Davys and Beddoe 2010). For social workers, reflective practice relates to assessing individual and community needs, relationships with others, agendas, and allocation of resources. The notion of reflective practice refers to how the practitioner can review their current actions by critical questioning and develop further planned strategies in their work (Taylor 2013). Different layers of reflection that lead to deeper critical understanding and transformation in learning and practice have been described by influential authors over the last 50 years (Argyris and Schön 1974; Boud et al. 1985; Brookfield 1995; Mezirow 1981). The *Reflective Practitioner* (Schön 1983) and the *Experiential Learning* model (Kolb 1984) have been key contributions towards learning and development and the exploration of alternatives in professional practice.

Critical reflection provides a deeper analysis of structures and omnipresence of power within society which influence individuals and relationships (Brookfield 2009). Through the process of critical reflection, the social worker widely examines the cultural, social, and political environment and, from an anti-oppressive perspective, promotes alternative strategies of action. Authors such as Fook and Gardner (2007) have highlighted critical reflection as essential to the core professional values of social work. This form of reflection provides social workers the opportunity to explore contemporary issues impacting on society and service users related to power, oppression, social justice, and human rights (Gray and Webb 2013; Taylor 2013). According to Fook and Gardner (2007), the process of critical reflection is achieved through a two-step process of deconstructing assumptions, values, discourses, and wider influences held by the professional in order for meaning to be reconstructed with changes in awareness and action. Fook and Gardner's approach to critical reflection exposes gaps between espoused and enacted theory and provides the opportunity to improve practice. For social workers to maintain their professional identity, ethics, and visibility within organizations and communities, critical reflection (including the wider systemic and contextual environment) needs to be continually developed in practice. Within the managerial and neoliberal pressures of meeting targets, risk, and mechanistic practice, social workers require a professional space for both reflective practice and critical reflection. Reflective supervision provides this space.

Reflective supervision

Supervision, as a space for critical examination, needs to promote the professional development of big-picture social workers (Noble et al. 2016) operating in an oppressive and complex environment. More importantly, the ability of social work practitioners to critically reflect on their work within supervision is expected to improve performance and produce better outcomes for the service users they work with (Carpenter et al. 2012; Mor Barak et al. 2009). Traditionally, the multi-faceted and structured nature of supervision has been identified through various functions: administrative, educative, supportive, and providing mediation for the supervisee (Kadushin and Harkness 2014; Morrison 2005). Such structural-functional approaches have provided a foundational understanding of what supervision is and what should be canvassed within sessions (Wilkins et al. 2016). However, according to Morrison (2005), it is also essential that supervision has a framework to assist staff to develop and use skills and knowledge within the ever-changing environment of modern social work. Reflective supervision is one of many supervisory approaches and affirms the practitioner in working towards linking their theory to practice, knowledge development, and transformation in practice (Davys and Beddoe 2010). Reflective supervision places emphasis on how learning takes place between the supervisor and supervisee within the session.

Models specific to reflective supervision have been developed from action and reflection. The reflective learning model describes a cyclic process, as identified by Kolb's (1984) experiential learning model, undertaken between supervisor and supervisee within supervision (Davys and Beddoe 2010). The reflective learning model depicts a set structure for supervision with a clearly defined beginning, key stages to learning and decision making, and ending with a conclusion (Davys and Beddoe 2010). Watkins et al. (2019) have developed an educational tool, the Supervision Session Pyramid (SSP), a step by step conceptual map that assists supervisors understand the reflective and cyclic nature of the session. Reflective supervision has also been described as transformative in that significant changes in thinking establish new behavior for the individual and the environment they work in (Shohet 2011; Weld 2012). Carroll (2010) has identified this process taking place in reflective supervision through four sequential levels moving towards transformational learning: problem solving (Level 1); changes in the behavior (Level 2); changes in the thinking (Level 3); and changes in the thinking behind the thinking (Level 4) (Carroll 2010, 2011). Within reflective supervision, part of the transformative aspect is that the supervisor, too, learns from the experiences that the supervisee brings to supervision. This ongoing learning creates fundamental shifts in behavior and ways of working with others in different contexts (Weld 2012).

Reflective supervision also encompasses an understanding of the wider contextual influences on practice. As Davys and Beddoe (2010, p. 56) note, "supervision does not occur in a professional vacuum" and is also located within broader political, socio-cultural, and structural contexts which influence the supervisory relationship (Hernández and McDowell 2010). This kind of supervision identifies the space to examine power dynamics, existing structures, and dominant discourses that impact on social workers and their work with service users (Rankine et al. 2018). Authors such as Noble et al. (2016) have developed a critical supervision and practice process which provides a strategic, contextual focus to supervision through the critical exploration of broader perspectives. The assumptions and tensions held within practice can be explored which leads to alternative action plans. In consideration of the wider perspectives influencing practice, Hair and O'Donoghue (2009) have emphasized the significance of social constructionism (where knowledge is created by individuals through their interaction with others) within reflective supervision. Predominantly Western discourses have influenced traditional supervision practices, and social constructionism supports diversity within the supervisory conversation so that anti-oppressive and culturally sensitive practice is encouraged (Hair and O'Donoghue 2009). Contextual knowledge, culture, and language, particularly from Indigenous perspectives require critical consideration (O'Donoghue 2003). The understanding of the wider context of practice within supervision has led to the development of alternative culturally specific approaches to supervision, for example, Kaupapa (principles) Māori supervision (Eruera 2012) and cross-cultural supervision (Tsui et al. 2014). Alternative frameworks in reflective supervision that are contextually specific need to be ongoing and relevant to meet the changes within, and demands of, practice. The four-layered practice model of reflective supervision provides a structure to critically explore various contextual layers of social work and develop social justice strategies for practice.

The four-layered practice model

This practice model was developed from previous research related to the current use of reflective supervision within community-based child welfare services in Aotearoa New Zealand (Rankine et al. 2018). Although social work practitioners discussed the significance of critical reflection, there was much speculation over this being common in practice – rather reflection in supervision was poor and on a superficial level. Further research was identified in order to support social workers in their self-awareness, critical thinking, and social justice informed strategies within reflective supervision (Rankine et al. 2018).

Once time has been taken to develop trust, openness, and an agreed way of working together, the process of reflective supervision can be clarified between the supervisor and supervisee (see Table 28.1). The supervisee has a role in being prepared for supervision in bringing specific agenda items for critical reflection. The supervisor has the task to facilitate the session and co-ordinate reflective questioning in relation to the supervisee's agenda item. The supervisor's approach needs to be one of a naïve enquirer in which openness and curiosity are essential so that practice experience, previously held assumptions, and the development of social justice informed plans for action can be developed. The supervisor is also required to navigate the critical discussion between different areas of the supervisee's practice.

The four-layered practice model of reflective supervision provides the supervisor and supervisee with a holistic examination of different areas of practice including a critical understanding of the social worker's self-awareness, their organization, relationships with others, and the wider environment where practice is undertaken (Rankine 2017). Each area of practice is identified in the model as a layer (see Table 28.1). When discussed sequentially in supervision (from layer one), each layer of practice offers a unique dimension for critical exploration of the agenda item that is being brought to the session. The model also highlights the connection between each layer of practice,

Table 28.1 The four-layered practice model of reflective supervision

Layer	Supervisee's and supervisor's agenda	Supervisor questions
Layer 1: Self and role	Self-care Feelings Cultural identity and reflexivity Role clarity	• What self-care strategies need to be implemented? • What feelings does this issue raise for you? Where do these feelings come from? • How do personal experiences and/or triggers connect to this issue? • How do your cultural values, beliefs, assumptions impact on the situation? How do these connect with your role? How could you respond differently? • What are the parameters of your role?
Layer 2: The organization	Function and purpose Funding Resources Meeting criteria Organizational culture Understanding tensions	• What is the purpose and function of the organization? • What are the parameters of the service? How is the service funded? What other resources are available? Who else may assist? • What are the protocols and policies of the organization? How do they impact on the issue? • What are the taken-for-granted meanings/assumptions/power dynamics within the organization? How could they be different? • What can you do to contribute towards changes being implemented in the organization? How can you be the facilitator of change?
Layer 3: Relationships with others	Discussion of supervisory process The use of supervision – internal and external Work with clients Work with professionals Work with colleagues Exploration of power, difference, and cross-cultural identities	• What accountabilities/responsibilities do we have to the supervision process? What are the parameters/power issues? How can we build a more effective relationship? • What are the power issues/assumptions/tensions/successes (in the identified relationship)? How do you think others perceive you? How do you engage with others? • How do your personal experiences/beliefs impact on this relationship? What changes in the relationship could be made?

(Continued)

Table 28.1 Continued

Layer	Supervisee's and supervisor's agenda	Supervisor questions
Layer 4: The socio-political and socio-cultural context	Public perception Power of social worker Socio-political and socio-cultural context Examination of dominant discourses and their impact on wider discourses Bi-culturalism Social justice Human rights	• What perspectives are you using when you consider this issue? What other perspectives are missing? How do these perspectives impact on your role? What would you want to change? • What are the social/cultural/ political contexts related to this issue? How do these broader contexts impact? • What needs to be considered from an (Indigenous) Aotearoa New Zealand/ bi-cultural perspective? • What social work theories/ standards/ethics/ research/protocols need to be considered? • What is the impact of dominant discourses and structures on this issue? What other discourses need to be considered? How can you support other discourses being heard? • What wider assumptions have been made and by whom? Where do these assumptions come from? What alternative actions can be considered?

Source: Rankine (2017, p.69–70) reprinted with permission of the Editor of the *Aotearoa New Zealand Social Work Journal.*

as experiences, perspectives, and assumptions operate at every level and require critical unpacking. Each layer of the model will be unpacked further to explore its relevance in the supervision discussion and how the model can be applied in practice through use of vignettes.

Layer one: Self and role

The first layer of the model provides the supervisee with the opportunity to develop their self-awareness and greater understanding of their role. The development of self-awareness is an ongoing journey within social work supervision and identifies the personal links with professional practice (Adamovich et al. 2014). As part of their agenda for supervision, the supervisee should regularly discuss their emotions related to their job and their self-care to ensure longevity in their role (Vito 2015). Supervisors need to be part of the social worker's system for the safe exploration and containment of strong emotions generated through the day-to-day practice with vulnerable populations and the implications this has for individual well-being. Supervisors are required to interpret how a supervisee might be feeling and manage giving and receiving feedback in this process (Davys and Beddoe 2010). In working with others, social workers can be triggered by their own personal histories of trauma and abuse which can lead to feelings of being overwhelmed. The safe expression of emotions in reflective supervision without judgement by the supervisor supports the supervisee towards the building of resilience, an acknowledgment of strengths, and the development of well-being strategies (Beddoe et al. 2014; Engelbrecht 2010).

Vignette one

Meghan wanted to use the time in supervision to discuss her strong feelings of being overwhelmed in her job over the last few weeks. As a result, Meghan felt incompetent in her role as a community mental health social worker. Meghan wanted to know what to do about this and have a plan to manage this.

Meghan's supervisor asked her questions where these feelings came from and slowly Meghan could identify she had been working on some complex situations with service users involving addictions. Through the supervisor probing further, Meghan could think back to growing up in a rural family where alcoholism was prevalent and how she would regularly get into arguments with her father about his drinking. In connecting to her role, Meghan saw how this personal issue had recently encroached into her professional role and had contributed to her feelings of being overwhelmed in working with some service users. She could also acknowledge that working with addictions was a common theme associated with her role and she had had similar feelings before. The supervisor highlighted Meghan's resilience in working in a very demanding area and asked Meghan what self-care strategies she needed to ensure were implemented. Meghan agreed that she had neglected this area of late and that she would organize purposeful time over the next weekend to connect with friends and partner.

Reflective supervision is also important in developing an ongoing awareness of how knowledge, values, culture, and diversity influence practice. The supervisor and supervisee have a responsibility to explore the assumptions and expectations that reinforce and influence repetitive, and potentially oppressive, ways of working (Beddoe and Davys 2016). In layer one, the supervisee needs to work collaboratively with the supervisor in understanding their own cultural identity, and the supervisor needs to provide the space in supervision through open questioning for this critical exploration.

Layer two: The organization

Layer two of the four-layered practice model provides the social worker with connection to their place of work. The environment and practices within an organization are influential to the development of every practitioner, and for learning to occur, reflective supervision needs to be part of this process (Karvinen-Niinikoski 2004). An understanding of the organizational structure and the impact of this on practice needs critical exploration. The supervisor's role is to assist the supervisee to articulate the context and parameters of their organization. In doing so, the supervisee is reminded of their position at work, the methods and programs they employ, and how this position influences professional interactions with others. In order to highlight possible tensions between professional practice and organizational imperatives, the supervisor encourages the supervisee to identify relevant policies and protocols of the organization (Hair 2015).

Vignette two

Andrew worked for statutory child protection services and raised in supervision how increasingly difficult it was to find the time to attend his reflective supervision sessions due to his complex caseload. After expressing his frustrations, Andrew realized that he wanted to be able to prioritize the time for supervision better in the future and have support from his organization.

His supervisor asked questions related to the purpose and the parameters of Andrew's organization to which Andrew replied "manage risk to children and ensure they are all kept safe from harm." The supervisor then asked Andrew about the policies in place regarding supervision. Andrew recalled that supervision needed to be monthly and the rationale for this being important to practice and the organization. When Andrew's supervisor queried what were the taken-for-granted assumptions held within the organization, Andrew realized how the bureaucratic nature of his work impacted on his views about reflective supervision — that it was seen as a luxury for those who were obviously not busy enough. With the supervisor's support, Andrew could identify that he needed to role model the importance of attending reflective supervision to his colleagues and that he would need to speak with his manager for support to ensure this process was not forgotten in the team's busy work schedule.

An organization's culture is significant towards learning and what may commonly be promoted, may not necessarily be part of the daily routines in the workplace (Davys and Beddoe 2010; Rankine et al. 2018). Developing an awareness of degenerate cultural patterns within an organization is essential in supervision and is the first step towards changing these (Hawkins and Shohet 2012). Reflective supervision provides the space to critically examine aspects of the organizational environment that are hindering policy and effective practice. The supervisee needs to raise the impact of high workload, high turnover, loss of resources, and lack of funding in reflective supervision in order to maintain a healthy level of functioning and resilience. The supervisor's task of open questioning is significant towards the supervisee's identification of unhealthy cultures and assumptions within organizations, impacting on learning. In addition, the supervisor encourages the supervisee to take ownership towards changes through the removal of existing barriers and exploration of alternative solutions within their control.

Layer three: Relationships

Relationships sit at the heart of social work, and supervision can be the space for competing discourses to be openly discussed and how they impact on practice (Saltiel 2016). The third layer in the four-layered practice model critically explores relationships with others. These relationships include the supervisor-supervisee relationship, working with service users, colleagues, and other professional relationships.

The key relationship that the social worker has is with their supervisor, as this provides an important socializing and structured process which determines how other working relationships are developed. Beddoe and Davys (2016) have referred to the isomorphic nature of supervision upon which a supervisee then builds other professional interactions. In order for reflective supervision to be effective for the supervisee, the supervisor needs to display key attributes that demonstrate empathy, congruence, and positive regard (Westergaard 2013). To explore power and the importance of culture, the supervisor needs to exhibit confidence in their abilities to ask critical questions, have good self-awareness, and be willing to encourage the supervisee to explore different perspectives.

Vignette three

Chloe placed her relationship with Tamara on top of her agenda for supervision. Chloe had been in her role as team leader at a community children's service for six months and had found Tamara in her team oppositional and defensive when she had engaged with her. These awkward interactions had kept Chloe awake at night. Chloe was aware that Tamara had had worked in the agency for many years and had struggled with learning difficulties and English not being her first language. Chloe wanted to discuss in supervision how she would address her concerns with Tamara.

The supervisor asked if Chloe had been in this situation before. Chloe remembered a previous working relationship with a staff member that had led to arguments and performance management issues. The supervisor asked if this experience impacted on the current relationship and Chloe disclosed that she was nervous of this negative experience happening all over again. Chloe's supervisor encouraged Chloe to identify the power issues associated with her role, how Tamara may perceive her coming into the team, and the different cultural assumptions that existed. Chloe was able to appreciate Tamara's situation further and separate out her own previous negative experiences and assumptions. This assisted Chloe to develop a more collaborative plan with Tamara but also to outline the professional expectations she had.

Significant in layer three of the model is the opportunity for the social worker to analyze the challenges when working with service users, colleagues, and other professional groups. Within any professional relationship, dominant discourses that privilege some, and disadvantage others, according to their role and responsibility present a common challenge. The supervisor's task becomes concerned with facilitating exploration of the power dynamics within the specific relationship. Hair and O'Donoghue (2009) have previously suggested a questioning stance by the supervisor in order to promote open dialogue. This is so the social worker has the opportunity to understand the complexity of the interaction, competing systems, forces, and how power impacts on the social worker's role. In addition, the supervisor encourages the supervisee to explore cross-cultural interactions and elements of diversity. This dialogue in supervision is important towards developing greater understandings of equity and justice in social work practice (Hernández and McDowell 2010). When reflective supervision is used in this way, the relationship the social worker has can be examined with compassion, more comprehensively for creative solutions, and assist with building more collaborative partnerships with others.

Layer four: The wider environment

The final layer of the four-layered practice model is the socio-political and socio-cultural context of practice. For reflective supervision to support social work values and ethics relating to social justice, critical analysis of wider systems and structures need discussion (Rankine 2017). Through this discussion, appropriate plans for change can be implemented. The supervisor's task is to assist the supervisee to appreciate the cultural, social, and political contexts of practice. The supervisor's questioning relates to the impact of dominant discourses and structures on the supervisee's issue. This level of critical examination assists the supervisee in making connections between individuals and their environment and how oppressive and dominant structures are maintained in society. Supervisees have the responsibility to critically analyze these wider questions related to the issue and how these impact on service users and their way of working with others. In addition, supervisors connect the supervisee to their professional social work values that include acknowledgment of Indigenous discourses, social justice, and oppression (Beddoe and Davys 2016). This process is important so that the supervisor can evaluate and develop areas of the supervisee's competence to promote culturally sensitive practice with diverse groups. Vignette four highlights this process in an Aotearoa New Zealand context where professional social work has a commitment to bi-cultural practice, ethics, and responsibilities towards supporting marginalized groups (ANZASW 2008; SWRB 2016).

Vignette four

Mark works with Hemi (a service user who identifies as Māori – an Indigenous group within Aotearoa New Zealand) at a community center offering support and education. In supervision, Mark discusses how he feels conflicted in working with Hemi – Hemi often does not turn up for arranged appointments and does not appear to be telling Mark everything he needs to know for his assessment. When asked by the supervisor if he had worked with Māori before, Mark said that he had, but they seemed to be avoiding the help offered and ultimately remaining in their disadvantaged situation. Mark wants to know how to support Hemi as he states he is on the point of giving up.

The supervisor asked about Mark's professional and organizational mandate attached to his role and whether any perspectives were missing. Mark noticed Hemi's voice was missing. Mark could reflect that, although as a social worker, he was attached to an ethical code of conduct that supported vulnerable and Indigenous perspectives, he was getting caught in ensuring needs of service users met the service criteria. The supervisor asked Mark to consider Hemi's situation from a bi-cultural perspective. Mark could then appreciate how Hemi may view the service as another oppressive structure where he feels unheard and not representing his views and needs as Māori. The supervisor affirmed the powerful learning moment for Mark. With his supervisor's support, Mark then planned how to develop a more constructive working relationship with Hemi.

The contribution of the model

Internationally, economic, social, and cultural factors have influenced social work practice. Similarly, these factors have altered the space of supervision in social work services from professional learning to focus solely on surveillance of caseloads, procedure, and work completion by social workers (Beddoe 2010). These influences have hampered the practitioner's ability to understand the importance of critical reflection to their work. Such mechanistic practices lead to repetition in service delivery, and risk discourses lead to reactive ways of working by the social worker (Noble and Irwin 2009). The roles of both the supervisee and supervisor become devalued within a one-size-fits-all approach to supervision and less about the diversity and critical exploration of professional social work (Beddoe 2015; O'Donoghue 2015).

Reflective supervision combats the contradictory managerial and neoliberal agendas that dominate many social service organizations in that for learning to occur, both the supervisor and supervisee have significant roles. The four-layered practice model identifies the supervisory relationship as a co-constructed partnership where the supervisor and supervisee have joint responsibilities in the agenda, task, and process for supervision. Although the supervisor has accountabilities to organizational and professional procedures, the main responsibility is to enable critical questioning of the supervisee's practice so that learning can occur. The supervisor's role is crucial towards facilitating conversations related to cultural awareness and social justice (Hair 2015). Equally, the supervisee has a professional and ethical responsibility to learn about good practices in supervision and consider the wider implications to their work (Rankine 2017). The exploration of ethics in supervision supports the practitioner with better decision making (Davys and Beddoe 2010). Critical conversations related to socio-cultural and socio-political issues influencing practice are often sidelined from supervision. Reflective models such as the four-layered practice model support social work codes of practice and foster a deeper understanding of power dynamics, Indigenous approaches, and cross-cultural ways of working. In doing so, the social worker learns to develop reflective practice and critical reflection. Such models are crucial in developing a deeper understanding of practice and wider socio-political and socio-cultural influences.

Reflective supervision is essential for the development of social work practice through critical thinking and exploring the connections and complexities in practice. The four-layered practice model of reflective supervision provides an examination of the interrelationship between the social worker, the organization they work for, relationships with others, and the wider systemic context of practice. In doing so, the supervisor and supervisee can view each perspective offering critical insight and uniqueness to an issue raised in the session but also at a multi-dimensional level where holistic influences on practice can be identified. The four-layered practice model has the potential to be adaptable to a range of social work fields of practice (such as mental health, children and family work, and corrections), as it is context-specific, and this provides the basis for critical exploration and strategies for action. The value of reflective supervision models, such as the four-layered practice model is that social workers are offered insight to develop a variety of skills in an ever-changing social work context. The significance of promoting social justice in social work supervision continues to be promoted in recent literature (Beddoe 2015; Hair and O'Donoghue 2009; Noble et al. 2016). Reflective supervision provides the ideal space for critical reflection to be actioned for the purpose of improving social work practice and work with service users.

Conclusion

Reflective supervision provides an essential space for the social worker to professionally develop and provide the best support to service users. The four-layered practice model highlights the importance of a co-constructed partnership between the supervisor and supervisee within the supervision session. Through deeper exploration of the four intersecting layers influencing practice, the social worker is supported by their supervisor to critically evaluate their practice and develop further action strategies. The tension associated with the current neoliberal environment reinforces the urgency for social workers to develop reflective models in supervision that enhance critical analysis and social justice in their work.

References

Adamowich, T., Kumsa, M.K., Rego, C., Stoddart, J., and Vito, R., 2014. Playing hide-and-seek: searching for the use of self in reflective social work practice. *Reflective Practice: International and Multidisciplinary Perspectives*, 15 (2), 131–143. doi:10.1080/14623943.2014.883312.

Aotearoa New Zealand Association of Social Workers. 2008. *ANZASW code of ethics*. 2nd rev ed. Christchurch: Aotearoa New Zealand Association of Social Workers.

Argyris, C., and Schön, D., 1974. *Theory in practice: increasing professional effectiveness*. San Francisco: Jossey Bass.

Beddoe, L., 2010. Surveillance or reflection: professional supervision in the risk society. *British Journal of Social Work*, 40 (4), 1279–1296. doi:10.1093/bjsw/bcq018.

Beddoe, L., 2015. Supervision and developing the profession: one supervision or many?. *China Journal of Social Work*, 8 (2), 150–163. doi:10.1080/17525098.2015.1039173.

Beddoe, L., and Davys, A., 2016. *Challenges in professional supervision. Current themes and models for practice*. London: Jessica Kingsley Publishers.

Beddoe, L., Davys, A., and Adamson, C., 2014. Never trust anybody who says 'i don't need supervision': practitioners' beliefs about social worker resilience. *Practice*, 26 (2), 113–130. doi:10.1080/09503153.2014.896888.

Boud, D., Keogh, R., and Walker, D., 1985. Promoting reflection in learning: a model. *In*: D. Boud, R. Keogh, and D. Walker, eds. *Reflection: turning experience into learning*. London: Kogan Page, 18–40.

Brookfield, S., 1995. *Becoming a critically reflective teacher*. San Francisco: Jossey-Bass.

Brookfield, S., 2009. The concept of critical reflection: promises and contradictions, *European Journal of Social Work*, 12 (3), 293–304. doi:10.1080/13691450902945215.

Carpenter, J., Webb, C., Bostock, L., and Coomber, C., 2012. *Effective supervision in social work and social care. Research briefing 43*. London: Social Care Institute for Excellence.

Carroll, M., 2010. Supervision: critical reflection for transformational learning (part 2). *The Clinical Supervisor*, 29 (1), 1–19. doi:10.1080/07325221003730301.

Carroll, M., 2011. Supervision: a journey of lifelong learning. *In*: R. Shohet, ed. *Supervision as transformation: a passion for learning*. London: Jessica Kingsley, 14–28.

Davys, A., and Beddoe, L., 2010. *Best practice in professional supervision: a guide for the helping professions*. London: Jessica Kingsley.

Engelbrecht, L.K., 2010. A strengths perspective on supervision of social workers: an alternative management paradigm within a social development context. *Social Work & Social Sciences Review*, 14 (1), 47–58. doi:10.1921/095352210X505490.

Eruera, M., 2012. He Korari, he Kete, he Korero. *Aotearoa New Zealand Social Work*, 24 (3/4), 12–19.

Fook, J., and Gardner, F., 2007. *Practising critical reflection: a resource handbook*. Maidenhead, UK: Open University Press.

Gray, M., and Webb, S., eds., 2013. *The new politics of social work*. Basingstoke, UK: Palgrave Macmillan.

Hair, H., 2015. Supervision conversations about social justice and social work practice. *Journal of Social Work*, 15 (4), 349–370, doi:10.1177/1468017314539082.

Hair, H., and O'Donoghue, K., 2009. Culturally relevant, socially just social work supervision: becoming visible through a social constructionist lens. *Journal of Ethnic and Cultural Diversity in Social Work*, 18 (1–2), 70–88, doi:10.1080/15313200902874979.

Hawkins, P., and Shohet, R., 2012. *Supervision in the helping professions*. 4th ed. Maidenhead, UK: Open University Press.

Hernández, P., and McDowell, T., 2010. Intersectionality, power, and relational safety in context: key concepts in clinical supervision. *Training and Education in Professional Psychology*, 4 (1), 29–35. doi:10.1037/a0017064.

Kadushin, A., and Harkness, D., 2014. *Supervision in social work*. 5th ed. New York: Columbia University Press.

Karvinen-Niinikoski, S., 2004. Social work supervision contributing to innovative knowledge production and open expertise. *In*: N. Gould and M. Baldwin, eds. *Social work, critical reflection and the learning organisation*, Farnham, UK: Ashgate, 23–39.

Kolb, D., 1984. *Experiential learning: experience as the source of learning and development*. Englewood Cliffs, NJ: Prentice Hall.

Mezirow, J., 1981. A critical theory of adult learning and education. *Adult Education Quarterly*, 32 (1), 3–24. doi:10.1177/074171368103200101.

Mor Barak, M.E., et al., 2009. The impact of supervision on worker outcomes: a meta-analysis. *Social Service Review*, 83 (1), 3–32, doi:10.1086/599028.

Morrison, T., 2005. *Staff supervision in social care: making a real difference for staff and service users*. Brighton: Pavilion.

Noble, C., Gray, M., and Johnston, L., 2016. *Critical supervision for the human services: a social model to promote learning and value-based practice*. London: Jessica Kingsley.

Noble, C., and Irwin, J., 2009. Social work supervision: an exploration of the current challenges in a rapidly changing social, economic and political environment. *Journal of Social Work*, 9 (3), 345–358. doi:10.1177/1468017309334848.

O'Donoghue, K., 2003. *Restorying social work supervision*. Palmerston North, New Zealand: Dunmore Press.

O'Donoghue, K., 2015. Issues and challenges facing social work supervision in the twenty-first century. *China Journal of Social Work*, 8 (2), 136–149. doi:10.1080/17525098.2015.1039172.

O'Donoghue, K., and Tsui, M.S., 2011. Towards a professional supervision culture: therapie development of social work supervision in Aotearoa New Zealand. International *Social Work,* 55 (1), 5–28. doi:10.1177/0020872810396109.

Rankine, M., 2017. Making the connections: a practice model for reflective supervision. *Aotearoa New Zealand Social Work*, 29 (3), 66–78.

Rankine, M., 2018. How critical are we? revitalising critical reflection in supervision. *Advances in Social Work and Welfare Education*, 20 (2), 31–46.

Rankine, M., et al., 2018. What's your Agenda? reflective supervision in community-based child welfare services. *European Journal of Social Work*, 21 (3), 428–440. doi:10.1080/13691457.2017.1326376.

Saltiel, D., 2016. Supervision: a contested space for learning and decision making. *Qualitative Social Work*, 16 (4), 533–549. doi:1473325016633445.

Schön, D., 1983. *The reflective practitioner: how professionals think in action.* New York: Basic Books.

Shohet, R., ed., 2011. *Supervision as transformation: a passion for learning.* London: Jessica Kingsley Publishers.

Social Workers Registration Board 2016. *Code of conduct.* Wellington: Social Workers Registration Board.

Taylor, C., 2013. Critically reflective practice. *In*: M. Gray and S. Webb, eds. *The new politics of social work.* Basingstoke, UK: Palgrave Macmillan, 79–97.

Tsui, M.S., O'Donoghue, K., and Ng, A.K.T., 2014. Culturally competent and diversity-sensitive clinical supervision. *In*: C.E. Watkins Jr and D.L. Milne, eds. *The Wiley international handbook of clinical supervision.* Chichester, UK: John Wiley and Sons, 238–254.

Vito, R., 2015. Leadership support of supervision in social work practice: challenges and enablers to achieving success. *Canadian Social Work Review/Revue Canadienne de Service Social*, 32 (1–2), 151–165. doi:10.7202/1034148ar.

Watkins, C., Callahan, J., and Vişcu, L., 2019. The common process of supervision process: the supervision session pyramid as a teaching tool in the beginning supervision seminar. *Journal of Contemporary Psychotherapy.* doi: 10.1007/s10879-019-09436-5.

Weld, N., 2012. *A practical guide to transformative supervision for the helping professions.* London: Jessica Kingsley.

Westergaard, J., 2013. Line management supervision in the helping professions: moving from external supervision to a line manager supervisor model. *The Clinical Supervisor*, 32 (2), 167–184. doi:10.1080/07325223.2013.846756.

Wilkins, D., Forrester, D., and Grant, L., 2016. What happens in child and family social work supervision?. *Child and Family Social Work*, 22 (2), 942–951. doi:10.1111/cfs.12314.

29

THE PASE SUPERVISION MODEL

Tracey Harris and Maddy Slattery

Introduction

Professional supervision plays a crucial role in social work. It ensures that social workers critically reflect on all aspects of their practice, maintain professional identity, and ensure that organizational requirements are met in line with their position description (Harris 2018). Carroll (2010) suggests that professional supervision provides the ideal environment for supervisees to analyze not only what they do to be accountable, but how they do it from a practice perspective. Supervision encourages supervisees to consciously use their ethical framework and engage in continual development throughout their career (Bernard and Goodyear 2009; Chiller and Crisp 2012; Harris 2018; Thomas 2010). When supervision has clear processes, a framework, and supervision model, it develops the supervisees' competence and influences quality client outcomes (Bambling et al. 2006; Lucock et al. 2006). Effective supervision also reduces the risk of stress and burnout and increases job satisfaction (Abu-Bader 2000; Kadushin and Harkness 2014; Kim and Lee 2009; Mor Barak et al. 2001).

Providing effective supervision is one of the significant challenges facing supervisors. Supervisors draw on a range of things including their competencies and different supervision models and approaches (Bogo and McKnight 2006; O'Donoghue et al. 2005). According to Sloan and Watson (2002, p. 41) supervision models and approaches provide a conceptual framework for supervisors that "highlight the different stages of the supervisory process, the functions of supervision, the supervisor's and supervisee's role and where to focus their attention," therefore how supervision is delivered can be influenced by the model and approach adopted by the supervisor. This chapter will briefly discuss a number of the more common supervision models and approaches used by social work supervisors and introduces the PASE supervision model which has been developed in Australia to support social work supervisors in their provision of supervision. The PASE model and its application to supervisory practice is also demonstrated using a practice example. The chapter concludes by suggesting that more research is required to consider how the PASE supervision model can positively influence the future of professional supervision practice, the Australian Association of Social Work supervision standards, and more broadly social work practice both in Australia and internationally.

Supervision models and approaches

Numerous supervision models and approaches have been developed over the years. A recent study of 231 social work supervisors (Harris 2017) in Australia found that the majority (59%) of respondents used supervision models and approaches to guide the supervision process and content of their supervision discussions. A New Zealand study surveyed 209 supervisors (O'Donoghue et al. 2005) and also found that social work supervisors use eclectic approaches in providing supervision. Both studies reported that supervisors were drawing on a wide range of models of supervision including orientation-specific, developmental, functional, systems, and integrated approaches in supervision. All of these models provide different approaches in which supervision is delivered in order for it to be focused and effective (Harris 2018; O'Donoghue and Tsui 2011). In an overview of the literature, Tsui (2005) suggests that supervisors often adopt theories in practice as a model of supervision and equally, supervision models can be derived from practice theory as evidenced in case work, group work, and peer supervision models (agency models). Other models around interactional processes and structural-functional models all support how social work occurs in practice.

Orientation-specific supervision models of supervision follow the same types of theories and tools that are used to work with clients in the practice context, for example, solution-focused therapy, strengths-based, narrative, and psychodynamic approaches (Basa 2017). The success of these models are associated with both the supervisor and supervisee having an adequate understanding of the therapeutic approach to use with the client and how it can be discussed and reflected upon in a supervision context. One of the more common orientation-specific supervision models used in social work is referred to as a strengths-based approach (O'Donoghue et al. 2005). When applying this approach, the supervisor uses strengths-based principles and language in supervision discussions. This is evidenced by identifying and externalizing the supervisee's personal and professional strengths and qualities and how these are applied in the supervisee's practice. Using this approach also provides a secure and supportive environment in which supervisees' can reflect on and reinforce their practice skills with confidence. The supervisor's role is to provide the space in which critical thinking can take place, which enhances reflection to build and maintain competence in the social worker's role based on their strengths (Calvert et al. 2017; Kadushin and Harkness 2014).

Developmental models of supervision are not aligned to any particular orientation, but are applicable to most, if not all, supervision approaches (Stoltenberg et al. 2014). Developmental models of supervision assume that supervisees progress through various stages of development in the practice context (novice through to advanced), and through the supervisor's capabilities, over time the supervisee transitions towards advanced practice (Stoltenberg 1981). When using a developmental model of supervision, supervisors assess the supervisee's developmental level (e.g. years of experience, qualifications, and competencies) and adjust their supervisory style accordingly to expedite the developmental process. For example, social work graduates may have limited knowledge and skills, therefore the supervisor imparts their expertise providing more direction to the supervisee in their work. It is assumed that more experienced social workers will have a clear understanding of their capabilities, use a professional practice framework to guide their practice, and be more independent in their role (Haynes et al. 2003; Stoltenberg and McNeill 2012). In a developmental model of supervision, supervisors provide supervisees with learning opportunities in each level so they can continue to further develop their capability (Dea 2016).

Over the last 40 years, the function of supervision approaches has been readily accepted as a preferred framework for supervision practice. Both Kadushin (1974) and Proctor's (1988) supervision framework proposed three functions. Kadushin's (1974) functional model proposed three domains of supervision: *administration* (e.g. supervisors ensuring that supervisees adhere to the organization's policies and procedures and meet the organizations requirements), *education* (e.g. supervisors helping supervisees to be more reflective in their work with clients to develop their full potential), and *support* (e.g. supervisors attending to their supervisee's expressed needs and providing psychological support to alleviate stress and burnout) (Kadushin 1974). Proctor (1988) developed a three-function model which also described the tasks and responsibilities of supervisors and supervisees. The three functions included: *normative* (e.g. where the supervisor supports the supervisee to reflect on their practice, deliver safe, ethical, and effective care to clients whilst maintaining professional accountability in their role), *formative* (e.g. the supervisor addresses the educational needs of the supervisee i.e. development of knowledge, skills, and attitudes, and identification of future training needs), and *restorative* (the supervisor develops a nurturing and supportive relationship with the supervisee and encourages their well-being through the use of self-care). Although presented as three separate functions, in practice these tasks and responsibilities overlap and intersect with each other in the organizational context (Bruncro & Stein-Parbury 2008). While there are similarities between Kadushin (1974) Proctor's (1988) three function models, each present their own perspectives of how to address the need for balancing the managerial aspects of supervision and support of the supervisee in practice.

Systems models such as Holloway's (1995) (SAS) Systems Approach to Supervision provides a useful context for the process of supervision and demonstrates the systemic nature of how it connects to the organizational business system. The SAS model was "designed to provide a visual road map for supervisors to strategically consider the numerous factors that impact on supervision both internal and external of the organisation environment" (Holloway 2016, p. 13). These factors include the learning that occurs in supervision, the client, supervisee, supervisor functions, the organization, and the supervisory alliance. To conceptualize the supervision process, Holloway (2016) created a matrix which defined the primary functions/roles for a supervisor as well as the learning tasks for supervisees (Johnston 2006). The functions in supervision included monitoring/evaluating (e.g. giving feedback), advising/instructing (e.g. sharing information), modeling (e.g. using role plays), consulting/exploring (e.g. encouraging reflection on practice), and supporting/sharing (e.g. being empathic) (Gaete and Ness 2015). The five learning tasks Holloway (2016) suggested that were important for supervisees included: focusing on counseling skills, case conceptualization, their professional role, emotional awareness, and self-evaluation (Lonneman Doroff 2012).

Given the extensive number of theories, models, and approaches that exist in providing supervision, integrated models of supervision have been developed that are eclectic, relying on more than one theory or approach. They are evidence-informed and consider the complexities of supervision (Haynes et al. 2003). An integrated supervision model that has been developed in Australia for social workers is the PASE supervision model. The PASE supervision model supports supervisors to consciously focus supervision sessions through an evidence informed framework that assists to integrate key aspects of their supervisory practice. The model considers the supervisor's capability, supervision tasks, organizational needs, and the supervisee's role. The PASE model ensures the focus of supervision discussions are more clearly defined and that time is used effectively in supervision sessions to ensure productive outcomes are achieved in an integrated manner (Harris 2018).

The PASE model

The PASE supervision model has been developed for social workers who are in a professional practice or clinical role. The model draws on common elements of the supervision models discussed in this chapter such as developmental and strengths-based models. The PASE model supports supervision to be highly transparent and use the discussion to evidence the supervisees' practice. It allows the supervisor to demonstrate key competencies and their supervisory style. The use of the PASE model is supported by social work research which has found that when supervision utilizes an evidence informed supervision model, it can result in supervisees feeling refocused and having more clarity about their work and practice. It also supports supervisees to be more satisfied with the supervision they receive and their role (O'Donoghue et al. 2018).

The PASE model is represented in a visual informed by a circle that is evenly divided into four quadrants: *Practice/Professional* (P), *Administrative/Line Management* (A), *Support/Person* (S), and *Educative/Professional Development* (E). Each of the quadrants reflect the important elements of what is typically discussed in supervision sessions. The PASE supervision model focuses on the social worker's professional practice (P), how the supervisee meets organizational requirements (A), explores how the supervisee is supported in their role (S), and how the supervisee continues to advance their knowledge and practice through evidence of professional excellence (E) (See Figure 29.1).

The PASE model allows supervision discussions to be purposeful, intentional, and meaningful in both intent and outcome, therefore increasing the reflexive process and productive outcomes. The model assists the supervisor and supervisee to easily set an agenda for each meeting through the words that act as prompts in each of the quadrants (see Figure 29.2). All four PASE quadrants do not need to be covered in every supervision session, but instead the model can be used more as a guide for what could be the focus for supervision discussions where the supervisor facilitates the discussion in the model as it aligns to the agenda. Agenda topics may come from any or all of the quadrants in the supervision session. Each of the four quadrants will now be discussed in more detail.

Quadrant one: Practice/Professional (P)

The Practice/Professional (P) quadrant focuses the supervision discussion on professional aspects of the social worker's role including how different practices and theoretical approaches are used in their role. Discussion in this quadrant typically focuses on: case conceptualization and case reviews, the supervisee's use of self in their role, and how they engage reflection on practice. Other topics in supervision include how the supervisee demonstrates their professional identity, ethical issues, decision making, and how the supervisee uses their professional practice framework to demonstrate their skills, knowledge, qualities, and professional identity in their work.

Quadrant two: Administrative/Line Management (A)

The Administrative/Line Management (A) quadrant focuses the supervision discussion on the line management aspects of the supervisee's role. This quadrant is used more often when the supervisor has a dual role of line manager and professional supervisor. Discussion in the *Administrative/Line Management* quadrant focuses on how the supervisee is meeting the require-

PASE™ Supervision Model

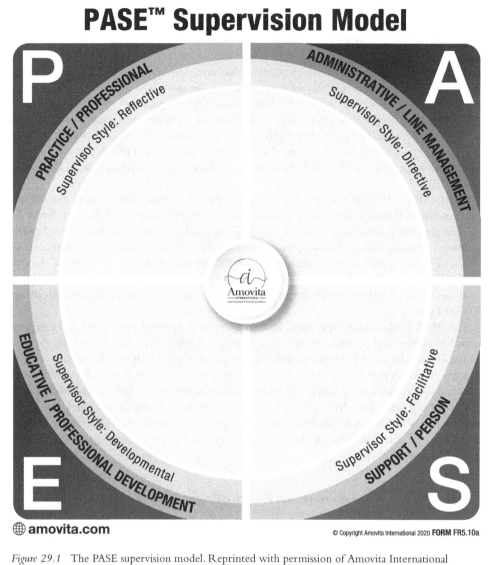

Figure 29.1 The PASE supervision model. Reprinted with permission of Amovita International

ments of the role, compliance, accreditation, risk management, client satisfaction, workflow, policies, and leave planning. This quadrant also focuses the supervision discussion on any performance issues. Initially they might be explored from the *Support/Person* quadrant to provide support but can also be discussed in the *Administrative/Line Management* quadrant to problem solve. Where issues continue around performance, the discussion is then taken outside of the supervision environment and addressed through the organization's performance management policy process (Harris 2018). This assists in maintaining the integrity of the supervisory relationship which can be fractured when the supervisor is both the line manager and professional supervisor. For this process to work effectively, the supervisor requires advanced supervisory skills including meta-competencies and specific supervisory training.

PASE™ Supervision Model

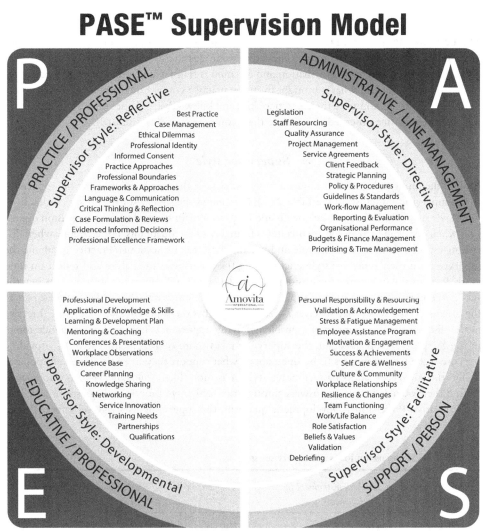

Figure 29.2 The PASE supervision model. Reprinted with permission of Amovita International

Quadrant three: Support/Person (S)

The Support/Person (S) quadrant focuses the supervision discussion on the supervisee's well-being, how self-care is maintained, engagement in professional relationships, and to acknowledge achievements. Other agenda items include how personal beliefs and values may intersect in their professional role, how to minimize fatigue and burnout in the role, and maintain resilience. This aspect of the discussion provides the supervisee with a debriefing mechanism where they can receive support, validation, encouragement and feel valued. When supervisees debrief in a supportive environment it increases trust and enables the supervisee to feel better connected to the supervisor/supervisee relationship and reduce the power differential that can exist in the supervisory alliance (Farmer 2009; Milne 2014; Miehls 2014).

Quadrant four: Educative/Professional Development (E)

The Educative/Professional Development (E) quadrant focuses on maintaining the supervisees' professional excellence in their role. The supervision agenda focuses on their developmental needs, career planning, how information and learning is transferred from supervision back into the supervisee's role, and what is brought from the practice context into supervision. It supports the supervisee to demonstrate their practice skills and knowledge and encourages the supervisee to have their practice observed to enhance their competencies (Harris 2018).

Supervisor style

Each of the four quadrants incorporate a supervisory style that can be adopted by the supervisor in the supervision discussion (see Table 29.1). This allows the supervisor to remain conscious of what style may suit the supervisee's needs and helps to remain focused in the supervision discussion when discussing any of the agenda items from any of the quadrants. For example, when discussing aspects of the supervisee's role and practice from the Professional/Practice quadrant, the supervisor can use a reflective style encouraging the supervisees to analyze and reflect on their work. It assists the supervisee to consider relevant language and communication style. When the supervisee uses a directive style of supervision in the Administrative/Line Management part of the discussion, the supervisee receives a clear message that the supervisor may be more directive in the discussion and use more of a problem-solving approach. When exploring agenda topics in the Support/Person quadrant, the supervisor takes more of a facilitative style by providing a secure space for supervisees to be open about what support they need through self-appraisal. When the supervisee adopts a facilitative style, it is more likely the supervisee is encouraged to find their own solutions or answers through the facilitative process and questions asked. In the Educative/Professional Development quadrant, the supervisor uses a developmental style

Table 29.1 PASE discussion focus and supervisor style

(P)Practice/Professional	(A)Administrative/Line Management	(S)Support/Person	(E)Educative/ Professional Development
DISCUSSION FOCUS			
Agenda items are focused on the professional and all aspects of their practice	The agenda is focused on meeting the organization's requirements in line with the supervisee's position description	Discussion is focused on the person in their role and offers the space for support, validation, and refueling	There is a focus on continual learning, growth, and professional development in the role
SUPERVISOR STYLE			
Reflective	**Directive**	**Facilitative**	**Developmental**
The supervisor guides a reflective discussion to promote practice excellence	The supervisor is outcome focused and solution focused, providing direction and clear outcomes	The supervisor's style provides a guided space to allow the supervisee to draw their own conclusions in the discussion	This style provides a developmental platform where the supervisee continually experiences growth and development

of supervision where the supervisee understands that the supervisor will use an approach that enhances the supervisee's knowledge and competencies. Having the supervisor's style listed in each of the quadrants demonstrates to the supervisee that different supervisory styles can be adopted in any of the quadrants throughout the discussion.

Using the PASE

The PASE supervision model can be utilized in either individual and group supervision and is used in every supervision session with the supervisee predominantly setting the agenda to meet their needs. At the beginning of the supervision meeting, the supervisor asks the supervisee what they would like to focus on in the discussion and from what quadrant. It is important that the supervisee understands the model and how to use it to be clear about from what perspective they would like to discuss their agenda items. The discussion then moves around the quadrants as relevant to make the discussion effective. The discussion does not need to be linear i.e. move from quadrant to quadrant, but the discussion can be more of a fluid process identifying where the discussion is focused as it occurs. Where supervisees prefer more of a linear process, the supervisor may discuss agenda items in each of the quadrants.

The PASE model incorporates a subjective evaluation process at the end of each supervision meeting that shows both parties where the focus of the discussion has been. The evaluation process uses a 10-point Likert scale, with 0 representing there has been no focus in that part of the quadrant discussion, and 10 represents there has been a significant discussion in that particular quadrant. If there are quadrants that are regularly focused on, or quadrants that are rarely focused on, this may require supervisors to review the supervision agenda and review why this might be occurring. The evaluation process is helpful for the supervisor to know where the focus of the supervision discussion has been over time and identify any trends i.e. there has been a significant focus in the Support/Person quadrant over time or where there has been no focus in a particular quadrant over time.

Normative evaluation approaches in supervision usually require the supervisee to provide verbal feedback about how supervision is going, for example, the supervisor may ask the supervisee how the supervision session was for them and what they got out of it. This can place unnecessary pressure on the supervisee to feel compelled to tell the supervisor how good supervision was or how skilled the supervisor is in their role (Falender and Shafranske 2017). Where the supervisee provides subjective feedback about the focus of the discussion rather than on how good the supervision was, it reduces the power differential in the supervisory relationship particularly where the supervisor has a dual role of line manager and professional supervisor. It allows the supervisee to provide authentic feedback that does not compromise any dual relationship in place i.e. where the supervisor is both the line management and professional supervisor (Harris 2018). The following example provides a useful overview of how the PASE supervision model's evaluation process can be used in supervision meetings.

Case example

To set the scene, Megan is an experienced social worker with a career spanning ten years. She is a senior social worker in a clinical mental health team undertaking clinical assessment services for organizations who work with children and youth in a therapeutic residential setting. Megan receives professional supervision from her line manager Matt. Both Megan and Matt have attended a PASE supervision training program (three days) separately just over a year ago. Matt provides formal supervision to Megan on a monthly basis.

Using the PASE model, Matt asks Megan what she would like to focus on in supervision. Megan advises from the Practice/Professional (P) quadrant she would like to discuss a complex case that she is having challenges with, from the Support/Person (S) quadrant she would like to discuss an ethical dilemma in relation to this case, and from the Administrative/Line Management (A) quadrant she would like to discuss her high workload as this has been impacting on her over the last few weeks.

Using the PASE supervision model to set the agenda ensures the conversation is focused and the supervisor has a clear idea of where to start the discussion. Megan can refer to the prompt words outlined in the each of the quadrants to set the agenda, and the discussion moves around the quadrants where relevant in a flexible and meaningful way rather than being a linear process as is often the case when setting the agenda in supervision.

The supervision discussion begins with Megan exploring a client case in an organization that is providing support to a twelve-year-old young person in a therapeutic residential setting. Megan overviews her concerns about the way some of the staff are engaging with the young person and the lack of trauma-informed practices in place. She discusses aspects of the case focused in the Practice/Professional quadrant, and because Megan has indicated that she wishes to start with the (P) quadrant initially, the supervisor now has a clear sense of where to focus the discussion. Knowing that the conversation is focused in the Practice/Professional quadrant allows the supervisor to adopt a reflective style through the use of relevant questions and communication techniques. When the case discussion focuses on the Practice/Professional quadrant, it also allows Megan to identify what aspects of her practice she is adopting through her professional practice framework and what professional strategies she can use with the organization to ensure a trauma-informed approach is taken. Through the supervisor's reflective style in this quadrant, questions are posed to Megan that raise her awareness in a way that minimizes the discussion being directive (as would typically be used in supervision which focuses on the Administrative/Line Management).

Megan has also included on her agenda an ethical dilemma she wishes to discuss from the Support/Person quadrant. Exploring the dilemma from this quadrant focuses the discussion on the impact the dilemma is having on Megan and what support she needs. She is likely to feel more supported by her supervisor having the discussion in this quadrant compared to having the discussion from the Administrative/Line Management quadrant. The supervisor adopts a line of questioning from an appreciative inquiry perspective that is facilitative rather than directive. The Support/Person quadrant discussion facilitates a space whereby the supervisee has the opportunity to resolve any dilemma given the facilitative approach taken in the discussion (Milne 2014). The supervisee contemplates the influence any dilemmas are having and seeks to understand the juncture between any personal and professional beliefs and values that may be evident (Harris 2018).

Megan's final agenda item were about workload challenges from an Administrative/Line Management perspective. Matt brainstorms with Megan relevant strategies to deal with her workload more effectively and discusses leave planning. Given the discussion is from the Administrative/Line Management quadrant, the supervisor will have more of a solution focused approach and provide direction if needed. As the meeting ends, Matt asks Megan to evaluate the focus of the discussion from each quadrant, and both parties assess where the focus of the discussion has been. Megan advises that she thought that the focus in the Practice/Professional quadrant was 8/10 and Matt agreed there had been a lot of discussion in that quadrant, so he rated the focus as a 7/10. In the Administrative/Line Management quadrant Megan stated she thought there was less focus in this quadrant so evaluated it as 3/10. Matt agreed it that there was a lower focus in this part of the discussion and evaluated the focus as a 4/10. When it came to evaluate the focus of the discussion in the Support/Person quadrant, Megan indicated she felt that she was able to resolve her ethical dilemma with support from Matt and they had a lot of discussion in this quadrant, so her evaluation was a 9/10. Matt indicated he thought it was a 7/10 for the same reason. Both parties made comment on their ratings and both agreed there had been no discussion in the Educative/Professional Development so both had 0/10. The ratings are included in the supervision minutes and compared over time from each meeting to see if any trends emerge. Where there is a discrepancy in the rating of more than three, both parties indicate why they believed what their rating was. It is normal when supervisees are getting to know the model and evaluation process for there to be differences in the supervisor and supervisee's evaluation. As both parties become familiar with using the model they align. Equally, the supervisor may evaluate a high focus in the Practice/Professional quadrant and the supervisee has a high evaluation in the Support/Person quadrant and vice versa. This can occur when there is a discussion about values and the supervisee is focused on personal values and the supervisor is focused in the discussion on professional values. There will be times where both parties are focused in different quadrants and this is noted in the supervision minutes.

PASE training

Supervisees and supervisors are encouraged to attend PASE supervision training either together or separately in understand how to use the model and undertake the evaluation process. The training includes how to move around the quadrants, how to set the agenda, the supervisor's style, and how to document discussions (Harris 2018). Training is delivered predominantly face-to-face, with an introductory (1 day), intermediate (2–3 days), and advanced training over three days. Depending on which training is attended, topics include: the context of supervision, how to undertake an intake process to ensure supervision is set up appropriately, use of appropriate documentation, how to record supervision discussions within an industrial context, developing an ethical decision-making framework and practice framework, as well as having open and challenging conversations. The training also explores how to evaluate the focus of each discussion and how to formally evaluate supervision. Participants receive a comprehensive PASE training manual and resources to use in supervision, for example, a professional excellence framework template, a range of reflective practice frameworks, ethical decision-making framework, and an ethical navigation process. In the advanced training, supervisors have their supervisory practice evaluated over the three days and benchmarked from beginner to advanced supervisory practice.

Evaluation of the PASE model

Over the last seven years, approximately 9,000 supervisors and supervisees have attended PASE training in Australia. Anecdotal feedback from many participants who have attended training indicates that the PASE supervision model is important to guide discussions and ensure supervision remains effective. After each training program, participants are invited to provide qualitative feedback that assists the facilitators to change any aspect of the training. For example, Peta provided feedback about the training, "this training is all about providing quality supervision. My mindset has changed about supervision and the PASE model has changed how I set the agenda and have discussions. The range of resources received in the training was incredible." Ben attended a three-day training,

> I thought I knew all there was about supervision having been a social worker for fifteen years and having been in senior roles. After attending the three-day PASE training,

> I now think differently about how I prepare for supervision, am far more present in the discussion and the PASE model has really changed how I have discussions. After training my supervisees in the model, they get more out of the discussion and are more interested in what they are achieving in their roles.

At the current time one formal research study has been undertaken (Allport 2018) in Australia to explore how supervisors learn and develop their supervision practice within the researcher's organization, a large non-government organization. The organizations training includes how to use the PASE supervision model in practice. The research found that the PASE model has a high level of recognition across the organization and Allport's (2018, p. 93) research indicated that the visual model is important as it ensure a consistent approach to supervision practice. Participants stated they valued the PASE model as it provided the necessary structure, and the four quadrants promoted consistency in discussions (Allport 2018). One respondent stated, "I use the PASE model. I love the PASE model because it's really easy to understand and it also helps guide the conversation." The research also found that the visual representation of the model assisted supervisees to feel their supervision was effective, with one participant stating, "I found it most useful being able to look visually at the PASE circle and the four different quadrants and unpacking which areas to focus on in supervision" (Allport 2018, p. 96).

With only one formal research study being undertaken that included aspects of the PASE supervision model, further research needs to be conducted to further validate the effectiveness of the model and its wider application to supervisory practice. As O'Donoghue et al. (2018) indicate, there continues to be a lack of empirically supported supervision models in social work, therefore it is important to be developing an evidence base for the use of supervision models such as PASE to support all aspects of the supervisees' role and to understand the competence and capability of supervisors in their supervisory practice (Bogo and McKnight 2006; Harris 2018).

Conclusion

The literature provides a clear picture of what supervision is, how it is defined, and the role it plays. There are various models and approaches that support supervisors to provide effective supervision. This chapter commenced with a review of some of the more common supervision models and approaches used in social work and provided an overview of the origins of the PASE supervision model, and the case examples demonstrated how to apply the PASE model in practice. The PASE supervision model contributes to the literature on social work supervision and the use of evidence-informed models to support effective outcomes. It also provides the Australian Association of Social Workers with the opportunity to update the supervision standards with a more contemporary approach about how supervision can be effective through the use of evidence informed models such as the PASE. Providing supervision is one of the critical elements in social work practice and one of the most neglected aspects in organizational systems. We will continue to evaluate the positive influence that the PASE model has in both supervision and social work practice and how social workers can look forward to their supervision discussions where they can define how supervision meets their needs.

References

Abu-Bader, S.H., 2000. Work satisfaction, burnout, and turnover among social workers in Israel: a causal diagram. *International Journal of Social Welfare*, 9 (3), 191–200.

Allport, B., 2018. *Study of the influence of training and work environment factors on learning and developing supervision practice within a human service organisation.* Thesis (MEd) Queensland University of Technology. Available from: https://eprints.qut.edu.au/116770/ [Accessed 13 Sept 2019].

Bambling, M., King, R., Raue, P., Schweitzer, R., and Lambert, W., 2006. Clinical supervision: its influence on client-related working alliance and client symptom reduction in the brief treatment of major depression. *Psychotherapy Research,* 16 (3), 317–331.

Basa, V., 2017. Models of supervision in therapy, brief defining features. *European Journal of Counselling Theory,* 1, 1–5.

Bernard, J., and Goodyear, R., 2009. *Fundamentals of clinical supervision.* 5th ed. New York: Pearson.

Bogo, M., and McKnight, K., 2006. Clinical supervision in social work: a review of the research literature. *The Clinical Supervisor,* 24 (1–2), 49–67.

Brunero, S., and Stein-Parbury, J., 2008. The effectiveness of clinical supervision in nursing: an evidence-based literature review. *Australian Journal of Advanced Nursing,* 25 (3), 86–94.

Calvert, F.L., Crowe, T.P., and Grenyer, B.F., 2017. An investigation of supervisory practices to develop relational and reflective competence in psychologists. *Australian Psychologist,* 52 (6), 467–479.

Carroll, M., 2010. Levels of reflection: on learning reflection. *Psychotherapy in Australia,* 16 (2), 24–31.

Chiller, P., and Crisp, B., 2012. Professional supervision: a workforce retention strategy for social work?. *Australian Social Work,* 65 (2), 232–242.

Dea, M., 2016. Guided paper on developmental supervision: critical review. *International Journal of Sciences: Basic and Applied Research,* 2 (1), 39–53.

Falender, C., and Shafranske, E., 2017. Competency-based supervision clinical supervision: status, opportunities, tensions and the future. *Australian Psychologist,* 52, 86–93.

Farmer, R., 2009. *Neuroscience and social work practice: the missing link.* Thousand Oaks, CA: SAGE Publications.

Gaete, J., and Ness, O., 2015. Supervision: from prescribed roles to preferred positionings. *The Clinical Supervisor,* 34 (1), 57–77.

Harris, T., 2017. *Excellence in supervisory practice:* developing *a supervisory capability framework for effective professional supervision in social work practice in Australia.* Unpublished thesis. Griffith University.

Harris, T., 2018. *Developing leadership excellence: a practical guide for the new professional supervisor.* New York: Routledge.

Haynes, R., Corey, G., and Moulton, P., 2003. *Clinical supervision in the helping professions: a practical guide.* Pacific Grove, CA: Brooks/Cole.

Holloway, E., 1995. *Clinical supervision: a systems approach.* Thousand Oaks, CA: SAGE.

Holloway, E., 2016. *Supervision essentials for a systems approach to supervision.* Washington, DC: American Psychological Association.

Johnston, K., 2006. *Defining the nature and outcomes of Australian professional supervision:* applying *Holloway's systems approach.* Thesis (PhD), Queensland University of Technology (QUT). Available from http://eprints.qut.edu.au/16383/ [Accessed 13 Sept 2019].

Kadushin, A., 1974. Supervisor supervisee: a survey. *Social Work,* 19 (3), 288–298.

Kadushin, A., and Harkness, D., 2014. *Supervision in social work.* 5th ed. New York: Columbia University Press.

Kim, H., and Lee, S.Y., 2009. Supervisory communication, burnout, and turnover intention among social workers in health care settings. *Social Work in Health Care,* 48 (4), 364–385.

Lonneman Doroff, T., 2012. *Supervision in applied counselling settings: a socially constructed grounded theory.* Thesis (PhD). University of Northern Colorado, USA. Available from: https://digscholarship.unco .edu/dissertations/197/?utm_source=digscholarship.unco.edu%2Fdissertations%2F197&utm_medium =PDF&utm_campaign=PDFCoverPages; https://digscholarship.unco.edu/dissertations/197/; https:// digscholarship.unco.edu/cgi/viewcontent.cgi?article=1197&context=dissertations [Accessed 17 August 2019].

Lucock, M.P., Hall, P., and Noble, R., 2006. A survey of influences on the practice of psychotherapists and clinical psychologists in training in the UK. *Clinical Psychology and Psychotherapy,* 13 (2), 123–130.

Miehls, D., 2014. Neuroscience insights that inform clinical supervision. *Smith College Studies in Social Work,* 84, (2–3), 367–384.

Milne, D., 2014. Beyond the acid test: a conceptual review and reformulation of outcome evaluation in clinical supervision. *American Journal of Psychotherapy,* 68 (2), 213–220.

Mor Barak, M., Nissly, J., and Levin, A., 2001. Antecedents to retention and turnover among child welfare, social work, and other human service employees: what can we learn from past research? A review and meta-analysis. *Social Service Review,* 75 (4), 625–661.

O'Donoghue, K., Munford, R., and Trlin, A., 2005. Mapping the territory: supervision within the association. *Social Work Review*, 17 (4), 46–64.

O'Donoghue, K., and Tsui, M-S., 2011. Towards a professional supervision culture: the development of social work supervision in New Zealand. *International Social Work*, 55 (1), 5–28.

O'Donoghue, K., Wong Yuh Ju, P., and Tsui, M-S., 2018. Constructing an evidence-informed social work supervision model. *European Journal of Social Work*, 21 (3), 348–358.

Proctor, B., 1988. Supervision: a co-operative exercise in accountability. *In*: M. Marken and M. Payne, eds. *Enabling and ensuring supervision in practice*. Leicester, UK: National Youth Bureau and Council for Education and Training in Youth and Community Work, 21–23.

Sloan, G., and Watson, H., 2002. Clinical supervision models for nursing: structure, research and limitations. *Nursing Standard*, 17 (4), 41–46.

Stoltenberg, C., 1981. Approaching supervision from a developmental perspective: the counsellor complexity model. *Journal of Counseling Psychology*, 28 (1), 59–65.

Stoltenberg, C., Bailey, K., Cruzan, C., Hart, J., and Ukuku, U., 2014. The integrative developmental model of supervision. *In*: D. Milne and C. Watkins. eds. *The Wiley international handbook of clinical supervision*. Oxford, UK: John Wiley & Sons Ltd, 576–597.

Stoltenberg, C.D., and McNeill, B.W., 2012. Supervision: research, models and competence. *In*: N.A. Fouad, J.A. Carter, and L.M. Subich. eds. *APA handbook of counselling psychology: vol. 1. Theories, research and methods*. Washington, DC: American Psychological Association, 295–327.

Thomas, J., 2010. *Ethical and legal issues in supervision and consultation*. Washington, DC: American Psychological Association.

Tsui, M.S., 2005. *Social work supervision: contexts and concepts*. CA: SAGE.

30

THE SNAP MODEL OF SUPERVISION

Karen Sewell

Introduction

Supervision for social work practice is highly valued for practitioners, a consensus that has been well established by the discipline (Beddoe and Wilkins 2019; Bogo and McKnight 2006). The value is based on the support provided by supervisors, and the reported knowledge and skill development that takes place within supervision (Beddoe and Wilkins 2019; Kadushin and Harkness 2014). However, the literature speaks to a lack of knowledge about what occurs within supervision in practice, and how supervision contributes to worker and client outcomes (Carpenter et al. 2013; Dorsey et al. 2017; O'Donoghue 2015). The literature is also clear that most workplace-based supervisors often perform their roles based on their experiences of supervision without specific training, access to supervision research or best practices, or guidance from models of supervision (Beddoe et al. 2016; Carpenter et al. 2013; Hoge et al. 2011; Kadushin and Harkness 2014). This has led social work supervision researchers to articulate the need for models of supervision to be specified with regard to content, processes, and frequency to guide practice and use in research to be able to evaluate effectiveness (Beddoe et al. 2016; Carpenter et al. 2013; Hoge et al. 2011; Milne 2014). Toward this end, a proposed model of clinical supervision for the SNAP (Stop Now and Plan) model is now presented.

The context and need for a SNAP model of supervision

The context for the proposed SNAP model of clinical supervision (CS model) is connected to children's mental health, the SNAP evidence-based interventions, and a Canadian national implementation strategy. Practice realities have further driven the need for the development of an intervention-specific model of supervision. This background information can be helpful in understanding an example of a structured approach to supervision that can benefit supervisors interested in practical ways to infuse theory and best practices into their supervision.

Disruptive behavior difficulties in childhood can lead to pervasive mental health issues, educational difficulties, delinquency, and unemployment (Fergusson et al. 2005; Wertz et al. 2018). In a recent Canadian provincial study using the DSM-IV-TR definition of behavioral disorders (i.e., comprising Attention-Deficit/Hyperactivity Disorder, Oppositional-Defiant Disorder, Conduct Disorder), the prevalence of these disorders for children aged 4–11 was 12%

(Georgiades et al. 2014). For this group of children and their families, involvement in mental health interventions to address their behavioral and socio-emotional needs can serve to ameliorate current and future mental health issues, support positive development, prevent problematic life trajectories, and reduce negative individual, family, and societal impact (Canadian Institute for Health Information 2015). Specific mental health programs have been identified as effective for this group of children based on empirical support (Kaminski and Claussen 2017).

Developed by the Child Development Institute, a children's mental health center in Toronto, Canada, the SNAP (Stop Now and Plan) model is an identified evidence-based intervention which includes two gender-specific programs offering multiple treatment components (e.g., individual, group, family counseling, community, school support, and advocacy) for children aged 6–11 with disruptive behaviors and their families (Augimeri et al. 2014). The interventions focus on the acquisition of emotion-regulation, self-control, and problem-solving skills. For children, involvement with SNAP has led to increased skills in these focus areas, as well as reduced anti-social behavior and aggression. For parents, involvement in SNAP has been shown to reduce stress, and support parenting efficacy. The evidence-base of these interventions includes randomized controlled trials (Augimeri et al. 2007; Burke and Loeber 2016, 2015; Walsh et al. 2002), multiple qualitative studies (e.g., Lipman et al. 2011), and a cost-benefit analysis (Farrington and Koegl 2015). In a private sector competition, this empirical support contributed to the SNAP model's selection as a social innovation to be backed by philanthropic financial and resource support. An implementation goal was set to reach approximately 14,000 children and families in affiliate intervention sites in 140 Canadian communities by 2022, referred to as "the SNAP Expansion" (Augimeri et al. 2018).

The "SNAP Expansion" comes at a time when there is a contemporary imperative to use the best available research evidence to inform interventions across disciplines and sectors (Fixsen et al. 2009), and specifically, the use of effective interventions in children's mental health (Waddell et al. 2019). However, in children's mental health services, the translation of research to practice and the implementation of effective interventions in community-based settings have had limited success (Barwick et al. 2019). Active processes to support the use of evidence in practice have been postulated as a solution, giving rise to the field of implementation science (Fixsen et al. 2009). The goals within the work of implementation science center on informing the real-world delivery of evidence-based processes, interventions, and policies through effective strategies that support sustainable benefits, and ultimately improve care (Bauer et al. 2015; Proctor 2017).

Successful implementation of new interventions is contingent upon behavioral change at multiple organizational levels, including among supervisors and staff (Fixsen et al. 2009). Supervisors have the ability to motivate and impact the attitudes of staff in adopting interventions as well as reduce perceived evidence-based intervention (EBI) burden through their leadership (Aarons et al. 2016; Brimhall et al. 2016). Supervision has been identified as a "key quality management strategy" (Bunger et al. 2017), with trained supervisors supporting clinician competence and EBI sustainability (Godley et al. 2011). Proctor and colleagues (2011) have identified sustainability of EBIs in community settings as the final stage of effective implementation, whereby EBIs attain viability and become regular practice within community-based organizations. While external consultants often provide consultation and training for the initial implementation, over time intervention sustainability is reliant on supervisors in the community settings who support staff through guidance, observation, and EBI skill practice (Bunger et al. 2017; Fixsen et al. 2009; Weisz et al. 2018).

Given there are many models of supervision available in the literature to provide guidance and direction for supervisors of students, trainees, and supervisors across helping professions (Bernard and Goodyear 2018; Pollock et al. 2017; Sewell 2018), it would be reasonable to wonder why a specific model of supervision would be needed, and what such a model could offer supervisors within the SNAP interventions. Intervention-specific supervision can be effective in supporting EBI delivery through incorporating active strategies (e.g., role playing, modeling) explicitly aimed at developing and maintaining practitioner competence needed for the intervention. Program developers can provide supervisor training, tools, and consultation aligned with the treatment approach, entrenching supervision policy in intervention licensure and thereby enhancing supervision being embedded in community-based agencies (Bearman et al. 2017; Hoge et al. 2014). Through surveying SNAP affiliate supervisors and practitioners in Canada, the need for a model of enhanced supervision was demonstrated. Participants reported receiving/providing supervision, yet the content and regular frequency of these supervisory sessions were variable (Sewell 2020a). Furthermore, strategies identified in the literature as supervisory best practices (e.g., reviewing work, skill practice) were not occurring regularly for participants (and in many cases were not occurring at all).

Developing a model of clinical supervision

In developing a model of clinical supervision, establishing the orientation and needed purpose were the first steps. Staff in the SNAP programs are interdisciplinary in nature and represent variety in educational backgrounds and experiences (Sewell 2020a). Social work is one of the key disciplines contributing to and represented in the development and delivery of the interventions. As such, a social work definition of supervision has been used to ground the purpose of the model, especially given the organizational context of the SNAP interventions. Kadushin and Harkness (2014, p. 11) define supervision in relation to the supervisor:

> A supervisor is a licensed social worker to whom authority is delegated to direct, coordinate, enhance, and evaluate the on-the-job performance of the supervisees for whose work he/she is held accountable. In implementing this responsibility, the supervisor performs administrative, educational and supportive functions in interaction with the supervisee in the context of a positive relationship. The supervisor's ultimate objective is to deliver to agency clients the best possible service, both quantitatively and qualitatively, in accordance with agency policies and procedures.

The next step in approaching the development of an evidence-informed model of supervision, was to become immersed in the supervision literature – social work, and that of related helping professions (e.g., psychology, nursing). Key social work texts and reviews provided grounding and direction. In particular, these texts included the work of Kadushin and Harkness (2014), Shulman (2010), and Munson (2002), which comprehensively explain supervisory purpose, functions, processes, and activities. The empirical literature was initially accessed through influential reviews – Bogo and McKnight's (2006) and O'Donoghue and Tsui's (2015) reviews summarizing supervision research from a social work perspective, and two meta-analyses by social workers providing insight into the state of supervision outcome research (Carpenter et al. 2013; Mor Barak et al. 2009). While not available at the time of developing the model, two additional social work reviews are informative, O'Donoghue et al.'s (2018) review constructing a social work supervision model of evidence-informed social work, and Wilkins (2019) review of social work reviews developing a theory of social work supervision. The interdisciplinary supervision literature was consulted and incorporated in the model as later described.

The literature provided an accepted, general theoretical proposition articulating the underlying tenets of supervision, stating that supervision functions to enhance worker outcomes and

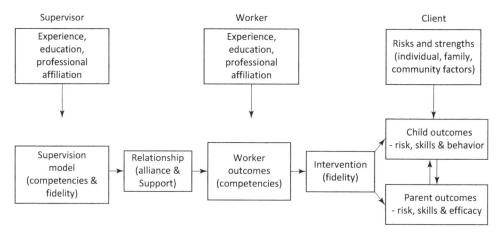

Figure 30.1 A conceptual model of the role of supervision with the SNAP interventions

thus service, which in turn enhances client outcomes (Bogo and McKnight 2006; Gonsalvez et al. 2017; Kadushin and Harkness 2014; Watkins 2011). The integrative functions of supervision have also widely been theorized. These functions – educative, supportive, and administrative – are employed toward the goal of improved services (Bogo and McKnight 2006; Kadushin and Harkness 2014). With foundational knowledge from the literature, a conceptual framework for the role of supervision within the SNAP interventions was developed, expanding on the general supervision theory of change to take into consideration theoretical influences from multiple system levels and findings from the empirical literature (see Figure 30.1: A conceptual model of the role of supervision with the SNAP interventions).

The literature was further directive in specifying the necessary dimensions and constructs required to develop the model (Jaccard and Jacoby 2010), which will be explained in this chapter.

An important step in the development of the model was the ongoing researcher-practitioner working relationship through which elements of the model were adjusted and enhanced in establishing value and fit for practice.

The SNAP model of supervision

The remainder of the chapter will focus on describing the CS model and tools that support supervision for the SNAP EBIs. The CS model is grounded in explanatory and practice theories, integrating best practices from disciplinary guidelines and complementary supervision practice models as they align with the SNAP intervention framework (Sewell 2017, see Figure 30.2: The SNAP Model of Supervision). The purpose of the CS model is "to provide the best possible service for clients through enhancing and supporting the implementation of the SNAP programs, while meeting the educational and emotional needs of staff" (Sewell 2017, p. 342). This is connected to a system's perspective, as described by Kadushin and Harkness (2014) where supervision comprises a sub-system of the supervisor and supervisee in which education and support occur, with the focus of this work on the practitioner-client dyad. The model includes an articulation of the structure of supervision, focusing predominately on standards which frame and support supervision within both the agency environment and the supervisor-supervisee

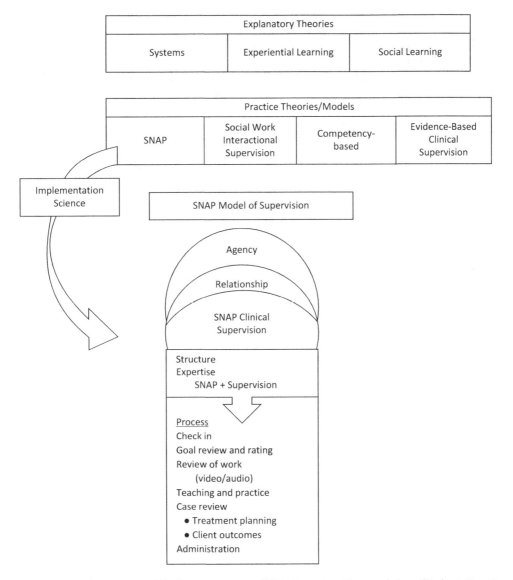

Figure 30.2 The SNAP Model of Supervision. Sewell (2017) reprinted by permission of Taylor & Francis Ltd.

dyad. The expertise dimension specifies the SNAP and generic supervision competencies—knowledge, skills, values/attitudes for supervisors. Integrating best practices from the identified practice theories and models, the process element specifies activities and methods occurring within supervisory sessions which both support the worker toward the development of competence and expertise, and ensure fidelity for the purpose of realizing beneficial client outcomes. The model is predicated on the supervisory relationship, and its importance in learning and enacting the SNAP intervention competencies to deliver the EBI (Beinart 2014; Kadushin and Harkness 2014; Tangen and Borders 2016; Watkins 2017).

Integrated theoretical underpinnings

Within the SNAP EBIs, there are identified core theories directing the work with children, families, and their environments. These include: systems, cognitive behavioral therapy, social interactional learning, and feminist and attachment theories (see Augimeri et al. 2014). As the CS model of supervision has been developed to support the theoretical orientation of the SNAP interventions, identifying and explicating relevant, complementary theories for supervision at the explanatory and practice levels provides a framework for understanding and directing supervisors in their practice (see Sewell 2017). At the explanatory level, systems, experiential learning, and social learning theories provide a way of understanding the importance and focus of supervision within the interventions, and supervisee learning within the larger children's mental health system within which the SNAP interventions operate. These explanatory theories also provide support for the dimensions of the CS model. Complementary supervision practice models (i.e., social work supervision, interactional supervision, competency-based supervision, and evidence-based clinical supervision) contribute key activities and processes that have been incorporated in the model, enhanced by and connected to the SNAP model framework and implementation science.

Structure

The model includes an articulation of the structure of supervision, focusing on standards which frame and support supervision within both the agency environment and the supervisor-supervisee dyad. While integrated in other dimensions of the CS model, a systems theory orientation is particularly salient in discussing the structure of supervision. The focus within this model is on the supervisee-supervisor, practitioner-client, agency, and implementation subsystems (Kadushin and Harkness 2014). It is through the implementation subsystem that the developers of SNAP can impact the structure and support for supervision with affiliate sites through standards for supervision, fidelity requirements and mechanisms, and licensure.

Hoge et al. (2014) developed standards of supervision for the Yale Program of Supervision which have largely been incorporated into the CS model. One of the standards that is being encouraged with the CS model is the use of a written supervision policy outlining the resources and specification of frequency and format for supervision. The structure also includes a contracting component between the practitioner and supervisor in order to provide clarity around expectations and set the conditions for establishing a productive supervisory relationship. A contract template directs a conversational process leading to documenting the contract and promotes accountability for supervision (see Figure 30.3, SNAP Supervision Contract). As is outlined in the contract, another aspect of the structure involves documentation of the supervisory sessions, again to promote accountability, provide a record of supervision and next steps to be revisited during subsequent sessions, and as a CS model fidelity mechanism.

Expertise

To enact the supervision model, the expertise dimension provides a clear articulation of the competencies deemed necessary to effectively supervise within the SNAP EBIs (see Figure 30.4 for the competencies as they are outlined in the SNAP Supervisor Competency Assessment and Goal Setting Form). Within the CS model, two sub-dimensions of competence are required: 1) that of the SNAP Intervention and 2) that of clinical supervision. For intervention competence, the competencies have been derived from the SNAP framework (Augimeri et al. 2014) which outlines intervention principles (e.g., client-centered, ecosystemic), the theoretical underpin-

SNAP® Supervision Contract

Between: _____ & _____
         (Staff member)   (Clinical Supervisor)

The following have been discussed:

☐ Approach to supervision

☐ Supervision experience, learning style and preferences

☐ Supervision roles and responsibilities:
   ☐ *Supervisee:*

- attend scheduled supervision regularly, or cancel and reschedule as agreed upon
- prepare agenda items for supervision
- identify work to review (videotape, written work, live observation)

- discuss support needs discuss client situations and outcomes
- practice skills
- bring forward issues that may interfere with work

_____

   ☐ *Supervisor:*

- attend scheduled supervision regularly, or cancel and reschedule as agreed upon
- prepare and bring agenda items for supervision
- bring forward identify work to review (videotape, written work, live observation)

- discuss and engage in ongoing assessment of learning and support needs
- review client outcomes with staff
- practice skills with staff member
- sign off on work
- keep log of supervisory sessions
- link to agency leadership

_____

☐ Confidentiality (and limits) within the supervisory relationship
- Duty to report; subpoenaed; if work is impacted-Director, HR, discussion of sharing of information if warranted

☐ Review purpose within SNAP programs

☐ Authority within the supervision relationship
- multiple supervisory roles (support, education, administration)
- scope of supervisory competence

☐ Evaluation:
- formal (probationary, yearly thereafter), completed by supervisor with input from supervisee
- informal: in supervision, following observations

☐ Frequency: _____

Figure 30.3 SNAP Supervision Contract. Reprinted by permission of Child Development Institute. All rights reserved. No part of this may be reproduced or transmitted in any form or by any means without written permission from Child Development Institute

☐ Duration: _____

☐ Scheduling, cancellation and rescheduling: _____

☐ Review structure, process, and content of supervision

☐ Preparation for supervision

☐ _____

☐ _____

Name: _____   Name: _____
       (Staff Member)   (Clinical Supervisor)

Date: _____   Date: _____

Figure 30.3 Continued

nings (e.g., social interactional learning, cognitive behavioral therapy), and the research-base of the interventions. In order to support and direct staff in work aimed at facilitating treatment goals, supervisors are expected to have knowledge of, and skills in, assessment and treatment as aligned with the intervention approach. Having knowledge and skills in these areas allow for supervisors to be seen as credible to staff, to model and coach skill practice appropriately, guide treatment planning and client outcome reviews, engage in co-counseling, and provide growth-oriented feedback. With respect to clinical supervision competence, consensus statements developed for the disciplines of social work (Association of Social Work Boards 2019) and psychology (Falender and Shafranske 2004) have greatly informed the identified, knowledge, skill, and value/attitude competencies included in the model (Sewell 2017). It is important to note, that in line with the current state of competency-based supervision (Falender and Shafranske 2017), these competencies are aspirational. Meaning, that through identifying competencies in the literature that support the SNAP EBIs and the stated purpose of supervision within the SNAP model, allows supervisors to self-assess and identify areas of competence and areas that require additional attention. For areas that are rated below the average level of competence, supervisors are able to set goals and determine developmental steps that can support learning in these areas (e.g., consultation, self-directed reading lists).

Process

The process element of the CS model provides guidance for the activities and content occurring within supervision, ensuring all three functions of supervision are met (i.e., support, education, and administration), supports practitioners toward the development of competence and expertise, and ensures fidelity for the purpose of realizing beneficial client outcomes. This element is connected to experiential learning principles of activating previous experience, abstract conceptualization, practice, and reflection, creating safe learning environments in supervision to transform experiences into learning (Kolb and Kolb 2005). It is also connected to social learning theory whereby learning and skill mastery toward self-efficacy takes place through modeling, goal setting and monitoring, skill practice, reinforcement, and the provision of feedback (Bandura 1977). Best practices and "gold star strategies" have been identified as connected to these learning theories and aligned with strategies promoted within implementation science (Accurso et al. 2011; Borders et al. 2014; Dorsey et al. 2013; Fixsen et al. 2005; Manthorpe et al. 2015; Milne et al. 2011; Shulman 2010). These activities/processes

SNAP® Supervisor Competency Assessment and Goal Setting Form

Name:_____   Date: _____

I – Knowledge	*(1= low level, 3= average level, 5= high level)*		
SNAP Model, research-base and underlying theories (Systems, Social Interactional Learning, Cognitive Behavioral Therapy, Attachment and Feminist theories)	1—2—3—4—5 n/a	Ethics and legal issues specific to working with children and families	1—2—3—4—5 n/a
Assessment, case planning, intervention, evaluation for children with behavior problems & their families; school and community systems	1—2—3—4—5 n/a	Diversity in all forms	1—2—3—4—5 n/a
CS structure (i.e. supervision contracting, staff assessment, evaluation)	1—2—3—4—5 n/a	Compassion fatigue, burnout and vicarious trauma	1—2—3—4—5 n/a
II-Skills	*(1– low ability, 3– average ability, 5– excellent ability)*		
Relationship skills (building supervisory relationship, communication)	1—2—3—4—5 n/a	Addressing parallel process	1—2—3—4—5 n/a
Assessing: competencies, learning style and needs, development level of supervisee	1—2—3—4—5 n/a	Encouraging and using evaluative feedback from the supervisee	1—2—3—4—5 n/a
Teaching and didactic skills	1—2—3—4—5 n/a	Conducting own self-assessment process	1—2—3—4—5 n/a
Promoting growth and self- assessment in the supervisee	1—2—3—4—5 n/a	Establishing and maintaining boundaries, and identify issues outside of supervisory competence and seeking	1—2—3—4—5 n/a
Evaluating: formative and summative (constructive feedback: validating effective performance and supporting areas of needed improvement)	1—2—3—4—5 n/a	Flexibility	
Addressing thoughts, feelings, and behaviors	1—2—3—4—5 n/a		
III- Values/Attitudes	*(1= low commitment, 3= average commitment, 5= high commitment)*		
Responsible for client and supervisee rests with supervisor	1—2—3—4—5 n/a	Committed to ethical principles, and guide supervisee in meeting	1—2—3—4—5 n/a
Both supportive and challenging	1—2—3—4—5 n/a	Committed to using evidence related to supervision	1—2—3—4—5 n/a
Respectful	1—2—3—4—5 n/a	Responsible for sensitivity to diversity in all its forms	1—2—3—4—5 n/a
Empowering	1—2—3—4—5 n/a	*Commitment to lifelong learning and professional growth*	1—2—3—4—5 n/a
Capable of balancing clinical work and training needs	1—2—3—4—5 n/a	*Commitment to knowing one's limitations*	1—2—3—4—5 n/a

Your supervisory goal:

_____

_____

Date: _____

Figure 30.4 SNAP Supervisor Competency Assessment and Goal Form. Adapted from Child Development Institute's SNAP Skills Competency Checklist (CCCO)

Steps Necessary to Achieve Goal:

1.

2.

3.

Goal Ratings:

How did you do on your goal?	(1= needs improvement, 3= some progress, 5= achieved)		
Date:_____	1—2—3—4—5 n/a	_____	1—2—3—4—5 n/a
Date:_____	1—2—3—4—5 n/a	_____	1—2—3—4—5 n/a
Date:_____	1—2—3—4—5 n/a	_____	1—2—3—4—5 n/a
Did you achieve your goal? Yes – No		Date: _____	

Figure 30.4   Continued

have been outlined in the Post Supervision Record (see Figure 30.5) and constitute a focus of the training for supervisors. The best practices and "gold star strategies" include the following: a check-in focusing on the relationship and agenda setting, practitioner goal review and rating, review of work, teaching and EBI skill practice including modeling and coaching, case review and conceptualization taking into consideration client outcomes, administration, and evaluation of the supervisory session. A semi-structured format allows supervisors to ensure integration of best practices, while tailoring the supervision as needed to the developmental level and case load needs of practitioners.

Training, tools, and consultation

Training for the CS model is intended to strengthen and build on supervisors' existing skills and knowledge in order to successfully implement the CS model with their staffing groups. As previously described (Sewell 2020b), the training content emphasizes the dimensions of the SNAP CS model (i.e., structure, expertise, and process), with a focus on supervisory best practices, and implementation of the model. The training highlights the theoretical underpinnings of the model and how these can be translated into practice. Content emphasis can be tailored to participants' goals related to their self-ratings of competence (e.g., managing relationships, delivering feedback, using skill rehearsal with staff). The SNAP Supervisor Competency Assessment and Goal form is completed by participants ahead of the training sessions for this purpose (see Figure 30.4). A variety of teaching/learning strategies are incorporated in the training, as identified in the supervision training literature, e.g., lecture-style presentations, group discussions, role-playing, and problem-based learning activities (Milne et al. 2011; Stuart et al. 2004). Following the CS model pilot (Sewell 2020b), additional voluntary consultation/coaching activities were added to the model to support supervisors (Egizio et al. 2019; Fixsen et al. 2009). This involves monthly phone consultations to discuss implementation of the supervisory model and problem-solving challenges related to real-world practice. Supervisors have the opportunity to add agenda items for the consultation related to their supervisory competency goals.

POST-SUPERVISION RECORD

Staff: _____   Supervisor: _____   Date of Session: _____

Process	Notes and Follow Up
Check in	
Goal Review and Rating: SNAP Competency Goal / Other Clinical Goal / Professional Development Goal	
Review of Work Digital Written	
Teaching-identify content: **Skill Practice-identify skill:**	
Case Review See attached for further details	Client Initials*: Assessment/formulation Tx Planning Critical Risk/Outcome Review
Administration	
Supervision session feedback	
Additional Notes:	

* Abridged. Reprinted by permission of Child Development Institute. All rights reserved. No part of this may be reproduced or transmitted in any form or by any means without written permission from Child Development Institute.

Figure 30.5   SNAP Post-Supervision Record. Abridged. Reprinted by permission of Child Development Institute. All rights reserved. No part of this may be reproduced or transmitted in any form or by any means without written permission from Child Development Institute

Support for the model

Initial support for the CS model can be associated with its theoretical grounding, connection to the literature, and incorporation of best practices. Additionally, support is linked to the process of establishing face validity with the SNAP Development Team and the model connection to the SNAP interventions and practice. However, the intent has been to stringently evaluate the model with respect to worker and client outcomes. The articulation of the CS model was the first step. As recommended by Carpenter and colleagues (2013), an incremental, evidence-building approach is being used. A multiple case study was conducted to assess implementation outcomes (Proctor et al. 2011) and determine if the model was acceptable to intervention supervisors, applicable to their work, adopted during a pilot period, and feasible (Sewell 2020b).

Three SNAP sites implemented the CS model for a period of three months during which time Post-Supervision Records documents were submitted (n= 64). Qualitative interviews were then conducted with supervisors from these sites with varying experience levels in conducting supervision, to explore their experiences in implementing the CS model (n=3). Findings indicate that the CS model was found to be acceptable and applicable, that it was adopted, and was generally feasible within the parameters of practice settings (e.g., vacation, position vacancies). These findings were related to the direction the CS model provided in establishing supervision structure, enhancing collaborative relationships, increasing focus in sessions, and integrating best practices in supervision.

A feasibility pilot study assessing the feasibility of processes (i.e., recruitment and retention rates), study management (i.e., challenges in managing the study requirements), and scientific impact (i.e., treatment effect; Thabane et al. 2010) is currently underway. The study is testing the hypothesis that adherence to the SNAP CS model will increase both workers' competencies related to delivery of the SNAP intervention and their perception of supervisory support following a six-month study period. Challenges with recruitment for a control group have impacted the ability to use a randomized controlled study design, however, preliminary results suggest the CS model contributes to practitioner competence and perceived support in intervention implementation. Interviews with supervisors and practitioners support the multiple case study findings in that the structure of the model is perceived to be beneficial, and there is a heightened focus on competence development. Furthermore, both supervisors and practitioners are reporting that supervision is occurring more frequently, and the quality is enhanced. Quantitative competence measures are being completed pre-post, along with a validated supervision measure capturing support, and fidelity is being tracked. Depending on the results of this study, the next step in the program of research will involve examining client outcomes related to the intervention as provided either by staff members who received supervision per the CS model, or practitioners whose supervisors did not participate in implementing the CS model.

Conclusion

In response to practice and implementation needs, the proposed SNAP CS model has been informed by the social work and interdisciplinary supervision literature and grounded in both explanatory and practice theories. Through an articulation of the model dimensions of structure, expertise, and process, guidance is provided to supervisors in implementing a structured approach to supervision. This guidance is furthered through model-specific training, consultation, and tools. The proposed model has been the focus of a multiple case study where it was adopted, deemed acceptable, appropriate, and predominately feasible by participants. A feasibility pilot is currently underway, examining the impact of the model on worker competence and perceived support.

References

Aarons, G.A., Ehrhart, M.G., Torres, E.M., Finn, N.K., and Roesch, S.C., 2016. Validation of the implementation leadership scale (ILS) in substance use disorder treatment organizations. *Journal of Substance Abuse Treatment*, 68, 31–35. https://doi.org/10.1016/j.jsat.2016.05.004

Accurso, E., Taylor, R., and Garland, A., 2011. Evidence-based practices addressed in community-based children's mental health clinical supervision. *Training and Education in Professional Psychology*, 5, 88–96. https://doi.org/10.1037/a0023537

Association of Social Work Boards 2019. *An analysis of supervision for social work licensure: guidelines on supervision for regulators and educators.* https://www.aswb.org/wp-content/uploads/2021/01/Supervision -Analysis.pdf [Accessed 4 March 2021].

Augimeri, L.K., et al., 2007. The SNAP™ under 12 outreach project: effects of a community based program for children with conduct problems. *Journal of Child and Family Studies*, 16, 799–807. https://doi .org/10.1007/s10826-006-9126-x

Augimeri, L.K., et al., 2014. Stop Now and Plan (SNAP®) model. *In*: *Encyclopedia of criminology and criminal justice.* Vol. 9. Springer Science+Business Media, 5053–5063.

Augimeri, L.K., Walsh, M., and Slater, N., 2018. *Scaling for social impact: taking an evidence-based program, SNAP, to scale.* Paper presented at the 2018 Annual Meeting of Children's Mental Health Ontario, Toronto, ON.

Bandura, A., 1977. *Social learning theory.* Englewood Cliffs, NJ: Prentice Hall.

Barwick, M., et al., 2019. Advancing implementation frameworks with a mixed methods case study in child behavioral health. *Translational Behavioral Medicine*, 1–20. https://doi.org/10.1093/tbm/ibz005

Bauer, M.S., et al., 2015. An introduction to implementation science for the non-specialist. *BMC Psychology*, 3, 32. https://doi.org/10.1186/s40359-015-0089-9

Bearman, S.K., Schneiderman, R.L., and Zoloth, E., 2017. Building an evidence base for effective supervision practices: an analogue experiment of supervision to increase EBT fidelity. *Administration and Policy in Mental Health and Mental Health Services Research*, 44 (2), 293–307.

Beddoe, L., et al., 2016. Towards an international consensus on a research agenda for social work supervision: report on the first survey of a Delphi study. *British Journal of Social Work*, 46, 1568–1586. https:// doi.org/10.1093/bjsw/bcv110

Beddoe, L., and Wilkins, D., 2019. Does the consensus about the value of supervision in social work stifle research and innovation?. *Aotearoa New Zealand Social Work*, 31, 1–6. http://dx.doi.org/10.11157/ anzswj-vol31iss3id643

Beinart, H., 2014. Building and sustaining the supervisory relationship. *In*: C.E. Watkins Jr and D.L. Milne, eds. *The Wiley international handbook of clinical supervision*. New York, NY: John Wiley and Sons, 255–281.

Bernard, J.M., and Goodyear, R.K., 2018. *Fundamentals of clinical supervision* 6th ed. Upper Saddle River, NJ: Pearson.

Bogo, M., and McKnight, K., 2006. Clinical supervision in social work: a review of the research literature. *The Clinical Supervisor*, 24, 49–67. https://doi.org/10.1300/J001v24n01_04

Borders, L.D., et al., 2014. Best practices in clinical supervision: evolution of a counseling specialty. *The Clinical Supervisor*, 33, 26–44. https://doi.org/10.1080/07325223.2014.905225

Brimhall, K.C., Fenwick, K., Farahnak, L.R., Hurlburt, M.S., Roesch, S.C., and Aarons, G.A., 2016. Leadership, organizational climate, and perceived burden of evidence-based practice in mental health services. *Administration and Policy in Mental Health and Mental Health Services Research*, 43 (5), 629–639. doi:10.1007/s10488-015-0670-9

Bunger, A.C., et al., 2017. Tracking implementation strategies: a description of a practical approach and early findings. *Health Research Policy and Systems*, 15. https://doi.org/10.1186/s12961-017-0175-y

Burke, J.D., and Loeber, R., 2015. The effectiveness of the Stop Now and Plan (SNAP) program for boys at risk for violence and delinquency. *Prevention Science*, 16, 242–253. https://doi.org/10.1007/s11121 -014-0490-2

Burke, J.D., and Loeber, R., 2016. Mechanisms of behavioral and affective treatment outcomes in a cognitive behavioral intervention for boys. *Journal of Abnormal Child Psychology*, 44, 179–189. https://doi.org /10.1007/s10802-015-9975-0

Canadian Institute for Health Information 2015. *Care for children and youth with mental disorders.* Ottawa, ON: Canadian Institute for Health Information.

Carpenter, J., Webb, C.M., and Bostock, L., 2013. The surprisingly weak evidence base for supervision: findings from a systematic review of research in child welfare practice (2000 2012). *Children and Youth Services Review*, 35, 1843–1853. https://doi.org/10.1016/j.childyouth.2013.08.014

Dorsey, S., et al., 2013. Improving practice in community-based settings: a randomized trial of supervision—study protocol. *Implementation Science*, 8, 1–12.

Dorsey, S., et al., 2017. The juggling act of supervision in community mental health : implications for supporting evidence-based treatment. *Administration and Policy in Mental Health and Mental Health Services Research*, 44, 838–852. https://doi.org/10.1007/s10488-017-0796-z

Egizio, L.L., et al., 2019. Field supervision training for a screening brief intervention and referral to treatment (SBIRT) implementation project. *Clinical Social Work Journal*, 47, 53–60. https://doi.org/10.1007 /s10615-018-0686-1

Falender, C.A., and Shafranske, E.P., 2004. *Clinical supervision: a competency-based approach.* Washington, DC: American Psychological Association (APA).

Falender, C.A., and Shafranske, E.P., 2017. Competency-based clinical supervision: status, opportunities, tensions, and the future: competency-based clinical supervision. *Australian Psychologist*, 52, 86–93. https://doi.org/10.1111/ap.12265

Farrington, D.P., and Koegl, C.J., 2015. Monetary benefits and costs of the Stop Now and Plan program for boys aged 6–11, based on the prevention of later offending. *Journal of Quantitative Criminology*, 31, 263–287. https://doi.org/10.1007/s10940-014-9240-7

Fergusson, D.M., Horwood, J.L., and Ridder, E.M., 2005. Show me the child at seven: the consequences of conduct problems in childhood for psychosocial functioning in adulthood. *Journal of Child Psychology and Psychiatry*, 46, 837–849. https://doi.org/10.1111/j.1469-7610.2004.00387.x

Fixsen, D.L., et al., 2005. *Implementation research: a synthesis of the literature (No. FMHI Publication #231).* University of South Florida, Louis de al Parte Florida Mental Health Institute, The National Implementation Research Network, Tampa, Florida.

Fixsen, D.L., et al., 2009. Core implementation components. *Research on Social Work Practice*, 19, 531–540. https://doi.org/10.1177/1049731509335549

Georgiades, K., et al., 2014. Ontario child health study team, 2019. Six-month prevalence of mental disorders and service contacts among children and youth in Ontario: evidence from the 2014 Ontario Child Health Study. *Canadian Journal of Psychiatry*, 64, 246–255. https://doi.org/10.1177/0706743719830024

Godley, S.H., et al., 2011. A large-scale dissemination and implementation model for evidence-based treatment and continuing care. *Clinical Psychology: Science and Practice* 18, 67–83.

Gonsalvez, C.J., Deane, F.P., and O'Donovan, A., 2017. Introduction to the special issue recent developments in professional supervision: challenges and practice implications. *Australian Psychologist*, 52, 83–85. https://doi.org/10.1111/ap.12276

Hoge, M.A., et al., 2011. Supervision in public sector behavioral health: a review. *The Clinical Supervisor*, 30, 183–203. https://doi.org/10.1080/07325223.2011.604276

Hoge, M.A., et al., 2014. Strengthening supervision in systems of care: exemplary practices in empirically supported treatments. *Clinical Social Work Journal*, 42, 171–181. https://doi.org/10.1007/s10615-013-0466-x

Jaccard, J., and Jacoby, J., 2010. *Theory construction and model-building skills: a practical guide for social scientists.* New York, NY: Guilford Press.

Kadushin, A., and Harkness, D., 2014. *Supervision in Social Work.* 5th ed. Columbia University Press.

Kaminski, J.W., and Claussen, A.H., 2017. Evidence base update for psychosocial treatments for disruptive behaviors in children. *Journal of Clinical Child & Adolescent Psychology*, 46, 477–499. https://doi.org/10.1080/15374416.2017.1310044

Kolb, A.Y., and Kolb, D.A., 2005. Learning styles and learning spaces: enhancing experiential learning in higher education. *Academy of Management Learning & Education*, 4, 193–212.

Lipman, E.L., et al., 2011. Helping boys at-risk of criminal activity: qualitative results of a multi-component intervention. *BMC Public Health*, 11, 364.

Manthorpe, J., et al., 2015. Content and purpose of supervision in social work practice in England: views of newly qualified social workers, managers and directors. *British Journal of Social Work*, 45, 52–68. https://doi.org/10.1093/bjsw/bct102

Milne, D.L., et al., 2011. Evidence-based training for clinical supervisors: a systematic review of 11 controlled studies. *The Clinical Supervisor*, 30, 53–71. https://doi.org/10.1080/07325223.2011.564955

Milne, D.L., 2014. Toward an evidence-based approach to clinical supervision. *In*: C.J. Watkins Jr. and D.L. Milne, eds. *The Wiley international handbook of clinical supervision.* New York, NY: Wiley-Blackwell, 38–60.

Mor Barak, M.E., et al., 2009. The impact of supervision on worker outcomes: a meta-analysis. *Social Service Review*, 83, 3–32. https://doi.org/10.1086/599028

Munson, C.E., 2002. *Handbook of clinical social work supervision.* Binghamton, NY: Haworth Press.

O'Donoghue, K.B., 2015. Issues and challenges facing social work supervision in the twenty-first century. *China Journal of Social Work*, 8, 136–149. https://doi.org/10.1080/17525098.2015.1039172

O'Donoghue, K.B., and Tsui, M.-S., 2015. Social work supervision research (1970–2010): the way we were and the way ahead. *British Journal of Social Work*, 45, 616–633. https://doi.org/10.1093/bjsw/bct115

O'Donoghue, K.B., Wong Yuh Ju, P., and Tsui, M.S., 2018. Constructing an evidence-informed social work supervision model. *European Journal of Social Work*, 21, 348–358. http://dx.doi.org/10.1080/13691457.2017.1341387

Pollock, A., Campbell, P., Deery, R., Fleming, M., Rankin, J., Sloan, G., and Cheyne, H., 2017. A systematic review of evidence relating to clinical supervision for nurses, midwives and allied health professionals. *Journal of advanced nursing*, 73 (8), 1825–1837. https://doi.org/10.1111/jan.13253

Proctor, E., 2017. The pursuit of quality for social work practice: three generations and counting. *Journal of the Society for Social Work and Research*, 8, 335–353. https://doi.org/10.1086/693431

Proctor, E., et al., 2011. Outcomes for implementation research: conceptual distinctions, measurement challenges, and research agenda. *Administration and Policy in Mental Health and Mental Health Services Research*, 38, 65–76. https://doi.org/10.1007/s10488-010-0319-7

Sewell, K.M., 2017. Theoretically grounded, evidence-informed clinical supervision for the SNAP programs: a model in development. *The Clinical Supervisor*, 36, 340–359. https://doi.org/10.1080/07325223.2017.1352549

Sewell, K.M., 2018. Social work supervision of staff: a primer and scoping review (2013–2017). *Clinical Social Work Journal*, 46, 252–265.

Sewell, K.M., 2020a. Exploring supervision in practice within an evidence-based intervention for children with severe disruptive behaviors. Manuscript submitted for publication.

Sewell, K.M., 2020b. Implementing a proposed model of clinical supervision in an evidence-based intervention: a multiple case study. Manuscript submitted for publication.

Shulman, L., 2010. *Interactional supervision*. 3rd ed. Washington, DC: National Association of Social Workers Press.

Stuart, G.W., Tondora, J., and Hoge, M.A., 2004. Evidence-based teaching practice: implications for behavioral health. *Administration and Policy in Mental Health and Mental Health Services Research*, 32, 107–130.

Tangen, J.L., and Borders, D., 2016. The supervisory relationship: a conceptual and psychometric review of measures. *Counselor Education and Supervision*, 55, 159–181. https://doi.org/10.1002/ceas.12043

Thabane, L., et al., 2010. A tutorial on pilot studies: the what, why and how. *BMC Medical Research Methodology*, 10, 1.

Waddell, C., et al., 2014. Ontario child health study team, 2019. 2014 Ontario child health study findings: policy implications for Canada. *Canadian Journal of Psychiatry*, 64, 227–231. https://doi.org/10.1177/0706743719830033

Walsh, M.M., Pepler, D., and Levene, K., 2002. A model intervention for girls with disruptive behaviour problems: the earlscourt girls connection. *Canadian Journal of Counselling*, 36, 297–311.

Watkins, C.E., 2011. Does psychotherapy supervision contribute to patient outcomes? considering thirty years of research. *The Clinical Supervisor*, 30, 235–256. https://doi.org/10.1080/07325223.2011.619417

Watkins, C.E., 2017. Convergence in psychotherapy supervision: a common factors, common processes, common practices perspective. *Journal of Psychotherapy Integration*, 27, 140–152. https://doi.org/10.1037/int0000040

Weisz, J.R., et al., 2018. When the torch is passed, does the flame still burn? testing a "train the supervisor" model for the Child STEPs treatment program. *Journal of Consulting and Clinical Psychology*, 86, 726–737. https://doi.org/10.1037/ccp0000331

Wertz, J., et al., 2018. From childhood conduct problems to poor functioning at age 18 years: examining explanations in a longitudinal cohort Study. *Journal of the American Academy of Child & Adolescent Psychiatry*, 57, 54–60. https://doi.org/10.1016/j.jaac.2017.09.437

Wilkins, D., 2019. Social work supervision in child and family services: developing a working theory of how and why it works. *Aotearoa New Zealand Social Work*, 31, 7–19. https://doi.org/10.11157/anzswj-vol31iss3id644

31

STRENGTHS-BASED SUPERVISION

Lambert Engelbrecht

Introduction

This chapter propounds strengths-based supervision in social work, which may find common ground in diverse contexts. A strengths-based perspective in social work practice is not a modern conception, and this chapter starts with conceptualizing a strengths-based perspective on social work intervention. It is argued that the significance of a strengths-based perspective does not attach exclusively to social work intervention; all practice-based social work interventions with service users cannot simply be paralleled or translated to supervision of social workers without some contextual modification; but the underlying philosophical roots should remain the same for intervention with service users and supervision of social workers. Particular strengths-based principles, processes, tasks, techniques, and tools can be devised and employed in strengths-based supervision. This is illustrated in this chapter by a vignette reflecting tangible examples of the composition of a strengths-based equation and assessment, associated tools, a supervision plan, and subsequent supervision sessions. Specific strengths-based supervision attributes were identified, which could be built on, adapted, and converted to fit unique contexts of a specific supervision equation as a proactive response to managerial demands.

A strengths-based perspective on social work intervention

The philosophical roots of a strengths-based perspective may be traced back to an Aristotelian teleological theory of *eudaimonia*, commonly translated into such modern positive psychology constructs as happiness, well-being, welfare, and human flourishing — all typically considered to be based on subjective elements and ideas of human virtues (compare Buckingham and Clifton 2001; Gray 2011; Seligman 2011). This philosophy presumes that all human beings have the ability to flourish by impelling innate capacities towards capabilities on a higher level, given the right conditions.

Eudaimonia denotes the fundamental philosophy of many disciplines of the social sciences, and influenced the ideas of most Western social work pioneers. However, many of the pioneering scholars who contributed to the body of knowledge of Western social work (cf. Hollis 1966; Perlman 1957; Richmond 1917), and who suggested that social workers should appreciate their clients' strengths, based their theories on the problems of individuals, groups, and communities, which were commonly regarded as the linchpin for assessments and interventions in social work. For instance, the universal inclination in social work intervention during the previous millennium to rely on problem-solving models, was embodied in the postulation of Compton and Galaway (1984, p. 11): "Intervention refers to deliberate, planned actions undertaken by the client and the worker to resolve a problem." Hence, the conventional hypothesis was that social workers should be able to compose an appropriate intervention plan (solution) for clients/service users (individuals, groups and communities), if they are able to assess and define problems accurately. Thus, throughout the mainstream evolution of the body of Western knowledge in social work, the emphasis and yardstick of effective professional social work rested ultimately on the abilities, capacities, and capabilities in problem identification and formulation of the academically trained social worker. These strengths of social workers as opposed to the deficits of service users formed part of the language used in social work and ascribed a position of professional authority to social workers. This central focus on service users' problems and deficits, however, potentially contributed to a general, discreet, underlying tension between the value base of social workers and their assessments of service users' problems, the eventual problem formulation, and their intervention plans for service users. For instance, the social work principle of the recognition of the inherent dignity of humanity (IASSW/AIETS 2018), which is perceived by many scholars to be inherent in conventional social work intervention, might have caused contentious ethical conundrums in problem-focused social work interventions (Engelbrecht 2019).

Therefore, "a dramatic departure from conventional social practice" (Saleebey 2002, p. 1) was embraced by social work academics and practitioners alike with a movement initiated largely by prominent scholars' revival of a strengths-based perspective in social work intervention (compare Weick et al. 1989). This movement was substantiated by "a more apt expression of some of the deepest values of social work" (Weick et al. 1989, p. 350). Proponents such as Saleebey (1996, 2002, 2008) and Chapin (1995) popularized the assumptions and principles of strengths-based social work practice with at-risk populations.

Against this background, Engelbrecht (2010, p. 49) synthesized a conceptualization of strengths-based practices, based on postulations of primary authors on the topic, such as Rapp (1998), Saleebey (1996), and Weick et al. (1989):

> ...the strengths perspective adheres to a multifaceted philosophy which moves away from pathology and deficits towards practices which focus on the strengths, assets, capacities, abilities, resilience and resources of people; and as such is based on key concepts such as empowerment, partnership, facilitation and participation; it concerns itself with a language of progressive change; it is compatible with social work's commitment to the person-in-environment; and it can be applied in a number of contexts and situations.

Saleebey (2002), as a proponent of a strengths perspective, nevertheless proclaims that these strengths-based practices may seem to be merely a mantra to encourage positive thinking and a disguised attempt at reframing misery. In a more explicit and critical analysis, Gray (2011) highlights the potential synergies between the strengths perspective and contemporary neoliberalism, exposed by the perspective's strong links with liberalism, social capital, and the subjective well-being movement. The most persuasive criticism levelled at strengths-based practices is however from Staudt et al. (2001), who suggest that it is unclear how strengths-based practices vary from conventional social work approaches. They found in their study that few evaluations of strengths-based interventions had been published and concluded that the "...strengths perspective is a value stance, but there is little support for it as a distinct and uniquely effective practice model" (Staudt et al. 2001, p. 1). This was echoed by Gray (2011, p. 10) who asserted that "…while appreciative of the value of the strengths perspective, it's not wise to be overly ambitious in claims about its potential." A rebuttal of these critical views may however be found in the original postulations by primary proponents of the strengths-based perspective, such as that the strengths perspective is not a theory (Rapp 1998) but merely a practice perspective in social work, and as such does not consist of a definite process of facilitation (Weick et al. 1989). Therefore, the strengths perspective is simply "…a way of thinking about what you do with whom you do it. It provides a distinctive lens for examining the world of practice" (Saleebey 2002, p. 20).

Notwithstanding its detractors, Guo and Tsui (2010) observed that since its introduction, the strengths perspective has been widely applied in cases related to child welfare, substance abuse, family services, and services for elderly people. A decade later, Mendenhall and Carney (2020, p. x) confirmed that the strengths perspective had become internationally pervasive in social work and that "strengths as a starting point are ubiquitous in our field." This observation underscores evidence provided by Roose et al. (2014) of contributions to the strengths perspective flowing from a myriad of theoretical and conceptual frameworks such as empowerment and anti-oppressive social work, constructive social work, social pedagogy, and the capabilities approach. Hence, the usefulness of a strengths perspective in a variety of social work contexts has been confirmed in a plethora of contemporary publications, such as those by Mendenhall and Carney (2020), who are lauding the strengths perspective in social work practice, social work education, on both micro and macro levels, and with diverse population groups.

Strengths-based supervision of social workers

As illustrated in the previous section, the significance of a strengths-based perspective is not confined to social work intervention. Since this perspective emerged as a philosophy, adopted by many disciplines in social sciences as a study of optimal human functioning, the perspective became a specialist terrain of study in positive psychology, observing positive aspects of human experiences such as personal potential, happiness, talents, subjective wellbeing, wellness, and satisfaction. Self-help books, such as one by Seligman (2011) titled *Flourish: A visionary new understanding of happiness and well-being*, became bestsellers and popular not only amongst the general public, but also in the academic fraternity concerned with organizational and management studies, where coaching and mentoring of team members became the norm in an increasingly neoliberal work environment (cf. Engelbrecht 2012, 2015).

The developments in positive psychology also found credence in the field of neurosciences. Another bestseller was by Buckingham and Clifton (2001): *Now, discover your strengths*. Subsequent to this publication, Donald Clifton developed CliftonStrengths, which is an online psychological assessment (Gallup 2020). By completing a Clifton StrengthsFinder assessment online, a unique combination of 34 CliftonStrengths themes will be uncovered, promising to maximize an individual's potential. Exploring this online product furthermore signifies a shift from performance management to performance development for participants. This shift is based on the rationale that organizations may discover that their current performance management systems are not motivating employees, and that the future of work is complex, digital, and more collaborative than ever before. These organizational challenges are being shaped by extraordinary changes in technology, globalization, and overwhelming information flow. In agile, fast-paced workplaces, some skills can become obsolete. Therefore, organizations need to equip employees with mindsets that would encourage success and contribute to their growth.

However, despite the worldwide appreciation of strengths-based practices in social work intervention and the prevalent, significant developments of these practices within a variety of disciplines and organizational contexts (as illustrated in the previous paragraphs), international publications on strengths-based practices within the context of social work management and supervision practices are surprisingly meagre and anecdotal. Worldwide, a relatively small number of authors have published on strengths-based social work supervision (see for example Brown 2019; Cohen 1999; Engelbrecht 2010, 2019; Engelbrecht and Ornellas 2015; Lietz and Rounds 2009; Lietz 2013; Lietz et al. 2014; Lietz and Julien-Chinn 2017; Mamaleka 2018). One reason for this is most probably that contemporary social issues and phenomena take precedence over supervision of social workers, with supervision therefore not necessarily being a mainstream topic in social work publications and at academic conferences as research dissemination platforms (Engelbrecht 2019). For instance, no references to supervision in any form were included in the themes and subthemes of the International Federation of Social Workers' 2020 online conference where the social work Global Agenda of 2020 to 2030 was discussed (IFSW 2020), although in the fourth report on the Global Agenda, feedback suggests that "….supervision of practitioners was thought to have been ignored" (IASSW, ICSW, IFSW 2020, p. 314).

Indeed, this is incomprehensible given the context of the parallel process between social work practices and supervision of the practitioners who execute those practices (Engelbrecht 2010, 2019). The minimal opportunities afforded to the dissemination of social work supervision practices do not however explain or justify the under-reporting of strengths-based supervision, in light of the worldwide use of strengths-based social work practices, which is generally presented as a basic point of departure in social work practice (cf. Engelbrecht 2010, 2019; Mendenhall and Carney 2020; Roose et al. 2014). In this regard scholars, and more specifically, Shulman (2006, p. 26) propose a "parallel process" between supervision and social work intervention and describe this process as an inherent part of the supervisory relationship and as "meaning the way in which the clinical supervisors interact with the supervisee models what the supervisor believes is at the core of any helping relationship." In addition, Cohen (1999) suggests that problem-solving supervision may undermine strengths-based practices, considering the parallels that exist between the process of supervision and the process of practice. He postulates that "…problem-centred supervision would render strengths-based practice very difficult indeed and could result in the strengths-oriented supervisee developing either a powerful resistance to the supervision or a grand confusion in his or her work with clients" (Cohen 1999, p. 462).

Thus, the disquieting lack of research publications on strengths-based social work supervision, despite the widely assumed common use thereof, and empirical evidence of its contribution to higher levels of satisfaction with supervision (cf. Lietz and Julien-Chinn 2017), may be ascribed to the fact that strengths-based practices originated in, and are primarily focused on, social work intervention. Moreover, it could be argued that all practice-based interventions with service users cannot simply be paralleled or translated to supervision practices without some contextual modification. The "crossover" from intervention *by* social workers to the supervision *of* social workers requires a deliberate appreciation of differences in context and application, as the ultimate aim of social work intervention with service users and supervision of social workers bears different nuances and cannot be ignored by using exactly the same "nomenclature" without adaptation (cf. Engelbrecht 2019; Mamaleka 2018). Nevertheless, the underlying philosophy of *eudaimonia*, the "way of thinking" and "distinctive lens" (Saleebey 2002, p. 20) of the strengths perspective could remain the same for and parallel to intervention by social workers and supervision of social workers.

Moreover, strengths-based supervision of social workers may be merely a disposition and value stance by the supervisor who uses this perspective as a neoliberal yardstick to measure the abilities, capacities, and capabilities of the supervisee (Engelbrecht 2015; Ornellas 2018; Ornellas and Engelbrecht 2020). Hence, as in the case of the problem-oriented social worker-service user dyad, the supervisor may retain the authority and power base, while the supervisee still reflects mere deficits. In an effort to address this issue, Mamaleka (2018, p. 213) suggests "collaborative" supervision by asking: "Your voice or our voices?" This is a fundamental question in efforts towards strengths-based supervision practices.

In an effort to establish strengths-based supervision practices, as opposed to supervision grounded on the supervisor's authority and power base, Engelbrecht and Ornellas (2015) examined the self-reported perceived signature strengths of 100 social work supervisors in South Africa and clustered their strengths in a registry of intrinsic strengths, strengths in their relations with supervisees, and strengths in their general supervision practices. Table 31.1 illustrates these strengths.

Although the scope of supervisors' signature strengths captured in Table 31.1 was not intended to measure success of any kind and to be exhaustive, the deduction drawn from this research was simply that some supervisors perceive that they indeed possess distinctive strengths and practice strengths-based supervision, and that these clusters of signature supervisory strengths could be used as benchmarks for social work supervisors in different contexts.

This particular study (Engelbrecht and Ornellas 2015) propelled three consecutive, interrelated qualitative studies to voice social work supervisees' experiences on what is in fact happening in supervision (Chibaya 2018; Brandt 2019; Wynne 2020). The findings of these three studies were used to determine the correlations between the supervisors' perceived strengths in supervision and the actual lived experiences of supervisees in approximately similar contexts. It was suggested that supervisees prefer and appreciate strengths-based supervision, and they were able to identify closely which elements in the supervision dyad were contributing to helpful and positive experiences. The characteristics they ascribed to strengths-oriented supervisors correlate in essence with the exposition in the registry of supervisors' perceived signature strengths as presented by Engelbrecht and Ornellas (2015) in Table 31.1.

Table 31.1 A registry of supervisors' perceived signature strengths (adapted from Engelbrecht and Ornellas 2015)

Intrinsic strengths	Strengths in relations with supervisees	Strengths in supervision practices
Confident/dynamic	Accessible/approachable/attentive	Competent
Creative/initiative	Communicative/assertive	Knowledgeable
Modest/grateful	Compassionate/kind/benevolent	Experienced
Emotionally mature	Patient/persevering	Accountable/responsible/
Independent/self-aware	Empathic/engaging	committed
Self-directed/self-regulation	Friendly/goodwill/helpful	Analytical/critical/evaluative
Energetic	Supportive	Reflective/practical
Positive attitude/optimistic	Discreet/respectful	Future-minded/ prudent/strategic
Honesty/integrity	Sincere/spontaneous	Hard-working/diligent/loyal
Humoristic	Transparent/trustworthy	Planning/organizing/coordinating/
Inquisitive/curious	Objective/fair	leading
Eager to learn/open-minded		Meticulous/multi-tasking/focused
Adaptable/open to change		Structured/systematic
Spiritual		Passionate/enthusiastic
		Open to criticism
		Team player

However, supervisees as participants in the studies of Chibaya (2018), Brandt (2019), and Wynne (2020) were also able to identify which aspects of supervision were not helpful (and even harmful) in the facilitation of their strengths and prohibited them from flourishing (compare Seligman 2011). Upon examination, these findings clearly suggest that the intention of strengths-oriented supervisors, who rely on a strengths-based perspective in supervision as "…a way of thinking" and a "distinctive lens for examining the world of practice" (Saleebey 2002, p. 20) may be "…overly ambitious in claims about its [strengths-based supervision's] potential" (Gray 2011, p. 10). One of the reasons for the response by participants in all three studies concerned, seems to be that supervisees could not identify the specific process followed by their supervisors in their supervision. More specifically, the participants in these studies suggested that they rather were constantly and acutely made aware of their own deficits owing to the (i) authority and power stance of the supervisor, and (ii) that this was exacerbated by the unstructured open-door policy and on-the-run nature of their supervision. These deductions are based on the fact that supervisees reported in the studies that they chiefly engaged with their supervisors when they needed advice, or could not execute a task, and when they were controlled, monitored, or reprimanded.

These lived experiences and perceptions of supervisees clearly indicate that intended strengths-based supervision should inherently display specific principles, a process, tasks, techniques, and thus a structure in operationalization for it to be successful, and that a mere philosophical reliance on a way of thinking and a lens for viewing the world, is not sufficient to reach the intended goal of supervision (cf. Engelbrecht 2019). This notion is supported by the growing interest of the global labor workforce in the interdisciplinary positive psychology and neuroscientific mind-sets of workers' strengths, as a shift from performance management to performance development, which acts as motivation for retention, growth, and flourishing in the contemporary, fast-changing complex work environments of the world (cf. Buckingham and Clifton 2001; Seligman 2011).

A vignette of structured strengths-based supervision

To illustrate the operationalization of strengths-based supervision in the unique context of the social work discipline, a vignette is offered here as an example of a practice framework for structured strengths-based supervision (as opposed to problem-oriented ambiguous supervision). The material for this vignette was initially inspired by the work of Botha (1985), a pioneer in the establishment of social work supervision in South Africa, both in academia and in practice. Botha (2002, p. 104) composed a supervision model based on Perlman's (1957) problem-solving process and Kadushin's (1976) exposition thereof, which "…comprises details related to the welfare organisation (place), the individuals, families, groups, communities (client system), the needs or problems of the client system (problems), the social work process (process), and the social worker (personnel)." This model provides a definite, comprehensive, and unique framework for holistic supervision practices, as generally practiced in South Africa in the 1980s and early 1990s. However, the philosophical underpinning of this model is problem-oriented, and with the worldwide interest and shift towards strengths-based social work practices, this model was modified by Engelbrecht's (2010, 2019) research on the operationalization of strengths-based supervision practices in South African social work agencies.

The point of departure for this vignette is "…the unpredictable, non-routined, non-standardised, highly individualised and imperceptible nature of social work practice, which in actual fact necessitated supervision…" (Botha 2002, p. 2), and which calls for paradigm shifts in supervision in a fast-changing world, characterized by constant change and uncertainties, brought about by resultant global challenges for the social work discipline. Therefore, the principles, process, tasks, and techniques of supervision displayed in this vignette endeavor to be relevant to contemporary developments in social work practices, and to provide certainty, clarity, direction, and structure to both supervisors and supervisees, as the foundation for collaborative, systems-oriented strengths-based supervision, parallel to social work intervention. The aim of this supervision remains to deliver the best possible services to the service user.

Brief context

Both the supervisor and supervisee are licensed social workers with some experience. The supervisee recently accepted an appointment as a frontline child protection social worker.

Engagement and clarification of fundamental principles

One of the first aspects that the supervisor and the supervisee clarified during their first engagement, is that the supervision dyad would be strengths-based in order to parallel the organization's strengths-based and systems perspective on its service delivery. They also determined that the scope of their supervision should be structured as far as possible and not be crisis-driven, as this would suggest a problem orientation; and both the supervisor and supervisee needed to assume a facilitation role by adopting a strengths vocabulary. They concurred that these fundamental principles ought not to be considered as a denial of the supervisee's developmental needs, but should rather be viewed as an effort to unlock the supervisee's intellectual, performance, personal, and consequence competencies (cf. Parker 2017).

The supervisor and supervisee also agreed that their supervision, from the onset, would be aimed at promoting both the supervisor's and supervisee's active participation in the supervision process. Therefore, the supervisor undertook to relinquish the power associated with the title of "supervisor," implying that she was assuming a facilitative, collaborative, and partnership role in supervision. This also suggested that the supervisee in turn accepted co-responsibility for her own development in supervision, and that both the supervisor and supervisee would learn from each other. Therefore, the supervisor conceded that she was not the all-knowing expert and made a concerted effort to acknowledge, appreciate, and utilize the supervisee's knowledge and experience.

In addition, the supervisor and supervisee recognized that their desire to determine what was missing or lacking appeared stronger than their wish to locate strengths. Therefore, they both acknowledged that the language they would use was important, as conventional social work language tends to be chiefly problem focused. Most importantly, they acknowledged that the supervisee was not accustomed to the responsibility of taking ownership of the supervision process, as she was more used to reflect on her own deficits in supervision.

The supervisor and supervisee consequently opted to be jointly involved in critical, reflective, and imaginative assessment, planning, and execution of supervision by giving each other equal opportunity to talk, to listen, and to do. This meant that they would make joint decisions, based on what was meaningful to both of them, and they would strive to discover and develop each other's strengths, instead of trying to control or to coerce each other into typical supervision games (cf. Kadushin and Harkness 2014; Tsui 2005). They explicitly embarked on a shared ownership of the supervision process, imbuing it with practical content by acknowledging that it would be idealistic to deny deficits, but also not beneficial to deny that which was possible. To reach this "balancing act," they compiled a strengths-based assessment consisting of various interrelated systemic components.

Strengths-based assessment

To encapsulate the fundamental principles as agreed upon in their initial engagement, based on the distinct systematic components of a strengths perspective on supervision, the supervisor and supervisee composed a supervision equation (see Figure 31.1). The equation starts with the challenges of service users (indicated with "C"), which need to be addressed by the best possible intervention. The intervention strengths (indicated with "In") refer to the culmination of strengths of the service users, organization, and supervisee (indicated with "SOS"). By drawing on her strengths, the supervisor (indicated with "Sup") has to facilitate administrative, educational, and supportive supervision functions (cf. Kadushin and Harkness 2014), aiming at the strengths of the supervisee, which in turn, are interrelated with strengths of the service users and organization. The challenges of service users ("C"); intervention strengths ("In"); service users', organization's, and supervisee's strengths ("SOS"); as well as the supervisor's strengths ("Sup") equals a specific supervision plan (why, what, how, when). Figure 31.1 illustrates this equation.

To structure the systemic components of the equation, a framework for a strengths-based assessment tool was designed and completed during the course of several supervision sessions, devoted to the assessment of all the systemic components as identified in the strengths-based supervision equation. An ecological systems perspective was primarily used as theoretical foundation (cf. Bronfenbrenner 1979) to assess the challenges of service users and the strengths of the intervention, service users, and the organization on micro, mezzo, and macro levels. Characteristics, knowledge, skills, and attitude (cf. Kraiger et al. 1993) served as frame of reference to assess the strengths of both the supervisee and supervisor.

It was specifically noted that a detailed distinction between the identified systemic components could become a mere superficial exercise owing to their overlapping nature and scope. In addition, although the assessment tool was viewed as a point of departure to compose a supervision plan, the tool was also seen as a constant work in progress and the systemic components were used merely as a framework to guide supervision sessions. The initial assessment was thus only anecdotal, but acquired more shape, detail, and momentum during the course of the supervision. Table 31.2 depicts the strengths-based assessment tool.

The supervisor and supervisee started to assess the myriad challenges facing the service users in the supervisee's work area. To this end, a community profile provided statistics and reports from various sources, including case files from the supervisee's designated caseload. The economic inequalities on a macro level, resulting in unemployment and families' alcohol misuse on a mezzo level, and a specific case of child abuse on a micro level, were identified as some challenges and as such noted in the assessment tool.

The next systemic component in the assessment tool focused on the potential strengths in the intervention by the social worker to address the challenges of service users on all levels. These

---

$\left\{ C < In = (SOS)Sup \right\} = $ (Supervision plan: why, what, how, when)

C: challenges of service users

In: intervention strengths

SOS: service users', organisation's and supervisee's strengths

Sup: supervisor's strengths

Figure 31.1 A strengths-based supervision equation

Table 31.2 A strengths-based assessment tool

Challenges of service users	Intervention strengths	Service users' strengths	Organization's strengths	Supervisee's strengths	Supervisor's strengths
Micro	Micro	Micro	Micro	Characteristics (enablers)	Characteristics (enablers)
Mezzo	Mezzo	Mezzo	Mezzo	Knowledge (know how)	Knowledge (know how)
Macro	Macro	Macro	Macro	Skills (know what)	Skills (know what)
				Attitude (know why)	Attitude (know why)

strengths included specific social work methods, theories, and perspectives that the supervisee may employ, such as prevention counseling, focusing on parenting skills with a single mother through a task-centered approach on a micro level, group work with foster-care parents on a mezzo level, and a community awareness program regarding gender-based violence on a macro level.

When implementing specific interventions, the supervisee needed to draw on strengths from different levels of the service users in her caseload and community, strengths of the organization employing her, and the strengths of her own characteristics, knowledge, skills, and attitudes as indicated in the assessment tool. The strengths of the service users were identified as the active collaboration by a specific family on the micro level, the practicing of *Ubuntu* (compassion and humanity) in the community on a mezzo level, and a range of supporting government social welfare policies on a macro level. The organization's strengths nested in its expertise as a designated child protection body on a micro level, the availability of resources, such as available foster parents in the community on a mezzo level, and a sophisticated Children's Act on a macro level. Empathy, innovation, and leadership potential were specific strengths identified as characteristics of the supervisee, in tandem with her knowledge of child protection, interviewing and report-writing skills, and compassionate attitude towards impoverished vulnerable people in the community she served. She specifically revealed the strengths in her learning style, which she typified as being an independent learner. This means that she was apt to determine her own educational content, she was open to learning from any supervision style, and would use the supervisor as a resource. She also learned by conceptualizing challenges of service users and to critically analyze these challenges to discern the relationship between theory and practice.

The final systemic component in the assessment tool, namely the strengths of the supervisor, is pertinent in a strengths-based assessment (as opposed to problem-oriented supervision, where the supervisor is the assessor and may have sole authority). Both the supervisor and supervisee acknowledged that the strengths of the supervisor in the supervision equation primarily encompassed those strengths on which the supervisor could draw in supervision of the supervisee. Therefore, matching the supervisor's supervision style with the strengths in the supervisee's preferred learning style was especially significant (cf. Kolb 1973). The supervisee's characteristic pattern of behavior in a learning environment was revealed in the way she absorbed, processed, comprehended, and retained information. The supervisor's supervision style was defined by the manner in which she approached the supervision dyad and may include how she directed, motivated, and communicated, and specifically fulfilled pertinent functions of education, support, and management.

The engagement of the supervisor and supervisee in dialogue on the strengths of their preferred styles in the supervision dyad, also determined specific roles that the supervisor had to fulfil (cf. Engelbrecht 2019). These roles could include, inter alia, being an administrator, educator, supporter, expert, motivator, enabler, broker, facilitator, empowerer, negotiator, mediator, advocate, and activist. Identifying these roles of the supervisor might provide, together with her matching supervision, a platform for drawing deliberately on her enabling characteristics that would enhance the strengths of the supervisee. The supervisor and supervisee agreed that the supervisor should focus at the onset of the supervision process, on fulfilling an educator role, owing to the fact that the supervisee was in a new environment with the main brief of child protection. The supervisor revealed that she was, inter alia, structured, patient, and compassionate (cf. Table 31.1), which might enable her to build on the strengths of the supervisee. Most importantly, she revealed that since the supervisee was an independent learner, she (as supervisor) had the knowledge (*know how*) to fulfil an educator role (based on the supervisor's knowledge of adult education), and possessed the skills (*know what*) to facilitate the supervisee's interventions by means of various supervision techniques. The supervisor also acknowledged that critical feedback would guide her attitude (*know why*) towards the supervisee and that she as supervisor was able to provide this in a fair, mutually beneficial, and mature manner.

During the course of the supervision sessions devoted to the strengths-based assessment, the systemic components discussed above were intertwined and were assessed as a coherent meaningful whole, while retaining specific content. Thus, although the strengths-based assessment is a structured process, its execution is not linear, because it is a multi-dimensional and exploratory process, based on reciprocity, openness, and mutual trust. Throughout this process, both the supervisor and supervisee reminded each other that the conclusive systemic component of the supervision equation remained the challenges of the service user, which should be overcome or alleviated by the best possible intervention. Therefore, to keep track of the goal of supervision, a specific supervision plan was composed, with the systemic components of the strengths-based assessment being the driving force.

Supervision plan

The supervisor and supervisee examined the various forms of supervision plans at their disposal. Initially, they considered Botha's (2002, p. 104) model, which comprises details related to the welfare organization, the client system, the needs or problems of the client system, the social work process, and the social worker as staff member. Although this model provides a definite, comprehensive, and unique framework for holistic supervision practice, they noted that the philosophical underpinning of this model is inherently problem-oriented, does not include the supervisor as a systemic component, and thus needs to be transformed to be compatible with a strengths perspective.

They also considered the exposition of a personal development plan by Engelbrecht (2010, 2019) in terms of a matrix indicating identified challenges (learning or development needs) in order of priority. In this matrix, specific competencies inform defined outcomes, which demonstrate reliable, valid, authentic, current, and sufficient achievements. The outcomes contain a verb to denote action, an object or noun, and a word or parameter qualifying each outcome. This personal development plan defines what the supervisee will learn (in terms of competencies and outcomes), how the supervisee will learn (with specific references to supervision activities in supervision sessions, indicating methods, techniques, and opportunities for demonstration), and how it will be assessed. However after completion of a trial, both supervisor and super-

Table 31.3 A strengths-based supervision plan

Challenges(why)	Supervision goals(what)	Supervision session's objectives(how)	Dates(when)
....	....	....	....
		....	....
		....	....
		....	....

visee found the outcome too complex and subsequently devised a more simplistic tool for a strengths-based supervision plan (see Table 31.2).

They agreed to start with the challenges of the service users (as indicated in their strengths-based assessment tool – see Table 31.2). They prioritized these challenges in an ethical, informed way according to aspects such as risks, needs, immediacy, and complexity, substantiated by a grounded rationale why these challenges should be tackled in supervision. Second, they decided on a broad basis which strengths, as identified in the strengths-based assessment (Table 31.2), might curb the challenges of the service users (this translates to the specific goal of a range of supervision sessions). Third, they formulated several objectives on how they would reach their desired supervision goal/s (each representing one or more supervision sessions). They expressed these objectives in simple language, but to be as specific, measurable, attainable, relevant, and timely as possible, including some techniques to be used in supervision sessions. Finally, they set some dates by which to complete the supervision plan. See Table 31.3.

This supervision plan holds that each supervision session has a specific objective, aimed at achieving a broader supervision goal in order to tackle challenges of service users, which have been formulated as part of the strengths-based supervision equation. The supervisor and the supervisee realized that in this strengths-based supervision process, they both needed to take responsibility for the structuring, monitoring, and evaluation of the supervision plan. They also noted the premise for this shared endeavor to be that the supervision plan should be user-friendly and a document in progress for everyday use; it should focus on what the supervisee can do; and in essence should be a document to celebrate achievements.

Supervision sessions

The strengths-based supervision sessions, which focused primarily on reaching the specific objective/s of the supervision plan, were based on the principles of adult education (compare Knowles 1971) towards a positive resolution. This implied that the supervisor respected the supervisee's self-concept and autonomy. In turn, the supervisee took co-ownership of the supervision process. In addition, both the supervisor and supervisee acknowledged each other's wealth of experience, which could stand them in good stead during intervention and the supervision process. They decided to embrace teaching and learning opportunities as they arose and accorded each other the opportunity to apply their strengths to what both regarded as immediately essential and of interest in supervision and intervention. This enhanced the motivation of both to be fully engaged in the supervision process, as both felt valued and appreciated. The fact that they collaborated and matched the unique strengths of their learning and supervision styles contributed to their experience that the content of all the systemic components of the supervision equation was helpful and meaningful.

During the course of the supervision sessions, both the supervisor and supervisee employed a range of strengths-oriented techniques which complemented their respective learning and supervision styles. They specifically used a mix of expository, didactic, and dialectical-hypothetical techniques such as reflections, discussions, questioning, brainstorming, self-study, report-writing, and different forms of role play. Of great importance was the way in which reciprocal feedback was framed throughout the strengths-based supervision process, as feedback to each other was provided systematically, explicitly, and timeously after actions were completed. They agreed that this feedback should be descriptive, hypothetically as an exchange of ideas, and not condemning, but focusing on how to enhance strengths and not entertain deficits.

In sum, for the supervisor and supervisee, the strengths-based supervision sessions provided opportunities to conduct self-observation, introspective-retrospective reviews of the social work interventions, and for analytical reflection. The purpose of these supervision sessions was to convert the initial strengths-based assessment into a structured strengths-based supervision plan; to transform the objectives of the strengths-based supervision plan into specific actions; and to eventually render the best possible service to the service user.

Conclusion: Strengths-based supervision attributes

The operationalization of strengths-based supervision, as illustrated in the preceding vignette, requires innovation, passion, and a scholarly understanding of supervision and the principles of a strengths-based perspective. These requirements may result in a strengths-based supervision process which many social work practitioners regard as too time-consuming, complex, intense, and inapplicable. A similar criticism has been levelled at Kadushin and Harkness (2002) in a complaint that they present an unrealistic, idealistic picture of supervision, focusing on how supervision should be and not on how it actually is. As a response Kadushin and Harkness (2002, preface xvii) commended: "There is, however, some justification for presenting a systematic synthesis of the best in social work supervision. It suggests the ideal against which we can measure our practice and reveals the direction in which changes need to be made." This notion is supported as social work supervision is regarded as a professional practice. Therefore, scholarly knowledge, skills, and attitudes of both the supervisor and the supervisee about supervision are essential for successful supervision.

In addition, Engelbrecht (2010) found that attempts to employ strengths-based supervision have transformative potential in the eco-systems of social work organizations, supervisors, frontline social workers, and service users alike: all systems have to regard each other as equally important and included in the supervision equation; and all systems have to change their vocabulary from a fixation on problems and deficits to that of strengths. It remains however a constant challenge to transform all applicable systems towards a strengths perspective as an alternative intervention, supervision, and management paradigm. This may be ascribed to two main factors.

First, in her research on social workers' reflections on the implications of neoliberal tenets for social work, Ornellas (2018) concludes that supervision was specifically raised by social workers and supervisors as an area of social work that was being particularly affected by neoliberal reform with a managerial agenda: supervision has become less clinical and more managerial in a variety of environments. This tendency is infiltrating the ultimate goal and functions of supervision, as there is simply not sufficient appreciation for the essential significance of social work supervision, with resulting insufficient budget allocations, time constraints, and overall incapacity to undertake effective supervision of frontline workers. Regular, structured, intensive supervision, focusing on all functions of supervision is generally acknowledged and appreciated, but is increasingly regarded by social work managers as an unrealistic expectation and an unaffordable luxury in comparison with the overwhelming needs of society, and inadequate funding for social service delivery. A mere managerial overseeing of social workers when the need arises, and a problem-focused "quick fix" are regarded as much more cost-effective by social work managers (Ornellas 2018; Ornellas and Engelbrecht 2020).

Second, Botha (2002) concurs in line with other commentators that supervisors and social workers are not peers, and that supervisors carry the primary responsibility for what transpires in supervision. This points not only to assuming ownership in supervision but also to the authority and power differences in the problem-oriented supervision dyad. Botha (2002, p. 130) also comments that the supervisor should attempt "…to create a structured learning situation for social workers that intends to provide and ensure maximum development for the individual strengths of each social worker.. Even with reference to the supervisee's strengths, this comment is still cemented in the context of problem-oriented supervision, where the supervisor is the lead, expert actor with the responsibility to create structure, learning, and development of the social worker. The effectiveness and success of supervision in such a context is thus primarily determined by the abilities of the supervisor, parallel to those of the problem-oriented social worker in intervention with the service user.

Conversely, in strengths-based supervision the sum of all aspects (such as abilities, capabilities, potential, assets, resilience, resources, competencies, and talents) contributing to strengths of both the supervisor and supervisee is needed to advance the effectiveness and success of supervision and to ultimately benefit the service user. Both the supervisor and supervisee are regarded as lead, expert actors in supervision with a mutual responsibility to create structure, learning, and development.

In conclusion, it would be vital to identify some specific strengths-based supervision attributes, based on the exposition in this chapter:

(i)   Strengths-based supervision suggests an equal, collaborative, participatory activity between the supervisor and supervisee, characterized by co-responsibility and co-ownership.
(ii) A coherent structure for supervision should be devised by the supervisor and supervisee, and should be operationalized in terms of tangible processes, tasks, techniques, and tools.
(iii) Applicable systemic components of a strengths-based supervision equation should be identified and assessed.
(iv) The systemic components of a strengths-based equation should be encapsulated in a holistic, detailed supervision plan.
(v)   Objectives of a supervision plan should guide supervision sessions, based on specific role allocations, principles of adult education, strengths-oriented techniques, and feedback according to the supervisee's and supervisor's respective learning and supervision styles.

With these attributes in mind, it is important to note that the tools displayed in the vignette are merely innovative examples in a specific context. The challenge is to likewise devise situation-relevant and supervisor-supervisee centered strengths-based processes, tasks, techniques, and tools with transformative potential as a proactive response to let supervision practices flourish, despite problem-oriented, managerial demands to do more (intervention) with less (supervision).

References

Botha, N.J., 1985. Onderrigmodel vir doeltreffende supervisie [The educational model for effective supervision]. *Social Work/Maatskaplike Werk*, 21 (4), 239–248.

Botha, N.J., 2002. *Supervision and consultation in social work.* Bloemfontein: Drufoma.

Brandt, S., 2019. *Beginner maatskaplike werkers se ervaring van volwasseneonderrig in supervisie [Beginner social workers' experiences of adult education principles in supervision].* Unpublished thesis. Stellenbosch University.

Bronfenbrenner, U., 1979. *The ecology of human development.* Cambridge, MA: Harvard University Press.

Brown, A., 2019. *A literature review on the development, implementation and evaluation of strengths-based and culturally-grounded supervision models in social work.* Victoria, BC: University of Victoria.

Buckingham, M., and Clifton, D.O., 2001. *Now, discover your strengths.* New York: Simon and Schuster.

Chapin, R.K., 1995. Social policy development: the strengths perspective. *Social Work*, 40 (4), 506–514.

Chibaya, N.H., 2018. *The execution of individual reflective supervision sessions: experiences of intermediate frontline social workers.* Unpublished thesis. Stellenbosch University.

Cohen, B.-Z., 1999. Intervention and supervision in strengths-based social work practice. *Families in Society*, 80 (5), 460–466.

Compton, B., and Galaway, B., 1984. *Social work processes.* Homewood: Dorsey Press.

Engelbrecht, L.K., 2010. A strengths perspective on supervision of social workers: an alternative management paradigm within a social development context. *Social Work and Social Sciences Review*, 14 (1), 47–58.

Engelbrecht, L.K., 2012. Coaching, mentoring and consultation: the same but different activities in supervision of social workers in South Africa?. *Social Work/Maatskaplike Werk*, 48 (3), 357–368.

Engelbrecht, L.K., 2015. Revisiting the esoteric question: can non-social workers manage and supervise social workers?. *Social Work/Maatskaplike Werk*, 51 (3), 310–331.

Engelbrecht, L.K., 2019. Processes, tasks, methods and activities in supervision. *In*: L.K. Engelbrecht, ed. *Management and supervision of social workers: issues and challenges within a social development paradigm.* 2nd ed. Andover: Cengage Learning EMEA Limited, 174–190.

Engelbrecht, L.K., and Ornellas, A., 2015. A conceptual framework for a strengths perspective on supervision of social workers within a mental health context: reflections from South Africa. *In*: A. Francis, P. La Rosa, L. Sankaran, and S.P. Rajeev, eds. *Social work practice in mental health: cross-cultural perspectives.* New Delhi: Allied Publishers, 19–40.

Gallup, 2020. *CliftonStrengths.* Available from: https://www.gallup.com/cliftonstrengths/en/home.aspx [Accessed 1 July 2020].

Gray, M., 2011. Back to basics: a critique of the strengths perspective in social work. *Families in Society: The Journal of Contemporary Social Services*, 92 (1), 5–11.

Guo, W.H., and Tsui, M.S., 2010. From resilience to resistance: a reconstruction of the strengths perspective in social work practice. *International Social Work*, 53 (2), 233–245.

Hollis, F., 1966. *Casework: a psychosocial therapy.* New York: Random House.

IASSW/AIETS 2018. *Global social work statement of ethical principles.* Available from: https://www.iassw-aiets.org/wp-content/uploads/2018/04/Global-Social-Work-Statement-of-Ethical-Principles-IASSW-27-April-2018-1.pdf [Accessed 1 March 2020].

IASSW, ICSW, IFSW 2020. *Global Agenda for social work and social development: fourth report. Strengthening recognition of the importance of human relationships.* (Ed. David, N. Jones), Rheinfelden, Switzerland: IFSW. Available from: https://www.iassw-aiets.org/wp-content/uploads/2020/07/2020-07-06-Global-Agenda-4th-Report-FINAL-1.pdf#page=312 [Accessed 20 July 2020].

IFSW (International Federation of Social Workers) 2020. *Online conference: the 2020 to 2030 Social Work Global Agenda, co-building social transformation.* Available from: https://www.ifsw.org/2020-conference/ [Accessed 20 July 2020].

Kadushin, A., 1976. *Supervision in social work.* New York: Columbia University Press.

Kadushin, A., and Harkness, D., 2002. *Supervision in social work.* 4th ed. New York: Columbia University Press.

Kadushin, A., and Harkness, D., 2014. *Supervision in social work.* 5th ed. New York: Columbia University Press.

Knowles, M.S., 1971. *The modern practice of adult education – andragogy versus pedagogy.* New York: Association Press.

Kolb, D.A., 1973. *An experiential learning theory. Experience as source of learning and development.* New York: Prentice Hall.

Kraiger, K., Ford, J.K., and Salas, E., 1993. Application of cognitive, skill-based, and affective theories of learning outcomes to new methods of training evaluation. *Journal of Applied Psychology*, 78 (2), 311–378.

Lietz, C.A., 2013. Strengths-based supervision: supporting implementation of family-centered practice through supervisory processes. *Journal of Family Strengths*, 13 (1), 1–16.

Lietz, C.A., Hayes, M.J., Cronin, T.W., and Julien-Chinn, F., 2014. Supporting family-centered practice through supervision: an evaluation of strengths-based supervision. *Families in Society*, 95 (4), 227–235.

Lietz, C.A., and Julien-Chinn, F.J., 2017. Do the components of strengths-based supervision enhance child welfare workers' satisfaction with supervision?. *Families in Society*, 98 (2), 146–155.

Lietz, C.A., and Rounds, T., 2009. Strengths-based supervision: a child welfare supervision training project. *The Clinical Supervisor*, 28 (2), 124–140.

Mamaleka, M.M., 2018. Towards collaborative social work supervision: your voice or our voices?. *In*: A.L. Shokane, J.C. Makhubele and L.V. Blitz, eds. *Issues around aligning theory, research and practice in social work education (Knowledge pathing: Multi-, inter- and trans-disciplining in social sciences series*. Vol. 1. Cape Town: AOSIS, 213–235.

Mendenhall, A.N., and Carney, M.M., eds., 2020. *Rooted in strengths*: celebrating *the strengths perspective in social work*. Lawrence: University of Kansas Libraries. Available from: https://kuscholarworks.ku.edu/handle/1808/30023 [Accessed 1 June 2020].

Ornellas, A., 2018. *Social workers' reflections on implications of neoliberal tenets for social work in South African Non-Governmental Organisations*. Unpublished thesis. Stellenbosch University.

Ornellas, A., and Engelbrecht, L.K., 2020. Neoliberal impact on social work in South African Non-Governmental Organisations. *Southern African Journal for Social Work and Social Development*, 32 (1), 1–21.

Parker, L., 2017. *Essential professional competencies of social work supervisors in a non-profit welfare organisation*. Unpublished thesis. Stellenbosch University.

Perlman, H.H., 1957. *Social casework: a problem-solving process*. Chicago: University of Chicago Press.

Rapp, C.A., 1998. *The strengths model: case management with people suffering from severe and persistent mental illness*. New York: Oxford University Press.

Richmond, M.E., 1917. *Social diagnosis*. New York: Russell Sage Foundation.

Roose, R., Roets, G., and Schiettecat, T., 2014. Implementing a strengths perspective in child welfare and protection: a challenge not to be taken lightly. *European Journal of Social Work*, 17 (1), 3–17.

Saleebey, D., 1996. The strengths perspective in social work practice: extensions and cautions. *Social Work*, 41 (3), 296–305.

Saleebey, D., 2002. *The strengths perspective in social work practice*. 3rd ed. Boston: Allyn & Bacon.

Saleebey, D., 2008. *The strengths perspective in social work practice*. 5th ed. Boston: Allyn & Bacon.

Seligman, M.E.P., 2011. *Flourish: a visionary new understanding of happiness and well-being*. New York: Free Press.

Shulman, L., 2006. The clinical supervisor-practitioner working alliance: a parallel process. *The Clinical Supervisor*, 24 (1–2), 23–47.

Staudt, M., Howard, M.O., and Drake, B., 2001. The operationalization, implementation, and effectiveness of the strengths perspective: a review of empirical studies. *Journal of Social Service Research*, 27 (33), 1–21.

Tsui, M., 2005. *Social work supervision. Contexts and concepts*. London: SAGE.

Weick, A., Rapp, C., Sullivan, W.P., and Kisthardt, W., 1989. A strengths perspective for social work practice. *Social Work*, 34 (6), 350–354.

Wynne, T., 2020. *Potential factors contributing to harmful supervision of social workers*. Unpublished thesis. Stellenbosch University.

32

TRANSFORMATIVE SUPERVISION

Nicki Weld

Social work requires a focused and conscious use of relationship and self, and in turn, supervisors must seek to provide supervision that provides for transformative development in these areas. Essential to doing this is the ability to facilitate a meaningful learning process for the supervisee through the skillful use of questioning and application of observations. This chapter will explore the transformative role in professional supervision to deepen both professional and personal development. This will be done through an analysis of an actual supervision session (with the identifying details changed). A brief overview of professional (reflective) supervision is provided including core relational components that support this and the importance of openness. Transformative supervision is then defined, along with indicators that evidence this. Ways to provide transformative supervision session are outlined using the practice example to illustrate these, including the use of observations, the application of emotions, and accessing intuition.

Professional (reflective supervision)

With the focus on the overall professional development of the supervisee, professional supervision attends to the worker in their role, their practice, and the possible impacts of the work (Inskipp and Proctor 1993). Professional supervision explores the emotional content of the work and enables the supervisee to integrate experiences into learning, thus building both professional and personal practice wisdom. It is a place where workers can pause and focus on their personal and professional learning with the overall goal of supporting professional development. I liken it to a "professional base camp" where supervises journey out from in order to undertake their work, then return to be revitalized, experience security, and replenish themselves to be re-energized to go back out to practice (Weld 2012, p. 22).

Professional supervision needs to be protected as a valued learning space and not become a place solely focused on organizational compliance where workers feel under surveillance. Davys and Beddoe (2010, p. 228) comment that supervision can become "process driven and dominated by case management." Care needs to be taken that line management supervision and professional supervision are not attempted within the same session. If a line management role is undertaken in professional supervision it will tend to dominate, especially in highly bureaucratic or compliance-based organizations. Supervisees can be also become protective of what they will share, knowing that the supervisor will have input into their performance appraisal or other human resource requirements. This can result in "guarding" (Herkt and Hocking 2007), where a supervisee becomes selective in what they share, or tend to avoid supervision.

The vulnerability of examining your practice with another person reinforces the importance of relational factors that enable supervisees to engage in in-depth analysis of their work. Supervision is essentially about a relationship, one that enables openness from both supervisee and supervisor. Factors that support openness include: warmth, humor, honesty, empathy, and highly developed active listening skills. Having a principled approach to providing supervision including valuing the learning offered by the supervisee and a commitment to their safety and wellbeing, also ensures a safe, respectful, and reflective space is provided. Care needs to be taken to separate the supervisee's behavior from their self as a person, which helps supervisees to not feel personally attacked or shamed. Beddoe (2010, p. 15) notes that professional supervision assists with "preserving practitioner confidence in the face of uncertainty, conflict, and competing interest and that trust is essential for this type of supervision to flourish and survive." A supervisory relationship that promotes openness is essential to undertake the transformative role of supervision.

Transformative supervision

The transformative role of supervision contributes to a worker engaging in personal and professional change. It is evidenced by shifts in self-awareness, ways of working, and overall amplifies insight which contributes to an action of change. Indicators of transformative work include:

- A deep sense of thoughtfulness that leads to a change or shift in values and beliefs
- A new behavior that is immediately put into action in the workplace
- A sense of excitement, passion, and motivation to do something differently following a connection to self "truth"
- A named breakthrough in thinking or a new realization that is connected to the workplace and self
- An expanded view or position to an issue or difficulty that connects to prior learning and contributes to future action

(Weld 2012)

Changes may occur immediately or afterwards when the supervisee has had further time to process and make sense of what has surfaced for them. The supervisor assists in this process through questions and observations that enable the supervisee to think "deeply and vulnerably about life and values" (Carroll 2001, p. 76) and advance their personal and professional development.

A concern for supervisors in engaging in transformative work is that they may cross the boundary of supervision and therapy. This can cause supervisors to avoid discussion of the worker's emotional responses to the work and instead focus simply on discussing the detail of "cases" and providing advice. The Indirect Trauma Sensitive Supervision (ITSS) model developed by Brian Miller (2018) encourages supervisors to be able to recognize and normalize strong emotional reactions with a reminder to not move into problem solving too quickly with time taken to attend to emotional content first. Attending to the emotional impacts of work is essential in supervision and can counter indirect trauma impacts such as compassion fatigue, secondary traumatic stress, and vicarious trauma. Transformative supervision is likely at times to provide a therapeutic experience related to the restorative function of professional supervision. Rather than be feared, this should be considered a valuable contribution to a worker especially when they are engaged in therapeutic work with others.

Practice example

Jenn (supervisee) wished to review a recent interaction with her manager regarding a request to change her work hours. The relationship between her and the manager had a history of communication difficulties resulting in Jenn often feeling frustrated. Jenn described the events following her request, which escalated to a meeting with the CEO of the service to try and resolve the issue. In describing what happened, Jenn became louder in her tone of voice, she sat forward in her chair, and spoke increasingly quickly, with little space for me to interject with questions or comments. She talked like this for about twenty minutes. When she had finished, I decided to explore the dynamic of the relationship as I noticed that as Jenn had pushed forward with her request and became rigid around this, the manager appeared to withdraw and become equally fixed in her decision.

I shared this observation with Jenn using an Emotion Focused Therapy description of pursuer and withdrawer, and Jenn agreed to some degree. I also shared what I had noticed when Jenn was recounting the story, namely how her tone of voice had become louder and faster, as almost to drive the point home. Jenn fell silent at this point. I explained that sometimes in interactions such as she described, a value or belief of our own is triggered, causing us to defend or argue our position. I asked Jenn if she could identify whether this had happened and if so, what the belief or value might be. Jenn began by saying it was because the manager was unclear in their reasoning about the decision, so therefore she could not accept the outcome. She said if a decision was spelled out as to why it could not happen she could cope with it better. I asked her to take that level of analysis one step further and look at what lay underneath that for her, was there a value or belief being activated? Jenn thought for a moment and said "Fairness!" She then said, "But fairness is really important and I really believe in it!"

At this point she physically started to get up from her chair as if to signal the conversation was over (we were close to the hour being up). I could see she was feeling uncomfortable and wanting the conversation to end. I deliberately remained seated and said calmly that while fairness was an important value sometimes it could become unhelpful. I shared a previous situation I had experienced with a worker for whom fairness was a value that had developed through being treated unfairly as a child. Over time the value of fairness had become dominant in her thinking, and contributed to her becoming antagonistic in her collegial relationships, causing serious conflict. I said that I wasn't saying this was necessarily happening for Jenn but it was always important to check that our beliefs and values were still serving us well. Jenn was now standing up and looked quite tense. She commented again about fairness and as I got up from my chair I said that perhaps it was important to consider that the other person may have a different viewpoint and believed what was being requested wasn't fair in some way. We were out of time and I closed the session by saying I admired how Jenn was prepared to examine the situation (even though I could tell she was not comfortable exploring a different viewpoint). We finished warmly and I felt confident we had enough trust in the supervisory relationship to carry on.

About fifteen minutes later, I received a text from Jenn that said:

> "That was really good for me Nicki, ha! Thanks, and you are right, there is always another side, have a good weekend!"

I responded with:

> "You have such compassion, commitment and sensitivity Jenn. Thank you for being able to step into discomfort and look...not easy to do. Good on you!"

She responded with:

> "Thanks Nicki. No definitely not but I have faith you help turn me into the best Jenn I can be!" She has continued to bring up this conversation in other supervision sessions and notes how it helps her reflect when she is feeling strongly about something and to pause and try and see the other person's viewpoint.

Techniques to enable the transformative role of supervision

Observations

Observations are a key factor in contributing to transformative moments in supervision, and result from consciously tuning in to the supervisee and their world (O'Donoghue 2003). Being able to name observations in what is being shared and also in the telling of the issue requires attending and attuning to the worker. This requires a process of slowing down, focusing, and noticing what is happening in the supervision session and for the supervisee. Named observations of emotional responses displayed through body language, voice tone, facial descriptions, and verbal descriptions can help the supervisee build further understanding of their reactions and responses. The use of observations also includes the supervisor attuning to their own emotions and intuition and observing how these are informing the situation. For example, in noticing Jenn was becoming uncomfortable I noted my own sense of a rising tension within myself almost in an empathetic response to what she was experiencing. This gave me clues to how Jenn may have been feeling, and indicated a level of care I needed to take in sharing my observations so these did not arrive as a form of criticism or scrutiny.

In noticing Jenn was uncomfortable, I was observing her body language, facial expression, tone, dropping eye contact, looking beyond me, and movement from her chair. All of this signaled she was wanting to exit from the conversation and she literally conveyed this by actively trying to move away from it. If there had been more time, I would have explored how she appeared uncomfortable and asked her what was happening for her right then in that moment as I continued with my direction of inquiry. Assisting people to identify what is happening in their body in the moment can be a powerful source of information. It can also help identify any incongruence between what is being said and what is being felt. Using questions that begin with "I'm noticing…" or "What emotions or reactions are you aware of in your body right now talking about this?" provide helpful clues that can in turn be useful moments of insight.

Honesty

In order to work transformatively as a supervisor we have to be able to tolerate holding a line of honest inquiry which may generate uncomfortableness. This is different from pursuing a line of inquiry that is becoming distressing. Being uncomfortable suggests moving out of one's comfort zone, a space less familiar, but one in which learning can occur. Supporting this requires a degree of direct honesty that aims to observe and surface an important issue or contributing factor to the difficulty being explored. Sometimes there can be a tendency to maintain a relationship to a degree that honesty occurs in a less direct way and may not achieve the same transformative result. In the practice example, I could have sided with Jenn and agreed the decision was unfair, and I suspect this confirmation/affirmation is what she wanted from me. However I saw an important opportunity for Jenn to explore her own way or responding, identify what was the driver behind this (so a value or belief), and then be able to recognize the dynamic of interaction she was engaging in (pursuing to "win"). I felt if she could look at this there was a rich learning opportunity to find alternative ways to engage instead of one that kept resulting in rigidity from both sides. I saw this as potentially beneficial for her present and future collegial relationships.

It is important to maintain a position of warmth and kindness when sharing observations or asking honest direct questions that are pushing for honest answers. This can help prevent the situation from becoming distressing or unbearable and relies on a conveying of acceptance of the supervisee. While I may be questioning an aspect of their work or their response, I am not criticizing or judging them as a person. It is important that this is conveyed, and yet the honest ground is held so the inquiry can continue. Often in the contracting phase of beginning a supervisory relationship, people will ask to be given honest or constructive feedback, or to be challenged. It is important that supervisors understand what this would look like in order for it to be received. Most people can cope with this type of feedback or questioning if there is existing openness in the supervisory relationship and the acceptance of the person is conveyed and remains foremost in the interaction.

Offering the unexpected

From observations we can form a hypothesis or wondering that can contribute to a transformative moment by disrupting the narrative. In the practice example this occurred when I suggested that in relation to fairness, it was possible the other person was experiencing Jenn's request as unfair. This statement was possibly unexpected by Jenn and linked her identified belief in fairness for herself to a bigger contemplation of how her need was perhaps unfair. This interrupted her story as having been treated unjustly or unfairly and offered a different way to look at what had happened.

Offering an unexpected view, idea, or question can provide a re-frame or a different perspective on the issue. It invites the supervisee to think about the issue differently, to consider it from a different angle or to see a part of it that they had not realized. Sometimes it helps to give a preliminary lead up to this such as "I'm going to ask you something or suggest something that may seem a little unusual" or with regard to a statement, simply naming it and being able to say what led to that idea or though if need be. The intention of offering the unexpected is to contribute to wider thinking on an issue or to cause a deeper reflection on what is informing it. Allowing silence after offering an unexpected comment or question is helpful, and the time taken by the supervisee to consider it can be an indicator that they are reflecting on it. As suggested in the Johari window model (Luft and Ingham 1955), this often opens the windows that may have been blind to the supervisee or hidden from others. Surfacing beliefs, feelings, and thoughts enables them to be further explored, and this contributes to the transformative role of supervision.

The application of emotions

Ensuring emotions are an integral conversation within supervision contributes to emotional awareness and self-knowledge, both of which contribute to professional and personal development. Emotional responses to the work provide a powerful source of information that can assist a supervisee and supervisor to explore barriers or challenges in practice situations. Simply being able to voice and talk through emotional responses can be cathartic – helping the supervisee to express what is happening for them so their responses do not become compounded, and instead clarity can be found.

As suggested, attending to the emotional content of the work helps prevent indirect trauma impacts and also professional dangerousness. Workers may inadvertently fail to take protective action if they overly or personally relate to what is occurring, leading to professional dangerousness. This may also occur when they are experiencing high levels of unmanaged anxiety and fear. Not having time to reflect and process emotions especially to upsetting or disturbing situations can contribute to vicarious trauma, compassion fatigue, and secondary traumatic stress. Left unattended, these responses can also contribute to professional dangerousness as workers inadvertently shift the protective intent for vulnerable people into a protective intention for themselves. Gray et al. (2010, p. 53) write:

> An endangered species in this pressured supervisory climate can be the management of emotion…if the emotion of our work is not managed there can be considerable impact on our effectiveness. We don't work well if we are frightened, depressed, grieving or frozen. Expression of negative emotion is crucial in allowing people to come to terms with a situation and move on from it…supervision must be a place where emotions can be expressed and explored.

Miller and Sprang (2017) note that compassion fatigue is less about experiencing intense feelings in response to hearing other people's pain, but instead, the effort related to inhibiting the intensity of feelings generated in response and the energy required to do this can contribute to fatigue. The intensity of feeling may be more acute for those workers with their own trauma history, who through a process of countertransference may in turn avoid or distance from their emotional reactions or even from the client. I had an experience of this with a mental health social worker who identified withdrawing from a 16-year-old client who was experiencing suicidal ideation linked to physical abuse in her childhood. The worker, on hearing the young woman's experiences, felt triggered into her own history and inadvertently shut the conversation down too soon in a self-protective action. She regretted this and chose to explore it in supervision. On beginning to discuss it with me she became very tearful in relation to her own experiences as a child, which I did not previously know. I gently affirmed her courage in sharing her story with me, and for recognizing what her countertransference had caused her to do. We then talked about identifying a safe place she could explore her own history again and also how to redress the situation with the young woman who had been left vulnerable. The importance of exploring emotional responses and supporting workers to fully experience these in the safe forum of supervision can therefore assist with both worker and client safety.

Compassion fatigue can also be related to empathy strain which Miller and Sprang (2017, p. 159) note is linked to "surface acting" where the practitioner may not feel a natural affinity or empathy for the person and therefore has to work hard to generate this for them. This can be observed in practitioners who work with people whose behavior they may find personally abhorrent or difficult such as sexual abuse towards a child. This creates "emotional labor" (Miller and Sprang 2017, p. 159) which over time can be exhausting for the practitioner. As a supervisor the importance of connecting the practitioner to a place of compassion or understanding may help ease this, along with revisiting core motivation for undertaking the work which can restore this empathetic connection. Helping restore worker confidence, curiosity, and connection to learning, can also help (Miller and Sprang 2017).

Ensuring that emotions can be expressed, explored, and integrated into learning, begins with asking reflective questions that openly inquire into the emotional response of the supervisee. A lack of emotional response may signal an inadvertent discounting of the situation or a reframing of it as a way for the worker to reduce their anxiety. Exploring an emotional response to an issue can also provide information on what the person one is working and engaging with could be experiencing and helps in the identification of transference and counter-transference. A clue to transference and countertransference is often an unbalanced emotional response to a situation, either experiencing too high a level of emotional response or an under response that may be self-protective.

In a later conversation with Jenn, we explored her emotional response to the manager through two counter-transference questions: "If you imagined her as an animal, what sort of animal would she be? "and "What sort of animal would you be in relation to her animal?" (adapted, Rothschild 1994). These elicited extremely useful information about the dynamic within the relationship and how the power imbalance (the power being with Jenn) could be addressed through her identifying how she wanted to be interacting with the manager. It provided a transformative moment where she gained further insight in how she did not like being so aggressive and this helped her move on to committing to finding a way forward and changing the dynamic.

The identification of emotions in supervision also supports recognizing thoughts that contribute to these, providing an opportunity to alter the thinking and influence the emotional response. This includes questioning the thinking for accuracy and assisting supervisees to bring greater analytic reasoning to the situation. This supports the tasks of emotional intelligence which include the ability to: label, perceive, and distinguish own and other's emotions, manage and control own emotions and impulses, marshal and use emotional knowledge in judgment, develop understanding and relate to others using emotional knowledge, and adapt and problem solve in an emotionally responsive and competent way (Bar-on 2005; Goleman 2004; Salovey and Mayer 1990; Weld 2012). Mastery of these areas supports critical reflection which in turn contributes to the transformative role of supervision.

Accessing intuition

As part of our reasoning process, we utilize both the analytic and intuitive parts of our brains (Munro 2008), bringing together both emotional information and logic. Exploring intuitive responses in supervision can help surface unnamed reactions and help workers to examine what has informed these. As intuitive reasoning tends to stem from the limbic center in the brain which guides emotions, arousal, and memories; it is often described as a feeling or "gut" reaction. A combination of non-verbal and verbal information can inform it which workers may initially struggle to describe. Workers may be drawing on previous client experiences, their own values and morals, their mental constructs, and even primitive survival mechanisms to quickly make sense of something. Supervision offers an opportunity to bring analytic reasoning to the intuitive response which includes slowing down and examining why the worker felt and or responded in the way they have. Munro (2008, p. 6) notes that "intuitive reasoning can be dominant, but workers need to take time later to stop and reflect in quieter circumstances." Supervision is the ideal place in which this reflection can occur.

Identifying and exploring intuitive responses often begins firstly by exploring emotional reactions, as emotions are often the voice of our intuition (Weld 2012). We can ask questions about feelings and thoughts that they have not named or are finding it difficult to name and explore these further and identify what these might be informed by (values, beliefs, mental models). The aim to help a supervisee question and explore their thinking may reveal fixed or rigid thinking that is affecting their ability to be open or curious. This can also surface reasoning that requires development or further exploration to ensure safe practice is occurring.

Other techniques to explore intuition include asking a direct question about the worker's intuitive reaction to a person or situation, such as "What is/was your intuition telling you about this?" This tends to immediately cause the supervisee to pause and reflect, as they listen inwardly and notice how their emotional based responses are informing their intuitive reasoning. It invites a process of slowing down and really looking and noticing what is driving decision making. With regard to finding a different way of responding or affirming the choice of action to take, ask "What would a wise person say to you about how to respond or think about this issue?" This question which I heard from a friend who attended the School of Philosophy in Wellington, brings the persons' own wisdom to bear, affirms this, and also tends to lower a highly emotional reactive response. It is a very calming and grounding question and one I use frequently as it connects workers to their existing wisdom.

As supervisors, we also rely on intuition to guide our questioning along with our analytic reasoning. In the session with Jenn, my intuitive reasoning was that an unspoken value or belief was fueling her need to "win" the situation with her manager. This may not have been correct, which confirms the need to bring analytic reasoning to intuitive responses. This may have been overly influenced by my previous experience of working with a supervisee who was overly reactive to perceived unfairness. It also may have been influenced by my own belief in taking time to consider other perspectives. It is always important to check for our own bias and determine if we have inadvertently become rigid or fixed in relation to this. It is not helpful to bring our own unexamined biases into the supervision session.

Conclusion

Professional supervision can provide a transformative function that ultimately benefits the people receiving services from workers. In order to achieve this, supervision must contain openness and a commitment to learn from both the supervisee and supervisor. Supervision needs to provide relational safety while requiring workers to critically examine what is personally and professionally informing their practice. Supervisors are required to apply the skilled use of observations, and be bold in their questioning, even if this becomes uncomfortable, in order to surface learning that supports professional and personal development. Enabling the transformative function in supervision is innovative and invigorating, and supports a reciprocity of learning that is rich and meaningful. Supervisors need to ensure their own supervision also provides for transformative work and embrace this with curiosity. Supervision then becomes not only a base camp to restore and support workers, but a place of discovery, one that enables both supervisee and supervisor to travel further on their journey of service to others.

References

Bar-On, R., 2005. *The Bar-On model of emotional social intelligence (ESI)*. Austin: University of Texas.

Beddoe, E., 2010. Surveillance or reflection: professional supervision in the 'risk society'. *British Journal of Social Work*, 40 (4), 1279–1296.

Carroll, M., 2001. The spirituality of supervision. *In*: Carroll, M., and Tholstrup, M., eds. *Integrative approaches to supervision*. London: Jessica Kingsley, 76–89.

Davys, A., and Beddoe, E., 2010. *Best practice in professional supervision. A guide for the helping professions*. London: Jessica Kingsley.

Goleman, D., 2004. *Emotional intelligence and working with emotional intelligence*. London: Bloomsbury.

Gray, I., Field, R., and Brown, K., 2010. *Effective leadership, management and supervision. Health and social care.* Exeter: Learning Matters Ltd.

Herkt, J., Hocking, C., 2007. Supervision in New Zealand; professional growth or maximising competence?. *New Zealand Journal of Occupational Therapy*, 54, (2), 24–30.

Inskipp, F., and Proctor, B., 1993. *The art, craft and tasks of counselling supervision. Part 1 Making the most of supervision.* Twickenham Middlesex: Cascade Publications.

Luft, J., and Ingham, H., 1955. *The Johari window, a graphic model of interpersonal awareness.* In the Proceedings of the Western Training Laboratory in Group Development. Los Angeles. CA: UCLA..

Miller, B., 2018. Indirect trauma sensitive supervision in child welfare. *In*: Strand, V.C, and Sprang, G., eds. *Trauma responsive child welfare systems.* Switzerland: Springer International, 299–314.

Miller, B., and Sprang, G., 2017. A components-based practice and supervision model for reducing compassion fatigue by affecting clinician experience. *Traumatology*, 23 (2), 153–164. http://dx.doi.org/10 .1037/trm0000058

Munro, E., 2008. Improving reasoning in supervision. *Social Work Now: The Practice Journal of Child, Youth and Family*, 40, 3–10.

O'Donoghue, K., 2003. *Re-storying social work supervision.* Palmerston North, New Zealand: Dunmore Press.

Rothschild, B., 1994. Transference and countertransference. A common sense perspective. *Energy and Character*, 25 (2), 8–12.

Salovey, P., and Mayer, J., 1990. Emotional intelligence. *Imagination, Cognition and Personality*, 9, (3), 185–211.

Weld, N., 2012. *A practical guide to transformative supervision for the helping professions. Amplifying insight.* London: Jessica Kingsley.

33

TRAUMA INFORMED SUPERVISION

Carolyn Knight

In 2001, Harris and Follett introduced the term, "trauma informed" (TI) to describe an approach to practice that recognized the likelihood that many clients were survivors of trauma. Since that time, there has been a veritable explosion in the conceptual, research, and practice literature that examines the nature of and benefits associated with the trauma informed formulation. A noteworthy gap in this literature has been the lack of attention to trauma informed supervision. This is surprising since a foundational assumption of the perspective is that TI *practice* – the services provided to clients – cannot exist without TI *care* – the organizational climate that supports it. Clinical supervision is an essential aspect of TI care. In this chapter, the author summarizes the TI formulation. The author then applies TI principles to supervision integrating the latest conceptual and empirical literature. Case examples illustrate core supervisory skills.

Prevalence of trauma

Findings from epidemiological studies indicate that a trauma informed orientation is warranted. International health surveys revealed that more than 70% of respondents reported experiencing at least one life-time trauma, and the average was three incidents per respondent (Atwoli et al. 2015; Kessler et al. 2017). A meta-analysis of clinical populations (Santiago et al. 2013) found that:

1. The predominant form of trauma among clinical populations was "intentional" trauma, the most common of which was childhood abuse, followed by rape and sexual assault, domestic violence, and community violence;
2. Three-quarters of clients in mental health settings had a history of trauma;
3. Three-quarters of women and at least 50% of men in substance abuse treatment have a history of trauma;
4. The majority of adult parents involved in the child welfare system had a history of trauma; and
5. The majority of refugees seeking asylum have a history of trauma, in addition to the trauma associated with their status.

Long-term sequelae of trauma

There are variations in the long-term sequelae of trauma exposure, but there also are notable commonalities. Documented long-term effects – especially when trauma involves interpersonal victimization in childhood – include substance abuse, self-harm/injury, chronic pain and somatic complaints, suicidal ideation, depression, and stress, anxiety, and dissociative disorders (O'Donnell et al. 2016; Dye 2018). Exposure to trauma – particularly in childhood – also results in neurobiological changes that affect individuals' ability to process and manage stress (Sperry 2016).

Contemporary research efforts focus on how individuals experience trauma and the influence of sociocultural and environmental forces (van der Kolk 2007). Constructivist self-development (CSD) theorists observe, "…the individual [is an] active agent in creating and construing his or her reality" (McCann and Pearlman 1990, pp. 5–6). CSD theorists also note that trauma exposure leads to changes in cognitive schema (Currier et al. 2015; Samuelson et al. 2017). Survivors of trauma often develop a worldview characterized by a lack of safety and predictability and view themselves as powerless. When the trauma is interpersonal in nature, mistrust of self and others also is common. CSD theorists also note that trauma exposure, especially when it is interpersonal in nature and occurs in childhood, compromises survivors' "self-capacities" which include the ability to self-soothe, manage affect, make decisions, and trust one's judgment.

Risk and protective factors and adversarial growth

Researchers have sought to identify risk and protective factors, the most significant of which are social support and prior emotional functioning (Carlson et al. 2016; Smith et al. 2017). Social support, including but not limited to, acknowledgment and understanding of trauma's impact, availability of resources, and acceptance and validation, has a mitigating effect and promotes resilience. In contrast, the absence of support, in the form of blame or accusation, lack of validation or acknowledgment, and an absence of resources exacerbates the impact of trauma. Pre-existing mental health problems also place individuals at greater risk.

Researchers also have examined the ways in which exposure to trauma promotes growth and well-being. "Adversarial" or "post-traumatic" growth includes: a reordering of priorities; a renewed or a new sense of spirituality; enhanced feelings of empathy and concern for others; and increased feelings of self-efficacy (Bonnano et al. 2011; Burton et al. 2015). Research does indicate that adversarial growth is harder for survivors of interpersonal violence in childhood to identify (Ulloa et al. 2016).

Indirect trauma

Clinicians engaged in working with trauma survivors have been found to be indirectly traumatized by their work. Indirect trauma is viewed as an inevitable occupational hazard for clinicians who work with survivors of trauma (Molnar et al. 2017). Three distinct reactions have been identified, two of which parallel those experienced by individuals directly exposed to trauma.

Secondary traumatic stress refers to persistent intrusive thoughts and images associated with survivors' experiences, re-experiencing clients' reactions and trauma, and hyper-arousal and vigilance (Bride 2004). For example, a social worker in child protective services observed[1]:

> Now that I have my own child, I find it a lot harder to turn off my thoughts about the kids on my caseload. I just finished an investigation involving allegations of physical and sexual abuse of a four-year-old boy. The child has signs of having been repeatedly sodomized and has a lot of physical injuries. I have a son who's five. I look at my son

and can't help but see this little boy, and all the other kids that I've seen over the years. This little kid, he's got these dead eyes. I keep seeing those dead eyes of his every time I look at my son.

The DSM-V (APA 2013) includes this reaction under the new diagnosis of Trauma and Stress Related Disorders. As a way of managing these symptoms, clinicians may adopt distancing strategies like denial, detachment, and emotional insulation.

Vicarious trauma refers to changes in cognition that parallel that of survivors of trauma (Pearlman and Saakvitne 1995). Clinicians develop a worldview characterized by mistrust, pessimism, and powerlessness. Consider the comments of a counselor in a rape crisis center[2]:

My daughter is now 16, and from the time she was old enough to walk, I was convinced that something horrible would happen. I was convinced that she would be molested or kidnapped. My husband would tell me I was being overprotective. I would tell him that he was being naïve, that he had no idea of the dangers that were out there. I still worry about her every day. Now, as I think about it, it really pisses me off that my views have been so distorted by my clients' experiences.

Practitioners that work with trauma survivors also may experience *compassion fatigue*. While not unique to working with trauma survivors, clinicians engaged in this work are at heightened risk (Figley 1995; Berzoff and Kita 2010). Survivors – particularly those who have experienced interpersonal victimization – often approach the helping relationship with mistrust and hostility and are, therefore, difficult to engage. In addition, the nature of survivors' trauma and the current problems in living with which they struggle may overwhelm clinicians, leading to a reduced capacity to empathize.

Indirect trauma is not the same as burnout or countertransference, but it can lead to both (Salston and Figley 2003; Berzoff and Kita 2010). Consider the following example:

Sharon works in a public elementary school. Many of her young clients lack stable homes. She makes frequent attempts to involve parents in her work, but generally finds them uninterested. She is particularly concerned about twins, Sandra and Samuel, age eight. They come to school hungry and in dirty, ripped clothes. Both are bullied for their appearance and body odor. They have been living with their invalid grandmother and their mother, who is a drug addict.

Sharon frequently has asked mother and/or grandmother to meet with her, but they have not kept appointments or been home when she visited. She is frustrated, sad, discouraged, and questions whether she can continue in her job. She feels like all she does is apply band aids to her clients' problems. Sharon also states that she is "furious" at the twins' family for "not caring."

Personal, background characteristics that increase the risk of indirect trauma include less education, newly employed, having extensive or minimal experience working with survivors, and having a large number of trauma survivors on one's caseload. Factors that lower the risk of indirect trauma include satisfaction with one's personal life and supportive personal and professional social networks; findings regarding the impact of a personal history of trauma are mixed (Hensel et al. 2015; Molnar et al. 2017).

Research indicates that organizational variables are both risk and protective factors (Dombo and Blome 2016; Sprang et al. 2017). Organizational support in the form of validation and normalization of clinicians' reactions, promotion of self-care, attention to caseloads, and opportunities for continuing education lessen the risk of indirect trauma.

In contrast, an unsupportive organizational climate that minimizes or denies the existence of indirect trauma and does not attend to caseload management increases the risk. Consider the following example of a clinician working in a halfway house for men recently released from prison with substance abuse problems. He describes his isolation which has been exacerbated by his supervisor's response:

> I have never thought it was acceptable to talk about how I feel about my clients. They aren't easy to work with. They have terrible stories to tell. I go from being frustrated with them for not wanting my help to angry at their situations and the lack of resources to furious at the people who screwed them up so much when they were younger.
>
> I mentioned to the clinical director, who is my supervisor, that I was having trouble dealing with my feelings about one particular client who was raped as a kid by his father and his father's friends. He became a prostitute to support his own addiction, served time in prison, and was sodomized there. The clinical director told me that we shouldn't be getting into our clients' past, that we had to focus on the present. She also told me that I needed to remember what it meant to be a professional, which was to not bring our own feelings into our work. Part of me knew that I shouldn't listen to her, but I still found myself feeling guilty and questioning my professionalism.

A second example reveals the negative impact of a lack of organizational support and reflects the phenomenon known as organizational contagion; manifestations of indirect trauma become pervasive among some or all staff (Wolf et al. 2014).

> Luis works in an alternative school setting with youth mandated to attend by the juvenile court, as an alternative to incarceration. During the current academic year, five students have been murdered, and three of Luis's clients lost loved ones to violence. On several occasions, he has brought up his sadness and feelings of despair and hopelessness with his supervisor, but she either avoids discussing this or subtly suggests he needs therapy himself. This has led Luis to worry that there is something wrong with him, a feeling exacerbated by the fact that other staff seem unaffected. He recently overheard another worker say about a client who had been murdered, "He wasn't going to amount to anything anyway. Thank goodness he's God's problem now, not ours!" This led others to laugh out-loud.

Analogous to resilience and adversarial growth, researchers have identified benefits associated with working with trauma survivors. "Vicarious resilience" or "vicarious post-traumatic growth" includes enhanced appreciation for one's advantages in life, re-ordering of personal goals and priorities, heightened capacity for empathy, and increased feelings of competence (Frey et al. 2017). Among clinicians with histories of trauma, enhanced appreciation of their strengths and resilience has been observed.

Trauma-informed formulation: Core principles

The trauma informed formulation reflects the "direct opposite" of the experiences of survivors (Hales et al. 2017) and applies to all aspects of service delivery. Five principles undergird the model: safety, trust, collaboration, choice, and empowerment.

Trauma informed practice

A therapeutic relationship that promotes safety and trust is an essential element of TI practice. Trauma survivors need assurance that they are both physically and emotionally safe with the practitioner and in the practitioner's office and agency. Survivors often need help in trusting themselves. This includes developing confidence in their judgment and their ability to manage affect, both of which are important self-capacities. When clinicians provide clear and consistent boundaries – including a clear explanation of role and purpose, limits of confidentiality, and the purpose of the intervention – this also promotes trust and safety.

Clinicians promote choice, collaboration, and empowerment through clear lines of communication, informed consent, and respecting survivors' cultural identities and the ways in which these shape their experiences of trauma. The therapeutic relationship is framed as a partnership in which survivors are the experts in their lives.

Trauma informed care

Trauma informed care begins with the physical environment of an organization that promotes comfort, safety, and privacy for staff and clients. A culture that promotes respectful relationships between staff at all levels and between staff and clients also reinforces safety and trust.

A TI organization provides clear expectations for employees and rewards excellence. TI care also recognizes and legitimizes the existence of indirect trauma and is proactive in providing staff with the resources to manage this. TI organizations promote choice, collaboration, and empowerment when staff and clients have an opportunity to have input into policies that impact them. Choice, collaboration, and empowerment also are promoted when staff are provided opportunities for continuing education and to improve upon their work, and recognized for their contributions.

Agency context and trauma informed practice and care

In many settings, treatment emphasis will be on current problems in living rather than the underlying trauma that they may reflect. In settings such as mental health, forensic/correctional, child welfare, substance abuse, and shelters for homeless individuals and victims of domestic violence, clients' past trauma is likely to be in the background not in the forefront. Clinicians may have limited capacity to address trauma. Yet, they are on the front-line of trauma work since survivors are more likely to be seen in these problem-focused settings than those that are trauma-focused (Wolf et al. 2014). Trauma-focused settings include rape crisis, hospital trauma centers, and human-made, natural disaster, and refugee relief.

The principles of TI practice will be applied differently in these two contexts. Both settings should promote survivors' self-capacities. In trauma-focused settings, the present trauma is by definition the focus of treatment – though any previous trauma may go unaddressed and unrecognized.

In problem-focused settings, clinicians must clarify with survivors what they can work on and what they cannot. Treatment emphasis will reflect an organization's mission, goals, and purpose and the need to avoid re-traumatizing survivors by raising issues they are not yet able to manage and/or that the clinician is unable to address due to agency constraints. In these settings, the treatment emphasis may be on helping survivors: understand the connection between present challenges and past trauma; manage these challenges; and identify next steps, each of which promote self-capacities.

TI care will be similar in both contexts. Research reveals that this formulation has not been widely adopted, even in settings with a trauma focus (Berliner and Kolko 2016). Adopting a

TI lens in problem-focused settings may be more challenging. Not all clients will be survivors of trauma, and many survivors of trauma may not reveal this, nor even recognize its association with their current difficulties. This reality may obscure survivors' needs. Clinicians' needs in these settings also may be overlooked; survivors' behaviors and problems will reflect their underlying trauma, even if the trauma has not been recognized.

Trauma-informed supervision: The missing link

The skills needed for trauma informed supervision are not new. What is required is for supervisors to: use these skills intentionally in ways that model trauma informed practice; proactively and appropriately address clinicians' affective reactions; and educate and support clinicians in their work with trauma survivors.

Relevant models of supervision

Four theoretical approaches to supervision lend themselves to developing a model of trauma informed supervision. Bernard and Goodyear's (2014) discrimination model distinguishes three roles that supervisors adopt. In the role of teacher, the supervisor enhances supervisees' understanding of trauma informed practice. When engaged in the consultant role, the supervisor offers suggestions and insights, but encourages supervisees to become more independent. These two roles reflect the underlying assumption that an essential responsibility of the supervisor is to help supervisees move from passive to active learners. As counselor, the supervisor assists clinicians in engaging in self-reflection and identifying and managing indirect trauma.

Relational approaches to supervision attend to the supervisory alliance, since this is the means through which clinicians enhance practice competence (Bennett et al. 2013). For example, a supervisor in Berger and Quiros' (2016) Delphi study of trauma informed supervision described the relationship as, "…an oasis within the chaos, [where the supervisor balances] being very attentive, gentle supportive, and nurturing, while also nudging workers to challenge themselves, hold them accountable, and yet create a safe place to struggle professional growth" (p. 149).

The interactional model of supervision (Shulman 2010) emphasizes the importance of the parallel process, adhering to the principle, "more is caught than taught." The supervisor's actions and the dynamics that surface in the supervisory relationship mirror those that exist in the therapeutic one (O'Donoghue 2014). Both relational and interactional models assume that, "the positive working relationship between supervisor and supervisee is the medium of supervisory influence" (Lawlor 2013, p. 180).

A solution-focused approach to supervision has received much less attention in the literature. However, its specific focus on building upon supervisees' strengths is consistent with the TI principle of empowerment. Supervisees' missteps and learning needs are not ignored; but emphasis is placed upon helping them identify what they are doing right and applying this to other clinical situations (Koob 2003; Trenhaile 2005; Thomas 2013).

Promoting trust and safety

Clarify expectations

Creating a supervisory relationship that promotes trust and safety begins with clarifying expectations and asking for supervisee feedback. Essentially, the supervisor is saying, "Here is how I suggest we work together. Does this make sense? What are your thoughts?" Supervisor and supervisee establish an agreement about basic issues like the frequency and length of meetings and supervisee' learning goals. Supervisors also explain their expectation that supervisees will take an increasingly active role in their learning. Supervisors must clarify the boundaries of the relationship. Many supervisors have administrative responsibilities such as evaluating their supervisees' performance and must establish where administrative responsibilities end, and the clinical supervision begins. The relationship is not a therapeutic one, but it is a place where supervisees examine their affective reactions. If, from the beginning, supervisors inform supervisees of this expectation, this sends a message that it is safe for supervisees to disclose their affective reactions.

Encourage open discussion

Given the administrative role that a supervisor often plays and supervisees' natural reluctance to admit to mistakes or a lack of knowledge, the supervisor actively encourages and models open and honest discussion. Research in clinical supervision reveals that clinicians are reluctant to discuss in supervision the issues that are most important, often their reactions to their work and mistakes they may have made (Best et al. 2014; Mehr et al. 2015). Research also reveals that when supervisors are transparent and disclose the struggles they have faced in their own clinical practice, this enhances supervisees' willingness to do the same (Petrila et al. 2015). Consider the following example:

> Sandy works in a housing and rehabilitation program for homeless veterans as a case manager. Her client, Tim, a 45-year-old army veteran, has been homeless for more than two years and has an addiction to opiates and alcohol. Sandy meets with him weekly to see how he is progressing on the goals that he and the clinical team have established. Tim has begun to share his memories of combat in the Mideast, which included seeing friends blown-up from improvised explosive devices and women and children killed by allied forces.
>
> When Sandy meets with her supervisor, Matthew, she tells him she does not know how to help Tim, saying, "I'm not a therapist, I'm *just a case manager*" [italics added for emphasis]. Sandy becomes teary-eyed as she relates some of the experiences that Tim shared with her. Matthew assures Sandy that she does have the skills needed to help Tim with what he has disclosed and validates how difficult it is to hear stories such as Tim's:

> *Matthew:* A lot of our clients have seen and done terrible things which is why they end up homeless and addicted. And it's really hard to hear their stories. Over the years, I've learned ways to deal with my feelings. I'm thinking we could take some time to help you do the same. No matter where you work or who you work with, your feelings can get the best of you. But, how about we first talk about how you are being helpful to Tim.
> *Sandy:* Great, because I feel like I'm not qualified to help him!
> *Matthew:* You're not giving yourself enough credit! First off, you listened to his recollections and expressed your concern for him and sadness for what he experienced, right? That means you validated his experience and what it meant for him. By letting him talk about this, you are helping him manage his feelings.
> *Sandy:* But he needs so much more than I can provide.
> *Matthew:* Well, I agree that your role doesn't allow you to provide him with in-depth counseling, but as his case manager, you do have the ability to validate his concerns, identify resources that can help him deal with his war experiences, and support the positive changes he has been making. Those are all incredibly important for Tim.

Matthew's actions reflect two "hats" the discrimination model identifies. Matthew adopts the teacher role as he helps Sandy understand how her efforts are beneficial to Tim. Theirs is a problem-focused practice context, so it is understandable that Sandy – who is relatively inexperienced and new to the job – does not appreciate this. Matthew's explanation reflects his understanding of what trauma informed practice means in his setting.

This example also illustrates the parallel process in action. Matthew uses the very skills in supervision that he is helping Sandy develop in her practice. He adopts the counselor role when he discloses his own struggles, inviting Sandy to share hers. Matthew maintains clear boundaries and avoids transforming the supervisory alliance into a therapeutic one.

Attend to supervisees' affective reactions

Making an "affective check-in" a routine aspect of supervision (Walker 2004) conveys to supervisees that their emotional reactions are legitimate topics for discussion. Supervisors may need to look for signs of indirect trauma like avoidance, numbness, and lack of empathy, since clinicians may not be fully aware of them or what they represent. To accomplish this, supervisors engage in "deep listening," entering the world of their supervisee without judgment (Vargehese et al. 2018).

Supervisor and supervisee focus on the manifestations of indirect trauma, *not* on the trauma histories of clients that precipitated them. Supervisors also must be prepared to help clinicians contain feelings (Collins-Camargo and Antle 2018). These two considerations reduce the likelihood that clinicians will be re-traumatized.

This focus also serves an important educational function. Through "targeted reflective supervision," supervisors help clinicians see how their thoughts and reactions connect with the needs of their clients (Collins-Camargo and Antle 2018). Essentially, the supervisor asks clinicians to consider the parallel process: "What am I thinking and feeling?" and "How do my reactions help me better understand my clients' needs?"

Research reveals that clinicians' dissatisfaction with clinical supervision increases when the relationship turns into – or is experienced as – therapy (Ladany et al. 2013; Ellis 2017). Consider the following example drawn from a rape crisis and sexual assault center:

> The social worker, Mae, began seeing a new client who had been raped by an ex-boyfriend. The client, Suanna, also disclosed that she had been sexually abused between the ages of five and ten by a series of her mother's boyfriends. Suanna described the abuse in detail: vaginal and anal penetration, gang rape, and penetration with objects.
>
> Mae had been working at the center for several months, but this was the first time she was working with a client who had a history of sexual abuse in addition to being a victim of rape. She herself had been sexually abused as a child, had been in therapy to address this, and believed that she was doing well. Because she experienced such a strong affective reaction to Suanna's disclosures, Mae worried that she might not be doing as well as she thought. She also was concerned that her ability to be helpful to Suanna might be compromised. In supervision, Mae described what her client had disclosed, and her concerns. The supervisor responded:
>
> *Diana (Supervisor):* I didn't know you were a survivor of sexual abuse. That can create boundary issues. Perhaps you need to think about why you chose to work in an agency like this. Maybe to resolve some of your personal issues?

Mae: Well…..uh…..I do want to work in this field because of my experience, but I don't think it's because I haven't worked through my own abuse. Until now, I thought I had. Suanna's abuse was just so awful!

Diana: Well, yes of course it is. But in our line of work, we have to be prepared to hear stories like hers. You're going to be hearing a lot of terrible things, so maybe we need to talk more about what happened to you, so that in the future, you're better able to handle these situations.

The supervisor's response to the clinician was both re-traumatizing and invalidating and reinforces Diana's reservations about herself. A more helpful and appropriate response would have been to normalize Mae's reactions. The supervisor could have used Mae's concerns and disclosure of her own history of sexual abuse to affirm her vicarious post-traumatic growth. Consider the following hypothetical response:

Diana: I'm glad you felt comfortable sharing your concerns with me. I understand that you are worried that your reaction might mean you have some unfinished work of your own. That's possible, but anyone who heard Suanna's story would be deeply impacted. I am close to tears thinking about it, and I'm not a survivor. I think one way we can help you is to identify how you can manage these reactions when they happen. The fact that you brought this up and are aware of how much Suanna's story affected you suggests how far you've come in your journey. But, if, after we've processed the case further, you're still thinking you have some work of your own to do, we can figure how where and how to do that.

The supervisor does not ignore the possibility that the clinician might have more work to do. But she focuses on the more likely possibility that the clinician's reactions are normal and expected.

Attend to the supervisory relationship

Trauma informed supervisors tailor their approach to the unique learning needs, interpersonal style, and cultural identity of their supervisees. They avoid adopting a "one style fits all" approach. They appreciate the social positions they themselves hold and help clinicians understand the implications for practice of the social identities and positions they and their clients hold. Of particular importance is the need for clinicians and supervisors to examine the role that power and privilege play in their relationship with one another and with their clients (Berger et al. 2018). In 1995; Fontes introduced the term "sharevision" to describe a supervisory alliance that is more egalitarian in nature. When the power differential is lessened between supervisors and clinicians, both are able to engage in more honest discussion and self-reflection.

TI supervisors consistently monitor the supervisory alliance and are prepared to directly address disruptions in the relationship since these will undermine clinicians' ability to learn from and use supervision. In yet another example of the parallel process, the supervisor's skills will mirror those clinicians use when they face a therapeutic impasse with clients. Essentially, the supervisor is willing to acknowledge, "I think there is something going on between us that is getting in the way of our ability to work together."

Consider the following example drawn from the forensic unit of an inpatient psychiatric facility[3]. The intern supervisor, Richard, addresses tension that has surfaced in his relationship with his student, Tanya, who has been working with Marcus. In previous sessions, Tanya tearfully described Marcus's childhood: he witnessed the murder of an older brother; was physically abused by his father; and was placed in numerous foster homes in which he was physically and sexually abused. In their latest supervisory meeting – that took place three weeks before Tanya's practicum ended – she reported to Richard that she had promised Marcus she would accompany him to a court hearing, which would occur after her placement ended:

Richard: Whoa, Tanya, we need to talk about this. I understand you want to be there for Marcus for his trial, but once you leave us, you're no longer his social worker.

Silence

Richard: Tanya.....so…what are you thinking? You look angry.

Tanya: Marcus has nobody! He told me that I'm the first person who has been there for him. I have to go to the hearing! It's not fair to not let me go!

Richard: I'm not keeping you from going. I am reminding you that, when you terminate, your work with your clients is over, and unfortunately that includes your work with Marcus.

Silence

Richard: Tanya, I know this is tough. I know you care about him. And I know that Marcus has had no one, and you have been there for him. You seem angry with me? Maybe for reminding you of boundaries?

Tanya: I just don't think boundaries should matter in this case. I have been his social worker for four months. You don't understand how hard it's been on him! I don't think you're being fair to him or me.

Richard: I understand that you're upset and that you can tell me this. I hope you'll consider the possibility that it's not really me you're angry at. Maybe you're angry at the situation – that you can't be there for him when he needs you to be. Angry at all those people that weren't there for him when he needed them. Maybe you're even feeling a little guilty? That you are "abandoning" him when he needs you the most?

Silence

Tanya: I'm sorry. I'm being disrespectful.

Richard: Nothing to apologize for! You care about Marcus, and you have to terminate with him at a critical juncture in his life.

The fact that Tanya could share her anger with Richard suggests that theirs is a solid supervisory alliance. He encourages Tanya to engage in self-reflection and suggests to her in a non-threatening way that her reactions to him – indicators of transference – might actually reflect her understandable anger at the unfairness of her client's life and current situation.

Promoting collaboration, choice, empowerment

For the ease of discussion, the author separated skills and responsibilities associated with trust and safety from those associated with these three principles. In fact, there is much overlap. Supervisors also promote collaboration, choice, and empowerment (CCE) as they engage in the four previous tasks when they:

1. Clarify expectations and ask for feedback and suggestions;
2. Convey the expectation that clinicians will take increased responsibility for their learning;
3. Address clinicians' affective reactions by sharing the challenges they have faced in their own practice; and

4. Reflect on the supervisory relationship and invite and attend to supervisees' feedback, which may lead to "recontracting" the expectations associated with their work together.

Additional supervisory skills and responsibilities directly promote CCE.

Encourage supervisees to take responsibility for their learning

From the beginning, the supervisor conveys the expectation that supervisees will actively participate in their learning. Collins-Camargo (2006) describes a process of "targeted questioning" in which supervisors ask supervisees to reflect on their work and their reactions. For example, rather than saying, "Perhaps the reason why the client reacted to you that way is…," the supervisor asks, "Why do you think the client might have reacted to you that way?" By refraining from immediately providing their insights, supervisors encourage clinicians to develop these on their own.

Identify and build upon supervisees' strengths

When supervisors adopt a solution-focused orientation, they are readily able to build upon supervisees' strengths. The supervisor explores with clinicians what they are doing right, in addition to identifying mistakes and missteps. The supervisor asks clinicians to think about times when their work with a particular client (or their work in general) was going well and identify what they did that led to their success. In a previous example, the supervisor, Matthew, reframes his supervisee's work in a way that illuminates her strengths. This, in turn, encourages her to more intentionally engage in similar interventions with future clients.

Clinicians' learning needs and areas for growth are not ignored; rather, the supervisor invites them to identify their successes and helps them apply this learning to future work. Supervisees may be reluctant to identify strengths out of fear of appearing immodest or they actually may have a hard time identifying what is going well in their practice, requiring persistence on the part of the supervisor.

Provide direct assistance in supervisees' practice

Research findings suggest that when supervisors are willing to involve themselves directly in clinicians' practice, this enhances satisfaction and enhances feelings of self-efficacy (Mor Barak et al. 2009). Supervisors work with clinicians to address challenges in their practice, they do not do this *for* them. In some instances, this might involve the supervisor participating in a session with a client; in others, supervisor and clinician engage in behavioral rehearsal or role play as the following example illustrates:

> The agency – an outpatient drug treatment program routinely screens for a history of sexual abuse in its intake procedures. Erin, a new social worker, will be conducting an intake for a new client, Sylvia, who is self-referred for an addiction to cocaine. Erin has observed and participated in several intake interviews with her supervisor, Susan, but this will be the first time she will conduct an intake on her own. Erin and Susan meet to prepare Erin for this client encounter.
>
> *Susan:* So, you're seeing Sylvia this afternoon. I'm wondering how you are feeling?
> *Erin:* Nervous! But also excited. I'm glad I've gotten to see how you do this. It makes me feel more like I won't mess up.

Susan: Good to hear! I'm wondering what your thoughts are about asking Sylvia about any possible abuse history? I've been conducting these interviews for a long time, but I still find it hard to ask about this. I hate to bring up a topic that might be painful for the client. I find myself holding my breath – hoping that when I ask, the client will say no!

Erin: I'm kind of feeling the same way. I know that if our clients have been abused, it's important we know about it as soon as possible to make it part of our treatment plan. But, I'm scared that if she tells me something did happen, I won't know what to say.

Susan: Okay, suppose Sylvia does disclose she was abused in some way? Where do you go from there? Remember we've talked about how important it is to validate our clients' experiences and feelings? That's a place to start. How might you go about doing that?

Erin: Well, I'm not sure. (*Hesitates*) I think I'm hoping she says she wasn't abused.

Susan: I understand, don't we all (*smiles*)? But since we can't control that, let's role play several possible responses Sylvia might provide. I'll be Sylvia.

Silence

Susan: I know this might seem awkward, but there's no need to feel funny. There's no right or wrong answer. Think of this as a dress rehearsal. We're giving you the chance to practice how to reply to Sylvia so that you can feel more confident and both you and Sylvia can feel more comfortable. Give it a try.

Erin: (*Takes a deep breath*). Okay… [to Susan] Sylvia, I'm going to ask you some questions that clients sometimes have a hard time answering, about whether you've ever been touched or abused sexually when you were a child or at any other point. So many of our clients have had something like this happen to them that we think it's important to know this so we can work with our clients to develop a plan that fully meets their needs.

The supervisor skillfully blends her responsibility as counselor when she addresses Erin's affective reactions with her responsibility as a consultant. She does not tell Erin how to conduct the intake, preferring instead to have Erin do this on her own.

Help supervisees manage affective reactions

Making an affective check in a routine aspect of supervision is accompanied by helping clinicians manage their reactions. Consistent with a solution-focused orientation, supervisors ask clinicians to reflect upon coping skills they already are using. Instead of saying, "When I find I can't stop thinking about my clients, I [fill in the blank]," the supervisor says, "When you can't stop thinking about something distressing, what have you done to push those thoughts away?" Supervisors explore with clinicians what coping skills they have previously employed when faced with challenges comparable to those that they are experiencing in their work.

Mediate between agency demands and needs of clients and clinicians

Supervisors have an important role to play in bridging the gap between the needs of clients and clinicians and decision makers within the organization. This typically involves helping the organization become more attuned and responsive to the needs of both constituencies. Consider the following example:

Shayla is a social worker in a transitional housing program for chronically mentally ill individuals being prepared to live in the community. One of her patients stopped taking her medications, resulting in the return of symptoms of paranoid schizophrenia. The patient attacked Shayla, believing Shayla was the "she-devil." [The patient had mentioned this before, and Shayla and other staff assumed "she-devil" referred to the patient's mother who had subjected the client to horrific physical abuse]. Shayla suffered a knee injury that required medical care and time off. When Shayla returned to work, she experienced much anxiety and was hesitant to interact with patients. The patient who had attacked her had been returned to a more secure unit, but Shayla worried that another patient might attack her. Other staff expressed similar concerns.

Shayla's supervisor immediately asked how she was doing. Shayla mentioned her anxiety about seeing clients, and the supervisor suggested they discuss how they could help Shayla resume her responsibilities and feel safe doing so. The supervisor also shared her intent to talk with her immediate superior – the clinical director – about what steps could be taken to ensure workers' safety, prevent another incident like this from happening again, and provide support to staff on an ongoing basis.

Challenges and future directions

Trauma informed supervision does not require a new way of working with clinicians. The skills and responsibilities the author identifies in this article reflect models of supervision that are widely known and utilized. What is new is that supervisors knowledgeably and intentionally operate from a trauma informed lens.

Supervisors face four challenges in their quest to operate from a trauma informed lens. First, they must understand:

1. Trauma informed practice, so that they can educate clinicians and assist them in their practice as needed;
2. Indirect trauma, so that they can appropriately respond to the needs of supervisees; and
3. Trauma informed care, so that they can advocate for the needs of clients and clinicians.

Since the trauma informed perspective is still not widely understood or employed in many practice settings, a significant challenge facing supervisors is their own lack of familiarity with the formulation.

Second, supervisors' administrative responsibilities often overshadow their clinical ones, making it difficult for them to create and maintain the supervisory alliance that trauma informed supervision requires. For practical as well as purposeful reasons, one way to address this challenge is employ group supervision. The obvious advantage is that less of the supervisor's time is required. Group TI supervision has the added benefit of promoting all five principles since it, "facilitates peer feedback, encourages support and validation of supervisees' experiences and reactions, and provides opportunities to learn from a broad range of cases and practice scenarios" (Knight 2017, p. 1). Limited attention has been directed towards adopting this modality in TI supervision, but authors agree it shows promise (Haans and Balke 2018; Radis 2019).

Yet, group supervision itself presents challenges to supervisors who employ it. Group supervision is much more than individual supervision in a group context and requires supervisors to use group work skills. Therefore, supervisors must not only understand the TI conceptualization, they also must be adept at the use of the group modality in clinical practice and its applications to supervision (Knight 2017).

Third, just as clinicians can be expected to experience indirect trauma as a result of their work with clients, supervisors also are likely to be impacted. Scant attention has been devoted to elaborating upon supervisors' experiences with indirect trauma, but several authors note the risk (Adamson 2018; Collins-Camargo and Antle 2018).

Finally, TI supervision in settings that are problem-focused can be difficult to implement, since clients' trauma may be unknown and only minimally addressed. Therefore, the need for trauma informed lens may go unrecognized. Yet, the author asserts that TI supervision epitomizes excellence in supervision and is appropriate in any setting and for all practitioners.

Future efforts must be directed towards addressing these challenges to expand the availability of TI supervision in all practice arenas. More generally, and equally important, continued efforts must focus on elaborating upon the requirements of TI practice, care, and supervision and encouraging their adoption in settings that are both trauma- and problem-focused.

Notes

1 This case example first appeared in Knight, C., 2009. *Introduction to working with adult survivors of childhood trauma.* Belmont CA: Thomson/Brooks Cole.
2 A version of this case example first appeared in Knight, C., 2009. *Introduction to working with adult survivors of childhood trauma.* Belmont CA: Thomson/Brooks Cole.
3 This example first appeared in Knight, C., 2019. Trauma informed practice and care: implications for field instruction. *Clinical Social Work Journal,* 47 (1), 79–89.

References

Adamson, C., 2018. Trauma-informed supervision in the disaster context. *Clinical Supervisor,* 37 (1), 221–240.

American Psychiatric Association (APA) 2013. *Diagnostic and statistical manual of mental disorders.* 5th ed. Washington, DC: APA.

Atwoli, L., Stein, D.J., Koenen, K.C., and McLaughlin, K.A., 2015. Epidemiology of posttraumatic stress disorder: prevalence, correlates and consequences. *Current Opinion in Psychiatry,* 28 (4), 307.

Bennett, S., Mohr, J., Deal, K.H., and Hwang, J., 2013. Supervisor attachment, supervisory working alliance, and affect in social work field instruction. *Research on Social Work Practice,* 23 (2), 199–209. https://doi .org/10.1177/1049731512468492

Berger, R., and Quiros, L., 2016. Best practices for training trauma-informed practitioners: supervisors' voice. *Traumatology,* 22 (2), 145–154. https://doi.org/10.1037/trm0000076

Berger, R., Quiros, L., and Benavidez-Hatzis, J.R., 2018. The intersection of identities in supervision for trauma-informed practice: challenges and strategies. *The Clinical Supervisor,* 37 (1), 122–141.

Berliner, L., and Kolko, D.J., 2016. Trauma informed care: a commentary and critique. *Child Maltreatment,* 21 (2), 168–172.

Bernard, J.M., and Goodyear, R.K., 2014. *Fundamentals of clinical supervision.* 5th ed. New York, NY: Pearson.

Berzoff, J., and Kita, E., 2010. Compassion fatigue and countertransference: two different concepts. *Clinical Social Work Journal,* 38 (3), 341–349. https://doi.org/10.1007/s10615-010-0271-8

Best, D., et al., 2014. A model for predicting clinician satisfaction with clinical supervision. *Alcoholism Treatment Quarterly,* 32 (1), 67–78.

Bonanno, G.A., Westphal, M., and Mancini, A.D., 2011. Resilience to loss and potential trauma. *Annual Review of Clinical Psychology,* 7, 511–535.

Bride, B., 2004. The impact of providing psychosocial services to traumatized populations. *Stress, Trauma, and Crisis,* 7 (1), 29–46.

Burton, M.S., Cooper, A.A., Feeny, N.C., and Zoellner, L.A., 2015. The enhancement of natural resilience in trauma interventions. *Journal of Contemporary Psychotherapy,* 45 (4), 193–204. https://doi.org/10.1007 /s10879-015-9302-7

Carlson, E.B., Palmieri, P.A., Field, N.P., Dalenberg, C.J., Macia, K.S., and Spain, D.A., 2016. Contributions of risk and protective factors to prediction of psychological symptoms after traumatic experiences. *Comprehensive Psychiatry*, 69, 106–115. https://doi.org/10.1016/j.comppsych.2016.04.022

Collins-Camargo, C., 2006. Clinical supervision in public child welfare: themes from a multi-site study. *Professional Development: Journal of Continuing Social Work Education*, 9 (2/3), 102–112.

Collins-Camargo, C., and Antle, B., 2018. Child welfare supervision: special issues related to trauma-trauma informed care in a unique environment. *The Clinical Supervisor*, 37 (1), 64–82.

Currier, J.M., Holland, J.M., Drescher, K., and Foy, D., 2015. Initial psychometric evaluation of the Moral Injury Questionnaire--Military version. *Clinical Psychology & Psychotherapy*, 22 (1), 54–63. https://doi.org/10.1002/cpp.1866

Dombo, E.A., and Blome, W., 2016. Vicarious trauma in child welfare workers: a study of organizational responses. *Journal of Public Child Welfare*, 10 (5), 505–523.

Dye, H., 2018. The impact and long-term effects of childhood trauma. *Journal of Human Behavior in the Social Environment*, 28 (3), 381–392.

Ellis, M.V., 2017. Narratives of harmful clinical supervision. *The Clinical Supervisor*, 36 (1), 20–87.

Figley, C., 1995. Compassion fatigue: toward a new understanding of the costs of caring. *In*: B. Stamm, ed. *Secondary trauma stress: self-care issues for clinicians, researchers, and educators*. Lutherville, MD: Sidran Press, 3–28.

Fontes, L., 1995. Sharevision: collaborative supervision and self-care strategies for working with trauma. *Family Journal*, 3, 249–254.

Frey, L.L., Beesley, D., Abbott, D., and Kendrick, E., 2017. Vicarious resilience in sexual assault and domestic violence advocates. *Psychological Trauma: Theory, Research, Practice, and Policy*, 9 (1), 44–51.

Haans, A., and Balke, N., 2018. Trauma-informed intercultural group supervision. *Clinical Supervisor*, 37 (1), 158–181.

Hales, T., Kusmaul, N., and Nochajski, T., 2017. Exploring the dimensionality of trauma-informed care: implications for theory and practice. *Human Service Organizations: Management, Leadership & Governance*, 41 (3), 317–325.

Harris, M., and Fallot, R., 2001. *Using trauma theory to design service systems: new directions for mental health services*. San Francisco, CA: Jossey Bass.

Hensel, J.M., Ruiz, C., Finney, C., and Dewa, C.S., 2015. Meta-analysis of risk factors for secondary traumatic stress in therapeutic work with trauma victims. *Journal of Traumatic Stress*, 28 (2), 83–91.

Kessler, R.C., Aguilar-Gaxiola, S., Alonso, J., Benjet, C., Bromet, E.J., Cardoso, G., Degenhardt, L., de Girolamo, G., Dinolova, R.V., Ferry, F., Florescu, S., Gureje, O., Haro, J.M., Huang, Y., Karam, E.G., Kawakami, N., Lee, S., Lepine, J.P., Levinson, D., Navarro-Mateu, F., Pennell, B.E., Piazza, M., Posada-Villa, J., Scott, K.M., Stein, D.J., Ten Have, M., Torres, Y., Viana, M.C., Petukhova, M.V., Sampson, N.A., Zaslavsky, A.M., and Koenen, K.C., 2017. Trauma and PTSD in the WHO world mental health surveys. *European Journal of Psychotraumatology*, 8 (sup5), 1353383. https://doi.org/10.1080/20008198.2017.1353383.

Knight, C., 2017. The mutual aid model of group supervision. *The Clinical Supervisor*, 36 (2), 259–281.

Koob, J.J., 2003. The effects of solution-focused supervision on the perceived self-efficacy of therapists in training. *The Clinical Supervisor*, 21 (2), 161–183.

Ladany, N., Mori, Y., and Mehr, K.E., 2013. Effective and ineffective supervision. *The Counseling Psychologist*, 41 (1), 28–47.

Lawlor, D., 2013. A transformation programme for children's social care managers using an interactional and reflective supervision model to develop supervision skills. *Journal of Social Work Practice*, 27 (2), 177–189.

McCann, I., and Pearlman, L., 1990. *Psychological trauma and the adult survivor*. New York, NY: Brunner/Mazel.

Mehr, K.E., Ladany, N., and Caskie, G.I.L., 2015. Factors influencing trainee willingness to disclose in supervision. *Training and Education in Professional Psychology*, 9 (1), 44–51.

Molnar, B. et al., 2017. Advancing science and practice for vicarious traumatization/secondary traumatic stress: a research agenda. *Traumatology*, 23 (2), 129–142.

Mor Barak, M.E., Travis, D., Pyun, H., and Xie, B., 2009. The impact of supervision on worker outcomes: a meta-analysis. *Social Service Review*, 83 (1), 3–32.

O'Donnell, M.L. et al., 2016. A longitudinal study of adjustment disorder after trauma exposure. *American Journal of Psychiatry*, 173 (12), 1231–1238.

O'Donoghue, K.B., 2014. Towards an interactional map of the supervision session: an exploration of supervisees' and supervisors' experiences. *Practice: Social Work in Action*, 26 (1), 53–70.

Pearlman, L., and Saakvitne, K., 1995. *Trauma and the therapist: countertransference and vicarious traumatization in psychotherapy with incest survivors.* New York, NY: Norton.

Petrila, A., Fireman, O., Fitzpatrick, L.S., Hodas, R.W., and Taussig, H.N., 2015. Student satisfaction with an innovative internship. *Journal of Social Work Education,* 51, 121–135.

Radis, B., 2019. Reflections on facilitating a trauma-informed clinical supervision group with housing first staff. *Social Work with Groups.* doi:10.1080/01609513.2019.1638654.

Salston, M., and Figley, C.R., 2003. Secondary traumatic stress effects of working with survivors of criminal victimization. *Journal of Traumatic Stress,* 16 (2), 167–174. https://doi.org/10.1023/A:1022899207206

Samuelson, K.W., Bartel, A., Valadez, R., and Jordan, J.T., 2017. PTSD symptoms and perception of cognitive problems: the roles of posttraumatic cognitions and trauma coping self-efficacy. *Psychological Trauma: Theory, Research, Practice and Policy,* 9 (5), 537–544. https://doi.org/10.1037/tra0000210

Santiago, P.N., et al., 2013. A systematic review of PTSD prevalence and trajectories in DSM-5 defined trauma exposed populations: intentional and non-intentional traumatic events. *PloS One,* 8 (4), 1–5.

Shulman, L., 2010. *Interactional supervision.* 3rd ed. Washington, DC: NASW Press.

Smith, A.J., Felix, E.D., Benight, C.C., and Jones, R.T., 2017. Protective factors, coping appraisals, and social barriers predict mental health following community violence: a prospective test of social cognitive theory. *Journal of Traumatic Stress,* 30 (3), 245–253. https://doi.org/10.1002/jts.22197

Sperry, L., 2016. Trauma, neurobiology, and personality dynamics: a primer. *Journal of Individual Psychology,* 72 (3), 161–167.

Sprang, G., Ross, L., Miller, B.C., Blackshear, K., and Ascienzo, S., 2017. Psychometric properties of the secondary traumatic stress–informed organizational assessment. *Traumatology,* 23 (2), 65–171.

Thomas, F.N., 2013. *Solution-focused supervision: a resource-oriented approach to developing clinical expertise.* Springer Science+Business Media.

Trenhaile, J.D., 2005. Solution-focused supervision: returning the focus to client goals. *Journal of Family Psychotherapy,* 16 (1/2), 223–228.

Ulloa, E.C., Hammett, J.F., O'Neal, D.N., Lydston, E.E., and Leon Aramburo, L.F., 2016. The big five personality traits and intimate partner violence: findings from a large, nationally representative sample. *Violence & Victims,* 31 (6), 1100–1115. doi:10.1891/0886-6708.VV-D-15-00055

van der Kolk, B.A., 2007. The history of trauma in psychiatry. *In:* M.J. Friedman, T.M. Keane, and P.A. Resick, eds. *Handbook of PTSD: science and practice.* The Guilford Press, 19–36.

Varghese, R., Quiros, L., and Berger, R., 2018. Reflective practices for engaging in trauma-informed culturally competent supervision. *Smith College Studies in Social Work,* 88 (2), 135–151.

Walker, M., 2004. Supervising practitioners working with survivors of childhood abuse: countertransference, secondary traumatization, and terror. *Psychodynamic Practice,* 10 (2), 173–193.

Wolf, M.R. et al., 2014. 'We're all civil servants': the status of trauma-informed care in the community. *Journal of Social Service Research,* 40 (1), 111–120.

34

ETHICAL EVIDENCE-INFORMED SUPERVISION

Kieran O'Donoghue

Social work and the supervision of social workers has been characterized as being both a practical moral and a rational-technical endeavor (Parton 2000; Parton and O'Byrne 2000; Wilkins 2019). The practical-moral basis is derived from the profession's values, ethics, and practices, whereas the rational-technical basis is drawn from its theory, practice wisdom, and research, or in other words the evidence that informs practice. Since the turn of 21st century, there have been developments in social work ethics and in the use of evidence to guide and inform social workers and supervisors (Barsky 2010; Nevo and Slonim-Nevo 2011; Gitterman and Knight 2013; Mullen 2016; Collins 2018; Reamer 2018). The advances in ethics concern ethical risk management, the ethical use of information and communications technology (ICT), and the emergence of care ethics in social work (Collins 2018; Reamer 2018). The developments concerning evidence have seen a more nuanced understanding of what evidence is and how it may be used to inform and guide practice, as well as greater recognition of the challenges pertaining to the evidence-informed argumentation and the translation of evidence into practice (Nevo and Slonim-Nevo 2011; Gitterman and Knight 2013; Mullen 2016). Despite both ethics and evidence having a key role in both social work practice and supervision it is uncommon that these two concepts are considered together or integrated into practice theory or supervision models. For example, McAuliffe and Chenoweth (2019) note that ethics is rarely integrated into the social work theory and practice literature. A similar point is apparent in social work supervision, with Wilkins (2019) identifying the absence of ethics in his working theory on how and why supervision works in child and family settings. Likewise, O'Donoghue and O'Donoghue (2019) noted ethics was in the background in supervision until an ethical issue was identified. They also identified a lack of research evidence pertaining to application of ethics within supervision and argued for a care ethics culture informed by the International Association of Schools of Social Work (IASSW) nine ethical principles (IASSW 2018) to be implemented by the profession and social services organizations.

Turning to the use evidence within social work supervision, which is described as being at an emerging stage, with O'Donoghue (2019) commenting that the work to date has involved making research evidence more accessible through research reviews, the inclusion of evidence-based practice models (i.e. motivational interviewing, solution-focused practice, and cognitive behavioral therapy) to support supervisory interventions, and the development of an evidence-informed social work supervision model. To date there has been no exploration concerning how ethics and evidence are connected in social work supervision. This is despite claims that care ethics sanctions "supervision as a practice that involves caring about social workers, their clients and the community" (O'Donoghue and O'Donoghue 2019, p. 354).

The discussion above raises the following questions regarding the evidence-informed social work supervision model: 1) To what extent does the evidence-informed social work supervision model include ethics? 2) How could care ethics inform the evidence-informed model? This chapter aims to examine the evidence-informed model of social work supervision by exploring how ethics is present within the model and considering how care ethics could inform the model (O'Donoghue et al. 2018; O'Donoghue and O'Donoghue 2019).

Evidence-informed social work supervision model

The evidence-informed social work supervision model was developed from an analysis of the results of 130 peer-reviewed empirical research articles, written in the English language, on social work supervision from 1958 to 2015 (O'Donoghue, et al. 2018; O'Donoghue 2019). The model attempts to apply the findings from international supervision research to supervisory practice through supervisors enacting three processes and focusing on two tasks. The three processes are: a) the construction of supervision; b) the supervision alliance; and c) the interactional process. The outcomes from these processes are the development of shared understanding, purpose, and expectations; a trusting and effective relationship; and positive communication within supervision. The two tasks are the supervision of practitioner and the supervision of their practice with clients. The goals these tasks seek to achieve are: to enhance the performance, well-being, and development of the practitioner; and to facilitate best practice with clients and improvements in client outcomes.

Figure 34.1 below illustrates the interrelationship between the processes and tasks within the model.

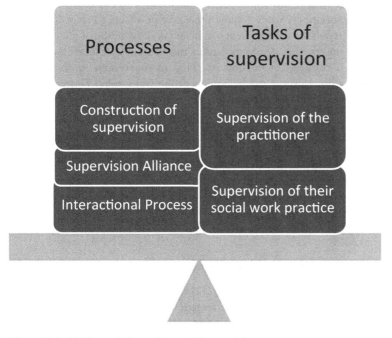

Figure 34.1   Evidence-informed supervision model

The application of both the processes and tasks in the model involves the supervisor drawing on the summaries of the research findings and applying them in supervision. As Figure 34.1 illustrates, the processes are integrally connected to the task of supervision to the extent that they form an integrated and dynamic model. However, since the purpose of this chapter is to explore how ethics are present in the model and then to consider how care ethics could be incorporated, each process and task will be discussed individually.

Construction of supervision

O'Donoghue et al. (2018) found that supervision is socially and personally constructed. This means that the construction of supervision is influenced by the context and narratives surrounding it and the participants' personal conceptualizations of supervision derived from their experiences and perceptions. In other words, while there is a consensus that supervision is composed of administrative, educative, and support functions and primarily practiced through individual sessions or meetings, with group supervision being either an adjunct or substitute for individual supervision. How supervision is practiced in a specific setting is shaped by the social, cultural, organizational, professional, and practice context within which it occurs, and the supervisors' and supervisees' understanding of supervision. According to O'Donoghue et al. (2018) supervisees prefer and benefit from supervision that is focused on their practice, education, and support rather than solely on administrative matters. Supervisors, on the other hand, understand and construct supervision as a relational and reflective process concerned with organizational and professional accountability, development, and support. The implications of this for supervisory practice are that supervisors need to develop with their supervisees a shared understanding of contextual influences within which supervision is immersed, as well as clarify roles, responsibilities, expectations, arrangements, accountabilities, and the sanctioning of supervision. In doing this the supervisor is mindful of the supervisee's preferences, as well as balancing the tasks of supervising the practitioner and their practice with clients within the relational and reflective process.

Despite ethics not being specifically named in the process of developing a shared construction of supervision, it is inferred in the development of a shared understanding of roles, responsibilities, accountabilities, and the sanctioning of supervision. Incorporating a care ethics approach into the process of a shared construction or understanding of supervision involves making ethics more overt through a discussion at the beginning of the relationship concerning how supervision involves caring about the supervisee, clients, and community (O'Donoghue and O'Donoghue 2019). This discussion might canvass how the IASSW's (2018) nine ethical principles, code of ethics, and other authorities, sanction and encapsulate the values and standards of care by which the profession aspires to and is held accountable for by the community (Rhodes 1986). The aim of the ethics discussion is to develop a shared understanding about how ethics is construed by the supervisor and supervisee and the implications of this for ethical social work practice with clients and the ethical processes and practices that occur within supervision. The agreements and understandings derived from the initial and subsequent discussions are recorded and included in the written supervision agreement.

Supervision alliance

The research summarized by O'Donoghue et al. (2018) concerning supervision alliance describes this relationship as a secure base that is characterized by trust, support, honesty, openness, and the ability to mutually navigate power relations, as well as respect social and cultural differences. The purpose of the supervision alliance is for the parties engaged in supervision to feel safe, participate fully, and work effectively in supervision to improve the performance, well-being, and development of the practitioner and to facilitate best practice with clients and improvements in client outcomes. The supervisor's contribution to the supervision alliance is by establishing and sustaining a constructive, considerate, culturally responsive, and caring relationship with supervisees, through demonstrating empathy, emotional intelligence, practice expertise, and relationship skills.

Whilst ethics is not specifically named in the supervision alliance it is nonetheless inferred in the characteristics of the relationship described above. O'Donoghue and O'Donoghue (2019) identify the hallmarks of a care ethics relationship within supervision as one that reflects ethical sensitivity by attending to the duty of care the relationship has to the supervisee, their clients, organization, profession, and the community. It also engages in ethical dialogue which involves constructive conversations that explore ethics and draw upon ethical theories, principles, and questions (e.g. What are the ethical considerations we need to be mindful of? To what extent have we fulfilled our duties of care? And how well have we met our ethical obligations to the client, organization, profession, and the community?). One principle of ethical dialogue that applies to the supervision alliance is partnership. Partnership means the supervisor and supervisee work together and there are clear and transparent processes for things that relate to them and their supervision relationship, such as the dual role of the supervisor when they are a line manager, the management of conflict, the recording, storage, and access of supervision records, the limits of confidentiality, the process of disclosure and reporting to others, as well as the process of consulting others outside of the relationship, such as ethics or cultural experts. These matters are also included in a written supervision agreement.

Interactional process

The interactional process in the evidence-informed model is described as formal and paralleling the social work interview process (O'Donoghue et al. 2018). The supervision session has a format through which the supervisee is involved in reflective discussion and problem-solving or solution-finding process. The rituals involved in this format vary in accordance with the type of supervision, the styles of the supervisor and supervisee, their cultural and ethnic diversity, and the intricacies of their communication (O'Donoghue 2019). The process is progressive and moves through stages of preparation, beginning, planning, working, and ending, with the interactional exchanges between the supervisor and supervisee being the means through which the route to the end of a session is achieved (O'Donoghue 2014). If the process becomes stuck or disrupted, the evidence indicates the supervisee may become disorientated or dissatisfied (O'Donoghue et al. 2018).

Although not specifically referred to in the research evidence, care ethics can be inferred in the participatory nature of the interactional process and through responsiveness to the supervisee's cultural and ethnic background, as well as through respectful and reflective dialogue in the progressive movement through the stages. That said, the model could be enhanced through more explicit reference to ethical dialogue. Ethical dialogue is an open interactional exchange process that involves reflection, exploration, learning, decision-making, action planning, review, and evaluation (O'Donoghue and O'Donoghue 2019). In the interactional process of the supervision session, ethical dialogue is most likely to occur in the working stage of the session. It is at this stage that the supervisor and supervisee are engaged in interactively processing and working through the specifics of an item on the supervision agenda. The ethical dialogue involves a conversation concerning how ethical theories, principles, and authorities such as codes of ethics apply to the situation. The conversation is analytical through the exploratory process of ethical dialogue, and evaluative in the decision-making and the follow up that occurs. The principle of ethical dialogue that aligns with the interactional process is ensuring participation. This involves both the supervisor and supervisee in contributing to what is right for the people involved and in relation to the situation that they are discussing.

In summary, the review of the three processes of the evidence-informed model, (i.e. construction of supervision, supervision alliance, and interactional process) has revealed that ethics are inferred in each of these processes. It has also identified that the processes within the model could be more specific and detailed regarding ethics. This could be achieved by an overt ethics discussion at the beginning of the relationship and through the development of shared understanding of how ethics is construed by the parties and regarding ethical social work practice and ethical supervision. The supervision alliance could also incorporate ethics through the development of ethical sensitivity and ethical dialogue, by engaging in a partnership concerning ethical matters that relate to the parties and their relationship. Similarly, the inclusion of ethical dialogue and the principle of participation could make ethics more apparent in the interactional process. The discussion now turns to the two tasks of the evidence-informed model, namely, the supervision of the practitioner and the supervision of their practice with clients.

Supervision of the practitioner

The research evidence concerning the supervision of the practitioner suggests that when supervisors provide practical help, social and emotional support, and professional development, the supervisees are more likely to be effective in their work, have higher job satisfaction, be more committed to staying in their organization, and be psychologically well (Mor Barak et al. 2009; O'Donoghue et al. 2018). The task of supervising the practitioner relies on creating a secure base that is safe for the practitioner to share, explore, grow, and develop regarding their emotions, perceptions, and values. This involves the practitioner being safe enough to share their vulnerabilities and fears. In other words, the supervisor provides a holding environment which reinforces the importance of the supervisee bringing their concerns and fears to supervision in order to help the supervisee contain them, problem solve and learn from them, as well as from the situation from which they arose. The supervisor also focuses on developing the practitioner's competence through supporting their learning and by role-modeling professional ethical standards, whilst making sure that their supervision is aligned to the developmental level of the supervisee (O'Donoghue 2019).

This task directly relates to the supervisor having a duty of care in relation to the supervisee. This duty of care concerns the supervisee's well-being, development, and competence as a social worker. However, the detail concerning how the model is used to develop the practitioner's competence, beyond providing support and role-modeling professional ethical standards, is not specific. According to O'Donoghue and O'Donoghue (2019, p. 348) social work supervision is "influential in ethical resolution, and contributes to practitioners' ethics education, behaviour and ethical development." Nevertheless, there is no empirical research regarding how supervisors help supervisees develop ethical sensitivity, ethical maturity, and ethical competence. In the absence of this research O'Donoghue and O'Donoghue (2019) identified the following ideas from the supervision and ethics literature as ways to develop ethical sensitivity, maturity, and competence through ethical conversations that:

- Discuss the Code of Ethics and the supervisee's understanding of it and how they apply it
- Refer to the Code of Ethics directly in supervision by asking questions like "What does the Code of Ethics say about this?" or "What guidance does the Code of Ethics give in this area?" (O'Donoghue and O'Donoghue 2019, p. 348)

- Explore with the supervisee their perspective, preferences, and understanding of ethical theories by asking questions in supervision concerning: rules or absolutes (ethical absolutism); consequences such as good outcomes or least harm (ethical relativism or consequentialism); intentions (virtue ethics); care responsibilities (care ethics); and community norms (communitarian ethics)
- Examine the supervisee's perspective, preferences, understanding, and use of the IASSW nine ethical principles (IASSW 2018), namely, Recognition of the Inherent Dignity of Humanity; Promoting Human Rights; Promoting Social Justice; Promoting the Right to Self-determination; Promoting the Right to Participation; Respect for Confidentiality and Privacy; Treating People as Whole Persons; Ethical Use of Technology and Social Media; and Professional Integrity.

Two other concepts, namely, ethical maturity and ethical risk-management are part of the supervisor's duty of care towards the supervisee. Ethical maturity was coined by Carroll (2011a, b), and consists of five elements, namely: ethical sensitivity; ethical discernment; ethical implementation; ethical accountability; and ethical sustainability and peace. Ethical maturity is essentially

> …having the reflective, rational and emotional capacity to decide actions are right and wrong or good and better, having the resilience and courage to implement those decisions, being accountable for ethical decisions made (publicly or privately), and being able to learn from and live with the experience.
>
> *(Carroll 2011a, p. 19)*

The concept of ethical maturity helps both the supervisee and supervisor to use supervision as a forum for moral and ethical learning and development. Essentially, it highlights the importance of the learning relationship within supervision and the duty of care the supervisor has pertaining to their supervisees. In addition, its challenges both the supervisor and supervisee to grow together in their shared ethical maturity regarding how they ought to act in relation to others and each other (Rhodes 1986). Ethical risk-management, on the other hand, is concerned with keeping the supervisee safe through being tuned into common ethics related risks as they relate to the supervisee's competence, any impairment, negligence, and conduct (Reamer 2015). Risk management strategies include detailed written supervision agreements; clear documentation of supervision meetings which details of what happened, what was agreed, or recommended; and the follow up that occurred. Reamer (2015) identifies that there are also ethical risks when supervising practitioners using information and communication technology. These risks concern privacy, confidentiality, and information security regarding the technology. There are also risks for the supervisor related to informed consent and the supervisor's competence using technology. If supervision is provided cross-nationally or involves more than one regulatory or licensing body, there is a risk related to competence in that jurisdiction. In relation to the supervisee there are risks related to the use of social media both personally and professionally and the maintenance of appropriate professional boundaries (Reamer 2015; O'Donoghue and O'Donoghue 2019). The risk reduction strategies include ensuring that both the supervisor and their supervisees understand fully the security limitations about electronic technology and have adequate security in the form of firewalls, malware protection, strong passwords, and use encryption software (Reamer 2015). It is also important that supervisors provide full informed consent to supervisees regarding the level of protection they have for the supervisees information and what they would do in the case of a privacy breach. Other risk management practices regarding technology include obtaining appropriate supervision and consultation, reviewing the relevant ethical standards, and regulations and laws, including social media policies and guidelines. As stated earlier it is important that these matters are detailed in supervision agreements and in the supervision session notes.

Supervision of the practice with clients

The evidence regarding the supervision of supervisee's practice with clients suggests that focused attention on the client's problems is more likely to result in better client outcomes, and that an emphasis on clinical practice and evidence-based practice within supervision and organizations results in better practice (O'Donoghue et al. 2018). In the evidence-informed model this task involves the supervisor facilitating a focused reflection with the supervisee upon the client's issues and situation with a view to envisioning the best possible outcomes. In this dialogue the supervisor encourages and critically explores with the supervisee the application of the available empirical research, together with other forms of knowledge (i.e. professional ethics, practice theory, cultural values, and practice wisdom) to the client's situation; the interventions proposed; and monitoring and evaluation of this in relation to best client outcomes (O'Donoghue et al. 2018).

In this task, professional ethics is included as a form of knowledge that is to be considered alongside the available empirical research in the process of envisioning the best possible outcomes for clients. In other words, professional ethics is seen as part of the evidence that informs the supervision of the social worker's practice with clients. That said, how professional ethics is used to inform the supervisee's practice with clients in the evidence-informed model could be elaborated on and further developed in three ways, namely, through a) sensitivity to ethics related risks to clients, b) ethical dialogue. and c) the principle the care and protection of vulnerable people (O'Donoghue and O'Donoghue 2019).

Developing sensitivity to ethics related risks to clients requires the supervisor and supervisee to be aware of and to attend to the common ethics risks related to direct practice with clients. These include violations of clients' rights, issues pertaining to confidentiality, privacy, duty to protect, informed consent, boundaries, conflict of interest, working within one's scope of practice, and termination of services (Reamer 2015). The development of ethical sensitivity in relation to these common ethics risks necessitates the supervisor and supervisee to develop a shared understanding of each of the common ethics risks. When discussing these ethics risks, they also need to discuss how these matters would be managed, worked through, and recorded in supervision. The key points from these discussions should also be included in the written supervision agreement. The use of ethics questions, ethical dialogue, and a structured ethical analysis and decision-making model in supervision supports the development of ethical sensitivity in relation to the supervisee's practice with clients. It does this by providing a means by which ethics can be explored, examined, and managed within supervision sessions. When engaging in ethical dialogue related to clients, supervisors also have a duty of care to the client and the community with which they live. According to O'Donoghue and O'Donoghue (2019), this duty relates to the principle care and protection of vulnerable people, which concerns ensuring the promotion of clients' and the community's human rights, dignity, and the promotion of social justice (IASSW 2018). Essentially, the key addition is to have a focus upon ethics as they pertain to the care of clients and the achievement of client outcomes whilst also fulfilling the duty of care to the community.

Overall, the review of the two tasks of the evidence-informed social work supervision model has shown that the tasks of supervising the practitioner and supervising their practice with clients could be further developed in relation to ethics. This further development concerns the need to focus on the supervisee's development of ethical sensitivity, maturity, and competence through ethical dialogue and risk-management, together with a focus on the ethics risks related to the care of clients and the community.

Integrating ethics and evidence in the model

This review of the processes and tasks of the evidence-informed social work supervision model has illustrated how ethics could be incorporated into the evidence-informed social work supervision model. It has also shown the importance of combining both the practical-moral basis of social work with the rational-technical basis in an integrated approach. In other words, questions concerning ethics (e.g. "How ought we act in relation to others?") and evidence (e.g. "What is most effective?") are complementary. This means that social work supervision should be informed by both ethics and evidence. One way in which this may be achieved is by evolving the evidence-informed social work supervision model into an ethical evidence-informed social work supervision model through integrating key ideas from care ethics, such as ethical sensitivity and ethical dialogue, within the processes and task of the model and revising the supervisory practice application. Figure 34.2 illustrates the emerging ethical evidence-informed social work supervision model, while Table 34.1 provides a summary of the ideas from care ethics, the research evidence, and supervisory practice application across the construction of supervision, the supervision alliance, the interactional process, the supervision of the practitioner, and the supervision of practice with clients.

The emerging ethical evidence-informed model has implications for supervisory practice, training, social service organizations, and research and evaluation. The main implication for supervisory practice is that the model helps supervisors keep ethics and evidence to the forefront of their practice. It also provides a way in which supervisors can focus on what is right as

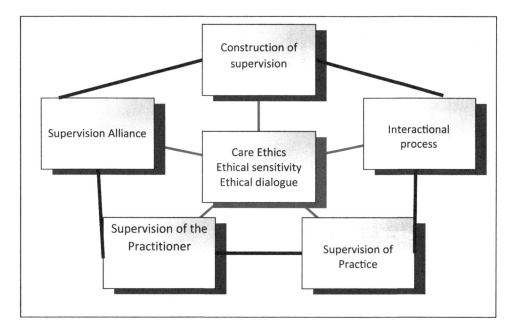

Figure 34.2   Ethical evidence-informed model of social work supervision

Table 34.1 Ethical evidence-informed supervision model

Aspect	Care ethics	Summary of the evidence	Supervisory practice application
Construction of supervision	• Supervision is concerned with caring about clients, supervisee, and the community. • Ethical codes, theories, principles and other authorities, sanction and summarize the values and standards of care by which the profession aspires to and is held accountable for by the community.	• Supervision is socially and personally constructed. • Supervision arrangements are influenced by the social, cultural, organizational, and practice contexts and are situation specific. • The regular practice of supervision mostly occurred through meetings or sessions between an individual supervisee and supervisor. • Group and team supervision occur mainly as substitutes or supplementary to individual supervision. • Supervisees and supervisors personally construct supervision from their experiences. • Supervisees prefer supervision that is focused on their practice, education, and support rather than administrative matters. • Supervisors construct supervision as a relational and reflective process that was concerned with organizational and professional accountability, development, and support.	• Work with the supervisee to develop a shared understanding of the social, cultural, organizational, professional, and practice context within which supervision is situated. • Clarify with the supervisee(s) the roles, responsibilities, arrangements, accountabilities, mandate, and sanctioning of the supervision. • Develop with the supervisee a shared understanding of IASSW (2018) nine ethical principles, code of ethics, and other authorities. • Develop a shared understanding about how ethics is construed and what this means in relation to ethical social work practice with clients and the ethical processes and practices that occur within supervision. • Clarify expectations and review with the supervisee their past supervision experience. • Be mindful and responsive to supervisees' preference for a focus on their practice, education, and support. • Maintain an awareness of the task of supervising the practitioner and their practice, as well as the process of supervision as a relational and reflective practice. • The agreements and shared understandings are recorded and included in the written supervision agreement.

Aspect	Care ethics	Summary of research evidence	Supervisory practice applications
Supervision alliance	• The relationship reflects ethical sensitivity and engages in ethical dialogue by attending to the duty of care to the supervisee, their clients, organization, profession, and the community. • The supervisor and supervisee work in partnership and have clear and transparent processes for things that relate to them and their supervision relationship.	• Supervisees prefer a relationship that provides them with a secure base and is characterized by trust, support, honesty, openness, the ability to collaboratively navigate power relations as well as respect for social and cultural differences, in order to feel safe and participate fully in supervision.	• Establish and sustain a constructive, considerate, culturally competent, and caring relationship with supervisees based upon empathy and emotional intelligence, practice expertise, and relationship skills. • Use ethical dialogue in partnership to manage dual roles, conflict, recording, storage and access of supervision records, the limits of confidentiality, processes of disclosure and reporting to others, and consulting others outside of the relationship, such as ethics or cultural experts. • Record matters related to the supervision relationship in the written supervision agreement.
Interactional process	• The interactional process involves an ethical dialogue that involves open interactional exchange process that involves reflection, exploration, learning, decision-making, action planning, review and evaluation. • Both the supervisor and supervisee participate in ethical dialogue by exploring what is right for the people involved and in relation to the specific situation.	• The process is both formal and mirrors the social work helping process. • The supervision session has a structure and engages the supervisee in an interactive reflective problem-solving process. • There are variations of the structure which are due to the type of supervision, the people involved, cultural and ethnic diversity, and the dynamics of the process. • Where the interactional process is unstructured and unproductive, supervisees are disorientated and dissatisfied with supervision.	• Use a clear structure for supervision session that involves preparation, beginning, planning, working, and ending phases. • Engage supervisees in a meaningful interactive problem-solving process wherein they explore, reflect, understand, and action plan. • Engage in a participatory ethical dialogue exploring how ethical theories, principles and authorities such as codes of ethics apply and inform decision-making and action plans. • Use listening, questioning, challenging, and summarizing skills in interaction with supervisee. • Acknowledge social, cultural and ethnic differences between supervisor and supervisee, and explore whether the supervisee wished to have their cultural worldview and practices incorporated into the supervision.

(Continued)

Table 34.1 Continued

Aspect	Care ethics	Summary of the evidence	Supervisory practice application

Supervision of practitioner	• Supervision is influential in practitioners' ethical resolution, and contributes to their ethics education, behavior, and ethical development.
	• This involves developing the practitioner's ethical sensitivity, maturity, and competence through supervision.
	• Creating safety through awareness and action in relation to common ethics risks.
		• When supervisees are helped with their work, professional development, and given social and emotional support, they are more likely to be satisfied and effective in their work, committed to the organization, and be well psychologically.	• Create a safe relational space for the supervisees to process and learn from their emotions and perceptions, particularly those pertaining to their safety, vulnerabilities, and fears.
			• Support learning by role-modeling ethical professional standards and ensure supervision matches the developmental level of the supervisee.
			• Maintain a focus on the supervisee as a person and an active interest in their well-being, emotions, and professional development.
			• Develop ethical sensitivity, maturity, and competence through conversations that:
			  ◦ Discuss the Code of Ethics and the supervisee's understanding and application
			  ◦ Refer to the Code of Ethics directly in supervision.
			• Explore with the supervisee their perspective, preferences, and understanding of ethical theories
			• Examine the supervisee's perspective, preferences, understanding, and use of the IASSW nine ethical principles (IASSW 2018)
			• Use risk management strategies such as written supervision agreements; documenting supervision meetings, including agreements actions and follow up.

| *Supervision of practice with clients* | • Ethical awareness and sensitivity to the common ethical risks related to practice with clients.
• The supervisor's duty of care to practice with clients.
• Enacting the principle care and protection of vulnerable people through the promotion of clients' and the community's human rights, dignity, and the promotion of social justice. | • Focused attention on the client's problems is more likely to result in better client outcomes.
• An emphasis on clinical practice and evidence-based practice within supervision and organization result in better practice. | • Engage in conversations concerning the common ethics risks related to direct practice with clients.
• Develop a shared understanding of the each of the common ethics risks and how these will be managed, worked through, and recorded in supervision and included in written supervision agreement.
• Facilitate with supervisees a dialogue focused reflection on exploring the client's issues and situation with a view to envisioning the best possible outcomes.
• This dialogue also uses ethics questions, and a structured ethical analysis and decision-making model in supervision
  • Encourage and explore with supervisees the application of relevant research, theory, and ethical principles in regard to:
  • How that may inform their understanding of the client and their situations;
  • How might that inform and assist their interventions; and
  • How to evaluate and monitor progress toward the best client outcomes. |

well as what works in the supervisee's practice with clients. The main implication for supervisory training is that this model brings together both the ethics and evidence strands of a supervisory curriculum, as well as provides, through its processes and tasks, a clear set of modules related to how supervision is constructed and defined, the supervision alliance, the interactional process, supervising practitioners, and supervising their practice with clients. For social service organizations, an implication of the model is that it could aid them in the development, refinement, and evaluation of their supervision policies, agreements, practices, and audit processes for supervision and ethics. The central implication concerning the research and evaluation of this model is that supervisors need to be trained in it, then following the training implement and evaluate the model's effectiveness in relation to ethics management, alongside practitioner and client outcomes. Finally, because the research evidence and ethics knowledge that informs the model is continually evolving, the model would need to be regularly updated, reviewed, and revised.

Conclusion

This chapter aimed to examine the evidence-informed model of social work supervision through exploring how ethics was present within the model and considering how care ethics could inform the model. The review of the processes and tasks of the evidence-informed model found that while ethics was inferred in the processes and tasks, the model could be strengthened by making ethics more overt and incorporating ethics into the processes and tasks. Ultimately, the review highlighted the need for both ethics and evidence to be integrated into an emergent ethical evidence-informed social work supervision model. In conclusion, the most significant message of this chapter is the importance for supervisors of keeping their focus on both ethics and evidence in their supervisory practice. The emergent ethical evidence-informed social work supervision model provides a way for supervisors to keep ethics and evidence to the forefront of their supervisory practice.

References

Barsky, A.E., 2010. *Ethics and values in social work: an integrated approach for a comprehensive curriculum*. New York: Oxford University Press.

Carroll, M., 2011a. Ethical maturity: compasses for life and work decisions–part I. *Psychotherapy in Australia*, 17 (3), 12–23.

Carroll, M., 2011b. Ethical maturity: making ethical decisions–part II. *Psychotherapy in Australia*, 17 (4), 40–51.

Collins, S., 2018. Ethics of care and statutory social work in the UK: critical perspectives and strengths. *Practice*, 30 (1), 3–18. https://doi.org/10.1080/09503153.2017.1339787

Gitterman, A., and Knight, C., 2013. Evidence-guided practice: integrating the science and art of social work. *Families in Society*, 94 (2), 70–78. https://doi.org/10.1606/1044-3894.4282

International Association of Schools of Social Work 2018. *Global social work statement of ethical principles (IASSW)*. Available from: https://www.iassw-aiets.org/wp-content/uploads/2018/04/Global-Social-Work-Statement-of-Ethical-Principles-IASSW-27-April-2018-1.pdf. [Accessed 11 January 2020]

McAuliffe, D., and Chenoweth, L., 2019. Repositioning ethical theory in social work education. *In*: R. Munford, and K. O'Donoghue, eds. *New theories for social work practice: ethical practice for working with individuals*. London: Jessica Kingsley, 291–308.

Mor Barak, M.E., Travis, D.J., Pyun, H., and Xie, B., 2009. The impact of supervision on worker outcomes: a meta-analysis. *Social Service Review*, 83 (1), 3–32.

Mullen, E.J., 2016. Reconsidering the 'idea' of evidence in evidence-based policy and practice. *European Journal of Social Work*, 19 (3–4), 310–335. https://doi.org/10.1080/13691457.2015.1022716

Nevo, I., and Slonim-Nevo, V., 2011. The myth of evidence-based practice: towards evidence-informed practice. *British Journal of Social Work*, 41, 1176–1197. https://doi.org/10.1093/bjsw/bcq149

O'Donoghue, K., 2019. Supervision and evidence-informed practice. *In*: R. Munford and K. O'Donoghue, eds. *New theories for social work practice: ethical practice for working with individuals, families and communities*. London: Jessica Kingsley, 271–288.

O'Donoghue, K.B., 2014. Towards an interactional map of the supervision session: an exploration of supervisees and supervisors experiences. *Practice*, 26 (1), 53–70. https://doi.org/10.1080/09503153.2013.869581

O'Donoghue, K., and O'Donoghue, R., 2019. The application of ethics within social work supervision: a selected literature and research review. *Ethics and Social Welfare*, 13 (4), 340–360. https://doi.org/10.1080/17496535.2019.1590438.

O'Donoghue, K., Wong Yuh Ju, P., and Tsui, M.S., 2018. Constructing an evidence-informed social work supervision model. *European Journal of Social Work*, 21 (3), 348–358. https://doi.org/10.1080/13691457.2017.1341387

Parton, N., 2000. Some thoughts on the relationship between theory and practice in and for social work. *British Journal of Social Work*, 30 (4), 449–463. https://doi.org/10.1093/bjsw/30.4.449

Parton, N., and O'Byrne, P., 2000. *Constructive social work: towards a new practice*. Basingstoke, UK: MacMillan.

Reamer, F., 2015. *Risk management in social work preventing professional malpractice, liability, and disciplinary action*. New York, NY: Columbia University Press.

Reamer, F., 2018. *Social work values and ethics*. 5th ed. New York NY: Columbia University Press.

Rhodes, M., 1986. *Ethical dilemmas in social work practice*. Milwaukee, WI: Family Service of America.

Wilkins, D., 2019. Social work supervision in child and family services: developing a working theory of how and why it works. *Aotearoa New Zealand Social Work*, 31 (3), 7–19. http://dx.doi.org/10.11157/anzswj-vol31iss3id644

PART V

The interactional process

35

INTERACTIONAL SUPERVISION

Shifting the guiding paradigm

Lawrence Shulman

Introduction

Social work and social work supervision borrowed a paradigm from medicine using a linear three-step model of practice: study-diagnosis-treatment. The Interactional Model of social work practice and supervision represents a paradigm shift that focuses on the moment-to-moment interaction between social worker and client, and the parallel process between the supervisor and the social worker, with each affecting and being affected by the other. This chapter describes and illustrates this dynamic process. The chapter also examines supervision and practice against the backdrop of time, the four phases of work – the Preliminary, Beginning, Middle, and the Ending/Transition phases.

Finally, the chapter challenges a number of false dichotomies that negatively affect practice and supervision. A false dichotomy is the perception that a choice has to be made between two apparently opposing ideas. In this chapter, I question a number of false dichotomies that I believe have a negative impact on practice and supervision. One example is when helping professionals appear to be making a choice between science, the most current research on Evidenced-Based Practice (EBP), and the use of the professional's unique personal artistry. This has become more of an issue in social work when such practices have a specific prescribed protocol, designed to guide the professional and require consistency in the implementation of the model.

I argue that effective supervision and practice emerges from using science to guide individual artistry rather than following rigidly prescribed actions and responses. Rather than adopting a specific model, I support using the EBP science to identify elements of practice that can enhance core social work practice and in turn, supervision.

Challenges facing new and experienced supervisors

There are a number of common challenges reported by supervisors in social service agencies (Shulman 2010, pp. 3–5). For example, a worker was promoted from within the agency to a supervisory role after six years of frontline work. On the first Monday morning in her new role, she walked into the common room for coffee and her former peers became quiet. Two of them had also applied for the job and were upset that they did not get it. She knew they were talking about her because she used to talk about the former supervisor with them. She wondered if this meant the end of her friendship with them. She also wondered how she would deal with the disappointed supervisees.

In another example, a new supervisor was brought into an agency from the outside. The administrator warned her that her department had experienced poor supervision and needed some shaking up. The administrator had turned down a male frontline worker, with more experience, who had also applied for the supervisor's job. He told the new supervisor in their first conference that the previous supervisor had left him alone to do his work. The supervisor felt a gut-tightening sensation as she wondered how she would deal with this obvious challenge to her authority.

In a third example, a supervisor had to confront a staff member for being far behind in submitting required paperwork. The staff member agreed immediately and said he would address the problem. As he said this, the supervisor felt it was a "New Year's Resolution" meant to be broken, but she remained silent. The staff member's work improved for a short period, but he soon fell behind again. The supervisor realized the staff member's earlier acceptance of the critique was a form of passive resistance. The worker had said exactly what he thought the supervisor wanted to hear, rather than sharing his real thoughts and feelings. Their conversation was what I will refer to as an "illusion of work" rather than a conversation of substance.

In a fourth and final example, a supervisor noted that a relatively new school social worker appeared to identify with a student having trouble in school and seemed to blame and be critical of the student's parents. She wondered how to help this social worker understand the "two client" concept and the importance of identifying with both the student and the parents at the same time without seeming to be overly critical.

These examples and the issues involved need to be addressed directly by the supervisor but often are not. In part, this is because the situations are confrontational and difficult. Supervisors often believe that if left alone the problem will eventually go away. More often, they do not, and in fact if ignored they magnify and become more complex.

Another factor that contributes to a supervisor's response may be the paradigm underlying our understanding of practice and supervision. The "medical model," mentioned earlier and described in the next section, tends to ignore the interactive nature of supervision and can lead to supervisors not trusting their moment-by-moment reactions, thus failing to respond directly or skillfully to such a situation. In the example above in which the supervisor senses passive resistance, she might directly confront the illusion of work as it repeats itself over time.

The Interactional Model described in this chapter encourages spontaneity and suggests that the supervisor should trust and use, rather than lose, his or her feelings in the moment (Shulman 1982, 2008, 2010, 2016). In this chapter, I explore these issues and examples in more detail. First, we need to understand the concept of a guiding paradigm.

Paradigms, paradigm shifts, and the medical model

A factor that de-emphasizes process discussions or the actual conversations between the worker and client or the supervisor and worker, is in part the diagnostic paradigm guiding professional practice. I am using the term "paradigm" in the way that Kuhn presented it in his groundbreaking book *The Structure of Scientific Revolution* (1962). He described a paradigm as an overarching model that guides a particular scientific discipline. For example, the idea that the earth was the center of the universe (Ptolemy) dominated the view of astronomers for hundreds of years. Paradigms guide the thinking process and the development of explanations for how the world of science (for example, chemistry and physics) views reality.

Events that seem to contradict a paradigm are anomalies, are eventually understood through further research. Of course, in the world of astronomy, the invention of the telescope and the work of Galileo and Copernicus led to the revolution in the paradigm, and the sun became the center of our universe. This resolved many, but not all, of the observable anomalies. Even this shift was followed by other evolutions in the paradigm over time.

So what does this have to do with supervision? The helping professions in general have operated for years using a paradigm borrowed from medicine. The medical model describes practice as a three-stage, linear process involving a study (obtaining a great deal of information about the client), followed by diagnosis (often referred to as an assessment), and then the development of a treatment plan. A fourth stage, evaluation, was introduced as a way of correcting either the diagnosis or the treatment plan if the original effort did not seem to be successful.

This paradigm focuses attention on the client, and heavily emphasizes the ability to obtain data in the study process. For example, when I participated in staff group case consultations, I have noted, following a worker's presentation of a first client interview, how much of the discussion centers on the worker's information about the client and how little attention is paid to the interaction between the two.

When I have intervened and asked the worker to describe his or her actual conversation with the client, for example, when the client was resistant or defensive, a different picture emerges. As I encourage the worker to do what I call "memory work," sharing some of the conversational content that took place with the client along with the worker's associated affect, the team can often see the client's behavior, in part, as a reaction to the worker's interventions. In addition, the worker's responses may be a direct result of the impact of the client's behavior on the worker. Rather than a linear, three- or four-step process to understand practice and supervision, an interactional paradigm may better explain the process and account for the practice anomalies, such as the client's noncompliance with a perfectly sound treatment plan.

The Interactional Model of practice and supervision

The Interactional Model of practice and supervision shifts the perspective from the client, or worker, to the moment-by-moment interaction between the two (Shulman 2018). It also places an emphasis on the affect – the feelings of both the client and the worker that affect the process. I call this the "feeling-doing-connection." I believe that the affect experienced by the helping professional directly affects how they respond to the client in practice, and in turn, how the supervisor responds to the worker. Instead of diagnosing the client, we shift to understanding the interaction. This shift has been taking place in medicine as well. The literature now refers to "behavioral medicine" where the interaction between the doctor and the patient is the center of attention. However, this same shift has not yet generally taken hold when considering the interaction between supervisor and supervisee.

The shift I am discussing is important since it requires attention to the process of practice and supervision as well as to the theory. Practice and supervision models that remain at a higher level of theory and do not connect directly to the process can leave the practitioner or supervisor unclear about what next steps to take in an interaction with the client or worker. Thus, after discussing the assessment of the client or a theoretical model, the social worker may still face the ultimate question: "So what do I do?"

The parallel process

Central to the Interactional Model of supervision is the concept of the parallel process. This suggests that a number of parallels exist between practice dynamics and interventions, and those in supervision. The content of supervision usually focusses on the following areas:

1. A supervisee's job management (e.g., timely submissions of required paper work)
2. Skillful professional impact in work with other professionals (e.g., avoiding a battle over "Who owns the client?")
3. Continued learning (e.g., use of the current literature, presentation of practice issues in supervision and case conferences)
4. Direct practice with clients (e.g., analysis of individual, family, group, and community interactions)

It is inappropriate to allow supervision to become a form of personal counseling and therapy. That boundary, which is related to the purpose of supervision and the role of the supervisor, is essential to maintain. For example, if a supervisee raises a personal problem in a supervision conference, it would be appropriate to listen and empathize, but then to make a referral to counseling if needed. The focus of the discussion should then turn to asking how this personal problem may be affecting the supervisee's work with clients. I call that "dealing with feelings in pursuit of purpose." That involves empathizing with the worker but staying focused on the business of supervision.

By doing so, the supervisor is also modeling an important practice principle. Clarity of purpose and role, which are elements of "contracting" in the beginning phase of practice, is crucial when working with a client. For example, a school social worker may work with parents of a child exhibiting problematic behaviors; however, the focus of the work is on the student and the issues in the school. While helping the parents to understand how a number of problems, for example conflicts between the parents, economic stress, etc., may be affecting the child at school, the school social worker should not begin family therapy. This is not the job of the school social worker.

In turn, by staying focused in supervision sessions on the social worker's practice, the supervisor is modeling how clarity of purpose and role provide a "structure" that actually creates "freedom" for both supervisor and social worker to create an effective "contract" and to guard that contract by respecting boundaries (Shulman 2010, 2018).

In another illustration of the parallel process, again involving the school social worker example, the worker in supervision may describes a difficult conference with the parents. The worker may suggest that he/she can now understand why the child reacts the way he/she does. In this conversation, the worker may be signaling that they have identified with the child and decided the problem is with the parents. Responding to the parents with mild critical comments and suggestions for how to change their behavior, the social worker may simply increase the parent's resistance and anger. The parents may believe that the worker is on their child's side and does not understand their feelings. In this case, the parents may be right.

Therefore, it is important in the supervision session that the worker describe the interview, the process, in some detail. What did the worker say to the client? What did the client say back? During this discussion, the supervisor may recognize the worker's over-identification with the child. If the supervisor simply points out that the worker may be missing the parents' feelings and over identifying with the child, the worker may now perceive the supervisor as critical. This can then result in the worker's resistance, often prefaced by "Yes, but…" This is a classic parallel process example of the supervisor identifying with the client and not appreciating the feelings of the worker. This models the opposite of effective supervision and practice.

If instead, the supervisor were to ask the worker, "How did it feel to you when the parents seemed so angry and resistant?", and then explores those feelings and how they affected the worker's response to the family, the supervisor is modeling how to stay connected with the worker and the parents at the same time. After genuinely empathizing with the worker, the supervisor may ask the social worker to consider how the parents may have felt, thus identifying the source of the resistance. This process increases the chance that the worker will hear the suggestion and be able to tune in to the parents as well as to their child. This can be an important integration of the "two client" concept: the importance of being emotionally with the parents and the child at exactly the same time.

The supervisor could continue by helping the social worker consider the next interview with the family members and catch the practice "mistake." For example, role-playing how to say to the parents I want to apologize since I believe at our last meeting I did not fully understand how your child's behavior was impacting both of you. It must have been difficult and stressful for you to hear about his behavior from the school staff. Let's try again and see if I can be more helpful.

Three important observations can be drawn from this example. First, the social worker is learning he or she can make mistakes, go back to the clients, and correct the mistakes. Analyzing and learning about your practice is a lifelong professional task in which we all make what I sometimes refer to as a "beautiful mistake" when it emerges from the worker's spontaneity. I then suggest that the task is to correct the mistake and then go on to make "more sophisticated mistakes."

Second, it is possible to move from a specific example to generalize about practice, which can be helpful when faced with a similar issue with another client. This also emphasizes the importance of "continued learning" on the part of all professionals, learning from mistakes rather than being closed and defensive.

Third, on another level of interaction, the social worker is actually modeling for the parents how to go back to their child and to explore and understand their child's feelings and how they may be influencing his trouble at school. This is the power of the parallel process with the social worker modeling skillful parental behaviors that can be helpful with the child. Rather than just being critical of their child, the parents can use the same interventions by trying to understand the child's feelings and their connection to his or her behavior. Another way of understanding this modeling and the parallel process is the expression "more is caught than taught." The client, social worker, and supervisor all learn more by how the worker and the supervisor acts than what they say.

The phases of work in practice and supervision

The Interactional Model also incorporates the importance of time and its impact on the dynamics and interactions in both practice and supervision. William Schwartz (1961) first described the four phases as the Preliminary (Preparatory), the Beginning (Contracting), the Middle (Work), and the Endings and Transitions Phases. This model has also been used to describe a single practice or supervision session (Shulman 2018).

For example, let us reach back to the common example described earlier in this chapter, of the new supervisor promoted from within. They might find it useful to use a specific skill in the Preliminary Phase termed "tuning in." This means the supervisor might put him or herself in the shoes of former colleagues now supervisees, and especially any of them who also applied for the position. This would involve attempting to understand what the unsuccessful colleague may be thinking or feeling about the change in the professional relationship. An associated skill would be the ability to respond directly to indirect communications.

Consider the following example of Fran, a new supervisor promoted from within, addressing these issues at a staff meeting. The staff group had developed a social as well as professional relationship and often went out together for lunch. The first time they asked Fran to go with them she was overwhelmed with her new administrative responsibilities and declined. The staff, interpreting this as a change in the relationship, simply stopped asking her to join them.

With some help in thinking through the dynamics, the supervisor, at the next staff meeting, directly addressed the change in the relationship as well as issues associated with her new role and her authority.

Fran: I wanted to take a few minutes to talk about something on my mind since I switched jobs and became a supervisor. I have always felt close to all of you and thought we had a good friendship, but recently it seems to have been strained. I have been trying to figure out how to still be friends with you while carrying out this supervisory job – and it has not been easy. I just know I value your relationship too much to lose it. How about you? Has it been on your mind too?

Louise: We felt things were more uncomfortable, but we figured you were just cutting yourself off now that you were a supervisor – you know, not wanting to have as much to do with us socially.

Terry: Frankly, it is not as easy to talk in front of you anymore. I mean, we used to be able to share all the dirt about what was going on – you know, the gossip about who was doing what or goofing off. Now, it would feel like squealing. It is hard enough already, knowing what you know about what we do around here.

Fran: You know, that is my problem, too. Those same conversations would have a different meaning for me now because I am responsible for that stuff.

Louise: Maybe we just have to sort out what we can talk about with you and what is so work-related that we need to separate it from the social part. Just knowing that you still want our friendship is important to me, because I felt a loss as well. (Shulman 2010, p. 59)

In another "new supervisor" example, Jane was appointed from the outside, coming from another agency. She decided to deal directly with the signals of resistance she was experiencing in her work with John, one of her front-line supervisees. He was a long-term worker at the agency who had applied for the supervisor's job and was rejected when Jane was hired. He was sending signals of resistance in the first weeks, ignoring her as his supervisor, not sharing his cases with her in conferences, missing conferences, or coming in late and apologizing. The following comes from her notes shared with participants in a supervision workshop (Shulman 2010, pp. 61–63).

I had asked John to meet with me to review his current caseload so I could be in touch with any problems he felt I should know about. He missed the first appointment, apologizing later and telling me he had forgotten. He was 10 minutes late for the second appointment and had not brought his case files with him, even though that was the usual procedure for reviewing cases. I was getting the distinct feeling that he was not too happy about meeting with me. Taking my courage in hand, I decided to try to get at the problem directly.

I told him I had the feeling he was not too anxious to talk with me about the cases – at least he certainly did not seem enthusiastic. He said he did not really see the need for the discussion because, as he told me before, there were no problems on his caseload that he needed help with right now. I told him I could appreciate that he had his caseload in order, but I felt that it was important for me to get a feel for the work that all of the staff was doing. He told me that Sam (the previous supervisor) had respected his competence and had left him alone to do his work.

John's response seems designed to put the supervisor on the spot. He is equating her doing her job, asking to be informed of his work, as an attack on his competency. No supervisor wants to be accused of not respecting staff, so he is attacking a vulnerable area. Her preparation in our workshop and her increasing frustration finally led her to take the plunge into the difficult issue of her getting the job for which he had also applied:

> At this point, I felt stuck and frustrated, as if we were going around in circles. I finally leveled with him and told him that I felt there was more to this than just a change in procedures. I told him I had felt some tension from him since I had received the appointment and I knew he had applied for the job. I was worried about what it meant. I told him I had felt uncomfortable about the whole situation. I had even avoided raising it with him – which was a mistake. I realized he was an experienced caseworker and had even been at the agency for a while, and yet I got the job. I was frankly afraid he would be mad at me, and that was what I was sensing.

Her response could be described as a "facilitative confrontation," which is an integration of support and confrontation, challenging another false dichotomy. She is opening the door for the discussion, recognizing he has understandable disappointment, and she is taking some responsibility for not raising it sooner. She directly addresses the indirect signals of anger. John denies the feelings. At a moment like this, most supervisors would be glad to drop the conversation. Having tuned in to her own discomfort, she was prepared to use the strategy of "coming back a second time," sending the signal that she really wanted to discuss this issue. The frequent mistake is to drop the issue when the supervisee denies there is such a problem. Doing so usually reflects the supervisor's discomfort and is not helpful long-term.

When Jane, the supervisor, pursues the issue, John does respond with anger – the anger he said he did not feel. From my perspective, the supervisor is in a better position with this active resistance and obvious anger than when John pretended it was not there and used passive resistance to send his message.

> He told me he did not understand what I was talking about. He was not angry with me, although he did not feel he had received completely fair treatment in the selection process. I asked him what he meant by that, and he responded by saying he did not want to talk about it; it was all over. I told him that I was feeling upset about their having to make the choice between us in the recruitment process for this position. Therefore, I would not have been surprised if he had some feelings as well.
>
> He got angry with me and said, "Look, if you feel people are angry at you for getting the job, that's your problem, not mine. Maybe you feel guilty about having gotten it in the first place." I told him I was not feeling guilty, just worried about how we would get along in these circumstances. He told me that if I let him alone, there should be no problems.
>
> I told him I could not do that and still feel comfortable about the job. We had better work out what we could expect from each other. I told him I would expect to be informed about his work, as I would with all staff. He could, however, expect that I would respect his competency and give him a good deal of leeway in the way he handled cases. In those situations in which I differed with him, and I thought there would be some, I would have to take responsibility for the final decision because that came with my job. I asked if he would make another appointment, and this time I would like him to bring the client folders. He said he would do that, and our conference ended.

449

I was glad because by this time, my knees were shaking so hard I was sure he must be able to hear them.

Although the session was difficult and although Jane did not think she was much further along with John, she had taken some important steps. First, she had declared the formally taboo subject of her authority as legitimate for discussion. Second, John actually had become angry with Jane, while simultaneously denying he felt any anger at all. It is possible that John was not in touch with how he felt in the situation and meant the denial. At any rate, the quarrel was out in the open, and it might be picked up later when John felt free to discuss it. Even if it were not raised again, simply pointing out the obstacle in this way might effectively diminish its effect.

Jane had confronted the issue of their working relationship and had made it clear that John would not intimidate her into pretending she was not his supervisor. This was important for John to hear; because now she had made it clear she would not just disappear; he was going to have to deal with her in one way or another. At the same time that she made this part of the contract clear, she stated her respect for his experience and competency, something that he also needed to hear – although his feelings might have made it hard for him to understand.

The supervision workshop group in which Jane presented this example offered support for her courage in the exchange. It was significant that she did not close the door because of John's first response. Often, a staff member needs time to think things over before being able to engage in a dialogue. It would be a mistake to assume that the question was closed forever or that John would not become more responsive as the work progressed. Jane would have to achieve the delicate balance of remaining sensitive to his feelings while not letting up on her demands and expectations.

I pointed out that it would be wise to document in writing her experiences since she had taken this job, and to include a summary of this conversation. I also suggested that she send a memo to her administrator indicating she was confronting John with this behavior and wished to have his support. Another key issue, I believe, was that she could not supervise John's work adequately if her administrator withheld support from her.

I also suggested that it might be helpful if the administrator could meet with John and explain why he had been passed over. I pointed out that she was on the receiving end of a great deal of anger that might actually be felt toward the agency and the administrator. I also felt that John's defensiveness and his behavior with Jane suggested a lack of professionalism that might emerge in his work with clients. I suggested that Jane take a close look at that possibility, since John had been able to avoid supervision for years with the former supervisor collaborating in the illusion of work.

Jane ended the discussion by saying that although it had been rough going in this case and although she still saw problems ahead, she felt strengthened by having at least confronted the problem and finding that the whole world did not collapse.

This is an important observation. It is often true that the problems we fear the most turn out to be less potent the moment we start to face them. As Jane pointed out, anything was better than how she felt avoiding John's resistance and his underlying anger. We all credited Jane with her courage, especially since she confronted him, as she pointed out, with her knees shaking. I suggested it would get easier with experience and that she had made a great start.

Summary and conclusion

This chapter has presented an alternative paradigm for guiding social work practice and supervision. It examined both against the backdrop of time – the Preliminary, Beginning, Middle, and Endings and Transitions. It also illustrates the parallel process by identifying and illustrating dynamics and skills central to both direct practice and supervision. Finally, it challenges a number of false dichotomies that appear to make social workers and supervisors choose between two apparent opposite choices rather than effectively integrating them.

References

Kuhn, T.H., 1962. *The structure of scientific revolution*. Chicago: University of Chicago Press.

Schwartz, W., 1961. The social worker in the group. *In*: B. Saunders, ed., *New perspectives on services to groups: theory, organization, practice*. New York: National Association of Social Workers, 7–34.

Shulman, L., 1982. *Skills of staff supervision and staff management*. Itasca, IL: F.E. Peacock Publishers.

Shulman, L., 2008. Supervision. *In*: T. Mizrahi, and L.E. Davis, eds.–in–Chief. *Encyclopedia of social work*. 20th ed., Vol. 4. Washington, DC; Oxford, NY: NASW Press and Oxford University Press, 186–190.

Shulman, L., 2010. *Interactional supervision*. 3rd ed. Washington, DC: National Association of Social Workers Press.

Shulman, L., 2016. Shifting the social work practice paradigm: the contribution of the interactional model. *Journal of Social Work Education*, 52 (sup1), S16–S27. doi:10.1080/10437797.2016.1174645

Shulman, L., 2018. *The skills of helping individual, families, groups and communities*. 8th edition enhanced. Boston, MA: Cengage Learning.

36

THE SUPERVISION SESSION

Kieran O'Donoghue

This chapter discusses the supervision session by drawing from research about the session. In the literature the supervision session is generally described as being a formal meeting or series of meetings between supervisors and supervisees (Munson 2002; Shulman 2010; Tsui 2005). It is the primary method through which supervision occurs and it mainly happens through individual face to face meetings that are usually an hour to an hour and a half long (O'Donoghue and Tsui 2015). Group sessions and sessions mediated through information and communication technology are less common, with the former being mostly used as an adjunct and substitute for individual sessions and the latter mainly being used where the supervisor and supervisee are at a distance (Mo and O'Donoghue 2019; O'Donoghue 2015). Historically, there are few studies that are specifically focused on the intricacies of the session, with most of the related research tending to focus on supervision generally, or an aspect, issue, or dynamic within supervision (O'Donoghue 2014). Prior to 2014, research on the session was mostly concerned with the frequency and length of sessions as well as the need to improve the structure of sessions and supervisory practices within it (O'Donoghue 2014). Since 2014 several studies conducted in Aotearoa New Zealand, Canada, China, and the United Kingdom have provided further insights into the supervision session (Davys et al. 2019; Hair 2015; Manthorpe et al. 2015; Mo and O'Donoghue 2019; O'Donoghue 2014, 2019a, b; Rankine and Thompson 2015; Wilkins and Antonopoulou 2019; Wilkins et al. 2017). The findings of these studies are discussed in this chapter with a specific focus upon how they contribute to understanding the frequency, length, content, structure, interactional process, and how to improve sessions.

Frequency and length of sessions

The first research studies on the frequency and length of sessions were the two national surveys conducted in the United States by Kadushin (1974, 1992). Kadushin (1974) found that regular sessions occurred between supervisors and supervisees three to four times a month with a duration between an hour and an hour and a half. The second survey reported findings concerning the average frequency and length of session with the majority of these being scheduled once a week and an hour to an hour and a half in duration (Kadushin 1992). Since 2014, the frequency of supervision and length of sessions have been examined in three studies (Manthorpe et al. 2015; O'Donoghue 2019a, Wilkins and Antonopoulou 2019). Manthorpe et al. (2015) surveyed newly qualified social workers (NQSWs) and their line-managers in England over a three-year period. They found that over two-thirds (82%) of 317 NQSWs had supervision sessions at least once a month, with slightly over a quarter (26%) having supervision sessions at least once a week or every two weeks. Manthorpe et al. (2015) also identified that this weekly or two weekly frequency was extended to monthly as the years of experience increased. The length of sessions was up to ninety minutes. The second study of O'Donoghue (2019a) was a national survey of the supervision of registered social workers (RSW) in Aotearoa New Zealand. O'Donoghue (2019a) found that most (88.4%) of the 276 social workers participated in sessions at least once a month. The majority (56.2%) had sessions monthly, over a fifth (22.6%) had fortnightly sessions, and nearly a tenth (9.6%) had weekly sessions. An additional finding was that social workers who worked in non-government organizations and statutory child welfare had more regular supervision (i.e., weekly and fortnightly) than those who worked in health, with the latter having a much great percentage of monthly supervision sessions. (O'Donoghue 2020). The average length of sessions for most (93.2%) RSW was between 31 minutes and 89 minutes. Half had sessions between 31 and 59 minutes, just over four tenths (43.3%) had sessions that were between 60 to 89 minutes. The most noticeable difference between areas of practice was that nearly two-thirds (63%) of those who worked in statutory child welfare had sessions between 31 and 59 minutes. The third study of Wilkins and Antonopoulou (2019) was an online survey of 315 social workers in child and adult services in the UK. The survey was concerned with social workers' perceptions of how supervision helped them. Wilkins and Antonopoulou (2019) found that the frequency of supervision varied with many of their respondents having supervision monthly (58.1%). This group was categorized as having a typical frequency. Those who had supervision less often than monthly were categorized as low frequency (28.8%) and those who had supervision more often than monthly were described as high frequency (11.4%). Amongst these groupings, Wilkins and Antonopoulou (2019) found significant differences between the frequency of supervision and its helpfulness in relation to quality of practice, analysis and reflection, focus on the client, child focus, clarity about risk, emotional support, and decision making. The differences indicated that the more frequent the supervision, the more it was perceived to be helpful. They also found that NQSWs had more frequent supervision than social workers and senior social workers and that nearly two-thirds of the NQSWs had group supervision sessions. Wilkins and Antonopoulou's (2019) findings concerning the length of sessions were that over two-thirds (68.5%) of their respondents had sessions that lasted between 60 and 120 minutes. They grouped the responses with sessions under 60 minutes being labelled as short duration (17.7%), between 60 and 90 minutes as typical (38.7%), between 90 and 120 minutes (29.8%) as long, and those greater than 120 minutes (13.3%) as very long. Significant differences were identified between long and short supervision concerning its helpfulness in terms of the quality of practice, analysis and reflection, focus on the client, child focus, emotional support, clarity about risk, and decision making. According to Wilkins and Antonopoulou (2019) the differences in the length of sessions indicate that at a certain point increases in the length of sessions are of less benefit to the overall helpfulness of supervision sessions.

The research discussed above indicates that the frequency and length of session varies, and that the social workers' years of experience and area of practice seemingly contribute to variations in both frequency and length of sessions. Wilkins and Antonopoulou's (2019) findings concerning variances in perceived helpfulness related to the frequency and length of supervision, highlight the need for further research related to the correlations between frequency and length of sessions with types of supervision, worker outcomes, and client outcomes. The research findings from all of the studies, which are based in the UK and Aotearoa New Zealand, also raise questions regarding to what extent the frequency and length of session vary internationally and why this occurs.

Content of sessions

Across the three studies that examined the content of supervision, the discussion of cases was the most prevalent content (Manthorpe et al. 2015; O'Donoghue 2019a, Wilkins et al. 2017). Manthorpe et al. (2015), asked NQSWs to identify from nine items the content usually covered in their supervision meetings. They found that the review of each case and advice and guidance on more difficult cases were the most common content identified as usually being covered by the most respondents. This was followed by matters pertaining to the NQSWs training needs, personal support, encouragement and appreciation, and closing cases. The least common matters identified by NQSWs were suggestions for developing reflection and self-awareness, help in applying theoretical approaches or explanations to practice, and performance against targets. O'Donoghue (2019a) used a five-point scale (with 1 = *not at all* and 5 = *almost always*) to identify how frequently 18 items were discussed in the RSW's supervision sessions. The most frequently discussed items were complex and challenging cases, the supervisee's concerns or matters, caseload review, workload, professional development, ethical issues, team issues, boundaries, and stress. The less commonly discussed matters were problems with the organization and management, the supervisor's concerns or matters, personal issues, problems with colleagues, cultural matters, performance management, and the supervision relationship. The third study of Wilkins et al. (2017) examined recordings of 34 case discussions in a child and family social service authority in London. Wilkins et al. (2017) identified that the content of the discussions were very similar across the recordings, with most starting with the social workers' well-being and discussion of administrative matters, then there was a list of families for discussion, followed by the discussion of each individual family. From these three studies, the general content of supervision sessions seemingly includes matters that relate to the supervisee's practice with clients, the supervisee's needs, their organizational setting, context, and relationships. However, in most sessions the core content is the supervisee's work with clients. Although focusing on the supervisee's work with clients in sessions is important, the studies referred to above only give us a picture of the content of supervision in England and Aotearoa New Zealand. Internationally we do not know whether the content of sessions is similar or different in other countries. Moreover, these studies do not interrogate what is not commonly discussed in supervision or what ought to be discussed in social work supervision. For example, Hair (2015), in her study concerned with social justice conversations within supervision, found that despite respondents wanting their sessions to have a social justice focus that they did not experience this in their sessions. This example together with the findings from the studies referred to above indicates that there are further questions to explore internationally regarding what content is discussed in supervision and what content is not discussed and why.

Structure of sessions

The structure of the supervision session is generally described in the literature as having a beginning, middle, and end (Kadushin 2014; Shulman 2010). The beginning involves engaging and preparing to focus on the work done in the middle, while the end concerns reviewing, closing the session, and disengaging. Morrison (2005) developed a one-page structure of specific aspects that occur in a session as a guide for supervisors. O'Donoghue et al. (2005) drew Morrison's structure in the development of an 11-item scale to measure the occurrence of specific aspects within supervisees' sessions. O'Donoghue et al. (2005) found that the aspects related to the work done in the middle (i.e., decision making and discussion) occurred more frequently than the aspects related to engagement and closure in sessions. O'Donoghue (2019a, b) completed an updated survey, this time from the standpoint of both supervisees and supervisors. In this survey the respondents (supervisee and supervisors) were asked to rate on a five-point scale (with 1 = *not at all* and 5 = *almost always*) the following 11 items: preparation, karakia (spiritual incantation or prayer, which is used to open and close a space or event to make it safe), checking-in, agenda setting, prioritization of items, discussion of item(s), decision-making, action planning, summarization and review, evaluation, and closure. Most of the above items commonly occurred in the supervisees' sessions with the discussion of item(s), action planning, decision-making, and checking-in being the most frequently occurring. Two aspects, namely evaluation and karakia were very infrequent (O'Donoghue 2019a). Significant differences were identified according to ethnicity in the occurrence of karakia, with Māori supervisees having a higher average occurrence than non-Māori. This revealed that the cultural practice of karakia occurred more often in sessions where the supervisee was Māori. For the supervisors, all items, except karakia, commonly occurred in their sessions. There were some differences in the order of prevalence with the most frequently occurring items being discussion of item(s), checking-in, action planning, and decision-making (O'Donoghue 2019b). There was a similar significant difference according to ethnicity in the occurrence of karakia, with Māori supervisors having a significantly higher average occurrence than non-Māori. This difference also highlights that karakia occurred more often in sessions when the supervisor was Māori. Comparing the prevalence of the aspects for both the supervisees and supervisors there were a few interesting differences, for example, amongst supervisors checking-in was second highest, while for supervisees it was fourth. Another was that supervisors' preparation was the eighth most prevalent aspect, whereas for supervisees it was the fifth. These differences reflected the different experiences and emphasis of each supervision role, with the supervisee role being focused on tasks in the session and the supervisor's role being more focused on process.

Two other studies refer to the structure of the session (Rankine and Thompson 2015; Wilkins et al. 2017). Rankine and Thompson (2015) describe the structure of the session similarly to Kadushin and Harkness (2014) with beginning, middle, and end stages. The beginning stage involves orientating to being in supervision and setting an agenda, the middle is where issues are explored, and the end stages is where the session is concluded and closed. In contrast, Wilkins et al. (2017, p. 947) describe the structure of case discussions within sessions as "beginning with a 'verbal deluge' by the social worker, followed by the identification of 'the problem' and the provision of a solution by the manager."

Overall, these studies show that there is a structure to a session and that this involves a stage of engagement and planning, a working stage in which matters are discussed, decisions made, and plans developed, and a concluding stage where the session is brought to a close and ends. That said, two areas for further research are evident. The first concerns the responsiveness of the session structure to cultural differences and practices. O'Donoghue's (2019a, b) findings about the prevalence of karakia raises questions about how culturally responsive supervision is in Aotearoa New Zealand, while the other studies make no reference to cultural practices in session (Rankine and Thompson 2015; Wilkins et al. 2017). This indicates the need for further research concerning culturally responsive sessions and decolonizing the supervision session. The second area for further research is the difference between the supervisors' and supervisees' experiences of the session and how the structure of the supervision session is experienced differently by the supervisee and supervisor and does this change over time or differ due to the experience or expertise of the supervisor and supervisee, and to what extent the structure of a session is shaped by organizational culture, field of practice, and supervisor training and qualifications.

The interactional process

The interactional process of the supervision session is often described as being isomorphic or a parallel process of the social work interview (Kadushin 2014; Shulman 2010). It is also depicted as an interactive problem-solving process that mirrors the practitioner-client interaction (Shulman 2010). The recent research on the interactive process has focused on mapping the interactive discursive exchange and co-constructed format, as well as the processes that facilitate reflection within supervision (O'Donoghue 2014). O'Donoghue (2014) interviewed 16 social workers and 18 supervisors about their recent supervision sessions. Each participant prior to interview completed a pre-interview guided self-reflection of a recent session which included their description of what happened, and their reflections on the experience and the process. At the interview, the participants were questioned about their experiences, thoughts, feelings, and reflections during the session and in supervision sessions generally. O'Donoghue (2014) found that the interactive process had a ritualized format that relied upon the supervisee and supervisor playing their part and cooperating in the interaction exchanges that occurred between them. He figuratively described the session as a dance, with the dancing (i.e., the sessional interactions) creating the dance (i.e., supervision session) and the type of dance depending on the dancers (i.e., the supervisee and supervisor) and how well they are in step with each other. According to O'Donoghue (2014), the stages of the session that the supervisee and supervisor work through are preparation, beginning, planning, working, and ending, with each party moving through phases which progressively advance the process (see Figure 36.1 below).

For the supervisee, their preparation starts by continually thinking about matters they might take to supervision and then closer to the session focusing on the specific things they wish to discuss. The supervisor's preparation, on the other hand, involves reviewing the supervision record for matters to follow up on or as a reminder, then thinking about the supervisee and what they might bring. This sometimes involves a quiet period of reflective preparation. As the time for the session draws near, the supervisor's attention turns to the physical setting and making sure there are no interruptions or that there is some water or other drink for the supervisee. The rituals of engagement at the beginning of the session were reflective of relationship and individuals involved.

For supervisees, there was a social engagement phase involving an exchange of greetings, a catch up about matters and events that have occurred since the last meeting, and a process of centering, which might involve cultural practices such as karakia, and attending to hospitality needs. Next, there is a transition to an orientation phase which involves checking-in and focusing. The checking-in entails the supervisee sharing about their current situation, while focusing involves a conversation about what they want to discuss or achieve from supervision. The supervisors' experiences mirrored that of the supervisees' with the start reflecting both the supervisors' and supervisees' preferences (O'Donoghue 2014). For the supervisors, the start began with the supervisee's arrival and brief time of centering, by way of prayer, karakia, or a moment of silence. This was followed by a checking-in phase wherein the supervisor enquired about feelings, well-being, and what was happening to them in their work. This checking-in phase could last between three to five minutes or a quarter of an hour and was dependent about what the supervisee raised and how they were feeling. The transition into focusing on supervision would occur through questions like, "Is this what you wanted to discuss today?" or "Is this part of your list?" or "What is on your list to discuss today?"

The planning phase was similar for both supervisees and supervisors and consisted of agenda setting and then prioritizing the list. The setting of the agenda was either a joint process or one that was supervisee focused. The joint process involved both the supervisee and supervisor

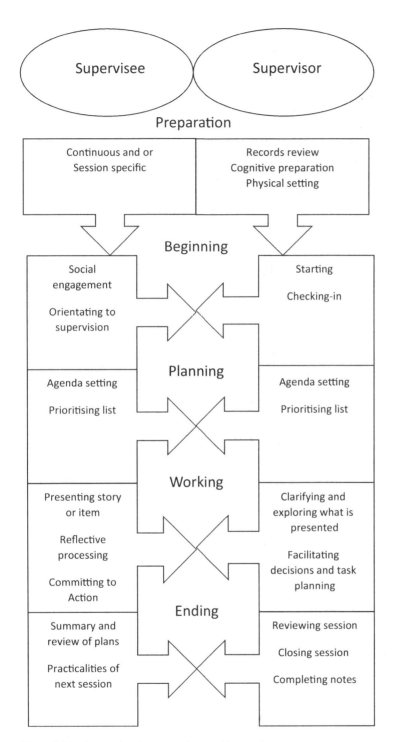

Figure 36.1   Interactional process of supervision session

contributing items whereas the supervisee-focused process was where the agenda was based solely on what the supervisee brought, and the supervisor did not add items. The prioritization of items was also a process that was either a joint decision or a decision that was made by the supervisee. Things that were considered by the supervisee and supervisors in prioritizing items were matters related to urgency and safety, the supervisee's wishes, what is easiest or quickest to deal with, and what the supervisor wanted to discuss. Some supervisors, rather than prioritizing the whole list, asked the supervisee for the most important item and then prioritized and worked on that item. Once they had finished the item, they would then prioritize again, and this occurred throughout the session. Once the items were prioritized, the first item would be explored, and this marked the start of the working stage.

The working stage is essentially an interactive problem-solving process that involves the supervisee's exploring, reflecting, developing an understanding, and action planning, with the supervisor supporting through listening, questioning, challenging, and summarizing. For supervisees, three phases occurred, the first was presenting the story or item. According to O'Donoghue (2014, p. 62), supervisees present their item or tell the story to "get it more refined" and with "a view to further discussion." In other words, supervisees tell their story to explore and reflect on it and for their supervisor to develop an understanding of the situation and the supervisee's experience of it. The second phase happens when the supervisor helps the supervisee to reflectively process the matter they have raised. This occurs through the supervisor using questions and reflective responses to help the supervisee organize and make sense of the issue, as well as explore it from a range of different angles or perspectives. The reflective processing phase ends when the supervisee and supervisor have obtained to a shared sense of the matter being discussed and the conversation shifts to one that focuses on decisions and plans. The third phase starts when the supervisee commits to action, and this involves identifying the specific actions to address the matter under discussion. This may take the form of specific actions or tasks or involve identifying a specific learning from that situation discussed that can be generally applied in the supervisee's practice. The supervisor's part in the working stage consists of two phases, namely, clarifying and exploring what is presented, and facilitating decisions and task planning. In the clarifying and exploring phase the supervisor firstly clarifies what is being presented using questions, reflective responses, paraphrasing, and summarizations. The supervisor does this to assist the supervisee to elaborate on the matter they presented, as well as to obtain an understanding of the story or item presented, and to work out the supervisee's needs concerning why this matter was brought to supervision. The exploration of the issue involves the use of a range of questioning and other techniques, such as using a whiteboard, diagrams (e.g., genograms and eco-maps), analogies, hypothetical cases, weighing up the pros and cons, and reframing techniques. The exploration phase ends at the point where the supervisee indicates that there is a way forward, which in turn starts the facilitating decisions and task planning phase. At this point the supervisor's focus shifts towards outcomes, strategies, and the learning from this situation. In facilitating decisions, the supervisor helps the supervisee to name the decision and commit to action. The task planning phase involves the identification of actions, the exploration of possible outcomes and responses to these, as well as the agreement of the tasks to be undertaken. When all matters on the agenda have been addressed or the time allotted for the session is close to being reached, the session moves into the ending stage.

The ending stage commences the ritual of disengagement that the supervisor and supervisee have either agreed or decided to enact. For the supervisees, ending the session consists of two phases. The first concerns summarizing and reviewing the session. The process of summarizing alerts supervisees that the session is drawing to a close and leads into a review of the discussion, and achievements. It also provides an opportunity for the supervisee to give feedback to the supervisor on their experience of the session. Following this, the practicalities regarding the next session are resolved before moving into a social discussion and/or ritual ending previously agreed by the supervisee and supervisor. For the supervisors the ending stage is like that of the supervisees, in that it starts with a review of the session, which in turn is followed by a discussion of the practicalities related to arranging another session. The supervisors would then initiate a closure of the session according to the agreed process with the supervisee. The final phase of the session for the supervisors is the completion of the supervision notes after the supervisee has left. Overall, the interactional process map of the supervision session details a way for supervisees and supervisors to navigate their way together through sessions. It also highlights the importance of cooperative engagement and partnership in the interactional process and co-construction of the session. That said, the interactional process map also demonstrates a need for further research in terms of how this process occurs in other countries and in relation to how interactional factors within supervision sessions affect the parties' perceptions and participation within their supervision relationships, as well as their learning and development, and the social worker's practice with clients.

Improving supervision sessions

The previous research concerned with improving supervision suggests that sessions could be improved firstly, through a more deliberate, definite process that included a ritualized opening and closing, a focus on the agenda and priorities, more in-depth discussion and reflection to explore issues, together with a process of review and evaluation in sessions (O'Donoghue 2008). A second area of improvement concerned the professionalism of supervisors in sessions. This included better clinical skills to listen and facilitate reflection, better personal management regarding timekeeping and preparation and more support for supervisees through being more available and attentive to supervisees' needs (O'Donoghue 2008). O'Donoghue (2008) recommended that in order to achieve these improvements, supervision sessions needed to be observed, discussed, and reflected through the supervision of supervisors' practice, and supervision sessions need to be evaluated both at the end of the session and throughout the relationship. Concerning the need to improve the professionalism of supervisors, O'Donoghue (2008) noted the importance of education and development for supervisors and the need for workforce planning that starts at the foundational entry level and progresses through to an advanced practitioner level. This education and development would require a progressive supervision curriculum, supervisory competencies, and course standards.

In recent studies, some new ways of potentially improving sessions have come to light through recording sessions and then reviewing them using a thinking out loud reflective process (Davys et al. 2019; Rankine and Thompson 2015). Rankine and Thompson (2015) audio-recorded and transcribed three standard supervision sessions and then independently reviewed the transcripts and recordings before meeting to share their reflections on the process, content, and meaning of the sessions. This reflection process was helpful to both parties in the supervision relationship and helped both the supervisee and supervisor to further improve how they worked together in the supervision session through providing greater insight into their interactions within supervision. Davys et al. (2019) further developed the thinking out loud process through a learning community reflective process which they called the koru model. This involved the audio recording of a supervision session. The next part of this recorded session was presented to a group of peer supervisors for feedback and review. The feedback and learning from it was then used by the members of the group in their supervision sessions. At the subsequent group meeting they would then share their reflections on the learning experience. All the group meetings were audio recorded. For the group involved, this process helped them all further develop their supervision practice. Davys et al. (2019)

also recommended that this process could be used to enhance supervisor education and competence. The strengths of this process are that it involves reflection and learning from the practice of supervising. In addition, the learning community provides support and development through the process of reviewing each member's supervisory practice over time. The challenges related to this approach concern the nature of the learning community and its reliance on collegial support and trust, which means the memberships and relationships are key. It is noted that all the members of Davys et al.'s (2019) group were longstanding colleagues who know each other relatively well prior to forming the group. The nature of the learning community may well be different amongst groups who do not have such previous relationships and who may need to establish trust, rather than build on an already established level of trust.

The other area of recent research concerns the evaluation of sessions. This has been explored at a descriptive level regarding the prevalence and process within sessions across two studies. The first was Davys et al. (2017) who reported that 27% of the 120 supervisees and 36.7% of 72 supervisors in their study were evaluated on a session-by-session basis, with the most common method of evaluation being an informal discussion between the supervisor and supervisee. The most common content of these evaluations was whether reflection occurred within sessions. The other study was that of O'Donoghue (2019a) who found that for 84.2% of 273 supervisees, evaluation occurred to some extent in their sessions and for 39.2% this occurred a lot or almost always. Among the 135 supervisors, O'Donoghue (2019b) found that for 96.2 % of them, evaluation occurred to some extent in their session and for 52.6% it occurred a lot, or almost always. From this research, the conclusions we can draw regarding evaluation within sessions is that it is variable and that there is no standard method of evaluation of supervision sessions.

Conclusion

This chapter has reviewed recent studies that have focused on the supervision session. From the research reviewed and discussed it is clear that frequency and length of session varies, with the practitioners' experience and area of practice being the main variations. It was also identified that further research is needed to explore the relationships between the frequency and length of sessions and different types of supervision, worker outcomes, and client outcomes. Regarding the content of supervision sessions, it was found that this primarily concerns the supervisee's practice with clients, with the supervisee's needs, their organizational setting, context, and relationships being discussed to a lesser extent. Further research areas were also identified concerning the content of sessions internationally and in relation to what content is discussed in supervision and what content is not discussed and why. A structure for the session that consists of stages of engagement, planning, working, and a conclusion was identified. Two areas for further research were identified concerning the structure of the session, the first concerns how responsive the structure is to culturally diverse practices, whereas, the second pertains to how the structure of the supervision session is experienced differently by the supervisee and supervisor across a range of areas and contexts. In relation to the interactional process, a map of the supervision session was reviewed. This map helps supervisees and supervisors navigate their way together through sessions. Further international research is needed regarding the interactional factors within supervision sessions and how these affect the parties' perceptions and participation within their supervision relationships, as well as their learning and development, and the social worker's practice with clients. Finally, the research concerned with improving supervision sessions suggested ways that recording and reflecting upon sessions can lead to improvement. This research also identified that evaluation has a part to play in the improvement of sessions. Nevertheless, further research is needed about the methods of improving sessions by way of observation, reflection, and through educative and supervisory processes. Likewise, further research is needed related to the development of a standard evaluation for sessions that encompass the interaction, the learning and development of the supervisee, the outcomes for the client, professional standards, and organizational requirements. In conclusion, this chapter has identified the knowledge base informing the supervision session; in doing so it has also highlighted the need for more international research that is directly related to the session. Since the session is the primary means through which supervision occurs, it is arguably imperative that supervisees and supervisors are informed by the best international research evidence available. In addition, it behooves future researchers and practitioners to ensure that the supervision session is at the heart of the research and evaluation agenda.

References

Davys, A., Howard, F., Rankine, M., and Thompson, A., 2019. Supervision under the microscope: critical conversations in a learning community. *Practice*, 31 (5), 359–374. doi:10.1080/09503153.2018.1558196

Davys, A.M., May, J., Burns, B., and O'Connell, M., 2017. Evaluating social work supervision. *Aotearoa New Zealand Social Work*, 29 (3), 108–121. doi:10.11157/anzswj-vol29iss3id314

Hair, H.J., 2015. Supervision conversations about social justice and social work practice. *Journal of Social Work*, 15 (4), 349–370. doi:10.1177/1468017314539082.

Kadushin, A., 1974. Supervisor supervisee: a survey. *Social Work*, 19 (3), 288–298.

Kadushin, A., 1992. Social work supervision: an updated survey. *The Clinical Supervisor*, 10 (2), 9–27.

Kadushin, A., and Harkness, D., 2014. *Supervision in social work*. 5th ed. New York: University of Columbia Press.

Manthorpe, J., Moriarty, J., Hussein, S., Stevens, M., and Sharpe, E., 2015. Content and purpose of supervision in social work practice in England: views of newly qualified social workers, managers and directors. *British Journal of Social Work*, 45 (1), 52–68. doi:10.1093/bjsw/bct102

Mo, Y.H., and O' Donoghue, K., 2019. A snapshot of cyber supervision in Mainland China. *Qualitative Social Work*. doi:10.1177/1473325019836714

Morrison, T., 2005. *Staff supervision in social care*. Brighton: Pavilion.

Munson, C.E., 2002. *Handbook of clinical social work supervision*. 3rd ed. New York: Haworth Press.

O'Donoghue, K., 2008. Towards improving social work supervision in Aotearoa New Zealand. *Aotearoa New Zealand Social Work Review*, 20 (1), 10–21.

O'Donoghue, K., 2014. Towards an interactional map of the supervision session: an exploration of supervisees and supervisors experiences. *Practice*, 26 (1), 53–70. doi:10.1080/09503153.2013.869581

O'Donoghue, K., 2015. Issues and challenges facing social work supervision in the twenty-first century. *China Journal of Social Work*, 8 (2), 136–149.

O'Donoghue, K., 2019a. The supervision of registered social workers in Aotearoa New Zealand: a national survey. *Aotearoa New Zealand Social Work*, 31 (3), 58–77. doi:10.11157/anzswj-vol31iss3id648

O'Donoghue, K., 2019b. Registered social workers who are supervisors: a national survey. *Aotearoa New Zealand Social Work*, 31 (3), 97–115. doi:10.11157/anzswj-vol31iss3id651

O'Donoghue, K., 2020. Area of practice variances in registered social workers supervision. Unpublished manuscript.

O'Donoghue, K., Munford, R., and Trlin, A., 2005. Mapping the territory: supervision within the association. *Social Work Review*, 17 (4), 46–64.

O'Donoghue, K., and Tsui, M.S., 2015. Social work supervision research (1970–2010): the way we were and the way ahead. *British Journal of Social Work*, 45 (2), 616–633. doi:10.1093/bjsw/bct115

Rankine, M., and Thompson, A., 2015. 'Swimming to shore': co-constructing supervision with a thinking-aloud process. *Reflective Practice*, 16 (4), 508–521. 10.1080/14623943.2015.1064377

Shulman, L., 2010. *Interactional supervision*. 3rd ed. Washington, DC: NASW Press.

Tsui, M.S., 2005. *Social work supervision: contexts and concepts*. Thousand Oaks, CA: SAGE.

Wilkins, D., and Antonopoulou, V., 2019. What does supervision help with? a survey of 315 social workers in the UK. *Practice*, 31 (1), 21–40. doi:10.1080/09503153.2018.1437398

Wilkins, D., Forrester, D., and Grant, L., 2017. What happens in child and family social work supervision?. *Child & Family Social Work*, 22 (2), 942–951. doi:10.1111/cfs.12314

37

EMOTIONALLY SENSITIVE SUPERVISION

Richard Ingram

Supervision in social work comes in many shapes and forms and there is a plethora of literature which debates the role, purpose, configuration, and content of effective supervision. It might seem intuitive to start this chapter by getting straight into these debates and, given the title of the chapter, championing the conceptions of supervision which best deliver emotional sensitivity and exploration. However, if we accept that supervision is ultimately to improve practice, well-being, and professional development (O'Donoghue 2015), then it seems better to begin with considering what we mean by emotions and the place that they may have within the practice of social workers. From that conceptual foundation we can then move into considering how best supervision may elucidate the opportunities, challenges, and contributions of the emotional content of practice.

Defining emotions

Emotions are a multifaceted and contested concept. A search for literature focused on emotions will pull you in many directions including neuroscience, cognitive psychology, socio cultural perspectives, and evolutionary science to name but a few. The scope of this chapter will not allow a thorough exploration of this literature, and it would be very useful to seek out the relevant papers and books contained in the list of references. The list below will introduce you to some the key dimensions of emotions and those which resonate significantly in the context of social work and this chapter.

- Making sense of situations – emotions are in part rooted in our previous experiences and provide working models of how the world works (Turner and Stets 2005). We respond to events and draw upon previous emotional markers to determine the nature, relevance, and future actions.
- Labeling and prioritizing – emotions help us to establish labels and categories to quickly appraise the importance of a range of stimuli (Lazarus and Lazarus 1994). For example, this helps us determine potential levels of risk to ourselves and others.
- Motivation and action – given the labeling function of emotions, this is then linked with a further cognitive step which lets us determine our motivation to act and in turn the nature of that action (Lane et al. 2000).

- Communicable between people – emotions are not only an internally experienced and "felt" phenomena but also something which we communicate to others through our verbal and non-verbal communication (Ingram 2015).
- Contextual – the way we may perceive and evaluate situations will be in part influenced by our context and role. This links also to the aforementioned emotional expression which may be moderated or controlled by the contexts in which we operate (Hochschild 1983; Mann 2004). For example, emotional regulation may be seen as important in social work relationships (Howe 2008).
- Conscious and unconscious – the rapid neurological processes which allow for the emotional labor to take place may not always involve immediately knowable origins (Clore and Ortony 2000). This means that at times our reactions are not easily explicable and in turn require further reflection to understand.

This list highlights how pervasive and central emotions are to how we operate as human beings. This does not cease when we adopt our professional personas as social workers, indeed it seems that their role is heightened further as we seek to engage in and understand complex situations and relationships. Let us turn our attention to the context of social work whilst maintaining a keen focus on the preceding facets of emotions.

Linking emotions and social work practice

Whilst it is difficult to generalize across the myriad of social work contexts locally and globally, there is at the core of the social work profession a commitment to working with individuals, groups, and communities to promote well-being, empowerment, and social justice (IFSW 2014). Regardless of service delivery context, and/or the pervasiveness of managerialist constrictions to practice, there is an importance placed on the relationships developed between social workers and the users of services with whom they work (Ruch, Turney and Ward 2018). This provides us with an important link to the preceding discussion about the centrality of emotions, as the relationships we build, the sense we make of situations, and the actions we subsequently take are all connected to our emotional responses.

Staempfli and Fairlough (2018) highlight how a relationship-based conception of practice recognizes that emotions, rationality, and the socio-political context are all at play within the interactions social workers engage in. This suggests that a focus solely on concrete knowledge and a managerialist proliferation of processes and procedures can only go so far to equip social workers to meet these challenges. The fluid and complex emotional aspects of practice are ever present for social workers and require focus and attention. Ruch and Turner (2016) highlight that the seminal Munro Report (2011) in the UK posited that intuitive knowledge and emotional responses were essential streams of information for child protection social workers when making the difficult and balanced judgments required in practice. They note the role supervision can have in allowing space for reflection and thinking, and perhaps crucially that emotions are a contributor to effective practice rather than simply a *response* to it. Even within social work practice contexts which privilege concrete knowledge and managerialist approaches, the emotional labor of practice remains as does its crucial contribution, it is only less valued and visible.

There is a further mandate for locating emotions at the heart of practice when we consider the clear messages arising from service user focused literature. Themes such as genuineness, empathy, warmth, and positivity emerge as perennial characteristics desired of social workers by the people who use services (Harding and Beresford 1995; McNeil et al. 2005; Hennessey 2011). To achieve such positive engagement, social workers must bring themselves into practice, which requires a degree of emotional exposure and interpersonal connection with service users (Hennessey 2011). Such emotional engagement is necessary if social workers are to be able express empathy within their practice and in turn meet the desire of service users *to be heard and understood* (Howe 2013; Ingram 2015). This genuine connection, albeit within the parameters of a professional role, requires social workers to exercise a degree of emotional intelligence. Emotional intelligence involves individuals understanding their own emotional responses and being able to regulate and manage these within their relationships. Furthermore, emotional intelligence involves individuals being motivated to then tune into the emotional worlds of others and to be able to communicate empathy and understand accordingly (Howe 2008).

This discussion suggests that social work practice involves a significant degree of relationship building which is underpinned by varying degrees of emotional attunement, exposure, and regulation. Such practice is inevitably impactful on all parties involved and for social workers this is no less significant. This leads us to recognizing the substantial contribution supervision may have in supporting social workers to use, manage, and understand the role of emotions in their practice.

Emotions and supervision

In this section we will explore the key characteristics of supervision which are most significant when considering emotional sensitivity and exploration. If we accept the purpose of supervision posited in the opening paragraph of this chapter, then it is helpful to use the *managerial*, *supportive*, and *educational* functions of supervision proposed by Kadushin (1985) as a way of understanding how supervision can be orientated and delivered. These functions can co-exist and may be fluid in terms of their relevancy depending on the needs of the social worker and the nature of the practice in which they are involved.

Emotionally sensitive supervision can straddle these three spheres, as all are as much part of a holistic picture of social work practice as the other. For example, emotionally sensitive supervision would help social workers to understand and be accountable for the decisions and judgments they make (or not) and to illicit the extent to which they are informed and guided by their emotions among other streams of knowledge. Additionally, such an approach to supervision is likely to be experienced as supportive, as it will require a trusting and open environment in which the supervisor can "be there" for the social worker (Smith 2000). Finally, emotionally sensitive supervision is about exploring the "knowable" and "unknowable" aspects of practice which can lead to significant self-knowledge and wider learning related to decision-making and the lives of the service users with whom we work. Lambley (2019) notes that for such supervision to be possible the time allocated to it needs to be confidential, ring-fenced, and a safe forum for discussion. Hair (2013) warns that the rise internationally of business management approaches to social work has threated the balance of these supervisory functions and can often privilege administrative needs (i.e. procedural case management) over practice focused needs (i.e. practitioner well-being and reflection). The contents of this chapter are intended to provide a counterbalance to such trends, passive or otherwise.

There is a plethora of literature relating to reflective social work practice (see: Ingram et al. 2014; Mantell and Scragg 2019), and reflection forms a core element of most social work qualifying and professional development programs globally. Reflection involves thinking about and reviewing one's practice and considering the context, knowledge, inter/intra personal dynamics, and outcomes at play and considering how this learning may impact on current understanding and future practice (Ingram 2015). This provides a further mandate for ensuring social workers receive opportunities to reflect upon and unpick their practice experiences to enhance practice and safeguard well-being (Lambley 2019). Supervision is a universally recognized forum for such reflection (whether individually or in group-based settings) and a focus on "self" is common across a range of models of reflection. This is heartening as it provides a robust and widely accepted approach to supervision which by its very nature opens the door for emotional reflection and also crucially how and in what ways it informs and impacts on practice. Furthermore, models of reflection require a feedback loop into future practice and actions to be meaningful and impactful (Ingram et al. 2014). This helps deliver on one of the core remits of supervision which is to improve outcomes for service users (O'Donoghue 2015). The cognitive aspect of reflection which involves deep thinking about events sits comfortably with work of Lazarus and Lazarus (1994) who emphasize the role of emotional appraisal and the heightened importance to be emotionally aware when one has a significant stake or investment in an event. This is never truer than for social workers and the importance and accountability of their professional practice.

The educative aspect of supervision sits within a wider sphere of learning cultures. The messages that social workers receive about the acceptability of exploring emotions in supervision and/or learning from practice more generally is crucial (Ingram 2013). These messages may be conveyed at a professional, organizational, or individual level and ideally will be echoed across all three spheres. Staempfli and Fairlough (2018) suggest that such a learning culture must arise from an acknowledgement of the complexity of the internal and external worlds of those involved in social work and that a compliance with a managerial culture which privileges certainties and evidence over uncertainty and complexity is an obstacle to realizing such a vision. Hair (2013) notes that once established, such a learning culture needs to be tangible and communicable at the individual level of supervisor/supervisee(s). Simply put, the structure and tone of supervision needs to facilitate the openness and lack of certainty that a learning culture must contain. Hair (2013) goes on to note that 90% of the social workers in her study felt that they needed supervision with emotional support embedded within it, and that due to the constantly fluid and unique nature of social work practice, such supervision was required throughout one's career. This is important as it emphasizes the continual nature of learning which does not arrive at a destination of knowingness when it is linked to practice, and also that practice is experienced at an emotional level and not only a practical or procedural one.

There are many parallels between the nature and content of a supervisory relationship and those that are experienced between a social worker and a service user. Clearly, there are very significant differences in terms of purpose, power, and function, but the skills and qualities utilized by a supervisor must allow for openness, trust, honesty, and empathy. To enable the sense of safety and trust that is required for emotional openness and expressions of uncertainty and doubt, there needs to be explicit reassurances (underpinned by effective relationship-based skills) that it is acceptable and not at risk of negative judgment and/or performance appraisal. This is the intersection between the managerial and supportive elements of supervision and are in many ways held in tension. This is not to suggest that poor practice or ill-informed decision making should be overlooked, but that there is an environment and quality of relationship established which manages this tension and allows space for social worker to be "held" and contained to allow for deep reflection and honesty. Containment in this context is the challenge for supervision to allow for uncertainty, and crucially to encourage curiosity to explore issues in depth (Ruch et al. 2018). Without this, the reflective element of supervision may become overly edited and selective and in turn less authentic. This then may lead to a reduction in genuine accountability as well as a more limited enhancement of practice. This links with the concept of negative capability (Cornish 2011). This refers to the ability to function effectively while being uncertain about certain aspects of one's practice. This requires a significant degree of openness and trust on both sides of the supervisory relationship as well as an acceptance that professional/self-knowledge is not static or indeed ever fully realized.

This section highlights many of the key elements required to create what could be called an emotionally inclusive supervisory environment. These elements are important and necessary across the range of supervisory approaches and configurations. Let us now turn to some examples of how this may be constructed and delivered in practice.

Emotionally sensitive supervision: Permissions, safety, and configurations

The contents of this book will highlight the breadth and depth of knowledge relating to social work supervision and will make clear that when we talk about supervision, we are talking about a process which may operate at a one-to-one level and a range of group configurations. There are also many variations in terms of the role and function of those charged with providing supervision and this in turn can have an impact on the potential for emotional sensitivity and exploration.

Ingram (2013) explored the experiences of social workers within supervision, and it emerged that there was significant variance in terms of the level of emotional content and focus. This was often attributed to either feeling "safe" or "not safe" to share such aspects of practice. This idea of safety related to a sense that exploring emotions and/or uncertainties in supervision could be perceived as incompetence or a symptom of stress. This brings us back to the idea that learning cultures need to be explicit. However, it was also evident that there was variance within organizations and teams which pointed to the importance of the bespoke relationships that supervisors and supervisees form regardless of the overarching culture. The desirability of establishing openness and clarity from the outset of a supervisory relationship is clear. Hafford-Letchfield (2009) suggests that a co-produced agreement between supervisor and supervisee can achieve the aforementioned clarity as well as setting boundaries and expectations. Jindal-Snape and Ingram (2013) developed a model which required the supervisor and supervisee to plot their expectations of supervision on a horizontal (emotional focus) and vertical (casework focus) axis. This generates a visual representation of initial positionality, and then can form the basis of a further discussion which allows both parties to explain their choices and to negotiate how/if the distance between any expectations can be reduced. This is a very useful approach as it involves the supervisee as a partner from the outset and allows for organizational constraints to be aired and understood rather than implied or hidden. This then allows the supervisory relationship to develop with a degree of trust and clarity which will provide an essential foundation for emotionally sensitive supervision. It also provides a marker for both parties to return to should the content of supervision begin to drift away from the agreed focus. O'Donoghue and Tsui (2011) highlight the importance of supervisors and supervisees "getting to know" each other as a building block of trust. This sits comfortably with the notion of a co-produced agreement and/or contract. Kadushin et al. (2009) note that the nature of one-to-one supervision varies over time and may evolve into something more akin to peer consultation as the experience of the supervisee increases.

The co-produced agreement described above could be utilized in both an individual one-to-one configuration and also group based approaches to supervision. The nature of the role of the supervisor will also have an impact on how this may work in practice. Kelly and Green (2019) note that supervisors may often be drawn for allied professions such as healthcare due to the way service delivery is configured in certain locations and contexts. This provides opportunities for incorporating different perspectives and may reduce the influence of the line-management element of the relationship which can raise the profile of the administrative aspects of the supervisory relationship. Beddoe (2010) highlighted the rise in externally sourced supervisors from outside the agency in which a social worker operates. This clearly has the advantage of largely sidestepping the line-management aspect of supervision and may reduce the impact of managerial agency level priorities taking center stage. Ingram (2015) argues that whilst there are merits in such an approach, there is also a risk of placing emotions at the periphery of the actual practice. Beddoe (2010) notes the need for a feedback loop into practice and agencies to avoid an "us and them" divide forming and perhaps difficult and competing messages from organizations and supervisors.

Lambley (2019) notes that increasingly social workers engage in group-based supervision. This can either be the sole mode of supervision or can more typically be part of a multi-modal approach to supervision in which it is combined with individual supervision too (Vassos, Harms, and Rose 2018). There are many potential elements of group-based supervision which may enhance the opportunities for emotional sensitivity:

- The sense of "safety in numbers" where there is a collective agreement to explore the complexities of practice
- Shared experience – the benefit of discussing issues with others who may have a first-hand knowledge of the issues that are most relevant.
- Diverse range of views – a core component of a learning culture
- Less focused on caseload management and more on generic issues or specific challenges

Of course these benefits are not guaranteed, which underlines that the discussion about conditions required for emotionally sensitive supervision in the preceding pages of this chapter must be considered alongside this. Group supervision should adhere to the group-work practice of establishing clear ground rules and purpose. This chimes with the preceding discussion relating to co-production, and is essential if the sense of safety and permission is to be felt within a group context. Vassos et al. (2018) note that the motivation to build in group based supervision can often be driven by resource issues such as time, space, and supervisor availability. This is a shaky foundation as it may lead to a need to focus on the immediate practical elements of casework rather than create the opportunity for deeper reflection. They also note that groups are experienced differently by individuals and may be beneficial for some but inhibitive for others. The issues of power and the supervisee/supervisor relationship may remain in group-based supervision which prompts consideration of a peer-led approach whereby there is not a "senior" facilitator but where the group is operated and developed among peers (Staempfli and Fairlough 2018). This would most likely complement individual supervision opportunities to safeguard the connections between supervision and organizational aims and accountability.

Emotionally sensitive approaches to supervision

This chapter has made the case that emotionally sensitive supervision requires a willingness from the supervisor and supervisee to engage in complex and uncertain discussions about practice and be able to commit themselves to a degree of emotional exposure. This requires motivation and security within the relationship to achieve this in order to allow the containment necessary to seek greater clarity about the dynamics of one's practice (Ruch et al. 2018). In this section we will cover some specific approaches which may stimulate emotionally sensitive supervision and take as a starting point that all the conditions and considerations posited elsewhere in this chapter have been heeded.

The place of reflection in social work is well established and the vast literature on the subject should be seen as a close companion to discussions about supervision. Turney and Ruch (2016) propose a cognitive interviewing approach for supervision which may provide a useful model for emotionally sensitive and exploratory supervision. This approach has its roots in forensic interviewing within the criminal justice system (Geiselman et al. 1986) and is well tested and evaluated in this arena (Stein and Memon 2006), the purpose being to seek as high a degree of accuracy and detail in witness accounts (Turney and Ruch 2016). The approach has four key aspects:

- Take oneself mentally back to the time, place, and environment of the event.
- Report all aspects of the event regardless of what seems important including thoughts, feelings and reactions.
- Re-order the events in different configurations.
- Consider a range of perspectives in terms of how the event may be viewed.

When we apply this to a social work supervision context, it can help to create an environment which is inclusive of all the information present rather than privileging certain types of information over others, and explicitly challenges the fragmentation of knowledge whereby emotions are seen as separate from concrete evidence (Munro 2011). The key in this approach is that it accepts the messiness of practice from the outset and does not rush towards clarity and conclusions. This of course requires the time and resources needed for emotionally sensitive supervision to be effective. The innovative re-ordering of events can shine light on otherwise hidden dynamics and relationships, and if conducted within a safe and trusting relationship, can also allow for the containment necessary to engage with difficult and painful aspects of practice. These new insights can help social workers understand the meanings and labels they attach to events and the reasons why they may do so. This arcs back to the start of this chapter in terms of the notion that emotions help us to understand and prioritize events but underline that these connections are not always immediately identifiable or retrievable. This application of cognitive interviewing to a supervisory context is cogent for emotionally sensitive supervision, and Turney and Ruch (2016) helpfully renamed it the Cognitive and Affective Supervisory Approach (CASA). Lombardo et al. (2009, p. 212) and note that this type of approach requires a "strong learning alliance" to exist within the supervisory relationship which is set up to accept and withstand confrontation and withdrawal during difficult discussions and be committed to collectively reflecting on these issues and repairing the relationship as required.

In a group supervision context, there are a range of models available which range from roundtable group discussion, semi-didactic professional development sessions, and peer led practice issue analysis. Staempfli and Fairtlough (2018) propose the "Intervision" approach to group supervision. They propose the method as being peer led without a formal supervisor, but equally the method would lend itself to a supervisor led approach accepting the impact that it may/may not have on trust and openness. Social workers get the opportunity to present practice issues to their peers to seek their support and insight, to clarify thinking, and enhance practice. Fook (2016) suggest that a peer based reflective discussion can build team cooperation as well as reducing stress and burnout. The Intervision model is based on the following key aspects:

- Three key roles – Facilitator, reflective team, and presenter. These roles rotate in order to benefit all members and to create a shared ownership of the process.
- The presenter shares a practice challenge/issue which is then clarified by questions from the reflective team. Through this process the presenter refines the key question.

- The reflective team discuss the issue (not directly involving the presenter) and produce hypotheses,
- A wider discussion may take place to complete the process.

The parallels between this approach and the preceding discussion in this chapter are manifest. The need for an explicit learning culture is at the root of the Intervision model. Additionally, the permissions and trust required to explore complex feelings and uncertainties are essential. The safety within one's peer group should not be taken as inevitable and may for some be even more difficult to attain in the dynamics of a group. The need for this environment to be self-reflective is important too, as group-based analysis needs to avoid becoming adversarial. The key benefit here, and essentially at the heart of emotionally sensitive supervision, is the opportunity for uncovering new understandings of one's self and complex practice situations.

The preceding examples reflect formal and semi-formal modes of supervision. There is a further forum which may prove to be helpful for social workers to explore the emotional content of practice, and that is purely informal discussion with peers. Ingram (2013) found that when asked where social workers felt most able to explore emotions, they identified informal support as being the most useful. The key aspects of such support included:

- Availability – support and advice could be available "on the spot" from colleagues.
- Shared experiences – the knowledge that colleagues had experienced similar situations was reassuring.
- Un-minuted – the lack of formality allowed issues to be explored without pressure to "get it right."
- Preparation – informal discussions could act as a pre-supervision exploration of issues.

Ingram (2015)

The peer-led modes of supervision are close to this as are some of the characteristics and benefits, but the informal support suggested here is essentially unstructured and opportunity-led interactions with colleagues. This is clearly best suited to complement more formal and structured support and supervision but reflects a wider learning culture and network. A key challenge of agencies and organizations is to consider if/how they can provide the physical spaces that encourage such interactions and/or the time with which to be able to engage effectively with colleagues.

Towards emotionally sensitive supervision

This chapter has established the role that emotions have in helping humans make sense of the world and in turn make decisions and judgments about behavior, relationships, and situations. This is equally true in a social work context, and the centrality of relationships and professional judgments makes emotional knowledge of supreme importance when thinking about the practice of social workers and the enhancement of outcomes for service users. The following points represent a checklist of conditions and considerations for any form of emotionally sensitive supervision arrangement:

- Trust
- Confidentiality
- Space for containment and uncertainty
- Explicit agreement and clarity about the nature and focus of supervision

- Ring-fenced and appropriate levels of time and resource allocated to it
- An acceptance and awareness of the positive contribution emotional knowledge can give to practice
- Value placed on the intersection between personal and professional identities

These conditions are not surprising but are not insignificant when placed within the context of competing pressures such as managerialism, limited resources, risk aversion, and worker's anxieties. Additionally, these conditions are rarely achieved permanently, and require constant attention and evaluation. However, they do represent important foundation stones for emotionally sensitive supervision and the establishment of learning cultures as well as raising the profile and contribution of emotions in social work practice.

References

Beddoe, L., 2010. Surveillance or reflection: professional supervision in a risk society. *British Journal of Social Work*, 40, 1279–1296.

Clore, G., and Ortony, A., 2000. Cognition in emotion: always sometimes or never? *In*: Lane, R., and Nadel, L., eds. *Cognitive neuroscience of emotions*. New York: Oxford University Press, 24–61.

Cornish, S., 2011. Negative capability and social work: insights from Keats, Bion and business. *Journal of Social Work Practice*, 25, 135–148.

Fook, J., 2016. *Social work: a critical approach to practice*. London: SAGE.

Geiselman, R., Fisher, R., MacKinnon, D., and Holland, H., 1986. Enhancement of eyewitness memory with the cognitive interview. *American Journal of Psychology*, 99, 385–401.

Hafford-Letchfield, T., 2009. *Management and organisations in social work*. Exeter: Learning Matters.

Hair, H., 2013. The purpose and duration of supervision, and the training and discipline of supervisors: what social workers say they need to provide effective services. *British Journal of Social Work*, 43, 1562–1588.

Harding, T., and Beresford, P., 1995. *The standards we expect: what service users and carers want from social workers*. London: National Institute of Social Work.

Hennessey, R., 2011. *Relationship skills in social work*. London: SAGE.

Hochschild, A.R., 1983. *The managed heart: commercialization of human feeling*. Los Angeles: University of California Press.

Howe, D., 2008. *The emotionally intelligent social worker*. Basingstoke: Palgrave.

Howe, D., 2013. *Empathy: what it is and why it matters*. Basingstoke: Palgrave.

Ingram, R., 2013. Exploring emotions within formal and informal forums: messages from social work practitioners. *British Journal of Social Work*, 45, 896–913.

Ingram, R., 2015. *Understanding emotions in social work: theory, practice and reflection*. Maidenhead: Open University Press.

Ingram, R., Fenton, J., Hodson, A., and Jindal-Snape, D., 2014. *Reflective social work practice*. Basingstoke: Palgrave.

International Federation of Social Workers (IFSW), 2014. Global definition of social work. Available from: https://www.ifsw.org/what-is-social-work/global-definition-of-social-work/ [Accessed 5 March 2021].

Jindal-Snape, D., and Ingram, R., 2013. Understanding and supporting triple transitions of international doctoral students: ELT and SuReCom models. *Journal of Perspectives in Applied Academic Practice*, 1, 17–24.

Kadushin, A., 1985. *Supervision in social work*. 2nd ed. New York: University of Columbia Press.

Kadushin, G., Berger, C., Gilbert, C., and St. Aubin, M.D., 2009. Models and Methods in Hospital Social Work Supervision. *The Clinical Supervisor*, 28 (2), 180–199. doi:10.1080/07325220903324660

Kelly, S., and Green, T., 2019. Seeing more, better sight: using an inter-professional model of supervision to support reflective child protection practice within the health setting. *British Journal of Social Work*. doi: 10.1093/bjsw/bcz030

Lambley, S., 2019. A semi-open supervision systems model for evaluating staff supervision in adult-care organizational settings: the research findings. *British Journal of Social Work*, 49, 391–410.

Lane, R., Nadel, L., Allen, J., and Kaszniak, A., 2000. The study of emotions from the perspective of cognitive neuroscience. *In*: R. Lane, and L. Nadel, eds. *Cognitive neuroscience of emotions*. New York: Oxford University Press, 3–11.

Lazarus, R., and Lazarus, B., 1994. *Passion and reason.* New York: Oxford University Press.

Lombardo, C., Milne, D., and Proctor, R., 2009. Getting to the heart of clinical supervision: a theoretical review of the role of emotions in professional development. *Behavioural and Cognitive Psychotherapy*, 37, 207–219.

McNeil, F., Batchelor, S., Burnett, R., and Knox, J., 2005. *Reducing reoffending - key practice skills.* Scottish Executive. Available from: https://www2.gov.scot/Publications/2005/04/21132007/20129 [Accessed 4 December 2019].

Mann, S., 2004. People work: emotion management, stress and coping. *British Journal of Guidance & Counselling*, 32 (2), 205–221.

Mantell, A., and Scragg, T., 2019. *Reflective practice in social work.* Basingstoke: Palgrave.

Munro, E.R., 2011. *Munro review of child protection: a child centred system.* Crown Copyright. Available from: https://assets.publishing.service.gov.uk/government/uploads/system/uploads/attachment_data/file/175391/Munro-Review.pdf [Accessed 4 December 2019].

O'Donoghue, K., 2015. Issues and challenges facing social work supervision in the 20th century. *China Journal of Social Work*, 8 (2), 136–149.

O'Donoghue, K., and Tsui, M., 2011. Towards a professional supervision culture: the development of social work supervision in Aotearoa New Zealand. *International Social Work*, 55, 5–28.

Ruch, G., Turney, D., and Ward, A., 2018. *Relationship based social work: getting to the heart of practice.* 2nd ed. London: Jessica Kingsley.

Smith, M., 2000. Supervision of fear in social work: a re-evaluation of reassurance. *Journal of Social Work Practice*, 14, 17–26.

Staempfli, A., and Fairtlough, A., 2018. Intervision and professional development: and exploration of a peer-group reflection method in social work education. *British Journal of Social Work.* doi:10.1093/bjsw/bcy096

Stein, L., and Memon, A., 2006. Testing the efficacy of the cognitive interview in a developing country. *Applied Cognitive Psychology*, 20, 597–605.

Turner, J., and Stets, J., 2005. *The sociology of emotions.* New York: Cambridge University Press.

Turney, D., and Ruch, G., 2016. Thinking about thinking after munro: the contribution of cognitive interviewing to child-care social work supervision and decision-making practices. *British Journal of Social Work*, 46, 669–685.

Vassos, S., Harms, L., and Rose, D., 2018. The value of mixing it up: student experiences of a multi-modal approach to supervision on placement. *British Journal of Social Work.* doi:10.1093/bjsw/bcy105

38

THINKING ALOUD IN SUPERVISION

An interactional process for critical reflection

Matt Rankine

Introduction

Central to positive and ethical social work practice are positive and pro-active relationships with others including colleagues, professionals, service users, and managers. However, being relational with their practice presents as a challenge for social workers in the current managerial environment. Social service organizations such as child welfare operate in an environment of efficiency and so outcomes where relationships and engagement with others are often not prioritized (Beddoe 2010). To comprehend this complex environment, social workers require the necessary space in order to learn about themselves, relationships in practice, and understand wider socio-cultural and socio-political implications impacting on their work.

Supervision is a starting place to promote and forge positive and professional relationships in social work (Mor Barak et al. 2009; Carpenter et al. 2012). The supervisor's skill set is vital in facilitating a climate of safe exploration for the supervisee's learning and development (Bond and Holland 2010). Davys and Beddoe (2010) discuss the significance of isomorphism (similarity between one system that influences another) in relation to strengths-based supervision. Isomorphism is significant to social workers in that ethical, critical practice, values, and social justice need to be replicated within every interaction that takes place. Supervision that is relational, promotes critical reflection, and professional development will foster the growth of these practices for practitioners in other social work relationships (Weld 2012). In doing so, social work will provide greater support to service users and advocacy for communities.

In this chapter, thinking aloud is argued as an effective process for developing critical reflection and engagement between social work researchers, supervisors, and supervisees. Thinking aloud allows participants to verbally articulate their thought processes by way of examining transcribed material for deeper reflection (Priede and Farrall 2011). The use of thinking aloud between the researcher, supervisor, and supervisee is illustrated by examples from two separate qualitative studies conducted with social workers operating in community-based child welfare (Rankine 2019) and the emerging results of a study within statutory child welfare in Aotearoa New Zealand. Thinking aloud provides a process of placing the supervision session under the microscope by analyzing the conversation, the supervisory relationship, and providing a rare opportunity to critically consider further strategies for change in practice.

Critical reflection in supervisory relationships

The term critical reflection involves an exploration of power within society that impacts on individuals and their relationships with others (Brookfield 2009). This investigation includes a social critique of social work practice which can change the interpretations that are held by practitioners about the world (Knapp 2010). The examination of disadvantage and oppression of people is particularly relevant to social workers so that alternative actions and strategies in practice can be developed (Fook and Gardner 2007; Beddoe and Egan 2009). Irrespective of a social worker's role (whether statutory or community-based), practitioners have an ethical responsibility that recognizes the importance of upholding social justice and human rights in their work with others and an analysis of structural and dominant political agendas (International Federation of Social Workers 2019).

Fook and Gardner (2007) have identified a two-staged process involving the deconstruction and reconstruction of meaning (which includes the wider cultural and social context) in order to unsettle existing assumptions and develop new insights. Deconstructing, stage one of Fook and Gardner's (2007) process, involves the unpacking of values, thoughts, attitudes, and theoretical factors that influence and permeate a social worker's practice. Reconstructing, in stage two, involves reconfiguring these thoughts and discourses with changes in awareness and action planning. This two-staged process has been applied in research involving professionals in different health and social care contexts (Fook and Gardner 2013). Being able to critically reflect enables the social worker to maintain fresh perspectives when working alongside colleagues, managers, professionals, and service users, and examine contemporary issues influencing society (Gray and Webb 2013). Critical reflection is a constant consideration for social workers in practice, and supervision provides the opportunity and place where critical reflection can happen.

Supervision needs to be strategic and interactional so that practice ethics and working alongside others remains central to social work. Within current managerial practices in organizations, there is a risk that supervision and the relationship between supervisor and the supervisee only canvass areas related to procedure and caseload instruction (Rankine 2018). This organizational environment compromises the ability of social work supervision to recognize the complexity and diversity of the work and the significance of critical reflection (Beddoe 2015; O'Donoghue 2015). Therefore, two underpinning epistemological influences are important to consider in the practice and research of social work supervision: social constructionism and critical realism. Social constructionism (the view that knowledge is created by people and their engagement with others) allows for an appreciation of diverse perspectives (for example, age, gender, and ethnicity) (Crotty 1998). This stance supports supervisees and supervisors to explore and understand different perspectives in their work together (Hair and O'Donoghue 2009; Hernández and McDowell 2010). Critical realism provides an understanding both that society is driven by injustices and supports strategic thinking (Baines 2017). The influence of social constructionism and critical realism challenge supervisees and supervisors to critique their existing practice and develop alternative action plans. Crucial for supervision is the exploration of these perspectives and how the wider context influences social justice in practice (Noble et al. 2016). In order to create ongoing learning, supervision must provide a "dialogical container…in the space between the supervisor and supervisee" (Hawkins and Shohet 2012, p. 238). The supervisor has a fundamental role in facilitating critical conversations related to social justice in the session (Hair 2015), and the supervisee needs to be open to considering the impact of the wider environment on their work.

As a way forward to promote better professional relationships, critical reflection in social work supervision requires ongoing analysis in research and opportunity within practice so it remains relevant to the contextual demands and realities of social work operating in a managerial environment (Beddoe 2015; Fook et al. 2015). Recently, critical reflection has also been utilized in research as a co-constructed endeavor between participants and researchers to highlight the significance of professional experiences towards transforming practice (Fook 2011; Fook and Gardner 2013; Rankine 2017). Social work supervision provides the ideal professional space to explore alternatives to practice and enhance creativity. However, very rarely is the supervision session examined closely for the discourses being discussed and highlighting the skills that practitioners utilize. Thinking aloud provides a process that identifies relational ways of working and enhances critical thinking about practice.

Thinking aloud

The antecedents of thinking aloud originally come from cognitive interviews where the aim was to understand cognitive processes of participants when answering survey questions in research (Beatty and Willis 2007). The questioning of specific participant responses was the strategy employed by the researcher to facilitate this understanding and maintain an attention to detail through the use of open-ended questions (Priede and Farrall 2011). As a cognitive interviewing technique, thinking aloud provides an opportunity for deeper reflection by participants and rich data to be collected by the researcher.

From studies undertaken in social work supervision, thinking aloud has provided an exceptional opportunity to critically review practice and the significance of the interactive process (Cooper 1999; Maidment and Cooper 2002; Rankine and Thompson 2015; Davys et al. 2019; Rankine 2019). In relation to their work, participants have verbally articulated their thoughts by way of examining transcribed material from their recorded supervision session. The researcher has assisted this thinking through the facilitation of a follow-up session and encouraging participants to track their responses and thoughts at the time through open questions. Thinking aloud was an important process for social work supervisors to identify the number of pedagogical techniques they used when supervising students on placement (Cooper 1999). Maidment and Cooper (2002) used thinking aloud to examine how areas of oppression and diversity were discussed between supervisors and students in their supervision sessions. In their study, the supervision session was audio recorded and transcribed. The thinking aloud process with the supervisor afterwards involved the analysis of the transcripts and assisted with a deeper understanding of techniques used to explore diversity in their session (Maidment and Cooper 2002). Thinking aloud has also been used as a process to critically reflect on the content of researchers' own audio-recorded supervision sessions and support their future professional development and relational practice. Rankine and Thompson (2015) identified the shared process that they used in their own supervision together, as well as the unearthing of shared meanings from the content of each recorded session. An interprofessional learning community developed by Davys et al. (2019) used thinking aloud to develop a "koru" model (an unfurling fern frond) which assisted in the promotion of critical reflection, learning, professional integrity, and competence within their supervision as supervisors. In this chapter, thinking aloud is described as a process between the researcher and social work practitioners to assist critical reflection within supervision. This process supports a positive and pro-active interactional engagement within the supervisory relationship.

Thinking aloud in statutory and community-based social work supervision: The case studies

A thinking aloud process was used within two separate studies including supervisor-supervisee dyads. One study involved eight dyads from different community-based child welfare services in Auckland, New Zealand (Rankine 2019). The other current study included statutory child welfare social workers from a small, semi-rural province in New Zealand where six dyads participated. As a significant field of practice in social work, child welfare promotes the well-being of a vulnerable population, provides essential services in diverse communities, and is dominated by governmental and organizational agendas. The purpose of using thinking aloud in these studies was to support a process of critical reflection and deepen analysis of the session by supervisors and supervisees. Appropriate human ethics was sought and approved for both studies from the University of Auckland, and participant names were changed or removed to protect anonymity.

The data were gathered from supervisor and supervisee participants from two audio-recorded and transcribed sessions: the supervision session between the supervisee and supervisor, and a follow-up thinking aloud session approximately a month later with the researcher. This two-staged technique was to provide the deconstruction of practice with the recorded session and reconstruction with new ways of working associated with Fook and Gardner's critical reflection model (2007). Arrangements were made with participants to audio record a supervision session, and the material was transcribed. Each participant received a copy of the transcript when available and were encouraged to read through and make notes related to their reflections. Prior to the second meeting, the researcher reviewed the transcript and completed an initial content analysis of the session. In order to aid facilitation of the follow-up thinking aloud session, the content was grouped into themes. The thinking aloud session was facilitated by the researcher and it too, was audio recorded. This recording was also transcribed and participants received a copy of this material.

The collaborative process of thinking aloud provided a space for the supervisor and supervisee to critically reflect on relationships and wider variables influencing their practice. Thinking aloud provided the opportunity for both the supervisor and supervisee to go deeper with their critical thinking in supervision and consider a number of variables related to their practice discussions. The researcher guided the process through the use of a range of facilitative skills such as open questioning, paraphrasing, and feedback to encourage reflection. As a result, the researcher was very much involved within the engagement of critical reflection with the participants. Two examples of thinking aloud are illustrated below. Examples of the thinking aloud process in practice from both of the studies are presented to illustrate the co-constructed interaction between supervisor, supervisee, and the researcher in promoting critical reflection. The perspectives of supervisors and supervisees are also analyzed regarding their partnership and experiences of thinking aloud.

The thinking aloud interactions

The first example of thinking aloud involves Penny (supervisor) and Nathan (supervisee) who are statutory child protection social workers. From the recorded transcript of the supervision session, Nathan is struggling to understand the decision making of the parents in a case where they are potentially putting their child at risk. Penny has attempted to engage Nathan in critically considering the wider factors influencing their choices. The researcher utilizes the recorded transcript to facilitate critical thinking of the interaction that enables Penny and Nathan to explore alternative perspectives:

Nathan: We operate in three spheres... personal and professional and the sphere that overlaps ... Is it my professional feelings that are being agitated or is it personal feelings of frustration that are being drawn out? Sitting here ... [it] is dawning on me and [critical reflection] is something I could apply going forward because that is important to the decisions that we make.

Researcher: [refers to the transcript] I'm just picking up some of the conversation and the language. So Nathan you were saying that if you had a child removed from you "I would be knocking the wall down trying to get my child back".

Nathan: That is the personal sphere coming forward ... I project myself into the shoes of the child at that point and I would expect that parents ... step up and do what they need to do to provide. Professionally I guess it disappoints me that people who are capable of achieving simple tasks don't.

Researcher: [referring to the transcript] You asked a question here Penny.

Penny: So that particular question is what does Nathan think the block for the parent is like ... what is going on for them?

Nathan: When I saw the mother that day she looked like she had been on something. I guess evidence shows it is not so easy for people to turn the page quickly as we would like them to.

Researcher: If you were at that moment again Penny in supervision what might you say differently?

Penny: What does Nathan think sits behind what appears to be this concrete behaviour by these parents that they are presenting in this way?...What is feeding into those decisions they are making?

Researcher: [Nathan] from a lens of a professional social worker, how would a question like that have been interpreted by you at that point?

Nathan: It probably would have changed the thinking I had at the time.

Penny: Put a different lens on it.

Researcher: What would you have arrived at?

Nathan: Talk to the parents, they are in a situation where [the] resources available to them are quite limited.

Penny: I wanted Nathan to see past their behaviour, I wanted him to see... what is in their background [and] it is everything the whole story that they bring to that current picture is what we need to [understand].

Researcher: If you were to ask that one question how might you ask that?

Penny: If you were in their shoes what do you think would be going on for you?

Nathan: A long history of emotional trauma, there would be obviously violence: all those things would all impact the way they behave today...So that is something that needs to be consistent in the future considering how the story behind the actions tie into historical stuff.

Jessica provides external supervision to Grace (a social worker in a community child welfare service). The issue discussed from the session involves the navigation of balancing procedures and ethics concerning a complex child protection issue as well as the responsibility to maintain relationships with family members and different agencies. The recorded transcript provided the researcher the space to openly enquire about the experience and the opportunities for critical reflection:

Researcher: You're talking Grace, [referring to transcript] about ... [discussing with] the caregivers first about the concerns and the grey areas... Is that something that you felt attention was needed [and had] potential for that relationship to be undermined?

Grace: Absolutely ... making a report to [child protection agency] is so loaded for people that could put up a wall... That's why I wanted to speak first to the parent to let them know... my responsibilities to the organisation but to just affirm that that doesn't mean that we stop anything that we are doing.

Researcher: What thoughts [did] you have Jessica about this point?

Jessica: I thought it was brave to go and have that conversation and it's really rewarding when... the family come on board and they understand what you've got to do, why you've got to do it and that it's all about the children – you learn from that.

Grace: Yeah... I do come back to relationship being the very foundation of the work... There was a moral kind of feeling as well.

Jessica: [referring to transcript] You say if the children are going home that night they wouldn't be safe... I had the sense that it wasn't just a mandatory reporting kind of situation; it was like...

Grace: <u>How</u> do we address this?

Jessica: Yeah, and the relationship that you've established with the grandmother is why you were able to have a good outcome.

Researcher: You touched on Jessica [in the transcript], about practice standards, personal qualities... why [did] you mention that?

Jessica: When you're asking yourself "Am I doing the right thing?" you've got your practice that you know but if you suddenly feel that you don't know then you go to things like your organisational policy and if that doesn't give you the answers then you go to your wider social work ethics... So it's about stepping back.

Researcher: What were your feelings Grace?

Grace: I felt it'd given me the opportunity to put the whole thing in perspective, seen myself as a person in the middle of something complex and with many interactions. And that I did not have to hold it all... and is not all about my responsibility.

Researcher: How do you think you would've managed this situation had you not had that space for [critical reflection] in supervision?

Grace: I think I would've just kept [the experience] right up here, close, and taken it into the next interaction with [child protection agency] or with those children... whereas the next interaction [could be] a fresh page... things were different now [and]... how I can do [the situation] differently. There [were] a lot of different things it affected.

The supervisor and supervisee perspectives

The range of perspectives from the supervisors and supervisees were analyzed regarding their thinking aloud experiences. Significant themes such as culture, language, skills, navigating professional relationships, and commitment to professional practice were highlighted as central in the interaction. Feedback related to the presence of the researcher as part of the co-constructed space was also viewed as positive towards achieving critical reflection of practice. Finally, the thinking aloud process was evaluated relative to how it could be developed in future supervision sessions.

Ohaki and Rangi (a Māori supervisor-supervisee dyad) provided an opportunity within the study to identify an Indigenous perspective in utilizing a thinking aloud process. The significance of their culture and language was a key reflection in the supervisory relationship:

It's really hard to find a Māori supervisor... [thinking aloud] was a surprise for me because... it really affirms for me that there is a place for Māori doing supervision together... For me that's about safety... I have a Pākehā [European] supervisor and... it's a very different feel with you because a lot of stuff gets unsaid.

(Ohaki)

I really feel a sense of being heard. I've been affirmed in what I do, a sense of enlightenment that I've talked about it, I feel I've been supported… I come in with cement boots and I go out with wings! … It's the sense of being able to connect [widely] with my ahua [character], my wairua [spirit]. Ohaki has that sense … we tackled some tough issues that were really important to keep me functioning in all areas of what I'm doing.

(Rangi)

To think aloud about the supervision session and evaluate the supervisory experience provided an exceptional opportunity for busy supervisors. Yvonne explained that, within supervision sessions, "you're kind of in the middle of it … and don't have that [thinking aloud] perspective coming from the outside." Jessica found that thinking aloud had "given me an overview, so when I read [the transcript] I can see how the [session] moved through that [reflective] cycle." For supervisors, thinking aloud enabled them to review the skills that they were using and ensure that they remain focused on creating a space for critical reflection for the supervisee rather than their own anxieties and assumptions.

[Thinking aloud] is really good and has allowed me to … go back and [see] how could I have done it differently… It gives me confidence that [supervision] is not a disaster, but I have [also] picked up things [that] I didn't realise I did. [Thinking aloud has helped] bring forward some of my thinking rather than trying to get people to a point where I'm at because I might not be right.

(Abraham)

For supervisees, thinking aloud affirmed the supervisor's pivotal position in facilitating critical reflection so that social work practice can be developed:

I'm really fortunate that I have a supervisor [who] really does understand the organisation and my thinking style … Because Debbie has a really good innate understanding and the questions she asks always make me think more.

(Jane)

Supervisees were able to identify more deeply with their learning from the supervision session through the process of recording, the written transcript, and then by thinking aloud about the session. Susan expressed this from the transcript:

It's really advantageous to be able to see it written down … this shows how important [supervision] is to my work, my practice, my personal and my professional development and [I am getting the things] that I wanted out of supervision.

(Susan)

Other supervisees were able to track their discussions in supervision when navigating complex professional relationships and come to a deeper realization of their situation. For Alice, thinking aloud assisted her with acknowledging her frustration directed towards another professional and to "figure out a different way" to address the existing power dynamic. Tracey realized from the thinking aloud process that, within her own supervision, "being more open where we come from [and] be[ing] more willing to explore … and realis[ing] … different perspectives" would assist her in acknowledging specific roles and accountabilities.

In addition, thinking aloud enabled the supervisee to understand the value in being prepared to use supervision to critically explore their practice and the "two-way" commitment required for this relationship.

> *I have appreciated [thinking aloud] because it has made me think more about the content of supervision and how I can use supervision in the future. We don't get this opportunity to actually unpack what is going on, how it is formulated and what the supervisor is thinking in comparison to what I was thinking [often enough].*
>
> *(Sue)*

The researcher's presence in facilitating the thinking aloud process for the supervisory dyads was also viewed favorably in creating a positive interactional experience and assisting with new learning that the supervisee and supervisor achieved together:

> *I do see the benefit in somebody looking into what is within that supervisor/supervisee relation-ship …and notice what was generated … [it enriches] the relationship.*
>
> *(Grace)*

> *The process is really good … to actually have someone from the outside, from a different perspec-tive to ask questions … and afterwards get the outcome.*
>
> *(Yvonne)*

Thinking aloud provided a learning tool within supervision for the supervisory dyads. A key strength identified from the studies was how this interaction had the potential to be replicated in the future.

For Penny and Nathan, the researcher's facilitation of the thinking aloud session brought pro-found learning in how supervision could be developed so further critical thinking and informed decision making could be achieved with families:

Penny: We can take aspects of what [the researcher] has done here today, recreate this process from the research [and] we record everything. We can do whatever we like with our supervision sessions … because [thinking aloud] helps Nathan to do his "reflection on reflection."
Researcher: Nathan by "reflecting on the reflection" what happens to your practice do you think?
Nathan: It ultimately improves my practice because … that process of reflecting on what I talked about is incorporated into the assessments I make [and decisions] which I would like to think is better for all parties [and the families] involved.

For supervisees, the transformative potential to think aloud and be supported in the supervisory relationship to develop and grow was enormous. Susan realized that thinking aloud was "good for everyone to be able to reflect and learn and how you can do better." Jackie also agreed that think-ing aloud needed to "happen more frequently" and as "another resource for professional learning."

The supervisors believed that thinking aloud provided a learning opportunity to review skills and interventions and needed further development in sessions:

> *It needs to be used more regularly as a learning tool and an opportunity to keep refreshed … just an extra pair of eyes on the value added [to] supervision and difference it is making.*
>
> *(Debbie)*

Evaluation of the supervision process is an area seldom considered and actioned by either party. Jessica, an experienced supervisor, felt that evaluating her interactions with supervisees was important and that thinking aloud provided a strategy to do so on an ongoing basis:

> *It's making me think about how we do supervision reviews, whether I should [periodically] be recording sessions and going back over them … I've been on a bit of a journey recently about how we evaluate supervision so it's contributed to that a lot.*

> *(Jessica)*

Thinking aloud as an interactional process

The importance of positive professional relationships in social work can be forgotten within the dominant managerial landscape of practice. The social work profession has become deeply affected by globalization, the need to be cost-effective, and manage ongoing risk and uncertainty in practice (Beddoe 2010; Gray and Webb 2013). Such a preoccupation by social workers on meeting targets and being overloaded with complex casework has had an impact on developing and maintaining relationships with others—essential to ethical, social work practice. Supervision holds the key as an essential relationship for the social worker to develop critical reflection and the place to harness the skills necessary to build meaningful interactions with others (Davys and Beddoe 2010; Noble et al. 2016). It is anticipated that this level of criticality and engagement achieved can then be replicated in other professional relationships.

Developing a critical perspective in social work is imperative for the survival of the profession (Gray and Webb 2013). The complex effect of the wider environment on social workers, service users, and organizations needs to be more fully understood so that social-justice-informed strategies can be implemented (Hair 2015). Within the context of supervision, supervisors and supervisees need to apply critical analysis in their discussions in order for supervision to be a site of discovery, replenishment, and transformational thinking.

Within research and practice, a greater understanding is required towards the importance of the supervisory relationship for the practitioner, the skills and interventions used within the session, and the essential contribution supervision has towards working with others and professional practice (Beddoe et al. 2015; O'Donoghue 2015).

Critical reflection is dialogic and interactive in analyzing diverse perspectives and promoting change (Fook 2011). As a research approach, critical reflection is still relatively new as a concept in how it is captured within qualitative research by researchers and developed alongside practitioners in different contexts (Fook et al. 2015). The role of the researcher as part of the co-constructed process towards transformational learning and change is pivotal to this interaction (Fook 2011). The researcher brings additional skill and experience into such practice interactions. Previously, Monzó (2013) has described co-construction in research as developing an awareness that subjectivities are always present between researcher and participants. For the researcher, critical reflection provides the platform to critically engage alongside practitioners, draw further meaning from the research experience and for additional knowledge to be created. This process is essential for the future of critical social work. Horsfall and Higgs (2011) describe that:

> Being in relationships, negotiating these relationships, and acknowledging how we and others are or might be feeling, are essential parts of the research process.

> *(p. 53)*

With supervision as the ideal platform for learning, social work researchers and practitioners have the opportunity to develop specific models and learning tools to explore and enhance knowledge and make changes to existing practices. Learning tools, such as thinking aloud, provide practitioners with the assistance to stop from the doing of their practice and place their practice under the microscope for examination and review (Davys et al. 2019), something which can usefully be introduced and taught in various situations to stimulate learning.

Thinking aloud, as used in these two qualitative studies, provided the innovative opportunity to cultivate critical reflection through a collaboration between social work researchers and the interaction between the supervisor and supervisee. Irrespective of the practice context, whether within a statutory or community-based environment, the co-construction between the supervisory dyads and the researcher allowed the space for a deeper appreciation of practice and greater understanding of socio-cultural and socio-political influences on social work and service users and alternative ways to practicing. The roles of the researcher, supervisor, and supervisee contributed equally to the unearthing of an alternative discourse that triggered transformative thinking, solutions, and professional development within the context of supervision. Although an uncommon opportunity within the day-to-day practice of social work supervision, thinking aloud on supervision enables an interactional and dialogical space to open up flexibility across a range of different practice contexts. In addition, there is scope for other professionals such as social work supervisors and managers with experience in critical reflection and different supervision approaches, to facilitate a thinking aloud process. The manager or consultant supervisor can achieve this through open questioning that supports the exploration of current supervision interventions, skills, agenda items and the impact of organizational and wider environmental issues on practice. The process could be adapted as part of a commitment towards ongoing professional development for supervisors and supervisees (every three months for example) that demonstrates critical reflection in supervision.

Conclusion

The opportunity for social workers to critically reflect on their practice is a rare occurrence in many practice environments within the current neoliberal and managerial constraints. Supervision, however, provides an important opportunity and a professional space in social work to develop practice and challenge existing discourses.

Critical reflection promotes diversity, evaluation of existing knowledge, and facilitates change in practice and research. Thinking aloud, as a tool to aid critical reflection, creates the space for the supervisor and supervisee to enhance their learning and promote transformative discourses in their practice. This co-constructed interaction in these studies was further enhanced by the involvement of the researcher to assist critical reflection through a curious and open approach to the dialogue occurring within the supervision session. Critical reflection and the development of learning tools that assist this interaction in supervision need to be fostered in different social work settings to explore the wider context of social work practice, develop relationships, and greater understanding of social justice.

References

Baines, D., 2017. *Doing anti-oppressive practice: social justice social work*. Halifax, NS: Fernwood.

Beatty, P.C., and Willis, G.B., 2007. Research synthesis: the practice of cognitive interviewing. *Public Opinion Quarterly*, 71 (2), 287–311.

Beddoe, L., 2010. Surveillance or reflection: professional supervision in the risk society. *British Journal of Social Work*, 40 (4), 1279–1296. doi:10.1093/bjsw/bcq018.

Beddoe, L., 2015. Supervision and developing the profession: one supervision or many?. *China Journal of Social Work*, 8 (2), 150–163. doi:10.1080/17525098.2015.1039173.

Beddoe, L., and Egan, R., 2009. Social work supervision. *In*: M. Connolly, and L. Harms, eds. *Social work: contexts and practice*. 2nd ed. Victoria, Australia: Oxford University Press, 410–422.

Beddoe, L., Karvinen-Niinikoski, S., Ruch, G., and Tsui, M.S., 2015. Towards an international consensus on a research agenda for social work supervision: report on the first survey of a Delphi study. *British Journal of Social Work*. doi:10.1093/bjsw/bcv110.

Bond, M., and Holland, S., 2010. *Skills of clinical supervision for nurses: a practical guide for supervisees, clinical supervisors and managers*. 2nd ed. Maidenhead, UK: Open University Press.

Brookfield, S., 2009. The concept of critical reflection: promises and contradictions. *European Journal of Social Work*, 12 (3), 293–304. doi:10.1080/13691450902945215.

Carpenter, J., Webb, C., Bostock, L., and Coomber, C., 2012. *Effective supervision in social work and social care: research briefing 43*. London, UK: Social Care Institute for Excellence.

Cooper, L., 1999. Pedagogical approaches to student supervision in social work: practical experiences in professional education. *QUT, Research Monograph*, 3, 87–102.

Crotty, M., 1998. *The foundations of social research: meaning and perspective in the* research process. New South Wales: Allen and Unwin.

Davys, A., and Beddoe, L., 2010. *Best practice in professional supervision: a guide for the helping professions*. London: Jessica Kingsley.

Davys, A., Howard, F., Rankine, M., and Thompson, A., 2019. Supervision under the microscope: critical conversations in a learning community. *Practice*, 31 (5), 359–374. doi:10.1080/09503153.2018.1558196.

Fook, J., 2011. Developing critical reflection as a research method. *In*: J. Higgs, et al., eds. *Creative spaces for qualitative researching: living research*. Vol. 5. Rotterdam, Netherlands: Sense Publishers, 55–64.

Fook, J., Collington, V., Ross, F., Ruch, G., and West, L., 2015. *Researching critical reflection: multidisciplinary perspectives*. London: Routledge.

Fook, J., and Gardner, F., 2007. *Practising critical reflection: a resource handbook*. Maidenhead: Open University Press.

Fook, J., and Gardner, F., eds., 2013. *Critical reflection in context: applications in health and social care*. Oxon, UK: Routledge.

Gray, M., and Webb, S., eds., 2013. *The new politics of social work*. Basingstoke: Palgrave Macmillan.

Hair, H., 2015. Supervision conversations about social justice and social work practice. *Journal of Social Work*, 15 (4), 349–370. doi:10.1177/1468017314539082.

Hair, H., and O'Donoghue, K., 2009. Culturally relevant, socially just social work supervision: becoming visible through a social constructionist lens. *Journal of Ethnic and Cultural Diversity in Social Work*, 18 (1–2), 70–88. doi:10.1080/15313200902874979.

Hawkins, P., and Shohet, R., 2012. *Supervision in the helping professions*. 4th ed. Maidenhead: Open University Press.

Hernández, P., and McDowell, T., 2010. Intersectionality, power, and relational safety in context: key concepts in clinical supervision. *Training and Education in Professional Psychology*, 4 (1), 29–35. doi:10.1037/a0017064.

Horsfall, D., and Higgs, J., 2011. Boundary riding and shaping research spaces. *In*: J. Higgs et al., eds. *Creative spaces for qualitative researching: living research*. Rotterdam, The Netherlands: Sense Publishers, 45–54.

International Federation of Social Workers 2019. *Global definition of social work*. Available from: https://www.ifsw.org/global-definition-of-social-work/

Knapp, R., 2010. Collective team learning process models: a conceptual review. *Human Resource Development Review*, 9 (3), 285–299.

Maidment, J., and Cooper, L., 2002. Acknowledgement of client diversity and oppression in social work student supervision. *Social Work Education*, 21 (4), 399–407. doi:10.1080/02615470220150366.

Monzó, L., 2013. Learning to follow: the ethnographer's tales of engagement. *In*: M. Berryman, S. Soohoo and A. Nevin, eds. *Cultural responsive methodologies*. Bingley, UK: Emerald, 371–387.

Mor Barak, M.E., et al., 2009. The impact of supervision on worker outcomes: a meta-analysis. *Social Service Review*, 83 (1), 3–32. doi:10.1086/599028.

Noble, C., Gray, M., and Johnston, L., 2016. *Critical supervision for the human services: a social model to promote learning and value-based practice*. London: Jessica Kingsley.

O'Donoghue, K., 2015. Issues and challenges facing social work supervision in the twenty-first century. *China Journal of Social Work*, 8 (2), 136–149. doi:10.1080/17525098.2015.1039172.

Priede, C., and Farrall, S., 2011. Comparing results from different styles of cognitive interviewing: "verbal probing" vs. "thinking aloud". *International Journal of Social Research Methodology*, 14 (4), 271–287. doi:10.1080/13645579.2010.523187.

Rankine, M., 2017. Making the connections: a practice model for reflective supervision. *Aotearoa New Zealand Social Work*, 29 (3), 66–78.

Rankine, M., 2018. How critical are we? revitalising critical reflection in supervision. *Advances in Social Work & Welfare Education*, 20 (2), 31–46.

Rankine, M., 2019. The "thinking aloud" process: a way forward in social work supervision. *Reflective Practice*, 20 (1), 97–110. doi:10.1080/14623943.2018.1564651.

Rankine, M., and Thompson, A., 2015. "Swimming to shore": co-constructing supervision with a thinking-aloud process. *Reflective Practice*, 16 (4), 508–521. doi:10.1080/14623943.2015.1064377.

Weld, N., 2012. *A practical guide to transformative supervision for the helping professions*. London: Jessica Kingsley.

39

LIVE PRACTICE OBSERVATION AND FEEDBACK

Allyson Davys and Liz Beddoe

To open one's practice to the observation of a supervisor (or a colleague) can be both an exhilarating and daunting experience, but the feedback gained in the process can lead to valuable, deep learning. The Negotiated Collaborative Model for live observation of practice (Davys and Beddoe 2015a, b) provides a clear, structured process for observing practice where the parameters of the observation, and the feedback process, are designed and agreed by both the observed and the observer. Whether live observation of practice is mandated by the organization or social work profession, or whether it is chosen by the practitioner, when live observation is negotiated the opportunity is presented for social workers to engage in, take ownership of, and learn from a focused reflective discussion about aspects of their practice. This chapter presents and details the four steps of the Negotiated Collaborative Model for live observation when it is conducted within a supervision relationship. The giving and receiving of feedback are considered and guidelines are provided to assist this to be a constructive experience for both supervisor and supervisee.

Observation of practice is a common experience for students on fieldwork placements as they develop their practice and progress through their social work qualification. These observations, which are generally prescribed by education providers, usually have an evaluative agenda where a predetermined focus for the feedback will have been designed to match educational targets and learning outcomes. Such experiences are well described and discussed in the student fieldwork and education literature (Beddoe et al. 2011; Kourgiantakis et al. 2018). This chapter will consider the opportunities which are available for the qualified (and often very experienced) social worker to open their practice to observation and feedback. Whilst live observation and feedback can be negotiated (and can be very effective) between peers and colleagues, it is the observation of a social worker's work, by that social worker's supervisor, which is considered here. An overview of the issues which accompany live observation in supervision is followed by a description of the Negotiated Collaborative Model as a framework for organizing and conducting that observation.

Live observation in practice

Live observation has been defined by the authors as "when a practitioner works with a service user in the presence of another practitioner or supervisor" (Davys and Beddoe 2015a, p. 4) and can also encompass situations where the observer accesses digital audio, or visual, recordings of the practitioner's session. Live observation is frequently confused both in the literature and in general discussion, with live supervision (Davys and Beddoe 2015a), and it is useful to distinguish between these similar but distinct processes. Possibly the clearest difference is the manner in which the observer participates in each of these events. In live observation the observer's role is passive and apart from general introductions, the observer does not interact within the session. When the session has ended and the service user has departed, the observer debriefs with the practitioner and provides feedback (Sexton et al. 2013). In live supervision the observer (the supervisor) however takes an active role. Either present in the room with the practitioner, or watching from behind a one-way screen, the supervisor may frequently intervene and influence the session (Bernard and Goodyear 2009; Champ and Kleist 2003).

Calls for the audit of skills and competence of qualified social workers to include empirical evidence from practice (Davys and Beddoe 2015a; Wilkins and Antonopoulou 2017) have led some organizations to also require such evidence to support annual performance appraisals and practice reviews although this is sparsely reported in the literature. Live observation of practice in these circumstances may be viewed with apprehension and concern by practitioners. Performance and evaluation anxiety can become entangled with past stressful experiences of having their practice observed, and social workers may feel little ownership of the observation process. If the focus and the process of the observation is chosen and negotiated however, even when the observation is a requirement, new opportunities arise and social workers can shape and claim agency of the observation, of the way in which it is conducted and of the sort of feedback offered. Social workers who are comfortable with observation report choosing live observation as a form of professional development to support and hone their professional practice (Davys et al. 2019)

The Negotiated Collaborative Model for live observation (Davys and Beddoe 2015a, b) is a model for observation of practice which was developed from the earlier work of Maidment (2000) and Beddoe et al. (2011). Initially trialed as a model for providing feedback to students on placement, subsequent development has positioned it as a framework for observation of practice at any level of practitioner experience and competence (Davys and Beddoe 2015a, b). The collaborative aspect of the model, which provides for learning to be identified by both the observed and the observer, means that this framework opens up opportunity for in-depth consideration of practice. This can be particularly beneficial to, and valued by, more experienced practitioners and their supervisors where there is an opportunity for mutual reflection and learning. As has been found in other studies (Hendrickson et al. 2002), supervisors can find challenge and helpful insights into their own professional and supervisory skills through the observation of their supervisees.

The intent or purpose which underpins a supervisor's observation of practice can be considered along a continuum of formality (Davys and Beddoe 2015b). At the one end is observation as a process of professional development. Here the social worker initiates the observation and negotiates with his or her supervisor to observe (live or recorded) practice. The observation is premised on a wish by the supervisee for feedback and critique of his or her work. At the other end of the continuum is observation by the supervisor for external audit of practice, competency credentialing, or performance management. Table 39.1 *Contexts for observation in supervision* summarizes this continuum of contexts.

The Negotiated Collaborative model, as presented in this chapter, will consider the first three contexts of Table 39.1. Live observation will be discussed as an aspect of the regular supervision of social workers where the observation has been initiated by either the supervisee or by the supervisor and where it is related to compliance. Observation which is related to performance

Table 39.1 Contexts for observation in supervision

Low formality

Supervisor role	Process	Purpose for supervisor	Benefits for supervisor	Purpose for supervisee	Benefits for supervisee
Context one: Observation initiated by supervisee.	Supervisee identifies areas for feedback. Observation focus, feedback, and debriefing process and roles mutually agreed	To participate in the professional and skill development of the supervisee by providing feedback and discussion	Opportunity to observe and understand the practice competence and developmental needs of a supervisee	To receive feedback and critique on practice in general or on a predetermined aspect of practice	To have an opportunity for targeted feedback which can become part of ongoing supervision discussion and professional development
Context two: Observation initiated by supervisor. May be specified in the supervision contract or in response to concerns or questions about a supervisee's practice in a certain area	Supervisor may identify areas for feedback. Supervisee may be invited to also identify areas for feedback. Observation focus, feedback, and debriefing process and roles mutually agreed	As an agreed process of supervision. To establish a baseline understanding of aspects of a supervisee's practice. To participate in the professional and skill development of the supervisee by providing feedback and discussion	Opportunity to observe and understand the practice competence and developmental needs of a supervisee.	To receive feedback and critique on practice in general or on a predetermined aspect of practice.	To have an opportunity for targeted feedback which can become part of ongoing supervision discussion and professional development
Context three: Observation initiated in compliance with an organizational or professional expectation	Some, or all, criteria may be predetermined. Opportunity for individual criteria to be included. Feedback and debriefing process and roles mutually agreed	To establish a baseline understanding of aspects of a supervisee's practice. Comply with organizational or professional expectations	Opportunity to observe and understand the practice competence and developmental needs of a supervisee.	To receive feedback and critique on practice in general or on a predetermined aspect of practice. Comply with organizational or professional expectations	To have an opportunity for targeted feedback which can become part of ongoing supervision discussion and professional development

High Formality

| Context four: Performance management | Explicit and transparent process. Criteria for observation and feedback explicit (may be non-negotiable) Where possible process and roles mutually agreed and negotiated | Provide evidence of supervisee's practice | With evidence of supervisee's practice the ability to provide targeted supervision, education, professional development and support | To demonstrate level of competence and skills | To have opportunity for focused feedback which can be used to provide a platform for development and focused support |

Adapted from Davys and Beddoe 2015a

concerns will not be specifically addressed. It is noted however, and discussed in more detail elsewhere (Davys and Beddoe 2015a), that when performance is an issue it is essentially the parameters of the observation and the formality or informality of the context which changes, rather than the application of the model.

Regardless of the quality of the supervision relationship and degree of trust on which this relationship is based, it is important to the success of live observation between a supervisor and a supervisee to acknowledge the power inherent in the supervision arrangement. The observer's responsibilities as a supervisor accompany them into the observation space. As has been noted in other studies however, when positional and role power are openly acknowledged and the individual expertise of both the supervisee and supervisor is recognized, "the power relations of supervision can be transformed" (Hair 2014, p. 111). A clear, negotiated supervision contract where power is acknowledged, where accountability is explicit, and where live observation is an agreed event, is therefore an essential platform for successful observation of practice (Davys and Beddoe 2015a).

Observation of practice however also requires the supervisor to have a broad awareness of both their role and of their skill to manage and facilitate the observation. Anxiety and lack of role clarity and have been identified as factors which can compromise the success of an observation of supervisees' practice (Davys and Beddoe 2015a). The supervisor requires the ability to hold the dual focus of knowing the responsibilities which accompany the role of a supervisor, while at the same time honoring the focus and intent of the observation. This means ensuring that, unless otherwise agreed, observation is not an evaluative or assessment exercise. The supervisor needs to be able to view the supervisee's work as a demonstration of that supervisee's practice in that moment, to be able to put aside personal "preferred" methods, and not to interrupt or take over a session. This will require supervisors to position themselves in a place of interest and enquiry, of critique but not judgement. For some supervisors this may require personal reflection on their current approach to observation and possibly lead to the development of new skills. For supervisees the major issue of live observation can be that the very process of being observed undermines their confidence and so affects their performance.

The Negotiated Collaborative Model for live observation is, as its title suggests, both negotiated and collaborative.

> It is negotiated in that the participants discuss and agree the criteria for observation, the processes by which the observation will be conducted and the manner in which the feedback will be delivered. The model is collaborative, in that the participants work together to achieve the agreed outcomes of the observation.
>
> *(Davys and Beddoe 2015b, p. 177)*

As such the model can be considered as an integral aspect of professional practice where the practitioner has agency in his or her professional development. Importantly, the model invites the observer to participate in the learning and to make connections between what they have observed and critiqued and their own practice. There is a mutual understanding and expectation that the feedback from live observation will be valued, considered, and integrated into future practice. The model is underpinned by four propositions:

1. That feedback criteria are overt and negotiated
2. That the feedback given is specific, appreciative, and strengths-based and is heard from both the observed (the practitioner) and the observer
3. That the discussion and reflections between practitioners and observer(s) following the feedback, create an opportunity for professional conversations and practice development

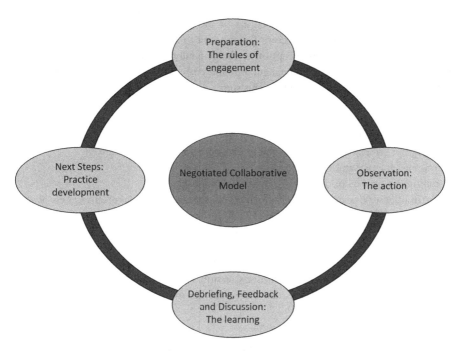

Figure 39.1 Negotiated Collaborative Model. Reprinted with permission by Taylor and Francis from Davys A. and Beddoe L. (2015) 'Going Live': A Negotiated Collaborative Model for Live Observation of Practice, *Practice,* 27 (3), 178, DOI: 10.1080/09503153.2015.1032234.

4. That the learning identified by all participants will be followed with a commitment to introduce it into future practice (Davys and Beddoe 2015a, pp. 11–13)

The Model

The Negotiated Collaborative Model comprises four steps: Preparation: "rules of engagement"; Observation: "the action"; Debriefing and Feedback: "the learning"; and Next Steps: "practice development." See Figure 39.1 Negotiated Collaborative Model.

Step one: Preparation – the rules of engagement

As with many professional exchanges, to create the optimum base for live observation, attention to preparation and negotiation is key (Goldsmith et al. 2011; Sexton et al. 2013). Through detailed consideration of the purpose and process of observation, both parties – the supervisee and the supervisor – can with confidence identify their needs and negotiate how these may be met in the observation. One of the most important questions to be addressed at this stage is therefore "What is the purpose of this observation?" Table 39.1 *Contexts for observation in supervision* identifies some of the most common reasons for observation.

Clarification and agreement of the purpose of the observation paves the way for discussion, negotiation, and agreement of the structure of the observation and for the parameters of the feedback which is to be provided. Safety and safe practice can also be considered. Whenever practice is observed it is important in the preliminary conversations to identify and agree to a process for addressing unsafe practice or risk as identified by the observer within the session.

This conversation may also identify what actions or interventions the supervisor may make in a session where they are physically present (as opposed to watching or listening to a digital recording). Such action would be an exception to the generally accepted role of the observer as a passive participant in the session. The engagement and consent of the service user can also be considered. Six tasks have been identified for this step:

- Determining the purpose of the observation
- Negotiating the role of the observer
- Identifying the criteria against which the practitioner's work will be viewed
- Agreeing safe practice and reporting
- Negotiating the process of debriefing, feedback, and discussion
- Considering the service user: gaining informed consent, suitability/appropriateness of situation to be observed, service-user rights regarding the information collected, and the process of observation (Davys and Beddoe 2015b, p. 182)

Importantly, step one is where the groundwork for the giving and receiving of constructive feedback occurs. What aspects of the supervisee's session will be the focus, and how will the feedback be given and received? These issues will be further discussed in step three: Debriefing and feedback – the learning.

Step two: Negotiated observation – the action

The second step of the model is the step where the supervisee's session is observed. It is here that action occurs. Following the detailed preparation of the previous step, the negotiated observation occurs within that planned framework.

Step three: Debriefing, feedback, and discussion – the learning

The third step of the model is pivotal to the observation process. The session is debriefed and feedback is given to the supervisee about the work which was observed. A final discussion draws together the perspectives and thoughts of both the supervisor and the supervisee, and is where the key points from the observation are identified for both. This opens up opportunity for new insights and learning to be identified.

Debriefing and feedback, which are both central to this step of the live observation model, although aligned, are nevertheless different processes. Where debriefing is described as a shared exchange, "an interactive, bidirectional, and reflective discussion or conversation" (Sawyer et al. 2016, p. 209), feedback, when given by the supervisor to the supervisee, is unidirectional. Feedback in this context can be defined as "information about performance provided [to the supervisees] ... with the intent to modify thinking and/or behavior to facilitate learning and improve future performance" (Sawyer et al. 2016, p. 209). Debriefing and feedback may occur together, or separately, in the third step of the negotiated collaborative model.

Ideally, following the observation of a live session, the supervisor and supervisee would combine the two processes of debriefing and feedback. A reflective discussion about the session would be followed by a more structured critique (feedback – as negotiated in step one) to the supervisee. Frequently however, in the busyness of practice, time constraints mean that it is not possible to combine both processes without compromising the quality of the feedback and learning. In these situations, supervisors and supervisees agree to separate debriefing from feedback. A debrief of the key elements of the session may occur immediately after the session. Here the supervisor and supervisee can share and discuss the most immediate issues, thoughts, and impressions of the session and possibly discuss any action which is consequent to the session. The supervisor and supervisee will then agree to meet later when feedback can be given (and received) in a more structured and considered manner. The time between the two events however is critical and, in order to preserve the detail and freshness of the recall and so to promote the conditions for accurate, specific, and detailed feedback and learning, it is recommended that the feedback session is within 24 hours of the actual observed session (Goldsmith et al. 2011; Sexton et al. 2013).

Feedback

Feedback, much canvassed in the literature on professional education (Kourgiantakis et al. 2018), is often regarded with apprehension by those both giving and receiving the feedback and can be considered to be a challenging and uncomfortable event (Voyer and Hatala 2015). Memories of feedback in early learning experiences, for many social workers as noted, can be carried into practice and can shape attitudes to subsequent feedback opportunities. In a refreshing approach, Hewson and Carroll (2016, p. 129) highlight feedback as a process where both parties, the giver and receiver, hold responsibility for ensuring that feedback is a constructive experience. "It does not matter how much authority or power a feedback giver has; the receivers are in control of what they let in." Feedback is thus as much an act of receiving as it is an act of giving.

Hewson and Carroll (2016) identify three types of feedback: killer, cricket, and collaborative. Killer feedback they describe as feedback that shames and is abusive. Learning does not occur through killer feedback and shaming feedback undermines effective supervision (Beddoe 2017). Cricket feedback, described as non-productive repetitive feedback which the receiver simply "bats" away, similarly does not result in learning. Still using the sporting metaphor, Hewson and Carroll (2016, p. 129) describe collaborative feedback as throwing "catchable feedback balls to someone who is ready, willing and able to catch them."

A key focus of the first step the Negotiated Collaborative Model of live observation is to prepare the ground so that the supervisee is indeed willing, ready, and able to catch the feedback which is accurately and appropriately "thrown" by the supervisor. The preparatory conversations in step one allow for individual agendas to be disclosed and for the supervisee to take ownership of the type and focus of the feedback they want to receive. The supervisor similarly can disclose those issues of practice that they wish to consider in the observation. Through this discussion and negotiation of the structure of the feedback process, trust can begin to develop which will provide the supervisee with the confidence that the feedback will be "catchable" and help the supervisor to know which balls to throw.

During the negotiations of step one, as well as identifying the focus of the feedback, the participants will also have detailed the process for the feedback exchange. While different models for giving and receiving feedback are identified in the literature, the authors have a preferred model which they have used for many years in education settings when viewing videos of student practice (Davys and Beddoe 2010, 2015a).

Two rules shape this feedback model. First, the positive and the negative feedback are kept apart. Feedback which identifies a need for change, or development, of the practice observed, is delivered separately from comments which affirm the aspects of practice which went well. Second, the person who has been observed provides a self-evaluation. The feedback process begins with the person who was observed, the supervisee. In a self-evaluation the supervisee identifies those aspects of the session which, in their opinion, did not go well and/or need to be developed. The supervisor then provides feedback in a similar vein. The process is then repeated, focusing on, and affirming, those areas which went well. The rationale for separating the two

Table 39.2 A feedback process

Supervisee:	What did I not like about this session?
	What would I like to develop?
Supervisor:	What did I think didn't go so well in this session?
	What would I like the supervisee to develop?
Supervisee:	What did I like about this session?
	What would I like to do more?
Supervisor:	What did I like about this session?
	What would I like the supervisee to do more of?

categories of feedback is to prevent the positive practice from being diluted or overshadowed by the practice to be developed. When affirming and development feedback are given together, the affirmation may be heard as a softener for the "hard" feedback which follows and may be dismissed or viewed with suspicion. Keeping them separate allows for each group of feedback to be considered for its own merits and learning.

The feedback process thus looks as follows in Table 39.2.

In order to prepare for the task of assembling and giving feedback, it may be useful for supervisors to recall the CORBS model (Hawkins and Shohet 2012, pp. 159–160). In this mnemonic (Clear, Owned, Regular, Balanced, and Specific), Hawkins and Shohet remind us that the feedback needs to be clearly focused and owned as the perception or opinion of the feedback provider. Feedback should be something which is offered regularly in the supervision relationship and there needs to be a balance between positive feedback and feedback on areas which need development. Finally, the feedback needs to be specific and to refer to concrete and behavioral events or interventions which have occurred in the practice under observation.

Learning

The final section of the third step is where the learning from the observation is brought together. The supervisee and the supervisor can engage in a discussion which adds depth and reflection to the feedback which has just been shared. With much in common with the debriefing discussed earlier in this section, this conversation however focuses on the feedback experience and learning rather than the client session. It is here that both the supervisor and supervisee can ponder their separate perceptions and those areas where they agreed and those areas where there may have been difference. The process of live observation should aim to "bring together the truths of all parties in as democratic a manner as possible, which will include making sense of any inconsistencies" (Humphrey 2007, p. 734).

This is an opportunity for "reflective or wondering feedback" (Davys and Beddoe 2010, p. 144) where the supervisee's practice may be considered and discussed with a wonder, with interest, with tentative suggestion or interpretation. These conversations can open up possibility and be moments of creativity and new insight. For Henderson (2009, p. 30), "wondering" provides an opportunity to "offer curiosity in the context of not knowing, and to tolerate ambiguity." The reflection on, and the wondering about, the observation cements the mutuality of the live observation model. This leads to the final step in the model which invites the participants to step back and consider the process and experience of the observation as well as the content. It is here that the supervisor and supervisee alike consider, from their different perspectives, what they have learned from the observation.

Step four: Next steps – practice development

Step four of the Negotiated Collaborative Model provides a platform from which the participants can identify their learning from the observed session and commit to transferring that learning into practice. The observer and the observed also consider their participation in the broader observation process and what they will take from that experience to use in subsequent professional work. Learning and insights can be matched to clear goals for practice development and change, thus providing both transparency and accountability. The focus in this step on both the supervisor and the supervisee, their learning, and its transfer to the practice, also acknowledges the collaboration and dual benefits of the observation process. This mutuality has the potential to shift some of the issues of power and authority which are inherently vested in supervision relationships (Davys and Beddoe 2015a).

Table 39.3 Action plan

Action plan		
Supervisee:	*Feedback*	*Actions to be taken:*
	Affirming	What do I want to do more of, develop, learn more about, or continue discussions about in the coming months?
	Developmental	What do I want to introduce, develop, learn more about, or continue discussions about in the coming months?
Supervisee:	*Observation process*	
		What have I learned from the process of the observation?
		What have I learned from the process of the debriefing and feedback?
		What will be the impact on my future practice/work/ observations?
		What changes do I want to suggest?
		What feedback do I have for the supervisor?
Supervisor:	*Observation process*	
	What have I learned	What have I learned from the live observation?
		What have I learned from the process of the debriefing and feedback?
		What will be the impact on my future practice/work/ observations?
		What changes do I want to suggest?
		How would I evaluate my role?
Supervisee:	*Follow-up reporting*	What time frames are there on the actions identified for me?
		What resources have been identified?
		How will resources be accessed?
		When will I bring this back to supervision for review?
Supervisor:	*Follow-up reporting*	What time frames are there on the actions for the supervisee?
		What resources have been identified?
		How can I assist access to those resources?
		What time frames are there on the actions I have identified for myself?
		What is useful or appropriate to discuss in supervision with this supervisee?
		What issues do I need to take to my own supervision?

Next Steps culminates in the production of a plan which has three components: actions to be followed consequent to the feedback; identification of the learning from the observation process and its implication for future practice; and a process for reporting back on the progress, or fulfilment, of the plan. The construction of the plan begins with the assembly of the issues which were identified from the debriefing and feedback from the observation. Individual issues can be prioritized and actions identified which will address, or begin to address, these issues. When considering the feedback, priority can be allocated to individual areas, and useful and/or necessary resources may be identified. It is important that the plan is balanced, allowing positive and affirming feedback to also feature. All too often development plans are dominated by the areas of deficit which need attention and stop short of encouraging the supervisee to develop and extend areas of strength.

When the actions, emanating from the live session, have been organized, the supervisor and supervisee together may consider both the *process* of the observation and the *process* of the feedback exchange. What was the observation experience like and how might it be developed or altered in future? How was the process of giving, and of receiving, the feedback experienced by each party? Are there changes required to the way this has occurred? Is there any aspect of observed practice which has caught the supervisor's attention, and which might be relevant to other practice situations? Finally, the plan needs to record and detail follow-up meetings and opportunities for progress reports. A summary of the action plan is in Table 39.3.

Conclusion

In our experience as supervision educators we are familiar with the plethora of concerns that greet attempts to normalize observation of practice in social work. These coalesce around concerns for the rights and comfort of service users, and the fear of managerial concerns overly dominating the supervision space. In this chapter we have not diminished the importance of those concerns, rather we see their consideration as central elements for negotiation, and thus significant in determining how effective this professional collaboration is. Attention to power, emotions, and respectful engagement in preparation for all involved parties creates the space for supervision to be strengthened as a key component of professional development for social workers. Readers are encouraged to use the model provided as a framework for enhancing their learning, at any stage of their career. Opening social work practice in this manner not only offers commentary and critique to the practitioner but also provides opportunity to deepen trust and to build social work expertise within agencies.

References

Beddoe, L., 2017. Harmful supervision: a commentary. *The Clinical Supervisor*, 36 (1), 88–101. doi:10.1080/07325223.2017.1295894.

Beddoe, L., Ackroyd, J., Chinnery, S.-A., and Appleton, C., 2011. Live supervision of students in field placement: more than just watching. *Social Work Education*, 30 (5), 512–528. doi:10.1080/02615479.2010.516358.

Bernard, J.M., and Goodyear, R.K., 2009. *Fundamentals of clinical supervision*. 4th ed. Upper Saddle River, NJ: Pearson.

Champ, J., and Kleist, M.D., 2003. Live supervision: a review of the research. *Family Journal: Counseling and Therapy for Couples and Families*, 11 (3), 268–275.

Davys, A., and Beddoe, L., 2010. *Best practice in professional supervision: a guide for the helping professions*. London: Jessica Kingsley.

Davys, A.M., and Beddoe, L., 2015a. 'Going live': a negotiated collaborative model for live observation of practice. *Practice*, 27 (3), 177–196. doi:10.1080/09503153.2015.1032234.

Davys, A.M., and Beddoe, L., 2015b. 'Going live': an exploration of models of peer, supervisor observation and observation for assessment. *Practice*, 28 (1), 3–20. doi:10.1080/09503153.2015.1053857.

Davys, A., Howard, F., Rankine, M., and Thompson, A., 2019. Supervision under the microscope: critical conversations in a learning community. *Practice*, 1–16. doi:10.1080/09503153.2015.1032234.

Goldsmith, C., Honeywell, C., and Mettler, G., 2011. Peer observed interaction and structured evaluation (POISE): a Canadian experience with peer supervision for genetic counselors. *Journal of Genetic Counseling*, 20 (2), 204–214. doi:10.1007/s10897-010-9341-x.

Hair, H.J., 2014. Power relations in supervision: preferred practices according to social workers. *Families in Society: The Journal of Contemporary Social Services*, 95 (2), 107–114. doi:10.1177/1468017314539082.

Hawkins, P., and Shohet, R., 2012. *Supervision in the helping professions*. Maidenhead, Berkshire, UK: Open University Press.

Henderson, P., 2009. *A different wisdom: reflections on supervision practice*. London: Karnac Books.

Hendrickson, S.M., Veach, P.M., and LeRoy, B.S., 2002. A qualitative investigation of student and supervisor perceptions of live supervision in genetic counseling. *Journal of Genetic Counseling*, 11 (1), 25–49.

Hewson, D., and Carroll, M., 2016. *Reflective practice in supervision: companion volume to the reflective practice toolkit*. Hazelbrook, NSW: MoshPit.

Humphrey, C., 2007. Observing students' practice (through the looking glass and beyond). *Social Work Education: The International Journal*, 26 (7), 723–736.

Kourgiantakis, T., Sewell, K.M., and Bogo, M., 2018. The importance of feedback in preparing social work students for field education. *Clinical Social Work Journal*, 47 (1), 124–133. doi:10.1007/s10615-018-0671-8.

Maidment, J., 2000. Strategies to promote student learning and integration of theory with practice in the field. *In:* L. Cooper, and L. Briggs, eds. *Fieldwork in the human services*. Sydney: Allen & Unwin, 205–215.

Sawyer, T., Eppich, W., Brett-Fleegler, M., Grant, V., and Cheng, A., 2016. More than one way to debrief. Simulation in healthcare. *The Journal of the Society for Simulation in Healthcare*, 11 (3), 209–217. doi:10.1097/SIH.0000000000000148.

Sexton, A., Hodgkin, L., Bogwitz, M., Bylstra, Y., Mann, K., Taylor, J., Hodgson, J., Sahhar, M., and Kentwell, M., 2013. A model for peer experiential and reciprocal supervision (PEERS) for genetic counselors: development and preliminary evaluation within clinical practice. *Journal of Genetic Counseling*, 22 (2), 175–187. doi:10.1007/s10897-012-9540-8.

Voyer, S., and Hatala, R., 2015. Debriefing and feedback. Simulation in healthcare *The Journal of the Society for Simulation in Healthcare*, 10 (2), 67–68. doi:10.1097/SIH.0000000000000075.

Wilkins, D., and Antonopoulou, V., 2017. How not to observe social workers in practice. *Social Work Education*, 36 (7), 837–843. doi:10.1080/02615479.2017.1340446.

40

MANAGING CONFLICT AND CHALLENGING PROCESSES IN SUPERVISION

Carolyn Cousins

Introduction

Some supervisory relationships provide reflective, professionally supportive, and psychologically safe spaces for growth, examination of practice, and exploration of clinical issues. Other supervisory relationships offer little more than time to be endured, where one or both parties would rather be anywhere else and are employing strategies to stay safe and avoid judgment. While much is written about the hoped-for positive versions of supervision, there can be significant challenges and judgment in these intense, closed door interactions. This chapter looks at situations where conflicts arise in supervisory relationships. It considers some of the causes and the use of power. It proposes questions both parties in the supervisory relationship might consider to examine dynamics and their roles in them. Managing and addressing challenges takes bravery and insight from both parties.

Stance to be taken

When there are challenges in a supervisory relationship it can be easy to find fault in the other party. This can lead to us taking a position of superiority, assuming our take is correct, and the other person is somehow in the wrong. This is rarely helpful for resolving tensions and conflict. Rather, it can be useful to interrogate the relationship; what has gone wrong in the relationship and what has been each party's contribution. This can lead towards a solution orientation and self-examination, as well as being curious about the position and stance of the other person. Ruptures can come from differences in understanding both the purpose and expectations. Part of resolution will be trying to take the perspective of the other and implement what Wiseman (1996, p. 1162) calls the four qualities of empathy: understanding their perspective as their truth; staying out of judgment; recognizing the others' emotions; and communicating that recognition.

Establishing safety

Creating a space in which genuine reflective supervision can occur is not straightforward. Quite often practitioners have learned that supervision can be unsafe and then enter a relationship defensively and with professional anxiety. There can be hopes for what supervision will provide, however as Wilkins and Antonopoulou (2019) argue, many practitioners do not feel their needs are being met. In the author's experience, many organizations assume that the provision of supervision is sufficient. Rarely are there checks on the quality of what is occurring in the sessions, nor an assessment as to whether the worker's or agency's needs are being addressed.

In line management supervisory relationships, rarely are the supervisors' abilities to provide skilled and nuanced supervision tested, or even made a priority, at the point of recruitment. Many supervisors have learned their skills or reference points for providing supervision primarily from being on the receiving end of supervision.

Safety exists when the supervisee can admit and explore mistakes without fear of judgment, consider alternatives to their ways of thinking and being, and be open to gentle challenge. It is the task of a supervisor to be encouraging and, when needed, challenging. As Klauber (2008, p. xxi) says,

> Bion's concept of containment … is one way of describing the establishment of a setting that is accepting but not passive, thought-provoking without being directly challenging, inclusive without being seeming to make everyone say or think the same thing. If this is achieved, then something transformative can happen.

Supervisory environments are not always comfortable. Reaching this transformative space could be described as a skill, an art, or a form of intuition. However, this safe reflection space does not happen easily, or commonly. Once safety has been established, it can be tenuous and fragile. Working through conflicts and tensions to achieve a successful resolution should be a key goal of effective supervision.

Where conflicts originate

Conflict in the supervisory relationship can arise from: relationships and fears brought in by supervisor or supervisee; imposter syndrome anxiety about "not knowing"; and/or dynamics in the clinical relationship that can spill into the supervisory relationship. Whatever the cause, challenges should be predicted, rather than seen as unusual.

Impact of past supervisory relationships

Far too many workers have experienced unsafe supervision in which supervisory games, as identified by Kadushin (1968), have been engaged to cope. For some, these games have then become habits, safeguards that manage the anxiety supervision can trigger.

The author's view is that having strong and positive supervision experiences early in your professional practice sets the scene for not only seeking, but utilizing those experiences in future supervision. Even when you encounter problematic supervision, those with prior positive experiences will continue to seek to have their needs met, either in their current supervisory relationship, or through another. However, early poor experiences will often lead to resistance, a lack of understanding of supervision benefits, and the enacting of games to avoid perceived risk (see for example, Cleak and Wilson 2013, p. 67).

Taking time to review past supervision experiences with a critical eye and identifying the impacts, both positive and potentially negative, on your view of supervision can be a beneficial exercise. This assists both supervisee and supervisor in being prepared to articulate their needs.

Supervisory relationships take time to develop their own rhythm, co-created by the participants. Once trust has been established, it is appropriate for the supervisor to initiate discussion of how it is developing, offering the chance to again explore the impact of past relationships and what may have been transferred, consciously or subconsciously, into this relationship.

Imposter syndrome

Imposter syndrome, a term coined by Clance and Imes (1978) is the idea that people doubt their accomplishments and have a persistent, internalized fear of being exposed as fraudulent or not knowing what they are doing. Both participants in supervision can feel the risk of exposure, resulting in feelings of shame and fear, that can be projected through hostility and resistance. Boland (2006, p. 25) outlines the impact of self-doubt and fear of failure on the part of the supervisee, pointing out ways in which supervisees can become afraid to attempt new challenges. Carroll (cited 2006 in Weld 2012, p. 34) also notes how supervisees with shame and fear struggle to reflect and learn, clinging to more abstract and theoretical constructs, resisting self-examination and employing games to avoid scrutiny. Weld (2012, p. 15) observes the importance of supervisors knowing they are not required to be subject matter experts in every aspect of practice; instead they are to be "skilled in eliciting and supporting other people's reflection, insight, and solution-finding capacities."

Clinical parallels and differences in approaches

The possibility of clinical dynamics paralleling within supervision should also be considered. For example, in youth teams, the relationship between staff and management can become reminiscent of an adolescent and their parents, and domestic violence services can see a dynamic of power and control play out through management and staff (see Webb 2011; Cousins 2018 for more discussion).

Where either supervisor or supervisee is attached to certain approaches, this can become a source of tension. Clinical practice rarely has one "right" approach, and some practitioners and agencies are better able to tolerate difference. It is important to seek clarity about what is required by policy or procedure and what is open to interpretation. There is often more than one way to reach the agency's goals or address client need; however, the supervisor might be accustomed to things being done "a certain way." The supervisee will be assessing how much challenge to their approach a supervisor can manage and which boundaries can be stretched. Areas that are held to be areas of justice, inequity, or feeling unheard on the part of the supervisee, if not able to be discussed and tolerated, can be sources of ongoing tension and resentment with battles, small and large, ensuing.

Specific conflicts arising in line management relationships

In many agencies where supervision is offered, supervisors and supervisees do not "choose" each other, but rather enter this key professional relationship because of the positions they hold. This makes for a complicated professional interaction, where power and role dynamics can impede the transaction being a genuine, ethical, and client-focused interaction (see Carroll 2012, for discussion). Internally provided supervision can impact the level of transparency a supervisee is able to show, limit exploration of areas, such as self-doubt, and make it hard to challenge agency-held beliefs or culture.

Line managers have a different level of power, and no matter how democratic the style the supervisor takes, they make the final decisions and have a greater communication with management. Weld (2012, p. 24) highlights how managers can struggle to create supervision as a learning environment, and supervision that becomes too closely linked with compliance measures and performance.

Kahn (1979, p. 521) notes that fears of inadequacy and criticism, as well as resistance to learning, come into play in all supervisory relationships. She cites research that while supervisors saw themselves as having relaxed, collegial attitudes, they were often seen by supervisees as "admired teachers but also feared and powerful judges." People learn early in life that there are some risks involved in being honest with authority figures.

Appointed line management supervisors need to be clear about what is required and in which areas the supervisee has choice, seeking permission from the supervisee about whether to be more challenging. See for example, Radley and Stanley (2018) about the difference between cooperative and detached supervisory experiences. Just as a client may be concerned about consequences and tell us a partial narrative, so supervisees may hide or distort their telling in order to present themselves in a certain way.

Research by Manthorpe (2014) and Cooper (2002) shows that much "in-house" supervision has become focused on management actions and organizational risk protection, leaving little space or appetite for reflective supervision. Weld (2012, p. 23) points out how "supervision by the line manager can become aimed at compliance with procedure and checklists to ensure tasks are done and safe, surface exploration." She adds this type of supervision becomes mundane and a "must do" rather than a "want to do." And depending on the way the supervisor aligns themselves with organizational views, it can also be difficult to honestly discuss organizational culture contributions to vicarious trauma. See Ashley-Binge and Cousins 2019; Reynolds 2011, for discussion of this.

Vicarious trauma and burnout

Where challenges could be stemming from vicarious trauma and burnout it often requires sensitivity to raise, and yet these can be very real sources of tensions arising in supervision. Weinbach (1984) identifies that supervisors are "available targets for the representation and frustration that cannot easily be directed at the organisation." Finding compassionate and sensitive ways to the vicarious trauma is vital, although Ashley-Binge and Cousins (2019) argue it must include organizational factors and the potential contribution of workplace culture, rather than just asking about self-care.

Addressing direct conflict

Where there are direct ruptures, hostilities, and even arguments, it is at least clear there is an issue to both parties. In external supervisory relationships, this will often result in the termination of the supervisory relationship, although where both parties are willing, a new level of contracting is possible. If both parties have the option of withdrawing, choosing to "stay in" usually means a commitment to transparently working through the conflict in a professional manner.

Direct conflict is far more problematic in line management relationships, where the parties may have no choice but to continue working and meeting. By their nature, these arrangements have the imbalance of power issues outlined. Even if the supervisor raises issues in a supportive manner, as Shulman (2010) points out, the worker may still respond defensively: "This may be the worker's pattern of handling any criticism in life, not just at work. If the supervisor recognizes this pattern, he or she needs to shift the discussion from the worker's practice to the worker's difficulty in dealing with criticism."

Naming the dynamics

Difficult interactions can trigger "flight fight freeze" responses for one or both parties, and heightened anxiety will mean neither party is bringing their best self. Finding ways to appropriately name, discuss, and unpack the dynamics away from the tension is challenging, and yet this is what is needed.

Considerations include using a different neutral physical space to where supervision occurs, to shift dynamics and avoid triggers. Discussing how to have a conversation about the dynamics, setting out intentions for fair resolution, and exploration with a view to learning about one another and creating a new and safer dynamic going forward should be considered. Tools that create distancing from the dynamics can be useful, especially those which normalize difference, such as a DISC profile, or Myers Briggs. Discussion of conflict and learning styles can also allow differences to be considered and new agreements reached. A session like this may need facilitating, depending on the level of conflict that has already occurred, but it should be solution and future focused rather than attributing blame or trying to justify past behaviors.

Ideally, this discussion should allow both parties to explore their expectations of supervision, how they prepare, and their styles. In exploring assumptions and expectations with empathy, areas of misunderstanding can be identified and new approaches negotiated. It is useful to discuss whether fight or dissociative responses have been enacted. If this is occurring, agreeing a way that either party can name increasing anxiety in supervision and call for a session break can be helpful. Many practitioners know the usefulness of these techniques clinically, and yet do not always think to bring this learning into their supervision.

Emotive outbursts

As outlined, some supervision interactions are enough to trigger a fight or flight response in either party. This can be accompanied by anger, tears, or other heightened emotions. While these are not accepted workplace responses, and apologies may be required, it is ideal that both parties step back after the "heat" of the interaction to consider individually, and then together, what the communications and needs behind such outbursts may have been. Aggressive or bullying behavior is not to be tolerated, and boundaries may need to be put in place. Yet where a party is able to own and examine their emotive response, there is good hope for working through the issues behind it. Where emotive outbursts are regular and/or extreme, consideration must be given to whether supervisory games are at play, and whether they should be able to continue.

Passive resistance and challenging processes

In 1964, psychiatrist Eric Berne identified the dynamics underlying human relationships leading to the practice of transactional analysis. Alfred Kadushin, in his seminal work (1968), used Berne's ideas applying them to "the kinds of recurrent interactional incidents between supervisor and supervisee that have a payoff for one of the parties in the transaction." O'Donoghue (2012) proposes we all engage in "games" at times and past experiences of supervision may have created defensive and/or preventative tactics that we continue to employ. Starting to name forms of passive resistance and exploring dynamics can begin to address them .

Table 40.1 Some examples – Supervisee games

Name	Tactic	Aim	Identified by
Two against the agency	Supervisee frustrated by agency procedures alludes to conflict between bureaucratic requirements and time with clients.	• Asks supervisor to allow them not to ignore bureaucratic requirements, e.g. record keeping, timeframes. • Reduction in administrative requirements/sanctioned rule breaking	Kadushin (1968)
Treat me don't beat me	Invites supervisor to assist them with personal problems as a diversion from work accountabilities	• Supervisor becomes therapist, making it hard to hold the worker accountable. • Work adjustments given	Kadushin (1968) expanded by Cousins (2010)
The perpetual "new worker"	Stays in "learner mode" longer than is reasonable, asks for support and advice	• Reduction in workload and expectations • Appeases and placates supervisor by taking one down position	Kadushin (1968)
Flattery	Strokes the ego of the supervisor	• Supervision focus is advice giving rather than supervisee's work or role • Reduction in accountability	Kadushin (1968)
Selective sharing	Picking topics and cases that are safe to talk about and prevent deeper analysis of work	• Reduces the threat of criticism and accountability • Reduced risk of exposing inadequacies	Kadushin (1968)
If you knew Dostoyevsky like I know Dostoyevsky ….	Relies on supervisor thinking they need to know as much or more as the supervisee	• Supervisee self-manages lest they expose lack of knowledge of supervisor • Can behave like a peer with reduced oversight	Kadushin (1968)
I'll just run this past you in the corridor / on email	Avoids sit down supervision	• Avoidance of scrutiny and depth	Kadushin (1968)
I have a little list…	Keeps the supervisor busy with topics they like to discuss and are safe for the supervisee	• Avoidance of scrutiny and depth • Reduction in anxiety	Kadushin (1968)
Let's be friends	Becomes friend to supervisor with "special privileges"	• Avoidance of evaluation • Creation of loyalty • Reduction in power differential	Kadushin (1968)

Addressing tactics and dynamics

The difficulty with many of these tactics is one of degrees. Even the most self-aware practitioner engages in some of these tactics at times. There is what Hawthorne (1975, p. 180) calls an "essential validity." Key indicators that a dynamic is becoming a problem are when it is affecting job satisfaction, productivity, or the outcomes for clients. Dill and Bogo (2009, p. 142) remind the supervisor that central to their role is ensuring agency clients get the best possible service, which sometimes means addressing these issues directly.

There are risks in naming and exposing tactics and their effects. It is akin to naming defensive mechanisms in clients: some weighing up of consequences is required. Kadushin (1968, p. 32) suggests first considering the "defensive significance" of the dynamic. This will engender empathy and highlight cautions, to ensure exposure of tactics is undertaken in a way that maintains dignity and offers options for change in moving forward. Weld (2012, p. 59) offers that in bringing forward prior emotional experiences to make an empathic connection, we can pay better attention to the emotional signals of ourselves and others, allowing greater connection.

It is important to remember that both parties have usually engaged in the dynamic, and "refusing to play" as Kadushin (1968, p. 31) puts it, can mean forfeiting certain advantages. For example, the supervisor must be willing to deal with potential supervisee rejection and hostility; willing to accept criticism, deny flattery, reject the voyeurism of acting as therapist; or be willing to openly admit ignorance on a subject.

Where the dynamics are initiated by the supervisor, Hawthorne (1975, p. 182) acknowledges the supervisee may be too vulnerable to address with the dynamic directly. One option is to regularly point out the approach in a light-hearted way, if the supervisory relationship will tolerate this. With the abdicating supervisor, Hawthorne (1975, p. 182) suggests the supervisee present their needs persistently, professionally, and in a non-threatening way.

With the supervisor using games of power, where the dynamics have become pronounced, or are bullying, it is wise to seek advice and consult workplace policies (Table 40.2). Addressing

Table 40.2 Some examples – Supervisor games

	Tactic	*Aim*	*Identified by*
Games of Power: • My Team: ownership reminders • It's for your own good: withholding information to "protect" the team • Analysis of practitioner rather than their practice	Reminds practitioner of their place and the power of the supervisor. Makes it less likely staff will challenge the supervisor, "I wonder why you said that?"	• Reduce challenge to supervisor or exposure of their sense of inadequacy	Hawthorne (1975)
Games of Abdication • They won't let me: says they are powerless to effect change • Tries to be friends with staff they supervise • Invitations to look after the stressed supervisor	Tries to devolve or ignore power of role. Pretends to be just like the supervisee. Either makes supervision about them or how put upon they are by the system	• To feel less embarrassed by the positional power • Prove they haven't "sold out" to management	Hawthorne (1975) Donovan and Jackson (1991)

supervisory difficulties and challenges takes two somewhat willing participants, and where one party is using "power over," directly addressing that abuse of power is unlikely to be successful. It is important to be realistic about whether the person with the least power can affect change. As Martin Luther King Jr (1963, p. 2) said, "Freedom is never given voluntarily by the oppressor." The cost of demanding freedom has to be weighed carefully. In these cases, it is the author's experience that it is useful to make alternative arrangements to ensure professional needs are met as you consider options.

Things to consider when it gets challenging

Conflict styles

It can be useful to explore supervisee and supervisor's styles of conflict management before ruptures occur. This includes considering when they tend to avoid conflict, around what issues, and if a need to be liked or seen as helpful is influencing the relationship. This can provide a hook to return to if needed. Understanding what conflict triggers in you, when and why you avoid it, and whether you see it as a positive learning opportunity is vital. Understanding the Drama Triangle (Karpman 1968), and whether you have a tendency towards rescuer (a common problem for supervisors) or victim (a common issue for supervisees) can also provide space for useful reflection (Figure 40.1).

Karpman (1968) proposed that people can quite unconsciously "enter the Drama Triangle." If the supervisee or supervisor adopts the persecutor position (perhaps because they are having a bad day and want to blame someone, bringing annoyance or frustration to the session) then they can prompt the other party into the victim position, where they will react to feeling unfairly persecuted or accused.

If the supervisee or supervisor is prone to adopt the victim position, bringing themes of being hard done by or put upon by either the clients or system, the other party is invited to assume the rescuer position in an attempt to reduce the distress. For those in the helping profes-

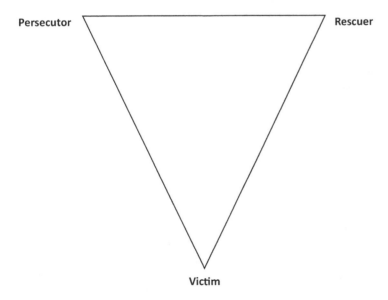

Figure 40.1 Drama Triangle

sions, this might be a familiar or even favored position in the triangle. Time and attention in the session will be taken with rescuing the other party, and this is then being reinforced through the feedback that it has been "so helpful."

Karpman (1968) proposed that even thought people may have a preferred starting position in the Drama Triangle, in a relationship (including presumably a supervisory one), people end up switching positions, sometimes repeatedly, meaning that the Drama Triangle ways of relating to each other can become an unhelpful cycle. When one party in the supervisory relationship, for example, is stuck in a victim narrative, "refusing" to be rescued, the other party may lose patience and move from willing rescuer, to persecutor.

Own blocks and resistance

Honesty about our areas of resistance can be challenging. Compassionate yet robust self-analysis should be part of any true reflection aimed at uncovering our part in difficult dynamics. As Trevithick (2011) argues, practitioners may be inclined not to critically reflect on their own behavior, and it can be preferable to blame others (psychological projection). Brookfield (1998, p. 197) points out that few of us can get very far reflecting on our own. Finding others don't just support our hypothesis but challenge us to consider alternative views is important.

> No matter how much we may think we have an accurate sense of ourselves, we are stymied by the fact that we are using our own interpretive filters to become aware of our own interpretive filters. ..... A self-confirming cycle often develops whereby our uncritically accepted assumptions shape actions that then only serve to confirm the truth of those assumptions.
>
> *(Brookfield 1998, p. 197).*

Things for supervisees to consider
Ability of the supervisor to meet needs

Considering the range of purposes supervision can be expected to address, it seems unlikely that one individual can meet all the needs and expectations. Where it is an imposed supervisory relationship, assessing what the relationship can offer, and tailoring supervision expectations to obtain these, can be useful for reducing frustration and disappointment. This does not mean you should not articulate your needs, or get them met, however it is important to recognize the limitations of the allocated supervisor and consider and assess where your needs in the professional world can be satisfied. This may be through peer support, reading and reflection, or through externally chosen supervision.

Trust to go deeper

Part of assessing a supervisor's ability to meet your needs is being clear on what you feel safe to reveal and whether you are willing to expose your vulnerabilities. It is important to ask whether you have a tendency to avoid scrutiny or accountability, whether you are keen to present a particular sort of "professional face" or level of competence, and whether you can challenge yourself to go deeper and reveal more. In each supervisory relationship, supervisees will be looking for signs of support or judgment. As Weld (2012, p. 34) points out, to "go into a room with someone who may hold greater experience, or perceived status than yourself, and freely talk about possible mistakes you have made in your work is no easy feat."

Wish to hold supervisor in high esteem

As part of your vulnerability, how much do you "look up" to the supervisor and does this affect the level of honesty you have about self-doubts, struggles, and areas of concern? Pondering this can reveal whether you perceive supervision as an educative environment, where you learn from someone with more knowledge. For others, it may reveal a psychological need to believe there are wiser, stronger, and better practitioners out there – providing a sense of psychological safety and calm in the work. While this is understandable, it is important to consider how this may prevent us owning our own developing professional competence.

Questions for supervisees to consider

- What would you conceal from a supervisor? What might prompt you to do this? How would you resist this?
- How do you decide what to bring? Has anything changed about the way you prepare?
- Do you see assessment and feedback as part of the supervisory relationship?
- How could you become more vulnerable and less defensive in supervision? If this is not possible in this supervisory relationship, where can you do this?
- Do you identity with the Drama Triangle? Do you tend to assign certain roles to yourself or others?
- Do you understand your own conflict style, as well as what you tend to avoid?

Things for the supervisor to consider

Where are you examining your own practice?

If supervisors' value the reflective practice and accountability supervision brings, they need to be in supervision themselves, examining their style and showing their commitment to growth and learning. This will include examining their reactions to different supervisees. Just as with clients, we will find some supervisees easier to work with. Supervisors need to discuss triggers in relation to age, gender, discipline, and types of roles of those they are supervising. Reflecting on this can reveal the need to pay continued attention to how we are adjusting our supervisory provision to meet the needs of the supervisee, rather than just offering what we know and prefer.

The motivation of supervisors vary. For some, it is simply because their work role or position requires it. For others, providing supervision is key to what led them to take a leadership role. Others choose supervision provision outside a work relationship, finding they enjoy it. Provision of supervision can provide a chance to share wisdom and knowledge, a place to watch others have "a-ha" moments, or to be admired. Becoming honest about our motivations can reveal new insights and areas for further exploration.

It is important for supervisors to resist becoming defensive. Donovan and Jackson (1991, p. 342) state that managers need to be able to depersonalize resistance and occasional hostility and be able to resist the urge to treat organizational relationships as therapeutic ones. They (1991, p. 342) suggest that to be a good manager, you need to be secure, without need to be universally loved.

Temptations to use "power over"

Examining with someone else the different ways we use or resist supervisory power, both overtly and subtly, is important for ethical, accountable, and examined supervisory provision. It can be tempting to tell a supervisee what to do, or use the power of greater experience or position to steer them to a particular outcome. Sometimes this is appropriate, but examining our motivations is key. Have you used power to direct a particular outcome because it is necessary for the client or to ensure the practitioner is operating within policy or legislation? Or was it easier or quicker than supporting the practitioner to reach a conclusion themselves? This short-circuits their learning and encourages dependence on the supervisor. Sometimes, the supervisor prefers things done their way and has the power to enforce this.

A particularly interesting dynamic can develop when a supervisee has become accustomed to a supervisor who uses power. These supervisees may behave in ways that require the supervisor to adopt a different style than their preferred style, or become the manager the worker expects based on past experiences. Boland (2006, p. 25) points out that past experiences can mean a practitioner "finds the experience of fair treatment hard to trust or tolerate," and they may respond by attempting to provoke their manager into behaving in more familiar and punitive ways that they expect.

Being honest about areas where we need to grow

While it is not impossible to become a good supervisor through experience and provision alone, to assume that simply having been a supervisee will mean a professional knows how to provide supervision to others is naïve. We don't assume that being a client means you can be a counselor, nor do we assume studying a subject means someone is qualified to teach it. And yet, too often, the assumption is made that practitioners know instinctively how to provide supervision. What most will have is some idea how to provide the style of supervision they themselves find helpful. This does not mean it will suit others.

Knowing your preferred learning style and understanding the range of learning styles of others is important to ensure you are not simply providing the supervision that would suit you. Similarly, understanding your preferred style of communication and those of others can unlock new options for how to provide supervision. It is the role of the supervisor to experiment and discuss with the supervisee a range of styles to see what will best facilitate growth. Zorga (2007) argues it is also the role of the supervisor to examine areas of supervision provision they will need in order to learn and grow and to seek out opportunities to create this growth.

Role of a supervisor in addressing personal and personality issues

Sometimes supervisors, as clinicians of old, are tempted to clinically assess and analyze supervisees, pondering their histories and triggers, moving into "counseling mode." Yet as far back as Kahn (1979, p. 520), there was recognition that the "resolution of a supervisee's personality problem is usually not seen as a supervisory responsibility." It can be tempting to therapize the practitioner, especially where we can see the clinical impact. Yet rarely has permission been given by the supervisee, and this shift will likely result in resistance or hostility. Wishing to preserve professional integrity and identity, most practitioners will react when they sense a shift from supervisor to therapist (with the exception of those who invite this game, as per Table 40.1, who will encourage it).

In some supervisory relationships, it can be important to address this directly, outlining that if needed, a referral can be made for personal counseling. Discussing early on the boundaries between supervision and counseling can avoid some dynamics. For example, the author has experience supervising Indigenous practitioners in an Australian context, where discussion of the personal self and its interaction with the professional self is often an agreed part of the supervisory space. However, this is always specifically discussed and negotiated, rather than assumed.

Questions for supervisors to consider

- In what ways has the style of your supervision provision changed and evolved? What about in each relationship?
- How are you developing your understanding of leadership in supervision?
- What are you doing to grow your self-awareness and interpersonal skills?
- How well do you know your own conflict style? Could you describe it if asked? Do you recognize your tendencies in the Drama Triangle?
- How do you use power? When are you tempted to operate from direction rather than collaboration or cooperation?
- If honest with yourself, do challenges to your authority produce frustration or a wish to "pull rank"?
- Do you see conflict as an of opportunity for growth? If not, could you?
- How many trusted challengers do you have – people who can tell it like it is, that you can hear?
- Do you try to "educate" in supervision? Do you like to be in a position of authority and held as wise? What does it mean for you if a supervisee has more experience than you in an area?

Proactive strategies for supervisors

It is important for supervisors to be kind to themselves and remember that even the most skilled supervisor cannot be perfect. Supervisors miss signals, overreact, are not supportive enough, fail to manage their own reactions, and sometimes use power when they shouldn't. It is important for the supervisor to be able to admit and apologize when they make a mistake. Cousins argues (2004) it is important for supervisees to see that their supervisor may not always get it right, or know what to do, all of the time. It is also important for the supervisor to not always know what is best for the situation, but to model seeking advice. Supervisors owning their contribution to difficult dynamics and apologizing for their contribution can open up safer and more transparent conversations about the style of supervision that has developed and what is needed, post tension.

Recognizing endings

It may seem obvious, but it is important to regularly assess your own supervisory needs and the various relationships in which you are having them met. Supervisory relationships should not be held onto simply because they are comfortable or because of professional loyalty. They should challenge us to learn, grow, and improve. Saying goodbye to one supervisory relationship and moving to a new one can be a healthy part of professional development.

Conclusion

Establishing enough psychological safety to create supervisory relationships that can tolerate challenging conversations and move past ruptures is not straightforward. People's past experiences can result in a range of conflicts, both overt and hidden. Addressing the challenging dynamics often happens in a state of heightened anxiety for both parties, and finding ways to step back, examine the influences and impacts, and identify a way forward takes commitment, empathy, and bravery.

By drawing together these ideas, it is hoped this chapter can be a useful reflection for supervisees and supervisors alike to examine their interactions and intentions. It takes bravery to question your own supervisory style and ask for feedback, and yet, seeking the feedback of other respected professionals in this area can be a catalyst for professional development and growth, leading to improved supervisory experiences.

References

Ashley-Binge, S., and Cousins, C., 2019. Individual and organisational practices addressing social workers' experiences of vicarious. *Journal of Trauma Practice*, 32 (3), 197–207. doi:10.1080/09503153.2019.1620201.

Berne, E., 1964. *Games people play: the psychology of human relationships*. New York: Ballantine Books.

Brookfield, S., 1998. Critically reflective practice. *Journal of Continuing Education in the Health Professions*, 18, 197–205.

Boland, C., 2006. Functional families: functional teams. *ANZJFT*, 27 (1), 22–28.

Carroll, M., and Shaw, E., 2012. *Ethical maturity in the helping professions*. Victoria. PsychOz Publications.

Clance, P.R., and Imes, S.A., 1978. The imposter phenomenon in high achieving women: dynamics and therapeutic intervention. *Psychotherapy: Theory, Research & Practice*, 15 (3), 241–247.

Cleak, H., and Wilson, J., 2013. *Making the most of field placement*. 3rd ed. Melbourne: Cengage.

Cooper, L., 2002. Social work supervision: a social justice perspective. *In*: M. McMahon and W. Patton, eds. *Supervision in the helping professions: a practical approach*, Sydney, Australia: Pearson Education, 185–195.

Cousins, C., 2004. Becoming a social work supervisor: a significant role transition. *Australian Social Work*, 57 (2), 175–185.

Cousins, C., 2010. 'Treat me don't beat me': exploring supervisory games and their effect on poor performance management. *Practice*, 22 (5), 281–292.

Cousins, C., 2018. Parallel process in domestic violence services: are we doing harm? *Australian Counselling Research Journal*, 12 (1), 23–28.

Dill, K., and Bogo, M., 2009., Moving beyond the administrative: supervisors' perspectives on clinical supervision in child welfare. *Journal of Public Child Welfare*, 3 (1), 87–105.

Donovan, F., and Jackson, A., 1991. *Human resource (personnel) management, managing human service organisations*. New York: Prentice Hall.

Hawthorne, L., 1975. Games supervisors play. *Social Work*, 20 (3), 179–183.

Kadushin, A., 1968. Games people play in supervision. *Social Work*, 13, 23–32.

Kahn, E., 1979. The parallel process in social worker treatment and supervision. *Social Casework: The Journal of Contemporary Social Work*, 60, 520–528.

Karpman, S., 1968. Fairy tales and script drama analysis. *Transactional Analysis Bulletin*, 7 (26), 39–43.

King, Martin Luther Jr., 1963. *Letter from Birmingham Jail, why we can't wait*. Avaiable at: https://kinginstitute.stanford.edu/encyclopedia/why-we-cant-wait [Accessed 14th January 2020].

Klauber, T., 2008. Foreword. *In*: M. Rustin and J. Bradley, eds. *Work discussion: learning from reflective practice in work with children and families*. London: Tavistock Clinic Series.

Manthorpe, J., Moriarty, J., Stevens, M., Hussein, S., and Sharpe, E., 2014. The 'making' of social workers: findings from interviews with managers of newly qualified social workers. *Practice*, 26 (2), 97–111.

O'Donoghue, K., 2012. Windows on the supervisee experience: an exploration of supervisees' supervision histories. *Australian Social Work*, 65 (2), 214–231. doi:10.1080/0312407x.2012.667816.

Radey, M., and Stanley, L., 2018. Hands on" vs. "empty": supervision experiences of frontline child welfare workers. *Children and Youth Services Review*, 91, 128–136.

Reynolds, V., 2011. Resisting burnout with justice doing. *International Journal of Narrative Therapy and Community Work*, 4, 15–18.

Shulman, L., 2010. *Interactional supervision*. 3rd ed. Washington: NASW Press.

Trevithick, P., and Wengraf, T., 2011. Understanding defences and defensiveness in social work. *Journal of Social Work Practice*, 25 (4), 389–412. doi:10.1080/02650533.2011.626642.

Webb, A., 2011. Exploring parallel process within post-separation service organisations: the client, worker and organisation divorce. *Psychotherapy in Australia*, 17 (4), 56–64.

Weinbach, R.W., 1984. Implementing change: insights and strategies for the supervisor. *Social Work*, 29 (3), 282–286. doi:10.1093/sw/29.3.282

Weld, N., 2012. *A practical guide to transformative supervision for the helping professions*. London: Jessica Kingsley.

Wilkins, D., and Antonopoulou, V., 2019. What does supervision help with? A survey of 315 social workers in the UK. *Practice*, 31 (1), 21–40.

Wiseman, T., 1996. A concept analysis of empathy. *Journal of Advanced Nursing*, 23 (6), 1162–1167.

Zorga, S., 2007. Stages of supervisor development. *Ljetopis socijalnog rada*, 14 (2), 433–441.

PART VI

Leading and managing supervision

41

LEADERSHIP AND SUPERVISION

John Lawler

Introduction

This chapter deals with two issues and their interrelationship – leadership and supervision. Both are commonly used terms, and there is an assumption that they have common understandings as to what they are and how they operate. It is important though, at the outset, to clarify significant fundamental and perhaps overlooked elements. Firstly, there is the issue of definition. In social work there is an argument that supervision does not have a common and agreed definition and that its interpretation (and therefore its practice) varies (Wilkins and Antonopoulou 2019). Similarly in the management and organization literature there is continuing debate about a definition of leadership (Rosenbach et al. 2018) and indeed some who argue that a common definition might be impossible to agree (Senge 1999) and might not be particularly helpful even if one could be found (Alvesson and Sveningsson 2003).

Secondly there is the evidential basis for each issue, that is, to what extent is there an evidence base which illustrates the effectiveness of social work supervision (on practice) and the effectiveness of leadership (on individual and organizational performance). In both cases the evidence, perhaps surprisingly to some, is very thin! In their systematic review of work from 2000–2012, Carpenter et al. (2013) found that supervision was related to social worker satisfaction and dealing effectively with stress but that there was little evidence of any quality in relation to the outcomes of supervision, particularly none relating to outcome for consumers. There is a similar picture regarding leadership. Despite the multiplicity of academic and other publications on the topic, the evidence base for the effect of leadership on individual and organizational performance is again weak (Thorpe et al. 2007).

West et al. (2015) note in the context of the United Kingdom (UK) National Health Service (NHS) that much of the writing on leadership and much of the emphasis on leadership development is "based on fads and fashions rather than hard evidence." Thus it is easy for practice in this area, and perhaps others, to be ill-informed. This echoes the earlier conclusion of Thorpe et al. (2007) that there is little research evidence to support the notion that single individuals (aka leaders) have "the kind of dramatic impact on organizational performance that is so often claimed." They note the work of Pfeffer and Jones (2006), whose findings replicate other earlier work over many years noting that the evidence for individual influence is generally modest at best. Obviously, taken together, these points do not mean that supervision and leadership are themselves without point – there is much anecdotal and experiential work which highlights their respective utility. But we need to recognize the weak evidence base for much discussion and conclude that much normative work exists on both topics and thus potentially informs practice. We need therefore to be cautious and questioning in dealing with both topics.

Two other aspects also need to be highlighted at this opening stage of the chapter, leading from the above points. Firstly, both supervision and leadership appear to be accepted in themselves as being beneficial – a "good thing." Supervision and leadership when practiced inadequately can have considerable negative outcomes (Beddoe 2017; Ciulla 2014). Secondly, and perhaps one of the reasons why they are difficult topics to research adequately, is both these processes are fundamentally relational, that is, they are almost entirely dependent for their effectiveness on the quality of the relationship between parties to the supervision process and to the leadership process respectively. Both or all parties involved in both supervision and leadership relationships are fully active members participating in and contributing to the process and to the quality of the relationship. In relation to leadership, there is in some of the literature an implicit assumption that people other than the "leader" are relatively passive – blank sheets as it were for the leader to make her/his imprint. This is reflected in the term "follower" ascribed to roles other than that of leader in the leadership process. Few of us are likely to wish to be so described! Social work perhaps is slightly more enlightened in expecting a more active role for the social worker in the supervision process, but the terms supervisor and supervisee assume a particular power dynamic. The supervisor and the leader are assumed to be "expert," and the "follower" or supervisee is developing. Contrast this with roles of e.g. mentor or coach, where the latter may have particular expertise and experience but the "expert practitioner" in the relationship is the person acting as counter to the mentor or coach in that relationship.

Over the past two decades the use of the word "leadership" has grown enormously in the area of management and organizational literature (Storey 2016) and arguably within more regular narratives in the work, social, and political contexts. More recently its use within the social work context has followed this general trend. It is one of those terms which in common parlance requires little definition as its common understanding is taken for granted. In general discussion, a common understanding of the term is assumed which is both a benefit and hindrance to communication. It is a benefit in that time is saved discussing the matter before moving on to other more important aspects of the issue. It can be a hindrance in that if the assumed common understanding is not accurate, different interpretations, arguments, and conclusions might be reached whilst all parties assume agreement. For example, members of the same team, division, or organization might agree with the assertion the "we need better/more effective leadership here" but different understandings might well occur. What might such an assertion mean: better decision-making? More inclusive communications? A greater sense of direction? More effective role models? A clearer ethical framework? The accumulation and distribution of more resources? If different interpretations of leadership exist, it is inevitable that disappointment will arise when some of these expectations are unrealized.

In order to avoid multiple misunderstandings in the context of social work supervision, the initial part of this chapter briefly charts the rise of the use of the word leadership and the different understandings of the term in the management and organizational literature. It also examines some of the possible reasons for this increase. The section concludes with comments on the interpretation of leadership in the social work context. This is important as the increase in the use of the term "leadership" occurs at different levels in social work, from the social policy level through to the level of service use. Allied to the issue of common (mis)understanding is the issue of what is anticipated of leadership: what is "more leadership" expected to achieve? What will be its outcomes? If our initial understandings differ, what is expected must also vary.

Growth of attention given to leadership

The broader social developments which provide a context for the increased attention given to leadership are considered next. There are several aspects to these developments including: the growth of individualization and that of consumerism; the changing roles of the state in the political and social realm; our current "post-deferential" society and the changing roles of service providers and service users and their mutual relationship; and the changing context within which social work services are provided i.e. austerity, changing expectations of social work, increased demand for cross organizational working. Each of these has contributed to the increase in attention given to leadership in its own different way. Each of these issues will be discussed in brief before we go to consider what more effective leadership might achieve, particularly in the social work supervision process.

Western society has seen a considerable increase in individualization in the second part of the twentieth century and into the twenty-first (Lawler 2016). This has taken place as a development away from more collective approaches to social interaction which preceded it. In an increasingly post-modern world, society has become more fragmented, identity is seen as being more fluid, we are no longer restrained by traditional expectations of gender, class, or ethnicity, we are increasingly responsible for who we are and whom we become, and we have increasing responsibility for how we exercise that choice (Bauman 2008). Individualization is seen as the dominant social phenomenon in current, post-modern society. Traditionally, society has been seen as a set of beliefs, social mores, values, and institutions which exercise a degree of collective control and authority over individual members who internalize those beliefs etc., influencing and perhaps constraining behavior. In the twenty-first century the role of the individual in society is developing in a more independent way. Beck and Beck-Gernsheim (2002) describe how we now are more "self-sufficient" and independent from one another than in previous generations. As a result, we are less bound by traditional bonds, hierarchies, and obligations. We are less constrained by traditional roles, traditional career trajectories, and traditional relationships (both inside and beyond work). Indeed, we now have greater independence over our own identities rather than being constrained by more traditional identities imposed on us – we are free to choose who we are and who we become.

With regard to greater consumerism, how might his effect leadership? In social work we no longer see the person who uses services as a client, or user but increasingly as the customer. The role of the customer is one which sees the individual as choosing whether or not to use one service or another; and as having greater power and influence in the relationship between provider and consumer and possibly making greater demands on providers that in a previous era.

This constitutes a change in direction for the delivery of public services, part of a process of "modernization" where service delivery organizations are seen as businesses and where services become increasingly individualized (O'Brien and Penna 1998). As such, public services are customized for individual service users or customers. In this way individualization as a process has a direct influence on service delivery and its customization.

The changing role of the state is pertinent in relation to this in that the state is no longer the provider of all services but a facilitator or, sometimes, as provider in a competitive market. Over the past recent decades, the role of the state has been increasingly questioned and the market has been seen to be the better provider for customer demands (Jones 2018). The state is not required to define need. Rather consumers are seen to be better placed to define their own requirements. Indeed, it is increasingly more likely for public bodies to commission services from private providers than to provide services itself. The expectation is that customer demands are met rather than that social needs are provided for. All these factors in combination result in situations of greater uncertainty and unpredictability, a situation in which we, as citizens/consumers/professional workers or whatever, are no longer "rule-followers" but "rule finders" (Fahmi 2017). Part of this societal change has been a decline in traditional deference – to professional workers, to organizations, to "experts," in short to a traditional hierarchy of authority (Sutcliffe-Braithwaite 2018).

The combination of redefining the role of the state and its agencies, together with a context of restrictions on spending for public services has had consequences for how public services are designed, organized, and delivered. The demand for services shows no diminution, so bodies delivering such services are increasingly to do more with the resources for which they are responsible. Additionally, there are increasing requirements for public service organization to work collaboratively with other agencies in the public and independent sectors, e.g. for social care agencies to work with health organizations; for police to collaborate with education (Sullivan and Skelcher 2002). This again means that traditional professional roles and boundaries become blurred and "rule-finding" gains pre-eminence. Other factors contribute to the need for additional organizational responses of ways of managing and organizing, because of the increase in reported levels of stress in professional service organizations, the increasing interest in individual performance, and the target-driven focus of many public service organizations.

All the above have implications for leadership and indeed may be influential in the increased attention given to leadership in organizational and professional discourse. Traditional relationships are changing; innovation and inspiration are required to maintain and improve service and practice; there is an increasing need for greater individual "discretionary effort" (Pendleton and Furnham 2016) that is, going beyond strict limitations of the job in question; cross-organizational working cannot rely exclusively on traditional organizational hierarchies but needs collaboration, respect, and trust between profession workers. All these pressures combine in the need for something beyond traditional organizational working and standard procedures and traditional management. It is within such a context that more effective "leadership" is increasingly seen as the primary means of dealing with these issues. Storey (2016) noted the exponential rise in academic articles over the past three decades, from under 200 citations on one business and management database in the 1970s, through tens of thousands in the 1990s, to millions in the twenty-first century. Perhaps this a reflection of the academic interest in means of responding to the increasing changes facing all organizations in the present era. In order to not be overwhelmed by the scale of work in this area, it is important to have a critical perspective in considering this growth and some of the approaches evident in this literature. This will be dealt with later in the chapter.

As part of this critical perspective, it is important to avoid seeing leadership as a silver bullet for organizational and professional shortcomings. The word "leadership" might need to be viewed with caution, similarly the use of the term "organizational culture," in that they may be seen as residual characteristics of organizations, teams, or professionals, when other issues have been dealt with, such as structure, policy, or resources. When it is unclear why effectiveness of the team or organization is not as it might be, it can be easily agreed that the blame can be placed on "leadership" or "culture" without actually clarifying what that might mean precisely. Without such clear understanding remedial action might be ineffective. The danger is, as noted above, in assuming a common understanding of the terms of the diagnosis and of the consequent actions required.

A short and rather simplified look at the development of leadership might be useful here before considering what the implications are of its increasing use on the supervision context. As part of this it is important to note that there is no dominant and accepted definition of leadership and despite the increased attention it receives, it remains highly unlikely there ever will be. This is echoed by writers over the decades: there are "As many definitions as writers on the subject" (Stogdill 1974, p. 7), and "A snowball's chance in hell of redefining leadership in this day and age" (Senge 1999, p. 90). And there is the suggestion that seeking a definition is a fruitless venture: "we doubt a common definition is possible, would not be helpful, does not hit the target and obstructs new ideas" (Alvesson and Sveningsson 2003, p. 362). Grint (2005) argues that leadership is an "eternally contested topic" and resolution will not be forthcoming. There are many different foci of attention in leadership research and different assumptions as to what leadership might be, from seeing leadership as a facet of personality, or as charisma or as decision-making, to seeing it as a set of behavioral traits, through to seeing it as a social construction, rather than an objective phenomenon. Grint (2005) provides a summary of approaches: seeing leadership as to do with the Person – WHO the leader is; or as a set of Results – WHAT the leader achieves; seeing leadership as to do with Position – WHERE leaders operate; to seeing leadership as a Process – HOW things get done. At this point in the twenty-first century this demonstrates some progress in our understanding of leadership. In earlier days of academic study into the topic, there initially was a focus on the "Great Man" (it was usually assumed the leader was a man!) or Trait approach to leadership (Fleenor 2006). Studies focused on someone in a position of leadership and attempts were made to see what behavioral and personality traits this person had which distinguished them from others. If these traits were identified, attempts could then be made to inculcate them in others in preparation for future leadership responsibilities. Further approaches were also taken which focused more precisely on behaviors – what effective leaders did – in the search to identify and them emulate effective leadership behaviors. When it was recognized that these approaches were unlikely to identify a universal or generalizable "essence" of leadership, as it were, it became more acceptable to argue that effective leadership depended on the context of operation – someone might be an effective leader in one situation or at one time, but this did not mean they would continue to be effective or that the leadership approach shown in that situation was transferable to other contexts – effective leadership was "contingent" on a number of contextual factors including resources, information, ability levels of staff, communication levels, etc. More recently there have been other approaches which take, in general, a more critical view of the concept of leadership, that is to say, approaches which problematize the concept and seek different understandings be they philosophical, psychological, sociological, or political. The common theme found amongst most of these approaches is one of the exercise of power and influence. It is interesting to note the development in the literature of the distinction between leadership and management. There are those who see these as distinct but related elements in organizational life; others who see them as synonymous; and others again who suggest that leadership is a part of management or indeed vice versa (Kotter 2001). The debate is unresolved, possibly in part because of the difficulty of definition noted above. Those who argue that they are distinct from one another and are both necessary for organization effectiveness note the need for management to establish processes and routines, and to aim for regulation, efficiency, and a degree of certainly or predictability. Leadership on the other hand is required in times or situations of unpredictability or uncertainty, when existing processes or regulations are no longer appropriate and new thinking or actions are required to respond. One particular aspect of the discussion which merits attention is that management carries with it a certain authority (i.e. power) which comes along with the role at the time of appointment. Leadership is not quite as straightforward, in that it is argued that leadership is ascribed to someone in a certain position by those others involved in the context – leadership is accorded or earned, according to this view (Grobler and Holtzhausen 2018). It does not come automatically with appointment to a particular post, nor is necessarily hierarchical. Thus, a manager might not be a leader and a leader might not be a manager. An effective trade union or professional association representative, for example might be seen as displaying effective leadership, without any hierarchical authority.

More recent approaches to leadership have also moved away from the notion that leadership is an individual phenomenon – that is, that leadership is exercised through an individual in any given situation. Such approaches see leadership as being distributed among various actors, possibly among all actors, in any particular context. Such approaches lead to the concept of "leaderful" organizations (Raelin 2011) which develop shared responsibilities, and which encourage widespread communication and innovation. This is not to suggest these approaches advocate egalitarian organizations but that there is much more potential for development and innovation and much more resilience and initiative in organizations that might traditionally be assumed.

Despite the continuing growth of research and literature on leadership, the underpinning evidence which highlights how effective leadership is in operation, is surprisingly sparse (Thorpe et al. 2007). With some notable exceptions, (e.g. Alimo-Metcalfe and Alban Metcalfe 2001) a considerable element of the literature is made up of rhetorical, anecdotal, or aspirational work which fails to define at the outset, its fundamental terms. Thus, it is a fair question to ask whether (more) leadership per se is a "good thing" if it can mean different things to different audiences. One important development in the literature over recent years was the distinction between "distant" and "nearby" leaders. As noted above, initial approaches focused on the "great" people who were familiar figures to much of the population – figures of national or international standing from politics, business, culture, and sport for example. Such leaders were unlikely to interact personally with the vast majority of those who regarded them as leaders, indeed they were unlikely to recognize most of them. The work of Shamir (1995) made the distinction between such people, recognized by much of the populace, and those who were not necessarily recognized beyond their own areas of operation – "nearby" leaders who interacted regularly with those around them and whose influence was mutually recognized.

The importance of the notion of the nearby leader is that it emphasized the inter-relational aspect of leadership, that is, that influence takes effect through the interactions of all those involved in the leadership relationship and that all parties have a role in these interactions. An implicit assumption in the literature is of leaders having the active role in any relations and others having a much more passive role. Thus, we see the traditional axis of leader as opposed to follower with an assumption that the latter are relatively inactive and waiting to be acted upon or energized by the leader, without whom little or nothing would occur. We shall return to this interactional or inter-relational aspect of leadership when we discuss the social work supervision context.

The distinction between distant and nearby leaders can be seen in relation to different aspects of the social work context. One might see distant leaders in this context as those who act as national or international policy makers, or developers and innovators of practice, or key analysts and researchers, or heads of national and international social work bodies. Such figures can be seen to be exercising leadership at a degree of distance from most others in practice in the professional field. They might be responsible for leading innovation, for developing standards, or for promoting a better understanding of the profession e.g. in relation to work with other professional groups or promoting the image or values of the profession in the broader public. At a nearby leadership level, we might see them interacting on a very regular and personal level with professional work colleagues, focusing on development and practice and operational effectiveness.

Purposes of supervision

According to British Association of Social Workers/ College of Social Work (BASW/CoSW) (2011), supervision in social work has several related facets including developing good relationships, good quality practice, good decision-making, and enhancing a learning culture within the organization and profession. It also highlights the combination of this with effective performance management. Two elements here merit further discussion in the context of leadership and supervision. The first is the performance management role and its relationship with supervision because, as we noted above, there is discussion in the organizational literature about the distinctions and commonalities of leadership and management. The second element to note is that of the different aspects of supervision referred to by BASW/CoSW and the extent to which the concept of leadership might apply.

Firstly then leadership and management: as mentioned above much of the literature notes the distinction between the two concepts with the emphasis of management on routinizing certain tasks with an emphasis on predictability, efficient use of resources, and the standardization of work routines and practices (see e.g. Thorpe et al. 2010). Leadership focuses more though on creativity and innovation, effectiveness rather than efficiency per se, and dealing with and in some cases provoking uncertainty through doing things differently. The functions of management and leadership are seen to overlap though, and many writers agree that both are necessary for effective organizations over the longer term. Within the context of social work supervision there is inevitably some tension, particularly as practice supervision is undertaken by one person – thus the leadership and management functions cannot be dealt with by different parties.

In a survey conducted some time ago (BASW 2011), just over half the respondents indicated they were dissatisfied with the frequency of supervision. About half the respondents in the same survey indicated that they felt supervision to be only fair or poor. Similar results appear more recently in a survey of social care workers (Wilkins and Antonopoulou 2019). The different functions of supervision need to be remembered here: The Formative function is developmental and looking at revision of practice, reinforcement of effective elements, and inclusion of elements which are missing. The Normative function focuses on performance in relation to objectives and expectations and looks at standards and their maintenance. Finally, the Restorative function focuses on support, encouragement, and the development of resilience (Inskipp and Proctor 1993). It is first and last of these functions which distinguish leadership from management in this context. The focus of the effective leader is on development and support, the manager on performance and standards. Whilst it not explicit in the above research, it would be reasonable to assume that it is the formative and restorative functions which are missed by the respondents and thus a limitation of leadership which is indicated.

There may be an imperative for social work managers to focus on the more objective and publicly visible function of supervision, the normative aspect at the expense of the other two functions. This is highlighted by Munro (2011) where she notes

> the conundrum facing managers is that the quick way of achieving a minimum standard of practice is through rule and process-driven practice, but this creates obstacles to the development of higher levels of practice. A simple example of how it inhibits learning is that it is a factor in driving staff away and retaining staff is a necessary step to help them achieve expertise.
>
> *(Munro 2011 p. 75)*

Carpenter et al. (2013) also note effective support in supervision as being key to retaining social work staff, particularly in an era where demoralization is reported in the profession (Rogowski 2011).

Leadership and supervision

The supervisor thus plays a key leadership role in retaining and developing individual social workers through supporting and encouraging professional learning and practice. Assuming a passive role for the social worker or "follower" in the leadership dynamic as noted above, s/he is assumed in much of the leadership literature as an inert party awaiting the action of leadership to energize or motivate. Alternatively, there might be the unarticulated assumption that social worker's attitude, commitment, and motivation will remain unchanged as supervision focuses more on enhanced performance and less on learning and support. The nature of social work as being a particularly stressful occupation (Wilberforce et al. 2014) highlights the deficiency of this approach. In similar vein, Beddoe (2017) notes how the focus on an external view of performance – a shift from internal to external regulation – presents a threat to the motivation and commitment of social workers.

In the introduction, we noted the relational aspect of both social work supervision and leadership. There are no universal prescriptions for these just as there are no universal prescriptions for how social work itself is delivered in the interactions between professionals and users, as noted by Munro (2011) among others. The key constituents though of effective relations, e.g. in the casework context, have been recognized (e.g. Biestek 1957), in particular personal contact and recognition, respect, and trust. In the supervisory context and in relation to the leadership process such constituents equally apply. The growth of individualization and the accompanying growth in managerialism in the public services is noted above. As such many private sector approaches have been advocated as being equally applicable to the public sphere. Masal and Vogel (2012) make interesting points in their analysis of the application of such techniques in the public service context. As also noted above, public service managers have increasingly been expected to provide high levels of service with diminishing resources, and more effective leadership is seen as being the means of achieving this. The distinction between normative supervision and formative/supportive is mirrored in Masal and Vogel's discussion of "structural leadership" and "interactional leadership." Structural leadership refers to the way in which individual action is prescribed by regulation, external standards, and targets. Individual discretion is limited by procedures and protocols. The structural framework expects particular activities. Interactional leadership on the other hand refers to the quality of the relationship between staff and manager – in our case between supervisor and social worker. Perhaps counter to expectations, they argue that in highly structured settings where discretion is limited, interactional leadership becomes more important.

> It is precisely those employees who work in a bureaucratic environment where there is apparently little freedom of action and few opportunities for development who need a personal meaningfulness in their everyday lives
>
> *(2012, p. 8).*

This echoes the notion that in some cases within social work, leadership performs an important counterbalance to increased managerialism (Lawler 2013).

Wilkins et al. (2017) point to the focus of supervision in their research as relating to the "what and when" of social work practice to the relative neglect of the "how and why." In Masal and Vogel's terms, this would indicate a preoccupation with structural rather than interactional leadership. There is a parallel here with the points above relating to management and leadership differences with the "what and when" being more managerial and the "how and why" more related to leadership. In that respect "structural leadership" might be viewed as management and "interactional leadership" more related to leadership. Wilkins et al. (2017) found in their research the focus of supervision and of practice to be action-orientated rather than developmental. They discuss the possible reasons for this, some of them being related to a context where resources might be stretched. They also discuss the possibility that supervisors themselves had little opportunity to learn about and reflect on supervision. For their own supervisory practice, they might rely on mirroring their own experiences of being supervised as practitioners and thus perpetuate a particular pragmatic model of supervision. The organization might expect "structural leadership" through its preoccupation with prescribing action, achieving targets, and maintaining standards. The supervisor however has the opportunity to engage in interactional leadership through using the potential in the supervision process to reflect on the emotional and developmental aspects of practice and supervision. The aim of sharing the supervisor's professional experience can be achieved though greater discussion of the "how and why" in reflective discussion of the social worker's practice. These authors also note that aspects of the supervision process take place outside the formal supervision session – through more general interaction and through the supervisor modeling professional and leadership practice in interactions with other professionals and with service consumers. In developing a more equal balance of structural and interactional leadership than is apparent in Wilkins et al.'s (2017) study, the organizations' priorities can be addressed together with professional practice development.

There appears to be a contrast in leadership styles between private and public sector organizations according to Hansen and Villadsen (2017) though it is important to avoid over-generalizations. One might expect a more collegial or participative approach in a professional organization, and this does appear to be the case to some extent. Vogel and Masal (2012) argue that in a professional organization dealing with complexity and uncertainty, a more participative rather than directive approach is advisable in order to encourage inter- and intra-professional learning and to enable innovation and adaptation, bearing in mind the need to maintain professional standards. In addition, public service organizations need to address the expectations of a varied and complex range of stakeholders and to combine often contrasting functions (e.g. care/control) and manage indeterminate outcomes. Participative approaches might lend themselves more appropriately to such contexts. Additionally, in the private service sector, extrinsic rewards in the form of additional pay and bonuses are more easily available and more related directly to individual actions and performance. In such situations a more directive leadership approach might be more accepted and understood.

There is interesting work which brings together the concepts of extrinsic rewards (pay, recognition, bonuses, promotion) with intrinsic rewards (satisfaction, pride, feelings of self-efficacy, and achievement) and which relates to the active nature of all participants in the leadership process. Such work notes that the individual is not a passive object waiting to be energized or motivated but that everyone brings bring her/his own personal experience, expectations, and motivations with them into the work environment. Writers such as Sandel (2012), Pink (2010), and Kohn (1993) argue that, perhaps counter-intuitively, an over-emphasis on extrinsic factors can damage intrinsic motivation rather than add to it. This is an important factor in professional organizations such as social work, where individual professionals are expected to enter the profession for reason other than pay alone. They may bring with them a commitment to equality of service and opportunity to helping others improve their life situations through their professional interventions, to individual development together with a commitment to civic values. The opportunity to engage in meaningful work is also noted as an important reason why people enter public service in general (Perry and Hondeghen 2008) and social work in particular (Baines 2010).

The above writers note the possibility that an over-reliance by leaders on extrinsic factors, can undermine or "crowd out" the intrinsic motivators individual professionals bring to their work. Frey (2000) emphasizes these notions and builds further on them such that we see encouragement to take full account of intrinsic factors to avoid such "crowding out" of commitment but also to "crowd in" such factors through encouraging their combination with other work-based factors. Issues such as self-determination and self-esteem, both intrinsic factors, are noted by Frey as being major individual motivators. Indeed, we see how importantly these factors are in social work as service users are encouraged to develop bother in and through their interactions with social workers and others.

The danger of an inappropriately over-directive, less participative approach to leadership in the supervisory context as well as elsewhere is that individuals feel their self-esteem and self-determination are bother eroded, as professional judgment and status might be perceived as being under threat.

It should be noted that over recent years there has been growing criticism of individualized models of "heroic" leaders and greater attention given to distributed models of leadership:

> Over the last 50 years, much research has focused on organizational forms of a hierarchical nature; wittingly or not, this reinforces the view that knowledge and direction trickle down from a notional "top" of the organization, and that leaders as individuals set the tone and make all the key decisions. These leaders are seen as acting as figureheads, for others (depicted as "followers") to look up to and to follow… Over this period, there has been a decided lack of research evidence for single individuals having the kind of dramatic impact on organizational performance that is so often claimed.
>
> *(Thorpe et al. 2011, p. 239)*

The implicit warning is that too much can be expected of individuals in leadership roles. In the social work supervision context, it is important to acknowledge the relational element of leadership, the need to challenge managerial models of control and compliance, and to promote relationships which encourage reflection, development, and commitment. Supervision presents the opportunity, beyond looking at organizational objectives, to encourage development, to reinforce commitment and the meaningfulness of professional work, to provide a channel for questioning and on occasion, dissent, and to promote reflection and learning and reflection both for the social worker and the supervisor.

Conclusion

It is important to recognize the somewhat problematic nature of the term "leadership" and that there is no generally accepted prescription for effective leadership. It is also important to consider the interactional nature of the leadership process, especially in the context of supervision, that is, it occurs in the interaction between those involved. We have noted pressures in supervision which influence the focus often to be on action, results, targets etc. but we must be mindful of the affective and developmental aspects of supervision and effective leadership. To recap, supervisors and managers more generally, can be appointed to their roles and positions but they need to earn respect and trust to be regarded as effective leaders by those for whom they are responsible. It is also important to recognize that professional social workers bring with them their own experiences, commitment, and motivations to their work and to their supervision. Those commitments and motivations are not a given: inadequate leadership and management put these in jeopardy. The positive potential of effective leadership in supervision is considerable though, both for the social worker – in present and in future practice – and ultimately for the service consumer.

References

Alimo-Metcalfe, B., and Alban-Metcalfe, R.J., 2001. The development of a new transformational leadership questionnaire. *Journal of Occupational and Organizational Psychology*, 74, 1–27.

Alvesson, M., and Sveningsson, S., 2003. The great disappearing act: difficulties in doing "leadership". *Leadership Quarterly*, 14, 359–381.

Baines, D., 2010. "If we don't get back to where we were before": working in the restructured non-profit social services. *British Journal of Social Work*, 40 (3), 928–945.

BASW/CoSW 2011. *England research on supervision in social work, with particular reference to supervision practice in multi-disciplinary teams, England document*. London: BASW/CoSW.

Bauman, Z., 2008. *Identity*. Cambridge: Polity Press.

Beck, U., and Beck-Gernsheim, E. eds., 2002. *Individualization: institutionalised individualism and its social and political consequences*. London: SAGE.

Beddoe, E., 2017. Harmful supervision: a commentary. *The Clinical Supervisor*, 36 (1), 88–101.

Biestek, F.P., 1957. *The casework relationship*. London: George Allen and Unwin.

Carpenter, J., Webb, C.M., and Bostock, L., 2013. The surprisingly weak evidence base for supervision: findings from a systematic review of research in child welfare practice (2000–2012). *Children and Youth Services Review*, 35 (11), 1843–1853.

Ciulla, J., ed., 2014. *Ethics: the heart of leadership*. Santa Barbara, CA: Praeger.

Fahmi, K., 2017. Social work practice and research as an emancipatory process. *In*: L. Davies, eds. *Social work in a corporate era: practices of power and resistance*. London: Routledge, 144–159.

Fleenor, J.W., 2006. *Trait approach to leadership: encyclopedia of industrial and organizational psychology*. London: SAGE.

Frey, B.S., 2000. Motivation and human behaviour. *In*: P. Taylor-Gooby, ed. *Risk, trust and welfare*. Basingstoke: Macmillan, 31–50.

Grint, K., 2005. *Leadership: limits and possibilities*. Basingstoke: Palgrave Macmillan.

Grobler, A., and Holtzhausen, M.M.E., 2018. Supervisory trust to be earned: the role of ethical leadership mediated by person-organisational fit. *South African Journal of Economic and Management Sciences*, 1 (1), 1–11.

Hansen, M.B., and Villadsen, A.R., 2017. The external networking behaviour of public managers - the missing link of weak ties. *Public Management Review*, 19 (10), 1556–1576. 10.1080/14719037.2017.1299200

Inskipp, F., and Proctor, B., 1993. *Making the most of supervision. Part 1*. Twickenham: Cascade.

Jones, R., 2018. *In whose interest?*. London: Policy Press.

Kohn, A., 1993. *Punished by rewards: the trouble with gold stars, incentive plans, a's, praise and other bribes*. Boston: Houghton Mifflin.

Kotter, J., 2001. What leaders really do. *Harvard Business Review*, 79 (11, December), 23–34. Reprint of article originally published in 1990.

Lawler, J., 2013. Critical management. *In*: M. Gray, and S.A. Webb, eds. *The new politics of critical social work*. London: Palgrave Macmillan, 98–115.

Lawler, J., 2016. Social care and social work leadership. *In*: J. Storey, ed. *Leadership in organizations: current issues and key trends*. 3rd ed. London: Routledge, 249–263.

Munro, E., 2011. *The 'Munro review' of child protection: final report, a child-centred system*. London: Stationery Office.

O'Brien, M., and Penna, S., 1998. *Theorising welfare: enlightenment and modern society*. London: Sage.

Pendleton, D., and Furnham, A., 2016. *Leadership: all you need to know*. 2nd ed. London: Palgrave Macmillan.

Perry, J.L., and Hondeghem, A., eds., 2008. *Motivation in public management: the call of public service*. Oxford: Oxford University Press.

Pfeffer, J., and Sutton, R.I., 2006. *Hard facts, dangerous half-truths, and total nonsense: profiting from evidence-based management*. Boston: Harvard Business School Press.

Pink, D.H., 2010. *Drive: the surprising truth about what motivates us*. Edinburgh: Canongate.

Raelin, J., 2011. From leadership-as-practice to leaderful practice. *Leadership*, 7 (2), 195–211.

Rosenbach, W.E., Taylor, R.L., and Youndt, M.A., eds., 2018. *Contemporary issues in leadership*. 7th ed. London & New York: Routledge.

Rogowski, S., 2011. Managers, managerialism and social work with children and families: the deformation of a profession? *Practice*, 23 (3), 157–167. doi: 10.1080/09503153.2011.569970

Sandel, M., 2012. *What money can't buy: the moral limits to markets*. London: Penguin Books.

Senge, P., 1999. The gurus speak (panel discussion): complexity and organizations. *Emergence*, 1 (1), 73–91.

Shamir, B., 1995. Social distance and charisma: theoretical notes and an exploratory study. *Leadership Quarterly*, 6 (1), 19–47.

Stogdill, R.M., 1974. *Handbook of leadership: a survey of theory and research*. New York: Free Press.

Storey, J. ed., 2016. *Leadership in organizations: current issues and key trends*. 3rd ed. London: Routledge.

Sullivan, H., and Skelcher, C., 2002. *Working across boundaries: collaboration in public services*. London: Palgrave Macmillan.

Sutcliffe-Braithwaite, F., 2018. *Class, politics and the decline of deference in England, 1968–2000*. Oxford: Oxford University Press.

Thorpe, R., Gold, J., and Lawler, J., 2011. Locating distributed leadership. *International Journal of Management Reviews Special Issue*, 13 (3), 239–250.

Thorpe, R., Gold, J., and Mumford, A., eds., 2010. *Gower handbook of leadership and management development*. London & New York: Gower.

Thorpe, R., Lawler, J., and Gold, J., 2007. *Systematic review*. Leeds: University of Leeds, Northern Leadership Academy.

Vogel, R., and Masal, D., 2012. Publicness, motivation and leadership: the dark side of private management concepts in the public sector. *Administration and Public Management*, 19, 6–15.

West, M., Armit, K., Loewenthal, L., Eckert, R., West, T., and Lee, A., 2015. *Leadership and leadership development in health care: the evidence base*. London: Kings Fund.

Wilberforce, M., Jacobs, S., Challis, D., Manthorpe, J., Stevens, M., Jasper, R., Fernandez, J.-L., et al. 2014. Revisiting the causes of stress in social work: sources of job demands, control and support in personalised adult social care. *British Journal of Social Work*, 44 (4): 812–830. doi: 10.1093/bjsw/bcs166

Wilkins, D., and Antonopoulou, V., 2019. What does supervision help with? a survey of 315 social workers in the UK. *Practice*, 31 (1), 21–40.

Wilkins, D., Forrester, D., and Grant, L., 2017. What happens in child and family supervision?. *Child and Family Social Work*, 22 (2), 942–951.

42

"RIDING THE JUGGERNAUT"

Tensions and opportunities in management supervision

Trish Hafford-Letchfield

Introduction

Over the past couple of decades, the impact of neo-liberalism, globalization, and austerity on public services have influenced a move towards increased inspection and surveillance of professional social work practice alongside calls for greater management control (Lawler and Bilson 2009; Hafford-Letchfield et al. 2014). There has been a resurgence of counter narratives as we learn more about the significance of relationships in our day-to-day work and what this means for moving towards creating a healthier organizational culture to improve quality (Rønningstad 2019). We are also accumulating increasing evidence on trauma-informed approaches when working in difficult contexts (Easki 2020) and realizing the potential that comes through working within flatter and more collaborative structures and processes which can better facilitate co-production (Jierk 2020). Within this context, professional supervision remains one of the main instruments of social work management and can be harnessed by managers in many different ways so as to promote their individual relationships with front line staff as well as providing a potential tool to mediate between staff and the organization's changing demands. More importantly, professional supervision has always been cited within the social work literature as one of the most effective tools for facilitating and supporting individuals to contain and work with the anxiety that naturally arises within social work practice and can be at the root of its many failings (Bourne and Hafford-Letchfield 2011; Hafford-Letchfield and Huss 2018). As we move to multi-professional, integrated arrangements in the UK, it has been important for social workers to be able to support and challenge decisions when working with other professionals (Department of Health and Social Care 2018). Through its different functions, supervision therefore provides an opportunity for managers to engage staff with the vision of the organization and become an arbiter of the quality and standards of professional practice within it (Hafford-Letchfield 2006).

This chapter reviews some of the relevant literature and research findings on the specific features of management supervision and what we might learn from such a review for contemporary practice. Paying attention to some of the strategies and practice of managers in supervision systems, relationships and outcomes can help to challenge tacit or taken-for-granted modes of supervision as well to challenge some of the negativity about the role that managers are seen to play and described in recent narratives of neo-liberalism (Lambley 2010). It is important to highlight the important functions of supervision that can be prioritized within management practice and the value given to creating a space for both managers and staff to reflect critically on the context in which they work and on the opportunities to lead change. Looking at supervision through a management lens highlights how supervision does not exist in a vacuum and at how wider organizational issues inevitably impact on the supervisory process. Giddens (1990, p. 53) used the term "riding the juggernaut," to characterize the complexity of institutional frameworks and rapidly expanding information/knowledge that comes with negotiating these. Cooper (2005) also pointed to clear tensions between surface and depth issues in social work often ignored in any ensuing critiques of social work practice following critical incidents. Cooper highlighted how managers may be only skimming the surface of some of the anxieties being contained in the organization around the often difficult, complex, and sometimes dangerous work that they and their staff are dealing with in social care. In this chapter therefore I will pay attention to some of the strategies that managers might use to mediate these uncertainties and to demonstrate balanced, nuanced, and compassionate supervision practices which are also framed within maintaining and supporting the best standards of social work possible.

Not all supervision is concerned with conceptualized risks in providing care services. An enabling management style involves shared values, purpose, and a collaborative culture as well as the sharing of authentic leadership – the value base of equality and empowerment underpinning social care which fits with this model of working (Haworth et al. 2019). It also fits with a strengths-based approach in the way that it values the voice of individuals and the experiences they bring to directly involve them in decision making processes.

Practitioners need to be able to shape strengths-based practice for people working with adults, families, and communities. This can happen if managers themselves model the behavior they want practitioners in the organization to emulate, by behaving in a way that is aligned with the strengths-based practice – so as to cultivate and reinforce a culture and ethos that is relationship based and strengths-based (Department of Health and Social Care 2019). As far back as the 1960s, Winnicott talked about creating a holding environment in which staff feel safe and supported in carrying out their work, and in which in turn benefits service users served by staff who feel well cared for (Winnicott 1965). Such containment refers to meeting the basic needs of, and providing physical care and safety for, the people within the environment. Using both structure and support managers provide a lynchpin for working in the organization in a way that is as predictable as possible organizing roles and responsibilities, involving people, and affirming their contribution. These should also be combined with support that includes kindness as the basis of a structure that fosters predictability and control.

Managers, managerialism, and marketization of care services

The social work literature has been resplendent in its numerous critiques of the impact of managerialism and the extensive marketization of care services (Clarke and Newman 1997; Harris 2002; Tsui and Cheung 2004; Hafford-Letchfield et al. 2014). The introduction of traditional management and leadership theory into environments where uncertainty, turbulence, and issues of inequality and power are at the core of most of its business have given rise to tensions for everyone involved (Lawler and Bilson 2009). Within this context, social work appears to be in a continuous state of fluctuation or always at the point of a major transformation (Higgins 2016a). In the UK for example, serious case reviews and national reports following critical incidents in social work have cited the importance of effective oversight of practice through skillful managerial and professional supervision (Stanley and Manthorpe 2004; Laming 2009) and have led to major reforms mostly in social work education (Social Work Task Force 2009; Munro 2011;

Narey 2014). The response has also given rise to reforms which seek to standardize practice for example in the many "Knowledge and Skills Statements" published in specialist areas thought necessary to guide future capabilities for the social work workforce (Department for Education 2015; Department of Health and Social Care 2018). These have resulted in a process-driven approach (Wilson 2013) rather than emphasizing quality and effectiveness (Higgins 2016a). This reduction of the complexity of social work knowledge and skills to a series of statements or their "commodification" (Brancaleone and O'Brien 2011) creates the illusion that all is needed is more guidance and standards and managers to oversee their implementation. Beck (1994) referred to these processes as "linear" learning. Higgins (2016b) has also critiqued the concepts of linear learning or so called "objective process of facts" and "right decisions" to reflect on what he sees as an uncontested and unambiguous approach to managing practice which is not always helpful nor authentic and can actually promote failure to translate findings into specific, realistic, and achievable goals.

One of the more important features coming out of reviews of critical incidents and failures in social work practice over the last decade is the need for closer scrutiny of those working at more senior levels in organizations with statutory responsibilities for safeguarding children and adults, and of accountability at this level (Sidebotham 2010; Francis 2013). Contributory factors such as the difficult conditions faced by practitioners working with complex and challenging situations in social care, together with criticisms about the decision-making and practice of front-line practitioners and their supervising managers in a range of professions for their failings to adequately safeguard vulnerable people in the front line, are also being challenged (Laming 2009; SCIE 2015). Poor working conditions on the frontline of services, in which inadequate support for social workers, poor communication, and even antagonistic relations between social workers and managers have to some extent worked against the capacity of managers to lead and manage services (Hafford-Letchfield et al. 2014). Sidebotham et al. (2010) for example in their study of learning from Serious Case Reviews recommended that engaging practitioners, and indeed organizations, with the process needs to be done in a constructive and supportive manner including effective mechanisms for feedback and debrief. The nature of the process can also feel threatening to organizations which may have an internal agenda to protect themselves, hence quality internal systems analysis may not occur. Further, the emotional impact of Serious Case Reviews on practitioners, and the need to support professionals through the process, so that they are able to learn from it places dual emphasis on learning and support being clearly embedded in any process.

All these issues point towards the need for continuous assessment and development of management skills and the opportunity for managers to be adequately supported for providing good quality supervision. In summary, management supervision is one of the most significant and meaningful ways in which managers can gain insight into the everyday work of social work staff, maximize the potential of different stakeholders, manage the process of delegation, and monitor and evaluate performance on behalf of the organization (Bourn and Hafford-Letchfield 2011). This goes hand in hand with a more compassionate and ethical approach (Hafford-Letchfield 2019).

Finally, Carpenter et al. (2012) found strong links between supervisory support and actual turnover and retention rates in social care and drew conclusions that good supervision can help workers to stay in their jobs, given that leavers often cite poor supervision as a reason for having left. This latter point is crucial when we think about the challenges facing the social work workforce (Wermerling 2013). The combination of effective supervision arrangements, together with a suitable working environment, manageable workloads, supportive management systems, and access to continuous learning, will help to ensure that social workers are able to provide good and responsive services for children, adults, and families. By creating these conditions, employers will help to provide a setting in which social workers choose to work and remain. The UK Government set out its vision to develop a confident, skilled, and capable profession which has received the best training; is supported through a clear, practice-based career pathway to enable progression from practitioner to supervisor to principal social worker or other senior practitioner or leadership roles; and has opportunities to specialize in key areas of practice and improve outcomes for people (Department of Health and Social Care 2018).

It is easy to forget that managers themselves may experience unmanageable workloads and unmet needs for support and continuing professional development (Hafford-Letchfield et al. 2014). Supervisors have reported that critical reflection and power issues were rarely considered within the context of their own supervision with senior managers despite the desire for a more open dialogue. Supervisors' own supervision tended to focus on administrative aspects, and modeling from their own managers is even more desirable (Bogo and Dill 2008). Experienced supervisors stressed the importance of receiving supervision themselves despite their knowledge particularly in respect of clinical decision making, critical thinking, parallel processes, and personal issues related to using their power and authority. However, they felt that these opportunities were rarely available to them (Bogo and Dill 2008).

Demarcating management and leadership

There is a demarcated process of interpersonal influence when talking about the differences between management and leadership (Alvesson and Jonsson 2016). Interpersonal leadership includes a wide variety of behaviors centering on the relationship between the manager supervisor and the supervisee, such as listening, discussing, and providing feedback (Rønningstad 2019). Rønningstad's research found that managers and supervisees or subordinates experienced managers' characteristics and behaviors as leadership, viewed leadership in relational terms, and characterized it as personable, emphatic, and showing engagement. These characteristics linked to their managers' interpersonal behaviors such as chatting and answering questions. This experience of supervisees who saw their supervising managers as leaders, illustrates this integration between management behaviors and leadership characteristics. Other examples given by Rønningstad (2019) included possession of knowledge, the evaluation of the quality of supervisees' work, and the combination of administration and decision making. What was stressed within these research findings was the importance of managers' reality or meaning-making influence which was found to be valuable in offering a structure for the supervisee's work and gave supervisees a framework within which to operate. Rønningstad (2019) concluded that it was these management structuring and controlling actions that were motivating from the supervisees' perspective, as it offered a means of acknowledging their contributions and provided feelings of security.

An unambiguous, clear, authoritative approach with clear expectations and willingness to help suggested in this study has been born out in government guidance:

> Practice supervisors should strike a balance between employing a managerial, task focussed approach and a reflective, enabling, leadership style to achieve efficient day-to-day functioning.
>
> *(Department for Health and Social Care 2018, p. 11)*

In conclusion, Rønningstad's (2019) findings illuminate how management behaviors such as deciding, controlling, and structuring the work create arenas for leadership and how these arenas vary with the standardization of work tasks. The findings connect employees' leadership experiences to their need for management, and thus challenge the assumption that management tasks are a hindrance to leadership in the public welfare sector.

What "works" in managerial supervision and its different functions?

The remainder of this chapter will look at some of the functions of supervision which have come to be known as the hard and soft knowledge and skills in the context of the literature providing evidence on what is working well or might work better.

Administrative functions and the use of power and authority

Managers should be able to explain to practitioners the full legal, regulatory, procedural and performance framework within which they operate and be accountable for their work within it. Structured supervision can provide opportunities for staff to give and receive constructive feedback on their performance and to respond by recognizing and commending hard work and excellent practice so as to support the social worker build confidence in their practice as well as to challenge complacency and holding poor practice to account.

Abraham and Vinarski-Peretz (2010) have advocated the use of skills such as diplomacy, tact, and persuasiveness by means of argument or entreaty by which socially skilled leaders are likely to design and shape healthy work relationships in their organizations and appropriate use of authority. They assert the value in these activities and associating costs with the investment in such skills for example, increased productivity, quality, and financial returns. Central to the supervisory role is the way in which power and authority are understood and used as supervisors balance organizational and administrative oversight with their commitment to the empowerment and professional development of frontline staff (Bogo and Dill 2008).

Some research has found that front-line workers will engage in tactics to bend (or sometimes break) program rules if they view that policies and procedures are misaligned with service user needs (Borry and Henderson 2020). Similarly, Bogo and Dill (2008) suggest that exercising administrative functions are crucial to encompassing accountability for workers' practice including those made which involve life-changing decisions for service users and the means by which the organization takes responsibility for these. Managers as supervisors have to account for such controversial decisions to the public, and in particular, senior managers need to account for decisions that result in negative consequences (see also Cooper 2005). According to Kadushin and Harkness (2002), using authority is legitimized in collaboration with directives to frontline workers.

Rai's (2013) research into management in long term care facilities suggests that staff want a certain amount of control exercised by upper hierarchal levels for direction, guidance, and coordination of different activities. His findings assert that both centralization and formalization of control can be positively correlated with job satisfaction and suggests that the use of rules and procedures may be healthy for the organization in these circumstances Further, Rai considers the Weberian formulation of bureaucracy, in which centralization and formalization may be positively correlated with each other and the two different forms of control used simultaneously. Rai (2013) concluded that hierarchy of authority and rules and procedures are essential for the smooth functioning of the organization. The findings from this study reveal that bureaucracy may not always be bad for all organizations. In the long-term care environment, staffs' perception of senior authority and the rules were positively related, and this served to enhance satisfaction for them. It also served to minimize role conflict by the communication of clear expectations.

The way the supervisor negotiates and demonstrates this power and authority affects the supervisor/supervisee working relationship through initial contracting and through their work together. There is a tension between the motivation and desire supervisors experience to be supportive, empowering, and respectful or when faced with instances where they need to set limits and hold workers accountable to organizational and professional expectations.

Research conducted by Bourn and Hafford-Letchfield (2011) looked at how managers conveyed expectations and mediated organizational culture. Organizational culture is commonly understood as "the way we do things around here." Handy (1976, p. 176) argues that "deep-set beliefs" about the way work should be organized and how authority should be exercised, and people rewarded and controlled are all parts of the culture of an organization. Front-line managers have a key role in mediating organizational culture through the way in which they manage their staff, reward, and control them and the extent to which they allow flexibility and initiative or expect obedience or compliance. Managers in Bourn and Hafford-Letchfield's study used devices such as the frequent use of humor, somewhat ironic apologies, or other tactics for diffusing conflict and aggravation or for gaining compliance with the implementation of otherwise unwelcome procedural changes. For example, managers often used the pronoun "we" as in "We need to…" or "I need you to …," clearly indicating that they were talking on behalf of the organization and reflecting some of the authority behind their supervisory role or they distanced themselves from the task required by indicating a lack of ownership so that the request was seen as cosmetic rather than a real meaningful "demand." This enabled them to assert a demand without any further explanation or sense of accountability – but nevertheless this was a "rule" which required compliance. Such tactics were used to reduce tension around issues such as time management and implementation of new policies, suggesting a "we're in this together" and "it has to be done" stance. However, many settings are likewise characterized by continuing policy and guidance, which renders the role of the supervisor challenging. Bogo and Dill's (2008) metaphor of "walking the tightrope" (p. 147) accurately depicts this rebalancing of support with agency demands. They suggested that managers do not generally perceive themselves to be agents of organizational change but rather more like conduits, or messengers, between senior managers and frontline workers. Organizational culture is therefore a powerful and determining factor related to how power and authority issues are played out in supervision. In research done by Bogo and Dill, participants identified a "culture of fear" (p. 148), seen in defensive and angry reactions to cases portrayed in a negative light in the media and thus reinforcing the message that accountability is the predominant driver in the supervisory relationship. Supervisors also reported that critical reflection and power issues were rarely considered within the context of their own supervision with senior managers despite the desire for a more open dialogue. Supervisors' own supervision tended to focus on administrative aspects, and modeling from their own managers was seen as desirable. Experienced supervisors stressed the importance of receiving supervision themselves despite their knowledge particularly in respect of decision making, critical thinking, parallel processes, and personal issues related to using their power and authority. However, they felt that these opportunities were rarely available. The sharing of authority through delegation of tasks and diffusing of power through this process has been suggested as one tactic (Conaway 2019).

Supervision strategies that enhance relationships with supervisees

As already stated, supervision offers a positive place where feelings of distress and anxiety can be expressed and the worker given appropriate support. Conaway (2019) found that trust was a feature of those supervisors sharing authority with supervisees in the belief that this promoted worker competence in decision making. Trust was also seen as a feature in unique relationships except where there were competency issues. Given that many supervisors have to trust in the information given and its accuracy, Conway found that the lack of trust influenced a supervisor's interactions with supervisees and eroded the capacity to develop an open and honest relationship.

As discussed earlier, hierarchical, competitive, power-based relationships discount the knowledge of the social worker and ignore larger social and political contexts (Tsui 1997; Hair and O'Donoghue 2009). Hair and O'Donoghue argue for a social constructionist lens which they say can help to shape supervisory relationships and thereby encourage transparency, collaboration, and an exchange of ideas. They also suggest that this can be strengthened when the supervisor is coming from a position of unknowing and curiosity. Similarly, Lusk et al. (2017) highlight the importance of incorporating the supervisee's cultural orientation, values, and social position into the practice of social work supervision in view of the profession becoming more diverse and the requisite for culturally competent and effective practice. They suggest that the incorporation of critical analysis of privilege, power, and intersectionality in both supervision and practice is one way to address the supervisor-worker relationship which can be fraught, with power differentials and distorted supervisory styles based on privilege. Asserting that cultural humility is at the foundation of critical cultural competence, Lusk et al. (2017) suggest taking steps to level the supervision relationship and taking steps to reframe this more in the terms of a peer professional partnership. This echoes the earlier theme of organizational culture, where the tone of supervision can mimic the organizational culture and becomes more didactic and thus nullify the rich intellectual discourse that supervision should reinforce. Lusk et al. (2017) also refer to managers who themselves may be from traditionally oppressed or marginalized groups. Such managers may have been acculturated to the dominant culture and traditional management styles which may lead them to acceptance and incorporation of dominant values and worldviews or to be worried about how they are perceived. Their findings from a survey of 262 social workers to assess their experiences with their workplace supervisors found room for improvement in how supervisors are able to respond to cultural diversity and appreciate and respect cultures and identities over business imperatives. Building further on the strengths-based approach stressed at the beginning of this chapter, it is reiterated that recognizing how the culture and identity of social workers are among the person's best assets will enable managers to operate from the perspective that the supervisee is already well trained, competent, and ethical and that the supervisor's role is to inspire, guide, and focus the work rather than to find fault. Further, Lusk et al. (2017) found a manager's belief that the supervisee is capable and qualified provides the potential to create an atmosphere of trust, safety, and shared leadership.

In an exploration of the use of compassion in practice supervision, Hafford-Letchfield (2019) utilized Nussbaum's (2017) seven dimensions of compassionate leadership to identify what can be used to support good social care practice. These included:

1. Attentiveness – to show an interest in others during a personal encounter
2. Active listening – stimulating the person to tell their story and share emotion
3. Naming of suffering – acknowledging what is going on, encouraging expressions of loss, paraphrasing a person's experiences, and recognizing the significance of these. This can be done both with the experiences of staff and people with lived experience
4. Involvement by sharing emotion and establishing mutuality and trust so the person feels safe
5. Helping and demonstrating an urge to be of value through one's actions
6. Being present both physically and emotionally and noticing what is important to the person
7. Having an understanding of suffering and loss and the emotions that go with it, drawing on professional skills of inquiry and knowledge to promote these.

Hafford-Letchfield (2019) also drew on research by Yuill and Mueller-Hirth (2019) which involved social workers describing their "compassionate self." The "compassionate self" is relevant to all professional caring roles. It may be formed early in life when recognizing the suffering of others. It can also emerge from a disenchantment with a previous work life where one goes on to seek greater meaning and purpose to make a meaningful difference to the lives of others. For example, sometimes people change direction and follow a career in caring – a career which involves using skills such as counseling and therapeutic techniques. Yuill and Mueller-Hirth's research revealed that despite the presence of some demoralizing and damaging factors at work, where staff positively framed compassionate moments and reflected on these made their job worthwhile. This positive reflection acted as a buffer against other less welcome demands in the job and kept people in the profession against the odds. Supervisors can support staff to balance job related demands with positive factors and to reflect on the impact compassionate moments have on them and the people they work with.

Hafford-Letchfield (2019) suggests that if people observe the systems they work in to be careless, with little social or emotional support, they may be reluctant to perceive themselves as a part of that organization and seek other employment. They may also be less likely to engage in compassion or in exercising compassionate leadership. West and Chowla (2017) published evidence from the NHS which suggested that hierarchical and top-down approaches to leadership are ineffective ways of managing in care organizations. Leaders who model a commitment to high-quality and compassionate care were shown to have a profound effect on clinical effectiveness; service user's safety and experience; the efficiency with which resources are used; and the health, wellbeing, and engagement of staff.

Understanding and respecting dignity at work has been defined by Hodson (2001) as "the ability to establish a sense of self-worth and self-respect and to appreciate the respect of others" (p. 3). Manager supervisors have an important influence and through this can model and encourage dignity, resistance, and resilience. Hodson talks about the idea of organizational citizenship where people pursue meaning and social relations at work. Being able to recognize the multi-dimensional nature of dignity is important for leading effective compassionate care services. Respecting the dignity of both people with lived experience and staff is important so as not to cause contradictions in the care environment. Staff dignity is as a critical factor in the development of healthy workplaces, work-life balance, and quality services.

Enabling coping, compassion, and resilience

At a micro level, compassion fatigue is a recognized phenomenon that may occur when social care professionals experience vicarious trauma related to the repeated exposure of working with people who experience traumatic events (Figley 1995). This can negatively affect people's personal and/or professional lives, coping capacity, and result in a decreased sense of accomplishment. This can negatively impact the capacity of staff to support the wellbeing of people with lived experience and may also increase staff turnover. Managers will need to consider the risk factors for staff that may have little experience in working with trauma or have their own history of trauma which may surface when they are exposed to traumatic events within their work. Getting to know staff well and recognizing and fostering compassion is important (Yuill and Mueller-Hirth 2019). Conaway (2019) and Hafford-Letchfield (2014, 2019) have both referred to the need for managers to also be able to work with the diversity of front-line staff identities and appreciate how these interact in complex ways that might also in turn differentially shape service users' experiences making these susceptible to discretionary decision-making that may result in divergent "treatments" even where there is a strong evidence-base. Mosely et al. (2019) further argues that combining a learning approach with a social work perspective that utilizes research alongside relationships, allows for individual interpretation, and the organizational realities will only be effectively done when organizations are open to learning, not held at knifepoint (see also Conaway 2019).

There is significant evidence of inequalities in opportunities for career progression and in the development of leadership more generally for people from diverse backgrounds. Factors include ethnicity, religion, gender and sexual identity, and disability (Hafford-Letchfield 2011; Spillet 2014; Ryan et al. 2016). The role of managers in nurturing staff from diverse communities to bring something unique to organizations, can make a contribution at many levels and can give a sense of achievement to individual staff as leaders in making a difference to their community (Spillet 2014, p. 34). Supervisors have a significant role in enabling discussions that promote equality and in providing opportunities and support to overcome barriers to taking up leadership opportunities. Compassionate managers take time to understand people's individual lives and experiences, to support them to identify their interests and make the most of leadership development opportunities (Hafford-Letchfield 2019).

To help develop resilience, Bourassa's (2012) study of nine social workers in adult safeguarding identified some protective factors for managers to be aware of in their supervision practice with staff experiencing challenges. Bourassa found workers with good training, that equipped them with knowledge and skills to make sense of the situations they were dealing with, were able to:

- Create boundaries, for example between their personal and work life and recognizing the importance of recognizing the roles of other professionals
- Provide co-worker support such as initiating peer groups that openly discussed the signs of compassion fatigue and provided opportunities to discuss issues in a safe non-confrontational environment
- Initiate self-care strategies such as taking exercise and holidays

Bogo and Dill (2008) have also highlighted the importance of supervisors' own professional development. Supervisors identified the value of experience and how they tended to be more self-conscious about their perceived power and authority over staff members, which then became more integrated as they grew with experience and developed a more assertive style of working. Collaborative models require skillful practitioners able to engage and work with service users in a way that shares and does not abdicate power.

Again, many of the managers in Bourn and Hafford-Letchfield's study (2011), whilst very skilled in active listening and clearly committed to a participatory style of supervision, succumbed to demands and pressures such as inputting data into their laptops during supervision meetings and collecting information for auditing purposes, and these diversions prevent managers from practically offering space for more reflective discussion and so inevitably impacts on the effective management of emotion in the workplace and ultimately affects staff morale. Busy managers need skills in balancing organizational and administrative oversight with a commitment to the empowerment of their staff and service.

Conclusion

This chapter has focused specifically on some of the unique functions and challenges for managers supervising social workers and has drawn on some of the relevant literature to make some distinctions here. Overall, the findings point to the central importance of relationships in supervision and the ability to create a supportive space for discussion and reflection and to balance these with other tensions encountered by supervisor managers which also talk to the different supervisory functions commonly described in the literature (Kadushin and Harkness 2002; Morrison 2006). As we learn more about what contributes to good relationships and thus organizational culture, one such tension is to ensure that staff support and development needs do not become more peripheral in the context of pressures on resources and the drive towards greater performance measurement and increasing management surveillance. These inevitably impact on the degree of trust and professional confidence within the supervisory relationship and will have a direct impact on their practice, service quality, and the experiences of service users.

Investment in a manager's own supervision as they develop and cultivate their management roles can grow with experience to facilitate a more assertive style of working so that they can work in a way that shares but does not abdicate power. As will have been rehearsed many times within the contributions to this handbook, supervision is traditionally seen as having three functions: administrative/managerial (to achieve competent accountable performance); welfare and personal (to support the professional in work which may be complex and emotionally challenging); and professional development (to ensure staff have the necessary knowledge, skills, values, and ethics (Kadushin and Harkness 2002). A fourth role relates to mediation (between the individual worker and the organization, and between other professions). Good quality supervision incorporates learning and support functions. Giving and receiving positive and also critical constructive feedback can create an atmosphere of learning, self-improvement, and strong sense of security whilst contributing to organizational objectives (Hafford-Letchfield et al. 2008, 2019). Rogers (2002) suggests that facilitation of learning rests upon certain attitudinal qualities that exist within the relationship. Kadushin and Harkness (2002) highlight the need for supervising managers to have a good professional knowledge of the field as well as skills in coordinating work, setting limits, and manageable goals, monitoring progress for front-line workers and creating a climate of belief and trust.

Despite the intentions towards good supervisory practice, however, research suggests that managers themselves are not only among the most stressed workers within social services departments but also consider themselves to be the least well-prepared and supported to do their current job (Balloch et al. 1995; Bourn and Hafford-Letchfield 2011; Department for Children, Schools and Families 2009).

Positive relationships, communication, and informal and supportive interactions are essential "riding the juggernaut" for effective supervisory relationships. Being valued, encouraged, positively reinforced, and appreciated are important for job satisfaction. Open communication between supervisors and social workers is a key element of empowerment strategies and allows social workers to access resources, information, and support in the organization to get the job done successfully (Hafford-Letchfield et al. 2014). Upward communication, job relevant communication, information exchange, and supportive relationships are thus empowerment factors for staff, enabling them to vent their feelings and express their concerns, views, and perceptions of the work and articulate service user needs.

References

Abraham, C., and Vinarski-Peretz, H., 2010. Linking leader social skills and organisational health to positive work relationships in local governments. *Local Government Studies*, 36 (1), 151–169.
Alvesson, M., and Jonsson, A., 2016. The bumpy road to exercising leadership: fragmentations in meaning and practice. *Leadership*, 14 (1), 40–57.
Balloch, S., Andrew, T., Ginn, T., McLean, J., and Williams, J., 1995. *Working in the social services*. London: National Institute Social Work Research Unit.

Beck, U., 1994. The reinvention of politics in: towards a theory of reflexive modernisation. *In*: U. Beck, A. Giddens, and S. Lash, eds. *Reflexive modernisation*. Cambridge: Polity Press, 1–55.

Bogo, M., and Dill, K., 2008. Walking the tightrope using power and authority in child welfare supervision. *Child Welfare*, 87 (6), 141–57.

Borry, E.L., and Henderson, A.C., 2020. Patients, protocols, and prosocial behavior: rule breaking in frontline health care. *The American Review of Public Administration*, 50 (1), 45–61. doi:10.1177/0275074019862680

Bourassa, D., 2012. Examining self-protection measures guarding adult protective services social workers against compassion fatigue. *Journal of Interpersonal Violence*, 27 (9), 1699–1715. https://doi.org/10.1177/0886260511430388

Bourn, D., and Hafford-Letchfield, T., 2011. Professional supervision in conditions of uncertainty. *International Journal of Knowledge, Culture and Change Management*, 10 (9), 41–56.

Brancaleone, D., and O'Brien, S., 2011. Educational commodification and the (economic) sign value of learning outcomes. *British Journal of Sociology of Education*, 32 (4), 501–519.

Carpenter, J., Webb, C., Bostock, L., and Coomber, C., 2012. *Effective supervision in social work and social care SCIE research briefing 43*. London: Social Care Institute for Excellence. Available from: https://www.scie.org.uk/publications/briefings/briefing43/ [Accessed 27 March 2020].

Clarke, J., and Newman, J., 1997. *The managerial state*. London: SAGE.

Conaway, C., 2019. *Maximizing research use in the world we actually live in: relationships, organizations, and interpretation*. (CALDER Policy Brief No. 14-0319-1). Washington, DC: National Center for Analysis of Longitudinal Data in Education Research. Available from: http://caldercouncil.org/wp-content/uploads/2020/03/CALDER-Policy-Brief-14-0319-1.pdf [Accessed 27 March 2020].

Cooper, A., 2005. Surface and depth in the Victoria Climbié inquiry report. *Child & Family Social Work*, 10, 1–9. doi:10.1111/j.1365-2206.2005.00350.x

Department for Children, Schools and Families, 2009. *The protection of children in England, action plan: the government's response to lord laming*. London: The Stationery Office.

Department of Health 2015. *Knowledge and skills statement for social workers in adult services*. London: DH. Available from: https://assets.publishing.service.gov.uk/government/uploads/system/uploads/attachment_data/file/411957/KSS.pdf [Accessed 27 March 2020].

Department for Health and Social Care 2018. *Post qualifying standards for social work practice supervisors in adult social care*. London: DHSC. Available from: https://assets.publishing.service.gov.uk/government/uploads/system/uploads/attachment_data/file/762818/Post-qualifying_standards_for_social_work_supervisors.pdf [Accessed 27 March 2020].

Department for Health and Social Care 2019. *Guidance: strengths-based social work: practice framework and handbook*. London: DHSC. Available from: https://assets.publishing.service.gov.uk/government/uploads/system/uploads/attachment_data/file/778134/stengths-based-approach-practice-framework-and-handbook.pdf [Accessed 27 March 2020].

Esaki, N., 2020. Trauma-responsive organizational cultures: how safe and supported do employees feel?. *Human Service Organizations: Management, Leadership & Governance*, 44 (1), 1–8.

Fabelo, H., O'Connor, M.K., Netting, F.E., and Wyche, A.K., 2013. When the paradoxical is ideal: employees' perceptions of their organizations, work units, and ideal workplaces. *Administration in Social Work*, 37 (4), 340–355. doi:10.1080/03643107.2012.693461

Figley, C.R., 1995. Compassion fatigue as secondary traumatic stress disorder: an overview. *In*: C.R. Figley, ed. *Compassion fatigue: coping with secondary traumatic stress disorder in those who treat the traumatized*. New York, NY: Brunner/Mazel, 1–20.

Francis, R., 2013. *Report of the mid staffordshire NHS foundation trust public inquiry executive summary*. London: HMSO. Available from: https://assets.publishing.service.gov.uk/government/uploads/system/uploads/attachment_data/file/279124/0947.pdf [Accessed 27 March 2020].

Giddens, A., 1990. *The consequences of modernity*. Cambridge: Polity Press.

Hafford-Letchfield, T., 2006. *Management and organisations in social work*. Exeter: Learning Matters Ltd.

Hafford-Letchfield, T., 2011. Sexuality and women in care organisations: negotiating boundaries within a gendered cultural script. *In*: P. Dunk-West, and T. Hafford-Letchfield, eds. *Sexual identities and sexuality in social work: research and reflections from women in the field*. Ashgate: Contemporary Social Work Studies, 11–30.

Hafford-Letchfield, T., 2019. *Leading with compassion: supervisors briefing*. Research in Practice for Adults, Totnes, RiPfA. Available from: https://strathprints.strath.ac.uk/71277/1/Hafford_Letchfield_RiPfA2019_Leading_compassion_supervisors_briefing.pdf [Accessed 27 March 2020].

Hafford-Letchfield, T., and Huss, E., 2018. Putting you in the picture: the use of visual imagery in social work supervision. *European Journal of Social Work*, 21 (3), 441–453. doi:10.1080/13691457.2018.1423546

Hafford-Letchfield, T., Chick, N.F., Leonard, K., and Begum, N., 2008. *Leadership and management in social care*. Thousand Islands, London: Sage.

Hafford-Letchfield, T., Lambley, S., Spolander, G., Daly, N., and Cocker, C., 2014. *Inclusive leadership: managing to make a difference in social work and social care*. Bristol: Policy Press.

Hair, H.J., and O'Donoghue, K., 2009. Culturally relevant, socially just social work supervision: becoming visible through a social constructionist lens. *Journal of Ethnic & Cultural Diversity in Social Work*, 18 (1–2), 70–88. doi:10.1080/15313200902874979

Handy, C., 1976. *Understanding organisations*. Penguin: Middlesex.

Harris, J., 2002. *The social work business*. London: Routledge.

Haworth, S., Miller, R., and Schaub, J., 2019. *Leadership* in social work (and can *it learn from clinical health-care?*). University of Birmingham, UK. Available from: https://www.birmingham.ac.uk/Documents/college-social-sciences/social-policy/Misc/leadership-in-social-work.pdf [Accessed 27 March 2020].

Higgins, M., 2016a. Cultivating our humanity. *Social Work Education*, 35 (5), 518–529.

Higgins, M., 2016b. How has the professional capabilities framework changed social work education and practice in England?. *British Journal of Social Work*, 46 (7), 1981–1996.

Hodson, R., 2001. *Dignity at work*. Cambridge: Cambridge University Press.

Jirek, S.L., 2020. Ineffective organizational responses to workers' secondary traumatic stress: a case study of the effects of an unhealthy organizational culture. *Human Service Organizations: Management, Leadership & Governance*, 1–19. doi:10.1080/23303131.2020.1722302

Kadushin, A., and Harkness, D., 2002. *Supervision in social work*. 4th ed. New York: Columbia University Press.

Lambley, S., 2010. Managers: are they really to blame for what's happening to social work?. *Social Work and Social Sciences Review*, 14 (2), 6–19.

Laming, H., 2009. *The* protection of children in england: action plan. London: Stationary Office. Available from: https://assets.publishing.service.gov.uk/government/uploads/system/uploads/attachment_data/file/327238/The_protection_of_children_in_England_-_action_plan.pdf [Accessed 27 March 2020].

Lawler, J., and Bilson, A., 2009. *Social work management and leadership: managing complexity with creativity*. London: Routledge.

Lusk, M., Terrazas, S., and Salcido, R., 2017. Critical cultural competence in social work supervision. *Human Service Organizations: Management, Leadership & Governance*, 41 (5), 464–476.

Manthorpe, J., and Stanley, N., 2004. *The age of the inquiry. Learning and blaming in health and social care*. Basingstoke: Routledge, 294.

Morrison, T., 2006. *Staff supervision in social care: making a real difference for staff and service users*. 3rd ed. Brighton, UK: Pavilion.

Mosley, J.E., Marwell, N.P., and Ybarra, M., 2019. How the "what works" movement is failing human service organizations, and what social work can do to fix it. *Human Service Organizations: Management, Leadership & Governance*, 43 (4), 326–335. doi:10.1080/23303131.2019.1672598

Munro, E., 2011. *Review of child protection: final report a child centred system*. Available from: https://assets.publishing.service.gov.uk/government/uploads/system/uploads/attachment_data/file/175391/Munro-Review.pdf [Accessed 27 March 2020]

Narey, M., 2014. *Making the education of social workers consistently effective*. Available from: https://www.gov.uk/government/uploads/system/uploads/attachment_data/file/278741/Social_worker_education_report.PDF [Accessed 27 March 2020].

Nussbaum, M., 2017. *Upheavals of thought: the intelligence of emotions*. Cambridge: Cambridge University Press.

Rai, G.S., 2013. Job satisfaction among long-term care staff: Bureaucracy isn't always bad. *Administration in Social Work*, 37 (1), 90–99. doi:10.1080/03643107.2012.657750

Rogers, C., 2002. The interpersonal relationship in the facilitation of learning. *In*:R. Harrison, F. Reeve, A. Hanson, and J. Clarke, eds. *Supporting lifelong learning, Vol 1: perspectives on learning*. London: Routledge, 25–39.

Rønningstad, C., 2019. How unstandardized work tasks create arenas for leadership. *Human Service Organizations: Management, Leadership & Governance*, 43 (2), 111–124. doi:10.1080/23303131.2019.1610130

Ryan, P., Edwards, M., Hafford-Letchfield, T., Bell, L., Carr, S., Puniskis, M., Hanna, S., and Jeewa, S., 2016. *Research on the experience of staff with disabilities within the NHS workforce*. Project Report. Middlesex University, London UK. Available from: http://eprints.mdx.ac.uk/18741/ [Accessed 27 March 2020].

Sidebotham, P., Brandon, M., Powell, C., Solebo, C., Koistinen, J., and Ellis, C., 2010. *Report of a research study on the methods of learning lessons nationally from serious case reviews.* Research Report DFE-RR037, London, Department for Education. Available from: https://assets.publishing.service.gov.uk/government/uploads/system/uploads/attachment_data/file/181618/DFE-RR037.pdf [Accessed 27 March 2020].

Social Work Task Force 2009. *Building a safe, confident future: the final report of the Social Work Task Force.* Available from: https://www.education.gov.uk/publications/eOrderingDownload/01114-2009DOM -EN.pdf [Accessed 27 March 2020].

Spillet, M., 2014. *Leadership imbalance: black and Asian leaders missing in action, a think piece.* ADCS Virtual Staff College. Available from: https://www.ppma.org.uk/wp-content/uploads/2017/12/Leadership-imbalance.pdf [Accessed 27 March 2020].

Tsui, M.S., 1997. Empirical research on social work supervision. *Journal of Social Service Research*, 23 (2), 39–54. doi:10.1300/J079v23n02_03

Tsui, M.S., and Cheung, F.C.G., 2004. Gone with the wind: the impact of managerialism on human services. *British Journal of Social Work*, 34 (3), 437–442.

Wermeling, L., 2013. Why social workers leave the profession: understanding the profession and workforce. *Administration in Social Work*, 37 (4), 329–339.

West, M.A., and Chowla, R., 2017. Compassionate leadership for compassionate health care. *In*: P. Gilbert, ed. *Compassion*. London: Routledge, 237–257.

Wilson, G., 2013. Evidencing reflective practice in social work education: theoretical uncertainties and practical challenges. *British Journal of Social Work*, 43 (1), 154–172.

Winnicott, D.W., 1965. *The maturational processes and the facilitating environment: studies in the theory of emotional development.* Oxford, England: International Universities Press.

Yuill, C., and Mueller-Hirth, N., 2019. Paperwork, compassion and temporal conflicts in British social work. *Time & Society*, 28 (4), 1532–1551. doi:10.1177/0961463X18785030

43

ENHANCING AND MANAGING PERFORMANCE THROUGH SUPERVISION

Lareen Cooper and Michael Dale

Social work staff are key to achieving human services organizational goals. It is their performance, their commitment to their jobs, and client groups, that support clients and communities through challenging times. But do we always understand the needs of staff and establish systems that support high performance?

For human services organizations (HSOs) to meet their goals, their staff are the most critical pathway to success. How well staff perform their roles is arguably the most important aspect of any HSO. To do this, HSOs must have highly performing teams and this is a challenge. Social work leaders must recruit and retain a motivated workforce and develop teams that excel in their work. Social work supervisors play a key leadership role in achieving these goals. This chapter explores the organizational context of supervision, examines the role of leadership especially as it relates to leading social work professionals, sets the scene for successful teams, performance improvement and management, and concludes with three case scenarios.

Organizational and practice context

Social work supervision takes place in highly complex human service organizations. Social work supervisors are leaders and managers in their organizations. Their role and challenge is in ensuring a positive organizational culture and climate, appointing and managing the right staff, leading ethical practice, and maintaining a focus on each of the macro, mezzo, and micro environment. Supervisors must understand the role social policy plays in determining what and how social services are delivered and how this is subject to change.

Social work leadership

Supervisors are leaders and managers in their teams. These terms are closely related but in much of the literature significantly differentiated. Leadership is often described as the inspirational side of management while management is seen as administration – the traditional list of the functions of management planning, leading, organizing, and controlling (Bartol et al. 2011). However, a more balanced view could be that managers are successful when "he or she exerts leadership capabilities such that people want to follow the directives of a good leader" (Weinbach 2008 cited Wilson and Lau 2011, p. 253). Or alternatively, "a collection of organizational, relational, and individual behaviors that effect positive change in order to address client and societal challenges through emotional competence and the full acceptance, validation, and trust of all individuals as capable human beings" (Colby Peters 2018, p. 41). The American National Network for Social Work Managers defines a number of competencies for social work leadership within four domains of executive leadership, resource management, strategic management, and community collaboration (2018). Holosko (2009, p. 454) describes the core attributes of social work leadership in this way:

1. Vision
   - Having one: *To have a description of a desired condition at some point in the future*
   - Implementing one: *To plan and put in place strategic steps to enact the vision*
2. Influencing others to act: *To inspire and enable others to take initiative, have a belief in a cause and to perform duties and responsibilities*
3. Teamwork/collaboration: *To work collectively and in partnership with others toward achieving a goal*
4. Problem-solving capacity: *To both anticipate problems and also act decisively on them when they occur*
5. Creating positive change: *Moving people in organizations to a better place than where they once were.*

De Groot (2016, p. 27) defines leadership as "a process by which an individual or individuals inspire the attitudes and behaviors of others to engage in value-based and purpose-critical efforts in order to complete a set of shared objectives."

A key issue arising in recent research is the lack of emphasis in social work foundational qualifications on leadership and organizational theory (Colby Peters 2018; Wilson and Lau 2011; Patterson 2015). Commonly, social workers move from direct practice to their first supervisory roles with little education in their social work qualifying programs or continuing formal education as a supervisor or practice leader. The strain on staff making this move should not be underestimated (Patterson 2015). While supervisors are often seen as effective street level bureaucrats that manage highly professional teams in spite of distant "head office" rules (Evans 2011), these same organizational constructs can be overwhelmingly negative, and stifle innovation, energy, and enthusiasm for helping clients to make change in their lives. (Raeymaeckers and Dierckx 2013).

Another challenge to social work leadership is the lack of social workers wanting to take up these roles (NASW 2018; Wilson and Lau 2011). Colby Peters (2018) and Holosko (2009) outline concerns that social work education is not covering key aspects of social work leadership. Colby Peters lists risk analysis, communication, conflict, and inter disciplinary teams as gaps. Further, they identify that the focus is on practice skills with individuals and families. The risk then is that social workers do not see leadership roles as an option, do not take them up and the profession then being managed by other professionals who will embrace leadership roles. We see this being particularly the case with nurses. Social workers without a depth of understanding of organizations and how they operate, or the role of professional leaders or supervisors, may lack real agency to make change or be influential in their practice at a wider level.

The lack of awareness of the importance of leadership and organizational contexts in basic training, the move from direct practice to supervision with very little training, and the complexity of the social work environment are significant issues. Social work leadership needs to encourage the move from direct practice to supervision but support it through effective supervision and training, with clear understanding of what leadership means in the sector.

Leading and managing professional staff

Social work is a profession and as such, subscribes to the general view of how professions are determined and defined. This includes requiring a recognized tertiary training program, and adherence to a code of ethics and/or code of conduct. Ongoing registration with a professional body is also most often a requirement of practice internationally. These bodies determine entry to the profession, set out standards for both training and conduct, along with the code of ethics and or conduct within their jurisdiction. Internationally, the professional status of social work is set out by the International Federation of Social Work and the International Association of Schools of Social Work. Social workers then are expected to practice in a professional and competent manner. The ability to do this is a core expectation of any professional. It supports the autonomous practice of professionals and thus determines in many ways the individual professional's practice responsibilities and accountabilities which sit alongside the management of organizations (Empson and Langley, cited Empson et al. 2015). Society expects that professionals work to serve the public good and that their commitment is above any financial or employment obligations (Raelin 2016; Dale 2006).

While professionals accept their accountabilities to their managers and organizations for the wider aspects of the organization, they will heavily resist direction as to their practice that comes from outside a professional perspective. The managerialist agenda since the 1980s has received significant pushback from many professionals regarding clinical or professional governance – who should direct practice? Supervisors must be cognizant of their role – is it a managerial role with these accountabilities, an internal professional leadership role, or an external professional supervisor's role? Each has different responsibilities, belief systems, and values. Clinical governance, for example in healthcare today, is most often viewed as a bottom up approach seeking to provide the best care and safety for patients. Its values are in teamwork, continuous improvement and learning, shared responsibilities, and collaboration across professions and management (Veenstra et al. 2017). The importance of this team approach is seen as essential to patient care in many health settings (Kennedy et al. 2017) and further, according to MacFarlane (2019), these are the pillars of care and must be present at all times. Professional supervisors and social workers are constantly part of inter or multi-disciplinary teams and must consider the role of supervision within this context.

Challenges in the work environment affecting performance

The work environment is closely linked to work performance. Retention of staff is a key issue in social work internationally. Role conflict and role stress are not new concepts to social work but are still prevalent.

Geisler et al. (2019) surveyed 725 Swedish social workers in relation to retention. Their findings make the link between work engagement, job satisfaction, and organizational commitment to retention. The importance of organizational resources to do the job and support from both supervisors and colleagues is important. Social workers also need to identify with the organization in terms of their personal values and the values of the organization. Their main finding is that the best predictors for retention include work engagement, job satisfaction, and commitment to the organization. These come from social workers feeling they are doing good work, with appropriate working conditions, role clarity, and excellent social support from both colleagues and managers. The feeling of having a social community at work is noted. Job satisfaction is also influenced by creating an inclusive environment that values staff in all their diversity. This leads to higher participation, innovation, and improved participation in quality improvement (Brimhall and Mor Barak 2018).

Rai (2016) defines role conflict arising where the role expectations are either incompatible or incongruent with the professional attributes of the social worker. Role ambiguity differs. This is where the worker is not clear about expectations or their own performance. Rai (2016) found that the principles that the organization operated by in terms of an organizational justice model could be a significant way to improve role conflict and ambiguity. These principles included fairness and formalization of processes that supported good patient care.

Another challenge to retaining staff is the rigidity of the workplace. In line with the discussion on professional autonomy, social workers need to feel they have the opportunity to practice creatively and innovatively (Glisson 2015). If they see the organizational context supporting working with clients in an autonomous way to best meet the unique needs of clients – trusting to the professional skills of the social worker rather than following rules and regulations in a rigid way – better outcomes for clients are likely. This fits with a clinical governance model well. It enhances outcomes for clients and ensures an ongoing continuous improvement environment. Glisson (2015) cautions that this model needs to be formalized and embedded into organizations as it will not happen on its own. Congruence between the expectations of workers and the organization do make a difference to retention and job satisfaction (Graham et al. 2016). Bottom up approaches with consultation and participation to ensure alignment between worker and organizational expectations are important. Where social workers work within an empowering practice model with a high degree of participation in decision-making and support from both colleagues and supervisors, better outcomes for clients are reached. Where this environment does not exist it more likely that social workers will just "tick the box" (Raeymaeckers and Dierckx 2013). The skills and attributes of the supervisor are key to this approach as they can discuss creative approaches, and peer supervision can help with this also.

The context for performance management and improvement is significant for supervisors to understand. They are then able to draw on techniques to assist social workers in their overall job performance.

Performance management

Performance management involves a range of activities and processes that seek to improve practitioner behavior and motivation, in alignment with organizational policy, legal requirements, and professional standards (Bartol et al. 2011; Leggat 2009). Additionally, performance management information supports reporting requirements by which organizations are accountable for the use of resources (Hafford-Letchfield 2010).

The organizational context of social work practice will influence the construction of practice within any field. For van Berkel and Knies (2016) the pervasive influence of New Public Management raises the question as to the degree that performance management may be seen to limit the autonomy of the professional. A focus upon performance measurement and accountability poses a challenge for supervisors who must balance the responsibility to support ethical, informed practice and offer guidance to social workers, with the requirement to conform with organizational rules and funder expectations.

Cheung and Yeung (2015) offer the prospect that a nurturing organizational culture may have a positive effect on worker job performance and mental health, identifying relational practices including recognition and appreciation of workers' skill and performance. Similarly, Gruman and Saks (2011) suggest that performance management that promotes employee engagement is likely to result in performance improvement.

Supervising and managing social workers requires specialized supervision that meets the needs of professional workers. As discussed earlier, professionals are distinguished by specialized knowledge, training, membership of an association, registration, autonomy, and accountability. Therefore, performance management should be tailored to meet the needs of professional social work practitioners.

Social worker effectiveness is linked to professional supervision that focuses upon professional skills and competence (Egan et al. 2016). This in turn is related to social worker performance and how service is provided to clients (Cousins 2010; van Berkel and Knies 2016). The social work supervisor has responsibility for organizing staff, assigning work, and ensuring that resources are available to support the achievement of the mission and goals of the agency (Kadushin and Harkness 2002).

The leadership behavior of the supervisor is important and can affect worker satisfaction and performance (Blosser et al. 2010). Wright (2017) suggests that supervisor capabilities are linked to staff performance, and advocates for a relationship characterized by co-participation and joint sense-making. While Leggat (2009) adds that the nature of the relationship between the supervisor and staff has impact on how negative feedback is received and responded to.

For Secka (2017), a servant leadership style places importance on the welfare and development of staff, offering a more ethical and people-centered model. Secka maintains that this approach is more likely to result in trust, ethical behavior, performance improvement, satisfaction, and commitment.

Performance management and improvement process

The performance management and improvement process involves five stages: (1) setting performance expectations, (2) supporting the achievement of desired performance, (3) reviewing and assessing performance, (4) providing feedback, and (5) taking required action.

Setting performance expectations

The foundation to effective performance management is establishing clear expectations regarding work tasks and behavior; these are usually found in a job description and person specification. There should be alignment between individual work tasks and the achievement of the goals of the organization, and importantly the social worker should understand not only the technical aspects of work tasks but also the rationale supporting the task requirement. At times there may be tension between organizational and individual needs that the supervisor must mediate with the social worker (Bartol et al. 2011; Coulshed et al. 2006; van Berkel and Knies 2016). Performance expectations are usually set out in a written performance agreement that specifies tasks, standards, timeframes, and review processes.

A key aspect of setting performance expectations is work allocation. The supervisor should consider a range of factors, including the social worker's: experience and capacity; workload (work equity is important); ability to manage work complexity; and need for development, challenge, and extension.

Kadushin and Harkness (2002) draw attention to the issue of worker autonomy and work delegation. Dependent upon social worker experience and competence, differing levels of practice autonomy may be delegated. Social workers who are able to exercise autonomy are likely to experience higher levels of job satisfaction, commitment, and productivity, and this approach is consistent with a professional construction of practice (Kadushin and Harkness 2002). Of course, there are organizational constraints within which practice autonomy must be exercised.

Supporting the achievement of desired performance

The second aspect of a successful performance management process surrounds supporting the social worker to achieve the desired level of performance. There are three activities that are central to providing support to the social worker: supervision, training, and staff development.

Supervision that incorporates regular review of performance expectations should also focus upon the social worker's practice competence. The social worker/supervisor relationship that is based on trust and respect will provide the context within which ongoing professional development can occur. It is important that the supervisor provides the social worker with specific feedback regarding the attainment of work tasks. The use of a clear feedback loop will assist both supervisor and social worker with clear direction regarding action that is required (Coulshed et al. 2006).

At times the supervisor may provide direct coaching to the social worker regarding a specific work task. The supervisor and social worker should also plan the specific training that is required to support and develop the social worker's practice. Any staff development strategy should align with the organizational strategic direction, and the social worker should be actively involved in the development of the training plan. Training and development can enhance employee motivation and satisfaction, and it is also important to ensure that the objectives from training should be applied in practice (Coulshed et al. 2006; Bartol et al. 2011).

Reviewing and assessing performance

Performance evaluation is also linked to promoting professional growth. Kadushin and Harkness (2002) suggest that monitoring, review, and evaluation supervision are important to ensure satisfactory service to the client. It is important to be clear regarding the purpose of evaluation.

Coulshed et al. (2006, p. 75) identify a range of purposes, including: measuring behaviors, assessing the performance of technical tasks, considering the knowledge and skills, and the attitudes and interaction of the social worker with work colleagues. How a performance appraisal is conducted is important as the social worker may feel defensive if there is the process is not clear, and there is not clear communication.

A number of appraisal techniques can be employed including self-review, peer feedback, and direct administration by the supervisor. In larger organizations performance appraisal is typically overseen by a Human Resources department, in smaller organizations this responsibility will fall upon line supervisors. While traditionally appraisal systems are hierarchical, the use of 360-degree feedback can be more effective in staff development, however the success of this approach will require a supportive structure to enable the social worker to have confidence in the process (Coulshed et al. 2006)

Leggat (2009) notes that relevant performance indicators should be identified, and these should be valid (measure what they say they measure), reliable (be consistent and repeatable), and be fair and equitable (they should not disadvantage any group) (Bartol et al. 2011, pp. 376–377). Rhamy (2013) notes the sources of information that can be used, including: data that has been collected and analyzed, error reports, information from external agencies, and client complaints. Account should also be taken of factors that may affect the social workers ability to cope, such as high workload, the impact of complexity, the impact of overregulation, and the nature of the work environment (Cousins 2010).

Provide feedback

The provision of feedback is crucial to the success of any performance evaluation, and this should include both positive information that reinforces practice, and areas where social worker performance can be enhanced. Clardy (2013) highlights the importance of exploring explanations of performance that may identify knowledge or skills deficit, and the need for training/education. Typically, feedback will be provided both in a written form, and also in dialogue with the social worker.

Taking required action

The final stage of the performance management and improvement process involves taking required action. The focus should be upon the actions that will support and strengthen the social worker's practice, and may address knowledge, skills, behaviors, and attitudes. Options may include coaching, mentoring, and training, and should be linked to a professional development plan.

A plan for action should be documented and prepared in consultation with the social worker. Clardy (2013) maintains that performance should be responded to with consequences, that both address performance deficits and reinforce achievements (for example, symbolic rewards such as recognition and thanks) and material rewards (for example, an award or increased remuneration). Examples of possible actions are outlined in the case studies that follow.

Managing poor performance and behavior

Weinbach and Taylor (2011) point to the supervisor's ethical responsibility to take action to address worker performance and behavior that does not meet the standards that have been set by the agency. This aspect of supervision can be both challenging and stressful, and supervisors may seek to avoid confronting poor performance (Wright 2017). This is also noted by Cousins (2010) who points to the need for supervisors to receive support from next level management, and to receive supervision themselves. It is important that staff are afforded the opportunity to change behavior, however the time allowed will vary depending upon the nature of the performance issue. Weinbach and Taylor (2011) identify three progressive steps: (1) the issue of a verbal reprimand that is linked to opportunity to improve (with support via supervision and training). They also advise against issuing "group reprimands" as this is likely to engender a negative response from staff who are performing well. It is better to directly confront the worker whose performance is at issue; (2) the issue of a written reprimand that is included on the staff member's file (this may be time limited depending upon the circumstances, and can be removed once satisfactory performance has been achieved); and (3) the issue of a formal warning that sets out clearly the issue and possible consequences if performance does not improve. The issue of a formal warning and subsequent steps may have implications for continuing employment. In all cases it important to maintain clear written records, and to receive guidance from a Human Resources adviser. There are a range of issues that will constitute gross misconduct (for example, sexual harassment, criminal conviction, and dishonesty), and in these cases a progressive approach will not be appropriate (Weinbach and Taylor 2011). Social workers and their supervisors work in complex environments. The context of the organization, its purpose, team structure, values, and any changes to it all influence practice. Challenges facing individual social workers will be influenced by these factors. The scenarios below give the opportunity to explore, from a supervisor perspective, reactions to issues and planning pathways for intervention. The questions posed allow supervisors to think deeply about their actions.

Scenarios

The following scenarios aim to provide professional supervisors with opportunities to think through issues for the development of a new practitioner, extending a senior practitioner, and managing poor performance.

Scenario one: Developing a new practitioner

Jane is a 24-year-old new graduate social worker. She completed a Bachelor of Social Work degree one year ago. She is working in a large public hospital. Appointed initially to work on a general medical ward, she worked mostly with older people and within the stroke unit of the ward. This was a multi-disciplinary team focus with most of her work being related to assessment and discharge planning. Patients had longer average time in hospital to allow for acute treatment and rehabilitation. However, six months into her role, the Medical Assessment and Planning Unit (MAPU) social worker was injured in an accident. In the absence of any other options, the Chief Social Worker asked Jane to take up this role for six months. MAPU patients are admitted to the Unit for short stay intervention. This is much more of an interdisciplinary team. It consists of a lead physician, other senior and junior medical staff, charge nurse and nursing staff, and a physiotherapist. Staff from other disciplines receive referrals from the Unit, as necessary.

The Unit has a Nurse Manager who coordinates the team and provides day-to-day management. Jane also receives supervision from the social work team from an experienced supervisor. There are 45 full time equivalent social workers across the hospital services.

Jane was excited to be appointed into this position although she misses the focus of working with elderly and the friendship groups she had made in the medical ward. She finds the pace of the MAPU challenging. Patients can only stay 24 hours. Decisions need to be made quickly, to keep patient turnover moving. She is the only social worker in the team, and this is her first experience of being in an interdisciplinary team. Most of the other staff are older and very experienced especially the nursing staff. Medical teams made up of the surgical team and the team from general medicine visit their patients at 8am daily to determine next steps. They all arrive at the same time. Jane is very nervous of speaking up with these groups.

Jane is daunted by the complexity of issues that the patient group have and is anxious that she does not understand the illnesses and treatments well. She worries about her work and this is impacting on her life at home. She is starting to work longer hours and taking longer to write up files. She feels everyone else on the team knows what they are doing but she does not, and she is worried about letting the team and the patients down. Jane's parents are concerned about her well-being.

Jane has decided to bring this to her next supervision session to discuss.

As you consider this scenario, what questions arise and how could Jane's supervisor support her through the supervisory process? This requires the supervisor to have prepared well for the supervision session. A starting point will be to investigate if Jane had a new position description on starting in the MAPU. On looking back to the time of her appointment, was this overlooked and did Jane receive any orientation into this new role? An important question might be to explore if Jane has been introduced to the concept of MAPU, and in this Unit, its values, operating model, and everyone's roles. A key feature in the supervisor's thinking will be to look back and see if Jane has had any continued professional development in working in an interdisciplinary team and into the evidence for the development of these Units along with the role of the social worker for these Units. When looking back at these few months and taking an ethical perspective, has Jane had enough support for her new role? A key discussion in supervision will be around Jane's self-care and if she has an active plan. This might help her to manage her stress. She may not have taken any annual leave in her time at the hospital this time to allow her time to rest and recuperate. Key to the success of working through the issues raised will be being prepared for supervision and providing a supportive environment for Jane to unpack the issues she is facing and to find a plan to move forward. Establishing an agreed understanding and pathway is critical to Jane's well-being personally and professionally and to providing a professional social work service. The supervisor and Jane will need to reflect on all the options that might be available to achieve this. This might include Jane taking leave, extra supervision, or access to the employee assistance program or counseling, moving to a different role, considering the workload Jane is carrying as a new graduate, and professional development. Ensuring a positive supervisory model quickly will support Jane to work through the challenges she is facing before this becomes a serious performance management issue.

Scenario two: Developing an experienced practitioner

Ian is forty-five years old and an experienced social worker. He completed his social work degree 20 years ago. He has been working in the local community mental health (CMH) team for fifteen years. Prior to this, he worked for a number of years as an inpatient mental health social worker and prior to this he worked in child protection. Ian has attended many in house training sessions over the years and completed a Master of Social Work degree about ten years ago. He meets the requirements for his continuing professional development for his practicing certificate. Recently, Ian has identified that he is feeling less motivated and excited by his job and that he has been in the role for too long. He reports that he starting to feel jaded about his work and beginning to feel that he is getting a bit cynical about his co-workers and his clients. He is concerned that his negative feelings are beginning to be evident in his team.

Ian works full-time during the day and is also rostered on call for the Emergency Mental Health Crisis Team at night and weekends. He has two children at university in another city and lives with his wife of twenty years who is a nurse.

Ian has signaled that he wants to talk with you about his future in his next supervisory session.

As you consider this scenario, what questions arise and how could Ian's supervisor support him through the supervisory process? This requires the supervisor to have prepared well for the supervision session. Ian has a busy workload working in the daytime as well as being on-call. An important question for the supervisor will be to consider if this workload is reasonable or if it has changed. The supervisor may already be aware of vacancies in the team or rapid turnover of staff with implications for other staff such as Ian. Wider community issues may have had an impact such as natural disasters, economic downturn, or the impact of the global pandemic Covid-19. These issues may have increased the number of or changed the nature of referrals to the service. The supervisor could reflect on whether there have ever been any complaints about Ian's practice and if he has been taking his annual leave. A key issue facing health services is often the inability to take leave due to staff shortages. Having considered these aspects fully, it may be that Ian would like to find a way to enrich his role through doing special project work on secondment. But job enrichment needs to be carefully considered alongside whether Ian is experiencing burn out. Ian and his supervisor both have responsibilities to reflect on Ian's current experience. Not dealing with these issues could have serious consequences for Ian and for clients. A supportive approach is needed to explore these issues with Ian and to develop an agreed plan to move forward which might include a move to a new area of practice and new challenges.

Scenario three: Dealing with disciplinary issues

Jasper is a 32-year-old social worker in a faith based non-government organization (NGO) in a large city. He qualified as a social worker about ten years ago and prior to this job worked in community corrections. The NGO provides family services particularly working with clients in poverty, with poor housing and food insecurity. Jasper is passionately committed to the allevia-tion of poverty related issues and works tirelessly for clients to find secure housing and income. These are both key issues in the community due to poor housing supply along with skyrocket-ing rents, and unemployment. Jasper also works at an advocacy level with his local body council and lobbies at a national level on housing. Jasper's values align with the values and goals of the organization. You have been supervising Jasper for several years and you are also his line manager and have never had reason to be concerned about his practice.

One of Jasper's co-workers has raised with you that Jasper was seen at the movies with a cli-ent and her children last Saturday at 5pm. You are concerned to hear this and want to meet with Jasper urgently. On checking the client file, you note that Jasper has visited this family weekly for several months.

Dealing with this type of allegation requires careful thought and preparation by the super-visor. Seeking the support of the human resources advisor and the supervisor's own manager will be critical, as this is potentially a disciplinary issue. In preparing to meet with Jasper, the supervisor will need to consider the issue of crossing professional boundaries in terms of the professional codes of conduct or ethics for the profession. The organization will have a formally constructed policy on relationships with clients and responding to allegations of this nature. These policies rest on the principles of natural justice and require the supervisor to advise Jasper as soon as possible of the allegations, to ensure he has the opportunity for accessing support e.g. from a union, and to ensure a process where he is able to respond to the allegations. As this is a potentially serious situation, advising Jasper of extra support such as the employee assistance program or union representation is required. An early suspension from duties may be considered. But it is important to consider if the allegation could be mistaken, false, or malicious. This will not be known until an investigation has taken place. It is also important to consider the safety and well-being of the client in this scenario. The appointment of a new social worker may be considered. Careful attention to keeping excellent notes is important in this type of investiga-tion. Even though this is a serious matter that could be a breach of conduct, establishing a transparent and supportive approach is essential to the successful conclusion of what could be a difficult situation. Whatever the outcome of the investigation, final decisions are delivered formally in writing to Jasper.

Conclusion

High performing social work teams do not happen by chance but are critical for HSOs to meet their goals. They occur when social work supervisors understand the wider environment they work in and their role as leaders within it. They must understand the challenges being faced by staff and communities, and work to recruit and retain social workers at differing career stages through good organizational practices and excellent supervision. These practices will incorporate establishing positive cultures, supporting the achievement of desired performance, setting clear performance expectations, and providing ongoing performance review. Managing performance that is below expectation is challenging and complex as shown by the scenarios above. This chapter has provided insight into the context of performance management along with steps that will both enhance good performance and manage performance that does not meet expectations.

References

Bartol, K., Tein, M., Matthews, M., Sharma, B., and Scott-Ladd, B., eds., 2011. *Management a pacific rim focus*. 6th ed. North Ryde, NSW, Australia: McGraw-Hill.

Blosser, J., Cadet, D., and Downs Jr., L., 2010. Factors that influence retention and professional development of social workers. *Administration in Social Work*, 34 (2), 168–177.

Brimhall, K., and Mor Barak, M., 2018. The critical role of workplace inclusion in fostering innovation, job satisfaction, and quality of care in a diverse human service organization. *Human Service Organizations: Management, Leadership & Governance*, 42 (5), 474–492. doi:10.1080/23303131.2018.1526151

Cheung, C., and Yeung, J., 2015. Enhancing job performance and mental health through organizational nurturing culture. *Human Service Organizations: Management, Leadership & Governance*, 39 (4), 251–266.

Clardy, A., 2013. A general framework for performance management systems: structure, design, and analysis. *Performance Improvement*, 52 (2), 5–15.

Colby Peters, S., 2018. Defining social work leadership: a theoretical and conceptual review and analysis. *Journal of Social Work Practice*, 32 (1), 31–44. doi:10.1080/02650533.2017.1300877

Coulshed, V., Mullender, A., Jones, D., and Thompson, N., 2006. *Management in social work*. 3rd ed. Hampshire, England: Palgrave Macmillan.

Cousins, C., 2010. 'Treat me don't beat me' ... exploring supervisory games and their effect on poor performance management. *Practice*, 22 (5), 281–292.

Dale, M.P., 2006. *Probation practice, leadership and effective service delivery; a qualitative study of the perspectives of probation officers and service managers in the New Zealand Probation Service*. Thesis (PhD). Massey University. Available from: http://hdl.handle.net/10179/1476 [Accessed 7 May 2020].

De Groot, S., 2016. *Responsive leadership in social services: a practical approach for optimizing engagement and performance*. Los Angeles: SAGE.

Egan, R., Maidment, J., and Connolly, M., 2016. Who is watching whom? Surveillance in Australian social work supervision. *The British Journal of Social Work*, 46 (6), 1617–1635. doi:10.1093/bjsw/bcv098

Empson, L., and Langley, A., 2015. Leadership and professionals. *In*: L. Empson, D. Muzio, J.P. Broschak and B. Hinings, eds. *The Oxford handbook of professional service firms*. Oxford: Oxford University Press, 163–169.

Evans, T., 2011. Professionals, managers and discretion: critiquing street-level bureaucracy. *British Journal of Social Work*, 41, 368–386. doi:10.1093/bjsw/bcq074

Geisler, M., Berthelsen, H., and Muhonen, T., 2019. Retaining social workers: the role of quality of work and psychosocial safety climate for work engagement, job satisfaction, and organizational commitment. *Human Service Organizations: Management, Leadership & Governance*, 43 (1), 1–15.

Glisson, C., 2015. The role of organizational culture and climate in innovation and effectiveness. *Human Service Organizations: Management, Leadership & Governance*, 39 (4), 245–250.

Graham, J., Shier, M., and Nicholas, D., 2016. Workplace congruence and occupational outcomes among social service workers. *British Journal of Social Work*, 46, 1096–1114. doi:10.1093/bjsw/bcu153

Gruman, J., and Saks, A., 2011. Performance management and employee engagement. *Human Resource Management Review*, 21 (2), 123–136.

Hafford-Letchfield, T., 2010. *Social care management, strategy and business planning*. London: Jessica Kingsley.

Holosko, M.J., 2009. Social work leadership: identifying core attributes. *Journal of Human Behavior in the Social Environment*, 19 (4), 448–459. doi: 10.1080/10911350902872395

Kadushin, A., and Harkness, D., 2002. *Supervision in social work*. 4th ed. New York: Columbia University Press.

Kennedy, M., Elcock, M., Ellis, E., and Tall, G., 2017. Pre-hospital and retrieval medicine: clinical governance and workforce models. *Emergency Medicine Australasia*, 29 (4), 467–469. doi:10.1111/1742-6723.12776

Leggat, S., 2009. A guide to performance management for the health information manager. *Health Information Management Journal*, 38 (3), 1833–3583.

MacFarlane, A.J., 2019. What is clinical governance?. *BJA Education*, 19 (6), 174–175. doi:10.1016/j.bjae.2019.02.003

Patterson, F., 2015. Transition and metaphor: crossing a bridge from direct practice to first line management in social services. *British Journal of Social Work*, 45, 2072–2088. doi:10.1093/bjsw/bcu034

Raelin, J.A., 2016. Imagine there are not leaders: reframing leadership as collaborative agency. *Leadership*, 12 (2), 131–158. doi:10.1177/1742715014558076

Raeymaeckers, P., and Dierckx, D., 2013. To work or not to work? The role of the organizational context for social workers' perceptions on activation. *British Journal of Social Work*, 43, 1170–1189.

Rai, G., 2016. Minimizing role conflict and role ambiguity: a virtuous organization approach. *Human Service Organizations: Management, Leadership & Governance*, 40 (5), 508–523.

Rhamy, J., 2013. Performance improvement: what gets measured gets managed. *Clinical Leadership & Management Review*, 27 (4), 16–19.

The Network for social work management 2018. *Human services management competencies*. USA, viewed 24 January 2020, Available from: https://socialworkmanager.org/wp-content/uploads/2018/12/HSMC -Guidebook-December-2018.pdf [Accessed 7 June 2020].

Secka, E., 2017. Servant leadership: the ultimate key designed for the success of political alliances and leadership. *Performance Improvement*, 56 (9), 40–45.

van Berkel, R., and Knies, E., 2016. Performance management, caseloads and the frontline provision of social services. *Social Policy & Administration*, 50 (1), 59–78.

Veenstra, G.L., Ahaus, K., Welker, G.A., Heineman, E., van der Laan, M.J., and Muntinghe, F.L., 2017. Rethinking clinical governance: healthcare professionals' views: a Delphi study. *BMJ Open*, 7 (1), e012591. doi:10.1136/ bmjopen-2016-012591

Weinbach, R., and Taylor, L., 2011. *The social worker as manager: a practical guide to success*. 6th ed. Boston, MA: Pearson.

Wilson, S., and Lau, B., 2011. Preparing tomorrow's leaders and administrators: evaluating a course in social work management. *Administration in Social Work*, 35 (3), 324–342. doi:10.1080/03643107.2011.575347

Wright, E., 2017. Dialogic development in the situational leadership style. *Performance Improvement*, 56 (90), 27–31.

44

FACILITATING FLOURISHING THROUGH STAFF SUPERVISION

Beth R. Crisp

Introduction

Like many others who seek careers in social work, I was attracted to a profession "that promotes social change and development, social cohesion, and the empowerment and liberation of people" (IFSW 2014). As my expertise developed, I was promoted into positions of responsibility, with the expectation that, with a little bit of in-house training, I would develop the expertise to supervise/manage staff (Bradley et al. 2010). This included ensuring staff were compliant to a myriad of organizational requirements, which at times has seemed a long way from my early career plans (see also Baines et al. 2014).

While there is agreement amongst social workers that supervision has administrative, educative, and supportive functions, the relative importance of these varies according to context (O'Donoghue et al. 2018). As a line manager in a university, administrative aspects of supervision are the key focus, but this is also the case for social work line managers in many agency settings (Bradley and Höjer 2009). If, as it has been claimed, the stressors on social work students are at least as much as those on beginning practitioners (Rajan-Rankin 2014), support for teaching staff is a critical aspect of my work. However, if my goals as a manager have been reduced to ensuring survival of both individual staff and the wider program, then I am succumbing to a neoliberal agenda in which flourishing is an optional extra (Baines et al. 2014; Bradley et al. 2010).

For social workers who are line managers (and despite working in a university I do regard myself as a social worker), the social work literature provides mixed messages as to what our role is. On the one hand, many social workers believe that line management and professional supervision should be separated and not undertaken by the same person. Moreover, there may be a preference for professional supervision to be provided by someone external to the organization to ensure that professional development is not obscured by organizational needs (Beddoe 2012). However, for many social workers, line management and professional supervision is provided by the same person with no distinction made between these roles (Bradley et al. 2010; Egan 2012).

Professional supervision and risk management

As a line manager, my responsibilities include the control and management of risk, and there are expectations that a key focus of staff supervision is on those aspects of the work that are most likely to be subject to organizational scrutiny or auditing (Brown et al. 2008). This includes ensuring staff conform to legal and ethical obligations as well as professional standards (Westergaard 2013). Indeed, I am notified and can be called to account if staff in my team have not complied with organizational requirements.

Discourses around risk and harm often shape and hinder professional practice (Baker 2010). In many areas of social work practice, there has been an emphasis on risk rather than care in legislation, policy, and practice guidance (Dixon 2010; Gillingham 2006). When "social problems are regarded once again as the result of individual pathology" the role of social work become "social control, policing and surveillance" (Noble and Irwin 2009, p. 350). Service users are no longer seen as virtuous (Pithouse et al. 2012) but as people who society believes require supervision.

In work social work practice the term "supervision" is frequently used in respect of needing to manage risk to individuals and/or the broader community. Those identified as requiring supervision include vulnerable children (Oak 2015; Rudolph et al. 2018) and adults (Ghesquiere et al. 2018), homeless youth (Robert et al. 2005) or those living in out of home care (Albertson et al. 2018), offenders released from prison on parole (Baker 2010; Borrill et al. 2017; Lee 2017; Watson and Vess 2007), and persons who have, or are alleged to have, committed a criminal act but have been detained under mental health provisions (Dixon 2010). Supervision may also be provided for those involved in direct caring work such as parents (Morrongiello et al. 2009) and foster carers (Jagger 2018).

Supervision has been proposed as a panacea for a wide range of problems facing social work practice (Magnussen 2018). In particular, supervision has gained favor as a means of quality assurance and ensuring professional staff are accountable. This includes preventing staff misconduct (Wurtele et al. 2019) and leads to interpretations of the role of the supervisor as providing guidance as to what are "defensible" actions from the perspective of the organization (Littlechild 2008, p. 665). In the case of encouraging parents to ensure their children are appropriately supervised, a punitive approach which incites guilt or blame is less effective than approaches which motivate change (Morrongiello et al. 2009). As supervision is "socially constructed by the contexts within which it is embedded and personally constructed by the participants' expectations, experiences and enactment" (O'Donoghue et al. 2018, p. 350), it is unsurprising that social workers who are struggling with the demands of their work often avoid seeking support from their supervisors as a way of avoiding being ridiculed or disparaged for lack of competence (Cooper 1998). Even for those who engage with a supervisor, the agenda in supervision may be to appear as competent which may mean that they do not get the most out of supervision (Sweeney et al. 2001b).

A supervisory emphasis on risk assessment and management designed to foster professional conformity is popular with policy makers and organizational management (Oak 2015) but can subject social workers to the same levels of surveillance which they are required to impose on various parts of the community (Westergaard 2013). As such, supervision becomes supervision of the practitioner rather than supervision of professional practice (O'Donoghue et al. 2018), and it is not surprising that such notions of professional supervision are rejected by social workers (Beddoe 2010). Supervision which has primary aims of safeguarding vulnerable clients and prevention of trouble for organizations can readily disregard the development needs of staff (Moore 2017; Reisel 2017). Indeed, it has been argued that a strong supervisory focus on risk "stifles professional growth" (Beddoe 2010, p. 1295).

Risk management also includes a responsibility to ensuring safe workplaces, and that policies and procedures to minimize the potential for risk to staff are followed. Ensuring staff are aware of, and follow, organizational protocols is the responsibility of supervisors. Apart from the threat of physical harm, constant dealing with people who are aggressive and combative can result in stress levels that compromise mental health to the point that staff are no longer able to perform the duties of their position (Littlechild 2005). Lack of contact with a supervisor can result in safety not being prioritized such as allocations of work where individual staff are placed in potentially dangerous situations (Butler et al. 2018).

The routinization of risk management as professional practice can result in some employers not acknowledging that staff, particularly those employed on a short-term basis, benefit from supervision (Manthorpe et al. 2012). The amount of supervision parents provide to their children reflects both the degree of risk perception and their capacity to provide the level of supervision they believe is required (Morrongiello et al. 2009). The same is true for supervision of professional staff. Social workers for whom professional supervision is more likely deemed essential are those whose work involves the management of risk rather than responding to requests for advice or assistance of a practical nature (Burke 1997). Moreover, the amount of time spent on topics in supervision, reflect the organizational agenda (Bradley et al. 2010). The need to manage growing numbers of clients perceived to be at risk, can put unreasonable pressure on individuals and organizations when no capacity for providing supervision has been made, and lead to supervision which is reductionist (Rodriguez-Keyes et al. 2012). Reduction of supervision to management of risk, reflects increasing demands on organizations to do more with the same or less funding. It also reflects a lack of understanding of the benefits to both staff and the organization of a wider role for supervision (Rankine et al. 2018).

Beyond risk

When supervision is just another task to be ticked off as having been undertaken, the experience can be uncomfortable and unproductive (Sweeney et al. 2001a). It may also be avoided as much as possible (Egan 2012), particularly if the focus of supervision is the reduction of risk, which social workers may perceive as a management concern rather than what mattered to them (Beddoe 2012). Moreover, "when the level of surveillance, control, and risk management within supervision was increased it was arguably counter-productive because of the effect it had in reducing supervisees' participation and ownership of their supervision" (O'Donoghue 2012, p. 228).

Supervision which focuses only on risk and what has gone wrong fails to provide recognition of the many things which are going well (Beddoe 2009). Moreover, it is not responsive to the very real challenges of the work (Foster 2013). Effective supervision can enable and foster the development of critically reflective practitioners who can make professional judgements (Oak 2015) by building professional confidence and expertise so that practitioners have the capacity to understand how theory and ethics inform their practice rather than just conforming to practice guidance (Rankine et al. 2018). As Noble and Irwin noted a decade ago,

> … the move to restrict supervision to monitoring worker performance at the expense of professional and intellectual growth is inhibiting the possibility of new and challenging practice dialogues and learning opportunities from emerging. Focusing on the tasks associated with management expectations and performance outcomes in supervision sessions closes off any opportunity to reflect on current issues and to develop strategic responses.
>
> *(Noble and Irwin 2009, p. 252)*

For supervisees, the agenda in supervision may be to appear as competent, which may mean that they do not get the most out of supervision (Sweeney et al. 2001b). When supervision sessions are spent only discussing cases, this may reflect overwhelming concerns about risk. However, it may also reflect an avoidance by supervisees to be able to enter into discussions in which they feel safe enough to discuss their professional practice at a deeper level. Alternately, if they have had no experience of supervision other than reviewing of difficult cases, then supervisees may have little understanding of what the process of supervision might be able offer them in respect of professional growth and development (O'Donoghue 2012).

Some organizations recognize the benefits of supervisory relationships which go beyond risk management. Managers can gain deeper insights as to how services are being delivered and be proactive in identifying issues that need addressing (Fleming and Taylor 2007) or ensuring maintenance of an organizational narrative in which social justice rather than risk is the central narrative (Rankine et al. 2018). Active management is particularly crucial when the work is changing rapidly (Pithouse et al. 2012).

In the short-term, supervision can also be a mechanism for identifying and supporting staff whose work leaves them at risk of being traumatized (Joubert et al. 2013; Knight 2013; Lee 2017). Over time, regular supervision can address burnout and stress, leading to improved capacity for decision-making (Wallbank and Hatton 2011). Lack of support from management is a key reason for staff turnover (Fleming and Taylor 2007). Staff considering leaving their current position are less attached to their supervisors and receive less guidance from them than those with an intention to stay (Yankeelov et al. 2009). Hence, in the longer term, regular supervision is seen as a way of redressing high staff turnover in both organizations and within a sector (Chenot et al. 2009).

The need for supervision is often not enshrined in organizational policies (Magnussen 2018) which can place it under risk. Being able to demonstrate that supervision has benefits and not just a luxurious use of time critical. Developing a supervision policy may be an important first step to changing an organizational culture which is primarily risk averse (Froggett 2000) to an organization which encourages professional and/or personal development (Clare 2001) and is supportive of staff (Littlechild 2005). However, the development of a supervision policy can lead to unrealistic expectations that supervision is a "quick-fix" for a range of issues (Clare 2001). How a policy is implemented is crucial, as some arrangements, such as group supervision, may be time efficient from an organizational perspective (O'Donoghue 2012) but may not meet the needs of all staff (Magnussen 2018). Yet in other contexts, group supervision may be valued by participants, particularly if it can provide a forum for discussion for staff working from different disciplinary paradigms (Bostock et al. 2018).

While it is often assumed that good practitioners make for good supervisors (Burke 1997), this may be an unfounded assumption (Sweeney et al. 2001a). Supervision which goes beyond risk management and compliance is more likely when supervisors have been trained to understand that developmental and supportive functions have a very real place in the supervisory relationship (Bradley et al. 2010; Rodrigues-Keyes et al. 2012). While for line managers with a background in social work, this may take us back to understandings of supervision in our professional training, a theoretical understanding of supervision is insufficient and training in supervisory practice may be required (Egan 2012). Line managers may also require administrative support to carry out their supervisory functions (Rodrigues-Keyes et al. 2012).

Facilitating flourishing

Like many people, I have had my share of workplace experiences when line management was merely functional and was not particularly interested in me or my needs. I have also been lucky enough to experience managers who have encouraged their staff to flourish and become accomplished in their work rather than just meeting performance standards (Yürür and Sarikaya 2012).

As with many words in the English language, multiple derivations have emerged, but when I refer to "flourishing," I am returning to a very early usage, which the *Oxford English Dictionary* (2019) reports was used as far back as the 14th century, referring to "thriving" or "prospering." In more recent times, the notion of flourishing is reflected in the World Health Organization's contention that "To reach a state of complete physical, mental and social wellbeing, an individual or group must be able to identify and to realize aspirations, to satisfy needs, and to change or cope with the environment" (World Health Organization 1986).

Importantly, this notion of well-being, or flourishing, is for everyone. Cicely Saunders' pioneering thinking a few decades ago remains influential in the provision of palliative care today. Instead of providing high doses of analgesics when dying patients reported high levels of pain, Cecily instituted a regime that involved providing regular low doses of medication with the aim of keeping pain in remission and improving quality of life:

> … they could now ease their patients' pain without making them comatose. … News of these changes began to reach the wider world; the inevitable comment of visitors being shown around the Hospice was, "But your patients look so serene, so alert and happy and no one looks as if they have pain". A nurse from a London hospital said as the end of a complete tour of the Hospice, "But we haven't been through your terminal wards yet". She had. In fact she had been talking to some of the patients in them.
> *(du Boulay and Raning 2007, p. 48)*

What this nurse had not realized was that even patients for whom death was imminent, could in their own way flourish. As a line manager, I hope that I am "making a difference" (Jagger 2018, p. 386) and encouraging staff not just to do what is required but to flourish. But is this possible if the role of a line manager is confined to the mechanics of keeping a program running by ensuring compliance and that staff have the resources, such as training and support, to do their work effectively? Reading the social work literature on supervision, one might easily come to that viewpoint. For example, it is often argued that professional supervision is most effective when decoupled from line management and is undertaken by someone from outside the organization (e.g. Beddoe 2012). In many situations, such arguments create an unhelpful binary which negate the expertise of the line manager and at the same time place all the responsibility for professional development on someone from outside the organization.

Despite organizational expectations that supervision is about ensuring compliance, effective supervisors facilitate development of knowledge and expertise (Canavera and Akesson 2018). In the rest of this chapter, I want to take that one step further and argue that it is the responsibility of an effective line manager to facilitate staff to flourish. That is not to say they must do it all themselves, because often staff will have others who contribute to their development. Indeed, there will be situations in which staff may have legitimate reservations about sharing their vulnerabilities with a line manager (Westergaard 2013) and should be encouraged to talk with others. For example, in the university setting, it is common for staff to have mentors, often former managers or supervisors of doctoral theses. In the school I work in, all junior staff are appointed a mentor from within the senior staff who is not their line manager, who they can consult with. Rather than viewing others who contribute to the development of the staff I manage as competitors, their inputs are valuable because they invariably challenge and develop staff in ways which I might not be able to. If, as the adage says, it takes a village to raise a child, then similarly it takes a professional community to raise and support its members.

As a line manager, there are some things which I can do to encourage the flourishing of staff which a supervisor external to my team or organization cannot do. Good supervision has a developmental component, in which supervisees are challenged to do better or take on new roles or tasks (O'Donoghue 2012). While an external supervisor may make recommendations about new responsibilities, as a line manager who is charged with allocating work across a team of people, I work with staff to develop workloads which seek to enable them to develop and flourish as far as possible within the organizational constraints. However, this requires me to have spent time with staff in getting to know them, including their future plans and areas in which they would like the opportunity to develop. As a line manager, one of my challenges is to take seriously the "importance of establishing and sustaining a constructive, considerate, culturally competent and caring relationship" (O'Donoghue et al. 2018, p. 351) with the staff in my team.

Supervision is only one strategy of many that a good workplace employs to facilitate staff well-being. Employment conditions are also critical (Butler et al. 2018). A line manager requires a good understanding of what the work entails and what organizational supports they need to ensure are provided to enable a staff member to do what is required (Westergaard 2013). Hence, if staff are to thrive or flourish, there is a role for the line manager to ensure workloads are manageable (Rose and Palattayil 2020). At times this may require telling staff that they may need to make choices as to what roles and tasks they are allocated, to reduce the likelihood of burnout (Yürür and Sarikaya 2012). Enabling staff as much choice as possible is important, as a culture in which staff have no role in making decisions and capacity to suggest alternative approaches is disempowering (Rodriguez-Keyes et al. 2012).

Many practitioners look to their line managers to facilitate their professional development, or at least provide clear directions as to how supervisees should proceed in their career development (Sweeney et al. 2001b). As a line manager, it is important that supervisory sessions are not just a talkfest but to recognize that I have a role in facilitating actions which have been determined. At the simplest level, the supervision may be limited if staff have no time to follow up on ideas raised during supervisory sessions (Magnussen 2018). Hence, allocations of time for supervision need to be longer than just the actual time a staff member spends with their supervisor. As a line manager, I also have a role in the approval processes for expenditure of funds for professional development, including conference attendance. While opportunities may be suggested by external supervisors, in many organizations, it is the line supervisor who has influence on how the, usually limited, funds for professional development are spent.

Furthermore, effective supervision from line managers does not just occur in designated supervisory space. Supervisors who model good practice in their day to day work, can also contribute to staff development (Foster 2013; Stevens et al. 2018). Good supervision also includes feedback on what has been well done (O'Donoghue 2012). A short passing comment to a staff member telling them something was done well which is timely may be as important, or more so, than waiting until the next formal meeting when the message may be lost in among the many issues discussed.

The experience of flourishing

When I think back to the various places I have worked over the last three and a half decades, those which hold most affection are those when I was in environments where there was an expectation or desire that everyone should flourish, although this did not mean we should all be carbon copies of each other. Rather, like a musical ensemble, we all had a part, and we were all performing well, the result was magnificent and much better than any of us could achieve by themselves. That does not mean it was all fun—in fact the process for achieving excellence can at times be excruciating, but these are mediated by the memories of celebration, and dare I say it, having fun.

I am now working in a position where I am flourishing, and it is one of my aims to try and ensure the staff in the program I manage flourish, and also hopefully our students. Earlier in my career I struggled to find positions in which I could be myself, let alone flourish. I have worked in organizations in which those who succeeded conformed to a culture which to me was not only foreign but unpalatable. I have worked in organizations in which staff have been mere pawns on a chessboard as those more senior set out to meet their next prize, and I have been subject to workplace abuse and had my career almost destroyed by prima donna senior managers who were threatened by any of their staff showing promise.

Thankfully, I have also had some excellent role models among the people I have worked for whose attitude was that the organization could not prosper unless all its members were thriving. Now while I find the term "asset management" somewhat disdainful in respect of human beings, working for someone who considers their staff to be their best assets and is prepared to invest in them, is wonderful, particularly when they believe in you and encourage you to take steps you would not dare have taken on your own. Such individuals have allowed me to be myself, but also to develop that self, including developing management skills that in turn challenge me to encourage the staff I manage to flourish.

It is perhaps difficult to envisage facilitating others to flourish if you are not flourishing. Most jobs will have aspects which one would rather not do, but for me, it is about making sure that on a regular basis I manage to do some of things which enable me to flourish, as well as those around me. The following suggestions as to some ways of moving towards flourishing come from my own reflections on what has been helpful for me and are offered to encourage the reader to think about what enables them to flourish:

- Identify what it is that will enable you to flourish.
- Do not just take a pathway because you think it is what is expected of you.
- Discerning the pathways which will enable you to flourish may involve taking some risks and trying things out of the box.
- If you find you are heading in a direction you do not want to go, consider other possibilities and do not treat the future as being inevitable.
- Just because you are flourishing or doing things to enable you to flourish, does not mean it will be easy.
- Having friends and supporters is essential.
- Find wise mentors. Ones who will listen to your story and dreams and either encourage you to realize these or if they consider them unrealistic have the gumption to tell you so.
- Recognize and respect the gifts and talents in those you work with and play your part in assisting them to flourish too.
- Believe it or not, courtesy and cooperation pay off, even in a world in which a competitive ethos predominates.
- Take time for self-care and nourishment of the soul now and do not think only of the future. Coffee and conversation, reading a novel, watching a film, or engaging in a hobby are not a waste of time if they form the fuel to keep working towards your goals.

Conclusions

In this chapter I have explored the extent to which the literature on professional supervision can provide guidance to social workers who are line managers. One perspective is that the role of the line manager is functional with responsibilities for ensuring compliance and risk management functions, while the role of the professional supervisor is to facilitate ongoing development as a social worker. However, such a rigid distinction is of little benefit to the majority of social workers who do not have a separate professional supervisor. Nor does such thinking encourage social workers who have line management responsibilities to be any more than functionaries.

Rather than placing the professional supervisor and line manager as competitors for the right to nurture professional development, it is proposed that both have responsibilities in this area. Moreover, the line manager, as well as the professional supervisor should not only be ensuring the supervisees are competent in performing their roles but facilitate flourishing of those for whom they provide professional oversight. However, this may require a radical rethinking of the rationale and methods for providing professional supervision, so that it is incorporated into, rather than divorced from, organizational leadership. Individuals who choose to have an external supervisor of their own choice should still have this option, but this should be considered by employers as additional, and not provide managers with an excuse for not contributing to staff development.

As was noted at the beginning of this chapter, the word flourishing dates back to the 14th century. Yet flourishing is as necessary in the 21st century as it ever has been for individual well-being as well as organizational thriving. For those of us who are line managers, facilitating flourishing needs to be on our agenda. If not, we are abdicating our responsibilities to the social workers we manage. Moreover, if our management is no different from that of managers of other professions, we are, in effect, suggesting that social workers would not benefit from having a manager from their own profession. So instead of continuing the argument that line management and professional supervision must be separated, as a profession the priority must be to ensure that all social workers have professional relationships with managers and/or supervisors who enable them to flourish. That will have immense benefits not only for our profession, but also for those to whom we provide services (Rankine et al. 2018).

References

Albertson, K.M., Crouch, J.M., Udell, W., Schimmel-Bristow, A., Serrano, J., and Ahrens, K.R., 2018. Caregiver perceived barriers to preventing unintended pregnancies and sexually transmitted infections among youth in foster care. *Children and Youth Services Review*, 94, 82–87.

Baines, D., Charlesworth, S., Turner, D., and O'Neill, L., 2014. Lean social care and worker identity: the role of outcomes, supervision and mission. *Critical Social Policy*, 34 (4), 433–453.

Baker, K., 2010. More harm than good? The language of public protection. *Howard Journal of Criminal Justice*, 49 (1), 42–53.

Beddoe, L., 2009. Creating continuous conversation: social workers and learning organizations. *Social Work Education*, 28 (7), 722–736.

Beddoe, L., 2010. Surveillance or reflection: professional supervision in 'the risk society'. *British Journal of Social Work*, 40 (4), 1279–1296.

Beddoe, L., 2012. External supervision in social work: power, space, risk, and the search for safety. *Australian Social Work*, 65 (2), 197–213.

Borrill, J., Cook, L., and Beck, A., 2017. Suicide and supervision: issues for probation practice. *Probation Journal*, 64 (1), 6–19.

Bostock, L., Lynch, A., Newlands, F., and Forrester, D., 2018. Diffusion theory and multi-disciplinary working in children's services. *Journal of Integrated Care*, 26 (2), 120–129.

Bradley, G., Engelbrecht, L., and Höjer, S., 2010. Supervision: a force for change? Three stories told. *International Social Work*, 53 (6), 773–790.

Bradley, G., and Höjer, S., 2009. Supervision reviewed: reflections on two different social work models in England and Sweden. *European Journal of Social Work*, 12 (1), 71–85.

Brown, B., Crawford, P., Nerlich, B., and Koteyko, N., 2008. The habitus of hygiene: discourses of cleanliness and infection control in nursing work. *Social Science and Medicine*, 67 (7), 1047–1055.

Burke, P., 1997. Risk and supervision: social work responses to referred user problems. *British Journal of Social Work*, 27 (1), 115–129.

Butler, M., Savic, M., Best, D.W., Manning, V., Mills, K.L., and Lubman, D.I., 2018. Wellbeing and coping strategies of alcohol and other drug therapeutic community workers: a qualitative study. *Therapeutic Communities*, 39 (3), 118–128.

Canavera, M., and Akesson, B., 2018. Supervision during social work education and training in Francophone West Africa: conceptual frameworks and empirical evidence from Burkina Faso and Côte d'Ivoire. *European Journal of Social Work*, 21 (3), 467–482.

Chenot, D., Benton, A.D., and Kim, H., 2009. The influence of supervisor support, peer support, and organizational culture among early career social workers in child welfare services. *Child Welfare Journal*, 88 (5), 129–147.

Clare, M., 2001. Operationalising professional supervision in this age of accountabilities. *Australian Social Work*, 54 (2), 69–79.

Cooper, L., 1998. I'm scared of being a wimp! Supervision: a view from beginning practitioners. *Practice*, 10 (4), 27–36.

Dixon, J., 2010. Social supervision, ethics and risk: an evaluation of how ethical frameworks might be applied within the social supervision process. *British Journal of Social Work*, 40 (8), 2398–2413.

du Boulay, S., and Rankin, M., 2007. *Cecily Saunders: the founder of the modern hospice movement*. London: SPCK.

Egan, R., 2012. Australian social work supervision practice in 2007. *Australian Social Work*, 65 (2), 171–184.

Fleming, G., and Taylor, B.J., 2007. Battle on the home front: perceptions of home care workers of factors influencing staff retention in Northern Ireland. *Health and Social Care in the Community*, 15 (1), 67–76.

Foster, A., 2013. The challenge of leadership in front line clinical teams struggling to meet current policy demands. *Journal of Social Work Practice*, 27 (2), 119–131.

Froggett, L., 2000. Staff supervision and dependency culture: a case study. *Journal of Social Work Practice*, 14 (1), 27–35.

Ghesquiere, A., Plichta, S.B., McAfee, C., and Rogers, G., 2018. Professional quality of life of adult protective service workers. *Journal of Elder Abuse and Neglect*, 30 (1), 1–19.

Gillingham, P., 2006. Risk assessment in child protection: problem rather than solution?. *Australian Social Work*, 59 (1), 86–98.

IFSW 2014. *Global definition of social work* [online]. Available from: https://www.ifsw.org/what-is-social-work/global-definition-of-social-work/ [Accessed 30 August 2019].

Jagger, C., 2018. The supervising social worker in an inner city: how practitioners perceive and experience their role. *Adoption and Fostering*, 42 (4), 383–399.

Joubert, L., Hocking, A., and Hampson, R., 2013. Social work in oncology: managing vicarious trauma: the positive impact of professional supervision. *Social Work in Health Care*, 52 (2–3), 296–310.

Knight, C., 2013. Indirect trauma: implications for self-care, supervision, the organization, and the academic institution. *The Clinical Supervisor*, 32 (2), 224–243.

Lee, R., 2017. The impact of engaging with clients' trauma stories: personal and organizational strategies to manage probation practitioners' risk of developing vicarious traumatization. *Probation Journal*, 64 (4), 372–387.

Littlechild, B., 2005. The nature and effects of violence against child-protection social workers: providing effective support. *British Journal of Social Work*, 35 (3), 387–401.

Littlechild, B., 2008. Child protection social work: risks of fears and fears of risks: impossible tasks from impossible goals?. *Social Policy and Administration*, 42 (6), 662–675.

Magnussen, J., 2018. Supervision in Denmark: an empirical account of experiences and practices. *European Journal of Social Work*, 21 (3), 359–373.

Manthorpe, J., Cornes, M., and Moriarty, J., 2012. Considering the safeguarding risks presented by agency or temporary social care staff: research findings and recommendations. *Journal of Adult Protection*, 14 (3), 122–130.

Moore, T.P., 2017. Children and young people's views on institutional safety: it's not just because we're little. *Child Abuse and Neglect*, 74, 73–85.

Morrongiello, B.A., Zdzieborski, D., Sandomierski, M., and Lasenby-Lessard, J., 2009. Video messaging: what works to persuade mothers to supervise young children more closely in order to reduce injury risk?. *Social Science and Medicine*, 68 (6), 1030–1037.

Noble, C., and Irwin, J., 2009. Social work supervision: an exploration of the current challenges in a rapidly changing social, economic and political environment. *Journal of Social Work*, 9 (3), 345–358.

Oak, E., 2015. A minority report for social work? The Predictive Risk Model (PRM) and the Tuituia Assessment Framework in addressing the needs of New Zealand's vulnerable children. *British Journal of Social Work*, 46 (5), 1208–1223.

O'Donoghue, K., 2012. Windows on the supervisee experience: an exploration of supervisees' supervision histories. *Australian Social Work*, 65 (2), 214–231.

O'Donoghue, K., Wong, P.Y.J., and Tsui, M.S., 2018. Constructing an evidence-informed social work supervision model. *European Journal of Social Work*, 21 (3), 348–358.

Oxford English Dictionary 2019. Oxford University Press.

Pithouse, A., Broadhurst, K., Hall, C., Peckover, S., Wastell, D., and White, S., 2012. Trust, risk and the (mis) management of contingency and discretion through new information technologies in children's services. *Journal of Social Work*, 12 (2), 158–178.

Rajan-Rankin, S., 2014. Self-identity, embodiment and the development of emotional resilience. *British Journal of Social Work*, 44 (8), 2426–2442.

Rankine, M., Beddoe, L., O'Brien, M., and Fouché, C., 2018. What's your agenda? Reflective supervision in community-based child welfare services. *European Journal of Social Work*, 21 (3), 428–440.

Reisel, A., 2017. Practitioner's perceptions and decision-making regarding child sexual exploitation: a qualitative vignette study. *Child and Family Social Work*, 22 (3), 1292–1301.

Robert, M., Pauze, R., and Fournier, L., 2005. Factors associated with homelessness of adolescents under supervision of the youth protection scheme. *Journal of Adolescence*, 28 (2), 215–230.

Rodriguez-Keyes, E., Gossart-Walker, S., and Rowland, C., 2012. Revitalizing the vision in supervision: supporting the supervisor in home-based therapy programs. *Smith College Studies in Social Work*, 82 (2–3), 276–288.

Rose, S., and Palattiyil, G., 2020. Surviving or thriving? Enhancing the emotional resilience of social workers in their organisational settings? *Journal of Social Work*, 20 (1), 23–42.

Rudolph, J., Zimmer-Gembeck, M.J., Shanley, D.C., and Hawkins, R., 2018. Child sexual abuse prevention opportunities: parenting, programs, and the reduction of risk. *Child Maltreatment*, 23 (1), 96–106.

Stevens, M., Woolham, J., Manthorpe, J., Aspinall, F., Hussein, S., Baxter, K., Samsi, K., and Ismail, M., 2018. Implementing safeguarding and personalisation in social work: findings from practice. *Journal of Social Work*, 18 (1), 3–22.

Sweeney, G., Webley, P., and Treacher, A., 2001a. Supervision in occupational therapy, part 1: the supervisor's anxieties. *British Journal of Occupational Therapy*, 64 (7), 337–345.

Sweeney, G., Webley, P., and Treacher, A., 2001b. Supervision in occupational therapy, part 2: the supervisee's dilemma. *British Journal of Occupational Therapy*, 64 (8), 380–386.

Wallbank, S., and Hatton, S., 2011. Reducing burnout and stress: the effectiveness of clinical supervision. *Community Practitioner*, 84 (7), 31–35.

Watson, T., and Vess, J., 2007. Risk assessment of child-victim sex offenders for extended supervision in New Zealand. *Journal of Forensic Psychiatry and Psychology*, 18 (2), 235–247.

Westergaard, J., 2013. Line management supervision in the helping professions: moving from external supervision to a line manager supervision model. *The Clinical Supervisor*, 32 (2), 167–184.

World Health Organization 1986. *The Ottawa charter for health promotion* [online]. Available from: http://www.who.int/healthpromotion/conferences/previous/ottawa/en/ [Accessed 1 May 2011].

Wurtele, S.K., Mathews, B., and Kenny, M.C., 2019. Keeping students put of harm's way: reducing risks of educator sexual misconduct. *Journal of Child Sexual Abuse*, 28 (2), 160–186.

Yankeelov, P., Barbee, A.P., Sullivan, D., and Antie, B.F., 2009. Individual and organizational factors in job retention in Kentucky's child welfare agency. *Children and Youth Services Review*, 31 (5), 547–554.

Yürür, S., and Sarikaya, M., 2012. The effects of workload, role ambiguity, and social support on burnout among social workers in Turkey. *Administration in Social Work*, 36 (5), 457–478.

45

EFFECTIVE SUPERVISION AND ORGANIZATIONAL CULTURE

Abigail Ornellas and Lambert Engelbrecht

Introduction

Social work is a demanding profession and the role of supervision is one which can mitigate complex and often overwhelming intervention tasks, through disseminating knowledge and support from seasoned workers to frontline staff (Egan et al. 2016). Supervision has been a long-standing practice within social work and is considered to be a core feature in the development of professional identity (Hafford-Letchfield and Engelbrecht 2018). Yet it can be argued that the supervisory role has not effectively evolved globally to fit into the broader changing organizational culture of the social work profession, which has shifted due to socio-political changes and demands. While these changes may be reflected in the global circumscribed parameters of the profession, such as the global definition of social work (IFSW and IASSW 2014) and the global agenda for social work and social development (IFSW, IASSW, and ICSW 2012), it appears that the global concept of supervision, one which is the very muscle of the profession, has become relatively stagnant. While the global value-culture of the profession has begun to shift towards a more collective, macro, and structural address, supervision remains focused on case management and output accountability. Research suggests that the role of supervision has been largely displaced worldwide by management activities (Engelbrecht 2019), with frontline social workers expressing concerns over a lack of meaningful support. This is affecting not only the quality of intervention delivered to social work service users, but also the mental health of social workers themselves.

In this regard, the role of social work supervision has been re-positioned "to serve more conservative and restrictive environments" (Hafford-Letchfield and Engelbrecht 2018, p. 329). Nevertheless, conflicts between the value-base of managerial and technicist approaches to supervision versus relationship-based approaches have become increasingly evident in social work practice (Engelbrecht 2019). When the roles of supervisors are no longer aligned with the value-culture of an organization or the profession at large, segregation between the objectives and practices of the organization can manifest, causing a confusion and ineffectiveness in supervision, as well as a conflict between professional and managerial values. To remain effective, supervision practices need to be aligned with the evolving value-culture of social work organizations.

In the chapter that follows, the changing role of supervision in social work will be reflected upon, alongside the shifts in the broader organizational and professional culture of social work as stated in the global definition of social work (IFSW and IASSW 2014). The misalignment between supervision and managerial outputs will be discussed. Finally, the chapter concludes with the suggestion of potential approaches which could be undertaken to better align the potentially stagnating role of supervision with the value-culture of the profession. While these suggestions are by no means conclusive or complete, it is the authors' hope that they will open a dialogue for further debate and research.

Understanding the role of social work supervision

Supervision has been an enduring practice within social work. It has developed globally parallel with the profession, assuming various forms and roles as social work itself evolved to fit changing socio-economic contexts and demands (Rabinowitz 1987; Ornellas 2018). This section of the chapter offers a brief overview of the historical shifts in the supervision role within the social work profession. It is noted that such shifts refer to trends in the global professional social work fraternity; the role of Indigenous knowledge would certainly have influenced supervisory practices in various country-specific contexts.

In the 1870s to the 1960s, supervision was primarily focused on organizational management and learning (Munson 1979; Kadushin 1992). The role of the supervisor was one of disseminating knowledge around clients, organizational standards, norms and practices, as well as staff interactions. Recognized as an important instrument in highlighting relevant debates in the profession, supervision allowed for professional knowledge to be translated into effective practice (Egan et al. 2016).

In the 1970s and 1980s, however, social service organizations began to experience increased fiscal pressure and accountability expectations, alongside changing socio-economic trends (Bamford 1982; O'Donoghue 2015). Thus, supervision became increasingly administrative in its function (Melichercik 1984; O'Donoghue 2003; Kadushin and Harkness 2014), overriding the educational role of the supervisor (Blake-Palmer and Connolly 1989). During this period, the supervisor began to act as a buffer between the frontline social worker and upper management (Bunker and Wijnberg 1988). According to Schaufeli et al. (2009), this period was also marked by an awareness of the concept of burnout within social service organizations, and the link between supportive supervision and social worker job satisfaction was highlighted (Rauktis and Koeske 1994). Thus, while the administrative role of supervision was intensified, attention continued to be paid to the importance of the supportive function in supervision of social workers. O'Donoghue (2015) outlines the role of supervision during this timeframe as being two-fold: that of administrative accountability as well as worker support.

In the 1990s, the global pressure for fiscal accountability continued to grow, with the global trend veering towards a more neoliberal and business-focused orientation in all arenas of life, including the public sector (Ornellas 2018). Social service organizations were increasingly being expected to manage costs, while still producing measurable results (Munson 2002). This effect was eventually referred to as managerialism (Tsui and Cheung 2004; Harris 2014; Ornellas 2018) and will be explored in more detail later in this chapter. In terms of shifts in the role of supervision, however, the managerial impact was three-fold:

- Supervision became constructed as an accountability process (Bruce and Austin 2001; Tsui 1997, 2005).

- The administrative and managerial role of supervision took precedence over other functions. This saw a focus on contractual agreements, task completion, and job performance (Engelbrecht 2015; Ornellas 2018).
- The differences between managers, social workers, and clients were reinforced (Gowdy et al. 1993), resulting in the growing appointment of generic managers without a social work background (Rees 1999; Engelbrecht 2015).

Such changes in the organizational culture of the social work profession began to usher in a decline of the more traditional supervision models which combined the administrative, educational, and supportive functions in equal measure (Berger and Mizrahi 2001; O'Donoghue 2015). Social workers began to note that their supervision experience was becoming dominated by case management and targets, with less opportunity for learning, reflection, and clinical support (Baginsky et al. 2009; Egan et al. 2016). With shifts toward a managerial role, supervision became saturated with compliance procedures (Noble and Irwin 2009; Beddoe 2010), outputs, and cost-efficiency (Engelbrecht 2015). This period also reflected an increase in peer-based supervision within social service organizations (Kadushin et al. 2009).

In more recent years, the organizational culture of the social work profession has once again begun to turn, moving away from a target-driven dominance toward a more collective and radical approach (Lawlor 2013; Ornellas et al. 2018). This new trend is highlighted in changes to the global definition of social work (IFSW and IASS 2014). The neoliberal influence on practice is being resisted and social workers are shifting their focus to a structural response (Ornellas et al. 2018). However, such a shift has not necessarily been taken on board by the supervisor. While historically, the supervision role has been at the forefront of knowledge transference within the profession, today it seems that the supervisor remains stuck in a managerial role (Manthorpe et al. 2015). While frontline social work continues to evolve, supervision has become relatively stagnant. O'Donoghue (2015, p. 136) highlights that regardless of its importance, "the issues and challenges pertaining to supervision in the twenty-first century have not been contextualized with regard to the evolving nature of supervision, the influence of organizational and professional change and the effect of the evidence-based discourse on supervision." The concern is that such a mismatch can hinder the necessary growth and change which social work supervision is attempting. As argued by Lawlor (2013, p. 178), change is difficult "unless it is integrated into a strategic organizational and culture change initiative."

The changing organizational culture of social work

Organizational culture can be defined as "a pattern of shared values and beliefs that help individuals understand organizational functioning and thus provide them norms for behaviour in the organisation" (Deshpande and Webster 1989, p. 4). Organizational culture can powerfully influence the identity of social workers, and the way in which they perceive themselves and their role within the organization, as well as the behavior and attitudes of workers. While research has shown the importance of the supervisory role in promoting positive work-related outcomes (Lee et al. 2010), a mismatch between the organizational value-culture of social work and the value promotion of supervision can have debilitating consequences, leaving social workers feeling uncertain on how to act. Conflicts between global, professional, organizational, and supervisory values and expectations can lead to low morale in frontline social workers and an organizational practice which is often in and of itself, largely ineffective.

The shift in the global organizational culture of social work was ontologically unpacked by Ornellas et al. (2018) in their review of the revised global definition of social work as established by the IFSW and IASSW in 2014. In their analysis, they argue that the new global definition, as reflected in the individual-centric international social work definition of 2010 (IFSW and IASSW 2010), shows a resistance to the managerial shifts of the 1990s. While the previous international definition (IFSW and IASSW 2010) continued to maintain the profession's commitment to social justice and human rights, it was criticized for holding a perceived Western bias (Paulsen 2012), overemphasis on individualism and case management (Ornellas 2018), and its failure to recognize issues of collective social stability and cohesion (Truell 2014). Ornellas et al. (2018) argued that the previous international definition (IFSW and IASSW 2010), which represented the global value-culture of the profession, fell into two ontological categories: that of the individual-reformist framework and the neoliberal-managerialist framework. The overall attitudes of these two approaches, based on the combined works of Howe (1987), Dominelli (2002), and Garrett (2013) are outlined in Figure 45.1.

The individual-reformist framework emphasizes social order, focuses on meeting individual needs, while maintaining a good fit between the individual and the environment (Ornellas et al. 2018). Rather than seeking social change or upheaval, this approach seeks to maintain the dominant social system (Dominelli 2002). The neoliberal-managerial framework is much like the supervisory shift of the 1990s as discussed earlier in this chapter. It holds elements of the maintenance approach in that it also seeks to maintain the status quo as established by the market. Acquiring personal control is central to intervention, and the individual is seen as being responsible for his/her own well-being.

Figure 45.2, on the other hand reflects a shift in the value-culture of the profession, with the underpinnings of the 2014 revised global definition (IFSW and IASSW 2014) moving towards a socialist-collectivist framework, while retaining some elements of the individual-reformist perspective. The socialist-collectivist framework holds the core belief that, "seeking personal and social fulfilment is impossible given the constraints that capitalism imposes" (Garrett 2013, p. 5). The role of the social work profession in this context is one whereby the empowerment of individuals is seen as a collective act achieved through broader social transformation. According to this view, the

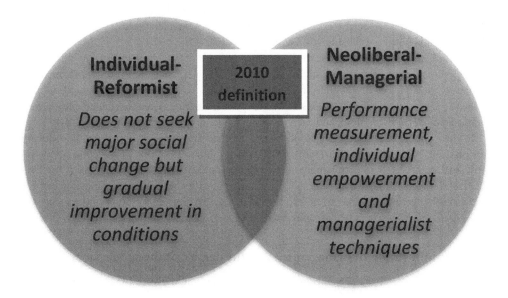

Figure 45.1 Frameworks underlying the 2010 international social work definition

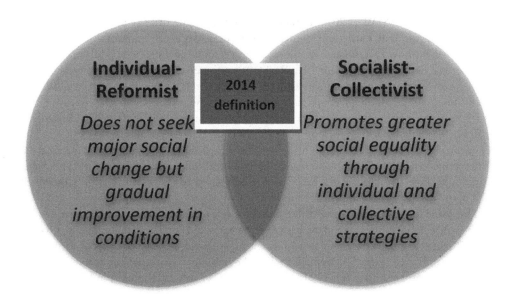

Figure 45.2 Frameworks underlying the 2014 global social work definition

socialist-collectivist aims to promote greater social equality through individual and collective strategies. Models of radical social work, critical social work, resistance social work, and developmental social work often fall in this category, as Dow and McDonald (2003, p. 7) assert: "The aim of social work is to structurally redistribute wealth and power through mobilizing collective action." Also, Ornellas et al. (2018) argue that this shift towards the collectivist framework of the revised definition (IFSW and IASSW 2014) is evident through its attention to the movement from individual to collective approaches and the increased emphasis on macro concepts and structural sources of inequality, as the new definition reads: "Principles of social justice, human rights, collective responsibility… are central to social work. … social work engages people and structures to address life challenges and enhance wellbeing" (IFSW and IASSW 2014).

It is thus apparent that this shift to the need for greater collectivism and macro-understandings is a direct result of changing socio-economic, political, spatial, and historical contexts and demands (Spolander et al. 2014). In implementing the new Global definition, the value-culture of the social work profession becomes centered upon addressing global social inequality, poverty, social exclusion, individualism, and the violation of human rights (Ornellas et al. 2018).

In the context of the above it could be argued that the global and professional value and organizational culture of the social work profession has shifted from one that was managerial and individual-centered to an increasingly more collective and structuralist perspective (Ornellas et al. 2018). However, it is questionable whether the supervisory role in many countries and contexts has yet effectively evolved to fit into the changing organizational culture of the social work profession, or whether it rather remains stagnant in its managerial and target-centric position.

The infiltration of management and the demise of the supervisory role

It can be concluded that the traditional supervisory role which evolved from the 1940s to the 1990s to combine support, education, and administration functions in social service organizations has currently been largely displaced by management roles and activities, despite the global shift to a more macro and collection-orientated approach in practice. This is affecting not only the quality of intervention delivered to service users, who are immersed in a global socio-economic world that prioritizes economic gain over social justice (Harvey 2005), but also the mental health of social workers themselves. Frontline social workers globally are expressing concerns over a lack of meaningful supervision and specifically debriefing (see for example Egan et al. 2016; Engelbrecht 2015; Fook 2012; Ornellas 2018).

As highlighted early in this chapter, the global neoliberal shift led to the infiltration by a managerial agenda in all spheres, including the public sector, and particularly, the role of the social work supervisor. With the market expectation for social service organizations to be run as businesses (Harris 2003), an emphasis on outputs, norms, procedures, standards, and cost-efficiency and accountability has served to limit, and often override the functions of the supervisor. Additionally, these expectations limit the practice of social workers themselves as they attempt to balance their professional values with organizational output demands (Engelbrecht 2015).

Outputs and statistics are emphasized over quality and intervention, and the supervision process has aligned itself with these priorities, and "...shifting from one of human agency and quality, to a management and monitoring of work output" (Ornellas 2018, p. 189). The latter author presents examples of where supervisors, in a South African context, are preoccupied with managerial tasks, reviewing outputs, procedures, norms, standards, and cost-efficiency measures, rather than allowing for a space for debriefing or support of social workers. Experiences of the South African frontline social workers correlate with other research in other contexts (Fook 2012; Harris 2014; Egan et al. 2016). To this end Sewpaul and Hölscher (2004) highlight two implications of managerialism within a context-specific but also in global social work practices that appear to be at play with the managerial supervisor:

- *Tunnel vision*: an emphasis on phenomena that are quantified in the performance management system at the expense of unquantified aspects of performance
- *Gaming*: minimizing the apparent scope for performance improvement to avoid increased expectations and higher targets in the future

Further still, the rising phenomenon of non-social workers taking on management and even supervisory posts, with little knowledge of the demands of the profession, suggests that when making critical decisions, it is likely that management knowledge will take priority over that of social work expertise. This preoccupation with business outputs, norms, and standards (Engelbrecht 2015) minimizes the human element of social work intervention and process (Harris and Unwin 2009; Harris 2014), while performance retains a particular importance within this system of organizational control (Clarke 2004). Hence, organizational objectives are measured through performance indicators and the reaching of targets over and above matters of social justice and collective orientation, as called for by the global definition (Harris and Unwin 2009; IFSW and IASSW 2014; Ornellas 2018). As a result, supervision has shifted from depth to surface work, as the professional functions of the supervisor are worn away by the effects of managerialism (O'Donoghue and Tsui 2012).

In their study, Dlamini and Sewpaul (2015) emphasize that in following such established managerial protocols, social workers often find themselves being deterred from advocating for vulnerable people, and fiscal efficiency often takes precedence in intervention decision-making. Sewpaul (2013, p. 22) maintained that such an emphasis on

> getting the job done at the lowest cost in the shortest space of time and with checks and balances, impacts on relationship building, the requisite empathic tuning into the

life worlds of people … and the use of emancipatory people-driven processes towards social change and development.

It is necessary to note here that this reference to the hindrance of managerial expectations on social work delivery, includes supervision. Dlamini and Sewpaul (2015) refer specifically to the alignment of oppressive managerial practices of a hierarchical and controlling supervisory practice.

The concern here is that supervisors, who should be presenting the role of knowledge dissemination and support, are themselves potentially detracting social workers from their professional role as laid out in the global definition (IFSW and IASSW 2014). If this holds true, it is less likely that social workers will challenge the status quo. The more likely outcome will be either the upholding of an individualized and neoliberal approach to practice, or a struggle between the supervisor expectation and larger global value-culture. As suggested by Fook (2012, p. 9): "Supervision thus becomes a political site, where the often-competing demands for managerial accountability, professional support and development are often played out in interpersonal interactions between supervisors and frontline workers."

Thus, there appears to be a growing contradiction and poor fit between the value-culture of the profession and the broader organization of social work, and with that of the supervisory approach. Social work professional values which promote principles of social justice and human rights are in contrast with the managerial discourse of accountability (Egan et al. 2016). When a managerial discourse is supported and perpetuated by the supervisor, the social worker is left unsupported and unhinged in an increasingly complex work environment. Thus, to remain effective, supervision practices need to be aligned with the evolving value-culture of social work organizations, which is becoming increasingly collective and complex in its approach, requiring increased supervisory support and knowledge dissemination.

To this end, Williams (2018) notes that in the social work profession, less emphasis has been placed on training interventions which target supervisors directly, to better enhance the supervisor-worker relationship. Research suggests a need to better understand performance within supervision (Egan et al. 2018) and to promote an organizational culture whereby workers are encouraged to develop their skills in a supportive and learning environment. As Williams (2018) asserts, such intervention is vital as it impacts on the wellbeing and effective practice of social workers, which in turn ensures better services for social work service users.

Approaches for aligning supervision practices with an evolving organizational culture

Engelbrecht (2019) highlights several approaches that would better align supervision and management with the value-culture of the organization and profession at large. The three approaches which appear to be most relevant in supporting an evolving organizational culture include the empowerment approach, the value-driven approach, and the learning organization approach.

With the *empowerment approach*, supervisors concern themselves with the provision of organizational structures and policies that better promote active participation of workers in decision-making. In this approach, supervision would inter alia aim to:

- Empower workers through more formalized participation in decision-making
- Promote partnerships with service users and workers as equal participants
- Involve service users in service delivery
- Encourage employee advocacy
- Use practice measures which aim to balance inclusion in organizational decision-making

Engelbrecht (2019) notes, however, that such an approach can be challenging to maintain by supervisors, without enough understanding of the value-culture of the organization and profession at large. Thus, the empowerment approach is further enhanced when implemented alongside a value-driven approach.

The *value-driven approach* constitutes supervision by values (Engelbrecht 2019), whereby actions and decisions of supervisors and managers alike are reflected upon, and aligned with, impact and long-term organizational values. Thus, supervision is based specifically upon the unique vision, mission; and mandate of the organization. Such an alignment when practiced in juxtaposition with the empowerment approach would ensure that the vision, mission, and mandate of the organization are determined through equal participation by an organization's workers. This approach to supervision holds elements of empowerment, while creating a uniform value-culture within the organization from which empowerment-based decision-making and management can be derived.

It is noted that the above would require an ongoing learning process, adapting to the evolving organizational culture of the specific organization as well as the profession. Thus, the use of a learning organization approach can be beneficial in ensuring supervisory approaches to remain relevant and not stagnate.

The *learning organization approach* is one whereby the organization, its workers, supervisors, and management are committed to lifelong learning and evolution, challenging assumptions (such as neoliberal individualism, by way of example), and continuously developing a shared organizational vision (Engelbrecht 2019). This approach encourages active dialogue and the promotion of systems thinking. Benefits for the supervisor-worker relationship are best found in embracing learning which is people-centered. The enhancement of personal functioning, strengthening of human capital, and a deep appreciation for aspects of social justice and human wellbeing are central to this learning organization approach.

Separating supervision and management roles

The above approaches could certainly provide an effective platform from which a better aligned supervision of social workers could be launched; however, the saturation of supervision with managerial functions may still not be sufficiently addressed. In this case, it is likely that the above empowering, value-based, and learning approaches by the supervisor will once again begin to be overrun by managerial functions and expectations.

Ideally, to better ensure supervisory capacity for learning and support, a separation between the supervisor function and the managerial function should be instigated where feasible (Bradley and Höjer 2009; Engelbrecht 2015; Egan et al. 2016). As recommended by Ornellas (2018), where possible, supervision should be clinical and supportive in its orientation, rather than being overly concerned with performance measurements or work outputs; these functions should instead be taken up by social work managers. Egan et al. (2016) accurately point out that given the continuing fiscal pressures of the neoliberal environment, managerial accountability and monitoring of performance will likely continue to be necessary within social service organizations, ad infinitum. Thus, separating the managerial and supervisory functions is likely the most ideal model; this model has been taken up by some Scandinavian and European models of supervision (Dellgran and Höjer 2005; Bradley et al. 2010). However, a wholly separate social work managerial position should not be defined by neoliberal or business standards, nor feed off existing supervision definitions (Ornellas 2018), but rather should develop a unique social work managerial approach which incorporates value-driven, empowerment, and learning organization approaches as highlighted in this chapter.

However, if such a model is not within the capacity of the organization, there is some value in considering the outsourcing of seasoned and experienced social workers for supervision rounds within the organization, "...to ensure that all social workers are receiving supervision, at the very least, that is meaningful and human-centered. This is however less desirable than the insourcing of social work supervisors" (Ornellas 2018, p. 220).

Engelbrecht (2015) suggests the balancing of supervisory and management considerations, rather than forgoing all administrative aspects of the supervisor, which are still necessary within social service organizations. Thus, shifting the role of the supervisor to one where administrative, supportive, and educational functions are equally represented and value-aligned may hold some benefits, though achieving such a balance can be challenging.

> Maintaining the pivotal centre in a balancing act is vital, and to move in either direction of the continuum would be to abandon both social development and management principles. Hence, the ideal manager and supervisor is one that combines expert social work education with a managerial role; and one who combines the normative background of social work as an academic discipline with the ability to operate as a specialist in an administrative capacity.
>
> *(Engelbrecht 2015, p. 325)*

Conclusion

The collective and macro-based shifts in the value-culture of the social work profession, as reflected in the global definition of social work (IFSW and IASSW 2014), occurred as a result of multinational debate and discussion. The resistance of the profession to neoliberal managerialism has risen out of social workers' commitment to social justice and human rights. To this end, Ornellas et al. (2018) argued that by critically reflecting on the significant definitional shifts towards macro understandings of oppression, collective solutions, and increased academic and indigenous integrity, the social work profession can continue to remain relevant and accountable to its commitment to promote social cohesion and social justice in today's challenging global world.

Thus, for the supervisory muscle of the profession to not align itself with this global value-culture is a matter of grave concern. While this chapter does not propose to offer a definitive roadmap to the realignment of the supervisory role, it does present suggested shifts in the supervision approach and overall framework of functioning, based on ideas which are of lasting import in social work and management literature. It invites consideration of the changes to the professional value-culture, and honest, critical reflections on both the value and stagnation of the supervisory role in social work.

References

Baginsky, M., Moriarty, J., Manthorpe, J., Stevens, M., MacInnes, T., and Nagendran, T., 2009. *Social workers' workload survey messages from the frontline: findings from the 2009 survey and interviews with senior managers.* Social Work Task Force. Available from: https://dera.ioe.ac.uk/1945/ [Accessed 02 September 2019].

Bamford, T., 1982. *Managing social work.* London: Tavistock.

Beddoe, L., 2010. Surveillance or reflection: professional supervision in "the risk society". *British Journal of Social Work*, 40 (4), 1279–1296.

Berger, C., and Mizrahi, T., 2001. An evolving paradigm of supervision within a changing health care environment. *Social Work in Health Care*, 32 (4), 1–18.

Blake-Palmer, L., and Connolly, M., 1989. Supervision - but not as we know it!. *Social Work Review*, 2 (2/3), 21–22.

Bradley, G., Engelbrecht, L.K., and Höjer, S., 2010. Supervision: a force for change? three stories told. *International Social Work*, 53 (6), 773–790.

Bradley, G., and Höjer, S., 2009. Supervision reviewed: reflections on two different social work models in England and Sweden. *European Journal of Social Work*, 12 (1), 71–85.

Bruce, E.J., and Austin, M.J., 2001. Social work supervision. *The Clinical Supervisor*, 19 (2), 85–107.

Bunker, D.R., and Wijnberg, M.H., 1988. *Supervision and performance: managing professionals in human service organizations*. San Francisco, CA: Jossey-Bass.

Clarke, J., 2004. Dissolving the public realm? The logics and limits of neo-liberalism. *Journal of Social Policy*, 33 (1), 27–48.

Dellgran, P., and Höjer, S., 2005. Privatisation as professionalisation? attitudes, motives and achievements among Swedish social workers. *European Journal of Social Work*, 8 (1), 39–62.

Deshpande, R., and Webster, F.E., 1989. Organizational culture and marketing: defining the research agenda. *Journal of Marketing*, 53 (1), 2–15.

Dlamini, T.T., and Sewpaul, V., 2015. Rhetoric versus reality in social work practice: political, neoliberal and new managerial influences. *Social Work/Maatskaplike Werk*, 50 (4), 467–481.

Dominelli, L., 2002. *Anti-oppressive social work theory and practice*. New York: Palgrave Macmillan.

Dow, B., and McDonald, J., 2003. Social support or structural change? Social work theory and research on care-giving. *Australian Social Work*, 56 (3), 197–208.

Egan, R., Maidment, J., and Connolly, M., 2016. Who is watching whom? Surveillance in Australian social work supervision. *British Journal of Social Work*, 46 (6), 1617–1635.

Egan, R., Maidment, J., and Connolly, M., 2018. Supporting quality supervision: insights for organisational practice. *International Social Work*, 61 (13), 353–367.

Engelbrecht, L.K., 2015. Revisiting the esoteric question: can non-social workers manage and supervise social workers?. *Social Work/Maatskaplike Werk*, 51 (3), 311–331.

Engelbrecht, L.K., 2019. Fundamental aspects of supervision. *In*: L.K. Engelbrecht, ed. *Management and supervision of social workers: issues and challenges within a social development paradigm*. 2nd ed. Andover: Cengage, 150–173.

Fook, J., 2012. Forward. *In*: N. Weld, ed. *A practice guide to transformative supervision for the helping professions. Amplifying insight*. London: Jessica Kingsley, 9–10.

Garrett, P.M., 2013. *Social work and social theory: making connections*. Bristol, UK: Policy Press.

Gowdy, E.A., Rapp, C.A., and Poertner, J., 1993. Management is performance. *Administration in Social Work*, 17 (1), 3–22.

Hafford-Letchfield, T., and Engelbrecht, L.K., 2018. Contemporary practices in social work supervision: time for new paradigms?. *European Journal of Social Work*, 21 (3), 329–332.

Harris, J., 2003. *The social work business*. London, UK and New York: Routledge.

Harris, J., 2014. (Against) neoliberal social work. *Critical and Radical Social Work*, 2 (1), 7–22.

Harris, J., and Unwin, P., 2009. Performance management in modernised social work. *In*: J. Harris, and V. White, eds. *Modernising social work: critical considerations*. Bristol: Policy Press, 9–30.

Harvey, D., 2005. *A brief history of neoliberalism*. Oxford, UK: Oxford University Press.

Howe, D., 1987. *An introduction to social work theory*. London, UK: Ashgate.

IFSW, IASSW, and ICSW 2012. Global Agenda for Social Work and Social Development. [Online] Available from: http://www.globalsocialagenda.org [Accessed 02 September 2019]. imited.

International Federation of Social Workers (IFSW) and International Association of Schools of Social Work (IASSW) 2010. *Definition of social work* [online]. Available from: http://www.eassw.org/definition.asp [Accessed 02 September 2019].

International Federation of Social Workers (IFSW) and International Association of Schools of Social Work (IASSW) 2014. *Global definition of social work* [online]. Available from: http://ifsw.org/policies/definition-of-social-work/ [Accessed 02 September 2019].

Kadushin, A., 1992. *Supervision in social work*. 3rd ed. New York: University of Columbia Press.

Kadushin, G., Berger, C., Gilbert, C., and St. Aubin, M.D., 2009. Models and methods in hospital social work supervision. *The Clinical Supervisor*, 28 (2), 180–199.

Kadushin, A., and Harkness, D., 2014. *Supervision in social work*. 5th ed. New York: Columbia University Press.

Lawlor, D., 2013. A transformation programme for children's social care managers using an interactional and reflective supervision model to develop supervision skills. *Journal of Social Work Practice*, 27 (2), 177–189.

Lee, J., Forster, M., and Rehner, T., 2010. The retention of public child welfare workers: the roles of professional organizational culture and coping strategies. *Children and Youth Services Review*, 33 (1), 102–109.

Manthorpe, J., Moriarty, J., Hussein, S., Stevens, M., and Sharpe, E., 2015. Content and purpose of supervision in social work practice in England: views of newly qualified social workers, managers and directors. *British Journal of Social Work*, 45 (1), 52–68.

Melichercik, J., 1984. Social work supervision in transition: an exploration of current supervisory practice. *The Social Worker*, 52 (3), 108–112.

Munson, C., 1979. An empirical study of structure and authority in social work supervision. *In*: C. Munson, ed. *Social work supervision: classic statements and critical issues*. New York: Free Press, 286–296.

Munson, C., 2002. *Handbook of clinical social work supervision*. 3rd ed. Binghamton, NY: Haworth Social Work Practice.

Noble, C., and Irwin, J., 2009. Social work supervision: an exploration of the current challenges in a rapidly changing social, economic and political environment. *Journal of Social Work*, 9 (3), 345–358.

O'Donoghue, K., 2003. *Restoring social work supervision*. Palmerston North, NZ: Dunmore Press.

O'Donoghue, K., 2015. Issues and challenges facing social work supervision in the twenty-first century. *China Journal of Social Work*, 8 (2), 136–149.

O'Donoghue, K., and Tsui, M.S., 2012. Towards a professional supervision culture: the development of social work supervision in Aotearoa New Zealand. *International Social Work*, 55 (1), 5–28.

Ornellas, A., 2018. *Social workers' reflections on implications of neoliberal tenets for social work in South African non-governmental organisations*. Thesis (PhD). University of Stellenbosch.

Ornellas, A., Spolander, G., and Engelbrecht, L.K., 2018. The global social work definition: ontology, implications and challenges. *Journal of Social Work*, 18 (2), 222–240.

Paulsen, N., 2012. *IFSW social work definition project report to the IFSW* [online]. Available from: http://cdn.ifsw.org/assets/ifsw:85554-5.pdf [Accessed 02 September 2019].

Rabinowitz, J., 1987. Why ongoing supervision in social casework. *The Clinical Supervisor*, 5 (3), 79–90.

Rauktis, M.E., and Koeske, G.F., 1994. Maintaining social worker morale: when supportive supervision is not enough. *Administration in Social Work*, 18 (1), 39–60.

Rees, S., 1999. Managerialism in social welfare: proposals for a humanitarian alternative – an Australian perspective. *European Journal of Social Work*, 2 (2), 193–202.

Schaufeli, W.B., Leiter, M.P., and Maslach, C., 2009. Burnout: 35 Years of research and practice. *Career Development International*, 14 (3), 204–220.

Sewpaul, V., 2013. Neoliberalism and social work in South Africa. *Critical and Radical Social Work*, 1 (1), 15–30.

Sewpaul, V., and Hölscher, D., eds., 2004. *Social work in times of neoliberalism: a postmodern discourse*. Pretoria: Van Schaik Publishers.

Spolander, G., et al., 2014. The implications of neoliberalism for social work: reflections from a six country international research collaboration. *International Social Work*, 57 (4), 300–311.

Truell, R., 2014. What is social work? [online]. *The Guardian*. Accessed from: http://www.theguar http://dian.com/social-care-network/2014/jul/07/what-is-social-work [Accessed 02 September 2019].

Tsui, M.S., 1997. The roots of social work supervision. *The Clinical Supervisor*, 15 (2), 191–198.

Tsui, M.S., 2005. *Social work supervision: contexts and concepts*. Thousand Oaks, CA: SAGE.

Tsui, M.S., and Cheung, F.C.H., 2004. Gone with the wind: the impacts of managerialism on human services. *British Journal of Social Work*, 34 (3), 437–442.

Williams, S.E., 2018. Organizational culture, supervision and retention of public child welfare workers. *Journal of Sociology and Social Work*, 6 (2), 1–5.

46

STRENGTHS-BASED SUPERVISION

Supporting effective implementation of family-centered practice in child welfare

Cynthia Lietz

Strengths-Based Supervision (SBS) (Lietz 2013) is a model of supervision that was developed to advance effective implementation of strengths-based, family-centered practice within public child welfare. The model encapsulates four components that provide an overall framework that guides supervisory practice. The development of this model has been an important development in child welfare practice in the United States for a few reasons. First, until recently, there was very little training provided to supervisors in child welfare. When training was provided, it often focused on human resource procedures and agency policy without teaching new supervisors important skills such as how to cultivate critical, analytical skills in the workforce through clinical supervision, how to provide effective supervisory support in the context of a stressful work environment, or effective use of supervisory authority. SBS is a specific model of supervision that includes defined concepts and skills that better prepare middle managers in child welfare to supervise their staff.

In addition to meeting general training needs in supervision, SBS was created to model the practice principles of Family-Centered Practice (FCP). FCP has been adopted as the guiding framework for practice with children and families in the United States for almost three decades (Briar-Lawson et al. 2001). Yet, implementation of these principles to real world practice has been slow and inconsistent (Lietz 2011; Michalopoulos et al. 2012; Sandau et al. 2002). Considering that supervision has been recognized as essential to advancing practice models (Frey et al. 2012), SBS was developed such that its activities encourage a supervisor to model FCP practice principles during supervisory conferences to leverage parallel process in translating strengths-based practice to real world practice. This chapter describes the development of this model with a brief description of its roll-out in child welfare settings in the United States, provides a summary of the model, and closes with a discussion of data that provide preliminary support for its use. For organizations seeking to advance strengths-based practice regardless of the field or location, SBS offers an option for enhancing effective implementation by developing supervisory processes that are theoretically coherent to these practice principles.

Model development

SBS was developed in 2008 for a large, public child welfare system in a southwestern state in the United States. Leaders at this organization expressed concerns that they were investing a great deal of resources to send their workforce to trainings in FCP, and yet, they felt these important practice principles were not being translated into everyday practice. For example, FCP is a collaborative process that infuses the voice of children, youth, and families in decision making. Approaches such as Family Group Decision Making (FGDM) and Team Decision Making (TDM) are good examples of specific interventions that were created to guide the decision-making process (Crampton 2007). The tenets of these approaches suggest that decision making is improved when clients, their families, and professionals come together to discuss next steps during pivotal moments in the life of a case. Despite sending their caseworkers and investigators to training on FCP and implementing the TDM process as one way of advancing this practice, leaders felt traditional methods of authoritative decision making continued to prevail in the everyday practice of their workforce.

Similarly, FCP principles include a focus on individualized, culturally-grounded practice that moves away from cookie-cutter case plans and instead develops goals and objectives that flow from a comprehensive strengths and risk assessment process. To advance this practice, the agency created a new assessment tool that provided a more holistic picture of the child and family and included a collection of data not just about risk, but also about strengths and protective capacities that could help the families to achieve their goals. Yet, agency leaders lamented that case plans too often continued to be developed in a similar fashion to the past despite efforts to shift this process.

As these concerns emerged, these conversations led to important reflection regarding the role of supervision in not just guiding, but also modeling practice principles. When new practices are rolled out across an organization, it is not uncommon to focus on the level of the workforce providing direct service to children and families. However, parallel process suggests that there are consistencies between the ways supervisees interact with their direct reports and the ways their direct reports interact with children, youth, and families (Shulman 2005). For example, if a supervisor tells a supervisee to be more strengths-based, but yet does so in an authoritative tone, that direct report will likely adopt what she observed rather than what she heard. This pattern was made most clear to me in my own parenting. I watched as I raised my own children, and it was striking to see how often they used words I used or handled situations in ways they had observed me doing so, even when I had never directly advised or taught my children to do so. When people, children or adults, observe the behavior of a leader, or someone who maintains authority over them, it is common to pick up the language, tone, and style of that person without even realizing it. And, when the behavior of the leader is consistent with specific direction or training content, that then makes the adoption of such practices quite likely. For example, if I tell my son to say, "thank you," he might pick up that behavior. But if I tell him to say "thank you," and he also sees me expressing gratitude to him and to the people in our lives, that dramatically increases the likelihood that he will pick up this behavior. As organizations seek to accomplish culture or climate change, training is only one step in this change process. Altering the way that supervision is handled such that supervisory practices remain theoretically consistent with the practice principles becomes essential to accomplishing organizational change at both the macro and micro levels.

As leaders were pondering their practice conundrum, they realized they sent their direct line staff to training in FCP without thinking about changing the supervision they were providing across this organization. By not fundamentally altering supervision, the training in many ways fell flat. Workers were excited about the ideas they were learning about FCP, but they then returned to their offices and experienced an organizational culture and climate that remained the same and most specifically, their supervision had not changed. Their supervision was not necessarily bad. However, it remained problem-focused and was grounded in an authoritative posture that suggested the supervisor maintained the expertise and therefore made the decisions. However, the agency was seeking to accomplish a paradigm shift from an incident-based, risk-only assessment approach. In this case, by not concurrently altering the process of supervision, the model of supervision became ineffective in that it contrasted the very practice principles the agency was seeking, a concern highlighted through Cohen's (1999) contention that "problem-centered supervision would render strengths-based practice very difficult" (p. 462).

There were several examples of these contradictions. For example, caseworkers were being training in the TDM process for collaborative decision making. Yet, when meeting with their supervisors, the modeling suggested otherwise, that decisions are made by those in authority, not through a collaborative process of dialog. The new strengths and risk assessment process sought to be more comprehensive. Yet, in many situations, decisions were being made solely on risk, protective capacities became just something listed on the tool, not a driving force in decision making. The workforce was sent to an initiative focused on advancing critical decision making by enhancing the analytical, critical thinking process. Yet, decisions were often made quickly without time to consider the impact of things like confirmation bias and overgeneralization and how common thinking errors increase reactive, biased decision making (Gambrill 2012). There were other factors impacting all of this. Caseloads were too high, and the economic downturn had impacted the number of positions authorized at the same time that the needs of children and youth in this state were growing. Although these factors yielded a substantial impact on this situation, they did not minimize the need for a new approach to supervision. To the contrary, these issues only furthered the need for having a model of supervision that guides and models practice principles the organization was seeking.

Supervisors are considered a key in the transfer of learning process. When direct reports attend training without the language and concepts of that training infused into supervisory conversation, it is likely that little of it will be adopted in daily practice. However, when staff members attend training and return to an office where those same concepts are talked about and encouraged, it increases the likelihood of that transfer. And, when those supervisors then model the very practice principles they are seeking in their staff, the organization has then set up an intentional, organizational plan for translation of practice principles to real world work with children and families. SBS was developed to meet this need. It offers a model of supervision that includes language that is consistent with family-centered, strengths-based practice principles. It reiterates the very concepts organizations are seeking to advance. And, it goes one step further. Grounded in the concept of parallel process, SBS models FCP practice principles in the way individual and group supervisory conferences are conducted, an idea also supported in the important work conducted by Landsman (2007).

After SBS was developed to advance FCP principles in one large state, a private non-profit organization that supports child welfare practice brought SBS to their organization that is located in five western states. Over the following ten years, leaders at four additional states asked that SBS be brought to their state and several public and private organizations across the United States adopted various elements of SBS in their supervisory program. The training program includes a two-day, twelve-hour professional development workshop in which content is presented about the model with various active learning activities to prompt application of the concepts. A website was also created (see: http://strengthsbasedsupervision.com/), where supervisors who participate in the SBS workshops can sign up to receive weekly tips that help remind attendees of the concepts they learned. Although the website exists to support transfer of learning for those who have attended the trainings, anyone can sign up for the weekly tips.

It is estimated that well over 2,000 supervisors have been trained in SBS in at least 14 different states. Although this model was initially focused on public child welfare, private child welfare agencies have cited the benefits of SBS, and organizations focused on strengths-based practice that fall outside of the child welfare field are also reporting its relevance to their work. Many countries outside of the United States are also working to adopt strengths-based, family-centered practice principles to social work practice (Briar-Lawson 2001; Crampton 2007; Oliver and Charles 2015). Because SBS is grounded in these theoretical principles which include the importance of remaining culturally-responsive and locally-embedded, this model offers application far beyond the United States.

The model

SBS is a model of supervision that involves integrating four primary components and a set of defined concepts and skills into one's supervisory practice. The four components expect that supervisors: (a) model family-centered practice in supervision, (b) incorporate both crisis-oriented and in-depth supervisory processes, (c) integrate the use of individual and group supervision modalities, and (d) fulfill the administrative, educational, and supportive functions of social service supervision. In Social Learning Theory, Bandura (1977) suggests that labeling a complicated cognitive construct can help one remember and apply that concept more efficiently once a word or phrase is attached to the overall idea. SBS training involves extensive labeling of supervisory processes to help supervisors become more intentional about how they structure the time they have with their direct reports. A list of some of the most important concepts that are discussed in SBS training are included in Table 46.1.

Table 46.1 Strengths-based supervision concepts

Parallel process	The idea that supervisory interactions are replicated when direct reports interact with the clients they serve.
Family-centered practice	A practice model that suggests clients are better served when their strengths guide the practice, when they and their families are included in decision-making, when practice is responsive to culture and identity, and when natural occurring community supports are engaged.
Critical thinking	The ability to delay action, manage bias, and consider/evaluate all reasonable options to support well-informed decisions.
Administrative supervision	A function of supervision that requires accountability, case assignment/ tracking, and review of adherence to policy and procedures
Education supervision	A function of supervision that involves providing mentoring, training, and the ability to develop critical, analytical thinking skills to support social work practice.
Supportive supervision	A function of supervision that involves developing respectful, give and take supervisory relationships. Supportive supervision involves providing both practical and emotional support.
Task-centered supervision	A more directive style of supervision that involves solving a problem and/or giving an answer.
Reflective supervision	A less directive, more discussion-oriented style of supervision that seeks to prompt critical, analytical thinking skills.
Clinical supervision	An approach used in supervision that involves supporting practice through in-depth, discussion-oriented case reviews.

The first component of SBS is to model strengths-based, family-centered practice principles in supervision. One of the primary purposes of this component is to increase intentionality in one's supervision to ensure the supervisory processes are theoretically coherent with the practice model. To accomplish this goal, supervisors are asked to reflect on their agency's practice model. They first summarize the principles of their practice model. Second, they describe what they would do or not do during their individual and group supervision if they were seeking to remain theoretically coherent with their organization's practice model. For example, if an agency adopted Motivational Interviewing (Miller and Rollnick 2012) as the primary approach to practice, a supervisor might act more like a coach, using reflective listening, and eliciting change talk when settings goals with a direct report. If an agency has adopted Family-Centered Practice (Briar-Lawson et al. 2001; Sandau-Beckler et al. 2002), a supervisor would ask questions about the family and would help direct reports consider all that could be done to maintain the family system. Regardless of the practice model, the first component of SBS suggests that, grounded in parallel process, it is essential that supervisors intentionally model the practice principles they seek from their direct reports.

The second component of SBS involves integrating both crisis and in-depth supervision. Crisis supervision requires that direct reports have access to supervision when there is a need for urgent decision-making. This is particularly relevant in child welfare settings considering the crisis-nature of this work, but in reality, just about every social work setting has some need to address emergencies that arise. Supervisees highly value the availability of their supervisor, particularly in moments that have serious implications for the health and well-being of client. Crisis supervision is often more task-centered and focuses on solving a problem or providing a quick answer. Sometimes things feel so urgent that supervisees track down their supervisor in a public place, sometimes known as *hallway* supervision. SBS acknowledges the importance of crisis supervision and offers some direction about how to engage in this process such as avoiding supervision that happens in a public place, remaining emotionally-grounded, and being clear and direct in one's communication when the implications of that decision represent risk to that client, the worker, and the organization.

Although crisis supervision is important, far too often this style of supervision becomes the norm. When all supervision occurs in a crisis, only cases that are facing an emergency get attention. This means that urgent matters always take precedent over case decisions that are important, yet not urgent. Some of the most serious situations live below the surface of what is an emergency. In SBS training, supervisors are encouraged to socialize their direct reports to what is urgent and what is important, yet non-urgent. To address the second, supervisors are encouraged to integrate crisis supervision with some scheduled, in-depth supervision. If all supervision is crisis in nature, a task-centered approach prevails. Although there are times task-centered supervision is appropriate, failing to have scheduled, in-depth supervisory conferences reinforces the authority of the supervisor and fails to model a collaborative, dialog-driven approach that is consistent with strengths-based practice. If supervision remains only or even primarily crisis-oriented, this style of supervision will undermine effective implementation of FCP.

The third component of SBS involves utilizing individual, one-on-one supervision while also implementing group supervision. Individual and group supervision modalities offer different benefits. Individual supervision is important for building a supervisor/supervisee relationship grounded in trust. The one-on-one supervisory conference allows supervisors the opportunity to get to know their direct reports, to understand their strengths and areas of growth. This also allows for in-depth case reviews, and is the right place for addressing any concerns regarding performance. Group supervision, on the other hand, allows the supervisor to develop a relationship with the team. Natural-occurring, peer driven support can emerge during group supervisory conferences. This modality is also helpful for prompting critical thinking in that it leverages the varied backgrounds, identities, perspectives, knowledge, and experience of the team in decision making. Not all supervisors oversee more than one direct report, but for those who supervise a group of people, bringing this team together using a reflective, dialog-driven process models the collaborative, group decision approach that is consistent with FCP.

The final component of SBS involves becoming mindful about fulfilling the three functions of social service supervision as described by Kadushin several decades ago (Kadushin and Harkness 2014). Kadushin's contention was that social service supervisors serve three fundamental functions: administrative, educational, and support. Administrative supervision involves monitoring the practice of another. The authority and hierarchical difference between supervisor and supervisee is embedded in this function. In administrative supervision, the supervisor evaluates practice. This means acknowledging good practice. It also means redirecting practice when it is not consistent with agency policy or procedures. In SBS training, supervisors are encouraged to implement administrative supervision in a way that mirrors their practice model. In the same way that supervisors have to collaborate to set goals and monitor goal progression with their direct reports, staff have to do this same thing with their clients. Demonstrating how to influence others and effectively exert authority while remaining collaborative and strengths-based offers important modeling for staff.

Second, supervisors serve an educational function. Even when an agency offers professional development opportunities, supervisors still maintain a responsibility for developing their staff. This sometimes involves teaching and explaining policy, procedures, and the practice model in a didactic fashion. At other times, the educational function is best served by asking questions and listening, similar to our work with clients. Clinical supervision is a good example of how educational supervision can involve a professional development activity that is dialog-driven. Clinical supervision can be used in individual or group supervision, and it involves having a direct report review a case with a supervisor and in group supervision, with the supervisor and also their peers. Clinical supervision helps the worker think more critically about the case, informing decision making for that case, but it also offers transfer of learning for similar cases on one's caseload. The adoption of clinical supervision within child welfare has become recognized as a best practice (Collins-Carmago and Millar 2010; Ferguson 2009; Lietz 2018). Discussing how to advance more supervision that is clinical in nature is a primary message delivered in the SBS workshops.

Finally, supervisors must also serve a support function. Research suggests that staff working in child welfare have higher job satisfaction (Barth et al. 2008) and are more likely to remain in their positions if they feel supported by their supervisor (Dickinson and Perry 2002; Nissly et al. 2005). The role of the supervisor in mediating vicarious trauma and helping direct reports to manage the stress of this work cannot be overstated. Helping supervisors to fulfill all three functions is the final component of SBS.

Most supervisors have natural strengths in one or two of these areas. Some are really supportive but feel uncomfortable with their authority in overseeing the quality of practice. Others embrace their administrative role but feel less comfortable in explaining concepts or prompting critical thinking through reflective dialog as required by the educational function. Some really enjoy teaching but feel less comfortable debriefing stress and supporting their staff when the work gets tough. During SBS training, supervisors are encouraged to reflect on their natural strengths regarding these three functions and also recognize the area for them that requires a bit of stretching beyond one's natural comfort zone. Having conducted SBS trainings for ten years now, it has been my experience that particularly for newer supervisors, it is fairly common to focus on the one or two functions with which they are most comfortable leading newer supervisors to avoid engaging in the third required function. Helping supervisors to understand that all three functions are essential, helps them to avoid this trap. Finally, it is important to note that in SBS training, we do not just discuss the what, meaning the importance of fulfilling all three functions. We also address the how, meaning that supervisors using SBS do more than fulfill all three functions, they approach these functions from a strengths perspective.

SBS is a model of supervision that labels supervisory activities in a way that increases one's intentionality regarding how supervision is implemented. When a supervisor is working for an organization where strengths-based, family-centered practice principles are adopted, developing a supervisory program that remains theoretically coherent to these ideas is necessary to ensure effective implementation of practice principles.

Evaluation of SBS training program

Preliminary data suggest supervisors have a high level of satisfaction with the SBS training program, and that supervisors and direct reports observe some tangible changes to the supervision conducted after their supervisors participate in SBS training. With that said, there are limitations to these findings, and further research is needed to develop SBS as an evidence-based practice.

Pre- and post-tests have been conducted in four of the states in which SBS was implemented. When given a course evaluation tool following the training, attendees report a high level of satisfaction. For example, SBS was recently delivered for all supervisors working in one region in a large southern state. Using a scale (6 = "Strongly Agree" to 1 = "Strongly Disagree"), respondents were asked to report their level of satisfaction with the training. On average, attendees agreed or strongly agreed that they were satisfied with the training on Day 1 ($m = 5.76$; $n = 46$) and on Day 2 ($m = 5.77$; $n = 47$). These data are consistent with other areas in which SBS was conducted.

In addition to course evaluations, when possible, pre- and post-test surveys were administered to (a) the supervisors who participated in the 12-hour SBS workshop series and (b) their direct reports through an anonymous, online survey. This allowed supervisors to self-report the degree to which they perceived they were implementing the elements of SBS after three months of implementation. The direct reports were included to assess the degree to which they observed changes in the supervision they received after their supervisors attended training.

Findings from the supervisor surveys indicate that supervisors perceive increases in some elements of their supervisory practice while some things remain relatively unchanged after participating in SBS training. For example, most supervisors do not see an increase in administrative or crisis-oriented supervision after SBS workshops. Administrative supervision is important. Supervisors do maintain a hierarchical difference between themselves and their direct reports. Appropriate use of supervisory authority is important. Child welfare and even many other fields within social work are crisis-oriented. As stated earlier, being available to a supervisee in a crisis situation is essential. With that said, research suggests that child welfare supervision has historically been more administrative and crisis-oriented (Zinn 2015). Therefore, it is not too surprising that training participants do not view an increase in these two functions, as many were already performing these functions consistently prior to attending SBS training. On the other hand, supervisors who participated in SBS training do report substantial improvements in the areas that are most highlighted in these workshops. They report an increase in the use of clinical supervision, group supervision, and in their ability to prompt critical thinking in the supervisory process (Lietz 2014, 2018). The fact that they report that some things stay the same whereas areas most focused on in SBS workshops improve suggests supervisors are able to integrate strengths-based supervisory practices with current practices relatively seamlessly.

Regarding the data collected from direct reports, in most locations, approximately 40% of the supervisees who respond to the surveys report observing positive changes to the supervision they receive after their supervisors have attended SBS training and been implementing the concepts for three months. Considering the challenges trainers face in achieving transfer of learning such that training concepts are quickly implemented in day to day practice, the fact that this percentage of direct reports observe positive changes offers preliminary support regarding the benefits of the SBS model and training program (Lietz 2014, 2018). Open ended comments offered by the direct reports corroborate the quantitative responses by both supervisors and supervisees as most of the responses express appreciation for more scheduled supervision, more clinical supervision, more group supervision, and a general sense that supervision is being conducted in an intentional fashion after supervisors start implementing SBS. These findings are consistent with other work that demonstrates that the components of SBS are associated with overall satisfaction with supervision (Lietz and Julien-Chinn 2017).

Although these findings are positive, future research is needed to develop SBS as an evidence-based practice. Moving forward, SBS should be implemented with a randomly assigned group of supervisors while another group receives practice as usual to test the degree to which change is observed or not observed in the treatment group when compared with a control group. This has been a challenging undertaking, considering public child welfare systems often seek SBS training when they recognize urgent needs in their workforce related to supervision training and particularly advancing supervisory practices that will support effective implementation of strengths-based, family-centered practice principles. In some ways, the roll-out of SBS has again demonstrated parallel process in that the process of implementing SBS in multiple states has occurred to meet urgent needs that sometimes stemmed from a crisis, similar to the field it seeks to transform. Next steps will involve advancing SBS in a way that remains consistent with its premise, intentionally, such that the implementation allows for rigorous testing, something that has been historically difficult in supervision research (Carpenter et al. 2013), but remains important as we seek to advance our ongoing understanding regarding the role of social work supervision in ensuring quality practice.

References

Bandura, A., 1977. *Social learning theory*. New York: General Learning Press.

Barth, R., Lloyd, E.C., Christ, S.L., Chapman, M.V., Dickinson, N.S., 2008. Child welfare worker characteristics and job satisfaction: a national study. *Social Work*, 53 (3), 199–209.

Briar-Lawson, K., Lawson, H.A., Hennon, C.B., and Jones, A.R., 2001. *Family-centered policies and practices: international implications*. New York: Columbia University Press.

Carpenter, J., Webb, C., and Bostock, L., 2013. The surprisingly weak evidence base for supervision: findings from a systematic review of research in child welfare practice (2000–2012). *Children and Youth Services Review*, 35, 1843–1853.

Cohen, B., 1999. Intervention and supervision in strengths-based social work practice. *Families in Society*, 80, 460–466.

Collins-Camargo, C., and Millar, K., 2010. The potential for a more clinical approach to child welfare supervision to promote practice and case outcomes: a qualitative study in four states. *The Clinical Supervisor*, 29, 164–187.

Crampton, D., 2007. Research review: family group decision-making: a promising practice in need of more programme theory and research. *Child and Family Social Work*, 12, 202–209.

Dickinson, N.S., and Perry, R.E., 2002. Factors influencing the retention of specially educated public child welfare workers. *Evaluation Research in Child Welfare*, 15 (3/4), 89–103.

Ferguson, S., 2009. Clinical supervision in child welfare. *In:* C. Potter and C. Brittain, eds. *Child welfare supervision*. Oxford: Oxford University Press, 296–329.

Frey, L., LeBeau, M., Kindler, D., Behan, C., Morales, I.M., and Freundlich, M., 2012. The pivotal role of child welfare supervision in implementing an agency's practice model. *Children and Youth Services Review*, 34, 273–1282.

Gambrill, E., 2012. *Critical thinking in clinical practice: improving the quality of judgments and decisions*. John Wiley & Sons.

Kadushin, A., and Harkness, D., 2014. *Supervision in social work*. New York: Columbia Press.

Landsman, M.J., 2007. Supporting child welfare supervisors to improve worker retention. *Child Welfare*, 86 (2), 105–124.

Lietz, C.A., 2011. Theoretical adherence to family centered practice: are strengths-based principles illustrated in families' descriptions of child welfare services?. *Children and Youth Services Review*, 33, 888–893.

Lietz, C.A., 2013. Strengths-based supervision: supporting implementation of family-centered practice through supervisory processes. *Journal of Family Strengths*, 13 (1). Article 6. Available from: https://digitalcommons.library.tmc.edu/jfs/vol13/iss1/6 [31 August 2019].

Lietz, C.A., 2018. Infusing clinical supervision throughout child welfare practice: advancing effective implementation of family-centered practice through supervisory processes. *Clinical Social Work Journal*, 46 (4), 331–340.

Lietz, C.A., Hayes, M., Cronin, T., and Julien-Chinn, F., 2014. Supporting family-centered practice through supervision: an evaluation of strengths-based supervision. *Families in Society*, 95 (4), 227–235.

Lietz, C.A., and Julien-Chinn, F.J., 2017. Do the components of strengths-based supervision enhance child welfare workers' satisfaction with supervision?. *Families in Society*, 98 (2), 146–155.

Michalopoulos, L., Ahn, H., Shaw, T.V., and O'Connor, J.,2012. Child welfare worker perception of the implementation of family-centered practice. *Research on Social Work Practice*, 22 (6), 656–664.

Miller, W.R., and Rollnick, S., 2012. *Motivational interviewing, helping people change*. 3rd ed. New York: Guilford Press.

Nissly, J.A., Mor Barak, M.E., and Levin, A., 2005. Stress, support, and workers' intentions to leave their jobs in public child welfare. *Administration in Social Work*, 29 (1), 79–100.

Oliver, C., and Charles, G., 2015. Enacting firm, fair and friendly practice: a model for strengths-based child protection relationships?. *British Journal of Social Work*, 46 (4), 1009–1026.

Sandau-Beckler, P., Salcido, R., Beckler, M.J., Mannes, M., and Beck, M., 2002. Infusing family-centered values into child protection practice. *Children and Youth Services Review*, 4 (9/10), 719–741.

Shulman, L., 2005. The clinical supervisor-practitioner working alliance: a parallel process. *The Clinical Supervisor*, 24, 23–47.

Zinn, A., 2015. A typology of supervision in child welfare: multilevel latent class and confirmatory analyses of caseworker–supervisor relationship type. *Children and Youth Services Review*, 48, 98–110.

47

EVALUATING SUPERVISION

Allyson Davys

Supervision is a core element of social work practice which, for many social workers, is clearly mandated by social work regulatory and/or professional bodies. The means by which the quality of that supervision is ensured, and how supervision is evaluated, is however less clear. This chapter considers how professional and regulatory bodies set the standards for supervision and how these standards, alongside organizational policy and culture, contribute to the practice of social work supervision. Ways in which social workers and their supervisors can promote and engage in best supervision practice and how they can evaluate their supervision relationship and the supervision process in which they engage are discussed. The importance for both the supervisor and the supervisee to take ownership of their roles within the supervision process is considered, as is the negotiation of the supervision contract and the ongoing maintenance of the supervision relationship.

Supervision is a core professional activity for many professionals (Hawkins and Shohet 2012) and described as "fundamental to the social work profession" (Wilkins et al. 2017, p. 1). Social work commentary on supervision supports these assertions with statements which attest to the effectiveness and value of supervision. For example:

> High quality supervision is one of the most important drivers in ensuring positive outcomes for people who use social care and children's services. It also has a crucial role to play in the development, retention and motivation of the workforce.
>
> *(Skills for Care and the Children's Workforce*
> *Development Council 2007, p. 2)*

Alongside such acclamation, supervision is shown through research and through anecdote to vary in both form and quality (Davys et al. 2017a; Kelly and Green 2019; Leggat et al. 2016; O'Donoghue et al. 2005), and the evidence to support such claims as those above has not been well established (Bernard and Goodyear 2009; Carpenter et al. 2013; O'Donoghue and Tsui 2013; Watkins 2011; Wheeler and Barkham 2014). While suggesting that it is to be expected that a professional practitioner will experience a range of good and not so good supervision over the course of their career (Beddoe 2017; Ladany et al. 2013), the supervision literature also warns that harmful and inadequate supervision "is neither an isolated nor rare incident" (McNamara et al. 2017, p. 124).

To date, the research and discussion of evaluation in the supervision literature, wrestling with questions of what should be the focus of evaluation and how should that evaluation take place, has largely considered the benefits of supervision in three areas: to the supervisee, to the organization, and to the clients (Davys et al. 2017a). Watkins (2011, p. 236), reviewing psychotherapy research, reports benefits to supervisees of "enhanced self-awareness, enhanced treatment knowledge, skill acquisition and utilization, enhanced self-efficacy, and strengthening of the supervisee–patient relationship," and Carpenter et al. (2013, p. 1843), exploring supervision for child welfare workers, note benefits of "job satisfaction, self-efficacy and [protection against] stress" for child welfare workers and "workload management, case analysis and retention" as benefits for organizations. Meanwhile in a meta-analysis of the research into the effectiveness of supervision in child welfare, social work, and mental health settings, Mor Barak et al. 2009, p. 3) identified a connection between effective supervision, including the "supervisory dimensions of task assistance, social and emotional support, and supervisory interpersonal interaction," and worker outcomes.

The literature is critical of the reliability of the evaluative research which has been reported and the ability to draw conclusions from it, particularly in relation to the relationship between supervision and client outcomes (Carpenter et al. 2013; Dawson et al. 2012; Wheeler and Barkham 2014; Watkins 2011). Wheeler and Barkham (2014) note a focus on pre-qualification supervision rather than on the supervision of experienced practitioners and an over reliance on self-report, which it has been noted elsewhere, "must be interpreted with caution" (Wilkins et al. 2018, p. 351). Meanwhile Bernard and Goodyear (2009, p. 301) observe that evaluation often rests on supervisee satisfaction, which they believe, though important, has imperfect "link[s] to outcomes such as supervisee skills, attitudes, and cognitions." Others (O'Donoghue and Tsui 2013), reviewing social work supervision research, identify a lack of empirical evidence and a reliance on retrospective accounts of supervision. Whether and how clients benefit from supervision is contentious. Watkins (2011) deemed it premature to draw any conclusions, while in the opinion of Carpenter et al. (2013, p. 1851) "the evidence for its [supervision's] effects on workers' practice is weak."

Despite, or possibly consequent to this critique, the need for and the importance of evaluation of supervision continues to be articulated in the social work literature (Beddoe 2016; O'Donoghue 2016; Sewell 2018), but again, such evaluation is confronted by the questions: what it is that is to be evaluated and against what standards?

Ellis et al. (2014, pp. 438–439) consulting the "requirements and standards for accreditation and licensure, certification, and guidelines and standards for clinical supervision" of a number of different professions in the United States (including social work), identified the "criteria for minimally adequate clinical supervision across disciplines." From the basis of these criteria Ellis et al. (2014) distinguished two further categories of supervision, inadequate supervision and harmful supervision. Inadequate supervision, they defined as being where the supervisor failed to meet the above standards for minimally adequate supervision, while harmful supervision they considered to be "supervisory practices that result in psychological, emotional, and/or physical harm or trauma to the supervisee" (Ellis et al. 2014, p. 440). In an assessment of the supervision of 363 supervisees in the United States, Ellis et al. (2014, p. 434) found that "93.0% were currently receiving inadequate supervision and 35.3% were currently receiving harmful supervision." In a subsequent study Ellis et al. (2015), again using above criteria for minimally adequate supervision, conducted a comparative exploration of the supervision of supervisees from both the Republic of Ireland and the United States. Whilst recognizing that the benchmarks for minimally adequate supervision, determined through examination of United States based standards and guidelines and which focused on prequalification supervision, were not all appropriate for the Republic of Ireland context, where 50% of the supervisee participants were post qualification, the researchers nevertheless found similar levels of inadequate supervision across these national groups. From the self-report of these supervisees, 79% of the Republic of Ireland supervisees and 70% of those from the United States categorized the supervision they were receiving as inadequate. Of more concern were the 40% of those from the Republic of Ireland and 25% of those from United States who said they were receiving harmful supervision. Such reports raise concern as to the experiences and quality of supervision.

In the global context of social work practice, where it is recognized that supervision for social workers is differently premised across geographical borders (Akesson and Canavera 2018; Antczak et al. 2019; Wilkins and Antonopoulou 2019), complexity is added. Antczak et al. (2019), describing social work supervision in Denmark, note that the main focus of supervision is on training and development and that the supervision is generally provided by a supervisor who is external to the organization. By way of contrast they describe social work supervision "in most English-speaking countries" as a "process whereby line managers oversee and support their staff" (Antczak et al. 2019, p. 2).

In these English speaking countries the link between supervision and line management is a long established feature of social work supervision (Beddoe 2010; Bogo and McKnight 2006; Hair 2014; O'Donoghue 2015), and definitions of social work supervision have traditionally considered supervision to include an evaluative activity linked to organizational purpose (Bogo and McKnight 2006; Mor Barak et al. 2009; Sewell 2018). The British Association of Social Work (BASW 2011, p. 8) addresses this in their policy document. "The word supervision has a specific meaning in the social work profession with interrelated functions including line management and accountability, professional supervision and continuing professional development."

Referencing a North American perspective, Bogo and McKnight (2006, p. 50) describe social work supervision as "primarily conceived of as an administrative function that aims to provide accountability in relation to the agency mandate." In Britain however, while acknowledging the interrelated functions mentioned earlier, calls have urged for the removal of practice audit and for social work supervision to regain a balance between oversight, critical reflection, learning, and support (Bartoli and Kennedy 2015; Laming 2009; Morrison and Wonnacott 2010). In response, and recognizing an "over emphasis ... on the managerial aspects of supervision," BASW (2011) note in their current policy that social work supervision must provide a "supportive environment for reflecting on practice and making well informed decisions using professional judgement and discretion" (BASW 2011, p. 8). Elsewhere, the Australian Association of Social Workers (AASW) adopted a definition of professional supervision in social work which explicitly names supervision as "a forum for reflection and learning" (AASW 2014). Notwithstanding these shifts, continuing reports by social workers of supervision agendas which deal primarily with management oversight, targets, and organizational outcomes (Bostock et al. 2017; Davys et al. 2017a; Egan et al. 2015; Manthorpe et al. 2015; Wilkins et al. 2017) suggest that creating and maintaining a space for reflection on practice within supervision remains a challenge for social workers.

Whether it is necessary to maintain this connection between line management on the one hand, and reflection and professional development on the other, in social work supervision has been questioned over past decades (Wong and Lee 2015) and the separation of the management function from the educative and supportive functions has been long promoted as one way in which to manage the consequent tension (Beddoe and Davys 1994; Payne 1994). Arguing that social work, as a profession, has been slow to respond to the developments of supervision practice and to recognize and incorporate the evidence which, to date, has emerged from research, O'Donoghue (2015) describes current models of social work supervision as outdated. He proposes that there is "a case for both the reconstruction in theory of what social work supervision is and for a revision of the mandate for supervision" (O'Donoghue 2015, p. 142). Specifically, he wonders if it is time for professional and organizational supervision to separate and for supervision to be provided in different formats by different people. This marks, he says, "a change from supervision occurring solely within an organization by a hierarchical supervisor, to a mixed provision involving both organizational and professional supervisors" (2015, p. 143).

The International Federation of Social Work (IFSW) offers no guidance for definition or expectations of social work supervision. The Global Social Work Statement of Ethical Principles (9.1) adjures social workers to "act in accordance with the current ethical code or guidelines in their country" while principle 9.6 states that "Social workers have a duty to take the necessary steps to care for themselves professionally and personally in the workplace, in their private lives and in society" (IFSW 2018). The practice of social work supervision thus returns, for definition, to the policies and practices of geographic regions, and the evaluation of social work supervision will be tempered by those definitions.

In the face of such debate and discussion, and until such time as social work as a profession, particularly in the English speaking countries, tackles some of the challenges inherent in its traditional model of supervision, what options are available to social workers and their supervisors to evaluate the quality of the supervision with which they engage? The framework for evaluation presented here provides a starting place to consider and discuss the practice, the structure, the value, and place of supervision as a professional requirement, as a professional practice within an organization, and as a relational, accountable practice between a supervisor and a supervisee. Such a process of evaluation has the benefit of situating supervision as a visible activity and its evaluation as a high order priority.

The framework considers supervision from three perspectives: professional mandate; organizational policy and practice; and supervisors' and supervisees' approach, practice, and relationship.

Professional mandate

Any evaluation of social work supervision needs to begin with a clear understanding and acknowledgement of the professional parameters of the supervision practice that is to be evaluated. These parameters will be intrinsically shaped by the overarching professional imperatives for supervision detailed in "the current ethical code or guidelines" (IFSW 2018) of the professional and or regulatory body of the country in which the social work is practiced. In short, how does the professional and or regulatory body for social work, in the country where social work is practiced, define supervision, and what do they direct regarding such things as frequency of supervision, focus or tasks of supervision, experience and/or training for supervisors etc. Following Ellis et al.'s (2014) lead, the question can be asked: what are the criteria for minimally adequate social work supervision as specified by the professional and regulatory dictates of the country where the social work supervision is taking place? Considering Ellis et al.'s (2014) criteria (see below) as a starting point, and accepting the limitations identified earlier, how well do the requirements for the social work supervision of specific countries, as defined and guided by policy of that country, match or address those items recorded by Ellis et al. (2014)? What is missing and what needs to be removed? Ellis et al.'s list asks whether the supervisor:

- Has the proper credentials as defined by the supervisor's discipline or profession;
- Has the appropriate knowledge of and skills for clinical supervision and an awareness of his or her limitations;
- Obtains a consent for supervision or uses a supervision contract;

- Provides a minimum of one hour of face-to-face individual supervision per week;
- Observes, reviews, or monitors supervisee's therapy/counseling sessions (or parts thereof);
- Provides evaluative feedback to the supervisee that is fair, respectful, honest, ongoing, and formal;
- Promotes and is invested in the supervisee's welfare, professional growth, and development;
- Is attentive to multicultural and diversity issues in supervision and in therapy/counseling;
- Maintains supervisee confidentiality (as appropriate); and
- Is aware of and attentive to the power differential (and boundaries) between the supervisee and supervisor and its effects (Ellis et al. 2014, p. 439).

As a starting place, identification of the higher order requirements for social work supervision enables further questions to be examined. When considering the above list, particularly in the context of the discussion of this chapter, the absence of any mention of evaluation or review stands out. Also absent is mention of any process to identify the supervisee's role and agency as a participant in the supervision process.

Understanding the professional requirements of social work supervision leads to the second focus of evaluation where two questions are posed: What are the organizational requirements and parameters for supervision? How, and to what extent, are the professional requirements for practice of supervision reflected, resourced, and supported by the organization?

Organizational policy and the practice of supervision

Social work practice typically occurs within the broader organizational context of health or social service provision. Here, no matter how social work supervision is defined or prescribed by the profession, the practice of supervision sits within a web of intersecting organizational policy, structures, and attitudes. Evaluation of supervision must therefore include examination of the dictates of these policies, the organizational structures, and the environment of practice. The first question to ask here may be to establish that the organization has a supervision policy, which according to Morrison (1993, p. 30) "is a necessity, not an optional extra."

After establishing that there is indeed an organizational supervision policy, the content of the policy can be considered. The alignment between organizational supervision policy and the professional or regulatory body requirements can be established, and the following questions may be usefully considered:

- What are the specific directives and provisions identified in the organizational supervision policy?
- How does the organizational supervision policy recognize, match, and resource the professional body and or regulatory body stipulations and/or regulations, including such things as frequency of supervision sessions, supervision training, and professional development?
- How does the policy articulate the relationship between supervision and line management?
- What opportunities are there for choice within supervision?
- How will conflict be managed should it occur?
- What happens to the information shared in supervision?
- How is confidentiality maintained for clients and supervisees?
- How does the policy reflect best supervision practice standards?
- How is supervision supported and resourced?
- What are the expectations for evaluation of supervision within the organization?

Supervision is a resource hungry activity (Davys et al. 2017b), and a lack of knowledge or understanding of the purpose of supervision, combined with the costs to the organization of resourcing supervision through time or money, may shape organizational responses and attitudes. It is therefore important that organizations understand and support supervision, particularly reflective supervision (Hewson and Carroll 2016). At the same time, the culture of the organization may affect the attitude towards, and practice of, supervision. The relationship between supervision and organizational culture, which is well addressed in the supervision literature (Davys and Beddoe 2010; Hawkins and Shohet 2012; Noble et al. 2016), is simply summed up by van Ooijen (2003, p. 221): "for supervision to work well within an organization, its culture needs to be favorable. If the culture is unhealthy it is likely that the supervision will be affected accordingly."

In a study conducted in Aotearoa New Zealand which explored how supervision was evaluated (Davys et al. 2017a), two social workers offered views which reflected how the organizational culture impacted on the practice and evaluation of their supervision.

> The organisation appears not to know what clinical supervision is, and to hold little value for [it]. There is a focus on administrative supervision to ensure KPI [key performance indicators] achieved, supervisors mostly untrained, do not understand or provide clinical supervision, therefore appear to see no reason to evaluate what they do provide, or its impact on practice (Social Worker).
>
> *(Davys et al. 2017a, p. 113)*

> Even if I had the opportunity to evaluate supervision, I would be concerned about how that information would be used by my team leader and/or manager … many of my colleagues also have similar feelings, however also fear repercussions if they speak out (Social Worker).
>
> *(Davys et al. 2017a, p. 117)*

It is beyond the scope of this chapter to do other than to raise awareness of organizational culture and to encourage social workers to think at this broader systemic level when evaluating social work supervision. Through consideration of their individual and collective roles social workers may identify what it is that they can contribute as a social worker or a supervisor to support, or challenge, the practice of supervision within their organization.

Supervisors' and supervisees' approach, practice, and relationship

Notwithstanding consideration of the higher order policies of supervision, it is important for supervision to be evaluated at the practice level between the supervisor and the supervisee. It is here that evaluation typically occurs. In the interprofessional study in Aotearoa New Zealand identified earlier, 329 supervisors, supervisees, and managers from the professions of counseling, mental health nursing, psychology, and social work reported the ways in which their supervision was evaluated. The responses, collected through an online survey, included the experiences and opinions of 145 social workers (Davys et al. 2017a). This study found that across the four professions, although there were no reported overarching practice or policies for evaluation, a majority of the participants evaluated supervision in some way.

The most common method of evaluation was an informal discussion between the supervisor and the supervisee, often at the time of the annual contract review. From a list of topics, generated from a pilot study which preceded this survey (Davys et al. 2017b), the participants indicated what they currently considered in their evaluation. Reflection was high on this list, and 90% of the social work supervisors and 73% of the social work supervisees indicated that they examined whether reflection occurred in supervision. Interestingly, while 81% of supervisors said they evaluated whether the supervisee goals were met, only 58% of supervisees identified this as an area of evaluation. Similarly, where 78% of social work supervisors said they evaluated the supervision relationship, only 60% of the supervisees recorded this response. The authors note that as it was not known if the supervisors and supervisees of the study were in a supervision relationship together (Davys et al. 2017a), the participants were considered to be describing separate supervision arrangements and this, in all likelihood, accounted for the differences in response. When asked what the ideal (rather than current) foci for evaluation should be, 90% of all social work respondents (supervisors, supervisees, and managers) named "impact on the supervisee's practice." Evaluating whether reflection occurred was important for 89% of respondents, 86% wanted to review whether supervisee goals are being met, and 85% thought that the supervision relationship should be evaluated (Davys et al. 2017a, p. 115).

The preference for areas for evaluation, as identified by the combined group of social work supervisors, supervisees, and managers, are presented in Table 47.1: What should be evaluated?

While this list may note aspects of the supervision process and content, another more personal audit can be considered by both the supervisor and the supervisee. This personal audit identifies the individual roles of the participants in supervision and promotes ownership and responsibility of the supervision process. While in many situations social work supervisees may

Table 47.1 What should be evaluated?

What should be evaluated	*Best*	*Practice*
	n	%
Impact on supervisee's practice	115	89.8
That reflection occurs	114	89.1
Whether supervisee goals are being met	110	85.9
Supervision relationship	109	85.2
Impact on supervisee's professional development	109	85.2
Level of support	106	82.8
Ethical considerations	105	82.0
Level of challenge	102	79.7
How learning is achieved	102	79.7
Supervisor's facilitation of skills	100	78.1
Supervisee's use	99	77.3
Risk management	99	77.3
Whether supervision fulfils professional requirements for supervisees	98	76.6
Supervisee's competence to practice	98	76.6
Supervision process	94	73.4
Cultural considerations of the supervisee's practice	91	71.1
Supervisee's attendance	90	70.3
Themes and content	75	58.6
Cultural identity of the supervisee	74	57.8
Other	7	5.5
None of the above	1	0.8
Don't know	0	0.0

Adapted from Davys et al. (2017a, p. 115) with kind permission of Aotearoa New Zealand Social Work.

Table 47.2 Supervisors' and supervisees' self-evaluation

Supervisor self-evaluation:	Supervisee self-evaluation:

Personal definition, values, and attributes

- What is the definition of supervision which guides my supervision practice?
- What is the model of supervision I use, and is it appropriate for the social workers I supervise?
- What do I see as my role and key responsibilities in the supervision process?
- How do I manage the tension between professional and organizational responsibilities?
- How do I ensure that supervision allows and encourages reflection and learning?
- How able am I to sit with "not knowing"?

- What is my definition and understanding of supervision?
- What is my role as a supervisee?
- What are my key responsibilities in the supervision process, and how do I honour those responsibilities?
- What choices do I have as a supervisee in terms of both role and behavior?
- How open am I to disclosing and exploring my practice?

Professional and Organizational Requirements

- What are the professional body and regulatory requirements of me as a supervisor?
- To what extent do I meet those requirements and expectations?
- What are the organizational requirements of me as a supervisor?
- To what extent do I meet those requirements and expectations?
- What are the organizational constraints? Where and how can I address those?
- What are the organizational opportunities? Do I take advantage of those opportunities?
- How aligned are the professional body and regulatory requirements and the organizational requirements?
- Are there any areas which need addressing or adjustment?
- How do I manage accountability in supervision: to the profession? to the organization?
- If I hold a dual role of line manager and supervisor, how do I manage the boundaries and keep those roles separate?

- What are the professional body and regulatory requirements of me as a social work supervisee?
- To what extent does my supervision meet those requirements and expectations?
- What needs to be addressed?
- What are the organizational requirements of me as a supervisee?
- To what extent do I meet those requirements and expectations?
- What are the organizational constraints? Where and how can I address those?
- What are the organizational opportunities? Do I take advantage of those opportunities?
- How aligned are the professional body and regulatory requirements and the organizational requirements?
- Are there any areas which need addressing or adjustment?
- How do I manage accountability in supervision: to the profession? to the organization?
- If my supervisor holds a dual role of line manager and supervisor, how are the boundaries of those roles maintained?

Supervision processes and relationship

- How do I negotiate a supervision contract with each supervisee? How do I ensure that the supervisee's needs and goals are included?
- How do I encourage reflection and learning in supervision?
- How do I provide feedback and challenge in supervision?

- Do I have a supervision contract?
- What was my contribution to developing that contract?
- What are my goals for supervision?
- How do I prepare for supervision?
- Am I facilitated to reflect on my practice?

(Continued)

587

Table 47.2 Continued

Supervisor self-evaluation:	Supervisee self-evaluation:
• How do I create a safe place and provide support in supervision?	• Am I assisted to identify the learning from my practice and my areas for development?
• How do I acknowledge diversity in supervision?	• How is feedback and challenge managed in supervision?
• How do I encourage the supervisee to provide feedback to me? How do I respond to feedback?	• Do I feel safe in supervision?
	• Do I feel heard?
	• How are my views and the cultural differences which I bring to supervision respected?
• How do I ensure the supervisee's needs are met in supervision?	• Am I able to provide feedback to my supervisor?
• Have we revisited the supervision contract? Is it still relevant?	• Are my supervision goals being met in supervision?
• How do we review and evaluate supervision?	• Am I getting the supervision I need?
• Is the review meaningful and honest?	• Have we revisited the supervision contract? Is it still relevant?
	• How do we review and evaluate supervision?
	• Is the review meaningful and honest?

Development

• What aspects of supervision practice present the greatest challenge to me?	• How open am I to the supervision process?
• What aspect of my supervision practice do I need to develop?	• How can I develop as a supervisee?
	• How has supervision changed my practice?
• What have I learned from supervision with the people I supervise?	
• How do I access my own supervision for the supervision that I provide?	

not have choice of supervisor, they do have a choice in how they behave (Davys 2007). The question is thus posed: What is my personal and professional responsibility for my participation in supervision and for the supervision which I receive or provide? This and a number of other questions which can be explored by both supervisors and supervisees are listed in Table 47.2: Supervisors' and supervisees' self-evaluation. Consideration of these questions may provide an independent personal evaluation for each party or may be in preparation for a focused evaluative discussion between both supervisor and supervisee. In either case the questions recognize that both supervisor and supervisee have agency in the supervision process.

Evaluation in, and of, supervision is a complex process which, as described earlier, is accompanied by considerable debate about method, focus, and results. This chapter has considered some of the parameters of evaluation of social work supervision, in particular the professional and organizational dictates which provide guidelines for basic standards for social work supervision and the organizational culture which influences the context of supervision practice. The inherent tension in social work supervision between line management roles and reflective supervision process has been identified. At the practice level a process for self-evaluation by both supervisor and supervisee provides a means of identifying the individual responsibilities and roles of the supervisor and the supervisee. This promotes ownership of the process for both parties and provides a beginning place for discussion. Evaluation of supervision inevitably turns to review what happens within the supervision session where the quality of supervision is fundamentally determined by the quality of the supervision relationship. "Relationship factors continue to be where the action is, literally. Everything else resolves around it" (Bernard 2006, p. 15).

References

AASW 2014. *AASW supervision standards*. Canberra ACT: Australian Association of Social Workers. Available from: https://www.aasw.asn.au/document/item/6027 [Accessed 23 September 2019].

Akesson, B., and Canavera, M., 2018. Expert understandings of supervision as a means to strengthen the social service workforce: results from a global Delphi study. *European Journal of Social Work*, 21 (3), 333–347.

Antczak, H.B., Mackrill, T., Steensbæk, S., and Ebsen, F., 2019. What works in video-based youth statutory caseworker supervision – caseworker and supervisor perspectives. *Social Work Education*, 1–16. doi:10.1 080/02615479.2019.1611757

Bartoli, A., and Kennedy, S., 2015. Tick if applicable: a critique of a national UK social work supervision. *Policy & Practice*, 27 (4), 239–250. doi:10.1080/09503153.2015.1048054

BASW 2011. *UK supervision policy*. British Association of Social Workers. Available from: https://www.basw .co.uk/system/files/resources/basw:73346-6_0.pdf [Accessed 23 September 2019].

Beddoe, L., 2010. Surveillance or reflection: professional supervision in 'the risk society'. *British Journal of Social Work*, 40 (4), 1279–1296. doi: 10.1093/bjsw/bcq018

Beddoe, L., 2016. Supervision in social work in Aotearoa New Zealand: challenges in changing contexts. *The Clinical Supervisor*, 35 (2), 156–174.

Beddoe, L., 2017. Harmful supervision: a commentary. *The Clinical Supervisor*, 36 (1), 88–101. doi:10.1080 /07325223.2017.1295894

Beddoe, L., and Davys, A., 1994. The status of supervision – reflections from a training perspective. *Social Work Review*, 6 (5/6), 16–21.

Bernard, J.M., 2006. Tracing the development of clinical supervision. *The Clinical Supervisor*, 24 (1), 3–21. doi:10.1300/J001v24n01_02

Bernard, J.M., and Goodyear, R.K., 2009. *Fundamentals of clinical supervision*. 4th ed. Upper Saddle River, NJ: Pearson.

Bogo, M., and McKnight, K., 2006. Clinical supervision in social work. *The Clinical Supervisor*, 24 (1–2), 49–67.

Bostock, L., Forrester, D., Patrizo, L., Godfrey, T., Zounouzi, M., Antonopoulou, V., Bird, H., and Tinarwo, M., 2017. *Scaling and deepening the reclaiming social work model*. Evaluation report. Cardiff, UK: Tilda Goldberg Centre for Social Work and Social Care, and CASCADE: Children's Social Research and Development Centre. Available from: https://assets.publishing.service.gov.uk/government/uploads /system/uploads/attachme   nt_data/file/625227/Scaling_and_deepening_the_Reclaiming_Social _Work_model.pd f [Accessed 23 September 2019].

Carpenter, J., Webb, C.M., and Bostock, L., 2013. The surprisingly weak evidence base for supervision: findings from a systematic review of research in child welfare practice (2000–2012). *Children and Youth Services Review*, 35 (11), 1843–1853.

Davys, A., 2007. Active participation in supervision: a supervisee's guide. *In*: D. Wepa, ed., *Clinical supervision in Aotearoa/New Zealand: a health perspective*. Auckland: Pearson Education, 26–42.

Davys, A., and Beddoe, L., 2010. *Best practice in professional supervision: a guide for the helping professions*. London: Jessica Kingsley.

Davys, A., May, J., Burns, B., and O'Connell, M., 2017a. Evaluating social work supervision. *Aotearoa New Zealand Social Work*, 29 (3), 108–121. doi:10.11157/anzswj-vol29iss3id314.

Davys, A.M., O'Connell, M., May, J., and Burns, B., 2017b. Evaluation of professional supervision in Aotearoa/New Zealand: an interprofessional study. *International Journal of Mental Health Nursing*, 26 (3), 249–258.

Dawson, M., Phillips, B., and Leggat, S.G., 2012. Effective clinical supervision for regional allied health professionals – The supervisee's perspective. *Australian Health Review*, 36 (1), 92–97.

Egan, R., Maidment, J., and Connolly, M., 2015. Who is watching whom? surveillance in Australian social work supervision. *British Journal of Social Work*, 46 (6), 1617–1635.

Ellis, M.V., Berger, L., Hanus, A.E., Ayala, E.E., Swords, B.A., and Siembor, M., 2014. Inadequate and harmful clinical supervision: testing a revised framework and assessing occurrence. *The Counseling Psychologist*, 42, 434–472.

Ellis, M.V., Creaner, M., Hutman, H.B., and Timulak, L., 2015. A comparative study of clinical supervision in the Republic of Ireland and the US. *Journal of Counseling Psychology*, 62, 621–631.

IFSW 2018. Global social work statement of ethical principles. International Federation of Social Workers. Available from: https://www.ifsw.org/global-social-work-statement-of-ethical-principles/ [Accessed 11 October 2019].

Hair, H., 2014. Power relations in supervision: preferred practices according to social workers. *Families in Society: The Journal of Contemporary Social Services*, 95 (2), 107–114. doi:10.1606/1044-3894.2014.95.14

Hawkins , P., and Shohet, R., 2012. *Supervision in the helping professions*. 4 ed. Maidenhead: Open University Press.

Hewson, D., and Carroll, M., 2016. *Reflective practice in supervision: companion volume to the reflective practice toolkit*. Hazelbrook, NSW: MoshPit.

Kelly, S., and Green, T., 2019. Seeing more, better sight: using an interprofessional model of supervision to support reflective child protection practice within the health setting. *British Journal of Social Work*. doi:10.1093/bjsw/bcz030

Ladany, N., Mori, Y., and Mehr, K.E., 2013. Effective and ineffective supervision. *The Counseling Psychologist*, 41 (1), 28–47.

Lamming, The Lord 2009. *The protection of children in England: a progress report*. London, UK: Stationery Office.

Leggat, S., Phillips, B., Pearce, P., Dawson, M., Schulz, D., and Smith, J., 2016. Clinical supervision for allied health staff: necessary but not sufficient. *Australian Health Review*, 40, 431–437. doi:https://org/10.1071/AH15080

Manthorpe, J., Moriarty, J., Hussein, S., Stevens, M., and Sharpe, E., 2015. Content and purpose of supervision in social work practice in England: views of newly qualified social workers, managers and directors. *British Journal of Social Work*, 45 (1), 52–68.

McNamara, M.L., Kangos, K.A., Corp, D.A., Ellis, M.V., and Taylor, E.J., 2017. Narratives of harmful clinical supervision: synthesis and recommendations. *The Clinical Supervisor*, 36 (1), 124–144. doi:10.1080/07325223.2017.1298488

Mor Barak, M.E., Travis, D.J., Pyun, H., and Xie, B., 2009. The impact of supervision on worker outcomes: a meta-analysis. *Social Service Review*, 83 (1), 3–32.

Morrison, T., 1993. *Staff supervision in social care: an action learning approach*. Brighton: Pavilion.

Morrison, T., and Wonnacott, J., 2010. Building foundations for best practice. Supervision: now or never, reclaiming reflective supervision in social work. Available from: http://www.in-trac.co.uk/supervision -now-or-never/ [Accessed 16 October 2019].

Noble, C., Gray, M., and Johnston, L., 2016. *Critical supervision for the human services: a social model to promote learning and value-based practice*. London: Jessica Kingsley.

O'Donoghue, K., 2015. Issues and challenges facing social work supervision in the twenty-first century. *China Journal of Social Work*, 8 (2), 136–149. doi:10.1080/17525098.2015.1039172

O'Donoghue, K., 2016. *An evaluation of clinical supervision of allied health professionals from two district health boards: a preliminary summary report*. (Unpublished report). Palmerston North, NZ: Massey University.

O'Donoghue, K., Munford, R., and Trlin, A., 2005. Mapping the territory : supervision within the association. *Social Work Review*, 17 (4), 46–64.

O'Donoghue, K., and Tsui, M.S., 2013. Social work supervision research (1970–2010): the way we were and the way ahead. *British Journal of Social Work*, 45 (2), 616–633.

Payne, M., 1994. Personal supervision in social work. *In*: A. Connor and S.E. Black, eds. *Performance review and quality in social care*. London: Jessica Kingsley, 43–58.

Sewell, K.M., 2018. Social work supervision of staff: a primer and scoping review (2013–2017). *Clinical Social Work Journal*, 46 (4), 252–265. doi:10.1007/ s10615-018-0679-0

Skills for Care and the Children's Workforce Development Council, 2007. *Providing effective supervision*. Available from: https://www.skillsforcare.org.uk/Document-library/Finding-and-keeping-workers/Supervision/Providing-Effective-Supervision.pdf [Accessed 9 March 2021].

Van Ooijen, E., 2003. *Clinical supervision made easy: the 3-step method*. UK: Churchill Livingstone.

Watkins, C.E., 2011. Does psychotherapy supervision contribute to patient outcomes? Considering thirty years of research. *The Clinical Supervisor*, 30 (2), 235–256.

Wilkins, D., and Antonopoulou, V., 2019. What does supervision help with? a survey of 315 social workers in the UK. *Practice*, 31 (1), 21–40. doi:10.1080/09503153.2018.1437398

Wilkins, D., Forrester, D., and Grant, L., 2017. What happens in child and family social work supervision?. *Child & Family Social Work*, 22 (2), 942–951. doi:10.1111/cfs.12314

Wilkins, D., Khan, M., Stabler, L., Newlands, F., and Mcdonnell, J., 2018. Evaluating the quality of social work supervision in UK children's services: comparing self-report and independent observations. *Clinical Social Work Journal*, 46 (4), 350–360.

Wheeler, S., and Barkham, M., 2014. A core evaluation battery for supervision. *In*: C.E. Watkins and D.L. Milne, eds. *Wiley international handbook of clinical supervision*. Chichester, UK: John Wiley and Sons, 367–467.

Wong, P.Y.J., and Lee, A.E.Y., 2015. Dual roles of social work supervisors: strain and strengths as managers and clinical supervisors. *China Journal of Social Work*, 8 (2), 164–181. doi:10.1080/17525098.2015.103 9168

48

DEVELOPING PROFESSIONAL SUPERVISION POLICIES, STANDARDS, AND PRACTICES

Priscalia Khosa and Lambert Engelbrecht

Introduction

Supervision as an essential element of the social work profession lays the foundation on which good practice is built. Although knowledge in social work supervision has evolved over time (Mo et al. 2020), a research gap on policies and standards that guide social work supervision practices still exists. Several authors observed that there are currently no universally accepted guidelines or best practices for social work supervision (Carpenter et al. 2012; Tkach and DiGirolamo 2017; O'Donoghue et al. 2018). This is also evident from the lack of recognition of values and ethics in social work supervision. O'Donoghue and O'Donoghue (2019) observed that social work ethics are not integrated into supervision processes and that the Global Social Work Statement of Ethical Principles (IASWW 2018) does not attach sufficient importance to ethics in supervision, as it is rarely mentioned in the statement. Hence, Tkach and DiGirolamo (2017) advocated for the development and agreement amongst researchers and practitioners on standardized measures to expand the supervision field in its understanding of what takes place in the supervision process. In social work supervision, this has been supported by the publication of policies and guidelines such as the British Association of Social Workers (BASW 2011) and the Australian Association of Social Workers (AASW 2014) that provide standards and statements of intent pertaining to supervision. However, such supervision standards and/or guidelines can be contentious if framed within a political agenda that focuses on reaching outcomes for auditing purposes, to the detriment of nurturing relationship-based supervisory styles (Ryan 2004). Bartoli and Kennedy (2015), Chibaya (2018), Engelbrecht (2019a), and Nickson et al. (2020) concur that the tick-box approaches to supervision versus relationship-based approaches have become increasingly evident in social work practice with the focus being placed rather on the attainment of targets than reflection on practice. This is despite the growth of evidence-based practice that has provoked discussion regarding modalities of supervision practice, and growing support for reflective supervision practices in order to meet the multifaceted needs of practitioners (Davys and Beddoe 2009; Turner-Daly and Jack 2017; O'Donoghue et al. 2018).

This chapter reviews supervision policies, standards, and guidelines developed in several countries, while recognizing that in such policies, the diverse cultures, settings, and needs of agencies must be acknowledged. The selection of the countries under discussion in this chapter serves merely as examples and is in no way intended to be complete and exhaustive, as the selection was based on (i) the national supervision policies or guidelines available in English online, while (ii) the supervision policy should focus only on social work practitioners per se and not interdisciplinary practitioners, as well as on (iii) existing, relevant and substantive publications by scholars about those countries in order to provide an empirical foundation and scholarly evidence. It was observed that different countries use different terminology to refer to documents that guide supervision practices, such as supervision "policy," "standards," "guidelines," "outcomes," and "frameworks." For the purposes of this chapter, the term "policy" and "standards" will be used as overarching concepts and to refer to all the documents under discussion that guide supervision practices. Essentially, all the supervision policy documents reviewed were aimed at providing a set of standards for social work supervision. The chapter first provides an overview on the ecology of supervision as context of policies for supervision. A discussion follows on supervision policies citing examples from various countries. In conclusion, potential best practices are outlined, drawn from different countries to develop policies that guide supervision practices.

Ecology of social work supervision

Social work supervision in itself is an ecosystem which centers on the interrelations between service users, practitioners, supervisors, and social service agencies (Engelbrecht 2019b). This implies that supervision does not only benefit practitioners, but also the agency, their clients, and the profession as a whole. However, sometimes the interconnectedness between the aforementioned is overlooked and overshadowed by tick-box managerial tendencies which may undermine the supervision policies developed in an effort to protect the wellbeing of clients while at the same time outlining the responsibilities of the agency, the worker, and the supervisor (Ornellas 2018). It is essential therefore, to acknowledge the role played by each system in the supervision process. For instance, supervision is important for agencies because it ideally ensures accountability in compliance with agency standards of service to the clients in an efficient and effective manner. In the same vein the profession maintains its standards of practice and enhances professional ethics amongst practitioners (AASW 2014; Kadushin and Harkness 2002). Social work practitioners also benefit from supervision because their needs for professional development and growth are met through supervisory relationships (Davys 2017; Sewell 2018). Moreover, these elements (agency, supervisor, supervisee, and client) are interwoven in the definition of social work supervision outlined in the seminal work of Kadushin. Kadushin (1992) refers to supervision as a process wherein the supervisor as an agency administrative staff member directs, coordinates, enhances, and evaluates the job performance of supervisees by implementing administrative, educational, and supportive functions in a positive supervisory relationship. The ultimate objective is to deliver the best possible service to clients, in accordance with agency policies and procedures. Shulman (2010) and O'Neill and Del Mar Fariña (2018) concur that the nature of the supervisory relationship and the process of supervision can have a profound impact on the social worker's attitudes toward the agency, as well as the social worker's direct practice and efforts toward the client system. Thus, all these interrelated elements make up the ecology of supervision which can be further espoused by adopting an ecosystems approach towards social work practice.

Lesser and Pope (2007) argue that due to the nature of social work practice and its perspective on human behavior, concepts from the systems and the ecological models are integrated in practice to create what is referred to as an ecosystems approach. This approach gained philosophical and intellectual momentum as a framework for social work practice due to its emphasis on person-in-environment (Bronfenbrenner 1979; Germain and Gitterman 1980; Johnson and

Yanca 2010). This applies to social work supervision in the sense that the goal of supervision is to oversee the ability of social workers to meet the goals of agencies where they work and to ensure that clients get the best quality service (Kadushin and Harkness 2002). Clients become part of the system when they seek social work services. Thus, clients, social workers, supervisors, and agencies employing social workers form interdependent systems. Hepworth et al. (2010) argue that an imbalance in one system contributes to an imbalance in others. For example, social workers' difficulties such as burnout influence how they relate to other people, including clients. On the other hand, environmental factors such as hostile working conditions can affect the social workers' interpersonal functioning. It is therefore imperative to view supervision as an ecosystem embracing specific systems, which have a direct impact on each other. Hence, when developing supervision policies, the role of each stakeholder in promoting effective supervision practices needs to be taken into account. This simplified interconnectedness is illustrated in Figure 48.1.

Figure 48.1 illustrates that social work supervision has four key interconnected elements. In a holistic view of the ecology of supervision, social work intervention is informed by the agency's goals, structures, policies, and the organizational climate which influence the process of supervision. For instance, most social work agencies regard supervision as a tool used to achieve organizational objectives because supervisors are required to report on the progress and outcomes of service delivery to top management, inter alia for accountability and funding purposes. Thus, the supervisor serves as a mediator and liaises between the agency and the supervisee. In addition, supervisors are expected not only to follow the agency's policies and procedures, but they also need to pay attention to the needs, morale, and satisfaction of supervisees in their supervisory relationship (Carpenter et al. 2013; Tsui 2005; Tsui et al. 2017). In terms of the supervisee and the client, a worker-client relationship is usually guided by the social work code

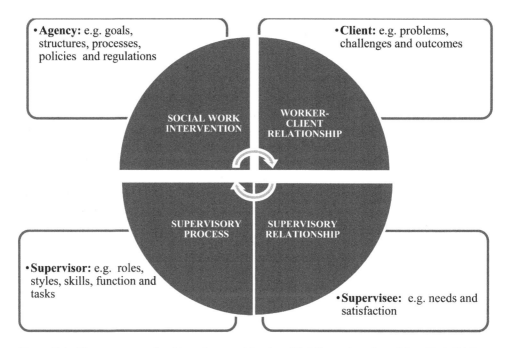

Figure 48.1 The ecosystem of social work supervision (modified illustration adapted from Tsui 2005)

of ethics and the agency policies. In this professional relationship, supervisees use the knowledge they acquired during their professional training and employ interventions supervised by their supervisors to achieve specific intervention objectives. This is also dependent on the supervisors' styles and how they implement specific supervision functions during the supervisory process. Furthermore, the agency must also account for and respond to the needs of clients, to achieve the common good in society (Tsui 2005; O'Donoghue 2010; Turner-Daly and Jack 2017). Therefore, effective client outcomes are the ultimate objective of social work supervision. In essence, this shows that failure in one system affects the whole system. For instance, if supervisors do not carry out their administrative, educational, and supportive roles successfully, supervisees will not be empowered to apply social work knowledge, skills, and values effectively to assist their clients. Consequently, clients will not receive quality and efficient social work services (Kadushin and Harkness 2014; O'Donoghue 2015). This means that agencies need to create an enabling environment for successful supervision practices such as preparation for assuming the supervisory role as well as the promotion of supportive supervision. Such an enabling environment can be realized by adopting supervision policies that take cognizance of all these systems, which are interconnected within the supervisory process.

The development and content of supervision policies and standards in some countries around the world

Across the world, it appears to be general practice that some aspects of supervision are mandated and prescribed in policies of professional bodies (Beddoe 2017; Engelbrecht 2019a). Although supervision practices do differ at regional and national levels (Beddoe 2016), Akesson and Canavera (2018) observed that supervision is likely to be subject to highly localized variations that will challenge attempts at creating universally applicable paradigms. For instance, countries such as Australia, Hong Kong, Singapore, New Zealand, United States, United Kingdom, and South Africa have introduced policies and standards to guide supervision in social work practice on a national level. However, there are different viewpoints regarding these standardized procedures. Some scholars argue that these standards augment bureaucracy and promote managerialism (Ryan 2004; Engelbrecht 2013), while some opponents state that it is essential to have some control over supervision practices in social work (Unguru and Sandu 2017). It is based on the latter assertion that various countries have developed supervision policies to guide supervision practices.

The process of developing supervision policies was led mainly by social work boards and/or associations of social workers in distinct countries. The rationale for this course of action was the fact that supervision forms an integral part of social work practice and is aimed at developing competent social workers, safeguarding and maintaining high professional standards and ensuring that quality services are delivered to clients. Most importantly, some of the associations of social workers recognized that the knowledge base of the social work profession has expanded, and due to the ever changing socio-economic and political climate, issues faced by clients have become more complex (see AASW 2014; BASW 2011, and NASW 2013). Hence social workers need to be equipped to handle such growing challenges, and supervision is one way of maintaining the best quality social work practice. This is why supervision standards are necessary to provide a framework that promotes uniformity in supervision practices and to reinforce the idea that supervision is an essential professional and ethical responsibility of all social workers (NASW 2013; SACSSP and DSD 2012; SWAAB 2017).

Nevertheless, some research has shown that a gap exists within low- and middle-income countries (LMIC) regarding the development of supervision standards and policies (Akesson and Canavera 2018; Unguru and Sandu 2018). South Africa is one example of a middle-income country exhibiting evidence of support for supervision. Scholars such as Botha (2002) noted that during the evolution of the social work profession in South Africa, several debates arose on the need for supervision in social work practice. With the enactment of the Social Service Professions Act (RSA, Act 110 of 1978) and the Policy Guidelines for the Course of Conduct, the Code of Ethics, and the Rules for Social Workers (SACSSP 2007), supervision of social workers in South Africa became statutorily mandated and guided by a constituted ethical code (Engelbrecht 2015). Owing to this legal mandate, the Department of Social Development (DSD), in partnership with the South African Council for Social Service Professions (SACSSP), developed a supervision framework for the social work profession in South Africa, noting the need for a policy to regulate supervision in the country (DSD and SACSSP 2012).

This supervision framework was developed after consultation with various role players in the social work field, where it was established that there is a decline in the productivity and quality of services rendered due to lack of supervision, as identified by Botha in 2002. This was owing to political and ideological shifts in the country, the result of high caseloads, high stress levels experienced by social workers due to personal and professional demands, as well as lack of resources to deliver services. The supervision framework intends to guide effective supervision of social workers and set out norms and standards in the execution of supervision. In this framework, the rationale, aim, and objectives of the policy document are outlined. This is followed by a distinction between key concepts relating to supervision, including management, consultation, and mentoring (DSD and SACSSP 2012). These concepts often overlap with supervision, and it would therefore be interesting to investigate their applicability within the South African context (Engelbrecht 2019a). Nevertheless, the political, socio-economic, or cultural context within which supervision is practiced in South Africa was not depicted in the supervision framework (Engelbrecht 2013). Some sections in the framework merely outlined the roles and responsibilities of supervisors and supervisees. It would have been informative to highlight what context informs supervision practices in South Africa. The framework concludes by pointing out the expected norms and standards when implementing supervision practices across social service agencies in South Africa (DSD and SACSSP 2012).

Akesson and Canavera (2018) maintain that South Africa's movement to support supervision in order to capacitate social workers and therefore benefit service users, serves as a model for other LMIC settings. Despite the existing framework, which may serve as an exemplary model for other countries, there are still challenges in social work supervision in South Africa. For example, one of the key standards outlined in the framework is that agencies employing social workers need to formulate their own supervision policy in alignment with the supervision framework. Specific requirements of what needs to be addressed in the organizational policies include the ratio of supervisor to supervisees, functions and methods of supervision, and requirements of a supervision contract (DSD and SACSSP 2012). However, the translation of these recommendations to the contexts of different welfare agencies employing social workers seems to be problematic. In her study, Silence (2016) found no supervision policy is evident in the Department of Health as one of the employers of social workers. This is not surprising as the national Department of Social Development itself also does not have an approved supervision policy. Despite this, the South African social development sector has adopted an inclusive approach to promote collaboration amongst different social service professions in line with the White Paper for Social Welfare (RSA 1997), which is the country's cornerstone for welfare service provision. This is evident through an ongoing process of developing a supervision framework for social service professions which seeks to include occupations in the social development sector, such as Community Development and Child and Youth Care Workers (DSD 2019), and which is unique to the South African context. However, Engelbrecht (2013, 2019b) cautions that the standardized South African supervision framework could potentially become the primary yardstick for measuring performances of agencies, supervisors, and supervisees.

Similar concerns regarding an over-emphasis on managerial tendencies of supervision were observed in the United Kingdom (BASW 2011). Scholars such as Bradley, Engelbrecht and Höjer (2010), Wonnacott (2012), and Wilkins and Antonopoulou (2018) noted that supervision in the United Kingdom (UK) has often assumed an administrative and management format wherein the focus is on compliance, practice audit, and task completion, with the goal of giving feedback to the government concerning outputs and achievements. This need to comply with government mandates, resulted in the production of reviews such as the Social Work Review Board [SWRB] (2010), which recommended that employers of social workers need to have clear binding standards that guide supervision. With the review's recommendations in mind, the SWRB introduced the Employer Standards and Supervision Framework (SWRB 2010) that set out expectations for employers, with an emphasis on good quality supervision as a vehicle to improve social services outcomes. The BASW (2011) observed that lack of reflective supervision practices and loss of professional judgement amongst practitioners led inadvertently to poor social service delivery. Against this backdrop the BASW developed a UK-wide supervision policy with the purpose to circumscribe the professional rights of social workers as well as the importance, purpose, and functions of supervision (BASW 2011; Bartoli and Kennedy 2015). This particular supervision policy embarked on providing a background and context, shaping how supervision is practiced in the UK. The policy further highlights the rationale and purpose of the policy as well as the principles guiding supervision practices, which are that social workers should receive supervision, engage in peer learning and participate in essential continuous professional development (BASW 2011). Although the aim of the policy is to clarify the responsibilities of the agency, the worker, and the supervisor, the policy mainly focuses on the role of the employer and neglects the responsibilities of social workers and supervisors. For instance, agencies are encouraged to have supervision policies which emphasize clear standards of acceptable supervision practices. This is pointed out in 12 policy statements that inform supervision practices in the UK (BASW 2011). Similar to the South African supervision framework, it however remains the responsibility of the employer to create an enabling working environment that promotes a positive supervisory culture.

Given that the UK supervision policy draws upon a consensus among some of the professional social work bodies in the United States and New Zealand, it is worth exploring supervision policies in these countries. The Aotearoa New Zealand Association for Social Workers (ANZASW) spearheaded the process of developing a policy for social work supervision. This development paralleled the development of social work and the recognition of a bicultural code of practice unique to the country's cultural diversity (O'Donoghue 2003; O'Donoghue and Tsui 2011; Beddoe 2016). Similar to South Africa and the UK, supervision in New Zealand became more managerially oriented due to the influences of social policies adopted in the country (O'Donoghue 2015; Beddoe 2016). Moreover, supervision was reduced to managerial oversight, with performance management and accountability systems replacing education, development, and critical reflection on the practitioner's use of self (O'Donoghue 2008; Beddoe 2016). Hence, the Aotearoa New Zealand Association of Social Workers (ANZASW) Supervision Policy set out the standards for social work supervision in order to ensure accountability of social workers and to protect clients' safety. In accordance with this policy, supervision is regarded as a process through which the supervisor facilitates the development of professional competence, responsible practice, and continuous professional development in order to enable supervisees to fulfil organizational, professional, and personal objectives (ANZASW 2015). Notably different from the supervision policies of South Africa and the UK, the policy of New Zealand promotes the ecology of supervision by outlining clearly the role of social workers, supervisors, and agencies. Furthermore, the policy emphasizes the importance of supervision in social work practice and points to the key principles guiding supervision in New Zealand, which are:

- Supervision recognizes cultural and ethnic diversity and is cognizant of specific *tangata whaiora*/client needs.
- Supervision ensures safety for participants.
- Supervision is a shared responsibility between the supervisee, the supervisor, and the agency.
- Supervision promotes anti-discriminatory practice.
- Supervision is based on the principle of adult learning. (ANZASW 2015, p. 1)

Echoing efforts in New Zealand to embrace diverse cultures, supervision in Hong Kong is also conducted, practiced, and influenced by the cultural context (Tsui 2004, 2006). Although some of the practices in Hong Kong have been adopted from North America and England, social work supervision in this country was often conducted informally and in an unstructured way. Hence in 2005, the Social Workers Registration Board (2009) conducted a large-scale survey of the practice of supervision among all social workers in Hong Kong wherein recommendations to formulate a set of guidelines for the practice of supervision were made. The main aim of the guidelines was to develop a set of recommended basic standards for practice in the social work field. In addition, the guidelines clarify the responsibility of agencies, social workers, and supervisors with regard to professional supervision. Unlike in other countries as discussed already, emphasis in Hong Kong is placed on the educational and supportive functions of supervision, in which emotional support and staff development are a priority (Tsui 2005, 2006). In the country's supervision guidelines, the fundamental aspects of social work supervision have been identified as the format, the purpose, the nature of the supervisory relationship, and the process of supervision, corresponding with the notions by Kadushin and Harkness (2014), Magnussen (2018), and Tsui (2004). In terms of the supervisory relationship, the supervision guidelines advocate for a collaborative relationship based on trust, openness, and mutual respect, taking into consideration sensitivity to gender, culture, and the context in which supervision is carried out. Moreover, regarding the purpose and functions of supervision in Hong Kong, the supervisor and the supervisee have the same professional goals, and the most distinctive feature of the supervisory relationship is a dual perspective on personal and professional building, which is maintained through reciprocity and consensus (Social Workers Registration Board 2009).

In Singapore, social work supervision guidelines are aimed at promoting effective supervision while supporting social workers to develop as competent professionals (Social Work Accreditation and Advisory Board [SWAAB] 2017). The guidelines were developed after a review of supervision guidelines in countries such as Hong Kong, New Zealand, United States, England, and Australia. The guidelines provide a general framework for developing supervision practices in order to ensure consistency and uniformity of practice for all social service agencies. Each agency employing social workers is required to contextualize the specifics of supervision in line with its own organizational culture. Agencies are also tasked to develop written supervision contracts defining the roles and responsibilities of both the supervisor and supervisee. The guidelines cover the functions of supervision, types of supervision, the supervisory relationship, and emphasize values of respect for diversity and social justice, to serve as a guide for supervisors and supervisees in managing ethical issues (SWAAB 2017).

In addition to supervision policies discussed above, supervision standards in the United States focus on the formative dimension of supervision and the transfer of skills in the supervision process. This is done by promoting a combination of administrative, supportive, and educational supervisory functions, to enhance competent and ethical services by social workers (National Association of Social Workers [NASW] 2013). In their supervision standards, the NASW (2013), as in the case of New Zealand and Hong Kong, draws attention to the importance of cultural context in substantiating the supervision process. Moreover, emphasis is placed on the supervision process to include responsibilities that contribute to increasing accountability for the outcomes of practice, which are meant to ensure that clients are protected during the intervention (NASW 2013; Unguru and Sandu 2018). Although interdisciplinary supervision seems to be unavoidable in the United States, in such situations, social workers are encouraged to seek clinical supervisory consultation outside of the agency on social work issues (NASW 2013). According to Bogo and McKnight (2006) due to the fact that clinical supervision is usually not agency-based and focuses more on the dynamics of the client, supervision in such a context tends to include only educational and supportive features, and focuses not so much on administration. The prioritization of these two supervision functions in the United States is commendable given that supervision policies in countries like South Africa and the UK focus much on the administrative function of supervision, which may promote a checklist mentality. Similar to supervision guidelines in Singapore, the NASW (2013) supervision standards uphold the principles of fairness, justice, and respect for others.

The supervisory standards introduced by the Australian Association of Social Workers (AASW) aim to convey the purpose, functions, and values of professional supervision for social workers. The standards outline the modes and processes of supervision deemed acceptable, as well as the requirements and responsibilities of supervisors and supervisees (AASW 2014). Supervision is defined by the AASW as a forum for reflection and learning based on interactive dialogue between supervisors and supervisees. The process of dialogue guides the evaluation, critical reflection, and re-planning of the professional work done by social workers. Congruent with the AASW's definition of supervision, mutual respect and confidentiality are cornerstone values in creating a platform for reflective practice in an Australian supervision context (Nickson et al. 2020). There is also an emphasis on a collaborative supervisory relationship built on trust, confidentiality, support, and empathic experiences (AASW 2014). In addition, the Australian standards are operationalized through indicators such as setting clear boundaries in the supervisory relationship by avoiding engaging in professional relationships of a social, business, or sexual nature (Unguru and Sandu 2017). Although the importance of supervision is clearly outlined and standards guiding supervision are specified, Nickson et al. (2020) contend that some of the agencies employing social workers do not prioritize supervision, making it inaccessible to some of the social workers in Australia, especially those based in rural areas.

An analysis of supervision policies across the world towards advancing supervision practices

It seems that national supervision policies in social work are relatively uniform throughout the world, and reflecting the evolution of the social work profession (Bartoli and Kennedy 2015; Unguru and Sandu 2018). What emerged from the review of the supervision policy documents in this chapter, was that national associations of social workers, national boards of social workers, or national social work agencies (hereafter referred to as national social work governing bodies) initiated the formulation of policies or standards required. It seems that in fact, a supervision policy does not only provide a context for supervision practices within a specific agency, but it also reveals the prominence afforded to social work supervision practices in a specific country (Morrison 1993).

On the development of supervision policies, Hawkins and Shohet (2006, p. 242) suggested a meaningful seven-stage cycle, which are:

i. Creating an appreciative inquiry into what supervision is already happening;
ii. Awakening the interest in developing supervision practice and policy;
iii. Initiating some experiments;
iv. Dealing with resistance to change;
v. Developing the supervision policies;
vi. Developing ongoing learning and development for supervisors and supervisees; and
vii. Having an ongoing audit and review process.

Although not all the policy documents reviewed in this chapter reflect specific steps in developing a supervision policy or standards, it appeared that most of the national social work governing bodies who initiated the development of national policies and standards, indeed utilized some of the steps as suggested by Hawkins and Shohet (2006). In addition, it seems that one or another consultancy process is evident in the development of the policies and standards by all countries. Various national and local key role players were consulted by all of the national social work governing bodies in order to arrive at the final product of the policy. For instance, in South Africa, America, Hong Kong, and Singapore task teams were appointed to spearhead the policy formulation process. What propelled the national social work governing bodies to develop supervision standards in the first instance, was that supervision has been neglected and conducted in an unstructured manner without clear guidelines. This is despite the fact that supervision plays an essential role in all the identified countries' training and continuing education required for the skillful development of professional social workers, to protect clients, and to ensure that professional standards and quality services are delivered by competent social workers (Social Workers Registration Board 2009; SACSSP and DSD 2012; NASW 2013; AASW 2014; ANZASW 2015; SWAAB 2017).

Before embarking on the formulation of supervision policies, some of the national social work governing bodies reviewed policy documents from other countries. However, the policies were then contextualized to fit the social work sector in that specific country. This allows social work practitioners to take ownership of their supervision policies and to acknowledge the benefits of such policies in advancing good supervision practices. Most of the national social work governing bodies in the different countries followed a bottom up approach in their efforts by listening to the social workers' discourses on their experiences and perceptions of supervision approaches. This was probably done, in line with Hawkins and Shohet's (2006) notion, to minimize resistance from practitioners, to involve them in the thinking and planning of the changes they need, to give them an opportunity to react, to understand their need for change, and to adapt to future necessities. However, it is unclear to what extent social work practitioners (frontline social workers, supervisors, and managers alike) in the respective countries actually bought into the final supervision policy product and were actively employing these policies in their specific contexts.

At the onset of developing the actual supervision policy documents, all the countries mentioned above complied with the recommendations by Hawkins and Shohet (2006). In their policy documents, these countries all set out the purpose of supervision. Overall, what was elicited from the policy documents reviewed for this chapter, is that supervision ensures that supervisees obtain advanced knowledge so that their skills and abilities can be applied to client populations in an ethical and competent manner. Supervision also engages social workers in ongoing professional learning that enhances capacities to respond effectively to complex and changing practice environments. Lastly, supervision of social workers assists in retaining social workers in agencies by supporting and resourcing them to provide quality, ethical, and accountable services in line with the agency's visions, goals, and policies.

Minimum standards of the content and conduct of supervision are also evident in all the reviewed policies. Guidelines in terms of minimum requirements for supervision contracts are, for example, included by all. Agencies are encouraged to present a statement of anti-discriminatory practice, and guidelines regarding ethics and principles in the supervisory relationship. Roles and responsibilities of both supervisor and supervisees are highlighted, although agencies such as the NASW (2013) focused mainly on the roles of supervisors, while the BASW (2011) did not explicitly state the role of supervisors and supervisees in their policy. In terms of conflict resolution, most of the supervision policies provide a mandate to employers to develop clear methods for resolving disagreements and the processes that need to be followed. However, it remains the key responsibility of employers of social workers to create an enabling environment for positive supervision practices to thrive. One way to achieve this is to establish ongoing training programs for supervisors. This is contained in most policy documents as a prerequisite for practitioners to take on supervisors' roles (AASW 2014; NASW 2013; Social Workers Registration Board 2009). However, Hawkins and Shohet (2006) caution that the best learning on how to supervise emerges from actual supervision practices. The first step towards becoming a skilled supervisor is to receive good supervision. Furthermore, in the same way that supervision of social workers is seen as a continuous developmental process by all the policies reviewed, likewise is the development of the supervision practices and policies in agencies. Thus, supervision policies need to be reviewed constantly. However, only Hong Kong specified the need to review their supervision guidelines periodically.

Nevertheless, it seems that all the reviewed policies are in agreement that the following aspects should be captured in one way or another in a specific agency's supervision policy:

- Definition of supervision, which clarifies the goal, format, scope, and context of the supervision process;
- Qualifications and experience of the supervisor;
- The priority that supervision should be given in relation to other tasks by both the supervisor and supervisee;
- Confidentiality and ethical conduct by both the supervisor and supervisee;
- Boundaries of the supervisor-supervisee relationship;
- Theoretical model/s underpinning supervision;
- Ratio of supervisor to supervisees;
- Statement on non-discriminatory practices;
- Functions of supervision;
- Methods of supervision (e.g. individual or group);
- A supervision contract between the supervisor and supervisee, which may include supervision outcomes, tasks, roles, responsibilities, mandates, and revision of the supervision contract;
- Requirements of supervision sessions, frequency thereof, duration, interruptions, cancellations, and supervision reports;
- Requirements of a personal development assessment of the supervisee based on essential competencies for practice;
- Requirements of a personal development (supervision) plan of the supervisee;
- Requirements of a performance management system;
- Methods for resolving dissatisfaction, disagreements, and breakdowns in the process;

- Responsibility of both the supervisee and supervisee in terms of continuing professional development, self-reliance, and self-preservation.

Following the discussion of the process of developing a supervision policy and its content, it is pivotal to point out that the implementation of such policies is often a challenge, which may create confusion around how these policies advance supervision practices. Some policies may present an illusion of what supervision is, more than the reality, which may be extremely complex and influenced by a number of variables (Engelbrecht 2013; Bartoli and Kennedy 2015). However, no study could be found which empirically investigated the success of the policies reviewed for the purpose of this chapter. This identified gap has propelled researchers such as Khosa (forthcoming) to investigate for instance, how agencies are implementing supervision policies, using a child protection agency in South Africa as a case study. What is evident though, from the policy documents reviewed in this chapter, is the fact that supervision policies should move beyond the practice of merely "ticking the box," and should rather create a foundation which enables supervisors to balance management and support functions of supervision (Engelbrecht 2013; Bartoli and Kennedy 2015).

Stemming from the latter comment, the question that begs an answer, is whether these policies are fit for purpose? This question emanates from the fact that some of the reviewed policies do not necessarily address issues which prevent ineffective or even harmful social work supervision (Wynne 2020). For instance, supervision of social workers is a mandatory practice in South Africa as determined by the country's Social Service Professions Act (RSA, Act 110 of 1978) and the supervision framework for the social service professions (SACSSP and DSD 2012). Nevertheless, research findings by Wynne (2020) reveal that some social workers experience supervision practices as more harmful than helpful, and sometimes supervisors who are contributing to harmful supervision practices even draw on the supervision framework to substantiate that they are indeed successfully following specific requirements of the policy document. The narratives of supervisees in this research show that the majority of participants find the process of supervision to be futile and only done in practice to tick a box. Specifically, a supervisee, as a research study participant, refers to the supervision framework's requirement of keeping supervision reports:

> So, the records, she types them up, I read through them and then I sign them and send them back to her. It's a waste of time for everybody involved. It's just … it's a one-page thing that she has to type… I'd rather have supervision where I'm not having to worry about, oh, I didn't sign this form or I didn't write this down, like it's just stupid.
>
> *(Wynne 2020, p. 69)*

The lack of support from a supervisor, but still executing a tick-box exercise to provide support, is illustrated by another supervisee in the study by Wynne (2020, p. 74):

> She asks me at the beginning of each supervision, how are you? But sometimes it feels more like a formality than really like, how are you, like how are you really?…And if I say, I'm not doing that well, like I'm quite anxious, it almost feels like there's not much focus on, why and how can we help you? It's sort of like, oh, you know, shame, okay, I hope you feel better quickly, like it's not heartfelt support.

Based on this feedback by supervisees regarding compliance with requirements in a supervision policy, an additional question can be raised: Is standardization sufficient to promote good supervision practices, or is there a need to allow agencies to function independently and operate with what works best for them in supervision? In this regard, Unguru and Sandu (2018) argue that supervision policies and standards do not consistently consider the national context to guide social work services sufficiently. For example, in South Africa, the supervision framework was adopted as one of the tools to address ineffective supervision. Despite the existence of such a framework since 2012, there are still numerous challenges as mentioned, which affect supervision practices that are not outlined in the supervision framework (Engelbrecht 2019a). As elucidated by Wynne's (2020) research, which captured some lived experiences of supervisees, challenges include instances where supervisors are preoccupied with managerial tasks, reviewing outputs, procedures, norms, standards, and cost-efficiency measures (in order to tick the boxes of the supervision policy), rather than allowing for a space to debrief or render emotional support to social workers. Hence, it is crucial to consider the context of all the systems in the ecology of supervision within which a supervision policy is developed; also, compliance with requirements in policies as evidence of accountability may defeat the purpose of supervision rather than advance the supervisor-supervisee relationship, and ultimately affect the quality of service rendering to clients.

Thus, a global neoliberal discourse (Spolander et al. 2014) may result, as described above, in the infiltration of a managerial agenda in all spheres of social work, and particularly the functions and role of the supervisor (Engelbrecht 2015; Ornellas 2018). With the market expectation for social service agencies to be run as businesses, an emphasis on outputs, norms, procedures, standards, cost-efficiency, and accountability have served to limit, and often override, the functions and role of the supervisor (Spolander et al. 2014) Additionally, managerial expectations limit the practice of social workers themselves as they attempt to balance their professional values with organizational output demands (Engelbrecht 2015; Magnussen 2018; Ornellas 2018). Stiglitz (2019) rightly argues that there is no magic bullet that can reverse the damage done by decades of neoliberalism. However, social workers and supervisors alongside agencies can dismantle this mentality by consciously functioning as an ecology, with all its parts being interdependent, in order to value the impact of each system on supervision practices.

Concluding remarks

In general, the content of most social work supervision policies across the world addresses four main areas namely: (i) social work practice, (ii) professional impact, (iii) continuous learning, and (iv) job management. These four areas clearly indicate that national supervision policies need be cognizant of the ecology of supervision in order to outline the specific role of each supervision system. However, the implementation of these standards and the translation of these policies into practice remain problematic. When developing supervision policies, it is essential to steer away from a mere tick-box approach to supervision, and rather deliberately move towards a humanizing supervision approach (Engelbrecht 2019a). Instead of social workers and supervisors having to comply with an unseen global neoliberal agenda (Ornellas and Engelbrecht 2020), they need to question the ideological intention of policies and assume a position which strives for social justice and human rights as the social work profession proclaims (Ornellas et al. 2018). Thus, although challenges arise from a global neoliberal discourse, affecting supervision of social workers with its managerial focus on control and accountability, the analysis of some country's supervision policies reveals that the power and core of supervision of social workers still reside within the supervisory relationship.

References

Akesson, B., and Canavera, M., 2018. Expert understandings of supervision as a means to strengthen the social service workforce: results from a global delphi study. *European Journal of Social Work*, 21 (3), 333–347.

Aotearoa New Zealand Association of Social Workers 2015. *ANZASW supervision policy*. Available from https://anzasw.nz/wp-content/uploads/ANZASW-Supervision-Policy-Updated-February-2015.pdf [Accessed 2 July 2019].

Australian Association of Social Workers 2014. *Supervision standards*. Australian Association of Social Workers. Available from: https://www.aasw.asn.au/document/item/6027 [Accessed 2 July 2019].

Bartoli, A., and Kennedy, S., 2015. Tick if applicable: a critique of a national UK social work supervision policy. *Practice*, 27 (4), 239–250.

BASW 2011. *UK supervision policy*. Available from: https://www.basw.co.uk/system/files/resources/basw :73346-6_0.pdf [Accessed 2 July 2019].

Beddoe, L., 2016. Supervision in social work in Aotearoa New Zealand: challenges in changing contexts. *The Clinical Supervisor*, 35 (2), 156–174.

Beddoe, L., 2017. Harmful supervision: a commentary. *The Clinical Supervisor*, 36 (1), 88–101.

Bogo, M., and McKnight, K., 2006. Clinical supervision in social work: a review of the research literature. *The Clinical Supervisor*, 1 (2), 49–67.

Botha, N.J., 2002. *Supervision and consultation in social work*. Bloemfontein: Drufoma.

Bradley, G., Engelbrecht, L., and Höjer, S., 2010. Supervision: a force for change? three stories told. *International Social Work*, 53 (6), 773–790.

Bronfenbrenner, U., 1979. *The ecology of human development*. Cambridge, MA: Harvard University Press.

Carpenter, J., Webb, C.M., and Bostock, L., 2013. The surprisingly weak evidence base for supervision: findings from a systematic review of research in child welfare practice (2000– 2012). *Children and Youth Services Review*, 35 (11), 1843–1853.

Carpenter, J., Webb, C., Bostock, L., and Coomber, C., 2012. *Effective supervision in social work and social care (SCIE Research Briefing 43)*. Available from: http://www.scie.org.uk/publications/briefings/briefing43/ [Accessed 12 May 2019].

Chibaya, N.H., 2018. *The execution of individual reflective supervision sessions: experiences of intermediate frontline social workers*. Unpublished thesis. Stellenbosch University.

Davys, A.M., 2017. Interprofessional supervision: a matter of difference. *Aotearoa New Zealand Social Work*, 29 (3), 79–94.

Davys, A.M., and Beddoe, L., 2009. The reflective learning model: supervision of social work students. *Social Work Education*, 28 (8), 919–933.

Department of Social Development (DSD) 2019. *Draft supervision framework for social service professions*. Unpublished document.

Department of Social Development and South African Council for Social Service Professions (DSD and SACSSP) 2012. *Supervision framework for the social work profession*. Department of Social Development.

Engelbrecht, L.K., 2013. Social work supervision policies and frameworks: playing notes or making music?. *Social Work/Maatskaplike Werk*, 49 (4), 456–468.

Engelbrecht, L.K., 2015. Revisiting the esoteric question: can non-social workers manage and supervise social workers?. *Social Work/Maatskaplike Werk*, 51 (3), 310–331.

Engelbrecht, L.K., 2019a. Towards authentic supervision of social workers in South Africa. *The Clinical Supervisor*, 1–24.

Engelbrecht, L.K., 2019b. Fundamental aspects of supervision. *In*: L.K. Engelbrecht, ed. *Management and supervision of social workers: issues and challenges within a social development paradigm*. 2nd ed. Andover: Cengage Learning EMEA Limited, 150–173.

Germain, C.B., and Gitterman, A., 1980. *The life model of social work practice*. New York: Columbia University Press.

Hawkins, P., and Shohet, R., 2006. *Supervision in the helping professions*. 3rd ed. Maidenhead: Open University Press.

Hepworth, D.H., Rooney, R.H., Rooney, G.D., Strom-Gottfried, K., and Larsen, J.A., 2010. *Direct social work practice: theory and skills*. 8th ed. Belmont, CA: Brooks/Cole.

International Association of Schools of Social Work 2018. *Global social work statement of ethical principles (IASSW)*. Available from: https://www.iassw-aiets.org/archive/ethics-in-social-work-statement-of -principles/ [Accessed 27 March 2020].

Johnson, L.C., and Yanca, S.J., 2010. *Social work practice. A generalist approach*. 8th ed. New York: Pearson Education.

Kadushin, A., 1992. *Supervision in social work*. 3rd ed. New York: Columbia University Press.

Kadushin, A., and Harkness, D., 2002. *Supervision in social work*. 4th ed. New York: Columbia University Press.

Kadushin, A., and Harkness, D., 2014. *Supervision in social work*. 5th ed. New York: Columbia University Press.

Khosa, P., Forthcoming. *Implementation of a supervision framework for the social work profession in South Africa by a designated child protection organisation*. Unpublished thesis. Stellenbosch University.

Lesser, J.G., and Pope, D.S., 2007. *Human behavior and the social environment: theory and practice*. 2nd ed. Boston: Allan and Bacon.

Magnussen, J., 2018. Supervision in Denmark: an empirical account of experiences and practices. *European Journal of Social Work*, 21 (3), 359–373.

Mo, K.Y., O'Donoghue, K., Wong, P.Y., and Tsui, M., 2020. The historical development of knowledge in social work supervision: finding new directions from the past. *International Social Work*. doi:10.1177/0020872819884995.

Morrison, T., 1993. *Staff supervision in social care. An action learning approach*. Harlow, Essex, England: Longman.

National Association of Social Workers 2013. *Best practice standards in social work supervision*. National Association of Social Workers. Available from: https://www.socialworkers.org/LinkClick.aspx?fileticket =GBrLbl4BuwI%3D&portalid=0 [Accessed 28 August 2019].

Nickson, A.M., Carter, M., and Francis, A.P., 2020. *Supervision and professional development in social work practice*. India: SAGE.

O'Donoghue, K., 2003. *Restorying social work supervision*. Palmerston North, New Zealand: Dunmore Press.

O'Donoghue, K., 2008. Towards improving social work supervision in Aotearoa New Zealand. *Aotearoa New Zealand Social Work Review*, 20 (1), 10–21.

O'Donoghue, K., 2010. *Towards the construction of social work supervision in Aotearoa New Zealand: a study of the perspectives of social work practitioners and supervisors*. Unpublished thesis. Massey University.

O'Donoghue, K., 2015. Issues and challenges facing social work supervision in the twenty-first century. *China Journal of Social Work*, 8 (2), 136–149.

O'Donoghue, K., Ju, P., and Tsui, M.S., 2018. Constructing an evidence-informed social work supervision model. *European Journal of Social Work*, 21 (3), 348–358.

O'Donoghue, K., and O'Donoghue, R., 2019. The application of ethics within social work supervision: a selected literature and research review. *Ethics and Social Welfare*, 13 (4), 340–360.

O'Donoghue, K., and Tsui, M., 2011. Towards a professional supervision culture: the development of social work supervision in Aotearoa New Zealand. *International Social Work*, 55 (1), 5–28.

O'Neill, P., and Del Mar Fariña, M., 2018. Constructing critical conversations in social work supervision: creating change. *Clinical Social Work Journal*, 46 (4), 298–309.

Ornellas, A., 2018. *Social workers' reflections on implications of neoliberal tenets for social work in South African Non-Governmental Organisations*. Unpublished thesis. Stellenbosch University.

Ornellas, A., and Engelbrecht, L.K., 2020. Neoliberal impact on social work in South African non-governmental organisations. *Southern African Journal for Social Work and Social Development*, 32 (1), 1–21.

Ornellas, A., Spolander, G., and Engelbrecht, L.K., 2018. The global social work definition: ontology, implications and challenges. *Journal of Social Work*, 18 (2), 222–240.

Republic of South Africa (RSA) 1978. *Social service professions act, Act 110 of 1978*. Pretoria: Government Printers.

Republic of South Africa (RSA) 1997. *Ministry for welfare and population development. White paper for social welfare*. Pretoria: Government Gazette.

Ryan, S., 2004. *Vital practice stories from the healing arts: the homeopathic and supervisory way*. Dorset: Sea Change.

Sewell, K.M., 2018. Social work supervision of staff: a primer and scoping review (2013–2017). *Clinical Social Work Journal*, 46 (4), 252–265.

Shulman, L., 2010. *Interactional supervision*. 3rd ed. Washington, DC: NASW Press.

Silence, E., 2016. *The significance of social work supervision in the department of health, Western Cape: social workers' experiences*. Unpublished thesis. University of Stellenbosch.

Social Work Accreditation and Advisory Board (SWAAB) 2017. *Social work supervision guidelines*. Singapore Association of Social Workers. Available from: https://www.sasw.org.sg/index.php?option=com_content&view=article&id=295&Itemid=235 [Accessed 26 March 2020].

Social Work Reform Board (SWRB) 2010. *Building a safe and confident future: one year on.* Norwich: Stationery Office.

Social Workers Registration Board, Hong Kong 2009. *Guidelines for social work supervision* [Online]. Available from: http://www.swrb.org.hk/documents/Supervision%20Guidelines_Eng.pdf [Accessed: 20 August 2019].

South African Council for Social Service Professions (SACSSP) 2007. *Policy guidelines for course of conduct, code of ethics and the rules for social workers* [Online]. Available from: http://www.sacssp.co.za/website/wp-content/uploads/2012/06/Code-of-Ethics.pdf [Accessed: 20 August 2019].

Spolander, G., et al., 2014. The implications of neoliberalism for social work: reflections from six country international research collaboration. *International Social Work*, 57 (4), 300–311.

Stiglitz, E.J., 2019. *After neoliberalism. International politics and society* [Online]. Available from: https://www.projectsyndicate.org/commentary/after-neoliberalism-progressivecapitalism-by-joseph-e-stiglitz-2019-05 [Accessed 12 August 2019].

Tkach, J., and DiGirolamo, J., 2017. The state and future of coaching supervision. *International Coaching Psychology Review*, 12 (1), 49–63.

Tsui, M., 2004. Supervision models in social work: from nature to culture. *Asian Journal of Counselling*, 11 (1–2), 7–55.

Tsui, M., 2005. *Social work supervision. Contexts and concepts.* London: SAGE.

Tsui, M., 2006. Hopes and dreams: ideal supervision for social workers in Hong Kong. *Asia Pacific Journal of Social Work and Development*, 16 (1), 33–42.

Tsui, M.S., O'Donoghue, K., Boddy, J., and Pak, C., 2017. From supervision to organisational learning: a typology to integrate supervision, mentorship, consultation and coaching. *British Journal of Social Work*, 47 (8), 2406–2420.

Turner-Daly, B., and Jack, G., 2017. Rhetoric vs. reality in social work supervision: the experiences of a group of child care social workers in England. *Child and Family Social Work*, 22, 36–46.

Unguru, E., and Sandu, A., 2017. Supervision from administrative control to continuous education and training of specialists in social work. *Revista Românească pentru Educație Multidimensională*, 9 (1), 17–35.

Unguru, E., and Sandu, A., 2018. Normative and institutional frameworks for the functioning of supervision in social work. *Revista Romaneasca pentru Educatie Multidimensionala*, 10 (2), 69–87.

Wilkins, D., and Antonopoulou, V., 2018. What does supervision help with? A survey of 315 social workers in the UK. *Practice*, 31, 1–20.

Wonnacott, J., 2012. *Mastering social work supervision.* London: Jessica Kingsley.

Wynne, T., 2020. *Potential factors contributing to harmful supervision of social workers.* Unpublished thesis. Stellenbosch University.

PART VII

Emerging areas

49

USING ARTS TO CONNECT BETWEEN PSYCHOLOGICAL AND SOCIAL THEORIES IN SOCIAL WORK SUPERVISION

Ephrat Huss

Introduction

Social work can be defined as sitting at the interface between individual and societal stress, and thus, its supervision helps social workers to intervene both at the micro (individual and family functioning) and macro (communities, organizations, institutions, and policy) systems levels. The aim of this chapter is to provide a theoretical understanding of how arts can enhance this integration between micro and macro in social work supervision. Firstly it will outline the inherent mechanisms in arts that help to address stress and strengthen resilience in social work supervision as well as address secondary trauma and burnout whilst also increasing post traumatic growth. Secondly, it will show how arts can embody and personalize social and critical theories in supervision, which embody the subjective experience of social context of both social workers and clients. The ability of art to hold these two different perspectives simultaneously is helpful in supervision and reflects the "person in context" focus of social work. In sum, art will be shown to be a methodology to embody and to integrate micro and macro, or psychological and social, understandings within supervision within a single image or gestalt (Bogo and McKnight 2006; Carpenter et al. 2013; Huss 2015; Sinding et al. 2014). The specific art mechanisms of art that enable this, and ways to utilize art for these aims, will be explained and illustrated.

Using arts to enhance resilience and encourage post traumatic growth in social workers' supervision

Social work supervision is a space to deal with the psychological impact of service users' problems on social workers. Social workers meet clients in dire situations with ongoing, intense, complex trauma. They often create an intense and embodied connection with them. Social practitioners' mental stress is documented as a major issue for the individual practitioner and for the organization, as well as for the quality of care received by service users (Shapiro et al. 2005; Bourbonnais et al. 2011). The arts are cited as a way to effectively deal with traumatic experiences because these are firstly encoded in visual and sensory parts of the brain. Arts help to re-encode new preverbal images and sensations, through distancing and mapping them out, and then, in the context of a safe relationship in supervision, finding more adaptive narratives and understandings of these experiences. Overall, the arts are an embodied experience that help to connect between sensations, emotions, and cognitions. (Kaye and Bleep 1997; Emerson and Smith 2000; Appleton 2001; Hass-Cohen 2003; Talwar 2007; Warren 2008; Sarid and Huss 2010; Munro 2011; Malchiodi 2012; Carpenter et al. 2013). This helps to bring the body, emotions, and sensations back into the supervision, and to counteract stress reactions such as fight, flight, freeze, or dissociation characteristic of stress, that create mechanistic social work engagement. Thus, the supervision can create enough distance to "observe" the experience as outside of the self, but at the same time, enough sensory stimuli to experience empathy towards the issue. (Huss et al. 2017; Huss and Hafford-Letchfield 2019).

In social or relational art, the focus is on the process of art making, and the meanings attribute to art, rather than to the final product as a separate entity. Thus, separating, uniting, or differently organizing shapes and colors can provide new perspectives (Huss and Sarid 2011, 2014).

For example an image drawn by a social worker in group supervision process for social workers during war (see Huss et al. 2010 for full case study), was followed by these comments from the social worker:

> *We were mostly needed to help put wounded people and people suffering from anxiety attacks into the ambulances. We were expected to talk to them and to calm them down. But it was terrifying for me to be there, to endanger my life. My mother criticized me for leaving my kids and risking my life in the middle of the war, all for a job.*

We see that through the tension between form and content, the social worker managed to express her feeling of being split between multiple roles. After explaining her drawing, she added new perceptions through filling in her body with the different colors stating that this is like Joseph's coat of many colors in the Bible. Joseph also managed to navigate stressful experiences. She stated that she can hold these different roles as a colorful magic coat and source of power. This can be a description of a situation of post traumatic growth through managing stress, by using the tension between form and content and symbols and metaphors to grow and develop beyond the stress and trauma. The meaning of the image shifted as she continued drawing and adding to it. This process can be taught in supervision and can be undertaken alone in moments of stress, using a small sketchbook.

The above example shows how the art enhances a sense of coherence (SOC) (Antonovsky 1979). That is, both meaning, manageability, and comprehension were shifted. Actively discussing the image as in supervision can help to enhance the aim of supervision in social work to actively create resilience. Art concretized the first component of SOC, that is manageability, through the element of actively "doing" something about the problem through drawing it. Art is an action-based activity in which the participant manages decisions about what and how to depict on the page, through focusing on figures, images, colors, and materials as well as their interpretation and explanation to the supervisor (Antonovsky 1979; Huss 2015; Zelizer 2003). The explanation of the image in supervision can enhance meaning making and comprehension by creating a hermeneutic and reflective space to integrate both emotional and cognitive components and to integrate new perspectives of the supervisor.

Using arts to intensify macro social work perspectives in supervision

In addition to dealing with stress in social work supervision, a central aim is to conceptualize service users' and social workers' problems through social theories rather than only through psychological theories. In other words, the subjective pain of clients is understood as emerging from social roles, stigmas, abuses of power, and lack of physical, symbolic, and social resources within those social systems. Social systems are at the interface between homeostasis and change, and the social worker utilizes this to address different forms of disempowerment of service users (Huss 2015). This also needs supervision, and as Mishna and Bogo (2007) posit, the emotional encounter (rather than classroom theorizing) with a social problem is messier than the theoretical social understanding. Arts help, as described above, creates a more emotional embodied space to work through these experiences that may be hidden under the intense intellectual socialization the students undergo toward social explanations of poverty. Additionally, personal interpretation and the engagement of the imagination are cited as techniques that enhance critical consciousness (Freire and Macedo 1987; Ramirez and Gallardo 2001). Thus, learners are "not passively educated but must find their own words and risk expressing themselves" (Freire and Macedo 1987). This enables one to bring social theories into supervision through a more phenomenological stand. The act of creating an image can be defined as a space that gives voice to socially silenced experience. It also shifts away from the power infused professional terms that may hide the social workers truth. The arts help to create an intermediate shift of power between supervisor (who is also often a manager) and social worker, through both shifting to the new visual language of feelings (Freire and Macedo 1987; Spivak and Guha 1988; Foster 2007; Huss 2012). This enables a space to co-produce new knowledge or terms in the supervising context in which the supervisor is not the "expert." The use of arts on this level can be understood as emancipatory within supervision as a way to help social workers access their own tacit knowledge, blind theories, or inner experience (Narhi and Matthies 2001; Kaufman et al. 2011). Tacit knowledge is often symbolic, narrative, and visual rather than based on abstract verbal concepts (Pascal 2010; Huss 2015). Arnhiem (1996) describes symbols as a medium that can hold multiple meanings; as such, the same symbol can be interpreted in different ways by different people without one side being right. (See also Sullivan 2001).

Through using symbols and metaphors which are a much broader hermeneutic or interpretive base than words, then there is space for the knowledge of both supervisor and social worker (or both social worker and service user). On this level arts are an emancipatory tool to diffuse the power imbalance of professional relationships. Compositionally, then arts can also help to understand the relationship between service user and context as an interactive one (Huss 2015). Social context can also work as a parallel process between supervisor, social worker, and service user. Huss and Hafford-Letchfield (2019) illustrate this through a case study in which a social worker's experience of her work overload is a background that "overwhelms" the figures in the foreground. This points to the parallels between social workers and their service users.

The ability of art to hold these two different perspectives simultaneously is helpful in supervision and reflects the "person in context" focus of social work. The image can be a gestalt that maps out multiple internal and external needs. The arts, from a neuro-biological perspective, are a way to group stimuli into a coherent gestalt or unit (Van der Kolk et al. 2001; Huss and Sarid 2014). Working memory selects and updates images and sensations that are most relevant to the individual. Thus, the "gestalt," in other words, the whole, at any given time, is made of a set of dominant and background needs (Huss 2015). This becomes a good way to concretize the often very complex cases that supervisors and social workers deal with. This broad spatial depiction of complicated cases may better suit the experience of practicing social workers rather than the more theoretical and linear knowledge of supervisors. At the same time because arts are metaphorical and symbolic as well as spatial, they can also encompass the past, present, and future – and show connections between them (Dokter 1994; Emerson and Smith 2000).

This can be enhanced through structured art directives that emerge from the supervision conversation, such as drawing bridges, creative genograms, and conflicting sides of issues. These can be depicted in art as in bridge drawings, in which the bridge, water, environment, and potential hazards and supports on the journey of crossing the bridge enable one to reach their goal. Similarly, creative genograms (Huss and Cwikel 2008) can help to see intergenerational connections and envisage more concretely where the service user and social worker are trying to go and how they can reach that place (Huss and Magos 2013).

Conclusion

The arts have been used in social work since the beginning of the profession, and yet, an articulation of a rationale for their use, that is, the ways that the mechanisms of visual art enhance social work supervision has been less articulated (Chamberlayn and Smith 2008; Huss 2015). The aim of this chapter was not to provide "recipes" for using arts as a distraction or leitmotif in supervision, but to provide a theoretical understanding of how the mechanisms inherent to arts can enhance social work supervision, in the ways outlined in the introduction. It has been argued that the arts can create an embodied, concrete dynamic transitional but also emancipatory space to integrate psychological and social theories in supervision. This is turn can help supervisees move beyond calming stress to enhancing post traumatic growth. The chapter has also showed how arts can help to address stress and to strengthen resilience and post traumatic growth, through helping to concretize elements of meaning, manageability, and comprehensibility, also known as sense of coherence (SOC). In addition, arts can help to embody and personalize critical theories, creating a space for silenced experience of social workers to be made manifest in power-infused contexts of supervision.

Most importantly for social work specifically, as stated in the introduction, is the ability of art to integrate the above psychological and social theories or to integrate between phenomenological experience and historical experience (Vodde and Gallant 2002). This translates into how the figure and background of an image help to construct each other. This creates a bridge between micro, or therapeutic social work based on psychological theories, and macro, or socially and community oriented social work based on social theories, and most importantly manages to hold them together at the same time. This can create a more complex understanding of service users' problems, and parallel processes with the social worker. Overall, the use of arts within social work supervision highlights the relevance of taking embodied, relational socially embedded aesthetic experiences in social work seriously and utilizing them as creative catalysts in supervision.

References

Antonovsky, A., 1979. *Health, stress, and coping: new perspectives on mental and physical well-being.* San Francisco, CA: Jossey-Bass Therapy.

Appleton, V., 2001. Avenues of hope: art therapy and the resolution of trauma. *Art Therapy*, 18 (1), 6–13.

Arnheim, R., 1996. *The split and the structure: twenty-eight essays.* Berkeley, CA: University of California Press.

Bogo, M., and McKnight, K., 2006. Clinical supervision in social work: a review of the research literature. *The Clinical Supervisor*, 24 (1–2), 49–67.

Bourbonnais, R., Brisson, C., and Vézina, M., 2011. Long-term effects of an intervention on psychosocial work factors among healthcare professionals in a hospital setting. *Occupational and Environmental Medicine*, 68 (7), 479–486.

Carpenter, J., Webb, C.M., and Bostock, L., 2013. The surprisingly weak evidence base for supervision: findings from a systematic review of research in child welfare practice (2000–2012). *Children and Youth Services Review*, 35 (11), 1843–1853.

Chamberlayn, P., and Smith, M., 2008. *Art creativity and imagination in social work practice*. London: Routledge.

Dokter, D., 1994. *Fragile bones: art therapies and clients with eating disorders*. Philadelphia, PA: Jessica Kingsley.

Emerson, M., and Smith, P., 2000. *Researching the visual: images, objects, contexts, and interactions in social*. London: SAGE.

Foster, V., 2007. Ways of knowing and showing: imagination and representation in feminist participatory social research. *Journal of Social Work Practice*, 21 (3), 361–376.

Freire, P., and Macedo, D., 1987. *Literacy, reading the word and the world*. London: Routledge.

Hass-Cohen, N., 2003. Art therapy mind body approaches. *Progress: Family Systems Research and Therapy*, 12, 24–38.

Huss, E., 2012. What we see and what we say: combining visual and verbal information within social work research. *British Journal of Social Work*, 42 (8), 1440–1459.

Huss, E., 2015. *A theory-based approach to art therapy*. London: Routledge.

Huss, E., and Cwikel, J., 2008. "It's hard to be the child of a fish and a butterfly": creative genograms bridging objective and subjective experiences. *Arts in Psychotherapy*, 35 (2), 171–180.

Huss, E., and Hafford-Letchfield, T., 2019. Using art to illuminate social workers' stress. *Journal of Social Work*, 19 (6), 751–768.

Huss, E., and Magos, M., 2013. Relationship between self-actualization and employment for at-risk young unemployed women. *Journal of Education and Work*, 4, 21–34.

Huss, E., and Sarid, O., 2011. Using imagery in health care settings: addressing physical and psychological trauma. *In*: C.A. Malchiodi, ed. *Art therapy and healthcare*. New York, NY: Guilford Press, 136–145.

Huss, E., and Sarid, O., 2014. Visually transforming artwork and guided imagery as a way to reduce work related stress: a quantitative pilot study. *The Arts in Psychotherapy*, 41 (4), 409–412.

Huss, E., Sarid, O., and Cwikel, J., 2010. Using art as a self-regulating tool in a war situation: a model for social workers. *Health and Social Work*, 35 (3), 201–211.

Huss, E., Yosef, K.B., and Zaccai, M., 2017. The meaning of flowers: a cultural and perceptual exploration of ornamental flowers. *The Open Psychology Journal*, 10 (1), 140–153.

Kaufman, R., Huss, E., and Segel-Englich, D., 2011. Social work students' changing perceptions of social problems after a year of community intervention. *Social Work Education*, 30 (8), 911–931.

Kaye, S., and Bleep, M., 1997. *Arts and healthcare*. London: Jessica Kingsley.

Malchiodi, C., ed., 2012. *Art therapy and healthcare*. New York, NY: Guilford Press.

Mishna, F., and Bogo, M., 2007. Reflective practice in contemporary social work classrooms. *Journal of Social Work Education*, 43 (3), 529–544.

Munro, E., 2011. *The Munro review of child protection: final report, a child-centred system*. Vol. 8062. London: Stationery Office.

Närhi, K., and Matthies, A.L., 2001. What is the ecological (self)consciousness of social work? Perspectives on the relationship between social work and ecology. *In*: A.-L. Matthies, K. Närhi, and D. Ward, eds. *Ecological social Approach in Social Work*. Jyväskylä: Sophi, 16–53.

Pascal, J., 2010. Phenomenology as a research method for social work contexts: understanding the lived experience of cancer survival. *Currents: Scholarship in the Human Services*, 9 (2), 1–23.

Ramirez, L., and Gallardo, O., eds., 2001. *Portraits of teachers in multicultural settings: a critical literacy approach*. Needham Heights, MA: Allyn and Bacon.

Sarid, O., and Huss, E., 2010. Trauma and acute stress disorder: a comparison between cognitive behavioral intervention and art therapy. *The Arts in Psychotherapy*, 37 (1), 8–12.

Shapiro, S.L., Astin, J.A., Bishop, S.R., and Cordova, M., 2005. Mindfulness-based stress reduction for health care professionals: results from a randomized trial. *International Journal of Stress Management*, 12 (2), 164–176.

Sinding, C., Warren, R., and Paton, C., 2014. Social work and the arts: images at the intersection. *Qualitative Social Work*, 13 (2), 187–202.

Spivak, G.C., and Guha, R., eds., 1988. *Selected subaltern studies*. New York, NY: Oxford University Press.

Sullivan, G., 2001. Artistic thinking as trans-cognitive practice: a reconciliation of the process–product dichotomy. *Visual Arts Research*, 27 (1), 2–12.

Talwar, S., 2007. Accessing traumatic memory through art making: an art therapy trauma protocol (ATTP). *The Arts in Psychotherapy*, 34 (1), 22–35.

van der Kolk, B.A., Hopper, J., and Osterman, J., 2001. Exploring the nature of traumatic memories: combining clinical knowledge with laboratory methods. *Journal of Aggression, Maltreatment and Trauma*, 4 (2), 9–31.

Vodde, R., and Gallant, J.P., 2002. Bridging the gap between micro and macro practice: large scale change and a unified model of narrative-deconstructive practice. *Journal of Social Work Education*, 38 (3), 439–458.

Warren, B., 2008. *Using the creative arts in therapy and healthcare*. London: Routledge.

Zelizer, C., 2003. The role of artistic processes in peacebuilding in Bosnia-Herzegovina. *Peace and Conflict Studies*, 10 (2), 62–75.

50

SUPERVISION AND SERVICE USER VOICE

Sharon Lambley

Introduction

This chapter considers the case for and against including service user voices in supervision. The case for excluding service user voice in supervision focuses upon professional concerns about how supervision would change if service user voices were included in supervision, and the practical problems of how to include service user voices in supervision. The case for including service user voice focuses upon the benefits of doing so, i.e., service user involvement would generate evidence of the impact from supervision and social work practice on service user outcomes and inform system improvements. Drawing from the research evidence, this chapter critically explores these positions, giving examples of key developments in research and practice settings that are addressing this issue.

The context for supervision and the service user voice

To consider the case for and against including service user voices in supervision we need to start with some assumptions. Firstly, giving people a voice in social work is at the heart of good social work practice (Ingram and Smith 2018). Secondly, service users do not usually participate directly in supervision, but their voices are represented in supervision by social workers (Lambley 2019). Thirdly, involving service users in decision making is beneficial but it may also be a requirement or "right" e.g., Article 12 of the UN Convention on the rights of the child requires children to be informed, heard, and involved in decision making proportionate to their age (Rap et al. 2019). Fourthly, supervision plays a role in supporting and developing social workers to deliver high quality social work practice, which in turn can support service improvements. These assumptions, however, can be misplaced in some care settings as highlighted in the following examples. Firstly, some service users say that their voices are not always heard e.g., one child in care said "I've been in care for a long time and I never get a say in what I would like. It's always what other people would like and I'm fed up with it" (Selwyn 2015, p. 22). Secondly, whilst service users acknowledge it is impractical for them to be in supervision meetings, they know that supervision is where decisions are made and therefore, "supervision is perceived as a threat to people who use services if it is not performed well, but is perceived as very useful if it works well" (SCIE 2013, p. 4). Thirdly, service users do not always participate in decision making, even when the decisions can have a significant impact on their lives. For example, Rap et al. (2019, p. 37) found "many obstacles exist that prevent effective participation in youth care and protection." Dutch municipalities have discretion in giving shape to child participation in access to voluntary and coercive youth care (Rap et al. 2019, p. 47). Fourthly, care systems do not always provide opportunities for service users to feedback on their social work experiences. For example, in mental health settings, service user feedback was "not a routine activity or requirement for service users" (Wilberforce et al. 2018, p. 3). In addition, Wilberforce et al. (2018, p. 1) said that "Despite being a profession dedicated to the empowerment of service users, empirical study of mental health social work appears dominated by the perspectives of social workers themselves. What service users value is less often reported." By finding such examples, it is possible to draw three conclusions. Firstly, supervisors have a role in making sure that service user voices are being heard, and secondly, supervisors need to educate and support good social work practice so that service user voices are heard. As Carpenter et al. (2012, p. 3) concluded in a literature review on supervision:

> The overall aim of professional supervision should be to provide the best possible support to service users in accordance with the organization's responsibilities and accountable professional standards…

Thirdly, there is a need to consider where service user voices can be heard in care settings and whether supervision has a role to play in this.

What service users say they want from social workers is broadly similar across service user groups, practice areas, and countries (Kam 2019; Caldwell et al. 2019; Wilberforce et al. 2018). Specifically, Kam (2019, p. 15) suggests that service users want "social workers to put aside professional authority, learn to share power with service users and increase their willingness to play the role of an ally who is keen to develop an equalitarian and partnership relationship with them." It is only by listening to service users that social workers can genuinely understand service user opinions, become more responsive to their needs, and work in more egalitarian ways (Kam 2019). Kam (2019, p. 4) also suggests that it is important that service user voices are heard in every care system, if such systems are to improve quality, performance, and service planning, suggesting that

> the major aim of service user participation is to make them feel that they have the right and power to influence the services provided to them and make them aware that, more than just a service consumer, they should be regarded as citizens with the right to participation.

However, before examining the case for and against service user voices in supervision, it is helpful to understand something of the history of service user voices in professional and managerial systems of care, and how the discourses in these systems impact on service users.

Service users have been labelled "client, patient, customer, consumer, expert by experience" (McLaughlin 2009, p. 1101). Such labels are important because labels "conjure up differing identities, identifying differing relationships and differing power dynamics" (McLaughlin 2009, p. 1102), and this affects "very practical and material outcomes" (McDonald 2006, p. 115). It is important therefore to deconstruct the meaning of these labels because labels are used to describe a person wanting a service "differently, with differing nuances and differing assumptions about the nature of the relationship" (McLaughlin 2009, p. 1102). For example, being a client is associated with being a passive recipient of social work, being a good person (the deserving poor) and "in need of help, because they lack either the necessary abilities or the capacity to help themselves, and thus need the specialist knowledge and skills of the social worker" (McLaughlin 2009, p. 1103). The label "client" is still used in many social work settings around the world, and Rollins (2019) has attached it to relationship-based practice. However, Rollins' (2019) study focuses on the social worker-client relationship from the social worker perspective, and so it is not possible to understand how people who use services view themselves in a social worker-client relationship. In many countries, the term client has been replaced with service user. McLaughlin (2009, p. 1107) suggests that whilst "service user involvement has become thoroughly embedded in social care" in many settings and in research, this term is problematic. The term "service user involvement is all too often 'tokenistic' and unproductive" (McLaughlin 2009, p. 1107). He goes on to say that "Wilson and Beresford (2000) also argue that service users' knowledge is being appropriated in areas like anti-oppressive practice, reinforcing oppression and the view of service users as passive whilst protecting professional power and legitimating controlling problematic practices" (McLaughlin 2009, p. 1107). McLaughlin (2009) carefully picks apart how power and control has become reasserted by professionals over people who use services. The term service user is associated with empowerment but in some practice settings professional power and control has become re-established in the relationships between social workers and service users. Clients and service user labels, however, are two of many other labels used around the world, e.g., customers, consumers, and co-producers. Flynn (2012) suggests that being a customer in a welfare service is on the face of it not too dissimilar to being a customer in other service industries. A customer orientation means setting and monitoring service standards, empowering customers by providing them with resources to choose and purchase a service, and training staff and services to respond to customer needs. However, Harris (2003) argues the relationship between social workers and customers is much more complex and that business labels are problematic because social work is a relationship practice. Payne (2005) suggests that it is how social work relationships are constructed in practice settings that gives the relationships meaning. For example, social workers who undertake an eligibility assessment can become engaged in short term transactional relationships, where personal histories, structural inequalities, and life challenges are of little or no concern to the social worker in the assessment process. This is not reflective of relationship based social work practice outlined by Ingram and Smith (2018). In customer settings, McLaughlin (2009) suggests that once approval for funding has been granted, customers can then source the services they need in care markets. Providing a good customer experience is associated with consumerism, which Harris (2003, p. 152) suggests is "concerned with modes of service delivery in ways that curtail that involvement to a universalized managerial set of expectations about what being treated well as a customer means." These ideas (customer and consumer) and the impact on the social work relationships have been introduced into social work practices and they are problematic. For example, Renouf and Bland (2005, p. 420) suggest that Australia's mental health strategy which focuses on "the importance of consumer participation in all aspects of mental health activity – from planning services with individual consumers, through to agency management and evaluation, and in the education and training of mental health professional" has stimulated the re-design of services and the introduction of evidence based practices (EBP). EBP make it difficult for social workers to "integrate critical, structural perspectives of power and change with clinical knowledge and theory" (Morley 2003), which is problematic (Renouf and Bland 2005, p. 425). There is "a tension evident between the demands of clinical expertise in general mental health practice……and the critical traditions of the profession" (Renouf and Bland 2005, p. 426). Social workers must decide whether to acquire the new skills and approaches in clinical settings or to challenge these approaches due to the links with scientific discourses, and the lack of structural considerations that are important to social workers (Renouf and Bland 2005). Renouf and Bland (2005, p. 426) suggest that "the challenge for the profession as a whole of course, is how to be both relevant and critical" whilst ensuring that managerial discourses do not distort service user feedback.

Co-production has emerged in recent years as a new way of labeling citizens in care systems. "People are not passive recipients of services and have assets and expertise which can help improve services" (Needham 2009, p. 1). However, co-production requires professionals to share "power, resources and partnerships, risks and outcomes" with people using services (Needham 2009, p. 1). Ingram and Smith (2018) adopt co-production as an approach to support relationship-based practice. Allen (2014) suggests that involving service users is beneficial for improving professional practice and services. They highlight how student social workers already collect data from service users about their practice, which is used in social work supervision. They suggest that there are many ways to capture service user voices in supervision, but supervisors need to re-conceptualize supervision and social work practice in ways that reflect the principles of co-production and develop practices.

McLaughlin (2009) suggests is that "we have now reached the point whereby we need to consider whether it really matters what label we use," and he argues that it does, because whatever label we use it "is descriptive not of a person, but of a relationship." How this relationship is supported in supervision and the wider care system needs to be better understood. Healy (2014, p. 8) makes the case for understanding discourses used in care settings and in supervision because "discourses shape knowledge and power relations in practice by influencing what counts as true and valid and who is recognized as authoritative," and the discourses used in supervision "constitute our understanding of service user needs and shape what is regarded as appropriate ways of understanding and responding to this needs, as well as legitimizing some kinds of knowledge and practice while devaluing others." (Healy 2014, p. 4). When we examine the dominant discourses in supervision, we can see that managerial discourses in supervision can undermine social work values, principles, and the purpose of social work. For example, in one local authority older people's team in England, a social worker said:

> (Social work values are) kind of discussed in supervision, but the choices you make are still very limited by services. I suppose we kind of always have the issues of user empowerment and choice and listening to the client up to a point. But at the same time, it's kind of restricted by what realistically we can offer.
>
> *(Evans 2010, p. 131)*

Trevithick (2014, p. 287) suggests that "the professional account of social work practice in which relationships play a central role appears to have been gradually stifled and replaced by a managerialist account that is fundamentally different." She goes on to say that social workers provide detailed assessments, collect evidence, and make plans, which emphasize the conscious, cognitive elements of the tasks, but there is less attention on helping staff acquire the skills to analyze the data they are collecting. This has a negative impact on social work and service users, not only in terms of what happens in supervision, but also within the wider welfare systems in which supervision is practiced. And this problem is a global one as managerialist discourses dominate welfare systems. For example, in China, Leung (2008, p. 543) describes how social work practice and service accountability was reconstructed "by the service providers as a provider-initiated process of information flow, in which a post hoc explanation of service-related decisions was a sufficient representation of accountability." This action neutralized any threat to the social work and management power base by reducing accountability "to the mere act of account giving" (Leung 2008, p. 543). This is at odds with the values of social work and the purpose of supervision which is to improve outcomes for service users (Harkness and Poertner 1989). Considering how service user voices are included and excluded at practice as well as at a systems level, it is time to consider the case for and against including service user voices in supervision.

The case for and against including service user voices in supervision

There are many arguments that can be made for and against including service user voices in supervision. Three arguments are considered here. The first two consider the relationships between service users and social workers and how this relationship is supported in supervision, whilst the final argument considers the challenges of managerialism.

The first argument is that social work supervision is focused on professional concerns, and that supervision would be changed if service user voices were included in supervision. This position assumes that service user voices are already heard in practice settings, and that it is the outcomes from this work that are examined in supervision. This allows supervisors to focus on professional concerns in supervision. Good supervision provides a safe space for social workers to reflect upon their practice, and to consider their own development and support needs (Rankine 2019). In organizations that provide supervision by external supervisors, Rankine (2019) suggests that social workers can access good opportunities for practice learning that support professional developmental opportunities without social workers becoming overwhelmed by managerial concerns, although this model of supervision is not without its challenges (Beddoe 2012). However, we also know that some service users do not always think that their voices are heard in social work practice (Selwyn 2015) and that service users can get little or no feedback from supervision where decisions have been taken that can significantly affect their lives (Lambley 2019). How can supervision be changed to improve on these practices, and what are the barriers?

One barrier is the professionalization of social work. "Professionalism is often associated with certainty, expertise and theoretical knowledge" (Broddie et al. 2008). Noddings (1996) however, distinguishes between professionalism and professionalization. She suggests that the latter is the result of codified and rule-bound conception of professionalism that derives from a quest for status. There is, however, little connection between such rule-bound professionalization and positive outcomes (Ingram and Smith 2018, p. 8).

Supervision that supports social work and is codified, rule bound, and protective of professional status can be a threat to good outcomes for service users. In such a scenario, it would be very difficult for a service user's voice to be heard. However, if service users could have some involvement in supervision there is "the potential to re-balance relationships between social worker and the person who uses services" (SCIE 2013, p. 6).

A second barrier is a reliance on professional expertise. Ingram and Smith, (2018, p. 9) suggest that current practice "may be unethical for both social workers and their clients, belying a message of inequality (that) is ultimately patronizing and disrespectful" (Alexander and Gra 2009, p. 19). Much of the social work literature recognizes the need for social workers to move away from being *the* expert to "one that seeks the views and involvement of individuals and communities, through what might be identified as co-production" (Ingram and Smith 2018, p. 5). "Co-production challenges the way in which client-professional relationships are constructed because it supports active inputs by people who use services, as well as – or instead of – those who traditionally provide them" (Needham 2009, p. 1). Service users said that the benefits of involving service users in delivering good outcomes for service users from supervision is that there is an opportunity for service users to give positive feedback – as well as improve things that are not working well (SCIE 2013).

A third barrier is the use of professional boundaries that may protect social workers and organizations but frustrate authentic relationship building. Relationship based approaches have "become a way of articulating the centrality of the relationship between social workers and service users" (Ingram and Smith 2018, p. 5). By embracing relationship-based practice, social workers are responding to a call "for a radical shift in how worker-client relationships are conceived" (Ingram and Smith 2018, p. 12). Ingram and Smith (2018, p. 9) suggest that social workers need to challenge practice traditions that support boundaries between service users and social workers because "it is important to distinguish between boundaries, which are dynamic, and can be deployed flexibly, and barriers, which are static and prioritize consistent application" (Ingram and Smith 2018, p. 9).

A fourth barrier is potentially the supervision model used in social work settings. There have been many supervision models developed for social work, and some include service users in the design, but few models have been empirically tested (Carpenter et al. 2012) or demonstrate how service user voices are heard in supervision. In a study funded by the Social Care Institute for Excellence (SCIE), the views of all stakeholders were captured using a semi-open supervision systems framework, developed from systems theory (Lambley 2018). The framework provides a conceptual map of any supervision system (see Figure 50.1).

The model can make service user contributions in supervision systems visible. For example, service user voices can be heard at a global and national level in the broader systems, e.g., in policy developments, laws, practice standards, and regulation systems, etc.. At the organizational level, supervision policies, trained supervisors, trained staff, resources, and service user contri-

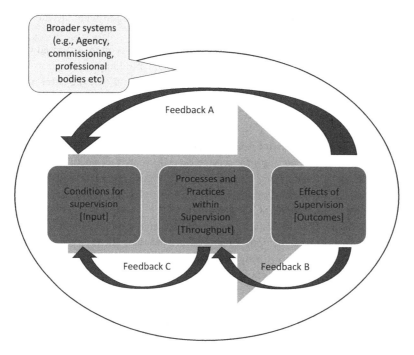

Figure 50.1 A semi-open supervision systems model. (Used with permission license number 4874220428674, from Lambley, S., 2018. A semi-open supervision systems model for evaluating staff supervision in adult care organizational settings: a conceptual framework. *European Journal of social work*, 21 (3), p. 393)

butions can be identified as *inputs* into the supervision system. Service user voices may also be present in supervision meetings along with professional voices and legal, management requirements etc. (*supervision throughputs*). Service user voices may be evidenced in the outcomes from supervision, whilst feedback in any part of the supervision system can be evidenced to demonstrate how the supervision system responds and changes (feedback loops).

This framework can be applied to a study by Bostock et al. (2017) on evaluating the "Reclaiming Social Work" model, which was introduced into five UK local authority social work children and family services. The reclaiming social work model was developed to address concerns over the impact of managerialist approaches in practice settings, and a need to reclaim social work practice. Service users were encouraged to provide feedback on the service. The study captures how service user focused social work practice and feedback from service users informed good practice and good outcomes. Specifically, feedback methods included interviews with staff and staff surveys; observations of systemic case discussions and direct practice, comparison of practice, service experiences, and outcomes between units and services; interviews with parents and children; as well as evaluation of data from computerized records and other secondary sources including impact of care entry and potential cost savings etc. Systemic case supervision was used in weekly unit meetings. Unit meetings lasted between two and four hours and consisted of a multi-skilled team and at times, an appropriately qualified clinician. Unit meetings were considered systemic if eight features were present, including the "child and family being present within the conversation." For example, a "unit generated hypothesis about why a teenager struggling to look after a baby" led a clinician to suggest several circular questions which "were designed to help the mother to think systemically about relationships within her family. For example, 'what would mum say if she was here?' and 'what would the baby say?'"Workers "welcomed the opportunity to discuss cases as a group; appreciated the safe space to discuss anxieties about risk to children, and actively sought out different perspectives to help them move forward with families" (Bostock et al. 2017, p. 51). Bostock et al. (2017, p. 10) identified three elements that families said they appreciated, including "whole family working where practice was empathetic and strengths based," being "part of the solution to their family's difficulties" and workers who were "skilled at respectfully exploring their situation with a view to improving fractured family relationships."

The second argument focuses on how service users' voices can be included in supervision, particularly when service users choose not to engage with social workers. For example, a person receiving end of life care may simply want social workers to provide a service, and they may ask a family member or a friend to liaise with the social worker on their behalf. A service user may be living a chaotic lifestyle, which affects their relationship with a social worker because they often miss appointments, or a service user may feel that the outcomes have already been decided for them, so they resist engaging with a social worker, etc. Cousins (2020) recognizes how a lack of control, loss of power or choice can affect working relationships so that service users resist change, choose not to engage with services, or appear compliant in order "to reduce the possibility of threat and to end the scrutiny" (Cousins 2020, p. 348). Understanding how power dynamics, transference, counter transference, issues of control, and the challenges surrounding difficult emotional conversations can give service users a voice in supervision as social workers and supervisors examine the lives of people using services and how this impacts on work with them. However, in recent years, there has been a growing interest in how practice with service users is measured and accountability demonstrated. Measures and accountability are not a "neutral" concept. Managerialism, which has been driving the need for measurement and accountability is "rooted in principles of economy, efficiency and effectiveness" and is evident in practice contexts where social work is turned into a technical and rational activity rather than an "ethical and relationship endeavour" because relationships "appear too woolly and difficult to measure and have become secondary to forms of practice," which are "increasingly framed around following procedures and ensuring compliance" (Lorenz 2016, p. 455). Where service users resist engaging with social workers, there are lessons from clinical settings that can be useful to social work particularly where outcomes are co-constructed with service users. The use of feedback and outcomes tools can become part of the intervention because "young people have talked about how difficult it is to really get their views across to practitioners in a way that feels safe and respected – even in therapy with practitioners who they experience as helpful and who listen" (Law and Woolpert 2014, p. 42). Law and Woolpert (2014, p. 43) suggest that the "one important reason for using outcomes measures is to improve the relationship between service users and therapists, and in turn, to enhance clinical practice." Lorenz (2016, p. 455) suggests that global neo-liberal social politics currently favor "a positivist meaning of evidence with implications of value neutrality" but social work practice needs "to address persons and their structural context equally." It is important therefore that any outcomes or accountability measures are co-constructed to ensure that social work colonizes managerialist tools for professional purposes.

The third argument is that supervision has become colonized by managerialism which reframes service user voices and is detrimental to good outcomes for service users. For example, Wilkins and Antonopoulou (2019, p. 36) engaged 315 social workers in a study to find out what they thought that social work supervision helped them with, and were dismayed to find that participants thought that supervision helped them primarily with management oversight and accountability in casework, and that supervision was least helpful

> for decision making, emotional support, analysis and reflection. It would have been better to find the exact opposite and it is hard to see how supervision that focuses on management oversight and accountability to the exclusion of much else can ever be truly helpful for people who use services.

Only a "small number of practitioners who received regular group supervision and those who received supervision more frequently said it helped with a much broader range of things" (Wilkins and Antonopoulou (2019, p. 36). In Hair's (2013) Canadian study of 636 social workers, one social worker described what supervision had become for them:

> I have sought and been told I was receiving clinical supervision, when it was quite evident that the primary needs being met were the organisations for compliance to policy and procedure. When an employee is inescapably caught in this kind of situation, it can be terribly damaging.

Participants in Hair's (2013, p. 1576) study suggested some solutions, including assigning two supervisors to deal with different aspects of the supervisory tasks, using external supervisors to support professional supervision, or training and development to ensure that supervisors can balance their responsibilities "with accountability to the code of ethics, legal parameters (and) agencies job requirements." Interestingly, feedback from participants suggested that there was a need for a protective mechanism to help ensure that supervisors would be accountable for their evaluation of supervisees. As one respondent noted, "I have seen countless managers and supervisors who break every standard in the college guidelines repeatedly and there is no recourse to the college or anyone else about their conduct" (Hair 2013, p. 1575).

In both these studies, managerialism colonizes social work practice and supervision and service user voices become lost. Feedback into care systems can become the only voices that care systems hear, and these may be concerned with whether the administrator made you feel welcome when you arrived at the office for a meeting (which is important!), but not ask you if your life has been transformed by the support, advice, and guidance that your worker gave you. Service users may want to talk about how they resisted help from a social worker because they were afraid, but it was a social worker who persisted with them and taught them that it was okay to be afraid and how to manage those fears, which changed their lives. Practice and research projects that seek to move beyond capturing the professional demise of social work are needed, if social work is to find solutions about how to work within often hostile care settings and to reinvigorate the profession in these challenging times. Such environments not only undermine social work, but organizations become sanitized of service user voices, which remind us why social work is needed at all. Supervisors play a key role in supporting good social work practice, as Bostock et al.'s (2017) study demonstrates. But much more research is needed to understand the contribution that supervision can make to changing hostile environments and how service user and social work voices together can transform these settings.

Conclusion

Lorenz (2016) suggests that the global neo-liberal context for social work practice is challenging. Supervisors need to understand how discourses arising from global change affects supervision, particularly in settings that have become increasingly hostile to social work (Healy 2014). Staying focused on service user voices in such settings remains important (Selwyn 2015). Service users are keen to help improve systems and to engage with social workers, but a new conceptualization and approach is needed in the field of supervision study to bring service user voices into supervision. Supervision is changed by such developments, but as professional and service user concerns become aligned in supervision, the colonization of social work can be halted, as demonstrated in the study by Bostock et al. (2017). This requires social workers and supervisors to accept that a paradigm change is underway, and that supervision needs to be focused on service users if it is to enable social work to evolve. The supportive and educational requirements of social workers need to be designed into new supervision models, and supervision research needs to consider how service user relationships can be developed and voices heard in supervision systems. Supervision has a role to play in developing measurements and accountability mechanisms that reflect the values and needs of service users and social workers, because leaving these activities to management is a threat to social work. Much more research is needed that asks service users what they think about social work and about supervision practice. Having feedback from the people who use social work services is critical for the development of the profession.

References

Alexandra, C., and Grant, C., 2009. Caring, mutuality and reciprocity in social worker-client relationships: rethinking principles of practice. *Journal of Social Work*, 9 (1), 5–22.

Allen, R., 2014. *The role of the social worker in adult mental health services*. London: College of Social Work.

Beddoe, L., 2012. External supervision in social work: power, space, risk, and the search for safety. *Australian Social Work*, 65 (2), 197–213.

Bostock, L., Forrester, D., Patrizo, L., Godfrey, T., Zonouzi, M., Antonopoulou, V., Bird, H., Tinarwo, M., 2017. *Scaling and deepening he reclaiming social work model, project report*. Department for Education. Available from: https://assets.publishing.service.gov.uk/government/uploads/system/uploads/attachment_data/file/625227/Scaling_and_deepening_the_Reclaiming_Social_Work_model.pdf, [Accessed 20 July 2020].

Brodie, I., Nottingham, C., and Plunkett, S., 2008. A tale of two reports: social work in Scotland from social work and the community (1966) to changing lives (2006). *British Journal of Social Work*, 38 (4), 697–715. doi:10.1093/bjsw/bcn035

Caldwell, J., McConvey, V., and Collins, M., 2019. Voices of the child – raising the volume of the voices of children and young people in care. *Child Care in Practice*, 25 (1), 1–5.

Carpenter, J., Webb, C., Bostock, L., and Coomber, C., 2012. *Effective supervision in social work and social care, research briefing 43*. London: SCIE.

Cousins, C., 2020. Supervising social workers in involuntary contexts: some considerations. *Australian Social Work*, 73 (3), 347–356. doi:10.1080/0312407X.2019.1695867

Evans, T., 2010. *Professional discretion in welfare services, beyond street level bureaucracy*. Surrey: Ashgate.

Flynn, N., 2012. *Public sector management*. London: SAGE.

Hair, H.J., 2013. The purpose and duration of supervision, and the training and discipline of supervisors: what social workers say they ned to provide effective services. *British Journal of Social Work*, 43, 1562–1588.

Harkness, D., and Poertner, J., 1989. Research and social work supervision: a conceptual review. *Social Work*, 34 (2), 115–119.

Harris, J., 2003. *The* social work business, the *state of welfare*. Oxen: Routledge.

Healy, K., 2014. *Social work theories in context, creating frameworks for practice*. Hampshire: Palgrave MacMillan.

Ingram, R., and Smith, M., 2018. Relationship-based practice: emergent themes in social work literature. *Insights 41*, IRISS. Available from: https://www.iriss.org.uk/resources/insights/relationship-based -practice-emergent-themes-social-work-literature [Accessed 20 July 2020].

Kam, P.K., 2019. 'Social work is not just a job': the qualities of social workers from the perspective of service users. *Journal of Social Work*. doi:10.1177/1468017319848109.

Lambley, S., 2018. A semi-open supervision systems model for evaluating staff supervision in adult care organisational settings: a conceptual framework. *European Journal of Social Work*, 21 (3), 389–399.

Lambley, S., 2019. A semi-open supervision systems model for evaluating staff supervision in adult care organisational settings: the research findings. *British Journal of Social Work*, 49, 391–410.

Law, D., and Woolpert, M., 2014. Guide to using outcomes and feedback tools with children, young people and families. *Press CAMHS*. Available from: https://www.corc.uk.net/media/1950/201404guide_to _using_outcomes_measures_and_feedback_tools-updated.pdf [Accessed 20 July 2020].

Leung, T.F.T., 2008. Accountability to welfare service users: challenges and responses of service providers. *British Journal of Social Work*, 38, 531–545.

Lorenz, W., 2016. Reaching the person-social work research as professional accountability. *European Journal of Social Work*, 19 (3/4), 455–467.

McDonald, C., 2006. *Challenging social work, the context of practice*. London: Palgrave McMillan.

McLaughlin, H., 2009. What's in a name: client, patient, customer, consumer, expert by experience – what's next?. *British Journal of Social Work*, 39, 1101–1117.

Morley, C., 2003. Towards critical social work practice in mental health: a review. *Journal of Progressive Human Services*, 14 (1), 61–84.

Needham, C. 2009. Co-Production: an emerging evidence base for adult social care transformation. Research Briefing no. 31, Social Care Institute for Excellence. Available from: http://www.scie.org.uk /publications/briefings/briefing31/index.asp [Accessed 24 June 2013].

Noddings, N., 1996. The caring professional. *In*: S. Gordon, P.Benner, and N. Noddings, eds. *Caregiving: readings in knowledge, practice, ethics and politics*. Philadelphia: University of Pennsylvania Press, 160–172.

Payne, M., 2005. *Modern social work theory*. 3rd ed. Hampshire: Palgrave MacMillan.

Rankine, M., 2019. The internal/external debate: the tensions within social work supervision. *Aotearoa New Zealand Social Work*, 31 (3), 32–45.

Rap, S., Verkroost, D., and Bruning, M., 2019. Children's participation in Dutch youth care practice: an exploratory study into the opportunities for child participation in youth care from professionals' perspective. *Child Care in Practice*, 25 (1), 37–50.

Renouf, N., and Bland, R., 2005. Navigating stormy waters: challenges and opportunities for social work in mental; health. *Australian Social Work*, 58 (4), 419–430.

Rollins, W., 2019. Social worker–client relationships: social worker perspectives. *Australian Social Work*. doi: 10.1080/0312407X.2019.1669687

SCIE 2013. *Service users and carer involvement in the supervision of health and social care workers: seminar report*. London: SCIE.

Selwyn, J., 2015. *Children and* young people's views on being in care: a literature review. Bristol: The Hadley Centre for Adoption and Foster Care Studies (and Coram Voice).

Trevithick, P., 2014. Humanising managerialism: reclaiming emotional reasoning, intuition, the relationship, and knowledge and skills in social work. *Journal of Social Work Practice*, 28 (3), 287–311.

Wilberforce, M., Abendstern, M., Batool, S., Boland, J., Challis, D., Christian, J., Hughes, J., Kinder, P., Lake-Jones, P., Mistry, M., Pitts, R., and Roberts, D., 2018. What do service users want from mental health social work? a best-worst scaling analysis. *British Journal of Social Work*. doi:10.1093/bjsw/bcz133

Wilkins, D., and Anotonopoulou, V., 2019. What does supervision help with? A survey of 315 social workers in the UK. *Practice*, 31 (1), 21–40.

Wilson, A., and Beresford, P., 2000. 'Anti-oppressive practice': emancipation or appropriation?. *British Journal of Social Work*, 30, 553–573.

51

SUPERVISION AND INFORMATION AND COMMUNICATION TECHNOLOGY (ICT)

Kitty Yuen Han Mo

This chapter examines how information and communication technology (ICT) is developing in supervision. One perspective on development suggests that both synchronous and asynchronous technologies play an important role in the development of cyber supervision. Another perspective suggests that the presence of ethical standards in some countries provides practice guidelines for people using technology-assisted supervision. Although applications of ICT in supervision practice seem to be increasing, there are still many issues to be explored in future. The issues include standardization of technology-assisted distance supervision, the measurement of e-supervision and e-learning outcomes, the building of a working relationship in an online supervision practice, and the supervision skills and approaches needed in technology-assisted distance supervision. The contemporary problems facing the development of cyber supervision include: 1) quality issues in using technology, and 2) insufficient understanding of the effectiveness and limitations of cyber supervision. Further research on technology-assisted supervision is needed.

The emergent practice in cyber supervision

Supervision using technology is an emergent supervision practice in the social work field (Reamer 2015). If a supervisor and a supervisee are separated from each other in two different locations, distance or remote supervision is an option for them. Distance supervision or remote supervision refers to supervision where either the supervisor or the supervisee is not in the same location or one or the other works in a remote or distant area (Rousmaniere and Renfro-Michel 2016). Telesupervision refers to the use of email, telephone, or video conferencing in supervision (Brandoff and Lombardi 2012). Cyber supervision means using synchronous (real time) and asynchronous (delayed time) technologies in supervision (Barnett 2011). Information and communications technology (ICT) means the integration of telecommunications and the exchange of information through the use of various kinds of technologies (Chan and Holosko 2016).

According to Chapman et al. (2011), the synchronous and asynchronous methods of ICT assisted supervision eliminate the need for direct face-to-face contact. Asynchronous communication allows the supervisor and supervisee to respond to messages at their own pace. Synchronous communication allows them to interact in real-time. Various technologies used in cyber supervision include email (Luke and Gordon 2016), videotape or audio recordings (Aveline 1992), chat rooms and computer-based live supervision (Harvey and Carlson 2003), web-based videoconferencing (Simpson 2005), and blackboard (Bushfield 2005). Recently, various social media and mobile applications have become popular in daily communication (Rashedul et al. 2010), learning and classroom teaching (Botzer and Yerushalmy 2007; Rousmaniere et al. 2014), and for building a mobile community to share knowledge (Tu and Corry 2003). Social media enables virtual contact between people and allows sharing of videos, photos, and documents. Currently, social media is not popular in formal learning (Chen and Bryer 2012).

Technology has changed supervision. Supervisors no longer need to have all the supervisees in one place to meet. They can communicate easily across different places and different time zones. Remote supervision or distance supervision is slowly becoming a new form of supervision practice. Advances in technologies such as smartphones and tablets allow distance supervision to become possible (Mishna et al. 2013). Watson (2003) reveals both the advantages and disadvantages of using cyber supervision. The advantages include more effective and efficient use of supervision time and a more flexible supervision schedule. Stebnicki and Glover (2001) found that supervisees felt more relaxed and that it was easier to communicate with their supervisors through email. Orr (2010) highlighted that having access to competent supervisors from around the world was an important learning opportunity for supervisees. However, supervision with remote methods and technologies is not without its challenges. Even now, the quality of real time communication is influenced by image quality, issues in voice quality, the transmission delay, or any feedback that occurs during the process (Marrow et al. 2002).

Different ways of using ICT in supervision/education/training

There are different ways of using ICT in supervision, education, and training. Technology has been used in supervision of counseling interns (Nelson et al. 2010), pre-service teachers (Dymond et al. 2008), and social work students (Pack 2014; Phelan 2015). Overall, supervisees benefit from technology in the following ways: (1) increased communication between supervisors and supervisees (Bushfield 2005); (2) reduced anxiety during counseling and practicing micro skills (Levitt and Jacques 2005); (3) the provision of access to education for students with disabilities (Leech and Holcomb 2004); (4) by enabling students in geographically remote locations to receive supervision and training (Wolfson et al. 2005); (5) the facilitation of online discussion and reflection among students (Oterholm 2009); (6) cost-effectiveness and time saving (Schmidt et al. 2015); and (7) supervisees receiving immediate help via social media platforms (Watson 2016).

Problems identified in using technology include poor internet connection, more time needed in equipment setup, poor knowledge about technology issues, and feasibility of using technology in certain conditions (Dymond et al. 2008). These problems highlight the importance of adequate technological support. Haythornthwaite et al. (2000) noted that supervisees felt isolated if they encountered obstacles when using technology to communicate with their supervisors. The use of technology creates ethical concerns such as the protection of privacy, confidentiality, and security (Panos et al. 2002). In addition, there are also limitations and difficulties in supervision concerning the observation of the nonverbal behaviors of supervisees during supervision (Stebnicki and Glover 2001). The following paragraphs illustrate the use of ICT in different areas.

Use of ICT in social work education

Many existing social work education programs in higher education incorporate technologies in their program delivery (Kurzman 2013). The need for online courses in undergraduate and graduate social work programs is common (Anderson-Meger 2011). An online social work education program requires students to be self-motivated and self-disciplined in study (Reardon 2010). Often the use of interactive online teaching is compatible with other face-to-face teaching methods such as classroom lectures and discussion (Regan and Freddolino 2008). Madoc-Jones and Parrott (2005) indicate that e-learning is as effective as face-to-face classroom learning. Garrison and Kanuka (2004) explain that e-learning in social work programs is generally used to offer more teaching flexibility, rather than to replace traditional classroom teaching. Phelan (2015) indicates that a blended learning environment in social work education brings benefits to students which include reducing financial burdens, increasing student's options, easier access to information, and flexibility in receiving supervision. Sandell and Hayes (2002) suggest that the use of ICT in social work education can be perceived either as a threat or an opportunity. The opportunity is to achieve pedagogical innovation in a social work program, increase competitiveness of the program, and increase students' access to technology resources. The threat is how to keep the online communication secure, to determine which kind of technology fits well with the curriculum, and to handle any complex issues arise from using the technology. Another future challenge is the development of effective multimedia web-based curricula (Shorkey and Uebel 2014).

Reamer (2019) summarizes the best practices of conducting online social work courses. These are: (1) lecturers are consistently present at the course site and provide frequent feedback, postings, and comments to students; (2) they engage students in a supportive online community by giving assignments and create opportunities for online discussion and dialogues; (3) they clearly spell out expectations for students such as the amount of time to spend on online assignments and activities, and offer timelines for completion of the assignments; (4) they employ a mixture of online teaching techniques such as use of video, audio recordings, online reading, or webcasts; (5) they make use of asynchronous and synchronous learning activities together; (6) they solicit feedback from students about online teaching and their feelings of online learning; (7) they actively invite students' questions, reflections, and responses through discussion posts; and (8) they make use of online activities to connect social work concepts with students' areas of interest.

Use of ICT in social work fieldwork practicum

The fieldwork practicum has played an essential role in the training and development of social workers. One of the challenges facing supervision in a fieldwork practicum has been how to deliver supervision at a distance. Advances in technology have enabled fieldwork programs to expand into distant areas and rural areas, both internationally and nationally. In addition, technology has decreased the time and expenses required to conduct on-site supervision. Videoconferencing is used most frequently in distance fieldwork supervision (Dudding and Justice 2004). Synchronous technologies support real time interaction during the supervision process (Reamer 2013). Asynchronous methods include journaling and providing access and support to materials. Pack (2014) for example, explored the use of online reflective journals in fieldwork training with social work placement students who were required to post their monthly e-journal with the content of fieldwork reflections. Their supervisors would then add their comments to the e-journal. The results indicated that the use of reflective online journals enhanced the student's practice confidence through reflection. Birkenmaier et al. (2005) examined a distance field education course that used WebCT to enable students' access to course materials at their convenience. They found that WebCT increased the amount of feedback the students provided regarding the course materials and supported their learning of theories and integration of knowledge.

Use of ICT in social work supervision and clinical supervision

Clinical supervision is a formal and continuous process of providing professional support and learning for frontline social workers, psychologists, counselors, therapists, and other professional practitioners. These practitioners are supported in developing their knowledge and skills through regular discussion, sharing with experienced supervisors and getting feedback and advice (Goodyear 2014). However, some practitioners are limited by geographic location and they cannot get direct access to qualified and competent supervisors (Miller et al. 2005). Technology assisted supervision becomes an affordable method for supervisees to gain access to supervisors with broader knowledge and experiences (Kanz 2001). Moreover, supervisees can upload their documents, pictures, papers, and presentations through real time social media and get an immediate response from supervisors (Priya et al. 2018). Glosoff et al. (2016) recognize the need to select online supervisory methods according to the supervisee's developmental level and learning style. Additionally, supervisors also need to choose appropriate technological products that provide opportunities to enhance the learning of supervisees.

Clinical supervision often involves cross-cultural issues, and it is necessary for supervisors to develop cultural awareness, cultural sensitivity, and supervise in a culturally appropriate manner (Burkard et al. 2006; Engelbrecht 2006). Apostolidou and Schweitzer (2017) explain that if a supervisor encourages a practitioner to develop cultural awareness and multicultural sensitivity, he or she can take the client's perspective. Deane et al. (2015) emphasize the importance of cultural competence when matching a distance supervisor and supervisee. Insensitivity to cross-cultural issues and concerns around gender, racial, and cultural differences creates problems in the supervisory relationship which in turn impacts on the effectiveness of supervision (Bryne and Hartley 2010).

Overall, technology enhances clinical learning if it is used ethically and legally (Bernard and Goodyear 2019). Webber and Deroche (2016) emphasize that hardware repairs and software upgrades are needed to maintain continuous implementation of online supervision. The availability of digital equipment is a prerequisite of conducting online supervision. Moreover, many older frontline practitioners who grew up without technology may not comfortable with technological devices. All these issues with technology need to be addressed in a working place.

Issues for further exploration and investigation

Applications of ICT in supervision practice seem to be increasing. Although many supervisors and supervisees have experimented with different types of technologically assisted supervision as a supplement to face-to-face supervision, ICT in supervision remains in its infancy. Rousmaniere (2014) reveals that there are unanswered issues in cyber supervision which include matters around cyber security, confidentiality, regulations, supervision process, and competences required in engaging technologically assisted supervision. There are still many issues to be explored in future. The following paragraphs discuss the issues requiring further investigation.

Standardization of technology-assisted distance supervision

There is an urgent need for standards to regulate technology-assisted distance supervision (McAdams and Wyatt 2010). Standardization of ICT distance supervision can minimize risks and keep practice safe. Brandoff and Lombardi (2012) recommend the use of password-protected and pseudonyms files to protect confidentiality. Carlisle et al. (2017) suggest that supervisees should be informed of the risks associated with sharing papers and documents online and the risks if any problem from technology failure arises. The National Association of Social Workers (2013) emphasizes the need to use technology in an ethical and lawful way. The practice of cyber supervision must fulfill the requirements stated in law, the organization's policy, and professional licensing rules.

Examples of existing regulations pertaining to technology-assisted distance supervision are listed below. In general, these regulations detail: (1) the risks associated with using technology in distance supervision; (2) ways to keep practice safe; (3) ways of avoiding malpractice and complaints; and (4) ethical conduct for cyber supervision practice.

- The American Counseling Association's Code of Ethics contains practice guidelines for counselors utilizing technology-assisted distance counseling and supervision (American Counseling Association 2005)
- Guidelines for the Practice of Telepsychology (American Psychological Association 2013)
- NASW, ASWB, CSWE, and CSWA Standards for Technology in Social Work Practice (National Association of Social Workers 2017)
- The ethical practice guidelines for web-counseling and web-supervision (National Board for Certified Counselors 2005)
- Ethics and practice guideline – social media, information, and communication technologies (Australian Association of Social Workers 2016)
- BASW Social media policy (British Association of Social Workers 2018)

Many countries do not have their own ethical standards and guidelines for the practice of cyber supervision (Reamer 2015). In the absence of standards, the responsibility lies with the individual supervisor and supervisee to determine the risks associated with each supervision practice (McAdams and Wyatt 2010). More research studies should be conducted in non-Western countries such as the Asian regions because these places may have their unique culture, regulations concerning cyber security, and attitudes towards data privacy or confidentiality. Priya et al. (2018) suggest that supervisors may need to be sensitive to the content they intend to share with their supervisees in cyberspace. In some countries, sensitive words should be avoided, such as the mentioning of names and personal matters of clients, internal data of an organization, or critical words about government policies (HNQQ 2013 November 16).

The measurement of online supervision outcomes and learning outcomes

The measurement of e-supervision and e-learning outcomes involves the selection of assessment methods which are appropriate to e-learning platforms. It is necessary to ensure that assessment methods are consistent with the intended learning outcomes. Coleman and Collins (2008) note that student impressions and satisfaction regarding technology do not imply that online teaching and learning is successful. Similarly, Davies and Graff (2005) found that online active participation by students does not necessarily translate into higher academic scores. Therefore, a specific assessment platform for assessing online supervision and learning outcomes is needed. Cicco

(2011) advocates the design of appropriate and realistic online evaluation methods for assessing learning outcomes in the courses that teach both skills and techniques. This ensures that quality online instruction has been achieved through facilitating solid skill development. Students need to have higher motivation and good self-discipline if they are engaged in online courses (Cicco 2011). Therefore, the abilities of students to use online resources independently and to work within a technological platform become a concern if the learning outcomes have to be measured. Individual learning styles and abilities of students to use technology also have to be seriously considered (Fearing and Riley 2005).

In the long run, the discussion of e-education or e-supervision as excellent alternatives to traditional classroom learning or face-to-face supervision is not enough. The effectiveness and outcomes must be assessed and evaluated more objectively. There is a need to consider a mixture of various online methods, or a combination of classroom and online learning to match the learning styles and development needs of each student or each supervisee.

The building of working relationships in an online supervision practice

Wright and Griffiths (2010) stress the importance of establishing a working agreement with supervisees which clarifies the expectation of both parties. Driscoll and Townsend (2007) propose a similar suggestion that both supervisor and supervisee gain an agreement beforehand in relation to issues about confidentiality, documentation, and time and length of online supervision. This preparation enhances the establishment of online supervisory relationships (Cook and Doyle 2002). Factors to promote the development of online supervisory relationships include: (1) technology skills and ease of use, which can reduce anxiety and increase trust in the working alliance (Webber and Deroche 2016); (2) a shared respect for the time and effort spent in online supervision., which is essential to the maintenance of supervisory relationship (Kasworm et al. 2010); (3) rapid asynchronous responses from supervisors, which can increase supervisee's satisfaction toward online supervision (Rudestam and Schoenholtz-Read 2010); and (4) demonstration of professional competence in supporting supervisees, encouraging self-reflection, and an accurate assessment of supervision outcomes (Cicco 2011).

The exploration of working relationships in an online supervision practice must also be extended to the consideration of gender, racial, and cultural issues. As suggested by Carrington (2004), supervision is a reciprocal learning process. The self-reflection of supervisors towards supervisees who come from different cultural backgrounds may facilitate supervisory professional development. It may also have a positive effect on strengthening supervisory relationships.

Supervision skills needed in technology-assisted distance supervision

Driscoll and Townsend (2007) note that online text language is open to cultural misinterpretation because there is an absence of visual clues. Moreover, the delay in receiving real time voice or text responses affects the flow of communication. Wright and Griffiths (2010) stress the importance of clear writing to convey a message or an idea in email or social media. It is necessary to ensure that the message receiver is clear about the meaning of the written text. If there is a misunderstanding of the message, immediate clarification is needed. Sometimes the text may be interpreted wrongly by the reader because he or she has his or her own preconceptions.

The development of "e-supervision skills" and "e-supervision process" is highly recommended. Mo and O'Donoghue (2018) examined the "e-supervision skills" which included immediate response, preparation, questioning, clarification, listening, and empathy. Supervisees expect supervisors react to their online messages quickly. Moreover, the questioning skills involved are frequently used to clarify messages, and explore deeper meanings, feelings, and opinions behind the messages. Supervisor also need to be sensitive to contextual factors and ask further questions to clarify the situation facing the supervisee. Welfel (2010) suggests that the first step of the "e-supervision process" is to get an informed consent to supervision. Time and location are important because the privacy and confidentiality of supervision must be protected. The next step is to have up to date technical equipment and software.

At present, the discussion about "e-supervision skills" and the "e-supervision process" in literature is scarce. A movement toward e-supervision can be facilitated by the emergence of different new e-supervision theories. In the long run, supervisors and supervisees need to draw on a range of knowledge to inform their practice. They are active knowledge makers, and their practice wisdom can be further developed to establish new approaches and theories in e-supervision.

The training for supervisors in the provision of ICT supervision

Currently, little effort has been made to provide training for supervisors in the provision of ICT supervision. A growing number of supervisors are already very comfortable with technologies for daily communication. But for those who are not familiar with using technologies, training on using new technology in supervision is recommended (Graf and Stebnicki 2002). Vaccaro and Lambie (2007) note that supervisors need to be specifically trained in using different kinds of ICT because they must know the strengths and limitations of using each kind of ICT. They have to know the limitations of using each ICT in advance in order to plan to mitigate the effect of these limitations on their supervision.

Moreover, supervisors must know how to set expectations for online supervision and the necessary responsibilities they have. Procedures and guidelines for online supervision are clearly stated in many existing guidelines such as NASW, ASWB, CSWE, and CSWA Standards for Technology in Social Work Practice (National Association of Social Workers 2017). Supervisors are reminded to be familiar with the guidelines about cyber supervision.

Concluding remarks

Many of the issues regarding the use of ICT in supervision have been discussed in this chapter. Based on advances in technology, there are a number of alternative ways of supervision open to supervisor and supervisee. Driscoll and Townsend (2007) propose that the utilization of technology may be the only option for receiving supervision in rural or remote areas. Although there is a growing awareness and implementation of ICT in supervision, there is room to further develop and theorize the applications of ICT in supervision at micro level, mezzo level, and macro level. Moreover, there is a need to include ICT in the education of supervisors. Supervisor education programs can make use of technologies to provide online training programs and through the inclusion of content on online supervision.

At the micro level this involves the development of "e-supervision skills" and "e-supervision process" as well as the formulation of theories and approaches in e-supervision. The mezzo level involves the outcomes and effectiveness of cyber supervision on personal growth, professional growth, and organizational growth. Evidence-based research on e-supervision outcomes and learning outcomes would also strengthen the development of future e-supervision. At the macro level the focus is on the discovery of distinctive e-supervision contexts and situations required for an effective e-supervision process, for example, the invention of technology in the future that would make e-supervision easier; the cultivation of an e-supervision culture; a collaborative environment between learning and technology; and the establishment of rules and regulations that give supervisors and supervisees continuous and open support to e-supervision.

Looking to the future, the use of technology in supervision is a developmental trend. For example, the Covid-19 pandemic and subsequent lockdown of societies internationally has provided an additional way that cyber-supervision can support social workers engaged in disaster work, particularly when face-to-face meetings may pose a risk to themselves and/or their supervisors. Clearly this emerging practice is an area for further research and development. The use of ICT in supervision has become highly relevant as web-based interventions and web-based supervision support are now more important than ever. In future, more studies can be undertaken to explore the possibility of using ICT in cyber-supervision to support frontline social workers.

Contemporary and future problems facing the development of cyber supervision must be further addressed (Bender and Dykeman 2016; Inman et al. 2019). These problems include: (1) ways to tackle quality issues in using technology; (2) ways to integrate different forms of modern mobile applications in supervision and learning; (3) the lack of universal standards for the ethical use of technology in supervision; (4) no established cyber supervision approach; (5) insufficient understanding of the effectiveness and limitations of cyber supervision; and (6) cyber supervision has not been popularized around the world.

References

American Counseling Association 2005. *ACA code of ethics* [online]. Available from: http://www.counseling .org/Resources/CodeOfEthics/TP/Home/CT2.aspx [Accessed 21 April 2018].

American Psychological Association 2013. *Guidelines for the practice of telepsychology* [online]. Available from: http://www.apapracticecentral.org/ce/guidelines/telepsychology-guidelines.pdf [Accessed 21 April 2018].

Anderson-Meger, J., 2011. Critical thinking and e-learning in social work education. *International Journal of Business, Humanities and Technology*, 1 (2), 17–27.

Apostolidou, Z., and Schweitzer, R., 2017. Practitioners' perspectives on the use of clinical supervision in their therapeutic engagement with asylum seekers and refugee clients. *British Journal of Guidance and Counselling*, 45 (1), 72–82.

Australian Association of Social Worker 2016. *Ethics and practice guideline—social media, information and communication technologies part 1 and 2* [online]. Available from: https://www.aasw.asn.au/practitioner -resources/ethical-guidelines [Accessed 21 April 2018].

Aveline, M., 1992. The use of audio and videotape recordings of therapy sessions in the supervision and practice of dynamic psychotherapy. *British Journal of Psychotherapy*, 8 (4), 347–358.

Barnett, J.E., 2011. Utilizing technological innovations to enhance psychotherapy supervision, training and outcomes. *Psychotherapy*, 48 (2), 103–108.

Bender, S., and Dykeman, C., 2016. Supervisees' perceptions of effective supervision: a comparison of fully synchronous cybersupervision to traditional methods. *Journal of Technology in Human Services*, 34 (4), 326–337.

Bernard, J.M., and Goodyear, R.K., 2019. *Fundamentals of clinical supervision*. 6th ed. Boston, MA: Pearson.

Birkenmaier, J., Wernet, S.P., Berg-Weger, M., Wilson, R.J., Banks, R., Olliges, R., and Delicath, T.A., 2005. Weaving a web: the use of internet technology in field education. *Journal of Teaching in Social Work*, 25, 3–19.

Botzer, G., and Yerushalmy, M., 2007. *Mobile application for mobile learning*. IADIS International Conference on Cognition and Exploratory Learning in Digital Age (CELDA 2007).

Brandoff, R., and Lombardi, R., 2012. Miles apart: two art therapists' experience of distance supervision. *American Art Therapy Association*, 29 (2), 93–96.

British Association of Social Workers 2018. *BASW policy: social media* [online]. Available from: https://www .basw.co.uk/resources/basws-social-media-policy [Accessed 21 April 2018].

Bryne, A.M., and Hartley, M.T., 2010. Digital technology in the 21st century: considerations for clinical supervision in rehabilitation education. *Rehabilitation Education*, 24 (1–2), 57–68.

Burkard, A.W., Johnson, A.J., Madson, M.B., Pruitt, N.T., Contreras-Tadych, D.A., Kozlowski, J.M., Hess, S.A., and Knox, S., 2006. Supervisor cultural responsiveness and unresponsiveness in cross-cultural supervision. *Journal of Counseling Psychology*, 53 (3): 288–301.

Bushfield, S.S., 2005. Field clusters online. *Journal of Technology in Human Services*, 23, 215–227.

Carlisle, R.M., Hays, D.G., Pribesh, S.L., and Wood, C.T., 2017. Educational technology and distance supervision in counselor education. *Counselor Education and Supervision*, 56 (1), 33–49.

Carrington, G., 2004. Supervision as a reciprocal learning process. *Educational Psychology in Practice*, 20 (1), 31–42.

Chan, C., and Holosko, M.J., 2016. A review of information and communication technology enhanced social work interventions. *Research on Social Work Practice*, 26 (1), 88–100.

Chapman, R.A., Baker, S.B., Nassar-McMillan, S.C., and Gerler, E.R., 2011. Cybersupervision: further examination of synchronous and asynchronous modalities in counseling practicum supervision. *Counselor Education and Supervision*, 50, 298–313.

Chen, B., and Bryer, T., 2012. Investigating instructional strategies for using social media in formal and informal learning. *The International Review of Research in Open and Distributed Learning*, 13 (1), 87–104.

Cicco, G., 2011. Assessment in online courses: how are counseling skills evaluated?. *Journal of Educational Technology*, 8 (2), 9–15.

Cook, J.E., and Doyle, C., 2002. Working alliance in online therapy as compared to face to-face therapy: preliminary results. *Cyber Psychology and Behavior*, 5, 95–105.

Coleman, H., and Collins, D., 2008. Technology in social work education: are we practicing what we preach?. *Currents: New Scholarship in the Human Services*, 7 (2), 1–17.

Davies, J., and Graff, M., 2005. Performance in e-learning: online participation and student grades. *British Journal of Educational Technology*, 36 (4), 657–663.

Deane, F.P., Gonsalvez, C.J., Blackman, R.J., Saffioti, D.F., and Andresen, R. 2015. Issues in the development of e-supervision in professional psychology: a review. *Australian Psychologist*, 50 (3), 241–247.

Driscoll, J., and Townsend, A., 2007. Alternative methods in clinical supervision: beyond the face-to-face encounter. *In*: Driscoll, J., ed. *Practising clinical supervision: a reflective approach for healthcare professionals*. 2nd ed. New York: Elsevier, 141–162.

Dudding, C.C., and Justice, L.M., 2004. An E-supervision model: videoconferencing as a clinical training tool. *Communication Disorders Quarterly*, 25 (3), 145–151.

Dymond, S.K., Renzaglia, A., Halle, J.W., Chadsey, J., and Bentz, J.L., 2008. An evaluation of videoconferencing as a supportive technology for practicum supervision. *Teacher Education and Special Education: The Journal of the Teacher Education Division of the Council*, 31 (4), 243–256.

Engelbrecht, L.K., 2006. Cultural friendliness as a foundation for the support function in the supervision of social work students in South Africa. *International Social Work*, 49 (2), 267–276.

Fearing, A., and Riley, M., 2005. Graduate students' perceptions of online teaching and relationship to preferred learning styles. *MEDSURG Nursing*, 14 (6), 383–389.

Garrison, D.R., and Kanuka, H., 2004. Blended learning: uncovering its transforming potential in higher education. *Internet and Higher Education*, 7 (2), 95–105.

Glosoff, H.L., Renfro-Michel, E., and Nagarajan, S., 2016. Ethical issues related to the use of technology in clinical supervision. *In*: Rousmaniere, T., and Renfro-Michel, E., eds. *Using technology to enhance clinical supervision*. Alexandria, VA: American Counselling Association, 31–46.

Goodyear, R.K., 2014. Supervision as pedagogy: attending to its essential instructional and learning processes. *The Clinical Supervisor*, 33 (1), 82–99.

Graf, N.M., and Stebnicki, M.A., 2002. Using e-mail for clinical supervision in practicum: a qualitative analysis. *Journal of Rehabilitation*, 68, 41–49.

Harvey, V.S., and Carlson, J.F., 2003. Ethical and professional issues with computer-related technology. *School Psychology Review*, 32, 92–104.

Haythornthwaite, C., Kazmer, M.M., Robbins, J., and Shoemaker, S., 2000. Community development among distance learners: temporal and technological dimensions. *Journal of Computer-Mediated Communication*, 6 (1), 1–24.

HNQQ 16 November 2013. *Tencent expert: wechat will not appear listening or leaking events* [online]. Available from: http://hn.qq.com/a/20131116/005424.htm [Accessed 26 April 2018].

Inman, A.G., Bashian, H., Pendse, A.C., and Luu, L.P., 2019. Publication trends in telesupervision: a content analysis study. *The Clinical Supervisor*, 38 (1), 97–115.

Kanz, J.E., 2001. Clinical-supervision.com: issues in the provision of online supervision. *Professional Psychology: Research and Practice*, 32 (4), 415–420.

Kasworm, C.E., Rose, A.D., and Ross-Gordon, J.M., eds., 2010. *Handbook of adult and continuing education.* Los Angeles: SAGE.

Kurzman, P.A., 2013. The evolution of distance learning and online education. *Journal of Teaching in Social Work*, 33 (4–5), 331–338.

Leech, L.L., and Holcomb, J.M., 2004. Leveling the playing field: the development of a distance education program in rehabilitation counseling. *Assistive Technology*, 16 (2), 135–143.

Levitt, D.H., and Jacques, J.D., 2005. Promoting tolerance for ambiguity in counselor training programs. *Journal of Humanistic Counseling, Education and Development*, 44, 46–54.

Luke, M., and Gordon, C., 2016. Clinical supervision via e-mail: a review of the literature and suggestions for practice. *In*: Rousmaniere, T., and Renfro-Michel, E., eds. *Using technology to enhance clinical supervision*. Chapter 8. Wiley, 115–134.

Madoc-Jones, I., and Parrott, L., 2005. Virtual social work education—theory and experience. *Social Work Education*, 24 (7), 755–768. doi:10.1080/02615470500238678

Marrow, C. E., Hollyoake, K., and Hamer, D., 2002. Clinical supervision using video conferencing technology: a reflective account. *Journal of Nursing Management*, 10, 275–282.

McAdams, C.R., and Wyatt, K.L., 2010. The regulation of technology-assisted distance counseling and supervision in the United States: an analysis of current extent, trends, and implications. *Counselor Education and Supervision*, 49 (3), 179–192.

Miller, T.W., Burton, D.C., Hill, K., Luftman, G., Veltkemp, L.J., and Swope, M., 2005. Telepsychiatry: critical dimensions for forensic services. *Journal of the American Academy of Psychiatry and the Law*, 33 (4), 539–546.

Mishna, F., Levine, D., Bogo, M., and Van Wert, M., 2013. Cyber counselling: an innovative field education pilot project. *Social Work Education*, 32 (4), 484–492.

Mo, Y.H., and O'Donoghue, K., 2018. A snapshot of cyber supervision in Mainland China. *Qualitative Social Work*, 0 (0): 1–18.

National Association of Social Workers 2013. Best practice standards in social work supervision [online]. Available from: https://www.socialworkers.org/LinkClick.aspx?fileticket=GBrLbl4BuwI%3D&portalid=0 [Accessed 29 April 2018].

National Association of Social Workers, Association of Social Work Boards, Association of Social Work Boards, Council on Social Work Education, Clinical Social Work Association 2017. *NASW, ASWB, CSWE and CSWA standards for technology in social work practice* [online]. Available from: https://www.socialworkers.org/includes/newIncludes/homepage/PRA-BRO-33617.TechStandards_FINAL_POSTING.pdf [Accessed 18 April 2018].

National Board for Certified Counselors 2005. *Code of ethics* [online]. Available from: http://www.nbcc.org/Assets/Ethics/nbcc-codeofethics.pdf [Accessed 18 April 2018].

Nelson, J.A., Nichter, M., and Henriksen, R., 2010. *On-line supervision and face-to-face supervision in the counseling internship: an exploratory study of similarities and differences.* [online]. Available from: http://counselingoutfitters.com/ vistas/vistas10/Article_46.pdf [Accessed 18 April 2018].

Orr, P.P., 2010. Distance supervision: research, findings, and considerations for art therapy. *The Arts in Psychotherapy*, 37 (2), 106–111.

Oterholm, I., 2009. Online critical reflection in social work education. *European Journal of Social Work*, 12 (3), 363–375.

Pack, M., 2014. Practice journeys: using online reflective journals in social work fieldwork education. *Reflective Practice International and Multidisciplinary Perspectives*, 15 (3), 404–412.

Panos, P.T., Panos, A., Cox, S.E., Roby, J.L., and Matheson, K.W., 2002. Ethical issues concerning the use of videoconferencing to supervise international social work field practicum students. *Journal of Social Work Education*, 38, 421–437.

Phelan, J.E., 2015. The use of E-learning in social work. *Journal of Education for Social Work*, 60 (3), 257–264.

Priya, M., Saravana, K., Lucylynn, L., 2018. Effective use of technology in clinical supervision. *Internet Interventions*, 8, 35–39.

Rashedul, M.I., Rofiqul, M.I., and Tahidul, A.M., 2010. Mobile application and its global impact. *International Journal of Engineering and Technology*, 10 (6), 72–78.

Reamer, F.G., 2013. Social work in a digital age: ethical and risk management challenges. *Social Work*, 58 (2), 163–172.

Reamer, F.G., 2015. *Risk management in social work preventing professional malpractice, liability, and disciplinary action.* New York, NY: Columbia University Press.

Reamer, F.G., 2019. Social work education in a digital world: technology standards for education and practice. *Journal of Social Work Education*, 55 (3), 420–432.

Reardon, C., 2010. Web-based social work education growing support, gaining ground. *Social Work Today*, 10 (5), 9–13.

Regan, A.R.C., and Freddolino, P.P., eds., 2008. *Integrating technology into the social work curriculum*. Alexandria, VA: Council on Social Work Education.

Rousmaniere, T., 2014. Using technology to enhance clinical supervision and training. *In*: C.E. Watkins and D. Milne, eds. *International handbook of clinical supervision*. New York: Wiley Publishers, 204–237.

Rousmaniere, T., Abbass, A., and Frederickson, J., 2014. New developments in technology-Assisted supervision and training: a practical overview. *Journal of Clinical Psychology*, 70 (11), 1082–1093.

Rousmaniere, T., and Renfro-Michel, E., 2016. *Using technology to enhance clinical supervision*. Alexandria, VA: American Counselling Association.

Rudestam, K.E., and Schoenholtz-Read, J., eds., 2010. *Handbook of online learning*. 2nd ed. Thousand Oaks, CA: SAGE.

Sandell, K., and Hayes, S., 2002. The web's impact on social work education: opportunities, challenges, and future directions. *Journal of Social Work Education*, 38, 85–99.

Schmidt, M., MacSuga Gage, A., Gage, N., Cox, P., and McLeskey, J., 2015. Bringing the field to the supervisor: innovation in distance supervision for field-based experiences using mobile technologies. *Rural Special Education Quarterly*, 34 (1), 37–43.

Shorkey, C.T., and Uebel, M., 2014. History and development of instructional technology and media in social work education. *Journal of Social Work Education*, 50 (2), 247–261.

Simpson, S., 2005. Video counseling and psychotherapy in practice. *In*: Goss, S., and Kate, A., eds. *Technology in counselling and psychotherapy: a practitioner's guide*. Basingstoke, NY: Palgrave.

Stebnicki, M.A., and Glover, N.M., 2001. E-supervision as a complementary approach to traditional face-to-face clinical supervision in rehabilitation counseling: problems and solutions. *Rehabilitation Education*, 15, 283–293.

Tu, C., and Corry, M., 2003. Building active online interaction via a collaborative learning community. *Computers in the Schools*, 20 (3), 51–59.

Vaccaro, N., and Lambie, G.W., 2007. Computer-based counselor-in-training supervision: ethical and practical implications for counselor educators and supervisors. *Counselor Education & Supervision*, 47, 46–57.

Watson, J.C., 2003. Computer-based supervision: implementing computer technology into the delivery of counseling supervision. *Journal of Technology in Counseling*, 3 (1). [online] Available from: http://jtc.colstate.edu/vol3_1/Watson/Watson.htm [Accessed 18 April 2018].

Watson, M.M., 2016. Social media (SM) use by technology education students on field placement. *Journal of Psychology in Africa*, 26 (2), 186–188.

Webber, J.M., and Deroche, M.D., 2016. Technology and accessibility in clinical supervision: challenges and solutions. *In*: Rousmaniere, T., and Renfro-Michel, E., eds., *Using technology to enhance clinical supervision*. Alexandria, VA: American Counselling Association, 67–86.

Welfel, E.R., 2010. *Ethics in counseling and psychotherapy: standards, research and emerging issues*. 4th ed. Belmont, CA: Brooks/Cole.

Wolfson, G., Magnuson, C., and Marson, G., 2005. Changing the nature of the discourse: teaching field seminars online. *Journal of Social Work Education*, 41, 355–361.

Wright, J., and Griffiths, F., 2010. Reflective practice at a distance: using technology in counselling supervision. *Reflective Practice*, 11 (5), 693–703.

52

ADVANCING THE SOCIAL WORK SUPERVISION RESEARCH AGENDA

Kieran O'Donoghue

This chapter aims to advance the social work supervision research agenda by reviewing recent research. It begins by examining the research reviews since 2012. This is followed by a description of the selection criteria and procedures used to review the research in peer-reviewed journals from January 2011 to September 2020. Next, the location, journals, design, participants, areas, and findings are reviewed. The chapter concludes with a discussion of the advances over the decade and then identifies a future research agenda.

Since 2012, there were three major reviews of social work supervision research. The first, Carpenter et al. (2013), reviewed 22 peer-review articles from 2000 to 2012, concerned with the outcomes from the supervision of child welfare workers. The review found some evidence that supervision was associated with positive outcomes for workers and organizations. The positive outcomes for workers were the mitigation of the effects of job stress and increased overall job satisfaction, whereas the positive outcomes for organizations concerned job retention and reducing staff turnover. Carpenter et al. (2013, p. 1852) also found no reliable evidence that supervision influenced consumer outcomes and they described the evidence-base for child welfare supervision as being "surprisingly limited." They concluded that more research on child welfare supervision is needed, with such research focusing on the development of evidence-based models that lead to improvements in worker, organizational, and client outcomes. O'Donoghue and Tsui (2015) undertook a comprehensive review of the research about the supervision of practicing social workers from 1970 to 2010. They selected and reviewed 86 peer reviewed journal articles and found the number of studies was doubled in each decade. They also observed an increasing geographical spread in the studies and that the research designs had become more diverse with the analysis more sophisticated. O'Donoghue and Tsui (2015) also asserted that the research evidence provided a knowledge base for supervision in social work and child welfare and demonstrated the influence supervision had on worker and client outcomes. They proposed a research agenda that focused on: 1) the evaluation of supervision practices and the development of empirically supported supervision; 2) client outcomes; and 3) international comparative studies. Sewell (2018) conducted a scoping review of 79 conceptual and research articles from 2013 to 2017 in which a social worker was the first author. She identified that the social work supervision literature was increasing with the articles being published in 36 journals and 16 countries across the continents of Australasia, North America, Europe, Asia, and

Africa, which revealed a shift from North American dominance to more global focus in the literature. Sewell (2018) identified 50 empirical articles and concluded that the recommendations from previous reviews regarding supervision knowledge still applied and that there was little movement toward evaluation of supervision practice, evidence-based models, and client outcomes. Overall, these reviews indicate firstly, that there is some evidence that supervision has positive outcomes for child welfare workers and their organizations and that there is a paucity of evidence of the influence of supervision on client outcomes in child welfare (Carpenter et al. 2013). Second, the research on social work supervision has spread geographically with the research designs being more varied with more sophisticated analysis. Third, the research has provided knowledge about social work supervision, child welfare supervision, and about the influence of supervision on social workers' outcomes and client outcomes. Having discussed the most recent research reviews, the focus now turns to the social work supervision research conducted over the decade from 2011 to 2020.

Selection criteria and procedures

Four criteria were used for identifying relevant studies. First, selection was limited to articles published in refereed journals between January 2011 and the end of September 2020. Second, since the focus is on the supervision of practicing social workers, any research on the supervision of social work students or fieldwork supervision was excluded. Third, the study reported empirical information on supervision. This means that articles that did not report results that were directly derived from supervision were excluded. Fourth, only articles published in the English language were selected.

The procedures used for selection of the articles were four-fold. First, the reference lists of the research reviews discussed above were scanned. Second, a search was conducted within the major social work and supervision journals that were cited in the research reviews. The third procedure involved a Google Scholar search using the terms: "social work supervision" research (2,120 items); "clinical social work supervision" research (283 items); and "professional social work supervision" research (54 items). These searches were scanned with the obvious items related to supervision of field education; other disciplines and those unrelated to supervision of social workers were excluded. The articles that remained on the list were subjected to a fourth procedure, which involved reviewing and reading each article to ascertain whether they met the criteria. During this stage the reference list of each article was checked for any further research articles that had not yet been identified. A total of 115 articles were identified as meeting the criteria. Table 52.1 below details the number of articles published each year.

The number of articles published between 2011 and 2020 surpasses the 86 published between 1970 and 2010 (O'Donoghue and Tsui 2015). There is also a doubling of the average number of articles per year from 4.4 for the 2000s to 11.5 for the past decade, continuing a trend that has occurred since the 1970s (O'Donoghue and Tsui 2015).

Development of supervision research

Since 2011 supervision research has increased both in terms of the number of studies reported, and the geographical spread of studies. The geographical spread revealed an increasing internationalization across the continents of Australasia, North America, Asia, Europe, and Africa. The largest amount of the studies (37) were conducted in Australasia, with most (25) occurring within Aotearoa New Zealand. Table 52.2 below provides an overview of the number of articles by geographical location. This table shows an increased number of locations with 17 countries

Table 52.1 Number of articles published each year

Year	Number of articles
2011	10
2012	9
2013	10
2014	8
2015	9
2016	8
2017	16
2018	16
2019	19
2020	10
Total	115

Table 52.2 Number of articles and geographical location

Location	N
Aotearoa New Zealand	25
United States	24
UK	18
Australia	12
Canada	7
China	6
Israel	5
Inter/multinational	4
Denmark	3
Romania	2
Germany	1
Hong Kong	1
Indonesia	1
Ireland	1
Italy	1
Norway	1
Singapore	1
Slovakia	1
South Africa	1
Total	115

reporting social work supervision research, as well as several international and multinational studies. The geographical spread and distribution of articles mirror the trend described by Sewell (2018).

The geographical spread is also apparent in the journals, with supervision research being published in 43 journals in Australasia, North America, Asia, Europe, and Africa. Table 52.3 shows in descending order the number of articles published in each journal. The number and range of journals has increased on that noted in previous reviews, with O'Donoghue and Tsui (2015) identifying 24 journals and Sewell (2018) identifying 36. It is notable that *The Clinical*

Table 52.3 The number of articles published in each journal 2011–2020

Journal	Number of articles
Aotearoa New Zealand Social Work	11
Australian Social Work	8
Journal of Social Work Practice	8
British Journal of Social Work	7
European Journal of Social Work	6
Practice	6
The Clinical Supervisor	5
Administration in Social Work which became Human Service Organizations: Management, Leadership & Governance from 2014	4
Child & Family Social Work	4
Children and Youth Services Review	4
Clinical Social Work Journal	4
Journal of Public Child Welfare	4
China Journal of Social Work	3
Families in Society: The Journal of Contemporary Social Services	3
International Social Work	3
Social Work Education	3
Administration and Policy in Mental Health and Mental Health Services Research	2
Journal of Social Work	2
Qualitative Social Work	2
Reflective Practice	2
Advances in Social Work and Welfare Education	1
Canadian Social Work Review	1
Child Abuse & Neglect	1
Children Australia	1
Child Welfare	1
Ethics and Social Welfare	1
International Journal of Advanced Science and Technology	1
International Journal of Knowledge, Culture and Change Management	1
International Journal of Mental Health Nursing	1
International Journal of Qualitative Studies on Health and Well-being	1
Journal of Children's Services	1
Journal of Evidence-Based Social Work	1
Journal of Family Strengths	1
Journal of Human Behavior in the Social Environment	1
Journal of Social Intervention: Theory and Practice	1
Journal of Workplace Behavioral Health	1
Postmodern Openings	1
Procedia – Social and Behavioral Sciences	1
Research on Social Work Practice	1
Smith College Studies in Social Work	1
Social Work	1
Social Work in Health Care	1
Social Work/Maatskaplike Werk	1
Total	**115**

Supervisor Journal was not the most prevalent source of social work supervision research despite being so in the previous decades (O'Donoghue and Tsui 2015). This is particularly apparent in the mean number of articles reducing in the past decade from 1 per year in previous decades to 0.5 per year. This indicates a preference for social work supervision researchers to publish within social work journals rather than interdisciplinary journals.

Review of the research

The research is reviewed through an examination of the research design, participants, areas, and findings.

Research design

The range of designs have continued to diversify over the last decade with studies reporting qualitative, quantitative, and mixed methods designs. Fifty-five (48%) studies used qualitative designs. Thirty-two were interview based with the majority using semi-structured interviews. Among the other studies some used focus groups (e.g. Bogo et al. 2011; Hanna and Potter 2012; Benton et al. 2017; Dempsey and Halton 2017), a few used action research methods including observations of sessions or reviews of recordings of sessions (e.g. Øien and Solheim 2015; Wilkins et al 2017), whereas others combined different qualitative methods, such as interviewing and focus groups (e.g. Mo and Tsui 2016), or observations (either in person or audio-recorded) and follow up interviews (e.g. Cooksey-Campbell et al. 2013; Saltiel 2017; Rankine 2019a; Calcaterra and Raineri 2020). Content analysis was used to analyze videos, reflections, supervision records, and participants' views (e.g. Bourn and Hafford-Letchfield 2011; Engelbrecht 2013; Wilkins 2017). A few researchers used auto-ethnography methods to reflect on their own experiences within supervision (e.g. Rankine and Thompson 2015; Lipscomb and Ashley 2017). Pre- and post-narrative evaluation was used in a study that was based upon a workshop that used the arts in supervision (Hafford-Letchfield and Huss 2018). Overall, the range of qualitative methods used over this decade have increased and become more sophisticated. There has been a particular increase in designs that involve observational methods. The credibility of the studies was for the most part good with researchers being clear about recruitment and selection of participants, the methods used to collect information, the type of analysis used, the ethical issues relevant to the study, and the limitations of the methodology and methods.

Thirty studies (26%) were quantitative, 28 were surveys, with the other two being experimental designs. Most surveys used online distribution methods with only four articles indicating the use of a postal survey (Ben-Porat and Itzhaky 2011; O'Donoghue 2019a, b; Quinn et al. 2019). Non-probability sampling was predominant with only two studies using probability sampling (i.e. random sampling) (O'Donoghue 2019a; Quinn et al. 2019). The non-probability samples mostly recruited respondents through professional bodies, organizations, professional forums, or networks. The sample sizes varied and ranged from 1460 (Zinn 2015) to 28 (Turner-Daly and Jack 2017). Twenty-two of the 28 surveys had sample sizes over 100, with 14 reporting samples larger than 200 respondents. Response rates were reported in 15 articles and these ranged from an estimated 93.4% (Zinn 2015) to 10.68% (Kuzyšin et al. 2020); the median response rate was 44% reported by Sweifach (2019). Turning to the analysis, almost half reported descriptive statistics, nine studies examined the relationship between variables through correlations and regression (Zinn 2015; Dagan et al. 2016; Julien-Chinn and Lietz 2016; Peled-Avram 2017; Kim et al. 2018; Weiss-Dagan et al. 2018; Griffiths et al. 2019a; Sweifach 2019; Cortis et al. 2020), whereas, five articles analyzed variances with four using bivariate analysis and one a multivariate analysis (Ben-Porat and Itzhaky 2011; Griffiths et al. 2019a; O'Donoghue 2019a, b; Wilkins and Antonopoulou 2019). One article used factor analysis to validate the perceptions of supervisory support scale (Fukui et al. 2014). The first article that used an experimental design was Lowe (2011), who tested the gender-sensitive case assignment practices of supervisors with regard to the exposure of male workers to client related violence by using vignettes with a control and an intervention group. The second article, Freund and Guez (2018) was a quasi-experimental design that involved a pre-test, intervention, and post-test evaluation which sought to identify the contributing factors in supervisors' intention to leave through a linear regression analysis. In general, the quantitative studies whilst variable in their rigor, reflect the trends of: (a) much greater use of online formats for recruitment and administration of instruments, and b) the use of larger samples and more sophisticated statistical analysis.

Thirty articles (26%) had mixed methods designs, over half (18) were combinations of surveys, interviews, and/or focus groups. Eight articles reported evaluation studies, which had various designs, with some using pre- and post-tests (e.g. Landsman and D'Aunno 2012; Bailey et al. 2014; Nickson et al. 2016), others used observations and rating scales and questionnaires (e.g. Magnussen 2018; Bostock et al. 2019a, b; Wilkins et al. 2018a, b). Two were part of a program evaluating aspects of strength-based supervision (Lietz et al. 2014; Lietz and Julien-Chinn 2017), whereas the others were an experiment to validate the Alliance Building: Learning to Engage (ABLE) model (Strickler et al. 2018) and a longitudinal study on the feasibility and impact of supervision training (Kraemer et al. 2011). Overall, the mixed methods studies mirrored the developments found in both the qualitative and quantitative designs. Interestingly only one study (Lietz and Julien-Chinn 2017) clearly identified the type of mixed method design used. That said, generally the research designs over the past decade have shown greater use of observational studies, online recruitment strategies, and wider use of mixed methods evaluation studies than previous decades.

Participants

The research participants were supervisees, supervisors, both supervisees and supervisors; and supervisees, supervisors, and clients. Forty-six (40%) articles were concerned with supervisees, while 25 (22%) articles solely focused on supervisors. Another 40 (35%) involved both supervisees and supervisors. Most of these studies collected data from each group separately, however, there were five articles in which the participants were identified as supervisee and supervisor dyads (Rankine and Thompson 2015; Mo and Tsui 2016; Rankine 2018; Mo and O'Donoghue 2019; Rankine 2019a). The dyad studies are an important advance in supervision research because they provide direct access to the interpersonal practices that occur within supervision. Another innovative study used a professional actor in the supervisee role in order to observe supervisors' skills and interactions in a supervision simulation (Wilkins et al. 2018). Four articles, all from the UK, reported included supervisor, supervisee, and clients as participants. Two were derived from a Social Care Institute for Excellence (SCIE) study on supervision with adult settings undertaken by Lambley (2018a, b). This study involved two service user focus groups that explored service user perceptions of the supervision system and service user experiences of its impact. The results from the service users were general and not specifically connected to information collected from supervisors or supervisees. The other two articles focused upon supervision within child and family social work settings and both involved families and connected the link between supervision, practice, and clients. Wilkins et al. (2018b) explored the relationship between supervision, practice, and family engagement in child and family social work through: a) observing and recording a group supervision session discussion about the family; b) the lead worker completing a case background questionnaire; c) observing and recording the worker's visit with the family; and d) interviewing family members about their experiences, relationship with the worker, and goals of the work. The second article, Bostock et al. (2019a) paired observations of systemic supervision with observations of the practice that occurred with service users. Bostock et al. (2019a) involved the social worker in recruiting the family into the study, then undertook a structured observation of the group supervision discussions. This was followed by the workers and family being observed and recorded in a home visit. To minimize bias, the researchers were blind to the pairing of supervision sessions and home visits. Overall, the developments over the last decade particularly those related to the use of dyads and the involvement of service users have contributed to advancing knowledge of the inner workings of supervision and have built on the previous work concerning the link between supervision, direct practice, and the impact on clients (Harkness and Hensley 1991; Harkness 1995, 1997).

Research areas and findings

The broad areas covered by the articles were categorized as experiences and perceptions of supervision generally, supervision within child welfare, and the influence of supervision on workers and organizations.

Experiences and perceptions of supervision

Sixty-two articles reported findings that were derived from the participants' experiences and perceptions of supervision. Fourteen were derived from supervisees' experiences of supervision. The areas explored in these included social workers' experiences of supervision nationally, and as migrants within in another country (Beddoe et al. 2012; O'Donoghue 2019a), as well as across a range of fields (e.g. refugees and asylum seekers, health, supportive housing, family violence and sexual assault, and social and legal protection) (Robinson 2013; Beddoe et al. 2014; Choy-Brown et al. 2016; Cortis et al. 2020; Kuzyšin et al. 2020). Some studies were focused on specific aspects of supervision and included studies on the purpose, duration, and training of supervisors; how power is experienced and perceived; the influence of supervision histories; the expression of emotion; the need for conversations about social justice and practice; and how supervision is used to navigate ethical challenges (Leung 2012; O'Donoghue 2012; Hair 2013, 2014, 2015; Ingram 2013; McCarthy et al. 2020).

The findings from the national studies and studies in specific fields suggested that the supervision supervisees participated in, whilst varied in its construction, was for the most part of good quality, helpful for their resilience, job retention, and met their expectations. Across these studies individual supervision was the most common type. There were concerns in some studies about the availability, frequency, cultural responsiveness, and attention given to social differences such as gender, sexual, and ethnic diversity. The findings from studies that focused on specific aspects of supervision indicated that for supervisees, the purpose of supervision was the development of knowledge and skills, as well as the provision of emotional support. Supervisees called for career-long supervision and their supervisors to be social workers and trained as supervisors (Hair 2015). The findings from the studies that were focused on power acknowledged the workplace positional power of supervisors but found that where supervisory authority was derived from expertise, this was associated with age and experience, which meant that perceived expertise changed overtime. Nonetheless, there was agreement that supervisors needed to be able to collaboratively work through power and authority issues in the relationship and where they were unsuccessful in achieving this, there was supervisee resistance (Leung 2012; Hair

2014). Supervisees' supervision histories influenced how they developed and participated in supervision in both positive and negative ways as well as established a map of the supervision relationship for supervisees (O'Donoghue 2012). The expression of emotion within supervision was dependent upon supervisees feeling safe and supervisors being emotionally competent (Ingram 2013). There was a desire for conversations about social justice and practice, however the conversations about social justice rarely happened (Hair 2015). Supervision was also used to navigate ethical challenges, however, this depended upon the supervisee's discretion about which ethical concerns they would bring to their supervision, with the power dynamics inherent to the supervisory relationship often shaping these decisions (McCarthy et al. 2020).

Ten articles examined interprofessional supervision, several explored general matters pertaining to the skills, processes, commonalities, differences, advantages, limitations, and evaluation methods used in interprofessional supervision (Bogo et al. 2011; Beddoe and Howard 2012; Howard et al. 2013; Pack 2014; Davys 2017; Davys et al. 2017a). Two studies explored supervisees' views, preferences, and suggestions about interprofessional supervision within an interprofessional agency setting (King et al. 2017; Sweifach 2019). Social workers' experiences and perspectives of interprofessional supervision were also examined in two articles (Geißler-Piltz 2011; Hutchings et al. 2014). The findings from interprofessional studies indicated that in mental health there was considerable agreement about the principles of interprofessional supervision. These included that it was regular, available in crisis for debriefing, and that the supervisors had specific clinical expertise and skills in teaching (Bogo et al. 2011; Pack 2014). Interprofessional supervision also helped practitioners bridge gaps in their knowledge, clinical skills, and to evaluate their practice. It gave supervisees an appreciation and respect for other professions, as well as a new appreciation of their own (Beddoe and Howard 2012; Howard et al. 2013). The evaluation of interprofessional supervision was undertaken idiosyncratically (Davys 2017). The main limitation of interprofessional supervision was its perceived lack of clinical accountability (Davys 2017). The findings from the studies conducted within agency settings indicated a mixed picture in which social work supervision was limited and was not the only form of advice and support (King et al. 2017; Sweifach 2019). While the findings from the studies focused solely on social workers' experiences, they also found that supervision within multi-professional teams reflected the professional hierarchy within health settings and that clear understandings of the purpose of interprofessional supervision amongst social workers, as well as practices guidelines, were needed (Geißler-Piltz 2011; Hutchings et al. 2014).

The perspectives and experiences of supervisors were discussed in eight articles which examined the supervisors' role development (Lam and Yan 2015; Schmidt and Kariuki 2019), experiences and reflectivity (O'Donoghue and Tsui 2011; Davys et al. 2019; O'Donoghue 2019b), and provision of dual role and external supervision (Beddoe 2011; Wong and Lee 2015; Mo and Tsui 2016). These articles provided insights into becoming a supervisor, supervisory training, how supervisors are informed, and how they use a thinking out loud process of reflection. They also identified the strengths and challenges of both dual-role supervision and external supervision.

Seven articles were internationally or nationally focused studies. Amongst these, three reported the results from two Delphi studies involving supervision experts (Beddoe et al. 2015; Akesson and Canavera 2018; Karvinen-Niinikoski et al. 2019), whereas the other four articles consisted of three derived from a doctoral study in Australia (Egan 2012; Egan et al. 2016, 2017) and an article on issues and challenges in the supervision of social workers in South Africa (Engelbrecht 2013). Generally, the findings from these articles emphasized the challenges that supervision faces internationally and nationally in the face of neoliberalism and managerialism, the need to balance managerial and reflective supervision and the risk of supervision becoming surveillance rather than being a method to enhance reflective practice, and worker and client outcomes. The findings also highlighted the need to strengthen the evidence base nationally and internationally, as well as the need for better structures and systems that support supervision.

Three articles were focused on evaluating the quality of supervision (Benton et al. 2017; Lambley 2018a, b), with two further articles examining evaluation methods (Fukui et al. 2014; Davys et al. 2017b; Wilkins et al. 2018a). The findings from the articles evaluating quality found that high quality supervision involves a supervisor who is skilled, and a trusting safe relationship. The content is balanced across functions and is reflective, as well as specific to the worker. The process has structure and keeps the focus on supervision and is enhanced by peer and group supervision. High quality supervision also improves service-user outcomes and worker support outcomes and is supported by organizational culture. In contrast, the findings concerning evaluation methods were mixed, with the perceptions of the supervisor support scale found to be a useful instrument for evaluating supervision (Fukui et al. 2014), whereas Wilkins et al. (2018a) found self-report to be more reliable than a simulated observation and noted that the development of an independent reliable measure to evaluate supervision was yet to be achieved. On the other hand, Davys et al. (2017b) found that despite evaluation occurring in some form there was no policy or culture of evaluation for supervision.

Supervision at a distance or in rural areas was another area researched. The findings from the articles showed that supervision in rural areas was needed and wanted in rural Romania (Sandu and Unguru 2013). While, in rural Australia, peer consultation and virtual peer supervision groups were helpful for practitioners and equivalent to traditional supervision (Bailey et al. 2014; Nickson et al. 2016). In China, cyber-supervision using a range of online media applications was an emerging area of supervision that provided supervisory support to social workers in isolated rural areas (Mo 2020; Mo and O'Donoghue 2020). Cultural differences were the focus of another group of articles with two articles focusing on Indigenous supervision for Māori in Aotearoa New Zealand (Eketone 2012; Wallace 2019), while a third article discussed an indigenized model of supervision in Shenzhen, China (Mo and Tsui 2019). The findings from these three articles reinforce the need for supervision to be decolonized and the development of Indigenous models, approaches, and supervision systems to be promoted. Two articles examined cross-cultural supervision and highlighted the need for further development in this area towards establishing cultural humility and responsiveness within agencies and amongst some supervisors, as well as the eradication of white privilege, tokenism, microaggressions, and culturally harmful supervision (Lipscomb and Ashley 2017; Lusk et al. 2017). The reflective and expressive process of supervision was the focus of four articles (O'Donoghue 2014; Øien and Solheim 2015; Rankine and Thompson 2015; Hafford-Letchfield and Huss 2018). The results from these studies reinforced supervision as an interactive exchange where participants reflect through expressing their thinking out loud, and this can be aided through the use of bodily movement, breathing, and visual imagery. The last group of articles in this section were three that reported the supervision experiences and perceptions of newly qualified social workers (Pack 2011; Manthorpe et al. 2015; Beddoe et al. 2020). The results from these articles highlighted the variability of supervision for beginning practitioners. They also reinforced the importance of regular supervision, that is developmentally focused and safe, which includes observation and feedback.

Supervision within child welfare

Thirty-nine articles examined supervision within child welfare. Thirteen were focused on evaluating various aspects of supervision. Nearly half of these explored general questions pertaining to what happened in supervision, how was supervision recorded, how it contributed to learning and decision making, what it helped with, and what effective supervision involved (McPherson et al. 2016; Saltiel 2017; Wilkins 2017; Wilkins et al. 2017; Weiss-Dagan et al. 2018; Wilkins and Antonopoulou 2019). These studies identified that case management discussions occurred in supervision and these discussions provided limited opportunity for reflection (Wilkins et al. 2017). The discussions were recorded as a descriptive narrative designed for management accountability rather than understanding professional decision-making and judgments (Wilkins 2017). Supervision was nonetheless found to be an important space for evaluating practitioners' accounts of their practice, as well as for learning and decision making (Saltiel 2017). Supervision was also found to help with management, oversight, and accountability (Wilkins and Antonopoulou 2019). Effective child welfare supervision was described as a safe supervisory relationship supported by knowledge and leadership within an empowering organizational and community context (McPherson et al. 2016). However, the ability to benefit from effective supervision could be impaired when social workers had high exposure to child abuse cases and role stress (Weiss-Dagan et al. 2018).

The other evaluation studies examined how particular factors impacted upon supervision and the outcomes arising from supervision. Kim et al. (2018) explored the effects of work experience and educational background on supervisory support and found that supervisory support steadily increased for qualified social workers, but sharply decreased as their work experience increased, which suggested that supervisors should provide individualized supervision that matches the needs and background of workers. Lietz et al. (2014) evaluated the transfer of learning of strength-based supervision training into supervisory practice and found that the changes in practice that occurred were positive and aligned with the training content. Landsman and D'Aunno (2012) also evaluated a supervisor training program and found that the skills learned about human resources and case practice supervision were transferred into practice with supervisors reporting increases in use of these skills after six months. The outcomes from the Scandinavian model of external supervision was the focus of Magnussen (2018) who found positive outcomes for clients, workers, and organizations. He argued that these outcomes were due to the reflective nature of this type of supervision. The relationship between supervision, practice, and clients was the focus of three studies (Wilkins et al. 2018b; Bostock et al. 2019a, b). The result from Wilkins et al.'s (2018b) study was that practice focused group supervision discussions were associated with more skillful social work practice and higher levels of parental engagement and goal agreement (Wilkins et al. 2018b). Similarly, Bostock et al. (2019a, b) found a significant association between systemic supervision discussions and the quality of direct practice with children's families. They also identified that strength of effective systemic supervision was its use of a "rehearsal space" to plan conversations with families (Bostock et al. 2019b, p. 522).

Nine articles reported studies involving supervision approaches with four articles exploring critical reflection (Rankine et al. 2018; Rankine 2018, 2019a, b). These articles detailed a model of critical reflective supervision and a thinking out loud process whilst also examining contextual factors and the risk environment's impact upon the capacity for reflective supervision. Turney and Ruch (2018) explored the application of the Cognitive and Affective Supervisory Approach (CASA) and found that it was not easily used by supervisors who had a preference for problem solving rather than active listening. Consequently, active listening was added as the fourth aspect of the reflective cycle alongside thinking, feeling, and doing, and was identified as integral to supervision. Observational video-based approaches for supervision were examined in two articles (Birkholm et al. 2017; Antczak et al. 2019). These approaches helped social workers assess their own practice in a more realistic way and improved the feedback from the supervisor and the workers' development of their practice. Peer supervision groups were the focus of two studies (Dempsey and Halton 2017; Calcaterra and Raineri 2020). These studies identified the importance of the practicalities, facilitation, and group process in the success of peer groups, as well as how these groups provide mutual aid and personal growth to group members.

Supervisees' experiences and perspectives were examined in nine articles. Six of these explored various aspects of supervision including: its role in professional development; satisfaction with strength-based supervision; the relationship between work self-efficacy and supervision; the supervision experiences of newly-hired workers; the supervision of social workers completing a post qualifying award; and the nature of child welfare supervision relationships (Caras and Sandu 2013; Zinn 2015; Julien-Chinn and Lietz 2016; Lietz and Julien-Chinn 2017; Turner-Daly and Jack 2017; Radey and Stanley 2018). The findings from these articles were that supervisees see a role for supervision in their professional development and that strength-based supervision contributed to supervisees' satisfaction (Caras and Sandu 2013; Lietz and Julien-Chinn 2017). There was a clear relationship between self-efficacy and supervision with this finding reinforcing that focused supervision tended to result in better client outcomes than unfocused supervision (Julien-Chinn and Lietz 2016). In the case of newly hired workers, there were expectations of regular supervision and that their supervisors were both available and knowledgeable (Radey and Stanley 2018). In contrast, the social workers undertaking the post graduate award predominately experienced supervision sessions focused on case management, with much less attention paid to the worker and opportunities for them to reflect on their practice (Turner-Daly and Jack 2017), while Zinn (2015) found child welfare supervision relationships varied and that this variation was attributed to the agency culture. Three articles reported studies about the impact of the environment upon supervisees and included studies about organizational change, secondary traumatization, and experiences of supervision following interactions with hostile and intimidating parents (Cooksey-Campbell et al. 2013; Dagan et al. 2016; Hunt et al. 2016). The findings from these studies were mixed with supervisees in the midst of organizational change wanting clear communication and support, whereas effective supervision was not found to contribute to secondary traumatization, but a lack of support was experienced by supervisees from their supervisors and organizations following stressful interactions with hostile and intimidating parents. The last two studies highlight a need for better supervision and support for workers' personal safety in this field.

Five articles were concerned with supervisors' experiences. Two reported contrasting findings concerning supervisory development with there being a lack of support for the development of supervisors in Canada (Blackman and Schmidt 2013) on the one hand, while on the other hand there was positive support for non-qualified child welfare supervisors to obtain a MSW degree in a US state and this improved their supervision (Falk 2020). Two articles looked at supervisors' well-being with Griffiths et al. (2019a) raising concerns about supervisors' job satisfaction and noting dissatisfaction with the level of recognition, workload impact, and salary. In another article Griffiths et al. (2019b) identified a range of worrying and unhealthy habits that supervisors had developed in response to job stress. The fifth article discussed the implementation of the education function of supervision by supervisors in Indonesia and noted that it was implemented in a limited way (Yuliani and Fahrudin 2020).

Three articles focused on child welfare supervision at team, unit, and organizational level. Claiborne and Lawson's (2011) case-study assisted the development of two supervisory teams and outlined a model for positive supervisory workforce development. In the second article, the characteristics of the effective child welfare unit supervisor were identified as being integrity, loyalty, and honesty, with these traits being embodied in people skills, organizational skills, and time management (Hanna and Potter 2012). An organizational study focused on the implementation of a trauma-responsive approach to child welfare and identified supervision as a key instrument for translating this approach into practice (Akin et al. 2019).

The influence of supervision on workers and organizations

Fourteen articles were concerned with the influence supervision had upon workers and organizations. Six discussed the impact of trauma, with the first of these being an examination of how supervision contributed to role competence, secondary traumatization, and burnout. Ben-Porat and Itzhaky (2011) found a significant positive correlation between satisfaction with supervision and role competence but did not find any between satisfaction with supervision and secondary traumatization, and burnout. The experience and management of vicarious trauma in a team of social workers at a specialist cancer hospital was the focus of Joubert et al. (2013). They highlighted the importance of supervision in reducing the risks associated with vicarious trauma and proposed a model for clinical social work supervision. The third article examined the contribution relational-oriented supervision had in mitigating the consequences of working with traumatized clients and found that the higher supervision was rated as effective and relational, the lower the level of vicarious traumatization. That said, supervision was not found to have a moderating effect on the risk factors that contribute to the development of vicarious traumatization (Peled-Avram 2017). The predictors of secondary traumatic stress among social workers was the focus of Quinn et al. (2019), who found that of the supervisory relationship, salary, caseload size, and personal anxiety to be factors that impact the development of secondary trauma among clinical social workers. They also identified that positive ratings of supervision and a higher income level were found to predict a substantial reduction in the level of secondary trauma symptoms experienced by social workers. Long (2020) examined supervisors' experiences of a model in which vicarious trauma and vicarious post-traumatic growth co-occurred and found that the supervisors used the model in a way that assisted social workers to process how their clients' trauma disclosures impacted on their levels of stress and changed their perception of self, their role, and their worldview. Long (2020) recommended that the socio-political context of refugee trauma and trauma recovery be added to the model as an additional component of supervision practice. The sixth article detailed the validation of the Alliance Building: Learning to Engage supervision tool which measured the supervisory working alliance (Strickler et al. 2018). The study also hypothesized that use of the tool might increase supervisees' outcomes pertaining to occupational self-efficacy, and professional quality of life (compassion satisfaction, and decreased burnout and traumatic stress) however, no increase in supervisees' outcomes were identified.

Three articles examined supervisory management and leadership and looked at case assignment practices, the importance of leadership support for supervision and how supervisors furthered the development of supervisees (Lowe 2011; Vito 2015; Mo and O'Donoghue 2019). The results of these articles indicated firstly that there was unequal case assignment, with male social workers being more exposed to potentially violent clients (Lowe 2011). Second, that social work leaders played an important role in supporting supervision by modeling values and creating a safe organizational culture (Vito 2015). The third article indicated that supervisors further the development of supervisees using a range of techniques including counseling skills, role modeling, and consultative advice (Mo and O'Donoghue 2019).

The remaining five articles examined organizational culture (Bourn and Hafford-Letchfield 2011; Egan et al. 2018), retention (Chiller and Crisp 2012; Freund and Guez 2018), and supervision training (Kraemer Tebes et al. 2011). The findings concerning organizational culture were that supervision contributed to achieving organizational objectives and influenced organizational culture, but it could be influenced by conflicting agendas and demands. Therefore, supervisors need to undertake a mediating role in which they create a reflective space for the exploration of issues and provide support whilst also meeting their organizational responsibilities (Bourn and Hafford-Letchfield 2011). In contrast, Egan et al. (2018) found a need to better understand performance within the practice and supervision, as well as create ways in which workers can be acknowledged to develop their skills in a supportive organizational environment. They claimed that the neoliberal environment presented real possibilities for professional supervision in the management of competing workplace demands. The two articles on retention explored the retention of social workers and the retention of supervisors. Chiller and Crisp (2011) found that supervision was important for social workers' well-being and one of the reasons the participants in their study were still social workers. They argued that regular professional supervision can increase the retention rate of social worker employees, and organizations should invest in it. In contrast, Freund and Guez (2018) found that supervisors' intention to leave the role, in their first year, was shaped by their attitude to supervision and intention to stay in the role. The other contributing factors they identified included organizational climate and work overload. Lastly, an article about supervisor training found that supervisory competency training was a feasible and effective approach that was associated with supervisor satisfaction and stress management (Kraemer Tebes et al. 2011).

Advances in supervision research

The supervision research discussed above reveals several advances in supervision research. From the supervision research derived from participants' experiences and perspectives of supervision, there are clear advances in national, cross-national, international, and field of practice studies, which illustrate the similarities and differences in supervision across these areas. These studies also highlighted the importance of cultural and social differences within supervision, as well as the need to decolonize cross-cultural supervision alongside supporting the indigenization of supervision. There have been several emerging research areas over the past decade, namely, newly qualified practitioners, interprofessional supervision, rural and supervision at a distance, cybersupervision, ethics, values, and power dynamics. Advances have also been made in terms of our understanding of emotion, expression, interaction, and reflection within supervision. There have also been advances in evaluative studies and in relation to the question of evaluating supervision, although to date no formal evaluation system or independent tool has yet been established (Davys et al. 2017b; Wilkins et al. 2018a).

The advances in child welfare supervision research have provided insights into what happens, how it is recorded, its contribution to decision-making, and what it helps with. Alongside these advances have been the prevalence of the risk environment and the influence of the managerial and neoliberal discourses upon social workers' ability to critically reflect on their knowing, decision-making, and actions. The development of strength-based, critical reflective, and peer group supervision, as well as the use of observation has advanced supervision practice. Another important advance is the finding that practice focused supervision improved outcomes for clients. The findings concerning the positive transfer of learning from supervision training are also new. However, the findings from studies concerning the impact of the work indicate a need for better supervision and support for workers' personal safety in the child welfare field. Likewise, the findings concerning supervisors' job satisfaction and well-being advance our understanding of the challenges and pressure supervisors face. This also demonstrates a pressing need for supervisory support and raises questions regard the supervision of supervisors.

The findings related to the influence of supervision on workers and organizations firstly advance our understanding of how supervision can mitigate the effects of vicarious and secondary trauma through effective and relationally supportive supervision. Another advance were the findings regarding supervisors' case assignment decisions and their potential impact on workers' safety which raises further questions about how risk and safety are considered in this process. The findings concerning the influence of organizational culture also reinforce the supervisor's role of mediating between the professional practice system and management. The results concerning supervisors' intentions to leave provide new insights in why supervisors leave the role and raise questions concerning support, training, and development of supervisors.

Future research agenda

The advances in supervision research discussed above have progressed the research agenda described by the previous reviews, which concerned the evaluation of supervision practices and the development of empirically supported supervision; the link between supervision and client outcomes; and the development of an international perspective and understanding of supervision. The research over the past decade has also highlighted new areas for further research, which are suggested as additions to the future research agenda. These suggestions are that the influence of cultural and social differences, the decolonization of supervision, and the development of Indigenous supervision models be advanced. Second, the emerging research areas of newly qualified practitioners, interprofessional supervision, rural and supervision at a distance, cyber-supervision, ethics, values, and power dynamics should be furthered. The third area is the role of supervision in supporting the personal safety of social workers, while the fourth concerns the impact of work and a trauma-informed approach to supervision. The final suggested addition to the supervision agenda concerns researching the support and supervision for supervisors.

Conclusion

This chapter aimed to advance the social work supervision research agenda by reviewing research from the past decade. This review has found that supervision research has increased and become more international. It has used more sophisticated methods and analysis in the research designs and has involved participants across the supervision system including service-users. The areas of research have included experiences and perspectives, supervision in child welfare, and the influence of supervision on workers and organizations. The findings from the research have advanced supervision research and progressed the research agenda outlined in previous reviews. Five areas have been suggested as additions to the research agenda in the hope that supervision may advance: a) in its responsiveness to cultural and social differences, decolonization, and indigenization; b) through furthering the emerging research areas of the last decade; c) by supporting the personal safety of social workers; d) through addressing the impact of the work and trauma-informed supervision; and e) by examining the support and supervision of supervisors. In conclusion, the challenge for the next generation of supervision researchers is to build upon the past and develop the knowledge-base of the human relational practice of social work supervision, so that it enhances and improves the well-being and development of all involved in the supervision system.

References

Akesson, B., and Canavera, M., 2018. Expert understandings of supervision as a means to strengthen the social service workforce: results from a global delphi study. *European Journal of Social Work*, 21 (3), 333–347. doi:10.1080/13691457.2017.1399352

Akin, B.A., Dunkerley, S., Brook, J., and Bruns, K., 2019. Driving organization and systems change toward trauma-responsive services in child welfare: supervisor and administrator perspectives on initial implementation. *Journal of Public Child Welfare*. doi:10.1080/15548732.2019.1652720

Antczak, H.B., Mackrill, T., Steensbæk, S., and Ebsen, F., 2019. What works in video-based youth statutory caseworker supervision – caseworker and supervisor perspectives. *Social Work Education*, 38 (8), 1025–1040. doi:10.1080/02615479.2019.1611757

Bailey, R., Bell, K., Kalle, W., and Pawar, M., 2014. Restoring meaning to supervision through a peer consultation group in rural Australia. *Journal of Social Work Practice*, 28 (4), 479–495. doi:10.1080/0265053 3.2014.896785

Beddoe, L., 2011. External supervision in social work: power, space, risk, and the search for safety. *Australian Social Work*, 65 (2), 197–213. doi:10.1080/0312407x.2011.591187

Beddoe, L., Ballantyne, N., Maidment, J., Hay, K., and Walker, S., 2020. Supervision, support and professional development for newly qualified social workers in Aotearoa New Zealand. *Aotearoa New Zealand Social Work*, 32 (2), 17–31. doi:https://doi.org/10.11157/anzswj-vol32iss2id738

Beddoe, L., Davys, A.M., and Adamson, C., 2014. 'Never trust anybody who says "i don't need supervision"': practitioners' beliefs about social worker resilience. *Practice*, 26 (2), 113–130. doi:10.1080/0950 3153.2014.896888

Beddoe, L., Fouché, C., Bartley, A., and Harington, P., 2012. Migrant social workers' experience in New Zealand: education and supervision issues. *Social Work Education*, 31 (8), 1012–1031. doi:10.1080/0261 5479.2011.633600

Beddoe, L., and Howard, F., 2012. Interprofessional supervision in social work and psychology: mandates and (inter) professional relationships. *The Clinical Supervisor*, 31 (2), 178–202. doi:10.1080/07325223. 2013.730471

Beddoe, L., Karvinen-Niinikoski, S., Ruch, G., and Tsui, M.S., 2015. Towards an international consensus on a research Agenda for social work supervision: report on the first survey of a delphi study. *British Journal of Social Work*, 46 (6), 1568–1586. doi:10.1093/bjsw/bcv110

Ben-Porat, A., and Itzhaky, H., 2011. The contribution of training and supervision to perceived role competence, secondary traumatization, and burnout among domestic violence therapists. *The Clinical Supervisor*, 30 (1), 95–108. doi:10.1080/07325223.2011.566089

Benton, A.D., Dill, K., and Williams, A.E., 2017. Sacred time: ensuring the provision of excellent supervision. *Journal of Workplace Behavioral Health*, 32 (4), 290–305. doi:10.1080/15555240.2017.1408416

Birkholm Antczak, H., Mackrill, T., Steensbæk, S., and Ebsen, F., 2017. Online video supervision for statutory youth caseworkers – a pilot study. *Journal of Children's Services*, 12 (2–3), 127–137. doi:10.1108/JCS-06-2017-0029

Blackman, K., and Schmidt, G., 2013. The development of child protection supervisors in northern British Columbia. *Child Welfare*, 92 (5), 87–105.

Bogo, M., Paterson, J., Tufford, L., and King, R., 2011. Interprofessional clinical supervision in mental health and addiction: toward identifying common elements. *The Clinical Supervisor*, 30 (1), 124–140. doi:10.1080/07325223.2011.56496

Bostock, L., Patrizo, L., Godfrey, T., and Forrester, D., 2019a. What is the impact of supervision on direct practice with families?. *Children and Youth Services Review*, 105, 104428. doi:10.1016/j.childyouth.2019.104428

Bostock, L., Patrizo, L., Godfrey, T., Munro, E., and Forrester, D., 2019b. How do we assess the quality of group supervision? developing a coding framework. *Children and Youth Services Review*, 100, 515–524. doi:10.1016/j.childyouth.2019.03.027

Bourn, D., and Hafford-Letchfield, T., 2011. The role of social work professional supervision in conditions of uncertainty. *International Journal of Knowledge, Culture and Change Management*, 10 (9), 41–56.

Calcaterra, V., and Raineri, M.L., 2020. Helping each other: a peer supervision group with facilitators of mutual aid groups. *Social Work with Groups*, 43 (4), 351–364. doi:10.1080/01609513.2019.1642829

Caras, A., and Sandu, A., 2013. The role of supervision in professional development of social work specialists. *Journal of Social Work Practice*, 28 (1), 75–94. doi:10.1080/02650533.2012.763024

Carpenter, J., Webb, C.M., and Bostock, L., 2013. The surprisingly weak evidence base for supervision: findings from a systematic review of research in child welfare practice (2000–2012). *Children and Youth Services Review*, 35 (11), 1843–1853. doi:10.1016/j.childyouth.2013.08.014

Chiller, P., and Crisp, B.R., 2012. Professional supervision: a workforce retention strategy for social work?. *Australian Social Work*, 65 (2), 232–242. doi:10.1080/0312407x.2011.625036

Choy-Brown, M., Stanhope, V., Tiderington, E., and Padgett, D.K., 2016. Unpacking clinical supervision in transitional and permanent supportive housing: scrutiny or support?. *Administration and Policy in Mental Health and Mental Health Services Research*, 43 (4), 546–554. doi:10.1007/s10488-015-0665-6

Claiborne, N., and Lawson, H.A., 2011. A two-site case study of consultation to develop supervisory teams in child welfare. *Administration in Social Work*, 35 (4), 389–411. doi:10.1080/03643107.2011.599749

Cooksey-Campbell, K., Folaron, G., and Sullenberger, S.W., 2013. Supervision during child welfare system reform: qualitative study of factors influencing case manager implementation of a new practice model. *Journal of Public Child Welfare*, 7 (2), 123–141. doi:10.1080/15548732.2012.740441

Cortis, N., Seymour, K., Natalier, K., and Wendt, S., 2020. Which models of supervision help retain staff? findings from australia's domestic and family violence and sexual assault workforces. *Australian Social Work*, 1–15. doi:10.1080/0312407X.2020.1798480

Dagan, S.W., Ben-Porat, A., and Itzhaky, H., 2016. Child protection workers dealing with child abuse: the contribution of personal, social and organizational resources to secondary traumatization. *Child Abuse & Neglect*, 51, 203–211. doi:10.1016/j.chiabu.2015.10.008

Davys, A.M., 2017. Interprofessional supervision: a matter of difference. *Aotearoa New Zealand Social Work*, 29 (3), 79–94. doi:10.11157/anzswj-vol29iss3id278

Davys, A., Howard, F., Rankine, M., and Thompson, A., 2019. Supervision under the microscope: critical conversations in a learning community. *Practice*, 31 (5), 359–374. doi:10.1080/09503153.2018.1558196

Davys, A.M., May, J., Burns, B., and O'Connell, M., 2017b. Evaluating social work supervision. *Aotearoa New Zealand Social Work*, 29 (3), 108–121. doi:10.11157/anzswj-vol29iss3id314

Davys, A.M., O'Connell, M., May, J., and Burns, B., 2017a. Evaluation of professional supervision in Aotearoa/New Zealand: an interprofessional study. *International Journal of Mental Health Nursing*, 26 (3), 249–258. doi:10.1111/inm.12254

Dempsey, M., and Halton, C., 2017. Construction of peer support groups in child protection social work: negotiating practicalities to enhance the professional self. *Journal of Social Work Practice*, 31 (1), 3–19. doi:10.1080/02650533.2016.1152958

Egan, R., 2012. Australian social work supervision practice in 2007. *Australian Social Work*, 65 (2), 171–184. doi:10.1080/0312407x.2011.653575

Egan, R., Maidment, J., and Connolly, M., 2016. Who is watching whom? surveillance in Australian social work supervision. *British Journal of Social Work*, 46 (6), 1617–1635. doi:10.1093/bjsw/bcv098

Egan, R., Maidment, J., and Connolly, M., 2017. Trust, power and safety in the social work supervisory relationship: results from Australian research. *Journal of Social Work Practice*, 31 (3), 307–321. doi:10.1080/02650533.2016.1261279

Egan, R., Maidment, J., and Connolly, M., 2018. Supporting quality supervision: insights for organisational practice. *International Social Work*, 61 (3), 353–367. doi:10.1177/0020872816637661

Eketone, A., 2012. The purposes of cultural supervision. *Aotearoa New Zealand Social Work*, 24 (3/4), 20–30.

Engelbrecht, L.K., 2013. Social Work supervision policies and frameworks: playing notes or making music?. *Social Work/Maatskaplike Werk*, 49 (4), 456–468.

Falk, D.S., 2020. Child welfare supervisors empowered through MSW education: graduates of a statewide title IV-E MSW program for public child welfare supervisors describe their learning. *Journal of Public Child Welfare*, doi:10.1080/15548732.2020.1802387

Freund, A., and Guez, G., 2018. Intentions to leave supervision among social work supervisors: contributing factors. *Social Work Education*, 37 (4), 458–471. doi:10.1080/02615479.2017.1422487

Fukui, S., Rapp, C.A., Goscha, R., Marty, D., and Ezell, M., 2014. The perceptions of supervisory support scale. *Administration and Policy in Mental Health and Mental Health Services Research*, 41 (3), 353–359. doi:10.1007/s10488-013-0470-z

Geißler-Piltz, B., 2011. How social workers experience supervision: results of an empirical study in the healthcare sector. *Journal of Social Intervention: Theory and Practice*, 20 (1), 5–22.

Griffiths, A., Harper, W., Desrosiers, P., Murphy, A., and Royse, D., 2019b. "The stress is indescribable": self-reported health implications from child welfare supervisors. *The Clinical Supervisor*, 38 (2), 183–201. doi:10.1080/07325223.2019.1643433

Griffiths, A., Murphy, A., Desrosiers, P., Harper, W., and Royse, D., 2019a. Factors influencing the turnover of frontline public child welfare supervisors. *Journal of Public Child Welfare*, 1–17. doi:10.1080/1554873 2.2019.1652719

Hafford-Letchfield, T., and Huss, E., 2018. Putting you in the picture: the use of visual imagery in social work supervision. *European Journal of Social Work*, 21 (3), 441–453. doi:10.1080/13691457.2018.1423 546

Hair, H.J., 2013. The purpose and duration of supervision, and the training and discipline of supervisors: what social workers say they need to provide effective services. *British Journal of Social Work*, 43 (8), 1562–1588. doi:10.1093/bjsw/bcs071

Hair, H., 2014. Power relations in supervision: preferred practices according to social workers. *Families in Society: The Journal of Contemporary Social Services*, 95 (2), 107–114. doi:10.1606/1044-3894.2014.95.14

Hair, H.J., 2015. Supervision conversations about social justice and social work practice. *Journal of Social Work*, 15 (4), 349–370. doi:10.1177/1468017314539082

Hanna, M.D., and Potter, C.C., 2012. The effective child welfare unit supervisor. *Administration in Social Work*, 36 (4), 409–425. doi:10.1080/03643107.2011.604403

Harkness, D., 1995. The art of helping in supervised practice: skills, relationships, and out-comes. *The Clinical Supervisor*, 13 (1), 63–76.

Harkness, D., 1997. Testing interactional social work theory: a panel analysis of super-vised practice and outcomes. *The Clinical Supervisor*, 15 (1), 33–50.

Harkness, D., and Hensley, H., 1991. Changing the focus of social work supervision: effects on client satis-faction and generalized contentment. *Social Work*, 37, 506–512.

Howard, F., Beddoe, L., and Mowjood, A., 2013. Interprofessional supervision in social work and psychol-ogy in Aotearoa New Zealand. *Aotearoa New Zealand Social Work*, 25 (4), 25–40.

Hunt, S., Goddard, C., Cooper, J., Littlechild, B., and Wild, J., 2016. 'If I feel like this, how does the child feel?' Child protection workers, supervision, management and organisationall response to parental vio-lence. *Journal of Social Work Practice*, 30 (1), 5–24. doi:10.1080/02650533.2015.1073145

Hutchings, J., Cooper, L., and O'Donoghue, K., 2014. Cross-disciplinary supervision amongst social work-ers in Aotearoa New Zealand. *Aotearoa New Zealand Social Work* Review, 26 (4), 53–64.

Ingram, R., 2013. Exploring emotions within formal and informal forums: messages from social work practitioners. *British Journal of Social Work*, 45 (3), 896–913. doi:10.1093/bjsw/bct166

Joubert, L., Hocking, A., and Hampson, R., 2013. Social work in oncology—managing vicarious trauma—the positive impact of professional supervision. *Social Work in Health Care*, 52 (2–3), 296–310. doi:10.1 080/00981389.2012.737902

Julien-Chinn, F.J., and Lietz, C.A., 2016. Permanency-focused supervision and workers' self-efficacy: exploring the link. *Social Work* 61 (1) 37–44. doi:10.1093/sw/swv043

Karvinen-Niinikoski, S., Beddoe, L., Ruch, G., and Tsui, M.S., 2019. Professional supervision and profes-sional autonomy. *Aotearoa New Zealand Social Work*, 31 (3), 87–96. doi:10.11157/anzswj-vol31iss3id650

Kim, J., Park, T., Pierce, B., and Hall, J.A., 2018. Child welfare workers' perceptions of supervisory support: a curvilinear interaction of work experience and educational background. *Human Service Organizations: Management, Leadership & Governance*, 42 (3), 285–299. doi:10.1080/23303131.2017.1395775

King, S., Carson, E., and Papatraianou, L.H., 2017. Self-managed supervision. *Australian Social Work*, 70 (1), 4–16. doi:10.1080/0312407X.2015.1134608

Kraemer Tebes, J., Matlin, S.L., Migdole, S.J., Farkas, M.S., Money, R.W., Shulman, L., and Hoge, M.A., 2011. Providing competency training to clinical supervisors through an interactional supervision approach. *Research on Social Work Practice*, 21 (2), 190–199. doi:10.1177/1049731510385827

Kuzyšin, B., Schavel, M., and Pavelková, J., 2020. Reflection of the specifics of the supervision process in the environment of social and legal protection of children. *Postmodern Openings*, 11 (1), 116–130. doi:10.18662/po/11.1sup1/126

Lam, C.M., and Yan, M.C., 2015. Driving ducks onto a perch: the experience of locally trained Shenzhen supervisor. *China Journal of Social Work*, 8 (2), 182–194. doi:10.1080/17525098.2015.1039169

Lambley, S., 2018a. A semi-open supervision systems model for evaluating staff supervision in adult care settings: a conceptual framework. *European Journal of Social Work*, 21 (3), 389–399. doi:10.1080/13691 457.2018.1441129

Lambley, S., 2018b. A semi-open supervision systems model for evaluating staff supervision in adult-care organisational settings: the research findings. *The British Journal of Social Work*, 49 (2), 391–410. doi:10.1093/bjsw/bcy069

Landsman, M., and D'Aunno, L., 2012. Developing a framework for child welfare supervision. *Journal of Family Strengths*, 12 (1), Article 10.

Leung, K.K.P., 2012. An exploration of the use of power in social work supervisory relationships in Hong Kong. *Journal of Social Work Practice*, 26 (2), 151–162. doi:10.1080/02650533.2010.536201

Lietz, C., Hayes, M., Cronin, T., and Julien-Chinn, F., 2014. Supporting family-centered practice through supervision: an evaluation of strengths-based supervision. *Families in Society: The Journal of Contemporary Social Services*, 95 (4), 227–235. doi:10.1606/1044-3894.2014.95.29

Lietz, C.A., and Julien-Chinn, F.J., 2017. Do the components of strengths-based supervision enhance child welfare workers' satisfaction with supervision?. *Families in Society: The Journal of Contemporary Social Services*, 98 (2), 146–155. doi:10.1606/1044-3894.2017.98.20

Lipscomb, A.E., and Ashley, W., 2017. Colorful disclosures: identifying identity-based differences and enhancing critical consciousness in supervision. *Smith College Studies in Social Work*, 87 (2–3), 220–237. doi:10.1080/00377317.2017.1324098

Long, S., 2020. Supervisors' perception of vicarious trauma and growth in australian refugee trauma counsellors. *Australian Social Work*, 73 (1), 105–117. doi:10.1080/0312407X.2018.1501587

Lowe, T.B., 2011. Practitioners' risk exposure to client violence: a test of gender-sensitive case assignment among supervisors. *The Clinical Supervisor*, 30 (1), 19–35. doi:10.1080/07325223.2011.564952

Lusk, M., Terrazas, S., and Salcido, R., 2017. Critical cultural competence in social work supervision. *Human Service Organizations: Management, Leadership & Governance*, 41 (5), 464–476. doi:10.1080/2330 3131.2017.1313801

Magnussen, J., 2018. Supervision in Denmark – an empirical account of experiences and practices. *European Journal of Social Work*, 21 (3), 359–373. doi:10.1080/13691457.2018.1451827

Manthorpe, J., Moriarty, J., Hussein, S., Stevens, M., and Sharpe, E., 2015. Content and purpose of supervision in social work practice in England: views of newly qualified social workers, managers and directors. *The British Journal of Social Work*, 45 (1), 52–68. doi:10.1093/bjsw/bct102

McCarthy, L.P., Imboden, R., Shdaimah, C.S., and Forrester, P., 2020. 'Ethics are messy': supervision as a tool to help social workers manage ethical challenges. *Ethics and Social Welfare*, 14 (1), 118–134. doi:10.1080/17496535.2020.1720265

McPherson, L., Frederico, M., and McNamara, P., 2016. Safety as a fifth dimension in supervision: stories from the frontline. *Australian Social Work*, 69 (1), 67–79. doi:10.1080/0312407X.2015.1024265

Mo, K.Y.H., and Tsui, M.S., 2016. External supervision for social workers in another socio-political context: a qualitative study in Shenzhen, China. *China Journal of Social Work*, 9 (1), 62–74. doi:10.1080/17 525098.2016.1141474

Mo, K.Y., and Tsui, M.S., 2019. Toward an indigenized external supervision approach in China. *International Social Work*, 62 (4), 1286–1303. doi:10.1177/0020872818778104

Mo, Y.H., 2020. In search of a cyber supervision process: from the perspective of social work supervisees in Mainland China. *Journal of Evidence-Based Social Work*. doi:10.1080/26408066.2020.1805383

Mo, Y.H., and O'Donoghue, K., 2019. Nurturing a budding flower: external supervisors' support of the developmental needs of Chinese social workers in Shenzhen, China. *International Social Work*, 62 (2), 950–964. doi:10.1177/0020872818755856

Mo, Y.H., and O'Donoghue, K., 2020. A snapshot of cyber supervision in Mainland China. *Qualitative Social Work*, 19 (4), 612–629. doi:10.1177/1473325019836714

Nickson, A., Gair, S., and Miles, D., 2016. Supporting isolated workers in their work with families in rural and remote Australia: exploring peer group supervision. *Children Australia*, 41 (4), 265–274. doi:10.1017/cha.2016.41

O'Donoghue, K., 2012. Windows on the supervisee experience: an exploration of supervisees' supervision histories. *Australian Social Work*, 65 (2), 214–231. doi:10.1080/0312407x.2012.667816

O'Donoghue, K., 2014. Towards an interactional map of the supervision session: an exploration of supervisees and supervisors experiences. *Practice*, 26 (1), 53–70. doi:10.1080/09503153.2013.869581

O'Donoghue, K., 2019a. The supervision of registered social workers in Aotearoa New Zealand: a national survey. *Aotearoa New Zealand Social Work*, 31 (3), 58–77. doi:10.11157/anzswj-vol31iss3id648

O'Donoghue, K., 2019b. Registered social workers who are supervisors: a national survey. *Aotearoa New Zealand Social Work*, 31 (3), 97–115. doi:10.11157/anzswj-vol31iss3id651

O'Donoghue, K., and Tsui, M.S., 2011. In search of an informed supervisory practice: an exploratory study. *Practice*, 24 (1), 3–20. doi:10.1080/09503153.2011.632678

O'Donoghue, K., and Tsui, M., 2015. Social work supervision research (1970–2010): the way we were and the way ahead. *British Journal of Social Work*, 45 (2), 616–633. doi:10.1093/bjsw/bct115

Øien, A.M., and Solheim, I.J., 2015. Supervision of professionals: interdependency between embodied experiences and professional knowledge. *International Journal of Qualitative Studies on Health and Well-being*, 10. doi:10.3402/qhw.v3410.28432; doi:10.3402/qhw.v10.28432

Pack, M., 2011. Two sides to every story: a phenomenological exploration of the meanings of clinical supervision from supervisee and supervisor perspectives. *Journal of Social Work Practice*, 26 (2), 163–179. doi:10.1080/02650533.2011.611302

Pack, M., 2014. 'Unsticking the stuckness': a qualitative study of the clinical supervisory needs of early-career health social workers. *British Journal of Social Work*, 45 (6), 1821–1836. doi:10.1093/bjsw/bcu069

Peled-Avram, M., 2017. The role of relational-oriented supervision and personal and work-related factors in the development of vicarious traumatization. *Clinical Social Work Journal*, 45 (1), 22–32. doi:10.1007/s10615-015-0573-y

Quinn, A., Ji, P., and Nackerud, L., 2019. Predictors of secondary traumatic stress among social workers: supervision, income, and caseload size. *Journal of Social Work*, 19 (4), 504–528. doi:10.1177/1468017318762450

Radey, M., and Stanley, L., 2018. "Hands on" versus "empty": supervision experiences of frontline child welfare workers. *Children and Youth Services Review*, 91, 128–136. doi:10.1016/j.childyouth.2018.05.037

Rankine, M., 2018. How critical are we? revitalising critical reflection in supervision. *Advances in Social Work and Welfare Education*, 20 (2), 31–46.

Rankine, M., 2019a. The 'thinking aloud' process: a way forward in social work supervision. *Reflective Practice*, 20 (1), 97–110. doi:10.1080/14623943.2018.1564651

Rankine, M., 2019b. The internal/external debate: the tensions within social work supervision. *Aotearoa New Zealand Social Work*, 31 (3), 32–45. doi:10.11157/anzswj-vol31iss3id646

Rankine, M., Beddoe, L., O'Brien, M., and Fouché, C., 2018. What's your agenda? reflective supervision in community-based child welfare services. *European Journal of Social Work*, 21 (3), 428–440. doi:10.1080/13691457.2017.1326376

Rankine, M., and Thompson, A., 2015. 'Swimming to shore': co-constructing supervision with a thinking-aloud process. *Reflective Practice*, 16 (4), 508–521. doi:10.1080/14623943.2015.1064377

Robinson, K., 2013. Supervision found wanting: experiences of health and social workers in non-government organisations working with refugees and asylum seekers. *Practice*, 25 (2), 87–103. doi:10.1080/09503153.2013.775238

Saltiel, D., 2017. Supervision: a contested space for learning and decision making. *Qualitative Social Work*, 16 (4), 533–549. doi:10.1177/1473325016633445

Sandu, A., and Unguru, E., 2013. Supervision of social work practice in north-eastern Romanian rural areas. *Procedia - Social and Behavioral Sciences*, 82, 386–391. doi:10.1016/j.sbspro.2013.06.280

Schmidt, G., and Kariuki, A., 2019. Pathways to social work supervision. *Journal of Human Behavior in the Social Environment*, 29 (3), 321–332. doi:10.1080/10911359.2018.1530160

Sewell, K.M., 2018. Social work supervision of staff: a primer and scoping review (2013–2017). *Clinical Social Work Journal*, 46 (4), 252–265. doi:10.1007/s10615-018-0679-0.

Strickler, A., Valenti, M.W., and Mihalo, J.R., 2018. Mechanisms for building working alliances in clinical supervision. *Clinical Social Work Journal*, 46 (4), 361–373. doi:10.1007/s10615-018-0684-3

Sweifach, J.S., 2019. A look behind the curtain at social work supervision in interprofessional practice settings: critical themes and pressing practical challenges. *European Journal of Social Work*, 22 (1), 59–68. doi:10.1080/13691457.2017.1357020

Turner-Daly, B., and Jack, G., 2017. Rhetoric vs. reality in social work supervision: the experiences of a group of child care social workers in England. *Child & Family Social Work*, 22 (1), 36–46. doi:10.1111/cfs.12191

Turney, D., and Ruch, G., 2018. What makes it so hard to look and to listen? exploring the use of the cognitive and affective supervisory approach with children's social work managers. *Journal of Social Work Practice*, 32 (2), 125–138. doi:10.1080/02650533.2018.1439460

Vito, R., 2015. Leadership support of supervision in social work practice: challenges and enablers to achieving success. *Canadian Social Work Review*, 32 (1–2), 151–165. doi:10.7202/1034148ar

Wallace, E., 2019. Ngā Aroro and social work supervision. *Aotearoa New Zealand Social Work*, 31 (3), 20–31. doi:10.11157/anzswj-vol31iss3id645

Weiss-Dagan, S., Ben-Porat, A., and Itzhaky, H., 2018. The contribution of role characteristics and supervisory functions to supervision effectiveness. *Clinical Social Work Journal*, 46 (4), 341–349. doi:10.1007/s10615-018-0675-4

Wilkins, D., 2017. How is supervision recorded in child and family social work? an analysis of 244 written records of formal supervision. *Child & Family Social Work*, 22 (3), 1130–1140. doi:10.1111/cfs.12330

Wilkins, D., and Antonopoulou, V., 2019. What does supervision help with? a survey of 315 social workers in the UK. *Practice*, 31 (1), 21–40. doi:10.1080/09503153.2018.1437398

Wilkins, D., Forrester, D., and Grant, L., 2017. What happens in child and family social work supervision?. *Child & Family Social Work*, 22 (2), 942–951. doi:10.1111/cfs.12314

Wilkins, D., Khan, M., Stabler, L., Newlands, F., and Mcdonnell, J., 2018a. Evaluating the quality of social work supervision in UK children's services: comparing self-report and independent observations. *Clinical Social Work Journal*, 46 (4), 350–360. doi:10.1007/s10615-018-0680-7

Wilkins, D., Lynch, A., and Antonopoulou, V., 2018b. A golden thread? The relationship between supervision, practice, and family engagement in child and family social work. *Child & Family Social Work*, 23 (3), 494–503. doi:10.1111/cfs.12442

Wong, P.Y.J., and Lee, A.E.Y., 2015. Dual roles of social work supervisors: strain and strengths as managers and clinical supervisors. *China Journal of Social Work*, 8 (2), 164–181. doi:10.1080/17525098.2015.1039168

Yuliani, D., and Fahrudin, A., 2020. Implementation of the education function on the supervision of child social worker in Indonesia. *International Journal of Advanced Science and Technology*, 29 (4), 2632–2643.

Zinn, A., 2015. A typology of supervision in child welfare: multilevel latent class and confirmatory analyses of caseworker–supervisor relationship type. *Children and Youth Services Review*, 48 (1), 98–110. doi:10.1016/j.childyouth.2014.12.004

INDEX

9781032009254